Publisher Provided Course Homepage

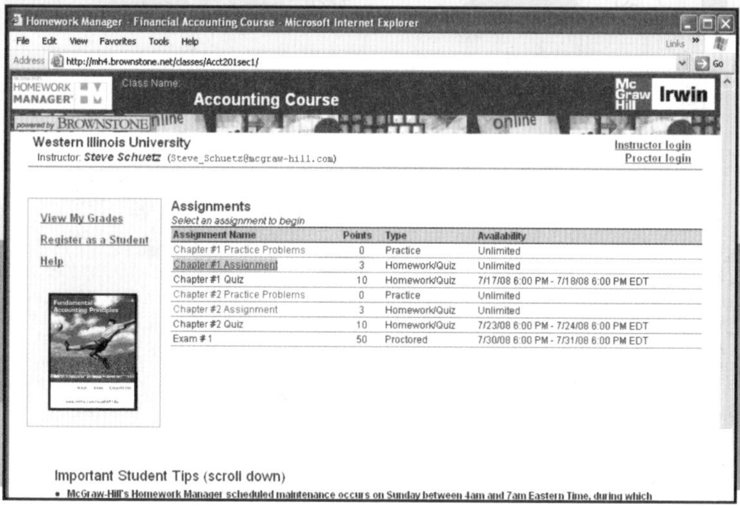

Easily Assign Online Homework

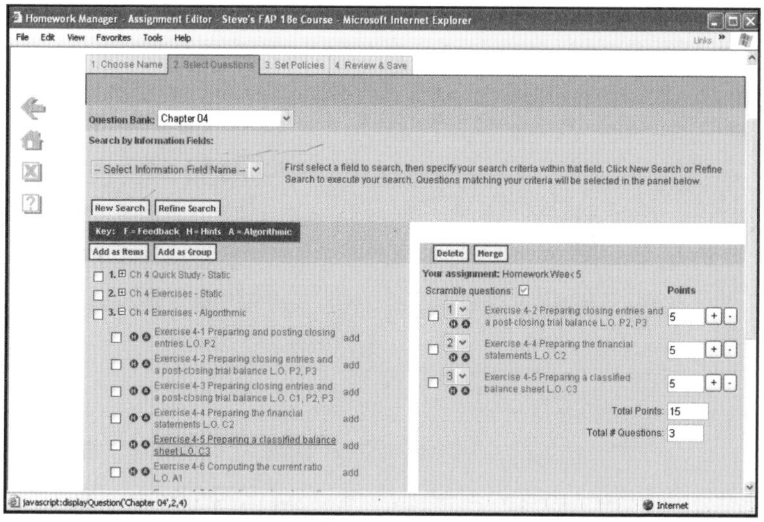

Track Student Results

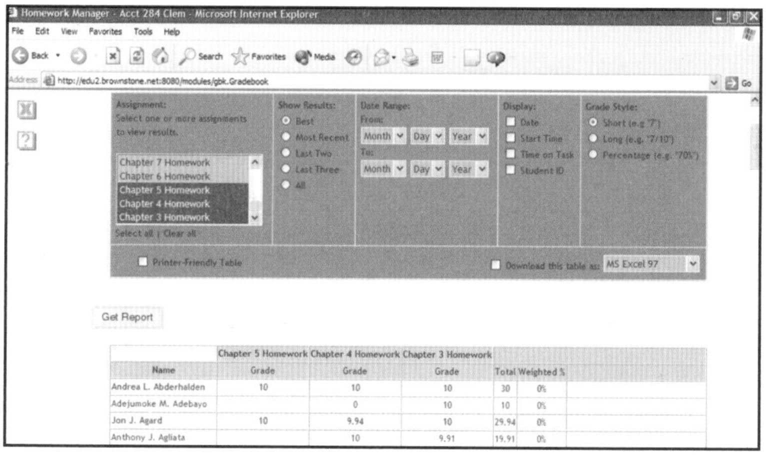

It's that easy.

Continuously Improving!

McGraw-Hill is committed to listening to our customers and making changes based on our customer desires; hence we are updating our system to bring you the following new features:

- Single Entry Point, Single Registration, Single Sign-on
- Local Time Zone Support
- Enhanced Grade Book Reporting Capabilities
  - Run reports on multiple sections at once
  - Export reports to WebCT and BlackBoard
- Enhanced Question Selection
  - Select by learning objective, AACSB Accreditation Criteria
- Enhanced Assignment Policies
- Enhanced eBook*
- Integrated eBook – Simple Toggle (no secondary log-in)
  - Topic Search
  - Adjustable text size
  - Jump to Page #
  - Print by Section
- Student Assignment Preview for Instructors

19

edition

Principles of Financial Accounting

John J. Wild
University of Wisconsin at Madison

Ken W. Shaw
University of Missouri at Columbia

Barbara Chiappetta
Nassau Community College

McGraw-Hill Irwin

Boston Burr Ridge, IL Dubuque, IA New York
San Francisco St. Louis Bangkok Bogotá Caracas Kuala Lumpur
Lisbon London Madrid Mexico City Milan Montreal New Delhi
Santiago Seoul Singapore Sydney Taipei Toronto

To my wife **Gail** and children, **Kimberly, Jonathan, Stephanie,** and **Trevor.**
To my wife **Linda** and children, **Erin, Emily,** and **Jacob.**
To my husband **Bob,** my sons **Michael** and **David,** and my **mother.**

McGraw-Hill Irwin

PRINCIPLES OF FINANCIAL ACCOUNTING

Published by McGraw-Hill/Irwin, a business unit of The McGraw-Hill Companies, Inc., 1221 Avenue of the Americas, New York, NY, 10020.

This book is printed on acid-free paper.

1 2 3 4 5 6 7 8 9 0 DOW/DOW 0 9 8

ISBN-13: 978-0-07-337954-8 (combined edition)
ISBN-10: 0-07-337954-9 (combined edition)
ISBN-13: 978-0-07-336629-6 (volume 1, chapters 1–12)
ISBN-10: 0-07-336629-3 (volume 1, chapters 1–12)
ISBN-13: 978-0-07-336628-9 (volume 2, chapters 12–25)
ISBN-10: 0-07-336628-5 (volume 2, chapters 12–25)
ISBN-13: 978-0-07-336630-2 (with working papers volume 1, chapters 1–12)
ISBN-10: 0-07-336630-7 (with working papers volume 1, chapters 1–12)
ISBN-13: 978-0-07-336631-9 (with working papers volume 2, chapters 12–25)
ISBN-10: 0-07-336631-5 (with working papers volume 2, chapters 12–25)
ISBN-13: 978-0-07-336627-2 (principles, chapters 1–17)
ISBN-10: 0-07-336627-7 (principles, chapters 1–17)

Vice president and editor-in-chief: *Brent Gordon*
Editorial director: *Stewart Mattson*
Publisher: *Tim Vertovec*
Executive editor: *Steve Schuetz*
Senior developmental editor: *Christina A. Sanders*
Executive marketing manager: *Sankha Basu*
Managing editor: *Lori Koetters*
Full service project manager: *Sharon Monday, Aptara®, Inc.*
Lead production supervisor: *Carol A. Bielski*
Lead designer: *Matthew Baldwin*
Senior photo research coordinator: *Lori Kramer*
Photo researcher: *Sarah Evertson*
Lead media project manager: *Brian Nacik*
Cover and interior design: *Matthew Baldwin*
Cover photo: *© Photolibrary*
Typeface: *10.5/12 Times Roman*
Compositor: *Aptara®, Inc.*
Printer: *R. R. Donnelley*

The Library of Congress has cataloged the single volume edition of this work as follows

Wild, John J.
Fundamental accounting principles / John J. Wild, Ken W. Shaw, Barbara Chiappetta.—19 ed.
p. cm.
Includes index.
ISBN-13: 978-0-07-337954-8 (combined edition : alk. paper)
ISBN-10: 0-07-337954-9 (combined edition : alk. paper)
ISBN-13: 978-0-07-336629-6 (volume 1 ch. 1–12 : alk. paper)
ISBN-10: 0-07-336629-3 (volume 1 ch. 1–12 : alk. paper)
[etc.]
1. Accounting. I. Shaw, Ken W. II. Chiappetta, Barbara. III. Title.
HF5635.P975 2009
657—dc22

2008035921

www.mhhe.com

Dear Colleagues/Friends,

As we roll out the new edition of *Fundamental Accounting Principles*, we thank each of you who provided suggestions to enrich this textbook. As teachers, we know how important it is to select the right book for our course. This new edition reflects the advice and wisdom of many dedicated reviewers, focus group participants, students, and instructors. Our book consistently rates number one in customer loyalty because of you. Together, we have created the most readable, concise, current, accurate, and innovative accounting book available today.

We are thrilled to welcome Ken Shaw to the *Fundamental Accounting Principles* team with this edition. Ken's teaching and work experience, along with his enthusiasm and dedication to students, fit nicely with our continuing commitment to develop cutting–edge classroom materials for instructors and students.

Throughout the writing process, we steered this book in the manner you directed. This path of development enhanced this book's technology and content, and guided its clear and concise writing.

Reviewers, instructors, and students say this book's enhanced technology caters to different learning styles and helps students better understand accounting. *Homework Manager Plus* offers new features to improve student learning and to assist instructor grading. Our *iPod* content lets students study on the go, while our *Algorithmic Test Bank* provides an infinite variety of exam problems. You and your students will find all these tools easy to apply.

We owe the success of this book to our colleagues who graciously took time to help us focus on the changing needs of today's instructors and students. We feel fortunate to have witnessed our profession's extraordinary devotion to teaching. Your feedback and suggestions are reflected in everything we write. Please accept our heartfelt thanks for your dedication in helping today's students understand and appreciate accounting.

With kindest regards,

John J. Wild   Ken W. Shaw   Barbara Chiappetta

#1 with Customers

Fundamental Accounting Principles rates #1 in Instructor and Student satisfaction over the prior three editions, and we are now proud to report that both independent research and development reviews show that *Fundamental Accounting Principles* is now #1 in customer loyalty!

#1 CUSTOMER LOYALTY

#1 in Accuracy
#1 in Assignments
#1 in Topic Coverage
#1 in Supplements
#1 in Readability
#1 in Organization
#1 in Overall Textbook Satisfaction

With ratings such as these, it is no surprise that *Fundamental Accounting Principles* is the fastest growing textbook in the accounting principles market. Take a look at **what instructors are saying** about *Fundamental Accounting Principles*.

Ken Coffey, Johnson County Community College
"There is nothing about this text that I do not like. We have been using it since I started teaching the course in 1971. We switched texts three times, but always went back to this one and I do not think we will try anything else."

Linda Rose, Westwood College
"Very thorough, readable, and graphically pleasant! Engages students in a variety of activities that create learning opportunities and [...link] materials to real-work scenarios and situations. End-of-chapter materials are engaging learning tools and broaden the learner's opportunity to practice and enhance retention of the chapter content."

Shafi Ullah, Broward CC
"The book contains detailed information with alternative exercises, problems, and cases with 'Beyond the Numbers'."

Marilyn Cilolino, Delgado CC
"I have always been a big fan of this book and praise it every chance I get. The authors are great people and are really concerned with their product. They listened to the instructors and take our comments and suggestions seriously. And they are always ready to help or answer any questions one might have."

Gloria Worthy, Southwest Tennessee CC
"FAP is a very good text and it is also good for our students because it addresses a variety of learning styles"

Phillip Lee, Nashville State Tech CC
"The Wild text packs more useful material into fewer pages than other principles of accounting textbooks."

John J. Wild is a distinguished professor of accounting at the University of Wisconsin at Madison. He previously held appointments at Michigan State University and the University of Manchester in England. He received his BBA, MS, and PhD from the University of Wisconsin.

Professor Wild teaches accounting courses at both the undergraduate and graduate levels. He has received numerous teaching honors, including the Mabel W. Chipman Excellence-in-Teaching Award, the departmental Excellence-in-Teaching Award, and the Teaching Excellence Award from the 2003 and 2005 business graduates at the University of Wisconsin. He also received the Beta Alpha Psi and Roland F. Salmonson Excellence-in-Teaching Award from Michigan State University. Professor Wild has received several research honors and is a past KPMG Peat Marwick National Fellow and is a recipient of fellowships from the American Accounting Association and the Ernst and Young Foundation.

Professor Wild is an active member of the American Accounting Association and its sections. He has served on several committees of these organizations, including the Outstanding Accounting Educator Award, Wildman Award, National Program Advisory, Publications, and Research Committees. Professor Wild is author of *Financial Accounting, Managerial Accounting,* and *College Accounting*, each published by McGraw-Hill/Irwin. His research articles on accounting and analysis appear in The Accounting Review, Journal of Accounting Research, Journal of Accounting and Economics, Contemporary Accounting Research, Journal of Accounting, Auditing and Finance, Journal of Accounting and Public Policy, and other journals. He is past associate editor of Contemporary Accounting Research and has served on several editorial boards including The Accounting Review.

Professor Wild, his wife, and four children enjoy travel, music, sports, and community activities.

Ken W. Shaw is an associate professor of accounting and the CBIZ/MHM Scholar at the University of Missouri. He previously was on the faculty at the University of Maryland at College Park. He received an accounting degree from Bradley University and an MBA and PhD from the University of Wisconsin. He is a Certified Public Accountant with work experience in public accounting.

Professor Shaw teaches financial accounting at the undergraduate and graduate levels. He received the Wiliams Keepers LLC Teaching Excellence award in 2007, was voted the "Most Influential Professor" by the 2005 and 2006 School of Accountancy graduating classes, and is a two-time recipient of the O'Brien Excellence in Teaching Award. He is the advisor to his School's chapter of Beta Alpha Psi, a national accounting fraternity.

Professor Shaw is an active member of the American Accounting Association and its sections. He has served on many committees of these organizations and presented his research papers at national and regional meetings. Professor Shaw's research appears in the Journal of Accounting Research; Contemporary Accounting Research; Journal of Financial and Quantitative Analysis; Journal of the American Taxation Association; Journal of Accounting, Auditing, and Finance; Journal of Financial Research; Research in Accounting Regulation; and other journals. He has served on the editorial boards of Issues in Accounting Education and the Journal of Business Research, and is treasurer of the American Accounting Association's FARS. Professor Shaw is co-author of *Financial and Managerial Accounting* and *College Accounting*, both published by McGraw-Hill.

In his leisure time, Professor Shaw enjoys tennis, cycling, music, and coaching his children's sports teams.

Barbara Chiappetta received her BBA in Accountancy and MS in Education from Hofstra University and is a tenured full professor at Nassau Community College. For the past two decades, she has been an active executive board member of the Teachers of Accounting at Two-Year Colleges (TACTYC), serving 10 years as vice president and as president from 1993 through 1999. As an active member of the American Accounting Association, she has served on the Northeast Regional Steering Committee, chaired the Curriculum Revision Committee of the Two-Year Section, and participated in numerous national committees.

Professor Chiappetta has been inducted into the American Accounting Association Hall of Fame for the Northeast Region. She had also received the Nassau Community College dean of instruction's Faculty Distinguished Achievement Award. Professor Chiappetta was honored with the State University of New York Chancellor's Award for Teaching Excellence in 1997. As a confirmed believer in the benefits of the active learning pedagogy, Professor Chiappetta has authored *Student Learning Tools*, an active learning workbook for a first-year accounting course, published by McGraw-Hill/Irwin.

In her leisure time, Professor Chiappetta enjoys tennis and participates on a U.S.T.A. team. She also enjoys the challenge of bridge. Her husband, Robert, is an entrepreneur in the leisure sport industry. She has two sons—Michael, a lawyer, specializing in intellectual property law in New York, and David, a composer, pursuing a career in music for film in Los Angeles.

Helping students achieve their goal!

Fundamental Accounting Principles 19e

Assist your students in achieving their goals by giving them what they need to succeed in today's accounting principles course.

Whether the goal is to become an accountant or a businessperson, or even just gain an understanding of the principles of accounting, *Fundamental Accounting Principles* (FAP) has helped generations of students succeed by giving them the support in the form of leading-edge accounting content that engages students, with state-of-the-art technology.

With FAP on your team, you'll be passed **engaging content** and a **motivating style** to help students see the relevance of accounting. Students are motivated when reading materials that are clear and relevant. FAP runs ahead of the field in engaging students. Its chapter-opening vignettes showcase dynamic, successful entrepreneurial individuals and companies guaranteed **to interest and excite students**. This edition's featured companies–Best Buy, Circuit City, RadioShack, and Apple–engage students with their annual reports, which are a pathway for learning financial statements. Further, this book's coverage of the accounting cycle fundamentals is widely praised for its clarity and effectiveness.

FAP also delivers innovative technology to help students succeed. **Homework Manager** provides students with instant grading and feedback for assignments that are completed online. **Homework Manager Plus** integrates an online version of the textbook with Homework Manager. Our algorithmic test bank in Homework Manager offers infinite variations of numerical test bank questions. FAP also offers students portable **iPod-ready content** to help students study and raise their scores.

We're confident you'll agree that **FAP will help your students achieve their goal**.

Engaging Content

FAP content continues to set the standard in the principles course. Take a look at Chapters 1, 2 and 3 and you'll see how *FAP* leads with the best coverage of the accounting cycle. We are the first book to cover equity transactions the way most instructors teach it and students learn it–by introducing the separate equity accounts upfront and not waiting until a chapter or two later. Chapter 2 has the time-tested 4-step approach to analyzing transactions: [1] Identify, [2] Analyze, [3] Record, and [4] Post. And Chapter 3 offers a new 3-step process to simplify adjusting accounts. *FAP* also motivates students with engaging chapter openers. Students identify with them and can even picture themselves as future entrepreneurs. Each book includes the financial statements of Best Buy, Circuit City, RadioShack, and Apple to further engage students.

State-of-the-Art Technology

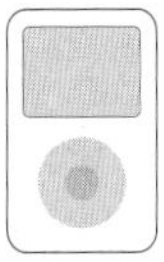

FAP offers the most advanced and comprehensive technology on the market in a seamless, easy-to-use platform. As students learn in different ways, *FAP* provides a technology smorgasbord that helps students learn more effectively and efficiently. Homework Manager, eBook options, and iPod content are some of the options. Homework Manager Plus takes learning to another level by integrating an online version of the book with all the power of Homework Manager. Technology offerings follow:

- Homework Manager
- Homework Manager Plus
- iPod content
- Algorithmic Test Bank
- Online Learning Center
- Carol Yacht's General Ledger
- ALEKS for the Accounting Cycle
- ALEKS for Financial Accounting

Premier Support

McGraw-Hill/Irwin has mobilized a new force of specialists committed to training and supporting the technology we offer. Our commitment to instructor service and support is top notch and leads the industry. Our new "McGraw-Hill Cares" program provides you with the fastest answers to your questions or solutions to your training needs. Ask your McGraw-Hill sales rep about our Key Media Support Plan and the McGraw-Hill Cares Program.

Through contemporary and engaging content, state-of-the-art technology, and committed service and support, *FAP* provides you and your students everything you need to achieve your goals!

How Technology helps

What Can McGraw-Hill Technology Offer You?

Whether you are just getting started with technology in your course, or you are ready to embrace the latest advances in electronic content delivery and course management, McGraw-Hill/Irwin has the technology you need, and provides training and support that will help you every step of the way.

Our most popular technologies, Homework Manager and Homework Manager Plus, are optional online Homework Management systems that will allow you to assign problems and exercises from the text for your students to work out in an online format. Student results are automatically graded, and the students receive instant feedback on their work. Homework Manager Plus adds an online version of the book.

Students can also use the Online Learning Center associated with this book to enhance their knowledge of accounting. Plus we now offer iPod content for students who want to study on the go.

For instructors, we provide all of the crucial instructor supplements on one easy to use Instructor CD-ROM; we can help build a custom class Website for your course using PageOut; we can deliver an online course cartridge for you to use in Blackboard, WebCT, or eCollege; and we have a technical support team that will provide training and support for our key technology products.

How Can Students Study on the Go Using Their iPod?

iPod Content

Harness the power of one of the most popular technology tools students use today–the Apple iPod. Our innovative approach allows students to download audio and video presentations right into their iPod and take learning materials with them wherever they go. Students just need to visit the Online Learning Center at **www.mhhe.com/wildFAP19e** to download our iPod content. For each chapter of the book they will be able to download audio narrated lecture presentations and financial accounting videos for use on various versions of iPods. iPod Touch users can even access self-quizzes.

It makes review and study time as easy as putting in headphones.

How Can My Students Use the Web to Complete Their Homework?

McGraw-Hill's Homework Manager®
is a Web-based supplement that duplicates problem structures directly from the end-of-chapter material in your textbook, using algorithms to provide a limitless supply of online self-graded assignments that can be used for student practice, homework, or testing. Each assignment has a unique solution. Say goodbye to cheating in your classroom; say hello to the power and flexibility you've been waiting for in creating assignments. Most Quick Studies, Exercises, and Problems are available with Homework Manager.

McGraw-Hill's Homework Manager is also a useful grading tool. All assignments can be delivered over the Web and are graded automatically, with the results stored in your private grade book. Detailed results let you see at a glance how each student does on an assignment or an individual problem—you can even see how many tries it took them to solve it.

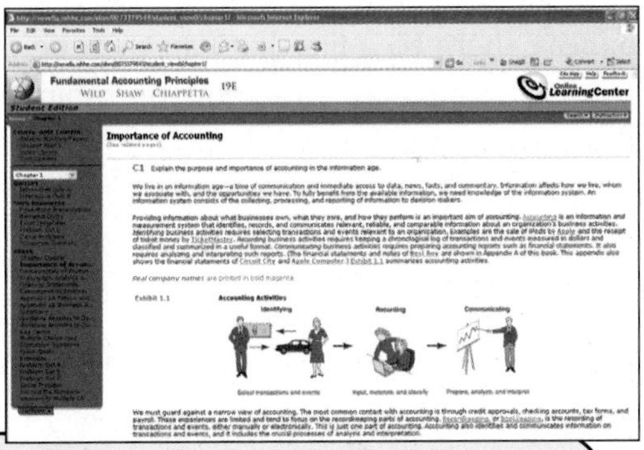

Barbara Gershowitz, Nashville State Technical Community College
"Very thorough . . . and there is a wide variety of supplemental materials that can be used by students. Homework Manager is a real time saver for instructors . . . as it provides immediate feedback to the students and gives them the opportunity to rework problems so that if they did not understand the concept the first time, they can repeat several times until they get it. Homework Manager Plus has worked very well for us. The instructors like it and I have lots of positive feedback from students."

Homework Manager Plus
is an extension of McGraw-Hill's popular Homework Manager System. With Homework Manager Plus you get all of the power of Homework Manager plus an integrated online version of the book. Students simply receive one single access code which provides access to all of the resources available through Homework Manager Plus.

Paula Ratliff, Arkansas State University
"I like the idea that there are online assignments that change algorithmically so that students can practice with them."

When students find themselves needing to reference the textbook to complete their homework, they can now simply click on hints and link directly to the most relevant materials associated with the problem or exercise they are working on.

Use EZ Test Online with Apple iPod® iQuiz to help students succeed.

Using our EZ Test Online you can make test and quiz content available for a student's Apple iPod®.

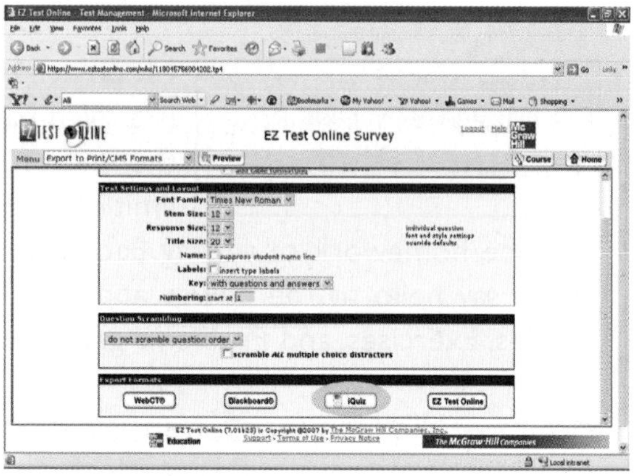

Students must purchase the iQuiz game application from Apple for 99¢ to use the iQuiz content. It works on the iPod fifth generation iPods and better.

Instructors only need EZ Test Online to produce iQuiz-ready content. Instructors take their existing tests and quizzes and export them to a file that can then be made available to the student to take as a self-quiz on their iPods. It's as simple as that.

How Can Text-Related Web Resources Enhance My Course?

Online Learning Center (OLC)

We offer an Online Learning Center (OLC) that follows *Fundamental Accounting Principles* chapter by chapter. It doesn't require any building or maintenance on your part. It's ready to go the moment you and your students type in the URL: **www.mhhe.com/wildFAP19e**.
As students study and learn from *Fundamental Accounting Principles*, they can visit the Student Edition of the OLC Website to work with a multitude of helpful tools:

- Generic Template Working Papers
- Chapter Learning Objectives
- Interactive Chapter Quizzes
- PowerPoint® Presentations
- Problem Set C
- Narrated PowerPoint® Presentations
- Video Library
- Excel Template Assignments
- Animated Demonstration Problems
- iPod Content
- Peachtree Templates

A secured Instructor Edition stores essential course materials to save you prep time before class. Everything you need to run a lively classroom and an efficient course is included. All resources available to students, plus . . .

- General Ledger and Peachtree Solution Files
- Problem Set C Solutions
- Instructor's Manual
- Solutions Manual
- Solutions to Excel Template Assignments
- Test Bank

The OLC Website also serves as a doorway to other technology solutions, like course management systems.

Lillian Grose, Delgado CC
"Logical, concise, comprehensive with excellent publisher support material."

Save money. Go green. McGraw-Hill eBooks.

Green…it's on everybody's mind these days. It's not only about saving trees, it's also about saving money. At 55% of the bookstore price, McGraw-Hill eBooks are an eco-friendly and cost-saving alternative to the traditional printed textbook. So, do some good for the environment…and do some good for your wallet.

CourseSmart

CourseSmart is a new way to find and buy eTextbooks. CourseSmart has the largest selection of eTextbooks available anywhere, offering thousands of the most commonly adopted textbooks from a wide variety of higher education publishers. CourseSmart eTextbooks are available in one standard online reader with full text search, notes, and highlighting, and email tools for sharing between classmates. Visit **www.CourseSmart.com** for more information on ordering.

McGraw-Hill's Homework Manager Plus

If you use Homework Manager in your course, your students can purchase McGraw-Hill's Homework Manager Plus for *FAP* 19e.

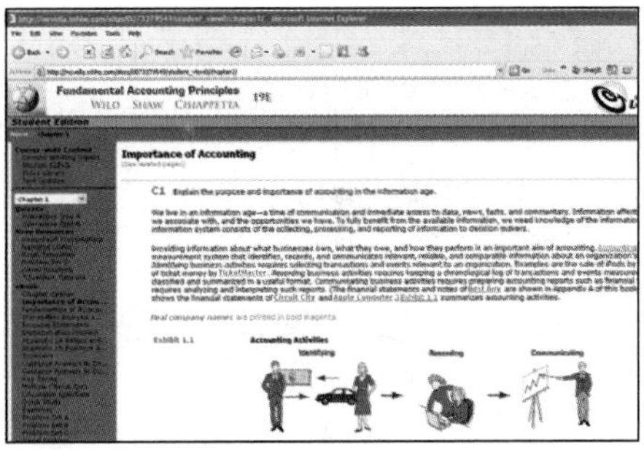

Homework Manager Plus gives students direct access to an online edition of the text while working assignments within Homework Manager. If you get stuck working a problem, simply click the "Hint" link and jump directly to relevant content in the online edition of the text.

Visit the Online Learning Center at www.mhhe.com/wildFAP19e to purchase McGraw-Hill's Homework Manager Plus.

McGraw-Hill/Irwin CARES

At McGraw-Hill/Irwin, we understand that getting the most from new technology can be challenging. That's why our services don't stop after you purchase our book. You can e-mail our Product Specialists 24 hours a day, get product training online, or search our knowledge bank of Frequently Asked Questions on our support Website.

McGraw-Hill/Irwin Customer Care Contact Information

For all Customer Support call **(800) 331-5094**
Email **be_support@mcgraw-hill.com**
Or visit **www.mhhe.com/support**
One of our Technical Support Analysts will be able to assist you in a timely fashion.

How Can McGraw-Hill Help Me Teach My Course Online?

ALEKS®

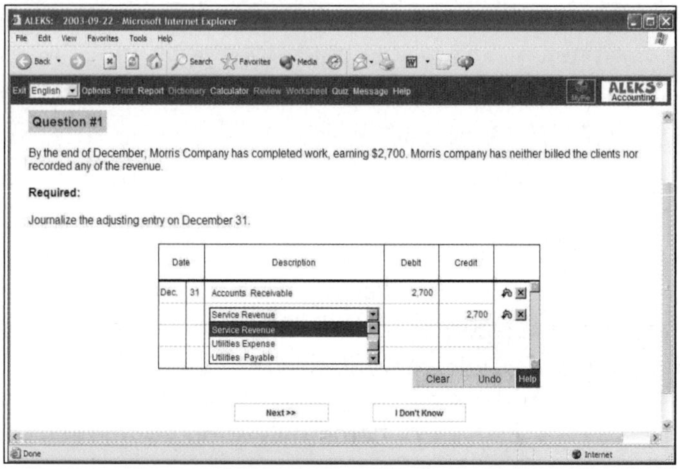

ALEKS® for the Accounting Cycle and ALEKS® for Financial Accounting
Available from McGraw-Hill over the World Wide Web, ALEKS (Assessment and LEarning in Knowledge Spaces) provides precise assessment and individualized instruction in the fundamental skills your students need to succeed in accounting.

ALEKS motivates your students because ALEKS can tell what a student knows, doesn't know, and is most ready to learn next. ALEKS does this using the ALEKS Assessment and Knowledge Space Theory as an artificial intelligence engine to exactly identify a student's knowledge of accounting. When students focus on precisely what they are ready to learn, they build the confidence and learning momentum that fuel success.

To learn more about adding ALEKS to your principles course, visit www.business.aleks.com.

Janice Stoudemire, Midlands Technical College
"The supplemental material that this principles accounting text provides is impressive: homework manager, the extensive online learning center, general ledger application software, as well as ALEKS."

How Can I Make My Classroom Discussions More Interactive?

CPS Classroom Performance System
This is a revolutionary system that brings ultimate interactivity to the classroom. CPS is a wireless response system that gives you immediate feedback from every student in the class. CPS units include easy-to-use software for creating and delivering questions and assessments to your class. With CPS you can ask subjective and objective questions. Then every student simply responds with their individual, wireless response pad, providing instant results. CPS is the perfect tool for engaging students while gathering important assessment data.

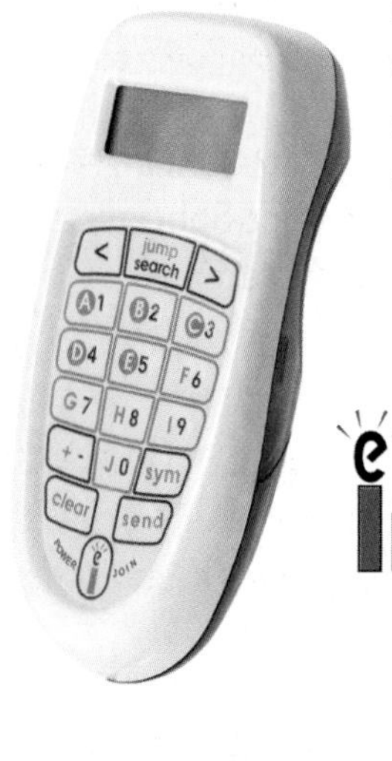

eInstruction®

Liz Ott, Casper College
"I originally adopted the book because of the tools that accompanied it: Homework Manager, ALEKS, CPS."

Online Course Management

No matter what online course management system you use (WebCT, BlackBoard, or eCollege), we have a course content ePack available for *FAP* 19e. Our new ePacks are specifically designed to make it easy for students to navigate and access content online. They are easier than ever to install on the latest version of the course management system available today.

Don't forget that you can count on the highest level of service from McGraw-Hill. Our online course management specialists are ready to assist you with your online course needs. They provide training and will answer any questions you have throughout the life of your adoption. So try our new ePack for *FAP* 19e and make online course content delivery easy and fun.

PageOut: McGraw-Hill's Course Management System

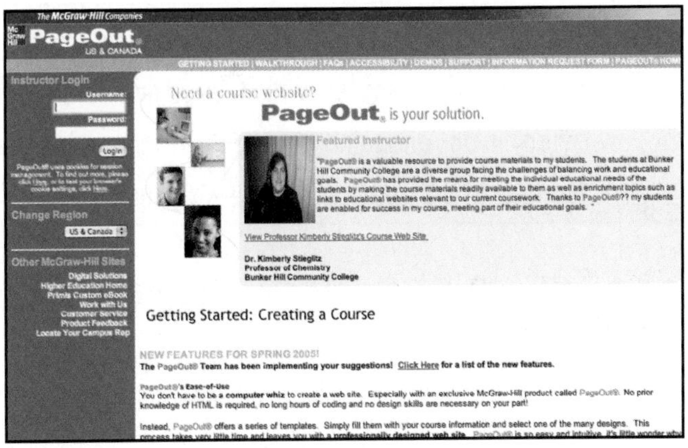

PageOut is the easiest way to create a Website for your accounting course. There is no need for HTML coding, graphic design, or a thick how-to book. Just fill in a series of boxes with simple English and click on one of our professional designs. In no time, your course is online with a Website that contains your syllabus!

Should you need assistance in preparing your Website, we can help. Our team of product specialists is ready to take your course materials and build a custom Website to your specifications. You simply need to call a McGraw-Hill/Irwin PageOut specialist to start the process. To learn more, please visit www.pageout.net and see "PageOut & Service" below.

Best of all, PageOut is free when you adopt *Fundamental Accounting Principles*!

PageOut Service

Our team of product specialists is happy to help you design your own course Website. Just call 1-800-634-3963, press 0, and ask to speak with a PageOut specialist. You will be asked to send in your course materials and then participate in a brief telephone consultation. Once we have your information, we build your Website for you, from scratch.

What tools bring Accounting to life

Decision Center

Whether we prepare, analyze, or apply accounting information, one skill remains essential: decision-making. To help develop good decision-making habits and to illustrate the relevance of accounting, *Fundamental Accounting Principles* 19e uses a unique pedagogical framework called the Decision Center. This framework is comprised of a variety of approaches and subject areas, giving students insight into every aspect of business decision-making. Answers to Decision Maker and Ethics boxes are at the end of each chapter.

Decision Insight

IFRSs IFRSs require that companies report the following four financial statements with explanatory notes:
—Balance sheet —Statement of changes in equity (or statement of recognized revenue and expense)
—Income statement —Statement of cash flows
IFRSs do not prescribe specific formats; and comparative information is required for the preceding period only.

Decision Analysis

A2 Compute the debt ratio and describe its use in analyzing financial condition.

An important business objective is gathering information t pay its debts. Companies finance their assets with either lia a relatively large portion of its assets with liabilities is sai *age*. Higher financial leverage involves greater risk because

Decision Ethics

Credit Manager As a new credit manager, you are being trained by the outgoing manager. She explains that the system prepares checks for amounts net of favorable cash discounts, and the checks are dated the last day of the discount period. She also tells you that checks are not mailed until five days later, adding that "the company gets free use of cash for an extra five days, and our department looks better. When a supplier complains, we blame the computer system and the mailroom." Do you continue this payment policy? [Answer—p. 203]

Decision Maker

Entrepreneur You open a wholesale business selling entertainment equipment to retail outlets. You find that most of your customers demand to buy on credit. How can you use the balance sheets of these customers to decide which ones to extend credit to? [Answer—p. 71]

"This text has the best introductions of any text that I have reviewed or used. Some texts simply summarize the chapter, which is boring to students. Research indicates that material needs to be written in an 'engaging manner.' That's what these vignettes do—they get the students interested."
Clarice McCoy, Brookhaven College

CAP Model

The Conceptual/Analytical/Procedural (CAP) Model allows courses to be specially designed to meet your teaching needs or those of a diverse faculty. This model identifies learning objectives, textual materials, assignments, and test items by C, A, or P, allowing different instructors to teach from the same materials, yet easily customize their courses toward a conceptual, analytical, or procedural approach (or a combination thereof) based on personal preferences.

Learning Objectives

CAP

Conceptual	Analytical	Procedural
C1 Explain the importance of periodic reporting and the time period assumption. *(p. 92)*	A1 Explain how accounting adjustments link to financial statements. *(p. 103)*	P1 Prepare and explain adjusting entries. *(p. 95)*
C2 Explain accrual accounting and how it improves financial statements. *(p. 93)*	A2 Compute profit margin and describe its use in analyzing company performance. *(p. 106)*	P2 Explain and prepare an adjusted trial balance. *(p. 104)*
C3 Identify the types of adjustments and their purpose. *(p. 94)*		P3 Prepare financial statements from an adjusted trial balance. *(p. 104)*
		P4 *Appendix 3A*—Explain the alternatives in accounting for prepaids. *(p. 110)*

LP3

Chapter Preview with Flow Chart

This feature provides a handy textual/visual guide at the start of every chapter. Students can now begin their reading with a clear understanding of what they will learn and when, allowing them to stay more focused and organized along the way.

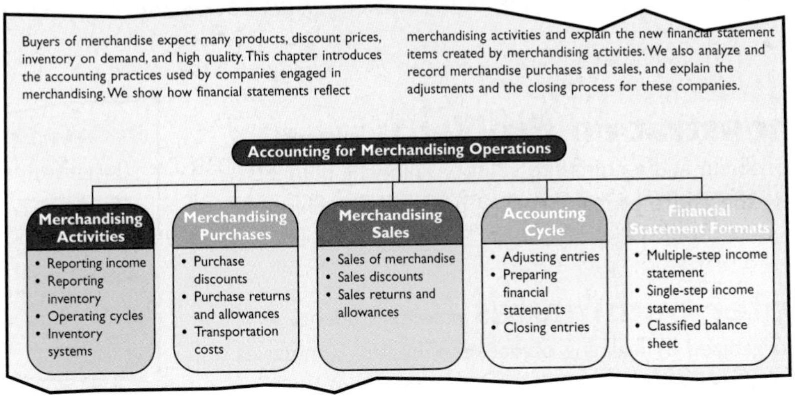

Quick Check

These short question/answer features reinforce the material immediately preceding them. They allow the reader to pause and reflect on the topics described, then receive immediate feedback before going on to new topics. Answers are provided at the end of each chapter.

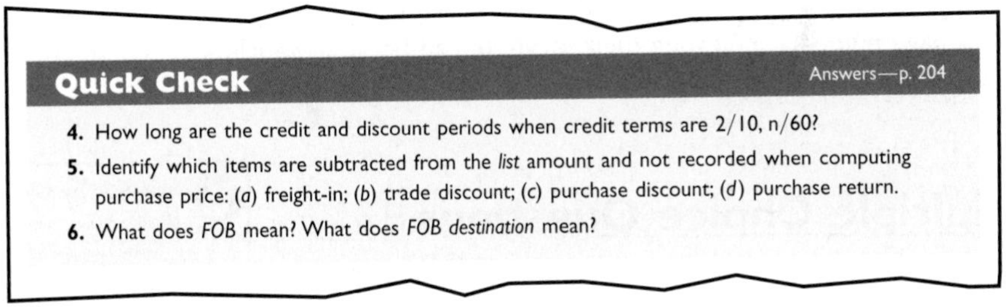

Quick Check Answers—p. 204

4. How long are the credit and discount periods when credit terms are 2/10, n/60?
5. Identify which items are subtracted from the *list* amount and not recorded when computing purchase price: (*a*) freight-in; (*b*) trade discount; (*c*) purchase discount; (*d*) purchase return.
6. What does *FOB* mean? What does *FOB destination* mean?

"(This book is) visually friendly with many illustrations. Good balance sheet presentation in margin."
Joan Cook, Milwaukee Area Technical College

Marginal Student Annotations

These annotations provide students with additional hints, tips, and examples to help them more fully understand the concepts and retain what they have learned. The annotations also include notes on global implications of accounting and further examples.

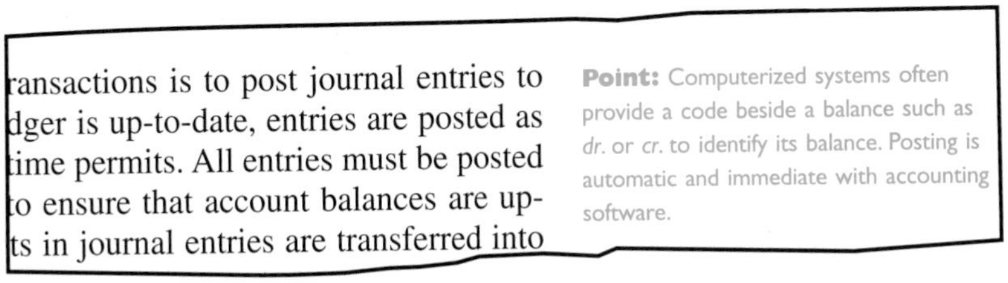

FastForward

FastForward is a case that takes students through the Accounting Cycle, chapters 1-4. The FastForward icon is placed in the margin when this case is discussed.

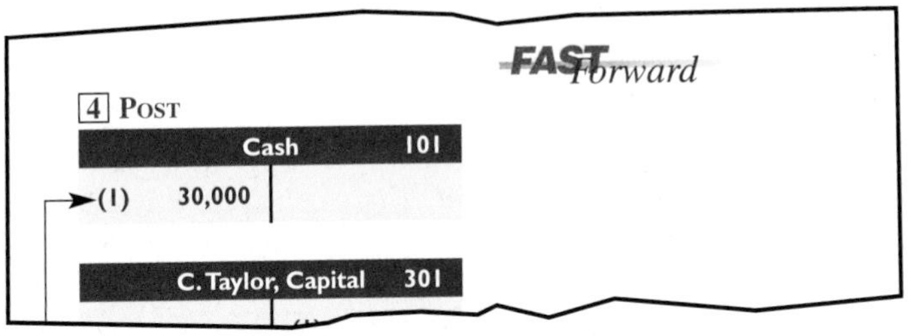

How are chapter concepts

Once a student has finished reading the chapter, how well he or she retains the material can depend greatly on the questions, exercises, and problems that reinforce it. This book leads the way in comprehensive, accurate assignments.

Demonstration Problems present both a problem and a complete solution, allowing students to review the entire problem-solving process and achieve success.

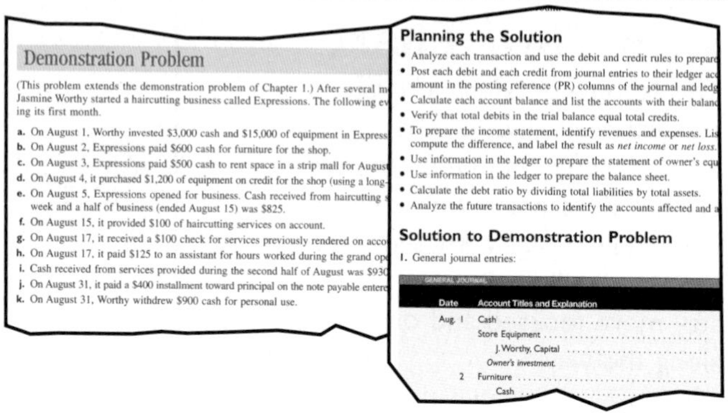

Chapter Summaries provide students with a review organized by learning objectives. Chapter Summaries are a component of the CAP model (see page xiv), which recaps each conceptual, analytical, and procedural objective.

Key Terms are bolded in the text and repeated at the end of the chapter with page numbers indicating their location. The book also includes a complete Glossary of Key Terms.

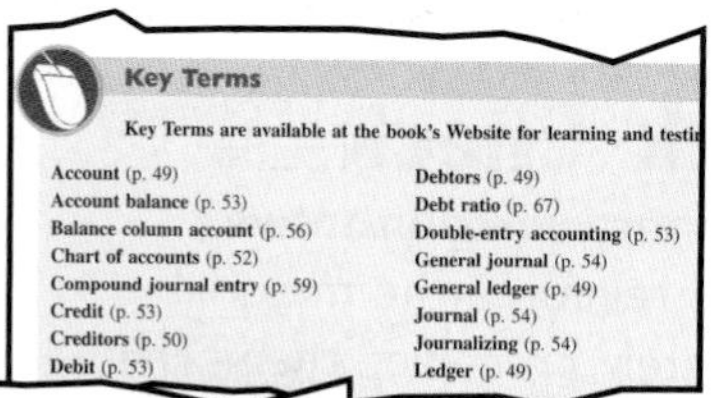

Multiple Choice Questions Multiple Choice Questions quickly test chapter knowledge before a student moves on to complete Quick Studies, Exercises, and Problems.

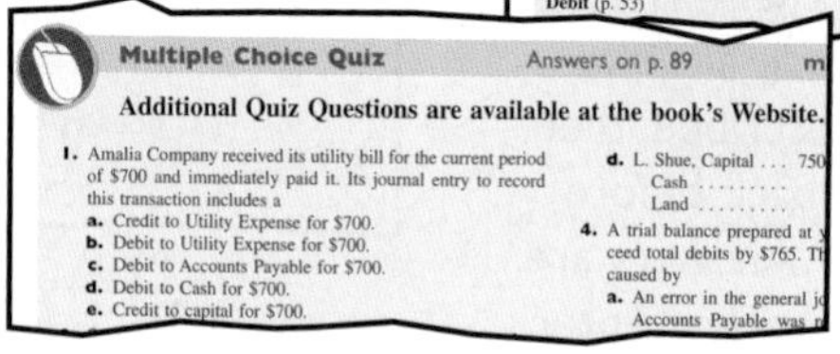

Quick Study assignments are short exercises that often focus on one learning objective. All are included in Homework Manager. There are usually 8-10 Quick Study assignments per chapter.

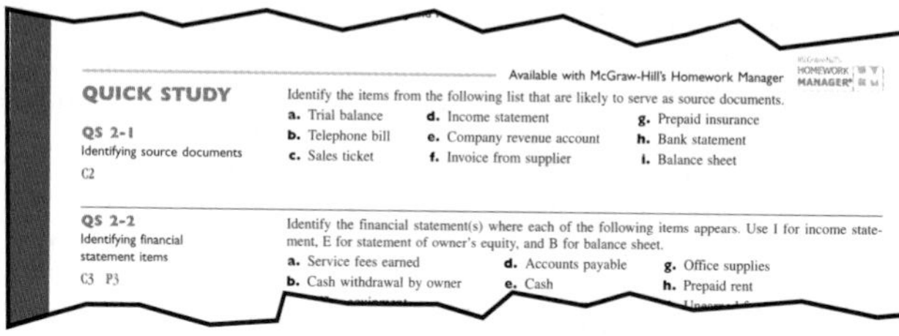

Exercises are one of this book's many strengths and a competitive advantage. There are about 10-15 per chapter and all are included in Homework Manager.

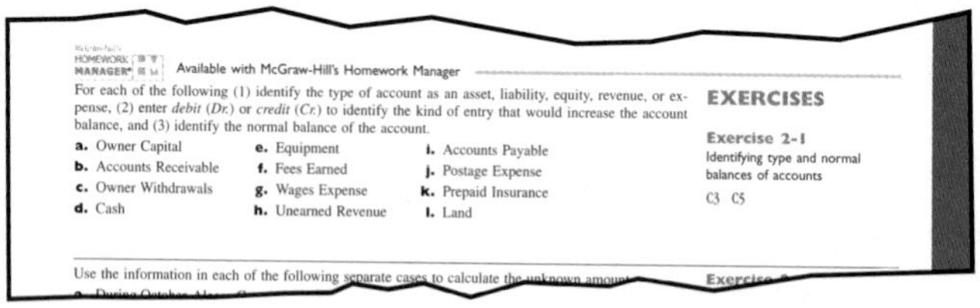

Problem Sets A & B are proven problems that can be assigned as homework or for in-class projects. Problem Set C is available on the book's Website. All problems are coded according to the CAP model (see page xiv), and Set A is included in Homework Manager.

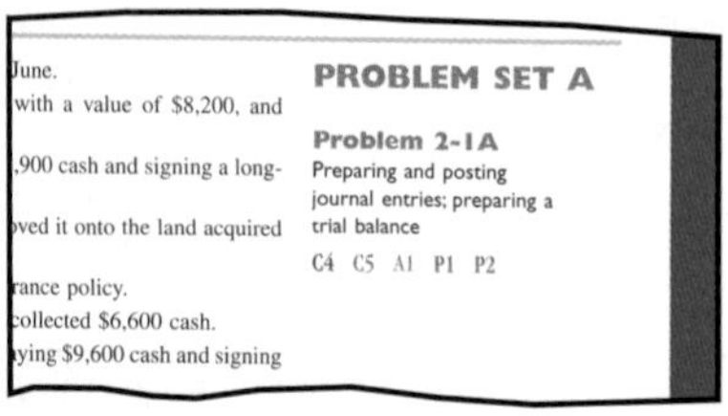

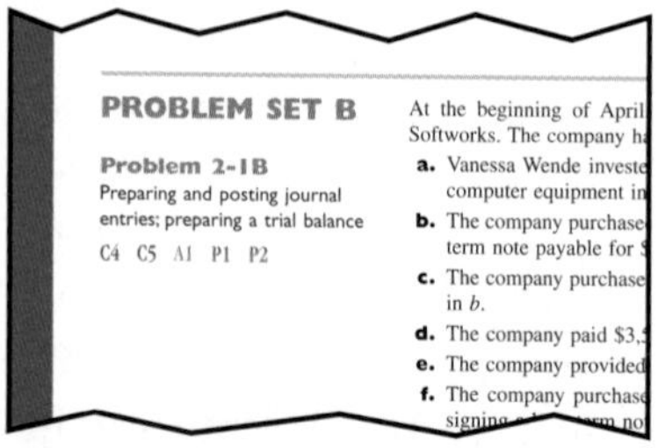

"One of the best features in FAP is the Serial Problem. I find the continuation of a company from a service to a merchandiser, to a manufacturing, and from a sole proprietorship form or business to a corporation, provides the student a real picture of a company's development. It also provides a consistency from one lesson to another."

Barbara Marotta, Northern Virginia Community College, Woodbridge

Beyond the Numbers exercises ask students to use accounting figures and understand their meaning. Students also learn how accounting applies to a variety of business situations. These creative and fun exercises are all new or updated, and are divided into sections:

- Reporting in Action
- Comparative Analysis
- Ethics Challenge
- Communicating in Practice
- Taking It To The Net
- Teamwork in Action
- Hitting the Road
- Entrepreneurial Decision
- Global Decision

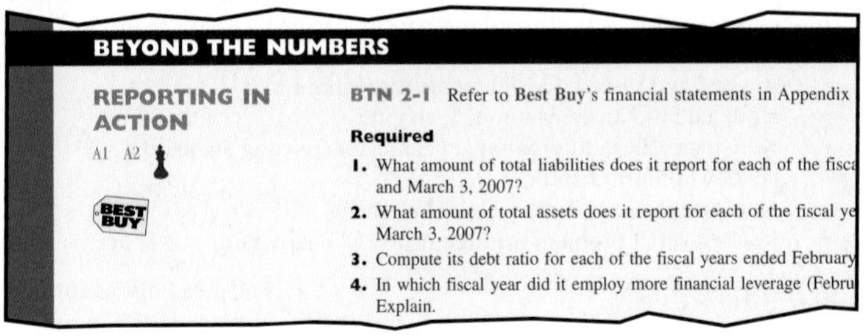

BEYOND THE NUMBERS

REPORTING IN ACTION
A1 A2

BTN 2-1 Refer to Best Buy's financial statements in Appendix

Required

1. What amount of total liabilities does it report for each of the fisca and March 3, 2007?
2. What amount of total assets does it report for each of the fiscal ye March 3, 2007?
3. Compute its debt ratio for each of the fiscal years ended February
4. In which fiscal year did it employ more financial leverage (Febru Explain.

Serial Problem uses a continuous running case study to illustrate chapter concepts in a familiar context. The Serial Problem can be followed continuously from the first chapter or picked up at any later point in the book; enough information is provided to ensure students can get right to work.

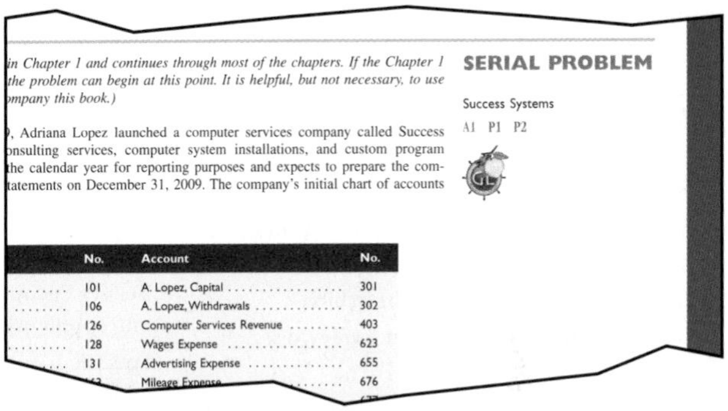

in Chapter 1 and continues through most of the chapters. If the Chapter 1 the problem can begin at this point. It is helpful, but not necessary, to use mpany this book.)

, Adriana Lopez launched a computer services company called Success nsulting services, computer system installations, and custom program he calendar year for reporting purposes and expects to prepare the com- tatements on December 31, 2009. The company's initial chart of accounts

SERIAL PROBLEM

Success Systems
A1 P1 P2

	No.	Account	No.
....	101	A. Lopez, Capital	301
....	106	A. Lopez, Withdrawals	302
....	126	Computer Services Revenue	403
....	128	Wages Expense	623
....	131	Advertising Expense	655
		Mileage Expense	676

"The best feature of this book is the use of real (financial) information in the Beyond the Numbers section. This is something that I do on my own, which can be very time consuming. I also like the Entrepreneurial questions, which are not even addressed in most textbooks."

Cindy Navaroli, Chaffey Community College

The End of the Chapter Is Only the Beginning

Our valuable and proven assignments aren't just confined to the book. From problems that require technological solutions to materials found exclusively online, this book's end-of-chapter material is fully integrated with its technology package.

- Quick Studies, Exercises, and Problems available on Homework Manager (see page ix) are marked with an icon.
- Problems supported by the General Ledger Application Software or Peachtree are marked with an icon.
- Online Learning Center (OLC) includes Interactive Quizzes, Excel template assignments, and more.
- Problems supported with Microsoft Excel template assignments are marked with an icon.

mhhe.com/wildFAP19e

- Material that receives additional coverage (slide shows, videos, audio, etc.) available in iPod ready format are marked with an icon.

Put Away Your Red Pen

We pride ourselves on the accuracy of this book's assignment materials. Independent research reports that instructors and reviewers point to the accuracy of this book's assignment materials as one of its key competitive advantages.

The authors extend a special thanks to accuracy checkers Barbara Schnathorst, The Write Solution, Inc.; Helen Roybark, Radford University; Beth Woods, CPA, Accuracy Counts; David Krug, Johnson Community College; ANSR Source; David Burba, Bowling Green State University; and Marilyn Sagrillo, University of Wisconsin - Green Bay.

Enhancements for FAP 19e

This edition's revisions are driven by feedback from instructors and students. Many of the revisions are summarized here. Feedback suggests that this is the book instructors want to teach from and students want to learn from. General revisions include:

- Revised and updated assignments throughout
- Updated ratio analyses for each chapter
- New material on International Financial Reporting Standards (IFRSs) in most chapters
- New and revised entrepreneurial elements
- Revised serial problem through nearly all chapters
- New art program, visual graphics, and text layout
- New Best Buy Annual Report with comparisons to Circuit City, RadioShack, Apple, and DSG (UK) with new assignments
- New graphics added to each chapter's analysis section
- New iPod content integrated and referenced in book

Chapter 1

Life is Good NEW opener with new entrepreneurial assignment

Revised section on accounting principles and assumptions

New visual layout on building blocks for GAAP

New graphic listing recent publicized accounting scandals

Transaction analysis with expanded accounting equation

Updated compensation data in exhibit

New discussion of conceptual framework linked to IFRSs

Chapter 2

SPANX NEW opener with new entrepreneurial assignment

New 4-step process to learn accounting for transactions: Identify, Analyze, Record, and Post

New sequential art layout for visualizing transaction accounting

New arrow lines link journal entries to the ledger

New material on financial statements related to IFRSs

Chapter 3

PopCap Games NEW opener with new entrepreneurial assignment

New 3-step process for accounting adjustments: (1) Determine what is, (2) Determine what should be, (3) Record adjustment

New summary tables show the accounting adjustment AND account balances before and after adjustment

New adjustment tables for prepaid expenses, including insurance, supplies, and depreciation

New adjustment tables for unearned revenue, accrued expenses, and accrued revenues

Chapter 4

Kathryn Kerrigan NEW opener with new entrepreneurial assignment

New graphic for learning the 4-step closing process

New graphic to aid learning of accounting cycle

Streamlined presentation of classified balance sheet

Chapter 5

BigBadToyStore NEW opener with new entrepreneurial assignment

Enhanced discussions on purchase allowances and purchase returns

Revised discussions on sales returns and sales allowances

Streamlined 4-step process for merchandisers' closing entries

New material on income statement formats for U.S. GAAP vis-à-vis IFRSs

Chapter 6

Beauty Encounter NEW opener with new entrepreneurial assignment

Specific Identification explanation revised for additional clarity

New explanation added to First-in, First-Out

Enhanced explanation to Last-in, First-Out

New description of weighted average

Enhanced explanations for LCM

New material on inventory methods for U.S. GAAP vis-à-vis IFRSs

Illustration of inventory errors is revised and enhanced

Revised exhibit on inventory errors for balance sheet

Appendix 6A, enhanced discussion of periodic inventory

Appendix 6A, expanded explanations of periodic FIFO, LIFO, and weighted average

Chapter 7

TerraCycle NEW opener with new entrepreneurial assignment

Enhanced exhibits for special journals and ledgers

New explanations for controlling and subsidiary ledgers

Updated discussion of enterprise resource planning

Chapter 8

Dylan's Candy Bar NEW opener with new entrepreneurial assignment

New material added on Sarbanes-Oxley and internal controls required

New section on cash management

Additional description of electronic funds transfer

Enhanced explanation of bank reconciliation with new assignments

New discussion of internal controls for IFRSs conversion

Chapter 9

Under Armor NEW opener with new entrepreneurial assignment

Reorganized sections on valuing accounts receivable

Enhanced explanation of recovering a bad debt

New material on assessing the direct write-off method

Reorganized section on estimating bad debts using percent of receivables

New enhanced summary Exhibit 9.13 on methods to estimate bad debts

Added new exercises on bad debts estimation

Chapter 10

Sambazon NEW opener with new entrepreneurial assignment

Updated all real world examples and graphics

Enhanced explanations on declining-balance and impairments

New description of ordinary repairs and its journal entry

Reorganized discussion of betterments and extraordinary repairs

New material on depreciation estimates for U.S. GAAP vis-à-vis IFRSs

Enhanced illustration for depletion including journal entry

Reorganized section on types of intangibles

Enhanced material related to franchises, licenses, trademarks and other intangibles

Enhanced explanation of exchanging plant assets

Chapter 11

Feed Granola Company NEW opener with new entrepreneurial assignment

Updated real world examples including those for Univision, Six Flags, AMF, and K2

New material on contingent liabilities for U.S. GAAP vis-à-vis IFRSs

Updated tax illustrations and assignments using the most recent rates

New section on "Who Pays What Payroll Taxes and Benefits"

Chapter 12

Samanta Shoes NEW opener with new entrepreneurial assignment

Updated real world examples including those for Macadamia Orchards and Big River

Productions

New example of partnership accounting using Trump Entertainment Resorts

Streamlined explanation of partnership liquidation

Chapter 13

Inogen NEW opener with new entrepreneurial assignment

New info graphic on subcategories of authorized stock

Updated many real world examples

New info graphic on stock splits

New material on preferred stock classification for U.S. GAAP vis-à-vis IFRSs

Additional explanation on closing process for corporations

Updated statement of stockholders' equity using Apple

Chapter 14

Rap Snacks NEW opener with new entrepreneurial assignment

Enhanced graphic and explanation of determining bond discount and premium

Revised bond illustration to use a 4-period bond

Streamlined bond illustration to show entire amortization process from issuance to maturity

Streamlined bond illustration for effective interest amortization

New material on bond interest computation for U.S. GAAP vis-à-vis IFRSs

Added new assignments that require accounting for bonds given an amortization table

Chapter 15

Tibi NEW opener with new entrepreneurial assignment

Updated real world examples and graphics including those for Gap, Pfizer, Starbucks, and Brunswick

Enhanced summary graphic on accounting for securities

Updated discussion related to FAS 157 and 159

New material on consolidation per U.S. GAAP vis-à-vis IFRSs

Chapter 16

Jungle Jim's NEW opener with new entrepreneurial assignment

Updated graphics for operating, investing and financing cash flows

Enhanced steps 1 through 5 for preparing the statement of cash flows

Simplified summary Exhibit 16.12 for indirect adjustments

Updated real world examples and graphics including that for Harley, Starbucks, and Nike

New info on indirect vs direct method for U.S. GAAP vis-à-vis IFRSs

Chapter 17

The Motley Fool REVISED opener with new entrepreneurial assignment

New Best Buy, Circuit City and RadioShack data throughout chapter, exhibits, and illustrations with comparative analysis

Enhanced presentation on comparative financial statements

Chapter 18

Kernel Season's NEW opener with new entrepreneurial assignment

New section on fraud and the role of ethics in managerial accounting

Added discussion on Institute of Management Accountants and its road-map for resolving ethical dilemmas

Updated real-world examples including that for Apple

Added balance sheet to exhibits that show cost flows across accounting reports

New discussion on role of nonfinancial information

Chapter 19

Sprinturf NEW opener with new entrepreneurial assignment

New info on custom design involving Nike

Enhanced exhibit on job order production activities

Added discussion linking accurate overhead application for jobs to both product pricing and performance evaluation

Streamlined explanation of closing over- and underapplied overhead

New discussion of employee payroll fraud schemes

Chapter 20

Hood River Juice Company NEW opener with new entrepreneurial assignment

New discussion on impact of automation for quality control and overhead application

Added explanation for use of a process cost summary in product pricing

Chapter 21

RockBottomGolf.com NEW opener with new entrepreneurial assignment

Enhanced explanation of evaluating investment center performance with financial measures

New discussion of residual income

Added explanation of economic value added

New section on evaluating investment center performance with nonfinancial measures including balanced scorecard

New Appendix 21A on transfer pricing

Decision Analysis: new explanation of investment center profit margin and investment turnover with new assignments

Chapter 22

Moe's Southwest Grill NEW opener with new entrepreneurial assignment

New section on working with changes in estimates for CVP analysis

New graphics illustrating how changes in estimates impact break-even analysis

New discussion on weighted average contribution margin in multiple product CVP analysis

New Appendix 22A on using Excel to estimate least squares regression

New assignments on break-even and changes in estimates

Chapter 23

Jibbitz NEW opener with new entrepreneurial assignment

Enhanced discussion of master budgets

New assignments on preparing budgets and budgeted financial statements

Chapter 24

Martin Guitar NEW opener with new entrepreneurial assignment

Reorganized discussion of overhead variance analysis

Revised graphics on framework for understanding overhead variances

New discussion of increased automation for overhead application

Revised explanation of journal entries for standard costing

Simplified discussion of closing variance accounts

New assignments on variance analysis

Added journal entries to chapter demonstration problem

Chapter 25

Prairie Sticks Bat Company NEW opener with new entrepreneurial assignment

New info graphic on cost of capital estimates across industries

Added discussion and example on use of profitability index to compare projects

New discussion on incorporating inflation in net present value calculations

Added explanation on conflicts between meeting analysts' forecasts and choosing profitable long-term projects

New Appendix 25A on using Excel to compute net present value and internal rate of return

New assignments on profitability index

Instructor Supplements

Assurance of Learning Ready

Assurance of learning is an important element of many accreditation standards. *Fundamental Accounting Principles* 19e is designed specifically to support your assurance of learning initiatives.

Each chapter in the book begins with a list of numbered learning objectives which appear throughout the chapter, as well as in the end-of-chapter problems and exercises. Every test bank question is also linked to one of these objectives, in addition to level of difficulty, AICPA skill area, and AACSB skill area. EZ Test, McGraw-Hill's easy-to-use test bank software, can search the test bank by these and other categories, providing an engine for targeted Assurance of Learning analysis and assessment.

AACSB Statement

The McGraw-Hill Companies is a proud corporate member of AACSB International. Understanding the importance and value of AACSB accreditation, *Fundamental Accounting Principles* 19e has sought to recognize the curricula guidelines detailed in the AACSB standards for business accreditation by connecting selected questions in the test bank to the general knowledge and skill guidelines found in the AACSB standards.

The statements contained in *Fundamental Accounting Principles* 19e are provided only as a guide for the users of this text. The AACSB leaves content coverage and assessment within the purview of individual schools, the mission of the school, and the faculty. While *Fundamental Accounting Principles* 19e and the teaching package make no claim of any specific AACSB qualification or evaluation, we have, within the *Fundamental Accounting Principles* 19e test bank labeled questions according to the six general knowledge and skills areas.

Instructor's Resource CD-ROM

FAP 19e, Chapters 1-25
ISBN13: 9780073366456
ISBN10: 0073366455

This is your all-in-one resource. It allows you to create custom presentations from your own materials or from the following text-specific materials provided in the CD's asset library:

- Instructor's Resource Manual
  Written by Barbara Chiappetta, Nassau Community College, and Patricia Walczak, Lansing Community College.
  This manual contains (for each chapter) a Lecture Outline, a chart linking all assignment materials to Learning Objectives, a list of relevant active learning activities, and additional visuals with transparency masters.
- Solutions Manual
- Test Bank, Computerized Test Bank
- PowerPoint® Presentations
  Prepared by Jon Booker, Charles Caldwell, and Susan Galbreth.
  Presentations allow for revision of lecture slides, and includes a viewer, allowing screens to be shown with or without the software.
- Link to PageOut

Test Bank

Vol. 1, Chapters 1-12
ISBN13: 9780073366524
ISBN10: 0073366528

Vol. 2, Chapters 13-25
ISBN13: 9780073366487
ISBN10: 007336648X

Revised by Barbara Gershowitz and Laurie Swanson of Nashville State Technical Community College.

Algorithmic Test Bank

ISBN13: 9780073366395
ISBN10: 0073366390

Solutions Manual

Vol. 1, Chapters 1-12
ISBN13: 9780073366517
ISBN10: 007336651X

Vol. 2, Chapters 13-25
ISBN13: 9780073366470
ISBN10: 0073366471

Written by John J. Wild, Ken W. Shaw, and Marilyn Sagrillo.

Geoffrey Heriot, Greenville Technical College
"The text is well presented and has excellent materials for both students and instructors. It is certainly one of the top texts in an entry level principles of accounting marketplace."

Excel Working Papers CD *(Chapters 1-25)*

ISBN13: 9780073366371
ISBN10: 0073366374

Written by John J. Wild.

Working Papers delivered in Excel spreadsheets. These Excel Working Papers are available on CD-ROM and can be bundled with the printed Working Papers; see your representative for information.

Working Papers

Vol. 1, Chapters 1-12
ISBN13: 9780077289515
ISBN10: 007728951X

Vol. 2, Chapters 12-25
ISBN13: 9780073366364
ISBN10: 0073366366

PFA, Chapters 1-17
ISBN13: 9780073366340
ISBN10: 007336634X

Written by John J. Wild.

Study Guide

Vol. 1, Chapters 1-12
ISBN13: 9780073366388
ISBN10: 0073366382

Vol. 2, Chapters 12-25
ISBN13: 9780073366357
ISBN10: 0073366358

Written by Barbara Chiappetta, Nassau Community College, and Patricia Walczak, Lansing Community College.

Covers each chapter and appendix with reviews of the learning objectives, outlines of the chapters, summaries of chapter materials, and additional problems with solutions.

Carol Yacht's General Ledger CD-ROM

ISBN13: 9780073366401
ISBN10: 0073366404

The CD-ROM includes fully functioning versions of McGraw-Hill's own General Ledger Application software. Problem templates prepared by Carol Yacht and student user guides are included that allow you to assign text problems for working in Yacht's General Ledger or Peachtree.

Contributing Author
The authors and book team wish to thank Marilyn Sagrillo for her excellent contributions.

Marilyn Sagrillo is an associate professor at the University of Wisconsin at Green Bay. She received her BA and MS from Northern Illinois University and her PhD from the University of Wisconsin at Madison. Her scholarly articles are published in *Accounting Enquiries*, *Journal of Accounting Case Research*, and the *Missouri Society of CPAs Casebook*. She is a member of the American Accounting Association and the Institute of Management Accountants. She previously received the UWGB Founder's Association Faculty Award for Excellence in Teaching. Professor Sagrillo is an active volunteer for the Midwest Renewable Energy Association. She also enjoys reading, traveling, and hiking.

Acknowledgments

John J. Wild, Ken W. Shaw, Barbara Chiappetta, and McGraw-Hill/Irwin would like to recognize the following instructors for their valuable feedback and involvement in the development of *Fundamental Accounting Principles* 19e. We are thankful for their suggestions, counsel, and encouragement.

Janet Adeyiga, Hampton University

Audrey Agnello, Niagara County Community College

John Ahmad, Northern Virginia Community College

Sylvia Allen, Los Angeles Valley College

Donna Altepeter, University of North Dakota

Juanita Ardavany, Los Angeles Valley College

Charles Baird, University of Wisconsin-Stout

Scott Barhight, Northampton Community College

Richard Barnhart, Grand Rapids Community College

Mary Barnum, Grand Rapids Community College

Allen Bealle, Delgado Community College

Susan Beasley, Community College of Baltimore County-Catonsville

Beverly Beatty, Anne Arundel Community College

Irene Bembenista, Davenport University

Laurel Berry, Bryant and Stratton College

Jaswinder Bhangal, Chabot College

Rick Bowden, Oakland Community College-Auburn Hills

Deborah Boyce, Mohawk Valley Community College

Nancy Boyd, Middle Tennessee State University

Debbie Branch, Surry Community College

Karen Brayden, Front Range Community College-Fort Collins

Nat Briscoe, Northwestern State University

Linda Bruff, Strayer University

Scott Butterfield, University of Colorado-Colorado Springs

James Capone, Kean University

Roy Carson, Anne Arundel Community College

Trudy Chiaravelli, Lansing Community College

Siu Chung, Los Angeles Valley College

Marilyn Ciolino, Delgado Community College

Ken Coffey, Johnson County Community College

Edwin Cohen, DePaul University

Kerry Colton, Aims Community College-Main Campus

James Cosby, John Tyler Community College

Kenneth Couvillion, San Joaquin Delta College

Ana Cruz, Miami-Dade College-Wolfson

Walter DeAguero, Saddleback College

Suryekaent Desai, Cedar Valley College-Lancaster

Mike Deschamps, Chaffey College

Susan Dickey, Motlow State Community College

Beth Dietz, South Texas College

Andy Dressler, Walla Walla College

Betty Driver, Murray State University

Michael Farina, Cerritos College

Jeannie Folk, College of DuPage

Jim Formosa, Nashville State Technical College

Ron Dustin, Fresno City College

Anthony Espisito, Community College of Baltimore County-Essex

Steve Fabian, Hudson County Community College

Patricia Feller, Nashville State Technical Community College

Anna Fitzpatrick, Gloucester City College

John Gabelman, Columbus State Community College

Dan Galvin, Diablo Valley College

Barbara Gershowitz, Nashville State Technical Community College

Lillian Grose, Delgado Community College

Betty Habershon, Prince George's Community College

Patricia Halliday, Santa Monica College

Jeff Hamm, University of Arkansas-Little Rock

John Hancock, University of California Davis

Jeannie Harrington, Middle Tennessee State University

Sara Harris, Arapahoe Community College

Laurie Hays, Western Michigan University-Kalamazoo

Kathy Hill, Leeward Community College

Patricia Holmes, Des Moines Area Community College

Constance Hylton, George Mason University

Vincent Huygen, North Greenville University

Bill Johnstone, Montgomery College

Jeffery Jones, Community College of Southern Nevada

Richard Irvine, Pensacola Jr. College

Irv Jason, Southwest Tennessee Community College-Macon Campus

Frank Jordan, Erie Community College South Campus-Orchard Park

Thomas Kam, Hawaii Pacific University

John Karbens, Hawaii Pacific University

George Katzt, Phillips College

Charles Kee, Kingsborough Community College

Howard Keller, Indiana University/Purdue University Indiana

Monique Kelly (Byrd), Fresno City College

Chula King, University of West Florida

Debra Kiss, Davenport University

Shirley Kleiner, Johnson County Community College

Robert Koch, St. Peter's College

Jerry Kreuze, Western Michigan University

David Krug, Johnson County Community College

Tara Laken, Joliet Junior College

Michael Landers, Middlesex County Community College

Sherman Layell, Surry Community College

Philip Lee, Nashville State Technical Community College

Paul Lee, Cleveland State University

Natasha Librizzi, Milwaukee Area Technical College

Danny Litt, University of California-Los Angeles

Steve Ludwig, Northwest Missouri State University

Maria Mari, Miami Dade College

Diane Marker, University of Toledo-Scott Park

Barbara Marotta, Northern Virginia Community College-Woodbridge

Brenda Mattison, Tri-County Technical College

Lynn Mazzola, Nassau County Community College

Cynthia McCall, Des Moines Area Community College

Patricia McClure, Springfield Technical Community College

Robert Mcwhorter, Northwest Vista College

Audrey Morrison, Pensacola Junior College

Andrea Murowski, Brookdale Community College

Tim Murphy, Diablo Valley College

Joe Nicassio, Westmoreland County Community College

Jamie O'Brien, South Dakota State University

Kathleen O'Donnell, Onondaga Community College

Ralph Ostrowski, Illinois Central College

Shelley Ota, Lee Ward Community College

Susan Pallas, Southeast Community College

Thomas Parker, Surry Community College

Ash Patel, Normandale Community College

Anahid Petrosian, South Texas College

Yvonne Phang, Boro of Manhattan Community College

Mary Phillips, Middle Tennessee State University

Gary Pieroni, Diablo Valley College

Greg Prescott, University of Southern Alabama

Paula Ratliff, Arkansas State University-State University

David Ravetch, University of California-Los Angeles

Jenny Resnick, Santa Monica College

Jim Riley, Palo Alto College

Richard Roding, Red Rocks Community College

Linda Rose, Westwood College

Al Ruggiero, Suffolk County Community College-Selden

Roger Sands, Milwaukee Area Tech-Milwaukee

Marilyn Sagrillo, University of Wisconsin-Green Bay

Richard Sarkisian, Camden County College

Wallace Satchell, St. Phillips College

Christine Schalow, University of Wisconsin-Stevens Point

William Schmalz, Sanford Brown College

Brad Smith, Des Moines Area Community College

Nancy Snow, University of Toledo

Laura Solano, Pueblo Community College

Charles Spector, State University of New York-Oswego

Gene Sullivan, Liberty University

Laurie Swanson, Nashville State Technical Community College

Larry Swisher, Muskegon County Community College

Margaret Tanner, University of Arkansas-Fort Smith

Domenico Tavella, Pittsburgh Technical Institute

Thomas G. Thompson, Madison Area Technical College

Debra Tyson, Bryant & Stratton College

Shafi Ullah, Broward Community College

Bob Urell, Irvine Valley College

Patricia Walczak, Lansing Community College

Valerie Walmsley, South Texas College

Keith Weidkamp, Sierra College

Dale Westfall, Midland College

Gloria Worthy, Southwest Tennessee Community College

Ray Wurzburger, New River Community College

Lynnette Yerbury, St. Louis Community College

Judith Zander, Grossmont College

In addition to the helpful and generous colleagues listed above, we thank the entire McGraw-Hill/Irwin *Fundamental Accounting Principles* 19e team, including Stewart Mattson, Tim Vertovec, Steve Schuetz, Christina Sanders, Sharon Monday of Aptara, Lori Koetters, Matthew Baldwin, Carol Bielski, and Brian Nacik. We also thank the great marketing and sales support staff, including Krista Bettino, Sankha Basu, and Randy Sealy. Many talented educators and professionals worked hard to create the supplements for this book, and for their efforts we're grateful. Finally, many more people we either did not meet or whose efforts we did not personally witness nevertheless helped to make this book everything that it is, and we thank them all.

John J. Wild *Ken W. Shaw* *Barbara Chiappetta*

Brief Contents

Contents

14 Long-Term Liabilities 548

15 Investments and International Operations 590

16 Reporting the Statement of Cash Flows 626

17 Analysis of Financial Statements 678

Principles of Financial Accounting

A Look at This Chapter

Accounting is crucial in our information age. In this chapter, we discuss the importance of accounting to different types of organizations and describe its many users and uses. We explain that ethics are essential to accounting. We also explain business transactions and how they are reflected in financial statements.

A Look Ahead

Chapter 2 describes and analyzes business transactions. We explain the analysis and recording of transactions, the ledger and trial balance, and the double-entry system. More generally, Chapters 2 through 4 show (via the accounting cycle) how financial statements reflect business activities.

Chapter 1 Accounting in Business

Learning Objectives

***Learning Objectives** are classified as conceptual, analytical, or procedural.*

CAP

Conceptual

C1 Explain the purpose and importance of accounting in the information age. *(p. 4)*

C2 Identify users and uses of accounting. *(p. 5)*

C3 Identify opportunities in accounting and related fields. *(p. 6)*

C4 Explain why ethics are crucial to accounting. *(p. 8)*

C5 Explain generally accepted accounting principles and define and apply several accounting principles. *(p. 9)*

C6 *Appendix 1B*—Identify and describe the three major activities of organizations. *(p. 24)*

Analytical

A1 Define and interpret the accounting equation and each of its components. *(p. 12)*

A2 Analyze business transactions using the accounting equation. *(p. 13)*

A3 Compute and interpret return on assets. *(p. 20)*

A4 *Appendix 1A*—Explain the relation between return and risk. *(p. 23)*

Procedural

P1 Identify and prepare basic financial statements and explain how they interrelate. *(p. 17)*

LP1

Decision Feature

*A **Decision Feature** launches each chapter showing the relevance of accounting for a real entrepreneur. An **Entrepreneurial Decision** problem at the end of the assignments returns to this feature with a mini-case.*

Life Is Good

"People are drawn to Jake usually with a grin or a big laugh . . . Jake rules!" — Bert Jacobs

BOSTON—Bert and John Jacobs launched their T-shirt company, **Life is good® (Lifeisgood.com),** with "nothing in our bank account and $78 in cash," explains Bert. Sales activities involved peddling T-shirts on college campuses and at street fairs. Although they lived and slept in their van and made only enough to pay for food and gas, they stayed the course. Then, Bert says, "We created Jake, and he showed us the way!"

Jake is the smiling stick figure that now adorns their products. Bert and John first drew Jake on their apartment wall and then printed him on a batch of T-shirts that sold within an hour at a Cambridge street fair. "It scared the hell out of us," says Bert. "We looked at each other and said, 'Oh my God, what do we have here?' " What they had was a Hollywood story in the making. Within a few years, Jake was adorning T-shirts, sweatshirts, and headwear and was producing millions in sales.

Bert and John have integrated their fun and quirky style into their business. A walk through the Life is good factory reveals blaring music, popcorn machines, free-roaming dogs, and giant murals on bright-colored walls. "We take our inspiration from Dr. Seuss," insists Bert. "We like to feel that in our own way we're having a positive impact . . . and having a lot of fun along the way." The brothers have successfully organized their business, set up accounting systems, learned to prepare and read financial reports, and apply financial analysis. Adds John, "Consistent performance is what has enhanced and strengthened [our products]."

The brothers' accounting system tracks all transactions, and they regularly prepare financial reports when making business decisions. Those accounting realities have been creatively merged with their fun-loving approach. In recent years, Life is good has held a factory talent show, bowling tournament, and watermelon seed–spitting contest. The brothers exude positive thinking. "The foundation of our brand is optimism," explains Bert, "and optimism is timeless."

[Sources: *Life is good Website*, January 2009; *SGB*, January 2006; *Boston Common*, Winter 2006; *Worthwhile Magazine*, 2005; *American Executive*, August 2005; *Inc.*, October 2006; *Entrepreneur*, May 2007]

*A **Preview** opens each chapter with a summary of topics covered.*

Today's world is one of information—its preparation, communication, analysis, and use. Accounting is at the core of this information age. Knowledge of accounting gives us career opportunities and the insight to take advantage of them. This book introduces concepts, procedures, and analyses that help us make better decisions, including career choices. In this chapter we describe accounting, the users and uses of accounting information, the forms and activities of organizations, and several accounting principles. We also introduce transaction analysis and financial statements.

Accounting in Business

Importance of Accounting
- Accounting information users
- Opportunities in accounting

Fundamentals of Accounting
- Ethics—key concept
- Generally accepted accounting principles

Transaction Analysis
- Accounting equation
- Transaction analysis—illustrated

Financial Statements
- Income statement
- Statement of owner's equity
- Balance sheet
- Statement of cash flows

Importance of Accounting

C1 Explain the purpose and importance of accounting in the information age.

Video1.1

Why is accounting so popular on campuses? Why are there so many accounting jobs for graduates? Why is accounting so important to companies? Why do politicians and business leaders focus on accounting regulations? The answer is that we live in an information age, where that information, and its reliability, impacts the financial well-being of us all.

Accounting is an information and measurement system that identifies, records, and communicates relevant, reliable, and comparable information about an organization's business activities. *Identifying* business activities requires selecting transactions and events relevant to an organization. Examples are the sale of iPods by **Apple** and the receipt of ticket money by **TicketMaster**. *Recording* business activities requires keeping a chronological log of transactions and events measured in dollars and classified and summarized in a useful format. *Communicating* business activities requires preparing accounting reports such as financial statements. It also requires analyzing and interpreting such reports. (The financial statements and notes of **Best Buy** are shown in Appendix A of this book. This appendix also shows the financial statements of **Circuit City**, **RadioShack**, and **Apple**.) Exhibit 1.1 summarizes accounting activities.

Real company names *are printed in bold magenta.*

We must guard against a narrow view of accounting. The most common contact with accounting is through credit approvals, checking accounts, tax forms, and payroll. These experiences are limited and tend to focus on the recordkeeping parts of accounting. **Recordkeeping,** or **bookkeeping,** is the recording of transactions and events, either manually or electronically. This

EXHIBIT 1.1
Accounting Activities

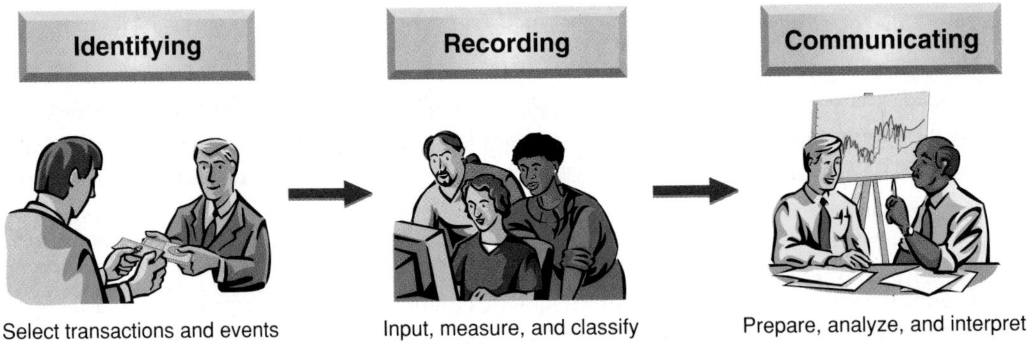

is just one part of accounting. Accounting also identifies and communicates information on transactions and events, and it includes the crucial processes of analysis and interpretation.

Technology is a key part of modern business and plays a major role in accounting. Technology reduces the time, effort, and cost of recordkeeping while improving clerical accuracy. Some small organizations continue to perform various accounting tasks manually, but even they are impacted by technology. As technology has changed the way we store, process, and summarize masses of data, accounting has been freed to expand. Consulting, planning, and other financial services are now closely linked to accounting. These services require sorting through data, interpreting their meaning, identifying key factors, and analyzing their implications.

***Margin notes** further enhance the textual material.*

Point: Technology is only as useful as the accounting data available, and users' decisions are only as good as their understanding of accounting. The best software and recordkeeping cannot make up for lack of accounting knowledge.

Users of Accounting Information

Accounting is often called the *language of business* because all organizations set up an accounting information system to communicate data to help people make better decisions. Exhibit 1.2 shows that the accounting information system serves many kinds of users (this is a partial listing) who can be divided into two groups: external users and internal users.

EXHIBIT 1.2

Users of Accounting Information

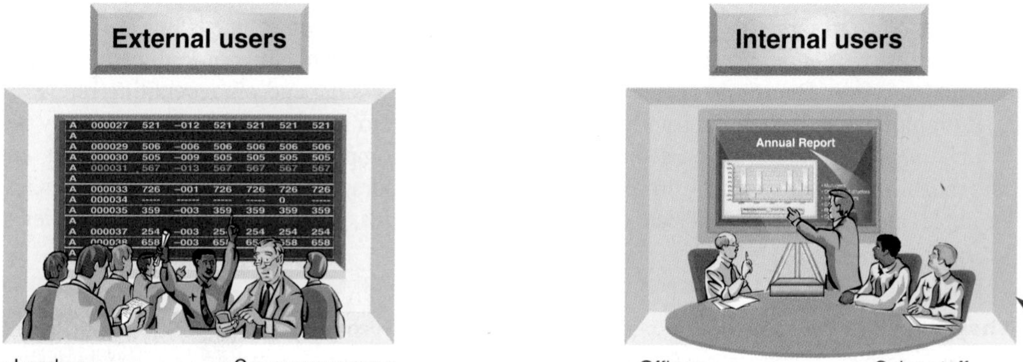

- Lenders
- Shareholders
- Governments
- Consumer groups
- External auditors
- Customers

- Officers
- Managers
- Internal auditors
- Sales staff
- Budget officers
- Controllers

***Infographics** reinforce key concepts through visual learning.*

C2 Identify users and uses of accounting.

External Information Users **External users** of accounting information are *not* directly involved in running the organization. They include shareholders (investors), lenders, directors, customers, suppliers, regulators, lawyers, brokers, and the press. External users have limited access to an organization's information. Yet their business decisions depend on information that is reliable, relevant, and comparable.

Financial accounting is the area of accounting aimed at serving external users by providing them with *general-purpose financial statements*. The term *general-purpose* refers to the broad range of purposes for which external users rely on these statements.

Each external user has special information needs depending on the types of decisions to be made. *Lenders* (creditors) loan money or other resources to an organization. Banks, savings and loans, co-ops, and mortgage and finance companies are lenders. Lenders look for information to help them assess whether an organization is likely to repay its loans with interest. *Shareholders* (investors) are the owners of a corporation. They use accounting reports in deciding whether to buy, hold, or sell stock. Shareholders typically elect a *board of directors* to oversee their interests in an organization. Since directors are responsible to shareholders, their information needs are similar. *External* (independent) *auditors* examine financial statements to verify that they are prepared according to generally accepted accounting principles. *Employees* and *labor unions* use financial statements to judge the fairness of wages, assess job prospects, and bargain for better wages. *Regulators* often have legal authority over certain activities of organizations. For example, the Internal Revenue Service (IRS) and other tax authorities require organizations to file accounting reports in computing taxes. Other regulators include utility boards that use accounting information to set utility rates and securities regulators that require reports for companies that sell their stock to the public.

Accounting serves the needs of many other external users. *Voters, legislators,* and *government officials* use accounting information to monitor and evaluate government receipts and expenses. *Contributors* to nonprofit organizations use accounting information to evaluate the use and impact of their donations. *Suppliers* use accounting information to judge the soundness of a customer before making sales on credit, and *customers* use financial reports to assess the staying power of potential suppliers.

Internal Information Users **Internal users** of accounting information are those directly involved in managing and operating an organization. They use the information to help improve the efficiency and effectiveness of an organization. **Managerial accounting** is the area of accounting that serves the decision-making needs of internal users. Internal reports are not subject to the same rules as external reports and instead are designed with the special needs of internal users in mind.

There are several types of internal users, and many are managers of key operating activities. *Research and development managers* need information about projected costs and revenues of any proposed changes in products and services. *Purchasing managers* need to know what, when, and how much to purchase. *Human resource managers* need information about employees' payroll, benefits, performance, and compensation. *Production managers* depend on information to monitor costs and ensure quality. *Distribution managers* need reports for timely, accurate, and efficient delivery of products and services. *Marketing managers* use reports about sales and costs to target consumers, set prices, and monitor consumer needs, tastes, and price concerns. *Service managers* require information on the costs and benefits of looking after products and services. Decisions of these and other internal users depend on accounting reports.

Both internal and external users rely on internal controls to monitor and control company activities. *Internal controls* are procedures set up to protect company property and equipment, ensure reliable accounting reports, promote efficiency, and encourage adherence to company policies. Examples are good records, physical controls (locks, passwords, guards), and independent reviews.

Decision Insight *boxes highlight relevant items from practice.*

Decision Insight

They Fought the Law Our economic and social welfare depends on reliable accounting information. A few managers forgot that and are now paying their dues. They include L. Dennis Kozlowski (in photo) of **Tyco**, convicted of falsifying accounting records; Bernard Ebbers of **WorldCom**, convicted of an $11 billion accounting scandal, Andrew Fastow of **Enron**, guilty of hiding debt and inflating income, and Joe Nacchio of **Qwest**, accused of falsely reporting sales.

Opportunities in Accounting

C3 Identify opportunities in accounting and related fields.

Accounting information affects many aspects of our lives. When we earn money, pay taxes, invest savings, budget earnings, and plan for the future, we are influenced by accounting. Accounting has four broad areas of opportunities: financial, managerial, taxation, and accounting-related. Exhibit 1.3 lists selected opportunities in each area.

EXHIBIT 1.3

Accounting Opportunities

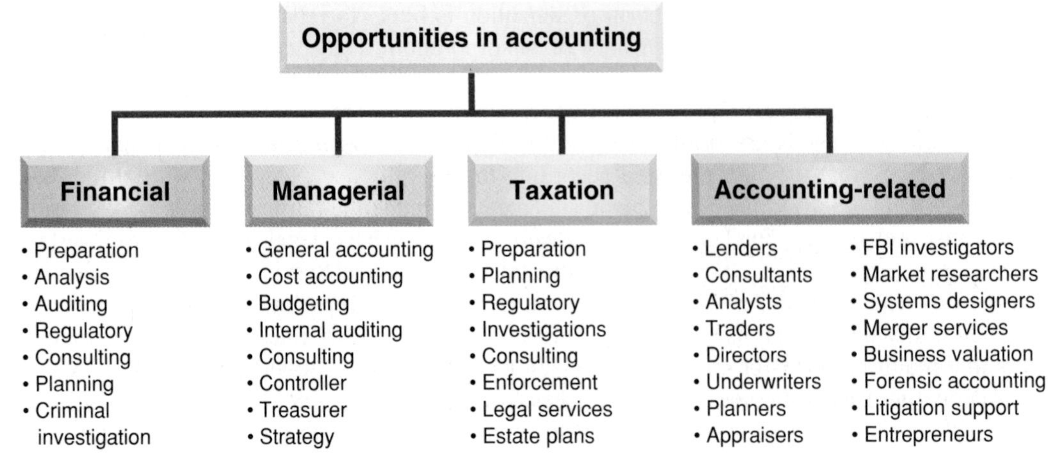

The majority of accounting opportunities are in *private accounting,* as shown in Exhibit 1.4. *Public accounting* offers the next largest number of opportunities. Still other opportunities exist in government (and not-for-profit) agencies, including business regulation and investigation of law violations.

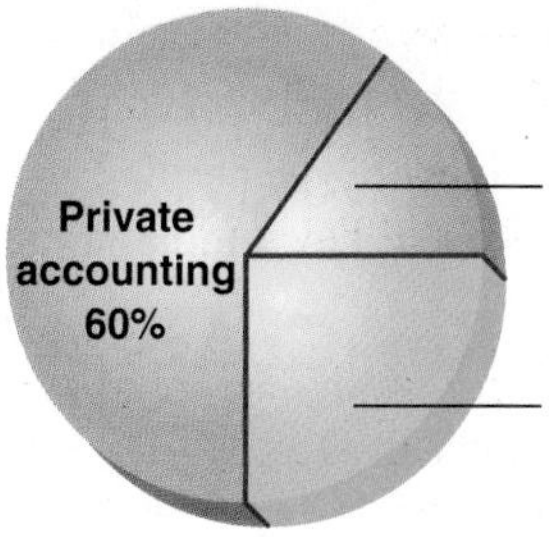

EXHIBIT 1.4

Accounting Jobs by Area

Accounting specialists are highly regarded. Their professional standing often is denoted by a certificate. Certified public accountants (CPAs) must meet education and experience requirements, pass an examination, and exhibit ethical character. Many accounting specialists hold certificates in addition to or instead of the CPA. Two of the most common are the certificate in management accounting (CMA) and the certified internal auditor (CIA). Employers also look for specialists with designations such as certified bookkeeper (CB), certified payroll professional (CPP), personal financial specialist (PFS), certified fraud examiner (CFE), and certified forensic accountant (CrFA).

Point: The largest accounting firms are Deloitte & Touche, Ernst & Young, PricewaterhouseCoopers, and KPMG.

Individuals with accounting knowledge are always in demand as they can help with financial analysis, strategic planning, e-commerce, product feasibility analysis, information technology, and financial management. Benefit packages can include flexible work schedules, telecommuting options, career path alternatives, casual work environments, extended vacation time, and child and elder care.

Demand for accounting specialists is booming. Exhibit 1.5 reports average annual salaries for several accounting positions. Salary variation depends on location, company size, professional designation, experience, and other factors. For example, salaries for chief financial officers (CFO) range from under $75,000 to more than $1 million per year. Likewise, salaries for bookkeepers range from under $30,000 to more than $80,000.

Point: Census Bureau (2007) reports that for workers 18 and over, higher education yields higher average pay:

Advanced degree	$79,946
Bachelor's degree	54,689
High school degree	29,448
No high school degree	19,915

EXHIBIT 1.5

Accounting Salaries for Selected Fields

Field	Title (experience)	2007 Salary	2012 Estimate*
Public Accounting	Partner	$190,000	$242,500
	Manager (6–8 years)	94,500	120,500
	Senior (3–5 years)	72,000	92,000
	Junior (0–2 years)	51,500	65,500
Private Accounting	CFO	232,000	296,000
	Controller/Treasurer	147,500	188,000
	Manager (6–8 years)	87,500	111,500
	Senior (3–5 years)	72,500	92,500
	Junior (0–2 years)	49,000	62,500
Recordkeeping	Full-charge bookkeeper	57,500	73,500
	Accounts manager	51,000	65,000
	Payroll manager	54,500	69,500
	Accounting clerk (0–2 years)	37,500	48,000

* Estimates assume a 5% compounded annual increase over current levels.

Point: For updated salary information:
www.AICPA.org
Abbott-Langer.com
Kforce.com

Quick Check

Answers—p. 26

Quick Check is a chance to stop and reflect on key points.

1. What is the purpose of accounting?
2. What is the relation between accounting and recordkeeping?
3. Identify some advantages of technology for accounting.
4. Who are the internal and external users of accounting information?
5. Identify at least five types of managers who are internal users of accounting information.
6. What are internal controls and why are they important?

Fundamentals of Accounting

Accounting is guided by principles, standards, concepts, and assumptions. This section describes several of these key fundamentals of accounting.

Ethics—A Key Concept

C4 Explain why ethics are crucial to accounting.

The goal of accounting is to provide useful information for decisions. For information to be useful, it must be trusted. This demands ethics in accounting. **Ethics** are beliefs that distinguish right from wrong. They are accepted standards of good and bad behavior.

Identifying the ethical path is sometimes difficult. The preferred path is a course of action that avoids casting doubt on one's decisions. For example, accounting users are less likely to trust an auditor's report if the auditor's pay depends on the success of the client's business. To avoid such concerns, ethics rules are often set. For example, auditors are banned from direct investment in their client and cannot accept pay that depends on figures in the client's reports. Exhibit 1.6 gives guidelines for making ethical decisions.

Point: Sarbanes-Oxley Act requires each issuer of securities to disclose whether it has adopted a code of ethics for its senior financial officers and the contents of that code.

EXHIBIT 1.6

Guidelines for Ethical Decision Making

Identify ethical concerns → **Analyze options** → **Make ethical decision**

Use personal ethics to recognize an ethical concern.

Consider all good and bad consequences.

Choose best option after weighing all consequences.

Providers of accounting information often face ethical choices as they prepare financial reports. These choices can affect the price a buyer pays and the wages paid to workers. They can even affect the success of products and services. Misleading information can lead to a wrongful closing of a division that harms workers, customers, and suppliers. There is an old saying: *Good ethics are good business.*

Some people extend ethics to *social responsibility,* which refers to a concern for the impact of actions on society. An organization's social responsibility can include donations to hospitals, colleges, community programs, and law enforcement. It also can include programs to reduce pollution, increase product safety, improve worker conditions, and support continuing education. These programs are not limited to large companies. For example, many small businesses offer discounts to students and senior citizens. Still others help sponsor events such as the Special Olympics and summer reading programs.

Point: The American Institute of Certified Public Accountants' *Code of Professional Conduct* is available at www.AICPA.org.

Decision Insight

Virtuous Returns Virtue is not always its own reward. Compare the S&P 500 with the Domini Social Index (DSI), which covers 400 companies that have especially good records of social responsibility. We see that returns for companies with socially responsible behavior are at least as high as those of the S&P 500.

Copyright © 2007 by KLD Research & Analytics, Inc. The "Domini 400 Social Index."

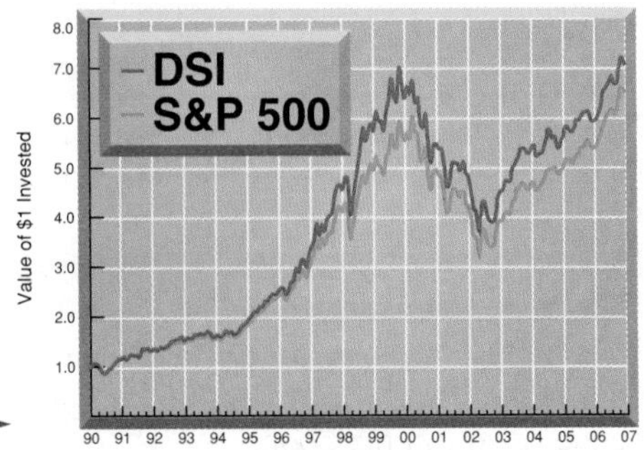

Graphical displays are often used to illustrate key points.

Generally Accepted Accounting Principles

Financial accounting practice is governed by concepts and rules known as **generally accepted accounting principles (GAAP).** To use and interpret financial statements effectively, we need to understand these principles, which can change over time in response to the demands of users. GAAP aims to make information in financial statements *relevant, reliable,* and *comparable.* Relevant information affects the decisions of its users. Reliable information is trusted by users. Comparable information is helpful in contrasting organizations.

C5 Explain generally accepted accounting principles and define and apply several accounting principles.

Setting Accounting Principles Two main groups establish generally accepted accounting principles in the United States. The **Financial Accounting Standards Board (FASB)** is the private group that sets both broad and specific principles. The **Securities and Exchange Commission (SEC)** is the government group that establishes reporting requirements for companies that issue stock to the public.

In today's global economy, there is increased demand by external users for comparability in accounting reports. This often arises when companies wish to raise money from lenders and investors in different countries. To that end, the **International Accounting Standards Board (IASB)** issues *International Financial Reporting Standards (IFRS)* that identify preferred accounting practices. The IASB hopes to create more harmony among accounting practices of different countries. If standards are harmonized, one company can potentially use a single set of financial statements in all financial markets. Many countries' standard setters support the IASB, and differences between U.S. GAAP and IASB's practices are fading. Yet, the IASB does not have authority to impose its standards on companies.

Point: State ethics codes require CPAs who audit financial statements to disclose areas where those statements fail to comply with GAAP. If CPAs fail to report noncompliance, they can lose their licenses and be subject to criminal and civil actions and fines.

Decision Insight

Principles and Scruples Auditors, directors, and lawyers are using principles to improve accounting reports. Examples include accounting restatements at **Navistar**, financial restatements at **Nortel**, accounting reviews at **Echostar**, and expense adjustments at **Electronic Data Systems**. Principles-based accounting has led accounting firms to drop clients deemed too risky. Examples include **Grant Thornton**'s resignation as auditor of **Fremont General** due to alleged failures in providing information when promised, and **Ernst and Young**'s resignation as auditor of **Catalina Marketing** due to alleged accounting errors.

Principles and Assumptions of Accounting Accounting principles (and assumptions) are of two types. *General principles* are the basic assumptions, concepts, and guidelines for preparing financial statements. *Specific principles* are detailed rules used in reporting business transactions and events. General principles stem from long-used accounting practices. Specific principles arise more often from the rulings of authoritative groups.

We need to understand both general and specific principles to effectively use accounting information. Several general principles are described in this section that are relied on in later chapters. General principles (in red font) and assumptions (in yellow font) are portrayed as building blocks of GAAP in Exhibit 1.7. The specific principles are described as we encounter them in the book.

EXHIBIT 1.7

Building Blocks for GAAP

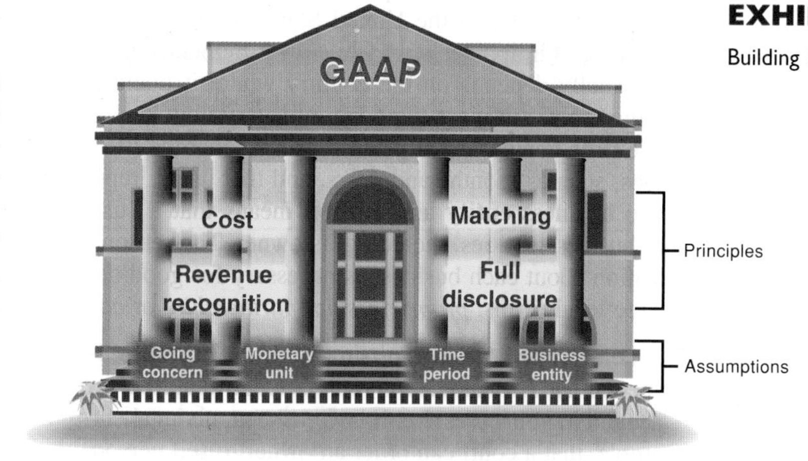

Accounting Principles General principles consist of at least four basic principles, four assumptions, and certain constraints. The **cost principle** means that accounting information is based on actual cost. Cost is measured on a cash or equal-to-cash basis. This means if cash is given for a service, its cost is measured as the amount of cash paid. If something besides cash is exchanged

Point: The cost principle is also called the *historical cost principle.*

A listing of some of the more publicized accounting scandals in recent years follows.

Company	Alleged Accounting Abuses
Enron	Inflated income, hid debt, and bribed officials
WorldCom	Understated expenses to inflate income and hid debt
Fannie Mae	Inflated income
Adelphia Communications	Understated expenses to inflate income and hid debt
AOL Time Warner	Inflated revenues and income
Xerox	Inflated income
Bristol-Myers Squibb	Inflated revenues and income
Nortel Networks	Understated expenses to inflate income
Global Crossing	Inflated revenues and income
Tyco	Hid debt, and CEO evaded taxes
Halliburton	Inflated revenues and income
Qwest Communications	Inflated revenues and income

To reduce the risk of accounting fraud, companies set up *governance systems.* A company's governance system includes its owners, managers, employees, board of directors, and other important stakeholders, who work together to reduce the risk of accounting fraud and increase confidence in accounting reports.

The impact of SOX regulations for accounting and business is discussed throughout this book. Ethics and investor confidence are key to company success. Lack of confidence in accounting numbers impacts company value as evidenced by huge stock price declines for **Enron**, **WorldCom**, **Tyco**, and **ImClone** after accounting misconduct was uncovered.

Decision Insight

IFRSs Like the FASB, the IASB uses a conceptual framework to aid in drafting standards. However, unlike the FASB, the IASB's conceptual framework is used as a reference when specific guidance is lacking. Also unlike the FASB, the IASB requires that transactions be accounted for according to their substance (not only their legal form).

Quick Check

Answers—p. 26

7. What three-step guidelines can help people make ethical decisions?
8. Why are ethics and social responsibility valuable to organizations?
9. Why are ethics crucial in accounting?
10. Who sets U.S. accounting rules?
11. How are U.S. companies affected by international accounting standards?
12. How are the objectivity concept and cost principle related?
13. Why is the business entity assumption important?
14. Why is the revenue recognition principle important?
15. What are the three basic forms of business organization?
16. Identify the owners of corporations and the terminology for ownership units.

Transaction Analysis and the Accounting Equation

To understand accounting information, we need to know how an accounting system captures relevant data about transactions, and then classifies, records, and reports data.

Accounting Equation

A1 Define and interpret the accounting equation and each of its components.

The accounting system reflects two basic aspects of a company: what it owns and what it owes. **Assets** are resources with future benefits that are owned or controlled by a company. Examples are cash, supplies, equipment, and land. The claims on a company's assets—what it owes—are separated into owner and nonowner claims. **Liabilities** are what a company owes its nonowners (creditors) in future payments, products, or services. **Equity** (also called owner's equity or capital) refers to the claims of its owner(s). Together, liabilities and equity are

EXHIBIT 1.8

Characteristics of Businesses

Characteristic	Proprietorship	Partnership	Corporation
Business entity	yes	yes	yes
Legal entity	no	no	yes
Limited liability	no*	no*	yes
Unlimited life	no	no	yes
Business taxed	no	no	yes
One owner allowed	yes	no	yes

* Proprietorships and partnerships that are set up as LLCs provide limited liability.

requirement is an agreement between partners to run a business together. The agreement can be either oral or written and usually indicates how income and losses are to be shared. A partnership, like a proprietorship, is *not* legally separate from its owners. This means that each partner's share of profits is reported and taxed on that partner's tax return. It also means *unlimited liability* for its partners. However, at least three types of partnerships limit liability. A *limited partnership* (*LP*) includes a general partner(s) with unlimited liability and a limited partner(s) with liability restricted to the amount invested. A *limited liability partnership* (*LLP*) restricts partners' liabilities to their own acts and the acts of individuals under their control. This protects an innocent partner from the negligence of another partner, yet all partners remain responsible for partnership debts. A *limited liability company* (*LLC*) offers the limited liability of a corporation and the tax treatment of a partnership (and proprietorship). Most proprietorships and partnerships are now organized as LLCs.

Point: Proprietorships and partnerships are usually managed by their owners. In a corporation, the owners (shareholders) elect a board of directors who appoint managers to run the business.

3. A **corporation** is a business legally separate from its owners, meaning it is responsible for its own acts and its own debts. Separate legal status means that a corporation can conduct business with the rights, duties, and responsibilities of a person. A corporation acts through its managers, who are its legal agents. Separate legal status also means that its owners, who are called **shareholders** (or **stockholders**), are not personally liable for corporate acts and debts. This limited liability is its main advantage. A main disadvantage is what's called *double taxation*—meaning that (1) the corporation income is taxed and (2) any distribution of income to its owners through dividends is taxed as part of the owners' personal income, usually at the 15% rate. (For lower income taxpayers, the dividend tax is less than 15%, and in some cases zero.) An *S corporation,* a corporation with special characteristics, does not owe corporate income tax. Owners of S corporations report their share of corporate income with their personal income. Ownership of all corporations is divided into units called **shares** or **stock.** When a corporation issues only one class of stock, we call it **common stock** (or *capital stock*).

***Decision Ethics** boxes are role-playing exercises that stress ethics in accounting and business.*

Decision Ethics

Entrepreneur You and a friend develop a new design for in-line skates that improves speed by 25% to 30%. You plan to form a business to manufacture and market those skates. You and your friend want to minimize taxes, but your prime concern is potential lawsuits from individuals who might be injured on these skates. What form of organization do you set up? [Answer—p. 25]

Sarbanes–Oxley (SOX)

Congress passed the **Sarbanes–Oxley Act,** also called *SOX,* to help curb financial abuses at companies that issue their stock to the public. SOX requires that these public companies apply both accounting oversight and stringent internal controls. The desired results include more transparency, accountability, and truthfulness in reporting transactions.

Point: An **audit** examines whether financial statements are prepared using GAAP. It does *not* attest to absolute accuracy of the statements.

Compliance with SOX requires documentation and verification of internal controls and increased emphasis on internal control effectiveness. Failure to comply can yield financial penalties, stock market delisting, and criminal prosecution of executives. Management must issue a report stating that internal controls are effective. CEOs and CFOs who knowingly sign off on bogus accounting reports risk millions of dollars in fines and years in prison. **Auditors** also must verify the effectiveness of internal controls.

Point: *BusinessWeek* reports that external audit costs run about $35,000 for startups, up from $15,000 pre-SOX.

A listing of some of the more publicized accounting scandals in recent years follows.

Company	Alleged Accounting Abuses
Enron	Inflated income, hid debt, and bribed officials
WorldCom	Understated expenses to inflate income and hid debt
Fannie Mae	Inflated income
Adelphia Communications	Understated expenses to inflate income and hid debt
AOL Time Warner	Inflated revenues and income
Xerox	Inflated income
Bristol-Myers Squibb	Inflated revenues and income
Nortel Networks	Understated expenses to inflate income
Global Crossing	Inflated revenues and income
Tyco	Hid debt, and CEO evaded taxes
Halliburton	Inflated revenues and income
Qwest Communications	Inflated revenues and income

To reduce the risk of accounting fraud, companies set up *governance systems*. A company's governance system includes its owners, managers, employees, board of directors, and other important stakeholders, who work together to reduce the risk of accounting fraud and increase confidence in accounting reports.

The impact of SOX regulations for accounting and business is discussed throughout this book. Ethics and investor confidence are key to company success. Lack of confidence in accounting numbers impacts company value as evidenced by huge stock price declines for **Enron**, **WorldCom**, **Tyco**, and **ImClone** after accounting misconduct was uncovered.

Decision Insight

IFRSs Like the FASB, the IASB uses a conceptual framework to aid in drafting standards. However, unlike the FASB, the IASB's conceptual framework is used as a reference when specific guidance is lacking. Also unlike the FASB, the IASB requires that transactions be accounted for according to their substance (not only their legal form).

Quick Check

Answers—p. 26

7. What three-step guidelines can help people make ethical decisions?
8. Why are ethics and social responsibility valuable to organizations?
9. Why are ethics crucial in accounting?
10. Who sets U.S. accounting rules?
11. How are U.S. companies affected by international accounting standards?
12. How are the objectivity concept and cost principle related?
13. Why is the business entity assumption important?
14. Why is the revenue recognition principle important?
15. What are the three basic forms of business organization?
16. Identify the owners of corporations and the terminology for ownership units.

Transaction Analysis and the Accounting Equation

To understand accounting information, we need to know how an accounting system captures relevant data about transactions, and then classifies, records, and reports data.

Accounting Equation

A1 Define and interpret the accounting equation and each of its components.

The accounting system reflects two basic aspects of a company: what it owns and what it owes. **Assets** are resources with future benefits that are owned or controlled by a company. Examples are cash, supplies, equipment, and land. The claims on a company's assets—what it owes—are separated into owner and nonowner claims. **Liabilities** are what a company owes its nonowners (creditors) in future payments, products, or services. **Equity** (also called owner's equity or capital) refers to the claims of its owner(s). Together, liabilities and equity are understand these principles, which can change over time in response to the demands of users. GAAP aims to make information in financial statements *relevant, reliable,* and *comparable.* Relevant information affects the decisions of its users. Reliable information is trusted by users. Comparable information is helpful in contrasting organizations.

C5 Explain generally accepted accounting principles and define and apply several accounting principles.

Setting Accounting Principles Two main groups establish generally accepted accounting principles in the United States. The **Financial Accounting Standards Board (FASB)** is the private group that sets both broad and specific principles. The **Securities and Exchange Commission (SEC)** is the government group that establishes reporting requirements for companies that issue stock to the public.

In today's global economy, there is increased demand by external users for comparability in accounting reports. This often arises when companies wish to raise money from lenders and investors in different countries. To that end, the **International Accounting Standards Board (IASB)** issues *International Financial Reporting Standards* (*IFRS*) that identify preferred accounting practices. The IASB hopes to create more harmony among accounting practices of different countries. If standards are harmonized, one company can potentially use a single set of financial statements in all financial markets. Many countries' standard setters support the IASB, and differences between U.S. GAAP and IASB's practices are fading. Yet, the IASB does not have authority to impose its standards on companies.

Point: State ethics codes require CPAs who audit financial statements to disclose areas where those statements fail to comply with GAAP. If CPAs fail to report noncompliance, they can lose their licenses and be subject to criminal and civil actions and fines.

Decision Insight

Principles and Scruples Auditors, directors, and lawyers are using principles to improve accounting reports. Examples include accounting restatements at **Navistar**, financial restatements at **Nortel**, accounting reviews at **Echostar**, and expense adjustments at **Electronic Data Systems**. Principles-based accounting has led accounting firms to drop clients deemed too risky. Examples include **Grant Thornton**'s resignation as auditor of **Fremont General** due to alleged failures in providing information when promised, and **Ernst and Young**'s resignation as auditor of **Catalina Marketing** due to alleged accounting errors.

Principles and Assumptions of Accounting Accounting principles (and assumptions) are of two types. *General principles* are the basic assumptions, concepts, and guidelines for preparing financial statements. *Specific principles* are detailed rules used in reporting business transactions and events. General principles stem from long-used accounting practices. Specific principles arise more often from the rulings of authoritative groups.

We need to understand both general and specific principles to effectively use accounting information. Several general principles are described in this section that are relied on in later chapters. General principles (in red font) and assumptions (in yellow font) are portrayed as building blocks of GAAP in Exhibit 1.7. The specific principles are described as we encounter them in the book.

EXHIBIT 1.7

Building Blocks for GAAP

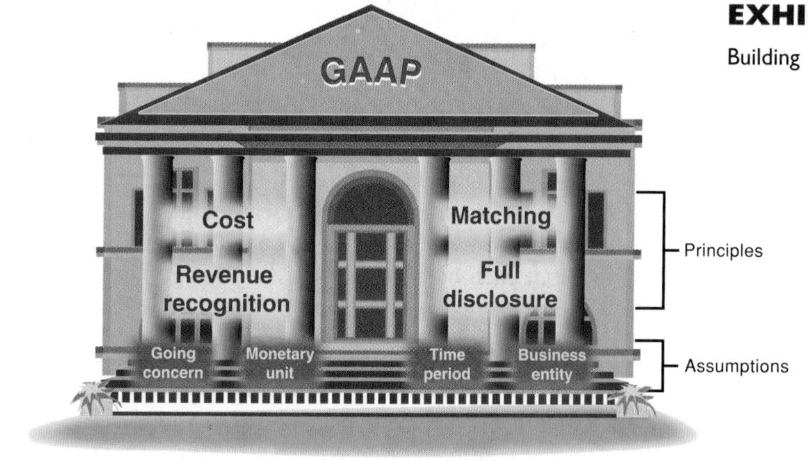

Accounting Principles General principles consist of at least four basic principles, four assumptions, and certain constraints. The **cost principle** means that accounting information is based on actual cost. Cost is measured on a cash or equal-to-cash basis. This means if cash is given for a service, its cost is measured as the amount of cash paid. If something besides cash is exchanged

Point: The cost principle is also called the *historical cost principle.*

(such as a car traded for a truck), cost is measured as the cash value of what is given up or received. The cost principle emphasizes reliability and verifiability, and information based on cost is considered objective. *Objectivity* means that information is supported by independent, unbiased evidence; it demands more than a person's opinion. To illustrate, suppose a company pays $5,000 for equipment. The cost principle requires that this purchase be recorded at a cost of $5,000. It makes no difference if the owner thinks this equipment is worth $7,000.

Revenue (sales) is the amount received from selling products and services. The **revenue recognition principle** provides guidance on when a company must recognize revenue. To *recognize* means to record it. If revenue is recognized too early, a company would look more profitable than it is. If revenue is recognized too late, a company would look less profitable than it is.

Three concepts are important to revenue recognition. (1) *Revenue is recognized when earned.* The earnings process is normally complete when services are performed or a seller transfers ownership of products to the buyer. (2) *Proceeds from selling products and services need not be in cash.* A common noncash proceed received by a seller is a customer's promise to pay at a future date, called *credit sales.* (3) *Revenue is measured by the cash received plus the cash value of any other items received.*

Example: When a bookstore sells a textbook on credit is its earnings process complete? *Answer:* A bookstore can record sales for these books minus an amount expected for returns.

The **matching principle** prescribes that a company must record its expenses incurred to generate the revenue reported. The **full disclosure principle** requires a company to report the details behind financial statements that would impact users' decisions. Those disclosures are often in footnotes to the statements.

Decision Insight

Revenues for the **San Diego Chargers** football team include ticket sales, television and cable broadcasts, radio rights, concessions, and advertising. Revenues from ticket sales are earned when the Chargers play each game. Advance ticket sales are not revenues; instead, they represent a liability until the Chargers play the game for which the ticket was sold. At that point, the liability is removed and revenues are reported.

Accounting Assumptions There are four accounting assumptions. The **going-concern assumption** means that accounting information reflects a presumption that the business will continue operating instead of being closed or sold. This implies, for example, that property is reported at cost instead of, say, liquidation values that assume closure.

The **monetary unit assumption** means that we can express transactions and events in monetary, or money, units. Money is the common denominator in business. Examples of monetary units are the dollar in the United States, Canada, Australia, and Singapore; and the peso in Mexico, the Philippines, and Chile. The monetary unit a company uses in its accounting reports usually depends on the country where it operates, but many companies today are expressing reports in more than one monetary unit.

Point: For currency conversion: cnnfn.com/markets/currencies

The **time period assumption** presumes that the life of a company can be divided into time periods, such as months and years, and that useful reports can be prepared for those periods.

The **business entity assumption** means that a business is accounted for separately from other business entities, including its owner. The reason for this assumption is that separate information about each business is necessary for good decisions. A business entity can take one of three legal forms: *proprietorship, partnership,* or *corporation.*

Point: Abuse of the entity assumption was a main culprit in **Enron**'s collapse.

1. A **sole proprietorship,** or simply **proprietorship,** is a business owned by one person. No special legal requirements must be met to start a proprietorship. It is a separate entity for accounting purposes, but it is *not* a separate legal entity from its owner. This means, for example, that a court can order an owner to sell personal belongings to pay a proprietorship's debt. This *unlimited liability* of a proprietorship is a disadvantage. However, an advantage is that a proprietorship's income is not subject to a business income tax but is instead reported and taxed on the owner's personal income tax return. Proprietorship characteristics are summarized in Exhibit 1.8, including those for partnerships and corporations.
2. A **partnership** is a business owned by two or more people, called *partners.* Like a proprietorship, no special legal requirements must be met in starting a partnership. The only

the source of funds to acquire assets. The relation of assets, liabilities, and equity is reflected in the following **accounting equation:**

Assets = Liabilities + Equity

Liabilities are usually shown before equity in this equation because creditors' claims must be paid before the claims of owners. (The terms in this equation can be rearranged; for example, Assets − Liabilities = Equity.) The accounting equation applies to all transactions and events, to all companies and forms of organization, and to all points in time. For example, **Best Buy**'s assets equal $13,570, its liabilities equal $7,369, and its equity equals $6,201 ($ in millions). Let's now look at the accounting equation in more detail.

Videos 1.1 & 1.2

Assets **Assets** are resources owned or controlled by a company. These resources are expected to yield future benefits. Examples are Web servers for an online services company, musical instruments for a rock band, and land for a vegetable grower. The term *receivable* is used to refer to an asset that promises a future inflow of resources. A company that provides a service or product on credit is said to have an account receivable from that customer.

Point: The phrases "on credit" and "on account" imply that cash payment will occur at a future date.

Liabilities **Liabilities** are creditors' claims on assets. These claims reflect company obligations to provide assets, products or services to others. The term *payable* refers to a liability that promises a future outflow of resources. Examples are wages payable to workers, accounts payable to suppliers, notes payable to banks, and taxes payable to the government.

Equity **Equity** is the owner's claim on assets. Equity is equal to assets minus liabilities. This is the reason equity is also called *net assets* or *residual equity*.

Equity for a noncorporate entity—commonly called owner's equity—increases and decreases as follows: owner investments and revenues *increase* equity, whereas owner withdrawals and expenses *decrease* equity. **Owner investments** are assets an owner puts into the company and are included under the generic account **Owner, Capital. Revenues** increase equity and are the assets earned from a company's earnings activities. Examples are consulting services provided, sales of products, facilities rented to others, and commissions from services. **Owner withdrawals** are assets an owner takes from the company for personal use. **Expenses** decrease equity and are the cost of assets or services used to earn revenues. Examples are costs of employee time, use of supplies, and advertising, utilities, and insurance services from others. In sum, equity is the accumulated revenues and owner investments less the accumulated expenses and withdrawals since the company began. This breakdown of equity yields the following **expanded accounting equation.**

*Key **terms** are printed in bold and defined again in the end-of-book **glossary.***

$$\text{Assets} = \text{Liabilities} + \overbrace{\text{Owner, Capital} - \text{Owner, Withdrawals} + \text{Revenues} - \text{Expenses}}^{\text{Equity}}$$

Net income occurs when revenues exceed expenses. Net income increases equity. A **net loss** occurs when expenses exceed revenues, which decreases equity.

Decision Insight

Web Info Most organizations maintain Websites that include accounting data—see **Best Buy (BestBuy.com)** as an example. The SEC keeps an online database called **EDGAR (www.sec.gov/edgar.shtml),** which has accounting information for thousands of companies that issue stock to the public. Information services such as **Finance.Google.com** and **Finance.Yahoo.com** offer additional online data and analysis.

Transaction Analysis

A2 Analyze business transactions using the accounting equation.

Business activities can be described in terms of transactions and events. **External transactions** are exchanges of value between two entities, which yield changes in the accounting equation. **Internal transactions** are exchanges within an entity; they can also affect the accounting equation. An example is a company's use of its supplies, which are reported as expenses when used.

Events refer to happenings that affect an entity's accounting equation *and* can be reliably measured. They include business events such as changes in the market value of certain assets and liabilities, and natural events such as floods and fires that destroy assets and create losses. They do not include, for example, the signing of service or product contracts, which by themselves do not impact the accounting equation.

This section uses the accounting equation to analyze 11 selected transactions and events of FastForward, a start-up consulting (service) business, in its first month of operations. Remember that each transaction and event leaves the equation in balance and that assets *always* equal the sum of liabilities and equity.

Point: There are 3 basic types of company operations: (1) **Services**—providing customer services for profit, (2) **Merchandisers**—buying products and re-selling them for profit, and (3) **Manufacturers**—creating products and selling them for profit.

Transaction 1: Investment by Owner On December 1, Chuck Taylor forms a consulting business focused on assessing the performance of athletic footwear and accessories, which he names FastForward. He sets it up as a proprietorship. Taylor owns and manages the business. The marketing plan for the business is to focus primarily on consulting with sports clubs, amateur athletes, and others who place orders for athletic footwear and accessories with manufacturers. Taylor personally invests $30,000 cash in the new company and deposits the cash in a bank account opened under the name of FastForward. After this transaction, the cash (an asset) and the owner's equity each equal $30,000. The source of increase in equity is the owner's investment, which is included in the column titled C. Taylor, Capital. (Owner investments are always included under the title *'Owner name,' Capital.*) The effect of this transaction on FastForward is reflected in the accounting equation as follows:

	Assets	=	Liabilities	+	Equity
	Cash	=			**C. Taylor, Capital**
(1)	+$30,000	=			+$30,000

Transaction 2: Purchase Supplies for Cash FastForward uses $2,500 of its cash to buy supplies of brand name athletic footwear for performance testing over the next few months. This transaction is an exchange of cash, an asset, for another kind of asset, supplies. It merely changes the form of assets from cash to supplies. The decrease in cash is exactly equal to the increase in supplies. The supplies of athletic footwear are assets because of the expected future benefits from the test results of their performance. This transaction is reflected in the accounting equation as follows:

	Assets			=	Liabilities	+	Equity
	Cash	+	**Supplies**	=			**C. Taylor, Capital**
Old Bal.	$30,000			=			$30,000
(2)	−2,500	+	$2,500				
New Bal.	$27,500	+	$ 2,500	=			$30,000
	$30,000				$30,000		

Transaction 3: Purchase Equipment for Cash FastForward spends $26,000 to acquire equipment for testing athletic footwear. Like transaction 2, transaction 3 is an exchange of one asset, cash, for another asset, equipment. The equipment is an asset because of its expected future benefits from testing athletic footwear. This purchase changes the makeup of assets but does not change the asset total. The accounting equation remains in balance.

	Assets					=	Liabilities	+	Equity
	Cash	+	**Supplies**	+	**Equipment**	=			**C. Taylor, Capital**
Old Bal.	$27,500	+	$2,500			=			$30,000
(3)	−26,000			+	$26,000				
New Bal.	$ 1,500	+	$2,500	+	$ 26,000	=			$30,000
			$30,000				$30,000		

Transaction 4: Purchase Supplies on Credit Taylor decides he needs more supplies of athletic footwear and accessories. These additional supplies total $7,100, but as we see from the accounting equation in transaction 3, FastForward has only $1,500 in cash. Taylor

arranges to purchase them on credit from CalTech Supply Company. Thus, FastForward acquires supplies in exchange for a promise to pay for them later. This purchase increases assets by $7,100 in supplies, and liabilities (called *accounts payable* to CalTech Supply) increase by the same amount. The effects of this purchase follow:

	Assets					=	Liabilities	+	Equity
	Cash	+	**Supplies**	+	**Equipment**	=	**Accounts Payable**	+	**C. Taylor, Capital**
Old Bal.	$1,500	+	$2,500	+	$26,000	=			$30,000
(4)		+	7,100				+$7,100		
New Bal.	$1,500	+	$9,600	+	$26,000	=	$ 7,100	+	$30,000
			$37,100					$37,100	

Example: If FastForward pays $500 cash in transaction 4, how does this partial payment affect the liability to CalTech? What would be FastForward's cash balance? *Answers:* The liability to CalTech would be reduced to $6,600 and the cash balance would be reduced to $1,000.

Transaction 5: Provide Services for Cash FastForward earns revenues by consulting with clients about test results on athletic footwear and accessories. It earns net income only if its revenues are greater than its expenses incurred in earning them. In one of its first jobs, FastForward provides consulting services to an athletic club and immediately collects $4,200 cash. The accounting equation reflects this increase in cash of $4,200 and in equity of $4,200. This increase in equity is identified in the far right column under Revenues because the cash received is earned by providing consulting services.

	Assets					=	Liabilities	+	Equity		
	Cash	+	**Supplies**	+	**Equipment**	=	**Accounts Payable**	+	**C. Taylor, Capital**	+	**Revenues**
Old Bal.	$1,500	+	$9,600	+	$26,000	=	$7,100	+	$30,000		
(5)	+4,200									+	$4,200
New Bal.	$5,700	+	$9,600	+	$26,000	=	$7,100	+	$30,000	+	$ 4,200
			$41,300						$41,300		

Transactions 6 and 7: Payment of Expenses in Cash FastForward pays $1,000 rent to the landlord of the building where its facilities are located. Paying this amount allows FastForward to occupy the space for the month of December. The rental payment is reflected in the following accounting equation as transaction 6. FastForward also pays the biweekly $700 salary of the company's only employee. This is reflected in the accounting equation as transaction 7. Both transactions 6 and 7 are December expenses for FastForward. The costs of both rent and salary are expenses, as opposed to assets, because their benefits are used in December (they have no future benefits after December). These transactions also use up an asset (cash) in carrying out FastForward's operations. The accounting equation shows that both transactions reduce cash and equity. The far right column identifies these decreases as Expenses.

By definition, increases in expenses yield decreases in equity.

	Assets					=	Liabilities	+	Equity				
	Cash	+	**Supplies**	+	**Equipment**	=	**Accounts Payable**	+	**C. Taylor, Capital**	+	**Revenues**	−	**Expenses**
Old Bal.	$5,700	+	$9,600	+	$26,000	=	$7,100	+	$30,000	+	$4,200		
(6)	−1,000											−	$1,000
Bal.	4,700	+	9,600	+	26,000	=	7,100	+	30,000	+	4,200	−	1,000
(7)	− 700											−	700
New Bal.	$4,000	+	$9,600	+	$26,000	=	$7,100	+	$30,000	+	$4,200	−	$ 1,700
			$39,600								$39,600		

Transaction 8: Provide Services and Facilities for Credit FastForward provides consulting services of $1,600 and rents its test facilities for $300 to an amateur sports club. The rental involves allowing club members to try recommended footwear and accessories at FastForward's testing area. The sports club is billed for the $1,900 total. This transaction results in a new asset, called *accounts receivable,* from this client. It also yields an increase in equity from the two revenue components reflected in the Revenues column of the accounting equation:

	Assets				= Liabilities +	Equity		
	Cash	+ Accounts Receivable	+ Supplies	+ Equipment	= Accounts Payable	+ C. Taylor, Capital	+ Revenues	− Expenses
Old Bal.	$4,000	+	+ $9,600	+ $26,000	= $7,100	+ $30,000	+ $4,200	− $1,700
(8)		**+ $1,900**					**+ 1,600**	
							+ 300	
New Bal.	$4,000	+ $ 1,900	+ $9,600	+ $26,000	= $7,100	+ $30,000	+ $6,100	− $1,700
	$41,500				$41,500			

Transaction 9: Receipt of Cash from Accounts Receivable The client in transaction 8 (the amateur sports club) pays $1,900 to FastForward 10 days after it is billed for consulting services. This transaction 9 does not change the total amount of assets and does not affect liabilities or equity. It converts the receivable (an asset) to cash (another asset). It does not create new revenue. Revenue was recognized when FastForward rendered the services in transaction 8, not when the cash is now collected. This emphasis on the earnings process instead of cash flows is a goal of the revenue recognition principle and yields useful information to users. The new balances follow:

Point: Receipt of cash is not always a revenue.

	Assets				= Liabilities +	Equity		
	Cash	+ Accounts Receivable	+ Supplies	+ Equipment	= Accounts Payable	+ C. Taylor, Capital	+ Revenues	− Expenses
Old Bal.	$4,000	+ $1,900	+ $9,600	+ $26,000	= $7,100	+ $30,000	+ $6,100	− $1,700
(9)	**+1,900**	**− 1,900**						
New Bal.	$5,900	+ $ 0	+ $9,600	+ $26,000	= $7,100	+ $30,000	+ $6,100	− $1,700
	$41,500				$41,500			

Transaction 10: Payment of Accounts Payable FastForward pays CalTech Supply $900 cash as partial payment for its earlier $7,100 purchase of supplies (transaction 4), leaving $6,200 unpaid. The accounting equation shows that this transaction decreases FastForward's cash by $900 and decreases its liability to CalTech Supply by $900. Equity does not change. This event does not create an expense even though cash flows out of FastForward (instead the expense is recorded when FastForward derives the benefits from these supplies).

	Assets				= Liabilities +	Equity		
	Cash	+ Accounts Receivable	+ Supplies	+ Equipment	= Accounts Payable	+ C. Taylor, Capital	+ Revenues	− Expenses
Old Bal.	$5,900	+ $ 0	+ $9,600	+ $26,000	= $7,100	+ $30,000	+ $6,100	− $1,700
(10)	**− 900**				**− 900**			
New Bal.	$5,000	+ $ 0	+ $9,600	+ $26,000	= $6,200	+ $30,000	+ $6,100	− $1,700
	$40,600				$40,600			

Transaction 11: Withdrawal of Cash by Owner The owner of FastForward withdraws $200 cash for personal use. Withdrawals (decreases in equity) are not reported as expenses because they are not part of the company's earnings process. Since withdrawals are not company expenses, they are not used in computing net income.

By definition, increases in withdrawals yield decreases in equity.

	Assets				= Liabilities +	Equity			
	Cash	+ Accounts Receivable	+ Supplies	+ Equipment	= Accounts Payable	+ C. Taylor, Capital	− C. Taylor, Withdrawals	+ Revenues	− Expenses
Old Bal.	$5,000	+ $ 0	+ $9,600	+ $26,000	= $6,200	+ $30,000		+ $6,100	− $1,700
(11)	**− 200**						**− $200**		
New Bal.	$4,800	+ $ 0	+ $9,600	+ $26,000	= $6,200	+ $30,000	− $200	+ $6,100	− $1,700
	$40,400				$40,400				

Summary of Transactions

We summarize in Exhibit 1.9 the effects of these 11 transactions of FastForward using the accounting equation. First, we see that the accounting equation remains in balance after each transaction. Second, transactions can be analyzed by their effects on components of the accounting equation. For example, in transactions 2, 3, and 9, one asset increased while another asset decreased by equal amounts.

Point: Knowing how financial statements are prepared improves our analysis of them. We develop the skills for analysis of financial statements throughout the book. Chapter 17 focuses on financial statement analysis.

EXHIBIT 1.9

Summary of Transactions Using the Accounting Equation

	Assets				=	Liabilities +	Equity			
	Cash	+ Accounts Receivable	+ Supplies	+ Equipment	=	Accounts Payable	+ C. Taylor, Capital	− C. Taylor, Withdrawals	+ Revenues	− Expenses
(1)	$30,000				=		$30,000			
(2)	− 2,500		+ $2,500							
Bal.	27,500		+ 2,500		=		30,000			
(3)	−26,000			+ $26,000						
Bal.	1,500		+ 2,500	+ 26,000	=		30,000			
(4)			+ 7,100			+$7,100				
Bal.	1,500		+ 9,600	+ 26,000	=	7,100	+ 30,000			
(5)	+ 4,200								+ $4,200	
Bal.	5,700		+ 9,600	+ 26,000	=	7,100	+ 30,000		+ 4,200	
(6)	− 1,000									− $1,000
Bal.	4,700		+ 9,600	+ 26,000	=	7,100	+ 30,000		+ 4,200	− 1,000
(7)	− 700									− 700
Bal.	4,000		+ 9,600	+ 26,000	=	7,100	+ 30,000		+ 4,200	− 1,700
(8)		+ $1,900							+ 1,600	
									+ 300	
Bal.	4,000	+ 1,900	+ 9,600	+ 26,000	=	7,100	+ 30,000		+ 6,100	− 1,700
(9)	+ 1,900	− 1,900								
Bal.	5,900	+ 0	+ 9,600	+ 26,000	=	7,100	+ 30,000		+ 6,100	− 1,700
(10)	− 900					− 900				
Bal.	5,000	+ 0	+ 9,600	+ 26,000	=	6,200	+ 30,000		+ 6,100	− 1,700
(11)	− 200							− $200		
Bal.	$ 4,800	+ $ 0	+ $ 9,600	+ $ 26,000	=	$ 6,200	+ $ 30,000	− $ 200	+ $6,100	− $ 1,700

Quick Check

Answers—p. 26

17. When is the accounting equation in balance, and what does that mean?
18. How can a transaction not affect any liability and equity accounts?
19. Describe a transaction increasing equity and one decreasing it.
20. Identify a transaction that decreases both assets and liabilities.

Financial Statements

P1 Identify and prepare basic financial statements and explain how they interrelate.

This section introduces us to how financial statements are prepared from the analysis of business transactions. The four financial statements and their purposes are:

1. **Income statement**—describes a company's revenues and expenses along with the resulting net income or loss over a period of time due to earnings activities.
2. **Statement of owner's equity**—explains changes in equity from net income (or loss) and from any owner investments and withdrawals over a period of time.

Video1.1

3. **Balance sheet**—describes a company's financial position (types and amounts of assets, liabilities, and equity) at a point in time.
4. **Statement of cash flows**—identifies cash inflows (receipts) and cash outflows (payments) over a period of time.

We prepare these financial statements using the 11 selected transactions of FastForward. (These statements are technically called *unadjusted*—we explain this in Chapters 2 and 3.)

Income Statement

FastForward's income statement for December is shown at the top of Exhibit 1.10. Information about revenues and expenses is conveniently taken from the Equity columns of Exhibit 1.9. Revenues are reported first on the income statement. They include consulting revenues of $5,800 from transactions 5 and 8 and rental revenue of $300 from transaction 8. Expenses are reported after revenues. (For convenience in this chapter, we list larger amounts first, but we can sort expenses in different ways.) Rent and salary expenses are from transactions 6 and 7. Expenses reflect the costs to generate the revenues reported. Net income (or loss) is reported at the bottom of the statement and is the amount earned in December. Owner's investments and withdrawals are *not* part of income.

Point: Net income is sometimes called *earnings* or *profit*.

Statement of Owner's Equity

Point: The statement of owner's equity is also called the *statement of changes in owner's equity*. Note: Beg. Capital + Net Income − Withdrawals = Ending Capital

The statement of owner's equity reports information about how equity changes over the reporting period. This statement shows beginning capital, events that increase it (owner investments and net income), and events that decrease it (withdrawals and net loss). Ending capital is computed in this statement and is carried over and reported on the balance sheet. FastForward's statement of owner's equity is the second report in Exhibit 1.10. The beginning capital balance is measured as of the start of business on December 1. It is zero because FastForward did not exist before then. An existing business reports a beginning balance equal to that as of the end of the prior reporting period (such as from November 30). FastForward's statement of owner's equity shows that Taylor's initial investment created $30,000 of equity. It also shows the $4,400 of net income earned during the period. This links the income statement to the statement of owner's equity (see line ①). The statement also reports Taylor's $200 cash withdrawal and FastForward's end-of-period capital balance.

Balance Sheet

FastForward's balance sheet is the third report in Exhibit 1.10. This statement refers to FastForward's financial condition at the close of business on December 31. The left side of the balance sheet lists FastForward's assets: cash, supplies, and equipment. The upper right side of the balance sheet shows that FastForward owes $6,200 to creditors. Any other liabilities (such as a bank loan) would be listed here. The equity (capital) balance is $34,200. Line ② shows the link between the ending balance of the statement of owner's equity and the equity balance on the balance sheet. (This presentation of the balance sheet is called the *account form:* assets on the left and liabilities and equity on the right. Another presentation is the *report form:* assets on top, followed by liabilities and then equity at the bottom. Either presentation is acceptable.)

***Decision Maker** boxes are role-playing exercises that stress the relevance of accounting.*

Decision Maker

Retailer You open a wholesale business selling entertainment equipment to retail outlets. You find that most of your customers demand to buy on credit. How can you use the balance sheets of these customers to help you decide which ones to extend credit to? [Answer—p. 26]

Statement of Cash Flows

Point: Statement of cash flows has three main sections: operating, investing, and financing.

Point: Payment for supplies is an operating activity because supplies are expected to be used up in short-term operations (typically less than one year).

FastForward's statement of cash flows is the final report in Exhibit 1.10. The first section reports cash flows from *operating activities*. It shows the $6,100 cash received from clients and the $5,100 cash paid for supplies, rent, and employee salaries. Outflows are in parentheses to denote subtraction. Net cash provided by operating activities for December is $1,000. If cash paid exceeded the $5,100 cash received, we would call it "cash used by operating activities." The second section

EXHIBIT 1.10

Financial Statements and Their Links

FASTFORWARD
Income Statement
For Month Ended December 31, 2009

Revenues		
Consulting revenue ($4,200 + $1,600)	$ 5,800	
Rental revenue	300	
Total revenues		$ 6,100
Expenses		
Rent expense	1,000	
Salaries expense	700	
Total expenses		1,700
Net income		$ 4,400

Point: A statement's heading identifies the company, the statement title, and the date or time period.

FASTFORWARD
Statement of Owner's Equity
For Month Ended December 31, 2009

C. Taylor, Capital, December 1, 2009		$ 0
Plus: Investments by owner	$30,000	
Net income	4,400	34,400
		34,400
Less: Withdrawals by owner		200
C. Taylor, Capital, December 31, 2009		$34,200

Point: Arrow lines show how the statements are linked. (1) Net income is used to compute equity. (2) Owner capital is used to prepare the balance sheet. (3) Cash from the balance sheet is used to reconcile the statement of cash flows.

FASTFORWARD
Balance Sheet
December 31, 2009

Assets		Liabilities	
Cash	$ 4,800	Accounts payable	$ 6,200
Supplies	9,600	Total liabilities	6,200
Equipment	26,000		
		Equity	
		C. Taylor, Capital	34,200
Total assets	$40,400	Total liabilities and equity	$ 40,400

Point: The income statement, the statement of owner's equity, and the statement of cash flows are prepared for a *period* of time. The balance sheet is prepared as of a *point* in time.

FASTFORWARD
Statement of Cash Flows
For Month Ended December 31, 2009

Cash flows from operating activities		
Cash received from clients ($4,200 + $1,900)	$ 6,100	
Cash paid for supplies ($2,500 + $900)	(3,400)	
Cash paid for rent	(1,000)	
Cash paid to employee	(700)	
Net cash provided by operating activities		$ 1,000
Cash flows from investing activities		
Purchase of equipment	(26,000)	
Net cash used by investing activities		(26,000)
Cash flows from financing activities		
Investments by owner	30,000	
Withdrawals by owner	(200)	
Net cash provided by financing activities		29,800
Net increase in cash		$ 4,800
Cash balance, December 1, 2009		0
Cash balance, December 31, 2009		$ 4,800

Point: A single ruled line denotes an addition or subtraction. Final totals are double underlined. Negative amounts are often in parentheses.

Point: Investing activities refer to long-term asset investments by the company, *not* to owner investments.

reports *investing activities,* which involve buying and selling assets such as land and equipment that are held for *long-term use* (typically more than one year). The only investing activity is the $26,000 purchase of equipment. The third section shows cash flows from *financing activities,* which include the *long-term* borrowing and repaying of cash from lenders and the cash investments from, and withdrawals by, the owner. FastForward reports $30,000 from the owner's initial investment and the $200 cash withdrawal. The net cash effect of all financing transactions is a $29,800 cash inflow. The final part of the statement shows FastForward increased its cash balance by $4,800 in December. Since it started with no cash, the ending balance is also $4,800—see line ③.

Quick Check

Answers—p. 26

21. Explain the link between the income statement and the statement of owner's equity.
22. Describe the link between the balance sheet and the statement of owner's equity.
23. Discuss the three major sections of the statement of cash flows.

***Decision Analysis** (a section at the end of each chapter) introduces and explains ratios helpful in decision making using real company data. Instructors can skip this section and cover all ratios in Chapter 17.*

Decision Analysis — Return on Assets

A *Decision Analysis* section at the end of each chapter is devoted to financial statement analysis. We organize financial statement analysis into four areas: (1) liquidity and efficiency, (2) solvency, (3) profitability, and (4) market prospects—Chapter 17 has a ratio listing with definitions and groupings by area. When analyzing ratios, we need benchmarks to identify good, bad, or average levels. Common benchmarks include the company's prior levels and those of its competitors.

A3 Compute and interpret return on assets.

This chapter presents a profitability measure: return on assets. Return on assets is useful in evaluating management, analyzing and forecasting profits, and planning activities. **Dell** has its marketing department compute return on assets for *every* order. **Return on assets (ROA),** also called *return on investment (ROI)*, is defined in Exhibit 1.11.

EXHIBIT 1.11

Return on Assets

$$\textbf{Return on assets} = \frac{\textbf{Net income}}{\textbf{Average total assets}}$$

Net income is from the annual income statement, and average total assets is computed by adding the beginning and ending amounts for that same period and dividing by 2. To illustrate, **Best Buy** reports net income of $1,377 million in 2007. At the beginning of fiscal 2007, its total assets are $11,864 million and at the end of fiscal 2007, they total $13,570 million. Best Buy's return on assets for 2007 is:

$$\text{Return on assets} = \frac{\$1{,}377 \text{ million}}{(\$11{,}864 \text{ million} + \$13{,}570 \text{ million})/2} = 10.8\%$$

Is a 10.8% return on assets good or bad for Best Buy? To help answer this question, we compare (benchmark) Best Buy's return with its prior performance, the returns of competitors (such as **Circuit City, RadioShack,** and **CompUSA**), and the returns from alternative investments. Best Buy's return for each of the prior five years is in the second column of Exhibit 1.12, which ranges from 1.3% to 10.8%.

EXHIBIT 1.12

Best Buy, Circuit City, and Industry Returns

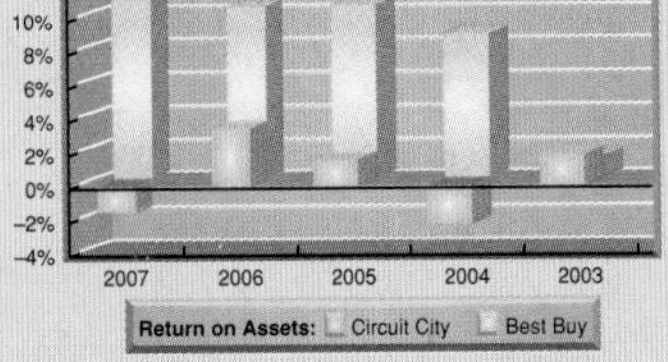

	Return on Assets		
Fiscal Year	**Best Buy**	**Circuit City**	**Industry**
2007	10.8%	(1.9)%	3.5%
2006	10.3	3.5	3.3
2005	10.4	1.6	3.2
2004	8.6	(2.3)	3.1
2003	1.3	1.9	3.0

Best Buy's returns show an increase in its productive use of assets in recent years. We also compute Circuit City's returns in the third column of Exhibit 1.12. In four of the five years, Best Buy's return exceeds Circuit City's, and its average return is higher for this period. We also compare Best Buy's return to the normal return for similar merchandisers of electronic products (fourth column). Industry averages are available from services such as **Dun & Bradstreet**'s *Industry Norms and Key Ratios* and **Robert Morris Associates**' *Annual Statement Studies*. When compared to the industry, Best Buy performs well.

*Each **Decision Analysis** section ends with a role-playing scenario to show the usefulness of ratios.*

Decision Maker

Business Owner You own a small winter ski resort that earns a 21% return on its assets. An opportunity to purchase a winter ski equipment manufacturer is offered to you. This manufacturer earns a 19% return on its assets. The industry return for this manufacturer is 14%. Do you purchase this manufacturer? [Answer—p. 26]

*The **Demonstration Problem** is a review of key chapter content. The* Planning the Solution *offers strategies in solving the problem.*

Demonstration Problem

After several months of planning, Jasmine Worthy started a haircutting business called Expressions. The following events occurred during its first month of business.

DP1

a. On August 1, Worthy invested $3,000 cash and $15,000 of equipment in Expressions.
b. On August 2, Expressions paid $600 cash for furniture for the shop.
c. On August 3, Expressions paid $500 cash to rent space in a strip mall for August.
d. On August 4, it purchased $1,200 of equipment on credit for the shop (using a long-term note payable).
e. On August 5, Expressions opened for business. Cash received from haircutting services in the first week and a half of business (ended August 15) was $825.
f. On August 15, it provided $100 of haircutting services on account.
g. On August 17, it received a $100 check for services previously rendered on account.
h. On August 17, it paid $125 cash to an assistant for hours worked during the grand opening.
i. Cash received from services provided during the second half of August was $930.
j. On August 31, it paid a $400 installment toward principal on the note payable entered into on August 4.
k. On August 31, Worthy made a $900 cash withdrawal from the company for personal use.

Required

1. Arrange the following asset, liability, and equity titles in a table similar to the one in Exhibit 1.9: Cash; Accounts Receivable; Furniture; Store Equipment; Note Payable; J. Worthy, Capital; J. Worthy, Withdrawals; Revenues; and Expenses. Show the effects of each transaction using the accounting equation.
2. Prepare an income statement for August.
3. Prepare a statement of owner's equity for August.
4. Prepare a balance sheet as of August 31.
5. Prepare a statement of cash flows for August.
6. Determine the return on assets ratio for August.

Planning the Solution

- Set up a table like Exhibit 1.9 with the appropriate columns for accounts.
- Analyze each transaction and show its effects as increases or decreases in the appropriate columns. Be sure the accounting equation remains in balance after each transaction.
- Prepare the income statement, and identify revenues and expenses. List those items on the statement, compute the difference, and label the result as *net income* or *net loss*.
- Use information in the Equity columns to prepare the statement of owner's equity.
- Use information in the last row of the transactions table to prepare the balance sheet.
- Prepare the statement of cash flows; include all events listed in the Cash column of the transactions table. Classify each cash flow as operating, investing, or financing.
- Calculate return on assets by dividing net income by average assets.

Solution to Demonstration Problem

1.

	Assets							=	Liabilities	+	Equity						
	Cash	+	**Accounts Receivable**	+	**Furniture**	+	**Store Equipment**	=	**Note Payable**	+	**J. Worthy, Capital**	−	**J. Worthy, Withdrawals**	+	**Revenues**	−	**Expenses**
a.	**$3,000**						**$15,000**				**$18,000**						
b.	**− 600**			+	**$600**												
Bal.	2,400	+		+	600	+	15,000	=			18,000						
c.	**− 500**															−	**$500**
Bal.	1,900	+		+	600	+	15,000	=			18,000					−	500
d.						+	**1,200**		**+$1,200**								
Bal.	1,900	+		+	600	+	16,200	=	1,200	+	18,000					−	500
e.	**+ 825**													+	**$ 825**		
Bal.	2,725	+		+	600	+	16,200	=	1,200	+	18,000			+	825	−	500
f.		+	**$100**											+	**100**		
Bal.	2,725	+	100	+	600	+	16,200	=	1,200	+	18,000			+	925	−	500
g.	**+ 100**	−	**100**														
Bal.	2,825	+	0	+	600	+	16,200	=	1,200	+	18,000			+	925	−	500
h.	**− 125**															−	**125**
Bal.	2,700	+	0	+	600	+	16,200	=	1,200	+	18,000			+	925	−	625
i.	**+ 930**													+	**930**		
Bal.	3,630	+	0	+	600	+	16,200	=	1,200	+	18,000			+	1,855	−	625
j.	**− 400**								**− 400**								
Bal.	3,230	+	0	+	600	+	16,200	=	800	+	18,000			+	1,855	−	625
k.	**− 900**											−	**$900**				
Bal.	$ 2,330	+	0	+	$600	+	$ 16,200	=	$ 800	+	$ 18,000	−	$900	+	$1,855	−	$625

2.

EXPRESSIONS
Income Statement
For Month Ended August 31

Revenues		
Haircutting services revenue		$1,855
Expenses		
Rent expense	$500	
Wages expense	125	
Total expenses		625
Net Income		$1,230

3.

EXPRESSIONS
Statement of Owner's Equity
For Month Ended August 31

J. Worthy, Capital, August 1*		$ 0
Plus: Investments by owner	$18,000	
Net income	1,230	19,230
		19,230
Less: Withdrawals by owner		900
J. Worthy, Capital, August 31		$18,330

* If Expressions had been an existing business from a prior period, the beginning capital balance would equal the Capital account balance from the end of the prior period.

4.

EXPRESSIONS
Balance Sheet
August 31

Assets		**Liabilities**	
Cash	$ 2,330	Note payable	$ 800
Furniture	600	**Equity**	
Store equipment	16,200	J. Worthy, Capital	18,330
Total assets	$19,130	Total liabilities and equity	$19,130

5.

EXPRESSIONS
Statement of Cash Flows
For Month Ended August 31

Cash flows from operating activities		
Cash received from customers	$1,855	
Cash paid for rent	(500)	
Cash paid for wages	(125)	
Net cash provided by operating activities		$1,230
Cash flows from investing activities		
Cash paid for furniture		(600)
Cash flows from financing activities		
Cash investments by owner	3,000	
Cash withdrawals by owner	(900)	
Partial repayment of (long-term) note payable	(400)	
Net cash provided by financing activities		1,700
Net increase in cash		$2,330
Cash balance, August 1		0
Cash balance, August 31		$2,330

6. $$\text{Return on assets} = \frac{\text{Net income}}{\text{Average assets}} = \frac{\$1{,}230}{(\$18{,}000^{*} + \$19{,}130)/2} = \frac{\$1{,}230}{\$18{,}565} = \mathbf{6.63\%}$$

* Uses the initial $18,000 investment as the beginning balance for the startup period only.

APPENDIX

1A Return and Risk Analysis

A4 Explain the relation between return and risk.

This appendix explains return and risk analysis and its role in business and accounting.

Net income is often linked to **return.** Return on assets (ROA) is stated in ratio form as income divided by assets invested. For example, banks report return from a savings account in the form of an interest return such as 4%. If we invest in a savings account or in U.S. Treasury bills, we expect a return of around 2% to 7%. We could also invest in a company's stock, or even start our own business. How do we decide among these investment options? The answer depends on our trade-off between return and risk.

Risk is the uncertainty about the return we will earn. All business investments involve risk, but some investments involve more risk than others. The lower the risk of an investment, the lower is our expected return. The reason that savings accounts pay such a low return is the low risk of not being repaid with interest (the government guarantees most savings accounts from default). If we buy a share of eBay or any other company, we might obtain a large return. However, we have no guarantee of any return; there is even the risk of loss.

EXHIBIT 1A.1

Average Returns for Bonds with Different Risks

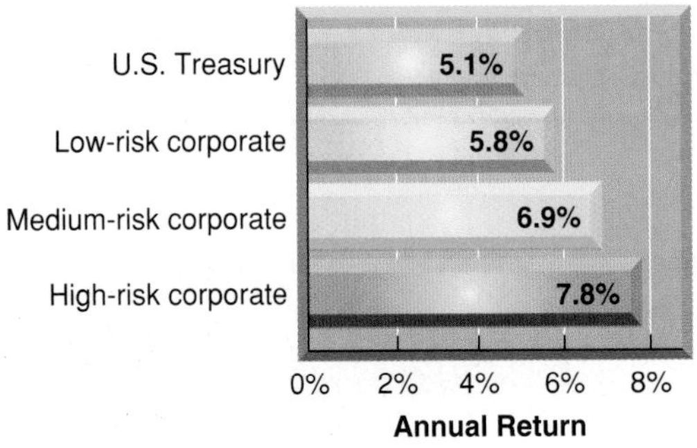

The bar graph in Exhibit 1A.1 shows recent returns for 30-year bonds with different risks. *Bonds* are written promises by organizations to repay amounts loaned with interest. U.S. Treasury bonds provide a low expected return, but they also offer low risk since they are backed by the U.S. government. High-risk corporate bonds offer a much larger potential return but with much higher risk.

The trade-off between return and risk is a normal part of business. Higher risk implies higher, but riskier, expected returns. To help us make better decisions, we use accounting information to assess both return and risk.

APPENDIX

1B Business Activities and the Accounting Equation

C6 Identify and describe the three major activities of organizations.

This appendix explains how the accounting equation is derived from business activities.

There are three major types of business activities: financing, investing, and operating. Each of these requires planning. *Planning* involves defining an organization's ideas, goals, and actions. Most public corporations use the *Management Discussion and Analysis* section in their annual reports to communicate plans. However, planning is not cast in stone. This adds *risk* to both setting plans and analyzing them.

Financing *Financing activities* provide the means organizations use to pay for resources such as land, buildings, and equipment to carry out plans. Organizations are careful in acquiring and managing financing activities because they can determine success or failure. The two sources of financing are owner and nonowner. *Owner financing* refers to resources contributed by the owner along with any income the owner leaves in the organization. *Nonowner* (or *creditor*) *financing* refers to resources contributed by creditors (lenders). *Financial management* is the task of planning how to obtain these resources and to set the right mix between owner and creditor financing.

Point: Management must understand accounting data to set financial goals, make financing and investing decisions, and evaluate operating performance.

Investing *Investing activities* are the acquiring and disposing of resources (assets) that an organization uses to acquire and sell its products or services. Assets are funded by an organization's financing. Organizations differ on the amount and makeup of assets. Some require land and factories to operate. Others need only an office. Determining the amount and type of assets for operations is called *asset management*.

Invested amounts are referred to as *assets*. Financing is made up of creditor and owner financing, which hold claims on assets. Creditors' claims are called *liabilities*, and the owner's claim is called *equity*. This basic equality is called the *accounting equation* and can be written as: Assets = Liabilities + Equity.

Point: Investing (assets) and financing (liabilities plus equity) totals are *always* equal.

Operating *Operating activities* involve using resources to research, develop, purchase, produce, distribute, and market products and services. Sales and revenues are the inflow of assets from selling products and services. Costs and expenses are the outflow of assets to support operating activities. *Strategic management* is the process of determining the right mix of operating activities for the type of organization, its plans, and its market.

Exhibit 1B.1 summarizes business activities. Planning is part of each activity and gives them meaning and focus. Investing (assets) and financing (liabilities and equity) are set opposite each other to stress their balance. Operating activities are below investing and financing activities to show that operating activities are the result of investing and financing.

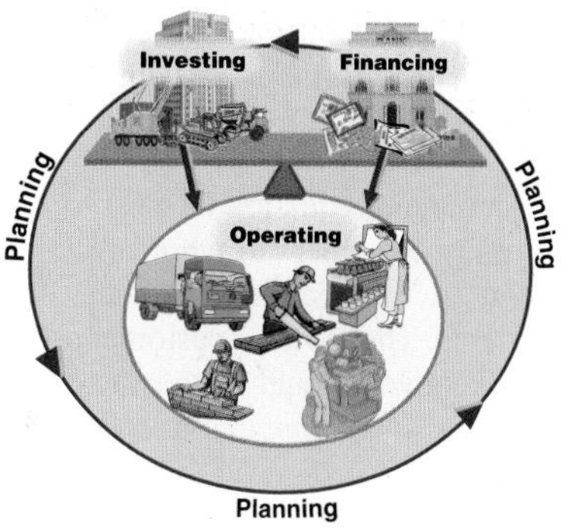

EXHIBIT 1B.1

Activities of Organizations

*A **Summary** organized by learning objectives concludes each chapter.*

Summary

C1 Explain the purpose and importance of accounting in the information age. Accounting is an information and measurement system that aims to identify, record, and communicate relevant, reliable, and comparable information about business activities. It helps assess opportunities, products, investments, and social and community responsibilities.

C2 Identify users and uses of accounting. Users of accounting are both internal and external. Some users and uses of accounting include (a) managers in controlling, monitoring, and planning; (b) lenders for measuring the risk and return of loans; (c) shareholders for assessing the return and risk of stock; (d) directors for overseeing management; and (e) employees for judging employment opportunities.

C3 Identify opportunities in accounting and related fields. Opportunities in accounting include financial, managerial, and tax accounting. They also include accounting-related fields such as lending, consulting, managing, and planning.

C4 Explain why ethics are crucial to accounting. The goal of accounting is to provide useful information for decision making. For information to be useful, it must be trusted. This demands ethical behavior in accounting.

C5 Explain generally accepted accounting principles and define and apply several accounting principles. Generally accepted accounting principles are a common set of standards applied by accountants. Accounting principles aid in producing relevant, reliable, and comparable information. Four principles underlying financial statements were introduced: cost, revenue recognition, matching, and full disclosure. Financial statements also reflect four assumptions: going-concern, monetary unit, time period, and business entity.

C6[B] Identify and describe the three major activities of organizations. Organizations carry out three major activities: financing, investing, and operating. Financing is the means used to pay for resources such as land, buildings, and machines. Investing refers to the buying and selling of resources used in acquiring and selling products and services. Operating activities are those necessary for carrying out the organization's plans.

A1 Define and interpret the accounting equation and each of its components. The accounting equation is: Assets = Liabilities + Equity. Assets are resources owned by a company. Liabilities are creditors' claims on assets. Equity is the owner's claim on assets (*the residual*). The expanded accounting equation is: Assets = Liabilities + [Owner Capital − Owner Withdrawals + Revenues − Expenses].

A2 Analyze business transactions using the accounting equation. A *transaction* is an exchange of economic consideration between two parties. Examples include exchanges of products, services, money, and rights to collect money. Transactions always have at least two effects on one or more components of the accounting equation. This equation is always in balance.

A3 Compute and interpret return on assets. Return on assets is computed as net income divided by average assets. For example, if we have an average balance of $100 in a savings account and it earns $5 interest for the year, the return on assets is $5/$100, or 5%.

A4[A] Explain the relation between return and risk. *Return* refers to income, and *risk* is the uncertainty about the return we hope to make. All investments involve risk. The lower the risk of an investment, the lower is its expected return. Higher risk implies higher, but riskier, expected return.

P1 Identify and prepare basic financial statements and explain how they interrelate. Four financial statements report on an organization's activities: balance sheet, income statement, statement of owner's equity, and statement of cash flows.

Guidance Answers to **Decision Maker** and **Decision Ethics**

Entrepreneur (p. 11) You should probably form the business as a corporation if potential lawsuits are of prime concern. The corporate form of organization protects your personal property from lawsuits directed at the business and places only the corporation's resources at risk. A downside of the corporate form is double taxation: The corporation must pay taxes on its income, and you normally must pay taxes on any money distributed to you from the business (even though the corporation already paid taxes on this money). You should also examine the ethical and socially responsible aspects of starting a business in which you anticipate injuries to others. Formation as an LLC or S corp. should also be explored.

Retailer (p. 18) You can use the accounting equation (Assets = Liabilities + Equity) to help identify risky customers to whom you would likely not want to extend credit. A balance sheet provides amounts for each of these key components. The lower a customer's equity is relative to liabilities, the less likely you would be to extend credit. A low equity means the business has little value that does not already have creditor claims to it.

Business Owner (p. 21) The 19% return on assets for the manufacturer exceeds the 14% industry return (and many others). This is a positive factor for a potential purchase. Also, the purchase of this manufacturer is an opportunity to spread your risk over two businesses as opposed to one. Still, you should hesitate to purchase a business whose return of 19% is lower than your current resort's return of 21%. You are probably better off directing efforts to increase investment in your resort, assuming you can continue to earn a 21% return.

Guidance Answers to **Quick Checks**

1. Accounting is an information and measurement system that identifies, records, and communicates relevant information to help people make better decisions.
2. Recordkeeping, also called *bookkeeping,* is the recording of financial transactions and events, either manually or electronically. Recordkeeping is essential to data reliability; but accounting is this and much more. Accounting includes identifying, measuring, recording, reporting, and analyzing business events and transactions.
3. Technology offers increased accuracy, speed, efficiency, and convenience in accounting.
4. External users of accounting include lenders, shareholders, directors, customers, suppliers, regulators, lawyers, brokers, and the press. Internal users of accounting include managers, officers, and other internal decision makers involved with strategic and operating decisions.
5. Internal users (managers) include those from research and development, purchasing, human resources, production, distribution, marketing, and servicing.
6. Internal controls are procedures set up to protect assets, ensure reliable accounting reports, promote efficiency, and encourage adherence to company policies. Internal controls are crucial for relevant and reliable information.
7. Ethical guidelines are threefold: (1) identify ethical concerns using personal ethics, (2) analyze options considering all good and bad consequences, and (3) make ethical decisions after weighing all consequences.
8. Ethics and social responsibility yield good behavior, and they often result in higher income and a better working environment.
9. For accounting to provide useful information for decisions, it must be trusted. Trust requires ethics in accounting.
10. Two major participants in setting rules include the SEC and the FASB. (*Note:* Accounting rules reflect society's needs, not those of accountants or any other single constituency.)
11. Most U.S. companies are not directly affected by international accounting standards. International standards are put forth as preferred accounting practices. However, stock exchanges and other parties are increasing the pressure to narrow differences in worldwide accounting practices. International accounting standards are playing an important role in that process.
12. The objectivity concept and cost principle are related in that most users consider information based on cost as objective. Information prepared using both is considered highly reliable and often relevant.
13. Users desire information about the performance of a specific entity. If information is mixed between two or more entities, its usefulness decreases.
14. The revenue recognition principle gives preparers guidelines on when to recognize (record) revenue. This is important; for example, if revenue is recognized too early, the statements report revenue sooner than it should and the business looks more profitable than it is. The reverse is also true.
15. The three basic forms of business organization are sole proprietorships, partnerships, and corporations.
16. Owners of corporations are called *shareholders* (or *stockholders*). Corporate ownership is divided into units called *shares* (or *stock*). The most basic of corporate shares is common stock (or capital stock).
17. The accounting equation is: Assets = Liabilities + Equity. This equation is always in balance, both before and after each transaction.
18. A transaction that changes the makeup of assets would not affect liability and equity accounts. FastForward's transactions 2 and 3 are examples. Each exchanges one asset for another.
19. Earning revenue by performing services, as in FastForward's transaction 5, increases equity (and assets). Incurring expenses while servicing clients, such as in transactions 6 and 7, decreases equity (and assets). Other examples include owner investments that increase equity and withdrawals that decrease equity.
20. Paying a liability with an asset reduces both asset and liability totals. One example is FastForward's transaction 10 that reduces a payable by paying cash.
21. An income statement reports a company's revenues and expenses along with the resulting net income or loss. A statement of owner's equity shows changes in equity, including that from net income or loss. Both statements report transactions occurring over a period of time.
22. The balance sheet describes a company's financial position (assets, liabilities, and equity) at a point in time. The equity amount in the balance sheet is obtained from the statement of owner's equity.
23. Cash flows from operating activities report cash receipts and payments from the primary business the company engages in. Cash flows from investing activities involve cash transactions from buying and selling long-term assets. Cash flows from financing activities include long-term cash borrowings and repayments to lenders and the cash investments from and withdrawals by the owner.

A list of key terms with page references concludes each chapter (a complete glossary is at the end of the book and also on the book's Website).

Key Terms mhhe.com/wildFAP19e

Key Terms are available at the book's Website for learning and testing in an online Flashcard Format.

Accounting (p. 4)
Accounting equation (p. 13)
Assets (p. 12)
Auditors (p. 11)
Balance sheet (p. 18)
Bookkeeping (p. 4)
Business entity assumption (p. 10)
Common stock (p. 11)
Corporation (p. 11)
Cost principle (p. 9)
Equity (p. 12)
Ethics (p. 8)
Events (p. 14)
Expanded accounting equation (p. 13)
Expenses (p. 13)
External transactions (p. 13)
External users (p. 5)
Financial accounting (p. 5)
Financial Accounting Standards Board (FASB) (p. 9)
Full disclosure principle (p. 10)
Generally Accepted Accounting Principles (GAAP) (p. 8)
Going-concern assumption (p. 10)
Income statement (p. 17)
Internal transactions (p. 13)
Internal users (p. 6)
International Accounting Standards Board (IASB) (p. 9)
Liabilities (p. 12)
Managerial accounting (p. 6)
Matching principle (p. 10)
Monetary unit assumption (p. 10)
Net income (p. 13)
Net loss (p. 13)
Owner, Capital (p. 13)
Owner investment (p. 13)
Owner withdrawals (p. 13)
Partnership (p. 10)
Proprietorship (p. 10)
Recordkeeping (p. 4)
Return (p. 23)
Return on assets (p. 20)
Revenue recognition principle (p. 10)
Revenues (p. 13)
Risk (p. 24)
Sarbanes–Oxley Act (p. 11)
Securities and Exchange Commission (SEC) (p. 9)
Shareholders (p. 11)
Shares (p. 11)
Sole proprietorship (p. 10)
Statement of cash flows (p. 18)
Statement of owner's equity (p. 17)
Stock (p. 11)
Stockholders (p. 11)
Time period assumption (p. 10)
Withdrawals (p. 13)

Multiple Choice Quiz

Answers on p. 45 mhhe.com/wildFAP19e

Additional Quiz Questions are available at the book's Website.

Quiz1

1. A building is offered for sale at $500,000 but is currently assessed at $400,000. The purchaser of the building believes the building is worth $475,000, but ultimately purchases the building for $450,000. The purchaser records the building at:
a. $50,000
b. $400,000
c. $450,000
d. $475,000
e. $500,000

2. On December 30, 2008, **KPMG** signs a $150,000 contract to provide accounting services to one of its clients in 2009. KPMG has a December 31 year-end. Which accounting principle or assumption requires KPMG to record the accounting services revenue from this client in 2009 and not 2008?
a. Business entity assumption
b. Revenue recognition principle
c. Monetary unit assumption
d. Cost principle
e. Going-concern assumption

3. If the assets of a company increase by $100,000 during the year and its liabilities increase by $35,000 during the same year, then the change in equity of the company during the year must have been:
a. An increase of $135,000.
b. A decrease of $135,000.
c. A decrease of $65,000.
d. An increase of $65,000.
e. An increase of $100,000.

4. **Brunswick** borrows $50,000 cash from Third National Bank. How does this transaction affect the accounting equation for Brunswick?
a. Assets increase by $50,000; liabilities increase by $50,000; no effect on equity.
b. Assets increase by $50,000; no effect on liabilities; equity increases by $50,000.
c. Assets increase by $50,000; liabilities decrease by $50,000; no effect on equity.
d. No effect on assets; liabilities increase by $50,000; equity increases by $50,000.
e. No effect on assets; liabilities increase by $50,000; equity decreases by $50,000.

5. **Geek Squad** performs services for a customer and bills the customer for $500. How would Geek Squad record this transaction?
a. Accounts receivable increase by $500; revenues increase by $500.
b. Cash increases by $500; revenues increase by $500.
c. Accounts receivable increase by $500; revenues decrease by $500.
d. Accounts receivable increase by $500; accounts payable increase by $500.
e. Accounts payable increase by $500; revenues increase by $500.

Superscript letter [A] ([B]) denotes assignments based on Appendix 1A (1B).

Discussion Questions

1. What is the purpose of accounting in society?
2. Technology is increasingly used to process accounting data. Why then must we study and understand accounting?
3. Identify four kinds of external users and describe how they use accounting information.
4. What are at least three questions business owners and managers might be able to answer by looking at accounting information?
5. Identify three actual businesses that offer services and three actual businesses that offer products.
6. Describe the internal role of accounting for organizations.
7. Identify three types of services typically offered by accounting professionals.
8. What type of accounting information might be useful to the marketing managers of a business?
9. Why is accounting described as a service activity?
10. What are some accounting-related professions?
11. How do ethics rules affect auditors' choice of clients?
12. What work do tax accounting professionals perform in addition to preparing tax returns?
13. What does the concept of *objectivity* imply for information reported in financial statements? Why?
14. A business reports its own office stationery on the balance sheet at its $400 cost, although it cannot be sold for more than $10 as scrap paper. Which accounting principle and/or assumption justifies this treatment?
15. Why is the revenue recognition principle needed? What does it demand?
16. Describe the three basic forms of business organization and their key characteristics.
17. Define (*a*) *assets,* (*b*) *liabilities,* (*c*) *equity,* and (*d*) *net assets.*
18. What events or transactions change equity?
19. Identify the two main categories of accounting principles.
20. What do accountants mean by the term *revenue?*
21. Define *net income* and explain its computation.
22. Identify the four basic financial statements of a business.
23. What information is reported in an income statement?
24. Give two examples of expenses a business might incur.
25. What is the purpose of the statement of owner's equity?
26. What information is reported in a balance sheet?
27. The statement of cash flows reports on what major activities?
28. Define and explain return on assets.
29.[A] Define return and risk. Discuss the trade-off between them.
30.[B] Describe the three major business activities in organizations.
31.[B] Explain why investing (assets) and financing (liabilities and equity) totals are always equal.
32. Refer to the financial statements of **Best Buy** in Appendix A near the end of the book. To what level of significance are dollar amounts rounded? What time period does its income statement cover?
33. Refer to **Circuit City**'s balance sheet in Appendix A near the end of the book. Confirm that its total assets equal its total liabilities plus total equity.
34. Identify the dollar amounts of **RadioShack**'s 2006 assets, liabilities, and equity as reported in its statements in Appendix A near the end of the book.
35. Access the SEC EDGAR database (www.SEC.gov) and retrieve **Apple**'s 2006 10-K (filed 12-29-2006). Identify its auditor. What responsibility does its independent auditor claim regarding Apple's financial statements?

Denotes Discussion Questions that involve decision making.

***Homework Manager** repeats assignments on the book's Website, which allows instructors to monitor, promote, and assess student learning. It can be used in practice, homework, or exam mode.*

***Quick Study** exercises give readers a brief test of key elements.*

Available with McGraw-Hill's Homework Manager

QUICK STUDY

QS 1-1
Identifying accounting users
C2

Identify the following users as either external users (E) or internal users (I).

a. Shareholders	**d.** FBI and IRS	**g.** Customers	**j.** Business press
b. Lenders	**e.** Consumer group	**h.** Suppliers	**k.** Managers
c. Controllers	**f.** Sales staff	**i.** Brokers	**l.** District attorney

QS 1-2
Identifying accounting terms
C1

Reading and interpreting accounting reports requires some knowledge of accounting terminology. (*a*) Identify the meaning of these accounting-related acronyms: GAAP, SEC, FASB and IASB. (*b*) Briefly explain the importance of the knowledge base or organization that is referred to for each of the accounting-related acronyms.

QS 1-3
Accounting opportunities
C3

There are many job opportunities for those with accounting knowledge. Identify at least three main areas of opportunities for accounting professionals. For each area, identify at least three job possibilities linked to accounting.

QS 1-4
Explaining internal control
C1

An important responsibility of many accounting professionals is to design and implement internal control procedures for organizations. Explain the purpose of internal control procedures. Provide two examples of internal controls applied by companies.

QS 1-5
Identifying accounting principles
C5

This icon highlights assignments that enhance decision-making skills.

Identify which accounting principle or assumption best describes each of the following practices:

a. In December 2009, Ace Landscaping received a customer's order and cash prepayment to install sod at a new house that would not be ready for installation until March 2010. Ace should record the revenue from the customer order in March 2010, not in December 2009.

b. If $51,000 cash is paid to buy land, the land is reported on the buyer's balance sheet at $51,000.

c. Jay Keren owns both Sailing Passions and Dockside Supplies. In preparing financial statements for Dockside Supplies, Keren makes sure that the expense transactions of Sailing Passions are kept separate from Dockside's statements.

QS 1-6
Identifying ethical concerns
C4

Accounting professionals must sometimes choose between two or more acceptable methods of accounting for business transactions and events. Explain why these situations can involve difficult matters of ethical concern.

QS 1-7
Applying the accounting equation
A1

Use the accounting equation to compute the missing financial statement amounts (*a*), (*b*), and (*c*).

Company	Assets	=	Liabilities	+	Equity
1	$375,000		$ (*a*)		$250,000
2	$ (*b*)		$90,000		$160,000
3	$185,000		$60,000		$ (*c*)

QS 1-8
Applying the accounting equation
A1

a. Total assets of Charter Company equal $500,000 and its equity is $320,000. What is the amount of its liabilities?

b. Total assets of Golfland equal $900,000 and its liabilities and equity amounts are equal to each other. What is the amount of its liabilities? What is the amount of its equity?

QS 1-9
Identifying and computing assets, liabilities, and equity
A2

Use **Apple**'s September 30, 2006, financial statements, in Appendix A near the end of the book, to answer the following:

a. Identify the dollar amounts of Apple's 2006 (1) assets, (2) liabilities, and (3) equity.

b. Using Apple's amounts from part *a*, verify that Assets = Liabilities + Equity.

QS 1-10
Identifying transactions and events
A2

Accounting provides information about an organization's business transactions and events that both affect the accounting equation and can be reliably measured. Identify at least two examples of both (*a*) business transactions and (*b*) business events that meet these requirements.

QS 1-11
Identifying items with financial statements
P1

Indicate in which financial statement each item would most likely appear: income statement (I), balance sheet (B), statement of owner's equity (OE), or statement of cash flows (CF).

a. Equipment
b. Expenses
c. Liabilities
d. Net decrease (or increase) in cash
e. Revenues
f. Total liabilities and equity
g. Assets
h. Cash from operating activities
i. Withdrawals

QS 1-12
Computing and interpreting return on assets
A3

In a recent year's financial statements, **Home Depot** reported the following results. Compute and interpret Home Depot's return on assets (assume competitors average a 12% return on assets).

Sales	$90,837 million
Net income	5,761 million
Average total assets	48,334 million

EXERCISES

Exercise 1-1
Identifying accounting users and uses
C2

Much of accounting is directed at servicing the information needs of those users that are external to an organization. (*a*) Identify at least three external users of accounting information and indicate two questions they might seek to answer through their use of accounting information. (*b*) Identify at least three internal users of accounting information and describe how each might use accounting information in their jobs.

Exercise 1-2
Describing accounting responsibilities
C2 C3

Many accounting professionals work in one of the following three areas:

A. Financial accounting **B.** Managerial accounting **C.** Tax accounting

Identify the area of accounting that is most involved in each of the following responsibilities:

_____ **1.** Investigating violations of tax laws.
_____ **2.** Planning transactions to minimize taxes.
_____ **3.** Preparing external financial statements.
_____ **4.** Reviewing reports for SEC compliance.
_____ **5.** Internal auditing.
_____ **6.** External auditing.
_____ **7.** Cost accounting.
_____ **8.** Budgeting.

Exercise 1-3
Identifying ethical concerns
C4

Assume the following role and describe a situation in which ethical considerations play an important part in guiding your decisions and actions:

a. You are an accounting professional with audit clients that are competitors in business.
b. You are an accounting professional preparing tax returns for clients.
c. You are a manager with responsibility for several employees.
d. You are a student in an introductory accounting course.

Exercise 1-4
Identifying accounting principles and assumptions
C5

Match each of the numbered descriptions with the principle or assumption it best reflects. Enter the letter for the appropriate principle or assumption in the blank space next to each description.

A. General accounting principle
B. Cost principle
C. Business entity assumption
D. Revenue recognition principle
E. Specific accounting principle
F. Full disclosure principle
G. Going-concern assumption
H. Matching principle

_____ **1.** Usually created by a pronouncement from an authoritative body.
_____ **2.** Financial statements reflect the assumption that the business continues operating.
_____ **3.** Derived from long-used and generally accepted accounting practices.
_____ **4.** Every business is accounted for separately from its owner or owners.
_____ **5.** Revenue is recorded only when the earnings process is complete.
_____ **6.** Information is based on actual costs incurred in transactions.
_____ **7.** A company reports details behind financial statements that would impact users' decisions.
_____ **8.** A company records the expenses incurred to generate the revenues reported.

Exercise 1-5
Distinguishing business organizations
C5

The following describe several different business organizations. Determine whether the description refers to a sole proprietorship, partnership, or corporation.

a. Wallingford is owned by Gary Malone, who is personally liable for the company's debts.
b. Ava Fong and Elijah Logan own Financial Services, a financial services provider. Neither Fong nor Logan has personal responsibility for the debts of Financial Services.
c. IBC Services does not have separate legal existence apart from the one person who owns it.
d. Computing Services pays its own income taxes and has two owners.
e. Ownership of Zander Company is divided into 1,000 shares of stock.
f. Emma Bailey and Dylan Kay own Speedy Packages, a courier service. Both are personally liable for the debts of the business.
g. Physio Products does not pay income taxes and has one owner.

Exercise 1-6
Using the accounting equation
A1

Determine the missing amount from each of the separate situations *a*, *b*, and *c* below.

	Assets	=	Liabilities	+	Equity
a.	?	=	$164,000	+	$16,000
b.	$ 90,000	=	$ 39,000	+	?
c.	$201,000	=	?	+	$62,000

Exercise 1-7
Learning the language of business
C1–C4

Match each of the numbered descriptions with the term or phrase it best reflects. Indicate your answer by writing the letter for the term or phrase in the blank provided.

A. Audit **C.** Ethics **E.** SEC **G.** Net income
B. GAAP **D.** Tax accounting **F.** Public accountants **H.** IASB

_______ **1.** An accounting area that includes planning future transactions to minimize taxes paid.
_______ **2.** Amount a business earns after paying all expenses and costs associated with its sales and revenues.
_______ **3.** Principles that determine whether an action is right or wrong.
_______ **4.** Accounting professionals who provide services to many clients.
_______ **5.** An examination of an organization's accounting system and records that adds credibility to financial statements.

Exercise 1-8
Using the accounting equation
A1 A2

Answer the following questions. (*Hint:* Use the accounting equation.)

a. Office Supplies has assets equal to $137,000 and liabilities equal to $110,000 at year-end. What is the total equity for Office Supplies at year-end?

b. At the beginning of the year, Addison Company's assets are $259,000 and its equity is $194,250. During the year, assets increase $80,000 and liabilities increase $52,643. What is the equity at the end of the year?

c. At the beginning of the year, Quasar Company's liabilities equal $57,000. During the year, assets increase by $60,000, and at year-end assets equal $190,000. Liabilities decrease $16,000 during the year. What are the beginning and ending amounts of equity?

Check (c) Beg. equity, $73,000

Exercise 1-9
Identifying effects of transactions on the accounting equation
A1 A2

Provide an example of a transaction that creates the described effects for the separate cases *a* through *g*.

a. Increases an asset and increases a liability.
b. Decreases a liability and increases a liability.
c. Decreases an asset and decreases a liability.
d. Increases an asset and decreases an asset.
e. Increases a liability and decreases equity.
f. Increases an asset and increases equity.
g. Decreases an asset and decreases equity.

Exercise 1-10
Analysis using the accounting equation
A1 A2

Zen began a new consulting firm on January 5. The accounting equation showed the following balances after each of the company's first five transactions. Analyze the accounting equation for each transaction and describe each of the five transactions with their amounts.

	Assets							=	Liabilities	+	Equity		
Transaction	Cash	+	Accounts Receivable	+	Office Supplies	+	Office Furniture	=	Accounts Payable	+	Zen, Capital	+	Revenues
a.	$20,000	+	$ 0	+	$ 0	+	$ 0	=	$ 0	+	$20,000	+	$ 0
b.	18,000	+	0	+	3,000	+	0	=	1,000	+	20,000	+	0
c.	10,000	+	0	+	3,000	+	8,000	=	1,000	+	20,000	+	0
d.	10,000	+	6,000	+	3,000	+	8,000	=	1,000	+	20,000	+	6,000
e.	11,000	+	6,000	+	3,000	+	8,000	=	1,000	+	20,000	+	7,000

Exercise 1-11
Identifying effects of transactions on accounting equation
A1 A2

The following table shows the effects of five transactions (*a* through *e*) on the assets, liabilities, and equity of Trista's Boutique. Write short descriptions of the probable nature of each transaction.

	Assets				= Liabilities +	Equity	
	Cash	+ Accounts Receivable	+ Office Supplies	+ Land	= Accounts Payable	+ Trista, Capital	+ Revenues
	$ 21,000	+ $ 0	+ $3,000	+ $ 19,000	= $ 0	+ $43,000	+ $ 0
a.	− 4,000			+ 4,000			
b.			+ 1,000		+1,000		
c.		+ 1,900					+ 1,900
d.	− 1,000				−1,000		
e.	+ 1,900	− 1,900					
	$ 17,900	+ $ 0	+ $4,000	+ $ 23,000	= $ 0	+ $43,000	+ $1,900

Exercise 1-12
Identifying effects of transactions using the accounting equation
A1 A2

Leora Diamond began a professional practice on June 1 and plans to prepare financial statements at the end of each month. During June, Diamond (the owner) completed these transactions:

a. Owner invested $70,000 cash in the company along with equipment that had a $20,000 market value.
b. The company paid $2,000 cash for rent of office space for the month.
c. The company purchased $25,000 of additional equipment on credit (payment due within 30 days).
d. The company completed work for a client and immediately collected the $3,000 cash earned.
e. The company completed work for a client and sent a bill for $9,500 to be received within 30 days.
f. The company purchased additional equipment for $5,000 cash.
g. The company paid an assistant $3,500 cash as wages for the month.
h. The company collected $6,500 cash as a partial payment for the amount owed by the client in transaction *e*.
i. The company paid $25,000 cash to settle the liability created in transaction *c*.
j. Owner withdrew $1,500 cash from the company for personal use.

Required

Create a table like the one in Exhibit 1.9, using the following headings for columns: Cash; Accounts Receivable; Equipment; Accounts Payable; L. Diamond, Capital; L. Diamond, Withdrawals; Revenues; and Expenses. Then use additions and subtractions to show the effects of the transactions on individual items of the accounting equation. Show new balances after each transaction.

Check Net income, $7,000

Exercise 1-13
Preparing an income statement
P1

On October 1, Keisha King organized Real Answers, a new consulting firm. On October 31, the company's records show the following items and amounts. Use this information to prepare an October income statement for the business.

Cash	$11,500	Cash withdrawals by owner	$ 2,000
Accounts receivable	12,000	Consulting fees earned	14,000
Office supplies	24,437	Rent expense	2,520
Land	46,000	Salaries expense	5,600
Office equipment	18,000	Telephone expense	760
Accounts payable	25,037	Miscellaneous expenses	580
Owner investments	84,360		

Check Net income, $4,540

Exercise 1-14
Preparing a statement of owner's equity P1

Use the information in Exercise 1-13 to prepare an October statement of owner's equity for Real Answers.

Exercise 1-15
Preparing a balance sheet P1

Use the information in Exercise 1-13 (if completed, you can also use your solution to Exercise 1-14) to prepare an October 31 balance sheet for Real Answers.

Exercise 1-16
Preparing a statement of cash flows
P1

Use the information in Exercise 1-13 to prepare an October 31 statement of cash flows for Real Answers. Also assume the following:

a. The owner's initial investment consists of $38,360 cash and $46,000 in land.
b. The company's $18,000 equipment purchase is paid in cash.
c. The accounts payable balance of $25,037 consists of the $24,437 office supplies purchase and $600 in employee salaries yet to be paid.
d. The company's rent, telephone, and miscellaneous expenses are paid in cash.
e. $2,000 has been collected on the $14,000 consulting fees earned.

Check Net increase in cash, $11,500

Exercise 1-17
Identifying sections of the statement of cash flows
P1

Indicate the section where each of the following would appear on the statement of cash flows.

O. Cash flows from operating activity
I. Cash flows from investing activity
F. Cash flows from financing activity

_____ **1.** Cash paid for rent
_____ **2.** Cash paid on an account payable
_____ **3.** Cash investment by owner
_____ **4.** Cash received from clients
_____ **5.** Cash paid for advertising
_____ **6.** Cash paid for wages
_____ **7.** Cash withdrawal by owner
_____ **8.** Cash purchase of equipment

Exercise 1-18
Analysis of return on assets
A3

Iowa Group reports net income of $36,000 for 2009. At the beginning of 2009, Iowa Group had $135,000 in assets. By the end of 2009, assets had grown to $185,000. What is Iowa Group's 2009 return on assets? How would you assess its performance if competitors average a 10% return on assets?

Exercise 1-19[B]
Identifying business activities
C6

Match each transaction or event to one of the following activities of an organization: financing activities (F), investing activities (I), or operating activities (O).

a. _____ An organization purchases equipment.
b. _____ An organization advertises a new product.
c. _____ The organization borrows money from a bank.
d. _____ An owner contributes resources to the business.
e. _____ An organization sells some of its land.

***Problem Set B** located at the end of **Problem Set A** is provided for each problem to reinforce the learning process.*

McGraw-Hill's HOMEWORK MANAGER® Available with McGraw-Hill's Homework Manager

PROBLEM SET A

Problem 1-1A
Computing missing information using accounting knowledge
A1 A2

The following financial statement information is from five separate companies:

	Company A	Company B	Company C	Company D	Company E
December 31, 2008					
Assets	$33,000	$25,740	$21,120	$58,740	$90,090
Liabilities	27,060	18,018	11,404	40,530	?
December 31, 2009					
Assets	36,000	25,920	?	65,520	99,360
Liabilities	?	17,625	11,818	31,449	78,494
During year 2009					
Owner investments	6,000	1,400	9,750	?	6,500
Net income (loss)	7,760	?	(1,289)	8,861	7,348
Owner cash withdrawals	3,500	2,000	5,875	0	11,000

Required

1. Answer the following questions about Company A:

a. What is the amount of equity on December 31, 2008?

b. What is the amount of equity on December 31, 2009?

c. What is the amount of liabilities on December 31, 2009?

2. Answer the following questions about Company B:

a. What is the amount of equity on December 31, 2008?

b. What is the amount of equity on December 31, 2009?

c. What is net income for year 2009?

3. Calculate the amount of assets for Company C on December 31, 2009.

4. Calculate the amount of owner investments for Company D during year 2009.

5. Calculate the amount of liabilities for Company E on December 31, 2008.

Check (1*b*) $16,200

(2*c*) $1,173

(3) $24,120

Problem 1-2A
Identifying effects of transactions on financial statements

A1 A2

Identify how each of the following separate transactions affects financial statements. For the balance sheet, identify how each transaction affects total assets, total liabilities, and total equity. For the income statement, identify how each transaction affects net income. For the statement of cash flows, identify how each transaction affects cash flows from operating activities, cash flows from financing activities, and cash flows from investing activities. For increases, place a "+" in the column or columns. For decreases, place a "−" in the column or columns. If both an increase and a decrease occur, place a "+/−" in the column or columns. The first transaction is completed as an example.

		Balance Sheet			Income Statement	Statement of Cash Flows		
	Transaction	Total Assets	Total Liab.	Total Equity	Net Income	Operating Activities	Financing Activities	Investing Activities
1	Owner invests cash in business	+		+			+	
2	Receives cash for services provided							
3	Pays cash for employee wages							
4	Incurs legal costs on credit							
5	Borrows cash by signing long-term note payable							
6	Buys land by signing note payable							
7	Provides services on credit							
8	Buys office equipment for cash							
9	Collects cash on receivable from (7)							
10	Owner withdraws cash							

Problem 1-3A
Preparing an income statement

P1

The following is selected financial information for Elko Energy Company for the year ended December 31, 2009: revenues, $66,000; expenses, $51,348; net income, $14,652.

Required

Prepare the 2009 calendar-year income statement for Elko Energy Company.

Problem 1-4A
Preparing a balance sheet

P1

The following is selected financial information for Amity Company as of December 31, 2009: liabilities, $54,244; equity, $87,756; assets, $142,000.

Required

Prepare the balance sheet for Amity Company as of December 31, 2009.

Problem 1-5A
Preparing a statement of cash flows
P1

Following is selected financial information of Fortune Co. for the year ended December 31, 2009.

Cash used by investing activities	$(3,250)
Net increase in cash	750
Cash used by financing activities	(4,050)
Cash from operating activities	8,050
Cash, December 31, 2008	4,100

Check Cash balance, Dec. 31, 2009, $4,850

Required

Prepare the 2009 statement of cash flows for Fortune Company.

Problem 1-6A
Preparing a statement of owner's equity
P1

Following is selected financial information for Atlee Co. for the year ended December 31, 2009.

A. Atlee, Capital, Dec. 31, 2009	$16,750	A. Atlee, Withdrawals	$ 2,000
Net income	7,750	A. Atlee, Capital, Dec. 31, 2008	11,000

Required

Prepare the 2009 statement of owner's equity for Atlee Company.

Problem 1-7A
Analyzing transactions and preparing financial statements
C5 A2 P1

excel
mhhe.com/wildFAP19e

Holden Graham started The Graham Co., a new business that began operations on May 1. The Graham Co. completed the following transactions during its first month of operations.

May 1 H. Graham invested $43,000 cash in the company.
1 The company rented a furnished office and paid $2,200 cash for May's rent.
3 The company purchased $1,940 of office equipment on credit.
5 The company paid $750 cash for this month's cleaning services.
8 The company provided consulting services for a client and immediately collected $5,800 cash.
12 The company provided $2,800 of consulting services for a client on credit.
15 The company paid $850 cash for an assistant's salary for the first half of this month.
20 The company received $2,800 cash payment for the services provided on May 12.
22 The company provided $4,000 of consulting services on credit.
25 The company received $4,000 cash payment for the services provided on May 22.
26 The company paid $1,940 cash for the office equipment purchased on May 3.
27 The company purchased $85 of advertising in this month's (May) local paper on credit; cash payment is due June 1.
28 The company paid $850 cash for an assistant's salary for the second half of this month.
30 The company paid $400 cash for this month's telephone bill.
30 The company paid $260 cash for this month's utilities.
31 H. Graham withdrew $2,000 cash from the company for personal use.

Required

1. Arrange the following asset, liability, and equity titles in a table like Exhibit 1.9: Cash; Accounts Receivable; Office Equipment; Accounts Payable; H. Graham, Capital; H. Graham, Withdrawals; Revenues; and Expenses.
2. Show effects of the transactions on the accounts of the accounting equation by recording increases and decreases in the appropriate columns. Do not determine new account balances after each transaction. Determine the final total for each account and verify that the equation is in balance.
3. Prepare an income statement for May, a statement of owner's equity for May, a May 31 balance sheet, and a statement of cash flows for May.

Check (2) Ending balances: Cash, $46,350; Expenses, $5,395

(3) Net income, $7,205; Total assets, $48,290

Problem 1-8A
Analyzing transactions and preparing financial statements
C5 A2 P1

excel
mhhe.com/wildFAP19e

Helga Anderson started a new business and completed these transactions during December.

Dec. 1 Helga Anderson transferred $68,800 cash from a personal savings account to a checking account in the name of Anderson Electric.
2 The company rented office space and paid $1,800 cash for the December rent.
3 The company purchased $13,000 of electrical equipment by paying $4,800 cash and agreeing to pay the $8,200 balance in 30 days.
5 The company purchased office supplies by paying $1,000 cash.
6 The company completed electrical work and immediately collected $1,600 cash for these services.
8 The company purchased $2,680 of office equipment on credit.
15 The company completed electrical work on credit in the amount of $6,000.
18 The company purchased $360 of office supplies on credit.
20 The company paid $2,680 cash for the office equipment purchased on December 8.
24 The company billed a client $1,000 for electrical work completed; the balance is due in 30 days.
28 The company received $6,000 cash for the work completed on December 15.
29 The company paid the assistant's salary of $1,500 cash for this month.
30 The company paid $570 cash for this month's utility bill.
31 H. Anderson withdrew $900 cash from the company for personal use.

Required

1. Arrange the following asset, liability, and equity titles in a table like Exhibit 1.9: Cash; Accounts Receivable; Office Supplies; Office Equipment; Electrical Equipment; Accounts Payable; H. Anderson, Capital; H. Anderson, Withdrawals; Revenues; and Expenses.
2. Use additions and subtractions to show the effects of each transaction on the accounts in the accounting equation. Show new balances after each transaction.
3. Use the increases and decreases in the columns of the table from part 2 to prepare an income statement, a statement of owner's equity, and a statement of cash flows—each of these for the current month. Also prepare a balance sheet as of the end of the month.

Check (2) Ending balances: Cash, $63,150, Accounts Payable, $8,560

(3) Net income, $4,730; Total assets, $81,190

Analysis Component

4. Assume that the owner investment transaction on December 1 was $49,000 cash instead of $68,800 and that Anderson Electric obtained another $19,800 in cash by borrowing it from a bank. Explain the effect of this change on total assets, total liabilities, and total equity.

Problem 1-9A
Analyzing effects of transactions
C5 P1 A1 A2

Inez Lopez started Wiz Consulting, a new business, and completed the following transactions during its first year of operations.

a. I. Lopez invests $67,000 cash and office equipment valued at $11,000 in the company.
b. The company purchased a $144,000 building to use as an office. Wiz paid $15,000 in cash and signed a note payable promising to pay the $129,000 balance over the next ten years.
c. The company purchased office equipment for $12,000 cash.
d. The company purchased $1,000 of office supplies and $1,700 of office equipment on credit.
e. The company paid a local newspaper $460 cash for printing an announcement of the office's opening.
f. The company completed a financial plan for a client and billed that client $2,400 for the service.
g. The company designed a financial plan for another client and immediately collected a $4,000 cash fee.
h. I. Lopez withdrew $3,025 cash from the company for personal use.
i. The company received $1,800 cash as partial payment from the client described in transaction *f*.
j. The company made a partial payment of $500 cash on the equipment purchased in transaction *d*.
k. The company paid $1,800 cash for the office secretary's wages for this period.

Required

1. Create a table like the one in Exhibit 1.9, using the following headings for the columns: Cash; Accounts Receivable; Office Supplies; Office Equipment; Building; Accounts Payable; Notes Payable; I. Lopez, Capital; I. Lopez, Withdrawals; Revenues; and Expenses.
2. Use additions and subtractions within the table created in part *1* to show the dollar effects of each transaction on individual items of the accounting equation. Show new balances after each transaction.
3. Once you have completed the table, determine the company's net income.

Check (2) Ending balances: Cash, $40,015; Expenses, $2,260; Notes Payable, $129,000

(3) Net income, $4,140

Problem 1-10A
Computing and interpreting return on assets
A3

Coca-Cola and PepsiCo both produce and market beverages that are direct competitors. Key financial figures (in $ millions) for these businesses over the past year follow.

Key Figures ($ millions)	Coca-Cola	PepsiCo
Sales	$24,088	$35,187
Net income	5,080	5,642
Average assets	29,695	30,829

Required

1. Compute return on assets for (*a*) Coca-Cola and (*b*) PepsiCo.

Check (1*a*) 17.1%; (1*b*) 18.3%

2. Which company is more successful in its total amount of sales to consumers?

3. Which company is more successful in returning net income from its assets invested?

Analysis Component

4. Write a one-paragraph memorandum explaining which company you would invest your money in and why. (Limit your explanation to the information provided.)

Problem 1-11A
Determining expenses, liabilities, equity, and return on assets
A1 A3

Notaro manufactures, markets, and sells cellular telephones. The average total assets for Notaro is $250,000. In its most recent year, Notaro reported net income of $64,000 on revenues of $468,000.

Required

1. What is Notaro's return on assets?

2. Does return on assets seem satisfactory for Notaro given that its competitors average a 9.5% return on assets?

3. What are total expenses for Notaro in its most recent year?

4. What is the average total amount of liabilities plus equity for Notaro?

Check (3) $404,000
(4) $250,000

Problem 1-12A[A]
Identifying risk and return
A4

All business decisions involve aspects of risk and return.

Required

Identify both the risk and the return in each of the following activities:

1. Investing $10,000 in Yahoo! stock.

2. Placing a $2,500 bet on your favorite sports team.

3. Investing $2,000 in a 5% savings account.

4. Taking out a $7,500 college loan to earn an accounting degree.

Problem 1-13A[B]
Describing organizational activities
C6

A start-up company often engages in the following transactions in its first year of operations. Classify those transactions in one of the three major categories of an organization's business activities.

F. Financing **I.** Investing **O.** Operating

______	**1.** Purchasing equipment.	______	**5.** Owner investing land in business.
______	**2.** Selling and distributing products.	______	**6.** Purchasing a building.
______	**3.** Paying for advertising.	______	**7.** Purchasing land.
______	**4.** Paying employee wages.	______	**8.** Borrowing cash from a bank.

Problem 1-14A[B]
Describing organizational activities C6

An organization undertakes various activities in pursuit of business success. Identify an organization's three major business activities, and describe each activity.

Required

1. Arrange the following asset, liability, and equity titles in a table like Exhibit 1.9: Cash; Accounts Receivable; Equipment; Accounts Payable; N. Benton, Capital; N. Benton, Withdrawals; Revenues; and Expenses.

Check (2) Ending balances: Cash, $43,790; Expenses, $5,230

2. Show the effects of the transactions on the accounts of the accounting equation by recording increases and decreases in the appropriate columns. Do not determine new account balances after each transaction. Determine the final total for each account and verify that the equation is in balance.

(3) Net income, $6,170; Total assets, $45,650

3. Prepare a June income statement, a June statement of owner's equity, a June 30 balance sheet, and a June statement of cash flows.

Problem 1-8B
Analyzing transactions and preparing financial statements
C5 A2 P1

Truro Excavating Co., owned by Raul Truro, began operations in July and completed these transactions during that first month of operations.

July	1	R. Truro invested $68,600 cash in the company.
	2	The company rented office space and paid $1,300 cash for the July rent.
	3	The company purchased excavating equipment for $14,600 by paying $6,400 cash and agreeing to pay the $8,200 balance in 30 days.
	6	The company purchased office supplies for $900 cash.
	8	The company completed work for a customer and immediately collected $2,000 cash for the work.
	10	The company purchased $2,720 of office equipment on credit.
	15	The company completed work for a customer on credit in the amount of $4,300.
	17	The company purchased $350 of office supplies on credit.
	23	The company paid $2,720 cash for the office equipment purchased on July 10.
	25	The company billed a customer $1,000 for work completed; the balance is due in 30 days.
	28	The company received $4,300 cash for the work completed on July 15.
	30	The company paid an assistant's salary of $1,900 cash for this month.
	31	The company paid $590 cash for this month's utility bill.
	31	R. Truro withdrew $900 cash from the company for personal use.

Required

1. Arrange the following asset, liability, and equity titles in a table like Exhibit 1.9: Cash; Accounts Receivable; Office Supplies; Office Equipment; Excavating Equipment; Accounts Payable; R. Truro, Capital; R. Truro, Withdrawals; Revenues; and Expenses.

Check (2) Ending balances: Cash, $60,190; Accounts Payable, $8,550

2. Use additions and subtractions to show the effects of each transaction on the accounts in the accounting equation. Show new balances after each transaction.

(3) Net income, $3,510; Total assets, $79,760

3. Use the increases and decreases in the columns of the table from part 2 to prepare an income statement, a statement of owner's equity, and a statement of cash flows—each of these for the current month. Also prepare a balance sheet as of the end of the month.

Analysis Component

4. Assume that the $14,600 purchase of excavating equipment on July 3 was financed from an owner investment of another $14,600 cash in the business (instead of the purchase conditions described in the transaction). Explain the effect of this change on total assets, total liabilities, and total equity.

Problem 1-9B
Analyzing effects of transactions
C5 P1 A1 A2

Nico Mitchell started a new business, Financial Management, and completed the following transactions during its first year of operations.

a. N. Mitchell invests $70,000 cash and office equipment valued at $12,000 in the company.

b. The company purchased a $141,000 building to use as an office. It paid $15,000 in cash and signed a note payable promising to pay the $126,000 balance over the next ten years.

c. The company purchased office equipment for $11,000 cash.

d. The company purchased $600 of office supplies and $1,300 of office equipment on credit.

e. The company paid a local newspaper $500 cash for printing an announcement of the office's opening.

f. The company completed a financial plan for a client and billed that client $2,400 for the service.

g. The company designed a financial plan for another client and immediately collected a $4,000 cash fee.

Problem 1-3B
Preparing an income statement
P1

Selected financial information for Onshore Co. for the year ended December 31, 2009, follows.

Revenues	$69,000	Expenses	$53,682	Net income	$15,318

Required

Prepare the 2009 income statement for Onshore Company.

Problem 1-4B
Preparing a balance sheet
P1

The following is selected financial information for NuTech Company as of December 31, 2009.

Liabilities	$46,222	Equity	$74,778	Assets	$121,000

Required

Prepare the balance sheet for NuTech Company as of December 31, 2009.

Problem 1-5B
Preparing a statement of cash flows
P1

Selected financial information of HalfLife Co. for the year ended December 31, 2009, follows.

Cash used by investing activities	$(3,750)
Net increase in cash	250
Cash used by financing activities	(4,550)
Cash from operating activities	8,550
Cash, December 31, 2008	3,700

Required

Prepare the 2009 statement of cash flows for HalfLife Company.

Problem 1-6B
Preparing a statement of owner's equity
P1

Following is selected financial information of Act First for the year ended December 31, 2009.

I. Firstact, Capital, Dec. 31, 2009	$10,500	I. Firstact, Withdrawals	$ 2,000
Net income	7,000	I. Firstact, Capital, Dec. 31, 2008	5,500

Required

Prepare the 2009 statement of owner's equity for Act First.

Problem 1-7B
Analyzing transactions and preparing financial statements
C5 A2 P1

Nikolas Benton launched a new business, Benton's Maintenance Co., that began operations on June 1. The following transactions were completed by the company during that first month.

June 1 N. Benton invested $41,000 cash in the company.
2 The company rented a furnished office and paid $2,200 cash for June's rent.
4 The company purchased $1,860 of equipment on credit.
6 The company paid $780 cash for this month's advertising of the opening of the business.
8 The company completed maintenance services for a customer and immediately collected $5,700 cash.
14 The company completed $2,400 of maintenance services for City Center on credit.
16 The company paid $810 cash for an assistant's salary for the first half of the month.
20 The company received $2,400 cash payment for services completed for City Center on June 14.
24 The company completed $3,300 of maintenance services for Build-It Coop on credit.
25 The company received $3,300 cash payment from Build-It Coop for the work completed on June 24.
26 The company made payment of $1,860 cash for the equipment purchased on June 4.
27 The company purchased $80 of product advertising in this month's (June) local newspaper on credit; cash payment is due July 1.
28 The company paid $810 cash for an assistant's salary for the second half of this month.
29 N. Benton withdrew $1,600 cash from the company for personal use.
30 The company paid $250 cash for this month's telephone bill.
30 The company paid $300 cash for this month's utilities.

Required

1. Arrange the following asset, liability, and equity titles in a table like Exhibit 1.9: Cash; Accounts Receivable; Equipment; Accounts Payable; N. Benton, Capital; N. Benton, Withdrawals; Revenues; and Expenses.
2. Show the effects of the transactions on the accounts of the accounting equation by recording increases and decreases in the appropriate columns. Do not determine new account balances after each transaction. Determine the final total for each account and verify that the equation is in balance.
3. Prepare a June income statement, a June statement of owner's equity, a June 30 balance sheet, and a June statement of cash flows.

Check (2) Ending balances: Cash, $43,790; Expenses, $5,230

(3) Net income, $6,170; Total assets, $45,650

Problem 1-8B
Analyzing transactions and preparing financial statements
C5 A2 P1

Truro Excavating Co., owned by Raul Truro, began operations in July and completed these transactions during that first month of operations.

July	1	R. Truro invested $68,600 cash in the company.
	2	The company rented office space and paid $1,300 cash for the July rent.
	3	The company purchased excavating equipment for $14,600 by paying $6,400 cash and agreeing to pay the $8,200 balance in 30 days.
	6	The company purchased office supplies for $900 cash.
	8	The company completed work for a customer and immediately collected $2,000 cash for the work.
	10	The company purchased $2,720 of office equipment on credit.
	15	The company completed work for a customer on credit in the amount of $4,300.
	17	The company purchased $350 of office supplies on credit.
	23	The company paid $2,720 cash for the office equipment purchased on July 10.
	25	The company billed a customer $1,000 for work completed; the balance is due in 30 days.
	28	The company received $4,300 cash for the work completed on July 15.
	30	The company paid an assistant's salary of $1,900 cash for this month.
	31	The company paid $590 cash for this month's utility bill.
	31	R. Truro withdrew $900 cash from the company for personal use.

Required

1. Arrange the following asset, liability, and equity titles in a table like Exhibit 1.9: Cash; Accounts Receivable; Office Supplies; Office Equipment; Excavating Equipment; Accounts Payable; R. Truro, Capital; R. Truro, Withdrawals; Revenues; and Expenses.
2. Use additions and subtractions to show the effects of each transaction on the accounts in the accounting equation. Show new balances after each transaction.
3. Use the increases and decreases in the columns of the table from part 2 to prepare an income statement, a statement of owner's equity, and a statement of cash flows—each of these for the current month. Also prepare a balance sheet as of the end of the month.

Check (2) Ending balances: Cash, $60,190; Accounts Payable, $8,550

(3) Net income, $3,510; Total assets, $79,760

Analysis Component

4. Assume that the $14,600 purchase of excavating equipment on July 3 was financed from an owner investment of another $14,600 cash in the business (instead of the purchase conditions described in the transaction). Explain the effect of this change on total assets, total liabilities, and total equity.

Problem 1-9B
Analyzing effects of transactions
C5 P1 A1 A2

Nico Mitchell started a new business, Financial Management, and completed the following transactions during its first year of operations.

a. N. Mitchell invests $70,000 cash and office equipment valued at $12,000 in the company.
b. The company purchased a $141,000 building to use as an office. It paid $15,000 in cash and signed a note payable promising to pay the $126,000 balance over the next ten years.
c. The company purchased office equipment for $11,000 cash.
d. The company purchased $600 of office supplies and $1,300 of office equipment on credit.
e. The company paid a local newspaper $500 cash for printing an announcement of the office's opening.
f. The company completed a financial plan for a client and billed that client $2,400 for the service.
g. The company designed a financial plan for another client and immediately collected a $4,000 cash fee.

Coca-Cola and PepsiCo both produce and market beverages that are direct competitors. Key financial figures (in $ millions) for these businesses over the past year follow.

Problem 1-10A
Computing and interpreting return on assets
A3

Key Figures ($ millions)	Coca-Cola	PepsiCo
Sales	$24,088	$35,187
Net income	5,080	5,642
Average assets	29,695	30,829

Required

1. Compute return on assets for (*a*) Coca-Cola and (*b*) PepsiCo.
2. Which company is more successful in its total amount of sales to consumers?
3. Which company is more successful in returning net income from its assets invested?

Check (1*a*) 17.1%; (1*b*) 18.3%

Analysis Component

4. Write a one-paragraph memorandum explaining which company you would invest your money in and why. (Limit your explanation to the information provided.)

Notaro manufactures, markets, and sells cellular telephones. The average total assets for Notaro is $250,000. In its most recent year, Notaro reported net income of $64,000 on revenues of $468,000.

Problem 1-11A
Determining expenses, liabilities, equity, and return on assets
A1 A3

Required

1. What is Notaro's return on assets?
2. Does return on assets seem satisfactory for Notaro given that its competitors average a 9.5% return on assets?
3. What are total expenses for Notaro in its most recent year?
4. What is the average total amount of liabilities plus equity for Notaro?

Check (3) $404,000
(4) $250,000

All business decisions involve aspects of risk and return.

Problem 1-12A[A]
Identifying risk and return
A4

Required

Identify both the risk and the return in each of the following activities:

1. Investing $10,000 in Yahoo! stock.
2. Placing a $2,500 bet on your favorite sports team.
3. Investing $2,000 in a 5% savings account.
4. Taking out a $7,500 college loan to earn an accounting degree.

A start-up company often engages in the following transactions in its first year of operations. Classify those transactions in one of the three major categories of an organization's business activities.

Problem 1-13A[B]
Describing organizational activities
C6

F. Financing **I.** Investing **O.** Operating

_____ **1.** Purchasing equipment.	_____ **5.** Owner investing land in business.
_____ **2.** Selling and distributing products.	_____ **6.** Purchasing a building.
_____ **3.** Paying for advertising.	_____ **7.** Purchasing land.
_____ **4.** Paying employee wages.	_____ **8.** Borrowing cash from a bank.

An organization undertakes various activities in pursuit of business success. Identify an organization's three major business activities, and describe each activity.

Problem 1-14A[B]
Describing organizational activities C6

PROBLEM SET B

Problem 1-1B
Computing missing information using accounting knowledge

A1 A2

The following financial statement information is from five separate companies.

	Company V	Company W	Company X	Company Y	Company Z
December 31, 2008					
Assets	$36,000	$ 28,080	$23,040	$64,080	$ 98,280
Liabilities	29,520	19,656	12,441	44,215	?
December 31, 2009					
Assets	39,000	28,080	26,130	?	107,640
Liabilities	21,450	?	12,803	34,070	85,035
During year 2009					
Owner investments	6,000	1,400	?	7,000	6,500
Net income or (loss)	?	1,162	(1,147)	10,045	7,449
Owner cash withdrawals	3,500	2,000	5,875	0	11,000

Required

1. Answer the following questions about Company V:
  a. What is the amount of equity on December 31, 2008?
  b. What is the amount of equity on December 31, 2009?
  c. What is the net income or loss for the year 2009?

2. Answer the following questions about Company W:
  a. What is the amount of equity on December 31, 2008?
  b. What is the amount of equity on December 31, 2009?
  c. What is the amount of liabilities on December 31, 2009?

3. Calculate the amount of owner investments for Company X during 2009.

4. Calculate the amount of assets for Company Y on December 31, 2009.

5. Calculate the amount of liabilities for Company Z on December 31, 2008.

Check (1*b*) $17,550

(2*c*) $19,094

(4) $70,980

Problem 1-2B
Identifying effects of transactions on financial statements

A1 A2

Identify how each of the following separate transactions affects financial statements. For the balance sheet, identify how each transaction affects total assets, total liabilities, and total equity. For the income statement, identify how each transaction affects net income. For the statement of cash flows, identify how each transaction affects cash flows from operating activities, cash flows from financing activities, and cash flows from investing activities. For increases, place a "+" in the column or columns. For decreases, place a "−" in the column or columns. If both an increase and a decrease occur, place "+/−" in the column or columns. The first transaction is completed as an example.

		Balance Sheet			Income Statement	Statement of Cash Flows		
	Transaction	Total Assets	Total Liab.	Total Equity	Net Income	Operating Activities	Financing Activities	Investing Activities
1	Owner invests cash in business	+		+			+	
2	Buys building by signing note payable							
3	Pays cash for salaries incurred							
4	Provides services for cash							
5	Pays cash for rent incurred							
6	Incurs utilities costs on credit							
7	Buys store equipment for cash							
8	Provides services on credit							
9	Collects cash on receivable from (8)							
10	Owner withdraws cash							

h. N. Mitchell withdrew $3,325 cash from the company for personal use.
i. The company received $1,750 cash as a partial payment from the client described in transaction *f.*
j. The company made a partial payment of $700 cash on the equipment purchased in transaction *d.*
k. The company paid $1,750 cash for the office secretary's wages.

Required

1. Create a table like the one in Exhibit 1.9, using the following headings for the columns: Cash; Accounts Receivable; Office Supplies; Office Equipment; Building; Accounts Payable; Notes Payable; N. Mitchell, Capital; N. Mitchell, Withdrawals; Revenues; and Expenses.
2. Use additions and subtractions within the table created in part *1* to show the dollar effects of each transaction on individual items of the accounting equation. Show new balances after each transaction.
3. Once you have completed the table, determine the company's net income.

Check (2) Ending balances: Cash, $43,475; Expenses, $2,250; Notes Payable, $126,000

(3) Net income, $4,150

Problem 1-10B
Computing and interpreting return on assets

A3

AT&T and **Verizon** produce and market telecommunications products and are competitors. Key financial figures (in $ millions) for these businesses over the past year follow.

Key Figures ($ millions)	AT&T	Verizon
Sales	$ 63,055	$ 84,144
Net income	7,356	6,197
Average assets	208,133	178,467

Required

1. Compute return on assets for (*a*) AT&T and (*b*) Verizon.
2. Which company is more successful in the total amount of sales to consumers?
3. Which company is more successful in returning net income from its assets invested?

Check (1*a*) 3.5%; (1*b*) 3.5%

Analysis Component

4. Write a one-paragraph memorandum explaining which company you would invest your money in and why. (Limit your explanation to the information provided.)

Problem 1-11B
Determining expenses, liabilities, equity, and return on assets

A1 A3

Carbondale Company manufactures, markets, and sells ATV and snowmobile equipment and accessories. The average total assets for Carbondale is $243,000. In its most recent year, Carbondale reported net income of $62,500 on revenues of $473,000.

Required

1. What is Carbondale Company's return on assets?
2. Does return on assets seem satisfactory for Carbondale given that its competitors average a 10% return on assets?
3. What are the total expenses for Carbondale Company in its most recent year?
4. What is the average total amount of liabilities plus equity for Carbondale Company?

Check (3) $410,500

(4) $243,000

Problem 1-12B[A]
Identifying risk and return

A4

All business decisions involve aspects of risk and return.

Required

Identify both the risk and the return in each of the following activities:

1. Investing $20,000 in Nike stock.
2. Placing a $250 bet on a horse running in the Kentucky Derby.
3. Stashing $500 cash under your mattress.
4. Investing $35,000 in U.S. Savings Bonds.

Problem 1-13B[B]
Describing organizational activities
C6

A start-up company often engages in the following activities during its first year of operations. Classify each of the following activities into one of the three major activities of an organization.

F. Financing **I.** Investing **O.** Operating

_____ **1.** Supervising workers.
_____ **2.** Owner investing money in business.
_____ **3.** Renting office space.
_____ **4.** Paying utilities expenses.
_____ **5.** Providing client services.
_____ **6.** Obtaining a bank loan.
_____ **7.** Purchasing machinery.
_____ **8.** Research for its products.

Problem 1-14B[B]
Describing organizational activities C6

Identify in outline format the three major business activities of an organization. For each of these activities, identify at least two specific transactions or events normally undertaken by the business's owners or its managers.

This serial problem starts in this chapter and continues throughout most chapters of the book. It is most readily solved if you use the Working Papers that accompany this book.

SERIAL PROBLEM

Success Systems

SP 1 On October 1, 2009, Adriana Lopez launched a computer services company, **Success Systems,** that is organized as a proprietorship and provides consulting services, computer system installations, and custom program development. Lopez adopts the calendar year for reporting purposes and expects to prepare the company's first set of financial statements on December 31, 2009.

Required

Create a table like the one in Exhibit 1.9 using the following headings for columns: Cash; Accounts Receivable; Computer Supplies; Computer System; Office Equipment; Accounts Payable; A. Lopez, Capital; A. Lopez, Withdrawals; Revenues; and Expenses. Then use additions and subtractions within the table created to show the dollar effects for each of the following October transactions for Success Systems on the individual items of the accounting equation. Show new balances after each transaction.

Oct. 1 Adriana Lopez invested $55,000 cash, a $20,000 computer system, and $8,000 of office equipment in the company.
3 The company purchased $1,420 of computer supplies on credit from Harris Office Products.
6 The company billed Easy Leasing $4,800 for services performed in installing a new Web server.
8 The company paid $1,420 cash for the computer supplies purchased from Harris Office Products on October 3.
10 The company hired Lyn Addie as a part-time assistant for $125 per day, as needed.
12 The company billed Easy Leasing another $1,400 for services performed.
15 The company received $4,800 cash from Easy Leasing as partial payment toward its account.
17 The company paid $805 cash to repair computer equipment damaged when moving it.
20 The company paid $1,940 cash for an advertisement in the local newspaper.
22 The company received $1,400 cash from Easy Leasing toward its account.
28 The company billed IFM Company $5,208 for services performed.
31 The company paid $875 cash for Lyn Addie's wages for seven days of work this month.
31 A. Lopez withdrew $3,600 cash from the company for personal use.

Check Ending balances: Cash, $52,560; Revenues, $11,408; Expenses, $3,620

Beyond the Numbers (BTN) *is a special problem section aimed to refine communication, conceptual, analysis, and research skills. It includes many activities helpful in developing an active learning environment.*

BEYOND THE NUMBERS

REPORTING IN ACTION

A1 A3 A4

BTN 1-1 Key financial figures for **Best Buy**'s fiscal year ended March 3, 2007, follow.

Key Figure	In Millions
Liabilities + Equity	$13,570
Net income	1,377
Revenues	35,934

Required

1. What is the total amount of assets invested in Best Buy?
2. What is Best Buy's return on assets? Its assets at February 25, 2006, equal $11,864 (in millions).
3. How much are total expenses for Best Buy for the year ended March 3, 2007?
4. Does Best Buy's return on assets seem satisfactory if competitors average an 8.1% return?

Check (2) 10.8%

Fast Forward

5. Access Best Buy's financial statements (Form 10-K) for fiscal years ending after March 3, 2007, from its Website (**BestBuy.com**) or from the SEC Website (**www.SEC.gov**) and compute its return on assets for those fiscal years. Compare the March 3, 2007, fiscal year-end return on assets to any subsequent years' returns you are able to compute, and interpret the results.

COMPARATIVE ANALYSIS

A1 A3 A4

BTN 1-2 Key comparative figures ($ millions) for both **Best Buy** and **RadioShack** follow.

Key Figure	Best Buy	RadioShack
Liabilities + Equity	$13,570	$2,070
Net income	1,377	73
Revenues and sales	35,934	4,778

Required

1. What is the total amount of assets invested in (*a*) Best Buy and (*b*) RadioShack?
2. What is the return on assets for (*a*) Best Buy and (*b*) RadioShack? Best Buy's beginning-year assets equal $11,864 (in millions) and RadioShack's beginning-year assets equal $2,205 (in millions).
3. How much are expenses for (*a*) Best Buy and (*b*) RadioShack?
4. Is return on assets satisfactory for (*a*) Best Buy and (*b*) RadioShack? (Assume competitors average an 8.1% return.)
5. What can you conclude about Best Buy and RadioShack from these computations?

Check (2b) 3.4%

ETHICS CHALLENGE

C4 C5

BTN 1-3 Liz Thorne works in a public accounting firm and hopes to eventually be a partner. The management of Allnet Company invites Thorne to prepare a bid to audit Allnet's financial statements. In discussing the audit fee, Allnet's management suggests a fee range in which the amount depends on the reported profit of Allnet. The higher its profit, the higher will be the audit fee paid to Thorne's firm.

Required

1. Identify the parties potentially affected by this audit and the fee plan proposed.
2. What are the ethical factors in this situation? Explain.
3. Would you recommend that Thorne accept this audit fee arrangement? Why or why not?
4. Describe some ethical considerations guiding your recommendation.

COMMUNICATING IN PRACTICE

A1 C2

BTN 1-4 Refer to this chapter's opening feature about **Life is good.**® Assume that Bert and John Jacobs desire to expand their manufacturing facilities to meet customer demand. They decide to meet with their banker to discuss a loan to allow them to expand.

Required

1. Prepare a half-page report outlining the information you would request from the Jacobs brothers if you were the loan officer.
2. Indicate whether the information you request and your loan decision are affected by the form of business organization for Life is good.

TAKING IT TO THE NET

A3

BTN 1-5 Visit the EDGAR database at (www.SEC.gov). Access the Form 10-K report of **Rocky Mountain Chocolate Factory** (ticker RMCF) filed on May 14, 2007, covering its 2007 fiscal year.

Required

1. Item 6 of the 10-K report provides comparative financial highlights of RMCF for the years 2004–2007. How would you describe the revenue trend for RMCF over this four-year period?
2. Has RMCF been profitable (see net income) over this four-year period? Support your answer.

TEAMWORK IN ACTION

C1

BTN 1-6 Teamwork is important in today's business world. Successful teams schedule convenient meetings, maintain regular communications, and cooperate with and support their members. This assignment aims to establish support/learning teams, initiate discussions, and set meeting times.

Required

1. Form teams and open a team discussion to determine a regular time and place for your team to meet between each scheduled class meeting. Notify your instructor via a memorandum or e-mail message as to when and where your team will hold regularly scheduled meetings.
2. Develop a list of telephone numbers and/or e-mail addresses of your teammates.

ENTREPRENEURIAL DECISION

A1 A2

BTN 1-7 Refer to this chapter's opening feature about **Life is good**. Assume that Bert and John Jacobs decide to open a new manufacturing facility to produce sunscreen. This new company will be called LifeScreen Manufacturing Company.

Required

1. LifeScreen Manufacturing obtains a $500,000 loan and the Jacobs brothers contribute $250,000 of their own assets in the new company.
   a. What is the new company's total amount of liabilities plus equity?
   b. What is the new company's total amount of assets?
2. If the new company earns $80,000 in net income in the first year of operation, compute its return on asset (assume average assets equal $750,000). Assess its performance if competitors average a 10% return.

Check (2) 10.7%

HITTING THE ROAD

C2

BTN 1-8 You are to interview a local business owner. (This can be a friend or relative.) Opening lines of communication with members of the business community can provide personal benefits of business networking. If you do not know the owner, you should call ahead to introduce yourself and explain your position as a student and your assignment requirements. You should request a thirty minute appointment for a face-to-face or phone interview to discuss the form of organization and operations of the business. Be prepared to make a good impression.

Required

1. Identify and describe the main operating activities and the form of organization for this business.
2. Determine and explain why the owner(s) chose this particular form of organization.
3. Identify any special advantages and/or disadvantages the owner(s) experiences in operating with this form of business organization.

BTN 1-9 **DSG international plc** (www.DSGiplc.com) is the leading European retailer of consumer electronics and competes with both **Best Buy** and **RadioShack**. Key financial figures for DSG follow.

GLOBAL DECISION

A1 A3 A4

DSG

BEST BUY

RadioShack.

Key Figure*	Pounds in Millions
Average assets	£4,048
Net income	207
Revenues	7,930
Return on assets	5.2%

* Figures prepared in accordance with International Financial Reporting Standards.

Required

1. Identify any concerns you have in comparing DSG's income and revenue figures to those of Best Buy and RadioShack (in BTN 1-2) for purposes of making business decisions.

2. Identify any concerns you have in comparing DSG's return on assets ratio to those of Best Buy and RadioShack (computed for BTN 1-2) for purposes of making business decisions.

ANSWERS TO MULTIPLE CHOICE QUIZ

1. c; $450,000 is the actual cost incurred.

2. b; revenue is recorded when earned.

3. d;

Assets	=	Liabilities	+	Equity
+$100,000	=	+35,000	+	?

Change in equity = $100,000 − $35,000 = $65,000

4. a

5. a

A Look Back

Chapter 1 defined accounting and introduced financial statements. We described forms of organizations and identified users and uses of accounting. We defined the accounting equation and applied it to transaction analysis.

A Look at This Chapter

This chapter focuses on the accounting process. We describe transactions and source documents, and we explain the analysis and recording of transactions. The accounting equation, T-account, general ledger, trial balance, and debits and credits are key tools in the accounting process.

A Look Ahead

Chapter 3 extends our focus on processing information. We explain the importance of adjusting accounts and the procedures in preparing financial statements.

Chapter 2 Analyzing and Recording Transactions

Learning Objectives

CAP

Conceptual

C1 Explain the steps in processing transactions. *(p. 48)*

C2 Describe source documents and their purpose. *(p. 48)*

C3 Describe an account and its use in recording transactions. *(p. 49)*

C4 Describe a ledger and a chart of accounts. *(p. 52)*

C5 Define *debits* and *credits* and explain double-entry accounting. *(p. 53)*

Analytical

A1 Analyze the impact of transactions on accounts and financial statements. *(p. 57)*

A2 Compute the debt ratio and describe its use in analyzing financial condition. *(p. 66)*

Procedural

P1 Record transactions in a journal and post entries to a ledger. *(p. 54)*

P2 Prepare and explain the use of a trial balance. *(p. 63)*

P3 Prepare financial statements from business transactions. *(p. 64)*

LP2

Decision Feature

The Bottom Line

"It has been a dream come true" — Sara Blakely

ATLANTA—"Working as a sales trainer by day and performing stand-up comedy at night, I didn't know the first thing about the pantyhose industry," admits Sara Blakely. "Except, I dreaded wearing most pantyhose." One night Sara cut the feet out of her pantyhose to wear with white pants and open-toed shoes, and at that moment, Sara knew she had a unique idea. Sara took $5,000 in savings and launched **SPANX (Spanx.com),** a manufacturer of footless pantyhose, slimming intimates, hosiery, and other women's apparel.

To pursue her business ambitions, Sara studied business activities and learned the value of accounting information. She established recordkeeping processes, transaction analysis, inventory accounting, and financial statement reporting. I had to get a handle on my financial situation, says Sara, as I wanted to remain self-funded. To this day, Sara remains self-funded and has a reliable accounting system to help her make good business decisions.

I had to account for product costs, office expenses, supplier payments, patent fees, and other expenses, says Sara. At the same time, Sara expanded sales and struggled to stay profitable. "I had no money to advertise, so I hit the road," laughs Sara. "For the entire first year, I did in-store rallies . . . staying all day introducing customers to Spanx."

In her first three months, Sara sold over 50,000 pairs of footless pantyhose. Today, just seven short years from her launch, Sara reports over $150 million in retail sales. "We are still a small company of women," claims Sara, "obsessed with inventing and improving comfortable undergarments." Sara continues to track and account for all revenues and expenses. She maintains that success requires proper accounting for and analysis of the financial side.

The bigger message of Spanx, says Sara, is promoting comfort and confidence for women. Insists Sara, "We believe all women deserve the opportunity to make the most of their assets!"

[Sources: *SPANX Website,* January 2009; *Entrepreneur,* May 2007; *Smart Money,* September 2002; *TV Guide,* July 2007; *Financial Times,* 2006; *ABC Television,* 2007]

Financial statements report on the financial performance and condition of an organization. Knowledge of their preparation, organization, and analysis is important. A main goal of this chapter is to illustrate how transactions are recorded, how they are reflected in financial statements, and how they impact analysis of financial statements. Debits and credits are introduced and identified as a tool in helping analyze and process transactions.

Analyzing and Recording Transactions

Analyzing and Recording Process
- Source documents
- The account and its analysis
- Types of accounts

Analyzing and Processing Transactions
- General ledger
- Double-entry accounting
- Journalizing and posting
- An illustration

Trial Balance
- Trial balance preparation
- Search for and correction of errors
- Trial balance use

Analyzing and Recording Process

C1 Explain the steps in processing transactions.

The accounting process identifies business transactions and events, analyzes and records their effects, and summarizes and presents information in reports and financial statements. These reports and statements are used for making investing, lending, and other business decisions. The steps in the accounting process that focus on *analyzing and recording* transactions and events are shown in Exhibit 2.1.

EXHIBIT 2.1

The Analyzing and Recording Process

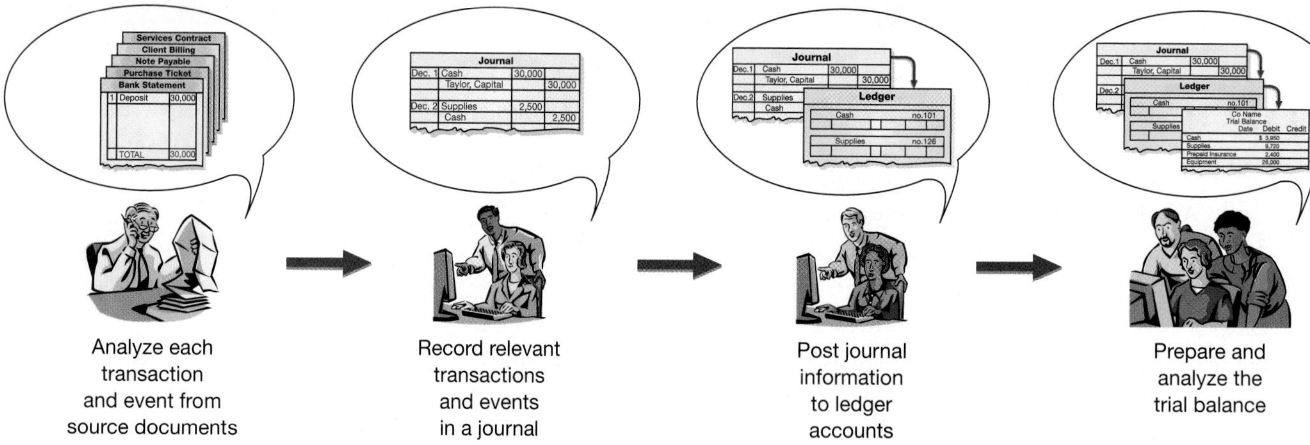

Business transactions and events are the starting points. Relying on source documents, the transactions and events are analyzed using the accounting equation to understand how they affect company performance and financial position. These effects are recorded in accounting records, informally referred to as the *accounting books,* or simply the *books*. Additional steps such as posting and then preparing a trial balance help summarize and classify the effects of transactions and events. Ultimately, the accounting process provides information in useful reports or financial statements to decision makers.

Source Documents

C2 Describe source documents and their purpose.

Source documents identify and describe transactions and events entering the accounting process. They are the sources of accounting information and can be in either hard copy or electronic form. Examples are sales tickets, checks, purchase orders, bills from suppliers, employee earnings records, and bank statements. To illustrate, when an item is purchased on credit, the seller usually prepares at least two copies of a sales invoice. One copy is given to the buyer. Another copy, often sent electronically, results in an entry in the seller's information system to record the sale. Sellers use invoices for recording sales and for control; buyers use them for recording purchases and for monitoring purchasing activity. Many cash registers record information for each sale on a tape or electronic file locked inside the register. This record can be used as a source document for recording sales in the accounting records. Source documents, especially if obtained from outside the organization, provide objective and reliable evidence about transactions and events and their amounts.

Point: To ensure that all sales are rung up on the register, most sellers require customers to have their receipts to exchange or return purchased items.

Decision Ethics

Cashier Your manager requires that you, as cashier, immediately enter each sale. Recently, lunch hour traffic has increased and the assistant manager asks you to avoid delays by taking customers' cash and making change without entering sales. The assistant manager says she will add up cash and enter sales after lunch. She says that, in this way, the register will always match the cash amount when the manager arrives at three o'clock. What do you do? [Answer—p. 71]

The Account and Its Analysis

C3 Describe an account and its use in recording transactions.

An **account** is a record of increases and decreases in a specific asset, liability, equity, revenue, or expense item. Information from an account is analyzed, summarized, and presented in reports and financial statements. The **general ledger,** or simply **ledger,** is a record containing all accounts used by a company. The ledger is often in electronic form. While most companies' ledgers contain similar accounts, a company often uses one or more unique accounts because of its type of operations. Accounts are arranged into three general categories (based on the accounting equation), as shown in Exhibit 2.2.

EXHIBIT 2.2

Accounts Organized by the Accounting Equation

Asset Accounts Assets are resources owned or controlled by a company and that have expected future benefits. Most accounting systems include (at a minimum) separate accounts for the assets described here.

A *Cash* account reflects a company's cash balance. All increases and decreases in cash are recorded in the Cash account. It includes money and any medium of exchange that a bank accepts for deposit (coins, checks, money orders, and checking account balances).

Accounts receivable are held by a seller and refer to promises of payment from customers to sellers. These transactions are often called *credit sales* or *sales on account* (or *on credit*). Accounts receivable are increased by credit sales and are decreased by customer payments. A company needs a separate record for each customer, but for now, we use the simpler practice of recording all increases and decreases in receivables in a single account called Accounts Receivable.

Point: Customers and others who owe a company are called its **debtors.**

A *note receivable,* or promissory note, is a written promise of another entity to pay a definite sum of money on a specified future date to the holder of the note. A company holding a promissory note signed by another entity has an asset that is recorded in a Note (or Notes) Receivable account.

Prepaid accounts (also called *prepaid expenses*) are assets that represent prepayments of future expenses (*not* current expenses). When the expenses are later incurred, the amounts in prepaid accounts are transferred to expense accounts. Common examples of prepaid accounts include prepaid insurance, prepaid rent, and prepaid services (such as club memberships). Prepaid accounts expire with the passage of time (such as with rent) or through use (such as with prepaid meal tickets). When financial statements are prepared, prepaid accounts are adjusted so that (1) all expired and used prepaid accounts are recorded as regular expenses and (2) all unexpired and unused prepaid accounts are recorded as assets (reflecting future use in

Point: A college parking fee is a prepaid account from the student's standpoint. At the beginning of the term, it represents an asset that entitles a student to park on or near campus. The benefits of the parking fee expire as the term progresses. At term-end, prepaid parking (asset) equals zero as it has been entirely recorded as parking expense.

Point: Prepaid accounts that apply to current and future periods are assets. These assets are adjusted at the end of each period to reflect only those amounts that have not yet expired, and to record as expenses those amounts that have expired.

future periods). To illustrate, when an insurance fee, called a *premium,* is paid in advance, the cost is typically recorded in the asset account Prepaid Insurance. Over time, the expiring portion of the insurance cost is removed from this asset account and reported in expenses on the income statement. Any unexpired portion remains in Prepaid Insurance and is reported on the balance sheet as an asset. (An exception exists for prepaid accounts that will expire or be used before the end of the current accounting period when financial statements are prepared. In this case, the prepayments *can* be recorded immediately as expenses.)

Supplies are assets until they are used. When they are used up, their costs are reported as expenses. The costs of unused supplies are recorded in a Supplies asset account. Supplies are often grouped by purpose—for example, office supplies and store supplies. *Office supplies* include stationery, paper, toner, and pens. *Store supplies* include packaging materials, plastic and paper bags, gift boxes and cartons, and cleaning materials. The costs of these unused supplies can be recorded in an Office Supplies or a Store Supplies asset account. When supplies are used, their costs are transferred from the asset accounts to expense accounts.

Point: Some assets are described as *intangible* because they do not have physical existence or their benefits are highly uncertain. A recent balance sheet for **Coca-Cola Company** shows nearly $1 billion in intangible assets.

Equipment is an asset. When equipment is used and gets worn down, its cost is gradually reported as an expense (called depreciation). Equipment is often grouped by its purpose—for example, office equipment and store equipment. *Office equipment* includes computers, printers, desks, chairs, and shelves. Costs incurred for these items are recorded in an Office Equipment asset account. The Store Equipment account includes the costs of assets used in a store, such as counters, showcases, ladders, hoists, and cash registers.

Buildings such as stores, offices, warehouses, and factories are assets because they provide expected future benefits to those who control or own them. Their costs are recorded in a Buildings asset account. When several buildings are owned, separate accounts are sometimes kept for each of them.

The cost of *land* owned by a business is recorded in a Land account. The cost of buildings located on the land is separately recorded in one or more building accounts.

Decision Insight

Women Entrepreneurs The Center for Women's Business Research reports that women-owned businesses, such as **SPANX**, are growing and that they

- Total approximately 11 million and employ nearly 20 million workers.
- Generate $2.5 trillion in annual sales and tend to embrace technology.
- Are philanthropic—70% of owners volunteer at least once per month.
- Are more likely funded by individual investors (73%) than venture firms (15%).

Liability Accounts Liabilities are claims (by creditors) against assets, which means they are obligations to transfer assets or provide products or services to other entities. **Creditors** are individuals and organizations that own the right to receive payments from a company. If a company fails to pay its obligations, the law gives creditors a right to force the sale of that company's assets to obtain the money to meet creditors' claims. When assets are sold under these conditions, creditors are paid first, but only up to the amount of their claims. Any remaining money, the residual, goes to the owners of the company. Creditors often use a balance sheet to help decide whether to loan money to a company. A loan is less risky if the borrower's liabilities are small in comparison to assets because this means there are more resources than claims on resources. Common liability accounts are described here.

Point: Accounts Payable are also called *Trade Payables.*

Accounts payable refer to oral or implied promises to pay later, which usually arise from purchases of merchandise. Payables can also arise from purchases of supplies, equipment, and services. Accounting systems keep separate records about each creditor. We describe these individual records in Chapter 5.

A *note payable* refers to a formal promise, usually denoted by the signing of a promissory note, to pay a future amount. It is recorded in either a short-term Note Payable account or a long-term Note Payable account, depending on when it must be repaid. We explain details of short- and long-term classification in Chapter 3.

Unearned Revenue refers to a liability that is settled in the future when a company delivers its products or services. When customers pay in advance for products or services (before revenue is earned), the revenue recognition principle requires that the seller consider this payment as unearned revenue. Examples of unearned revenue include magazine subscriptions collected in advance by a publisher, sales of gift certificates by stores, and season ticket sales by sports teams. The seller would record these in liability accounts such as Unearned Subscriptions, Unearned Store Sales, and Unearned Ticket Revenue. When products and services are later delivered, the earned portion of the unearned revenue is transferred to revenue accounts such as Subscription Fees, Store Sales, and Ticket Sales.[1]

Point: If a subscription is canceled, the publisher is expected to refund the unused portion to the subscriber.

Accrued liabilities are amounts owed that are not yet paid. Examples are wages payable, taxes payable, and interest payable. These are often recorded in separate liability accounts by the same title. If they are not large in amount, one or more ledger accounts can be added and reported as a single amount on the balance sheet. (Financial statements often have amounts reported that are a summation of several ledger accounts.)

Decision Insight

Revenue Spread The **Chicago Bears** have *Unearned Revenues* of about $60 million in advance ticket sales. When the team plays its home games, it settles this liability to its ticket holders and then transfers the amount earned to *Ticket Revenues.*

Equity Accounts The owner's claim on a company's assets is called *equity* or *owner's equity.* Equity is the owner's *residual interest* in the assets of a business after deducting liabilities. Equity is impacted by four types of accounts: owner's capital, owner's withdrawals, revenues, and expenses. We show this visually in Exhibit 2.3 by expanding the accounting equation.

Point: Equity is also called *net assets.*

EXHIBIT 2.3

Expanded Accounting Equation

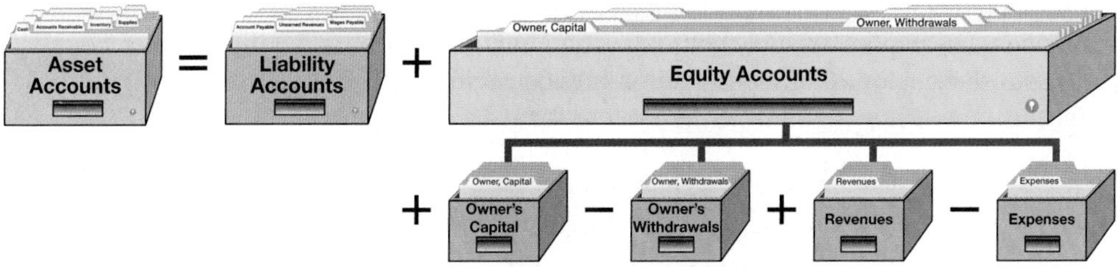

When an owner invests in a company, the invested amount is recorded in an account titled **Owner, Capital** (where the owner's name is inserted in place of "owner"). The account titled *C. Taylor, Capital* is used for FastForward. Any further owner investments are recorded in this account. When an owner withdraws assets for personal use it decreases both company assets and total equity. Withdrawals are not expenses of the business; they are simply the opposite of owner investments. The **Owner, Withdrawals** account is used to record asset distributions to the owner. The account titled *C. Taylor, Withdrawals* is used for FastForward. (Owners of proprietorships cannot receive company salaries because they are not legally separate from their companies; and they cannot enter into company contracts with themselves.)

Point: The Owner's Withdrawals account is a *contra equity* account because it reduces the normal balance of equity.

Point: The withdrawal of assets by the owners of a corporation is called a *dividend.*

Revenues and expenses also impact equity. Examples of revenue accounts are Sales, Commissions Earned, Professional Fees Earned, Rent Earned, and Interest Revenue. *Revenues increase equity* and result from products and services provided to customers. Examples of expense accounts are Advertising Expense, Store Supplies Expense, Office Salaries Expense, Office Supplies Expense, Rent Expense, Utilities Expense, and Insurance Expense. *Expenses decrease equity* and result from assets and services used in a company's operations. The variety of revenues and expenses can be seen by looking at the *chart of accounts* that follows the index

[1] In practice, account titles vary. As one example, Subscription Fees is sometimes called Subscription Fees Revenue, Subscription Fees Earned, or Earned Subscription Fees. As another example, Rent Earned is sometimes called Rent Revenue, Rental Revenue, or Earned Rent Revenue. We must use good judgment when reading financial statements because titles can differ even within the same industry. For example, product sales are called *revenue* at **Best Buy**, but *net sales and operating revenues* at **Circuit City**. Generally, the term *revenues* or *fees* is more commonly used with service businesses, and *net sales* or *sales* with product businesses.

at the back of this book. (Different companies sometimes use different account titles than those in this book's chart of accounts. For example, some might use Interest Revenue instead of Interest Earned, or Rental Expense instead of Rent Expense. It is important only that an account title describe the item it represents.)

Decision Insight

Sporting Accounts The **San Antonio Spurs** have the following major revenue and expense accounts:

Revenues	**Expenses**
Basketball ticket sales	Team salaries
TV & radio broadcast fees	Game costs
Advertising revenues	NBA franchise costs
Basketball playoff receipts	Promotional costs

Analyzing and Processing Transactions

This section explains several tools and processes that comprise an accounting system. These include a ledger, T-account, debits and credits, double-entry accounting, journalizing, and posting.

Ledger and Chart of Accounts

C4 Describe a ledger and a chart of accounts.

The collection of all accounts for an information system is called a *ledger* (or *general ledger*). If accounts are in files on a hard drive, the sum of those files is the ledger. If the accounts are pages in a file, that file is the ledger. A company's size and diversity of operations affect the number of accounts needed. A small company can get by with as few as 20 or 30 accounts; a large company can require several thousand. The **chart of accounts** is a list of all accounts a company uses and includes an identification number assigned to each account. A small business might use the following numbering system for its accounts:

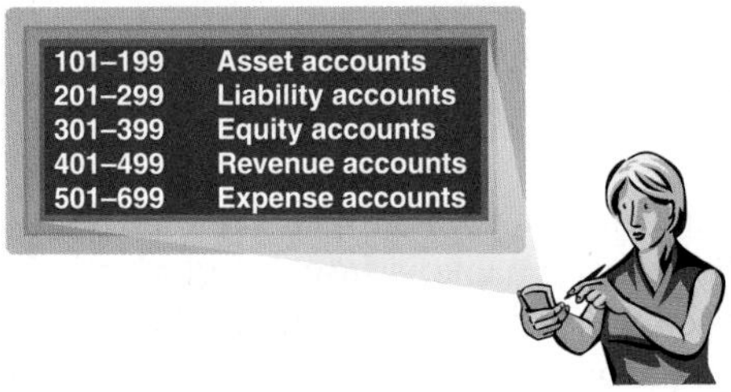

These numbers provide a three-digit code that is useful in recordkeeping. In this case, the first digit assigned to asset accounts is a 1, the first digit assigned to liability accounts is a 2, and so on. The second and third digits relate to the accounts' subcategories. Exhibit 2.4 shows a partial chart of accounts for FastForward, the focus company of Chapter 1. (Please review the more complete chart of accounts that follows the index at the back of this book.)

EXHIBIT 2.4

Partial Chart of Accounts for FastForward

Account Number	Account Name
101	Cash
106	Accounts receivable
126	Supplies
128	Prepaid insurance
167	Equipment
201	Accounts payable
236	Unearned consulting revenue

Account Number	Account Name
301	C. Taylor, Capital
302	C. Taylor, Withdrawals
403	Consulting revenue
406	Rental revenue
622	Salaries expense
637	Insurance expense
640	Rent expense
652	Supplies expense
690	Utilities expense

Debits and Credits

C5 Define *debits* and *credits* and explain double-entry accounting.

A **T-account** represents a ledger account and is a tool used to understand the effects of one or more transactions. Its name comes from its shape like the letter **T**. The layout of a T-account, shown in Exhibit 2.5, is (1) the account title on top, (2) a left, or debit side, and (3) a right, or credit, side.

EXHIBIT 2.5

The T-Account

Account Title	
(Left side) *Debit*	(Right side) *Credit*

The left side of an account is called the **debit** side, often abbreviated *Dr*. The right side is called the **credit** side, abbreviated *Cr*.[2] To enter amounts on the left side of an account is to *debit* the account. To enter amounts on the right side is to *credit* the account. Do not make the error of thinking that the terms *debit* and *credit* mean increase or decrease. Whether a debit or a credit is an increase or decrease depends on the account. For an account where a debit is an increase, the credit is a decrease; for an account where a debit is a decrease, the credit is an increase. The difference between total debits and total credits for an account, including any beginning balance, is the **account balance.** When the sum of debits exceeds the sum of credits, the account has a *debit balance*. It has a *credit balance* when the sum of credits exceeds the sum of debits. When the sum of debits equals the sum of credits, the account has a *zero balance*.

Point: Think of *debit* and *credit* as accounting directions for left and right.

Double-Entry Accounting

Double-entry accounting requires that each transaction affect, and be recorded in, at least two accounts. It also means the *total amount debited must equal the total amount credited* for each transaction. Thus, the sum of the debits for all entries must equal the sum of the credits for all entries, and the sum of debit account balances in the ledger must equal the sum of credit account balances.

The system for recording debits and credits follows from the usual accounting equation—see Exhibit 2.6. Two points are important here. First, like any simple mathematical relation, net increases or decreases on one side have equal net effects on the other side. For example, a net increase in assets must be accompanied by an identical net increase on the liabilities and equity side. Recall that some transactions affect only one side of the equation, meaning that two or more accounts on one side are affected, but their net effect on this one side is zero. Second, the left side is the *normal balance* side for assets, and the right side is the *normal balance* side for liabilities and equity. This matches their layout in the accounting equation where assets are on the left side of this equation, and liabilities and equity are on the right.

EXHIBIT 2.6

Debits and Credits in the Accounting Equation

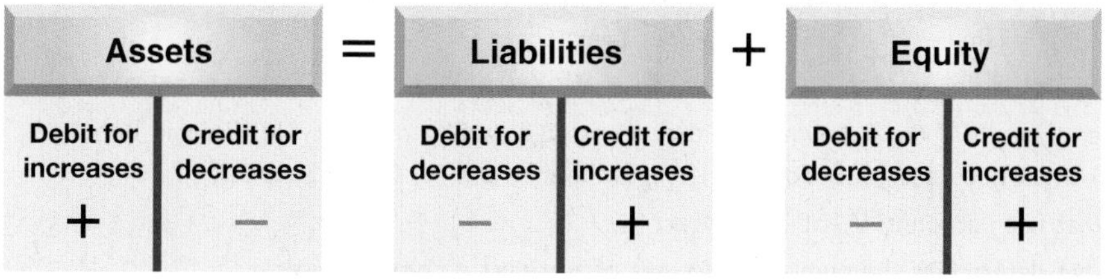

Recall that equity increases from revenues and owner investments and it decreases from expenses and owner withdrawals. These important equity relations are conveyed by expanding the accounting equation to include debits and credits in double-entry form as shown in Exhibit 2.7.

Increases (credits) to owner's capital and revenues *increase* equity; increases (debits) to withdrawals and expenses *decrease* equity. The normal balance of each account (asset, liability, capital, withdrawals, revenue, or expense) refers to the left or right (debit or credit) side where *increases* are recorded. Understanding these diagrams and rules is required to prepare, analyze, and interpret financial statements.

Point: Debits and credits do not mean favorable or unfavorable. A debit to an asset increases it, as does a debit to an expense. A credit to a liability increases it, as does a credit to a revenue.

[2] These abbreviations are remnants of 18th-century English recordkeeping practices where the terms *debitor* and *creditor* were used instead of *debit* and *credit*. The abbreviations use the first and last letters of these terms, just as we still do for Saint (St.) and Doctor (Dr.).

EXHIBIT 2.7

Debit and Credit Effects for Component Accounts

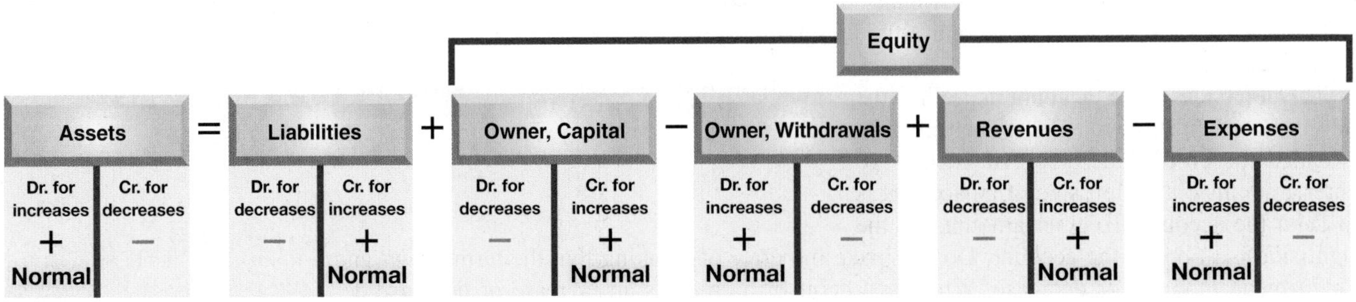

The T-account for FastForward's Cash account, reflecting its first 11 transactions (from Exhibit 1.9), is shown in Exhibit 2.8. The total increases in its Cash account are $36,100, the total decreases are $31,300, and the account's debit balance is $4,800. (We illustrate use of T-accounts later in this chapter.)

EXHIBIT 2.8

Computing the Balance for a T-Account

Point: The ending balance is on the side with the larger dollar amount.

Cash			
Investment by owner	30,000	Purchase of supplies	2,500
Consulting services revenue earned	4,200	Purchase of equipment	26,000
Collection of account receivable	1,900	Payment of rent	1,000
		Payment of salary	700
		Payment of account payable	900
		Withdrawal by owner	200
Balance	**4,800**		

Quick Check

Answers—p. 72

1. Identify examples of accounting source documents.
2. Explain the importance of source documents.
3. Identify each of the following as either an asset, a liability, or equity: (*a*) Prepaid Rent, (*b*) Unearned Fees, (*c*) Building, (*d*) Wages Payable, and (*e*) Office Supplies.
4. What is an account? What is a ledger?
5. What determines the number and types of accounts a company uses?
6. Does *debit* always mean increase and *credit* always mean decrease?
7. Describe a chart of accounts.

Journalizing and Posting Transactions

P1 Record transactions in a journal and post entries to a ledger.

Processing transactions is a crucial part of accounting. The four usual steps of this process are depicted in Exhibit 2.9. Steps 1 and 2—involving transaction analysis and double-entry accounting—were introduced in prior sections. This section extends that discussion and focuses on steps 3 and 4 of the accounting process. Step 3 is to record each transaction in a journal. A **journal** gives a complete record of each transaction in one place. It also shows debits and credits for each transaction. The process of recording transactions in a journal is called **journalizing.** Step 4 is to transfer (or *post*) entries from the journal to the ledger. The process of transferring journal entry information to the ledger is called **posting.**

Journalizing Transactions The process of journalizing transactions requires an understanding of a journal. While companies can use various journals, every company uses a **general journal.** It can be used to record any transaction and includes the following information about each transaction: (1) date of transaction, (2) titles of affected accounts, (3) dollar amount of each

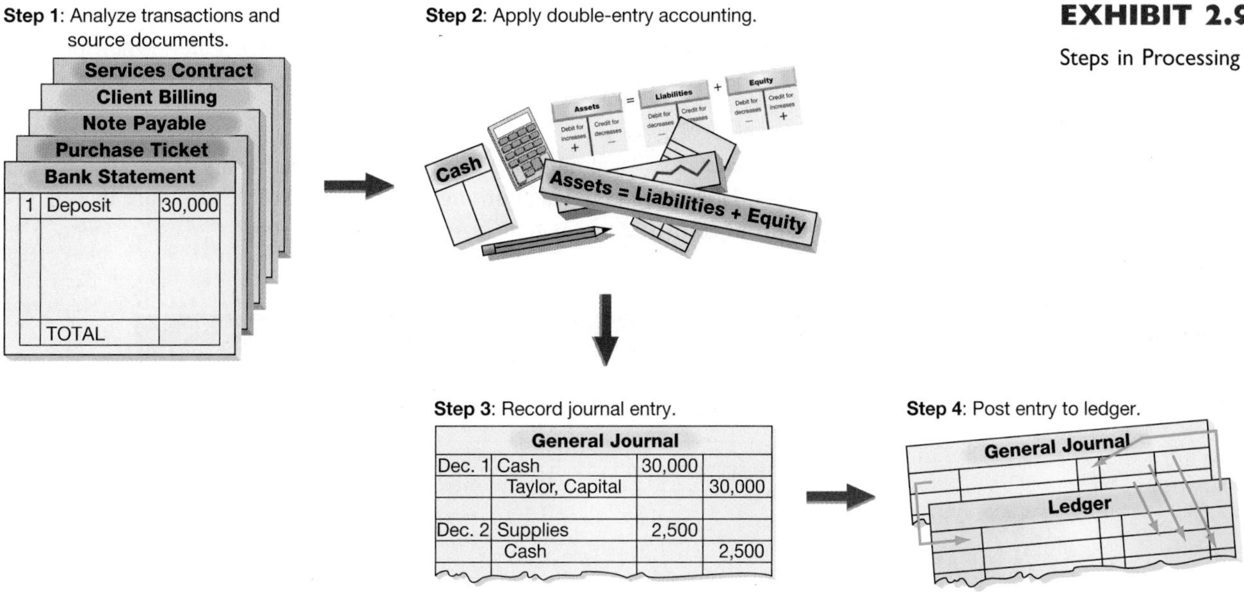

EXHIBIT 2.9

Steps in Processing Transactions

debit and credit, and (4) explanation of the transaction. Exhibit 2.10 shows how the first two transactions of FastForward are recorded in a general journal. This process is similar for manual and computerized systems. Computerized journals are often designed to look like a manual journal page, and also include error-checking routines that ensure debits equal credits for each entry. Shortcuts allow recordkeepers to select account names and numbers from pull-down menus.

EXHIBIT 2.10

Partial General Journal for FastForward

GENERAL JOURNAL

Date	Account Titles and Explanation	PR	Debit	Page 1 Credit
2009 Dec. 1	Cash		30,000	
	C. Taylor, Capital			30,000
	Investment by owner.			
Dec. 2	Supplies		2,500	
	Cash			2,500
	Purchased supplies for cash.			

To record entries in a general journal, apply these steps; refer to the entries in Exhibit 2.10 when reviewing these steps. ① Date the transaction: Enter the year at the top of the first column and the month and day on the first line of each journal entry. ② Enter titles of accounts debited and then enter amounts in the Debit column on the same line. Account titles are taken from the chart of accounts and are aligned with the left margin of the Account Titles and Explanation column. ③ Enter titles of accounts credited and then enter amounts in the Credit column on the same line. Account titles are from the chart of accounts and are indented from the left margin of the Account Titles and Explanation column to distinguish them from debited accounts. ④ Enter a brief explanation of the transaction on the line below the entry (it often references a source document). This explanation is indented about half as far as the credited account titles to avoid confusing it with accounts, and it is italicized.

Point: There are no exact rules for writing journal entry explanations. An explanation should be short yet describe why an entry is made.

Decision Insight

IFRSs IFRSs require that companies report the following four financial statements with explanatory notes:

—Balance sheet —Statement of changes in equity (or statement of recognized revenue and expense)

—Income statement —Statement of cash flows

IFRSs do not prescribe specific formats; and comparative information is required for the preceding period only.

A blank line is left between each journal entry for clarity. When a transaction is first recorded, the **posting reference (PR) column** is left blank (in a manual system). Later, when posting entries to the ledger, the identification numbers of the individual ledger accounts are entered in the PR column.

Balance Column Account T-accounts are simple and direct means to show how the accounting process works. However, actual accounting systems need more structure and therefore use **balance column accounts,** such as that in Exhibit 2.11.

EXHIBIT 2.11

Cash Account in Balance Column Format

		Cash			Account No. 101
Date	**Explanation**	**PR**	**Debit**	**Credit**	**Balance**
2009					
Dec. 1		G1	30,000		30,000
Dec. 2		G1		2,500	27,500
Dec. 3		G1		26,000	1,500
Dec. 10		G1	4,200		5,700

The balance column account format is similar to a T-account in having columns for debits and credits. It is different in including transaction date and explanation columns. It also has a column with the balance of the account after each entry is recorded. To illustrate, FastForward's Cash account in Exhibit 2.11 is debited on December 1 for the $30,000 owner investment, yielding a $30,000 debit balance. The account is credited on December 2 for $2,500, yielding a $27,500 debit balance. On December 3, it is credited again, this time for $26,000, and its debit balance is reduced to $1,500. The Cash account is debited for $4,200 on December 10, and its debit balance increases to $5,700; and so on.

Point: Explanations are typically included in ledger accounts only for unusual transactions or events.

The heading of the Balance column does not show whether it is a debit or credit balance. Instead, an account is assumed to have a *normal balance*. Unusual events can sometimes

EXHIBIT 2.12

Posting an Entry to the Ledger

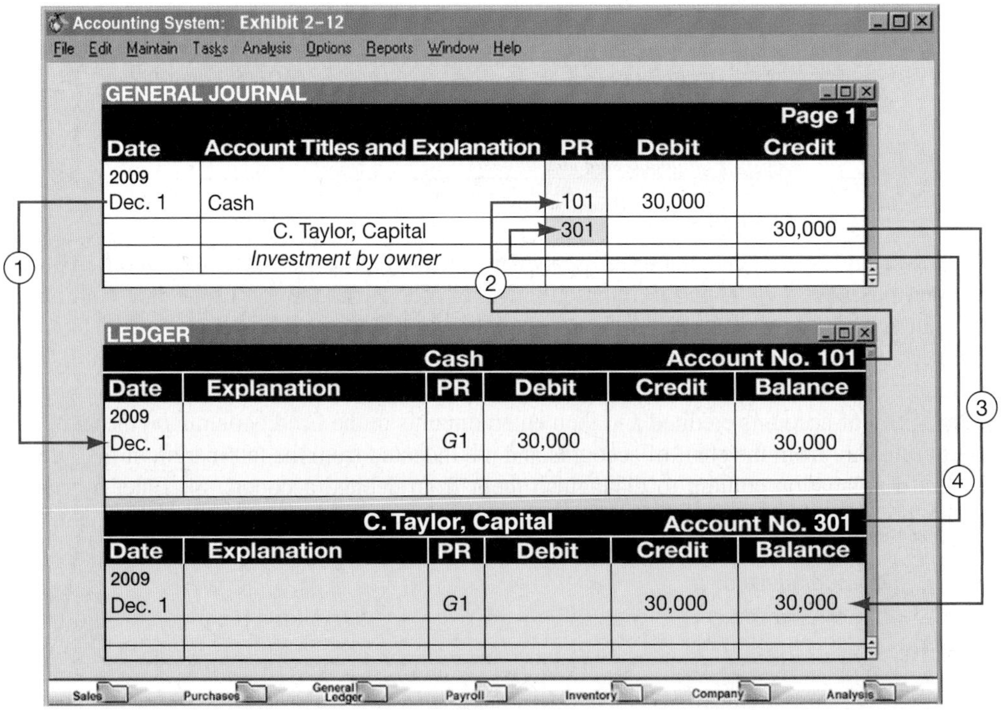

Key: (1) Identify debit account in Ledger: enter date, journal page, amount, and balance.
(2) Enter the debit account number from the Ledger in the PR column of the journal.
(3) Identify credit account in Ledger: enter date, journal page, amount, and balance.
(4) Enter the credit account number from the Ledger in the PR column of the journal.

Point: The fundamental concepts of a manual (pencil-and-paper) system are identical to those of a computerized information system.

temporarily give an account an abnormal balance. An *abnormal balance* refers to a balance on the side where decreases are recorded. For example, a customer might mistakenly overpay a bill. This gives that customer's account receivable an abnormal (credit) balance. An abnormal balance is often identified by circling it or by entering it in red or some other unusual color. A zero balance for an account is usually shown by writing zeros or a dash in the Balance column to avoid confusion between a zero balance and one omitted in error.

Posting Journal Entries Step 4 of processing transactions is to post journal entries to ledger accounts (see Exhibit 2.9). To ensure that the ledger is up-to-date, entries are posted as soon as possible. This might be daily, weekly, or when time permits. All entries must be posted to the ledger before financial statements are prepared to ensure that account balances are up-to-date. When entries are posted to the ledger, the debits in journal entries are transferred into ledger accounts as debits, and credits are transferred into ledger accounts as credits. Exhibit 2.12 shows the *four steps to post a journal entry*. First, identify the ledger account that is debited in the entry; then, in the ledger, enter the entry date, the journal and page in its PR column, the debit amount, and the new balance of the ledger account. (The letter *G* shows it came from the General Journal.) Second, enter the ledger account number in the PR column of the journal. Steps 3 and 4 repeat the first two steps for credit entries and amounts. The posting process creates a link between the ledger and the journal entry. This link is a useful cross-reference for tracing an amount from one record to another.

Point: Computerized systems often provide a code beside a balance such as *dr.* or *cr.* to identify its balance. Posting is automatic and immediate with accounting software.

Point: A journal is often referred to as the *book of original entry.* The ledger is referred to as the *book of final entry* because financial statements are prepared from it.

Analyzing Transactions—An Illustration

We return to the activities of FastForward to show how double-entry accounting is useful in analyzing and processing transactions. Analysis of each transaction follows the four steps of Exhibit 2.9. First, we review the transaction and any source documents. Second, we analyze the transaction using the accounting equation. Third, we use double-entry accounting to record the transaction in journal entry form. Fourth, the entry is posted (for simplicity, we use T-accounts to represent ledger accounts). Study each transaction thoroughly before proceeding to the next. The first 11 transactions are from Chapter 1, and we analyze five additional December transactions of FastForward (numbered 12 through 16) that were omitted earlier.

A1 Analyze the impact of transactions on accounts and financial statements.

FASTforward

1. Investment by Owner

1 IDENTIFY Chuck Taylor invests $30,000 cash in FastForward.

2 ANALYZE

Assets	=	Liabilities	+	Equity
Cash				C. Taylor, Capital
+30,000	=	0	+	30,000

3 RECORD

(1)	Cash	101	30,000	
	C. Taylor, Capital	301		30,000

4 POST

Cash	101
(1) 30,000	

C. Taylor, Capital	301
	(1) 30,000

2. Purchase Supplies for Cash

1 IDENTIFY FastForward pays $2,500 cash for supplies.

2 ANALYZE

Assets		=	Liabilities	+	Equity
Cash	Supplies				
−2,500	+2,500	=	0	+	0

Changes the composition of assets but not the total.

3 RECORD

(2)	Supplies	126	2,500	
	Cash	101		2,500

4 POST

Supplies	126
(2) 2,500	

Cash	101
(1) 30,000	(2) 2,500

3. Purchase Equipment for Cash

1 IDENTIFY FastForward pays $26,000 cash for equipment.

2 ANALYZE

Assets		=	Liabilities	+	Equity
Cash	**Equipment**				
−26,000	+26,000	=	0	+	0

Changes the composition of assets but not the total.

3 RECORD

(3)	Equipment	167	26,000	
	Cash	101		26,000

4 POST

Equipment 167

(3)	26,000		

Cash 101

(1)	30,000	(2)	2,500
		(3)	26,000

4. Purchase Supplies on Credit

1 IDENTIFY FastForward purchases $7,100 of supplies on credit from a supplier.

2 ANALYZE

Assets	=	Liabilities	+	Equity
Supplies		**Accounts Payable**		
+7,100	=	+7,100	+	0

3 RECORD

(4)	Supplies	126	7,100	
	Accounts Payable	201		7,100

4 POST

Supplies 126

(2)	2,500		
(4)	7,100		

Accounts Payable 201

		(4)	7,100

5. Provide Services for Cash

1 IDENTIFY FastForward provides consulting services and immediately collects $4,200 cash.

2 ANALYZE

Assets	=	Liabilities	+	Equity
Cash				**Consulting Revenue**
+4,200	=	0		+4,200

3 RECORD

(5)	Cash	101	4,200	
	Consulting Revenue	403		4,200

4 POST

Cash 101

(1)	30,000	(2)	2,500
(5)	4,200	(3)	26,000

Consulting Revenue 403

		(5)	4,200

6. Payment of Expense in Cash

1 IDENTIFY FastForward pays $1,000 cash for December rent.

2 ANALYZE

Assets	=	Liabilities	+	Equity
Cash				**Rent Expense**
−1,000	=	0		−1,000

3 RECORD

(6)	Rent Expense	640	1,000	
	Cash	101		1,000

4 POST

Rent Expense 640

(6)	1,000		

Cash 101

(1)	30,000	(2)	2,500
(5)	4,200	(3)	26,000
		(6)	1,000

7. Payment of Expense in Cash

Point: *Salary* usually refers to compensation for an employee who receives a fixed amount for a given time period, whereas *wages* usually refers to compensation based on time worked.

1 IDENTIFY FastForward pays $700 cash for employee salary.

2 ANALYZE

Assets	=	Liabilities	+	Equity
Cash				**Salaries Expense**
−700	=	0		−700

3 RECORD

(7)	Salaries Expense	622	700	
	Cash	101		700

4 POST

Salaries Expense 622

(7)	700		

Cash 101

(1)	30,000	(2)	2,500
(5)	4,200	(3)	26,000
		(6)	1,000
		(7)	700

8. Provide Consulting and Rental Services on Credit

1 IDENTIFY FastForward provides consulting services of $1,600 and rents its test facilities for $300. The customer is billed $1,900 for these services.

2 ANALYZE

Assets	=	Liabilities	+	Equity	
Accounts Receivable				**Consulting Revenue**	**Rental Revenue**
+1,900	=	0		+1,600	+300

3 RECORD

(8)	Accounts Receivable	106	1,900	
	Consulting Revenue	403		1,600
	Rental Revenue	406		300

4 POST

Accounts Receivable 106			
(8)	1,900		

Consulting Revenue 403			
		(5)	4,200
		(8)	1,600

Rental Revenue 406			
		(8)	300

Point: Transaction 8 is a **compound journal entry,** which affects three or more accounts.

9. Receipt of Cash on Account

1 IDENTIFY FastForward receives $1,900 cash from the client billed in transaction 8.

2 ANALYZE

Assets		=	Liabilities	+	Equity
Cash	**Accounts Receivable**				
+1,900	−1,900	=	0	+	0

3 RECORD

(9)	Cash	101	1,900	
	Accounts Receivable	106		1,900

4 POST

Cash 101			
(1)	30,000	(2)	2,500
(5)	4,200	(3)	26,000
(9)	1,900	(6)	1,000
		(7)	700

Accounts Receivable 106			
(8)	1,900	(9)	1,900

Point: The *revenue recognition principle* requires revenue to be recognized when earned, which is when the company provides products and services to a customer. This is not necessarily the same time that the customer pays. A customer can pay before or after products or services are provided.

10. Partial Payment of Accounts Payable

1 IDENTIFY FastForward pays CalTech Supply $900 cash toward the payable of transaction 4.

2 ANALYZE

Assets	=	Liabilities	+	Equity
Cash		**Accounts Payable**		
−900	=	−900	+	0

3 RECORD

(10)	Accounts Payable	201	900	
	Cash	101		900

4 POST

Accounts Payable 201			
(10)	900	(4)	7,100

Cash 101			
(1)	30,000	(2)	2,500
(5)	4,200	(3)	26,000
(9)	1,900	(6)	1,000
		(7)	700
		(10)	900

11. Withdrawal of Cash by Owner

1 IDENTIFY Chuck Taylor withdraws $200 cash from FastForward for personal use.

2 ANALYZE

Assets	=	Liabilities	+	Equity
Cash				**C. Taylor, Withdrawals**
−200	=	0		−200

3 RECORD

(11)	C. Taylor, Withdrawals	302	200	
	Cash	101		200

4 POST

C. Taylor, Withdrawals 302			
(11)	200		

Cash 101			
(1)	30,000	(2)	2,500
(5)	4,200	(3)	26,000
(9)	1,900	(6)	1,000
		(7)	700
		(10)	900
		(11)	200

12. Receipt of Cash for Future Services

1 IDENTIFY FastForward receives $3,000 cash in advance of providing consulting services to a customer.

2 ANALYZE

Assets	=	Liabilities	+	Equity
Cash		Unearned Consulting Revenue		
+3,000	=	+3,000	+	0

Accepting $3,000 cash obligates FastForward to perform future services and is a liability. No revenue is earned until services are provided.

3 RECORD

(12)	Cash	101	3,000	
	Unearned Consulting Revenue	236		3,000

4 POST

Cash			101
(1)	30,000	(2)	2,500
(5)	4,200	(3)	26,000
(9)	1,900	(6)	1,000
(12)	**3,000**	(7)	700
		(10)	900
		(11)	200

Unearned Consulting Revenue			236
		(12)	**3,000**

Point: Luca Pacioli, a 15th-century monk, is considered a pioneer in accounting and the first to devise double-entry accounting.

13. Pay Cash for Future Insurance Coverage

1 IDENTIFY FastForward pays $2,400 cash (insurance premium) for a 24-month insurance policy. Coverage begins on December 1.

2 ANALYZE

Assets		=	Liabilities	+	Equity
Cash	Prepaid Insurance				
−2,400	+2,400	=	0	+	0

Changes the composition of assets from cash to prepaid insurance. Expense is incurred as insurance coverage expires.

3 RECORD

(13)	Prepaid Insurance	128	2,400	
	Cash	101		2,400

4 POST

Prepaid Insurance			128
(13)	**2,400**		

Cash			101
(1)	30,000	(2)	2,500
(5)	4,200	(3)	26,000
(9)	1,900	(6)	1,000
(12)	3,000	(7)	700
		(10)	900
		(11)	200
		(13)	**2,400**

14. Purchase Supplies for Cash

1 IDENTIFY FastForward pays $120 cash for supplies.

2 ANALYZE

Assets		=	Liabilities	+	Equity
Cash	Supplies				
−120	+120	=	0	+	0

3 RECORD

(14)	Supplies	126	120	
	Cash	101		120

4 POST

Supplies			126
(2)	2,500		
(4)	7,100		
(14)	**120**		

Cash			101
(1)	30,000	(2)	2,500
(5)	4,200	(3)	26,000
(9)	1,900	(6)	1,000
(12)	3,000	(7)	700
		(10)	900
		(11)	200
		(13)	2,400
		(14)	**120**

15. Payment of Expense in Cash

1 IDENTIFY FastForward pays $230 cash for December utilities expense.

2 ANALYZE

Assets	=	Liabilities	+	Equity
Cash				**Utilities Expense**
−230	=	0		−230

3 RECORD

(15)	Utilities Expense	690	230	
	Cash	101		230

4 POST

Utilities Expense 690

(15)	230		

Cash 101

(1)	30,000	(2)	2,500
(5)	4,200	(3)	26,000
(9)	1,900	(6)	1,000
(12)	3,000	(7)	700
		(10)	900
		(11)	200
		(13)	2,400
		(14)	120
		(15)	**230**

16. Payment of Expense in Cash

1 IDENTIFY FastForward pays $700 cash in employee salary for work performed in the latter part of December.

2 ANALYZE

Assets	=	Liabilities	+	Equity
Cash				**Salaries Expense**
−700	=	0		−700

3 RECORD

(16)	Salaries Expense	622	700	
	Cash	101		700

4 POST

Salaries Expense 622

(7)	700		
(16)	700		

Cash 101

(1)	30,000	(2)	2,500
(5)	4,200	(3)	26,000
(9)	1,900	(6)	1,000
(12)	3,000	(7)	700
		(10)	900
		(11)	200
		(13)	2,400
		(14)	120
		(15)	230
		(16)	**700**

Point: We could merge transactions 15 and 16 into one *compound entry.*

Debit and Credit Rules

Accounts	Increase (normal bal.)	Decrease
Asset	Debit	Credit
Liability	Credit	Debit
Capital	Credit	Debit
Withdrawals	Debit	Credit
Revenue	Credit	Debit
Expense	Debit	Credit

Accounting Equation Analysis

Exhibit 2.13 shows the ledger accounts (in T-account form) of FastForward after all 16 transactions are recorded and posted and the balances computed. The accounts are grouped into three major columns corresponding to the accounting equation: assets, liabilities, and equity. Note several important points. First, as with each transaction, the totals for the three columns must obey the accounting equation. Specifically, assets equal $42,470 ($4,350 + $0 + $9,720 + $2,400 + $26,000); liabilities equal $9,200 ($6,200 + $3,000); and equity equals $33,270 ($30,000 − $200 + $5,800 + $300 − $1,400 − $1,000 − $230). These numbers prove the accounting equation: Assets of $42,470 = Liabilities of $9,200 + Equity of $33,270. Second, the capital, withdrawals, revenue, and expense accounts reflect the transactions that change equity. These account categories underlie the statement of owner's equity. Third, the revenue and expense account balances will be summarized and reported in the income statement. Fourth, increases and decreases in the cash account make up the elements reported in the statement of cash flows.

Point: Technology does not provide the judgment required to analyze most business transactions. Analysis requires the expertise of skilled and ethical professionals.

EXHIBIT 2.13

Ledger for FastForward (in T-Account Form)

Assets = Liabilities + Equity

Assets

Cash			101
(1)	30,000	(2)	2,500
(5)	4,200	(3)	26,000
(9)	1,900	(6)	1,000
(12)	3,000	(7)	700
		(10)	900
		(11)	200
		(13)	2,400
		(14)	120
		(15)	230
		(16)	700
Balance	**4,350**		

Accounts Receivable			106
(8)	1,900	(9)	1,900
Balance	**0**		

Supplies			126
(2)	2,500		
(4)	7,100		
(14)	120		
Balance	**9,720**		

Prepaid Insurance			128
(13)	**2,400**		

Equipment			167
(3)	**26,000**		

Liabilities

Accounts Payable			201
(10)	900	(4)	7,100
		Balance	**6,200**

Unearned Consulting Revenue			236
		(12)	**3,000**

Equity

C. Taylor, Capital			301
		(1)	**30,000**

C. Taylor, Withdrawals			302
(11)	**200**		

Consulting Revenue			403
		(5)	4,200
		(8)	1,600
		Balance	**5,800**

Rental Revenue			406
		(8)	**300**

Salaries Expense			622
(7)	700		
(16)	700		
Balance	**1,400**		

Rent Expense			640
(6)	**1,000**		

Utilities Expense			690
(15)	**230**		

Accounts in this white area reflect those reported on the income statement.

$42,470 = $9,200 + $33,270

Quick Check

Answers—p. 72

8. What types of transactions increase equity? What types decrease equity?

9. Why are accounting systems called *double-entry?*

10. For each transaction, double-entry accounting requires which of the following? (*a*) Debits to asset accounts must create credits to liability or equity accounts, (*b*) a debit to a liability account must create a credit to an asset account, or (*c*) total debits must equal total credits.

11. An owner invests $15,000 cash along with equipment having a market value of $23,000 in a company. Prepare the necessary journal entry.

12. Explain what a compound journal entry is.

13. Why are posting reference numbers entered in the journal when entries are posted to ledger accounts?

Trial Balance

Double-entry accounting requires the sum of debit account balances to equal the sum of credit account balances. A trial balance is used to verify this. A **trial balance** is a list of accounts and their balances at a point in time. Account balances are reported in the appropriate debit or credit column of a trial balance. Exhibit 2.14 shows the trial balance for FastForward after its 16 entries have been posted to the ledger. (This is an *unadjusted* trial balance—Chapter 3 explains the necessary adjustments.)

Video2.1

EXHIBIT 2.14

Trial Balance (Unadjusted)

Accounting System: Exhibit 2-14

File Edit Maintain Tasks Analysis Options Reports Window Help

FASTFORWARD
Trial Balance
December 31, 2009

	Debit	Credit
Cash	$ 4,350	
Accounts receivable	0	
Supplies	9,720	
Prepaid insurance	2,400	
Equipment	26,000	
Accounts payable		$ 6,200
Unearned consulting revenue		3,000
C. Taylor, Capital		30,000
C. Taylor, Withdrawals	200	
Consulting revenue		5,800
Rental revenue		300
Salaries expense	1,400	
Rent expense	1,000	
Utilities expense	230	
Totals	$ 45,300	$ 45,300

Sales Purchases General Ledger Payroll Inventory Company Analysis

Point: The ordering of accounts in a trial balance typically follows their identification number from the chart of accounts.

Preparing a Trial Balance

P2 Prepare and explain the use of a trial balance.

Preparing a trial balance involves three steps:

1. List each account title and its amount (from ledger) in the trial balance. If an account has a zero balance, list it with a zero in its normal balance column (or omit it entirely).
2. Compute the total of debit balances and the total of credit balances.
3. Verify (*prove*) total debit balances equal total credit balances.

The total of debit balances equals the total of credit balances for the trial balance in Exhibit 2.14. Equality of these two totals does not guarantee that no errors were made. For example, the column totals still will be equal when a debit or credit of a correct amount is made to a wrong account. Another error that does not cause unequal column totals is when equal debits and credits of an incorrect amount are entered.

Point: A trial balance is *not* a financial statement but a mechanism for checking equality of debits and credits in the ledger. Financial statements do not have debit and credit columns.

Searching for and Correcting Errors If the trial balance does not balance (when its columns are not equal), the error (or errors) must be found and corrected. An efficient

Example: If a credit to Unearned Revenue was incorrectly posted from the journal as a credit to the Revenue ledger account, would the ledger still balance? Would the financial statements be correct? *Answers:* The ledger would balance, but liabilities would be understated, equity would be overstated, and income would be overstated (all because of overstated revenues).

way to search for an error is to check the journalizing, posting, and trial balance preparation in *reverse order.* Step 1 is to verify that the trial balance columns are correctly added. If step 1 fails to find the error, step 2 is to verify that account balances are accurately entered from the ledger. Step 3 is to see whether a debit (or credit) balance is mistakenly listed in the trial balance as a credit (or debit). A clue to this error is when the difference between total debits and total credits equals twice the amount of the incorrect account balance. If the error is still undiscovered, Step 4 is to recompute each account balance in the ledger. Step 5 is to verify that each journal entry is properly posted. Step 6 is to verify that the original journal entry has equal debits and credits. At this point, the errors should be uncovered.[3]

If an error in a journal entry is discovered before the error is posted, it can be corrected in a manual system by drawing a line through the incorrect information. The correct information is written above it to create a record of change for the auditor. Many computerized systems allow the operator to replace the incorrect information directly.

Point: The IRS requires companies to keep records that can be audited.

If an error in a journal entry is not discovered until after it is posted, we do not strike through both erroneous entries in the journal and ledger. Instead, we correct this error by creating a *correcting entry* that removes the amount from the wrong account and records it to the correct account. As an example, suppose a $100 purchase of supplies is journalized with an incorrect debit to Equipment, and then this incorrect entry is posted to the ledger. The Supplies ledger account balance is understated by $100, and the Equipment ledger account balance is overstated by $100. The correcting entry is: debit Supplies and credit Equipment (both for $100).

Using a Trial Balance to Prepare Financial Statements

P3 Prepare financial statements from business transactions.

This section shows how to prepare *financial statements* from the trial balance in Exhibit 2.14 and from information on the December transactions of FastForward. These statements differ from those in Chapter 1 because of several additional transactions. These statements are also more precisely called *unadjusted statements* because we need to make some further accounting adjustments (described in Chapter 3).

EXHIBIT 2.15

Links between Financial Statements across Time

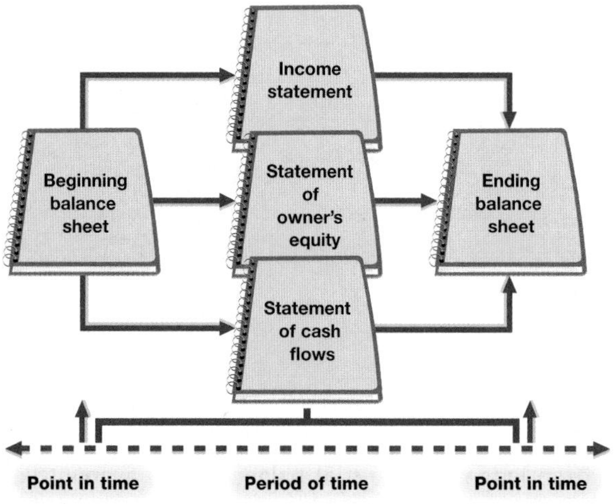

How financial statements are linked in time is illustrated in Exhibit 2.15. A balance sheet reports on an organization's financial position at a *point in time*. The income statement, statement of owner's equity, and statement of cash flows report on financial performance over a *period of time*. The three statements in the middle column of Exhibit 2.15 link balance sheets from the beginning to the end of a reporting period. They explain how financial position changes from one point to another.

---

[3] *Transposition* occurs when two digits are switched, or transposed, within a number. If transposition is the only error, it yields a difference between the two trial balance totals that is evenly divisible by 9. For example, assume that a $691 debit in an entry is incorrectly posted to the ledger as $619. Total credits in the trial balance are then larger than total debits by $72 ($691 − $619). The $72 error is *evenly* divisible by 9 (72/9 = 8). The first digit of the quotient (in our example it is 8) equals the difference between the digits of the two transposed numbers (the 9 and the 1). The number of digits in the quotient also tells the location of the transposition, starting from the right. The quotient in our example had only one digit (8), so it tells us the transposition is in the first digit. Consider another example where a transposition error involves posting $961 instead of the correct $691. The difference in these numbers is $270, and its quotient is 30 (270/9). The quotient has two digits, so it tells us to check the second digit from the right for a transposition of two numbers that have a difference of 3.

Preparers and users (including regulatory agencies) determine the length of the reporting period. A one-year, or annual, reporting period is common, as are semiannual, quarterly, and monthly periods. The one-year reporting period is known as the *accounting,* or *fiscal, year*. Businesses whose accounting year begins on January 1 and ends on December 31 are known as *calendar-year* companies. Many companies choose a fiscal year ending on a date other than December 31. **Best Buy** is a *noncalendar-year* company as reflected in the headings of its March 3 year-end financial statements in Appendix A near the end of the book.

Point: A statement's heading lists the 3 W's: **Who**—name of organization, **What**—name of statement, **When**—statement's point in time or period of time.

Income Statement An income statement reports the revenues earned less the expenses incurred by a business over a period of time. FastForward's income statement for December is shown at the top of Exhibit 2.16. Information about revenues and expenses is conveniently taken from the trial balance in Exhibit 2.14. Net income of $3,470 is reported at the bottom of the statement. Owner investments and withdrawals are *not* part of income.

Statement of Owner's Equity The statement of owner's equity reports information about how equity changes over the reporting period. FastForward's statement of owner's

EXHIBIT 2.16

Financial Statements and Their Links

FASTFORWARD
Income Statement
For Month Ended December 31, 2009

Revenues		
Consulting revenue ($4,200 + $1,600)	$ 5,800	
Rental revenue	300	
Total revenues		$ 6,100
Expenses		
Rent expense	1,000	
Salaries expense	1,400	
Utilities expense	230	
Total expenses		2,630
Net income		$ 3,470

Point: Arrow lines show how the statements are linked.

FASTFORWARD
Statement of Owner's Equity
For Month Ended December 31, 2009

C. Taylor, Capital, December 1, 2009		$ 0
Plus: Investments by owner	$30,000	
Net income	3,470	33,470
		33,470
Less: Withdrawals by owner		200
C. Taylor, Capital, December 31, 2009		$33,270

FASTFORWARD
Balance Sheet
December 31, 2009

Assets		Liabilities	
Cash	$ 4,350	Accounts payable	$ 6,200
Supplies	9,720	Unearned revenue	3,000
Prepaid insurance ..	2,400	Total liabilities	9,200
Equipment	26,000	**Equity**	
		C. Taylor, Capital	33,270
Total assets	$42,470	Total liabilities and equity .	$ 42,470

Point: To *foot* a column of numbers is to add them.

equity is the second report in Exhibit 2.16. It shows the $30,000 owner investment, the $3,470 of net income, the $200 withdrawal, and the $33,270 end-of-period (capital) balance. (The beginning balance in the statement of owner's equity is rarely zero; an exception is for the first period of operations. The beginning capital balance in January 2010 is $33,270, which is December's ending balance.)

Point: An income statement is also called an *earnings statement*, *a statement of operations*, or a *P&L* (profit and loss) *statement*. A balance sheet is also called a *statement of financial position*.

Point: While revenues increase equity, and expenses decrease equity, the amounts are not reported in detail in the statement of owner's equity. Instead, their effects are reflected through net income.

Balance Sheet The balance sheet reports the financial position of a company at a point in time, usually at the end of a month, quarter, or year. FastForward's balance sheet is the third report in Exhibit 2.16. This statement refers to financial condition at the close of business on December 31. The left side of the balance sheet lists its assets: cash, supplies, prepaid insurance, and equipment. The upper right side of the balance sheet shows that it owes $6,200 to creditors and $3,000 in services to customers who paid in advance. The equity section shows an ending balance of $33,270. Note the link between the ending balance of the statement of owner's equity and the capital balance here. (Recall that this presentation of the balance sheet is called the *account form:* assets on the left and liabilities and equity on the right. Another presentation is the *report form:* assets on top, followed by liabilities and then equity. Either presentation is acceptable.)

Decision Maker

Entrepreneur You open a wholesale business selling entertainment equipment to retail outlets. You find that most of your customers demand to buy on credit. How can you use the balance sheets of these customers to decide which ones to extend credit to? [Answer—p. 71]

Point: Knowing how financial statements are prepared improves our analysis of them.

Presentation Issues Dollar signs are not used in journals and ledgers. They do appear in financial statements and other reports such as trial balances. The usual practice is to put dollar signs beside only the first and last numbers in a column. **Best Buy**'s financial statements in Appendix A show this. When amounts are entered in a journal, ledger, or trial balance, commas are optional to indicate thousands, millions, and so forth. However, commas are always used in financial statements. Companies also commonly round amounts in reports to the nearest dollar, or even to a higher level. Best Buy is typical of many companies in that it rounds its financial statement amounts to the nearest million. This decision is based on the perceived impact of rounding for users' business decisions.

Quick Check

Answers—p. 72

14. Where are dollar signs typically entered in financial statements?

15. If a $4,000 debit to Equipment in a journal entry is incorrectly posted to the ledger as a $4,000 credit, and the ledger account has a resulting debit balance of $20,000, what is the effect of this error on the Trial Balance column totals?

16. Describe the link between the income statement and the statement of owner's equity.

17. Explain the link between the balance sheet and the statement of owner's equity.

18. Define and describe revenues and expenses.

19. Define and describe assets, liabilities, and equity.

Decision Analysis — Debt Ratio

A2 Compute the debt ratio and describe its use in analyzing financial condition.

An important business objective is gathering information to help assess a company's risk of failing to pay its debts. Companies finance their assets with either liabilities or equity. A company that finances a relatively large portion of its assets with liabilities is said to have a high degree of *financial leverage*. Higher financial leverage involves greater risk because liabilities must be repaid and often require regular interest payments (equity financing does not). The risk that a company might not be able to meet such required payments is higher if it has more liabilities (is more highly leveraged). One way to assess the risk associated with a company's use of liabilities is to compute the **debt ratio** as in Exhibit 2.17.

$$\textbf{Debt ratio} = \frac{\textbf{Total liabilities}}{\textbf{Total assets}}$$

EXHIBIT 2.17

Debt Ratio

To see how to apply the debt ratio, let's look at **Skechers**'s liabilities and assets. The company designs, markets, and sells footwear for men, women, and children under the Skechers brand. Exhibit 2.18 computes and reports its debt ratio at the end of each year from 2002 to 2006.

Point: Compare the equity amount to the liability amount to assess the extent of owner versus nonowner financing.

EXHIBIT 2.18

Computation and Analysis of Debt Ratio

$ in millions	2006	2005	2004	2003	2002
Total liabilities	$288	$238	$224	$211	$224
Total assets	$737	$582	$519	$467	$483
Debt ratio	**0.39**	**0.41**	**0.43**	**0.45**	**0.46**
Industry debt ratio	0.48	0.47	0.48	0.46	0.45

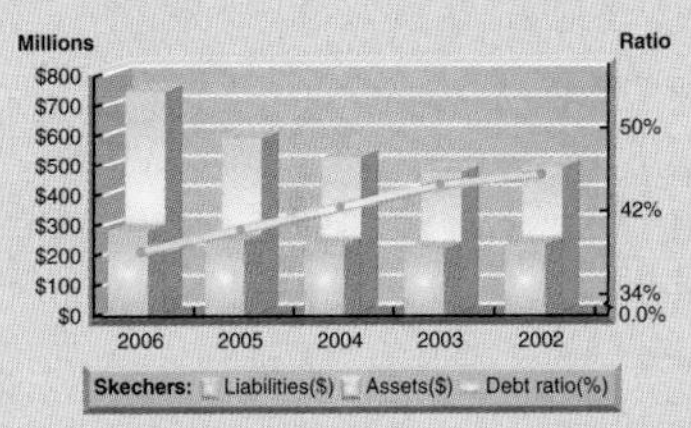

Skechers's debt ratio ranges from a low of 0.39 to a high of 0.46—also, see graph in margin. Its ratio is slightly lower, and has been declining, compared with the industry ratio. This analysis implies a low risk from its financial leverage. Is financial leverage good or bad for Skechers? To answer that question we need to compare the company's return on the borrowed money to the rate it is paying creditors. If the company's return is higher, it is successfully borrowing money to make more money. A company's success with making money from borrowed money can quickly turn unprofitable if its own return drops below the rate it is paying creditors.

Decision Maker

Investor You consider buying stock in **Converse**. As part of your analysis, you compute its debt ratio for 2006, 2007, and 2008 as: 0.35, 0.74, and 0.94, respectively. Based on the debt ratio, is Converse a low-risk investment? Has the risk of buying Converse stock changed over this period? (The industry debt ratio averages 0.40.) [Answer—p. 71]

Demonstration Problem

DP2

(This problem extends the demonstration problem of Chapter 1.) After several months of planning, Jasmine Worthy started a haircutting business called Expressions. The following events occurred during its first month.

a. On August 1, Worthy invested $3,000 cash and $15,000 of equipment in Expressions.
b. On August 2, Expressions paid $600 cash for furniture for the shop.
c. On August 3, Expressions paid $500 cash to rent space in a strip mall for August.
d. On August 4, it purchased $1,200 of equipment on credit for the shop (using a long-term note payable).
e. On August 5, Expressions opened for business. Cash received from haircutting services in the first week and a half of business (ended August 15) was $825.
f. On August 15, it provided $100 of haircutting services on account.
g. On August 17, it received a $100 check for services previously rendered on account.
h. On August 17, it paid $125 to an assistant for hours worked during the grand opening.
i. Cash received from services provided during the second half of August was $930.
j. On August 31, it paid a $400 installment toward principal on the note payable entered into on August 4.
k. On August 31, Worthy withdrew $900 cash for personal use.

Required

1. Open the following ledger accounts in balance column format (account numbers are in parentheses): Cash (101); Accounts Receivable (102); Furniture (161); Store Equipment (165); Note Payable (240); J. Worthy, Capital (301); J. Worthy, Withdrawals (302); Haircutting Services Revenue (403); Wages Expense (623); and Rent Expense (640). Prepare general journal entries for the transactions.
2. Post the journal entries from (1) to the ledger accounts.
3. Prepare a trial balance as of August 31.
4. Prepare an income statement for August.
5. Prepare a statement of owner's equity for August.
6. Prepare a balance sheet as of August 31.
7. Determine the debt ratio as of August 31.

Extended Analysis

8. In the coming months, Expressions will experience a greater variety of business transactions. Identify which accounts are debited and which are credited for the following transactions. (*Hint:* We must use some accounts not opened in part 1.)
   a. Purchase supplies with cash.
   b. Pay cash for future insurance coverage.
   c. Receive cash for services to be provided in the future.
   d. Purchase supplies on account.

Planning the Solution

- Analyze each transaction and use the debit and credit rules to prepare a journal entry for each.
- Post each debit and each credit from journal entries to their ledger accounts and cross-reference each amount in the posting reference (PR) columns of the journal and ledger.
- Calculate each account balance and list the accounts with their balances on a trial balance.
- Verify that total debits in the trial balance equal total credits.
- To prepare the income statement, identify revenues and expenses. List those items on the statement, compute the difference, and label the result as *net income* or *net loss*.
- Use information in the ledger to prepare the statement of owner's equity.
- Use information in the ledger to prepare the balance sheet.
- Calculate the debt ratio by dividing total liabilities by total assets.
- Analyze the future transactions to identify the accounts affected and apply debit and credit rules.

Solution to Demonstration Problem

1. General journal entries:

GENERAL JOURNAL — Page 1

Date	Account Titles and Explanation	PR	Debit	Credit
Aug. 1	Cash	101	3,000	
	Store Equipment	165	15,000	
	J. Worthy, Capital	301		18,000
	Owner's investment.			
2	Furniture	161	600	
	Cash	101		600
	Purchased furniture for cash.			
3	Rent Expense	640	500	
	Cash	101		500
	Paid rent for August.			
4	Store Equipment	165	1,200	
	Note Payable	240		1,200
	Purchased additional equipment on credit.			

[continued on next page]

[continued from previous page]

15	Cash	101	825	
	Haircutting Services Revenue	403		825
	Cash receipts from first half of August.			
15	Accounts Receivable	102	100	
	Haircutting Services Revenue	403		100
	To record revenue for services provided on account.			
17	Cash	101	100	
	Accounts Receivable	102		100
	To record cash received as payment on account.			
17	Wages Expense	623	125	
	Cash	101		125
	Paid wages to assistant.			
31	Cash	101	930	
	Haircutting Services Revenue	403		930
	Cash receipts from second half of August.			
31	Note Payable	240	400	
	Cash	101		400
	Paid an installment on the note payable.			
31	J. Worthy, Withdrawals	302	900	
	Cash	101		900
	Cash withdrawal by owner.			

2. Post journal entries from part 1 to the ledger accounts:

General Ledger

Cash — Account No. 101

Date	PR	Debit	Credit	Balance
Aug. 1	G1	3,000		3,000
2	G1		600	2,400
3	G1		500	1,900
15	G1	825		2,725
17	G1	100		2,825
17	G1		125	2,700
31	G1	930		3,630
31	G1		400	3,230
31	G1		900	2,330

Accounts Receivable — Account No. 102

Date	PR	Debit	Credit	Balance
Aug. 15	G1	100		100
17	G1		100	0

Furniture — Account No. 161

Date	PR	Debit	Credit	Balance
Aug. 2	G1	600		600

Store Equipment — Account No. 165

Date	PR	Debit	Credit	Balance
Aug. 1	G1	15,000		15,000
4	G1	1,200		16,200

Note Payable — Account No. 240

Date	PR	Debit	Credit	Balance
Aug. 4	G1		1,200	1,200
31	G1	400		800

J. Worthy, Capital — Account No. 301

Date	PR	Debit	Credit	Balance
Aug. 1	G1		18,000	18,000

J. Worthy, Withdrawals — Account No. 302

Date	PR	Debit	Credit	Balance
Aug. 31	G1	900		900

Haircutting Services Revenue — Account No. 403

Date	PR	Debit	Credit	Balance
Aug. 15	G1		825	825
15	G1		100	925
31	G1		930	1,855

Wages Expense — Account No. 623

Date	PR	Debit	Credit	Balance
Aug. 17	G1	125		125

Rent Expense — Account No. 640

Date	PR	Debit	Credit	Balance
Aug. 3	G1	500		500

3. Prepare a trial balance from the ledger:

EXPRESSIONS
Trial Balance
August 31

	Debit	Credit
Cash	$ 2,330	
Accounts receivable	0	
Furniture	600	
Store equipment	16,200	
Note payable		$ 800
J. Worthy, Capital		18,000
J. Worthy, Withdrawals	900	
Haircutting services revenue		1,855
Wages expense	125	
Rent expense	500	
Totals	$20,655	$20,655

4.

EXPRESSIONS
Income Statement
For Month Ended August 31

Revenues		
Haircutting services revenue		$1,855
Operating expenses		
Rent expense	$500	
Wages expense	125	
Total operating expenses		625
Net income		$1,230

5.

EXPRESSIONS
Statement of Owner's Equity
For Month Ended August 31

J. Worthy, Capital, August 1		$ 0
Plus: Investments by owner	$18,000	
Net income	1,230	19,230
		19,230
Less: Withdrawals by owner		900
J. Worthy, Capital, August 31		$18,330

6.

EXPRESSIONS
Balance Sheet
August 31

Assets		**Liabilities**	
Cash	$ 2,330	Note payable	$ 800
Furniture	600	**Equity**	
Store equipment	16,200	J. Worthy, Capital	18,330
Total assets	$19,130	Total liabilities and equity	$19,130

7. $$\text{Debt ratio} = \frac{\text{Total liabilities}}{\text{Total assets}} = \frac{\$800}{\$19{,}130} = \mathbf{4.18\%}$$

8a. Supplies *debited*
Cash *credited*

8b. Prepaid Insurance *debited*
Cash *credited*

8c. Cash *debited*
Unearned Services Revenue *credited*

8d. Supplies *debited*
Accounts Payable *credited*

Summary

C1 **Explain the steps in processing transactions.** The accounting process identifies business transactions and events, analyzes and records their effects, and summarizes and prepares information useful in making decisions. Transactions and events are the starting points in the accounting process. Source documents help in their analysis. The effects of transactions and events are recorded in journals. Posting along with a trial balance helps summarize and classify these effects.

C2 **Describe source documents and their purpose.** Source documents identify and describe transactions and events. Examples are sales tickets, checks, purchase orders, bills, and bank statements. Source documents provide objective and reliable evidence, making information more useful.

C3 **Describe an account and its use in recording transactions.** An account is a detailed record of increases and decreases in a specific asset, liability, equity, revenue, or expense. Information from accounts is analyzed, summarized, and presented in reports and financial statements for decision makers.

C4 **Describe a ledger and a chart of accounts.** The ledger (or general ledger) is a record containing all accounts used by a company and their balances. It is referred to as the *books*. The chart of accounts is a list of all accounts and usually includes an identification number assigned to each account.

C5 **Define *debits* and *credits* and explain double-entry accounting.** *Debit* refers to left, and *credit* refers to right. Debits increase assets, expenses, and withdrawals while credits decrease them. Credits increase liabilities, owner capital, and revenues; debits decrease them. Double-entry accounting means each transaction affects at least two accounts and has at least one debit and one credit. The system for recording debits and credits follows from the accounting equation. The left side of an account is the normal balance for assets, withdrawals, and expenses, and the right side is the normal balance for liabilities, capital, and revenues.

A1 **Analyze the impact of transactions on accounts and financial statements.** We analyze transactions using concepts of double-entry accounting. This analysis is performed by determining a transaction's effects on accounts. These effects are recorded in journals and posted to ledgers.

A2 **Compute the debt ratio and describe its use in analyzing financial condition.** A company's debt ratio is computed as total liabilities divided by total assets. It reveals how much of the assets are financed by creditor (nonowner) financing. The higher this ratio, the more risk a company faces because liabilities must be repaid at specific dates.

P1 **Record transactions in a journal and post entries to a ledger.** Transactions are recorded in a journal. Each entry in a journal is posted to the accounts in the ledger. This provides information that is used to produce financial statements. Balance column accounts are widely used and include columns for debits, credits, and the account balance.

P2 **Prepare and explain the use of a trial balance.** A trial balance is a list of accounts from the ledger showing their debit or credit balances in separate columns. The trial balance is a summary of the ledger's contents and is useful in preparing financial statements and in revealing recordkeeping errors.

P3 **Prepare financial statements from business transactions.** The balance sheet, the statement of owner's equity, the income statement, and the statement of cash flows use data from the trial balance (and other financial statements) for their preparation.

Guidance Answers to **Decision Maker** and **Decision Ethics**

Cashier The advantages to the process proposed by the assistant manager include improved customer service, fewer delays, and less work for you. However, you should have serious concerns about internal control and the potential for fraud. In particular, the assistant manager could steal cash and simply enter fewer sales to match the remaining cash. You should reject her suggestion without the manager's approval. Moreover, you should have an ethical concern about the assistant manager's suggestion to ignore store policy.

Entrepreneur We can use the accounting equation (Assets = Liabilities + Equity) to help us identify risky customers to whom we would likely not want to extend credit. A balance sheet provides amounts for each of these key components. The lower a customer's equity is relative to liabilities, the less likely you would extend credit. A low equity means the business has little value that does not already have creditor claims to it.

Investor The debt ratio suggests the stock of Converse is of higher risk than normal and that this risk is rising. The average industry ratio of 0.40 further supports this conclusion. The 2008 debt ratio for Converse is twice the industry norm. Also, a debt ratio approaching 1.0 indicates little to no equity.

Guidance Answers to **Quick Checks**

1. Examples of source documents are sales tickets, checks, purchase orders, charges to customers, bills from suppliers, employee earnings records, and bank statements.

2. Source documents serve many purposes, including recordkeeping and internal control. Source documents, especially if obtained from outside the organization, provide objective and reliable evidence about transactions and their amounts.

3.

Assets	Liabilities	Equity
a,c,e	b,d	—

4. An account is a record in an accounting system that records and stores the increases and decreases in a specific asset, liability, equity, revenue, or expense. The ledger is a collection of all the accounts of a company.

5. A company's size and diversity affect the number of accounts in its accounting system. The types of accounts depend on information the company needs to both effectively operate and report its activities in financial statements.

6. No. Debit and credit both can mean increase or decrease. The particular meaning in a circumstance depends on the *type of account*. For example, a debit increases the balance of asset, withdrawals, and expense accounts, but it decreases the balance of liability, capital, and revenue accounts.

7. A chart of accounts is a list of all of a company's accounts and their identification numbers.

8. Equity is increased by revenues and by owner investments. Equity is decreased by expenses and owner withdrawals.

9. The name *double-entry* is used because all transactions affect at least two accounts. There must be at least one debit in one account and at least one credit in another account.

10. The answer is (*c*).

11.

Cash	15,000	
Equipment	23,000	
Owner, Capital		38,000
Investment by owner of cash and equipment.		

12. A compound journal entry affects three or more accounts.

13. Posting reference numbers are entered in the journal when posting to the ledger as a cross-reference that allows the recordkeeper or auditor to trace debits and credits from one record to another.

14. At a minimum, dollar signs are placed beside the first and last numbers in a column. It is also common to place dollar signs beside any amount that appears after a ruled line to indicate that an addition or subtraction has occurred.

15. The Equipment account balance is incorrectly reported at $20,000—it should be $28,000. The effect of this error understates the trial balance's Debit column total by $8,000. This results in an $8,000 difference between the column totals.

16. An income statement reports a company's revenues and expenses along with the resulting net income or loss. A statement of owner's equity reports changes in equity, including that from net income or loss. Both statements report transactions occurring over a period of time.

17. The balance sheet describes a company's financial position (assets, liabilities, and equity) at a point in time. The capital amount in the balance sheet is obtained from the statement of owner's equity.

18. Revenues are inflows of assets in exchange for products or services provided to customers as part of the main operations of a business. Expenses are outflows or the using up of assets that result from providing products or services to customers.

19. Assets are the resources a business owns or controls that carry expected future benefits. Liabilities are the obligations of a business, representing the claims of others against the assets of a business. Equity reflects the owner's claims on the assets of the business after deducting liabilities.

Key Terms

mhhe.com/wildFAP19e

Key Terms are available at the book's Website for learning and testing in an online Flashcard Format.

Account (p. 49)
Account balance (p. 53)
Balance column account (p. 56)
Chart of accounts (p. 52)
Compound journal entry (p. 59)
Credit (p. 53)
Creditors (p. 50)
Debit (p. 53)
Debtors (p. 49)
Debt ratio (p. 67)
Double-entry accounting (p. 53)
General journal (p. 54)
General ledger (p. 49)
Journal (p. 54)
Journalizing (p. 54)
Ledger (p. 49)
Posting (p. 54)
Posting reference (PR) column (p. 56)
Source documents (p. 48)
T-account (p. 53)
Trial balance (p. 63)
Unearned revenue (p. 50)

Multiple Choice Quiz

Answers on p. 89 mhhe.com/wildFAP19e

Additional Quiz Questions are available at the book's Website.

Quiz2

1. Amalia Company received its utility bill for the current period of $700 and immediately paid it. Its journal entry to record this transaction includes a

a. Credit to Utility Expense for $700.
b. Debit to Utility Expense for $700.
c. Debit to Accounts Payable for $700.
d. Debit to Cash for $700.
e. Credit to capital for $700.

2. On May 1, Mattingly Lawn Service collected $2,500 cash from a customer in advance of five months of lawn service. Mattingly's journal entry to record this transaction includes a

a. Credit to Unearned Lawn Service Fees for $2,500.
b. Debit to Lawn Service Fees Earned for $2,500.
c. Credit to Cash for $2,500.
d. Debit to Unearned Lawn Service Fees for $2,500.
e. Credit to capital for $2,500.

3. Liang Shue contributed $250,000 cash and land worth $500,000 to open his new business, Shue Consulting. Which of the following journal entries does Shue Consulting make to record this transaction?

a.	Cash Assets	750,000	
	L. Shue, Capital		750,000
b.	L. Shue, Capital	750,000	
	Assets		750,000
c.	Cash	250,000	
	Land	500,000	
	L. Shue, Capital		750,000
d.	L. Shue, Capital . . .	750,000	
	Cash		250,000
	Land		500,000

4. A trial balance prepared at year-end shows total credits exceed total debits by $765. This discrepancy could have been caused by

a. An error in the general journal where a $765 increase in Accounts Payable was recorded as a $765 decrease in Accounts Payable.
b. The ledger balance for Accounts Payable of $7,650 being entered in the trial balance as $765.
c. A general journal error where a $765 increase in Accounts Receivable was recorded as a $765 increase in Cash.
d. The ledger balance of $850 in Accounts Receivable was entered in the trial balance as $85.
e. An error in recording a $765 increase in Cash as a credit.

5. Bonaventure Company has total assets of $1,000,000, liabilities of $400,000, and equity of $600,000. What is its debt ratio (rounded to a whole percent)?

a. 250%
b. 167%
c. 67%
d. 150%
e. 40%

Discussion Questions

1. Provide the names of two (*a*) asset accounts, (*b*) liability accounts, and (*c*) equity accounts.

2. What is the difference between a note payable and an account payable?

3. Discuss the steps in processing business transactions.

4. What kinds of transactions can be recorded in a general journal?

5. Are debits or credits typically listed first in general journal entries? Are the debits or the credits indented?

6. If assets are valuable resources and asset accounts have debit balances, why do expense accounts also have debit balances?

7. Should a transaction be recorded first in a journal or the ledger? Why?

8. Why does the recordkeeper prepare a trial balance?

9. If an incorrect amount is journalized and posted to the accounts, how should the error be corrected?

10. Identify the four financial statements of a business.

11. What information is reported in an income statement?

12. Why does the user of an income statement need to know the time period that it covers?

13. What information is reported in a balance sheet?

14. Define (*a*) *assets,* (*b*) *liabilities,* (*c*) *equity,* and (*d*) *net assets.*

15. Which financial statement is sometimes called the *statement of financial position?*

16. Review the **Best Buy** balance sheet in Appendix A. Identify three accounts on its balance sheet that carry debit balances and three accounts on its balance sheet that carry credit balances.

17. Refer to **Circuit City**'s balance sheet in Appendix A. What does Circuit City title its current liability for the purchase of merchandise?

18. Review the **RadioShack** balance sheet in Appendix A. Identify an asset with the word *receivable* in its account title and a liability with the word *payable* in its account title.

19. Locate **Apple**'s income statement in Appendix A. What is the title of its revenue account?

Denotes Discussion Questions that involve decision making.

Available with McGraw-Hill's Homework Manager

McGraw-Hill's HOMEWORK MANAGER®

QUICK STUDY

QS 2-1
Identifying source documents
C2

Identify the items from the following list that are likely to serve as source documents.

a. Trial balance
b. Telephone bill
c. Sales ticket
d. Income statement
e. Company revenue account
f. Invoice from supplier
g. Prepaid insurance
h. Bank statement
i. Balance sheet

QS 2-2
Identifying financial statement items
C3 P3

Identify the financial statement(s) where each of the following items appears. Use I for income statement, E for statement of owner's equity, and B for balance sheet.

a. Service fees earned
b. Cash withdrawal by owner
c. Office equipment
d. Accounts payable
e. Cash
f. Utilities expenses
g. Office supplies
h. Prepaid rent
i. Unearned fees

QS 2-3
Identifying normal balance
C5

Identify the normal balance (debit or credit) for each of the following accounts.

a. Office supplies
b. Owner Withdrawals
c. Fees Earned
d. Wages Expense
e. Cash
f. Prepaid Insurance
g. Wages Payable
h. Building
i. Owner Capital

QS 2-4
Linking debit or credit with normal balance
C5

Indicate whether a debit or credit *decreases* the normal balance of each of the following accounts.

a. Repair Services Revenue
b. Interest Payable
c. Accounts Receivable
d. Salaries Expense
e. Owner Capital
f. Prepaid Insurance
g. Buildings
h. Interest Revenue
i. Owner Withdrawals
j. Unearned Revenue
k. Accounts Payable
l. Office Supplies

QS 2-5
Analyzing debit or credit by account
C5 A1

Identify whether a debit or credit yields the indicated change for each of the following accounts.

a. To increase Land
b. To decrease Cash
c. To increase Utilities Expense
d. To increase Fees Earned
e. To decrease Unearned Revenue
f. To decrease Prepaid Insurance
g. To increase Notes Payable
h. To decrease Accounts Receivable
i. To increase Owner Capital
j. To increase Store Equipment

QS 2-6
Preparing journal entries
P1

Prepare journal entries for each of the following selected transactions.

a. On January 13, DeShawn Tyler opens a landscaping company called Elegant Lawns by investing $80,000 cash along with equipment having a $30,000 value.
b. On January 21, Elegant Lawns purchases office supplies on credit for $820.
c. On January 29, Elegant Lawns receives $8,700 cash for performing landscaping services.
d. On January 30, Elegant Lawns receives $4,000 cash in advance of providing landscaping services to a customer.

QS 2-7
Identifying a posting error
P2

A trial balance has total debits of $20,000 and total credits of $24,500. Which one of the following errors would create this imbalance? Explain.

a. A $2,250 credit to Consulting Fees Earned in a journal entry is incorrectly posted to the ledger as a $2,250 debit, leaving the Consulting Fees Earned account with a $6,300 credit balance.
b. A $4,500 debit to Salaries Expense in a journal entry is incorrectly posted to the ledger as a $4,500 credit, leaving the Salaries Expense account with a $750 debit balance.
c. A $2,250 debit to Rent Expense in a journal entry is incorrectly posted to the ledger as a $2,250 credit, leaving the Rent Expense account with a $3,000 debit balance.
d. A $2,250 debit posting to Accounts Receivable was posted mistakenly to Cash.
e. A $4,500 debit posting to Equipment was posted mistakenly to Supplies.
f. An entry debiting Cash and crediting Notes Payable for $4,500 was mistakenly not posted.

QS 2-8
Classifying accounts in financial statements
P3

Indicate the financial statement on which each of the following items appears. Use I for income statement, E for statement of owner's equity, and B for balance sheet.

a. Rental Revenue
b. Insurance Expense
c. Services Revenue
d. Interest Payable
e. Accounts Receivable
f. Salaries Expense
g. Equipment
h. Prepaid Insurance
i. Buildings
j. Interest Revenue
k. Owner Withdrawals
l. Office Supplies

McGraw-Hill's HOMEWORK MANAGER® Available with McGraw-Hill's Homework Manager

EXERCISES

Exercise 2-1
Identifying type and normal balances of accounts
C3 C5

For each of the following (1) identify the type of account as an asset, liability, equity, revenue, or expense, (2) enter *debit* (*Dr.*) or *credit* (*Cr.*) to identify the kind of entry that would increase the account balance, and (3) identify the normal balance of the account.

a. Owner Capital
b. Accounts Receivable
c. Owner Withdrawals
d. Cash
e. Equipment
f. Fees Earned
g. Wages Expense
h. Unearned Revenue
i. Accounts Payable
j. Postage Expense
k. Prepaid Insurance
l. Land

Exercise 2-2
Analyzing account entries and balances
A1

Use the information in each of the following separate cases to calculate the unknown amount.

a. During October, Alcorn Company had $104,750 of cash receipts and $101,607 of cash disbursements. The October 31 Cash balance was $17,069. Determine how much cash the company had at the close of business on September 30.

b. On September 30, Mordish Co. had a $83,250 balance in Accounts Receivable. During October, the company collected $75,924 from its credit customers. The October 31 balance in Accounts Receivable was $85,830. Determine the amount of sales on account that occurred in October.

c. Strong Co. had $148,000 of accounts payable on September 30 and $137,492 on October 31. Total purchases on account during October were $271,876. Determine how much cash was paid on accounts payable during October.

Exercise 2-3
Analyzing effects of transactions on accounts
A1

Nology Co. bills a client $65,000 for services provided and agrees to accept the following three items in full payment: (1) $12,000 cash, (2) computer equipment worth $90,000, and (3) to assume responsibility for a $37,000 note payable related to the computer equipment. The entry Nology makes to record this transaction includes which one or more of the following?

a. $37,000 increase in a liability account
b. $12,000 increase in the Cash account
c. $12,000 increase in a revenue account
d. $65,000 increase in an asset account
e. $65,000 increase in a revenue account
f. $37,000 increase in an equity account

Exercise 2-4
Preparing general journal entries
A1 P1

Prepare general journal entries for the following transactions of a new company called Special Pics.

Aug.	1	Madison Harris, the owner, invested $14,250 cash and $61,275 of photography equipment in the company.
	2	The company paid $3,300 cash for an insurance policy covering the next 24 months.
	5	The company purchased office supplies for $2,707 cash.
	20	The company received $3,250 cash in photography fees earned.
	31	The company paid $871 cash for August utilities.

Exercise 2-5
Preparing T-accounts (ledger) and a trial balance
C3 P2

Use the information in Exercise 2-4 to prepare an August 31 trial balance for Special Pics. Begin by opening these T-accounts: Cash; Office Supplies; Prepaid Insurance; Photography Equipment; M. Harris, Capital; Photography Fees Earned; and Utilities Expense. Then, post the general journal entries to these T-accounts (which will serve as the ledger), and prepare the trial balance.

Exercise 2-6
Recording effects of transactions in T-accounts
C5 A1

Record the transactions below for Amena Company by recording the debit and credit entries directly in the following T-accounts: Cash; Accounts Receivable; Office Supplies; Office Equipment; Accounts Payable; S. Amena, Capital; S. Amena, Withdrawals; Fees Earned; and Rent Expense. Use the letters beside each transaction to identify entries. Determine the ending balance of each T-account.

a. Sergey Amena, owner, invested $14,000 cash in the company.
b. The company purchased office supplies for $406 cash.
c. The company purchased $7,742 of office equipment on credit.
d. The company received $1,652 cash as fees for services provided to a customer.
e. The company paid $7,742 cash to settle the payable for the office equipment purchased in transaction *c*.
f. The company billed a customer $2,968 as fees for services provided.
g. The company paid $510 cash for the monthly rent.
h. The company collected $1,246 cash as partial payment for the account receivable created in transaction *f*.
i. S. Amena withdrew $1,200 cash from the company for personal use.

Check Cash ending balance, $7,040

Exercise 2-7
Preparing a trial balance P2

After recording the transactions of Exercise 2-6 in T-accounts and calculating the balance of each account, prepare a trial balance. Use May 31, 2009, as its report date.

Exercise 2-8
Analyzing and journalizing expense transactions
A1 P1

Examine the following transactions and identify those that create expenses for Thomas Services. Prepare general journal entries to record those expense transactions and explain why the other transactions did not create expenses.

a. The company paid $12,200 cash for office supplies that were purchased more than 1 year ago.
b. The company paid $1,233 cash for the just completed two-week salary of the receptionist.
c. The company paid $39,200 cash for equipment purchased.
d. The company paid $870 cash for this month's utilities.
e. Owner (Thomas) withdrew $4,500 cash from the company for personal use.

Exercise 2-9
Analyzing and journalizing revenue transactions
A1 P1

Examine the following transactions and identify those that create revenues for Thomas Services, a company owned by Brina Thomas. Prepare general journal entries to record those revenue transactions and explain why the other transactions did not create revenues.

a. Brina Thomas invests $39,350 cash in the company.
b. The company provided $2,300 of services on credit.
c. The company provided services to a client and immediately received $875 cash.
d. The company received $10,200 cash from a client in payment for services to be provided next year.
e. The company received $3,500 cash from a client in partial payment of an account receivable.
f. The company borrowed $120,000 cash from the bank by signing a promissory note.

Exercise 2-10
Preparing an income statement
C4 P3

On October 1, Diondre Shabazz organized a new consulting firm called Tech Talk. On October 31, the company's records show the following accounts and amounts. Use this information to prepare an October income statement for the business.

Cash	$ 12,614	D. Shabazz, Withdrawals	$ 2,000
Accounts receivable	25,648	Consulting fees earned	25,620
Office supplies	4,903	Rent expense	6,859
Land	69,388	Salaries expense	12,405
Office equipment	27,147	Telephone expense	560
Accounts payable	12,070	Miscellaneous expenses	280
D. Shabazz, Capital	124,114		

Check Net income, $5,516

Exercise 2-11
Preparing a statement of owner's equity P3

Use the information in Exercise 2-10 to prepare an October statement of owner's equity for Tech Talk. (The owner invested $124,114 to launch the company.)

Exercise 2-12
Preparing a balance sheet P3

Use the information in Exercise 2-10 (if completed, you can also use your solution to Exercise 2-11) to prepare an October 31 balance sheet for Tech Talk.

Exercise 2-13
Computing net income
A1 P3

A company had the following assets and liabilities at the beginning and end of a recent year.

	Assets	Liabilities
Beginning of the year	$131,000	$56,159
End of the year	180,000	72,900

Determine the net income earned or net loss incurred by the business during the year for each of the following *separate* cases:

a. Owner made no investments in the business and no withdrawals were made during the year.
b. Owner made no investments in the business but withdrew $650 cash per month for personal use.
c. No withdrawals were made during the year but the owner invested an additional $45,000 cash.
d. Withdrew $650 cash per month for personal use and the owner invested an additional $25,000 cash.

Exercise 2-14
Analyzing changes in a company's equity
C5 P3

Compute the missing amount in each of the following separate companies *a* through *d*.

		(a)	(b)	(c)	(d)
2	Equity, December 31, 2008	$ 0	$ 0	$ 0	$ 0
3	Owner investments during the year	112,500	?	85,347	201,871
4	Owner withdrawals during the year	?	(51,000)	(8,000)	(53,000)
5	Net income (loss) for the year	27,000	78,000	(6,000)	?
6	Equity, December 31, 2009	94,500	91,665	?	101,871

Exercise 2-15
Interpreting and describing transactions from T-accounts
C1 A1

Assume the following T-accounts reflect Belle Co.'s general ledger and that seven transactions *a* through *g* are posted to them. Provide a short description of each transaction. Include the amounts in your descriptions.

Cash			
(a)	12,000	(b)	4,800
(e)	9,000	(c)	2,000
		(f)	4,600
		(g)	820

Office Supplies			
(c)	2,000		
(d)	300		

Prepaid Insurance			
(b)	4,800		

Equipment			
(a)	15,200		
(d)	9,700		

Automobiles			
(a)	24,000		

Accounts Payable			
(f)	4,600	(d)	10,000

D. Belle, Capital			
		(a)	51,200

Delivery Services Revenue			
		(e)	9,000

Gas and Oil Expense			
(g)	820		

Exercise 2-16
Preparing general journal entries A1 P1

Use information from the T-accounts in Exercise 2-15 to prepare general journal entries for each of the seven transactions *a* through *g*.

Exercise 2-17
Identifying effects of posting errors on the trial balance A1 P2

Several posting errors are identified in the following table. In column (1), enter the amount of the difference between the two trial balance columns (debit and credit) due to the error. In column (2), identify the trial balance column (debit or credit) with the larger amount if they are not equal. In column (3), identify the account(s) affected by the error. In column (4), indicate the amount by which the account(s) in column (3) is under- or overstated. Item (a) is completed as an example.

	Description of Posting Error	(1) Difference between Debit and Credit Columns	(2) Column with the Larger Total	(3) Identify Account(s) Incorrectly Stated	(4) Amount that Account(s) is Over- or Understated
a.	$1,870 debit to Rent Expense is posted as a $1,780 debit.	$90	Credit	Rent Expense	Rent Expense understated $90
b.	$3,560 credit to Cash is posted twice as two credits to Cash.				
c.	$7,120 debit to the Withdrawals account is debited to Owner's Capital.				
d.	$1,630 debit to Prepaid Insurance is posted as a debit to Insurance Expense.				
e.	$31,150 debit to Machinery is posted as a debit to Accounts Payable.				
f.	$4,460 credit to Services Revenue is posted as a $446 credit.				
g.	$820 debit to Store Supplies is not posted.				

Exercise 2-18
Analyzing a trial balance error
A1 P2

You are told the column totals in a trial balance are not equal. After careful analysis, you discover only one error. Specifically, a correctly journalized credit purchase of a computer for $11,250 is posted from the journal to the ledger with a $11,250 debit to Office Equipment and another $11,250 debit to Accounts Payable. The Office Equipment account has a debit balance of $26,663 on the trial balance. Answer each of the following questions and compute the dollar amount of any misstatement.

a. Is the debit column total of the trial balance overstated, understated, or correctly stated?

b. Is the credit column total of the trial balance overstated, understated, or correctly stated?

c. Is the Office Equipment account balance overstated, understated, or correctly stated in the trial balance?

d. Is the Accounts Payable account balance overstated, understated, or correctly stated in the trial balance?

e. If the debit column total of the trial balance is $236,250 before correcting the error, what is the total of the credit column before correction?

Exercise 2-19
Interpreting the debt ratio and return on assets
A2

a. Calculate the debt ratio and the return on assets using the year-end information for each of the following six separate companies ($ thousands).

Case	Assets	Liabilities	Average Assets	Net Income
Company 3	$ 90,500	$ 12,000	$ 100,000	$ 20,000
Company 5	64,000	47,000	40,000	3,800
Company 6	32,500	26,500	50,000	660
Company 1	147,000	56,000	200,000	21,000
Company 4	92,000	31,000	40,000	7,500
Company 2	104,500	51,500	70,000	12,000

b. Of the six companies, which business relies most heavily on creditor financing?

c. Of the six companies, which business relies most heavily on equity financing?

d. Which two companies indicate the greatest risk?

e. Which two companies earn the highest return on assets?

f. Which one company would investors likely prefer based on the risk–return relation?

McGraw-Hill's HOMEWORK MANAGER® Available with McGraw-Hill's Homework Manager

PROBLEM SET A

Problem 2-1A
Preparing and posting journal entries; preparing a trial balance

C4 C5 A1 P1 P2

Lancet Engineering completed the following transactions in the month of June.

a. Jenna Lancet, the owner, invested $195,000 cash, office equipment with a value of $8,200, and $80,000 of drafting equipment to launch the company.
b. The company purchased land worth $52,000 for an office by paying $8,900 cash and signing a long-term note payable for $43,100.
c. The company purchased a portable building with $55,000 cash and moved it onto the land acquired in *b*.
d. The company paid $2,300 cash for the premium on an 18-month insurance policy.
e. The company completed and delivered a set of plans for a client and collected $6,600 cash.
f. The company purchased $24,000 of additional drafting equipment by paying $9,600 cash and signing a long-term note payable for $14,400.
g. The company completed $14,500 of engineering services for a client. This amount is to be received in 30 days.
h. The company purchased $1,100 of additional office equipment on credit.
i. The company completed engineering services for $23,000 on credit.
j. The company received a bill for rent of equipment that was used on a recently completed job. The $1,410 rent cost must be paid within 30 days.
k. The company collected $8,000 cash in partial payment from the client described in transaction *g*.
l. The company paid $2,500 cash for wages to a drafting assistant.
m. The company paid $1,100 cash to settle the account payable created in transaction *h*.
n. The company paid $970 cash for minor maintenance of its drafting equipment.
o. J. Lancet withdrew $10,450 cash from the company for personal use.
p. The company paid $2,000 cash for wages to a drafting assistant.
q. The company paid $2,400 cash for advertisements in the local newspaper during June.

Required

1. Prepare general journal entries to record these transactions (use the account titles listed in part 2).

2. Open the following ledger accounts—their account numbers are in parentheses (use the balance column format): Cash (101); Accounts Receivable (106); Prepaid Insurance (108); Office Equipment (163); Drafting Equipment (164); Building (170); Land (172); Accounts Payable (201); Notes Payable (250); J. Lancet, Capital (301); J. Lancet, Withdrawals (302); Engineering Fees Earned (402); Wages Expense (601); Equipment Rental Expense (602); Advertising Expense (603); and Repairs Expense (604). Post the journal entries from part 1 to the accounts and enter the balance after each posting.

3. Prepare a trial balance as of the end of June.

Check (2) Ending balances: Cash, $114,380; Accounts Receivable, $29,500; Accounts Payable, $1,410

(3) Trial balance totals, $386,210

Problem 2-2A
Preparing and posting journal entries; preparing a trial balance

C4 C5 A1 P1 P2

eXcel
mhhe.com/wildFAP19e

Denzel Brooks opens a Web consulting business called Venture Consultants and completes the following transactions in March.

March	1	Brooks invested $180,000 cash along with $30,000 of office equipment in the company.
	2	The company prepaid $8,000 cash for six months' rent for an office. (*Hint:* Debit Prepaid Rent for $8,000.)
	3	The company made credit purchases of office equipment for $3,300 and office supplies for $1,400. Payment is due within 10 days.
	6	The company completed services for a client and immediately received $6,000 cash.
	9	The company completed a $9,200 project for a client, who must pay within 30 days.
	12	The company paid $4,700 cash to settle the account payable created on March 3.
	19	The company paid $7,500 cash for the premium on a 12-month insurance policy.
	22	The company received $4,300 cash as partial payment for the work completed on March 9.
	25	The company completed work for another client for $3,590 on credit.
	29	Brooks withdrew $4,900 cash from the company for personal use.
	30	The company purchased $1,700 of additional office supplies on credit.
	31	The company paid $500 cash for this month's utility bill.

Required

Check (2) Ending balances: Cash, $164,700; Accounts Receivable, $8,490; Accounts Payable, $1,700

(3) Total debits, $230,490

1. Prepare general journal entries to record these transactions (use the account titles listed in part 2).
2. Open the following ledger accounts—their account numbers are in parentheses (use the balance column format): Cash (101); Accounts Receivable (106); Office Supplies (124); Prepaid Insurance (128); Prepaid Rent (131); Office Equipment (163); Accounts Payable (201); D. Brooks, Capital (301); D. Brooks, Withdrawals (302); Services Revenue (403); and Utilities Expense (690). Post the journal entries from part 1 to the ledger accounts and enter the balance after each posting.
3. Prepare a trial balance as of the end of March.

Problem 2-3A
Preparing and posting journal entries; preparing a trial balance
C4 C5 A1 P1 P2

Jayden Lanelle opens a computer consulting business called Viva Consultants and completes the following transactions in its first month of operations.

April 1 Lanelle invests $95,000 cash along with office equipment valued at $22,800 in the company.
2 The company prepaid $7,200 cash for twelve months' rent for office space. (*Hint:* Debit Prepaid Rent for $7,200.)
3 The company made credit purchases for $11,400 in office equipment and $2,280 in office supplies. Payment is due within 10 days.
6 The company completed services for a client and immediately received $2,000 cash.
9 The company completed a $7,600 project for a client, who must pay within 30 days.
13 The company paid $13,680 cash to settle the account payable created on April 3.
19 The company paid $6,000 cash for the premium on a 12-month insurance policy. (*Hint:* Debit Prepaid Insurance for $6,000.)
22 The company received $6,080 cash as partial payment for the work completed on April 9.
25 The company completed work for another client for $2,640 on credit.
28 Lanelle withdrew $6,200 cash from the company for personal use.
29 The company purchased $760 of additional office supplies on credit.
30 The company paid $700 cash for this month's utility bill.

Required

Check (2) Ending balances: Cash, $69,300; Accounts Receivable, $4,160; Accounts Payable, $760

(3) Total debits, $130,800

1. Prepare general journal entries to record these transactions (use account titles listed in part 2).
2. Open the following ledger accounts—their account numbers are in parentheses (use the balance column format): Cash (101); Accounts Receivable (106); Office Supplies (124); Prepaid Insurance (128); Prepaid Rent (131); Office Equipment (163); Accounts Payable (201); J. Lanelle, Capital (301); J. Lanelle, Withdrawals (302); Services Revenue (403); and Utilities Expense (690). Post journal entries from part 1 to the ledger accounts and enter the balance after each posting.
3. Prepare a trial balance as of April 30.

Problem 2-4A
Computing net income from equity analysis, preparing a balance sheet, and computing the debt ratio
C3 A1 A2 P3

mhhe.com/wildFAP19e

The accounting records of Faviana Shipping show the following assets and liabilities as of December 31, 2008 and 2009.

December 31	2008	2009
Cash	$ 47,867	$ 8,154
Accounts receivable	25,983	20,370
Office supplies	4,098	3,002
Office equipment	125,816	134,018
Trucks	49,236	58,236
Building	0	164,124
Land	0	40,956
Accounts payable	68,310	33,879
Note payable	0	85,080

Late in December 2009, the business purchased a small office building and land for $205,080. It paid $120,000 cash toward the purchase and an $85,080 note payable was signed for the balance. Ms. Faviana had to invest $34,000 cash in the business to enable it to pay the $120,000 cash. The owner withdraws $2,400 cash per month for personal use.

Required

1. Prepare balance sheets for the business as of December 31, 2008 and 2009. (*Hint:* Report only total equity on the balance sheet and remember that total equity equals the difference between assets and liabilities.)

2. By comparing equity amounts from the balance sheets and using the additional information presented in this problem, prepare a calculation to show how much net income was earned by the business during 2009.

3. Compute the 2009 year-end debt ratio for the business.

Check (2) Net income, $120,011

(3) Debt ratio, 27.7%

Problem 2-5A
Analyzing account balances and reconstructing transactions

C1 C4 A1 P2

Yi Min started an engineering firm called Min Engineering. He began operations and completed seven transactions in May, which included his initial investment of $18,000 cash. After those seven transactions, the ledger included the following accounts with normal balances.

Cash	$44,132
Office supplies	1,090
Prepaid insurance	4,700
Office equipment	11,200
Accounts payable	11,200
Y. Min, Capital	18,000
Y. Min, Withdrawals	4,328
Engineering fees earned	44,000
Rent expense	7,750

Required

1. Prepare a trial balance for this business as of the end of May.

Check (1) Trial balance totals, $73,200

Analysis Components

2. Analyze the accounts and their balances and prepare a list that describes each of the seven most likely transactions and their amounts.

3. Prepare a report of cash received and cash paid showing how the seven transactions in part 2 yield the $44,132 ending Cash balance.

(3) Cash paid, $17,868

Problem 2-6A
Recording transactions; posting to ledger; preparing a trial balance

C4 A1 P1 P2

Business transactions completed by Alanna Emitt during the month of September are as follows.

a. Emitt invested $82,000 cash along with office equipment valued at $22,000 in a new company named AE Consulting.
b. The company purchased land valued at $40,000 and a building valued at $165,000. The purchase is paid with $25,000 cash and a long-term note payable for $180,000.
c. The company purchased $1,700 of office supplies on credit.
d. Emitt invested her personal automobile in the company. The automobile has a value of $16,800 and is to be used exclusively in the business.
e. The company purchased $5,900 of additional office equipment on credit.
f. The company paid $1,500 cash salary to an assistant.
g. The company provided services to a client and collected $7,600 cash.
h. The company paid $630 cash for this month's utilities.
i. The company paid $1,700 cash to settle the account payable created in transaction *c*.

j. The company purchased $20,200 of new office equipment by paying $20,200 cash.
k. The company completed $6,750 of services for a client, who must pay within 30 days.
l. The company paid $2,000 cash salary to an assistant.
m. The company received $4,000 cash in partial payment on the receivable created in transaction *k*.
n. Emitt withdrew $2,900 cash from the company for personal use.

Required

1. Prepare general journal entries to record these transactions (use account titles listed in part 2).
2. Open the following ledger accounts—their account numbers are in parentheses (use the balance column format): Cash (101); Accounts Receivable (106); Office Supplies (108); Office Equipment (163); Automobiles (164); Building (170); Land (172); Accounts Payable (201); Notes Payable (250); A. Emitt, Capital (301); A. Emitt, Withdrawals (302); Fees Earned (402); Salaries Expense (601); and Utilities Expense (602). Post the journal entries from part 1 to the ledger accounts and enter the balance after each posting.
3. Prepare a trial balance as of the end of September.

Check (2) Ending balances: Cash, $39,670; Office Equipment, $48,100

(3) Trial balance totals, $321,050

PROBLEM SET B

Problem 2-1B
Preparing and posting journal entries; preparing a trial balance
C4 C5 A1 P1 P2

At the beginning of April, Vanessa Wende launched a custom computer solutions company called Softworks. The company had the following transactions during April.

a. Vanessa Wende invested $155,000 cash, office equipment with a value of $5,100, and $78,000 of computer equipment in the company.
b. The company purchased land worth $55,000 for an office by paying $8,700 cash and signing a long-term note payable for $46,300.
c. The company purchased a portable building with $59,000 cash and moved it onto the land acquired in *b*.
d. The company paid $3,500 cash for the premium on a two-year insurance policy.
e. The company provided services to a client and immediately collected $7,000 cash.
f. The company purchased $26,000 of additional computer equipment by paying $11,800 cash and signing a long-term note payable for $14,200.
g. The company completed $16,500 of services for a client. This amount is to be received within 30 days.
h. The company purchased $1,800 of additional office equipment on credit.
i. The company completed client services for $28,000 on credit.
j. The company received a bill for rent of a computer testing device that was used on a recently completed job. The $1,685 rent cost must be paid within 30 days.
k. The company collected $10,000 cash in partial payment from the client described in transaction *i*.
l. The company paid $1,300 cash for wages to an assistant.
m. The company paid $1,800 cash to settle the payable created in transaction *h*.
n. The company paid $985 cash for minor maintenance of the company's computer equipment.
o. V. Wende withdrew $10,230 cash from the company for personal use.
p. The company paid $1,300 cash for wages to an assistant.
q. The company paid $4,300 cash for advertisements in the local newspaper during April.

Required

1. Prepare general journal entries to record these transactions (use account titles listed in part 2).
2. Open the following ledger accounts—their account numbers are in parentheses (use the balance column format): Cash (101); Accounts Receivable (106); Prepaid Insurance (108); Office Equipment (163); Computer Equipment (164); Building (170); Land (172); Accounts Payable (201); Notes Payable (250); V. Wende, Capital (301); V. Wende, Withdrawals (302); Fees Earned (402); Wages Expense (601); Computer Rental Expense (602); Advertising Expense (603); and Repairs Expense (604). Post the journal entries from part 1 to the accounts and enter the balance after each posting.
3. Prepare a trial balance as of the end of April.

Check (2) Ending balances: Cash, $69,085; Accounts Receivable, $34,500; Accounts Payable, $1,685

(3) Trial balance totals, $351,785

Problem 2-2B

Preparing and posting journal entries; preparing a trial balance

C4 C5 A1 P1 P2

Kylan Management Services opens for business and completes these transactions in November.

Nov. 1 Rollie Kylan, the owner, invested $190,000 cash along with $29,000 of office equipment in the company.
2 The company prepaid $10,000 cash for six months' rent for an office. (*Hint:* Debit Prepaid Rent for $10,000.)
4 The company made credit purchases of office equipment for $4,300 and of office supplies for $2,100. Payment is due within 10 days.
8 The company completed work for a client and immediately received $7,000 cash.
12 The company completed a $9,200 project for a client, who must pay within 30 days.
13 The company paid $6,400 cash to settle the payable created on November 4.
19 The company paid $4,100 cash for the premium on a 24-month insurance policy.
22 The company received $3,700 cash as partial payment for the work completed on November 12.
24 The company completed work for another client for $4,010 on credit.
28 R. Kylan withdrew $6,300 cash from the company for personal use.
29 The company purchased $1,200 of additional office supplies on credit.
30 The company paid $1,100 cash for this month's utility bill.

Required

1. Prepare general journal entries to record these transactions (use account titles listed in part 2).

2. Open the following ledger accounts—their account numbers are in parentheses (use the balance column format): Cash (101); Accounts Receivable (106); Office Supplies (124); Prepaid Insurance (128); Prepaid Rent (131); Office Equipment (163); Accounts Payable (201); R. Kylan, Capital (301); R. Kylan, Withdrawals (302); Services Revenue (403); and Utilities Expense (690). Post the journal entries from part 1 to the ledger accounts and enter the balance after each posting.

3. Prepare a trial balance as of the end of November.

Check (2) Ending balances: Cash, $172,800; Accounts Receivable, $9,510; Accounts Payable, $1,200

(3) Total debits, $240,410

Problem 2-3B

Preparing and posting journal entries; preparing a trial balance

C4 C5 A1 P1 P2

Hassan Management Services opens for business and completes these transactions in September.

Sept. 1 Jamal Hassan, the owner, invests $130,000 cash along with office equipment valued at $31,200 in the company.
2 The company prepaid $7,200 cash for 12 months' rent for office space. (*Hint:* Debit Prepaid Rent for $7,200.)
4 The company made credit purchases for $15,600 in office equipment and $3,120 in office supplies. Payment is due within 10 days.
8 The company completed work for a client and immediately received $2,000 cash.
12 The company completed a $10,400 project for a client, who must pay within 30 days.
13 The company paid $18,720 cash to settle the payable created on September 4.
19 The company paid $6,000 cash for the premium on an 18-month insurance policy. (*Hint:* Debit Prepaid Insurance for $6,000.)
22 The company received $8,320 cash as partial payment for the work completed on September 12.
24 The company completed work for another client for $2,640 on credit.
28 J. Hassan withdrew $6,200 cash from the company for personal use.
29 The company purchased $1,040 of additional office supplies on credit.
30 The company paid $700 cash for this month's utility bill.

Required

1. Prepare general journal entries to record these transactions (use account titles listed in part 2).

2. Open the following ledger accounts—their account numbers are in parentheses (use the balance column format): Cash (101); Accounts Receivable (106); Office Supplies (124); Prepaid Insurance (128); Prepaid Rent (131); Office Equipment (163); Accounts Payable (201); J. Hassan, Capital (301); J. Hassan, Withdrawals (302); Service Fees Earned (401); and Utilities Expense (690). Post journal entries from part 1 to the ledger accounts and enter the balance after each posting.

3. Prepare a trial balance as of the end of September.

Check (2) Ending balances: Cash, $101,500; Accounts Receivable, $4,720; Accounts Payable, $1,040

(3) Total debits, $177,280

Problem 2-4B
Computing net income from equity analysis, preparing a balance sheet, and computing the debt ratio

C3 A1 A2 P3

The accounting records of Trinity Co. show the following assets and liabilities as of December 31, 2008 and 2009.

December 31	2008	2009
Cash	$ 54,773	$ 10,629
Accounts receivable	29,731	23,309
Office supplies	4,689	3,435
Office equipment	$143,968	153,353
Machinery	56,339	65,339
Building	0	187,802
Land	0	46,864
Accounts payable	78,165	38,767
Note payable	0	114,666

Late in December 2009, the business purchased a small office building and land for $234,666. It paid $120,000 cash toward the purchase and a $114,666 note payable was signed for the balance. Ms. Trinity, the owner, had to invest an additional $35,000 cash to enable it to pay the $120,000 cash toward the purchase. The owner withdraws $4,000 cash per month for personal use.

Required

1. Prepare balance sheets for the business as of December 31, 2008 and 2009. (*Hint:* Report only total equity on the balance sheet and remember that total equity equals the difference between assets and liabilities.)

Check (2) Net income, $138,963

2. By comparing equity amounts from the balance sheets and using the additional information presented in the problem, prepare a calculation to show how much net income was earned by the business during 2009.

(3) Debt ratio, 31.3%

3. Calculate the December 31, 2009, debt ratio for the business.

Problem 2-5B
Analyzing account balances and reconstructing transactions

C1 C4 A1 P2

Roshaun Gould started a Web consulting firm called Gould Solutions. He began operations and completed seven transactions in April that resulted in the following accounts, which all have normal balances.

Cash	$46,518
Office supplies	850
Prepaid rent	4,700
Office equipment	11,300
Accounts payable	11,300
R. Gould, Capital	22,500
R. Gould, Withdrawals	4,172
Consulting fees earned	43,000
Operating expenses	9,260

Required

Check (1) Trial balance total, $76,800

1. Prepare a trial balance for this business as of the end of April.

Analysis Component

2. Analyze the accounts and their balances and prepare a list that describes each of the seven most likely transactions and their amounts.

(3) Cash paid, $18,982

3. Prepare a report of cash received and cash paid showing how the seven transactions in part 2 yield the $46,518 ending Cash balance.

Problem 2-6B
Recording transactions; posting to ledger; preparing a trial balance
C4 A1 P1 P2

Witter Consulting completed the following transactions during June.

a. D. Witter, the owner, invested $82,000 cash along with office equipment valued at $23,000 in the new company.
b. The company purchased land valued at $50,000 and a building valued at $165,000. The purchase is paid with $30,000 cash and a long-term note payable for $185,000.
c. The company purchased $2,200 of office supplies on credit.
d. D. Witter invested his personal automobile in the company. The automobile has a value of $16,800 and is to be used exclusively in the business.
e. The company purchased $5,100 of additional office equipment on credit.
f. The company paid $1,500 cash salary to an assistant.
g. The company provided services to a client and collected $8,000 cash.
h. The company paid $630 cash for this month's utilities.
i. The company paid $2,200 cash to settle the payable created in transaction *c*.
j. The company purchased $20,400 of new office equipment by paying $20,400 cash.
k. The company completed $6,500 of services for a client, who must pay within 30 days.
l. The company paid $2,000 cash salary to an assistant.
m. The company received $4,000 cash in partial payment on the receivable created in transaction *k*.
n. D. Witter withdrew $2,700 cash from the company for personal use.

Required

1. Prepare general journal entries to record these transactions (use account titles listed in part 2).
2. Open the following ledger accounts—their account numbers are in parentheses (use the balance column format): Cash (101); Accounts Receivable (106); Office Supplies (108); Office Equipment (163); Automobiles (164); Building (170); Land (172); Accounts Payable (201); Notes Payable (250); D. Witter, Capital (301); D. Witter, Withdrawals (302); Fees Earned (402); Salaries Expense (601); and Utilities Expense (602). Post the journal entries from part 1 to the ledger accounts and enter the balance after each posting.
3. Prepare a trial balance as of the end of June.

Check (2) Ending balances: Cash, $34,570; Office Equipment, $48,500

(3) Trial balance totals, $326,400

SERIAL PROBLEM

Success Systems
A1 P1 P2

(This serial problem started in Chapter 1 and continues through most of the chapters. If the Chapter 1 segment was not completed, the problem can begin at this point. It is helpful, but not necessary, to use the Working Papers that accompany this book.)

SP 2 On October 1, 2009, Adriana Lopez launched a computer services company called Success Systems, which provides consulting services, computer system installations, and custom program development. Lopez adopts the calendar year for reporting purposes and expects to prepare the company's first set of financial statements on December 31, 2009. The company's initial chart of accounts follows.

Account	No.	Account	No.
Cash	101	A. Lopez, Capital	301
Accounts Receivable	106	A. Lopez, Withdrawals	302
Computer Supplies	126	Computer Services Revenue	403
Prepaid Insurance	128	Wages Expense	623
Prepaid Rent	131	Advertising Expense	655
Office Equipment	163	Mileage Expense	676
Computer Equipment	167	Miscellaneous Expenses	677
Accounts Payable	201	Repairs Expense—Computer	684

2. Form *expert teams* of individuals who selected the same component in part 1. Expert teams are to draft a report that each expert will present to his or her learning team addressing the following:

a. Identify for its component the (i) increase and decrease side of the account and (ii) normal balance side of the account.

b. Describe a transaction, with amounts, that increases its component.

c. Using the transaction and amounts in (*b*), verify the equality of the accounting equation and then explain any effects on the income statement and statement of cash flows.

d. Describe a transaction, with amounts, that decreases its component.

e. Using the transaction and amounts in (*d*), verify the equality of the accounting equation and then explain any effects on the income statement and statement of cash flows.

3. Each expert should return to his/her learning team. In rotation, each member presents his/her expert team's report to the learning team. Team discussion is encouraged.

ENTREPRENEURIAL DECISION

A1 A2 P3

BTN 2-7 Angel Fender is a young entrepreneur who operates Fender Music Services, offering singing lessons and instruction on musical instruments. Fender wishes to expand but needs a $30,000 loan. The bank requests Fender to prepare a balance sheet and key financial ratios. Fender has not kept formal records but is able to provide the following accounts and their amounts as of December 31, 2009.

Cash	$ 3,600	Accounts Receivable	$ 9,600	Prepaid Insurance	$ 1,500
Prepaid Rent	9,400	Store Supplies	6,600	Equipment	50,000
Accounts Payable	2,200	Unearned Lesson Fees	15,600	Total Equity*	62,900
Annual net income	40,000				

* The total equity amount reflects all owner investments, withdrawals, revenues, and expenses as of December 31, 2009.

Required

1. Prepare a balance sheet as of December 31, 2009, for Fender Music Services. (Report only the total equity amount on the balance sheet.)

2. Compute Fender's debt ratio and its return on assets (the latter ratio is defined in Chapter 1). Assume average assets equal its ending balance.

3. Do you believe the prospects of a $30,000 bank loan are good? Why or why not?

A1 A2 P3

BTN 2-8 Assume Sara Blakely of **SPANX** plans on expanding her business to accommodate more product lines. She is considering financing her expansion in one of two ways: (1) contributing more of her own funds to the business or (2) borrowing the funds from a bank.

Required

Identify the issues that Blakely should consider when trying to decide on the method for financing her expansion.

HITTING THE ROAD

C1

BTN 2-9 Obtain a recent copy of the most prominent newspaper distributed in your area. Research the classified section and prepare a report answering the following questions (attach relevant classified clippings to your report). Alternatively, you may want to search the Web for the required information. One suitable Website is **CareerOneStop** (**www.CareerOneStop.org**). For documentation, you should print copies of Websites accessed.

1. Identify the number of listings for accounting positions and the various accounting job titles.

2. Identify the number of listings for other job titles, with examples, that require or prefer accounting knowledge/experience but are not specifically accounting positions.

3. Specify the salary range for the accounting and accounting-related positions if provided.

4. Indicate the job that appeals to you, the reason for its appeal, and its requirements.

COMPARATIVE ANALYSIS

A1 A2

BTN 2-2 Key comparative figures for **Best Buy**, **Circuit City**, and **RadioShack** follow.

	Best Buy		Circuit City		RadioShack	
($ millions)	Current Year	Prior Year	Current Year	Prior Year	Current Year	Prior Year
Total liabilities	$ 7,369	$ 6,607	$2,216	$2,114	$1,416	$1,616
Total assets	13,570	11,864	4,007	4,069	2,070	2,205

1. What is the debt ratio for Best Buy in the current year and for the prior year?
2. What is the debt ratio for Circuit City in the current year and for the prior year?
3. What is the debt ratio for RadioShack in the current year and for the prior year?
4. Which of the three companies has the highest degree of financial leverage? What does this imply?

ETHICS CHALLENGE

C1 C2

BTN 2-3 Review the *Decision Ethics* case from the first part of this chapter involving the cashier. The guidance answer suggests that you should not comply with the assistant manager's request.

Required

Propose and evaluate two other courses of action you might consider, and explain why.

COMMUNICATING IN PRACTICE

C1 C3 A1 P3

BTN 2-4 Mora Stanley is an aspiring entrepreneur and your friend. She is having difficulty understanding the purposes of financial statements and how they fit together across time.

Required

Write a one-page memorandum to Stanley explaining the purposes of the four financial statements and how they are linked across time.

TAKING IT TO THE NET

A1

BTN 2-5 Access EDGAR online (www.SEC.gov) and locate the 2006 year 10-K report of **Amazon.com** (ticker AMZN) filed on February 16, 2007. Review its financial statements reported for years ended 2006, 2005, and 2004 to answer the following questions.

Required

1. What are the amounts of its net income or net loss reported for each of these three years?
2. Do Amazon's operations provide cash or use cash for each of these three years?
3. If Amazon has a 2005 net income, how is it possible that its cash balance at December 31, 2005, shows a decrease relative to its balance at December 31, 2004?

TEAMWORK IN ACTION

C1 C3 C5 A1

BTN 2-6 The expanded accounting equation consists of assets, liabilities, capital, withdrawals, revenues, and expenses. It can be used to reveal insights into changes in a company's financial position.

Required

1. Form *learning teams* of six (or more) members. Each team member must select one of the six components and each team must have at least one expert on each component: (*a*) assets, (*b*) liabilities, (*c*) capital, (*d*) withdrawals, (*e*) revenues, and (*f*) expenses.

2. Form *expert teams* of individuals who selected the same component in part 1. Expert teams are to draft a report that each expert will present to his or her learning team addressing the following:
   a. Identify for its component the (i) increase and decrease side of the account and (ii) normal balance side of the account.
   b. Describe a transaction, with amounts, that increases its component.
   c. Using the transaction and amounts in (*b*), verify the equality of the accounting equation and then explain any effects on the income statement and statement of cash flows.
   d. Describe a transaction, with amounts, that decreases its component.
   e. Using the transaction and amounts in (*d*), verify the equality of the accounting equation and then explain any effects on the income statement and statement of cash flows.
3. Each expert should return to his/her learning team. In rotation, each member presents his/her expert team's report to the learning team. Team discussion is encouraged.

ENTREPRENEURIAL DECISION

A1 A2 P3

BTN 2-7 Angel Fender is a young entrepreneur who operates Fender Music Services, offering singing lessons and instruction on musical instruments. Fender wishes to expand but needs a $30,000 loan. The bank requests Fender to prepare a balance sheet and key financial ratios. Fender has not kept formal records but is able to provide the following accounts and their amounts as of December 31, 2009.

Cash	$ 3,600	Accounts Receivable	$ 9,600	Prepaid Insurance	$ 1,500
Prepaid Rent	9,400	Store Supplies	6,600	Equipment	50,000
Accounts Payable	2,200	Unearned Lesson Fees	15,600	Total Equity*	62,900
Annual net income	40,000				

* The total equity amount reflects all owner investments, withdrawals, revenues, and expenses as of December 31, 2009.

Required

1. Prepare a balance sheet as of December 31, 2009, for Fender Music Services. (Report only the total equity amount on the balance sheet.)
2. Compute Fender's debt ratio and its return on assets (the latter ratio is defined in Chapter 1). Assume average assets equal its ending balance.
3. Do you believe the prospects of a $30,000 bank loan are good? Why or why not?

A1 A2 P3

BTN 2-8 Assume Sara Blakely of **SPANX** plans on expanding her business to accommodate more product lines. She is considering financing her expansion in one of two ways: (1) contributing more of her own funds to the business or (2) borrowing the funds from a bank.

Required

Identify the issues that Blakely should consider when trying to decide on the method for financing her expansion.

HITTING THE ROAD

C1

BTN 2-9 Obtain a recent copy of the most prominent newspaper distributed in your area. Research the classified section and prepare a report answering the following questions (attach relevant classified clippings to your report). Alternatively, you may want to search the Web for the required information. One suitable Website is **CareerOneStop** (**www.CareerOneStop.org**). For documentation, you should print copies of Websites accessed.

1. Identify the number of listings for accounting positions and the various accounting job titles.
2. Identify the number of listings for other job titles, with examples, that require or prefer accounting knowledge/experience but are not specifically accounting positions.
3. Specify the salary range for the accounting and accounting-related positions if provided.
4. Indicate the job that appeals to you, the reason for its appeal, and its requirements.

Problem 2-6B
Recording transactions; posting to ledger; preparing a trial balance
C4 A1 P1 P2

Witter Consulting completed the following transactions during June.

a. D. Witter, the owner, invested $82,000 cash along with office equipment valued at $23,000 in the new company.

b. The company purchased land valued at $50,000 and a building valued at $165,000. The purchase is paid with $30,000 cash and a long-term note payable for $185,000.

c. The company purchased $2,200 of office supplies on credit.

d. D. Witter invested his personal automobile in the company. The automobile has a value of $16,800 and is to be used exclusively in the business.

e. The company purchased $5,100 of additional office equipment on credit.

f. The company paid $1,500 cash salary to an assistant.

g. The company provided services to a client and collected $8,000 cash.

h. The company paid $630 cash for this month's utilities.

i. The company paid $2,200 cash to settle the payable created in transaction *c*.

j. The company purchased $20,400 of new office equipment by paying $20,400 cash.

k. The company completed $6,500 of services for a client, who must pay within 30 days.

l. The company paid $2,000 cash salary to an assistant.

m. The company received $4,000 cash in partial payment on the receivable created in transaction *k*.

n. D. Witter withdrew $2,700 cash from the company for personal use.

Required

1. Prepare general journal entries to record these transactions (use account titles listed in part 2).

2. Open the following ledger accounts—their account numbers are in parentheses (use the balance column format): Cash (101); Accounts Receivable (106); Office Supplies (108); Office Equipment (163); Automobiles (164); Building (170); Land (172); Accounts Payable (201); Notes Payable (250); D. Witter, Capital (301); D. Witter, Withdrawals (302); Fees Earned (402); Salaries Expense (601); and Utilities Expense (602). Post the journal entries from part 1 to the ledger accounts and enter the balance after each posting.

3. Prepare a trial balance as of the end of June.

Check (2) Ending balances: Cash, $34,570; Office Equipment, $48,500

(3) Trial balance totals, $326,400

SERIAL PROBLEM

Success Systems
A1 P1 P2

(This serial problem started in Chapter 1 and continues through most of the chapters. If the Chapter 1 segment was not completed, the problem can begin at this point. It is helpful, but not necessary, to use the Working Papers that accompany this book.)

SP 2 On October 1, 2009, Adriana Lopez launched a computer services company called Success Systems, which provides consulting services, computer system installations, and custom program development. Lopez adopts the calendar year for reporting purposes and expects to prepare the company's first set of financial statements on December 31, 2009. The company's initial chart of accounts follows.

Account	No.	Account	No.
Cash	101	A. Lopez, Capital	301
Accounts Receivable	106	A. Lopez, Withdrawals	302
Computer Supplies	126	Computer Services Revenue	403
Prepaid Insurance	128	Wages Expense	623
Prepaid Rent	131	Advertising Expense	655
Office Equipment	163	Mileage Expense	676
Computer Equipment	167	Miscellaneous Expenses	677
Accounts Payable	201	Repairs Expense—Computer	684

Required

1. Prepare journal entries to record each of the following transactions for Success Systems.

Oct. 1 Lopez invested $55,000 cash, a $20,000 computer system, and $8,000 of office equipment in the company.
2 The company paid $3,300 cash for four months' rent. (*Hint:* Debit Prepaid Rent for $3,300.)
3 The company purchased $1,420 of computer supplies on credit from Harris Office Products.
5 The company paid $2,220 cash for one year's premium on a property and liability insurance policy. (*Hint:* Debit Prepaid Insurance for $2,220.)
6 The company billed Easy Leasing $4,800 for services performed in installing a new Web server.
8 The company paid $1,420 cash for the computer supplies purchased from Harris Office Products on October 3.
10 The company hired Lyn Addie as a part-time assistant for $125 per day, as needed.
12 The company billed Easy Leasing another $1,400 for services performed.
15 The company received $4,800 cash from Easy Leasing as partial payment on its account.
17 The company paid $805 cash to repair computer equipment that was damaged when moving it.
20 The company paid $1,940 cash for an advertisement in the local newspaper.
22 The company received $1,400 cash from Easy Leasing on its account.
28 The company billed IFM Company $5,208 for services performed.
31 The company paid $875 cash for Lyn Addie's wages for seven days' work.
31 A. Lopez withdrew $3,600 cash from the company for personal use.

Nov. 1 The company reimbursed Lopez in cash for business automobile mileage allowance (Lopez logged 1,000 miles at $0.32 per mile).
2 The company received $4,633 cash from Liu Corporation for computer services performed.
5 The company purchased computer supplies for $1,125 cash from Harris Office Products.
8 The company billed Gomez Co. $5,668 for services performed.
13 The company received notification from Alex's Engineering Co. that Success Systems' bid of $3,950 for an upcoming project is accepted.
18 The company received $2,208 cash from IFM Company as partial payment of the October 28 bill.
22 The company donated $250 cash to the United Way in the company's name.
24 The company completed work for Alex's Engineering Co. and sent it a bill for $3,950.
25 The company sent another bill to IFM Company for the past-due amount of $3,000.
28 The company reimbursed Lopez in cash for business automobile mileage (1,200 miles at $0.32 per mile).
30 The company paid $1,750 cash for Lyn Addie's wages for 14 days' work.
30 A. Lopez withdrew $2,000 cash from the company for personal use.

Check (2) Cash, Nov. 30 bal., $48,052

(3) Trial bal. totals, $108,659

2. Open ledger accounts (in balance column format) and post the journal entries from part 1 to them.

3. Prepare a trial balance as of the end of November.

BEYOND THE NUMBERS

REPORTING IN ACTION

A1 A2

BTN 2-1 Refer to **Best Buy**'s financial statements in Appendix A for the following questions.

Required

1. What amount of total liabilities does it report for each of the fiscal years ended February 25, 2006, and March 3, 2007?

2. What amount of total assets does it report for each of the fiscal years ended February 25, 2006, and March 3, 2007?

3. Compute its debt ratio for each of the fiscal years ended February 25, 2006, and March 3, 2007.

4. In which fiscal year did it employ more financial leverage (February 25, 2006, or March 3, 2007)? Explain.

Fast Forward

5. Access its financial statements (10-K report) for a fiscal year ending after March 3, 2007, from its Website (BestBuy.com) or the SEC's EDGAR database (www.SEC.gov). Recompute its debt ratio for any subsequent year's data and compare it with the February 25, 2006, debt ratio.

BTN 2-10 DSG international plc (www.DSGiplc.com) competes with several companies, including **Best Buy** and **RadioShack**. Key financial ratios for the current fiscal year follow.

GLOBAL DECISION

A2

DSG

BEST BUY

RadioShack.

Key Figure	DSG	Best Buy	RadioShack
Return on assets	5.2%	10.8%	3.4%
Debt ratio	67.2%	54.3%	68.4%

Required

1. Which company is most profitable according to its return on assets?
2. Which company is most risky according to the debt ratio?
3. Which company deserves increased investment based on a joint analysis of return on assets and the debt ratio? Explain.

ANSWERS TO MULTIPLE CHOICE QUIZ

1. b; debit Utility Expense for $700, and credit Cash for $700.
2. a; debit Cash for $2,500, and credit Unearned Lawn Service Fees for $2,500.
3. c; debit Cash for $250,000, debit Land for $500,000, and credit L. Shue, Capital for $750,000.
4. d
5. e; Debt ratio = $400,000/$1,000,000 = 40%

A Look Back

Chapter 2 explained the analysis and recording of transactions. We showed how to apply and interpret company accounts, T-accounts, double-entry accounting, ledgers, postings, and trial balances.

A Look at This Chapter

This chapter explains the timing of reports and the need to adjust accounts. Adjusting accounts is important for recognizing revenues and expenses in the proper period. We describe the adjusted trial balance and how it is used to prepare financial statements.

A Look Ahead

Chapter 4 highlights the completion of the accounting cycle. We explain the important final steps in the accounting process. These include closing procedures, the post-closing trial balance, and reversing entries.

Chapter 3 Adjusting Accounts and Preparing Financial Statements

Learning Objectives

CAP

Conceptual

C1 Explain the importance of periodic reporting and the time period assumption. *(p. 92)*

C2 Explain accrual accounting and how it improves financial statements. *(p. 93)*

C3 Identify the types of adjustments and their purpose. *(p. 94)*

Analytical

A1 Explain how accounting adjustments link to financial statements. *(p. 103)*

A2 Compute profit margin and describe its use in analyzing company performance. *(p. 106)*

Procedural

P1 Prepare and explain adjusting entries. *(p. 95)*

P2 Explain and prepare an adjusted trial balance. *(p. 104)*

P3 Prepare financial statements from an adjusted trial balance. *(p. 104)*

P4 *Appendix 3A*—Explain the alternatives in accounting for prepaids. *(p. 110)*

LP3

Decision Feature

High Score

"Get a good accountant"—Jason Kapalka (from left: John Vechey, Brian Feite, Jason Kapalka)

SEATTLE—Jason Kapalka met John Vechey and Brian Feite, both 19 at the time, after the two had created an online game. "We hit it off really well," explains Jason. "We were all a little unhappy with our jobs. We thought, 'Hey, we could start our own company.'" Their startup company, **PopCap Games (PopCap.com),** is a creator and provider of downloadable games. Jason recalls that their friends considered them crazy.

Undaunted, the three scraped together the little cash they had. Jason explains that each worked out of their respective apartments to save money. "We survived," admits Jason, "because we didn't have many expenses." The young trio quickly developed a system to account for everything, including cash, revenues, receivables and payables. They also adjusted to the deferral and accrual of revenues and expenses. Setting up a good accounting system is an important part of success, explains Jason. "Don't wait until . . . everything is a big mess."

Most of PopCap's sales are paid for in advance of game delivery. This means few uncollectible accounts. The team also defers payment of their expenses to the time permitted—which is good management. "We're trying to keep a very simple business model," insists Jason. The team continues to fine-tune their accounting system as they remain focused on revenues, income, assets, and liabilities. "No matter what you do," argues Jason, "there's always something that you haven't done."

Financial statements preparation and analysis are a process that the three continue to work on. Although they insist on timely and accurate accounting reports, Jason says "it really helped us to keep things simple." To help make it simple, they took time to understand accounting adjustments and their effects. It is part of the larger picture. "You're not going to get breaks unless you're working hard."

Today, PopCap is a success story. "Now we can afford Mac and Cheese, and the occasional bottle of water," laughs Jason. "Life is good!"

[Sources: *PopCap Website*, January 2009; *Entrepreneur*, February 2008; *Wired*, March 2008; *2o2p Magazine*, September 2006; *Washington Post*, March 2008]

Financial statements reflect revenues when earned and expenses when incurred. This is known as *accrual accounting,* which was the focus of Chapter 2. We showed how companies use accounting systems to collect information about *external* transactions and events. We also explained how journals, ledgers, and other tools are useful in preparing financial statements. This chapter describes the accounting process for producing useful information involving *internal* transactions and events. An important part of this process is adjusting the account balances so that financial statements at the end of a reporting period reflect the effects of all transactions. We then explain the important steps in preparing financial statements.

Adjusting Accounts and Preparing Financial Statements

Timing and Reporting
- Accounting period
- Accrual versus cash
- Recognition of revenues and expenses

Adjusting Accounts
- Prepaid expenses
- Unearned revenues
- Accrued expenses
- Accrued revenues
- Adjusted trial balance

Preparing Financial Statements
- Income statement
- Statement of owner's equity
- Balance sheet

Timing and Reporting

This section describes the importance of reporting accounting information at regular intervals and its impact for recording revenues and expenses.

The Accounting Period

C1 Explain the importance of periodic reporting and the time period assumption.

The value of information is often linked to its timeliness. Useful information must reach decision makers frequently and promptly. To provide timely information, accounting systems prepare reports at regular intervals. This results in an accounting process impacted by the time period (or periodicity) assumption. The **time period assumption** presumes that an organization's activities can be divided into specific time periods such as a month, a three-month quarter, a six-month interval, or a year. Exhibit 3.1 shows various **accounting,** or *reporting,* **periods.** Most organizations use a year as their primary accounting period. Reports covering a one-year period are known as **annual financial statements.** Many organizations also prepare **interim financial statements** covering one, three, or six months of activity.

"Best Buy announces income of . . ."

Video3.1

EXHIBIT 3.1

Accounting Periods

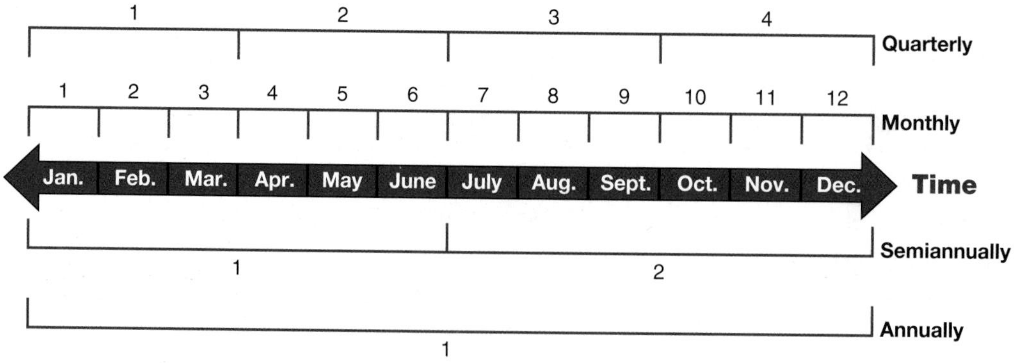

The annual reporting period is not always a calendar year ending on December 31. An organization can adopt a **fiscal year** consisting of any 12 consecutive months. It is also acceptable to adopt an annual reporting period of 52 weeks. For example, **Gap**'s fiscal year consistently ends the final week of January or the first week of February each year.

Companies with little seasonal variation in sales often choose the calendar year as their fiscal year. For example, the financial statements of **Marvel Enterprises** (the company that controls characters such as Spider-Man, Fantastic Four, and Shang-Chi) reflect a fiscal year that ends on December 31. Companies experiencing seasonal variations in sales often choose a **natural business year** end, which is when sales activities are at their lowest level for the year. The natural business year for retailers such as **Wal-Mart**, **Target**, and **Macy's** usually ends around January 31, after the holiday season.

Accrual Basis versus Cash Basis

C2 Explain accrual accounting and how it improves financial statements.

After external transactions and events are recorded, several accounts still need adjustments before their balances appear in financial statements. This need arises because internal transactions and events remain unrecorded. **Accrual basis accounting** uses the adjusting process to recognize revenues when earned and expenses when incurred (matched with revenues).

Cash basis accounting recognizes revenues when cash is received and records expenses when cash is paid. This means that cash basis net income for a period is the difference between cash receipts and cash payments. Cash basis accounting is not consistent with generally accepted accounting principles.

It is commonly held that accrual accounting better reflects business performance than information about cash receipts and payments. Accrual accounting also increases the *comparability* of financial statements from one period to another. Yet cash basis accounting is useful for several business decisions—which is the reason companies must report a statement of cash flows.

To see the difference between these two accounting systems, let's consider FastForward's Prepaid Insurance account. FastForward paid $2,400 for 24 months of insurance coverage beginning on December 1, 2009. Accrual accounting requires that $100 of insurance expense be reported on December 2009's income statement. Another $1,200 of expense is reported in year 2010, and the remaining $1,100 is reported as expense in the first 11 months of 2011. Exhibit 3.2 illustrates this allocation of insurance cost across these three years. The accrual basis balance sheet reports any unexpired premium as a Prepaid Insurance asset.

EXHIBIT 3.2

Accrual Accounting for Allocating Prepaid Insurance to Expense

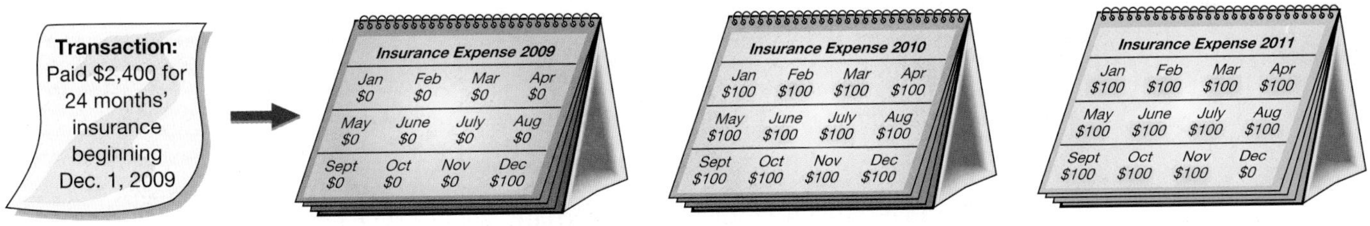

Alternatively, a cash basis income statement for December 2009 reports insurance expense of $2,400, as shown in Exhibit 3.3. The cash basis income statements for years 2010 and 2011 report no insurance expense. The cash basis balance sheet never reports an insurance asset because it is immediately expensed. This shows that cash basis income for 2009–2011 fails to match the cost of insurance with the insurance benefits received for those years and months.

EXHIBIT 3.3

Cash Accounting for Allocating Prepaid Insurance to Expense

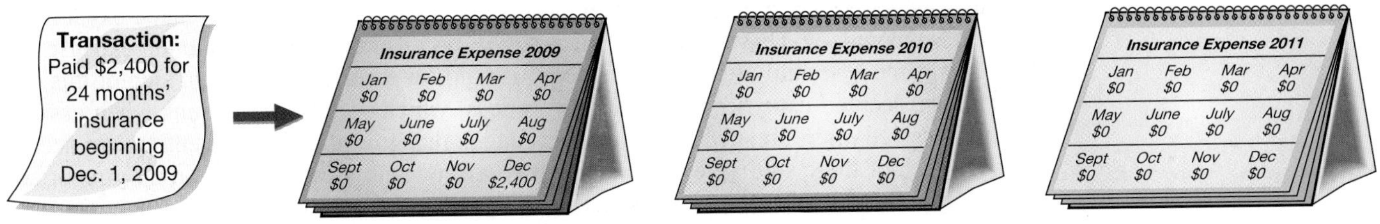

Recognizing Revenues and Expenses

Point: Recording revenue early overstates current-period revenue and income; recording it late understates current-period revenue and income.

Point: Recording expense early overstates current-period expense and understates current-period income; recording it late understates current-period expense and overstates current-period income.

We use the time period assumption to divide a company's activities into specific time periods, but not all activities are complete when financial statements are prepared. Thus, adjustments often are required to get correct account balances.

We rely on two principles in the adjusting process: revenue recognition and matching. Chapter 1 explained that the *revenue recognition principle* requires that revenue be recorded when earned, not before and not after. Most companies earn revenue when they provide services and products to customers. A major goal of the adjusting process is to have revenue recognized (reported) in the time period when it is earned. The **matching principle** aims to record expenses in the same accounting period as the revenues that are earned as a result of those expenses. This matching of expenses with the revenue benefits is a major part of the adjusting process.

Matching expenses with revenues often requires us to predict certain events. When we use financial statements, we must understand that they require estimates and therefore include measures that are not precise. **Walt Disney**'s annual report explains that its production costs from movies, such as *Pirates of the Caribbean,* are matched to revenues based on a ratio of current revenues from the movie divided by its predicted total revenues.

Decision Insight

Improper Adjustments Revenue recognition and expense matching are key to recording accounting adjustments. Good adjustments require good management judgment. Failure in judgment led to improper adjustments at **Fannie Mae, AOL Time Warner, WorldCom,** and **Xerox.**

Quick Check

Answers—p. 113

1. Describe a company's annual reporting period.
2. Why do companies prepare interim financial statements?
3. What two accounting principles most directly drive the adjusting process?
4. Is cash basis accounting consistent with the matching principle? Why or why not?
5. If your company pays a $4,800 premium on April 1, 2009, for two years' insurance coverage, how much insurance expense is reported in 2010 using cash basis accounting?

Adjusting Accounts

Adjusting accounts is a 3-step process:

Step 1: **Determine the current account balance.**

Step 2: **Determine what the current account balance *should be.***

Step 3: **Record an adjusting entry to get from step *1* to step *2.***

Framework for Adjustments

C3 Identify the types of adjustments and their purpose.

Adjustments are necessary for transactions and events that extend over more than one period. It is helpful to group adjustments by the timing of cash receipt or cash payment in relation to the recognition of the related revenues or expenses. Exhibit 3.4 identifies four types of adjustments.

The left side of this exhibit shows prepaid expenses (including depreciation) and unearned revenues, which reflect transactions when cash is paid or received *before* a related expense or revenue is recognized. They are also called *deferrals* because the recognition of an expense (or revenue) is *deferred* until after the related cash is paid (or received). The right side of this exhibit shows accrued expenses and accrued revenues, which reflect transactions when cash is paid or received *after* a related expense or revenue is recognized. Adjusting entries are necessary for each of these so that revenues, expenses, assets, and liabilities are correctly reported. It is helpful to remember that each adjusting entry affects one or more income statement accounts *and* one or more balance sheet accounts (but never the Cash account).

Point: Source documents provide information for most daily transactions, and in many businesses the recordkeepers record them. Adjustments require more knowledge and are usually handled by senior accounting professionals.

EXHIBIT 3.4

Types of Adjustments

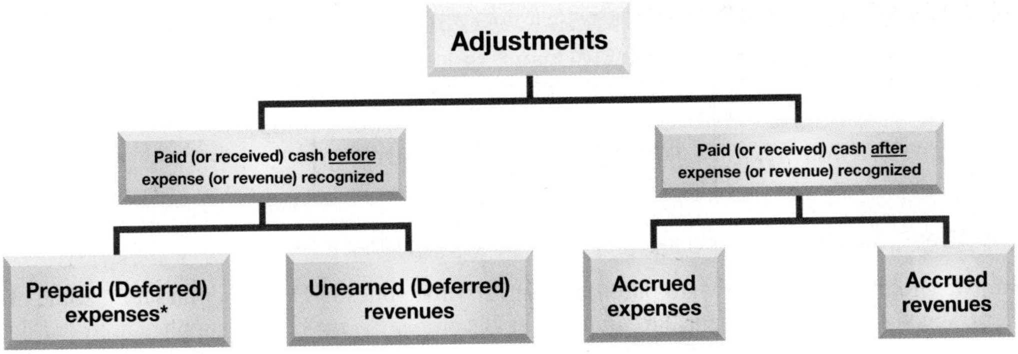

*Includes depreciation.

Prepaid (Deferred) Expenses

P1 Prepare and explain adjusting entries.

Prepaid expenses refer to items *paid for* in advance of receiving their benefits. Prepaid expenses are assets. When these assets are used, their costs become expenses. Adjusting entries for prepaids increase expenses and decrease assets as shown in the T-accounts of Exhibit 3.5. Such adjustments reflect transactions and events that use up prepaid expenses (including passage of time). To illustrate the accounting for prepaid expenses, we look at prepaid insurance, supplies, and depreciation.

EXHIBIT 3.5

Adjusting for Prepaid Expenses

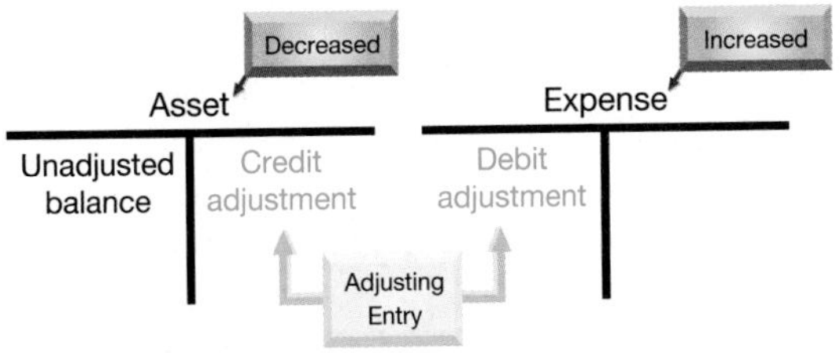

Prepaid Insurance We use our 3-step process for this and all accounting adjustments.

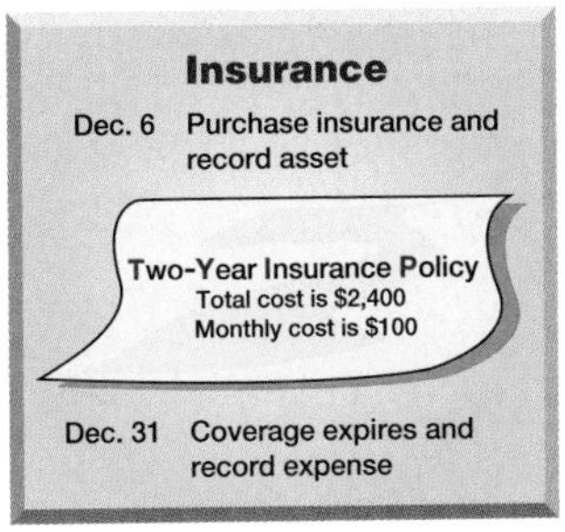

Step 1: We determine the current balance of FastForward's prepaid insurance to be equal to its payment of $2,400 for 24 months of insurance benefits beginning on December 1, 2009.

Step 2: With the passage of time, the benefits of the insurance gradually expire and a portion of the Prepaid Insurance asset becomes expense. For instance, one month's insurance coverage expires by December 31, 2009. This expense is $100, or 1/24 of $2,400.

Step 3: The adjusting entry to record this expense and reduce the asset, along with T-account postings, follows:

Adjustment (*a*)

Dec. 31	Insurance Expense	100	
	Prepaid Insurance		100
	To record first month's expired insurance.		

Assets	=	Liabilities	+	Equity
−100				−100

Insurance Expense 637

Dec. 31	100		

Prepaid Insurance 128

Dec. 6	2,400	Dec. 31	100
Balance	2,300		

Explanation After adjusting and posting, the $100 balance in Insurance Expense and the $2,300 balance in Prepaid Insurance are ready for reporting in financial statements. *Not* making the adjustment on or before December 31 would (1) understate expenses by $100 and overstate net income by $100 for the December income statement and (2) overstate both prepaid insurance (assets) and equity (because of net income) by $100 in the December 31 balance sheet. Exhibit 3.2 showed that 2010's adjustments must transfer a total of $1,200 from Prepaid Insurance to Insurance Expense, and 2011's adjustments must transfer the remaining $1,100 to Insurance Expense. The following table highlights the December 31 adjustment for prepaid insurance.

Point: Many companies record adjusting entries only at the end of each year because of the time and cost necessary.

Before Adjustment	Adjustment	After Adjustment
Prepaid Insurance = $2,400	**Deduct $100 from Prepaid Insurance** **Add $100 to Insurance Expense**	**Prepaid Insurance = $2,300**
Reports $2,400 policy for 24-months' coverage.	Record current month's $100 insurance expense and $100 reduction in prepaid amount.	Reports $2,300 in coverage for remaining 23 months.

Supplies Supplies are a prepaid expense requiring adjustment.

Step 1: Recall that FastForward purchased $9,720 of supplies in December and used some of them. When financial statements are prepared at December 31, the cost of supplies used during December must be recognized.

Step 2: When FastForward computes (takes physical count of) its remaining unused supplies at December 31, it finds $8,670 of supplies remaining of the $9,720 total supplies. The $1,050 difference between these two amounts is December's supplies expense.

Step 3: The adjusting entry to record this expense and reduce the Supplies asset account, along with T-account postings, follows:

Assets	=	Liabilities	+	Equity
−1,050				−1,050

Adjustment (*b*)

Dec. 31	Supplies Expense	1,050	
	Supplies		1,050
	To record supplies used.		

Supplies Expense 652

Dec. 31	**1,050**		

Supplies 126

Dec. 2	2,500	**Dec. 31**	**1,050**
6	7,100		
26	120		
Balance	8,670		

Explanation The balance of the Supplies account is $8,670 after posting—equaling the cost of the remaining supplies. *Not* making the adjustment on or before December 31 would (1) understate expenses by $1,050 and overstate net income by $1,050 for the December income statement and (2) overstate both supplies and equity (because of net income) by $1,050 in the December 31 balance sheet. The following table highlights the adjustment for supplies.

Before Adjustment	Adjustment	After Adjustment
Supplies = $9,720	**Deduct $1,050 from Supplies** **Add $1,050 to Supplies Expense**	**Supplies = $8,670**
Reports $9,720 in supplies.	Record $1,050 in supplies used and $1,050 as supplies expense.	Reports $8,670 in supplies.

Point: We assume that prepaid and unearned items are recorded in balance sheet accounts. An alternative is to record them in income statement accounts; Appendix 3A discusses this alternative. The adjusted financial statements are identical.

Other Prepaid Expenses Other prepaid expenses, such as Prepaid Rent, are accounted for exactly as Insurance and Supplies are. We should note that some prepaid expenses are both paid for and fully used up within a single accounting period. One example is when a company pays monthly rent on the first day of each month. This payment creates a prepaid expense on the first day of each month that fully expires by the end of the month. In these special cases, we can record the cash paid with a debit to an expense account instead of an asset account. This practice is described more completely later in the chapter.

Decision Maker

Investor A small publishing company signs a well-known athlete to write a book. The company pays the athlete $500,000 to sign plus future book royalties. A note to the company's financial statements says that "prepaid expenses include $500,000 in author signing fees to be matched against future expected sales." Is this accounting for the signing bonus acceptable? How does it affect your analysis? [Answer—p. 112]

Depreciation A special category of prepaid expenses is **plant assets,** which refers to long-term tangible assets used to produce and sell products and services. Plant assets are expected to provide benefits for more than one period. Examples of plant assets are buildings, machines, vehicles, and fixtures. All plant assets, with a general exception for land, eventually wear out or decline in usefulness. The costs of these assets are deferred but are gradually reported as expenses in the income statement over the assets' useful lives (benefit periods). **Depreciation** is the process of allocating the costs of these assets over their expected useful lives. Depreciation expense is recorded with an adjusting entry similar to that for other prepaid expenses.

Point: Depreciation does not necessarily measure decline in market value.

Point: An asset's expected value at the end of its useful life is called *salvage value.*

Step 1: Recall that FastForward purchased equipment for $26,000 in early December to use in earning revenue. This equipment's cost must be depreciated.

Step 2: The equipment is expected to have a useful life (benefit period) of four years and to be worth about $8,000 at the end of four years. This means the *net* cost of this equipment over its useful life is $18,000 ($26,000 − $8,000). We can use any of several methods to allocate this $18,000 net cost to expense. FastForward uses a method called **straight-line depreciation,** which allocates equal amounts of the asset's net cost to depreciation during its useful life. Dividing the $18,000 net cost by the 48 months in the asset's useful life gives a monthly cost of $375 ($18,000/48).

Depreciation

Dec. 3 Purchase equipment and record asset

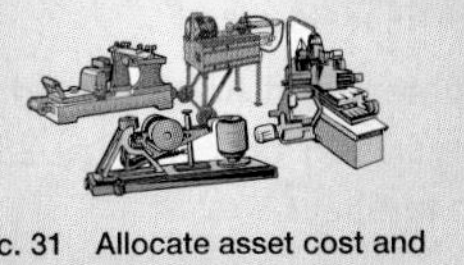

Dec. 31 Allocate asset cost and record depreciation

Step 3: The adjusting entry to record monthly depreciation expense, along with T-account postings, follows:

Adjustment (c)

Dec. 31	Depreciation Expense	375	
	Accumulated Depreciation—Equipment		375
	To record monthly equipment depreciation.		

Assets = Liabilities + Equity
−375 −375

Depreciation Expense—Equipment 612	
Dec. 31 375	

Equipment 167	
Dec. 3 26,000	

Accumulated Depreciation—Equipment 168	
	Dec. 31 375

Explanation After posting the adjustment, the Equipment account ($26,000) less its Accumulated Depreciation ($375) account equals the $25,625 net cost of the 47 remaining months in the benefit period. The $375 balance in the Depreciation Expense account is reported in the December income statement. *Not* making the adjustment at December 31 would (1) understate expenses by $375 and overstate net income by $375 for the December income statement and (2) overstate both assets and equity (because of income) by $375 in the December 31 balance sheet. The following table highlights the adjustment for depreciation.

Before Adjustment	Adjustment	After Adjustment
Equipment, net = $26,000	**Deduct $375 from Equipment, net Add $375 to Depreciation Expense**	**Equipment, net = $25,625**
Reports $26,000 in equipment.	Record $375 in depreciation and $375 as accumulated depreciation, which is deducted from equipment.	Reports $25,625 in equipment, net of accumulated depreciation.

Accumulated depreciation is kept in a separate contra account. A **contra account** is an account linked with another account, it has an opposite normal balance, and it is reported as a subtraction from that other account's balance. For instance, FastForward's contra account of Accumulated Depreciation—Equipment is subtracted from the Equipment account in the balance sheet (see Exhibit 3.7). This contra account allows balance sheet readers to know both the full costs of assets and the total depreciation.

The title of the contra account, *Accumulated Depreciation,* indicates that this account includes total depreciation expense for all prior periods for which the asset was used. To illustrate, the Equipment and the Accumulated Depreciation accounts appear as in Exhibit 3.6 on February 28, 2010, after three months of adjusting entries. The $1,125 balance in the accumulated depreciation account can be subtracted from its related $26,000 asset cost. The difference ($24,875) between these two balances is the cost of the asset that has not yet been

Point: The cost principle requires an asset to be initially recorded at acquisition cost. Depreciation causes the asset's book value (cost less accumulated depreciation) to decline over time.

EXHIBIT 3.6

Accounts after Three Months of Depreciation Adjustments

Equipment		167	
Dec. 3	26,000		

Accumulated Depreciation—Equipment		168
	Dec. 31	375
	Jan. 31	375
	Feb. 28	375
	Balance	1,125

Point: The net cost of equipment is also called the *depreciable basis.*

depreciated. This difference is called the **book value,** or the *net amount,* which equals the asset's costs less its accumulated depreciation.

These account balances are reported in the assets section of the February 28 balance sheet in Exhibit 3.7.

EXHIBIT 3.7

Equipment and Accumulated Depreciation on February 28 Balance Sheet

Assets (at February 28, 2010)		
Cash		$ ____
⋮		
Equipment	**$26,000**	
Less accumulated depreciation	**1,125**	**24,875**
Total Assets		$

Commonly titled *Equipment, net*

Decision Maker

Entrepreneur You are preparing an offer to purchase a family-run restaurant. The depreciation schedule for the restaurant's building and equipment shows costs of $175,000 and accumulated depreciation of $155,000. This leaves a net for building and equipment of $20,000. Is this information useful in helping you decide on a purchase offer? [Answer—p. 113]

Unearned (Deferred) Revenues

The term **unearned revenues** refers to cash received in advance of providing products and services. Unearned revenues, also called *deferred revenues,* are liabilities. When cash is accepted, an obligation to provide products or services is accepted. As products or services are provided, the unearned revenues become *earned* revenues. Adjusting entries for unearned revenues involve increasing revenues and decreasing unearned revenues, as shown in Exhibit 3.8.

EXHIBIT 3.8

Adjusting for Unearned Revenues

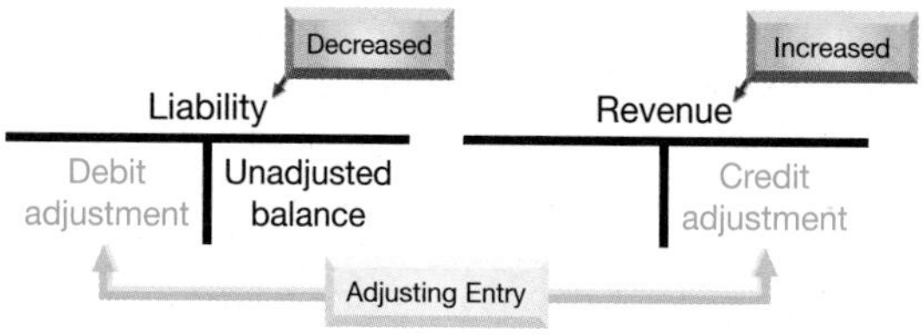

Point: To *defer* is to postpone. We postpone reporting amounts received as revenues until they are earned.

An example of unearned revenues is from **The New York Times Company**, which reports unexpired (unearned) subscriptions of nearly $80 million: "Proceeds from . . . subscriptions are deferred at the time of sale and are recognized in earnings on a pro rata basis over the terms of the subscriptions." Unearned revenues are nearly 10% of the current liabilities for the Times. Another example comes from the **Boston Celtics**. When the Celtics receive cash from advance ticket sales and broadcast fees, they record it in an unearned revenue account called *Deferred Game Revenues.* The Celtics recognize this unearned revenue with adjusting entries on a game-by-game basis. Since the NBA regular season begins in October and ends in April, revenue recognition is mainly limited to this period. For a recent season, the Celtics' quarterly revenues were $0 million for July–September; $34 million for October–December; $48 million for January–March; and $17 million for April–June.

Unearned Revenues

Dec. 26 Cash received in advance and record liability

Dec. 31 Provided services and record revenue

FastForward has unearned revenues. It agreed on December 26 to provide consulting services to a client for a fixed fee of $3,000 for 60 days.

Step 1: On December 26, the client paid the 60-day fee in advance, covering the period December 27 to February 24. The entry to record the cash received in advance is

Dec. 26	Cash	3,000	
	Unearned Consulting Revenue		3,000
	Received advance payment for services over the next 60 days.		

Assets	=	Liabilities	+	Equity
+3,000		+3,000		

This advance payment increases cash and creates an obligation to do consulting work over the next 60 days.

Step 2: As time passes, FastForward earns this payment through consulting. By December 31, it has provided five days' service and earned 5/60 of the $3,000 unearned revenue. This amounts to $250 ($3,000 × 5/60). The *revenue recognition principle* implies that $250 of unearned revenue must be reported as revenue on the December income statement.

Step 3: The adjusting entry to reduce the liability account and recognize earned revenue, along with T-account postings, follows:

Adjustment (*d*)

Dec. 31	Unearned Consulting Revenue	250	
	Consulting Revenue		250
	To record earned revenue that was received in advance ($3,000 × 5/60).		

Assets	=	Liabilities	+	Equity
		−250		+250

Unearned Consulting Revenue 236

Dec. 31	**250**	Dec. 26	3,000
		Balance	2,750

Consulting Revenue 403

		Dec. 5	4,200
		12	1,600
		31	**250**
		Balance	6,050

Explanation The adjusting entry transfers $250 from unearned revenue (a liability account) to a revenue account. *Not* making the adjustment (1) understates revenue and net income by $250 in the December income statement and (2) overstates unearned revenue and understates equity by $250 on the December 31 balance sheet. The following highlights the adjustment for unearned revenue.

Before Adjustment	Adjustment	After Adjustment
Unearned Consulting Revenue = $3,000	**Deduct $250 from Unearned Consulting Revenue** **Add $250 to Consulting Revenue**	**Unearned Consulting Revenue = $2,750**
Reports $3,000 in unearned revenue for consulting services promised for 60 days.	Record 5 days of earned consulting revenue, which is 5/60 of unearned amount.	Reports $2,750 in unearned revenue for consulting services owed over next 55 days.

Accounting for unearned revenues is crucial to many companies. For example, the **National Retail Federation** reports that gift card sales, which are unearned revenues for sellers, exceed $20 billion annually. Gift cards are now the top selling holiday gift.

Accrued Expenses

Accrued expenses refer to costs that are incurred in a period but are both unpaid and unrecorded. Accrued expenses must be reported on the income statement of the period when incurred. Adjusting entries for recording accrued expenses involves increasing expenses and increasing liabilities as shown in Exhibit 3.9. This adjustment recognizes expenses incurred in a period but not yet paid. Common examples of accrued expenses are salaries, interest,

EXHIBIT 3.9

Adjusting for Accrued Expenses

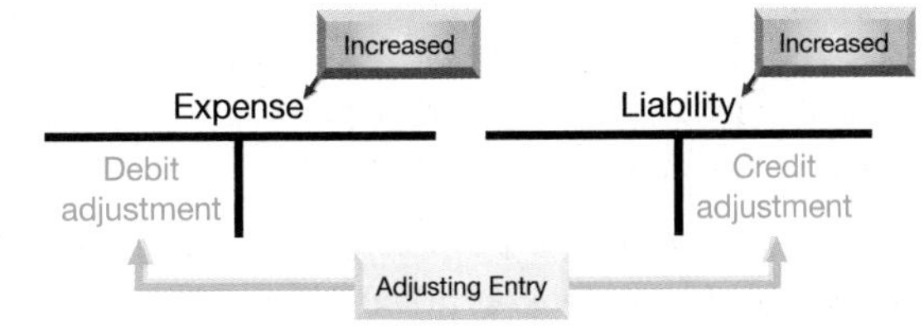

Point: Accrued expenses are also called accrued liabilities.

rent, and taxes. We use salaries and interest to show how to adjust accounts for accrued expenses.

Accrued Salaries Expense FastForward's employee earns $70 per day, or $350 for a five-day workweek beginning on Monday and ending on Friday.

Step 1: Its employee is paid every two weeks on Friday. On December 12 and 26, the wages are paid, recorded in the journal, and posted to the ledger.

Step 2: The calendar in Exhibit 3.10 shows three working days after the December 26 payday (29, 30, and 31). This means the employee has earned three days' salary by the close of

EXHIBIT 3.10

Salary Accrual and Paydays

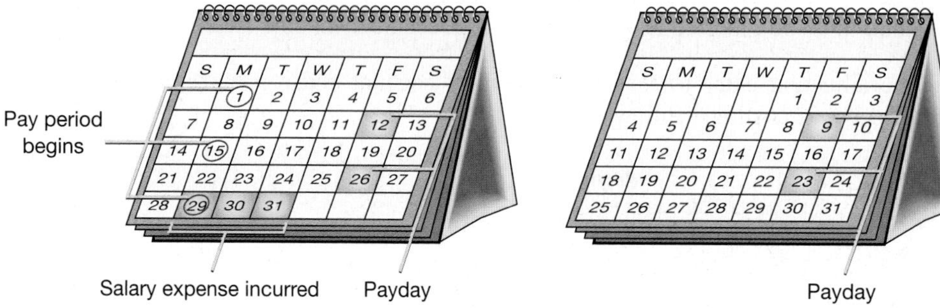

Point: An employer records salaries expense and a vacation pay liability when employees earn vacation pay.

business on Wednesday, December 31, yet this salary cost is not paid or recorded. The financial statements would be incomplete if FastForward fails to report the added expense and liability to the employee for unpaid salary from December 29, 30, and 31.

Step 3: The adjusting entry to account for accrued salaries, along with T-account postings, follows:

Assets = Liabilities + Equity
+210 −210

	Adjustment (e)		
Dec. 31	Salaries Expense	210	
	Salaries Payable		210
	To record three days' accrued salary (3 × $70).		

Salaries Expense		622
Dec. 12	700	
26	700	
31	**210**	
Balance	1,610	

Salaries Payable		209
	Dec. 31	**210**

Point: Instead, assume: (1) the last payday for the year is Dec. 19, (2) the next payday is Jan. 2, and (3) Dec. 25 is a paid holiday. Record the Dec. 31 adjusting entry. *Answer:* We must accrue pay for 8 working days (8 × $70):
Salaries Expense . . . 560
Salaries Payable 560

Explanation Salaries expense of $1,610 is reported on the December income statement and $210 of salaries payable (liability) is reported in the balance sheet. *Not* making the adjustment (1) understates salaries expense and overstates net income by $210 in the December income statement and (2) understates salaries payable (liabilities) and overstates equity by $210 on the December 31 balance sheet. The following highlights the adjustment for salaries incurred.

Before Adjustment	Adjustment	After Adjustment
Salaries Payable = $0	**Add $210 to Salaries Payable Add $210 to Salaries Expense**	**Salaries Payable = $210**
Reports $0 from employee salaries incurred but not yet paid in cash.	Record 3 days' salaries owed to employee, but not yet paid, at $70 per day.	Reports $210 salaries payable to employee but not yet paid.

Accrued Interest Expense Companies commonly have accrued interest expense on notes payable and other long-term liabilities at the end of a period. Interest expense is incurred with the passage of time. Unless interest is paid on the last day of an accounting period, we need to adjust for interest expense incurred but not yet paid. This means we must accrue interest cost from the most recent payment date up to the end of the period. The formula for computing accrued interest is:

Principal amount owed × Annual interest rate × Fraction of year since last payment date.

To illustrate, if a company has a \$6,000 loan from a bank at 6% annual interest, then 30 days' accrued interest expense is \$30—computed as \$6,000 × 0.06 × 30/360. The adjusting entry would be to debit Interest Expense for \$30 and credit Interest Payable for \$30.

Point: Interest computations assume a 360-day year; known as the *bankers' rule.*

Future Payment of Accrued Expenses Adjusting entries for accrued expenses foretell cash transactions in future periods. Specifically, accrued expenses at the end of one accounting period result in *cash payment* in a *future period*(s). To illustrate, recall that FastForward recorded accrued salaries of \$210. On January 9, the first payday of the next period, the following entry settles the accrued liability (salaries payable) and records salaries expense for seven days of work in January:

Jan. 9	Salaries Payable (3 days at \$70 per day)	210	
	Salaries Expense (7 days at \$70 per day)	490	
	Cash		700
	Paid two weeks' salary including three days accrued in December.		

Assets	=	Liabilities	+	Equity
−700		−210		−490

The \$210 debit reflects the payment of the liability for the three days' salary accrued on December 31. The \$490 debit records the salary for January's first seven working days (including the New Year's Day holiday) as an expense of the new accounting period. The \$700 credit records the total amount of cash paid to the employee.

Accrued Revenues

The term **accrued revenues** refers to revenues earned in a period that are both unrecorded and not yet received in cash (or other assets). An example is a technician who bills customers only when the job is done. If one-third of a job is complete by the end of a period, then the technician must record one-third of the expected billing as revenue in that period—even though there is no billing or collection. The adjusting entries for accrued revenues increase assets and increase revenues as shown in Exhibit 3.11. Accrued revenues commonly arise from services, products, interest, and rent. We use service fees and interest to show how to adjust for accrued revenues.

Point: Accrued revenues are also called *accrued assets.*

EXHIBIT 3.11

Adjusting for Accrued Revenues

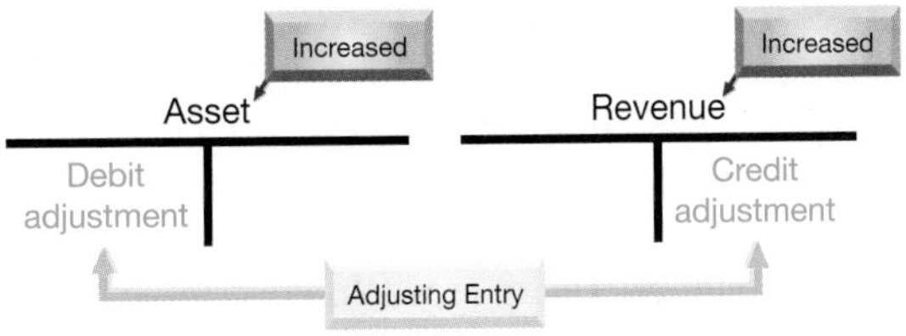

Accrued Services Revenue Accrued revenues are not recorded until adjusting entries are made at the end of the accounting period. These accrued revenues are earned but unrecorded because either the buyer has not yet paid for them or the seller has not yet billed the buyer. FastForward provides an example.

Step 1: In the second week of December, it agreed to provide 30 days of consulting services to a local sports club for a fixed fee of \$2,700. The terms of the initial agreement call for FastForward to provide services from December 12, 2009, through January 10, 2010, or 30 days of service. The club agrees to pay FastForward \$2,700 on January 10, 2010, when the service period is complete.

Step 2: At December 31, 2009, 20 days of services have already been provided. Since the contracted services are not yet entirely provided, FastForward has neither billed the club nor recorded the services already provided. Still, FastForward has earned two-thirds of the 30-day fee, or $1,800 ($2,700 × 20/30). The *revenue recognition principle* implies that it must report the $1,800 on the December income statement. The balance sheet also must report that the club owes FastForward $1,800.

Step 3: The year-end adjusting entry to account for accrued services revenue is

Assets	= Liabilities +	Equity
+1,800		+1,800

Adjustment (*f*)

Dec. 31	Accounts Receivable.	1,800	
	Consulting Revenue.		1,800
	To record 20 days' accrued revenue.		

Accounts Receivable 106

Dec. 12	1,900	Dec. 22	1,900
31	**1,800**		
Balance	1,800		

Consulting Revenue 403

		Dec. 5	4,200
		12	1,600
		31	250
		31	**1,800**
		Balance	7,850

Example: What is the adjusting entry if the 30-day consulting period began on December 22? *Answer:* One-third of the fee is earned:
Accounts Receivable . . . 900
Consulting Revenue . . . 900

Explanation Accounts receivable are reported on the balance sheet at $1,800, and the $7,850 total of consulting revenue is reported on the income statement. *Not* making the adjustment would understate (1) both consulting revenue and net income by $1,800 in the December income statement and (2) both accounts receivable (assets) and equity by $1,800 on the December 31 balance sheet. The following table highlights the adjustment for accrued revenue.

Before Adjustment	Adjustment	After Adjustment
Accounts Receivable = $0	**Add $1,800 to Accounts Receivable** **Add $1,800 to Consulting Revenue**	**Accounts Receivable = $1,800**
Reports $0 from revenue earned but not yet received in cash.	Record 20 days of earned consulting revenue, which is 20/30 of total contract amount.	Reports $1,800 in accounts receivable from consulting services provided.

Accrued Interest Revenue In addition to the accrued interest expense we described earlier, interest can yield an accrued revenue when a debtor owes money (or other assets) to a company. If a company is holding notes or accounts receivable that produce interest revenue, we must adjust the accounts to record any earned and yet uncollected interest revenue. The adjusting entry is similar to the one for accruing services revenue. Specifically, we debit Interest Receivable (asset) and credit Interest Revenue.

Future Receipt of Accrued Revenues Accrued revenues at the end of one accounting period result in *cash receipts* in a *future period*(s). To illustrate, recall that FastForward made an adjusting entry for $1,800 to record 20 days' accrued revenue earned from its consulting contract. When FastForward receives $2,700 cash on January 10 for the entire contract amount, it makes the following entry to remove the accrued asset (accounts receivable) and recognize the revenue earned in January. The $2,700 debit reflects the cash received. The $1,800 credit reflects the removal of the receivable, and the $900 credit records the revenue earned in January.

Assets	= Liabilities +	Equity
+2,700		+900
−1,800		

Jan. 10	Cash	2,700	
	Accounts Receivable (20 days at $90 per day)		1,800
	Consulting Revenue (10 days at $90 per day)		900
	Received cash for the accrued asset and recorded earned consulting revenue for January.		

Decision Maker

Loan Officer The owner of an electronics store applies for a business loan. The store's financial statements reveal large increases in current-year revenues and income. Analysis shows that these increases are due to a promotion that let consumers buy now and pay nothing until January 1 of next year. The store recorded these sales as accrued revenue. Does your analysis raise any concerns? [Answer—p. 113]

Links to Financial Statements

A1 Explain how accounting adjustments link to financial statements.

The process of adjusting accounts is intended to bring an asset or liability account balance to its correct amount. It also updates a related expense or revenue account. These adjustments are necessary for transactions and events that extend over more than one period. (Adjusting entries are posted like any other entry.)

Exhibit 3.12 summarizes the four types of transactions requiring adjustment. Understanding this exhibit is important to understanding the adjusting process and its importance to financial statements. Remember that each adjusting entry affects one or more income statement accounts *and* one or more balance sheet accounts (but never cash).

EXHIBIT 3.12

Summary of Adjustments and Financial Statement Links

	BEFORE Adjusting		
Category	**Balance Sheet**	**Income Statement**	**Adjusting Entry**
Prepaid expenses†	Asset overstated Equity overstated	Expense understated	**Dr. Expense** **Cr. Asset***
Unearned revenues†	Liability overstated Equity understated	Revenue understated	Dr. Liability Cr. Revenue
Accrued expenses	Liability understated Equity overstated	Expense understated	**Dr. Expense** **Cr. Liability**
Accrued revenues	Asset understated Equity understated	Revenue understated	Dr. Asset Cr. Revenue

* For depreciation, the credit is to Accumulated Depreciation (contra asset).

† Exhibit assumes that prepaid expenses are initially recorded as assets and that unearned revenues are initially recorded as liabilities.

Information about some adjustments is not always available until several days or even weeks after the period-end. This means that some adjusting and closing entries are recorded later than, but dated as of, the last day of the period. One example is a company that receives a utility bill on January 10 for costs incurred for the month of December. When it receives the bill, the company records the expense and the payable as of December 31. Other examples include long-distance phone usage and costs of many Web billings. The December income statement reflects these additional expenses incurred, and the December 31 balance sheet includes these payables, although the amounts were not actually known on December 31.

Decision Ethics

Financial Officer At year-end, the president instructs you, the financial officer, not to record accrued expenses until next year because they will not be paid until then. The president also directs you to record in current-year sales a recent purchase order from a customer that requires merchandise to be delivered two weeks after the year-end. Your company would report a net income instead of a net loss if you carry out these instructions. What do you do? [Answer—p. 113]

Quick Check

Answers—p. 113

6. If an adjusting entry for accrued revenues of $200 at year-end is omitted, what is this error's effect on the year-end income statement and balance sheet?
7. What is a contra account? Explain its purpose.
8. What is an accrued expense? Give an example.
9. Describe how an unearned revenue arises. Give an example.

Adjusted Trial Balance

P2 Explain and prepare an adjusted trial balance.

An **unadjusted trial balance** is a list of accounts and balances prepared *before* adjustments are recorded. An **adjusted trial balance** is a list of accounts and balances prepared *after* adjusting entries have been recorded and posted to the ledger.

Exhibit 3.13 shows both the unadjusted and the adjusted trial balances for FastForward at December 31, 2009. The order of accounts in the trial balance is usually set up to match the order in the chart of accounts. Several new accounts arise from the adjusting entries.

EXHIBIT 3.13

Unadjusted and Adjusted Trial Balances

FASTFORWARD
Trial Balances
December 31, 2009

Acct. No.	Account Title	Unadjusted Trial Balance Dr.	Unadjusted Trial Balance Cr.	Adjustments Dr.	Adjustments Cr.	Adjusted Trial Balance Dr.	Adjusted Trial Balance Cr.
101	Cash	$ 4,350				$ 4,350	
106	Accounts receivable	0		(f) $1,800		1,800	
126	Supplies	9,720			(b) $1,050	8,670	
128	Prepaid insurance	2,400			(a) 100	2,300	
167	Equipment	26,000				26,000	
168	Accumulated depreciation—Equip.		$ 0		(c) 375		$ 375
201	Accounts payable		6,200				6,200
209	Salaries payable		0		(e) 210		210
236	Unearned consulting revenue		3,000	(d) 250			2,750
301	C. Taylor, Capital		30,000				30,000
302	C. Taylor, Withdrawals	200				200	
403	Consulting revenue		5,800		(d) 250		7,850
					(f) 1,800		
406	Rental revenue		300				300
612	Depreciation expense—Equip.	0		(c) 375		375	
622	Salaries expense	1,400		(e) 210		1,610	
637	Insurance expense	0		(a) 100		100	
640	Rent expense	1,000				1,000	
652	Supplies expense	0		(b) 1,050		1,050	
690	Utilities expense	230				230	
	Totals	$45,300	$45,300	$3,785	$3,785	$47,685	$47,685

Each adjustment (see middle columns) is identified by a letter in parentheses that links it to an adjusting entry explained earlier. Each amount in the Adjusted Trial Balance columns is computed by taking that account's amount from the Unadjusted Trial Balance columns and adding or subtracting any adjustment(s). To illustrate, Supplies has a $9,720 Dr. balance in the unadjusted columns. Subtracting the $1,050 Cr. amount shown in the adjustments columns yields an adjusted $8,670 Dr. balance for Supplies. An account can have more than one adjustment, such as for Consulting Revenue. Also, some accounts might not require adjustment for this period, such as Accounts Payable.

Preparing Financial Statements

P3 Prepare financial statements from an adjusted trial balance.

We can prepare financial statements directly from information in the *adjusted* trial balance. An adjusted trial balance (see the right-most columns in Exhibit 3.13) includes all accounts and balances appearing in financial statements, and is easier to work from than the entire ledger when preparing financial statements.

Point: Sarbanes-Oxley Act requires that financial statements filed with the SEC be certified by the CEO and CFO, including a declaration that the statements fairly present the issuer's operations and financial condition. Violators can receive fines and/or prison terms.

Exhibit 3.14 shows how revenue and expense balances are transferred from the adjusted trial balance to the income statement (red lines). The net income and the withdrawals amount are then used to prepare the statement of owner's equity (black lines). Asset and liability balances on the adjusted trial balance are then transferred to the balance sheet (blue lines). The ending capital is determined on the statement of owner's equity and transferred to the balance sheet (green lines).

EXHIBIT 3.14

Preparing Financial Statements (Adjusted Trial Balance from Exhibit 3.13)

FASTFORWARD
Adjusted Trial Balance
December 31, 2009

Acct. No.	Account Title	Debit	Credit
101	Cash	$ 4,350	
106	Accounts receivable	1,800	
126	Supplies	8,670	
128	Prepaid insurance	2,300	
167	Equipment	26,000	
168	Accumulated depreciation—Equip.		$ 375
201	Accounts payable		6,200
209	Salaries payable		210
236	Unearned consulting revenue		2,750
301	C. Taylor, Capital		30,000
302	C. Taylor, Withdrawals	200	
403	Consulting revenue		7,850
406	Rental revenue		300
612	Depreciation expense—Equip.	375	
622	Salaries expense	1,610	
637	Insurance expense	100	
640	Rent expense	1,000	
652	Supplies expense	1,050	
690	Utilities expense	230	
	Totals	$47,685	$47,685

Step 3 Prepare balance sheet

FASTFORWARD
Balance Sheet
December 31, 2009

Assets		
Cash		$ 4,350
Accounts receivable		1,800
Supplies		8,670
Prepaid insurance		2,300
Equipment	$26,000	
Less accumulated depreciation	375	25,625
Total assets		$ 42,745
Liabilities		
Accounts payable		$ 6,200
Salaries payable		210
Unearned consulting revenue		2,750
Total liabilities		9,160
Equity		
C. Taylor, Capital		33,585
Total liabilities and equity		$ 42,745

Step 2 Prepare statement of owner's equity

FASTFORWARD
Statement of Owner's Equity
For Month Ended December 31, 2009

C. Taylor, Capital, December 1		$ 0
Plus: Investments by owner	$30,000	
Net income	3,785	
		33,785
Less: Withdrawals by owner		200
C. Taylor, Capital, December 31		$33,585

Step 1 Prepare income statement

FASTFORWARD
Income Statement
For Month Ended December 31, 2009

Revenues		
Consulting revenue	$7,850	
Rental revenue	300	
Total revenues		$8,150
Expenses		
Depreciation expense—Equip.	375	
Salaries expense	1,610	
Insurance expense	100	
Rent expense	1,000	
Supplies expense	1,050	
Utilities expense	230	
Total expenses		4,365
Net income		$3,785

We usually prepare financial statements in the following order: income statement, statement of owner's equity, and balance sheet. This order makes sense because the balance sheet uses information from the statement of owner's equity, which in turn uses information from the income statement. The statement of cash flows is usually the final statement prepared.

Quick Check

Answers—p. 113

10. Music-Mart records $1,000 of accrued salaries on December 31. Five days later, on January 5 (the next payday), salaries of $7,000 are paid. What is the January 5 entry?

11. Jordan Air has the following information in its unadjusted and adjusted trial balances. What are the adjusting entries that Jordan Air likely recorded?

	Unadjusted		Adjusted	
	Debit	Credit	Debit	Credit
Prepaid insurance	$6,200		$5,900	
Salaries payable		$ 0		$1,400

12. What accounts are taken from the adjusted trial balance to prepare an income statement?

13. In preparing financial statements from an adjusted trial balance, what statement is usually prepared second?

Decision Analysis — Profit Margin

A2 Compute profit margin and describe its use in analyzing company performance.

A useful measure of a company's operating results is the ratio of its net income to net sales. This ratio is called **profit margin,** or *return on sales,* and is computed as in Exhibit 3.15.

EXHIBIT 3.15

Profit Margin

$$\textbf{Profit margin} = \frac{\textbf{Net income}}{\textbf{Net sales}}$$

This ratio is interpreted as reflecting the percent of profit in each dollar of sales. To illustrate how we compute and use profit margin, let's look at the results of **Limited Brands, Inc.**, in Exhibit 3.16 for the period 2004 through 2007.

EXHIBIT 3.16

Limited Brands' Profit Margin

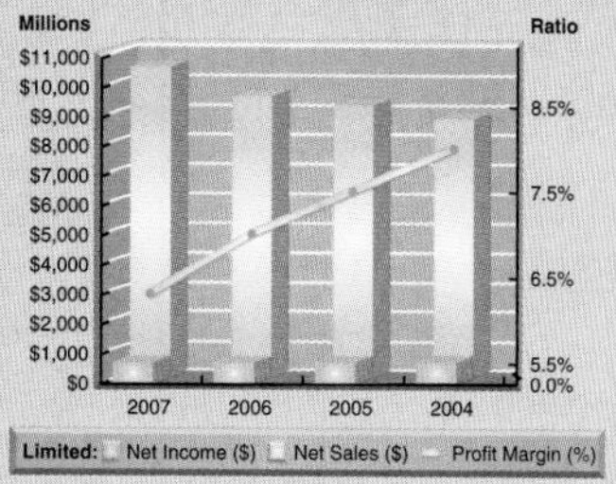

$ in millions	2007	2006	2005	2004
Net income	$ 676	$ 683	$ 705	$ 717
Net sales	$10,671	$9,699	$9,408	$8,934
Profit margin	**6.3%**	**7.0%**	**7.5%**	**8.0%**
Industry profit margin	1.6%	1.5%	1.4%	1.5%

The Limited's average profit margin is 7.2% during this period. This favorably compares to the average industry profit margin of 1.5%. However, Limited's profit margin has declined in recent years—from 8.0% in 2004 to 6.3% in 2007 (see margin graph). Future success depends on Limited maintaining and preferably increasing its profit margin.

Demonstration Problem 1

DP3

The following information relates to Fanning's Electronics on December 31, 2009. The company, which uses the calendar year as its annual reporting period, initially records prepaid and unearned items in balance sheet accounts (assets and liabilities, respectively).

a. The company's weekly payroll is $8,750, paid each Friday for a five-day workweek. Assume December 31, 2009, falls on a Monday, but the employees will not be paid their wages until Friday, January 4, 2010.

b. Eighteen months earlier, on July 1, 2008, the company purchased equipment that cost $20,000. Its useful life is predicted to be five years, at which time the equipment is expected to be worthless (zero salvage value).

c. On October 1, 2009, the company agreed to work on a new housing development. The company is paid $120,000 on October 1 in advance of future installation of similar alarm systems in 24 new homes. That amount was credited to the Unearned Services Revenue account. Between October 1 and December 31, work on 20 homes was completed.

d. On September 1, 2009, the company purchased a 12-month insurance policy for $1,800. The transaction was recorded with an $1,800 debit to Prepaid Insurance.

e. On December 29, 2009, the company completed a $7,000 service that has not been billed and not recorded as of December 31, 2009.

Required

1. Prepare any necessary adjusting entries on December 31, 2009, in relation to transactions and events *a* through *e*.
2. Prepare T-accounts for the accounts affected by adjusting entries, and post the adjusting entries. Determine the adjusted balances for the Unearned Revenue and the Prepaid Insurance accounts.
3. Complete the following table and determine the amounts and effects of your adjusting entries on the year 2009 income statement and the December 31, 2009, balance sheet. Use up (down) arrows to indicate an increase (decrease) in the Effect columns.

Entry	Amount in the Entry	Effect on Net Income	Effect on Total Assets	Effect on Total Liabilities	Effect on Total Equity

Planning the Solution

- Analyze each situation to determine which accounts need to be updated with an adjustment.
- Calculate the amount of each adjustment and prepare the necessary journal entries.
- Show the amount of each adjustment in the designated accounts, determine the adjusted balance, and identify the balance sheet classification of the account.
- Determine each entry's effect on net income for the year and on total assets, total liabilities, and total equity at the end of the year.

Solution to Demonstration Problem 1

1. Adjusting journal entries.

(a) Dec. 31	Wages Expense	1,750	
	Wages Payable		1,750
	To accrue wages for the last day of the year ($8,750 × 1/5).		
(b) Dec. 31	Depreciation Expense—Equipment	4,000	
	Accumulated Depreciation—Equipment		4,000
	To record depreciation expense for the year ($20,000/5 years = $4,000 per year).		
(c) Dec. 31	Unearned Services Revenue	100,000	
	Services Revenue		100,000
	To recognize services revenue earned ($120,000 × 20/24).		
(d) Dec. 31	Insurance Expense	600	
	Prepaid Insurance		600
	To adjust for expired portion of insurance ($1,800 × 4/12).		
(e) Dec. 31	Accounts Receivable	7,000	
	Services Revenue		7,000
	To record services revenue earned.		

2. T-accounts for adjusting journal entries *a* through *e*.

Wages Expense			
(a)	1,750		

Wages Payable			
		(a)	1,750

Depreciation Expense—Equipment			
(b)	4,000		

Accumulated Depreciation—Equipment			
		(b)	4,000

Unearned Revenue			
		Unadj. Bal.	120,000
(c)	100,000		
		Adj. Bal.	20,000

Services Revenue			
		(c)	100,000
		(e)	7,000
		Adj. Bal.	107,000

Insurance Expense			
(d)	600		

Prepaid Insurance			
Unadj. Bal.	1,800		
		(d)	600
Adj. Bal.	1,200		

Accounts Receivable			
(e)	7,000		

3. Financial statement effects of adjusting journal entries.

Entry	Amount in the Entry	Effect on Net Income	Effect on Total Assets	Effect on Total Liabilities	Effect on Total Equity
a	$ 1,750	$ 1,750 ↓	No effect	$ 1,750 ↑	$ 1,750 ↓
b	4,000	4,000 ↓	$4,000 ↓	No effect	4,000 ↓
c	100,000	100,000 ↑	No effect	$100,000 ↓	100,000 ↑
d	600	600 ↓	$ 600 ↓	No effect	600 ↓
e	7,000	7,000 ↑	$7,000 ↑	No effect	7,000 ↑

Demonstration Problem 2

Use the following adjusted trial balance to answer questions 1–3.

CHOI COMPANY
Adjusted Trial Balance
December 31

	Debit	Credit
Cash	$ 3,050	
Accounts receivable	400	
Prepaid insurance	830	
Supplies	80	
Equipment	217,200	
Accumulated depreciation—Equipment		$ 29,100
Wages payable		880

[continued on next page]

[continued from previous page]

Interest payable		3,600
Unearned rent		460
Long-term notes payable		150,000
M. Choi, Capital		40,340
M. Choi, Withdrawals	21,000	
Rent earned		57,500
Wages expense	25,000	
Utilities expense	1,900	
Insurance expense	3,200	
Supplies expense	250	
Depreciation expense—Equipment	5,970	
Interest expense	3,000	
Totals	$281,880	$281,880

1. Prepare the annual income statement from the adjusted trial balance of Choi Company.

Answer:

CHOI COMPANY
Income Statement
For Year Ended December 31

Revenues		
Rent earned		$57,500
Expenses		
Wages expense	$25,000	
Utilities expense	1,900	
Insurance expense	3,200	
Supplies expense	250	
Depreciation expense—Equipment	5,970	
Interest expense	3,000	
Total expenses		39,320
Net income		$18,180

2. Prepare a statement of owner's equity from the adjusted trial balance of Choi Company. Choi's capital account balance of $40,340 consists of a $30,340 balance from the prior year-end, plus a $10,000 owner investment during the current year.

Answer:

CHOI COMPANY
Statement of Owner's Equity
For Year Ended December 31

M. Choi, Capital, December 31 prior year-end		$30,340
Plus: Owner investments	$10,000	
Net income	18,180	28,180
		58,520
Less: Withdrawals by owner		21,000
M. Choi, Capital, December 31 current year-end		$37,520

3. Prepare a balance sheet from the adjusted trial balance of Choi Company.

Answer:

CHOI COMPANY
Balance Sheet
December 31

Assets		
Cash		$ 3,050
Accounts receivable		400
Prepaid insurance		830
Supplies		80
Equipment	$217,200	
Less accumulated depreciation	29,100	188,100
Total assets		$192,460
Liabilities		
Wages payable		$ 880
Interest payable		3,600
Unearned rent		460
Long-term notes payable		150,000
Total liabilities		154,940
Equity		
M. Choi, Capital		37,520
Total liabilities and equity		$192,460

APPENDIX

3A Alternative Accounting for Prepayments

This appendix explains an alternative in accounting for prepaid expenses and unearned revenues.

Recording the Prepayment of Expenses in Expense Accounts

P4 Explain the alternatives in accounting for prepaids.

An alternative method is to record *all* prepaid expenses with debits to expense accounts. If any prepaids remain unused or unexpired at the end of an accounting period, then adjusting entries must transfer the cost of the unused portions from expense accounts to prepaid expense (asset) accounts. This alternative method is acceptable. The financial statements are identical under either method, but the adjusting entries are different. To illustrate the differences between these two methods, let's look at FastForward's cash payment of December 6 for 24 months of insurance coverage beginning on December 1. FastForward recorded that payment with a debit to an asset account, but it could have recorded a debit to an expense account. These alternatives are shown in Exhibit 3A.1.

EXHIBIT 3A.1

Alternative Initial Entries for Prepaid Expenses

		Payment Recorded as Asset		Payment Recorded as Expense	
Dec. 6	Prepaid Insurance	2,400			
	Cash		2,400		
Dec. 6	Insurance Expense			2,400	
	Cash				2,400

At the end of its accounting period on December 31, insurance protection for one month has expired. This means $100 ($2,400/24) of insurance coverage expired and is an expense for December. The adjusting entry depends on how the original payment was recorded. This is shown in Exhibit 3A.2.

EXHIBIT 3A.2

Adjusting Entry for Prepaid Expenses for the Two Alternatives

		Payment Recorded as Asset		Payment Recorded as Expense	
Dec. 31	Insurance Expense	100			
	Prepaid Insurance		100		
Dec. 31	Prepaid Insurance			2,300	
	Insurance Expense				2,300

When these entries are posted to the accounts in the ledger, we can see that these two methods give identical results. The December 31 adjusted account balances in Exhibit 3A.3 show Prepaid Insurance of $2,300 and Insurance Expense of $100 for both methods.

EXHIBIT 3A.3

Account Balances under Two Alternatives for Recording Prepaid Expenses

Payment Recorded as Asset

Prepaid Insurance			128
Dec. 6	2,400	Dec. 31	100
Balance	**2,300**		

Insurance Expense			637
Dec. 31	**100**		

Payment Recorded as Expense

Prepaid Insurance			128
Dec. 31	**2,300**		

Insurance Expense			637
Dec. 6	2,400	Dec. 31	2,300
Balance	**100**		

Recording the Prepayment of Revenues in Revenue Accounts

As with prepaid expenses, an alternative method is to record *all* unearned revenues with credits to revenue accounts. If any revenues are unearned at the end of an accounting period, then adjusting entries must transfer the unearned portions from revenue accounts to unearned revenue (liability) accounts. This alternative method is acceptable. The adjusting entries are different for these two alternatives, but the financial statements are identical. To illustrate the accounting differences between these two methods, let's look at FastForward's December 26 receipt of $3,000 for consulting services covering the period December 27 to February 24. FastForward recorded this transaction with a credit to a liability account. The alternative is to record it with a credit to a revenue account, as shown in Exhibit 3A.4.

EXHIBIT 3A.4

Alternative Initial Entries for Unearned Revenues

		Receipt Recorded as Liability		Receipt Recorded as Revenue	
Dec. 26	Cash	3,000			
	Unearned Consulting Revenue		3,000		
Dec. 26	Cash			3,000	
	Consulting Revenue				3,000

By the end of its accounting period on December 31, FastForward has earned $250 of this revenue. This means $250 of the liability has been satisfied. Depending on how the initial receipt is recorded, the adjusting entry is as shown in Exhibit 3A.5.

EXHIBIT 3A.5

Adjusting Entry for Unearned Revenues for the Two Alternatives

		Receipt Recorded as Liability		Receipt Recorded as Revenue	
Dec. 31	Unearned Consulting Revenue	250			
	Consulting Revenue		250		
Dec. 31	Consulting Revenue			2,750	
	Unearned Consulting Revenue				2,750

After adjusting entries are posted, the two alternatives give identical results. The December 31 adjusted account balances in Exhibit 3A.6 show unearned consulting revenue of $2,750 and consulting revenue of $250 for both methods.

EXHIBIT 3A.6

Account Balances under Two Alternatives for Recording Unearned Revenues

Receipt Recorded as Liability

Unearned Consulting Revenue			236
Dec. 31	250	Dec. 26	3,000
		Balance	**2,750**

Consulting Revenue			403
		Dec. 31	**250**

Receipt Recorded as Revenue

Unearned Consulting Revenue			236
		Dec. 31	**2,750**

Consulting Revenue			403
Dec. 31	2,750	Dec. 26	3,000
		Balance	**250**

Summary

C1 **Explain the importance of periodic reporting and the time period assumption.** The value of information is often linked to its timeliness. To provide timely information, accounting systems prepare periodic reports at regular intervals. The time period assumption presumes that an organization's activities can be divided into specific time periods for periodic reporting.

C2 **Explain accrual accounting and how it improves financial statements.** Accrual accounting recognizes revenue when earned and expenses when incurred—not necessarily when cash inflows and outflows occur. This information is valuable in assessing a company's financial position and performance.

C3 **Identify the types of adjustments and their purpose.** Adjustments can be grouped according to the timing of cash receipts and cash payments relative to when they are recognized as revenues or expenses as follows: prepaid expenses, unearned revenues, accrued expenses, and accrued revenues. Adjusting entries are necessary so that revenues, expenses, assets, and liabilities are correctly reported.

A1 **Explain how accounting adjustments link to financial statements.** Accounting adjustments bring an asset or liability account balance to its correct amount. They also update related expense or revenue accounts. Every adjusting entry affects one or more income statement accounts *and* one or more balance sheet accounts. An adjusting entry never affects cash.

A2 **Compute profit margin and describe its use in analyzing company performance.** *Profit margin* is defined as the reporting period's net income divided by its net sales. Profit margin reflects on a company's earnings activities by showing how much income is in each dollar of sales.

P1 **Prepare and explain adjusting entries.** *Prepaid expenses* refer to items paid for in advance of receiving their benefits. Prepaid expenses are assets. Adjusting entries for prepaids involve increasing (debiting) expenses and decreasing (crediting) assets. *Unearned* (or *prepaid*) *revenues* refer to cash received in advance of providing products and services. Unearned revenues are liabilities. Adjusting entries for unearned revenues involves increasing (crediting) revenues and decreasing (debiting) unearned revenues. *Accrued expenses* refer to costs incurred in a period that are both unpaid and unrecorded. Adjusting entries for recording accrued expenses involve increasing (debiting) expenses and increasing (crediting) liabilities. *Accrued revenues* refer to revenues earned in a period that are both unrecorded and not yet received in cash. Adjusting entries for recording accrued revenues involve increasing (debiting) assets and increasing (crediting) revenues.

P2 **Explain and prepare an adjusted trial balance.** An adjusted trial balance is a list of accounts and balances prepared after recording and posting adjusting entries. Financial statements are often prepared from the adjusted trial balance.

P3 **Prepare financial statements from an adjusted trial balance.** Revenue and expense balances are reported on the income statement. Asset, liability, and equity balances are reported on the balance sheet. We usually prepare statements in the following order: income statement, statement of owner's equity, balance sheet, and statement of cash flows.

P4[A] **Explain the alternatives in accounting for prepaids.** Charging all prepaid expenses to expense accounts when they are purchased is acceptable. When this is done, adjusting entries must transfer any unexpired amounts from expense accounts to asset accounts. Crediting all unearned revenues to revenue accounts when cash is received is also acceptable. In this case, the adjusting entries must transfer any unearned amounts from revenue accounts to unearned revenue accounts.

Guidance Answers to **Decision Maker** and **Decision Ethics**

Investor Prepaid expenses are items paid for in advance of receiving their benefits. They are assets and are expensed as they are used up. The publishing company's treatment of the signing bonus is acceptable provided future book sales can at least match the $500,000 expense. As an investor, you are concerned about the risk of future book sales. The riskier the likelihood of future book sales is, the more likely your analysis is to treat the $500,000, or a portion of it, as an expense, not a prepaid expense (asset).

Entrepreneur Depreciation is a process of cost allocation, not asset valuation. Knowing the depreciation schedule is not especially useful in your estimation of what the building and equipment are currently worth. Your own assessment of the age, quality, and usefulness of the building and equipment is more important.

Loan Officer Your concern in lending to this store arises from analysis of current-year sales. While increased revenues and income are fine, your concern is with collectibility of these promotional sales. If the owner sold products to customers with poor records of paying bills, then collectibility of these sales is low. Your analysis must assess this possibility and recognize any expected losses.

Financial Officer Omitting accrued expenses and recognizing revenue early can mislead financial statement users. One action is to request a second meeting with the president so you can explain that accruing expenses when incurred and recognizing revenue when earned are required practices. If the president persists, you might discuss the situation with legal counsel and any auditors involved. Your ethical action might cost you this job, but the potential pitfalls for falsification of statements, reputation and personal integrity loss, and other costs are too great.

Guidance Answers to **Quick Checks**

1. An annual reporting (or accounting) period covers one year and refers to the preparation of annual financial statements. The annual reporting period is not always a calendar year that ends on December 31. An organization can adopt a fiscal year consisting of any consecutive 12 months or 52 weeks.

2. Interim-financial statements (covering less than one year) are prepared to provide timely information to decision makers.

3. The revenue recognition principle and the matching principle lead most directly to the adjusting process.

4. No. Cash basis accounting is not consistent with the matching principle because it reports revenue when received, not necessarily when earned, and expenses when paid, not necessarily in the period when the expenses were incurred as a result of the revenues earned.

5. No expense is reported in 2010. Under cash basis accounting, the entire $4,800 is reported as an expense in April 2009 when the premium is paid.

6. If the accrued revenues adjustment of $200 is not made, then both revenues and net income are understated by $200 on the current year's income statement, and both assets and equity are understated by $200 on the balance sheet.

7. A contra account is an account that is subtracted from the balance of a related account. Use of a contra account provides more information than simply reporting a net amount.

8. An accrued expense is a cost incurred in a period that is both unpaid and unrecorded prior to adjusting entries. One example is salaries earned but not yet paid at period-end.

9. An unearned revenue arises when a firm receives cash (or other assets) from a customer before providing the services or products to the customer. A magazine subscription paid in advance is one example; season ticket sales is another.

10.

Salaries Payable	1,000	
Salaries Expense	6,000	
Cash		7,000
Paid salary including accrual from December.		

11. The probable adjusting entries of Jordan Air are:

Insurance Expense	300	
Prepaid Insurance		300
To record insurance expired.		
Salaries Expense	1,400	
Salaries Payable		1,400
To record accrued salaries.		

12. Revenue accounts and expense accounts.

13. Statement of owner's equity.

Key Terms

mhhe.com/wildFAP19e

Key Terms are available at the book's Website for learning and testing in an online Flashcard Format.

Accounting period (p. 92)
Accrual basis accounting (p. 93)
Accrued expenses (p. 99)
Accrued revenues (p. 101)
Adjusted trial balance (p. 104)
Adjusting entry (p. 94)
Annual financial statements (p. 92)
Book value (p. 98)
Cash basis accounting (p. 93)
Contra account (p. 97)
Depreciation (p. 97)
Fiscal year (p. 93)
Interim financial statements (p. 92)
Matching principle (p. 94)
Natural business year (p. 93)
Plant assets (p. 97)
Prepaid expenses (p. 95)
Profit margin (p. 106)
Straight-line depreciation method (p. 97)
Time period assumption (p. 92)
Unadjusted trial balance (p. 104)
Unearned revenues (p. 98)

Multiple Choice Quiz

Answers on p. 133

mhhe.com/wildFAP19e

Additional Quiz Questions are available at the book's Website.

1. A company forgot to record accrued and unpaid employee wages of $350,000 at period-end. This oversight would

a. Understate net income by $350,000.
b. Overstate net income by $350,000.
c. Have no effect on net income.
d. Overstate assets by $350,000.
e. Understate assets by $350,000.

2. Prior to recording adjusting entries, the Supplies account has a $450 debit balance. A physical count of supplies shows $125 of unused supplies still available. The required adjusting entry is:

a. Debit Supplies $125; Credit Supplies Expense $125.
b. Debit Supplies $325; Credit Supplies Expense $325.
c. Debit Supplies Expense $325; Credit Supplies $325.
d. Debit Supplies Expense $325; Credit Supplies $125.
e. Debit Supplies Expense $125; Credit Supplies $125.

3. On May 1, 2009, a two-year insurance policy was purchased for $24,000 with coverage to begin immediately. What is the amount of insurance expense that appears on the company's income statement for the year ended December 31, 2009?

a. $4,000
b. $8,000
c. $12,000
d. $20,000
e. $24,000

Quiz3

4. On November 1, 2009, Stockton Co. receives $3,600 cash from Hans Co. for consulting services to be provided evenly over the period November 1, 2009, to April 30, 2010—at which time Stockton credited $3,600 to Unearned Consulting Fees. The adjusting entry on December 31, 2009 (Stockton's year-end) would include a

a. Debit to Unearned Consulting Fees for $1,200.
b. Debit to Unearned Consulting Fees for $2,400.
c. Credit to Consulting Fees Earned for $2,400.
d. Debit to Consulting Fees Earned for $1,200.
e. Credit to Cash for $3,600.

5. If a company had $15,000 in net income for the year, and its sales were $300,000 for the same year, what is its profit margin?

a. 20%
b. 2,000%
c. $285,000
d. $315,000
e. 5%

Superscript letter ^A denotes assignments based on Appendix 3A.

Discussion Questions

1. What is the difference between the cash basis and the accrual basis of accounting?

2. Why is the accrual basis of accounting generally preferred over the cash basis?

3. What type of business is most likely to select a fiscal year that corresponds to its natural business year instead of the calendar year?

4. What is a prepaid expense and where is it reported in the financial statements?

5. What type of assets require adjusting entries to record depreciation?

6. What contra account is used when recording and reporting the effects of depreciation? Why is it used?

7. What is unearned revenue and where is it reported in financial statements?

8. What is an accrued revenue? Give an example.

9.[A] If a company initially records prepaid expenses with debits to expense accounts, what type of account is debited in the adjusting entries for those prepaid expenses?

10. Review the balance sheet of **Best Buy** in Appendix A. Identify the asset accounts that require adjustment before annual financial statements can be prepared. What would be the effect on the income statement if these asset accounts were not adjusted?

11. Review the balance sheet of **Circuit City** in Appendix A. In addition to Prepayments, identify two accounts (either assets or liabilities) requiring adjusting entries.

12. Refer to **RadioShack**'s balance sheet in Appendix A. What year-end adjusting entry is necessary for accrued interest earned from its notes receivable listed under current assets?

13. Refer to **Apple**'s balance sheet in Appendix A. If it made an adjustment for unpaid wages at year-end, where would the accrued wages expense be reported on its balance sheet?

Denotes Discussion Questions that involve decision making.

McGraw-Hill's HOMEWORK MANAGER® Available with McGraw-Hill's Homework Manager

QUICK STUDY

QS 3-1
Computing accrual and cash income
P1 C2

In its first year of operations, Case Co. earned $60,000 in revenues and received $52,000 cash from these customers. The company incurred expenses of $37,500 but had not paid $6,000 of them at year-end. The company also prepaid $3,250 cash for expenses that would be incurred the next year. Calculate the first year's net income under both the cash basis and the accrual basis of accounting.

QS 3-2
Identifying accounting adjustments
P1

Classify the following adjusting entries as involving prepaid expenses (PE), unearned revenues (UR), accrued expenses (AE), or accrued revenues (AR).

a. ______ To record wages expense incurred but not yet paid (nor recorded).
b. ______ To record expiration of prepaid insurance.
c. ______ To record revenue earned that was previously received as cash in advance.
d. ______ To record annual depreciation expense.
e. ______ To record revenue earned but not yet billed (nor recorded).

QS 3-3
Recording and analyzing adjusting entries
A1

Adjusting entries affect at least one balance sheet account and at least one income statement account. For the following entries, identify the account to be debited and the account to be credited. Indicate which of the accounts is the income statement account and which is the balance sheet account.

a. Entry to record revenue earned that was previously received as cash in advance.
b. Entry to record wage expenses incurred but not yet paid (nor recorded).
c. Entry to record revenue earned but not yet billed (nor recorded).
d. Entry to record expiration of prepaid insurance.
e. Entry to record annual depreciation expense.

QS 3-4
Adjusting prepaid expenses
P1

a. On July 1, 2009, Rendex Company paid $3,000 for six months of insurance coverage. No adjustments have been made to the Prepaid Insurance account, and it is now December 31, 2009. Prepare the journal entry to reflect expiration of the insurance as of December 31, 2009.
b. Indus Company has a Supplies account balance of $900 on January 1, 2009. During 2009, it purchased $4,000 of supplies. As of December 31, 2009, a supplies inventory shows $750 of supplies available. Prepare the adjusting journal entry to correctly report the balance of the Supplies account and the Supplies Expense account as of December 31, 2009.

QS 3-5
Adjusting for depreciation
P1

a. Andrews Company purchases $45,000 of equipment on January 1, 2009. The equipment is expected to last five years and be worth $3,000 at the end of that time. Prepare the entry to record one year's depreciation expense of $8,400 for the equipment as of December 31, 2009.
b. Fortel Company purchases $40,000 of land on January 1, 2009. The land is expected to last indefinitely. What depreciation adjustment, if any, should be made with respect to the Land account as of December 31, 2009?

QS 3-6
Accruing salaries
A1 P1

Lakia Rowell employs one college student every summer in her coffee shop. The student works the five weekdays and is paid on the following Monday. (For example, a student who works Monday through Friday, June 1 through June 5, is paid for that work on Monday, June 8.) Rowell adjusts her books monthly, if needed, to show salaries earned but unpaid at month-end. The student works the last week of July—Friday is August 1. If the student earns $100 per day, what adjusting entry must Rowell make on July 31 to correctly record accrued salaries expense for July?

QS 3-7
Adjusting for unearned revenues
A1 P1

a. Fortune Co. receives $30,000 cash in advance for 4 months of legal services on October 1, 2009, and records it by debiting Cash and crediting Unearned Revenue both for $30,000. It is now December 31, 2009, and Fortune has provided legal services as planned. What adjusting entry should Fortune make to account for the work performed from October 1 through December 31, 2009?
b. Warner Co. started a new publication called *Contest News*. Its subscribers pay $24 to receive 12 issues. With every new subscriber, Warner debits Cash and credits Unearned Subscription Revenue for

the amounts received. The company has 100 new subscribers as of July 1, 2009. It sends *Contest News* to each of these subscribers every month from July through December. Assuming no changes in subscribers, prepare the journal entry that Warner must make as of December 31, 2009, to adjust the Subscription Revenue account and the Unearned Subscription Revenue account.

QS 3-8
Preparing adjusting entries
C3 P1

During the year, Sonoma Co. recorded prepayments of expenses in asset accounts, and cash receipts of unearned revenues in liability accounts. At the end of its annual accounting period, the company must make three adjusting entries: (1) accrue salaries expense, (2) adjust the Unearned Services Revenue account to recognize earned revenue, and (3) record services revenue earned for which cash will be received the following period. For each of these adjusting entries (1), (2), and (3), indicate the account from *a* through *i* to be debited and the account to be credited.

a. Unearned Services Revenue
b. Accounts Receivable
c. Accounts Payable
d. Prepaid Salaries
e. Salaries Expense
f. Services Revenue
g. Salaries Payable
h. Equipment
i. Cash

QS 3-9
Interpreting adjusting entries
C2 P2

The following information is taken from Booker Company's unadjusted and adjusted trial balances.

	Unadjusted		Adjusted	
	Debit	Credit	Debit	Credit
Prepaid insurance	$4,100		$3,700	
Interest payable		$ 0		$800

Given this information, which of the following is likely included among its adjusting entries?

a. A $400 debit to Insurance Expense and an $800 debit to Interest Expense.
b. A $400 debit to Insurance Expense and an $800 debit to Interest Payable.
c. A $400 credit to Prepaid Insurance and an $800 debit to Interest Payable.

QS 3-10
Determining effects of adjusting entries
C3 A1

In making adjusting entries at the end of its accounting period, Chao Consulting failed to record $1,600 of insurance coverage that had expired. This $1,600 cost had been initially debited to the Prepaid Insurance account. The company also failed to record accrued salaries expense of $1,000. As a result of these two oversights, the financial statements for the reporting period will [choose one] (1) understate assets by $1,600; (2) understate expenses by $2,600; (3) understate net income by $1,000; or (4) overstate liabilities by $1,000.

QS 3-11
Analyzing profit margin
A2

Miller Company reported net income of $78,750 and net sales of $630,000 for the current year. Calculate the company's profit margin and interpret the result. Assume that its competitors earn an average profit margin of 15%.

QS 3-12[A]
Preparing adjusting entries
C3 P4

Bevin Consulting initially records prepaid and unearned items in income statement accounts. Given this company's accounting practices, which of the following applies to the preparation of adjusting entries at the end of its first accounting period?

a. Unpaid salaries are recorded with a debit to Prepaid Salaries and a credit to Salaries Expense.
b. The cost of unused office supplies is recorded with a debit to Supplies Expense and a credit to Office Supplies.
c. Unearned fees (on which cash was received in advance earlier in the period) are recorded with a debit to Consulting Fees Earned and a credit to Unearned Consulting Fees.
d. Earned but unbilled (and unrecorded) consulting fees are recorded with a debit to Unearned Consulting Fees and a credit to Consulting Fees Earned.

McGraw-Hill's HOMEWORK MANAGER® Available with McGraw-Hill's Homework Manager

EXERCISES

Exercise 3-1
Classifying adjusting entries
C3

In the blank space beside each adjusting entry, enter the letter of the explanation *A* through *F* that most closely describes the entry.

A. To record accrued interest revenue.
B. To record accrued interest expense.
C. To record the earning of previously unearned income.
D. To record this period's depreciation expense.
E. To record accrued salaries expense.
F. To record this period's use of a prepaid expense.

_____	1.	Interest Expense	2,208	
		Interest Payable		2,208
_____	2.	Insurance Expense	3,180	
		Prepaid Insurance		3,180
_____	3.	Unearned Professional Fees	19,250	
		Professional Fees Earned		19,250
_____	4.	Interest Receivable	3,300	
		Interest Revenue		3,300
_____	5.	Depreciation Expense	38,217	
		Accumulated Depreciation		38,217
_____	6.	Salaries Expense	13,280	
		Salaries Payable		13,280

Exercise 3-2
Preparing adjusting entries
P1

Prepare adjusting journal entries for the year ended (date of) December 31, 2009, for each of these separate situations. Assume that prepaid expenses are initially recorded in asset accounts. Also assume that fees collected in advance of work are initially recorded as liabilities.

a. Depreciation on the company's equipment for 2009 is computed to be $16,000.
b. The Prepaid Insurance account had a $6,000 debit balance at December 31, 2009, before adjusting for the costs of any expired coverage. An analysis of the company's insurance policies showed that $640 of unexpired insurance coverage remains.
c. The Office Supplies account had a $325 debit balance on December 31, 2008; and $3,480 of office supplies were purchased during the year. The December 31, 2009, physical count showed $383 of supplies available.
d. One-fifth of the work related to $15,000 of cash received in advance was performed this period.
e. The Prepaid Insurance account had a $6,800 debit balance at December 31, 2009, before adjusting for the costs of any expired coverage. An analysis of insurance policies showed that $6,160 of coverage had expired.
f. Wage expenses of $2,700 have been incurred but are not paid as of December 31, 2009.

Check (c) Dr. Office Supplies Expense, $3,422; (e) Dr. Insurance Expense, $6,160

Exercise 3-3
Preparing adjusting entries
P1

For each of the following separate cases, prepare adjusting entries required of financial statements for the year ended (date of) December 31, 2009. (Assume that prepaid expenses are initially recorded in asset accounts and that fees collected in advance of work are initially recorded as liabilities.)

a. One-third of the work related to $15,000 cash received in advance is performed this period.
b. Wages of $7,500 are earned by workers but not paid as of December 31, 2009.
c. Depreciation on the company's equipment for 2009 is $17,251.
d. The Office Supplies account had a $240 debit balance on December 31, 2008. During 2009, $6,102 of office supplies are purchased. A physical count of supplies at December 31, 2009, shows $660 of supplies available.
e. The Prepaid Insurance account had a $4,000 balance on December 31, 2008. An analysis of insurance policies shows that $1,300 of unexpired insurance benefits remain at December 31, 2009.
f. The company has earned (but not recorded) $1,400 of interest from investments in CDs for the year ended December 31, 2009. The interest revenue will be received on January 10, 2010.
g. The company has a bank loan and has incurred (but not recorded) interest expense of $2,000 for the year ended December 31, 2009. The company must pay the interest on January 2, 2010.

Check (e) Dr. Insurance Expense, $2,700; (*f*) Cr. Interest Revenue, $1,400

Exercise 3-4
Adjusting and paying accrued wages
C1 P1

Arton Management has five part-time employees, each of whom earns $165 per day. They are normally paid on Fridays for work completed Monday through Friday of the same week. They were paid in full on Friday, December 28, 2009. The next week, the five employees worked only four days because New Year's Day was an unpaid holiday. Show (*a*) the adjusting entry that would be recorded on Monday, December 31, 2009, and (*b*) the journal entry that would be made to record payment of the employees' wages on Friday, January 4, 2010.

Exercise 3-5
Determining cost flows through accounts
C1 A1 P1

Determine the missing amounts in each of these four separate situations *a* through *d*.

	a	b	c	d
Supplies available—prior year-end	$ 350	$1,855	$ 1,576	?
Supplies purchased during the current year	2,450	6,307	?	$6,907
Supplies available—current year-end	800	?	2,056	800
Supplies expense for the current year	?	1,555	11,507	7,482

Exercise 3-6
Adjusting and paying accrued expenses
A1 P1

Check (*b*) May 20 Dr. Interest Expense, $3,800

The following three separate situations require adjusting journal entries to prepare financial statements as of April 30. For each situation, present both the April 30 adjusting entry and the subsequent entry during May to record the payment of the accrued expenses.

a. On April 1, the company retained an attorney at a flat monthly fee of $4,500. This amount is payable on the 12th of the following month.

b. A $760,000 note payable requires $5,700 of interest to be paid at the 20th day of each month. The interest was last paid on April 20 and the next payment is due on May 20. As of April 30, $1,900 of interest expense has accrued.

c. Total weekly salaries expense for all employees is $12,000. This amount is paid at the end of the day on Friday of each five-day workweek. April 30 falls on Tuesday of this year, which means that the employees had worked two days since the last payday. The next payday is May 3.

Exercise 3-7
Determining assets and expenses for accrual and cash accounting
C2

Check 2009 insurance expense: Accrual, $5,100; Cash, $0. Dec. 31, 2009, asset: Accrual, $4,250; Cash, $0.

On November 1, 2007, a company paid a $15,300 premium on a 36-month insurance policy for coverage beginning on that date. Refer to that policy and fill in the blanks in the following table.

Balance Sheet Prepaid Insurance Asset Using			Insurance Expense Using		
	Accrual Basis	Cash Basis		Accrual Basis	Cash Basis
Dec. 31, 2007	$_____	$_____	2007	$_____	$_____
Dec. 31, 2008	_____	_____	2008	_____	_____
Dec. 31, 2009	_____	_____	2009	_____	_____
Dec. 31, 2010	_____	_____	2010	_____	_____
			Total	$_____	$_____

Exercise 3-8
Analyzing and preparing adjusting entries
A1 P1 P3

Following are two income statements for Vix Co. for the year ended December 31. The left column is prepared before any adjusting entries are recorded, and the right column includes the effects of adjusting entries. The company records cash receipts and payments related to unearned and prepaid items in balance sheet accounts. Analyze the statements and prepare the ten adjusting entries that likely were recorded. (*Note:* 30% of the $6,600 adjustment for Fees Earned has been earned but not billed, and the other 70% has been earned by performing services that were paid for in advance.)

VIX CO. Income Statements For Year Ended December 31	Unadjusted	Adjusted
Revenues		
Fees earned	$24,000	$30,600
Commissions earned	36,500	36,500
Total revenues	$60,500	67,100
Expenses		
Depreciation expense—Computers	0	1,650
Depreciation expense—Office furniture	0	1,925
Salaries expense	12,500	15,195
Insurance expense	0	1,430
Rent expense	3,800	4,500
Office supplies expense	0	528
Advertising expense	2,500	3,000
Utilities expense	1,250	1,327
Total expenses	20,050	29,555
Net income	$40,450	$37,545

Exercise 3-9
Computing and interpreting profit margin

A2

Use the following information to compute profit margin for each separate company *a* through *e*.

	Net Income	Net Sales		Net Income	Net Sales
a.	$ 6,039	$ 52,970	**d.**	$67,140	$1,721,520
b.	100,890	471,430	**e.**	84,780	513,800
c.	106,880	301,920			

Which of the five companies is the most profitable according to the profit margin ratio? Interpret that company's profit margin ratio.

Exercise 3-10^A
Adjusting for prepaids recorded as expenses and unearned revenues recorded as revenues

P4

Lowes Construction began operations on December 1. In setting up its accounting procedures, the company decided to debit expense accounts when it prepays its expenses and to credit revenue accounts when customers pay for services in advance. Prepare journal entries for items *a* through *d* and the adjusting entries as of its December 31 period-end for items *e* through *g*.

a. Supplies are purchased on December 1 for $2,000 cash.

b. The company prepaid its insurance premiums for $1,540 cash on December 2.

c. On December 15, the company receives an advance payment of $13,000 cash from a customer for remodeling work.

d. On December 28, the company receives $3,700 cash from another customer for remodeling work to be performed in January.

e. A physical count on December 31 indicates that Lowes has $1,840 of supplies available.

f. An analysis of the insurance policies in effect on December 31 shows that $340 of insurance coverage had expired.

g. As of December 31, only one remodeling project has been worked on and completed. The $5,570 fee for this project had been received in advance.

Check (*f*) Cr. Insurance Expense, $1,200; (*g*) Dr. Remodeling Fees Earned, $11,130

Exercise 3-11^A
Recording and reporting revenues received in advance

P4

Colgate Company experienced the following events and transactions during July.

July	1	Received $2,800 cash in advance of performing work for Vivian Solana.
	6	Received $8,100 cash in advance of performing work for Iris Haru.
	12	Completed the job for Solana.
	18	Received $7,300 cash in advance of performing work for Amina Jordan.
	27	Completed the job for Haru.
	31	None of the work for Jordan has been performed.

a. Prepare journal entries (including any adjusting entries as of the end of the month) to record these events using the procedure of initially crediting the Unearned Fees account when payment is received from a customer in advance of performing services.

b. Prepare journal entries (including any adjusting entries as of the end of the month) to record these events using the procedure of initially crediting the Fees Earned account when payment is received from a customer in advance of performing services.

Check (c) Fees Earned, $10,900

c. Under each method, determine the amount of earned fees reported on the income statement for July and the amount of unearned fees reported on the balance sheet as of July 31.

Available with McGraw-Hill's Homework Manager — McGraw-Hill's HOMEWORK MANAGER®

PROBLEM SET A

Problem 3-1A
Identifying adjusting entries with explanations
C3 P1

For each of the following entries, enter the letter of the explanation that most closely describes it in the space beside each entry. (You can use letters more than once.)

A. To record an accrued revenue.
B. To record this period's use of a prepaid expense.
C. To record payment of a prepaid expense.
D. To record this period's depreciation expense.
E. To record receipt of unearned revenue.
F. To record this period's earning of prior unearned revenue.
G. To record payment of an accrued expense.
H. To record receipt of an accrued revenue.
I. To record an accrued expense.

____	1.	Interest Expense	1,000	
		Interest Payable		1,000
____	2.	Depreciation Expense	4,000	
		Accumulated Depreciation		4,000
____	3.	Unearned Professional Fees	3,000	
		Professional Fees Earned		3,000
____	4.	Insurance Expense	4,200	
		Prepaid Insurance		4,200
____	5.	Salaries Payable	1,400	
		Cash		1,400
____	6.	Prepaid Rent	4,500	
		Cash		4,500
____	7.	Salaries Expense	6,000	
		Salaries Payable		6,000
____	8.	Interest Receivable	5,000	
		Interest Revenue		5,000
____	9.	Cash	9,000	
		Accounts Receivable (from consulting)		9,000
____	10.	Cash	7,500	
		Unearned Professional Fees		7,500
____	11.	Cash	2,000	
		Interest Receivable		2,000
____	12.	Rent Expense	2,000	
		Prepaid Rent		2,000

Problem 3-2A
Preparing adjusting and subsequent journal entries
C1 A1 P1

Hormel Co. follows the practice of recording prepaid expenses and unearned revenues in balance sheet accounts. The company's annual accounting period ends on December 31, 2009. The following information concerns the adjusting entries to be recorded as of that date.

a. The Office Supplies account started the year with a $2,900 balance. During 2009, the company purchased supplies for $11,977, which was added to the Office Supplies account. The inventory of supplies available at December 31, 2009, totaled $2,552.

b. An analysis of the company's insurance policies provided the following facts.

Policy	Date of Purchase	Months of Coverage	Cost
A	April 1, 2008	24	$11,640
B	April 1, 2009	36	10,440
C	August 1, 2009	12	9,240

The total premium for each policy was paid in full (for all months) at the purchase date, and the Prepaid Insurance account was debited for the full cost. (Year-end adjusting entries for Prepaid Insurance were properly recorded in all prior years.)

c. The company has 15 employees, who earn a total of $1,830 in salaries each working day. They are paid each Monday for their work in the five-day workweek ending on the previous Friday. Assume that December 31, 2009, is a Tuesday, and all 15 employees worked the first two days of that week. Because New Year's Day is a paid holiday, they will be paid salaries for five full days on Monday, January 6, 2010.

d. The company purchased a building on January 1, 2009. It cost $800,000 and is expected to have a $45,000 salvage value at the end of its predicted 40-year life. Annual depreciation is $18,875.

e. Since the company is not large enough to occupy the entire building it owns, it rented space to a tenant at $3,000 per month, starting on November 1, 2009. The rent was paid on time on November 1, and the amount received was credited to the Rent Earned account. However, the tenant has not paid the December rent. The company has worked out an agreement with the tenant, who has promised to pay both December and January rent in full on January 15. The tenant has agreed not to fall behind again.

f. On November 1, the company rented space to another tenant for $2,718 per month. The tenant paid five months' rent in advance on that date. The payment was recorded with a credit to the Unearned Rent account.

Required

1. Use the information to prepare adjusting entries as of December 31, 2009.

2. Prepare journal entries to record the first subsequent cash transaction in 2010 for parts *c* and *e*.

Check (1*b*) Dr. Insurance Expense, $12,280 (1*d*) Dr. Depreciation Expense, $18,875

Problem 3-3A
Preparing adjusting entries, adjusted trial balance, and financial statements
A1 P1 P2 P3

excel

mhhe.com/wildFAP19e

Wells Teaching Institute (WTI), a school owned by Tracey Wells, provides training to individuals who pay tuition directly to the school. WTI also offers training to groups in off-site locations. Its unadjusted trial balance as of December 31, 2009, follows. WTI initially records prepaid expenses and unearned revenues in balance sheet accounts. Descriptions of items *a* through *h* that require adjusting entries on December 31, 2009, follow.

Additional Information Items

a. An analysis of the school's insurance policies shows that $3,000 of coverage has expired.

b. An inventory count shows that teaching supplies costing $2,000 are available at year-end 2009.

c. Annual depreciation on the equipment is $10,000.

d. Annual depreciation on the professional library is $5,000.

e. On November 1, the school agreed to do a special six-month course (starting immediately) for a client. The contract calls for a monthly fee of $2,500, and the client paid the first five months' fees in advance. When the cash was received, the Unearned Training Fees account was credited. The fee for the sixth month will be recorded when it is collected in 2010.

f. On October 15, the school agreed to teach a four-month class (beginning immediately) for an individual for $1,600 tuition per month payable at the end of the class. The services are being provided as agreed, and no payment has yet been received.

g. The school's two employees are paid weekly. As of the end of the year, two days' salaries have accrued at the rate of $120 per day for each employee.

h. The balance in the Prepaid Rent account represents rent for December.

	WELLS TEACHING INSTITUTE Unadjusted Trial Balance December 31, 2009		
2		Debit	Credit
3	Cash	$ 28,064	
4	Accounts receivable	0	
5	Teaching supplies	11,000	
6	Prepaid insurance	16,000	
7	Prepaid rent	2,178	
8	Professional library	33,000	
9	Accumulated depreciation—Professional library		$ 10,000
10	Equipment	75,800	
11	Accumulated depreciation—Equipment		15,000
12	Accounts payable		39,500
13	Salaries payable		0
14	Unearned training fees		12,500
15	T. Wells, Capital		71,000
16	T. Wells, Withdrawals	44,000	
17	Tuition fees earned		111,000
18	Training fees earned		41,000
19	Depreciation expense—Professional library	0	
20	Depreciation expense—Equipment	0	
21	Salaries expense	52,000	
22	Insurance expense	0	
23	Rent expense	23,958	
24	Teaching supplies expense	0	
25	Advertising expense	8,000	
26	Utilities expense	6,000	
27	Totals	$ 300,000	$ 300,000
28			

Required

1. Prepare T-accounts (representing the ledger) with balances from the unadjusted trial balance.

2. Prepare the necessary adjusting journal entries for items *a* through *h* and post them to the T-accounts. Assume that adjusting entries are made only at year-end.

3. Update balances in the T-accounts for the adjusting entries and prepare an adjusted trial balance.

4. Prepare Wells Teaching Institute's income statement and statement of owner's equity for the year 2009 and prepare its balance sheet as of December 31, 2009.

Check (2e) Cr. Training Fees Earned, $5,000; (2*f*) Cr. Tuition Fees Earned, $4,000; (3) Adj. Trial balance totals, $319,480; (4) Net income, $41,384; Ending T. Wells, Capital $68,384

Problem 3-4A

Interpreting unadjusted and adjusted trial balances, and preparing financial statements

C3 A1 P1 P2 P3

excel

mhhe.com/wildFAP19e

A six-column table for KLJ Company follows. The first two columns contain the unadjusted trial balance for the company as of July 31, 2009. The last two columns contain the adjusted trial balance as of the same date.

Required

Analysis Component

1. Analyze the differences between the unadjusted and adjusted trial balances to determine the eight adjustments that likely were made. Show the results of your analysis by inserting these adjustment amounts in the table's two middle columns. Label each adjustment with a letter *a* through *h* and provide a short description of it at the bottom of the table.

Preparation Component

2. Use the information in the adjusted trial balance to prepare the company's (*a*) income statement and its statement of owner's equity for the year ended July 31, 2009 (*note:* K. Jenkins, Capital at July 31, 2008, was $46,000, and the current-year withdrawals were $10,000), and (*b*) the balance sheet as of July 31, 2009.

Check (2) Net income, $34,460; K. Jenkins, Capital (7/31/2009), $70,460; Total assets, $178,960

	Unadjusted Trial Balance		Adjustments		Adjusted Trial Balance	
Cash	$ 86,000				$ 86,000	
Accounts receivable	15,000				19,000	
Office supplies	17,800				9,000	
Prepaid insurance	6,040				3,960	
Office equipment	87,000				87,000	
Accum. depreciation—Office equip.		$ 24,000				$ 26,000
Accounts payable		9,100				24,000
Interest payable		0				2,500
Salaries payable		0				15,000
Unearned consulting fees		20,000				13,000
Long-term notes payable		54,000				54,000
K. Jenkins, Capital		46,000				46,000
K. Jenkins, Withdrawals	10,000				10,000	
Consulting fees earned		165,000				176,000
Depreciation expense—Office equip.	0				2,000	
Salaries expense	67,990				82,990	
Interest expense	1,270				3,770	
Insurance expense	0				2,080	
Rent expense	14,540				14,540	
Office supplies expense	0				8,800	
Advertising expense	12,460				27,360	
Totals	$318,100	$318,100			$356,500	$356,500

Problem 3-5A
Preparing financial statements from the adjusted trial balance and calculating profit margin

P3 A1 A2

The adjusted trial balance for Clarita Company as of December 31, 2009, follows.

	Debit	Credit
Cash	$149,000	
Accounts receivable	50,000	
Interest receivable	22,600	
Notes receivable (due in 90 days)	171,500	
Office supplies	16,000	
Automobiles	171,000	
Accumulated depreciation—Automobiles		$ 75,000
Equipment	146,000	
Accumulated depreciation—Equipment		23,000
Land	79,000	
Accounts payable		101,000
Interest payable		20,000
Salaries payable		42,000
Unearned fees		36,000
Long-term notes payable		140,000
S. Clarita, Capital		295,800
S. Clarita, Withdrawals	47,000	
Fees earned		534,000
Interest earned		20,000

[continued on next page]

[continued from previous page]

Depreciation expense—Automobiles	26,500	
Depreciation expense—Equipment	19,500	
Salaries expense	184,000	
Wages expense	43,000	
Interest expense	35,600	
Office supplies expense	33,800	
Advertising expense	65,500	
Repairs expense—Automobiles	26,800	
Totals	$1,286,800	$1,286,800

Required

Check (1) Total assets, $707,100

1. Use the information in the adjusted trial balance to prepare (*a*) the income statement for the year ended December 31, 2009; (*b*) the statement of owner's equity for the year ended December 31, 2009; and (*c*) the balance sheet as of December 31, 2009.
2. Calculate the profit margin for year 2009.

Problem 3-6A[A]
Recording prepaid expenses and unearned revenues
P1 P4

Riso Co. had the following transactions in the last two months of its year ended December 31.

Nov.	1	Paid $2,000 cash for future newspaper advertising.
	1	Paid $2,466 cash for 12 months of insurance through October 31 of the next year.
	30	Received $4,200 cash for future services to be provided to a customer.
Dec.	1	Paid $2,400 cash for a consultant's services to be received over the next three months.
	15	Received $7,250 cash for future services to be provided to a customer.
	31	Of the advertising paid for on November 1, $1,300 worth is not yet used.
	31	A portion of the insurance paid for on November 1 has expired. No adjustment was made in November to Prepaid Insurance.
	31	Services worth $1,600 are not yet provided to the customer who paid on November 30.
	31	One-third of the consulting services paid for on December 1 have been received.
	31	The company has performed $4,350 of services that the customer paid for on December 15.

Required

1. Prepare entries for these transactions under the method that records prepaid expenses as assets and records unearned revenues as liabilities. Also prepare adjusting entries at the end of the year.
2. Prepare entries for these transactions under the method that records prepaid expenses as expenses and records unearned revenues as revenues. Also prepare adjusting entries at the end of the year.

Analysis Component

3. Explain why the alternative sets of entries in requirements 1 and 2 do not result in different financial statement amounts.

PROBLEM SET B

Problem 3-1B
Identifying adjusting entries with explanations
C3 P1

For each of the following entries, enter the letter of the explanation that most closely describes it in the space beside each entry. (You can use letters more than once.)

A. To record this period's earning of prior unearned revenue.
B. To record an accrued expense.
C. To record payment of an accrued expense.
D. To record an accrued revenue.
E. To record receipt of accrued revenue.
F. To record payment of a prepaid expense.
G. To record this period's use of a prepaid expense.
H. To record this period's depreciation expense.
I. To record receipt of unearned revenue.

______	1.	Interest Receivable	3,500	
		Interest Revenue		3,500
______	2.	Salaries Payable	9,000	
		Cash		9,000
______	3.	Depreciation Expense	8,000	
		Accumulated Depreciation		8,000
______	4.	Cash	9,000	
		Unearned Professional Fees		9,000
______	5.	Insurance Expense	4,000	
		Prepaid Insurance		4,000
______	6.	Interest Expense	5,000	
		Interest Payable		5,000
______	7.	Cash	1,500	
		Accounts Receivable (from services)		1,500
______	8.	Salaries Expense	7,000	
		Salaries Payable		7,000
______	9.	Cash	1,000	
		Interest Receivable		1,000
______	10.	Prepaid Rent	3,000	
		Cash		3,000
______	11.	Rent Expense	7,500	
		Prepaid Rent		7,500
______	12.	Unearned Professional Fees	6,000	
		Professional Fees Earned		6,000

Problem 3-2B
Preparing adjusting and subsequent journal entries
C1 A1 P1

Wu-Tang Co. follows the practice of recording prepaid expenses and unearned revenues in balance sheet accounts. The company's annual accounting period ends on October 31, 2009. The following information concerns the adjusting entries that need to be recorded as of that date.

a. The Office Supplies account started the fiscal year with a $3,950 balance. During the fiscal year, the company purchased supplies for $16,313, which was added to the Office Supplies account. The supplies available at October 31, 2009, totaled $3,476.

b. An analysis of the company's insurance policies provided the following facts.

Policy	Date of Purchase	Months of Coverage	Cost
A	April 1, 2008	24	$10,824
B	April 1, 2009	36	9,540
C	August 1, 2009	12	8,424

The total premium for each policy was paid in full (for all months) at the purchase date, and the Prepaid Insurance account was debited for the full cost. (Year-end adjusting entries for Prepaid Insurance were properly recorded in all prior fiscal years.)

c. The company has 15 employees, who earn a total of $2,610 for each workday. They are paid each Monday for their work in the five-day workweek ending on the previous Friday. Assume that October 31, 2009, is a Tuesday, and all five employees worked the first day of that week. They will be paid salaries for five full days on Monday, November 7, 2009.

d. The company purchased a building on November 1, 2008, that cost $695,000 and is expected to have a $41,000 salvage value at the end of its predicted 30-year life. Annual depreciation is $21,800.

e. Since the company does not occupy the entire building it owns, it rented space to a tenant at $3,200 per month, starting on September 1, 2009. The rent was paid on time on September 1, and the amount received was credited to the Rent Earned account. However, the October rent has not been paid. The company has worked out an agreement with the tenant, who has promised to pay both October and November rent in full on November 15. The tenant has agreed not to fall behind again.

f. On September 1, the company rented space to another tenant for $2,899 per month. The tenant paid five months' rent in advance on that date. The payment was recorded with a credit to the Unearned Rent account.

Check (1*b*) Dr. Insurance Expense, $9,373; (1*d*) Dr. Depreciation Expense, $21,800.

Required

1. Use the information to prepare adjusting entries as of October 31, 2009.

2. Prepare journal entries to record the first subsequent cash transaction in November 2009 for parts *c* and *e*.

Problem 3-3B

Preparing adjusting entries, adjusted trial balance, and financial statements

A1 P1 P2 P3

Following is the unadjusted trial balance for Augustus Institute as of December 31, 2009, which initially records prepaid expenses and unearned revenues in balance sheet accounts. The Institute provides one-on-one training to individuals who pay tuition directly to the business and offers extension training to groups in off-site locations. Shown after the trial balance are items *a* through *h* that require adjusting entries as of December 31, 2009.

AUGUSTUS INSTITUTE
Unadjusted Trial Balance
December 31, 2009

		Debit	Credit
3	Cash	$ 27,000	
4	Accounts receivable	0	
5	Teaching supplies	10,000	
6	Prepaid insurance	16,000	
7	Prepaid rent	2,073	
8	Professional library	31,000	
9	Accumulated depreciation—Professional library		$ 9,000
10	Equipment	72,719	
11	Accumulated depreciation—Equipment		17,000
12	Accounts payable		35,600
13	Salaries payable		0
14	Unearned training fees		13,000
15	C. Augustus, Capital		66,000
16	C. Augustus, Withdrawals	41,000	
17	Tuition fees earned		106,000
18	Training fees earned		39,000
19	Depreciation expense—Professional library	0	
20	Depreciation expense—Equipment	0	
21	Salaries expense	50,000	
22	Insurance expense	0	
23	Rent expense	22,808	
24	Teaching supplies expense	0	
25	Advertising expense	7,000	
26	Utilities expense	6,000	
27	Totals	$ 285,600	$ 285,600

Additional Information Items

a. An analysis of the Institute's insurance policies shows that $3,000 of coverage has expired.

b. An inventory count shows that teaching supplies costing $3,000 are available at year-end 2009.

c. Annual depreciation on the equipment is $17,000.

d. Annual depreciation on the professional library is $6,000.

e. On November 1, the Institute agreed to do a special six-month course (starting immediately) for a client. The contract calls for a $2,600 monthly fee, and the client paid the first five months' fees in advance. When the cash was received, the Unearned Training Fees account was credited. The last one month's fees will be recorded when collected in 2010.

f. On October 15, the Institute agreed to teach a four-month class (beginning immediately) to an individual for $3,900 tuition per month payable at the end of the class. The class started on October 15, but no payment has yet been received.

g. The Institute's only employee is paid weekly. As of the end of the year, two days' wages have accrued at the rate of $170 per day.

h. The balance in the Prepaid Rent account represents rent for December.

Required

1. Prepare T-accounts (representing the ledger) with balances from the unadjusted trial balance.

2. Prepare the necessary adjusting journal entries for items *a* through *h*, and post them to the T-accounts. Assume that adjusting entries are made only at year-end.

3. Update balances in the T-accounts for the adjusting entries and prepare an adjusted trial balance.

4. Prepare the company's income statement and statement of owner's equity for the year 2009, and prepare its balance sheet as of December 31, 2009.

Check (2e) Cr. Training Fees Earned, $5,200; (2*f*) Cr. Tuition Fees Earned, $9,750; (3) Adj. trial balance totals, $318,690; (4) Net income, $38,729; Ending C. Augustus, Capital, $63,729

Problem 3-4B
Interpreting unadjusted and adjusted trial balances, and preparing financial statements

C3 A1 P1 P2 P3

A six-column table for Fresno Consulting Company follows. The first two columns contain the unadjusted trial balance for the company as of December 31, 2009, and the last two columns contain the adjusted trial balance as of the same date.

	Unadjusted Trial Balance		Adjustments		Adjusted Trial Balance	
Cash	$106,890				$106,890	
Accounts receivable	9,000				18,500	
Office supplies	16,600				9,000	
Prepaid insurance	9,040				3,960	
Office equipment	85,000				85,000	
Accumulated depreciation— Office equip.		$ 24,000				$ 34,000
Accounts payable		11,100				22,000
Interest payable		0				1,500
Salaries payable		0				9,000
Unearned consulting fees		22,000				18,000
Long-term notes payable		56,000				56,000
Y. Fresno, Capital		54,000				54,000
Y. Fresno, Withdrawals	7,500				7,500	
Consulting fees earned		162,000				175,500
Depreciation expense— Office equip.	0				10,000	
Salaries expense	67,070				76,070	
Interest expense	1,230				2,730	
Insurance expense	0				5,080	
Rent expense	14,620				14,620	
Office supplies expense	0				7,600	
Advertising expense	12,150				23,050	
Totals	$329,100	$329,100			$370,000	$370,000

Required

Analysis Component

1. Analyze the differences between the unadjusted and adjusted trial balances to determine the eight adjustments that likely were made. Show the results of your analysis by inserting these adjustment amounts in the table's two middle columns. Label each adjustment with a letter *a* through *h* and provide a short description of it at the bottom of the table.

Preparation Component

Check (2) Net income, $36,350; Y. Fresno, Capital (12/31/09), $82,850; Total assets, $189,350

2. Use the information in the adjusted trial balance to prepare this company's (*a*) income statement and its statement of owner's equity for the year ended December 31, 2009 (*note:* Y. Fresno, Capital at December 31, 2008, was $54,000, and the current-year withdrawals were $7,500), and (*b*) the balance sheet as of December 31, 2009.

Problem 3-5B
Preparing financial statements from the adjusted trial balance and calculating profit margin
P3 A1 A2

The adjusted trial balance for Rapid Courier as of December 31, 2009, follows.

	Debit	Credit
Cash	$109,000	
Accounts receivable	55,000	
Interest receivable	23,000	
Notes receivable (due in 90 days)	171,000	
Office supplies	16,000	
Trucks	174,000	
Accumulated depreciation—Trucks		$ 80,000
Equipment	144,000	
Accumulated depreciation—Equipment		44,000
Land	81,000	
Accounts payable		98,000
Interest payable		20,000
Salaries payable		22,000
Unearned delivery fees		32,000
Long-term notes payable		156,000
R. Rapid, Capital		311,800
R. Rapid, Withdrawals	55,000	
Delivery fees earned		474,000
Interest earned		32,000
Depreciation expense—Trucks	25,500	
Depreciation expense—Equipment	22,000	
Salaries expense	187,000	
Wages expense	43,000	
Interest expense	36,200	
Office supplies expense	35,600	
Advertising expense	63,500	
Repairs expense—Trucks	29,000	
Totals	$1,269,800	$1,269,800

Required

Check (1) Total assets, $649,000

1. Use the information in the adjusted trial balance to prepare (*a*) the income statement for the year ended December 31, 2009, (*b*) the statement of owner's equity for the year ended December 31, 2009, and (*c*) the balance sheet as of December 31, 2009.

2. Calculate the profit margin for year 2009.

Problem 3-6B[A]
Recording prepaid expenses and unearned revenues
P1 P4

Jazz Co. had the following transactions in the last two months of its fiscal year ended May 31.

Apr.	1	Paid $2,600 cash to an accounting firm for future consulting services.
	1	Paid $2,484 cash for 12 months of insurance through March 31 of the next year.
	30	Received $4,600 cash for future services to be provided to a customer.
May	1	Paid $2,700 cash for future newspaper advertising.
	23	Received $7,450 cash for future services to be provided to a customer.

31 Of the consulting services paid for on April 1, $1,700 worth has been received.
31 A portion of the insurance paid for on April 1 has expired. No adjustment was made in April to Prepaid Insurance.
31 Services worth $1,400 are not yet provided to the customer who paid on April 30.
31 One-third the advertising paid for on May 1 has not yet been provided.
31 The company has performed $3,000 of services that the customer paid for on May 23.

Required

1. Prepare entries for these transactions under the method that records prepaid expenses and unearned revenues in balance sheet accounts. Also prepare adjusting entries at the end of the year.

2. Prepare entries for these transactions under the method that records prepaid expenses and unearned revenues in income statement accounts. Also prepare adjusting entries at the end of the year.

Analysis Component

3. Explain why the alternative sets of entries in parts 1 and 2 do not result in different financial statement amounts.

SERIAL PROBLEM

Success Systems

This serial problem began in Chapter 1 and continues through most of the book. If previous chapter segments were not completed, the serial problem can still begin at this point. It is helpful, but not necessary, to use the Working Papers that accompany the book.

SP 3 After the success of the company's first two months, Adriana Lopez continues to operate Success Systems. (Transactions for the first two months are described in the serial problem of Chapter 2.) The November 30, 2009, unadjusted trial balance of Success Systems (reflecting its transactions for October and November of 2009) follows.

No.	Account Title	Debit	Credit
101	Cash	$ 48,052	
106	Accounts receivable	12,618	
126	Computer supplies	2,545	
128	Prepaid insurance	2,220	
131	Prepaid rent	3,300	
163	Office equipment	8,000	
164	Accumulated depreciation—Office equipment		$ 0
167	Computer equipment	20,000	
168	Accumulated depreciation—Computer equipment		0
201	Accounts payable		0
210	Wages payable		0
236	Unearned computer services revenue		0
301	A. Lopez, Capital		83,000
302	A. Lopez, Withdrawals	5,600	
403	Computer services revenue		25,659
612	Depreciation expense—Office equipment	0	
613	Depreciation expense—Computer equipment	0	
623	Wages expense	2,625	
637	Insurance expense	0	
640	Rent expense	0	
652	Computer supplies expense	0	
655	Advertising expense	1,940	
676	Mileage expense	704	
677	Miscellaneous expenses	250	
684	Repairs expense—Computer	805	
	Totals	$108,659	$108,659

Success Systems had the following transactions and events in December 2009.

Dec. 2 Paid $1,025 cash to Hillside Mall for Success Systems' share of mall advertising costs.
3 Paid $500 cash for minor repairs to the company's computer.
4 Received $3,950 cash from Alex's Engineering Co. for the receivable from November.
10 Paid cash to Lyn Addie for six days of work at the rate of $125 per day.
14 Notified by Alex's Engineering Co. that Success's bid of $7,000 on a proposed project has been accepted. Alex's paid a $1,500 cash advance to Success Systems.
15 Purchased $1,100 of computer supplies on credit from Harris Office Products.
16 Sent a reminder to Gomez Co. to pay the fee for services recorded on November 8.
20 Completed a project for Liu Corporation and received $5,625 cash.
22–26 Took the week off for the holidays.
28 Received $3,000 cash from Gomez Co. on its receivable.
29 Reimbursed Lopez's business automobile mileage (600 miles at $0.32 per mile).
31 A. Lopez withdrew $1,500 cash from the company for personal use.

The following additional facts are collected for use in making adjusting entries prior to preparing financial statements for the company's first three months:

a. The December 31 inventory count of computer supplies shows $580 still available.
b. Three months have expired since the 12-month insurance premium was paid in advance.
c. As of December 31, Lyn Addie has not been paid for four days of work at $125 per day.
d. The company's computer is expected to have a four-year life with no salvage value.
e. The office equipment is expected to have a five-year life with no salvage value.
f. Three of the four months' prepaid rent has expired.

Required

1. Prepare journal entries to record each of the December transactions and events for Success Systems. Post those entries to the accounts in the ledger.
2. Prepare adjusting entries to reflect *a* through *f*. Post those entries to the accounts in the ledger.
3. Prepare an adjusted trial balance as of December 31, 2009.
4. Prepare an income statement for the three months ended December 31, 2009.
5. Prepare a statement of owner's equity for the three months ended December 31, 2009.
6. Prepare a balance sheet as of December 31, 2009.

Check (3) Adjusted trial balance totals, $119,034

(6) Total assets, $93,248

BEYOND THE NUMBERS

REPORTING IN ACTION

C1 C2 A1 A2

BEST BUY

BTN 3-1 Refer to **Best Buy**'s financial statements in Appendix A to answer the following.

1. Identify and write down the revenue recognition principle as explained in the chapter.
2. Research Best Buy's footnotes to discover how it applies the revenue recognition principle. Report what you discover.
3. What is Best Buy's profit margin for fiscal years ended March 3, 2007, and February 25, 2006.

Fast Forward

4. Access Best Buy's financial statements (10-K) for fiscal years ending after March 3, 2007, at its Website (BestBuy.com) or the SEC's EDGAR database (www.SEC.gov). Compare the March 3, 2007, fiscal year profit margin to any subsequent year's profit margin that you are able to calculate.

COMPARATIVE ANALYSIS

A2

BEST BUY RadioShack

BTN 3-2 Key figures for the recent two years of both **Best Buy** and **RadioShack** follow.

Key Figures ($ millions)	Best Buy		RadioShack	
	Current Year	Prior Year	Current Year	Prior Year
Net income	$ 1,377	$ 1,140	$ 73	$ 270
Net sales	35,934	30,848	4,778	5,082

Required

1. Compute profit margins for (*a*) Best Buy and (*b*) RadioShack for the two years of data shown.
2. Which company is more successful on the basis of profit margin? Explain.

ETHICS CHALLENGE

C1 C2 A1

BTN 3-3 Jerome Boland works for Sea Biscuit Co. He and Farah Smith, his manager, are preparing adjusting entries for annual financial statements. Boland computes depreciation and records it as

Depreciation Expense—Equipment	123,000	
Accumulated Depreciation—Equipment		123,000

Smith agrees with his computation but says the credit entry should be directly to the Equipment account. She argues that while accumulated depreciation is technically correct, "it is less hassle not to use a contra account and just credit the Equipment account directly. And besides, the balance sheet shows the same amount for total assets under either method."

Required

1. How should depreciation be recorded? Do you support Boland or Smith?
2. Evaluate the strengths and weaknesses of Smith's reasons for preferring her method.
3. Indicate whether the situation Boland faces is an ethical problem. Explain.

COMMUNICATING IN PRACTICE

C1 A2

BTN 3-4 The class should be divided into teams. Teams are to select an industry (such as automobile manufacturing, airlines, defense contractors), and each team member is to select a different company in that industry. Each team member is to acquire the annual report of the company selected. Annual reports can be downloaded from company Websites or from the SEC's EDGAR database at (www.SEC.gov).

Required

1. Use the annual report to compute the return on assets, debt ratio, and profit margin.
2. Communicate with team members via a meeting, e-mail, or telephone to discuss the meaning of the ratios, how different companies compare to each other, and the industry norm. The team must prepare a single memo reporting the ratios for each company and identifying the conclusions or consensus of opinion reached during the team's discussion. The memo is to be copied and distributed to the instructor and all classmates.

TAKING IT TO THE NET

C1 A2

BTN 3-5 Access the **Gap**'s Website (GapInc.com) to answer the following requirements.

Required

1. What are Gap's main brands?
2. Access Gap's 2007 annual report (10-K) either at the company's Website or at www.SEC.gov. What is Gap's fiscal year-end?
3. What is Gap's net sales for the period ended February 2, 2008?
4. What is Gap's net income for the period ended February 2, 2008?
5. Compute Gap's profit margin for the year ended February 2, 2008.
6. Do you believe Gap's decision to use a year-end of early February or late January relates to its natural business year? Explain.

TEAMWORK IN ACTION

C3 A1 P1

BTN 3-6 Four types of adjustments are described in the chapter: (1) prepaid expenses, (2) unearned revenues, (3) accrued expenses, and (4) accrued revenues.

Required

1. Form *learning teams* of four (or more) members. Each team member must select one of the four adjustments as an area of expertise (each team must have at least one expert in each area).
2. Form *expert teams* from the individuals who have selected the same area of expertise. Expert teams are to discuss and write a report that each expert will present to his or her learning team addressing the following:
   a. Description of the adjustment and why it's necessary.
   b. Example of a transaction or event, with dates and amounts, that requires adjustment.
   c. Adjusting entry(ies) for the example in requirement *b*.
   d. Status of the affected account(s) before and after the adjustment in requirement *c*.
   e. Effects on financial statements of not making the adjustment.
3. Each expert should return to his or her learning team. In rotation, each member should present his or her expert team's report to the learning team. Team discussion is encouraged.

ENTREPRENEURIAL DECISION

A2

BTN 3-7 Review the opening feature of this chapter dealing with **PopCap Games**.

Required

1. Assume that PopCap sells a $300 gift certificate to a customer, collecting the $300 cash in advance. Prepare the journal entry for the (*a*) collection of the cash for delivery of the gift certificate to the customer and (*b*) revenue from the subsequent delivery of games when the gift certificate is used.
2. How can keeping no inventories help to improve PopCap profit margin?
3. PopCap understands that many companies carry inventories, and the owners are thinking of carrying an inventory of games on CDs. The owners desire your advice on the pros and cons of carrying such inventory. Provide at least one reason for and one reason against carrying inventories.

HITTING THE ROAD

C1

BTN 3-8 Visit the Website of a major company that interests you. Use the Investor Relations link at the Website to obtain the toll-free telephone number of the Investor Relations Department. Call the company, ask to speak to Investor Relations, and request a copy of the company's most recent annual report. You should receive the requested report within one to two weeks. Once you have received your report, use it throughout the term to see that the principles you are learning in class are being applied in practice.

GLOBAL DECISION

A2 C1 C2

DSG

BTN 3-9 **DSG international plc** is the United Kingdom's largest retailer of consumer electronics. Access its financial statements for the year ended April 28, 2007, at the company's Website (www.DSGiplc.com).

Required

1. Locate the notes to its financial statements, and read note *1.3 Revenue.* When is sales revenue recognized by DSG?
2. What is DSG's profit margin for the year ended April 28, 2007?
3. Compute DSG's current ratio for both the current year and the prior year. (DSG's balance sheet is in a slightly different format than the examples in the text: current assets follow fixed assets, and current liabilities follow current assets.)

ANSWERS TO MULTIPLE CHOICE QUIZ

1. b; the forgotten adjusting entry is: *dr*. Wages Expense, *cr*. Wages Payable.
2. c; Supplies used = \$450 − \$125 = \$325
3. b; Insurance expense = \$24,000 × (8/24) = \$8,000; adjusting entry is: *dr.* Insurance Expense for \$8,000, *cr.* Prepaid Insurance for \$8,000.
4. a; Consulting fees earned = \$3,600 × (2/6) = \$1,200; adjusting entry is: *dr.* Unearned Consulting Fee for \$1,200, *cr.* Consulting Fees Earned for \$1,200.
5. e; Profit margin = \$15,000/\$300,000 = 5%

A Look Back

Chapter 3 explained the timing of reports. We described why adjusting accounts is key for recognizing revenues and expenses in the proper period. We prepared an adjusted trial balance and used it to prepare financial statements.

A Look at This Chapter

This chapter emphasizes the final steps in the accounting process and reviews the entire accounting cycle. We explain the closing process, including accounting procedures and the use of a post-closing trial balance. We show how a work sheet aids in preparing financial statements.

A Look Ahead

Chapter 5 looks at accounting for merchandising activities. We describe the sale and purchase of merchandise and their implications for preparing and analyzing financial statements.

Chapter 4 Completing the Accounting Cycle

Learning Objectives

CAP

Conceptual

C1 Explain why temporary accounts are closed each period. *(p. 140)*

C2 Identify steps in the accounting cycle. *(p. 144)*

C3 Explain and prepare a classified balance sheet. *(p. 145)*

Analytical

A1 Compute the current ratio and describe what it reveals about a company's financial condition. *(p. 147)*

Procedural

P1 Prepare a work sheet and explain its usefulness. *(p. 136)*

P2 Describe and prepare closing entries. *(p. 141)*

P3 Explain and prepare a post-closing trial balance. *(p. 142)*

P4 *Appendix 4A*—Prepare reversing entries and explain their purpose. *(p. 153)*

LP4

Decision Feature

Walk in Her Shoes

"Stay true to your vision and your mission"
—Kathryn Kerrigan

CHICAGO—As a teenager, Kathryn Kerrigan wore a size 11 shoe and found shopping for shoes grueling. "I remember driving with my dad to every shopping mall looking for shoes," recalls Kathryn. "It's embarrassing and it doesn't have to be." Kathryn decided to do something about it. She wrote a business plan for a college project and executed that plan with her dad's encouragement. Her start-up company, **Kathryn Kerrigan (KathrynKerrigan.com),** now provides stylish women's shoes through size 14.

Success, however, requires Kathryn to monitor costs. "We had to create the molds for every shoe size," explains Kathryn. "These cost about $2,000 each." She set up an accounting system to track revenues and control costs, but it is a constant struggle as her business grows. Kathryn says that properly applying the accounting cycle, preparing classified financial statements, and acting on that information increase the odds of success. However, at times, admits Kathryn, "I had to find humility and ask for help."

Kathryn has successfully controlled materials costs while monitoring both revenues and customer needs. She uses the accounting system and closing entries to help identify and match costs with revenues for specific time periods. Kathryn says she relies on classified balance sheets to know when to pay bills. But what pulls her through, admits Kathryn, is knowing that "we're putting out a product that's missing in the marketplace."

Kathryn is on a mission. "What keeps me going," explains Kathryn, "are all the women who keep coming up to me . . . asking for shoes that fit." To make that happen, she tracks the accounting numbers to be sure it is a money-making venture. "It's important for entrepreneurs to be realistic," insists Kathryn. Yet she adds, "A great pair of shoes can make all the difference!"

[Sources: *Kathryn Kerrigan Website,* January 2009; *Success Magazine,* February 2008; *Inc.com,* July 2007; *Beep,* October 2007; *Chicago Sun-Times,* February 2008]

Many of the important steps leading to financial statements were explained in earlier chapters. We described how transactions and events are analyzed, journalized, and posted. This chapter explains the closing process that readies revenue, expense, and withdrawal accounts for the next reporting period and updates the capital account. A work sheet is shown to be a useful tool for these final steps and in preparing financial statements. It also explains how accounts are classified on a balance sheet to increase their usefulness to decision makers.

Completing the Accounting Cycle

- **Work Sheet**
  - Benefits of a work sheet
  - Use of a work sheet
- **Closing Process**
  - Temporary and permanent accounts
  - Closing entries
  - Post-closing trial balance
- **Accounting Cycle**
  - Definition of accounting cycle
  - Review of accounting cycle
- **Classified Balance Sheet**
  - Classification structure
  - Classification categories

Work Sheet as a Tool

Information preparers use various analyses and internal documents when organizing information for internal and external decision makers. Internal documents are often called **working papers.** One widely used working paper is the **work sheet,** which is a useful tool for preparers in working with accounting information. It is usually not available to external decision makers.

Benefits of a Work Sheet

P1 Prepare a work sheet and explain its usefulness.

A work sheet is *not* a required report, yet using a manual or electronic work sheet has several potential benefits. Specifically, a work sheet

- Aids the preparation of financial statements.
- Reduces the possibility of errors when working with many accounts and adjustments.
- Links accounts and adjustments to their impacts in financial statements.
- Assists in planning and organizing an audit of financial statements—as it can be used to reflect any adjustments necessary.
- Helps in preparing interim (monthly and quarterly) financial statements when the journalizing and posting of adjusting entries are postponed until year-end.
- Shows the effects of proposed or "what-if" transactions.

Decision Insight

High-Tech Work Sheet An electronic work sheet using spreadsheet software such as Excel allows us to easily change numbers, assess the impact of alternative strategies, and quickly prepare financial statements at less cost. It can also increase the available time for analysis and interpretation.

Use of a Work Sheet

Point: Since a work sheet is *not* a required report or an accounting record, its format is flexible and can be modified by its user to fit his/her preferences.

When a work sheet is used to prepare financial statements, it is constructed at the end of a period before the adjusting process. The complete work sheet includes a list of the accounts, their balances and adjustments, and their sorting into financial statement columns. It provides two columns each for the unadjusted trial balance, the adjustments, the adjusted trial balance, the income statement, and the balance sheet (including the statement of owner's equity). To describe and interpret the work sheet, we use the information from FastForward. Preparing the work sheet has five important steps. Each step, 1 through 5, is color-coded and explained with reference to Exhibits 4.1 and 4.2.

1 Step 1. Enter Unadjusted Trial Balance

Refer to Exhibit 4.1. The first step in preparing a work sheet is to list the title of every account and its account number that is expected to appear on its financial statements. This includes all accounts in the ledger plus any new ones from adjusting entries. Most adjusting entries—including expenses from salaries, supplies, depreciation, and insurance—are predictable and recurring. The unadjusted balance for each account is then entered in the appropriate Debit or Credit column of the unadjusted trial balance columns. The totals of these two columns must be equal. Exhibit 4.1 shows FastForward's work sheet after completing this first step. Sometimes blank lines are left on the work sheet based on past experience to indicate where lines will be needed for adjustments to certain accounts. Exhibit 4.1 shows Consulting Revenue as one example. An alternative is to squeeze adjustments on one line or to combine the effects of two or more adjustments in one amount. In the unusual case when an account is not predicted, we can add a new line for such an account following the *Totals* line.

2 Step 2. Enter Adjustments

Refer to Exhibit 4.1a (turn over first transparency). The second step in preparing a work sheet is to enter adjustments in the Adjustments columns. The adjustments shown are the same ones shown in Exhibit 3.13. An identifying letter links the debit and credit of each adjusting entry. This is called *keying* the adjustments. After preparing a work sheet, adjusting entries must still be entered in the journal and posted to the ledger. The Adjustments columns provide the information for those entries.

Point: A recordkeeper often can complete the procedural task of journalizing and posting adjusting entries by using a work sheet and the guidance that *keying* provides.

3 Step 3. Prepare Adjusted Trial Balance

Refer to Exhibit 4.1b (turn over second transparency). The adjusted trial balance is prepared by combining the adjustments with the unadjusted balances for each account. As an example, the Prepaid Insurance account has a $2,400 debit balance in the Unadjusted Trial Balance columns. This $2,400 debit is combined with the $100 credit in the Adjustments columns to give Prepaid Insurance a $2,300 debit in the Adjusted Trial Balance columns. The totals of the Adjusted Trial Balance columns confirm the equality of debits and credits.

Point: To avoid omitting the transfer of an account balance, start with the first line (cash) and continue in account order.

4 Step 4. Sort Adjusted Trial Balance Amounts to Financial Statements

Refer to Exhibit 4.1c (turn over third transparency). This step involves sorting account balances from the adjusted trial balance to their proper financial statement columns. Expenses go to the Income Statement Debit column and revenues to the Income Statement Credit column. Assets and withdrawals go to the Balance Sheet & Statement of Owner's Equity Debit column. Liabilities and owner's capital go to the Balance Sheet & Statement of Owner's Equity Credit column.

5 Step 5. Total Statement Columns, Compute Income or Loss, and Balance Columns

Refer to Exhibit 4.1d (turn over fourth transparency). Each financial statement column (from Step 4) is totaled. The difference between the totals of the Income Statement columns is net income or net loss. This occurs because revenues are entered in the Credit column and expenses in the Debit column. If the Credit total exceeds the Debit total, there is net income. If the Debit total exceeds the Credit total, there is a net loss. For FastForward, the Credit total exceeds the Debit total, giving a $3,785 net income.

The net income from the Income Statement columns is then entered in the Balance Sheet & Statement of Owner's Equity Credit column. Adding net income to the last Credit column implies that it is to be added to owner's capital. If a loss occurs, it is added to the Debit column. This implies that it is to be subtracted from owner's capital. The ending balance of owner's capital does not appear in the last two columns as a single amount, but it is computed in the

[continued on p. 140]

EXHIBIT 4.1

Work Sheet with Unadjusted Trial Balance

FastForward
Work Sheet
For Month Ended December 31, 2009

(1)

No.	Account	Unadjusted Trial Balance Dr.	Unadjusted Trial Balance Cr.	Adjustments Dr.	Adjustments Cr.	Adjusted Trial Balance Dr.	Adjusted Trial Balance Cr.	Income Statement Dr.	Income Statement Cr.	Balance Sheet & Statement of Owner's Equity Dr.	Balance Sheet & Statement of Owner's Equity Cr.
101	Cash	4,350									
106	Accounts receivable	0									
126	Supplies	9,720									
128	Prepaid insurance	2,400									
167	Equipment	26,000									
168	Accumulated depreciation—Equip.		0								
201	Accounts payable		6,200								
209	Salaries payable		0								
236	Unearned consulting revenue		3,000								
301	C. Taylor, Capital		30,000								
302	C. Taylor, Withdrawals	200									
403	Consulting revenue		5,800								
406	Rental revenue		300								
612	Depreciation expense—Equip.	0									
622	Salaries expense	1,400									
637	Insurance expense	0									
640	Rent expense	1,000									
652	Supplies expense	0									
690	Utilities expense	230									
	Totals	45,300	45,300								

List all accounts from the ledger and those expected to arise from adjusting entries.

Enter all amounts available from ledger accounts. Column totals must be equal.

A work sheet collects and summarizes information used to prepare adjusting entries, financial statements, and closing entries.

EXHIBIT 4.2

Financial Statements Prepared from the Work Sheet

FASTFORWARD
Income Statement
For Month Ended December 31, 2009

Revenues		
Consulting revenue	$ 7,850	
Rental revenue	300	
Total revenues		$ 8,150
Expenses		
Depreciation expense—Equipment	375	
Salaries expense	1,610	
Insurance expense	100	
Rent expense	1,000	
Supplies expense	1,050	
Utilities expense	230	
Total expenses		4,365
Net income		$ 3,785

FASTFORWARD
Statement of Owner's Equity
For Month Ended December 31, 2009

C. Taylor, Capital, December 1		$ 0
Add: Investment by owner	$30,000	
Net income	3,785	33,785
		33,785
Less: Withdrawals by owner		200
C. Taylor, Capital, December 31		$33,585

FASTFORWARD
Balance Sheet
December 31, 2009

Assets		
Cash		$ 4,350
Accounts receivable		1,800
Supplies		8,670
Prepaid insurance		2,300
Equipment	$26,000	
Accumulated depreciation—Equipment	(375)	25,625
Total assets		$42,745
Liabilities		
Accounts payable		$ 6,200
Salaries payable		210
Unearned consulting revenue		2,750
Total liabilities		9,160
Equity		
C. Taylor, Capital		33,585
Total liabilities and equity		$42,745

statement of owner's equity using these account balances. When net income or net loss is added to the proper Balance Sheet & Statement of Owner's Equity column, the totals of the last two columns must balance. If they do not, one or more errors have been made. The error can either be mathematical or involve sorting one or more amounts to incorrect columns.

Decision Maker

Entrepreneur You make a printout of the electronic work sheet used to prepare financial statements. There is no depreciation adjustment, yet you own a large amount of equipment. Does the absence of depreciation adjustment concern you? [Answer—p. 153]

Work Sheet Applications and Analysis

A work sheet does not substitute for financial statements. It is a tool we can use at the end of an accounting period to help organize data and prepare financial statements. FastForward's financial statements are shown in Exhibit 4.2. Its income statement amounts are taken from the Income Statement columns of the work sheet. Similarly, amounts for its balance sheet and its statement of owner's equity are taken from the Balance Sheet & Statement of Owner's Equity columns of the work sheet.

Information from the Adjustments columns of a work sheet can be used to journalize adjusting entries. It is important to remember that a work sheet is not a journal. This means that even when a work sheet is prepared, it is necessary to both journalize adjustments and post them to the ledger.

Work sheets are also useful in analyzing the effects of proposed, or what-if, transactions. This is done by entering financial statement amounts in the Unadjusted (what-if) columns. Proposed transactions are then entered in the Adjustments columns. We then compute "adjusted" amounts from these proposed transactions. The extended amounts in the financial statement columns show the effects of these proposed transactions. These financial statement columns yield **pro forma financial statements** because they show the statements *as if* the proposed transactions occurred.

Video4.1

Quick Check

Answers—p. 154

1. Where do we get the amounts to enter in the Unadjusted Trial Balance columns of a work sheet?
2. What are the advantages of using a work sheet to help prepare adjusting entries?
3. What are the overall benefits of a work sheet?

Closing Process

C1 Explain why temporary accounts are closed each period.

The **closing process** is an important step at the end of an accounting period *after* financial statements have been completed. It prepares accounts for recording the transactions and the events of the *next* period. In the closing process we must (1) identify accounts for closing, (2) record and post the closing entries, and (3) prepare a post-closing trial balance. The purpose of the closing process is twofold. First, it resets revenue, expense, and withdrawals account balances to zero at the end of each period. This is done so that these accounts can properly measure income and withdrawals for the next period. Second, it helps in summarizing a period's revenues and expenses. This section explains the closing process.

Temporary Accounts
- Revenues
- Expenses
- Owner Withdrawals
- Income Summary

Permanent Accounts
- Assets
- Liabilities
- Owner Capital

Temporary and Permanent Accounts

Temporary (or *nominal*) **accounts** accumulate data related to one accounting period. They include all income statement accounts, the withdrawals account, and the Income Summary account. They are temporary because the accounts are opened at the beginning of a period, used to record transactions and events for that period, and then closed at the end of the period. *The closing process applies only to temporary accounts.* **Permanent** (or *real*) **accounts** report on activities related to one or more future accounting periods. They carry their ending balances into the next period and generally consist of all balance sheet accounts. These asset, liability, and equity accounts are not closed.

Recording Closing Entries

To record and post **closing entries** is to transfer the end-of-period balances in revenue, expense, and withdrawals accounts to the permanent capital account. Closing entries are necessary at the end of each period after financial statements are prepared because

- Revenue, expense, and withdrawals accounts must begin each period with zero balances.
- Owner's capital must reflect prior periods' revenues, expenses, and withdrawals.

An income statement aims to report revenues and expenses for a *specific accounting period.* The statement of owner's equity reports similar information, including withdrawals. Since revenue, expense, and withdrawals accounts must accumulate information separately for each period, they must start each period with zero balances. To close these accounts, we transfer their balances first to an account called *Income Summary*. **Income Summary** is a temporary account (only used for the closing process) that contains a credit for the sum of all revenues (and gains) and a debit for the sum of all expenses (and losses). Its balance equals net income or net loss and it is transferred to the capital account. Next the withdrawals account balance is transferred to the capital account. After these closing entries are posted, the revenue, expense, withdrawals, and Income Summary accounts have zero balances. These accounts are then said to be *closed* or *cleared.*

Point: To understand the closing process, focus on its *outcomes—updating* the capital account balance to its proper ending balance, and getting *temporary accounts* to show *zero balances* for purposes of accumulating data for the next period.

Exhibit 4.3 uses the adjusted account balances of FastForward (from the Adjusted Trial Balance columns of Exhibit 4.1 or from the left side of Exhibit 4.4) to show the four steps necessary to close its temporary accounts. We explain each step.

EXHIBIT 4.3

Four-Step Closing Process

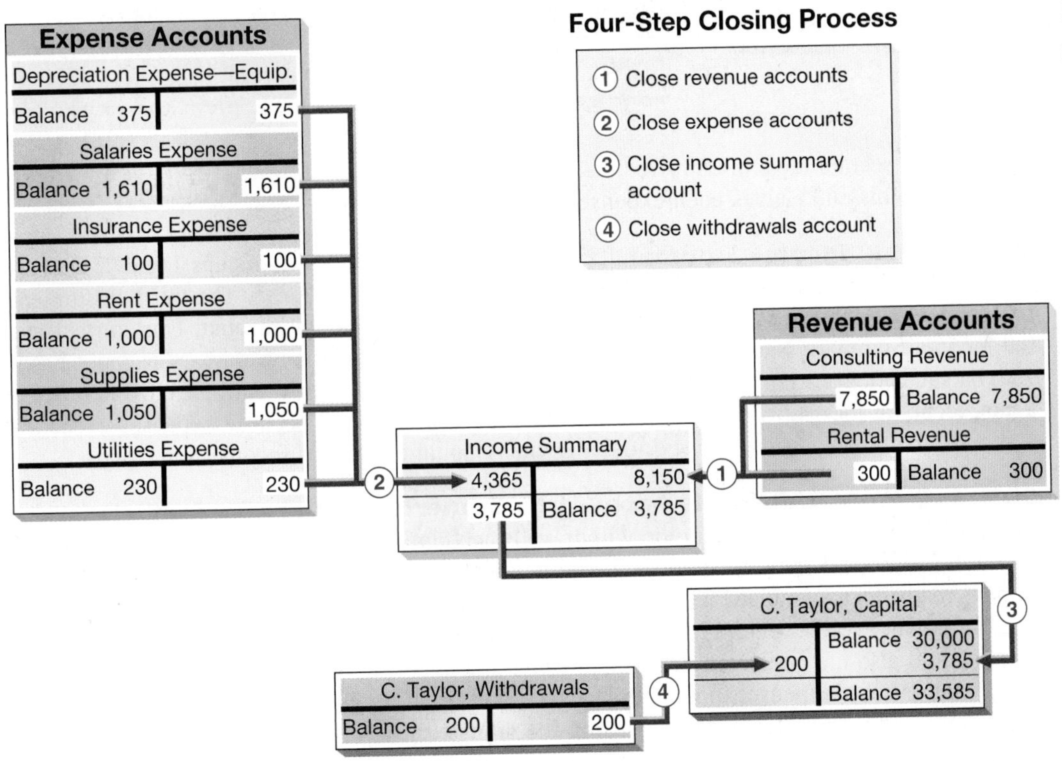

Point: C. Taylor, Capital is the only *permanent account* in Exhibit 4.3.

Step 1: Close Credit Balances in Revenue Accounts to Income Summary The first closing entry transfers credit balances in revenue (and gain) accounts to the Income Summary account. We bring accounts with credit balances to zero by debiting them. For FastForward, this journal entry is step 1 in Exhibit 4.4. This entry closes revenue accounts and leaves them with zero balances. The accounts are now ready to record revenues when they occur in the next period. The $8,150 credit entry to Income Summary equals total revenues for the period.

P2 Describe and prepare closing entries.

Step 2: Close Debit Balances in Expense Accounts to Income Summary The second closing entry transfers debit balances in expense (and loss) accounts to the Income Summary account. We bring expense accounts' debit balances to zero by crediting them. With a balance of zero, these accounts are ready to accumulate a record of expenses for the next

Point: It is possible to close revenue and expense accounts directly to owner's capital. Computerized accounting systems do this.

FASTFORWARD
Adjusted Trial Balance
December 31, 2009

	Debit	Credit
Cash	$ 4,350	
Accounts receivable	1,800	
Supplies	8,670	
Prepaid insurance	2,300	
Equipment	26,000	
Accumulated depreciation—Equip.		$ 375
Accounts payable		6,200
Salaries payable		210
Unearned consulting revenue		2,750
C. Taylor, Capital		30,000
C. Taylor, Withdrawals	200	
Consulting revenue		7,850
Rental revenue		300
Depreciation expense—Equip.	375	
Salaries expense	1,610	
Insurance expense	100	
Rent expense	1,000	
Supplies expense	1,050	
Utilities expense	230	
Totals	$47,685	$47,685

General Journal

Step 1:			
Dec. 31	Consulting Revenue	7,850	
	Rental Revenue	300	
	Income Summary		8,150
	To close revenue accounts.		
Step 2:			
Dec. 31	Income Summary	4,365	
	Depreciation Expense—Equipment		375
	Salaries Expense		1,610
	Insurance Expense		100
	Rent Expense		1,000
	Supplies Expense		1,050
	Utilities Expense		230
	To close expense accounts.		
Step 3:			
Dec. 31	Income Summary	3,785	
	C. Taylor, Capital		3,785
	To close Income Summary account.		
Step 4:			
Dec. 31	C. Taylor, Capital	200	
	C. Taylor, Withdrawals		200
	To close the withdrawals account.		

EXHIBIT 4.4

Preparing Closing Entries

period. This second closing entry for FastForward is step 2 in Exhibit 4.4. Exhibit 4.3 shows that posting this entry gives each expense account a zero balance.

Step 3: Close Income Summary to Owner's Capital After steps 1 and 2, the balance of Income Summary is equal to December's net income of $3,785. The third closing entry transfers the balance of the Income Summary account to the capital account. This entry closes the Income Summary account–see step 3 in Exhibit 4.4. The Income Summary account has a zero balance after posting this entry. It continues to have a zero balance until the closing process again occurs at the end of the next period. (If a net loss occurred because expenses exceeded revenues, the third entry is reversed: debit Owner Capital and credit Income Summary.)

Step 4: Close Withdrawals Account to Owner's Capital The fourth closing entry transfers any debit balance in the withdrawals account to the owner's capital account—see step 4 in Exhibit 4.4. This entry gives the withdrawals account a zero balance, and the account is now ready to accumulate next period's withdrawals. This entry also reduces the capital account balance to the $33,585 amount reported on the balance sheet.

We could also have selected the accounts and amounts needing to be closed by identifying individual revenue, expense, and withdrawals accounts in the ledger. This is illustrated in Exhibit 4.4 where we prepare closing entries using the adjusted trial balance.[1] (Information for closing entries is also in the financial statement columns of a work sheet.)

Post-Closing Trial Balance

P3 Explain and prepare a post-closing trial balance.

Exhibit 4.5 shows the entire ledger of FastForward as of December 31 after adjusting and closing entries are posted. (The transaction and adjusting entries are in Chapters 2 and 3.) The temporary accounts (revenues, expenses, and withdrawals) have ending balances equal to zero.

[1] The closing process has focused on proprietorships. It is identical for partnerships with the exception that each owner has separate capital and withdrawals accounts (for steps 3 and 4). The closing process for a corporation is similar with the exception that it uses a Retained Earnings account instead of a Capital account, and a Dividend account instead of a Withdrawals account.

EXHIBIT 4.5

General Ledger after the Closing Process for FastForward

Asset Accounts

Cash — Acct. No. 101

Date	Explan.	PR	Debit	Credit	Balance
2009					
Dec. 1		G1	30,000		30,000
2		G1		2,500	27,500
3		G1		26,000	1,500
5		G1	4,200		5,700
6		G1		2,400	3,300
12		G1		1,000	2,300
12		G1		700	1,600
22		G1	1,900		3,500
24		G1		900	2,600
24		G1		200	2,400
26		G1	3,000		5,400
26		G1		120	5,280
26		G1		230	5,050
26		G1		700	**4,350**

Accounts Receivable — Acct. No. 106

Date	Explan.	PR	Debit	Credit	Balance
2009					
Dec. 12		G1	1,900		1,900
22		G1		1,900	0
31	Adj.	G1	1,800		**1,800**

Supplies — Acct. No. 126

Date	Explan.	PR	Debit	Credit	Balance
2009					
Dec. 2		G1	2,500		2,500
6		G1	7,100		9,600
26		G1	120		9,720
31	Adj.	G1		1,050	**8,670**

Prepaid Insurance — Acct. No. 128

Date	Explan.	PR	Debit	Credit	Balance
2009					
Dec. 6		G1	2,400		2,400
31	Adj.	G1		100	**2,300**

Equipment — Acct. No. 167

Date	Explan.	PR	Debit	Credit	Balance
2009					
Dec. 3		G1	26,000		**26,000**

Accumulated Depreciation—Equipment — Acct. No. 168

Date	Explan.	PR	Debit	Credit	Balance
2009					
Dec. 31	Adj.	G1		375	**375**

Liability and Equity Accounts

Accounts Payable — Acct. No. 201

Date	Explan.	PR	Debit	Credit	Balance
2009					
Dec. 6		G1		7,100	7,100
24		G1	900		**6,200**

Salaries Payable — Acct. No. 209

Date	Explan.	PR	Debit	Credit	Balance
2009					
Dec. 31	Adj	G1		210	**210**

Unearned Consulting Revenue — Acct. No. 236

Date	Explan.	PR	Debit	Credit	Balance
2009					
Dec. 26		G1		3,000	3,000
31	Adj.	G1	250		**2,750**

C. Taylor, Capital — Acct. No. 301

Date	Explan.	PR	Debit	Credit	Balance
2009					
Dec. 1		G1		30,000	30,000
31	**Closing**	**G1**		**3,785**	**33,785**
31	**Closing**	**G1**	**200**		**33,585**

C. Taylor, Withdrawals — Acct. No. 302

Date	Explan.	PR	Debit	Credit	Balance
2009					
Dec. 24		G1	200		200
31	**Closing**	**G1**		**200**	**0**

Revenue and Expense Accounts (Including Income Summary)

Consulting Revenue — Acct. No. 403

Date	Explan.	PR	Debit	Credit	Balance
2009					
Dec. 5		G1		4,200	4,200
12		G1		1,600	5,800
31	Adj.	G1		250	6,050
31	Adj.	G1		1,800	7,850
31	**Closing**	**G1**	**7,850**		**0**

Rental Revenue — Acct. No. 406

Date	Explan.	PR	Debit	Credit	Balance
2009					
Dec. 12		G1		300	300
31	**Closing**	**G1**	**300**		**0**

Depreciation Expense—Equipment — Acct. No. 612

Date	Explan.	PR	Debit	Credit	Balance
2009					
Dec. 31	Adj.	G1	375		375
31	**Closing**	**G1**		**375**	**0**

Salaries Expense — Acct. No. 622

Date	Explan.	PR	Debit	Credit	Balance
2009					
Dec. 12		G1	700		700
26		G1	700		1,400
31	Adj.	G1	210		1,610
31	**Closing**	**G1**		**1,610**	**0**

Insurance Expense — Acct. No. 637

Date	Explan.	PR	Debit	Credit	Balance
2009					
Dec. 31	Adj.	G1	100		100
31	**Closing**	**G1**		**100**	**0**

Rent Expense — Acct. No. 640

Date	Explan.	PR	Debit	Credit	Balance
2009					
Dec. 12		G1	1,000		1,000
31	**Closing**	**G1**		**1,000**	**0**

Supplies Expense — Acct. No. 652

Date	Explan.	PR	Debit	Credit	Balance
2009					
Dec. 31	Adj.	G1	1,050		1,050
31	**Closing**	**G1**		**1,050**	**0**

Utilities Expense — Acct. No. 690

Date	Explan.	PR	Debit	Credit	Balance
2009					
Dec. 26		G1	230		230
31	**Closing**	**G1**		**230**	**0**

Income Summary — Acct. No. 901

Date	Explan.	PR	Debit	Credit	Balance
2009					
Dec. 31	**Closing**	**G1**		**8,150**	**8,150**
31	**Closing**	**G1**	**4,365**		**3,785**
31	**Closing**	**G1**	**3,785**		**0**

A **post-closing trial balance** is a list of permanent accounts and their balances from the ledger after all closing entries have been journalized and posted. It lists the balances for all accounts not closed. These accounts comprise a company's assets, liabilities, and equity, which are identical to those in the balance sheet. The aim of a post-closing trial balance is to verify that (1) total debits equal total credits for permanent accounts and (2) all temporary accounts have zero balances. FastForward's post-closing trial balance is shown in Exhibit 4.6. The post-closing trial balance usually is the last step in the accounting process.

EXHIBIT 4.6

Post-Closing Trial Balance

FASTFORWARD
Post-Closing Trial Balance
December 31, 2009

	Debit	Credit
Cash	$ 4,350	
Accounts receivable	1,800	
Supplies	8,670	
Prepaid insurance	2,300	
Equipment	26,000	
Accumulated depreciation—Equipment		$ 375
Accounts payable		6,200
Salaries payable		210
Unearned consulting revenue		2,750
C. Taylor, Capital		33,585
Totals	$43,120	$43,120

Accounting Cycle

C2 Identify steps in the accounting cycle.

The term **accounting cycle** refers to the steps in preparing financial statements. It is called a *cycle* because the steps are repeated each reporting period. Exhibit 4.7 shows the 10 steps in the cycle, beginning with analyzing transactions and ending with a post-closing trial balance

EXHIBIT 4.7

Steps in the Accounting Cycle*

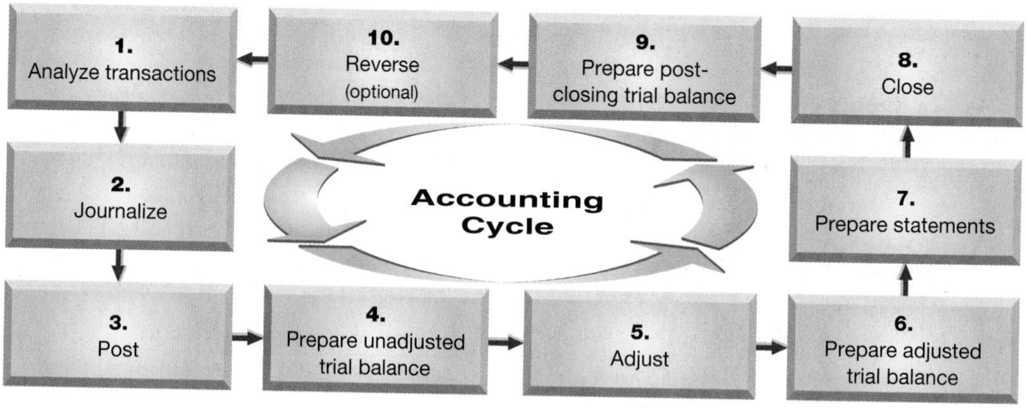

Video4.1

Explanations

1. Analyze transactions	Analyze transactions to prepare for journalizing.
2. Journalize	Record accounts, including debits and credits, in a journal.
3. Post	Transfer debits and credits from the journal to the ledger.
4. Prepare unadjusted trial balance	Summarize unadjusted ledger accounts and amounts.
5. Adjust	Record adjustments to bring account balances up to date; journalize and post adjustments.
6. Prepare adjusted trial balance	Summarize adjusted ledger accounts and amounts.
7. Prepare statements	Use adjusted trial balance to prepare financial statements.
8. Close	Journalize and post entries to close temporary accounts.
9. Prepare post-closing trial balance	Test clerical accuracy of the closing procedures.
10. Reverse (optional)	Reverse certain adjustments in the next period—optional step; see Appendix 4A.

* Steps 4, 6, and 9 can be done on a work sheet. A work sheet is useful in planning adjustments, but adjustments (step 5) must always be journalized and posted. Steps 3, 4, 6, and 9 are automatic with a computerized system.

or reversing entries. Steps 1 through 3 usually occur regularly as a company enters into transactions. Steps 4 through 9 are done at the end of a period. *Reversing entries* in step 10 are optional and are explained in Appendix 4A.

Quick Check Answers—p. 154

4. What are the major steps in preparing closing entries?
5. Why are revenue and expense accounts called *temporary?* Identify and list the types of temporary accounts.
6. What accounts are listed on the post-closing trial balance?

Classified Balance Sheet

C3 Explain and prepare a classified balance sheet.

Our discussion to this point has been limited to unclassified financial statements. This section describes a classified balance sheet. The next chapter describes a classified income statement. An **unclassified balance sheet** is one whose items are broadly grouped into assets, liabilities, and equity. One example is FastForward's balance sheet in Exhibit 4.2. A **classified balance sheet** organizes assets and liabilities into important subgroups that provide more information to decision makers.

Classification Structure

Video4.1

A classified balance sheet has no required layout, but it usually contains the categories in Exhibit 4.8. One of the more important classifications is the separation between current and noncurrent items for both assets and liabilities. Current items are those expected to come due (either collected or owed) within one year or the company's operating cycle, whichever is longer. The **operating cycle** is the time span from when *cash is used* to acquire goods and services until *cash is received* from the sale of goods and services. "Operating" refers to company operations and "cycle" refers to the circular flow of cash used for company inputs and then cash received from its outputs. The length of a company's operating cycle depends on its activities. For a service company, the operating cycle is the time span between (1) paying employees who perform the services and (2) receiving cash from customers. For a merchandiser selling products, the operating cycle is the time span between (1) paying suppliers for merchandise and (2) receiving cash from customers.

EXHIBIT 4.8

Typical Categories in a Classified Balance Sheet

Assets	Liabilities and Equity
Current assets	Current liabilities
Noncurrent assets	Noncurrent liabilities
Long-term investments	Equity
Plant assets	
Intangible assets	

Most operating cycles are less than one year. This means most companies use a one-year period in deciding which assets and liabilities are current. A few companies have an operating cycle longer than one year. For instance, producers of certain beverages (wine) and products (ginseng) that require aging for several years have operating cycles longer than one year. A balance sheet lists current assets before noncurrent assets and current liabilities before noncurrent liabilities. This consistency in presentation allows users to quickly identify current assets that are most easily converted to cash and current liabilities that are shortly coming due. Items in current assets and current liabilities are listed in the order of how quickly they will be converted to, or paid in, cash.

Classification Categories

This section describes the most common categories in a classified balance sheet. The balance sheet for Snowboarding Components in Exhibit 4.9 shows the typical categories. Its assets are

EXHIBIT 4.9

Example of a Classified Balance Sheet

SNOWBOARDING COMPONENTS
Balance Sheet
January 31, 2009

Assets		
Current assets		
Cash	$ 6,500	
Short-term investments	2,100	
Accounts receivable, net	4,400	
Merchandise inventory	27,500	
Prepaid expenses	2,400	
Total current assets		$ 42,900
Long-term investments		
Notes receivable	1,500	
Investments in stocks and bonds	18,000	
Land held for future expansion	48,000	
Total long-term investments		67,500
Plant assets		
Equipment and buildings	203,200	
Less accumulated depreciation	53,000	150,200
Land		73,200
Total plant assets		223,400
Intangible assets		10,000
Total assets		$343,800
Liabilities		
Current liabilities		
Accounts payable	$ 15,300	
Wages payable	3,200	
Notes payable	3,000	
Current portion of long-term liabilities	7,500	
Total current liabilities		$ 29,000
Long-term liabilities (net of current portion)		150,000
Total liabilities		179,000
Equity		
T. Hawk, Capital		164,800
Total liabilities and equity		$343,800

classified as either current or noncurrent. Its noncurrent assets include three main categories: long-term investments, plant assets, and intangible assets. Its liabilities are classified as either current or long-term. Not all companies use the same categories of assets and liabilities for their balance sheets. **K2 Inc.**'s balance sheet lists only three asset classes: current assets; property, plant and equipment; and other assets.

Current Assets **Current assets** are cash and other resources that are expected to be sold, collected, or used within one year or the company's operating cycle, whichever is longer. Examples are cash, short-term investments, accounts receivable, short-term notes receivable, goods for sale (called *merchandise* or *inventory*), and prepaid expenses. The individual prepaid expenses of a company are usually small in amount compared to many other assets and are often combined and shown as a single item. The prepaid expenses in Exhibit 4.9 likely include items such as prepaid insurance, prepaid rent, office supplies, and store supplies. Prepaid expenses are usually listed last because they will not be converted to cash (instead, they are used).

Point: Current is also called *short-term*, and noncurrent is also called *long-term*.

Long-Term Investments A second major balance sheet classification is **long-term** (or *noncurrent*) **investments.** Notes receivable and investments in stocks and bonds are long-term assets when they are expected to be held for more than the longer of one year or the operating cycle. Land held for future expansion is a long-term investment because it is *not* used in operations.

Plant Assets Plant assets are tangible assets that are both *long-lived* and *used to produce* or *sell products and services.* Examples are equipment, machinery, buildings, and land that are used to produce or sell products and services. The order listing for plant assets is usually from most liquid to least liquid such as equipment and machinery to buildings and land.

Point: Plant assets are also called *fixed assets; property, plant and equipment;* or *long-lived assets.*

Intangible Assets **Intangible assets** are long-term resources that benefit business operations, usually lack physical form, and have uncertain benefits. Examples are patents, trademarks, copyrights, franchises, and goodwill. Their value comes from the privileges or rights granted to or held by the owner. **K2, Inc.**, reports intangible assets of $228 million, which is nearly 20 percent of its total assets. Its intangibles include trademarks, patents, and licensing agreements.

Current Liabilities **Current liabilities** are obligations due to be paid or settled within one year or the operating cycle, whichever is longer. They are usually settled by paying out current assets such as cash. Current liabilities often include accounts payable, notes payable, wages payable, taxes payable, interest payable, and unearned revenues. Also, any portion of a long-term liability due to be paid within one year or the operating cycle, whichever is longer, is a current liability. Unearned revenues are current liabilities when they will be settled by delivering products or services within one year or the operating cycle, whichever is longer. Current liabilities are reported in the order of those to be settled first.

Point: Many financial ratios are distorted if accounts are not classified correctly.

Long-Term Liabilities **Long-term liabilities** are obligations *not* due within one year or the operating cycle, whichever is longer. Notes payable, mortgages payable, bonds payable, and lease obligations are common long-term liabilities. If a company has both short- and long-term items in each of these categories, they are commonly separated into two accounts in the ledger.

Equity Equity is the owner's claim on assets. For a proprietorship, this claim is reported in the equity section with an owner's capital account. (For a partnership, the equity section reports a capital account for each partner. For a corporation, the equity section is divided into two main subsections, common stock and retained earnings.)

Quick Check

Answers—p. 154

7. Classify the following assets as (1) current assets, (2) plant assets, or (3) intangible assets: (*a*) land used in operations, (*b*) office supplies, (*c*) receivables from customers due in 10 months, (*d*) insurance protection for the next 9 months, (*e*) trucks used to provide services to customers, (*f*) trademarks.
8. Cite two examples of assets classified as investments on the balance sheet.
9. Explain the operating cycle for a service company.

Decision Analysis

Current Ratio

A1 Compute the current ratio and describe what it reveals about a company's financial condition.

An important use of financial statements is to help assess a company's ability to pay its debts in the near future. Such analysis affects decisions by suppliers when allowing a company to buy on credit. It also affects decisions by creditors when lending money to a company, including loan terms such as interest rate, due date, and collateral requirements. It can also affect a manager's decisions about using cash to pay debts when they come due. The **current ratio** is one measure of a company's ability to pay its short-term obligations. It is defined in Exhibit 4.10 as current assets divided by current liabilities.

EXHIBIT 4.10

Current Ratio

$$\text{Current ratio} = \frac{\text{Current assets}}{\text{Current liabilities}}$$

Using financial information from **Limited Brands, Inc.**, we compute its current ratio for the recent four-year period. The results are in Exhibit 4.11.

EXHIBIT 4.11

Limited Brands' Current Ratio

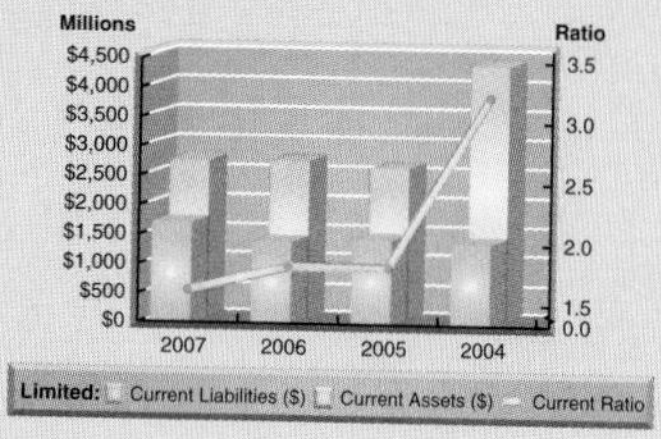

$ in millions	2007	2006	2005	2004
Current assets	$2,771	$2,784	$2,684	$4,433
Current liabilities	$1,709	$1,575	$1,451	$1,388
Current ratio	**1.6**	**1.8**	**1.8**	**3.2**
Industry current ratio	2.3	2.4	2.5	2.7

Limited Brands' current ratio averaged 2.1 for 2004 through 2007. The current ratio for each of these years suggests that the company's short-term obligations can be covered with its short-term assets. However, if its ratio would approach 1.0, Limited would expect to face challenges in covering liabilities. If the ratio were *less* than 1.0, current liabilities would exceed current assets, and the company's ability to pay short-term obligations could be in doubt.

Decision Maker

Analyst You are analyzing the financial condition of a company to assess its ability to meet upcoming loan payments. You compute its current ratio as 1.2. You also find that a major portion of accounts receivable is due from one client who has not made any payments in the past 12 months. Removing this receivable from current assets lowers the current ratio to 0.7. What do you conclude? [Answer—p. 153]

Demonstration Problem

DP4

The partial work sheet of Midtown Repair Company at December 31, 2009, follows.

	Adjusted Trial Balance		Income Statement		Balance Sheet and Statement of Owner's Equity	
	Debit	Credit	Debit	Credit	Debit	Credit
Cash	95,600					
Notes receivable (current)	50,000					
Prepaid insurance	16,000					
Prepaid rent	4,000					
Equipment	170,000					
Accumulated depreciation—Equipment		57,000				
Accounts payable		52,000				
Long-term notes payable		63,000				
C. Trout, Capital		178,500				
C. Trout, Withdrawals	30,000					
Repair services revenue		180,800				
Interest revenue		7,500				
Depreciation expense—Equipment	28,500					
Wages expense	85,000					
Rent expense	48,000					
Insurance expense	6,000					
Interest expense	5,700					
Totals	538,800	538,800				

Required

1. Complete the work sheet by extending the adjusted trial balance totals to the appropriate financial statement columns.
2. Prepare closing entries for Midtown Repair Company.
3. Set up the Income Summary and the C. Trout, Capital account in the general ledger (in balance column format) and post the closing entries to these accounts.
4. Determine the balance of the C. Trout, Capital account to be reported on the December 31, 2009, balance sheet.
5. Prepare an income statement, statement of owner's equity, and classified balance sheet (in report form) as of December 31, 2009.

Planning the Solution

- Extend the adjusted trial balance account balances to the appropriate financial statement columns.
- Prepare entries to close the revenue accounts to Income Summary, to close the expense accounts to Income Summary, to close Income Summary to the capital account, and to close the withdrawals account to the capital account.
- Post the first and second closing entries to the Income Summary account. Examine the balance of income summary and verify that it agrees with the net income shown on the work sheet.
- Post the third and fourth closing entries to the capital account.
- Use the work sheet's two right-most columns and your answer in part 4 to prepare the classified balance sheet.

Solution to Demonstration Problem

1. Completing the work sheet.

	Adjusted Trial Balance		Income Statement		Balance Sheet and Statement of Owner's Equity	
	Debit	Credit	Debit	Credit	Debit	Credit
Cash	95,600				95,600	
Notes receivable (current)	50,000				50,000	
Prepaid insurance	16,000				16,000	
Prepaid rent	4,000				4,000	
Equipment	170,000				170,000	
Accumulated depreciation—Equipment		57,000				57,000
Accounts payable		52,000				52,000
Long-term notes payable		63,000				63,000
C. Trout, Capital		178,500				178,500
C. Trout, Withdrawals	30,000				30,000	
Repair services revenue		180,800		180,800		
Interest revenue		7,500		7,500		
Depreciation expense—Equipment	28,500		28,500			
Wages expense	85,000		85,000			
Rent expense	48,000		48,000			
Insurance expense	6,000		6,000			
Interest expense	5,700		5,700			
Totals	538,800	538,800	173,200	188,300	365,600	350,500
Net income			15,100			15,100
Totals			188,300	188,300	365,600	365,600

2. Closing entries.

Dec. 31	Repair Services Revenue	180,800	
	Interest Revenue	7,500	
	Income Summary		188,300
	To close revenue accounts.		

[continued on next page]

[continued from previous page]

Dec. 31	Income Summary	173,200	
	Depreciation Expense—Equipment		28,500
	Wages Expense		85,000
	Rent Expense		48,000
	Insurance Expense		6,000
	Interest Expense		5,700
	To close expense accounts.		
Dec. 31	Income Summary	15,100	
	C. Trout, Capital		15,100
	To close the Income Summary account.		
Dec. 31	C. Trout, Capital	30,000	
	C. Trout, Withdrawals		30,000
	To close the withdrawals account.		

3. Set up the Income Summary and the capital ledger accounts and post the closing entries.

Income Summary — Account No. 901

Date	Explanation	PR	Debit	Credit	Balance
2009					
Jan. 1	Beginning balance				0
Dec. 31	Close revenue accounts			188,300	188,300
31	Close expense accounts		173,200		15,100
31	Close income summary		15,100		0

C. Trout, Capital — Account No. 301

Date	Explanation	PR	Debit	Credit	Balance
2009					
Jan. 1	Beginning balance				178,500
Dec. 31	Close Income Summary			15,100	193,600
31	Close C. Trout, Withdrawals		30,000		163,600

4. The final capital balance of $163,600 (from part 3) will be reported on the December 31, 2009, balance sheet. The final capital balance reflects the increase due to the net income earned during the year and the decrease for the owner's withdrawals during the year.

5.

MIDTOWN REPAIR COMPANY
Income Statement
For Year Ended December 31, 2009

Revenues		
Repair services revenue	$180,800	
Interest revenue	7,500	
Total revenues		$188,300
Expenses		
Depreciation expense—Equipment	28,500	
Wages expense	85,000	
Rent expense	48,000	
Insurance expense	6,000	
Interest expense	5,700	
Total expenses		173,200
Net income		$ 15,100

MIDTOWN REPAIR COMPANY
Statement of Owner's Equity
For Year Ended December 31, 2009

C. Trout, Capital, December 31, 2008		$178,500
Add: Investment by owner	$ 0	
Net income	15,100	15,100
		193,600
Less: Withdrawals by owner		30,000
C. Trout, Capital, December 31, 2009		$163,600

MIDTOWN REPAIR COMPANY
Balance Sheet
December 31, 2009

Assets		
Current assets		
Cash		$ 95,600
Notes receivable		50,000
Prepaid insurance		16,000
Prepaid rent		4,000
Total current assets		165,600
Plant assets		
Equipment	$170,000	
Less: Accumulated depreciation—Equipment	(57,000)	
Total plant assets		113,000
Total assets		$278,600
Liabilities		
Current liabilities		
Accounts payable		$ 52,000
Long-term liabilities		
Long-term notes payable		63,000
Total liabilities		115,000
Equity		
C. Trout, Capital		163,600
Total liabilities and equity		$278,600

APPENDIX

Reversing Entries 4A

Reversing entries are optional. They are recorded in response to accrued assets and accrued liabilities that were created by adjusting entries at the end of a reporting period. The purpose of reversing entries is to simplify a company's recordkeeping. Exhibit 4A.1 shows an example of FastForward's reversing entries. The top of the exhibit shows the adjusting entry FastForward recorded on December 31 for its employee's earned but unpaid salary. The entry recorded three days' salary of $210, which increased December's total salary expense to $1,610. The entry also recognized a liability of $210. The expense is reported on December's income statement. The expense account is then closed. The ledger on January 1,

Point: As a general rule, adjusting entries that create new asset or liability accounts are likely candidates for reversing.

EXHIBIT 4A.1

Reversing Entries for an Accrued Expense

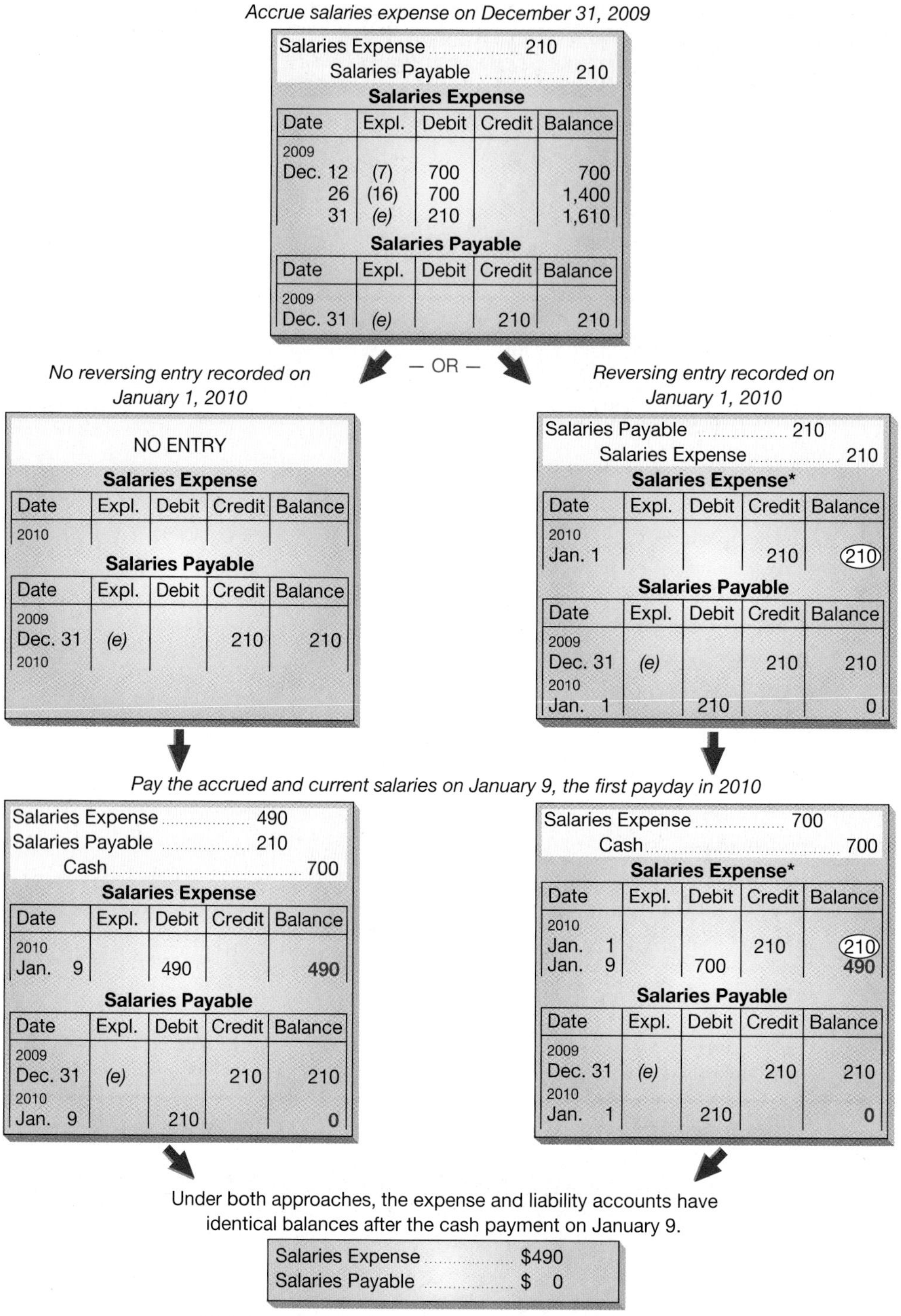

*Circled numbers in the *Balance* column indicate abnormal balances.

2010, shows a $210 liability and a zero balance in the Salaries Expense account. At this point, the choice is made between using or not using reversing entries.

Accounting *without* Reversing Entries

The path down the left side of Exhibit 4A.1 is described in the chapter. To summarize here, when the next payday occurs on January 9, we record payment with a compound entry that debits both the expense and liability accounts and credits Cash. Posting that entry creates a $490 balance in the expense account and reduces the liability account balance to zero because the debt has been settled. The disadvantage of this approach is the slightly more complex entry required on January 9. Paying the accrued liability means that this entry differs from the routine entries made on all other paydays. To construct the proper entry on January 9, we must recall the effect of the December 31 adjusting entry. Reversing entries overcome this disadvantage.

Accounting *with* Reversing Entries

P4 Prepare reversing entries and explain their purpose.

The right side of Exhibit 4A.1 shows how a reversing entry on January 1 overcomes the disadvantage of the January 9 entry when not using reversing entries. A reversing entry is the exact opposite of an adjusting entry. For FastForward, the Salaries Payable liability account is debited for $210, meaning that this account now has a zero balance after the entry is posted. The Salaries Payable account temporarily understates the liability, but this is not a problem since financial statements are not prepared before the liability is settled on January 9. The credit to the Salaries Expense account is unusual because it gives the account an *abnormal credit balance*. We highlight an abnormal balance by circling it. Because of the reversing entry, the January 9 entry to record payment is straightforward. This entry debits the Salaries Expense account and credits Cash for the full $700 paid. It is the same as all other entries made to record 10 days' salary for the employee. Notice that after the payment entry is posted, the Salaries Expense account has a $490 balance that reflects seven days' salary of $70 per day (see the lower right side of Exhibit 4A.1). The zero balance in the Salaries Payable account is now correct. The lower section of Exhibit 4A.1 shows that the expense and liability accounts have exactly the same balances whether reversing entries are used or not. This means that both approaches yield identical results.

Summary

C1 Explain why temporary accounts are closed each period. Temporary accounts are closed at the end of each accounting period for two main reasons. First, the closing process updates the capital account to include the effects of all transactions and events recorded for the period. Second, it prepares revenue, expense, and withdrawals accounts for the next reporting period by giving them zero balances.

C2 Identify steps in the accounting cycle. The accounting cycle consists of 10 steps: (1) analyze transactions, (2) journalize, (3) post, (4) prepare an unadjusted trial balance, (5) adjust accounts, (6) prepare an adjusted trial balance, (7) prepare statements, (8) close, (9) prepare a post-closing trial balance, and (10) prepare (optional) reversing entries.

C3 Explain and prepare a classified balance sheet. Classified balance sheets report assets and liabilities in two categories: current and noncurrent. Noncurrent assets often include long-term investments, plant assets, and intangible assets. Owner's equity for proprietorships (and partnerships) report the capital account balance. A corporation separates equity into common stock and retained earnings.

A1 Compute the current ratio and describe what it reveals about a company's financial condition. A company's current ratio is defined as current assets divided by current liabilities. We use it to evaluate a company's ability to pay its current liabilities out of current assets.

P1 Prepare a work sheet and explain its usefulness. A work sheet can be a useful tool in preparing and analyzing financial statements. It is helpful at the end of a period in preparing adjusting entries, an adjusted trial balance, and financial statements. A work sheet usually contains five pairs of columns: Unadjusted Trial Balance, Adjustments, Adjusted Trial Balance, Income Statement, and Balance Sheet & Statement of Owner's Equity.

P2 Describe and prepare closing entries. Closing entries involve four steps: (1) close credit balances in revenue (and gain) accounts to Income Summary, (2) close debit balances in expense (and loss) accounts to Income Summary, (3) close Income Summary to the capital account, and (4) close withdrawals account to owner's capital.

P3 Explain and prepare a post-closing trial balance. A post-closing trial balance is a list of permanent accounts and their balances after all closing entries have been journalized and posted. Its purpose is to verify that (1) total debits equal total credits for permanent accounts and (2) all temporary accounts have zero balances.

P4[A] Prepare reversing entries and explain their purpose. Reversing entries are an optional step. They are applied to accrued expenses and revenues. The purpose of reversing entries is to simplify subsequent journal entries. Financial statements are unaffected by the choice to use or not use reversing entries.

Guidance Answers to **Decision Maker** and **Decision Ethics**

Entrepreneur Yes, you are concerned about the absence of a depreciation adjustment. Equipment does depreciate, and financial statements must recognize this occurrence. Its absence suggests an error or a misrepresentation (there is also the possibility that equipment is fully depreciated).

Analyst A current ratio of 1.2 suggests that current assets are sufficient to cover current liabilities, but it implies a minimal buffer in case of errors in measuring current assets or current liabilities. Removing the past due receivable reduces the current ratio to 0.7. Your assessment is that the company will have some difficulty meeting its loan payments.

Guidance Answers to Quick Checks

1. Amounts in the Unadjusted Trial Balance columns are taken from current account balances in the ledger. The balances for new accounts expected to arise from adjusted entries can be left blank or set at zero.
2. A work sheet offers the advantage of listing on one page all necessary information to make adjusting entries.
3. A work sheet can help in (a) accounting efficiency and avoiding errors, (b) linking transactions and events to their effects in financial statements, (c) showing adjustments for audit purposes, (d) preparing interim financial statements, and (e) showing effects from proposed, or what-if, transactions.
4. The major steps in preparing closing entries are to close (1) credit balances in revenue accounts to Income Summary, (2) debit balances in expense accounts to Income Summary, (3) Income Summary to owner's capital, and (4) any withdrawals account to owner's capital.
5. Revenue (and gain) and expense (and loss) accounts are called *temporary* because they are opened and closed each period. The Income Summary and owner's withdrawals accounts are also temporary.
6. Permanent accounts make up the post-closing trial balance, which consist of asset, liability, and equity accounts.
7. Current assets: (*b*), (*c*), (*d*). Plant assets: (*a*), (*e*). Item (*f*) is an intangible asset.
8. Investment in common stock, investment in bonds, and land held for future expansion.
9. For a service company, the operating cycle is the usual time between (1) paying employees who do the services and (2) receiving cash from customers for services provided.

Key Terms

mhhe.com/wildFAP19e

Key Terms are available at the book's Website for learning and testing in an online Flashcard Format.

Accounting cycle (p. 144)
Classified balance sheet (p. 145)
Closing entries (p. 141)
Closing process (p. 140)
Current assets (p. 146)
Current liabilities (p. 147)
Current ratio (p. 147)
Income Summary (p. 141)
Intangible assets (p. 147)
Long-term investments (p. 147)
Long-term liabilities (p. 147)
Operating cycle (p. 145)
Permanent accounts (p. 140)
Post-closing trial balance (p. 144)
Pro forma financial statements (p. 140)
Reversing entries (p. 151)
Temporary accounts (p. 140)
Unclassified balance sheet (p. 145)
Working papers (p. 136)
Work sheet (p. 136)

Multiple Choice Quiz

Answers on p. 175

mhhe.com/wildFAP19e

Additional Quiz Questions are available at the book's Website.

1. G. Venda, owner of Venda Services, withdrew $25,000 from the business during the current year. The entry to close the withdrawals account at the end of the year is:

a.	G. Venda, Withdrawals	25,000	
	G. Venda, Capital		25,000
b.	Income Summary	25,000	
	G. Venda, Capital		25,000
c.	G. Venda, Withdrawals	25,000	
	Cash		25,000
d.	G. Venda, Capital	25,000	
	Salary Expense		25,000
e.	G. Venda, Capital	25,000	
	G. Venda, Withdrawals		25,000

2. The following information is available for the R. Kandamil Company before closing the accounts. After all of the closing entries are made, what will be the balance in the R. Kandamil, Capital account?

Quiz4

Total revenues	$300,000
Total expenses	195,000
R. Kandamil, Capital	100,000
R. Kandamil, Withdrawals	45,000

a. $360,000
b. $250,000
c. $160,000
d. $150,000
e. $60,000

3. Which of the following errors would cause the balance sheet and statement of owner's equity columns of a work sheet to be out of balance?
   a. Entering a revenue amount in the balance sheet and statement of owner's equity debit column.
   b. Entering a liability amount in the balance sheet and statement of owner's equity credit column.
   c. Entering an expense account in the balance sheet and statement of owner's equity debit column.
   d. Entering an asset account in the income statement debit column.
   e. Entering a liability amount in the income statement credit column.

4. The temporary account used only in the closing process to hold the amounts of revenues and expenses before the net difference is added or subtracted from the owner's capital account is called the
   a. Closing account.
   b. Nominal account.
   c. Income Summary account.
   d. Balance Column account.
   e. Contra account.

5. Based on the following information from Repicor Company's balance sheet, what is Repicor Company's current ratio?

Current assets	$ 75,000
Investments	30,000
Plant assets	300,000
Current liabilities	50,000
Long-term liabilities	60,000
D. Repicor, Capital	295,000

   a. 2.10
   b. 1.50
   c. 1.00
   d. 0.95
   e. 0.67

Superscript letter A denotes assignments based on Appendix 4A.

Discussion Questions

1. What accounts are affected by closing entries? What accounts are not affected?

2. What two purposes are accomplished by recording closing entries?

3. What are the steps in recording closing entries?

4. What is the purpose of the Income Summary account?

5. Explain whether an error has occurred if a post-closing trial balance includes a Depreciation Expense account.

6. What tasks are aided by a work sheet?

7. Why are the debit and credit entries in the Adjustments columns of the work sheet identified with letters?

8. What is a company's operating cycle?

9. What classes of assets and liabilities are shown on a typical classified balance sheet?

10. How is unearned revenue classified on the balance sheet?

11. What are the characteristics of plant assets?

12.[A] How do reversing entries simplify recordkeeping?

13.[A] If a company recorded accrued salaries expense of $500 at the end of its fiscal year, what reversing entry could be made? When would it be made?

14. Refer to the balance sheet for **Best Buy** in Appendix A. What five noncurrent asset categories are used on its classified balance sheet?

15. Refer to **Circuit City**'s balance sheet in Appendix A. Identify the accounts listed as current liabilities.

16. Refer to **RadioShack**'s balance sheet in Appendix A. Identify the accounts listed as current assets.

17. Refer to **Apple**'s financial statements in Appendix A. What journal entry was likely recorded as of September 30, 2006, to close its Income Summary account?

Denotes Discussion Questions that involve decision making.

McGraw-Hill's HOMEWORK MANAGER® Available with McGraw-Hill's Homework Manager

QUICK STUDY

QS 4-1
Determining effects of closing entries
C1 P2

Irvine Company began the current period with a $35,000 credit balance in the M. Irvine, Capital account. At the end of the period, the company's adjusted account balances include the following temporary accounts with normal balances.

Service fees earned	$42,000	Interest revenue	$8,000
Salaries expense	31,000	M. Irvine, Withdrawals	9,200
Depreciation expense	11,000	Utilities expense	5,000

After closing the revenue and expense accounts, what will be the balance of the Income Summary account? After all closing entries are journalized and posted, what will be the balance of the M. Irvine, Capital account?

QS 4-2
Identifying the accounting cycle
C2

List the following steps of the accounting cycle in their proper order.

a. Preparing the financial statements.
b. Preparing the unadjusted trial balance.
c. Journalizing transactions and events.
d. Preparing the post-closing trial balance.
e. Posting the journal entries.
f. Journalizing and posting adjusting entries.
g. Preparing the adjusted trial balance.
h. Journalizing and posting closing entries.
i. Analyzing transactions and events.

QS 4-3
Classifying balance sheet items
C3

The following are common categories on a classified balance sheet.

A. Current assets
B. Long-term investments
C. Plant assets
D. Intangible assets
E. Current liabilities
F. Long-term liabilities

For each of the following items, select the letter that identifies the balance sheet category where the item typically would appear.

_____ **1.** Accounts payable
_____ **2.** Store equipment
_____ **3.** Wages payable
_____ **4.** Cash
_____ **5.** Land not currently used in operations
_____ **6.** Notes payable (due in three years)
_____ **7.** Accounts receivable
_____ **8.** Trademarks

QS 4-4
Identifying current accounts and computing the current ratio
C3 A1

Compute Palmolive Company's current ratio using the following information.

Accounts receivable	$18,000	Long-term notes payable	$21,000
Accounts payable	11,000	Office supplies	2,860
Buildings	45,000	Prepaid insurance	3,500
Cash	7,000	Unearned services revenue	3,000

QS 4-5
Interpreting a work sheet
P1

The following selected information is taken from the work sheet for Fischer Company as of December 31, 2009. Using this information, determine the amount for J. Fischer, Capital, that should be reported on its December 31, 2009, balance sheet.

	Income Statement		Balance Sheet and Statement of Owner's Equity	
	Dr.	Cr.	Dr.	Cr.
⋮				
J. Fischer, Capital				36,000
J. Fischer, Withdrawals			18,000	
⋮				
Totals	61,000	90,000		

QS 4-6
Applying a work sheet
P1

In preparing a work sheet, indicate the financial statement Debit column to which a normal balance in the following accounts should be extended. Use I for the Income Statement Debit column and B for the Balance Sheet and Statement of Owner's Equity Debit column.

_____ **a.** Depreciation expense—Equipment
_____ **b.** Accounts receivable
_____ **c.** Insurance expense
_____ **d.** Equipment
_____ **e.** Owner, Withdrawals
_____ **f.** Prepaid rent

QS 4-7
Ordering work sheet steps
P1

List the following steps in preparing a work sheet in their proper order by writing numbers 1–5 in the blank spaces provided.

a. ______ Prepare an unadjusted trial balance on the work sheet.
b. ______ Prepare an adjusted trial balance on the work sheet.
c. ______ Enter adjustments data on the work sheet.
d. ______ Total the statement columns, compute net income (loss), and complete work sheet.
e. ______ Extend adjusted balances to appropriate financial statement columns.

QS 4-8
Preparing a partial work sheet
P1

The ledger of Edgardo Company includes the following unadjusted normal balances: Prepaid Rent $4,000, Services Revenue $65,000, and Wages Expense $30,000. Adjusting entries are required for **(a)** prepaid rent expense expired, $800; **(b)** accrued services revenue $950; and **(c)** accrued wages expense $750. Enter these unadjusted balances and the necessary adjustments on a work sheet and complete the work sheet for these accounts. *Note:* Also include the following accounts: Accounts Receivable, Wages Payable, and Rent Expense.

QS 4-9
Prepare closing entries from the ledger P2

The ledger of Simms Company includes the following accounts with normal balances: P. Simms, Capital $18,000; P. Simms, Withdrawals $1,600; Services Revenue $26,000; Wages Expense $16,800; and Rent Expense $3,200. Prepare the necessary closing entries from the available information at December 31.

QS 4-10
Identify post-closing accounts P3

Identify the accounts listed in QS 4-9 that would be included in a post-closing trial balance.

QS 4-11^A
Reversing entries
P4

On December 31, 2008, Yates Co. prepared an adjusting entry for $24,000 of earned but unrecorded management fees. On January 16, 2009, Yates received $37,500 cash in management fees, which included the accrued fees earned in 2008. Assuming the company uses reversing entries, prepare the January 1, 2009, reversing entry and the January 16, 2009, cash receipt entry.

EXERCISES

McGraw-Hill's HOMEWORK MANAGER® Available with McGraw-Hill's Homework Manager

Exercise 4-1
Preparing and posting closing entries
P2

Use the March 31 fiscal year-end information from the following ledger accounts (assume that all accounts have normal balances) to prepare closing journal entries and then post those entries to the appropriate ledger accounts.

General Ledger

R. Cruz, Capital Acct. No. 301

Date	PR	Debit	Credit	Balance
Mar. 31	G2			65,000

R. Cruz, Withdrawals Acct. No. 302

Date	PR	Debit	Credit	Balance
Mar. 31	G2			46,770

Services Revenue Acct. No. 401

Date	PR	Debit	Credit	Balance
Mar. 31	G2			114,530

Depreciation Expense Acct. No. 603

Date	PR	Debit	Credit	Balance
Mar. 31	G2			17,000

Salaries Expense Acct. No. 622

Date	PR	Debit	Credit	Balance
Mar. 31	G2			32,500

Insurance Expense Acct. No. 637

Date	PR	Debit	Credit	Balance
Mar. 31	G2			4,420

Rent Expense Acct. No. 640

Date	PR	Debit	Credit	Balance
Mar. 31	G2			9,440

Income Summary Acct. No. 901

Date	PR	Debit	Credit	Balance

Check R. Cruz, Capital (ending balance), $69,400

Exercise 4-2
Preparing closing entries and a post-closing trial balance
P2 P3

The adjusted trial balance for Santara Marketing Co. follows. Complete the four right-most columns of the table by first entering information for the four closing entries (keyed *1* through *4*) and second by completing the post-closing trial balance.

No.	Account Title	Adjusted Trial Balance Dr.	Adjusted Trial Balance Cr.	Closing Entry Information Dr.	Closing Entry Information Cr.	Post-Closing Trial Balance Dr.	Post-Closing Trial Balance Cr.
101	Cash	$ 11,900					
106	Accounts receivable	24,000					
153	Equipment	41,000					
154	Accumulated depreciation—Equipment		$ 16,500				
193	Franchise	30,000					
201	Accounts payable		14,000				
209	Salaries payable		3,200				
233	Unearned fees		2,600				
301	T. Santara, Capital		66,701				
302	T. Santara, Withdrawals	14,400					
401	Marketing fees earned		83,000				
611	Depreciation expense—Equipment	11,000					
622	Salaries expense	33,034					
640	Rent expense	12,616					
677	Miscellaneous expenses	8,051					
901	Income summary						
	Totals	$186,001	$186,001				

Exercise 4-3
Preparing closing entries and a post-closing trial balance
C1 P2 P3

The following adjusted trial balance contains the accounts and balances of Ferrara Company as of December 31, 2009, the end of its fiscal year. (1) Prepare the December 31, 2009, closing entries for Ferrara Company. (2) Prepare the December 31, 2009, post-closing trial balance for Ferrara Company.

No.	Account Title	Debit	Credit
101	Cash	$18,000	
126	Supplies	13,900	
128	Prepaid insurance	2,000	
167	Equipment	23,000	
168	Accumulated depreciation—Equipment		$ 6,500
301	N. Ferrara, Capital		48,168
302	N. Ferrara, Withdrawals	6,000	
404	Services revenue		37,200
612	Depreciation expense—Equipment	2,000	
622	Salaries expense	21,687	
637	Insurance expense	1,562	
640	Rent expense	2,492	
652	Supplies expense	1,227	
	Totals	$91,868	$91,868

Check (2) N. Ferrara, Capital (ending), $50,400; Total debits, $56,900

Exercise 4-4
Preparing the financial statements
C2

Use the following adjusted trial balance of Resource Trucking Company to prepare the (1) income statement, and (2) statement of owner's equity, for the year ended December 31, 2009. The J. Reso, Capital account balance is $161,901 at December 31, 2008.

Account Title	Debit	Credit
Cash	$ 5,800	
Accounts receivable	17,500	
Office supplies	3,000	
Trucks	156,000	
Accumulated depreciation—Trucks		$ 32,136
Land	85,000	
Accounts payable		9,800
Interest payable		4,000
Long-term notes payable		53,000
J. Reso, Capital		161,901
J. Reso, Withdrawals	20,000	
Trucking fees earned		121,000
Depreciation expense—Trucks	20,727	
Salaries expense	56,749	
Office supplies expense	6,655	
Repairs expense—Trucks	10,406	
Totals	$381,837	$381,837

Exercise 4-5
Preparing a classified balance sheet C3

Use the information in the adjusted trial balance reported in Exercise 4-4 to prepare Resource Trucking Company's classified balance sheet as of December 31, 2009.

Check Total assets, $235,164; J. Reso, Capital, $168,364

Exercise 4-6
Computing the current ratio
A1

Use the information in the adjusted trial balance reported in Exercise 4-4 to compute the current ratio as of the balance sheet date (round the ratio to one decimal). Interpret the current ratio for the Resource Trucking Company. (Assume that the industry average for the current ratio is 1.5.)

Exercise 4-7
Computing and analyzing the current ratio
A1

Calculate the current ratio in each of the following separate cases (round the ratio to two decimals). Identify the company case with the strongest liquidity position. (These cases represent competing companies in the same industry.)

	Current Assets	Current Liabilities
Case 1	$ 76,000	$26,666
Case 2	101,080	64,351
Case 3	42,863	41,204
Case 4	82,308	69,156
Case 5	58,444	84,638

Exercise 4-8
Preparing adjusting entries from a work sheet
P1

Use the following information from the Adjustments columns of a 10-column work sheet to prepare the necessary adjusting journal entries (*a*) through (*e*).

No.	Account Title	Adjustments Debit	Adjustments Credit
109	Interest receivable	(*d*) $ 636	
124	Office supplies		(*b*) $1,729
128	Prepaid insurance		(*a*) 979

[continued on next page]

[continued from previous page]

164	Accumulated depreciation—Office equipment		(c) 3,300
209	Salaries payable		(e) 716
409	Interest revenue		(d) 636
612	Depreciation expense—Office equipment	(c) 3,300	
620	Office salaries expense	(e) 716	
636	Insurance expense—Office equipment	(a) 470	
637	Insurance expense—Store equipment	(a) 509	
650	Office supplies expense	(b) 1,729	
	Totals	$7,360	$7,360

Exercise 4-9
Extending adjusted account balances on a work sheet
P1

These 16 accounts are from the Adjusted Trial Balance columns of a company's 10-column work sheet. In the blank space beside each account, write the letter of the appropriate financial statement column (A, B, C, or D) to which a normal account balance is extended.

A. Debit column for the Income Statement columns.

B. Credit column for the Income Statement columns.

C. Debit column for the Balance Sheet and Statement of Owner's Equity columns.

D. Credit column for the Balance Sheet and Statement of Owner's Equity columns.

_____ **1.** Accounts Receivable
_____ **2.** Accumulated Depreciation
_____ **3.** Office Supplies
_____ **4.** Insurance Expense
_____ **5.** Interest Receivable
_____ **6.** Cash
_____ **7.** Rent Expense
_____ **8.** Wages Payable
_____ **9.** Interest Revenue
_____ **10.** Machinery
_____ **11.** Owner, Withdrawals
_____ **12.** Depreciation Expense
_____ **13.** Accounts Payable
_____ **14.** Service Fees Revenue
_____ **15.** Owner, Capital
_____ **16.** Interest Expense

Exercise 4-10
Extending accounts in a work sheet
P1

The Adjusted Trial Balance columns of a 10-column work sheet for Linn Company follow. Complete the work sheet by extending the account balances into the appropriate financial statement columns and by entering the amount of net income for the reporting period.

No.	Account Title	Debit	Credit
101	Cash	$ 8,200	
106	Accounts receivable	35,834	
153	Trucks	41,500	
154	Accumulated depreciation—Trucks		$ 16,683
183	Land	30,000	
201	Accounts payable		19,106
209	Salaries payable		4,370
233	Unearned fees		3,770
301	D. Linn, Capital		69,012
302	D. Linn, Withdrawals	15,534	
401	Plumbing fees earned		84,000
611	Depreciation expense—Trucks	5,561	
622	Salaries expense	39,312	
640	Rent expense	12,768	
677	Miscellaneous expenses	8,232	
	Totals	$196,941	$196,941

Check Net income, $18,127

Exercise 4-11
Completing the income statement columns and preparing closing entries

P1 P2

These partially completed Income Statement columns from a 10-column work sheet are for Johnson's Bike Rental Company. (1) Use the information to determine the amount that should be entered on the net income line of the work sheet. (2) Prepare the company's closing entries. The owner, C. Johnson, did not make any withdrawals this period.

Account Title	Debit	Credit
Rent earned		90,000
Salaries expense	39,960	
Insurance expense	5,670	
Office supplies expense	13,230	
Bike repair expense	2,790	
Depreciation expense—Bikes	17,190	
Totals		
Net income		
Totals		

Check Net income, $11,160

Exercise 4-12
Preparing a work sheet and recording closing entries

P1 P2

The following unadjusted trial balance contains the accounts and balances of Santaga Delivery Company as of December 31, 2009, its first year of operations.

(1) Use the following information about the company's adjustments to complete a 10-column work sheet for Dylan.

a. Unrecorded depreciation on the trucks at the end of the year is $16,000.

b. The total amount of accrued interest expense at year-end is $8,000.

c. The cost of unused office supplies still available at the year-end is $500.

(2) Prepare the year-end closing entries for this company, and determine the capital amount to be reported on its year-end balance sheet.

Account Title	Debit	Credit
Cash	$ 15,000	
Accounts receivable	33,000	
Office supplies	4,000	
Trucks	340,000	
Accumulated depreciation—Trucks		$112,000
Land	150,000	
Accounts payable		23,550
Interest payable		6,000
Long-term notes payable		104,000
D. Santaga, Capital		272,770
D. Santaga, Withdrawals	38,000	
Delivery fees earned		274,350
Depreciation expense—Truck	48,000	
Salaries expense	128,670	
Office supplies expense	14,000	
Interest expense	6,000	
Repairs expense—trucks	16,000	
Totals	$792,670	$792,670

Check Adj. trial balance totals, $810,670; Net income, $40,180

Exercise 4-13A
Preparing reversing entries

P4

The following two events occurred for Tankwell Co. on October 31, 2009, the end of its fiscal year.

a. Tankwell rents a building from its owner for $3,300 per month. By a prearrangement, the company delayed paying October's rent until November 5. On this date, the company paid the rent for both October and November.

b. Tankwell rents space in a building it owns to a tenant for $1,050 per month. By prearrangement, the tenant delayed paying the October rent until November 8. On this date, the tenant paid the rent for both October and November.

Required

1. Prepare adjusting entries that the company must record for these events as of October 31.

2. Assuming Tankwell does *not* use reversing entries, prepare journal entries to record Tankwell's payment of rent on November 5 and the collection of rent on November 8 from Tankwell's tenant.

3. Assuming that the company uses reversing entries, prepare reversing entries on November 1 and the journal entries to record Tankwell's payment of rent on November 5 and the collection of rent on November 8 from Tankwell's tenant.

Exercise 4-14[A]
Preparing reversing entries
P4

Scholl Company records prepaid assets and unearned revenues in balance sheet accounts. The following information was used to prepare adjusting entries for the company as of August 31, the end of the company's fiscal year.

a. The company has earned $4,500 in unrecorded service fees.

b. The expired portion of prepaid insurance is $3,750.

c. The company has earned $2,100 of its Unearned Service Fees account balance.

d. Depreciation expense for office equipment is $2,600.

e. Employees have earned but have not been paid salaries of $2,700.

Prepare any necessary reversing entries for the accounting adjustments *a* through *e* assuming that the company uses reversing entries in its accounting system.

Available with McGraw-Hill's Homework Manager — McGraw-Hill's HOMEWORK MANAGER®

PROBLEM SET A

Problem 4-1A
Determining balance sheet classifications
C3

In the blank space beside each numbered balance sheet item, enter the letter of its balance sheet classification. If the item should not appear on the balance sheet, enter a *Z* in the blank.

A. Current assets
B. Long-term investments
C. Plant assets
D. Intangible assets
E. Current liabilities
F. Long-term liabilities
G. Equity

_____ **1.** Accumulated depreciation—Trucks
_____ **2.** Cash
_____ **3.** Buildings
_____ **4.** Store supplies
_____ **5.** Office equipment
_____ **6.** Land (used in operations)
_____ **7.** Repairs expense
_____ **8.** Office supplies
_____ **9.** Current portion of long-term note payable
_____ **10.** Unearned services revenue
_____ **11.** Long-term investment in stock
_____ **12.** Depreciation expense—Building
_____ **13.** Prepaid rent
_____ **14.** Interest receivable
_____ **15.** Taxes payable
_____ **16.** Automobiles
_____ **17.** Notes payable (due in 3 years)
_____ **18.** Accounts payable
_____ **19.** Prepaid insurance
_____ **20.** Owner, Capital

Problem 4-2A
Applying the accounting cycle
C1 C2 P2 P3
eXcel
mhhe.com/wildFAP19e

On April 1, 2009, Jiro Nozomi created a new travel agency, Adventure Travel. The following transactions occurred during the company's first month.

April	1	Nozomi invested $32,000 cash and computer equipment worth $26,000 in the company.
	2	The company rented furnished office space by paying $1,300 cash for the first month's (April) rent.
	3	The company purchased $2,500 of office supplies for cash.
	10	The company paid $2,502 cash for the premium on a 12-month insurance policy. Coverage begins on April 11.
	14	The company paid $2,300 cash for two weeks' salaries earned by employees.
	24	The company collected $16,000 cash on commissions from airlines on tickets obtained for customers.
	28	The company paid $2,400 cash for two weeks' salaries earned by employees.
	29	The company paid $750 cash for minor repairs to the company's computer.
	30	The company paid $550 cash for this month's telephone bill.
	30	Nozomi withdrew $1,200 cash from the company for personal use.

The company's chart of accounts follows:

101	Cash	405	Commissions Earned
106	Accounts Receivable	612	Depreciation Expense—Computer Equip.
124	Office Supplies	622	Salaries Expense
128	Prepaid Insurance	637	Insurance Expense
167	Computer Equipment	640	Rent Expense
168	Accumulated Depreciation—Computer Equip.	650	Office Supplies Expense
209	Salaries Payable	684	Repairs Expense
301	J. Nozomi, Capital	688	Telephone Expense
302	J. Nozomi, Withdrawals	901	Income Summary

Required

1. Use the balance column format to set up each ledger account listed in its chart of accounts.
2. Prepare journal entries to record the transactions for April and post them to the ledger accounts. The company records prepaid and unearned items in balance sheet accounts.
3. Prepare an unadjusted trial balance as of April 30.
4. Use the following information to journalize and post adjusting entries for the month:
   a. Two-thirds of one month's insurance coverage has expired.
   b. At the end of the month, $700 of office supplies are still available.
   c. This month's depreciation on the computer equipment is $500.
   d. Employees earned $720 of unpaid and unrecorded salaries as of month-end.
   e. The company earned $3,050 of commissions that are not yet billed at month-end.
5. Prepare the income statement and the statement of owner's equity for the month of April and the balance sheet at April 30, 2009.
6. Prepare journal entries to close the temporary accounts and post these entries to the ledger.
7. Prepare a post-closing trial balance.

Check (3) Unadj. trial balance totals, $74,000

(4*a*) Dr. Insurance Expense, $139

(5) Net income, $8,591; J. Nozomi, Capital (4/30/2009), $65,391; Total assets, $66,111

(7) P-C trial balance totals, $66,611

Problem 4-3A
Preparing trial balances, closing entries, and financial statements

C3 P2 P3

eXcel
mhhe.com/wildFAP19e

The adjusted trial balance of Charon Repairs on December 31, 2009, follows.

CHARON REPAIRS
Adjusted Trial Balance
December 31, 2009

No.	Account Title	Debit	Credit
101	Cash	$ 16,100	
124	Office supplies	1,300	
128	Prepaid insurance	2,800	
167	Equipment	50,000	
168	Accumulated depreciation—Equipment		$ 5,000
201	Accounts payable		12,000
210	Wages payable		1,400
301	L. Charon, Capital		33,000
302	L. Charon, Withdrawals	16,000	
401	Repair fees earned		98,600
612	Depreciation expense—Equipment	5,000	
623	Wages expense	39,000	
637	Insurance expense	800	
640	Rent expense	13,000	
650	Office supplies expense	3,100	
690	Utilities expense	2,900	
	Totals	$150,000	$150,000

Check (1) Ending capital balance, $51,800; net income, $34,800

(2) P-C trial balance totals, $70,200

Required

1. Prepare an income statement and a statement of owner's equity for the year 2009, and a classified balance sheet at December 31, 2009. There are no owner investments in 2009.

2. Enter the adjusted trial balance in the first two columns of a six-column table. Use columns three and four for closing entry information and the last two columns for a post-closing trial balance. Insert an Income Summary account as the last item in the trial balance.

3. Enter closing entry information in the six-column table and prepare journal entries for it.

Analysis Component

4. Assume for this part only that

a. None of the $800 insurance expense had expired during the year. Instead, assume it is a prepayment of the next period's insurance protection.

b. There are no earned and unpaid wages at the end of the year. (*Hint:* Reverse the $1,400 wages payable accrual.)

Describe the financial statement changes that would result from these two assumptions.

Problem 4-4A
Preparing closing entries, financial statements, and ratios

C3 A1 P2

The adjusted trial balance for Tamar Construction as of December 31, 2009, follows.

TAMAR CONSTRUCTION
Adjusted Trial Balance
December 31, 2009

No.	Account Title	Debit	Credit
101	Cash	$ 7,000	
104	Short-term investments	23,500	
126	Supplies	8,200	
128	Prepaid insurance	7,500	
167	Equipment	45,000	
168	Accumulated depreciation—Equipment		$ 22,500
173	Building	162,000	
174	Accumulated depreciation—Building		54,000
183	Land	66,770	
201	Accounts payable		17,000
203	Interest payable		2,900
208	Rent payable		3,500
210	Wages payable		2,100
213	Property taxes payable		900
233	Unearned professional fees		7,100
251	Long-term notes payable		66,000
301	E. Tamar, Capital		131,700
302	E. Tamar, Withdrawals	11,000	
401	Professional fees earned		102,000
406	Rent earned		15,000
407	Dividends earned		3,000
409	Interest earned		2,200
606	Depreciation expense—Building	11,880	
612	Depreciation expense—Equipment	6,750	
623	Wages expense	30,500	
633	Interest expense	4,700	
637	Insurance expense	8,900	
640	Rent expense	10,900	
652	Supplies expense	5,500	
682	Postage expense	2,500	
683	Property taxes expense	5,000	
684	Repairs expense	6,200	
688	Telephone expense	3,100	
690	Utilities expense	3,000	
	Totals	$429,900	$429,900

E. Tamar invested $7,000 cash in the business during year 2009 (the December 31, 2008, credit balance of the E. Tamar, Capital account was $124,700). Tamar Construction is required to make a $7,500 payment on its long-term notes payable during 2010.

Required

1. Prepare the income statement and the statement of owner's equity for the calendar year 2009 and the classified balance sheet at December 31, 2009.
2. Prepare the necessary closing entries at December 31, 2009.
3. Use the information in the financial statements to compute these ratios: (*a*) return on assets (total assets at December 31, 2008, was $200,000), (*b*) debt ratio, (*c*) profit margin ratio (use total revenues as the denominator), and (*d*) current ratio.

Check (1) Total assets (12/31/2009), $243,470; Net income, $23,270

Problem 4-5A
Preparing a work sheet, adjusting and closing entries, and financial statements

C3 P1 P2

The following unadjusted trial balance is for Archer Construction Co. as of the end of its 2009 fiscal year. The June 30, 2008, credit balance of the owner's capital account was $55,800, and the owner invested $27,000 cash in the company during the 2009 fiscal year.

ARCHER CONSTRUCTION CO.
Unadjusted Trial Balance
June 30, 2009

No.	Account Title	Debit	Credit
101	Cash	$ 17,000	
126	Supplies	7,000	
128	Prepaid insurance	5,500	
167	Equipment	149,200	
168	Accumulated depreciation—Equipment		$ 25,500
201	Accounts payable		5,200
203	Interest payable		0
208	Rent payable		0
210	Wages payable		0
213	Property taxes payable		0
251	Long-term notes payable		20,000
301	G. Archer, Capital		82,800
302	G. Archer, Withdrawals	31,500	
401	Construction fees earned		141,000
612	Depreciation expense—Equipment	0	
623	Wages expense	40,000	
633	Interest expense	2,200	
637	Insurance expense	0	
640	Rent expense	11,000	
652	Supplies expense	0	
683	Property taxes expense	4,900	
684	Repairs expense	2,900	
690	Utilities expense	3,300	
	Totals	$ 274,500	$ 274,500

Required

1. Prepare a 10-column work sheet for fiscal year 2009, starting with the unadjusted trial balance and including adjustments based on these additional facts.
   a. The supplies available at the end of fiscal year 2009 had a cost of $2,520.
   b. The cost of expired insurance for the fiscal year is $3,465.
   c. Annual depreciation on equipment is $8,300.
   d. The June utilities expense of $560 is not included in the unadjusted trial balance because the bill arrived after the trial balance was prepared. The $560 amount owed needs to be recorded.
   e. The company's employees have earned $1,900 of accrued wages at fiscal year-end.
   f. The rent expense incurred and not yet paid or recorded at fiscal year-end is $500.
   g. Additional property taxes of $700 have been assessed for this fiscal year but have not been paid or recorded in the accounts.

h. The long-term note payable bears interest at 12% per year. The unadjusted Interest Expense account equals the amount paid for the first 11 months of the 2009 fiscal year. The $200 accrued interest for June has not yet been paid or recorded. (Note that the company is required to make a $4,500 payment toward the note payable during the 2010 fiscal year.)

2. Use the work sheet to enter the adjusting and closing entries; then journalize them.

3. Prepare the income statement and the statement of owner's equity for the year ended June 30 and the classified balance sheet at June 30, 2009.

Check (3) Total assets, $136,955; Current liabilities, $13,560; Net income, $56,595

Analysis Component

4. Analyze the following separate errors and describe how each would affect the 10-column work sheet. Explain whether the error is likely to be discovered in completing the work sheet and, if not, the effect of the error on the financial statements.

a. Assume that the adjustment for supplies used consisted of a credit to Supplies for $2,520 and a debit for $2,520 to Supplies Expense.

b. When the adjusted trial balance in the work sheet is completed, assume that the $17,000 Cash balance is incorrectly entered in the Credit column.

Problem 4-6A[A]

Preparing adjusting, reversing, and next period entries

P4

The following six-column table for Hunter Golf Range includes the unadjusted trial balance as of December 31, 2009.

HUNTER GOLF RANGE
December 31, 2009

Account Title	Unadjusted Trial Balance		Adjustments		Adjusted Trial Balance	
	Dr.	Cr.	Dr.	Cr.	Dr.	Cr.
Cash	$ 10,000					
Accounts receivable	0					
Supplies	4,230					
Equipment	102,000					
Accumulated depreciation—Equipment		$ 19,584				
Interest payable		0				
Salaries payable		0				
Unearned member fees		10,770				
Notes payable		57,000				
A. J. Hunter, Capital		28,893				
A. J. Hunter, Withdrawals	15,000					
Member fees earned		40,800				
Depreciation expense—Equipment	0					
Salaries expense	21,542					
Interest expense	4,275					
Supplies expense	0					
Totals	$157,047	$157,047				

Required

1. Complete the six-column table by entering adjustments that reflect the following information.

a. As of December 31, 2009, employees had earned $689 of unpaid and unrecorded salaries. The next payday is January 4, at which time $1,226 of salaries will be paid.

b. The cost of supplies still available at December 31, 2009, is $2,076.

c. The notes payable requires an interest payment to be made every three months. The amount of unrecorded accrued interest at December 31, 2009, is $1,425. The next interest payment, at an amount of $1,710, is due on January 15, 2010.

d. Analysis of the unearned member fees account shows $4,308 remaining unearned at December 31, 2009.

e. In addition to the member fees included in the revenue account balance, the company has earned another $6,936 in unrecorded fees that will be collected on January 31, 2010. The company is also expected to collect $8,000 on that same day for new fees earned in January 2010.

f. Depreciation expense for the year is $9,792.

2. Prepare journal entries for the adjustments entered in the six-column table for part 1.

3. Prepare journal entries to reverse the effects of the adjusting entries that involve accruals.

4. Prepare journal entries to record the cash payments and cash collections described for January.

Check (1) Adjusted trial balance totals, $175,889

PROBLEM SET B

Problem 4-1B
Determining balance sheet classifications
C3

In the blank space beside each numbered balance sheet item, enter the letter of its balance sheet classification. If the item should not appear on the balance sheet, enter a *Z* in the blank.

A. Current assets
B. Long-term investments
C. Plant assets
D. Intangible assets
E. Current liabilities
F. Long-term liabilities
G. Equity

_____ **1.** Rent receivable
_____ **2.** Salaries payable
_____ **3.** Income taxes payable
_____ **4.** Owner, Capital
_____ **5.** Office supplies
_____ **6.** Interest payable
_____ **7.** Rent revenue
_____ **8.** Notes receivable (due in 120 days)
_____ **9.** Land (used in operations)
_____ **10.** Depreciation expense—Trucks
_____ **11.** Commissions earned
_____ **12.** Interest receivable
_____ **13.** Long-term investment in stock
_____ **14.** Prepaid insurance
_____ **15.** Machinery
_____ **16.** Notes payable (due in 15 years)
_____ **17.** Copyrights
_____ **18.** Current portion of long-term note payable
_____ **19.** Accumulated depreciation—Trucks
_____ **20.** Office equipment

Problem 4-2B
Applying the accounting cycle
C1 C2 P2 P3

On July 1, 2009, Carl Park created a new self-storage business, Safe Storage Co. The following transactions occurred during the company's first month.

July	1	Park invested $34,000 cash and buildings worth $175,000 in the company.
	2	The company rented equipment by paying $1,500 cash for the first month's (July) rent.
	5	The company purchased $1,300 of office supplies for cash.
	10	The company paid $3,600 cash for the premium on a 12-month insurance policy. Coverage begins on July 11.
	14	The company paid an employee $1,280 cash for two weeks' salary earned.
	24	The company collected $11,500 cash for storage fees from customers.
	28	The company paid $1,320 cash for two weeks' salary earned by an employee.
	29	The company paid $250 cash for minor repairs to a leaking roof.
	30	The company paid $850 cash for this month's telephone bill.
	31	Park withdrew $2,400 cash from the company for personal use.

The company's chart of accounts follows:

101	Cash	401	Storage Fees Earned
106	Accounts Receivable	606	Depreciation Expense—Buildings
124	Office Supplies	622	Salaries Expense
128	Prepaid Insurance	637	Insurance Expense
173	Buildings	640	Rent Expense
174	Accumulated Depreciation—Buildings	650	Office Supplies Expense
209	Salaries Payable	684	Repairs Expense
301	C. Park, Capital	688	Telephone Expense
302	C. Park, Withdrawals	901	Income Summary

Required

1. Use the balance column format to set up each ledger account listed in its chart of accounts.

2. Prepare journal entries to record the transactions for July and post them to the ledger accounts. Record prepaid and unearned items in balance sheet accounts.

Check (3) Unadj. trial balance totals, $220,500

(4*a*) Dr. Insurance Expense, $200

(5) Net income, $5,630; C. Park, Capital (7/31/2009), $212,230; Total assets, $212,800

(7) P-C trial balance totals, $214,550

3. Prepare an unadjusted trial balance as of July 31.
4. Use the following information to journalize and post adjusting entries for the month:
   a. Two-thirds of one month's insurance coverage has expired.
   b. At the end of the month, $800 of office supplies are still available.
   c. This month's depreciation on the buildings is $1,750.
   d. An employee earned $570 of unpaid and unrecorded salary as of month-end.
   e. The company earned $2,350 of storage fees that are not yet billed at month-end.
5. Prepare the income statement and the statement of owner's equity for the month of July and the balance sheet at July 31, 2009.
6. Prepare journal entries to close the temporary accounts and post these entries to the ledger.
7. Prepare a post-closing trial balance.

Problem 4-3B
Preparing trial balances, closing entries, and financial statements
C3 P2 P3

Goldsmith Company's adjusted trial balance on December 31, 2009, follows.

GOLDSMITH COMPANY
Adjusted Trial Balance
December 31, 2009

No.	Account Title	Debit	Credit
101	Cash	$ 10,300	
125	Store supplies	1,400	
128	Prepaid insurance	2,200	
167	Equipment	52,000	
168	Accumulated depreciation—Equipment		$ 9,000
201	Accounts payable		17,000
210	Wages payable		1,300
301	N. Goldsmith, Capital		33,400
302	N. Goldsmith, Withdrawals	16,500	
401	Repair fees earned		91,500
612	Depreciation expense—Equipment	8,500	
623	Wages expense	41,500	
637	Insurance expense	1,000	
640	Rent expense	11,400	
651	Store supplies expense	4,400	
690	Utilities expense	3,000	
	Totals	$152,200	$152,200

Required

Check (1) Ending capital balance, $38,600

(2) P-C trial balance totals, $65,900

1. Prepare an income statement and a statement of owner's equity for the year 2009, and a classified balance sheet at December 31, 2009. There are no owner investments in 2009.
2. Enter the adjusted trial balance in the first two columns of a six-column table. Use the middle two columns for closing entry information and the last two columns for a post-closing trial balance. Insert an Income Summary account (No. 901) as the last item in the trial balance.
3. Enter closing entry information in the six-column table and prepare journal entries for it.

Analysis Component

4. Assume for this part only that
   a. None of the $1,000 insurance expense had expired during the year. Instead, assume it is a prepayment of the next period's insurance protection.
   b. There are no earned and unpaid wages at the end of the year. (*Hint:* Reverse the $1,300 wages payable accrual.)

   Describe the financial statement changes that would result from these two assumptions.

The adjusted trial balance for Myra Co. as of December 31, 2009, follows.

Problem 4-4B
Preparing closing entries, financial statements, and ratios
C3 A1 P2

MYRA COMPANY
Adjusted Trial Balance
December 31, 2009

No.	Account Title	Debit	Credit
101	Cash	$ 7,500	
104	Short-term investments	23,500	
126	Supplies	8,100	
128	Prepaid insurance	8,600	
167	Equipment	40,000	
168	Accumulated depreciation—Equipment		$ 20,000
173	Building	177,000	
174	Accumulated depreciation—Building		59,000
183	Land	68,120	
201	Accounts payable		17,000
203	Interest payable		3,000
208	Rent payable		3,500
210	Wages payable		2,500
213	Property taxes payable		1,300
233	Unearned professional fees		7,900
251	Long-term notes payable		64,500
301	S. Myra, Capital		132,600
302	S. Myra, Withdrawals	10,300	
401	Professional fees earned		104,000
406	Rent earned		18,000
407	Dividends earned		2,500
409	Interest earned		2,300
606	Depreciation expense—Building	12,980	
612	Depreciation expense—Equipment	6,000	
623	Wages expense	27,500	
633	Interest expense	3,800	
637	Insurance expense	7,700	
640	Rent expense	11,300	
652	Supplies expense	6,100	
682	Postage expense	2,800	
683	Property taxes expense	3,400	
684	Repairs expense	6,900	
688	Telephone expense	3,200	
690	Utilities expense	3,300	
	Totals	$438,100	$438,100

S. Myra invested $7,500 cash in the business during year 2009 (the December 31, 2008, credit balance of the S. Myra, Capital account was $125,100). Myra Company is required to make a $6,000 payment on its long-term notes payable during 2010.

Required

1. Prepare the income statement and the statement of owner's equity for the calendar year 2009 and the classified balance sheet at December 31, 2009.

Check (1) Total assets (12/31/2009), $253,820; Net income, $31,820

2. Prepare the necessary closing entries at December 31, 2009.

3. Use the information in the financial statements to calculate these ratios: (*a*) return on assets (total assets at December 31, 2008, were $200,000), (*b*) debt ratio, (*c*) profit margin ratio (use total revenues as the denominator), and (*d*) current ratio.

Problem 4-5B
Preparing a work sheet, adjusting and closing entries, and financial statements

C3 P1 P2

The following unadjusted trial balance is for Brawn Demolition Company as of the end of its April 30, 2009, fiscal year. The April 30, 2008, credit balance of the owner's capital account was $51,610, and the owner invested $30,000 cash in the company during the 2009 fiscal year.

BRAWN DEMOLITION COMPANY
Unadjusted Trial Balance
April 30, 2009

No.	Account Title	Debit	Credit
101	Cash	$ 17,000	
126	Supplies	9,500	
128	Prepaid insurance	6,500	
167	Equipment	140,460	
168	Accumulated depreciation—Equipment		$ 22,000
201	Accounts payable		6,000
203	Interest payable		0
208	Rent payable		0
210	Wages payable		0
213	Property taxes payable		0
251	Long-term notes payable		25,000
301	J. Brawn, Capital		81,610
302	J. Brawn, Withdrawals	25,500	
401	Demolition fees earned		140,000
612	Depreciation expense—Equipment	0	
623	Wages expense	48,000	
633	Interest expense	2,750	
637	Insurance expense	0	
640	Rent expense	15,400	
652	Supplies expense	0	
683	Property taxes expense	4,400	
684	Repairs expense	2,100	
690	Utilities expense	3,000	
	Totals	$ 274,610	$ 274,610

Required

1. Prepare a 10-column work sheet for fiscal year 2009, starting with the unadjusted trial balance and including adjustments based on these additional facts.

a. The supplies available at the end of fiscal year 2009 had a cost of $3,420.

b. The cost of expired insurance for the fiscal year is $4,095.

c. Annual depreciation on equipment is $11,000.

d. The April utilities expense of $580 is not included in the unadjusted trial balance because the bill arrived after the trial balance was prepared. The $580 amount owed needs to be recorded.

e. The company's employees have earned $1,500 of accrued wages at fiscal year-end.

f. The rent expense incurred and not yet paid or recorded at fiscal year-end is $1,400.

g. Additional property taxes of $500 have been assessed for this fiscal year but have not been paid or recorded in the accounts.

h. The long-term note payable bears interest at 12% per year. The unadjusted Interest Expense account equals the amount paid for the first 11 months of the 2009 fiscal year. The $250 accrued interest for April has not yet been paid or recorded. (Note that the company is required to make a $5,000 payment toward the note payable during the 2010 fiscal year.)

2. Enter the adjusting and closing entry information in the work sheet; then journalize it.

3. Prepare the income statement and the statement of owner's equity for the year ended April 30 and the classified balance sheet at April 30, 2009.

Check (3) Total assets, $130,285; current liabilities, $15,230; Net income, $38,945

Analysis Component

4. Analyze the following separate errors and describe how each would affect the 10-column work sheet. Explain whether the error is likely to be discovered in completing the work sheet and, if not, the effect of the error on the financial statements.

a. Assume the adjustment for expiration of the insurance coverage consisted of a credit to Prepaid Insurance for $2,405 and a debit for $2,405 to Insurance Expense.

b. When the adjusted trial balance in the work sheet is completed, assume that the $2,100 Repairs Expense account balance is extended to the Debit column of the balance sheet columns.

Problem 4-6B^A
Preparing adjusting, reversing, and next period entries

P4

The following six-column table for Oberst Co. includes the unadjusted trial balance as of December 31, 2009.

OBERST COMPANY
December 31, 2009

Account Title	Unadjusted Trial Balance		Adjustments		Adjusted Trial Balance	
	Dr.	Cr.	Dr.	Cr.	Dr.	Cr.
Cash	$ 18,500					
Accounts receivable	0					
Supplies	7,825					
Machinery	188,700					
Accumulated depreciation—Machinery		$ 36,230				
Interest payable		0				
Salaries payable		0				
Unearned rental fees		19,924				
Notes payable		54,000				
B. Oberst, Capital		101,044				
B. Oberst, Withdrawals	27,750					
Rental fees earned		75,480				
Depreciation expense—Machinery	0					
Salaries expense	39,853					
Interest expense	4,050					
Supplies expense	0					
Totals	$286,678	$286,678				

Required

1. Complete the six-column table by entering adjustments that reflect the following information:

a. As of December 31, 2009, employees had earned $1,275 of unpaid and unrecorded wages. The next payday is January 4, at which time $2,269 in wages will be paid.

b. The cost of supplies still available at December 31, 2009, is $3,842.

c. The notes payable requires an interest payment to be made every three months. The amount of unrecorded accrued interest at December 31, 2009, is $1,350. The next interest payment, at an amount of $1,620, is due on January 15, 2010.

d. Analysis of the unearned rental fees shows that $7,969 remains unearned at December 31, 2009.

e. In addition to the machinery rental fees included in the revenue account balance, the company has earned another $12,831 in unrecorded fees that will be collected on January 31, 2010. The company is also expected to collect $8,000 on that same day for new fees earned in January 2010.

f. Depreciation expense for the year is $18,115.

2. Prepare journal entries for the adjustments entered in the six-column table for part 1.

3. Prepare journal entries to reverse the effects of the adjusting entries that involve accruals.

4. Prepare journal entries to record the cash payments and cash collections described for January.

Check (1) Adjusted trial balance totals, $320,249

SERIAL PROBLEM

Success Systems P2 P3

(This serial problem began in Chapter 1 and continues through most of the book. If previous chapter segments were not completed, the serial problem can begin at this point. It is helpful, but not necessary, to use the Working Papers that accompany the book.)

SP 4 The December 31, 2009, adjusted trial balance of Success Systems (reflecting its transactions from October through December of 2009) follows.

No.	Account Title	Debit	Credit
101	Cash	$ 58,160	
106	Accounts receivable	5,668	
126	Computer supplies	580	
128	Prepaid insurance	1,665	
131	Prepaid rent	825	
163	Office equipment	8,000	
164	Accumulated depreciation—Office equipment		$ 400
167	Computer equipment	20,000	
168	Accumulated depreciation—Computer equipment		1,250
201	Accounts payable		1,100
210	Wages payable		500
236	Unearned computer services revenue		1,500
301	A. Lopez, Capital		83,000
302	A. Lopez, Withdrawals	7,100	
403	Computer services revenue		31,284
612	Depreciation expense—Office equipment	400	
613	Depreciation expense—Computer equipment	1,250	
623	Wages expense	3,875	
637	Insurance expense	555	
640	Rent expense	2,475	
652	Computer supplies expense	3,065	
655	Advertising expense	2,965	
676	Mileage expense	896	
677	Miscellaneous expenses	250	
684	Repairs expense—Computer	1,305	
901	Income summary		0
	Totals	$119,034	$119,034

Required

1. Record and post the necessary closing entries for Success Systems.
2. Prepare a post-closing trial balance as of December 31, 2009.

Check Post-closing trial balance totals, $94,898

BEYOND THE NUMBERS

REPORTING IN ACTION

C1 P2

BTN 4-1 Refer to **Best Buy**'s financial statements in Appendix A to answer the following.

Required

1. For the fiscal year ended March 3, 2007, what amount is credited to Income Summary to summarize its revenues earned?
2. For the fiscal year ended March 3, 2007, what amount is debited to Income Summary to summarize its expenses incurred?

3. For the fiscal year ended March 3, 2007, what is the balance of its Income Summary account before it is closed?

4. In its statement of cash flows for the year ended March 3, 2007, what amount of cash is paid in dividends to common stockholders?

Fast Forward

5. Access Best Buy's annual report for fiscal years ending after March 3, 2007, at its Website (BestBuy.com) or the SEC's EDGAR database (www.SEC.gov). How has the amount of net income closed to Income Summary changed in the fiscal years ending after March 3, 2007? How has the amount of cash paid as dividends changed in the fiscal years ending after March 3, 2007?

COMPARATIVE ANALYSIS

A1

BTN 4-2 Key figures for the recent two years of **Best Buy** and **RadioShack** follow.

Key Figures ($ thousands)	Best Buy		RadioShack	
	Current Year	Prior Year	Current Year	Prior Year
Current assets	$9,081	$7,985	$1,600	$1,627
Current liabilities	6,301	6,056	984	986

Required

1. Compute the current ratio for both years for both companies.

2. Which company has the better ability to pay short-term obligations according to the current ratio?

3. Analyze and comment on each company's current ratios for the past two years.

4. How do Best Buy's and RadioShack's current ratios compare to their industry average ratio of 1.6?

ETHICS CHALLENGE

C2

BTN 4-3 On January 20, 2009, Tamira Nelson, the accountant for Picton Enterprises, is feeling pressure to complete the annual financial statements. The company president has said he needs up-to-date financial statements to share with the bank on January 21 at a dinner meeting that has been called to discuss Picton's obtaining loan financing for a special building project. Tamira knows that she will not be able to gather all the needed information in the next 24 hours to prepare the entire set of adjusting entries that must be posted before the financial statements accurately portray the company's performance and financial position for the fiscal period ended December 31, 2008. Tamira ultimately decides to estimate several expense accruals at the last minute. When deciding on estimates for the expenses, she uses low estimates because she does not want to make the financial statements look worse than they are. Tamira finishes the financial statements before the deadline and gives them to the president without mentioning that several account balances are estimates that she provided.

Required

1. Identify several courses of action that Tamira could have taken instead of the one she took.

2. If you were in Tamira's situation, what would you have done? Briefly justify your response.

COMMUNICATING IN PRACTICE

C1 P2

BTN 4-4 Assume that one of your classmates states that a company's books should be ongoing and therefore not closed until that business is terminated. Write a half-page memo to this classmate explaining the concept of the closing process by drawing analogies between (1) a scoreboard for an athletic event and the revenue and expense accounts of a business or (2) a sports team's record book and the capital account. (*Hint:* Think about what would happen if the scoreboard is not cleared before the start of a new game.)

TAKING IT TO THE NET

A1

BTN 4-5 Access **Motley Fool**'s discussion of the current ratio at Fool.com/School/Valuation/CurrentAndQuickRatio.htm. (If the page changed, search that site for the *current ratio*.)

Required

1. What level for the current ratio is generally regarded as sufficient to meet near-term operating needs?
2. Once you have calculated the current ratio for a company, what should you compare it against?
3. What are the implications for a company that has a current ratio that is too high?

TEAMWORK IN ACTION

P1 P2 P3

BTN 4-6 The unadjusted trial balance and information for the accounting adjustments of Noseworthy Investigators follow. Each team member involved in this project is to assume one of the four responsibilities listed. After completing each of these responsibilities, the team should work together to prove the accounting equation utilizing information from teammates (1 and 4). If your equation does not balance, you are to work as a team to resolve the error. The team's goal is to complete the task as quickly and accurately as possible.

Unadjusted Trial Balance

Account Title	Debit	Credit
Cash	$16,000	
Supplies	12,000	
Prepaid insurance	3,000	
Equipment	25,000	
Accumulated depreciation—Equipment		$ 7,000
Accounts payable		3,000
D. Noseworthy, Capital		34,000
D. Noseworthy, Withdrawals	6,000	
Investigation fees earned		33,000
Rent expense	15,000	
Totals	$77,000	$77,000

Additional Year-End Information

a. Insurance that expired in the current period amounts to $2,200.
b. Equipment depreciation for the period is $4,000.
c. Unused supplies total $5,000 at period-end.
d. Services in the amount of $800 have been provided but have not been billed or collected.

Responsibilities for Individual Team Members

1. Determine the accounts and adjusted balances to be extended to the balance sheet columns of the work sheet for Noseworthy. Also determine total assets and total liabilities.
2. Determine the adjusted revenue account balance and prepare the entry to close this account.
3. Determine the adjusted account balances for expenses and prepare the entry to close these accounts.
4. Prepare T-accounts for both D. Noseworthy, Capital (reflecting the unadjusted trial balance amount) and Income Summary. Prepare the third and fourth closing entries. Ask teammates assigned to parts 2 and 3 for the postings for Income Summary. Obtain amounts to complete the third closing entry and post both the third and fourth closing entries. Provide the team with the ending capital account balance.
5. The entire team should prove the accounting equation using post-closing balances.

ENTREPRENEURIAL DECISION

A1 C3 P2

BTN 4-7 Review this chapter's opening feature involving Kathryn Kerrigan and her shoe business.

1. Explain how a classified balance sheet can help Kathryn Kerrigan know what bills are due when, and whether she has the resources to pay those bills.

2. Why is it important for Kathryn Kerrigan to match costs and revenues in a specific time period? How do closing entries help her in this regard?

3. What objectives are met when Kathryn Kerrigan applies closing procedures each fiscal year-end?

HITTING THE ROAD

C2

BTN 4-8 Select a company that you can visit in person or interview on the telephone. Call ahead to the company to arrange a time when you can interview an employee (preferably an accountant) who helps prepare the annual financial statements. Inquire about the following aspects of its *accounting cycle:*

1. Does the company prepare interim financial statements? What time period(s) is used for interim statements?

2. Does the company use the cash or accrual basis of accounting?

3. Does the company use a work sheet in preparing financial statements? Why or why not?

4. Does the company use a spreadsheet program? If so, which software program is used?

5. How long does it take after the end of its reporting period to complete annual statements?

GLOBAL DECISION

A1

DSG

BTN 4-9 **DSG international plc** is the United Kingdom's largest retailer of consumer electronics. Access its financial statements for the year ended April 28, 2007, at the company's Website (www.DSGiplc.com). The following selected information is available from DSG's financial statements.

(£ millions)	Current Year	Prior Year
Current assets	£2,067	£2,094
Current liabilities	1,869	1,749

Required

1. Compute DSG's current ratio for both the current year and the prior year.

2. Comment on any change from the prior year to the current year for the current ratio.

ANSWERS TO MULTIPLE CHOICE QUIZ

1. e

2. c

3. a

4. c

5. b

A Look Back

Chapters 3 and 4 focused on the final steps of the accounting process. We explained the importance of proper revenue and expense recognition and described the adjusting and closing processes. We also prepared financial statements.

A Look at This Chapter

This chapter emphasizes merchandising activities. We explain how reporting merchandising activities differs from reporting service activities. We also analyze and record merchandise purchases and sales transactions, and explain the adjustments and closing process for merchandisers.

A Look Ahead

Chapter 6 extends our analysis of merchandising activities and focuses on the valuation of inventory. Topics include the items in inventory, costs assigned, costing methods used, and inventory estimation techniques.

Chapter 5 Accounting for Merchandising Operations

Learning Objectives

CAP

Conceptual

C1 Describe merchandising activities and identify income components for a merchandising company. *(p. 178)*

C2 Identify and explain the inventory asset of a merchandising company. *(p. 179)*

C3 Describe both perpetual and periodic inventory systems. *(p. 179)*

C4 Analyze and interpret cost flows and operating activities of a merchandising company. *(p. 187)*

Analytical

A1 Compute the acid-test ratio and explain its use to assess liquidity. *(p. 193)*

A2 Compute the gross margin ratio and explain its use to assess profitability. *(p. 193)*

Procedural

P1 Analyze and record transactions for merchandise purchases using a perpetual system. *(p. 180)*

P2 Analyze and record transactions for merchandise sales using a perpetual system. *(p. 185)*

P3 Prepare adjustments and close accounts for a merchandising company. *(p. 188)*

P4 Define and prepare multiple-step and single-step income statements. *(p. 191)*

P5 *Appendix 5A*—Record and compare merchandising transactions using both periodic and perpetual inventory systems. *(p. 198)*

LP5

Decision Feature

Toy Story

"I've always been a gambler... but we were also growing exponentially the first few years" — Joel Boblit

SOMERSET, WI—Joel Boblit says his first and greatest business challenge was "being teased by my friends." But now Joel is having the time of his life. His retail business, **BigBadToyStore (BigBadToyStore.com),** deals in new and old action figures. Launched from his parents' basement, the store now projects over $4 million in annual sales.

But the early years were not easy. "I mortgaged everything I owned for the first two years," explains Joel. The business required a merchandising accounting system that Joel says needed to account for purchases and sales transactions. Inventory was especially important to account for. "Many of the store's customers offered inventory suggestions," explains Joel.

To succeed, Joel needed to make smart business decisions. He set up an accounting system to capture and communicate costs and sales information. Tracking merchandising activities was necessary to set prices and to manage discounts, allowances, and returns of both sales and purchases. A perpetual inventory system enabled Joel to stock the right type and amount of merchandise and to avoid the costs of out-of-stock and excess inventory. "We're [now] able to make much more efficient use of the space we have," recounts Joel.

Mastering accounting for merchandising is a means to an end for Joel. He says he loves his business and enjoys the nostalgia of childhood toys. Joel insists, however, that he will continue to take risks. "I've always been a gambler," insists Joel, and "I've always [believed] . . . that the harder you work, the more you'll be paid."

[Sources: *BigBadToyStore Website,* January 2009; *Entrepreneur,* December and October 2005; *St. Croix Chronicle,* March–April 2005; *Alma Matters,* Fall 2005; *YouMakeMillions.blogspot.com*, May 2007]

Buyers of merchandise expect many products, discount prices, inventory on demand, and high quality. This chapter introduces the accounting practices used by companies engaged in merchandising. We show how financial statements reflect merchandising activities and explain the new financial statement items created by merchandising activities. We also analyze and record merchandise purchases and sales, and explain the adjustments and the closing process for these companies.

Accounting for Merchandising Operations

Merchandising Activities
- Reporting income
- Reporting inventory
- Operating cycles
- Inventory systems

Merchandising Purchases
- Purchase discounts
- Purchase returns and allowances
- Transportation costs

Merchandising Sales
- Sales of merchandise
- Sales discounts
- Sales returns and allowances

Accounting Cycle
- Adjusting entries
- Preparing financial statements
- Closing entries

Financial Statement Formats
- Multiple-step income statement
- Single-step income statement
- Classified balance sheet

Merchandising Activities

C1 Describe merchandising activities and identify income components for a merchandising company.

Previous chapters emphasized the accounting and reporting activities of service companies. A merchandising company's activities differ from those of a service company. **Merchandise** consists of products, also called *goods,* that a company acquires to resell to customers. A **merchandiser** earns net income by buying and selling merchandise. Merchandisers are often identified as either wholesalers or retailers. A **wholesaler** is an *intermediary* that buys products from manufacturers or other wholesalers and sells them to retailers or other wholesalers. A **retailer** is an intermediary that buys products from manufacturers or wholesalers and sells them to consumers. Many retailers sell both products and services.

Video5.1

Reporting Income for a Merchandiser

Net income for a merchandiser equals revenues from selling merchandise minus both the cost of merchandise sold to customers and the cost of other expenses for the period, see Exhibit 5.1.

EXHIBIT 5.1

Computing Income for a Merchandising Company versus a Service Company

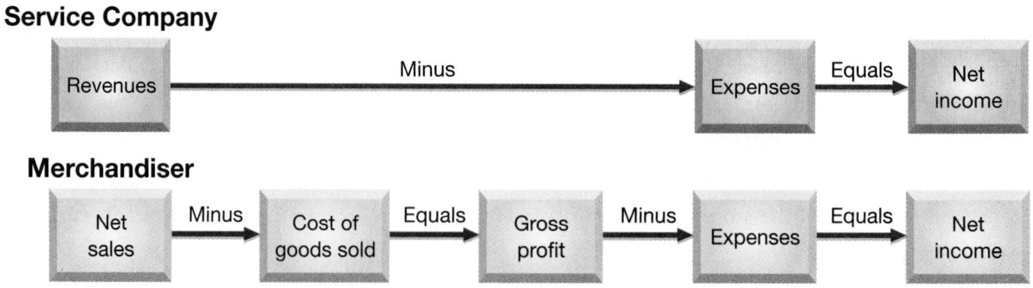

The usual accounting term for revenues from selling merchandise is *sales,* and the term used for the expense of buying and preparing the merchandise is **cost of goods sold.** (Some service companies use the term *sales* instead of revenues; and cost of goods sold is also called *cost of sales.*)

The income statement for Z-Mart in Exhibit 5.2 illustrates these key components of a merchandiser's net income. The first two lines show that products are acquired at a cost of $230,400 and sold for $314,700. The third line shows an $84,300 **gross profit,** also called

Point: Fleming, SuperValu, and SYSCO are wholesalers. Gap, Oakley, Target, and Wal-Mart are retailers.

EXHIBIT 5.2

Merchandiser's Income Statement

Z-MART Income Statement For Year Ended December 31, 2009	
Net sales	$314,700
Cost of goods sold	**230,400**
Gross profit	**84,300**
Expenses	71,400
Net income	$ 12,900

gross margin, which equals net sales less cost of goods sold. Additional expenses of $71,400 are reported, which leaves $12,900 in net income.

Point: Analysis of gross profit is important to effective business decisions, and is described later in the chapter.

Reporting Inventory for a Merchandiser

C2 Identify and explain the inventory asset of a merchandising company.

A merchandiser's balance sheet includes a current asset called *merchandise inventory,* an item not on a service company's balance sheet. **Merchandise inventory,** or simply *inventory,* refers to products that a company owns and intends to sell. The cost of this asset includes the cost incurred to buy the goods, ship them to the store, and make them ready for sale.

Operating Cycle for a Merchandiser

A merchandising company's operating cycle begins by purchasing merchandise and ends by collecting cash from selling the merchandise. The length of an operating cycle differs across the types of businesses. Department stores often have operating cycles of two to five months. Operating cycles for grocery merchants usually range from two to eight weeks.

Exhibit 5.3 illustrates an operating cycle for a merchandiser with credit sales. The cycle moves from (*a*) cash purchases of merchandise to (*b*) inventory for sale to (*c*) credit sales to (*d*) accounts receivable to (*e*) cash. Companies try to keep their operating cycles short because assets tied up in inventory and receivables are not productive. Cash sales shorten operating cycles.

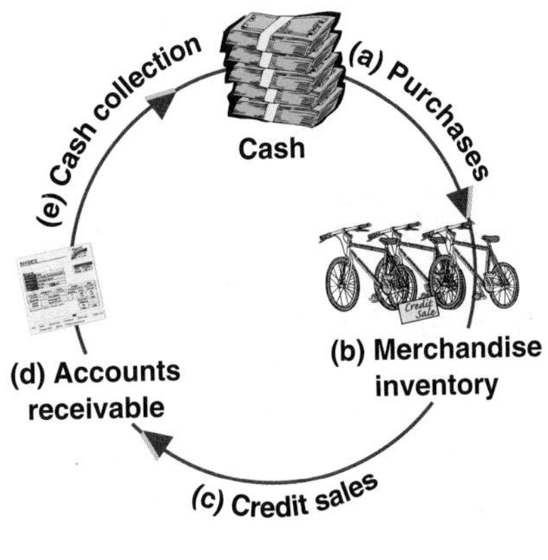

EXHIBIT 5.3

Merchandiser's Operating Cycle

Inventory Systems

C3 Describe both perpetual and periodic inventory systems.

Cost of goods sold is the cost of merchandise sold to customers during a period. It is often the largest single expense on a merchandiser's income statement. **Inventory** refers to products a company owns and expects to sell in its normal operations. Exhibit 5.4 shows that a company's merchandise available for sale consists of what it begins with (beginning

EXHIBIT 5.4

Merchandiser's Cost Flow for a Single Time Period

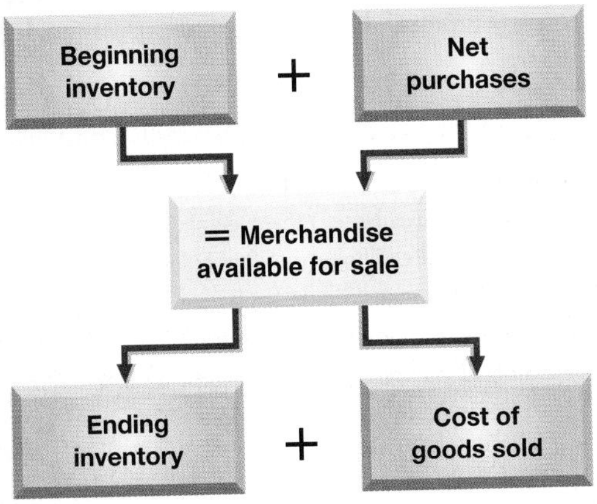

inventory) and what it purchases (net purchases). The merchandise available is either sold (cost of goods sold) or kept for future sales (ending inventory).

Two alternative inventory accounting systems can be used to collect information about cost of goods sold and cost of inventory: *perpetual system* or *periodic system*. The **perpetual inventory system** continually updates accounting records for merchandising transactions—specifically, for those records of inventory available for sale and inventory sold. The **periodic inventory system** updates the accounting records for merchandise transactions only at the *end of a period*. Technological advances and competitive pressures have dramatically increased the use of the perpetual system. (Some companies use a *hybrid* system where the perpetual system is used for tracking units available and the periodic system is used to compute cost of sales.)

Point: Growth of superstores such as **Costco** and **Sam's** is fueled by efficient use of perpetual inventory.

Quick Check Answers—p. 204

1. Describe a merchandiser's cost of goods sold.
2. What is gross profit for a merchandising company?
3. Explain why use of the perpetual inventory system has dramatically increased.

The following sections on purchasing, selling, and adjusting merchandise use the perpetual system. Appendix 5A uses the periodic system (with the perpetual results on the side). An instructor can choose to cover either one or both inventory systems.

Accounting for Merchandise Purchases

P1 Analyze and record transactions for merchandise purchases using a perpetual system.

The cost of merchandise purchased for resale is recorded in the Merchandise Inventory asset account. To illustrate, Z-Mart records a $1,200 cash purchase of merchandise on November 2 as follows:

Nov. 2	Merchandise Inventory	1,200	
	Cash		1,200
	Purchased merchandise for cash.		

Assets = Liabilities + Equity
+1,200
−1,200

The invoice for this merchandise is shown in Exhibit 5.5. The buyer usually receives the original invoice, and the seller keeps a copy. This *source document* serves as the purchase invoice of Z-Mart (buyer) and the sales invoice for Trex (seller). The amount recorded for merchandise inventory includes its purchase cost, shipping fees, taxes, and any other costs necessary to make it ready for sale. This section explains how we compute the recorded cost of merchandise purchases.

Point: The Merchandise Inventory account reflects the cost of goods available for resale.

Decision Insight

Trade Discounts When a manufacturer or wholesaler prepares a catalog of items it has for sale, it usually gives each item a **list price,** also called a *catalog price*. However, an item's intended *selling price* equals list price minus a given percent called a **trade discount.** The amount of trade discount usually depends on whether a buyer is a wholesaler, retailer, or final consumer. A wholesaler buying in large quantities is often granted a larger discount than a retailer buying in smaller quantities. A buyer records the net amount of list price minus trade discount. For example, in the November 2 purchase of merchandise by Z-Mart, the merchandise was listed in the seller's catalog at $2,000 and Z-Mart received a 40% trade discount. This meant that Z-Mart's purchase price was $1,200, computed as $2,000 − (40% × $2,000).

EXHIBIT 5.5

Invoice

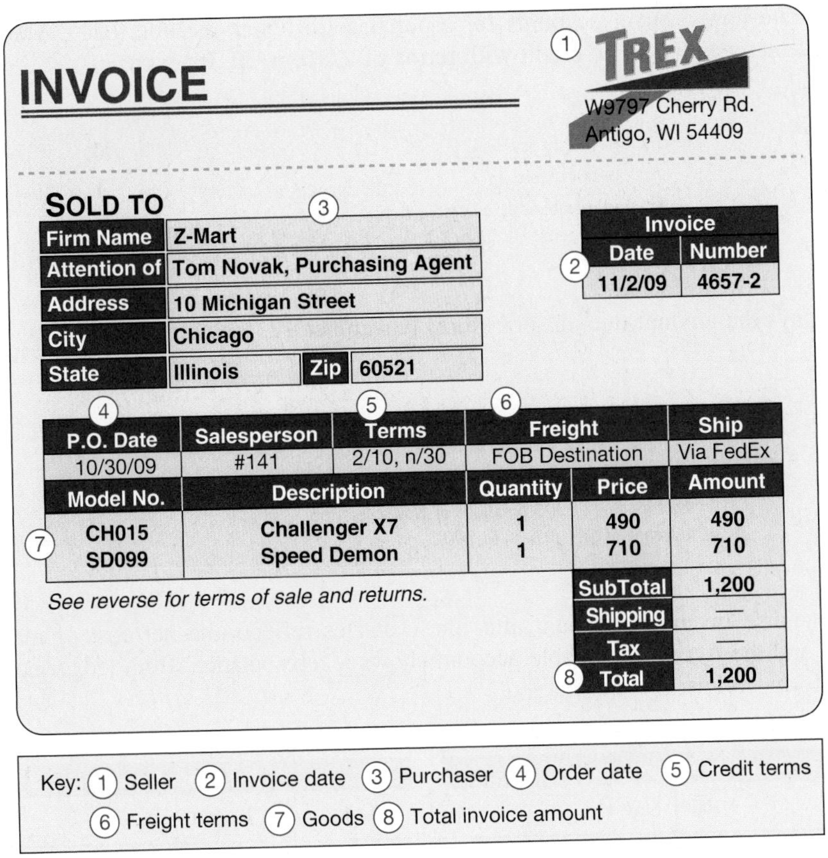
INVOICE

(1) TREX
W9797 Cherry Rd.
Antigo, WI 54409

SOLD TO (3)

Firm Name	Z-Mart
Attention of	Tom Novak, Purchasing Agent
Address	10 Michigan Street
City	Chicago
State	Illinois — Zip 60521

(2)

Invoice Date	Invoice Number
11/2/09	4657-2

P.O. Date (4)	Salesperson	Terms (5)	Freight (6)	Ship
10/30/09	#141	2/10, n/30	FOB Destination	Via FedEx

Model No.	Description	Quantity	Price	Amount
(7) CH015	Challenger X7	1	490	490
SD099	Speed Demon	1	710	710

See reverse for terms of sale and returns.

SubTotal	1,200
Shipping	—
Tax	—
(8) Total	1,200

Key: (1) Seller (2) Invoice date (3) Purchaser (4) Order date (5) Credit terms (6) Freight terms (7) Goods (8) Total invoice amount

Purchase Discounts

The purchase of goods on credit requires a clear statement of expected future payments and dates to avoid misunderstandings. **Credit terms** for a purchase include the amounts and timing of payments from a buyer to a seller. Credit terms usually reflect an industry's practices. To illustrate, when sellers require payment within 10 days after the end of the month of the invoice date, the invoice will show credit terms as "n/10 EOM," which stands for net 10 days after end of month (**EOM**). When sellers require payment within 30 days after the invoice date, the invoice shows credit terms of "n/30," which stands for *net 30 days*.

Exhibit 5.6 portrays credit terms. The amount of time allowed before full payment is due is called the **credit period.** Sellers can grant a **cash discount** to encourage buyers to pay earlier. A buyer views a cash discount as a **purchase discount.** A seller views a cash discount as a **sales discount.** Any cash discounts are described in the credit terms on the invoice. For example, credit terms of "2/10, n/60" mean that full payment is due within a 60-day credit period, but the buyer can deduct 2% of the invoice amount if payment is made within 10 days of the invoice date. This reduced payment applies only for the **discount period.**

Point: Since both the buyer and seller know the invoice date, this date is used in setting the discount and credit periods.

EXHIBIT 5.6

Credit Terms

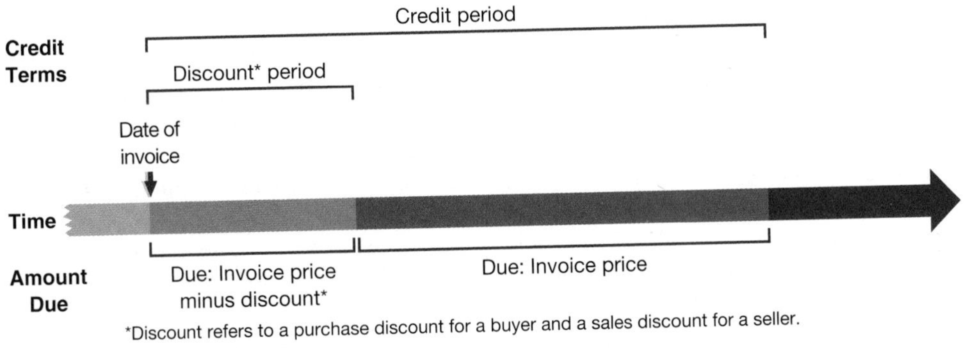

Point: Appendix 5A repeats journal entries *a* through *f* using a periodic inventory system.

To illustrate how a buyer accounts for a purchase discount, assume that Z-Mart's $1,200 purchase of merchandise is on credit with terms of 2/10, n/30. Its entry is

Assets	= Liabilities	+ Equity
+1,200	+1,200	

(a) Nov. 2	Merchandise Inventory	1,200	
	Accounts Payable		1,200
	Purchased merchandise on credit, invoice dated Nov. 2, terms 2/10, n/30.		

If Z-Mart pays the amount due on (or before) November 12, the entry is

Assets	= Liabilities	+ Equity
−24	−1,200	
−1,176		

(b) Nov. 12	Accounts Payable	1,200	
	Merchandise Inventory		24
	Cash		1,176
	Paid for the $1,200 purchase of Nov. 2 less the discount of $24 (2% × $1,200).		

Point: These entries illustrate what is called the *gross method* of accounting for purchases with discount terms.

The Merchandise Inventory account after these entries reflects the net cost of merchandise purchased, and the Accounts Payable account shows a zero balance. Both ledger accounts, in T-account form, follow:

Merchandise Inventory			
Nov. 2	1,200	Nov. 12	24
Balance	1,176		

Accounts Payable			
Nov. 12	1,200	Nov. 2	1,200
		Balance	0

A buyer's failure to pay within a discount period can be expensive. To illustrate, if Z-Mart does not pay within the 10-day 2% discount period, it can delay payment by 20 more days. This delay costs Z-Mart $24, computed as 2% × $1,200. Most buyers take advantage of a purchase discount because of the usually high interest rate implied from not taking it.[1] Also, good cash management means that no invoice is paid until the last day of the discount or credit period.

Decision Maker

Entrepreneur You purchase a batch of products on terms of 3/10, n/90, but your company has limited cash and you must borrow funds at an 11% annual rate if you are to pay within the discount period. Do you take advantage of the purchase discount? [Answer—p. 203]

Purchase Returns and Allowances

Point: The sender (maker) of a *debit memorandum* will debit the account of the memo's receiver. The memo's receiver will credit the sender's account.

Purchase returns refer to merchandise a buyer acquires but then returns to the seller. A *purchase allowance* is a reduction in the cost of defective or unacceptable merchandise that a buyer acquires. Buyers often keep defective but still marketable merchandise if the seller grants an acceptable allowance. When a buyer returns or takes an allowance on merchandise, the buyer issues a **debit memorandum** to inform the seller of a debit made to the seller's account in the buyer's records.

[1] The *implied annual interest rate* formula is:

(365 days ÷ [Credit period − Discount period]) × Cash discount rate.

For terms of 2/10, n/30, missing the 2% discount for an additional 20 days is equal to an annual interest rate of 36.5%, computed as (365 days/[30 days − 10 days]) × 2% discount rate. *Favorable purchase discounts* are those with implied annual interest rates that exceed the purchaser's annual rate for borrowing money.

Purchase Allowances To illustrate purchase allowances, assume that on November 15, Z-Mart (buyer) issues a $300 debit memorandum for an allowance from Trex for defective merchandise. Z-Mart's November 15 entry to update its Merchandise Inventory account to reflect the purchase allowance is

(c) Nov. 15	Accounts Payable	300	
	Merchandise Inventory.		300
	Allowance for defective merchandise.		

Assets = Liabilities + Equity
−300 −300

The buyer's allowance for defective merchandise is usually offset against the buyer's current account payable balance to the seller. When cash is refunded, the Cash account is debited instead of Accounts Payable.

Purchase Returns Returns are recorded at the net costs charged to buyers. To illustrate the accounting for returns, suppose Z-Mart purchases $1,000 of merchandise on June 1 with terms 2/10, n/60. Two days later, Z-Mart returns $100 of goods before paying the invoice. When Z-Mart later pays on June 11, it takes the 2% discount only on the $900 remaining balance. When goods are returned, a buyer can take a purchase discount on only the remaining balance of the invoice. The resulting discount is $18 (2% × $900) and the cash payment is $882 ($900 − $18). The following entries reflect this illustration.

June 1	Merchandise Inventory	1,000	
	Accounts Payable		1,000
	Purchased merchandise, invoice dated June 1, terms 2/10, n/60.		
June 3	Accounts Payable	100	
	Merchandise Inventory.		100
	Returned merchandise to seller.		
June 11	Accounts Payable	900	
	Merchandise Inventory	18	
	Cash		882
	Paid for $900 merchandise ($1,000 − $100) less $18 discount (2% × $900).		

Example: Assume Z-Mart pays $980 cash for $1,000 of merchandise purchased within its 2% discount period. Later, it returns $100 of the original $1,000 merchandise. The return entry is
Cash 98
Merchandise Inventory . . . 98

Decision Ethics

Credit Manager As a new credit manager, you are being trained by the outgoing manager. She explains that the system prepares checks for amounts net of favorable cash discounts, and the checks are dated the last day of the discount period. She also tells you that checks are not mailed until five days later, adding that "the company gets free use of cash for an extra five days, and our department looks better. When a supplier complains, we blame the computer system and the mailroom." Do you continue this payment policy? [Answer—p. 203]

Transportation Costs and Ownership Transfer

The buyer and seller must agree on who is responsible for paying any freight costs and who bears the risk of loss during transit for merchandising transactions. This is essentially the same as asking at what point ownership transfers from the seller to the buyer. The point of transfer is called the **FOB** (*free on board*) point, which determines who pays transportation costs (and often other incidental costs of transit such as insurance).

Exhibit 5.7 identifies two alternative points of transfer. (1) *FOB shipping point,* also called *FOB factory,* means the buyer accepts ownership when the goods depart the seller's place of business. The buyer is then responsible for paying shipping costs and bearing the risk of damage or loss when goods are in transit. The goods are part of the buyer's inventory when they are in transit since ownership has transferred to the buyer. **Cannondale**, a bike manufacturer,

EXHIBIT 5.7

Ownership Transfer and Transportation Costs

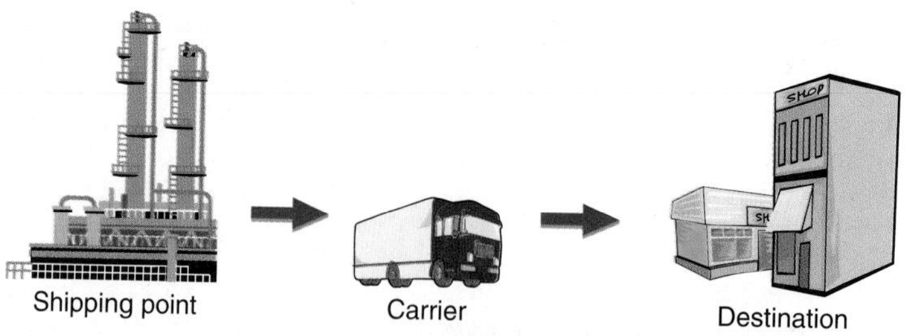

	Ownership Transfers when Goods Passed to	Transportation Costs Paid by
FOB shipping point	Carrier	Buyer
FOB destination	Buyer	Seller

Point: The party not responsible for shipping costs sometimes pays the carrier. In these cases, the party paying these costs either bills the party responsible or, more commonly, adjusts its account payable or account receivable with the other party. For example, a buyer paying a carrier when terms are FOB destination can decrease its account payable to the seller by the amount of shipping cost.

uses FOB shipping point. (2) *FOB destination* means ownership of goods transfers to the buyer when the goods arrive at the buyer's place of business. The seller is responsible for paying shipping charges and bears the risk of damage or loss in transit. The seller does not record revenue from this sale until the goods arrive at the destination because this transaction is not complete before that point.

Z-Mart's $1,200 purchase on November 2 is on terms of FOB destination. This means Z-Mart is not responsible for paying transportation costs. When a buyer is responsible for paying transportation costs, the payment is made to a carrier or directly to the seller depending on the agreement. The cost principle requires that any necessary transportation costs of a buyer (often called *transportation-in* or *freight-in*) be included as part of the cost of purchased merchandise. To illustrate, Z-Mart's entry to record a $75 freight charge from an independent carrier for merchandise purchased FOB shipping point is

Assets = Liabilities + Equity
+75
−75

(*d*) Nov. 24	Merchandise Inventory	75	
	Cash		75
	Paid freight costs on purchased merchandise.		

A seller records the costs of shipping goods to customers in a Delivery Expense account when the seller is responsible for these costs. Delivery Expense, also called *transportation-out* or *freight-out,* is reported as a selling expense in the seller's income statement.

In summary, purchases are recorded as debits to Merchandise Inventory. Any later purchase discounts, returns, and allowances are credited (decreases) to Merchandise Inventory. Transportation-in is debited (added) to Merchandise Inventory. Z-Mart's itemized costs of merchandise purchases for year 2009 are in Exhibit 5.8.

EXHIBIT 5.8

Itemized Costs of Merchandise Purchases

Z-MART
Itemized Costs of Merchandise Purchases
For Year Ended December 31, 2009

Invoice cost of merchandise purchases	$235,800
Less: Purchase discounts received	(4,200)
Purchase returns and allowances	(1,500)
Add: Costs of transportation-in	2,300
Total cost of merchandise purchases	**$232,400**

Point: Some companies have separate accounts for purchase discounts, returns and allowances, and transportation-in. These accounts are then transferred to Merchandise Inventory at period-end. This is a *hybrid system* of perpetual and periodic. That is, Merchandise Inventory is updated on a perpetual basis but only for purchases and cost of goods sold.

The accounting system described here does not provide separate records (accounts) for total purchases, total purchase discounts, total purchase returns and allowances, and total transportation-in. Yet nearly all companies collect this information in supplementary records because managers need this information to evaluate and control each of these cost elements. **Supplementary records,** also called *supplemental records,* refer to information outside the usual general ledger accounts.

Quick Check

Answers—p. 204

4. How long are the credit and discount periods when credit terms are 2/10, n/60?
5. Identify which items are subtracted from the *list* amount and not recorded when computing purchase price: (*a*) freight-in; (*b*) trade discount; (*c*) purchase discount; (*d*) purchase return.
6. What does *FOB* mean? What does *FOB destination* mean?

Accounting for Merchandise Sales

Merchandising companies also must account for sales, sales discounts, sales returns and allowances, and cost of goods sold. A merchandising company such as Z-Mart reflects these items in its gross profit computation, as shown in Exhibit 5.9. This section explains how this information is derived from transactions.

EXHIBIT 5.9

Gross Profit Computation

Z-MART
Computation of Gross Profit
For Year Ended December 31, 2009

Sales		$321,000
Less: Sales discounts	$4,300	
Sales returns and allowances	2,000	6,300
Net sales		314,700
Cost of goods sold		230,400
Gross profit		**$ 84,300**

Sales of Merchandise

P2 Analyze and record transactions for merchandise sales using a perpetual system.

Each sales transaction for a seller of merchandise involves two parts. One part is the revenue received in the form of an asset from a customer. The second part is the recognition of the cost of merchandise sold to a customer. Accounting for a sales transaction under the perpetual system requires recording information about both parts. This means that each sales transaction for merchandisers, whether for cash or on credit, requires two entries: one for revenue and one for cost. To illustrate, Z-Mart sold $2,400 of merchandise on credit on November 3. The revenue part of this transaction is recorded as

(e) Nov. 3	Accounts Receivable	2,400	
	Sales		2,400
	Sold merchandise on credit.		

Assets = Liabilities + Equity
+2,400 +2,400

This entry reflects an increase in Z-Mart's assets in the form of an accounts receivable. It also shows the increase in revenue (Sales). If the sale is for cash, the debit is to Cash instead of Accounts Receivable.

The cost part of each sales transaction ensures that the Merchandise Inventory account under a perpetual inventory system reflects the updated cost of the merchandise available for sale. For example, the cost of the merchandise Z-Mart sold on November 3 is $1,600, and the entry to record the cost part of this sales transaction is

(e) Nov. 3	Cost of Goods Sold	1,600	
	Merchandise Inventory		1,600
	To record the cost of Nov. 3 sale.		

Assets = Liabilities + Equity
−1,600 −1,600

Decision Insight

Suppliers and Demands Large merchandising companies often bombard suppliers with demands. These include discounts for bar coding and technology support systems, and fines for shipping errors. Merchandisers' goals are to reduce inventories, shorten lead times, and eliminate errors.

Sales Discounts

Sales discounts on credit sales can benefit a seller by decreasing the delay in receiving cash and reducing future collection efforts. At the time of a credit sale, a seller does not know whether a customer will pay within the discount period and take advantage of a discount. This means the seller usually does not record a sales discount until a customer actually pays within the discount period. To illustrate, Z-Mart completes a credit sale for $1,000 on November 12 with terms of 2/10, n/60. The entry to record the revenue part of this sale is

Assets	= Liabilities	+ Equity
+1,000		+1,000

Nov. 12	Accounts Receivable	1,000	
	Sales		1,000
	Sold merchandise under terms of 2/10, n/60.		

This entry records the receivable and the revenue as if the customer will pay the full amount. The customer has two options, however. One option is to wait 60 days until January 11 and pay the full $1,000. In this case, Z-Mart records that payment as

Assets	= Liabilities	+ Equity
+1,000		
−1,000		

Jan. 11	Cash	1,000	
	Accounts Receivable		1,000
	Received payment for Nov. 12 sale.		

The customer's second option is to pay $980 within a 10-day period ending November 22. If the customer pays on (or before) November 22, Z-Mart records the payment as

Assets	= Liabilities	+ Equity
+980		−20
−1,000		

Nov. 22	Cash	980	
	Sales Discounts	20	
	Accounts Receivable		1,000
	Received payment for Nov. 12 sale less discount.		

Sales Discounts is a contra revenue account, meaning the Sales Discounts account is deducted from the Sales account when computing a company's net sales (see Exhibit 5.9). Management monitors Sales Discounts to assess the effectiveness and cost of its discount policy.

Sales Returns and Allowances

Point: Published income statements rarely disclose sales discounts, returns and allowances.

Sales returns refer to merchandise that customers return to the seller after a sale. Many companies allow customers to return merchandise for a full refund. *Sales allowances* refer to reductions in the selling price of merchandise sold to customers. This can occur with damaged or defective merchandise that a customer is willing to purchase with a decrease in selling price. Sales returns and allowances usually involve dissatisfied customers and the possibility of lost future sales, and managers monitor information about returns and allowances.

Sales Returns To illustrate, recall Z-Mart's sale of merchandise on November 3 for $2,400 that had cost $1,600. Assume that the customer returns part of the merchandise on November 6, and the returned items sell for $800 and cost $600. The revenue part of this transaction must reflect the decrease in sales from the customer's return of merchandise as follows:

Assets	= Liabilities	+ Equity
−800		−800

(f) Nov. 6	Sales Returns and Allowances	800	
	Accounts Receivable		800
	Customer returns merchandise of Nov. 3 sale.		

If the merchandise returned to Z-Mart is not defective and can be resold to another customer, Z-Mart returns these goods to its inventory. The entry to restore the cost of such goods to the Merchandise Inventory account is

Nov. 6	Merchandise Inventory	600	
	Cost of Goods Sold		600
	Returned goods added to inventory.		

Assets	=	Liabilities	+	Equity
+600				+600

This entry changes if the goods returned are defective. In this case the returned inventory is recorded at its estimated value, not its cost. To illustrate, if the goods (costing $600) returned to Z-Mart are defective and estimated to be worth $150, the following entry is made: Dr. Merchandise Inventory for $150, Dr. Loss from Defective Merchandise for $450, and Cr. Cost of Goods Sold for $600.

Decision Insight

Return to Sender Book merchandisers such as **Barnes & Noble, Borders Books, Books-A-Million,** and **Waldenbooks** can return unsold books to publishers at purchase price. Publishers say returns of new hardcover books run between 35% and 50%.

Sales Allowances To illustrate sales allowances, assume that $800 of the merchandise Z-Mart sold on November 3 is defective but the buyer decides to keep it because Z-Mart offers a $100 price reduction. Z-Mart records this allowance as follows:

Nov. 6	Sales Returns and Allowances	100	
	Accounts Receivable		100
	To record sales allowance on Nov. 3 sale.		

Assets	=	Liabilities	+	Equity
−100				−100

The seller usually prepares a credit memorandum to confirm a buyer's return or allowance. A seller's **credit memorandum** informs a buyer of the seller's credit to the buyer's Account Receivable (on the seller's books).

Point: The sender (maker) of a credit memorandum will *credit* the account of the receiver. The receiver of a credit memorandum will *debit* the sender's account.

Quick Check

Answers—p. 204

7. Why are sales discounts and sales returns and allowances recorded in contra revenue accounts instead of directly in the Sales account?
8. Under what conditions are two entries necessary to record a sales return?
9. When merchandise is sold on credit and the seller notifies the buyer of a price allowance, does the seller create and send a credit memorandum or a debit memorandum?

Completing the Accounting Cycle

Exhibit 5.10 shows the flow of merchandising costs during a period and where these costs are reported at period-end. Specifically, beginning inventory plus the net cost of purchases is the merchandise available for sale. As inventory is sold, its cost is recorded in cost of goods sold on the income statement; what remains is ending inventory on the balance sheet. A period's ending inventory is the next period's beginning inventory.

C4 Analyze and interpret cost flows and operating activities of a merchandising company.

EXHIBIT 5.10

Merchandising Cost Flow in the Accounting Cycle

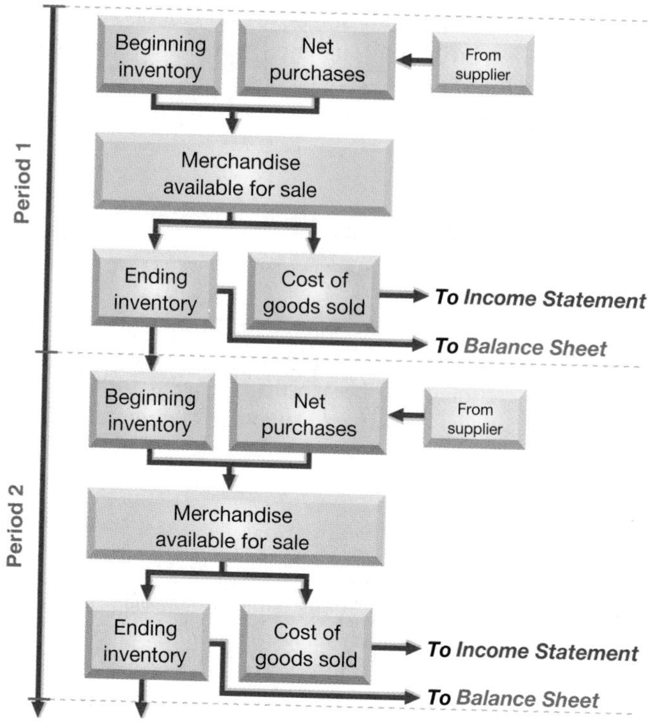

Adjusting Entries for Merchandisers

P3 Prepare adjustments and close accounts for a merchandising company.

Each of the steps in the accounting cycle described in the prior chapter for a service company applies to a merchandiser. This section and the next two further explain three steps of the accounting cycle for a merchandiser—adjustments, statement preparation, and closing.

Adjusting entries are generally the same for merchandising companies and service companies, including those for prepaid expenses (including depreciation), accrued expenses, unearned revenues, and accrued revenues. However, a merchandiser using a perpetual inventory system is usually required to make another adjustment to update the Merchandise Inventory account to reflect any loss of merchandise, including theft and deterioration. **Shrinkage** is the term used to refer to the loss of inventory and it is computed by comparing a physical count of inventory with recorded amounts. A physical count is usually performed at least once annually.

Point: About two-thirds of shoplifting losses are thefts by employees.

To illustrate, Z-Mart's Merchandise Inventory account at the end of year 2009 has a balance of $21,250, but a physical count reveals that only $21,000 of inventory exists. The adjusting entry to record this $250 shrinkage is

Assets = Liabilities + Equity
−250 −250

Dec. 31	Cost of Goods Sold	250	
	Merchandise Inventory.		250
	To adjust for $250 shrinkage revealed by a physical count of inventory.		

Preparing Financial Statements

The financial statements of a merchandiser, and their preparation, are similar to those for a service company described in Chapters 2 through 4. The income statement mainly differs by the inclusion of *cost of goods sold* and *gross profit.* Also, net sales is affected by discounts, returns, and allowances, and some additional expenses are possible such as delivery expense and loss from defective merchandise. The balance sheet mainly differs by the inclusion of *merchandise inventory* as part of current assets. The statement of owner's equity is unchanged. A work sheet can be used to help prepare these statements, and one is illustrated in Appendix 5B for Z-Mart.

Point: Staples's costs of shipping merchandise to its stores is included in its costs of inventories as required by the cost principle.

Closing Entries for Merchandisers

Closing entries are similar for service companies and merchandising companies using a perpetual system. The difference is that we must close some new temporary accounts that arise from merchandising activities. Z-Mart has several temporary accounts unique to merchandisers: Sales (of goods), Sales Discounts, Sales Returns and Allowances, and Cost of Goods Sold. Their existence in the ledger means that the first two closing entries for a merchandiser are slightly different from the ones described in the prior chapter for a service company. These differences are set in **red boldface** in the closing entries of Exhibit 5.11.

Point: The Inventory account is not affected by the closing process under a perpetual system.

EXHIBIT 5.11

Closing Entries for a Merchandiser

Step 1: Close Credit Balances in Temporary Accounts to Income Summary.

Dec. 31	**Sales**	321,000	
	Income Summary		321,000
	To close credit balances in temporary accounts.		

Step 2: Close Debit Balances in Temporary Accounts to Income Summary.

Dec. 31	Income Summary	308,100	
	Sales Discounts		**4,300**
	Sales Returns and Allowances		**2,000**
	Cost of Goods Sold		**230,400**
	Depreciation Expense		3,700
	Salaries Expense		43,800
	Insurance Expense		600
	Rent Expense		9,000
	Supplies Expense		3,000
	Advertising Expense		11,300
	To close debit balances in temporary accounts.		

Step 3: Close Income Summary to Owner's Capital.

The third closing entry is identical for a merchandising company and a service company. The $12,900 amount is net income reported on the income statement.

Dec. 31	Income Summary	12,900	
	K. Marty, Capital		12,900
	To close the Income Summary account.		

Step 4: Close Withdrawals Account to Owner's Capital.

The fourth closing entry is identical for a merchandising company and a service company. It closes the Withdrawals account and adjusts the Owner's Capital account to the amount shown on the balance sheet.

Dec. 31	K. Marty, Capital	4,000	
	K. Marty, Withdrawals		4,000
	To close the Withdrawals account.		

Summary of Merchandising Entries

Exhibit 5.12 summarizes the key adjusting and closing entries of a merchandiser (using a perpetual inventory system) that are different from those of a service company described in prior chapters (the Demonstration Problem 2 illustrates these merchandising entries).

EXHIBIT 5.12

Summary of Merchandising Entries

	Merchandising Transactions	Merchandising Entries	Dr.	Cr.
Purchases	Purchasing merchandise for resale.	Merchandise Inventory	#	
		Cash or Accounts Payable		#
	Paying freight costs on purchases; FOB shipping point.	Merchandise Inventory	#	
		Cash		#
	Paying within discount period.	Accounts Payable	#	
		Merchandise Inventory		#
		Cash		#
	Recording purchase returns or allowances.	Cash or Accounts Payable	#	
		Merchandise Inventory		#
Sales	Selling merchandise.	Cash or Accounts Receivable	#	
		Sales		#
		Cost of Goods Sold	#	
		Merchandise Inventory		#
	Receiving payment within discount period.	Cash	#	
		Sales Discounts	#	
		Accounts Receivable		#
	Granting sales returns or allowances.	Sales Returns and Allowances	#	
		Cash or Accounts Receivable		#
		Merchandise Inventory	#	
		Cost of Goods Sold		#
	Paying freight costs on sales; FOB destination.	Delivery Expense	#	
		Cash		#
	Merchandising Events	**Adjusting and Closing Entries**		
Adjusting	Adjusting due to shrinkage (occurs when recorded amount larger than physical inventory).	Cost of Goods Sold	#	
		Merchandise Inventory		#
Closing	Closing temporary accounts with credit balances.	Sales	#	
		Income Summary		#
	Closing temporary accounts with debit balances.	Income Summary	#	
		Sales Returns and Allowances		#
		Sales Discounts		#
		Cost of Goods Sold		#
		Delivery Expense		#
		"Other Expenses"		#

Quick Check

Answers—p. 204

10. When a merchandiser uses a perpetual inventory system, why is it sometimes necessary to adjust the Merchandise Inventory balance with an adjusting entry?

11. What temporary accounts do you expect to find in a merchandising business but not in a service business?

12. Describe the closing entries normally made by a merchandising company.

Financial Statement Formats

Generally accepted accounting principles do not require companies to use any one presentation format for financial statements so we see many different formats in practice. This section describes two common income statement formats: multiple-step and single-step. The classified balance sheet of a merchandiser is also explained.

Multiple-Step Income Statement

A **multiple-step income statement** format shows detailed computations of net sales and other costs and expenses, and reports subtotals for various classes of items. Exhibit 5.13 shows a multiple-step income statement for Z-Mart. The statement has three main parts: (1) *gross profit,* determined by net sales less cost of goods sold, (2) *income from operations,* determined by gross profit less operating expenses, and (3) *net income,* determined by income from operations adjusted for nonoperating items.

P4 Define and prepare multiple-step and single-step income statements.

EXHIBIT 5.13

Multiple-Step Income Statement

Z-MART
Income Statement
For Year Ended December 31, 2009

Sales		$321,000	Gross profit computation
Less: Sales discounts	$ 4,300		
Sales returns and allowances	2,000	6,300	
Net sales		314,700	
Cost of goods sold		230,400	
Gross profit		84,300	
Operating Expenses			Income from operations computation
Selling expenses			
Depreciation expense—Store equipment	3,000		
Sales salaries expense	18,500		
Rent expense—Selling space	8,100		
Store supplies expense	1,200		
Advertising expense	11,300		
Total selling expenses	42,100		
General and administrative expenses			
Depreciation expense—Office equipment	700		
Office salaries expense	25,300		
Insurance expense	600		
Rent expense—Office space	900		
Office supplies expense	1,800		
Total general and administrative expenses	29,300		
Total operating expenses		71,400	
Income from operations		12,900	
Other revenues and gains (expenses and losses)			Nonoperating activities computation
Interest revenue	1,000		
Gain on sale of building	2,500		
Interest expense	(1,500)		
Total other revenue and gains (expenses and losses)		2,000	
Net income		$ 14,900	

Operating expenses are classified into two sections. **Selling expenses** include the expenses of promoting sales by displaying and advertising merchandise, making sales, and delivering goods to customers. **General and administrative expenses** support a company's overall operations and include expenses related to accounting, human resource management, and financial management. Expenses are allocated between sections when they contribute to more than one. Z-Mart allocates rent expense of $9,000 from its store building between two sections: $8,100 to selling expense and $900 to general and administrative expense.

Nonoperating activities consist of other expenses, revenues, losses, and gains that are unrelated to a company's operations. *Other revenues and gains* commonly include interest revenue, dividend revenue, rent revenue, and gains from asset disposals. *Other expenses and losses* commonly include interest expense, losses from asset disposals, and casualty losses. When a company has no reportable nonoperating activities, its income from operations is simply labeled net income.

Point: Z-Mart did not have any nonoperating activities; however, Exhibit 5.13 includes some for illustrative purposes.

Single-Step Income Statement

A **single-step income statement** is another widely used format, and is shown in Exhibit 5.14 for Z-Mart. It lists cost of goods sold as another expense and shows only one subtotal for total expenses. Expenses are grouped into very few, if any, categories. Many companies use formats that combine features of both the single- and multiple-step statements. Provided that income statement items are shown sensibly, management can choose the format. (In later chapters, we describe some items, such as extraordinary gains and losses, that must be reported in certain locations on the income statement.) Similar presentation options are available for the statement of owner's equity and statement of cash flows.

Point: Many companies report interest expense and interest revenue in separate categories after operating income and before subtracting income tax expense. As one example, see **Circuit City**'s income statement in Appendix A.

EXHIBIT 5.14

Single-Step Income Statement

Z-MART
Income Statement
For Year Ended December 31, 2009

Revenues		
Net sales		$314,700
Interest revenue		1,000
Gain on sale of building		2,500
Total revenues		318,200
Expenses		
Cost of goods sold	$230,400	
Selling expenses	42,100	
General and administrative expenses	29,300	
Interest expense	1,500	
Total expenses		303,300
Net income		$ 14,900

Classified Balance Sheet

The merchandiser's classified balance sheet reports merchandise inventory as a current asset, usually after accounts receivable according to an asset's nearness to liquidity. Inventory is usually less liquid than accounts receivable because inventory must first be sold before cash can be received; but it is more liquid than supplies and prepaid expenses. Exhibit 5.15 shows the current asset section of Z-Mart's classified balance sheet (other sections are as shown in Chapter 4).

EXHIBIT 5.15

Classified Balance Sheet (partial) of a Merchandiser

Z-MART
Balance Sheet (partial)
December 31, 2009

Assets	
Cash	$ 8,200
Accounts receivable	11,200
Merchandise inventory	**21,000**
Office supplies	550
Store supplies	250
Prepaid insurance	300
Total current assets	$ 41,500

Decision Insight

IFRSs There is no prescribed format for the income statement under IFRSs. This differs from the U.S. in that SEC regulations prescribe a basic format. IFRSs also prescribe that expenses be identified by their nature or function on the income statement. U.S. SEC regulations have no such requirement. IFRSs also allow alternative measures of income on the income statement. U.S. standards prohibit disclosure of alternative income measures in financial statements.

Acid-Test and Gross Margin Ratios

Decision Analysis

Acid-Test Ratio

A1 Compute the acid-test ratio and explain its use to assess liquidity.

For many merchandisers, inventory makes up a large portion of current assets. Inventory must be sold and any resulting accounts receivable must be collected before cash is available. Chapter 4 explained that the current ratio, defined as current assets divided by current liabilities, is useful in assessing a company's ability to pay current liabilities. Since it is sometimes unreasonable to assume that inventories are a source of payment for current liabilities, we look to other measures.

One measure of a merchandiser's ability to pay its current liabilities (referred to as its *liquidity*) is the acid-test ratio. It differs from the current ratio by excluding less liquid current assets such as inventory and prepaid expenses that take longer to be converted to cash. The **acid-test ratio,** also called *quick ratio,* is defined as *quick assets* (cash, short-term investments, and current receivables) divided by current liabilities—see Exhibit 5.16.

EXHIBIT 5.16

Acid-Test (Quick) Ratio

$$\textbf{Acid-test ratio} = \frac{\textbf{Cash and cash equivalents + Short-term investments + Current receivables}}{\textbf{Current liabilities}}$$

Exhibit 5.17 shows both the acid-test and current ratios of retailer **JCPenney** for fiscal years 2005 through 2007—also see margin graph. JCPenney's acid-test ratio reveals a general decrease from 2005 through 2007 that exceeds the industry average. Further, JCPenney's current ratio (never less than 1.9) suggests that its short-term obligations can be confidently covered with short-term assets.

EXHIBIT 5.17

JCPenney's Acid-Test and Current Ratios

($ millions)	2007	2006	2005
Total quick assets	$3,010	$3,286	$4,923
Total current assets	$6,648	$6,702	$8,232
Total current liabilities	$3,492	$2,762	$3,297
Acid-test ratio	**0.86**	**1.19**	**1.49**
Current ratio	**1.90**	**2.43**	**2.50**
Industry acid-test ratio	0.56	0.61	0.66
Industry current ratio	2.43	2.55	2.67

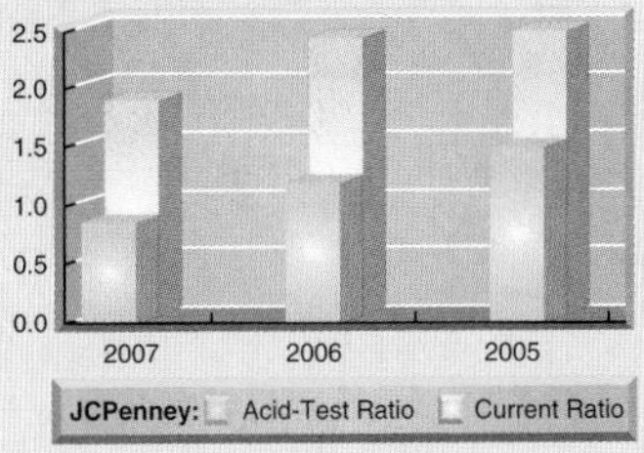

An acid-test ratio less than 1.0 means that current liabilities exceed quick assets. A rule of thumb is that the acid-test ratio should have a value near, or higher than, 1.0 to conclude that a company is unlikely to face near-term liquidity problems. A value much less than 1.0 raises liquidity concerns unless a company can generate enough cash from inventory sales or if much of its liabilities are not due until late in the next period. Similarly, a value slightly larger than 1.0 can hide a liquidity problem if payables are due shortly and receivables are not collected until late in the next period. Analysis of JCPenney reveals a slight concern with its liquidity in 2007. However, in all years, JCPenney's acid-test ratios exceed the norm and are at reasonable levels (and its inventory is fairly liquid).

Point: Successful use of a just-in-time inventory system can narrow the gap between the acid-test ratio and the current ratio.

Decision Maker

Supplier A retailer requests to purchase supplies on credit from your company. You have no prior experience with this retailer. The retailer's current ratio is 2.1, its acid-test ratio is 0.5, and inventory makes up most of its current assets. Do you extend credit? [Answer—p. 203]

Gross Margin Ratio

A2 Compute the gross margin ratio and explain its use to assess profitability.

The cost of goods sold makes up much of a merchandiser's expenses. Without sufficient gross profit, a merchandiser will likely fail. Users often compute the gross margin ratio to help understand this relation. It differs from the profit margin ratio in that it excludes all costs except cost of goods sold. The **gross margin ratio** (also called *gross profit ratio*) is defined as *gross margin* (net sales minus cost of goods sold) divided by net sales—see Exhibit 5.18.

EXHIBIT 5.18

Gross Margin Ratio

$$\textbf{Gross margin ratio} = \frac{\textbf{Net sales} - \textbf{Cost of goods sold}}{\textbf{Net sales}}$$

Point: The power of a ratio is often its ability to identify areas for more detailed analysis.

Exhibit 5.19 shows the gross margin ratio of **JCPenney** for fiscal years 2005 through 2007. For JCPenney, each $1 of sales in 2007 yielded about 39¢ in gross margin to cover all other expenses and still produce a net income. This 39¢ margin is up from 37.5¢ in 2005. This increase is an important (and positive) development. Success for merchandisers such as JCPenney depends on adequate gross margin.

EXHIBIT 5.19

JCPenney's Gross Margin Ratio

($ millions)	2007	2006	2005
Gross margin	$ 7,825	$ 7,191	$ 6,792
Net sales	$19,903	$18,781	$18,096
Gross margin ratio	**39.3%**	**38.3%**	**37.5%**

Decision Maker

Financial Officer Your company has a 36% gross margin ratio and a 17% net profit margin ratio. Industry averages are 44% for gross margin and 16% for net profit margin. Do these comparative results concern you? [Answer—p. 204]

Demonstration Problem 1

DP5

Use the following adjusted trial balance and additional information to complete the requirements.

KC ANTIQUES
Adjusted Trial Balance
December 31, 2009

	Debit	Credit
Cash	$ 7,000	
Accounts receivable	13,000	
Merchandise inventory	60,000	
Store supplies	1,500	
Equipment	45,600	
Accumulated depreciation—Equipment		$ 16,600
Accounts payable		9,000
Salaries payable		2,000
K. Carter, Capital		79,000
K. Carter, Withdrawals	10,000	
Sales		343,250
Sales discounts	5,000	
Sales returns and allowances	6,000	
Cost of goods sold	159,900	
Depreciation expense—Store equipment	4,100	
Depreciation expense—Office equipment	1,600	
Sales salaries expense	30,000	
Office salaries expense	34,000	
Insurance expense	11,000	
Rent expense (70% is store, 30% is office)	24,000	
Store supplies expense	5,750	
Advertising expense	31,400	
Totals	$449,850	$449,850

KC Antiques' *supplementary records* for 2009 reveal the following itemized costs for merchandising activities:

Invoice cost of merchandise purchases	$150,000
Purchase discounts received	2,500
Purchase returns and allowances	2,700
Cost of transportation-in	5,000

Required

1. Use the supplementary records to compute the total cost of merchandise purchases for 2009.
2. Prepare a 2009 multiple-step income statement. (Inventory at December 31, 2008, is $70,100.)
3. Prepare a single-step income statement for 2009.
4. Prepare closing entries for KC Antiques at December 31, 2009.
5. Compute the acid-test ratio and the gross margin ratio. Explain the meaning of each ratio and interpret them for KC Antiques.

Planning the Solution

- Compute the total cost of merchandise purchases for 2009.
- To prepare the multiple-step statement, first compute net sales. Then, to compute cost of goods sold, add the net cost of merchandise purchases for the year to beginning inventory and subtract the cost of ending inventory. Subtract cost of goods sold from net sales to get gross profit. Then classify expenses as selling expenses or general and administrative expenses.
- To prepare the single-step income statement, begin with net sales. Then list and subtract the expenses.
- The first closing entry debits all temporary accounts with credit balances and opens the Income Summary account. The second closing entry credits all temporary accounts with debit balances. The third entry closes the Income Summary account to the capital account, and the fourth entry closes the withdrawals account to the capital account.
- Identify the quick assets on the adjusted trial balance. Compute the acid-test ratio by dividing quick assets by current liabilities. Compute the gross margin ratio by dividing gross profit by net sales.

Solution to Demonstration Problem 1

1.

Invoice cost of merchandise purchases	$150,000
Less: Purchases discounts received	2,500
Purchase returns and allowances	2,700
Add: Cost of transportation-in	5,000
Total cost of merchandise purchases	$149,800

2. Multiple-step income statement

KC ANTIQUES
Income Statement
For Year Ended December 31, 2009

Sales		$343,250
Less: Sales discounts	$ 5,000	
Sales returns and allowances	6,000	11,000
Net sales		332,250
Cost of goods sold*		159,900
Gross profit		172,350
Expenses		
Selling expenses		
Depreciation expense—Store equipment	4,100	
Sales salaries expense	30,000	
Rent expense—Selling space	16,800	
Store supplies expense	5,750	
Advertising expense	31,400	
Total selling expenses	88,050	

[continued on next page]

[continued from previous page]

General and administrative expenses		
Depreciation expense—Office equipment	1,600	
Office salaries expense	34,000	
Insurance expense	11,000	
Rent expense—Office space	7,200	
Total general and administrative expenses	53,800	
Total operating expenses		141,850
Net income		$ 30,500

* Cost of goods sold can also be directly computed (applying concepts from Exhibit 5.4):

Merchandise inventory, December 31, 2008	$ 70,100
Total cost of merchandise purchases (from part 1)	149,800
Goods available for sale	219,900
Merchandise inventory, December 31, 2009	60,000
Cost of goods sold	$159,900

3. Single-step income statement

KC ANTIQUES
Income Statement
For Year Ended December 31, 2009

Net sales		$332,250
Expenses		
Cost of goods sold	$159,900	
Selling expenses	88,050	
General and administrative expenses	53,800	
Total expenses		301,750
Net income		$ 30,500

4.

Dec. 31	Sales	343,250	
	Income Summary		343,250
	To close credit balances in temporary accounts.		
Dec. 31	Income Summary	312,750	
	Sales Discounts		5,000
	Sales Returns and Allowances		6,000
	Cost of Goods Sold		159,900
	Depreciation Expense—Store Equipment		4,100
	Depreciation Expense—Office Equipment		1,600
	Sales Salaries Expense		30,000
	Office Salaries Expense		34,000
	Insurance Expense		11,000
	Rent Expense		24,000
	Store Supplies Expense		5,750
	Advertising Expense		31,400
	To close debit balances in temporary accounts.		
Dec. 31	Income Summary	30,500	
	K. Carter, Capital		30,500
	To close the Income Summary account.		
Dec. 31	K. Carter, Capital	10,000	
	K. Carter, Withdrawals		10,000
	To close the Withdrawals account.		

5. Acid-test ratio = (Cash and equivalents + Short-term investments + Current receivables)/Current liabilities
= (Cash + Accounts receivable/(Accounts payable + Salaries payable)
= ($7,000 + $13,000)/($9,000 + $2,000) = $20,000/$11,000 = 1.82

Gross margin ratio = Gross profit/Net sales = $172,350/$332,250 = 0.52 (or 52%)

KC Antiques has a healthy acid-test ratio of 1.82. This means it has more than \$1.80 in liquid assets to satisfy each \$1.00 in current liabilities. The gross margin of 0.52 shows that KC Antiques spends 48¢ (\$1.00 − \$0.52) of every dollar of net sales on the costs of acquiring the merchandise it sells. This leaves 52¢ of every dollar of net sales to cover other expenses incurred in the business and to provide a net profit.

Demonstration Problem 2

Prepare journal entries to record the following merchandising transactions for both the seller (BMX) and buyer (Sanuk).

May 4 BMX sold \$1,500 of merchandise on account to Sanuk, terms FOB shipping point, n/45, invoice dated May 4. The cost of the merchandise was \$900.

May 6 Sanuk paid transportation charges of \$30 on the May 4 purchase from BMX.

May 8 BMX sold \$1,000 of merchandise on account to Sanuk, terms FOB destination, n/30, invoice dated May 8. The cost of the merchandise was \$700.

May 10 BMX paid transportation costs of \$50 for delivery of merchandise sold to Sanuk on May 8.

May 16 BMX issued Sanuk a \$200 credit memorandum for merchandise returned. The merchandise was purchased by Sanuk on account on May 8. The cost of the merchandise returned was \$140.

May 18 BMX received payment from Sanuk for purchase of May 8.

May 21 BMX sold \$2,400 of merchandise on account to Sanuk, terms FOB shipping point, 2/10, n/EOM. BMX prepaid transportation costs of \$100, which were added to the invoice. The cost of the merchandise was \$1,440.

May 31 BMX received payment from Sanuk for purchase of May 21, less discount (2% × \$2,400).

Solution to Demonstration Problem 2

Date	BMX (Seller)	Debit	Credit	Sanuk (Buyer)	Debit	Credit
May 4	Accounts Receivable—Sanuk	1,500		Merchandise Inventory	1,500	
	Sales		1,500	Accounts Payable—BMX		1,500
	Cost of Goods Sold	900				
	Merchandise Inventory		900			
6	No entry.			Merchandise Inventory	30	
				Cash		30
8	Accounts Receivable—Sanuk	1,000		Merchandise Inventory	1,000	
	Sales		1,000	Accounts Payable—BMX		1,000
	Cost of Goods Sold	700				
	Merchandise Inventory		700			
10	Delivery Expense	50		No entry.		
	Cash		50			
16	Sales Returns & Allowances	200		Accounts Payable—BMX	200	
	Accounts Receivable—Sanuk		200	Merchandise Inventory		200
	Merchandise Inventory	140				
	Cost of Goods Sold		140			
18	Cash	800		Accounts Payable—BMX	800	
	Accounts Receivable—Sanuk		800	Cash		800
21	Accounts Receivable—Sanuk	2,400		Merchandise Inventory	2,500	
	Sales		2,400	Accounts Payable—BMX		2,500
	Accounts Receivable—Sanuk	100				
	Cash		100			
	Cost of Goods Sold	1,440				
	Merchandise Inventory		1,440			
31	Cash	2,452		Accounts Payable—BMX	2,500	
	Sales Discounts	48		Merchandise Inventory		48
	Accounts Receivable—Sanuk		2,500	Cash		2,452

APPENDIX

5A Periodic Inventory System

A **periodic inventory system** requires updating the inventory account only at the *end of a period* to reflect the quantity and cost of both the goods available and the goods sold. Thus, during the period, the Merchandise Inventory balance remains unchanged. It reflects the beginning inventory balance until it is updated at the end of the period. During the period the cost of merchandise is recorded in a temporary *Purchases* account. When a company sells merchandise, it records revenue ***but not the cost of the goods sold.*** At the end of the period when a company prepares financial statements, it takes a *physical count of inventory* by counting the quantities and costs of merchandise available. The cost of goods sold is then computed by subtracting the ending inventory amount from the cost of merchandise available for sale.

Recording Merchandise Transactions

P5 Record and compare merchandising transactions using both periodic and perpetual inventory systems.

Under a periodic system, purchases, purchase returns and allowances, purchase discounts, and transportation-in transactions are recorded in separate temporary accounts. At period-end, each of these temporary accounts is closed and the Merchandise Inventory account is updated. To illustrate, journal entries under the periodic inventory system are shown for the most common transactions (codes ***a*** through ***f*** link these transactions to those in the chapter, and we drop explanations for simplicity). For comparison, perpetual system journal entries are shown to the right of each periodic entry, where differences are in gray font.

Purchases The periodic system uses a temporary *Purchases* account that accumulates the cost of all purchase transactions during each period. Z-Mart's November 2 entry to record the purchase of merchandise for $1,200 on credit with terms of 2/10, n/30 is

(a)

Periodic			Perpetual		
Purchases	1,200		Merchandise Inventory	1,200	
Accounts Payable		1,200	Accounts Payable		1,200

Purchase Discounts The periodic system uses a temporary *Purchase Discounts* account that accumulates discounts taken on purchase transactions during the period. If payment in (*a*) is delayed until after the discount period expires, the entry is to debit Accounts Payable and credit Cash for $1,200 each. However, if Z-Mart pays the supplier for the previous purchase in (*a*) within the discount period, the required payment is $1,176 ($1,200 × 98%) and is recorded as

(b)

Periodic			Perpetual		
Accounts Payable	1,200		Accounts Payable	1,200	
Purchase Discounts		24	Merchandise Inventory		24
Cash		1,176	Cash		1,176

Purchase Returns and Allowances Z-Mart returned merchandise purchased on November 2 because of defects. In the periodic system, the temporary *Purchase Returns and Allowances* account accumulates the cost of all returns and allowances during a period. The recorded cost (including discounts) of the defective merchandise is $300, and Z-Mart records the November 15 return with this entry:

(c)

Periodic			Perpetual		
Accounts Payable	300		Accounts Payable	300	
Purchase Returns and Allowances		300	Merchandise Inventory		300

Transportation-In Z-Mart paid a $75 freight charge to transport merchandise to its store. In the periodic system, this cost is charged to a temporary *Transportation-In* account.

(d)

Periodic			Perpetual		
Transportation-In	75		Merchandise Inventory	75	
Cash		75	Cash		75

Sales Under the periodic system, the cost of goods sold is *not* recorded at the time of each sale. (We later show how to compute total cost of goods sold at the end of a period.) Z-Mart's November 3 entry to record sales of $2,400 in merchandise on credit (when its cost is $1,600) is:

(e)

Periodic			Perpetual		
Accounts Receivable	2,400		Accounts Receivable	2,400	
Sales		2,400	Sales		2,400
			Cost of Goods Sold	1,600	
			Merchandise Inventory		1,600

Sales Returns A customer returned part of the merchandise from the transaction in (*e*), where the returned items sell for $800 and cost $600. (*Recall:* The periodic system records only the revenue effect, not the cost effect, for sales transactions.) Z-Mart restores the merchandise to inventory and records the November 6 return as

(f)

Periodic			Perpetual		
Sales Returns and Allowances	800		Sales Returns and Allowances	800	
Accounts Receivable ...		800	Accounts Receivable		800
			Merchandise Inventory	600	
			Cost of Goods Sold		600

Sales Discounts To illustrate sales discounts, assume that the remaining $1,600 of receivables (computed as $2,400 from ***e*** less $800 for ***f***) has credit terms of 3/10, n/90 and that customers all pay within the discount period. Z-Mart records this payment as

Periodic			Perpetual		
Cash	1,552		Cash	1,552	
Sales Discounts ($1,600 × .03)	48		Sales Discounts ($1,600 × .03) ..	48	
Accounts Receivable ...		1,600	Accounts Receivable		1,600

Adjusting and Closing Entries

The periodic and perpetual inventory systems have slight differences in adjusting and closing entries. The period-end Merchandise Inventory balance (unadjusted) is $19,000 under the periodic system and $21,250 under the perpetual system. Since the periodic system does not update the Merchandise Inventory balance during the period, the $19,000 amount is the beginning inventory. However, the $21,250 balance under the perpetual system is the recorded ending inventory before adjusting for any inventory shrinkage.

A physical count of inventory taken at the end of the period reveals $21,000 of merchandise available. The adjusting and closing entries for the two systems are shown in Exhibit 5A.1. The periodic system records the ending inventory of $21,000 in the Merchandise Inventory account (which includes

EXHIBIT 5A.1

Comparison of Adjusting and Closing Entries—Periodic and Perpetual

PERIODIC			PERPETUAL		
Adjusting Entry—Shrinkage			Adjusting Entry—Shrinkage		
None			Cost of Goods Sold	250	
			Merchandise Inventory		250

[continued on next page]

[continued from previous page]

PERIODIC — Closing Entries		
(1) Sales	321,000	
Merchandise Inventory	**21,000**	
Purchase Discounts	**4,200**	
Purchase Returns and Allowances	**1,500**	
Income Summary		347,700
(2) Income Summary	334,800	
Sales Discounts		4,300
Sales Returns and Allowances		2,000
Merchandise Inventory		**19,000**
Purchases		**235,800**
Transportation-In		**2,300**
Depreciation Expense		3,700
Salaries Expense		43,800
Insurance Expense		600
Rent Expense		9,000
Supplies Expense		3,000
Advertising Expense		11,300
(3) Income Summary	12,900	
K. Marty, Capital		12,900
(4) K. Marty, Capital	4,000	
K. Marty, Withdrawals		4,000

PERPETUAL — Closing Entries		
(1) Sales	321,000	
Income Summary		321,000
(2) Income Summary	308,100	
Sales Discounts		4,300
Sales Returns and Allowances		2,000
Cost of Goods Sold		**230,400**
Depreciation Expense		3,700
Salaries Expense		43,800
Insurance Expense		600
Rent Expense		9,000
Supplies Expense		3,000
Advertising Expense		11,300
(3) Income Summary	12,900	
K. Marty, Capital		12,900
(4) K. Marty, Capital	4,000	
K. Marty, Withdrawals		4,000

shrinkage) in the first closing entry and removes the $19,000 beginning inventory balance from the account in the second closing entry.[2]

By updating Merchandise Inventory and closing Purchases, Purchase Discounts, Purchase Returns and Allowances, and Transportation-In, the periodic system transfers the cost of goods sold amount to Income Summary. Review the periodic side of Exhibit 5A.1 and notice that the **boldface** items affect Income Summary as follows.

Credit to Income Summary in the first closing entry includes amounts from:	
Merchandise inventory (ending)	$ 21,000
Purchase discounts	4,200
Purchase returns and allowances	1,500
Debit to Income Summary in the second closing entry includes amounts from:	
Merchandise inventory (beginning)	(19,000)
Purchases	(235,800)
Transportation-in	(2,300)
Net effect on Income Summary	**$(230,400)**

This $230,400 effect on Income Summary is the cost of goods sold amount. The periodic system transfers cost of goods sold to the Income Summary account but without using a Cost of Goods Sold account. Also, the periodic system does not separately measure shrinkage. Instead, it computes cost of goods

[2] This approach is called the *closing entry method.* An alternative approach, referred to as the *adjusting entry method,* would not make any entries to Merchandise Inventory in the closing entries of Exhibit 5A.1, but instead would make two adjusting entries. Using Z-Mart data, the two adjusting entries would be: (1) Dr. Income Summary and Cr. Merchandise Inventory for $19,000 each, and (2) Dr. Merchandise Inventory and Cr. Income Summary for $21,000 each. The first entry removes the beginning balance of Merchandise Inventory, and the second entry records the actual ending balance.

available for sale, subtracts the cost of ending inventory, and defines the difference as cost of goods sold, which includes shrinkage.

Preparing Financial Statements

The financial statements of a merchandiser using the periodic system are similar to those for a service company described in prior chapters. The income statement mainly differs by the inclusion of *cost of goods sold* and *gross profit*—of course, net sales is affected by discounts, returns, and allowances. The cost of goods sold section under the periodic system follows

Calculation of Cost of Goods Sold
For Year Ended December 31, 2009

Beginning inventory	$ 19,000
Cost of goods purchased	232,400
Cost of goods available for sale	251,400
Less ending inventory	21,000
Cost of goods sold	$230,400

The balance sheet mainly differs by the inclusion of *merchandise inventory* in current assets—see Exhibit 5.15. The statement of owner's equity is unchanged. A work sheet can be used to help prepare these statements. The only differences under the periodic system from the work sheet illustrated in Appendix 5B using the perpetual system are highlighted as follows in **blue boldface** font.

File Edit View Insert Format Tools Data Accounting Window Help

1			Unadjusted Trial Balance		Adjustments		Adjusted Trial Balance		Income Statement		Balance Sheet	
2	No.	Account	Dr.	Cr.	Dr.	Cr.	Dr.	Cr.	Dr.	Cr.	Dr.	Cr.
3	101	Cash	8,200				8,200				8,200	
4	106	Accounts receivable	11,200				11,200				11,200	
5	**119**	**Merchandise Inventory**	**19,000**				**19,000**		**19,000**	**21,000**	**21,000**	
6	126	Supplies	3,800			(b) 3,000	800				800	
7	128	Prepaid insurance	900			(a) 600	300				300	
8	167	Equipment	34,200				34,200				34,200	
9	168	Accumulated depr.—Equip.		3,700		(c) 3,700		7,400				7,400
10	201	Accounts payable		16,000				16,000				16,000
11	209	Salaries payable				(d) 800		800				800
12	301	K. Marty, Capital		42,600				42,600				42,600
13	302	K. Marty, Withdrawals	4,000				4,000				4,000	
14	413	Sales		321,000				321,000		321,000		
15	414	Sales returns and allowances	2,000				2,000		2,000			
16a	415	Sales discounts	4,300				4,300		4,300			
16b	**505**	**Purchases**	**235,800**				**235,800**		**235,800**			
16c	**506**	**Purchases returns & allowance**		**1,500**				**1,500**		**1,500**		
16d	**507**	**Purchases discounts**		**4,200**				**4,200**		**4,200**		
17	**508**	**Transportation-in**	**2,300**				**2,300**		**2,300**			
18	612	Depreciation expense—Equip.			(c) 3,700		3,700		3,700			
19	622	Salaries expense	43,000		(d) 800		43,800		43,800			
20	637	Insurance expense			(a) 600		600		600			
21	640	Rent expense	9,000				9,000		9,000			
22	652	Supplies expense			(b) 3,000		3,000		3,000			
23	655	Advertising expense	11,300				11,300		11,300			
24		Totals	389,000	389,000	8,100	8,100	393,500	393,500	334,800	347,700	79,700	66,800
25		Net income							12,900			12,900
26		Totals							347,700	347,700	79,700	79,700

Sheet1 / Sheet2 / Sheet3

Quick Check Answers—p. 204

13. What account is used in a perpetual inventory system but not in a periodic system?

14. Which of the following accounts are temporary accounts under a periodic system? (*a*) Merchandise Inventory; (*b*) Purchases; (*c*) Transportation-In.

15. How is cost of goods sold computed under a periodic inventory system?

16. Do reported amounts of ending inventory and net income differ if the adjusting entry method of recording the change in inventory is used instead of the closing entry method?

APPENDIX

5B Work Sheet—Perpetual System

Exhibit 5B.1 shows the work sheet for preparing financial statements of a merchandiser. It differs slightly from the work sheet layout in Chapter 4—the differences are in **red boldface**. Also, the adjustments in the work sheet reflect the following: (*a*) Expiration of $600 of prepaid insurance. (*b*) Use of $3,000 of supplies. (*c*) Depreciation of $3,700 for equipment. (*d*) Accrual of $800 of unpaid salaries. (*e*) Inventory shrinkage of $250. Once the adjusted amounts are extended into the financial statement columns, the information is used to develop financial statements.

EXHIBIT 5B.1

Work Sheet for Merchandiser (using a perpetual system)

			Unadjusted Trial Balance		Adjustments		Adjusted Trial Balance		Income Statement		Balance Sheet	
1												
2	**No.**	**Account**	**Dr.**	**Cr.**	**Dr.**	**Cr.**	**Dr.**	**Cr.**	**Dr.**	**Cr.**	**Dr.**	**Cr.**
3	101	Cash	8,200				8,200				8,200	
4	106	Accounts receivable	11,200				11,200				11,200	
5	**119**	**Merchandise Inventory**	**21,250**			**(*g*) 250**	**21,000**				**21,000**	
6	126	Supplies	3,800			(*b*) 3,000	800				800	
7	128	Prepaid insurance	900			(*a*) 600	300				300	
8	167	Equipment	34,200				34,200				34,200	
9	168	Accumulated depr.—Equip.		3,700		(*c*) 3,700		7,400				7,400
10	201	Accounts payable		16,000				16,000				16,000
11	209	Salaries payable				(*d*) 800		800				800
12	301	K. Marty, Capital		42,600				42,600				42,600
13	302	K. Marty, Withdrawals	4,000				4,000				4,000	
14	**413**	**Sales**		**321,000**				**321,000**		**321,000**		
15	**414**	**Sales returns and allowances**	**2,000**				**2,000**		**2,000**			
16	**415**	**Sales discounts**	**4,300**				**4,300**		**4,300**			
17	**502**	**Cost of goods sold**	**230,150**		**(*g*) 250**		**230,400**		**230,400**			
18	612	Depreciation expense—Equip.			(*c*) 3,700		3,700		3,700			
19	622	Salaries expense	43,000		(*d*) 800		43,800		43,800			
20	637	Insurance expense			(*a*) 600		600		600			
21	640	Rent expense	9,000				9,000		9,000			
22	652	Supplies expense			(*b*) 3,000		3,000		3,000			
23	655	Advertising expense	11,300				11,300		11,300			
24		Totals	383,300	383,300	8,350	8,350	387,800	387,800	308,100	321,000	79,700	66,800
25		Net income							12,900			12,900
26		Totals							321,000	321,000	79,700	79,700
27												

Summary

C1 Describe merchandising activities and identify income components for a merchandising company. Merchandisers buy products and resell them. Examples of merchandisers include Wal-Mart, Home Depot, The Limited, and Barnes & Noble. A merchandiser's costs on the income statement include an amount for cost of goods sold. Gross profit, or gross margin, equals sales minus cost of goods sold.

C2 Identify and explain the inventory asset of a merchandising company. The current asset section of a merchandising company's balance sheet includes *merchandise inventory,* which refers to the products a merchandiser sells and are available for sale at the balance sheet date.

C3 Describe both perpetual and periodic inventory systems. A perpetual inventory system continuously tracks the cost of goods available for sale and the cost of goods sold. A periodic system accumulates the cost of goods purchased during the period and does not compute the amount of inventory or the cost of goods sold until the end of a period.

C4 Analyze and interpret cost flows and operating activities of a merchandising company. Cost of merchandise purchases flows into Merchandise Inventory and from there to Cost of Goods Sold on the income statement. Any remaining inventory is reported as a current asset on the balance sheet.

A1 Compute the acid-test ratio and explain its use to assess liquidity. The acid-test ratio is computed as quick assets (cash, short-term investments, and current receivables) divided by current liabilities. It indicates a company's ability to pay its current liabilities with its existing quick assets. An acid-test ratio equal to or greater than 1.0 is often adequate.

A2 Compute the gross margin ratio and explain its use to assess profitability. The gross margin ratio is computed as gross margin (net sales minus cost of goods sold) divided by net sales. It indicates a company's profitability before considering other expenses.

P1 Analyze and record transactions for merchandise purchases using a perpetual system. For a perpetual inventory system, purchases of inventory (net of trade discounts) are added to the Merchandise Inventory account. Purchase discounts and purchase returns and allowances are subtracted from Merchandise Inventory, and transportation-in costs are added to Merchandise Inventory.

P2 Analyze and record transactions for merchandise sales using a perpetual system. A merchandiser records sales at list price less any trade discounts. The cost of items sold is transferred from Merchandise Inventory to Cost of Goods Sold. Refunds or credits given to customers for unsatisfactory merchandise are recorded in Sales Returns and Allowances, a contra account to Sales. If merchandise is returned and restored to inventory, the cost of this merchandise is removed from Cost of Goods Sold and transferred back to Merchandise Inventory. When cash discounts from the sales price are offered and customers pay within the discount period, the seller records Sales Discounts, a contra account to Sales.

P3 Prepare adjustments and close accounts for a merchandising company. With a perpetual system, it is often necessary to make an adjustment for inventory shrinkage. This is computed by comparing a physical count of inventory with the Merchandise Inventory balance. Shrinkage is normally charged to Cost of Goods Sold. Temporary accounts closed to Income Summary for a merchandiser include Sales, Sales Discounts, Sales Returns and Allowances, and Cost of Goods Sold.

P4 Define and prepare multiple-step and single-step income statements. Multiple-step income statements include greater detail for sales and expenses than do single-step income statements. They also show details of net sales and report expenses in categories reflecting different activities.

P5[A] Record and compare merchandising transactions using both periodic and perpetual inventory systems. Transactions involving the sale and purchase of merchandise are recorded and analyzed under both the periodic and perpetual inventory systems. Adjusting and closing entries for both inventory systems are illustrated and explained.

Guidance Answers to **Decision Maker** and **Decision Ethics**

Entrepreneur For terms of 3/10, n/90, missing the 3% discount for an additional 80 days equals an implied annual interest rate of 13.69%, computed as (365 days ÷ 80 days) × 3%. Since you can borrow funds at 11% (assuming no other processing costs), it is better to borrow and pay within the discount period. You save 2.69% (13.69% − 11%) in interest costs by paying early.

Credit Manager Your decision is whether to comply with prior policy or to create a new policy and not abuse discounts offered by suppliers. Your first step should be to meet with your superior to find out if the late payment policy is the actual policy and, if so, its rationale. If it is the policy to pay late, you must apply your own sense of ethics. One point of view is that the late payment policy is unethical. A deliberate plan to make late payments means the company lies when it pretends to make payment within the discount period. Another view is that the late payment policy is acceptable. In some markets, attempts to take discounts through late payments are accepted as a continued phase of "price negotiation." Also, your company's suppliers can respond by billing your company for the discounts not accepted because of late payments. However, this is a dubious viewpoint, especially since the prior manager proposes that you dishonestly explain late payments as computer or mail problems and since some suppliers have complained.

Supplier A current ratio of 2.1 suggests sufficient current assets to cover current liabilities. An acid-test ratio of 0.5 suggests, however, that quick assets can cover only about one-half of current liabilities. This implies that the retailer depends on money from sales of inventory to pay current liabilities. If sales of inventory decline or profit margins decrease, the likelihood that this retailer will default on its payments increases. Your decision is probably not to extend credit. If you do extend credit, you are likely to closely monitor the retailer's financial condition. (It is better to hold unsold inventory than uncollectible receivables.)

Financial Officer Your company's net profit margin is about equal to the industry average and suggests typical industry performance. However, gross margin reveals that your company is paying far more in cost of goods sold or receiving far less in sales price than competitors. Your attention must be directed to finding the problem with cost of goods sold, sales, or both. One positive note is that your company's expenses make up 19% of sales (36% − 17%). This favorably compares with competitors' expenses that make up 28% of sales (44% − 16%).

Guidance Answers to **Quick Checks**

1. Cost of goods sold is the cost of merchandise purchased from a supplier that is sold to customers during a specific period.
2. Gross profit (or gross margin) is the difference between net sales and cost of goods sold.
3. Widespread use of computing and related technology has dramatically increased the use of the perpetual inventory system.
4. Under credit terms of 2/10, n/60, the credit period is 60 days and the discount period is 10 days.
5. (*b*) trade discount.
6. *FOB* means "free on board." It is used in identifying the point when ownership transfers from seller to buyer. *FOB destination* means that the seller transfers ownership of goods to the buyer when they arrive at the buyer's place of business. It also means that the seller is responsible for paying shipping charges and bears the risk of damage or loss during shipment.
7. Recording sales discounts and sales returns and allowances separately from sales gives useful information to managers for internal monitoring and decision making.
8. When a customer returns merchandise *and* the seller restores the merchandise to inventory, two entries are necessary. One entry records the decrease in revenue and credits the customer's account. The second entry debits inventory and reduces cost of goods sold.
9. Credit memorandum—seller credits accounts receivable from buyer.
10. Merchandise Inventory may need adjusting to reflect shrinkage.
11. Sales (of goods), Sales Discounts, Sales Returns and Allowances, and Cost of Goods Sold (and maybe Delivery Expense).
12. Four closing entries: (1) close credit balances in temporary accounts to Income Summary, (2) close debit balances in temporary accounts to Income Summary, (3) close Income Summary to owner's capital, and (4) close withdrawals account to owner's capital.
13. Cost of Goods Sold.
14. (*b*) Purchases and (*c*) Transportation-In.
15. Under a periodic inventory system, the cost of goods sold is determined at the end of an accounting period by adding the net cost of goods purchased to the beginning inventory and subtracting the ending inventory.
16. Both methods report the same ending inventory and income.

Key Terms

mhhe.com/wildFAP19e

Key Terms are available at the book's Website for learning and testing in an online Flashcard Format.

Acid-test ratio (p. 193)
Cash discount (p. 181)
Cost of goods sold (p. 178)
Credit memorandum (p. 187)
Credit period (p. 181)
Credit terms (p. 181)
Debit memorandum (p. 182)
Discount period (p. 181)
EOM (p. 181)
FOB (p. 183)
General and administrative expenses (p. 191)
Gross margin (p. 179)
Gross margin ratio (p. 193)
Gross profit (p. 178)
Inventory (p. 179)
List price (p. 180)
Merchandise (p. 178)
Merchandise inventory (p. 179)
Merchandiser (p. 178)
Multiple-step income statement (p. 191)
Periodic inventory system (pp. 180, 198)
Perpetual inventory system (p. 180)
Purchase discount (p. 181)
Retailer (p. 178)
Sales discount (p. 181)
Selling expenses (p. 191)
Shrinkage (p. 188)
Single-step income statement (p. 192)
Supplementary records (p. 184)
Trade discount (p. 180)
Wholesaler (p. 178)

Multiple Choice Quiz

Answers on p. 221 mhhe.com/wildFAP19e

Additional Quiz Questions are available at the book's Website.

Quiz5

1. A company has $550,000 in net sales and $193,000 in gross profit. This means its cost of goods sold equals
   - **a.** $743,000
   - **b.** $550,000
   - **c.** $357,000
   - **d.** $193,000
   - **e.** $(193,000)
2. A company purchased $4,500 of merchandise on May 1 with terms of 2/10, n/30. On May 6, it returned $250 of that merchandise. On May 8, it paid the balance owed for merchandise, taking any discount it is entitled to. The cash paid on May 8 is
   - **a.** $4,500
   - **b.** $4,250
   - **c.** $4,160
   - **d.** $4,165
   - **e.** $4,410
3. A company has cash sales of $75,000, credit sales of $320,000, sales returns and allowances of $13,700, and sales discounts of $6,000. Its net sales equal
   - **a.** $395,000
   - **b.** $375,300
   - **c.** $300,300
   - **d.** $339,700
   - **e.** $414,700
4. A company's quick assets are $37,500, its current assets are $80,000, and its current liabilities are $50,000. Its acid-test ratio equals
   - **a.** 1.600
   - **b.** 0.750
   - **c.** 0.625
   - **d.** 1.333
   - **e.** 0.469
5. A company's net sales are $675,000, its costs of goods sold are $459,000, and its net income is $74,250. Its gross margin ratio equals
   - **a.** 32%
   - **b.** 68%
   - **c.** 47%
   - **d.** 11%
   - **e.** 34%

Superscript letter A (B) denotes assignments based on Appendix 5A (5B).

Discussion Questions

1. In comparing the accounts of a merchandising company with those of a service company, what additional accounts would the merchandising company likely use, assuming it employs a perpetual inventory system?
2. What items appear in financial statements of merchandising companies but not in the statements of service companies?
3. ♝ Explain how a business can earn a positive gross profit on its sales and still have a net loss.
4. ♝ Why do companies offer a cash discount?
5. How does a company that uses a perpetual inventory system determine the amount of inventory shrinkage?
6. Distinguish between cash discounts and trade discounts. Is the amount of a trade discount on purchased merchandise recorded in the accounts?
7. What is the difference between a sales discount and a purchase discount?
8. ♝ Why would a company's manager be concerned about the quantity of its purchase returns if its suppliers allow unlimited returns?
9. Does the sender (maker) of a debit memorandum record a debit or a credit in the recipient's account? What entry (debit or credit) does the recipient record?
10. What is the difference between the single-step and multiple-step income statement formats?
11. ♝ Refer to the balance sheet and income statement for **Best Buy** in Appendix A. What does the company title its inventory account? Does the company present a detailed calculation of its cost of goods sold?
12. Refer to **Circuit City**'s balance sheet in Appendix A. What title does it use for cost of goods sold?
13. Refer to the income statement for **RadioShack** in Appendix A. What does RadioShack title its cost of goods sold account?
14. Refer to the income statement of **Apple** in Appendix A. Does its income statement report a gross profit figure? If yes, what is the amount?
15. ♝ Buyers negotiate purchase contracts with suppliers. What type of shipping terms should a buyer attempt to negotiate to minimize freight-in costs?

♝ ***Denotes Discussion Questions that involve decision making.***

Available with McGraw-Hill's Homework Manager McGraw-Hill's HOMEWORK MANAGER®

QUICK STUDY

QS 5-1
Recording purchases—perpetual system P1

Prepare journal entries to record each of the following purchases transactions of a merchandising company. Show supporting calculations and assume a perpetual inventory system.

Mar. 5 Purchased 1,000 units of product at a cost of $12 per unit. Terms of the sale are 2/10, n/60; the invoice is dated March 5.
Mar. 7 Returned 50 defective units from the March 5 purchase and received full credit.
Mar. 15 Paid the amount due from the March 5 purchase, less the return on March 7.

QS 5-2
Recording sales—perpetual system
P2

Prepare journal entries to record each of the following sales transactions of a merchandising company. Show supporting calculations and assume a perpetual inventory system.

Apr. 1 Sold merchandise for $5,000, granting the customer terms of 2/10, EOM; invoice dated April 1. The cost of the merchandise is $3,000.
Apr. 4 The customer in the April 1 sale returned merchandise and received credit for $1,000. The merchandise, which had cost $600, is returned to inventory.
Apr. 11 Received payment for the amount due from the April 1 sale less the return on April 4.

QS 5-3
Computing and analyzing gross margin
C1 A2

Compute net sales, gross profit, and the gross margin ratio for each separate case *a* through *d.* Interpret the gross margin ratio for case *a.*

	a	b	c	d
Sales	$140,000	$378,000	$42,500	$593,000
Sales discounts	1,700	6,000	400	2,500
Sales returns and allowances	9,000	17,000	3,400	15,300
Cost of goods sold	82,493	222,230	28,676	451,532

QS 5-4
Accounting for shrinkage—perpetual system
P3

Crystal Company's ledger on July 31, its fiscal year-end, includes the following selected accounts that have normal balances (Crystal uses the perpetual inventory system).

Merchandise inventory	$ 42,000	Sales returns and allowances	$ 7,600
B. Crystal, Capital	124,900	Cost of goods sold	115,000
Sales	275,300	Depreciation expense	12,000
Sales discounts	5,200	Salaries expense	45,000
		Miscellaneous expenses	7,000

A physical count of its July 31 year-end inventory discloses that the cost of the merchandise inventory still available is $40,600. Prepare the entry to record any inventory shrinkage.

QS 5-5
Closing entries P3

Refer to QS 5-4 and prepare journal entries to close the balances in temporary revenue and expense accounts. Remember to consider the entry for shrinkage that is made to solve QS 5-4.

QS 5-6
Computing and interpreting acid-test ratio
A1

Use the following information on current assets and current liabilities to compute and interpret the acid-test ratio. Explain what the acid-test ratio of a company measures.

Cash	$ 3,000	Prepaid expenses	$ 1,400
Accounts receivable	5,580	Accounts payable	11,500
Inventory	12,000	Other current liabilities	1,700

QS 5-7
Contrasting liquidity ratios A1

Identify similarities and differences between the acid-test ratio and the current ratio. Compare and describe how the two ratios reflect a company's ability to meet its current obligations.

QS 5-8A
Contrasting periodic and perpetual systems
C3

Identify whether each description best applies to a periodic or a perpetual inventory system.

a. Requires an adjusting entry to record inventory shrinkage.
b. Markedly increased in frequency and popularity in business within the past decade.
c. Provides more timely information to managers.
d. Records cost of goods sold each time a sales transaction occurs.
e. Updates the inventory account only at period-end.

QS 5-9^A
Recording purchases—periodic system P5

Refer to QS 5-1 and prepare journal entries to record each of the merchandising transactions assuming that the periodic inventory system is used.

QS 5-10^A
Recording purchases—periodic system P5

Refer to QS 5-2 and prepare journal entries to record each of the merchandising transactions assuming that the periodic inventory system is used.

McGraw-Hill's HOMEWORK MANAGER® Available with McGraw-Hill's Homework Manager

EXERCISES

Exercise 5-1
Recording entries for merchandise purchases
P1

Prepare journal entries to record the following transactions for a retail store. Assume a perpetual inventory system.

Apr. 2 Purchased merchandise from Johns Company under the following terms: $5,900 price, invoice dated April 2, credit terms of 2/15, n/60, and FOB shipping point.
3 Paid $330 for shipping charges on the April 2 purchase.
4 Returned to Johns Company unacceptable merchandise that had an invoice price of $900.
17 Sent a check to Johns Company for the April 2 purchase, net of the discount and the returned merchandise.
18 Purchased merchandise from William Corp. under the following terms: $12,250 price, invoice dated April 18, credit terms of 2/10, n/30, and FOB destination.
21 After negotiations, received from William a $3,250 allowance on the April 18 purchase.
28 Sent check to William paying for the April 18 purchase, net of the discount and allowance.

Check April 28, Cr. Cash $8,820

Exercise 5-2
Analyzing and recording merchandise transactions—both buyer and seller
P1 P2

Fortuna Company purchased merchandise for resale from Lemar Company with an invoice price of $30,000 and credit terms of 2/10, n/60. The merchandise had cost Lemar $20,100. Fortuna paid within the discount period. Assume that both buyer and seller use a perpetual inventory system.

1. Prepare entries that the buyer should record for (*a*) the purchase and (*b*) the cash payment.
2. Prepare entries that the seller should record for (*a*) the sale and (*b*) the cash collection.
3. Assume that the buyer borrowed enough cash to pay the balance on the last day of the discount period at an annual interest rate of 8% and paid it back on the last day of the credit period. Compute how much the buyer saved by following this strategy. (Assume a 365-day year and round dollar amounts to the nearest cent.)

Check (3) $278 savings (rounded)

Exercise 5-3
Applying merchandising terms
C1

Enter the letter for each term in the blank space beside the definition that it most closely matches.

A. Cash discount
B. Credit period
C. Discount period
D. FOB destination
E. FOB shipping point
F. Gross profit
G. Merchandise inventory
H. Purchase discount
I. Sales discount
J. Trade discount

_____ **1.** Time period in which a cash discount is available.
_____ **2.** Reduction below list or catalog price that is negotiated in setting the price of goods.
_____ **3.** Reduction in a receivable or payable if it is paid within the discount period.
_____ **4.** Time period that can pass before a customer's payment is due.
_____ **5.** Difference between net sales and the cost of goods sold.
_____ **6.** Ownership of goods is transferred when the seller delivers goods to the carrier.
_____ **7.** Ownership of goods is transferred when delivered to the buyer's place of business.
_____ **8.** Goods a company owns and expects to sell to its customers.
_____ **9.** Purchaser's description of a cash discount received from a supplier of goods.
_____ **10.** Seller's description of a cash discount granted to buyers in return for early payment.

Exercise 5-4
Recording sales returns and allowances P2

Mechanic Parts was organized on May 1, 2009, and made its first purchase of merchandise on May 3. The purchase was for 1,200 units at a price of $7 per unit. On May 5, Mechanic Parts sold 720 of the units for $11 per unit to Radica Co. Terms of the sale were 2/10, n/60. Prepare entries for Mechanic Parts to record the May 5 sale and each of the following separate transactions *a* through *c* using a perpetual inventory system.

a. On May 7, Radica returns 251 units because they did not fit the customer's needs. Mechanic Parts restores the units to its inventory.

b. On May 8, Radica discovers that 60 units are damaged but are still of some use and, therefore, keeps the units. Mechanic Parts sends Radica a credit memorandum for $180 to compensate for the damage.

c. On May 15, Radica discovers that 72 units are the wrong color. Radica keeps 43 of these units because Mechanic sends a $92 credit memorandum to compensate. However, Radica returns the remaining 29 units to Mechanic. Mechanic restores the 29 returned units to its inventory.

Check (c) Dr. Sales Returns and Allowances $411

Exercise 5-5
Recording purchase returns and allowances P1

Refer to Exercise 5-4 and prepare the appropriate journal entries for Radica Co. to record the May 5 purchase and each of the three separate transactions *a* through *c*. Radica is a retailer that uses a perpetual inventory system and purchases these units for resale.

Exercise 5-6
Analyzing and recording merchandise transactions—both buyer and seller

P1 P2

On May 11, York Co. accepts delivery of $38,000 of merchandise it purchases for resale from Troy Corporation. With the merchandise is an invoice dated May 11, with terms of 3/10, n/90, FOB shipping point. The goods cost Troy $25,460. When the goods are delivered, York pays $520 to Express Shipping for delivery charges on the merchandise. On May 12, York returns $2,000 of goods to Troy, who receives them one day later and restores them to inventory. The returned goods had cost Troy $1,393. On May 20, York mails a check to Troy Corporation for the amount owed. Troy receives it the following day. (Both York and Troy use a perpetual inventory system.)

Check (1) May 20, Cr. Cash $34,920

1. Prepare journal entries that York Co. records for these transactions.

2. Prepare journal entries that Troy Corporation records for these transactions.

Exercise 5-7
Sales returns and allowances

C1 P2

Business decision makers desire information on sales returns and allowances. (1) Explain why a company's manager wants the accounting system to record customers' returns of unsatisfactory goods in the Sales Returns and Allowances account instead of the Sales account. (2) Explain whether this information would be useful for external decision makers.

Exercise 5-8
Computing revenues, expenses, and income

C1 C4

Using your accounting knowledge, fill in the blanks in the following separate income statements *a* through *e*. Identify any negative amount by putting it in parentheses.

	a	b	c	d	e
Sales	$82,800	$58,622	$50,094	$?	$32,540
Cost of goods sold					
Merchandise inventory (beginning)	7,866	3,507	10,519	9,902	3,351
Total cost of merchandise purchases	35,439	?	?	45,252	7,439
Merchandise inventory (ending)	?	(3,714)	(12,019)	(9,527)	?
Cost of goods sold	34,950	21,932	?	?	8,359
Gross profit	?	?	4,606	62,013	?
Expenses	9,000	10,650	14,923	32,600	6,100
Net income (loss)	$?	$26,040	$(10,317)	$29,413	$?

Exercise 5-9
Recording effects of merchandising activities

C4

The following supplementary records summarize Tandy Company's merchandising activities for year 2009. Set up T-accounts for Merchandise Inventory and Cost of Goods Sold. Then record the summarized activities in those T-accounts and compute account balances.

Cost of merchandise sold to customers in sales transactions	$296,000
Merchandise inventory, December 31, 2008	42,979
Invoice cost of merchandise purchases	303,459
Shrinkage determined on December 31, 2009	790
Cost of transportation-in	3,034
Cost of merchandise returned by customers and restored to inventory	2,700
Purchase discounts received	2,427
Purchase returns and allowances	3,900

Check Merchandise Inventory Dec. 31, $49,055

Exercise 5-10
Preparing adjusting and closing entries for a merchandiser
P3

The following list includes selected permanent accounts and all of the temporary accounts from the December 31, 2009, unadjusted trial balance of Yamiko Co., a business owned by Kumi Yamiko. Use these account balances along with the additional information to journalize (*a*) adjusting entries and (*b*) closing entries. Yamiko Co. uses a perpetual inventory system.

	Debit	Credit
Merchandise inventory	$ 30,200	
Prepaid selling expenses	4,000	
K. Yamiko, Withdrawals	1,600	
Sales		$543,600
Sales returns and allowances	20,656	
Sales discounts	5,783	
Cost of goods sold	267,451	
Sales salaries expense	59,796	
Utilities expense	17,395	
Selling expenses	46,749	
Administrative expenses	120,135	

Additional Information

Accrued sales salaries amount to $1,700. Prepaid selling expenses of $1,600 have expired. A physical count of year-end merchandise inventory shows $29,626 of goods still available.

Check Entry to close Income Summary: Cr. K. Yamiko, Capital $1,761

Exercise 5-11
Interpreting a physical count error as inventory shrinkage
A1 A2 P3

A retail company recently completed a physical count of ending merchandise inventory to use in preparing adjusting entries. In determining the cost of the counted inventory, company employees failed to consider that $5,000 of incoming goods had been shipped by a supplier on December 31 under an FOB shipping point agreement. These goods had been recorded in Merchandise Inventory as a purchase, but they were not included in the physical count because they were in transit. Explain how this overlooked fact affects the company's financial statements and the following ratios: return on assets, debt ratio, current ratio, profit margin ratio, and acid-test ratio.

Exercise 5-12
Computing and analyzing acid-test and current ratios
A1

Compute the current ratio and acid-test ratio for each of the following separate cases. Which company case is in the best position to meet short-term obligations? Explain.

	Case X	Case Y	Case Z
Cash	$ 920	$ 1,046	$1,220
Short-term investments	0	0	500
Current receivables	0	1,126	890
Inventory	2,300	1,136	4,600
Prepaid expenses	1,200	679	900
Total current assets	$4,420	$3,987	$8,110
Current liabilities	$2,563	$1,281	$4,254

Exercise 5-13
Preparing journal entries—perpetual system
P1 P2

Journalize the following merchandising transactions for Chiller Systems assuming it uses a perpetual inventory system.

1. On November 1, Chiller Systems purchases merchandise for $2,800 on credit with terms of 2/5, n/30, FOB shipping point; invoice dated November 1.
2. On November 5, Chiller Systems pays cash for the November 1 purchase.
3. On November 7, Chiller Systems discovers and returns $100 of defective merchandise purchased on November 1 for a cash refund.
4. On November 10, Chiller Systems pays $140 cash for transportation costs with the November 1 purchase.
5. On November 13, Chiller Systems sells merchandise for $3,024 on credit. The cost of the merchandise is $1,512.
6. On November 16, the customer returns merchandise from the November 13 transaction. The returned items sell for $205 and cost $115.

Exercise 5-14[A]
Recording purchases—periodic system P5

Refer to Exercise 5-1 and prepare journal entries to record each of the merchandising transactions assuming that the periodic inventory system is used.

Exercise 5-15[A]
Recording purchases and sales—periodic system P5

Refer to Exercise 5-2 and prepare journal entries to record each of the merchandising transactions assuming that the periodic inventory system is used by both the buyer and the seller. (Skip the part 3 requirement.)

Exercise 5-16[A]
Buyer and seller transactions—periodic system P5

Refer to Exercise 5-6 and prepare journal entries to record each of the merchandising transactions assuming that the periodic inventory system is used by both the buyer and the seller.

Exercise 5-17[A]
Recording purchases—periodic system P5

Refer to Exercise 5-13 and prepare journal entries to record each of the merchandising transactions assuming that the periodic inventory system is used.

Available with McGraw-Hill's Homework Manager — McGraw-Hill's HOMEWORK MANAGER®

PROBLEM SET A

Problem 5-1A
Preparing journal entries for merchandising activities—perpetual system

P1 P2

Prepare journal entries to record the following merchandising transactions of Flora Company, which applies the perpetual inventory system. (*Hint:* It will help to identify each receivable and payable; for example, record the purchase on July 1 in Accounts Payable—Arch.)

July 1 Purchased merchandise from Arch Company for $6,400 under credit terms of 1/15, n/30, FOB shipping point, invoice dated July 1.

2 Sold merchandise to Driver Co. for $900 under credit terms of 1/10, n/60, FOB shipping point, invoice dated July 2. The merchandise had cost $533.

3 Paid $130 cash for freight charges on the purchase of July 1.

8 Sold merchandise that had cost $1,700 for $2,100 cash.

9 Purchased merchandise from Kew Co. for $2,200 under credit terms of 1/15, n/60, FOB destination, invoice dated July 9.

11 Received a $200 credit memorandum from Kew Co. for the return of part of the merchandise purchased on July 9.

12 Received the balance due from Driver Co. for the invoice dated July 2, net of the discount.

16 Paid the balance due to Arch Company within the discount period.

19 Sold merchandise that cost $800 to Surtis Co. for $1,200 under credit terms of 1/15, n/60, FOB shipping point, invoice dated July 19.

21 Issued a $200 credit memorandum to Surtis Co. for an allowance on goods sold on July 19.

24 Paid Kew Co. the balance due after deducting the discount.

30 Received the balance due from Surtis Co. for the invoice dated July 19, net of discount.

31 Sold merchandise that cost $5,200 to Driver Co. for $6,900 under credit terms of 1/10, n/60, FOB shipping point, invoice dated July 31.

Check July 12, Dr. Cash $891
July 16, Cr. Cash $6,336
July 24, Cr. Cash $1,980
July 30, Dr. Cash $990

Problem 5-2A
Preparing journal entries for merchandising activities—perpetual system

P1 P2

Prepare journal entries to record the following merchandising transactions of Gore Company, which applies the perpetual inventory system. (*Hint:* It will help to identify each receivable and payable; for example, record the purchase on August 1 in Accounts Payable—Arotek.)

Aug. 1 Purchased merchandise from Arotek Company for $7,800 under credit terms of 1/10, n/30, FOB destination, invoice dated August 1.

4 At Arotek's request, Gore paid $270 cash for freight charges on the August 1 purchase, reducing the amount owed to Arotek.

5 Sold merchandise to Larton Corp. for $5,460 under credit terms of 2/10, n/60, FOB destination, invoice dated August 5. The merchandise had cost $3,898.

8 Purchased merchandise from Frees Corporation for $7,100 under credit terms of 1/10, n/45, FOB shipping point, invoice dated August 8. The invoice showed that at Gore's request, Frees paid the $240 shipping charges and added that amount to the bill. (*Hint:* Discounts are not applied to freight and shipping charges.)

9 Paid $120 cash for shipping charges related to the August 5 sale to Larton Corp.

10 Larton returned merchandise from the August 5 sale that had cost Gore $649 and been sold for $910. The merchandise was restored to inventory.

Check Aug. 9, Dr. Delivery Expense, $120

12 After negotiations with Frees Corporation concerning problems with the merchandise purchased on August 8, Gore received a credit memorandum from Frees granting a price reduction of $1,100.
15 Received balance due from Larton Corp. for the August 5 sale less the return on August 10.
18 Paid the amount due Frees Corporation for the August 8 purchase less the price reduction granted.
19 Sold merchandise to Jones Co. for $4,680 under credit terms of 1/10, n/30, FOB shipping point, invoice dated August 19. The merchandise had cost $3,247.
22 Jones requested a price reduction on the August 19 sale because the merchandise did not meet specifications. Gore sent Jones a $780 credit memorandum to resolve the issue.
29 Received Jones's cash payment for the amount due from the August 19 sale.
30 Paid Arotek Company the amount due from the August 1 purchase.

Aug. 18, Cr. Cash $6,180

Aug. 29, Dr. Cash $3,861

Problem 5-3A
Preparing adjusting entries and income statements; and computing gross margin, acid-test, and current ratios

A1 A2 P3 P4

excel
mhhe.com/wildFAP19e

The following unadjusted trial balance is prepared at fiscal year-end for Helix Company.

	HELIX COMPANY Unadjusted Trial Balance January 31, 2009		
1		Debit	Credit
2	Cash	$ 28,750	
3	Merchandise inventory	13,000	
4	Store supplies	5,500	
5	Prepaid insurance	2,400	
6	Store equipment	42,600	
7	Accumulated depreciation—Store equipment		$ 19,750
8	Accounts payable		14,000
9	A. Helix, Capital		39,000
10	A. Helix, Withdrawals	2,000	
11	Sales		115,800
12	Sales discounts	1,900	
13	Sales returns and allowances	2,300	
14	Cost of good sold	38,000	
15	Depreciation expense—Store equipment	0	
16	Salaries expense	27,400	
17	Insurance expense	0	
18	Rent expense	15,000	
19	Store supplies expense	0	
20	Advertising expense	9,700	
21	Totals	$ 188,550	$ 188,550
22			

Rent expense and salaries expense are equally divided between selling activities and the general and administrative activities. Helix Company uses a perpetual inventory system.

Required

1. Prepare adjusting journal entries to reflect each of the following:
   a. Store supplies still available at fiscal year-end amount to $2,550.
   b. Expired insurance, an administrative expense, for the fiscal year is $1,450.
   c. Depreciation expense on store equipment, a selling expense, is $1,975 for the fiscal year.
   d. To estimate shrinkage, a physical count of ending merchandise inventory is taken. It shows $10,300 of inventory is still available at fiscal year-end.

2. Prepare a multiple-step income statement for fiscal year 2009.

3. Prepare a single-step income statement for fiscal year 2009.

4. Compute the current ratio, acid-test ratio, and gross margin ratio as of January 31, 2009.

Check (2) Gross profit, $70,900; (3) Total expenses, $99,175; Net income, $12,425

Problem 5-4A
Computing merchandising amounts and formatting income statements
C4 P4

Rusio Company's adjusted trial balance on August 31, 2009, its fiscal year-end, follows.

	Debit	Credit
Merchandise inventory	$ 43,500	
Other (noninventory) assets	174,000	
Total liabilities		$ 50,242
C. Rusio, Capital		142,036
C. Rusio, Withdrawals	8,000	
Sales		297,540
Sales discounts	4,552	
Sales returns and allowances	19,637	
Cost of goods sold	114,571	
Sales salaries expense	40,762	
Rent expense—Selling space	13,984	
Store supplies expense	3,570	
Advertising expense	25,290	
Office salaries expense	37,192	
Rent expense—Office space	3,570	
Office supplies expense	1,190	
Totals	$489,818	$489,818

On August 31, 2008, merchandise inventory was $35,104. Supplementary records of merchandising activities for the year ended August 31, 2009, reveal the following itemized costs.

Invoice cost of merchandise purchases	$127,890
Purchase discounts received	2,685
Purchase returns and allowances	6.138
Costs of transportation-in	3,900

Required

1. Compute the company's net sales for the year.

2. Compute the company's total cost of merchandise purchased for the year.

3. Prepare a multiple-step income statement that includes separate categories for selling expenses and for general and administrative expenses.

4. Prepare a single-step income statement that includes these expense categories: cost of goods sold, selling expenses, and general and administrative expenses.

Check (2) $122,967;
(3) Gross profit, $158,780; Net income, $33,222;
(4) Total expenses, $240,129

Problem 5-5A
Preparing closing entries and interpreting information about discounts and returns
C4 P3

Use the data for Rusio Company in Problem 5-4A to complete the following requirements.

Required

1. Prepare closing entries as of August 31, 2009 (the perpetual inventory system is used).

Analysis Component

2. The company makes all purchases on credit, and its suppliers uniformly offer a 3% sales discount. Does it appear that the company's cash management system is accomplishing the goal of taking all available discounts? Explain.

3. In prior years, the company experienced a 4% returns and allowance rate on its sales, which means approximately 4% of its gross sales were eventually returned outright or caused the company to grant allowances to customers. How do this year's results compare to prior years' results?

Check (1) $33,222 Dr. to close Income Summary
(3) Current-year rate, 6.6%

Problem 5-6A[B]
Preparing a work sheet for a merchandiser
P3

Refer to the data and information in Problem 5-3A.

Required

Prepare and complete the entire 10-column work sheet for Helix Company. Follow the structure of Exhibit 5B.1 in Appendix 5B.

PROBLEM SET B

Problem 5-1B
Preparing journal entries for merchandising activities—perpetual system
P1 P2

Prepare journal entries to record the following merchandising transactions of Yarvelle Company, which applies the perpetual inventory system. (*Hint:* It will help to identify each receivable and payable; for example, record the purchase on May 2 in Accounts Payable—Pearl.)

May 2 Purchased merchandise from Pearl Co. for $6,600 under credit terms of 3/15, n/30, FOB shipping point, invoice dated May 2.
4 Sold merchandise to Miller Co. for $1,000 under credit terms of 3/10, n/60, FOB shipping point, invoice dated May 4. The merchandise had cost $550.
5 Paid $120 cash for freight charges on the purchase of May 2.
9 Sold merchandise that had cost $1,900 for $2,300 cash.
10 Purchased merchandise from Verte Co. for $2,500 under credit terms of 3/15, n/60, FOB destination, invoice dated May 10.
12 Received a $500 credit memorandum from Verte Co. for the return of part of the merchandise purchased on May 10.
14 Received the balance due from Miller Co. for the invoice dated May 4, net of the discount.
17 Paid the balance due to Pearl Co. within the discount period.
20 Sold merchandise that cost $800 to Stephen Co. for $1,200 under credit terms of 3/15, n/60, FOB shipping point, invoice dated May 20.
22 Issued a $100 credit memorandum to Stephen Co. for an allowance on goods sold from May 20.
25 Paid Verte Co. the balance due after deducting the discount.
30 Received the balance due from Stephen Co. for the invoice dated May 20, net of discount and allowance.
31 Sold merchandise that cost $5,400 to Miller Co. for $7,100 under credit terms of 3/10, n/60, FOB shipping point, invoice dated May 31.

Check May 14, Dr. Cash $970
May 17, Cr. Cash $6,402
May 30, Dr. Cash $1,067

Problem 5-2B
Preparing journal entries for merchandising activities—perpetual system
P1 P2

Prepare journal entries to record the following merchandising transactions of Allou Company, which applies the perpetual inventory system. (*Hint:* It will help to identify each receivable and payable; for example, record the purchase on July 3 in Accounts Payable—Magar.)

July 3 Purchased merchandise from Magar Corp. for $4,100 under credit terms of 1/10, n/30, FOB destination, invoice dated July 3.
4 At Magar's request, Allou paid $500 cash for freight charges on the July 3 purchase, reducing the amount owed to Magar.
7 Sold merchandise to Konop Co. for $2,870 under credit terms of 2/10, n/60, FOB destination, invoice dated July 7. The merchandise had cost $2,049.
10 Purchased merchandise from Payak Corporation for $3,400 under credit terms of 1/10, n/45, FOB shipping point, invoice dated July 10. The invoice showed that at Allou's request, Payak paid the $240 shipping charges and added that amount to the bill. (*Hint:* Discounts are not applied to freight and shipping charges.)
11 Paid $120 cash for shipping charges related to the July 7 sale to Konop Co.
12 Konop returned merchandise from the July 7 sale that had cost Allou $341 and been sold for $470. The merchandise was restored to inventory.
14 After negotiations with Payak Corporation concerning problems with the merchandise purchased on July 10, Allou received a credit memorandum from Payak granting a price reduction of $500.
17 Received balance due from Konop Co. for the July 7 sale less the return on July 12.
20 Paid the amount due Payak Corporation for the July 10 purchase less the price reduction granted.
21 Sold merchandise to Vescio for $2,460 under credit terms of 1/10, n/30, FOB shipping point, invoice dated July 21. The merchandise had cost $1,707.
24 Vescio requested a price reduction on the July 21 sale because the merchandise did not meet specifications. Allou sent Vescio a credit memorandum for $360 to resolve the issue.
30 Received Vescio's cash payment for the amount due from the July 21 sale.
31 Paid Magar Corp. the amount due from the July 3 purchase.

Check July 17, Dr. Cash $2,344
July 20, Cr. Cash $3,111
July 30, Dr. Cash $2,029

Problem 5-3B
Preparing adjusting entries and income statements; and computing gross margin, acid-test, and current ratios
A1 A2 P3 P4

The following unadjusted trial balance is prepared at fiscal year-end for Giaccio Products Company.

GIACCIO PRODUCTS COMPANY
Unadjusted Trial Balance
October 31, 2009

		Debit	Credit
2	Cash	$ 30,150	
3	Merchandise inventory	13,000	
4	Store supplies	5,300	
5	Prepaid insurance	2,700	
6	Store equipment	42,900	
7	Accumulated depreciation—Store equipment		$ 19,900
8	Accounts payable		15,000
9	G. Giaccio, Capital		38,000
10	G. Giaccio, Withdrawals	2,050	
11	Sales		116,250
12	Sales discounts	1,950	
13	Sales returns and allowances	2,300	
14	Cost of goods sold	39,000	
15	Depreciation expense—Store equipment	0	
16	Salaries expense	26,000	
17	Insurance expense	0	
18	Rent expense	14,000	
19	Store supplies expense	0	
20	Advertising expense	9,800	
21	Totals	$189,150	$189,150

Rent expense and salaries expense are equally divided between selling activities and the general and administrative activities. Giaccio Products Company uses a perpetual inventory system.

Required

1. Prepare adjusting journal entries to reflect each of the following.
   a. Store supplies still available at fiscal year-end amount to $1,650.
   b. Expired insurance, an administrative expense, for the fiscal year is $1,300.
   c. Depreciation expense on store equipment, a selling expense, is $1,990 for the fiscal year.
   d. To estimate shrinkage, a physical count of ending merchandise inventory is taken. It shows $11,600 of inventory is still available at fiscal year-end.
2. Prepare a multiple-step income statement for fiscal year 2009.
3. Prepare a single-step income statement for fiscal year 2009.
4. Compute the current ratio, acid-test ratio, and gross margin ratio as of October 31, 2009.

Check (2) Gross profit, $71,600; (3) Total expenses, $97,140; Net income, $14,860

Problem 5-4B
Computing merchandising amounts and formatting income statements
C1 C4 P4

Frisco Company's adjusted trial balance on March 31, 2009, its fiscal year-end, follows.

	Debit	Credit
Merchandise inventory	$ 34,500	
Other (noninventory) assets	138,000	
Total liabilities		$ 39,847
N. Frisco, Capital		115,110
N. Frisco, Withdrawals	8,000	

[continued on next page]

[continued from previous page]

Sales		235,980
Sales discounts	3,610	
Sales returns and allowances	15,574	
Cost of goods sold	91,673	
Sales salaries expense	32,329	
Rent expense—Selling space	11,091	
Store supplies expense	2,831	
Advertising expense	20,058	
Office salaries expense	29,497	
Rent expense—Office space	2,831	
Office supplies expense	943	
Totals	$390,937	$390,937

On March 31, 2008, merchandise inventory was $27,841. Supplementary records of merchandising activities for the year ended March 31, 2009, reveal the following itemized costs.

Invoice cost of merchandise purchases	$101,430
Purchase discounts received	2,130
Purchase returns and allowances	4,868
Costs of transportation-in	3,900

Required

1. Calculate the company's net sales for the year.
2. Calculate the company's total cost of merchandise purchased for the year.
3. Prepare a multiple-step income statement that includes separate categories for selling expenses and for general and administrative expenses.
4. Prepare a single-step income statement that includes these expense categories: cost of goods sold, selling expenses, and general and administrative expenses.

Check (2) $98,332;

(3) Gross profit, $125,123; Net income, $25,543;

(4) Total expenses, $191,253

Problem 5-5B
Preparing closing entries and interpreting information about discounts and returns
C4 P3

Use the data for Frisco Company in Problem 5-4B to complete the following requirements.

Required

1. Prepare closing entries as of March 31, 2009 (the perpetual inventory system is used).

Analysis Component

2. The company makes all purchases on credit, and its suppliers uniformly offer a 3% sales discount. Does it appear that the company's cash management system is accomplishing the goal of taking all available discounts? Explain.
3. In prior years, the company experienced a 5% returns and allowance rate on its sales, which means approximately 5% of its gross sales were eventually returned outright or caused the company to grant allowances to customers. How do this year's results compare to prior years' results?

Check (1) $25,543 Dr. to close Income Summary

(3) Current-year rate, 6.6%

Problem 5-6B[B]
Preparing a work sheet for a merchandiser
P3

Refer to the data and information in Problem 5-3B.

Required

Prepare and complete the entire 10-column work sheet for Giaccio Products Company. Follow the structure of Exhibit 5B.1 in Appendix 5B.

SERIAL PROBLEM

Success Systems

(This serial problem began in Chapter 1 and continues through most of the book. If previous chapter segments were not completed, the serial problem can begin at this point. It is helpful, but not necessary, to use the Working Papers that accompany the book.)

SP 5 Adriana Lopez created Success Systems on October 1, 2009. The company has been successful, and its list of customers has grown. To accommodate the growth, the accounting system is modified to set up separate accounts for each customer. The following chart of accounts includes the account number used for each account and any balance as of December 31, 2009. Lopez decided to add a fourth digit with a decimal point to the 106 account number that had been used for the single Accounts Receivable account. This change allows the company to continue using the existing chart of accounts.

No.	Account Title	Dr.	Cr.
101	Cash	$58,160	
106.1	Alex's Engineering Co.	0	
106.2	Wildcat Services	0	
106.3	Easy Leasing	0	
106.4	IFM Co.	3,000	
106.5	Liu Corp.	0	
106.6	Gomez Co.	2,668	
106.7	Delta Co.	0	
106.8	KC, Inc.	0	
106.9	Dream, Inc.	0	
119	Merchandise inventory	0	
126	Computer supplies	580	
128	Prepaid insurance	1,665	
131	Prepaid rent	825	
163	Office equipment	8,000	
164	Accumulated depreciation—Office equipment		400
167	Computer equipment	20,000	
168	Accumulated depreciation—Computer equipment		1,250
201	Accounts payable		1,100

No.	Account Title	Dr.	Cr.
210	Wages payable		500
236	Unearned computer services revenue		1,500
301	A. Lopez, Capital		90,148
302	A. Lopez, Withdrawals	0	
403	Computer services revenue		0
413	Sales		0
414	Sales returns and allowances	0	
415	Sales discounts	0	
502	Cost of goods sold	0	
612	Depreciation expense—Office equipment	0	
613	Depreciation expense—Computer equipment	0	
623	Wages expense	0	
637	Insurance expense	0	
640	Rent expense	0	
652	Computer supplies expense	0	
655	Advertising expense	0	
676	Mileage expense	0	
677	Miscellaneous expenses	0	
684	Repairs expense—Computer	0	

In response to requests from customers, Lopez will begin selling computer software. The company will extend credit terms of 1/10, n/30, FOB shipping point, to all customers who purchase this merchandise. However, no cash discount is available on consulting fees. Additional accounts (Nos. 119, 413, 414, 415, and 502) are added to its general ledger to accommodate the company's new merchandising activities. Also, Success Systems does not use reversing entries and, therefore, all revenue and expense accounts have zero beginning balances as of January 1, 2010. Its transactions for January through March follow:

Jan. 4 The company paid cash to Lyn Addie for five days' work at the rate of $125 per day. Four of the five days relate to wages payable that were accrued in the prior year.

5 Adriana Lopez invested an additional $25,000 cash in the company.

7 The company purchased $5,800 of merchandise from Kansas Corp. with terms of 1/10, n/30, FOB shipping point, invoice dated January 7.

9 The company received $2,668 cash from Gomez Co. as full payment on its account.

11 The company completed a five-day project for Alex's Engineering Co. and billed it $5,500, which is the total price of $7,000 less the advance payment of $1,500.

13 The company sold merchandise with a retail value of $5,200 and a cost of $3,560 to Liu Corp., invoice dated January 13.

15 The company paid $600 cash for freight charges on the merchandise purchased on January 7.

Check Jan. 11, Dr. Unearned Computer Services Revenue $1,500

16 The company received $4,000 cash from Delta Co. for computer services provided.
17 The company paid Kansas Corp. for the invoice dated January 7, net of the discount.
20 Liu Corp. returned $500 of defective merchandise from its invoice dated January 13. The returned merchandise, which had a $320 cost, is discarded. (The policy of Success Systems is to leave the cost of defective products in cost of goods sold.)
22 The company received the balance due from Liu Corp., net of both the discount and the credit for the returned merchandise.
24 The company returned defective merchandise to Kansas Corp. and accepted a credit against future purchases. The defective merchandise invoice cost, net of the discount, was $496.
26 The company purchased $9,000 of merchandise from Kansas Corp. with terms of 1/10, n/30, FOB destination, invoice dated January 26.
26 The company sold merchandise with a $4,640 cost for $5,800 on credit to KC, Inc., invoice dated January 26.
29 The company received a $496 credit memorandum from Kansas Corp. concerning the merchandise returned on January 24.
31 The company paid cash to Lyn Addie for 10 days' work at $125 per day.
Feb. 1 The company paid $2,475 cash to Hillside Mall for another three months' rent in advance.
3 The company paid Kansas Corp. for the balance due, net of the cash discount, less the $496 amount in the credit memorandum.
5 The company paid $600 cash to the local newspaper for an advertising insert in today's paper.
11 The company received the balance due from Alex's Engineering Co. for fees billed on January 11.
15 Adriana Lopez withdrew $4,800 cash from the company for personal use.
23 The company sold merchandise with a $2,660 cost for $3,220 on credit to Delta Co., invoice dated February 23.
26 The company paid cash to Lyn Addie for eight days' work at $125 per day.
27 The company reimbursed Adriana Lopez for business automobile mileage (600 miles at $0.32 per mile).
Mar. 8 The company purchased $2,730 of computer supplies from Harris Office Products on credit, invoice dated March 8.
9 The company received the balance due from Delta Co. for merchandise sold on February 23.
11 The company paid $960 cash for minor repairs to the company's computer.
16 The company received $5,260 cash from Dream, Inc., for computing services provided.
19 The company paid the full amount due to Harris Office Products, consisting of amounts created on December 15 (of $1,100) and March 8.
24 The company billed Easy Leasing for $8,900 of computing services provided.
25 The company sold merchandise with a $2,002 cost for $2,800 on credit to Wildcat Services, invoice dated March 25.
30 The company sold merchandise with a $1,100 cost for $2,220 on credit to IFM Company, invoice dated March 30.
31 The company reimbursed Adriana Lopez for business automobile mileage (400 miles at $0.32 per mile).

Check Jan. 20, No entry to Cost of Goods Sold

The following additional facts are available for preparing adjustments on March 31 prior to financial statement preparation:

a. The March 31 amount of computer supplies still available totals $2,005.

b. Three more months have expired since the company purchased its annual insurance policy at a $2,220 cost for 12 months of coverage.

c. Lyn Addie has not been paid for seven days of work at the rate of $125 per day.

d. Three months have passed since any prepaid rent has been transferred to expense. The monthly rent expense is $825.

e. Depreciation on the computer equipment for January 1 through March 31 is $1,250.

f. Depreciation on the office equipment for January 1 through March 31 is $400.

g. The March 31 amount of merchandise inventory still available totals $704.

Required

1. Prepare journal entries to record each of the January through March transactions.

2. Post the journal entries in part 1 to the accounts in the company's general ledger. (*Note:* Begin with the ledger's post-closing adjusted balances as of December 31, 2009.)

Check (2) Ending balances: Cash, $77,845; Sales, $19,240;

(3) Unadj. totals, $161,198; Adj. totals, $163,723;

3. Prepare a partial work sheet consisting of the first six columns (similar to the one shown in Exhibit 5B.1) that includes the unadjusted trial balance, the March 31 adjustments (*a*) through (*g*), and the adjusted trial balance. Do not prepare closing entries and do not journalize the adjustments or post them to the ledger.

(4) Net income, $18,686;

4. Prepare an income statement (from the adjusted trial balance in part 3) for the three months ended March 31, 2010. Use a single-step format. List all expenses without differentiating between selling expenses and general and administrative expenses.

(5) A. Lopez, Capital (3/31/10), $129,034;

5. Prepare a statement of owner's equity (from the adjusted trial balance in part 3) for the three months ended March 31, 2010.

(6) Total assets, $129,909

6. Prepare a classified balance sheet (from the adjusted trial balance) as of March 31, 2010.

BEYOND THE NUMBERS

REPORTING IN ACTION

C4 A1

BTN 5-1 Refer to **Best Buy**'s financial statements in Appendix A to answer the following.

Required

1. Assume that the amounts reported for inventories and cost of sales reflect items purchased in a form ready for resale. Compute the net cost of goods purchased for the fiscal year ended March 3, 2007.

2. Compute the current ratio and acid-test ratio as of March 3, 2007, and February 25, 2006. Interpret and comment on the ratio results. How does Best Buy compare to the industry average of 1.6 for the current ratio and 0.7 for the acid-test ratio?

Fast Forward

3. Access Best Buy's financial statements (form 10-K) for fiscal years ending after March 3, 2007, from its Website (BestBuy.com) or the SEC's EDGAR database (www.SEC.gov). Recompute and interpret the current ratio and acid-test ratio for these current fiscal years.

COMPARATIVE ANALYSIS

A2

BTN 5-2 Key comparative figures for both **Best Buy**, **Circuit City**, and **RadioShack** follow.

($ millions)	Best Buy		Circuit City		RadioShack	
	Current Year	Prior Year	Current Year	Prior Year	Current Year	Prior Year
Revenues (net sales)	$35,934	$30,848	$12,430	$11,514	$4,778	$5,082
Cost of sales	27,165	23,122	9,501	8,704	2,544	2,706

Required

1. Compute the dollar amount of gross margin and the gross margin ratio for the two years shown for each of these companies.

2. Which company earns more in gross margin for each dollar of net sales? How do they compare to the industry average of 27.5%?

3. Did the gross margin ratio improve or decline for these companies?

ETHICS CHALLENGE

C1 P2

BTN 5-3 Ashton Martin is a student who plans to attend approximately four professional events a year at her college. Each event necessitates a financial outlay of $100 to $200 for a new suit and accessories. After incurring a major hit to her savings for the first event, Ashton developed a different approach. She buys the suit on credit the week before the event, wears it to the event, and returns it the next week to the store for a full refund on her charge card.

Required

1. Comment on the ethics exhibited by Ashton and possible consequences of her actions.
2. How does the merchandising company account for the suits that Ashton returns?

COMMUNICATING IN PRACTICE

C3 C4 P3

BTN 5-4 You are the financial officer for Music Plus, a retailer that sells goods for home entertainment needs. The business owner, Jamie Madsen, recently reviewed the annual financial statements you prepared and sent you an e-mail stating that he thinks you overstated net income. He explains that although he has invested a great deal in security, he is sure shoplifting and other forms of inventory shrinkage have occurred, but he does not see any deduction for shrinkage on the income statement. The store uses a perpetual inventory system.

Required

Prepare a brief memorandum that responds to the owner's concerns.

TAKING IT TO THE NET

A2 C1

BTN 5-5 Access the SEC's EDGAR database (www.SEC.gov) and obtain the April 19, 2007, filing of its fiscal 2007 10-K report (for year ended February 3, 2007) for **J. Crew Group, Inc.**

Required

Prepare a table that reports the gross margin ratios for J. Crew using the revenues and cost of goods sold data from J. Crew's income statement for each of its most recent three years. Analyze and comment on the trend in its gross margin ratio.

TEAMWORK IN ACTION

C1 C4

BTN 5-6 Best Brands' general ledger and supplementary records at the end of its current period reveal the following.

Sales	$600,000	Merchandise inventory (beginning of period)	$ 98,000
Sales returns	20,000	Invoice cost of merchandise purchases	360,000
Sales discounts	13,000	Purchase discounts received	9,000
Cost of transportation-in	22,000	Purchase returns and allowances	11,000
Operating expenses	50,000	Merchandise inventory (end of period)	84,000

Required

1. *Each* member of the team is to assume responsibility for computing *one* of the following items. You are not to duplicate your teammates' work. Get any necessary amounts to compute your item from the appropriate teammate. Each member is to explain his or her computation to the team in preparation for reporting to the class.
   - **a.** Net sales
   - **b.** Total cost of merchandise purchases
   - **c.** Cost of goods sold
   - **d.** Gross profit
   - **e.** Net income
2. Check your net income with the instructor. If correct, proceed to step 3.
3. Assume that a physical inventory count finds that actual ending inventory is $76,000. Discuss how this affects previously computed amounts in step 1.

Point: In teams of four, assign the same student *a* and *e*. Rotate teams for reporting on a different computation and the analysis in step 3.

ENTREPRENEURIAL DECISION

C1 C4 P4

BTN 5-7 Refer to the opening feature about **BigBadToyStore**. Assume that Joel Boblit reports current annual sales at approximately $10 million and discloses the following income statement.

BigBadToyStore Income Statement For Year Ended January 31, 2008	
Net sales	$10,000,000
Cost of sales	6,100,000
Expenses (other than cost of sales)	2,000,000
Net income	$ 1,900,000

Joel Boblit sells to various individuals and retailers, ranging from small shops to large chains. Assume that Joel currently offers credit terms of 1/15, n/60, and ships FOB destination. To improve his cash flow, Joel is considering changing his credit terms to 3/10, n/30. In addition, he proposes to change his shipping terms to FOB shipping point. He expects that the increase in discount rate will increase his net sales by 9%, but his gross margin ratio (and ratio of cost of sales divided by net sales) is expected to remain unchanged. He also expects that his delivery expenses will be zero under this proposal; thus, his expenses other than cost of sales are expected to increase only 6%.

Required

1. Prepare a forecasted income statement for the year ended January 31, 2009, based on the proposal.
2. Based on the forecasted income statement alone (from your part 1 solution), do you recommend that Joel implement the new sales policies? Explain.
3. What else should Joel consider before he decides whether or not to implement the new policies? Explain.

HITTING THE ROAD

C1

Point: This activity complements the Ethics Challenge assignment.

BTN 5-8 Arrange an interview (in person or by phone) with the manager of a retail shop in a mall or in the downtown area of your community. Explain to the manager that you are a student studying merchandising activities and the accounting for sales returns and sales allowances. Ask the manager what the store policy is regarding returns. Also find out if sales allowances are ever negotiated with customers. Inquire whether management perceives that customers are abusing return policies and what actions management takes to counter potential abuses. Be prepared to discuss your findings in class.

GLOBAL DECISION

A2 P4

BTN 5-9 DSG (www.DSGiplc.com), **Best Buy**, **Circuit City**, and **RadioShack** are all competitors in the global marketplace. Key comparative figures for each company follow.

	Net Sales	Cost of Sales
DSG*	£ 7,930	£ 7,285
Best Buy†	$35,934	$27,165
Circuit City†	$12,430	$ 9,501
RadioShack†	$ 4, 778	$ 2,544

* £ millions for DSG.

† $ millions for Best Buy, Circuit City, and RadioShack.

Required

1. Rank the four companies (highest to lowest) based on the gross margin ratio.
2. Which of the companies uses a multiple-step income statement format? (Access DSG's annual report from its Website to answer this; the other three companies' reports are in Appendix A.)
3. Which company's income statement would likely be most easily interpreted by potential investors? Provide a brief justification for your choice.

ANSWERS TO MULTIPLE CHOICE QUIZ

1. c; Gross profit = \$550,000 − \$193,000 = \$357,000
2. d; (\$4,500 − \$250) × (100% − 2%) = \$4,165
3. b; Net sales = \$75,000 + \$320,000 − \$13,700 − \$6,000 = \$375,300
4. b; Acid-test ratio = \$37,500/\$50,000 = 0.750
5. a; Gross margin ratio = (\$675,000 − \$459,000)/\$675,000 = 32%

A Look Back

Chapter 5 focused on merchandising activities and how they are reported. We analyzed and recorded purchases and sales and explained accounting adjustments and closing for merchandisers.

A Look at This Chapter

This chapter emphasizes accounting for inventory. We describe methods for assigning costs to inventory and we explain the items and costs making up merchandise inventory. We also discuss methods of estimating and measuring inventory.

A Look Ahead

Chapter 7 emphasizes accounting information systems. We describe system principles, the system components, use of special journals and subsidiary ledgers, and technology-based systems.

Chapter 6 Inventories and Cost of Sales

Learning Objectives

CAP

Conceptual

C1 Identify the items making up merchandise inventory. *(p. 224)*

C2 Identify the costs of merchandise inventory. *(p. 225)*

Analytical

A1 Analyze the effects of inventory methods for both financial and tax reporting. *(p. 232)*

A2 Analyze the effects of inventory errors on current and future financial statements. *(p. 235)*

A3 Assess inventory management using both inventory turnover and days' sales in inventory. *(p. 236)*

LP6

Procedural

P1 Compute inventory in a perpetual system using the methods of specific identification, FIFO, LIFO, and weighted average. *(p. 226)*

P2 Compute the lower of cost or market amount of inventory. *(p. 233)*

P3 *Appendix 6A*—Compute inventory in a periodic system using the methods of specific identification, FIFO, LIFO, and weighted average. *(p. 242)*

P4 *Appendix 6B*—Apply both the retail inventory and gross profit methods to estimate inventory. *(p. 247)*

Decision Feature

Scent of Success

"Believe in yourself, your product and services"
—Jacquelyn Tran

HUNTINGTON BEACH, CA—As U.S. immigrants, Jacquelyn Tran and her family had no money and did not speak English. "They [her family] took the risk," explains Jacquelyn, in the hope of opportunity. A few years passed and Jacquelyn caught a glimpse of her future. "I saw an opportunity to take . . . the retail perfume business to the next level." She launched **Beauty Encounter (BeautyEncounter.com)** to provide perfume and beauty products to consumers.

The entrepreneurial road was rough at times. Jacquelyn struggled with inventory and sales, and had to deal with discounts, returns, and allowances. A major challenge was maintaining appropriate inventories while controlling costs. "I made plenty of mistakes," admits Jacquelyn. "I just had to throw myself in there and learn."

Learn she did. Applying modern inventory management, and trial and error, Jacquelyn learned to fill orders, collect money, and stock the right inventory. "We have something for everyone," explains Jacquelyn, and her perpetual inventory system accounts for inventory sales and purchases in real time. "It's really important for customers to be able to find products . . . [and for me] to give them what they want."

But business success requires more than good products and perpetual inventory management, insists Jacquelyn. "[It] requires a lot of patience, energy and faith." We focus on customer satisfaction, says Jacquelyn. As a result, "we have very loyal customers."

Although Jacquelyn continues to measure, monitor, and manage inventories and costs, her success and growth are pushing her to a more managerial role. "We are moving into a larger warehouse, allowing us to expand our selection," explains Jacquelyn. Her inventory procedures contribute to her success and allow her customers to know which products are hot. "I never imagined I would be where I am today," says Jacquelyn. "It is really cool."

[Sources: *Beauty Encounter Website,* January 2009; *USA Today,* April 2008; *CNN Money,* June 2005; *Inc.com,* July 2007; *Entrepreneur,* December 2007; *MyWomanOwnedBusiness.com,* August 2007]

Chapter Preview

Merchandisers' activities include the purchasing and reselling of merchandise. We explained accounting for merchandisers in Chapter 5, including that for purchases and sales. In this chapter, we extend the study and analysis of inventory by explaining the methods used to assign costs to merchandise inventory *and* to cost of goods sold. Retailers, wholesalers, and other merchandising companies that purchase products for resale use the principles and methods described here. Understanding inventory accounting helps in the analysis and interpretation of financial statements and helps people run their businesses.

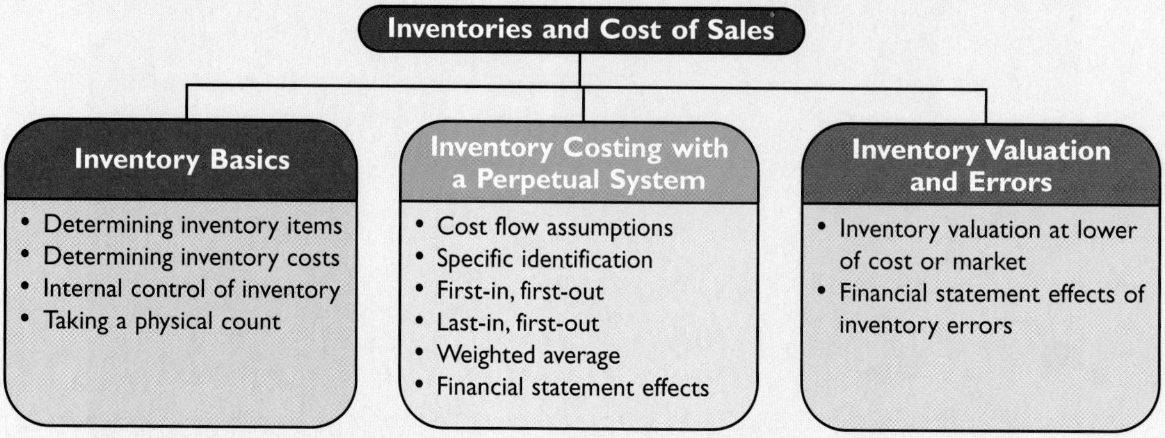

Inventory Basics

This section identifies the items and costs making up merchandise inventory. It also describes the importance of internal controls in taking a physical count of inventory.

Determining Inventory Items

C1 Identify the items making up merchandise inventory.

Merchandise inventory includes all goods that a company owns and holds for sale. This rule holds regardless of where the goods are located when inventory is counted. Certain inventory items require special attention, including goods in transit, goods on consignment, and goods that are damaged or obsolete.

Goods in Transit Does a purchaser's inventory include goods in transit from a supplier? The answer is that if ownership has passed to the purchaser, the goods are included in the purchaser's inventory. We determine this by reviewing the shipping terms: *FOB destination* or *FOB shipping point.* If the purchaser is responsible for paying freight, ownership passes when goods are loaded on the transport vehicle. If the seller is responsible for paying freight, ownership passes when goods arrive at their destination.

Goods on Consignment Goods on consignment are goods shipped by the owner, called the **consignor,** to another party, the **consignee.** A consignee sells goods for the owner. The consignor continues to own the consigned goods and reports them in its inventory. **Upper Deck,** for instance, pays sports celebrities such as Tiger Woods to sign memorabilia, which are offered to shopping networks on consignment. Upper Deck, the consignor, must report these items in its inventory until sold.

Goods Damaged or Obsolete Damaged and obsolete (and deteriorated) goods are not counted in inventory if they cannot be sold. If these goods can be sold at a reduced price, they are included in inventory at a conservative estimate of their **net realizable value.** Net realizable value is sales price minus the cost of making the sale. The period when damage or obsolescence (or deterioration) occurs is the period when the loss in value is reported.

Decision Insight

A wireless portable device with a two-way radio allows clerks to quickly record inventory by scanning bar codes and to instantly send and receive inventory data. It gives managers access to up-to-date information on inventory and its location.

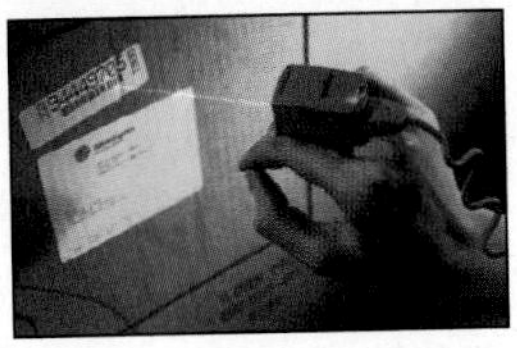

Determining Inventory Costs

C2 Identify the costs of merchandise inventory.

Merchandise inventory includes costs of expenditures necessary, directly or indirectly, to bring an item to a salable condition and location. This means that the cost of an inventory item includes its invoice cost minus any discount, and plus any incidental costs necessary to put it in a place and condition for sale. Incidental costs can include import duties, freight, storage, insurance, and costs incurred in an aging process (for example, aging wine or cheese).

Accounting principles prescribe that incidental costs be added to inventory. Also, the *matching principle* states that inventory costs should be recorded against revenue in the period when inventory is sold. However, some companies use the *materiality constraint* (*cost-to-benefit constraint*) to avoid assigning some incidental costs of acquiring merchandise to inventory. Instead, they expense them when incurred. These companies argue either that those incidental costs are immaterial or that the effort in assigning them outweighs the benefit.

Internal Controls and Taking a Physical Count

The Inventory account under a perpetual system is updated for each purchase and sale, but events can cause the Inventory account balance to differ from the actual inventory available. Such events include theft, loss, damage, and errors. Thus, nearly all companies take a *physical count of inventory* at least once each year—informally called *taking an inventory.* This often occurs at the end of a fiscal year or when inventory amounts are low. This physical count is used to adjust the Inventory account balance to the actual inventory available.

A company applies internal controls when taking a physical count of inventory that usually includes the following:

- *Prenumbered inventory tickets* are prepared and distributed to the *counters*—each ticket must be accounted for.
- Counters of inventory are assigned and do not include those responsible for inventory.
- Counters confirm the validity of inventory, including its existence, amount, and quality.
- A second count is taken by a different counter.
- A manager confirms that all inventories are ticketed once, and only once.

Point: The Inventory account is a controlling account for the inventory subsidiary ledger. This *subsidiary ledger* contains a separate record (units and costs) for each separate product, and it can be in electronic or paper form. Subsidiary records assist managers in planning and monitoring inventory.

Quick Check Answers—p. 250

1. What accounting principle most guides the allocation of cost of goods available for sale between ending inventory and cost of goods sold?
2. If **Skechers** sells goods to **Target** with terms FOB shipping point, which company reports these goods in its inventory while they are in transit?
3. An art gallery purchases a painting for $11,400 on terms FOB shipping point. Additional costs in obtaining and offering the artwork for sale include $130 for transportation in, $150 for import duties, $100 for insurance during shipment, $180 for advertising, $400 for framing, and $800 for office salaries. For computing inventory, what cost is assigned to the painting?

Inventory Costing Under a Perpetual System

Accounting for inventory affects both the balance sheet and the income statement. A major goal in accounting for inventory is to properly match costs with sales. We use the *matching principle* to decide how much of the cost of the goods available for sale is deducted from sales and how much is carried forward as inventory and matched against future sales.

Management decisions in accounting for inventory involve the following:

- Items included in inventory and their costs.
- Costing method (specific identification, FIFO, LIFO, or weighted average).
- Inventory system (perpetual or periodic).
- Use of market values or other estimates.

Video6.1

The first point was explained on the prior two pages. The second and third points will be addressed now. The fourth point is the focus at the end of this chapter. Decisions on these points affect the reported amounts for inventory, cost of goods sold, gross profit, income, current assets, and other accounts.

One of the most important issues in accounting for inventory is determining the per unit costs assigned to inventory items. When all units are purchased at the same unit cost, this process is simple. When identical items are purchased at different costs, however, a question arises as to which amounts to record in cost of goods sold and which amounts remain in inventory.

Four methods are commonly used to assign costs to inventory and to cost of goods sold: (1) specific identification; (2) first-in, first-out; (3) last-in, first-out; and (4) weighted average. Exhibit 6.1 shows the frequency in the use of these methods.

EXHIBIT 6.1

Frequency in Use of Inventory Methods

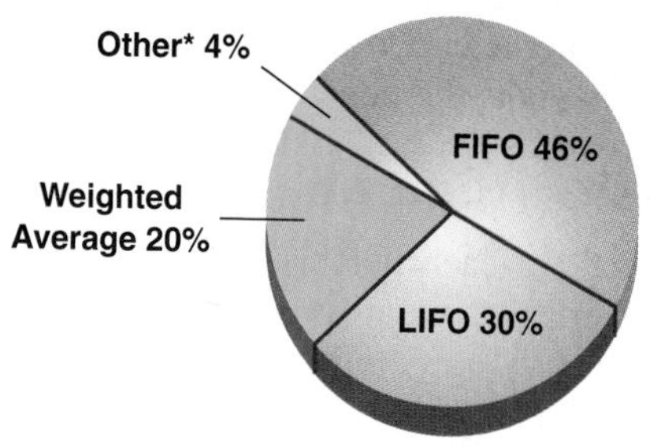

*Includes specific identification.

Each method assumes a particular pattern for how costs flow through inventory. Each of these four methods is acceptable whether or not the actual physical flow of goods follows the cost flow assumption. Physical flow of goods depends on the type of product and the way it is stored. (Perishable goods such as fresh fruit demand that a business attempt to sell them in a first-in, first-out physical flow. Other products such as crude oil and minerals such as coal, gold, and decorative stone can be sold in a last-in, first-out physical flow.) **Physical flow and cost flow need not be the same.**

Inventory Cost Flow Assumption

P1 Compute inventory in a perpetual system using the methods of specific identification, FIFO, LIFO, and weighted average.

Point: It is helpful to recall the cost flow of inventory from Exhibit 5.4.

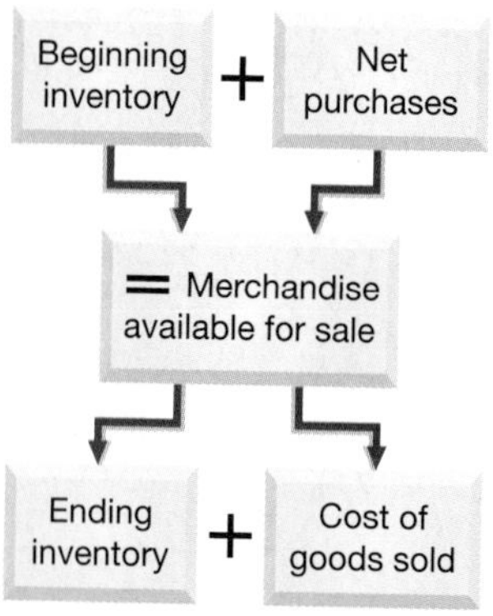

This section introduces inventory cost flow assumptions. For this purpose, assume that three identical units are purchased separately at the following three dates and costs: May 1 at $45, May 3 at $65, and May 6 at $70. One unit is then sold on May 7 for $100. Exhibit 6.2 gives a visual layout of the flow of costs to either the gross profit section of the income statement or the inventory reported on the balance sheet for FIFO, LIFO, and weighted average.

(1) *FIFO assumes costs flow in the order incurred.* The unit purchased on May 1 for $45 is the earliest cost incurred—it is sent to cost of goods sold on the income statement first. The remaining two units ($65 and $70) are reported in inventory on the balance sheet.

(2) *LIFO assumes costs flow in the reverse order incurred.* The unit purchased on May 6 for $70 is the most recent cost incurred—it is sent to cost of goods sold on the income statement. The remaining two units ($45 and $65) are reported in inventory on the balance sheet.

(3) *Weighted average assumes costs flow at an average of the costs available.* The units available at the May 7 sale average $60 in cost, computed as ($45 + $65 + $70)/3. One unit's $60 average cost is sent to cost of goods sold on the income statement. The remaining two units' average costs are reported in inventory at $120 on the balance sheet.

Cost flow assumptions can markedly impact gross profit and inventory numbers. Exhibit 6.2 shows that gross profit as a percent of net sales ranges from 30% to 55% due to nothing else but the cost flow assumption.

The following sections on inventory costing use the perpetual system. Appendix 6A uses the periodic system. An instructor can choose to cover either one or both systems. If the perpetual system is skipped, then read Appendix 6A and return to the section (seven pages ahead) titled "Valuing Inventory at LCM and . . ."

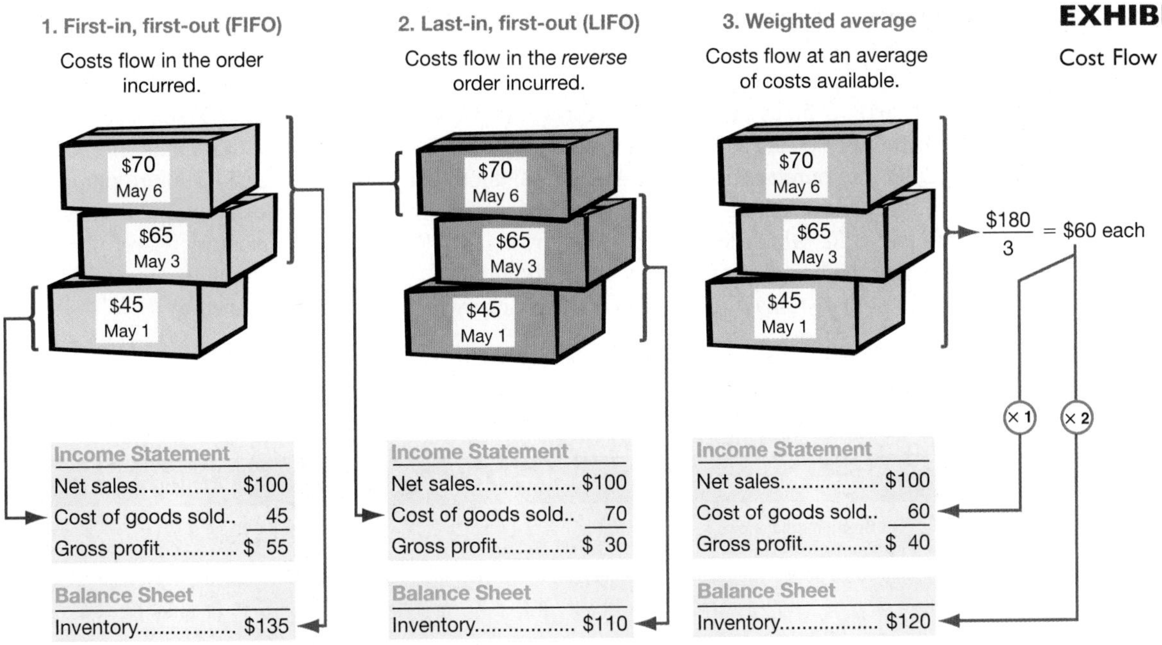

EXHIBIT 6.2

Cost Flow Assumptions

Inventory Costing Illustration

This section provides a comprehensive illustration of inventory costing methods. We use information from Trekking, a sporting goods store. Among its many products, Trekking carries one type of mountain bike whose sales are directed at resorts that provide inexpensive mountain bikes for complimentary guest use. Its customers usually purchase in amounts of 10 or more bikes. We use Trekking's data from August. Its mountain bike (unit) inventory at the beginning of August and its purchases and sales during August are shown in Exhibit 6.3. It ends August with 12 bikes remaining in inventory.

EXHIBIT 6.3

Purchases and Sales of Goods

Date	Activity	Units Acquired at Cost	Units Sold at Retail	Unit Inventory
Aug. 1	Beginning inventory	10 units @ $ 91 = $ 910		10 units
Aug. 3	Purchases	15 units @ $106 = $ 1,590		25 units
Aug. 14	Sales		20 units @ $130	5 units
Aug. 17	Purchases	20 units @ $115 = $ 2,300		25 units
Aug. 28	Purchases	10 units @ $119 = $ 1,190		35 units
Aug. 31	Sales		23 units @ $150	12 units
	Totals	55 units $5,990	43 units	

Point: The perpetual inventory system is now the most dominant system for U.S. businesses.

Point: Cost of goods sold plus ending inventory equals cost of goods available for sale.

Trekking uses the perpetual inventory system, which means that its merchandise inventory account is continually updated to reflect purchases and sales. **(Appendix 6A describes the assignment of costs to inventory using a periodic system.)** Regardless of what inventory method or system is used, cost of goods available for sale must be allocated between cost of goods sold and ending inventory.

Specific Identification

When each item in inventory can be identified with a specific purchase and invoice, we can use **specific identification** (also called *specific invoice inventory pricing*) to assign costs. We also need sales records that identify exactly which items were sold and when. Trekking's internal documents reveal the following specific unit sales:

August 14	Sold 8 bikes costing $91 each and 12 bikes costing $106 each
August 31	Sold 2 bikes costing $91 each, 3 bikes costing $106 each, 15 bikes costing $115 each, and 3 bikes costing $119 each

Point: Three key variables determine the dollar value of ending inventory: (1) inventory quantity, (2) costs of inventory, and (3) cost flow assumption.

Applying specific identification, and using the information above and from Exhibit 6.3, we prepare Exhibit 6.4. This exhibit starts with 10 bikes at $91 each in beginning inventory. On August 3, 15 more bikes are purchased at $106 each for $1,590. Inventory available now consists of 10 bikes at $91 each and 15 bikes at $106 each, for a total of $2,500. On August 14 (see sales above), 20 bikes costing $2,000 are sold—leaving 5 bikes costing $500 in inventory. On August 17, 20 bikes costing $2,300 are purchased, and on August 28, another 10 bikes costing $1,190 are purchased, for a total of 35 bikes costing $3,990 in inventory. On August 31 (see sales above), 23 bikes costing $2,582 are sold, which leaves 12 bikes costing $1,408 in ending inventory. Carefully study this exhibit and the boxed explanations to see the flow of costs both in and out of inventory. Each unit, whether sold or remaining in inventory, has its own specific cost attached to it.

EXHIBIT 6.4

Specific Identification Computations

"goods in" → Goods Purchased; "goods out" → Cost of Goods Sold; "what's left" → Inventory Balance

Date	Goods Purchased	Cost of Goods Sold		Inventory Balance	
Aug. 1	Beginning balance			10 @ $ 91	= $ 910
Aug. 3	15 @ $106 = $1,590			10 @ $ 91 15 @ $106	= $2,500
Aug. 14		8 @ $ 91 = $ 728 12 @ $106 = $1,272	= $2,000*	2 @ $ 91 3 @ $106	= $ 500
Aug. 17	20 @ $115 = $2,300			2 @ $ 91 3 @ $106 20 @ $115	= $2,800
Aug. 28	10 @ $119 = $1,190			2 @ $ 91 3 @ $106 20 @ $115 10 @ $119	= $3,990
Aug. 31		2 @ $ 91 = $ 182 3 @ $106 = $ 318 15 @ $115 = $1,725 3 @ $119 = $ 357	= $2,582*	5 @ $115 7 @ $119	= $1,408
			$4,582		

For the 20 units sold on Aug. 14, the company specifically identified that 8 of those had cost $91 and 12 had cost $106.

For the 23 units sold on Aug. 31, the company specifically identified each bike sold and its acquisition cost from prior purchases.

* Identification of items sold (and their costs) is obtained from internal documents that track each unit from its purchase to its sale.

When using specific identification, Trekking's cost of goods sold reported on the income statement totals **$4,582**, the sum of $2,000 and $2,582 from the third column of Exhibit 6.4. Trekking's ending inventory reported on the balance sheet is **$1,408**, which is the final inventory balance from the fourth column of Exhibit 6.4.

Point: Specific identification is usually practical only for companies with expensive, custom-made inventory.

The purchases and sales entries for Exhibit 6.4 follow (the colored boldface numbers are those impacted by the cost flow assumption).

Purchases

Aug. 3	Merchandise Inventory	1,590	
	Accounts Payable		1,590
17	Merchandise Inventory	2,300	
	Accounts Payable		2,300
28	Merchandise Inventory	1,190	
	Accounts Payable		1,190

Sales

Aug. 14	Accounts Receivable	2,600	
	Sales		2,600
14	Cost of Goods Sold	**2,000**	
	Merchandise Inventory		**2,000**
31	Accounts Receivable	3,450	
	Sales		3,450
31	Cost of Goods Sold	**2,582**	
	Merchandise Inventory		**2,582**

First-In, First-Out

The **first-in, first-out (FIFO)** method of assigning costs to both inventory and cost of goods sold assumes that inventory items are sold in the order acquired. When sales occur, the costs of the earliest units acquired are charged to cost of goods sold. This leaves the costs from the most recent purchases in ending inventory. Use of FIFO for computing the cost of inventory and cost of goods sold is shown in Exhibit 6.5.

This exhibit starts with beginning inventory of 10 bikes at $91 each. On August 3, 15 more bikes costing $106 each are bought for $1,590. Inventory now consists of 10 bikes at $91 each and 15 bikes at $106 each, for a total of $2,500. On August 14, 20 bikes are sold—applying FIFO, the first 10 sold cost $91 each and the next 10 sold cost $106 each, for a total cost of $1,970. This leaves 5 bikes costing $106 each, or $530, in inventory. On August 17, 20 bikes costing $2,300 are purchased, and on August 28, another 10 bikes costing $1,190 are purchased, for a total of 35 bikes costing $4,020 in inventory. On August 31, 23 bikes are sold—applying FIFO, the first 5 bikes sold cost $530 and the next 18 sold cost $2,070, which leaves 12 bikes costing $1,420 in ending inventory.

Point: The "Goods Purchased" column is identical for all methods. Data are taken from Exhibit 6.3.

EXHIBIT 6.5

FIFO Computations—Perpetual System

Date	Goods Purchased	Cost of Goods Sold		Inventory Balance	
Aug. 1	Beginning balance			10 @ $ 91	= $ 910
Aug. 3	15 @ $106 = $1,590			10 @ $ 91 15 @ $106	= $2,500
Aug. 14		10 @ $ 91 = $ 910 10 @ $106 = $1,060	= $1,970	5 @ $106	= $ 530
Aug. 17	20 @ $115 = $2,300			5 @ $106 20 @ $115	= $2,830
Aug. 28	10 @ $119 = $1,190			5 @ $106 20 @ $115 10 @ $119	= $4,020
Aug. 31		5 @ $106 = $ 530 18 @ $115 = $2,070	= $2,600	2 @ $115 10 @ $119	= $1,420
			$4,570		

For the 20 units sold on Aug. 14, the first 10 sold are assigned the earliest cost of $91 (from beg. bal.). The next 10 sold are assigned the next earliest cost of $106.

For the 23 units sold on Aug. 31, the first 5 sold are assigned the earliest available cost of $106 (from Aug. 3 purchase). The next 18 sold are assigned the next earliest cost of $115 (from Aug. 17 purchase).

Trekking's FIFO cost of goods sold reported on its income statement (reflecting the 43 units sold) is **$4,570** ($1,970 + $2,600), and its ending inventory reported on the balance sheet (reflecting the 12 units unsold) is **$1,420**.

Point: Under FIFO, a unit sold is assigned the earliest (oldest) cost from inventory. This leaves the most recent costs in ending inventory.

The purchases and sales entries for Exhibit 6.5 follow (the colored boldface numbers are those affected by the cost flow assumption).

Purchases

Aug. 3	Merchandise Inventory	1,590	
	Accounts Payable		1,590
17	Merchandise Inventory	2,300	
	Accounts Payable		2,300
28	Merchandise Inventory	1,190	
	Accounts Payable		1,190

Sales

Aug. 14	Accounts Receivable.	2,600	
	Sales		2,600
14	Cost of Goods Sold.	**1,970**	
	Merchandise Inventory. . . .		**1,970**
31	Accounts Receivable.	3,450	
	Sales		3,450
31	Cost of Goods Sold.	**2,600**	
	Merchandise Inventory. . . .		**2,600**

Last-In, First-Out

The **last-in, first-out (LIFO)** method of assigning costs assumes that the most recent purchases are sold first. These more recent costs are charged to the goods sold, and the costs of the earliest purchases are assigned to inventory. As with other methods, LIFO is acceptable even when

Point: Under LIFO, a unit sold is assigned the most recent (latest) cost from inventory. This leaves the oldest costs in inventory.

the physical flow of goods does not follow a last-in, first-out pattern. One appeal of LIFO is that by assigning costs from the most recent purchases to cost of goods sold, LIFO comes closest to matching current costs of goods sold with revenues (compared to FIFO or weighted average).

Exhibit 6.6 shows the LIFO computations. It starts with beginning inventory of 10 bikes at $91 each. On August 3, 15 more bikes costing $106 each are bought for $1,590. Inventory now consists of 10 bikes at $91 each and 15 bikes at $106 each, for a total of $2,500. On August 14, 20 bikes are sold—applying LIFO, the first 15 sold are from the most recent purchase costing $106 each, and the next 5 sold are from the next most recent purchase costing $91 each, for a total cost of $2,045. This leaves 5 bikes costing $91 each, or $455, in inventory. On August 17, 20 bikes costing $2,300 are purchased, and on August 28, another 10 bikes costing $1,190 are purchased, for a total of 35 bikes costing $3,945 in inventory. On August 31, 23 bikes are sold—applying LIFO, the first 10 bikes sold are from the most recent purchase costing $1,190, and the next 13 sold are from the next most recent purchase costing $1,495, which leaves 12 bikes costing $1,260 in ending inventory.

EXHIBIT 6.6

LIFO Computations—Perpetual System

For the 20 units sold on Aug. 14, the first 15 sold are assigned the most recent cost of $106. The next 5 sold are assigned the next most recent cost of $91.

For the 23 units sold on Aug. 31, the first 10 sold are assigned the most recent cost of $119. The next 13 sold are assigned the next most recent cost of $115.

Date	Goods Purchased	Cost of Goods Sold	Inventory Balance
Aug. 1	Beginning balance		10 @ $ 91 = $ 910
Aug. 3	15 @ $106 = $1,590		10 @ $ 91 15 @ $106 } = $ 2,500
Aug. 14		15 @ $106 = $1,590 5 @ $ 91 = $ 455 } = $2,045	5 @ $ 91 = $ 455
Aug. 17	20 @ $115 = $2,300		5 @ $ 91 20 @ $115 } = $ 2,755
Aug. 28	10 @ $119 = $1,190		5 @ $ 91 20 @ $115 10 @ $119 } = $ 3,945
Aug. 31		10 @ $119 = $1,190 13 @ $115 = $1,495 } = $2,685 $4,730	5 @ $ 91 7 @ $115 } = $1,260

Trekking's LIFO cost of goods sold reported on the income statement is **$4,730** ($2,045 + $2,685), and its ending inventory reported on the balance sheet is **$1,260**.

The purchases and sales entries for Exhibit 6.6 follow (the colored boldface numbers are those affected by the cost flow assumption).

Purchases

Aug. 3	Merchandise Inventory	1,590	
	Accounts Payable		1,590
17	Merchandise Inventory	2,300	
	Accounts Payable		2,300
28	Merchandise Inventory	1,190	
	Accounts Payable		1,190

Sales

Aug. 14	Accounts Receivable	2,600	
	Sales		2,600
14	Cost of Goods Sold	**2,045**	
	Merchandise Inventory		**2,045**
31	Accounts Receivable	3,450	
	Sales		3,450
31	Cost of Goods Sold	**2,685**	
	Merchandise Inventory		**2,685**

Weighted Average

The **weighted average** (also called **average cost**) method of assigning cost requires that we use the weighted average cost per unit of inventory at the time of each sale. Weighted average cost per unit at the time of each sale equals the cost of goods available for sale divided by the units available. The results using weighted average (WA) for Trekking are shown in Exhibit 6.7.

This exhibit starts with beginning inventory of 10 bikes at $91 each. On August 3, 15 more bikes costing $106 each are bought for $1,590. Inventory now consists of 10 bikes at $91 each and 15 bikes at $106 each, for a total of $2,500. The average cost per bike for that inventory

EXHIBIT 6.7

Weighted Average Computations—Perpetual System

Date	Goods Purchased	Cost of Goods Sold	Inventory Balance
Aug. 1	Beginning balance		10 @ $ 91 = $ 910
Aug. 3	15 @ $106 = $1,590		10 @ $ 91 15 @ $106 } = $2,500 (or $100 per unit)[a]
Aug. 14		20 @ $100 = **$2,000**	5 @ $100 = $ 500 (or $100 per unit)[b]
Aug. 17	20 @ $115 = $2,300		5 @ $100 20 @ $115 } = $2,800 (or $112 per unit)[c]
Aug. 28	10 @ $119 = $1,190		5 @ $100 20 @ $115 10 @ $119 } = $3,990 (or $114 per unit)[d]
Aug. 31		23 @ $114 = **$2,622**	12 @ $114 = **$1,368** (or $114 per unit)[e]
		$4,622	

For the 20 units sold on Aug. 14, the cost assigned is the $100 *average cost* per unit from the inventory balance column at the time of sale.

For the 23 units sold on Aug. 31, the cost assigned is the $114 *average cost* per unit from the inventory balance column at the time of sale.

[a] $100 per unit = ($2,500 inventory balance ÷ 25 units in inventory).
[b] $100 per unit = ($500 inventory balance ÷ 5 units in inventory).
[c] $112 per unit = ($2,800 inventory balance ÷ 25 units in inventory).
[d] $114 per unit = ($3,990 inventory balance ÷ 35 units in inventory).
[e] $114 per unit = ($1,368 inventory balance ÷ 12 units in inventory).

is $100, computed as $2,500/(10 bikes + 15 bikes). On August 14, 20 bikes are sold—applying WA, the 20 sold are assigned the $100 average cost, for a total cost of $2,000. This leaves 5 bikes with an average cost of $100 each, or $500, in inventory. On August 17, 20 bikes costing $2,300 are purchased, and on August 28, another 10 bikes costing $1,190 are purchased, for a total of 35 bikes costing $3,990 in inventory at August 28. The average cost per bike for the August 28 inventory is $114, computed as $3,990/(5 bikes + 20 bikes + 10 bikes). On August 31, 23 bikes are sold—applying WA, the 23 sold are assigned the $114 average cost, for a total cost of $2,622. This leaves 12 bikes costing $1,368 in ending inventory.

Trekking's cost of goods sold reported on the income statement (reflecting the 43 units sold) is **$4,622** ($2,000 + $2,622), and its ending inventory reported on the balance sheet (reflecting the 12 units unsold) is **$1,368**.

Point: Under weighted average, a unit sold is assigned the average cost of all items currently available for sale at the date of each sale.

The purchases and sales entries for Exhibit 6.7 follow (the colored boldface numbers are those affected by the cost flow assumption).

Purchases

Aug. 3	Merchandise Inventory	1,590	
	Accounts Payable		1,590
17	Merchandise Inventory	2,300	
	Accounts Payable		2,300
28	Merchandise Inventory	1,190	
	Accounts Payable		1,190

Sales

Aug. 14	Accounts Receivable	2,600	
	Sales		2,600
14	Cost of Goods Sold	**2,000**	
	Merchandise Inventory		**2,000**
31	Accounts Receivable	3,450	
	Sales		3,450
31	Cost of Goods Sold	**2,622**	
	Merchandise Inventory		**2,622**

Advances in technology have greatly reduced the cost of a perpetual inventory system. Many companies are now asking whether they can afford *not* to have a perpetual inventory system because timely access to inventory information is a competitive advantage and it can help reduce the level of inventory, which reduces costs.

Decision Insight

Inventory Control SOX demands that companies safeguard inventory and properly report it. Safeguards include restricted access, use of authorized requisitions, security measures, and controlled environments to prevent damage. Proper accounting includes matching inventory received with purchase order terms and quality requirements, preventing misstatements, and controlling access to inventory records.

Financial Statement Effects of Costing Methods

A1 Analyze the effects of inventory methods for both financial and tax reporting.

When purchase prices do not change, each inventory costing method assigns the same cost amounts to inventory and to cost of goods sold. When purchase prices are different, however, the methods nearly always assign different cost amounts. We show these differences in Exhibit 6.8 using Trekking's data.

EXHIBIT 6.8

Financial Statement Effects of Inventory Costing Methods

TREKKING COMPANY
For Month Ended August 31

	Specific Identification	FIFO	LIFO	Weighted Average
Income Statement				
Sales	$6,050	$6,050	$6,050	$6,050
Cost of goods sold	4,582	4,570	4,730	4,622
Gross profit	1,468	1,480	1,320	1,428
Expenses	450	450	450	450
Income before taxes	1,018	1,030	870	978
Income tax expense (30%)	305	309	261	293
Net income	$ 713	$ 721	$ 609	$ 685
Balance Sheet				
Inventory	$1,408	$1,420	$1,260	$1,368

This exhibit reveals two important results. First, when purchase costs *regularly rise,* as in Trekking's case, the following occurs:

- FIFO assigns the lowest amount to cost of goods sold—yielding the highest gross profit and net income.
- LIFO assigns the highest amount to cost of goods sold—yielding the lowest gross profit and net income, which also yields a temporary tax advantage by postponing payment of some income tax.
- Weighted average yields results between FIFO and LIFO.
- Specific identification always yields results that depend on which units are sold.

Point: FIFO is preferred when costs are rising *and* managers have incentives to report higher income for reasons such as bonus plans, job security, and reputation.

Point: LIFO inventory is often less than the inventory's replacement cost because LIFO inventory is valued using the oldest inventory purchase costs.

Second, when costs *regularly decline,* the reverse occurs for FIFO and LIFO. Namely, FIFO gives the highest cost of goods sold—yielding the lowest gross profit and income. However, LIFO then gives the lowest cost of goods sold—yielding the highest gross profit and income.

All four inventory costing methods are acceptable. However, a company must disclose the inventory method it uses in its financial statements or notes. Each method offers certain advantages as follows:

- FIFO assigns an amount to inventory on the balance sheet that approximates its current cost; it also mimics the actual flow of goods for most businesses.
- LIFO assigns an amount to cost of goods sold on the income statement that approximates its current cost; it also better matches current costs with revenues in computing gross profit.
- Weighted average tends to smooth out erratic changes in costs.
- Specific identification exactly matches the costs of items with the revenues they generate.

Decision Maker

Financial Planner One of your clients asks if the inventory account of a company using FIFO needs any "adjustments" for analysis purposes in light of recent inflation. What is your advice? Does your advice depend on changes in the costs of these inventories? [Answer—p. 249]

Tax Effects of Costing Methods Trekking's segment income statement in Exhibit 6.8 includes income tax expense (at a rate of 30%) because it was formed as a corporation. Since inventory costs affect net income, they have potential tax effects. Trekking gains a temporary tax advantage by using LIFO. Many companies use LIFO for this reason.

Companies can and often do use different costing methods for financial reporting and tax reporting. *The only exception is when LIFO is used for tax reporting; in this case, the IRS requires that it also be used in financial statements*—called the LIFO conformity rule.

Consistency in Using Costing Methods

The **consistency concept** prescribes that a company use the same accounting methods period after period so that financial statements are comparable across periods—the only exception is when a change from one method to another will improve its financial reporting. The *full-disclosure principle* prescribes that the notes to the statements report this type of change, its justification, and its effect on income.

The consistency concept does *not* require a company to use one method exclusively. For example, it can use different methods to value different categories of inventory.

Decision Ethics

Inventory Manager Your compensation as inventory manager includes a bonus plan based on gross profit. Your superior asks your opinion on changing the inventory costing method from FIFO to LIFO. Since costs are expected to continue to rise, your superior predicts that LIFO would match higher current costs against sales, thereby lowering taxable income (and gross profit). What do you recommend? [Answer—p. 249]

Quick Check

Answers—p. 250

4. Describe one advantage for each of the inventory costing methods: specific identification, FIFO, LIFO, and weighted average.
5. When costs are rising, which method reports higher net income—LIFO or FIFO?
6. When costs are rising, what effect does LIFO have on a balance sheet compared to FIFO?
7. A company takes a physical count of inventory at the end of 2009 and finds that ending inventory is understated by $10,000. Would this error cause cost of goods sold to be overstated or understated in 2009? In year 2010? If so, by how much?

Valuing Inventory at LCM and the Effects of Inventory Errors

This section examines the role of market costs in determining inventory on the balance sheet and also the financial statement effects of inventory errors.

Lower of Cost or Market

P2 Compute the lower of cost or market amount of inventory.

We explained how to assign costs to ending inventory and cost of goods sold using one of four costing methods (FIFO, LIFO, weighted average, or specific identification). However, *accounting principles require that inventory be reported at the market value (cost) of replacing inventory when market value is lower than cost.* Merchandise inventory is then said to be reported on the balance sheet at the **lower of cost or market (LCM).**

Computing the Lower of Cost or Market *Market* in the term *LCM* is defined as the current replacement cost of purchasing the same inventory items in the usual manner. A decline in replacement cost reflects a loss of value in inventory. When the recorded cost of inventory is higher than the replacement cost, a loss is recognized. When the recorded cost is lower, no adjustment is made.

LCM is applied in one of three ways: (1) to each individual item separately, (2) to major categories of items, or (3) to the whole of inventory. The less similar the items that make up inventory, the more likely companies are to apply LCM to individual items or categories. To illustrate, we apply LCM to the ending inventory of a motorsports retailer in Exhibit 6.9.

Video6.1

LCM to Whole When LCM is applied to the *whole* inventory, it is determined from *one* comparison. We compare the $295,000 total from the Total Cost column with the $287,000 total from the Total Market column and select the lower amount. This yields a $287,000 reported inventory on the balance sheet.

EXHIBIT 6.9

Lower of Cost or Market Computations

Items: $140,000 is the lower of $160,000 or $140,000

Categories: $200,000 is the lower of $210,000 or $200,000

Whole: $287,000 is the lower of $295,000 or $287,000

Inventory Items	Units	Per Unit Cost	Per Unit Market	Total Cost	Total Market	LCM Applied to Items	LCM Applied to Categories	LCM Applied to Whole
Cycles								
Roadster	20	$8,000	$7,000	$160,000	$140,000	$ 140,000		
Sprint	10	5,000	6,000	50,000	60,000	50,000		
Category subtotal				210,000	200,000		$ 200,000	
Off-Road								
Trax-4	8	5,000	6,500	40,000	52,000	40,000		
Blazer	5	9,000	7,000	45,000	35,000	35,000		
Category subtotal				85,000	87,000		85,000	
Totals				$295,000	$287,000	**$265,000**	**$285,000**	**$287,000**

Reported inventory depends on which of the 3 different LCM methods are applied

LCM to Categories When LCM is applied to the major *categories* of inventory, it is computed from two comparisons, where the number of comparisons equals the number of categories. First, for cycles, $200,000 is the lower of the $210,000 cost and the $200,000 market. Second, for off-road, $85,000 is the lower of the $85,000 cost and the $87,000 market. This yields a $285,000 reported inventory, computed from $200,000 for category one plus $85,000 for category two.

LCM to Items When LCM is applied to individual *items* of inventory, the number of comparisons equals the number of items. For Roadster, $140,000 is the lower of the $160,000 cost and the $140,000 market. For Sprint, $50,000 is the lower of the $50,000 cost and the $60,000 market. For Trax-4, $40,000 is the lower of the $40,000 cost and the $52,000 market. For Blazer, $35,000 is the lower of the $45,000 cost and the $35,000 market. This yields a $265,000 reported inventory, computed from $140,000 for Roadster plus $50,000 for Sprint plus $40,000 for Trax-4 plus $35,000 for Blazer.

Point: Advances in technology encourage the individual-item approach for LCM.

Any one of these three applications of LCM is acceptable. The retailer **Best Buy** applies LCM and reports that its "merchandise inventories are recorded at the lower of average cost or market."

Recording the Lower of Cost or Market Inventory must be adjusted downward when market is less than cost. To illustrate, if LCM is applied to the individual items of inventory in Exhibit 6.9, the Merchandise Inventory account must be adjusted from the $295,000 recorded cost down to the $265,000 market amount as follows.

Cost of Goods Sold	30,000	
Merchandise Inventory		30,000
To adjust inventory cost to market.		

Accounting rules require that inventory be adjusted to market when market is less than cost, but inventory normally cannot be written up to market when market exceeds cost. If recording inventory down to market is acceptable, why are companies not allowed to record inventory up to market? One view is that a gain from a market increase should not be realized until a sales transaction verifies the gain. However, this problem also applies when market is less than cost. A second and primary reason is the **conservatism constraint,** which prescribes the use of the less optimistic amount when more than one estimate of the amount to be received or paid exists and these estimates are about equally likely.

Decision Insight

IFRSs Use of the LIFO method is prohibited under IFRSs. Also under IFRSs, if inventory that previously had been written down to market subsequently increases in value, the write-down is reversed.

Financial Statement Effects of Inventory Errors

A2 Analyze the effects of inventory errors on current and future financial statements.

Companies must take care in both taking a physical count of inventory and in assigning a cost to it. An inventory error causes misstatements in cost of goods sold, gross profit, net income, current assets, and equity. It also causes misstatements in the next period's statements because ending inventory of one period is the beginning inventory of the next. As we consider the financial statement effects in this section, it is helpful if we recall the following *inventory relation.*

Beginning inventory + Net purchases − Ending inventory = Cost of goods sold

Income Statement Effects Exhibit 6.10 shows the effects of inventory errors on key amounts in the current and next periods' income statements. Let's look at row 1 and year 1. We see that understating ending inventory overstates cost of goods sold. This can be seen from the above inventory relation where we subtract a smaller ending inventory amount in computing cost of goods sold. Then a higher cost of goods sold yields a lower income.

To understand year 2 of row 1, remember that an understated ending inventory for year 1 becomes an understated beginning inventory for year 2. Using the above inventory relation, we see that if beginning inventory is understated, then cost of goods sold is understated (because we are starting with a smaller amount). A lower cost of goods sold yields a higher income.

Turning to overstatements, let's look at row 2 and year 1. If ending inventory is overstated, we use the inventory relation to see that cost of goods sold is understated. A lower cost of goods sold yields a higher income.

For year 2 of row 2, we again recall that an overstated ending inventory for year 1 becomes an overstated beginning inventory for year 2. If beginning inventory is overstated, we use the inventory relation to see that cost of goods sold is overstated. A higher cost of goods sold yields a lower income.

EXHIBIT 6.10

Effects of Inventory Errors on the Income Statement

	Year 1		Year 2	
Ending Inventory	Cost of Goods Sold	Net Income	Cost of Goods Sold	Net Income
Understated	Overstated	Understated	Understated	Overstated
Overstated*	Understated	Overstated	Overstated	Understated

* This error is less likely under a perpetual system because it implies more inventory than is recorded (or less shrinkage than expected). Management will normally follow up and discover and correct this error before it impacts any accounts.

To illustrate, consider an inventory error for a company with $100,000 in sales for each of the years 2008, 2009, and 2010. If this company maintains a steady $20,000 inventory level during this period and makes $60,000 in purchases in each of these years, its cost of goods sold is $60,000 and its gross profit is $40,000 each year.

Ending Inventory Understated—Year 1 Assume that this company errs in computing its 2008 ending inventory and reports $16,000 instead of the correct amount of $20,000. The effects of this error are shown in Exhibit 6.11. The $4,000 understatement of 2008 ending inventory causes a $4,000 overstatement in 2008 cost of goods sold and a $4,000 understatement in both gross profit and net income for 2008. We see that these effects match the effects predicted in Exhibit 6.10.

Ending Inventory Understated—Year 2 The 2008 understated ending inventory becomes the 2009 understated *beginning* inventory. We see in Exhibit 6.11 that this error causes an understatement in 2009 cost of goods sold and a $4,000 overstatement in both gross profit and net income for 2009.

Ending Inventory Understated—Year 3 Exhibit 6.11 shows that the 2008 ending inventory error affects only that period and the next. It does not affect 2010 results or any period thereafter. An inventory error is said to be *self-correcting* because it always yields an offsetting error in the next period. This does not reduce the severity of inventory errors. Managers, lenders, owners, and others make important decisions from analysis of income and costs.

Point: A former internal auditor at **Coca-Cola** alleges that just before midnight at the 2002 period-end, fully loaded Coke trucks were ordered to drive about 2 feet away from the loading dock so that Coke could record millions of dollars in extra sales.

EXHIBIT 6.11

Effects of Inventory Errors on Three Periods' Income Statements

Correct income is $30,000 for each year

Income Statements	2008		2009		2010	
Sales		$100,000		$100,000		$100,000
Cost of goods sold						
Beginning inventory	$20,000		$16,000*		$20,000	
Cost of goods purchased	60,000		60,000		60,000	
Goods available for sale	80,000		76,000		80,000	
Ending inventory	16,000*		20,000		20,000	
Cost of goods sold		64,000†		56,000†		60,000
Gross profit		36,000		44,000		40,000
Expenses		10,000		10,000		10,000
Net income		$ 26,000		$ 34,000		$ 30,000

* Correct amount is $20,000. † Correct amount is $60,000.

Example: If 2008 ending inventory in Exhibit 6.11 is overstated by $3,000 (not understated by $4,000), what is the effect on cost of goods sold, gross profit, assets, and equity? *Answer:* Cost of goods sold is understated by $3,000 in 2008 and overstated by $3,000 in 2009. Gross profit and net income are overstated in 2008 and understated in 2009. Assets and equity are overstated in 2008.

We can also do an analysis of beginning inventory errors. The income statement effects are the opposite of those for ending inventory.

Balance Sheet Effects Balance sheet effects of an inventory error can be seen by considering the accounting equation: Assets = Liabilities + Equity. For example, understating ending inventory understates both current and total assets. An understatement in ending inventory also yields an understatement in equity because of the understatement in net income. Exhibit 6.12 shows the effects of inventory errors on the current period's balance sheet amounts. Errors in *beginning* inventory do not yield misstatements in the end-of-period balance sheet, but they do affect that current period's income statement.

EXHIBIT 6.12

Effects of Inventory Errors on Current Period's Balance Sheet

Ending Inventory	Assets	Equity
Understated	Understated	Understated
Overstated	Overstated	Overstated

Quick Check

Answers—p. 250

8. Use LCM applied separately to the following individual items to compute ending inventory.

Product	Units	Unit Recorded Cost	Unit Market Cost
A	20	$ 6	$ 5
B	40	9	8
C	10	12	15

Decision Analysis — Inventory Turnover and Days' Sales in Inventory

A3 Assess inventory management using both inventory turnover and days' sales in inventory.

Inventory Turnover

Earlier chapters described two important ratios useful in evaluating a company's short-term liquidity: current ratio and acid-test ratio. A merchandiser's ability to pay its short-term obligations also depends on how quickly it sells its merchandise inventory. **Inventory turnover,** also called *merchandise inventory turnover,* is one ratio used to assess this and is defined in Exhibit 6.13.

EXHIBIT 6.13

Inventory Turnover

$$\text{Inventory turnover} = \frac{\text{Cost of goods sold}}{\text{Average inventory}}$$

This ratio reveals how many *times* a company turns over (sells) its inventory during a period. If a company's inventory greatly varies within a year, average inventory amounts can be computed from interim periods such as quarters or months.

Users apply inventory turnover to help analyze short-term liquidity and to assess whether management is doing a good job controlling the amount of inventory available. A low ratio compared to that of competitors suggests inefficient use of assets. The company may be holding more inventory than it needs to support its sales volume. Similarly, a very high ratio compared to that of competitors suggests inventory might be too low. This can cause lost sales if customers must back-order merchandise. Inventory turnover has no simple rule except to say *a high ratio is preferable provided inventory is adequate to meet demand.*

Point: We must take care when comparing turnover ratios across companies that use different costing methods (such as FIFO and LIFO).

Days' Sales in Inventory

To better interpret inventory turnover, many users measure the adequacy of inventory to meet sales demand. **Days' sales in inventory,** also called *days' stock on hand,* is a ratio that reveals how much inventory is available in terms of the number of days' sales. It can be interpreted as the number of days one can sell from inventory if no new items are purchased. This ratio is often viewed as a measure of the buffer against out-of-stock inventory and is useful in evaluating liquidity of inventory. It is defined in Exhibit 6.14.

Point: Inventory turnover is higher and days' sales in inventory is lower for industries such as foods and other perishable products. The reverse holds for nonperishable product industries.

EXHIBIT 6.14

Days' Sales in Inventory

$$\textbf{Days' sales in inventory} = \frac{\textbf{Ending inventory}}{\textbf{Cost of goods sold}} \times 365$$

Days' sales in inventory focuses on ending inventory and it estimates how many days it will take to convert inventory at the end of a period into accounts receivable or cash. Days' sales in inventory focuses on *ending* inventory whereas inventory turnover focuses on *average* inventory.

Point: Days' sales in inventory for many Ford models has risen: Freestyle, 122 days; Montego, 109 days; Five Hundred, 118 days. The industry average is 73 days. (*BusinessWeek* 2005)

Decision Insight

Dell-ocity From its roots in a college dorm room, **Dell** now sells over 50 million dollars' worth of computers each day from its Website. The speed of Web technology has allowed Dell to slash inventories. Dell's inventory turnover is 88 and its days' sales in inventory is 5 days. Michael Dell asserts, "Speed is everything in this business."

Analysis of Inventory Management

Inventory management is a major emphasis for merchandisers. They must both plan and control inventory purchases and sales. **Toys "R" Us** is one of those merchandisers. Its inventory in fiscal year 2007 was $1,690 million. This inventory constituted 59% of its current assets and 20% of its total assets. We apply the analysis tools in this section to Toys "R" Us, as shown in Exhibit 6.15—also see margin graph.

EXHIBIT 6.15

Inventory Turnover and Days' Sales in Inventory for Toys "R" Us

($ millions)	2007	2006	2005	2004
Cost of goods sold	$8,638	$7,652	$7,506	$7,646
Ending inventory	$1,690	$1,488	$1,884	$2,094
Inventory turnover	**5.4** times	**4.5** times	**3.8** times	**3.6** times
Industry inventory turnover	3.0 times	2.8 times	2.6 times	2.6 times
Days' sales in inventory	**71** days	**71** days	**92** days	**100** days
Industry days' sales in inventory	129 days	135 days	139 days	141 days

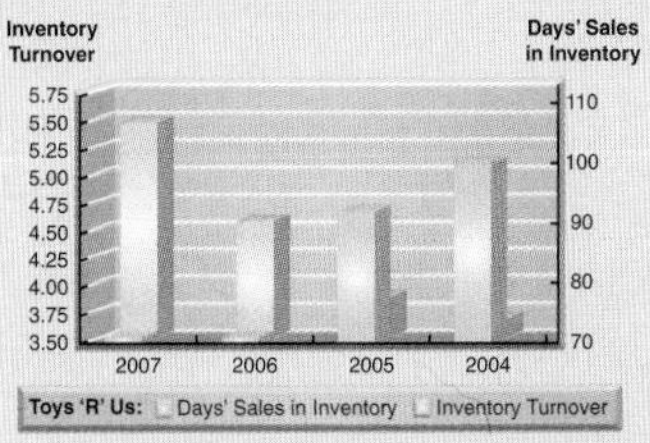

Its 2007 inventory turnover of 5.4 times means that Toys "R" Us turned over its inventory 5.4 times per year, or once every 68 days (365 days ÷ 5.4). We prefer inventory turnover to be high provided inventory is not out of stock and the company is not losing customers. The 2007 days' sales in inventory of 71 days reveals that it was carrying 71 days of sales in inventory. This inventory buffer seems more than adequate. Toys "R" Us would benefit from further management efforts to increase inventory turnover and reduce inventory levels.

Decision Maker

Entrepreneur Analysis of your retail store yields an inventory turnover of 5.0 and a days' sales in inventory of 73 days. The industry norm for inventory turnover is 4.4 and for days' sales in inventory is 74 days. What is your assessment of inventory management? [Answer—p. 249]

DILBERT reprinted by permission of United Feature Syndicate, Inc.

Demonstration Problem

DP6

Craig Company uses a perpetual inventory system for its one product. Its beginning inventory, purchases, and sales during calendar year 2009 follow.

Date	Activity	Units Acquired at Cost	Units Sold at Retail	Unit Inventory
Jan. 1	Beg. Inventory . .	400 units @ $14 = $ 5,600		400 units
Jan. 15	Sale		200 units @ $30	200 units
March 10	Purchase	200 units @ $15 = $ 3,000		400 units
April 1	Sale		200 units @ $30	200 units
May 9	Purchase	300 units @ $16 = $ 4,800		500 units
Sept. 22	Purchase	250 units @ $20 = $ 5,000		750 units
Nov. 1	Sale		300 units @ $35	450 units
Nov. 28	Purchase	100 units @ $21 = $ 2,100		550 units
	Totals	1,250 units $20,500	700 units	

Additional tracking data for specific identification: (1) January 15 sale—200 units @ $14, (2) April 1 sale—200 units @ $15, and (3) November 1 sale—200 units @ $14 and 100 units @ $20.

Required

1. Calculate the cost of goods available for sale.
2. Apply the four different methods of inventory costing (FIFO, LIFO, weighted average, and specific identification) to calculate ending inventory and cost of goods sold under each method.
3. Compute gross profit earned by the company for each of the four costing methods in part 2. Also, report the inventory amount reported on the balance sheet for each of the four methods.
4. In preparing financial statements for year 2009, the financial officer was instructed to use FIFO but failed to do so and instead computed cost of goods sold according to LIFO. Determine the impact on year 2009's income from the error. Also determine the effect of this error on year 2010's income. Assume no income taxes.
5. Management wants a report that shows how changing from FIFO to another method would change net income. Prepare a table showing (1) the cost of goods sold amount under each of the four methods, (2) the amount by which each cost of goods sold total is different from the FIFO cost of goods sold, and (3) the effect on net income if another method is used instead of FIFO.

Planning the Solution

- Compute cost of goods available for sale by multiplying the units of beginning inventory and each purchase by their unit costs to determine the total cost of goods available for sale.
- Prepare a perpetual FIFO table starting with beginning inventory and showing how inventory changes after each purchase and after each sale (see Exhibit 6.5).
- Prepare a perpetual LIFO table starting with beginning inventory and showing how inventory changes after each purchase and after each sale (see Exhibit 6.6).
- Make a table of purchases and sales recalculating the average cost of inventory prior to each sale to arrive at the weighted average cost of ending inventory. Total the average costs associated with each sale to determine cost of goods sold (see Exhibit 6.7).
- Prepare a table showing the computation of cost of goods sold and ending inventory using the specific identification method (see Exhibit 6.4).
- Compare the year-end 2009 inventory amounts under FIFO and LIFO to determine the misstatement of year 2009 income that results from using LIFO. The errors for year 2009 and 2010 are equal in amount but opposite in effect.
- Create a table showing cost of goods sold under each method and how net income would differ from FIFO net income if an alternate method is adopted.

Solution to Demonstration Problem

1. Cost of goods available for sale (this amount is the same for all methods).

Date			Units	Unit Cost	Cost
Jan.	1	Beg. Inventory	400	$14	$ 5,600
March	10	Purchase	200	15	3,000
May	9	Purchase	300	16	4,800
Sept.	22	Purchase	250	20	5,000
Nov.	28	Purchase	100	21	2,100
Total goods available for sale			1,250		$20,500

2a. FIFO perpetual method.

Date	Goods Purchased	Cost of Goods Sold	Inventory Balance	
Jan. 1	Beginning balance		400 @ $14	= $ 5,600
Jan. 15		200 @ $14 = $2,800	200 @ $14	= $ 2,800
Mar. 10	200 @ $15 = $3,000		200 @ $14 200 @ $15	= $ 5,800
April 1		200 @ $14 = $2,800	200 @ $15	= $ 3,000
May 9	300 @ $16 = $4,800		200 @ $15 300 @ $16	= $ 7,800
Sept. 22	250 @ $20 = $5,000		200 @ $15 300 @ $16 250 @ $20	= $12,800
Nov. 1		200 @ $15 = $3,000 100 @ $16 = $1,600	200 @ $16 250 @ $20	= $ 8,200
Nov. 28	100 @ $21 = $2,100		200 @ $16 250 @ $20 100 @ $21	= $10,300
Total cost of goods sold		**$10,200**		

Note to students: **In a classroom situation,** once we compute cost of goods available for sale, we can compute the amount for either cost of goods sold or ending inventory—it is a matter of preference. **In practice,** the costs of items sold are identified as sales are made and immediately transferred from the inventory account to the cost of goods sold account. The previous solution showing the line-by-line approach illustrates actual application in practice. The following alternate solutions illustrate that, once the concepts are understood, other solution approaches are available. Although this is only shown for FIFO, it could be shown for all methods.

Alternate Methods to Compute FIFO Perpetual Numbers

[FIFO Alternate No. 1: Computing cost of goods sold first]

Cost of goods available for sale (from part 1)			$ 20,500
Cost of goods sold			
Jan. 15	Sold (200 @ $14)	$2,800	
April 1	Sold (200 @ $14)	2,800	
Nov. 1	Sold (200 @ $15 and 100 @ $16)	4,600	10,200
Ending inventory			**$10,300**

[FIFO Alternate No. 2: Computing ending inventory first]

Cost of goods available for sale (from part 1)			$ 20,500
Ending inventory*			
Nov. 28	Purchase (100 @ $21)	$2,100	
Sept. 22	Purchase (250 @ $20)	5,000	
May 9	Purchase (200 @ $16)	3,200	
Ending inventory			**10,300**
Cost of goods sold			**$10,200**

* Since FIFO assumes that the earlier costs are the first to flow out, we determine ending inventory by assigning the most recent costs to the remaining items.

2b. LIFO perpetual method.

Date	Goods Purchased	Cost of Goods Sold	Inventory Balance	
Jan. 1	Beginning balance		400 @ $14	= $ 5,600
Jan. 15		200 @ $14 = $2,800	200 @ $14	= $ 2,800
Mar. 10	200 @ $15 = $3,000		200 @ $14 200 @ $15	= $ 5,800
April 1		200 @ $15 = $3,000	200 @ $14	= $ 2,800
May 9	300 @ $16 = $4,800		200 @ $14 300 @ $16	= $ 7,600
Sept. 22	250 @ $20 = $5,000		200 @ $14 300 @ $16 250 @ $20	= $12,600
Nov. 1		250 @ $20 = $5,000 50 @ $16 = $ 800	200 @ $14 250 @ $16	= $ 6,800
Nov. 28	100 @ $21 = $2,100		200 @ $14 250 @ $16 100 @ $21	= **$ 8,900**
Total cost of goods sold		**$11,600**		

2c. Weighted average perpetual method.

Date	Goods Purchased	Cost of Goods Sold	Inventory Balance	
Jan. 1	Beginning balance		400 @ $14	= $ 5,600
Jan. 15		200 @ $14 = $2,800	200 @ $14	= $ 2,800
Mar. 10	200 @ $15 = $3,000		200 @ $14 200 @ $15 (avg. cost is $14.5)	= $ 5,800
April 1		200 @ $14.5 = $2,900	200 @ $14.5	= $ 2,900
May 9	300 @ $16 = $4,800		200 @ $14.5 300 @ $16 (avg. cost is $15.4)	= $ 7,700
Sept. 22	250 @ $20 = $5,000		200 @ $14.5 300 @ $16 250 @ $20 (avg. cost is $16.93)	= $ 12,700
Nov. 1		300 @ $16.93 = $5,079	450 @ $16.93	= $ 7,618.5
Nov. 28	100 @ $21 = $2,100		450 @ $16.93 100 @ $21	= $9,718.5
Total cost of goods sold*		**$10,779**		

* The cost of goods sold ($10,779) plus ending inventory ($9,718.5) is $2.5 less than the cost of goods available for sale ($20,500) due to rounding.

2d. Specific identification method.

Date	Goods Purchased	Cost of Goods Sold	Inventory Balance	
Jan. 1	Beginning balance		400 @ $14	= $ 5,600
Jan. 15		200 @ $14 = $2,800	200 @ $14	= $ 2,800
Mar. 10	200 @ $15 = $3,000		200 @ $14 200 @ $15	= $ 5,800
April 1		200 @ $15 = $3,000	200 @ $14	= $ 2,800
May 9	300 @ $16 = $4,800		200 @ $14 300 @ $16	= $ 7,600
Sept. 22	250 @ $20 = $5,000		200 @ $14 300 @ $16 250 @ $20	= $12,600
Nov. 1		200 @ $14 = $2,800 100 @ $20 = $2,000	300 @ $16 150 @ $20	= $ 7,800
Nov. 28	100 @ $21 = $2,100		300 @ $16 150 @ $20 100 @ $21	= $ 9,900
Total cost of goods sold		**$10,600**		

3.

	FIFO	LIFO	Weighted Average	Specific Identification
Income Statement				
Sales*	$ 22,500	$22,500	$ 22,500	$22,500
Cost of goods sold	10,200	11,600	10,779	10,600
Gross profit	$ 12,300	$10,900	$ 11,721	$11,900
Balance Sheet				
Inventory	$10,300	$ 8,900	$9,718.5	$ 9,900

* Sales = (200 units × $30) + (200 units × $30) + (300 units × $35) = $22,500

4. Mistakenly using LIFO when FIFO should have been used overstates cost of goods sold in year 2009 by $1,400, which is the difference between the FIFO and LIFO amounts of ending inventory. It understates income in 2009 by $1,400. In year 2010, income is overstated by $1,400 because of the understatement in beginning inventory.
5. Analysis of the effects of alternative inventory methods.

	Cost of Goods Sold	Difference from FIFO Cost of Goods Sold	Effect on Net Income If Adopted Instead of FIFO
FIFO	$10,200	—	—
LIFO	11,600	+$1,400	$1,400 lower
Weighted average	10,779	+ 579	579 lower
Specific identification	10,600	+ 400	400 lower

APPENDIX 6A Inventory Costing Under a Periodic System

P3 Compute inventory in a periodic system using the methods of specific identification, FIFO, LIFO, and weighted average.

The basic aim of the periodic system and the perpetual system is the same: to assign costs to inventory and cost of goods sold. The same four methods are used to assign costs under both systems: specific identification; first-in, first-out; last-in, first-out; and weighted average. We use information from Trekking to show how to assign costs using these four methods with a periodic system. Data for sales and purchases are in Exhibit 6A.1. Also, recall that we explained the accounting entries under a periodic system in Appendix 5A.

EXHIBIT 6A.1

Purchases and Sales of Goods

Date	Activity	Units Acquired at Cost	Units Sold at Retail	Unit Inventory
Aug. 1	Beginning inventory	10 units @ $ 91 = $ 910		10 units
Aug. 3	Purchases	15 units @ $106 = $ 1,590		25 units
Aug. 14	Sales		20 units @ $130	5 units
Aug. 17	Purchases	20 units @ $115 = $ 2,300		25 units
Aug. 28	Purchases	10 units @ $119 = $ 1,190		35 units
Aug. 31	Sales		23 units @ $150	12 units
	Totals	55 units $5,990	43 units	

Specific Identification

We use the above sales and purchases information and the specific identification method to assign costs to ending inventory and units sold. Trekking's internal data reveal the following specific unit sales:

August 14 Sold 8 bikes costing $91 each and 12 bikes costing $106 each

August 31 Sold 2 bikes costing $91 each, 3 bikes costing $106 each, 15 bikes costing $115 each, and 3 bikes costing $119 each

Applying specific identification and using the information above, we prepare Exhibit 6A.2. This exhibit starts with 10 bikes at $91 each in beginning inventory. On August 3, 15 more bikes are purchased at $106 each for $1,590. Inventory available now consists of 10 bikes at $91 each and 15 bikes at $106 each, for a total of $2,500. On August 14 (see specific sales data above), 20 bikes costing $2,000 are sold—leaving 5 bikes costing $500 in inventory. On August 17, 20 bikes costing $2,300 are purchased, and on August 28, another 10 bikes costing $1,190 are purchased, for a total of 35 bikes costing $3,990 in inventory. On August 31 (see specific sales above), 23 bikes costing $2,582 are sold, which leaves 12 bikes costing $1,408 in ending inventory. Carefully study Exhibit 6A.2 to see the flow of costs both in and out of inventory. Each unit, whether sold or remaining in inventory, has its own specific cost attached to it.

EXHIBIT 6A.2

Specific Identification Computations

	"goods in"	"goods out"		"what's left"	
Date	**Goods Purchased**	**Cost of Goods Sold**		**Inventory Balance**	
Aug. 1	Beginning balance			10 @ $ 91	= $ 910
Aug. 3	15 @ $106 = $1,590			10 @ $ 91 15 @ $106	= $2,500
Aug. 14		8 @ $ 91 = $ 728 12 @ $106 = $1,272	= $2,000*	2 @ $ 91 3 @ $106	= $ 500
Aug. 17	20 @ $115 = $2,300			2 @ $ 91 3 @ $106 20 @ $115	= $2,800
Aug. 28	10 @ $119 = $1,190			2 @ $ 91 3 @ $106 20 @ $115 10 @ $119	= $3,990
Aug. 31		2 @ $ 91 = $ 182 3 @ $106 = $ 318 15 @ $115 = $1,725 3 @ $119 = $ 357	= $2,582*	5 @ $115 7 @ $119	= $1,408
			$4,582		

For the 20 units sold on Aug. 14, the company specifically identified that 8 of those had cost $91 and 12 had cost $106.

For the 23 units sold on Aug. 31, the company specifically identified each bike sold and its acquisition cost from prior purchases.

* Identification of items sold (and their costs) is obtained from internal documents that track each unit from its purchase to its sale.

When using specific identification, Trekking's cost of goods sold reported on the income statement totals **$4,582**, the sum of $2,000 and $2,582 from the third column of Exhibit 6A.2. Trekking's ending inventory reported on the balance sheet is **$1,408**, which is the final inventory balance from the fourth column. The purchases and sales entries for Exhibit 6A.2 follow (the colored boldface numbers are those affected by the cost flow assumption).

Point: The assignment of costs to the goods sold and to inventory using specific identification is the same for both the perpetual and periodic systems.

Purchases

Aug. 3	Purchases	1,590	
	Accounts Payable		1,590
17	Purchases	2,300	
	Accounts Payable		2,300
28	Purchases	1,190	
	Accounts Payable		1,190

Sales

Aug. 14	Accounts Receivable	2,600	
	Sales		2,600
31	Accounts Receivable	3,450	
	Sales		3,450

Adjusting Entry

31	Merchandise Inventory	**1,408**	
	Income Summary		498
	Merchandise Inventory		**910**

First-In, First-Out

The first-in, first-out (FIFO) method of assigning costs to inventory assumes that inventory items are sold in the order acquired. When sales occur, the costs of the earliest units acquired are charged to cost of goods sold. This leaves the costs from the most recent purchases in ending inventory. Use of FIFO for computing the cost of inventory and cost of goods sold is shown in Exhibit 6A.3.

This exhibit starts with computing $5,990 in total units available for sale—this is given to us at the start of this appendix. Applying FIFO, we know that the 12 units in ending inventory will be reported at the cost of the most recent 12 purchases. Reviewing purchases in reverse order, we assign costs to the 12 bikes in ending inventory as follows: $119 cost to 10 bikes and $115 cost to 2 bikes. This yields 12 bikes costing $1,420 in ending inventory. We then subtract this $1,420 in ending inventory from $5,990 in cost of goods available to get $4,570 in cost of goods sold.

EXHIBIT 6A.3

FIFO Computations—Periodic System

Exhibit 6A.1 shows that the 12 units in ending inventory consist of 10 units from the latest purchase on Aug. 28 and 2 units from the next latest purchase on Aug. 17.

Total cost of 55 units available for sale (from Exhibit 6A.1)		$5,990
Less ending inventory priced using FIFO		
10 units from August 28 purchase at $119 each	$1,190	
2 units from August 17 purchase at $115 each	230	
Ending inventory		1,420
Cost of goods sold		$4,570

Trekking's ending inventory reported on the balance sheet is **$1,420**, and its cost of goods sold reported on the income statement is **$4,570**. These amounts are the same as those computed using the perpetual system. This always occurs because the most recent purchases are in ending inventory under both systems. The purchases and sales entries for Exhibit 6A.3 follow (the colored boldface numbers are those affected by the cost flow assumption).

Point: The assignment of costs to the goods sold and to inventory using FIFO is the same for both the perpetual and periodic systems.

Purchases

Aug. 3	Purchases	1,590	
	Accounts Payable		1,590
17	Purchases	2,300	
	Accounts Payable		2,300
28	Purchases	1,190	
	Accounts Payable		1,190

Sales

Aug. 14	Accounts Receivable	2,600	
	Sales		2,600
31	Accounts Receivable	3,450	
	Sales		3,450
	Adjusting Entry		
31	Merchandise Inventory	**1,420**	
	Income Summary		510
	Merchandise Inventory		**910**

Last-In, First-Out

The last-in, first-out (LIFO) method of assigning costs assumes that the most recent purchases are sold first. These more recent costs are charged to the goods sold, and the costs of the earliest purchases are assigned to inventory. LIFO results in costs of the most recent purchases being assigned to cost of goods sold, which means that LIFO comes close to matching current costs of goods sold with revenues. Use of LIFO for computing cost of inventory and cost of goods sold is shown in Exhibit 6A.4.

This exhibit starts with computing $5,990 in total units available for sale—this is given to us at the start of this appendix. Applying LIFO, we know that the 12 units in ending inventory will be reported at the cost of the earliest 12 purchases. Reviewing the earliest purchases in order, we assign costs to the 12 bikes in ending inventory as follows: $91 cost to 10 bikes and $106 cost to 2 bikes. This yields 12 bikes costing $1,122 in ending inventory. We then subtract this $1,122 in ending inventory from $5,990 in cost of goods available to get $4,868 in cost of goods sold.

EXHIBIT 6A.4

LIFO Computations—Periodic System

Total cost of 55 units available for sale (from Exhibit 6A.1)		$5,990
Less ending inventory priced using LIFO		
10 units in beginning inventory at $91 each	$910	
2 units from August 3 purchase at $106 each	212	
Ending inventory		1,122
Cost of goods sold		$4,868

Exhibit 6A.1 shows that the 12 units in ending inventory consist of 10 units from the earliest purchase (beg. inv.) and 2 units from the next earliest purchase on Aug. 3.

Trekking's ending inventory reported on the balance sheet is **$1,122**, and its cost of goods sold reported on the income statement is **$4,868**. When LIFO is used with the periodic system, cost of goods sold is assigned costs from the most recent purchases for the period. With a perpetual system, cost of goods sold is assigned costs from the most recent purchases at the point of *each sale.* The purchases and sales entries for Exhibit 6A.4 follow (the colored boldface numbers are those affected by the cost flow assumption).

Purchases

Aug. 3	Purchases	1,590	
	Accounts Payable		1,590
17	Purchases	2,300	
	Accounts Payable		2,300
28	Purchases	1,190	
	Accounts Payable		1,190

Sales

Aug. 14	Accounts Receivable	2,600	
	Sales		2,600
31	Accounts Receivable	3,450	
	Sales		3,450

Adjusting Entry

31	Merchandise Inventory	**1,122**	
	Income Summary		212
	Merchandise Inventory		**910**

Weighted Average

The **weighted average** or **WA** (also called **average cost**) method of assigning cost requires that we use the average cost per unit of inventory at the end of the period. Weighted average cost per unit equals the cost of goods available for sale divided by the units available. The weighted average method of assigning cost involves three important steps. The first two steps are shown in Exhibit 6A.5. First, multiply the per unit cost for beginning inventory and each particular purchase by the corresponding number of units (from Exhibit 6A.1). Second, add these amounts and divide by the total number of units available for sale to find the weighted average cost per unit.

EXHIBIT 6A.5

Weighted Average Cost per Unit

Step 1:	10 units @ $ 91 =	$ 910
	15 units @ $106 =	1,590
	20 units @ $115 =	2,300
	10 units @ $119 =	1,190
	55	$5,990
Step 2:	$5,990/55 units = **$108.91** weighted average cost per unit	

Example: In Exhibit 6A.5, if 5 more units had been purchased at $120 each, what would be the weighted average cost per unit?
Answer: $109.83 ($6,590/60)

The third step is to use the weighted average cost per unit to assign costs to inventory and to the units sold as shown in Exhibit 6A.6.

EXHIBIT 6A.6

Weighted Average Computations—Periodic

Step 3:	Total cost of 55 units available for sale (from Exhibit 6A.1)	$ 5,990
	Less **ending inventory** priced on a weighted average cost basis: 12 units at $108.91 each (from Exhibit 6A.5)	1,307
	Cost of goods sold	$4,683

Trekking's ending inventory reported on the balance sheet is **$1,307**, and its cost of goods sold reported on the income statement is **$4,683** when using the weighted average (periodic) method. The purchases

Point: Weighted average usually yields different results for the perpetual and the periodic systems because under a perpetual system it recomputes the per unit cost prior to each sale, whereas under a periodic system, the per unit cost is computed only at the end of a period.

and sales entries for Exhibit 6A.6 follow (the colored boldface numbers are those affected by the cost flow assumption).

Purchases

Aug. 3	Purchases	1,590	
	Accounts Payable		1,590
17	Purchases	2,300	
	Accounts Payable		2,300
28	Purchases	1,190	
	Accounts Payable		1,190

Sales

Aug. 14	Accounts Receivable	2,600	
	Sales		2,600
31	Accounts Receivable	3,450	
	Sales		3,450
	Adjusting Entry		
31	Merchandise Inventory	**1,307**	
	Income Summary		397
	Merchandise Inventory		**910**

Financial Statement Effects

Point: LIFO inventory is often less than the inventory's replacement cost because LIFO inventory is valued using the oldest inventory purchase costs.

When purchase prices do not change, each inventory costing method assigns the same cost amounts to inventory and to cost of goods sold. When purchase prices are different, however, the methods nearly always assign different cost amounts. We show these differences in Exhibit 6A.7 using Trekking's data.

EXHIBIT 6A.7

Financial Statement Effects of Inventory Costing Methods

TREKKING COMPANY
For Month Ended August 31

	Specific Identification	FIFO	LIFO	Weighted Average
Income Statement				
Sales	$ 6,050	$ 6,050	$ 6,050	$ 6,050
Cost of goods sold	**4,582**	**4,570**	**4,868**	**4,683**
Gross profit	1,468	1,480	1,182	1,367
Expenses	450	450	450	450
Income before taxes	1,018	1,030	732	917
Income tax expense (30%)	305	309	220	275
Net income	**$ 713**	**$ 721**	**$ 512**	**$ 642**
Balance Sheet				
Inventory	**$1,408**	**$1,420**	**$1,122**	**$1,307**

This exhibit reveals two important results. First, when purchase costs *regularly rise,* as in Trekking's case, observe the following:

- FIFO assigns the lowest amount to cost of goods sold—yielding the highest gross profit and net income.
- LIFO assigns the highest amount to cost of goods sold—yielding the lowest gross profit and net income, which also yields a temporary tax advantage by postponing payment of some income tax.
- Weighted average yields results between FIFO and LIFO.
- Specific identification always yields results that depend on which units are sold.

Second, when costs *regularly decline,* the reverse occurs for FIFO and LIFO. FIFO gives the highest cost of goods sold—yielding the lowest gross profit and income. And LIFO gives the lowest cost of goods sold—yielding the highest gross profit and income.

All four inventory costing methods are acceptable in practice. A company must disclose the inventory method it uses. Each method offers certain advantages as follows:

- FIFO assigns an amount to inventory on the balance sheet that approximates its current cost; it also mimics the actual flow of goods for most businesses.
- LIFO assigns an amount to cost of goods sold on the income statement that approximates its current cost; it also better matches current costs with revenues in computing gross profit.
- Weighted average tends to smooth out erratic changes in costs.
- Specific identification exactly matches the costs of items with the revenues they generate.

Quick Check

Answers—p. 250

9. A company reports the following beginning inventory and purchases, and it ends the period with 30 units in inventory.

Beginning inventory	100 units at $10 cost per unit
Purchase 1	40 units at $12 cost per unit
Purchase 2	20 units at $14 cost per unit

a. Compute ending inventory using the FIFO periodic system.
b. Compute cost of goods sold using the LIFO periodic system.

APPENDIX

Inventory Estimation Methods 6B

Inventory sometimes requires estimation for two reasons. First, companies often require **interim statements** (financial statements prepared for periods of less than one year), but they only annually take a physical count of inventory. Second, companies may require an inventory estimate if some casualty such as fire or flood makes taking a physical count impossible. Estimates are usually only required for companies that use the periodic system. Companies using a perpetual system would presumably have updated inventory data.

This appendix describes two methods to estimate inventory.

P4 Apply both the retail inventory and gross profit methods to estimate inventory.

Retail Inventory Method

To avoid the time-consuming and expensive process of taking a physical inventory each month or quarter, some companies use the **retail inventory method** to estimate cost of goods sold and ending inventory. Some companies even use the retail inventory method to prepare the annual statements. **Home Depot**, for instance, says in its annual report: "Inventories are stated at the lower of cost (first-in, first-out) or market, as determined by the retail inventory method." A company may also estimate inventory for audit purposes or when inventory is damaged or destroyed.

Point: When a retailer takes a physical inventory, it can restate the retail value of inventory to a cost basis by applying the cost-to-retail ratio. It can also estimate the amount of shrinkage by comparing the inventory computed with the amount from a physical inventory.

The retail inventory method uses a three-step process to estimate ending inventory. We need to know the amount of inventory a company had at the beginning of the period in both *cost* and *retail* amounts. We already explained how to compute the cost of inventory. The *retail amount of inventory* refers to its dollar amount measured using selling prices of inventory items. We also need to know the net amount of goods purchased (minus returns, allowances, and discounts) in the period, both at cost and at retail. The amount of net sales at retail is also needed. The process is shown in Exhibit 6B.1.

The reasoning behind the retail inventory method is that if we can get a good estimate of the cost-to-retail ratio, we can multiply ending inventory at retail by this ratio to estimate ending inventory at cost. We show in Exhibit 6B.2 how these steps are applied to estimate ending inventory for a typical company. First, we find that

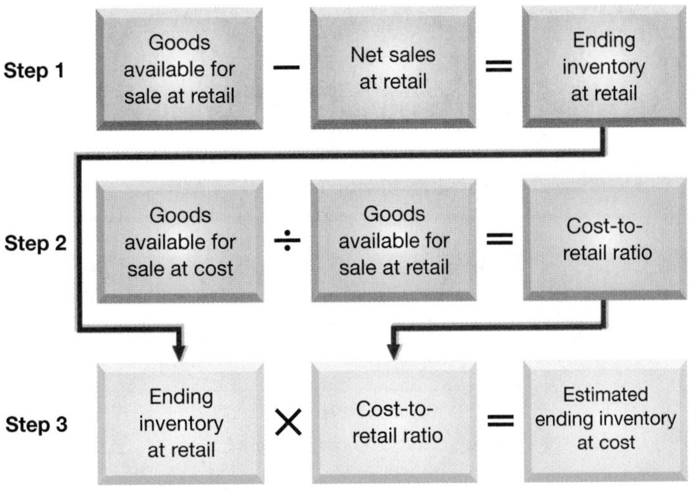

EXHIBIT 6B.1

Retail Inventory Method of Inventory Estimation

EXHIBIT 6B.2

Estimated Inventory Using the Retail Inventory Method

		At Cost	At Retail
	Goods available for sale		
	Beginning inventory	$ 20,500	$ 34,500
	Cost of goods purchased	39,500	65,500
Step 1:	Goods available for sale	60,000	100,000
	Deduct net sales at retail		**70,000**
	Ending inventory at retail		**$ 30,000**
Step 2:	**Cost-to-retail ratio: ($60,000 ÷ $100,000) = 60%**		
Step 3:	**Estimated ending inventory at cost ($30,000 × 60%)**	**$18,000**	

Example: What is the cost of ending inventory in Exhibit 6B.2 if the cost of beginning inventory is $22,500 and its retail value is $34,500? *Answer:* $30,000 × 62% = $18,600

$100,000 of goods (at retail selling prices) were available for sale. We see that $70,000 of these goods were sold, leaving $30,000 (retail value) of merchandise in ending inventory. Second, the cost of these goods is 60% of the $100,000 retail value. Third, since cost for these goods is 60% of retail, the estimated cost of ending inventory is $18,000.

Gross Profit Method

The **gross profit method** estimates the cost of ending inventory by applying the gross profit ratio to net sales (at retail). This type of estimate often is needed when inventory is destroyed, lost, or stolen. These cases require an inventory estimate so that a company can file a claim with its insurer. Users also apply this method to see whether inventory amounts from a physical count are reasonable. This method uses the historical relation between cost of goods sold and net sales to estimate the proportion of cost of goods sold making up current sales. This cost of goods sold estimate is then subtracted from cost of goods available for sale to estimate the ending inventory at cost. These two steps are shown in Exhibit 6B.3.

EXHIBIT 6B.3

Gross Profit Method of Inventory Estimation

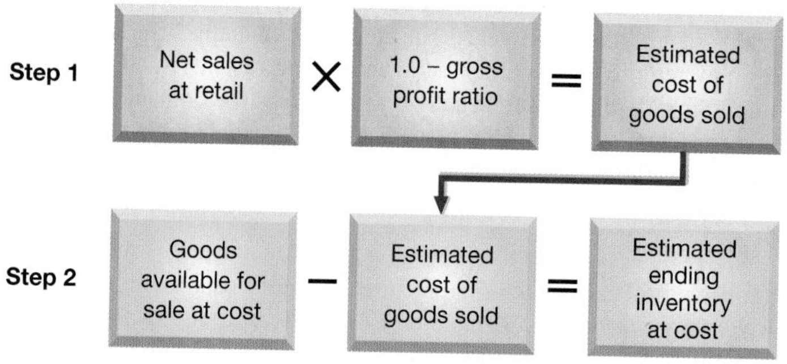

Point: A fire or other catastrophe can result in an insurance claim for lost inventory or income. Backup and off-site storage of data help ensure coverage for such losses.

Point: Reliability of the gross profit method depends on a good estimate of the gross profit ratio.

To illustrate, assume that a company's inventory is destroyed by fire in March 2009. When the fire occurs, the company's accounts show the following balances for January through March: sales, $31,500; sales returns, $1,500; inventory (January 1, 2009), $12,000; and cost of goods purchased, $20,500. If this company's gross profit ratio is 30%, then 30% of each net sales dollar is gross profit and 70% is cost of goods sold. We show in Exhibit 6B.4 how this 70% is used to estimate lost inventory of $11,500. To understand this exhibit, think of subtracting the cost of goods sold from the goods available for sale to get the ending inventory.

EXHIBIT 6B.4

Estimated Inventory Using the Gross Profit Method

	Goods available for sale		
	Inventory, January 1, 2009	$12,000	
	Cost of goods purchased	20,500	
	Goods available for sale (at cost)	32,500	
	Net sales at retail ($31,500 – $1,500)		$30,000
Step 1:	**Estimated cost of goods sold ($30,000 × 70%)**	**(21,000)**	× 0.70
Step 2:	**Estimated March inventory at cost**	**$11,500**	

Quick Check Answer—p. 250

10. Using the retail method and the following data, estimate the cost of ending inventory.

	Cost	Retail
Beginning inventory	$324,000	$530,000
Cost of goods purchased	195,000	335,000
Net sales		320,000

Summary

C1 Identify the items making up merchandise inventory. Merchandise inventory refers to goods owned by a company and held for resale. Three special cases merit our attention. Goods in transit are reported in inventory of the company that holds ownership rights. Goods on consignment are reported in the consignor's inventory. Goods damaged or obsolete are reported in inventory at their net realizable value.

C2 Identify the costs of merchandise inventory. Costs of merchandise inventory include expenditures necessary to bring an item to a salable condition and location. This includes its invoice cost minus any discount plus any added or incidental costs necessary to put it in a place and condition for sale.

A1 Analyze the effects of inventory methods for both financial and tax reporting. When purchase costs are rising or falling, the inventory costing methods are likely to assign different costs to inventory. Specific identification exactly matches costs and revenues. Weighted average smooths out cost changes. FIFO assigns an amount to inventory closely approximating current replacement cost. LIFO assigns the most recent costs incurred to cost of goods sold and likely better matches current costs with revenues.

A2 Analyze the effects of inventory errors on current and future financial statements. An error in the amount of ending inventory affects assets (inventory), net income (cost of goods sold), and equity for that period. Since ending inventory is next period's beginning inventory, an error in ending inventory affects next period's cost of goods sold and net income. Inventory errors in one period are offset in the next period.

A3 Assess inventory management using both inventory turnover and days' sales in inventory. We prefer a high inventory turnover, provided that goods are not out of stock and customers are not turned away. We use days' sales in inventory to assess the likelihood of goods being out of stock. We prefer a small number of days' sales in inventory if we can serve customer needs and provide a buffer for uncertainties.

P1 Compute inventory in a perpetual system using the methods of specific identification, FIFO, LIFO, and weighted average. Costs are assigned to the cost of goods sold account *each time* a sale occurs in a perpetual system. Specific identification assigns a cost to each item sold by referring to its actual cost (for example, its net invoice cost). Weighted average assigns a cost to items sold by dividing the current balance in the inventory account by the total items available for sale to determine cost per unit. We then multiply the number of units sold by this cost per unit to get the cost of each sale. FIFO assigns cost to items sold assuming that the earliest units purchased are the first units sold. LIFO assigns cost to items sold assuming that the most recent units purchased are the first units sold.

P2 Compute the lower of cost or market amount of inventory. Inventory is reported at market cost when market is *lower* than recorded cost, called the *lower of cost or market* (*LCM*) *inventory.* Market is typically measured as replacement cost. Lower of cost or market can be applied separately to each item, to major categories of items, or to the entire inventory.

P3^A Compute inventory in a periodic system using the methods of specific identification, FIFO, LIFO, and weighted average. Periodic inventory systems allocate the cost of goods available for sale between cost of goods sold and ending inventory *at the end of a period.* Specific identification and FIFO give identical results whether the periodic or perpetual system is used. LIFO assigns costs to cost of goods sold assuming the last units purchased for the period are the first units sold. The weighted average cost per unit is computed by dividing the total cost of beginning inventory and net purchases for the period by the total number of units available. Then, it multiplies cost per unit by the number of units sold to give cost of goods sold.

P4^B Apply both the retail inventory and gross profit methods to estimate inventory. The retail inventory method involves three steps: (1) goods available at retail minus net sales at retail equals ending inventory at retail, (2) goods available at cost divided by goods available at retail equals the cost-to-retail ratio, and (3) ending inventory at retail multiplied by the cost-to-retail ratio equals estimated ending inventory at cost. The gross profit method involves two steps: (1) net sales at retail multiplied by 1 minus the gross profit ratio equals estimated cost of goods sold, and (2) goods available at cost minus estimated cost of goods sold equals estimated ending inventory at cost.

Guidance Answers to **Decision Maker** and **Decision Ethics**

Financial Planner The FIFO method implies that the oldest costs are the first ones assigned to cost of goods sold. This leaves the most recent costs in ending inventory. You report this to your client and note that in most cases, the ending inventory of a company using FIFO is reported at or near its replacement cost. This means that your client need not in most cases adjust the reported value of inventory. Your answer changes only if there are major increases in replacement cost compared to the cost of recent purchases reported in inventory. When major increases in costs occur, your client might wish to adjust inventory (for internal reports) for the difference between the reported cost of inventory and its replacement cost. (*Note:* Decreases in costs of purchases are recognized under the lower of cost or market adjustment.)

Inventory Manager It seems your company can save (or at least postpone) taxes by switching to LIFO, but the switch is likely to reduce bonus money that you think you have earned and deserve. Since the U.S. tax code requires companies that use LIFO for tax reporting also to use it for financial reporting, your options are further constrained. Your best decision is to tell your superior about the tax savings with LIFO. You also should discuss your bonus plan and how this is likely to hurt you unfairly. You might propose to compute inventory under the LIFO method for reporting purposes but use the FIFO method for your bonus calculations. Another solution is to revise the bonus plan to reflect the company's use of the LIFO method.

Entrepreneur Your inventory turnover is markedly higher than the norm, whereas days' sales in inventory approximates the norm. Since your turnover is already 14% better than average, you are probably best served by directing attention to days' sales in inventory. You should see whether you can reduce the level of inventory while maintaining service to customers. Given your higher turnover, you should be able to hold less inventory.

Guidance Answers to **Quick Checks**

1. The matching principle.
2. Target reports these goods in its inventory.
3. Total cost assigned to the painting is $12,180, computed as $11,400 + $130 + $150 + $100 + $400.
4. Specific identification exactly matches costs and revenues. Weighted average tends to smooth out cost changes. FIFO assigns an amount to inventory that closely approximates current replacement cost. LIFO assigns the most recent costs incurred to cost of goods sold and likely better matches current costs with revenues.
5. FIFO—it gives a lower cost of goods sold, a higher gross profit, and a higher net income when costs are rising.
6. When costs are rising, LIFO gives a lower inventory figure on the balance sheet as compared to FIFO. FIFO's inventory amount approximates current replacement costs.
7. Cost of goods sold would be overstated by $10,000 in 2009 and understated by $10,000 in year 2010.
8. The reported LCM inventory amount (using items) is $540, computed as [(20 × $5) + (40 × $8) + (10 × $12)].

9.[A] a. FIFO periodic inventory = (20 × $14) + (10 × $12) = $400

b. LIFO periodic cost of goods sold = (20 × $14) + (40 × $12) + (70 × $10) = $1,460

10.[B] Estimated ending inventory (at cost) is $327,000. It is computed as follows:

Step 1: ($530,000 + $335,000) − $320,000 = $545,000

Step 2: $\frac{\$324,000 + \$195,000}{\$530,000 + \$335,000} = 60\%$

Step 3: $545,000 × 60% = $327,000

Key Terms

mhhe.com/wildFAP19e

Key Terms are available at the book's Website for learning and testing in an online Flashcard Format.

Average cost (pp. 230, 245)
Conservatism constraint (p. 234)
Consignee (p. 224)
Consignor (p. 224)
Consistency concept (p. 233)
Days' sales in inventory (p. 237)
First-in, first-out (FIFO) (p. 229)
Gross profit method (p. 248)
Interim statements (p. 247)
Inventory turnover (p. 236)
Last-in, first-out (LIFO) (p. 229)
Lower of cost or market (LCM) (p. 233)
Net realizable value (p. 224)
Retail inventory method (p. 247)
Specific identification (p. 227)
Weighted average (pp. 230, 245)

Multiple Choice Quiz

Answers on p. 265

mhhe.com/wildFAP19e

Additional Quiz Questions are available at the book's Website.

Quiz6

Use the following information from Marvel Company for the month of July to answer questions 1 through 4.

July 1	Beginning inventory	75 units @ $25 each
July 3	Purchase	348 units @ $27 each
July 8	Sale	300 units
July 15	Purchase	257 units @ $28 each
July 23	Sale	275 units

1. Assume that Marvel uses a perpetual FIFO inventory system. What is the dollar value of its ending inventory?
   a. $2,940
   b. $2,685
   c. $2,625
   d. $2,852
   e. $2,705
2. Assume that Marvel uses a perpetual LIFO inventory system. What is the dollar value of its ending inventory?
   a. $2,940
   b. $2,685
   c. $2,625
   d. $2,852
   e. $2,705
3. Assume that Marvel uses a perpetual specific identification inventory system. Its ending inventory consists of 20 units from beginning inventory, 40 units from the July 3 purchase, and 45 units from the July 15 purchase. What is the dollar value of its ending inventory?
   a. $2,940
   b. $2,685
   c. $2,625
   d. $2,852
   e. $2,840
4.[A] Assume that Marvel uses a *periodic* FIFO inventory system. What is the dollar value of its ending inventory?
   a. $2,940
   b. $2,685
   c. $2,625
   d. $2,852
   e. $2,705
5. A company has cost of goods sold of $85,000 and ending inventory of $18,000. Its days' sales in inventory equals:
   a. 49.32 days
   b. 0.21 days
   c. 4.72 days
   d. 77.29 days
   e. 1,723.61 days

Superscript letter [A] ([B]) denotes assignments based on Appendix 6A (6B).

Discussion Questions

1. Describe how costs flow from inventory to cost of goods sold for the following methods: (*a*) FIFO and (*b*) LIFO.
2. Where is the amount of merchandise inventory disclosed in the financial statements?
3. Why are incidental costs sometimes ignored in inventory costing? Under what accounting constraint is this permitted?
4. If costs are declining, will the LIFO or FIFO method of inventory valuation yield the lower cost of goods sold? Why?
5. What does the full-disclosure principle prescribe if a company changes from one acceptable accounting method to another?
6. Can a company change its inventory method each accounting period? Explain.
7. Does the accounting concept of consistency preclude any changes from one accounting method to another?
8. If inventory errors are said to correct themselves, why are accounting users concerned when such errors are made?
9. Explain the following statement: "Inventory errors correct themselves."
10. What is the meaning of *market* as it is used in determining the lower of cost or market for inventory?
11. What guidance does the accounting constraint of conservatism offer?
12. What factors contribute to (or cause) inventory shrinkage?
13. [A]What accounts are used in a periodic inventory system but not in a perpetual inventory system?
14. Refer to **Best Buy**'s financial statements in Appendix A. On March 3, 2007, what percent of current assets is represented by inventory?
15. Refer to **Circuit City**'s financial statements in Appendix A. Compute its cost of goods available for sale for the year ended February 28, 2007.
16. Refer to **RadioShack**'s financial statements in Appendix A and compute its cost of goods available for sale for the year ended December 31, 2006.
17. Refer to **Apple**'s financial statements in Appendix A. What percent of its current assets are inventory as of September 30, 2006, and as of September 24, 2005?
18. [B]When preparing interim financial statements, what two methods can companies utilize to estimate cost of goods sold and ending inventory?

Denotes Discussion Questions that involve decision making.

McGraw-Hill's HOMEWORK MANAGER® Available with McGraw-Hill's Homework Manager

QUICK STUDY

QS 6-1
Inventory costing methods—perpetual system
P1

A company reports the following beginning inventory and purchases for the month of January. On January 26, the company sells 360 units. What is the cost of the 155 units that remain in ending inventory at January 31, assuming costs are assigned based on a perpetual inventory system and use of (*a*) FIFO, (*b*) LIFO, and (*c*) weighted average? (Round per unit costs to three decimals, but inventory balances to the dollar.)

	Units	Unit Cost
Beginning inventory on January 1	320	$6.00
Purchase on January 9	85	6.40
Purchase on January 25	110	6.60

Check (c) $960

QS 6-2
Computing goods available for sale
P1

Rosen Company reports beginning inventory of 10 units at $28 each. Every week for four weeks it purchases an additional 10 units at respective costs of $30, $31, $32, and $34 per unit for weeks 1 through 4. Calculate the cost of goods available for sale and the units available for sale for this four-week period. Assume that no sales occur during those four weeks.

QS 6-3
Assigning costs to inventory—perpetual system
P1

Mercedes Brown starts a merchandising business on December 1 and enters into three inventory purchases:

December 7	10 units @ $ 9 cost
December 14	20 units @ $10 cost
December 21	15 units @ $12 cost

Brown sells 18 units for $35 each on December 15. Seven of the sold units are from the December 7 purchase and eleven are from the December 14 purchase. Brown uses a perpetual inventory system. Determine the costs assigned to the December 31 ending inventory based on (*a*) FIFO, (*b*) LIFO, (*c*) weighted average, and (*d*) specific identification. (Round per unit costs to three decimals, but inventory balances to the dollar.)

Check (c) $296

QS 6-4
Contrasting inventory costing methods
A1

Identify the inventory costing method best described by each of the following separate statements. Assume a period of increasing costs.

1. Results in a balance sheet inventory amount approximating replacement cost.
2. The preferred method when each unit of product has unique features that markedly affect cost.
3. Matches recent costs against net sales.
4. Yields a balance sheet inventory amount often markedly less than its replacement cost.
5. Provides a tax advantage (deferral) to a corporation when costs are rising.

QS 6-5
Inventory ownership
C1

Homestead Crafts, a distributor of handmade gifts, operates out of owner Emma Flynn's house. At the end of the current period, Emma reports she has 800 units (products) in her basement, 10 of which were damaged by water and cannot be sold. She also has another 400 units in her van, ready to deliver per a customer order, terms FOB destination, and another 100 units out on consignment to a friend who owns a retail store. How many units should Emma include in her company's period-end inventory?

QS 6-6
Inventory ownership
C1

1. Jabar Company has shipped $600 of goods to Chi Co., and Chi Co. has arranged to sell the goods for Jabar. Identify the consignor and the consignee. Which company should include any unsold goods as part of its inventory?
2. At year-end, Liu Co. had shipped $750 of merchandise FOB destination to Kwon Co. Which company should include the $750 of merchandise in transit as part of its year-end inventory?

QS 6-7
Inventory costs
C2

Rivers Associates, antique dealers, purchased the contents of an estate for $75,000. Terms of the purchase were FOB shipping point, and the cost of transporting the goods to Rivers Associates' warehouse was $1,800. Rivers Associates insured the shipment at a cost of $300. Prior to putting the goods up for sale, they cleaned and refurbished them at a cost of $1,750. Determine the cost of the inventory acquired from the estate.

QS 6-8
Inventory costs
C2

A car dealer acquires a used car for $17,500, terms FOB shipping point. Additional costs in obtaining and offering the car for sale include $300 for transportation-in, $1,000 for import duties, $250 for insurance during shipment, $400 for advertising, and $3,000 for sales staff salaries. For computing inventory, what cost is assigned to the used car?

QS 6-9
Applying LCM to inventories
P2

Paoli Trading Co. has the following products in its ending inventory. Compute lower of cost or market for inventory (*a*) as a whole and (*b*) applied separately to each product.

Product	Quantity	Cost per Unit	Market per Unit
Mountain bikes	20	$650	$500
Skateboards	22	400	450
Gliders	40	850	790

QS 6-10
Inventory errors
A2

In taking a physical inventory at the end of year 2009, Peña Company erroneously forgot to count certain units. Explain how this error affects the following: (*a*) 2009 cost of goods sold, (*b*) 2009 gross profit, (*c*) 2009 net income, (*d*) 2010 net income, (*e*) the combined two-year income, and (*f*) income for years after 2010.

QS 6-11
Analyzing inventory A3

Civic Company begins the year with $75,075 of goods in inventory. At year-end, the amount in inventory has increased to $89,925. Cost of goods sold for the year is $602,250. Compute Civic's inventory turnover and days' sales in inventory. Assume that there are 365 days in the year.

QS 6-12A
Costing methods—periodic system P3

Refer to QS 6-1 and assume the periodic inventory system is used. Determine the costs assigned to the ending inventory when costs are assigned based on (*a*) FIFO, (*b*) LIFO, and (*c*) weighted average. (Round per unit costs to three decimals, but inventory balances to the dollar.)

QS 6-13A
Costing methods—periodic system P3

Refer to QS 6-3 and assume the periodic inventory system is used. Determine the costs assigned to the December 31 ending inventory when costs are assigned based on (*a*) FIFO, (*b*) LIFO, (*c*) weighted average, and (*d*) specific identification. (Round per unit costs to three decimals, but inventory balances to the dollar.)

QS 6-14B
Estimating inventories—gross profit method
P4

Kaysee Store's inventory is destroyed by a fire on September 5, 2009. The following data for year 2009 are available from the accounting records. Estimate the cost of the inventory destroyed.

Jan. 1 inventory	$230,000
Jan. 1 through Sept. 5 purchases (net)	$492,000
Jan. 1 through Sept. 5 sales (net)	$850,000
Year 2009 estimated gross profit rate	37%

McGraw-Hill's HOMEWORK MANAGER® Available with McGraw-Hill's Homework Manager

EXERCISES

Exercise 6-1
Inventory costing methods—perpetual
P1

Liberty Company reported the following January purchases and sales data for its only product.

Date	Activities	Units Acquired at Cost		Units Sold at Retail
Jan. 1	Beginning inventory	140 units @ $7.00 =	$ 980	
Jan. 10	Sales			90 units @ $15
Jan. 20	Purchase	220 units @ $6.00 =	1,320	
Jan. 25	Sales			145 units @ $15
Jan. 30	Purchase	100 units @ $5.00 =	500	
	Totals	460 units	$2,800	235 units

Liberty uses a perpetual inventory system. Ending inventory consists of 225 units, 100 from the January 30 purchase, 80 from the January 20 purchase, and 45 from beginning inventory. Determine the cost assigned to ending inventory and to cost of goods sold using (*a*) specific identification, (*b*) weighted average, (*c*) FIFO, and (*d*) LIFO. (Round per unit costs to three decimals, but inventory balances to the dollar.)

Check Ending inventory: LIFO, $1,300; WA, $1,273

Exercise 6-2
Income effects of inventory methods
A1

Use the data in Exercise 6-1 to prepare comparative income statements for the month of January for Liberty Company similar to those shown in Exhibit 6.8 for the four inventory methods. Assume expenses are $1,250, and that the applicable income tax rate is 30%.

1. Which method yields the highest net income?
2. Does net income using weighted average fall between that using FIFO and LIFO?
3. If costs were rising instead of falling, which method would yield the highest net income?

Exercise 6-3 ✓
Inventory costing methods (perpetual)—FIFO and LIFO
P1

net sales - COGS / net sales

180 - 13

Harper Co. reported the following current-year purchases and sales data for its only product.

Date	Activities	Units Acquired at Cost		Units Sold at Retail
Jan. 1	Beginning inventory	126 units @ $8 =	$ 1,008	
Jan. 10	Sales			113 units @ $40
Mar. 14	Purchase	315 units @ $13 =	4,095	
Mar. 15	Sales			180 units @ $40
July 30	Purchase	250 units @ $18 =	4,500	
Oct. 5	Sales			378 units @ $40
Oct. 26	Purchase	50 units @ $23 =	1,150	
	Totals	741 units	$10,753	671 units

Harper uses a perpetual inventory system. Determine the costs assigned to ending inventory and to cost of goods sold using (*a*) FIFO and (*b*) LIFO. Compute the gross margin for each method.

Check Ending inventory: LIFO, $1,345

Exercise 6-4
Specific identification P1

Refer to the data in Exercise 6-3. Assume that ending inventory is made up of 5 units from the March 14 purchase, 15 units from the July 30 purchase, and all the units of the October 26 purchase. Using the specific identification method, calculate (*a*) the cost of goods sold and (*b*) the gross profit.

Exercise 6-5
Lower of cost or market P2

Maya Company's ending inventory includes the following items. Compute the lower of cost or market for ending inventory (*a*) as a whole and (*b*) applied separately to each product.

		Per Unit	
Product	Units	Cost	Market
Helmets	19	$45	$49
Bats	12	73	67
Shoes	33	90	86
Uniforms	37	31	31

Check (*b*) $5,644

Exercise 6-6
Analysis of inventory errors
A2

Abco Company had $1,100,000 of sales in each of three consecutive years 2008–2010, and it purchased merchandise costing $700,000 in each of those years. It also maintained a $280,000 physical inventory from the beginning to the end of that three-year period. In accounting for inventory, it made an error at the end of year 2008 that caused its year-end 2008 inventory to appear on its statements as $262,000 rather than the correct $280,000.

Check 2008 reported gross profit, $382,000

1. Determine the correct amount of the company's gross profit in each of the years 2008–2010.

2. Prepare comparative income statements as in Exhibit 6.11 to show the effect of this error on the company's cost of goods sold and gross profit for each of the years 2008–2010.

Exercise 6-7
Inventory turnover and days' sales in inventory
A3

Use the following information for Palmer Co. to compute inventory turnover for 2009 and 2008, and its days' sales in inventory at December 31, 2009 and 2008. (Round answers to one decimal.) Comment on Palmer's efficiency in using its assets to increase sales from 2008 to 2009.

	2009	2008	2007
Cost of goods sold	$667,134	$442,104	$405,600
Ending inventory	92,232	87,840	97,600

Exercise 6-8
Comparing LIFO numbers to FIFO numbers; ratio analysis
A1 A3

Cook Company uses LIFO for inventory costing and reports the following financial data. It also recomputed inventory and cost of goods sold using FIFO for comparison purposes.

	2009	2008
LIFO inventory	$110	$177
LIFO cost of goods sold	760	828
FIFO inventory	270	457
FIFO cost of goods sold	680	645
Current assets (using LIFO)	250	200
Current liabilities	225	180

Check (1) FIFO: Current ratio, 1.8; Inventory turnover, 1.9 times

1. Compute its current ratio, inventory turnover, and days' sales in inventory for 2009 using (*a*) LIFO numbers and (*b*) FIFO numbers. (Round answers to one decimal.)

2. Comment on and interpret the results of part 1.

Exercise 6-9^A^
Inventory costing—periodic system P3

Refer to Exercise 6-1 and assume the periodic inventory system is used. Determine the costs assigned to ending inventory and to cost of goods sold using (*a*) specific identification, (*b*) weighted average, (*c*) FIFO, and (*d*) LIFO. (Round per unit costs to three decimals, but inventory balances to the dollar.)

Exercise 6-10^A^
Inventory costing—periodic system P3

Refer to Exercise 6-3 and assume the periodic inventory system is used. Determine the costs assigned to ending inventory and to cost of goods sold using (*a*) FIFO and (*b*) LIFO. Compute the gross margin for each method.

Exercise 6-11[A]
Alternative cost flow assumptions—periodic
P3

Martinez Co. reported the following current-year data for its only product. The company uses a periodic inventory system, and its ending inventory consists of 405 units—135 from each of the last three purchases. Determine the cost assigned to ending inventory and to cost of goods sold using (*a*) specific identification, (*b*) weighted average, (*c*) FIFO, and (*d*) LIFO. (Round per unit costs to three decimals, but inventory balances to the dollar.) Which method yields the highest net income?

Jan. 1	Beginning inventory	270 units @ $1.90 =	$ 513
Mar. 7	Purchase	540 units @ $2.05 =	1,107
July 28	Purchase	1,350 units @ $2.30 =	3,105
Oct. 3	Purchase	1,230 units @ $2.60 =	3,198
Dec. 19	Purchase	390 units @ $2.70 =	1,053
	Totals	3,780 units	$8,976

Check Inventory; LIFO, $790; FIFO, $1,092

Exercise 6-12[A]
Alternative cost flow assumptions—periodic
P3

Genesis Gifts reported the following current-year data for its only product. The company uses a periodic inventory system, and its ending inventory consists of 360 units—120 from each of the last three purchases. Determine the cost assigned to ending inventory and to cost of goods sold using (*a*) specific identification, (*b*) weighted average, (*c*) FIFO, and (*d*) LIFO. (Round per unit costs to three decimals, but inventory balances to the dollar.) Which method yields the lowest net income?

Jan. 1	Beginning inventory	290 units @ $2.80 =	$ 812
Mar. 7	Purchase	610 units @ $2.70 =	1,647
July 28	Purchase	810 units @ $2.40 =	1,944
Oct. 3	Purchase	1,110 units @ $2.20 =	2,442
Dec. 19	Purchase	260 units @ $1.90 =	494
	Totals	3,080 units	$7,339

Check Inventory: LIFO, $1,001; FIFO, $714

Exercise 6-13[B]
Estimating ending inventory—retail method
P4

In 2009, Dakota Company had net sales (at retail) of $219,800. The following additional information is available from its records at the end of 2009. Use the retail inventory method to estimate Dakota's 2009 ending inventory at cost.

	At Cost	At Retail
Beginning inventory	$ 57,100	$108,200
Cost of goods purchased	97,740	168,300

Check End. Inventory, $31,752

Exercise 6-14[B]
Estimating ending inventory—gross profit method
P4

On January 1, Java Shop had $360,000 of inventory at cost. In the first quarter of the year, it purchased $1,267,200 of merchandise, returned $11,450, and paid freight charges of $18,100 on purchased merchandise, terms FOB shipping point. The company's gross profit averages 34%, and the store had $1,594,800 of net sales (at retail) in the first quarter of the year. Use the gross profit method to estimate its cost of inventory at the end of the first quarter.

McGraw-Hill's HOMEWORK MANAGER® Available with McGraw-Hill's Homework Manager

PROBLEM SET A

Problem 6-1A
Alternative cost flows—perpetual
P1

Ammons Company uses a perpetual inventory system. It entered into the following purchases and sales transactions for January.

Date	Activities	Units Acquired at Cost	Units Sold at Retail
Jan. 1	Beginning inventory	5 units @ $500/unit	
Jan. 5	Purchase	20 units @ $550/unit	
Jan. 9	Sales		21 units @ $850/unit
Jan. 18	Purchase	6 units @ $600/unit	
Jan. 25	Purchase	10 units @ $620/unit	
Jan. 29	Sales		8 units @ $950/unit
	Totals	41 units	29 units

Required

1. Compute cost of goods available for sale and the number of units available for sale.

2. Compute the number of units in ending inventory.

3. Compute the cost assigned to ending inventory using (*a*) FIFO, (*b*) LIFO, (*c*) weighted average, and (*d*) specific identification. (Round per unit costs to three decimals, but inventory balances to the dollar.) For specific identification, the January 9 sale consisted of 4 units from beginning inventory and 17 units from the January 5 purchase; the January 29 sale consisted of 2 units from the January 18 purchase and 6 units from the January 25 purchase.

4. Compute gross profit earned by the company for each of the four costing methods in part 3.

Check (3) Ending Inventory: FIFO, $7,400; LIFO, $6,840, WA, $7,176

(4) LIFO gross profit, $8,990

Problem 6-2A
Alternative cost flows—perpetual

P1

Marlow Company uses a perpetual inventory system. It entered into the following calendar-year 2009 purchases and sales transactions.

Date	Activities	Units Acquired at Cost	Units Sold at Retail
Jan. 1	Beginning inventory	770 units @ $50/unit	
Feb. 10	Purchase	420 units @ $41/unit	
Mar. 13	Purchase	260 units @ $25/unit	
Mar. 15	Sales		770 units @ $75/unit
Aug. 21	Purchase	180 units @ $49/unit	
Sept. 5	Purchase	585 units @ $42/unit	
Sept. 10	Sales		650 units @ $75/unit
	Totals	2,215 units	1,420 units

Required

1. Compute cost of goods available for sale and the number of units available for sale.

2. Compute the number of units in ending inventory.

3. Compute the cost assigned to ending inventory using (*a*) FIFO, (*b*) LIFO, (*c*) specific identification—units sold consist of 95 units from beginning inventory, 175 from the February 10 purchase, 70 from the March 13 purchase, and 455 from the September 5 purchase, and (*d*) weighted average. (Round per unit costs to three decimals, but inventory balances to the dollar.)

4. Compute gross profit earned by the company for each of the four costing methods in part 3.

Check (3) Ending inventory: FIFO, $34,140; LIFO, $39,635; WA, $34,424;

(4) LIFO gross profit, $50,525

Analysis Component

5. If the company's manager earns a bonus based on a percent of gross profit, which method of inventory costing will the manager likely prefer?

Problem 6-3A
Lower of cost or market

P2

A physical inventory of SoundLand Company taken at December 31 reveals the following.

		Per Unit	
Item	**Units**	**Cost**	**Market**
Audio equipment			
Receivers	343	$ 88	$ 96
CD players	255	109	98
MP3 players	323	84	93
Speakers	198	50	39
Video equipment			
Handheld LCDs	481	148	123
VCRs	288	91	82
Camcorders	206	308	320
Car audio equipment			
Satellite radios	179	68	82
CD/MP3 radios	164	95	103

Required

Calculate the lower of cost or market for the inventory (*a*) as a whole, (*b*) by major category, and (*c*) applied separately to each item.

Check (*b*) $271,462; (*c*) $264,007

Problem 6-4A
Analysis of inventory errors
A2

excel
mhhe.com/wildFAP19e

Nikita Company's financial statements show the following. The company recently discovered that in making physical counts of inventory, it had made the following errors: Inventory on December 31, 2008, is understated by $56,000, and inventory on December 31, 2009, is overstated by $25,000.

For Year Ended December 31	2008	2009	2010
(*a*) Cost of goods sold	$ 623,000	$ 955,000	$ 780,000
(*b*) Net income	230,000	275,000	250,000
(*c*) Total current assets	1,247,000	1,360,000	1,230,000
(*d*) Total equity	1,387,000	1,580,000	1,245,000

Required

1. For each key financial statement figure—(*a*), (*b*), (*c*), and (*d*) above—prepare a table similar to the following to show the adjustments necessary to correct the reported amounts.

Figure: ______	2008	2009	2010
Reported amount	______	______	______
Adjustments for: 12/31/2008 error	______	______	______
12/31/2009 error	______	______	______
Corrected amount	______	______	______

Check (1) Corrected net income: 2008, $286,000; 2009, $194,000; 2010, $275,000

Analysis Component

2. What is the error in total net income for the combined three-year period resulting from the inventory errors? Explain.

3. Explain why the understatement of inventory by $56,000 at the end of 2008 results in an understatement of equity by the same amount in that year.

Problem 6-5A[A]
Alternative cost flows—periodic
P3

Austin Company began year 2009 with 33,000 units of product in its January 1 inventory costing $17 each. It made successive purchases of its product in year 2009 as follows. The company uses a periodic inventory system. On December 31, 2009, a physical count reveals that 40,000 units of its product remain in inventory.

Mar. 7	38,000 units @ $19 each
May 25	34,000 units @ $22 each
Aug. 1	26,000 units @ $26 each
Nov. 10	22,000 units @ $30 each

Required

1. Compute the number and total cost of the units available for sale in year 2009.

2. Compute the amounts assigned to the 2009 ending inventory and the cost of goods sold using (*a*) FIFO, (*b*) LIFO, and (*c*) weighted average. (Round per unit costs to three decimals, but inventory balances to the dollar.)

Check (2) Cost of goods sold: FIFO, $2,239,000; LIFO, $2,673,000; WA, $2,486,720

Problem 6-6A[A]
Income comparisons and cost flows—periodic
A1 P3

Bay Corp. sold 6,500 units of its product at $50 per unit in year 2009 and incurred operating expenses of $5 per unit in selling the units. It began the year with 900 units in inventory and made successive purchases of its product as follows.

Jan. 1	Beginning inventory	900 units @ $21 per unit
Feb. 20	Purchase	1,950 units @ $22 per unit
May 16	Purchase	1,050 units @ $25 per unit
Oct. 3	Purchase	700 units @ $26 per unit
Dec. 11	Purchase	2,750 units @ $27 per unit
	Total	7,350 units

Check (1) Net income: FIFO, $80,970; LIFO, $77,910; WA, $79,724

Required

1. Prepare comparative income statements similar to Exhibit 6.8 for the three inventory costing methods of FIFO, LIFO, and weighted average. (Round per unit costs to three decimals, but inventory balances to the dollar.) Include a detailed cost of goods sold section as part of each statement. The company uses a periodic inventory system, and its income tax rate is 40%.
2. How would the financial results from using the three alternative inventory costing methods change if Bay had been experiencing declining costs in its purchases of inventory?
3. What advantages and disadvantages are offered by using (*a*) LIFO and (*b*) FIFO? Assume the continuing trend of increasing costs.

Problem 6-7A^B
Retail inventory method
P4

excel
mhhe.com/wildFAP19e

The records of Ultra Company provide the following information for the year ended December 31.

	At Cost	At Retail
January 1 beginning inventory	$ 476,600	$ 927,950
Cost of goods purchased	3,481,060	6,401,050
Sales		5,565,800
Sales returns		49,800

Check (1) Inventory, $979,020 cost; (2) Inventory shortage at cost, $55,134

Required

1. Use the retail inventory method to estimate the company's year-end inventory at cost.
2. A year-end physical inventory at retail prices yields a total inventory of $1,710,900. Prepare a calculation showing the company's loss from shrinkage at cost and at retail.

Problem 6-8A^B
Gross profit method
P4

Optek Company wants to prepare interim financial statements for the first quarter. The company wishes to avoid making a physical count of inventory. Optek's gross profit rate averages 39%. The following information for the first quarter is available from its records.

January 1 beginning inventory	$ 312,580
Cost of goods purchased	944,040
Sales	1,391,160
Sales returns	8,760

Check Estimated ending inventory, $413,356

Required

Use the gross profit method to estimate the company's first-quarter ending inventory.

PROBLEM SET B

Problem 6-1B
Alternative cost flows—perpetual
P1

Sheila Company uses a perpetual inventory system. It entered into the following purchases and sales transactions for May.

Date	Activities	Units Acquired at Cost	Units Sold at Retail
May 1	Beginning inventory	150 units @ $300/unit	
May 6	Purchase	350 units @ $350/unit	
May 9	Sales		180 units @ $1,200/unit
May 17	Purchase	80 units @ $450/unit	
May 25	Purchase	100 units @ $458/unit	
May 30	Sales		300 units @ $1,400/unit
	Total	690 units	480 units

Required

1. Compute cost of goods available for sale and the number of units available for sale.
2. Compute the number of units in ending inventory.

3. Compute the cost assigned to ending inventory using (*a*) FIFO, (*b*) LIFO, (*c*) weighted average, and (*d*) specific identification. (Round per unit costs to three decimals, but inventory balances to the dollar.) For specific identification, the May 9 sale consisted of 80 units from beginning inventory and 100 units from the May 6 purchase; the May 30 sale consisted of 200 units from the May 6 purchase and 100 units from the May 25 purchase.

Check (3) Ending inventory: FIFO, $88,800; LIFO, $62,500; WA, $75,600;

4. Compute gross profit earned by the company for each of the four costing methods in part 3.

(4) LIFO gross profit, $449,200

Problem 6-2B
Alternative cost flows—perpetual
P1

Hawaii Pacific Company uses a perpetual inventory system. It entered into the following calendar-year 2009 purchases and sales transactions.

Date	Activities	Units Acquired at Cost	Units Sold at Retail
Jan. 1	Beginning inventory	520 units @ $45/unit	
Jan. 10	Purchase	350 units @ $50/unit	
Feb. 13	Purchase	200 units @ $51/unit	
Feb. 15	Sales		620 units @ $75/unit
July 21	Purchase	260 units @ $52/unit	
Aug. 5	Purchase	595 units @ $53/unit	
Aug. 10	Sales		660 units @ $75/unit
	Total	1,925 units	1,280 units

Required

1. Compute cost of goods available for sale and the number of units available for sale.

2. Compute the number of units in ending inventory.

3. Compute the cost assigned to ending inventory using (*a*) FIFO, (*b*) LIFO, (*c*) specific identification—units sold consist of 105 units from beginning inventory, 140 units from the January 10 purchase, 105 units from the February 13 purchase, 50 units from the July 21 purchase, and 245 units from the August 5 purchase, and (*d*) weighted average. (Round per unit costs to three decimals, but inventory balances to the dollar.)

Check (3) Ending inventory: FIFO, $34,135; LIFO, $30,390; WA, $32,890;

4. Compute gross profit earned by the company for each of the four costing methods in part 3.

(4) LIFO gross profit, $30,235

Analysis Component

5. If the company's manager earns a bonus based on a percent of gross profit, which method of inventory costing will the manager likely prefer?

Problem 6-3B
Lower of cost or market
P2

A physical inventory of Office Mart taken at December 31 reveals the following.

	Item	Units	Per Unit Cost	Per Unit Market
3	Office furniture			
4	Desks	376	$231	$239
5	Credenzas	280	198	207
6	Chairs	725	36	33
7	Bookshelves	218	103	99
8	Filing cabinets			
9	Two-drawer	136	85	82
10	Four-drawer	317	129	126
11	Lateral	92	114	118
12	Office equipment			
13	Fax machines	352	55	65
14	Copiers	430	405	396
15	Telephones	515	63	61

Required

Compute the lower of cost or market for the inventory (*a*) as a whole, (*b*) by major category, and (*c*) applied separately to each item.

Check (b) $477,375; (c) $470,440

Problem 6-4B
Analysis of inventory errors
A2

Watson Company's financial statements show the following. The company recently discovered that in making physical counts of inventory, it had made the following errors: Inventory on December 31, 2008, is overstated by $64,000, and inventory on December 31, 2009, is understated by $35,000.

For Year Ended December 31	2008	2009	2010
(*a*) Cost of goods sold	$ 615,000	$ 957,000	$ 786,000
(*b*) Net income	225,000	285,000	244,000
(*c*) Total current assets	1,251,000	1,360,000	1,265,000
(*d*) Total equity	1,387,000	1,520,000	1,250,000

Required

1. For each key financial statement figure—(*a*), (*b*), (*c*), and (*d*) above—prepare a table similar to the following to show the adjustments necessary to correct the reported amounts.

Figure: ________	2008	2009	2010
Reported amount			
Adjustments for: 12/31/2008 error			
12/31/2009 error			
Corrected amount			

Check (1) Corrected net income: 2008, $161,000; 2009, $384,000; 2010, $209,000

Analysis Component

2. What is the error in total net income for the combined three-year period resulting from the inventory errors? Explain.

3. Explain why the overstatement of inventory by $64,000 at the end of 2008 results in an overstatement of equity by the same amount in that year.

Problem 6-5B[A]
Alternative cost flows—periodic
P3

Solaris Co. began year 2009 with 39,000 units of product in its January 1 inventory costing $21 each. It made successive purchases of its product in year 2009 as follows. The company uses a periodic inventory system. On December 31, 2009, a physical count reveals that 40,000 units of its product remain in inventory.

Jan. 4	34,000 units @ $20 each
May 18	32,000 units @ $19 each
July 9	18,000 units @ $16 each
Nov. 21	36,000 units @ $14 each

Required

1. Compute the number and total cost of the units available for sale in year 2009.

2. Compute the amounts assigned to the 2009 ending inventory and the cost of goods sold using (*a*) FIFO, (*b*) LIFO, and (*c*) weighted average. (Round per unit costs to three decimals, but inventory balances to the dollar.)

Check (2) Cost of goods sold: FIFO, $2,331,000; LIFO, $2,060,000; WA, $2,169,680

Problem 6-6B[A]
Income comparisons and cost flows—periodic
A1 P3

Shasta Company sold 6,850 units of its product at $63 per unit in year 2009 and incurred operating expenses of $5 per unit in selling the units. It began the year with 1,100 units in inventory and made successive purchases of its product as follows.

Jan. 1	Beginning inventory	1,100 units @ $23 per unit
April 2	Purchase	2,100 units @ $24 per unit
June 14	Purchase	1,250 units @ $25 per unit
Aug. 29	Purchase	1,200 units @ $27 per unit
Nov. 18	Purchase	2,250 units @ $29 per unit
	Total	7,900 units

Required

1. Prepare comparative income statements similar to Exhibit 6.8 for the three inventory costing methods of FIFO, LIFO, and weighted average. (Round per unit costs to three decimals, but inventory balances to the dollar.) Include a detailed cost of goods sold section as part of each statement. The company uses a periodic inventory system, and its income tax rate is 30%.
2. How would the financial results from using the three alternative inventory costing methods change if the company had been experiencing decreasing prices in its purchases of inventory?
3. What advantages and disadvantages are offered by using (*a*) LIFO and (*b*) FIFO? Assume the continuing trend of increasing costs.

Check (1) Net income: LIFO, $151,795; FIFO, $156,205; WA, $153,926

Problem 6-7B^B
Retail inventory method
P4

The records of Mercury Co. provide the following information for the year ended December 31.

	At Cost	At Retail
January 1 beginning inventory	$ 468,010	$ 934,950
Cost of goods purchased	3,383,110	6,471,050
Sales		5,573,800
Sales returns		48,800

Required

1. Use the retail inventory method to estimate the company's year-end inventory.
2. A year-end physical inventory at retail prices yields a total inventory of $1,701,900. Prepare a calculation showing the company's loss from shrinkage at cost and at retail.

Check (1) Inventory, $978,120 cost; (2) Inventory shortage at cost, $93,132

Problem 6-8B^B
Gross profit method
P4

Tacita Equipment Co. wants to prepare interim financial statements for the first quarter. The company wishes to avoid making a physical count of inventory. Tacita's gross profit rate averages 40%. The following information for the first quarter is available from its records.

January 1 beginning inventory	$ 301,580
Cost of goods purchased	941,040
Sales	1,401,160
Sales returns	9,100

Required

Use the gross profit method to estimate the company's first quarter ending inventory.

Check Estim. ending inventory, $407,384

SERIAL PROBLEM

Success Systems

(This serial problem began in Chapter 1 and continues through most of the book. If previous chapter segments were not completed, the serial problem can begin at this point.)

SP 6

Part A

Adriana Lopez of Success Systems is evaluating her inventory to determine whether it must be adjusted based on lower of cost or market rules. Lopez has three different types of software in her inventory and the following information is available for each.

		Per Unit	
Inventory Items	**Units**	**Cost**	**Market**
Office productivity	3	$ 76	$ 74
Desktop publishing	2	103	100
Accounting	3	90	96

Data

The company uses a perpetual inventory system. It had the following beginning inventory and current year purchases of its product.

Jan.	1	Beginning inventory	50 units @ $100 =	$ 5,000
Jan.	14	Purchase	150 units @ $120 =	18,000
Apr.	30	Purchase	200 units @ $150 =	30,000
Sept.	26	Purchase	300 units @ $200 =	60,000

The company transacted sales on the following dates at a $350 per unit sales price.

Jan. 10	30 units	(specific cost: 30 @ $100)
Feb. 15	100 units	(specific cost: 100 @ $120)
Oct. 5	350 units	(specific cost: 100 @ $150 and 250 @ $200)

Concepts and Procedures to Illustrate in Expert Presentation

a. Identify and compute the costs to assign to the units sold. (Round per unit costs to three decimals.)

b. Identify and compute the costs to assign to the units in ending inventory. (Round inventory balances to the dollar.)

c. How likely is it that this inventory costing method will reflect the actual physical flow of goods? How relevant is that factor in determining whether this is an acceptable method to use?

d. What is the impact of this method versus others in determining net income and income taxes?

e. How closely does the ending inventory amount reflect replacement cost?

4. Re-form learning teams. In rotation, each expert is to present to the team the presentation developed in part 3. Experts are to encourage and respond to questions.

ENTREPRENEURIAL DECISION

A3

BTN 6-7 Review the chapter's opening feature highlighting Jacquelyn Tran and her company, **Beauty Encounter**. Assume that Beauty Encounter consistently maintains an inventory level of $300,000, meaning that its average and ending inventory levels are the same. Also assume its annual cost of sales is $1,200,000. To cut costs, Jacquelyn proposes to slash inventory to a constant level of $150,000 with no impact on cost of sales. She plans to work with suppliers to get quicker deliveries and to order smaller quantities more often.

Required

1. Compute the company's inventory turnover and its days' sales in inventory under (*a*) current conditions and (*b*) proposed conditions.

2. Evaluate and comment on the merits of Jacquelyn's proposal given your analysis for part 1. Identify any concerns you might have about the proposal.

HITTING THE ROAD

C1 C2

BTN 6-8 Visit four retail stores with another classmate. In each store, identify whether the store uses a bar-coding system to help manage its inventory. Try to find at least one store that does not use bar-coding. If a store does not use bar-coding, ask the store's manager or clerk whether he or she knows which type of inventory method the store employs. Create a table that shows columns for the name of store visited, type of merchandise sold, use or nonuse of bar-coding, and the inventory method used if bar-coding is not employed. You might also inquire as to what the store's inventory turnover is and how often physical inventory is taken.

ETHICS CHALLENGE

A1

BTN 6-3 Golf Depot is a retail sports store carrying golf apparel and equipment. The store is at the end of its second year of operation and is struggling. A major problem is that its cost of inventory has continually increased in the past two years. In the first year of operations, the store assigned inventory costs using LIFO. A loan agreement the store has with its bank, its prime source of financing, requires the store to maintain a certain profit margin and current ratio. The store's owner is currently looking over Golf Depot's preliminary financial statements for its second year. The numbers are not favorable. The only way the store can meet the required financial ratios agreed on with the bank is to change from LIFO to FIFO. The store originally decided on LIFO because of its tax advantages. The owner recalculates ending inventory using FIFO and submits those numbers and statements to the loan officer at the bank for the required bank review. The owner thankfully reflects on the available latitude in choosing the inventory costing method.

Required

1. How does Golf Depot's use of FIFO improve its net profit margin and current ratio?
2. Is the action by Golf Depot's owner ethical? Explain.

COMMUNICATING IN PRACTICE

A1

BTN 6-4 You are a financial adviser with a client in the wholesale produce business that just completed its first year of operations. Due to weather conditions, the cost of acquiring produce to resell has escalated during the later part of this period. Your client, Javonte Cruz, mentions that because her business sells perishable goods, she has striven to maintain a FIFO flow of goods. Although sales are good, the increasing cost of inventory has put the business in a tight cash position. Cruz has expressed concern regarding the ability of the business to meet income tax obligations.

Required

Prepare a memorandum that identifies, explains, and justifies the inventory method you recommend your client, Ms. Cruz, adopt.

TAKING IT TO THE NET

A3

BTN 6-5 Access the 2006 annual 10-K report for **Oakley, Inc.** (Ticker OO), filed on March 9, 2007, from the EDGAR filings at www.sec.gov.

Required

1. What product does Oakley sell that is especially popular with college students?
2. What inventory method does Oakley use? (*Hint:* See the notes to its financial statements.)
3. Compute Oakley's gross margin and gross margin ratio for the 2006 calendar year. Comment on your computations—assume an industry average of 35% for the gross margin ratio.
4. Compute Oakley's inventory turnover and days' sales in inventory for the year ended December 31, 2006. Comment on your computations—assume an industry average of 3.9 for inventory turnover.

TEAMWORK IN ACTION

A1 P1

BTN 6-6 Each team member has the responsibility to become an expert on an inventory method. This expertise will be used to facilitate teammates' understanding of the concepts relevant to that method.

1. Each learning team member should select an area for expertise by choosing one of the following inventory methods: specific identification, LIFO, FIFO, or weighted average.
2. Form expert teams made up of students who have selected the same area of expertise. The instructor will identify where each expert team will meet.
3. Using the following data, each expert team must collaborate to develop a presentation that illustrates the relevant concepts and procedures for its inventory method. Each team member must write the presentation in a format that can be shown to the learning team.

Point: Step 1 allows four choices or areas for expertise. Larger teams will have some duplication of choice, but the specific identification method should not be duplicated.

Data

The company uses a perpetual inventory system. It had the following beginning inventory and current year purchases of its product.

Jan. 1	Beginning inventory	50 units @ $100 =	$ 5,000
Jan. 14	Purchase	150 units @ $120 =	18,000
Apr. 30	Purchase	200 units @ $150 =	30,000
Sept. 26	Purchase	300 units @ $200 =	60,000

The company transacted sales on the following dates at a $350 per unit sales price.

Jan. 10	30 units	(specific cost: 30 @ $100)
Feb. 15	100 units	(specific cost: 100 @ $120)
Oct. 5	350 units	(specific cost: 100 @ $150 and 250 @ $200)

Concepts and Procedures to Illustrate in Expert Presentation

a. Identify and compute the costs to assign to the units sold. (Round per unit costs to three decimals.)

b. Identify and compute the costs to assign to the units in ending inventory. (Round inventory balances to the dollar.)

c. How likely is it that this inventory costing method will reflect the actual physical flow of goods? How relevant is that factor in determining whether this is an acceptable method to use?

d. What is the impact of this method versus others in determining net income and income taxes?

e. How closely does the ending inventory amount reflect replacement cost?

4. Re-form learning teams. In rotation, each expert is to present to the team the presentation developed in part 3. Experts are to encourage and respond to questions.

ENTREPRENEURIAL DECISION

A3

BTN 6-7 Review the chapter's opening feature highlighting Jacquelyn Tran and her company, **Beauty Encounter**. Assume that Beauty Encounter consistently maintains an inventory level of $300,000, meaning that its average and ending inventory levels are the same. Also assume its annual cost of sales is $1,200,000. To cut costs, Jacquelyn proposes to slash inventory to a constant level of $150,000 with no impact on cost of sales. She plans to work with suppliers to get quicker deliveries and to order smaller quantities more often.

Required

1. Compute the company's inventory turnover and its days' sales in inventory under (*a*) current conditions and (*b*) proposed conditions.

2. Evaluate and comment on the merits of Jacquelyn's proposal given your analysis for part 1. Identify any concerns you might have about the proposal.

HITTING THE ROAD

C1 C2

BTN 6-8 Visit four retail stores with another classmate. In each store, identify whether the store uses a bar-coding system to help manage its inventory. Try to find at least one store that does not use bar-coding. If a store does not use bar-coding, ask the store's manager or clerk whether he or she knows which type of inventory method the store employs. Create a table that shows columns for the name of store visited, type of merchandise sold, use or nonuse of bar-coding, and the inventory method used if bar-coding is not employed. You might also inquire as to what the store's inventory turnover is and how often physical inventory is taken.

Required

1. Prepare comparative income statements similar to Exhibit 6.8 for the three inventory costing methods of FIFO, LIFO, and weighted average. (Round per unit costs to three decimals, but inventory balances to the dollar.) Include a detailed cost of goods sold section as part of each statement. The company uses a periodic inventory system, and its income tax rate is 30%.
2. How would the financial results from using the three alternative inventory costing methods change if the company had been experiencing decreasing prices in its purchases of inventory?
3. What advantages and disadvantages are offered by using (*a*) LIFO and (*b*) FIFO? Assume the continuing trend of increasing costs.

Check (1) Net income: LIFO, $151,795; FIFO, $156,205; WA, $153,926

Problem 6-7B[B]
Retail inventory method
P4

The records of Mercury Co. provide the following information for the year ended December 31.

	At Cost	At Retail
January 1 beginning inventory	$ 468,010	$ 934,950
Cost of goods purchased	3,383,110	6,471,050
Sales		5,573,800
Sales returns		48,800

Required

1. Use the retail inventory method to estimate the company's year-end inventory.
2. A year-end physical inventory at retail prices yields a total inventory of $1,701,900. Prepare a calculation showing the company's loss from shrinkage at cost and at retail.

Check (1) Inventory, $978,120 cost; (2) Inventory shortage at cost, $93,132

Problem 6-8B[B]
Gross profit method
P4

Tacita Equipment Co. wants to prepare interim financial statements for the first quarter. The company wishes to avoid making a physical count of inventory. Tacita's gross profit rate averages 40%. The following information for the first quarter is available from its records.

January 1 beginning inventory	$ 301,580
Cost of goods purchased	941,040
Sales	1,401,160
Sales returns	9,100

Required

Use the gross profit method to estimate the company's first quarter ending inventory.

Check Estim. ending inventory, $407,384

SERIAL PROBLEM

Success Systems

(This serial problem began in Chapter 1 and continues through most of the book. If previous chapter segments were not completed, the serial problem can begin at this point.)

SP 6

Part A

Adriana Lopez of Success Systems is evaluating her inventory to determine whether it must be adjusted based on lower of cost or market rules. Lopez has three different types of software in her inventory and the following information is available for each.

		Per Unit	
Inventory Items	Units	Cost	Market
Office productivity	3	$ 76	$ 74
Desktop publishing	2	103	100
Accounting	3	90	96

Required

1. Compute the lower of cost or market for ending inventory assuming Lopez applies the lower of cost or market rule to inventory as a whole. Must Lopez adjust the reported inventory value? Explain.
2. Assume that Lopez had instead applied the lower of cost or market rule to each product in inventory. Under this assumption, must Lopez adjust the reported inventory value? Explain.

Part *B*

Selected accounts and balances for the three months ended March 31, 2010, for Success Systems follow.

January 1 beginning inventory	$ 0
Cost of goods sold	14,052
March 31 ending inventory	704

Required

1. Compute inventory turnover and days' sales in inventory for the three months ended March 31, 2010.
2. Assess the company's performance if competitors average 10 times for inventory turnover and 29 days for days' sales in inventory.

BEYOND THE NUMBERS

REPORTING IN ACTION

C2 A3

BTN 6-1 Refer to **Best Buy**'s financial statements in Appendix A to answer the following.

Required

1. What amount of inventories did Best Buy report as a current asset on March 3, 2007? On February 25, 2006?
2. Inventories represent what percent of total assets on March 3, 2007? On February 25, 2006?
3. Comment on the relative size of Best Buy's inventories compared to its other types of assets.
4. What accounting method did Best Buy use to compute inventory amounts on its balance sheet?
5. Compute inventory turnover for fiscal year ended March 3, 2007, and days' sales in inventory as of March 3, 2007.

Fast Forward

6. Access Best Buy's financial statements for fiscal years ended after March 3, 2007, from its Website (BestBuy.com) or the SEC's EDGAR database (www.SEC.gov). Answer questions 1 through 5 using the current Best Buy information and compare results to those prior years.

COMPARATIVE ANALYSIS

A3

BTN 6-2 Comparative figures for **Best Buy**, **Circuit City**, and **RadioShack** follow.

	Best Buy			Circuit City			RadioShack		
($ millions)	Current Year	One Year Prior	Two Years Prior	Current Year	One Year Prior	Two Years Prior	Current Year	One Year Prior	Two Years Prior
Inventory	$ 4,028	$ 3,338	$ 2,851	$1,637	$1,698	$1,455	$ 752	$ 965	$1,004
Cost of sales ...	27,165	23,122	20,938	9,501	8,704	7,861	2,544	2,706	2,407

Required

1. Compute inventory turnover for each company for the most recent two years shown.
2. Compute days' sales in inventory for each company for the three years shown.
3. Comment on and interpret your findings from parts 1 and 2. Assume an industry average for inventory turnover of 6.3.

BTN 6-9 Key figures (£ millions) for **DSG international plc** (**www.DSGiplc.com**) follow.

GLOBAL DECISION

A3

DSG | BEST BUY | circuit city | RadioShack.

£ Millions	Current Year	One Year Prior	Two Years Prior
Inventory	1,031	873	811
Cost of sales	7,285	6,379	6,325

Required

1. Use these data and those from BTN 6-2 to compute (*a*) inventory turnover and (*b*) days' sales in inventory for the most recent two years shown for **DSG**, **Best Buy**, **Circuit City**, and **RadioShack**.

2. Comment on and interpret your findings from part 1.

ANSWERS TO MULTIPLE CHOICE QUIZ

1. a; FIFO perpetual

Date	Goods Purchased	Cost of Goods Sold		Inventory Balance	
July 1				75 units @ $25	= $ 1,875
July 3	348 units @ $27 = $9,396			75 units @ $25 348 units @ $27	= $ 11,271
July 8		75 units @ $25 225 units @ $27	= $ 7,950	123 units @ $27	= $ 3,321
July 15	257 units @ $28 = $7,196			123 units @ $27 257 units @ $28	= $ 10,517
July 23		123 units @ $27 152 units @ $28	= $ 7,577	105 units @ $28	= $ 2,940
			$15,527		

2. b; LIFO perpetual

Date	Goods Purchased	Cost of Goods Sold		Inventory Balance	
July 1				75 units @ $25	= $ 1,875
July 3	348 units @ $27 = $9,396			75 units @ $25 348 units @ $27	= $ 11,271
July 8		300 units @ $27	= $ 8,100	75 units @ $25 48 units @ $27	= $ 3,171
July 15	257 units @ $28 = $7,196			75 units @ $25 48 units @ $27 257 units @ $28	= $ 10,367
July 23		257 units @ $28 18 units @ $27	= $ 7,682	75 units @ $25 30 units @ $27	= $ 2,685
			$15,782		

3. e; Specific identification perpetual—Ending inventory computation.

20 units @ $25	$ 500
40 units @ $27	1,080
45 units @ $28	1,260
105 units	$2,840

4. a; FIFO periodic—Ending inventory computation.
105 units @ $28 each = $2,940; The FIFO periodic inventory computation is identical to the FIFO perpetual inventory computation (see question 1).

5. d; Days' sales in inventory = (Ending inventory/Cost of goods sold × 365)
= ($18,000/$85,000) × 365 = 77.29 days

A Look Back

Chapters 5 and 6 focused on merchandising activities and accounting for inventory. We explained inventory systems, accounting for inventory transactions, and assigning costs to inventory.

A Look at This Chapter

This chapter emphasizes accounting information systems. We describe fundamental system principles, the system's components, use of special journals and subsidiary ledgers, and technology-based systems.

A Look Ahead

Chapter 8 focuses on internal controls and accounting for cash and cash equivalents. We explain good internal control procedures and their importance.

Chapter 7 Accounting Information Systems

Learning Objectives

CAP

Conceptual

C1 Identify fundamental principles of accounting information systems. *(p. 268)*

C2 Identify components of accounting information systems. *(p. 269)*

C3 Explain the goals and uses of special journals. *(p. 271)*

C4 Describe the use of controlling accounts and subsidiary ledgers. *(p. 272)*

C5 Explain how technology-based information systems impact accounting. *(p. 282)*

Analytical

A1 Compute segment return on assets and use it to evaluate segment performance. *(p. 284)*

Procedural

P1 Journalize and post transactions using special journals. *(p. 274)*

P2 Prepare and prove the accuracy of subsidiary ledgers. *(p. 275)*

P3 *Appendix 7A*—Journalize and post transactions using special journals in a periodic inventory system. *(p. 288)*

LP7

Decision Feature

Trash to Treasure

"Push the envelope beyond the expected"—Tom Szaky

TRENTON, NJ—Tom Szaky could not shake the idea of making a product from trash. His dream product was biological waste, or what Tom affectionately calls "worm poop," which he would package in used soda bottles. Consumers would then apply it to their plants as liquid fertilizer. His start-up company, **TerraCycle (TerraCycle.net),** is successfully applying what Tom refers to as "upcycling," which is using existing recyclables in a saleable product.

Tom collects his bottling recyclables from dorms, schools, and even agreeable manufacturers. He also uses company rejects and overruns for everything from cardboard boxes to trigger spray tops. In the process, Tom set up accounting systems to measure, track, summarize, and report on operations. "There are so many areas in which you need to make good decisions," explains Tom. "The scary thing is you are always making decisions without knowing the future. Should we invest in more machinery, or stay with more labor? Should we build a large inventory, or try to fill re-orders as they come in?" These business decisions fundamentally shape Tom's accounting system.

"I've always learned on-the-job," says Tom. That on-the-job learning includes applying internal controls, special journals, accounting ledgers, and systems technology. TerraCycle maintains special journals for its sales, cash receipts, purchases, and cash disbursements. Its purchases system is especially unique in that it uses others' trash and, in some cases, gets paid for it. "It's a total paradigm shift," explains Tom. "You get paid for your raw materials and then you're paid for your finished product." Developing his accounting system to capture those operations is no easy task, but well worth the effort. "If people are willing to pay us for our raw materials," insists Tom, "there's really no limit to what TerraCycle can do. Garbage is just something we hadn't been creative enough to solve yet."

Tom's company is riding high with the right systems and operations for long run success. "I love being an entrepreneur . . . hunker down, work very hard, and wish for a little luck," advises Tom. "That luck has come our way every time!"

[Sources: *TerraCycle Website,* January 2009; *Enterprising Solutions,* July 2008; *Inc.com,* July 2007; *Brand Packaging,* June 2008; *Peregrin Pages,* June 2008]

With increases in the number and complexity of business activities, the demands placed on accounting information systems increase. Accounting information systems must meet this challenge in an efficient and effective manner. In this chapter, we learn about fundamental principles guiding information systems, and we study components making up these systems. We also explain procedures that use special journals and subsidiary ledgers to make accounting information systems more efficient. An understanding of the details of accounting reports makes us better decision makers when using financial information, and it improves our ability to analyze and interpret financial statements.

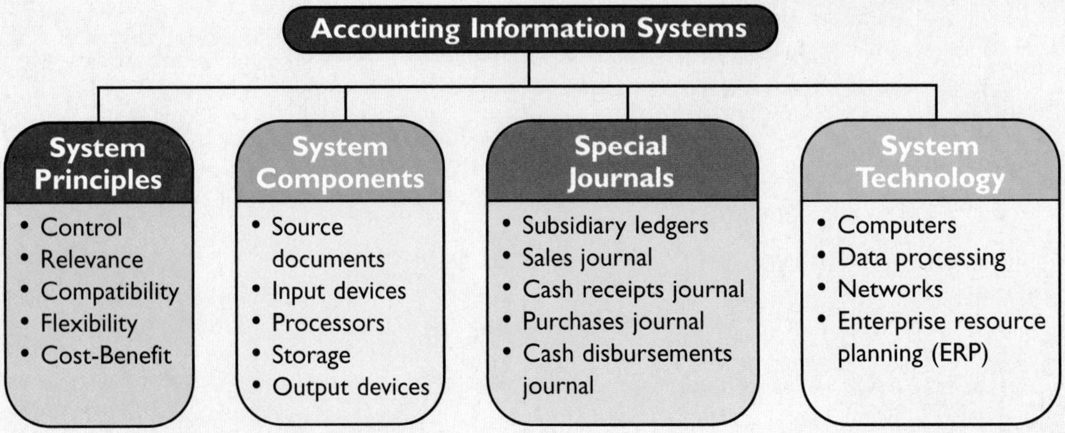

Fundamental System Principles

C1 Identify fundamental principles of accounting information systems.

Accounting information systems collect and process data from transactions and events, organize them in useful reports, and communicate results to decision makers. With the increasing complexity of business and the growing need for information, accounting information systems are more important than ever. All decision makers need to have a basic knowledge of how accounting information systems work. This knowledge gives decision makers a competitive edge as they gain a better understanding of information constraints, measurement limitations, and potential applications. It allows them to make more informed decisions and to better balance the risks and returns of different strategies. This section explains five basic principles of accounting information systems, shown in Exhibit 7.1.

EXHIBIT 7.1

System Principles

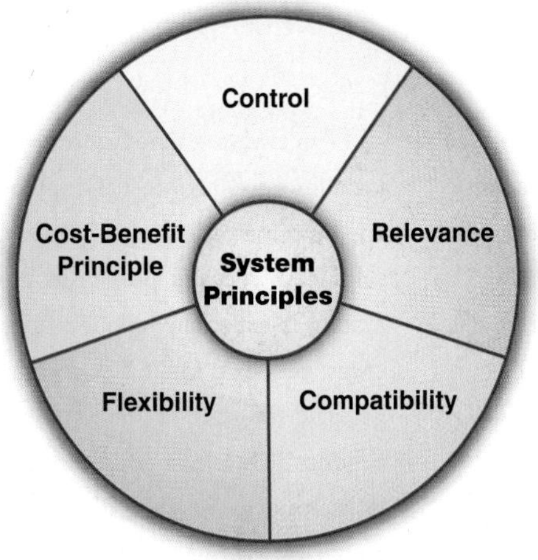

Control Principle

Managers need to control and monitor business activities. The **control principle** prescribes that an accounting information system have internal controls. **Internal controls** are methods and procedures allowing managers to control and monitor business activities. They include policies to direct operations toward common goals, procedures to ensure reliable financial reports, safeguards to protect company assets, and methods to achieve compliance with laws and regulations.

Point: A hacker stole 300,000 credit card numbers from online music retailer CDUniverse due to internal control failure.

Relevance Principle

Decision makers need relevant information to make informed decisions. The **relevance principle** prescribes that an accounting information system report useful, understandable, timely, and pertinent information for effective decision making. The system must be designed to capture data that make a difference in decisions. To ensure this, we must consider all decision makers when identifying relevant information for disclosure.

Compatibility Principle

Accounting information systems must be consistent with the aims of a company. The **compatibility principle** prescribes that an accounting information system conform with a company's activities, personnel, and structure. It also must adapt to a company's unique characteristics. The system must not be intrusive but must work in harmony with and be driven by company goals. Most start-up entrepreneurs require only a simple information system. **Harley-Davidson**, on the other hand, demands both a merchandising and a manufacturing information system able to assemble data from its global operations.

Flexibility Principle

Accounting information systems must be able to adjust to changes. The **flexibility principle** prescribes that an accounting information system be able to adapt to changes in the company, business environment, and needs of decisions makers. Technological advances, competitive pressures, consumer tastes, regulations, and company activities constantly evolve. A system must be designed to adapt to these changes.

Cost-Benefit Principle

The **cost-benefit principle** prescribes that the benefits from an activity in an accounting information system outweigh the costs of that activity. The costs and benefits of an activity such as producing a specific report will impact the decisions of both external and internal users. Decisions regarding other systems principles (control, relevance, compatibility, and flexibility) are also affected by the cost-benefit principle.

Point: Law requires that *all* employers destroy credit-check and other employee records *before* tossing them. A cross-cut shredder is the tool of choice.

Decision Insight

Digital Is Forever E-communications have helped bring down many employees, including the CEO of **Boeing**. To comply with Sarbanes-Oxley, more and more companies now archive and monitor e-mails, instant messages, blog postings, and Net-based phone calls. Using natural-language software, companies sift through digital communications in milliseconds, checking for trade secrets, bad language, porn, and pirated files.

Components of Accounting Systems

Accounting information systems consist of people, records, methods, and equipment. The systems are designed to capture information about a company's transactions and to provide output including financial, managerial, and tax reports. All accounting information systems have these same goals, and thus share some basic components. These components apply whether or not a system is heavily computerized, yet the components of computerized systems usually provide more accuracy, speed, efficiency, and convenience than those of manual systems.

The five basic **components of accounting systems** are source documents, input devices, information processors, information storage, and output devices. Exhibit 7.2 shows these components as a series of steps, yet we know that much two-way communication occurs between many of these components. We briefly describe each of these key components in this section.

C2 Identify components of accounting information systems.

EXHIBIT 7.2

Accounting System Components

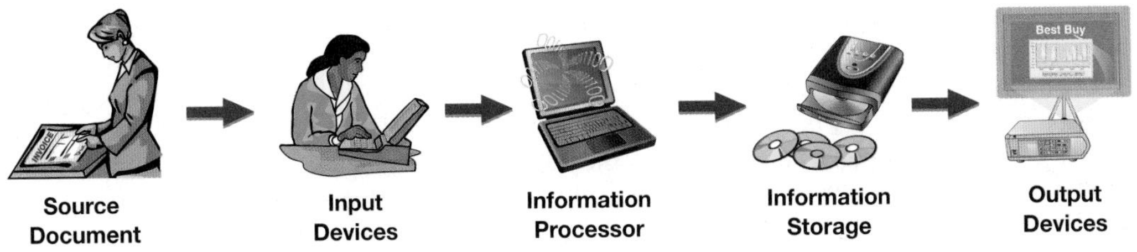

Source Documents

We introduced source documents in Chapters 1 and 2 and explained their importance for both business transactions and information collection. Source documents provide the basic information processed by an accounting system. Examples of source documents include bank statements and checks, invoices from suppliers, billings to customers, cash register files, and employee earnings records. Source documents can be paper, although they increasingly are taking the form of electronic files and Web communications. A growing number of companies are sending documents directly from their systems to their customers' and suppliers' systems. The Web is playing a major role in this transformation from paper-based to *paperless* systems.

Accurate source documents are crucial to accounting information systems. Input of faulty or incomplete information seriously impairs the reliability and relevance of the information system. We commonly refer to this as "garbage in, garbage out." Information systems are set up with attention on control procedures to limit the possibility of entering faulty data in the system.

Input Devices

Input devices capture information from source documents and enable its transfer to the system's information processing component. These devices often involve converting data on source documents from written or electronic form to a form usable for the system. Journal entries, both electronic and paper based, are a type of input device. Keyboards, scanners, and modems are some of the most common input devices in practice today. For example, bar code readers capture code numbers and transfer them to the organization's computer for processing. Moreover, a scanner can capture writing samples and other input directly from source documents.

Point: Understanding a manual accounting system is useful in understanding an electronic system.

Controls are used to ensure that only authorized individuals input data to the system. Controls increase the system's reliability and allow information to be traced back to its source.

Decision Insight

Geek Chic Cyberfashion pioneers are creating geek chic, a kind of wearable computer. Cyberfashion draws on digital cellular phones, lithium batteries, and miniature monitors. Special thread is woven into clothing to carry low-voltage signals from one part of the system to another, and fabric keyboards are sewn into clothes. These creations give new meaning to the term *software*.

Information Processors

Information processors are systems that interpret, transform, and summarize information for use in analysis and reporting. An important part of an information processor in accounting systems is professional judgment. Accounting principles are never so structured that they limit the need for professional judgment. Other parts of an information processor include journals, ledgers, working papers, and posting procedures. Each assists in transforming raw data to useful information.

Point: *BusinessWeek* (2005) reports that 75% of all e-mail traffic is spam.

Increasingly, computer technology (both computing hardware and software) is assisting manual information processors. This assistance is freeing accounting professionals to take on increased analysis, interpretive, and managerial roles. Web-based application service providers (ASPs) offer another type of information processor.

Information Storage

Information storage is the accounting system component that keeps data in a form accessible to information processors. After being input and processed, data are stored for use in future analyses and reports. The database must be accessible to preparers of periodic financial reports. Auditors rely on this database when they audit both financial statements and a company's controls. Companies also maintain files of source documents.

Point: A financial accounting database can be designed to support a wide range of internal reports for management.

Older systems consisted almost exclusively of paper documents, but most modern systems depend on electronic storage devices. Advances in information storage enable accounting systems to increasingly store more detailed data. This means managers have more data to access and work with in planning and controlling business activities. Information storage can be online, meaning that data can be accessed whenever, and from wherever, it is needed. Off-line storage means access often requires assistance and authorization. Information storage is increasingly augmented by Web sources such as SEC databases, benchmarking services, and financial and product markets.

Decision Insight

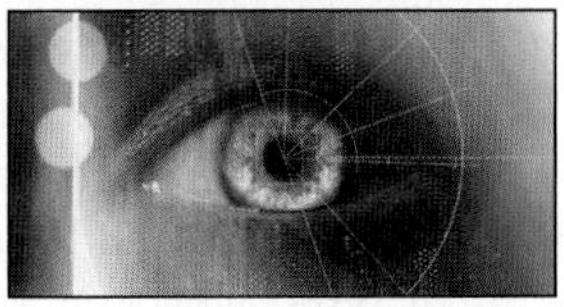

Direct Output A screenless computer display, called *virtual retinal display* (VRD), scans rows of pixels directly onto the user's retina by means of a laser. VRDs can simulate three-dimensional virtual worlds, including 3D financial graphics.

Output Devices

Output devices are the means to take information out of an accounting system and make it available to users. Common output devices are printers, monitors, LCD projectors, and Web communications. Output devices provide users a variety of items including graphics, analysis reports, bills to customers, checks to suppliers, employee paychecks, financial statements, and internal reports. When requests for output occur, an information processor takes the needed data from a database and prepares the necessary report, which is then sent to an output device. A special type of output is an electronic funds transfer (EFT). One example is the transfer of payroll from the company's bank account to its employees' bank accounts. This requires an interface to allow a company's accounting system to send payroll data directly to the bank's accounting system. This interface can involve a company recording its payroll data on CD and forwarding it to the bank. The bank then uses this output to transfer wages earned to employees' accounts.

Decision Ethics

Accountant Your client requests advice in purchasing software for its accounting system. You have been offered a 10% commission by a software company for each purchase of its system by one of your clients. Does this commission arrangement affect your evaluation of software? Do you tell your client about the commission arrangement? [Answer—p. 293]

Quick Check

Answers—p. 293

1. Identify the five primary components of an accounting information system.
2. What is the aim of information processors in an accounting system?
3. How are data in the information storage component of an accounting system used?

Special Journals in Accounting

This section describes the underlying records of accounting information systems. Designed correctly, these records support efficiency in processing transactions and events. They are part of all systems in various forms and are increasingly electronic. Even in technologically advanced systems, a basic understanding of the records we describe in this section aids in using, interpreting, and applying accounting information. It also improves our knowledge of computer-based systems. Remember that all accounting systems have common purposes and internal workings whether or not they depend on technology.

This section focuses on special journals and subsidiary ledgers that are an important part of accounting systems. We describe how special journals are used to capture transactions, and we explain how subsidiary ledgers are set up to capture details of accounts. This section uses a

C3 Explain the goals and uses of special journals.

perpetual inventory system, and the special journals are set up using this system. Appendix 7A describes the change in special journals required for a *periodic* system. We also include a note at the bottom of each of the special journals explaining the change required if a company uses a periodic system.

Basics of Special Journals

Point: Companies can use as many special journals as necessary given their unique business activities.

Point: A specific transaction is recorded in only *one* journal.

A **general journal** is an all-purpose journal in which we can record any transaction. Use of a general journal for all transactions is usually more costly for a business *and* is a less effective control procedure. Moreover, for less technologically advanced systems, use of a general journal requires that each debit and each credit entered be individually posted to its respective ledger account. To enhance internal control and reduce costs, transactions are organized into common groups. A **special journal** is used to record and post transactions of similar type. Most transactions of a merchandiser, for instance, can be categorized into the journals shown in Exhibit 7.3. This section assumes the use of these four special journals along with the general journal. The general journal continues to be used for transactions not covered by special journals and for adjusting, closing, and correcting entries. We show in the following discussion that special journals are *efficient tools in helping journalize and post transactions.* This is done, for instance, by accumulating debits and credits of similar transactions, which allows posting of amounts as column *totals* rather than as individual amounts. The advantage of this system increases as the number of transactions increases. Special journals allow an *efficient division of labor,* which is also an effective control procedure.

EXHIBIT 7.3

Using Special Journals with a General Journal

It is important to note that special journals and subsidiary ledgers *are designed in a manner that is best suited for each business.* The most likely candidates for special journal status are recurring transactions—for many businesses those are sales, cash receipts, purchases, and cash disbursements. However, good systems design for a business could involve collapsing sales and cash receipts in one journal, or purchases and cash disbursement in another. It could also involve adding more special journals or additional subsidiary ledgers for other recurring transactions. This design decision extends to journal and ledger format. That is, the selection on number of columns, column headings, and so forth is based on what is best suited for each business. Thus, read the following sections as one example of a common systems design, but not the only design.

Subsidiary Ledgers

C4 Describe the use of controlling accounts and subsidiary ledgers.

To understand special journals, it is necessary to understand the workings of a **subsidiary ledger,** which is a list of individual accounts with a common characteristic. A subsidiary ledger contains detailed information on specific accounts in the general ledger. Information systems often include several subsidiary ledgers. Two of the most important are:

- *Accounts receivable ledger*—stores transaction data of individual customers.
- *Accounts payable ledger*—stores transaction data of individual suppliers.

Individual accounts in subsidiary ledgers are often arranged alphabetically, which is the approach taken here. We describe accounts receivable and accounts payable ledgers in this section. Our discussion of special journals uses these ledgers.

Accounts Receivable Ledger When we recorded credit sales in prior chapters, we debited (increased) Accounts Receivable. When a company has more than one credit customer, the accounts receivable records must show how much *each* customer purchased, paid, and has yet to pay. This information is collected by keeping a separate account receivable for each credit customer. A separate account for each customer *could* be kept in the general ledger with the other financial statement accounts, but this is uncommon. Instead, the general ledger usually has a single Accounts Receivable account, and a *subsidiary ledger* is set up to keep a separate account for each customer. This subsidiary ledger is called the **accounts receivable ledger** (also called *accounts receivable subsidiary ledger* or *customers ledger*), and it can exist in electronic or paper form.

Exhibit 7.4 shows the relation between the Accounts Receivable account and its individual accounts in the subsidiary ledger. After all items are posted, the balance in the Accounts Receivable account must equal the sum of all balances of its customers' accounts. The Accounts Receivable account is said to control the accounts receivable ledger and is called a **controlling account.** Since the accounts receivable ledger is a supplementary record controlled by an account in the general ledger, it is called a *subsidiary* ledger.

Point: When a general ledger account has a subsidiary ledger, any transaction that impacts one of them also impacts the other—some refer to this as *general and subsidiary ledgers kept in tandem.*

EXHIBIT 7.4

Accounts Receivable Controlling Account and Its Subsidiary Ledger

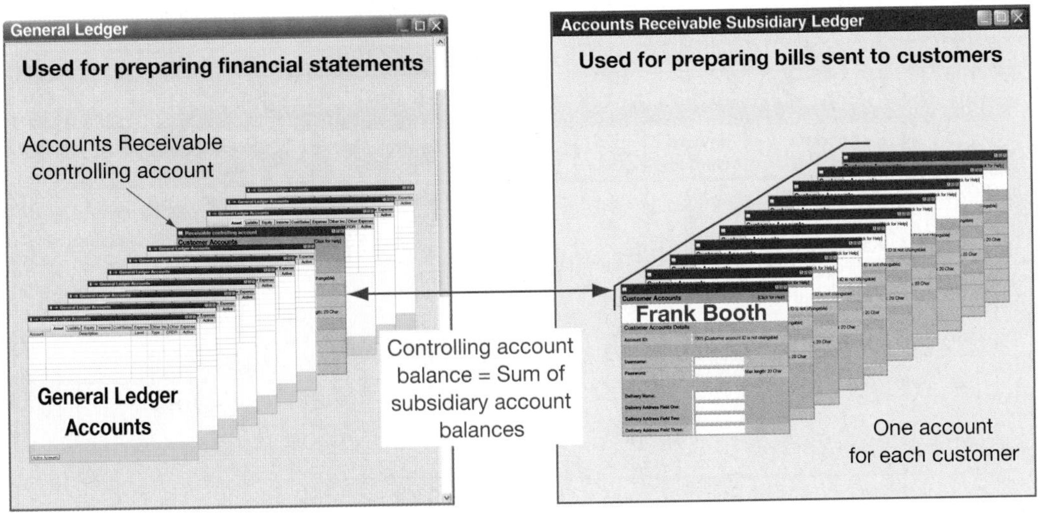

Accounts Payable Ledger There are other controlling accounts and subsidiary ledgers. We know, for example, that many companies buy on credit from several suppliers. This means that companies must keep a separate account for each supplier by keeping an Accounts Payable controlling account in the general ledger and a separate account for each supplier (creditor) in an **accounts payable ledger** (also called *accounts payable subsidiary ledger* or *creditors ledger*).

Point: Subsidiary ledgers: (1) remove excessive details from general ledger, (2) provide up-to-date info on customer or other specific account balances, (3) aid in error identification for individual accounts, and (4) help with division of labor (recordkeeping tasks).

Other Subsidiary Ledgers Subsidiary ledgers are common for several other accounts. A company with many classes of equipment, for example, might keep only one Equipment account in its general ledger, but its Equipment account would control a subsidiary ledger in which each class of equipment is recorded in a separate account. Similar treatment is common for investments, inventory, and any accounts needing separate detailed records. **Brunswick** reports sales information by product line in its annual report. Yet its accounting system keeps much more detailed sales records. Brunswick, for instance, sells hundreds of different products and must be able to analyze the sales performance of each. This detail can be captured by many different general ledger sales accounts but is instead captured by using supplementary records that function like subsidiary ledgers. Overall, subsidiary ledgers are applied in many different ways to ensure that the accounting system captures sufficient details to support analyses that decision makers need.

Sales Journal

P1 Journalize and post transactions using special journals.

A typical **sales journal** is used to record sales of inventory *on credit.* Sales of inventory for cash are not recorded in a sales journal but in a cash receipts journal. Sales of noninventory assets on credit are recorded in the general journal.

Journalizing Credit sale transactions are recorded with information about each sale entered separately in a sales journal. This information is often taken from a copy of the sales ticket or invoice prepared at the time of sale. The top portion of Exhibit 7.5 shows a typical sales journal from a merchandiser. It has columns for recording the date, customer's name, invoice number, posting reference, and the retail and cost amounts of each credit sale. The sales journal in this exhibit is called a **columnar journal,** which is any journal with more than one column.

Each transaction recorded in the sales journal yields an entry in the "Accounts Receivable Dr., Sales Cr." column. We usually need only one column for these two accounts. (An exception is when managers need more information about taxes, returns, and other sales details.) Each transaction in the sales journal also yields an entry in the "Cost of Goods Sold Dr., Inventory Cr." column. This entry reflects the perpetual inventory system of tracking costs with each sale. To illustrate, on February 2, this company sold merchandise on account to Jason Henry for $450. The invoice number is 307, and the cost of this merchandise is $315. This information is captured on

Point: Each transaction in the sales journal includes a debit to accounts receivable and a credit to sales.

EXHIBIT 7.5

Sales Journal with Posting*

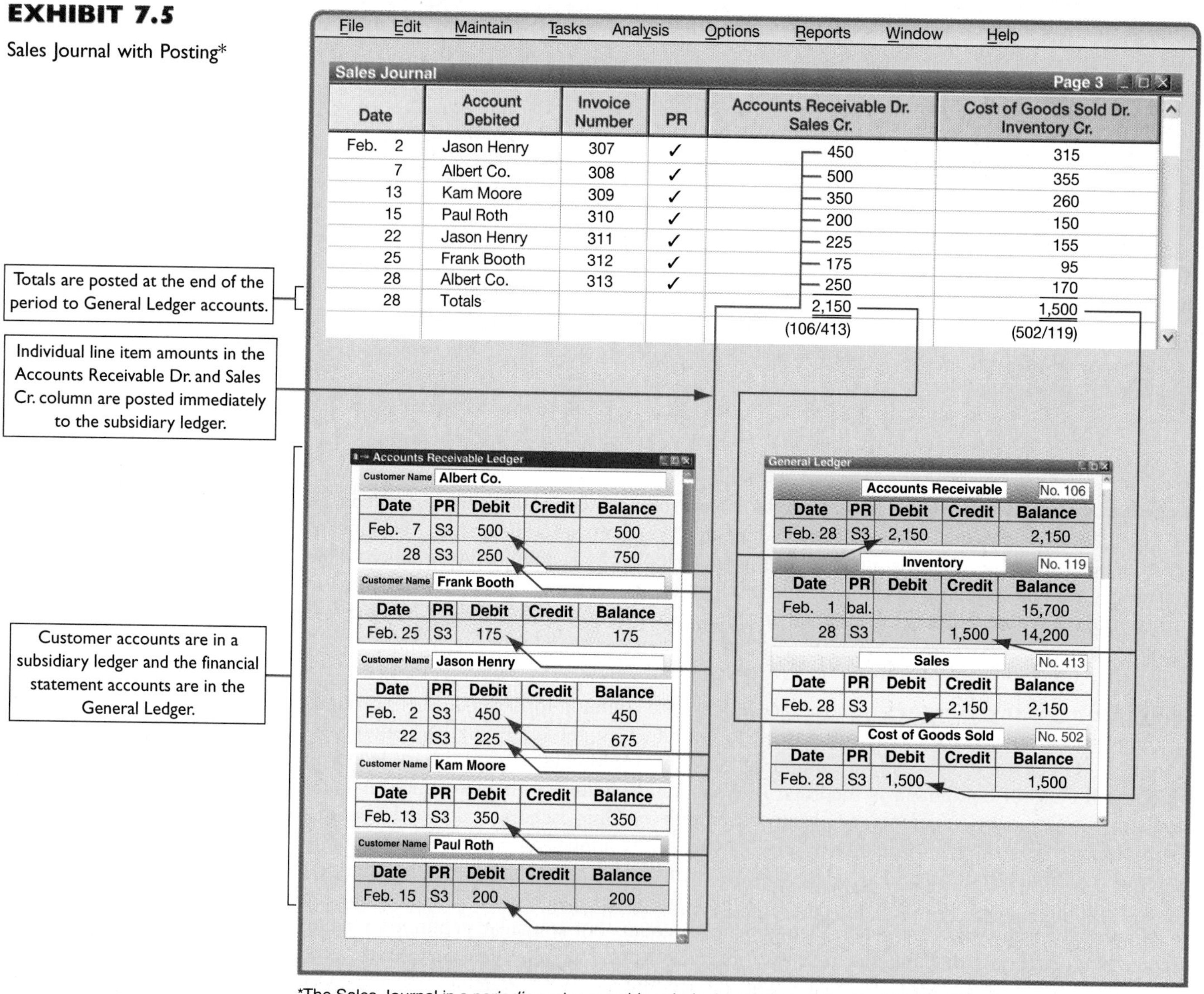

Date	Account Debited	Invoice Number	PR	Accounts Receivable Dr. Sales Cr.	Cost of Goods Sold Dr. Inventory Cr.
Feb. 2	Jason Henry	307	✓	450	315
7	Albert Co.	308	✓	500	355
13	Kam Moore	309	✓	350	260
15	Paul Roth	310	✓	200	150
22	Jason Henry	311	✓	225	155
25	Frank Booth	312	✓	175	95
28	Albert Co.	313	✓	250	170
28	Totals			2,150	1,500
				(106/413)	(502/119)

Accounts Receivable Ledger

Customer Name: Albert Co.

Date	PR	Debit	Credit	Balance
Feb. 7	S3	500		500
28	S3	250		750

Customer Name: Frank Booth

Date	PR	Debit	Credit	Balance
Feb. 25	S3	175		175

Customer Name: Jason Henry

Date	PR	Debit	Credit	Balance
Feb. 2	S3	450		450
22	S3	225		675

Customer Name: Kam Moore

Date	PR	Debit	Credit	Balance
Feb. 13	S3	350		350

Customer Name: Paul Roth

Date	PR	Debit	Credit	Balance
Feb. 15	S3	200		200

General Ledger

Accounts Receivable — No. 106

Date	PR	Debit	Credit	Balance
Feb. 28	S3	2,150		2,150

Inventory — No. 119

Date	PR	Debit	Credit	Balance
Feb. 1	bal.			15,700
28	S3		1,500	14,200

Sales — No. 413

Date	PR	Debit	Credit	Balance
Feb. 28	S3		2,150	2,150

Cost of Goods Sold — No. 502

Date	PR	Debit	Credit	Balance
Feb. 28	S3	1,500		1,500

*The Sales Journal in a *periodic* system would exclude the column on the far right titled "Cost of Goods Sold Dr., Inventory Cr." (see Exhibit 7A.1).

one line in the sales journal. No further explanations or entries are necessary, saving time and effort. Moreover, this sales journal is consistent with most inventory systems that use bar codes to record both sales and costs with each sale transaction. Note that the Posting Reference (PR) column is not used when entering transactions but instead is used when posting.

Point: Continuously updated customer accounts provide timely information for customer inquiries on those accounts and on current amounts owed.

Posting A sales journal is posted as reflected in the arrow lines of Exhibit 7.5. Two types of posting can be identified: (1) posting to the subsidiary ledger(s) and (2) posting to the general ledger.

Posting to subsidiary ledger. Individual transactions in the sales journal are posted regularly (typically concurrently) to customer accounts in the accounts receivable ledger. These postings keep customer accounts up-to-date, which is important for the person granting credit to customers. When sales recorded in the sales journal are individually posted to customer accounts in the accounts receivable ledger, check marks are entered in the sales journal's PR column. Check marks are used rather than account numbers because customer accounts usually are arranged alphabetically in the accounts receivable ledger. Note that posting debits to Accounts Receivable twice—once to Accounts Receivable and once to the customer's subsidiary account—does not violate the accounting equation of debits equal credits. The equality of debits and credits is always maintained in the general ledger.

Point: PR column is only checked *after* the amount(s) is posted.

Posting to general ledger. The sales journal's account columns are totaled at the end of each period (the month of February in this case). For the "sales" column, the $2,150 total is debited to Accounts Receivable and credited to Sales in the general ledger (see Exhibit 7.5). For the "cost" column, the $1,500 total is debited to Cost of Goods Sold and credited to Inventory in the general ledger. When totals are posted to accounts in the general ledger, the account numbers are entered below the column total in the sales journal for tracking. For example, we enter (106/413) below the total in the sales column after this amount is posted to account number 106 (Accounts Receivable) and account number 413 (Sales).

Point: Postings are automatic in a computerized system.

A company identifies in the PR column of its subsidiary ledgers the journal and page number from which an amount is taken. We identify a journal by using an initial. Items posted from the sales journal carry the initial ***S*** before their journal page numbers in a PR column. Likewise, items from the cash receipts journal carry the initial ***R***; items from the cash disbursements journal carry the initial ***D***; items from the purchases journal carry the initial ***P***; and items from the general journal carry the initial ***G***.

P2 Prepare and prove the accuracy of subsidiary ledgers.

Proving the Ledgers Account balances in the general ledger and subsidiary ledgers are periodically proved (or reviewed) for accuracy after posting. To do this we first prepare a trial balance of the general ledger to confirm that debits equal credits. Second, we test a subsidiary ledger by preparing a *schedule* of individual accounts and amounts. A **schedule of accounts receivable** lists each customer and the balance owed. If this total equals the balance of the Accounts Receivable controlling account, the accounts in the accounts receivable ledger are assumed correct. Exhibit 7.6 shows a schedule of accounts receivable drawn from the accounts receivable ledger of Exhibit 7.5.

EXHIBIT 7.6
Schedule of Accounts Receivable

Schedule of Accounts Receivable February 28	
Albert Co.	$ 750
Frank Booth	175
Jason Henry	675
Kam Moore	350
Paul Roth	200
Total accounts receivable	$2,150

Additional Issues We consider three additional issues with the sales journal: (1) recording sales taxes, (2) recording sales returns and allowances, and (3) using actual sales invoices as a journal.

Point: In accounting, the word *schedule* generally means a list.

Sales taxes. Governmental agencies such as cities and states often require sellers to collect sales taxes from customers and to periodically send these taxes to the appropriate agency. When using a columnar sales journal, we can keep a record of taxes collected by adding a Sales Taxes Payable column as follows.

File Edit Maintain Tasks Analysis Options Reports Window Help

Sales Journal — Page 3

Date	Account Debited	Invoice Number	PR	Accounts Receivable Dr.	Sales Taxes Payable Cr.	Sales Cr.	Cost of Goods Sold Dr. Inventory Cr.
Dec. 1	Favre Co.	7-1698		103	3	100	75

Individual amounts in the Accounts Receivable column would continue to be posted immediately to customer accounts in the accounts receivable ledger. Individual amounts in the Sales Taxes Payable and Sales columns are not posted. Column totals would continue to be posted as usual. (A company that collects sales taxes on its cash sales can also use a Sales Taxes Payable column in its cash receipts journal.)

Sales returns and allowances. A company with only a few sales returns and allowances can record them in a general journal with an entry such as the following:

Assets = Liabilities + Equity
−175 −175

May 17	Sales Returns and Allowances	414	175	
	Accounts Receivable—Ray Ball	106/✓		175
	Customer returned merchandise.			

The debit in this entry is posted to the Sales Returns and Allowances account (no. 414). The credit is posted to both the Accounts Receivable controlling account (no. 106) and to the customer's account. When we enter the account number and the check mark, 106/✓, in the PR column on the credit line, this means both the Accounts Receivable controlling account in the general ledger and the Ray Ball account in the accounts receivable ledger are credited for $175. [*Note:* If the returned goods can be resold to another customer, the company would debit (increase) the Inventory account and credit (decrease) the Cost of Goods Sold account. If the returned goods are defective (worthless), the company could simply leave their costs in the Cost of Goods Sold account (see Chapter 5).] A company with a large number of sales returns and allowances can save time by recording them in a separate sales returns and allowances journal.

Sales invoices as a sales journal. To save costs, some small companies avoid using a sales journal for credit sales and instead post each sales invoice amount directly to the customer's account in the accounts receivable ledger. They then put copies of invoices in a file. At the end of the period, they total all invoices for that period and make a general journal entry to debit Accounts Receivable and credit Sales for the total amount. The file of invoice copies acts as a sales journal. This is called *direct posting of sales invoices.*

Quick Check

Answers—p. 294

4. When special journals are used, where are cash payments by check recorded?
5. How does a columnar journal save posting time and effort?
6. How do debits and credits remain equal when credit sales are posted twice (once to Accounts Receivable and once to the customer's subsidiary account)?
7. How do we identify the journal from which an amount in a ledger account was posted?
8. How are sales taxes recorded in the context of special journals?
9. What is direct posting of sales invoices?

Cash Receipts Journal

A **cash receipts journal** is typically used to record all receipts of cash. Exhibit 7.7 shows one common form of the cash receipts journal.

Journalizing and Posting Cash receipts can be separated into one of three types: (1) cash from credit customers in payment of their accounts, (2) cash from cash sales, and

EXHIBIT 7.7

Cash Receipts Journal with Posting*

File Edit Maintain Tasks Analysis Options Reports Window Help

Cash Receipts Journal — Page 2

Date	Account Credited	Explanation	PR	Cash Dr.	Sales Discount Dr.	Accounts Receivable Cr.	Sales Cr.	Other Accounts Cr.	Cost of Goods Sold Dr. Inventory Cr.
Feb. 7	Sales	Cash sales	✗	4,450			4,450		3,150
12	Jason Henry	Invoice, 2/2	✓	441	9	450			
14	Sales	Cash sales	✗	3,925			3,925		2,950
17	Albert Co.	Invoice, 2/7	✓	490	10	500			
20	Notes Payable	Note to bank	245	750				750	
21	Sales	Cash sales	✗	4,700			4,700		3,400
22	Interest revenue	Bank account	409	250				250	
23	Kam Moore	Invoice, 2/13	✓	343	7	350			
25	Paul Roth	Invoice, 2/15	✓	196	4	200			
28	Sales	Cash sales	✗	4,225			4,225		3,050
28	Totals			19,770	30	1,500	17,300	1,000	12,550
				(101)	(415)	(106)	(413)	(✗)	(502/119)

Individual line item amounts in the Other Accounts Cr. column and the Accounts Receivable Cr. column are posted immediately.

Column totals are posted at the end of the period.

Accounts Receivable Ledger

Customer Name: Albert Co.

Date	PR	Debit	Credit	Balance
Feb. 7	S3	500		500
17	R2		500	0
28	S3	250		250

Customer Name: Frank Booth

Date	PR	Debit	Credit	Balance
Feb. 25	S3	175		175

Customer Name: Jason Henry

Date	PR	Debit	Credit	Balance
Feb. 2	S3	450		450
12	R2		450	0
22	S3	225		225

Customer Name: Kam Moore

Date	PR	Debit	Credit	Balance
Feb. 13	S3	350		350
23	R2		350	0

Customer Name: Paul Roth

Date	PR	Debit	Credit	Balance
Feb. 15	S3	200		200
25	R2		200	0

General Ledger

Cash — No. 101

Date	PR	Debit	Credit	Balance
Feb. 28	R2	19,770		19,770

Accounts Receivable — No. 106

Date	PR	Debit	Credit	Balance
Feb. 28	S3	2,150		2,150
28	R2		1,500	650

Inventory — No. 119

Date	PR	Debit	Credit	Balance
Feb. 1	bal.			15,700
28	S3		1,500	14,200
28	R2		12,550	1,650

Notes Payable — No. 245

Date	PR	Debit	Credit	Balance
Feb. 20	R2		750	750

Interest Revenue — No. 409

Date	PR	Debit	Credit	Balance
Feb. 22	R2		250	250

Sales — No. 413

Date	PR	Debit	Credit	Balance
Feb. 28	S3		2,150	2,150
28	R2		17,300	19,450

Sales Discounts — No. 415

Date	PR	Debit	Credit	Balance
Feb. 28	R2	30		30

Cost of Goods Sold — No. 502

Date	PR	Debit	Credit	Balance
Feb. 28	S3	1,500		1,500
28	R2	12,550		14,050

*The Cash Receipts Journal in a *periodic* system would exclude the column on the far right titled "Cost of Goods Sold Dr., Inventory Cr." (see Exhibit 7A.2).

Point: Each transaction in the cash receipts journal involves a debit to Cash. Credit accounts will vary.

(3) cash from other sources. The cash receipts journal in Exhibit 7.7 has a separate credit column for each of these three sources. We describe how to journalize transactions from each of these three sources. (An Explanation column is included in the cash receipts journal to identify the source.)

Cash from credit customers. *Journalizing.* To record cash received in payment of a customer's account, the customer's name is first entered in the Account Credited column—see transactions dated February 12, 17, 23, and 25. Then the amounts debited to both Cash and the Sales Discount (if any) are entered in their respective columns, and the amount credited to the customer's account is entered in the Accounts Receivable Cr. column.

Posting. Individual amounts in the Accounts Receivable Cr. column are posted immediately to customer accounts in the subsidiary accounts receivable ledger. The $1,500 column total is posted at the end of the period (month in this case) as a credit to the Accounts Receivable controlling account in the general ledger.

Cash sales. *Journalizing.* The amount for each cash sale is entered in the Cash Dr. column and the Sales Cr. column. The February 7, 14, 21, and 28 transactions are examples. (Cash sales are usually journalized daily or at point of sale, but are journalized weekly in Exhibit 7.7 for brevity.) Each cash sale also yields an entry to Cost of Goods Sold Dr. and Inventory Cr. for the cost of merchandise—see the far right column.

Point: Some software packages put cash sales in the sales journal.

Posting. For cash sales, we place an *x* in the PR column to indicate that its amount is not individually posted. We do post the $17,300 Sales Cr. total and the $12,550 total from the "cost" column.

Example: Record in the cash receipts journal a $700 cash sale of land when the land carries a $700 original cost. *Answer:* Debit the Cash column for $700, and credit the Other Accounts column for $700 (the account credited is Land).

Cash from other sources. *Journalizing.* Examples of cash from other sources are money borrowed from a bank, cash interest received on account, and cash sale of noninventory assets. The transactions of February 20 and 22 are illustrative. The Other Accounts Cr. column is used for these transactions.

Posting. Amounts from these transactions are immediately posted to their general ledger accounts and the PR column identifies those accounts.

Point: Subsidiary ledgers and their controlling accounts are *in balance* only after all posting is complete.

Footing, Crossfooting, and Posting To be sure that total debits and credits in a columnar journal are equal, we often crossfoot column totals before posting them. To *foot* a column of numbers is to add it. To *crossfoot* in this case is to add the Debit column totals, then add the Credit column totals, and compare the two sums for equality. Footing and crossfooting of the numbers in Exhibit 7.7 results in the report in Exhibit 7.8.

EXHIBIT 7.8

Footing and Crossfooting Journal Totals

Debit Columns		Credit Columns	
Cash Dr.	$19,770	Accounts Receivable Cr.	$ 1,500
Sales Discounts Dr.	30	Sales Cr.	17,300
Cost of Goods Sold Dr.	12,550	Other Accounts Cr.	1,000
		Inventory Cr.	12,550
Total	$32,350	Total	$32,350

At the end of the period, after crossfooting the journal to confirm that debits equal credits, the total amounts from the columns of the cash receipts journal are posted to their general ledger accounts. The Other Accounts Cr. column total is not posted because the individual amounts are directly posted to their general ledger accounts. We place an *x* below the Other Accounts Cr. column to indicate that this column total is not posted. The account numbers for the column totals that are posted are entered in parentheses below each column. (*Note:* Posting items immediately from the Other Accounts Cr. column with a delayed posting of their offsetting items in the Cash column total causes the general ledger to be out of balance during the period. Posting the Cash Dr. column total at the end of the period corrects this imbalance in the general ledger before the trial balance and financial statements are prepared.)

Decision Maker

Entrepreneur You want to know how promptly customers are paying their bills. This information can help you decide whether to extend credit and to plan your cash payments. Where do you find this information? [Answer—p. 293]

Purchases Journal

A **purchases journal** is typically used to record all credit purchases, including those for inventory. Purchases for cash are recorded in the Cash Disbursements Journal.

Journalizing Entries in the purchases journal in Exhibit 7.9 reflect purchase invoices or other source documents. We use the invoice date and terms to compute the date when payment for each purchase is due. The Accounts Payable Cr. column is used to record the amounts owed to each creditor. Inventory purchases are recorded in the Inventory Dr. column.

To illustrate, inventory costing $200 is purchased from Ace Manufacturing on February 5. The creditor's name (Ace) is entered in the Account column, the invoice date is entered in the Date of Invoice column, the purchase terms are entered in the Terms column, and the $200 amount is entered in the Accounts Payable Cr. and the Inventory Dr. columns. When a purchase involves an amount recorded in the Other Accounts Dr. column, we use the Account column to identify the general ledger account debited. For example, the February 28 transaction

Point: The number of special journals and the design of each are based on a company's specific needs.

Point: Each transaction in the purchases journal has a credit to Accounts Payable. Debit accounts will vary.

EXHIBIT 7.9

Purchases Journal with Posting*

File Edit Maintain Tasks Analysis Options Reports Window Help

Purchases Journal Page 1

Date	Account	Date of Invoice	Terms	PR	Accounts Payable Cr.	Inventory Dr.	Office Supplies Dr.	Other Accounts Dr.
Feb. 3	Horning Supply Co.	2/2	n/30	✓	350	275	75	
5	Ace Mfg. Co.	2/5	2/10, n/30	✓	200	200		
13	Wynet & Co.	2/10	2/10, n/30	✓	150	150		
20	Smite Co.	2/18	2/10, n/30	✓	300	300		
25	Ace Mfg. Co.	2/24	2/10, n/30	✓	100	100		
28	Store Supplies/ITT Co.	2/28	n/30	125/✓	225	125	25	75
28	Totals				1,325	1,150	100	75
					(201)	(119)	(124)	(✗)

Individual amounts in the Other Accounts Dr. column and the Accounts Payable Cr. column are posted immediately.

Column totals, except for Other Accounts Dr. column, are posted at the end of the period.

Accounts Payable Ledger

Company Name: Ace Mfg. Company

Date	PR	Debit	Credit	Balance
Feb. 5	P1		200	200
25	P1		100	300

Company Name: Horning Supply Company

Date	PR	Debit	Credit	Balance
Feb. 3	P1		350	350

Company Name: ITT Company

Date	PR	Debit	Credit	Balance
Feb. 28	P1		225	225

Company Name: Smite Company

Date	PR	Debit	Credit	Balance
Feb. 20	P1		300	300

Company Name: Wynet and Company

Date	PR	Debit	Credit	Balance
Feb. 13	P1		150	150

General Ledger

Inventory — No. 119

Date	PR	Debit	Credit	Balance
Feb. 1	bal.			15,700
28	S3		1,500	14,200
28	R2		12,550	1,650
28	P1	1,150		2,800

Office Supplies — No. 124

Date	PR	Debit	Credit	Balance
Feb. 28	P1	100		100

Store Supplies — No. 125

Date	PR	Debit	Credit	Balance
Feb. 28	P1	75		75

Accounts Payable — No. 201

Date	PR	Debit	Credit	Balance
Feb. 28	P1		1,325	1,325

*The Purchases Journal in a *periodic* system replaces "Inventory Dr." with "Purchases Dr." (see Exhibit 7A.3).

involves purchases of inventory, office supplies, and store supplies from ITT. The journal has no column for store supplies, so the Other Accounts Dr. column is used. In this case, Store Supplies is entered in the Account column along with the creditor's name (ITT). This purchases journal also includes a separate column for credit purchases of office supplies. A separate column such as this is useful when several transactions involve debits to the same account. Each company uses its own judgment in deciding on the number of separate columns necessary.

Point: The Other Accounts Dr. column allows the purchases journal to be used for any purchase on credit.

Posting The amounts in the Accounts Payable Cr. column are immediately posted to individual creditor accounts in the accounts payable subsidiary ledger. Individual amounts in the Other Accounts Dr. column are immediately posted to their general ledger accounts. At the end of the period, all column totals except the Other Accounts Dr. column are posted to their general ledger accounts.

Proving the Ledger Accounts payable balances in the subsidiary ledger are proved after posting the purchases journal. We prove the subsidiary ledger by preparing a **schedule of accounts payable,** which is a list of accounts from the accounts payable ledger with their balances and the total. If this total equals the balance of the Accounts Payable controlling account, the accounts in the accounts payable ledger are assumed correct. Exhibit 7.10 shows a schedule of accounts payable drawn from the accounts payable ledger of Exhibit 7.9.

Point: The balance in the Accounts Payable controlling account must equal the sum of the individual account balances in the accounts payable subsidiary ledger after posting.

EXHIBIT 7.10

Schedule of Accounts Payable

Schedule of Accounts Payable February 28	
Ace Mfg. Company	$ 300
Horning Supply Company	350
ITT Company	225
Smite Company	300
Wynet & Company	150
Total accounts payable	$1,325

Cash Disbursements Journal

A **cash disbursements journal,** also called a *cash payments journal,* is typically used to record all cash payments.

Journalizing The cash disbursements journal shown in Exhibit 7.11 illustrates repetitive entries to the Cash Cr. column of this journal (reflecting cash payments). Also note the frequent credits to Inventory (which reflect purchase discounts) and the debits to Accounts Payable. For example, on February 15, the company pays Ace on account (credit terms of 2/10, n/30—see February 5 transaction in Exhibit 7.9). Since payment occurs in the discount period, the company pays $196 ($200 invoice less $4 discount). The $4 discount is credited to Inventory. Note that when this company purchases inventory for cash, it is recorded using the Other Accounts Dr. column and the Cash Cr. column as illustrated in the February 3 and 12 transactions. Generally, the Other Accounts column is used to record cash payments on items for which no column exists. For example, on February 15, the company pays salaries expense of $250. The title of the account debited (Salaries Expense) is entered in the Account Debited column.

Point: Each transaction in the cash disbursements journal involves a credit to Cash. Debit accounts will vary.

The cash disbursements journal has a column titled Ck. No. (check number). For control over cash disbursements, all payments except for those of small amounts are made by check. Checks should be prenumbered and each check's number entered in the journal in numerical order in the column headed Ck. No. This makes it possible to scan the numbers in the column for omitted checks. When a cash disbursements journal has a column for check numbers, it is sometimes called a **check register.**

Posting Individual amounts in the Other Accounts Dr. column of a cash disbursements journal are immediately posted to their general ledger accounts. Individual amounts in the Accounts

EXHIBIT 7.11

Cash Disbursements Journal with Posting*

File Edit Maintain Tasks Analysis Options Reports Window Help

Cash Disbursements Journal — Page 2

Date	Ck. No.	Payee	Account Debited	PR	Cash Cr.	Inventory Cr.	Other Accounts Dr.	Accounts Payable Dr.
Feb. 3	105	L. & N. Railroad	Inventory	119	15		15	
12	106	East Sales Co.	Inventory	119	25		25	
15	107	Ace Mfg. Co.	Ace Mfg. Co.	✓	196	4		200
15	108	Jerry Hale	Salaries Expense	622	250		250	
20	109	Wynet & Co.	Wynet & Co.	✓	147	3		150
28	110	Smite Co.	Smite Co.	✓	294	6		300
28		Totals			927	13	290	650
					(101)	(119)	(✗)	(201)

Individual amounts in the Other Accounts Dr. column and the Accounts Payable Dr. column are posted immediately.

Column totals, except for Other Accounts column, are posted at the end of the period.

General Ledger

Cash — No. 101

Date	PR	Debit	Credit	Balance
Feb. 28	R2	19,770		19,770
28	D2		927	18,843

Inventory — No. 119

Date	PR	Debit	Credit	Balance
Feb. 1	bal.			15,700
3	D2	15		15,715
12	D2	25		15,740
28	S3		1,500	14,240
28	R2		12,550	1,690
28	P1	1,150		2,840
28	D2		13	2,827

Accounts Payable — No. 201

Date	PR	Debit	Credit	Balance
Feb. 28	P1		1,325	1,325
28	D2	650		675

Salaries Expense — No. 622

Date	PR	Debit	Credit	Balance
Feb. 15	D2	250		250

Accounts Payable Ledger

Company Name: Ace Mfg. Company

Date	PR	Debit	Credit	Balance
Feb. 5	P1		200	200
15	D2	200		0
25	P1		100	100

Company Name: Horning Supply Company

Date	PR	Debit	Credit	Balance
Feb. 3	P1		350	350

Company Name: ITT Company

Date	PR	Debit	Credit	Balance
Feb. 28	P1		225	225

Company Name: Smite Company

Date	PR	Debit	Credit	Balance
Feb. 20	P1		300	300
28	D2	300		0

Company Name: Wynet & Company

Date	PR	Debit	Credit	Balance
Feb. 13	P1		150	150
20	D2	150		0

*The Cash Disbursements Journal in a *periodic* system replaces "Inventory Cr." with "Purchases Discounts Cr." (see Exhibit 7A.4).

Payable Dr. column are also immediately posted to creditors' accounts in the subsidiary Accounts Payable ledger. At the end of the period, we crossfoot column totals and post the Accounts Payable Dr. column total to the Accounts Payable controlling account. Also, the Inventory Cr. column total is posted to the Inventory account, and the Cash Cr. column total is posted to the Cash account.

Decision Maker

Controller You wish to analyze your company's cash payments to suppliers and its purchases discounts. Where do you find this information? [Answer—p. 293]

General Journal Transactions

When special journals are used, we still need a general journal for adjusting, closing, and any other transactions for which no special journal has been set up. Examples of these other transactions might include purchases returns and allowances, purchases of plant assets by issuing a note payable, sales returns if a sales returns and allowances journal is not used, and receipt of a note receivable from a customer. We described the recording of transactions in a general journal in Chapters 2 and 3.

Quick Check Answers—p. 294

10. What are the normal recording and posting procedures when using special journals and controlling accounts with subsidiary ledgers?
11. What is the process for posting to a subsidiary ledger and its controlling account?
12. How do we prove the accuracy of account balances in the general ledger and subsidiary ledgers after posting?
13. Why does a company need a general journal when using special journals for sales, purchases, cash receipts, and cash disbursements?

Technology-Based Accounting Systems

C5 Explain how technology-based information systems impact accounting.

Accounting information systems are supported with technology, which can range from simple calculators to advanced computerized systems. Since technology is increasingly important in accounting information systems, we discuss the impact of computer technology, how data processing works with accounting data, and the role of computer networks.

Computer Technology in Accounting

Computer technology provides accuracy, speed, efficiency, and convenience in performing accounting tasks. A program can be written, for instance, to process customers' merchandise orders. Multipurpose off-the-shelf software applications exist for a variety of business operations. These include familiar accounting programs such as Peachtree® and QuickBooks®. Off-the-shelf programs are designed to be user friendly and menu driven, and many operate more efficiently as *integrated* systems. In an integrated system, actions taken in one part of the system automatically affect related parts. When a credit sale is recorded in an integrated system, for instance, several parts of the system are automatically updated, such as posting.

Point: Companies that have reported missing or stolen employee data such as Social Security numbers include Time Warner, Polo Ralph Lauren, Lexis/Nexis, ChoicePoint, and DSW Shoes.

Computer technology can dramatically reduce the time and effort devoted to recordkeeping. Less effort spent on recordkeeping means more time for accounting professionals to concentrate on analysis and managerial decision making. These advances have created a greater demand for accounting professionals who understand financial reports and can draw insights and information from mountains of processed data. Accounting professionals have expertise in determining relevant and reliable information for decision making. They also can assess the effects of transactions and events on a company and its financial statements.

Decision Insight

Middleware is software allowing different computer programs in a company or across companies to work together. It allows transfer of purchase orders, invoices, and other electronic documents between accounting systems. For example, suppliers can monitor inventory levels of their buyers for production and shipping purposes.

Data Processing in Accounting

Accounting systems differ with regard to how input is entered and processed. **Online processing** enters and processes data as soon as source documents are available. This means that databases are immediately updated. **Batch processing** accumulates source documents for a period of time and then processes them all at once such as daily, weekly, or monthly. The advantage of online processing is timeliness. This often requires additional costs related to both software and hardware requirements. Companies such as **Intuit** (**Intuit.com**) are making online processing of accounting data a reality for many businesses. The advantage of batch processing is that it requires only periodic updating of databases. Records used to send bills to customers, for instance, might require updating only once a month. The disadvantage of batch processing is the lack of updated databases for management to use when making business decisions.

Computer Networks in Accounting

Networking, or linking computers with each other, can create information advantages (and cost efficiencies). **Computer networks** are links among computers giving different users and different computers access to common databases, programs, and hardware. Many college computer labs, for instance, are networked. A small computer network is called a *local area network (LAN)*; it links machines with *hard-wire* hookups. Large computer networks extending over long distances often rely on *modem* or *wireless* communication.

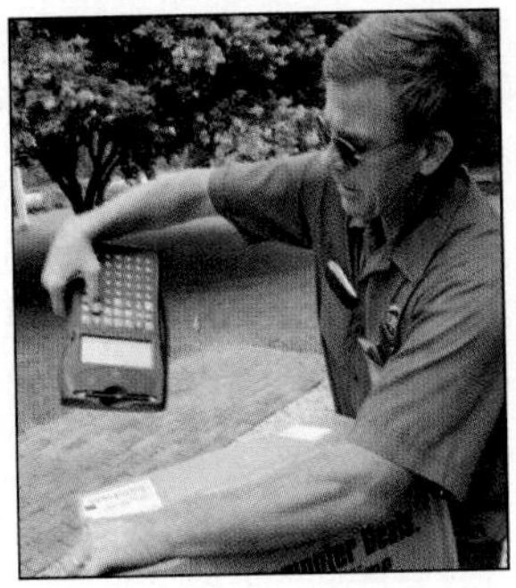

Demand for information sometimes requires advanced networks such as the systems **Federal Express** and **UPS** use to track packages and bill customers and the system **Wal-Mart** uses to monitor inventory levels in its stores. These networks include many computers and satellite communications to gather information and to provide ready access to its databases from all locations.

Enterprise Resource Planning Software

Enterprise resource planning (ERP) software includes the programs that manage a company's vital operations. They extend from order taking to manufacturing to accounting. When working properly, these integrated programs can speed decision making, identify costs for reduction, and give managers control over operations with the click of a mouse. For many managers, ERP software allows them to scrutinize business, identify where inventories are piling up, and see what plants are most efficient. The software is designed to link every part of a company's operations. This software allowed **Monsanto** to slash production planning from six weeks to three, trim its inventories, and increase its bargaining power with suppliers. Monsanto estimates that this software saves the company $200 million per year.

ERP has several suppliers. **SAP** leads the market, with **Oracle**, which gobbled up PeopleSoft and J. D. Edwards, a distant second (*AMR Research*). SAP software is used by more than half of the world's 500 largest companies. It links ordering, inventory, production, purchasing, planning, tracking, and human resources. A transaction or event triggers an immediate chain reaction of events throughout the enterprise. It is making companies more efficient and profitable.

Total ERP Market: About $30 Billion

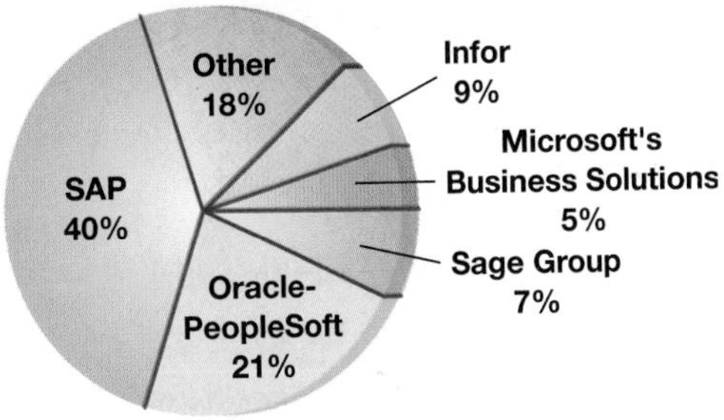

ERP is pushing into cyberspace and customer relationship management (CRM). Now companies can share data with customers and suppliers. Applesauce maker **Mott's** is using SAP so that distributors can check the status of orders and place them over the Net, and the **Coca-Cola Company** uses it to ship soda on time. ERP is also increasingly used by small business. For example, **NetSuite**'s accounting services to small and medium businesses are powered by Oracle's system.

Decision Insight

A new generation of accounting support is available. With the touch of a key, users can create real-time inventory reports showing all payments, charges, and credit limits at any point in the accounting cycle. Many services also include "alert signals" notifying the company when, for example, a large order exceeds a customer's credit limit or when purchases need to be made or when a bank balance is running low. These alerts occur via e-mail, fax, PDA, or phone.

Quick Check

Answers—p. 294

14. Identify an advantage of an integrated computer-based accounting system.

15. What advantages do computer systems offer over manual systems?

16. Identify an advantage of computer networks.

17. Describe ERP software and its potential advantages to businesses.

Decision Analysis

Segment Return on Assets

A1 Compute segment return on assets and use it to evaluate segment performance.

Good accounting information systems collect financial data for a company's various segments. A *segment* refers to a part of a company that is separately identified by its products or services, or by the geographic market it serves. **Harley-Davidson** reports that it operates in two business segments: (1) motorcycles and (2) financial services. Users of financial statements are especially interested in segment information to better understand a company's activities because segments often vary on profitability, risk, and growth.

Companies must report segment information, including their sales, operating income, identifiable assets, capital expenditures, and depreciation. However, managers are reluctant to release information that can harm competitive position. Exhibit 7.12 shows survey results on the number of companies with different (reported) segments.

EXHIBIT 7.12

Companies Reporting Operations by These Segments*

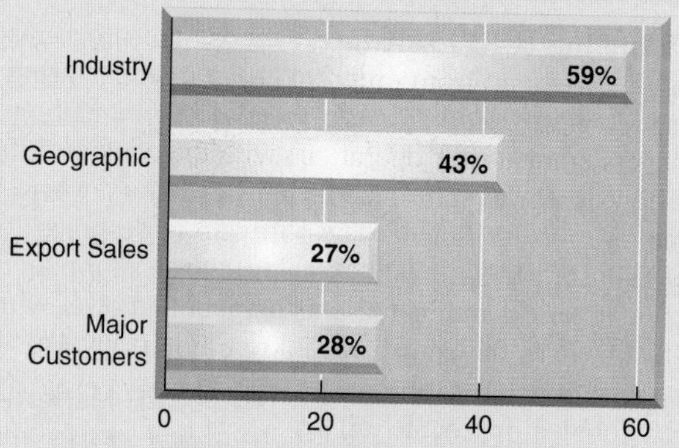

*Total exceeds 100% because companies can report more than one type of segment.

One measure of success for business segments is the **segment return on assets** ratio defined as follows.

$$\textbf{Segment return on assets} = \frac{\textbf{Segment operating income}}{\textbf{Segment average assets}}$$

This ratio reflects on the profitability of a segment. Exhibit 7.13 shows the segments' operating income, average assets, and return on assets for Harley-Davidson.

EXHIBIT 7.13

Harley-Davidson's Segment Return on Assets ($ millions)

	2006			2005			2004
Segment*	Operating Income	Average Assets	Return on Assets	Operating Income	Average Assets	Return on Assets	Return on Assets
Motorcycles	$1,414	$1,765	80%	$1,300	$1,746	74%	70%
Financial services	211	2,658	8%	192	2,294	8%	9%

* A segment's operating income is usually measured as income before taxes, and assets is usually measured as identifiable assets.

The trend in Harley's segment return on assets is increasing for its motorcycle segment, but not for its financial services segment. Also, its motorcycle segment is much more profitable (80%) than its financial services (8%) segment. Harley should consider further investment in its motorcycle segment if such returns can be sustained. Analysis can also be extended to geographical segments and any other segments that companies report.

Decision Maker

Banker A bicycle merchandiser requests a loan from you to expand operations. Its net income is $220,000, reflecting a 10% increase over the prior year. You ask about segment results. The owner reports that $160,000 of net income is from Cuban operations, reflecting a 60% increase over the prior year. The remaining $60,000 of net income is from U.S. operations, reflecting a 40% decrease. Does this segment information impact your loan decision? [Answer—p. 293]

Demonstration Problem—Perpetual System

Pepper Company completed the following selected transactions and events during March of this year. (Terms of all credit sales for the company are 2/10, n/30.)

DP7

Mar. 4 Sold merchandise on credit to Jennifer Nelson, Invoice No. 954, for $16,800 (cost is $12,200).

6 Purchased $1,220 of office supplies on credit from Mack Company. Invoice dated March 3, terms n/30.

6 Sold merchandise on credit to Dennie Hoskins, Invoice No. 955, for $10,200 (cost is $8,100).

11 Purchased $52,600 of merchandise, invoice dated March 6, terms 2/10, n/30, from Defore Industries.

12 Borrowed $26,000 cash by giving Commerce Bank a long-term promissory note payable.

14 Received cash payment from Jennifer Nelson for the March 4 sale less the discount (Invoice No. 954).

16 Received a $200 credit memorandum from Defore Industries for unsatisfactory merchandise Pepper purchased on March 11 and later returned.

16 Received cash payment from Dennie Hoskins for the March 6 sale less the discount (Invoice No. 955).

18 Purchased $22,850 of store equipment on credit from Schmidt Supply, invoice dated March 15, terms n/30.

20 Sold merchandise on credit to Marjorie Allen, Invoice No. 956, for $5,600 (cost is $3,800).

21 Sent Defore Industries Check No. 516 in payment of its March 6 dated invoice less the return and the discount.

22 Purchased $41,625 of merchandise, invoice dated March 18, terms 2/10, n/30, from Welch Company.

26 Issued a $600 credit memorandum to Marjorie Allen for defective merchandise Pepper sold on March 20 and Allen later returned.

31 Issued Check No. 517, payable to Payroll, in payment of $15,900 sales salaries for the month. Cashed the check and paid the employees.

31 Cash sales for the month are $134,680 (cost is $67,340). (Cash sales are recorded daily but are recorded only once here to reduce repetitive entries.)

Required

1. Open the following selected general ledger accounts: Cash (101), Accounts Receivable (106) Inventory (119), Office Supplies (124), Store Equipment (165), Accounts Payable (201), Long-Term Notes Payable (251), Sales (413), Sales Returns and Allowances (414), Sales Discounts (415), Cost of Goods Sold (502), and Sales Salaries Expense (621). Open the following accounts receivable ledger accounts: Marjorie Allen, Dennie Hoskins, and Jennifer Nelson. Open the following accounts payable ledger accounts: Defore Industries, Mack Company, Schmidt Supply, and Welch Company.
2. Enter the transactions using a sales journal, a purchases journal, a cash receipts journal, a cash disbursements journal, and a general journal similar to the ones illustrated in the chapter. Regularly post to the individual customer and creditor accounts. Also, post any amounts that should be posted as individual amounts to general ledger accounts. Foot and crossfoot the journals and make the month-end postings. *Pepper Co. uses the perpetual inventory system.*
3. Prepare a trial balance for the selected general ledger accounts in part 1 and prove the accuracy of subsidiary ledgers by preparing schedules of accounts receivable and accounts payable.

Planning the Solution

- Set up the required general ledger, the subsidiary ledger accounts, and the five required journals as illustrated in the chapter.

- Read and analyze each transaction and decide in which special journal (or general journal) the transaction is recorded.
- Record each transaction in the proper journal (and post the appropriate individual amounts).
- Once you have recorded all transactions, total the journal columns. Post from each journal to the appropriate ledger accounts.
- Prepare a trial balance to prove the equality of the debit and credit balances in your general ledger.
- Prepare schedules of accounts receivable and accounts payable. Compare the totals of these schedules to the Accounts Receivable and Accounts Payable controlling account balances, making sure that they agree.

Solution to Demonstration Problem — Perpetual System

Sales Journal — Page 2

Date	Account Debited	Invoice Number	PR	Accounts Receivable Dr. Sales Cr.	Cost of Goods Sold Dr. Inventory Cr.
Mar. 4	Jennifer Nelson	954	✓	16,800	12,200
6	Dennie Hoskins	955	✓	10,200	8,100
20	Marjorie Allen	956	✓	5,600	3,800
31	Totals			32,600	24,100
				(106/413)	(502/119)

Cash Receipts Journal — Page 3

Date	Account Credited	Explanation	PR	Cash Dr.	Sales Discount Dr.	Accounts Receivable Cr.	Sales Cr.	Other Accounts Cr.	Cost of Goods Sold Dr. Inventory Cr.
Mar. 12	L.T. Notes Payable	Note to bank	251	26,000				26,000	
14	Jennifer Nelson	Invoice 954, 3/4	✓	16,464	336	16,800			
16	Dennie Hoskins	Invoice 955, 3/6	✓	9,996	204	10,200			
31	Sales	Cash sales	x	134,680			134,680		67,340
31	Totals			187,140	540	27,000	134,680	26,000	67,340
				(101)	(415)	(106)	(413)	(x)	(502/119)

Purchases Journal — Page 3

Date	Account	Date of Invoice	Terms	PR	Accounts Payable Cr.	Inventory Dr.	Office Supplies Dr.	Other Accounts Dr.
Mar. 6	Office Supplies/Mack Co	3/3	n/30	✓	1,220		1,220	
11	Defore Industries	3/6	2/10, n/30	✓	52,600	52,600		
18	Store Equipment/Schmidt Supp	3/15	n/30	165/✓	22,850			22,850
22	Welch Company	3/18	2/10, n/30	✓	41,625	41,625		
31	Totals				118,295	94,225	1,220	22,850
					(201)	(119)	(124)	(x)

Cash Disbursements Journal — Page 3

Date	Ck. No.	Payee	Account Debited	PR	Cash Cr.	Inventory Cr.	Other Accounts Dr.	Accounts Payable Dr.
Mar. 21	516	Defore Industries	Defore Industries	✓	51,352	1,048		52,400
31	517	Payroll	Sales Salaries Expense	621	15,900		15,900	
31		Totals			67,252	1,048	15,900	52,400
					(101)	(119)	(x)	(201)

General Journal — Page 2

Date	Account Titles and Explanation	PR	Debit	Credit
Mar. 16	Accounts Payable—Defore Industries	201/✓	200	
	Inventory	119		200
	To record credit memorandum received.			
26	Sales Returns and Allowances	414	600	
	Accounts Receivable—Marjorie Allen	106/✓		600
	To record credit memorandum issued.			

Accounts Receivable Ledger

Marjorie Allen

Date	PR	Debit	Credit	Balance
Mar. 20	S2	5,600		5,600
26	G2		600	5,000

Dennie Hoskins

Date	PR	Debit	Credit	Balance
Mar. 6	S2	10,200		10,200
16	R3		10,200	0

Jennifer Nelson

Date	PR	Debit	Credit	Balance
Mar. 4	S2	16,800		16,800
14	R3		16,800	0

Accounts Payable Ledger

Defore Industries

Date	PR	Debit	Credit	Balance
Mar. 11	P3		52,600	52,600
16	G2	200		52,400
21	D3	52,400		0

Mack Company

Date	PR	Debit	Credit	Balance
Mar. 6	P3		1,220	1,220

Schmidt Supply

Date	PR	Debit	Credit	Balance
Mar. 18	P3		22,850	22,850

Welch Company

Date	PR	Debit	Credit	Balance
Mar. 22	P3		41,625	41,625

General Ledger (Partial Listing)

Cash Acct. No. 101

Date	PR	Debit	Credit	Balance
Mar. 31	R3	187,140		187,140
31	D3		67,252	119,888

Accounts Receivable Acct. No. 106

Date	PR	Debit	Credit	Balance
Mar. 26	G2		600	(600)
31	S2	32,600		32,000
31	R3		27,000	5,000

Inventory Acct. No. 119

Date	PR	Debit	Credit	Balance
Mar. 16	G2		200	(200)
21	D3		1,048	(1,248)
31	P3	94,225		92,977
31	S2		24,100	68,877
31	R3		67,340	1,537

Office Supplies Acct. No. 124

Date	PR	Debit	Credit	Balance
Mar. 31	P3	1,220		1,220

Store Equipment Acct. No. 165

Date	PR	Debit	Credit	Balance
Mar. 18	P3	22,850		22,850

Accounts Payable Acct. No. 201

Date	PR	Debit	Credit	Balance
Mar. 16	G2	200		(200)
31	P3		118,295	118,095
31	D3	52,400		65,695

Long-Term Notes Payable Acct. No. 251

Date	PR	Debit	Credit	Balance
Mar. 12	R3		26,000	26,000

Sales Acct. No. 413

Date	PR	Debit	Credit	Balance
Mar. 31	S2		32,600	32,600
31	R3		134,680	167,280

Sales Returns and Allowances Acct. No. 414

Date	PR	Debit	Credit	Balance
Mar. 26	G2	600		600

Sales Discounts Acct. No. 415

Date	PR	Debit	Credit	Balance
Mar. 31	R3	540		540

Cost of Goods Sold Acct. No. 502

Date	PR	Debit	Credit	Balance
Mar. 31	R3	67,340		67,340
31	S2	24,100		91,440

Sales Salaries Expense Acct. No. 621

Date	PR	Debit	Credit	Balance
Mar. 31	D3	15,900		15,900

PEPPER COMPANY
Trial Balance (partial)
March 31

	Debit	Credit
Cash	$119,888	
Accounts receivable	5,000	
Inventory	1,537	
Office supplies	1,220	
Store equipment	22,850	
Accounts payable		$ 65,695
Long-term notes payable		26,000
Sales		167,280
Sales returns and allowances	600	
Sales discounts	540	
Cost of goods sold	91,440	
Sales salaries expense	15,900	
Totals	$258,975	$258,975

reconciled

PEPPER COMPANY
Schedule of Accounts Receivable
March 31

Marjorie Allen	$5,000
Total accounts receivable	$5,000

reconciled

PEPPER COMPANY
Schedule of Accounts Payable
March 31

Mack Company	$ 1,220
Schmidt Supply	22,850
Welch Company	41,625
Total accounts payable	$65,695

APPENDIX

7A Special Journals under a Periodic System

P3 Journalize and post transactions using special journals in a periodic inventory system.

This appendix describes special journals under a periodic inventory system. Each journal is slightly impacted. The sales journal and the cash receipts journal both require one less column (namely that of Cost of Goods Sold Dr., Inventory Cr.). The Purchases Journal replaces the Inventory Dr. column with a Purchases Dr. column in a periodic system. The cash disbursements journal replaces the Inventory Cr. column with a Purchases Discounts Cr. column in a periodic system. These changes are illustrated.

Sales Journal

The sales journal using the periodic inventory system is shown in Exhibit 7A.1. The difference in the sales journal between the perpetual and periodic system is the exclusion of the column to record cost of goods sold and inventory amounts for each sale. The periodic system does *not* record the increase in cost of goods sold and the decrease in inventory at the time of each sale.

EXHIBIT 7A.1

Sales Journal—Periodic System

Sales Journal — Page 3

Date	Account Debited	Invoice Number	PR	Accounts Receivable Dr. Sales Cr.
Feb. 2	Jason Henry	307	✓	450
7	Albert Co.	308	✓	500
13	Kam Moore	309	✓	350
15	Paul Roth	310	✓	200
22	Jason Henry	311	✓	225
25	Frank Booth	312	✓	175
28	Albert Co.	313	✓	250
28	Total			2,150
				(106/413)

Cash Receipts Journal

The cash receipts journal using the periodic system is shown in Exhibit 7A.2. Note the absence of the column on the far right side to record debits to Cost of Goods Sold and credits to Inventory for the cost of merchandise sold (seen under the perpetual system). Consistent with the cash receipts journal shown in Exhibit 7.7, we show only the weekly (summary) cash sale entries.

EXHIBIT 7A.2

Cash Receipts Journal—Periodic System

Cash Receipts Journal — Page 2

Date	Account Credited	Explanation	PR	Cash Dr.	Sales Discount Dr.	Accounts Receivable Cr.	Sales Cr.	Other Accounts Cr.
Feb. 7	Sales	Cash sales	x	4,450			4,450	
12	Jason Henry	Invoice 307, 2/2	✓	441	9	450		
14	Sales	Cash sales	x	3,925			3,925	
17	Albert Co.	Invoice 308, 2/7	✓	490	10	500		
20	Notes Payable	Note to bank	245	750				750
21	Sales	Cash sales	x	4,700			4,700	
22	Interest revenue	Bank account	409	250				250
23	Kam Moore	Invoice 309, 2/13	✓	343	7	350		
25	Paul Roth	Invoice 310, 2/15	✓	196	4	200		
28	Sales	Cash sales	x	4,225			4,225	
28	Totals			19,770	30	1,500	17,300	1,000
				(101)	(415)	(106)	(413)	(x)

Purchases Journal

The purchases journal using the periodic system is shown in Exhibit 7A.3. This journal under a perpetual system included an Inventory column where the periodic system now has a Purchases column.

EXHIBIT 7A.3

Purchases Journal—Periodic System

Purchases Journal — Page 1

Date	Account	Date of Invoice	Terms	PR	Accounts Payable Cr.	Purchases Dr.	Office Supplies Dr.	Other Accounts Dr.
Feb. 3	Horning Supply Co.	2/2	n/30	✓	350	275	75	
5	Ace Mfg. Co.	2/5	2/10, n/30	✓	200	200		
13	Wynet and Co.	2/10	2/10, n/30	✓	150	150		
20	Smite Co.	2/18	2/10, n/30	✓	300	300		
25	Ace Mfg. Co.	2/24	2/10, n/30	✓	100	100		
28	Store Supplies/ITT Co.	2/28	n/30	125/✓	225	125	25	75
28	Totals				1,325	1,150	100	75
					(201)	(505)	(124)	(x)

Cash Disbursements Journal

The cash disbursements journal using a periodic system is shown in Exhibit 7A.4. This journal under the perpetual system included an Inventory column where the periodic system now has the Purchases Discounts column.

QS 7-2
Accounting information system
C2

Fill in the blanks to complete the following descriptions.

1. With ______ processing, source documents are accumulated for a period and then processed all at the same time, such as once a day, week, or month.
2. A computer ______ allows different computer users to share access to data and programs.
3. A ______ is an input device that captures writing and other input directly from source documents.
4. ______ ______ ______ software comprises programs that help manage a company's vital operations, from manufacturing to accounting.

QS 7-3
Accounting information system components
C2

Identify the most likely role in an accounting system played by each of the numbered items 1 through 12 by assigning a letter from the list A through E on the left.

A. Source documents
B. Input devices
C. Information processors
D. Information storage
E. Output devices

______ **1.** Bar code reader
______ **2.** Digital camera
______ **3.** Invoice from a supplier
______ **4.** Zip drive
______ **5.** Computer scanner
______ **6.** Filing cabinet
______ **7.** Computer keyboard
______ **8.** Computer printer
______ **9.** Computer monitor
______ **10.** MP3 player
______ **11.** Bank statement
______ **12.** Computer software

QS 7-4
Identifying the special journal of entry
C3

Weber Electronics uses a sales journal, a purchases journal, a cash receipts journal, a cash disbursements journal, and a general journal as illustrated in this chapter. Weber recently completed the following transactions *a* through *h*. Identify the journal in which each transaction should be recorded.

a. Sold merchandise for cash.
b. Purchased merchandise on credit.
c. Purchased inventory for cash.
d. Paid cash to a creditor.
e. Sold merchandise on credit.
f. Purchased shop supplies on credit.
g. Paid an employee's salary in cash.
h. Borrowed cash from the bank.

QS 7-5
Entries in the general journal
C3

Adrian Gifts uses a sales journal, a purchases journal, a cash receipts journal, a cash disbursements journal, and a general journal as illustrated in this chapter. Journalize its November transactions that should be recorded in the general journal. For those not recorded in the general journal, identify the special journal where each should be recorded.

Nov.	2	The company purchased $2,600 of merchandise on credit from the Midwest Co., terms 2/10, n/30.
	12	The owner, R. Adrian, contributed an automobile worth $17,000 to the company.
	16	The company sold $1,200 of merchandise (cost is $800) on credit to L. Norton, terms n/30.
	19	L. Norton returned $175 of (worthless) merchandise to the company originally purchased on November 16 (assume the cost of this merchandise is left in cost of goods sold).

QS 7-6
Analyzing segment reports
A1

Apple reports the following income (and average assets in parentheses) for each of its geographic segments—$ millions: Americas, $1,665 ($800); Europe, $607 ($380); and Japan, $201 ($173). Apple also reports the following sales (only) by product segments: iPod, $7,676; Desktops, $3,319; Portables, $4,056; Other, $1,885. Compute Apple's return on assets for each of its geographic segments, and assess the relative performance of these segments. Compute the percentage of total sales for each of its four product segments.

3. The ledger that contains the financial statement accounts of a company is the
- **a.** General journal
- **b.** Column balance journal
- **c.** Special ledger
- **d.** General ledger
- **e.** Special journal

4. A subsidiary ledger that contains a separate account for each supplier (creditor) to the company is the
- **a.** Controlling account
- **b.** Accounts payable ledger
- **c.** Accounts receivable ledger
- **d.** General ledger
- **e.** Special journal

5. Enterprise resource planning software
- **a.** Refers to programs that help manage company operations.
- **b.** Is another name for spreadsheet programs.
- **c.** Uses batch processing of business information.
- **d.** Is substantially declining in use.
- **e.** Is another name for database programs.

Superscript letter A denotes assignments based on Appendix 7A.

Discussion Questions

1. What are the five fundamental principles of accounting information systems?

2. What are five basic components of an accounting system?

3. What are source documents? Give two examples.

4. What is the purpose of an input device? Give examples of input devices for computer systems.

5. What is the difference between data that are stored off-line and data that are stored online?

6. What purpose is served by the output devices of an accounting system?

7. When special journals are used, they are usually used to record each of four different types of transactions. What are these four types of transactions?

8. What notations are entered into the Posting Reference column of a ledger account?

9. When a general journal entry is used to record sales returns, the credit of the entry must be posted twice. Does this cause the trial balance to be out of balance? Explain.

10. Describe the procedures involving the use of copies of a company's sales invoices as a sales journal.

11. Credits to customer accounts and credits to Other Accounts are individually posted from a cash receipts journal such as the one in Exhibit 7.7. Why not put both types of credits in the same column and save journal space?

12. Why should sales to and receipts of cash from credit customers be recorded and posted immediately?

13. Locate the note that discusses **Best Buy**'s operations by segments in Appendix A. In what two segments does it predominantly operate?

14. Does the income statement of **Circuit City** in Appendix A indicate the net income earned by its business segments? If so, list them.

15. Locate the note that discusses **RadioShack**'s segments from its 2006 annual report on its Website. What two reportable segments does RadioShack have?

16. Does the balance sheet of **Apple** in Appendix A indicate the identifiable assets owned by its business segments? If so, list them.

Denotes Discussion Questions that involve decision making.

McGraw-Hill's HOMEWORK MANAGER® Available with McGraw-Hill's Homework Manager

For account titles and numbers, use the Chart of Accounts at the end of the book.

QUICK STUDY

QS 7-1
Accounting information system principles
C1

Enter the letter of each system principle in the blank next to its best description.

A. Flexibility principle
B. Cost-benefit principle
C. Control principle
D. Relevance principle
E. Compatibility principle

1. _______ The principle prescribes the accounting information system to help monitor activities.

2. _______ The principle prescribes the accounting information system to adapt to the unique characteristics of the company.

3. _______ The principle prescribes the accounting information system to change in response to technological advances and competitive pressures.

4. _______ The principle that affects all other accounting information system principles.

5. _______ The principle prescribes the accounting information system to provide timely information for effective decision making.

QS 7-2
Accounting information system
C2

Fill in the blanks to complete the following descriptions.

1. With ______ processing, source documents are accumulated for a period and then processed all at the same time, such as once a day, week, or month.

2. A computer ______ allows different computer users to share access to data and programs.

3. A ______ is an input device that captures writing and other input directly from source documents.

4. ______ ______ ______ software comprises programs that help manage a company's vital operations, from manufacturing to accounting.

QS 7-3
Accounting information system components
C2

Identify the most likely role in an accounting system played by each of the numbered items 1 through 12 by assigning a letter from the list A through E on the left.

A. Source documents	______	**1.** Bar code reader
B. Input devices	______	**2.** Digital camera
C. Information processors	______	**3.** Invoice from a supplier
D. Information storage	______	**4.** Zip drive
E. Output devices	______	**5.** Computer scanner
	______	**6.** Filing cabinet
	______	**7.** Computer keyboard
	______	**8.** Computer printer
	______	**9.** Computer monitor
	______	**10.** MP3 player
	______	**11.** Bank statement
	______	**12.** Computer software

QS 7-4
Identifying the special journal of entry
C3

Weber Electronics uses a sales journal, a purchases journal, a cash receipts journal, a cash disbursements journal, and a general journal as illustrated in this chapter. Weber recently completed the following transactions *a* through *h*. Identify the journal in which each transaction should be recorded.

a. Sold merchandise for cash.
b. Purchased merchandise on credit.
c. Purchased inventory for cash.
d. Paid cash to a creditor.
e. Sold merchandise on credit.
f. Purchased shop supplies on credit.
g. Paid an employee's salary in cash.
h. Borrowed cash from the bank.

QS 7-5
Entries in the general journal
C3

Adrian Gifts uses a sales journal, a purchases journal, a cash receipts journal, a cash disbursements journal, and a general journal as illustrated in this chapter. Journalize its November transactions that should be recorded in the general journal. For those not recorded in the general journal, identify the special journal where each should be recorded.

Nov.	2	The company purchased $2,600 of merchandise on credit from the Midwest Co., terms 2/10, n/30.
	12	The owner, R. Adrian, contributed an automobile worth $17,000 to the company.
	16	The company sold $1,200 of merchandise (cost is $800) on credit to L. Norton, terms n/30.
	19	L. Norton returned $175 of (worthless) merchandise to the company originally purchased on November 16 (assume the cost of this merchandise is left in cost of goods sold).

QS 7-6
Analyzing segment reports
A1

Apple reports the following income (and average assets in parentheses) for each of its geographic segments—$ millions: Americas, $1,665 ($800); Europe, $607 ($380); and Japan, $201 ($173). Apple also reports the following sales (only) by product segments: iPod, $7,676; Desktops, $3,319; Portables, $4,056; Other, $1,885. Compute Apple's return on assets for each of its geographic segments, and assess the relative performance of these segments. Compute the percentage of total sales for each of its four product segments.

3. Data saved in information storage are used to prepare periodic financial reports and special-purpose internal reports as well as source documentation for auditors.

4. All cash payments by check are recorded in the cash disbursements journal.

5. Columnar journals allow us to accumulate repetitive debits and credits and post them as column totals rather than as individual amounts from each entry.

6. The equality of debits and credits is kept within the general ledger. The subsidiary ledger keeps the customer's individual account and is used only for supplementary information.

7. An initial and the page number of the journal from which the amount was posted are entered in the PR column next to the amount.

8. A separate column for Sales Taxes Payable can be included in both the cash receipts journal and the sales journal.

9. This refers to a procedure of using copies of sales invoices as a sales journal. Each invoice amount is posted directly to the customer's account. All invoices are totaled at period-end for posting to the general ledger accounts.

10. The normal recording and posting procedures are threefold. First, transactions are entered in a special journal if applicable. Second, individual amounts are posted to any subsidiary ledger accounts. Third, column totals are posted to general ledger accounts if not already individually posted.

11. Controlling accounts are debited periodically for an amount or amounts equal to the sum of their respective debits in the subsidiary ledgers (equals journal column totals), and they are credited periodically for an amount or amounts equal to the sum of their respective credits in the subsidiary ledgers (from journal column totals).

12. Tests for accuracy of account balances in the general ledger and subsidiary ledgers are twofold. First, we prepare a trial balance of the general ledger to confirm that debits equal credits. Second, we prove the subsidiary ledgers by preparing schedules of accounts receivable and accounts payable.

13. The general journal is still needed for adjusting, closing, and correcting entries and for special transactions such as sales returns, purchases returns, and certain asset purchases.

14. Integrated systems can save time and minimize errors. This is so because actions taken in one part of the system automatically affect and update related parts.

15. Computer systems offer increased accuracy, speed, efficiency, and convenience.

16. Computer networks can create advantages by linking computers, and giving different users and different computers access to common databases, programs, and hardware.

17. ERP software involves integrated programs, from order taking to manufacturing to accounting. It can speed decision making, help identify costs for reduction, and aid managers in controlling operations.

Key Terms

mhhe.com/wildFAP19e

Key Terms are available at the book's Website for learning and testing in an online Flashcard Format.

Accounting information systems (p. 268)
Accounts payable ledger (p. 273)
Accounts receivable ledger (p. 273)
Batch processing (p. 282)
Cash disbursements journal (p. 280)
Cash receipts journal (p. 277)
Check register (p. 280)
Columnar journal (p. 274)
Compatibility principle (p. 269)
Components of accounting systems (p. 269)
Computer networks (p. 283)
Controlling account (p. 273)
Control principle (p. 268)
Cost-benefit principle (p. 269)
Enterprise resource planning (ERP) software (p. 283)
Flexibility principle (p. 269)
General journal (p. 272)
Information processors (p. 270)
Information storage (p. 270)
Input devices (p. 270)
Internal controls (p. 268)
Online processing (p. 282)
Output devices (p. 271)
Purchases journal (p. 279)
Relevance principle (p. 268)
Sales journal (p. 274)
Schedule of accounts payable (p. 280)
Schedule of accounts receivable (p. 275)
Segment return on assets (p. 284)
Special journal (p. 272)
Subsidiary ledger (p. 272)

Multiple Choice Quiz

Answers on p. 311

mhhe.com/wildFAP19e

Additional Quiz Questions are available at the book's Website.

1. The sales journal is used to record
   a. Credit sales
   b. Cash sales
   c. Cash receipts
   d. Cash purchases
   e. Credit purchases

2. The purchases journal is used to record
   a. Credit sales
   b. Cash sales
   c. Cash receipts
   d. Cash purchases
   e. Credit purchases

Summary

C1 Identify fundamental principles of accounting information systems. Accounting information systems are governed by five fundamental principles: control, relevance, compatibility, flexibility, and cost-benefit.

C2 Identify components of accounting information systems. The five basic components of an accounting information system are source documents, input devices, information processors, information storage, and output devices.

C3 Explain the goals and uses of special journals. Special journals are used for recording transactions of similar type, each meant to cover one kind of transaction. Four of the most common special journals are the sales journal, cash receipts journal, purchases journal, and cash disbursements journal. Special journals are efficient and cost-effective tools in the journalizing and posting processes.

C4 Describe the use of controlling accounts and subsidiary ledgers. A general ledger keeps controlling accounts such as Accounts Receivable and Accounts Payable, but details on individual accounts making up the controlling account are kept in subsidiary ledgers (such as an accounts receivable ledger). The balance in a controlling account must equal the sum of its subsidiary account balances after posting is complete.

C5 Explain how technology-based information systems impact accounting. Technology-based information systems aim to increase the accuracy, speed, efficiency, and convenience of accounting procedures.

A1 Compute segment return on assets and use it to evaluate segment performance. A business segment is a part of a company that is separately identified by its products or services or by the geographic market it serves. Analysis of a company's segments is aided by the segment return on assets (segment operating income divided by segment average assets).

P1 Journalize and post transactions using special journals. Each special journal is devoted to similar kinds of transactions. Transactions are journalized on one line of a special journal, with columns devoted to specific accounts, dates, names, posting references, explanations, and other necessary information. Posting is threefold: (1) individual amounts in the Other Accounts column are posted to their general ledger accounts on a regular (daily) basis, (2) individual amounts in a column whose total is *not* posted to a controlling account at the end of a period (month) are posted regularly (daily) to their general ledger accounts, and (3) total amounts for all columns except the Other Accounts column are posted at the end of a period (month) to their column's account title in the general ledger.

P2 Prepare and prove the accuracy of subsidiary ledgers. Account balances in the general ledger and its subsidiary ledgers are tested for accuracy after posting is complete. This procedure is twofold: (1) prepare a trial balance of the general ledger to confirm that debits equal credits and (2) prepare a schedule to confirm that the controlling account's balance equals the subsidiary ledger's balance.

P3[A] Journalize and post transactions using special journals in a periodic inventory system. Transactions are journalized and posted using special journals in a periodic system. The methods are similar to those in a perpetual system; the primary difference is that both cost of goods sold and inventory are not adjusted at the time of each sale. This usually results in the deletion (or renaming) of one or more columns devoted to these accounts in each special journal.

Guidance Answers to **Decision Maker** and **Decision Ethics**

Accountant The main issue is whether commissions have an actual or perceived impact on the integrity and objectivity of your advice. You probably should not accept a commission arrangement (the AICPA Code of Ethics prohibits it when you perform the audit or a review). In any event, you should tell the client of your commission arrangement. Also, you need to seriously examine the merits of agreeing to a commission arrangement when you are in a position to exploit it.

Entrepreneur The accounts receivable ledger has much of the information you need. It lists detailed information for each customer's account, including the amounts, dates for transactions, and dates of payments. It can be reorganized into an "aging schedule" to show how long customers wait before paying their bills.

Controller Much of the information you need is in the accounts payable ledger. It contains information for each supplier, the amounts due, and when payments are made. This subsidiary ledger along with information on credit terms should enable you to conduct your analyses.

Banker This merchandiser's segment information is likely to greatly impact your loan decision. The risks associated with the company's two sources of net income are quite different. While net income is up by 10%, U.S. operations are performing poorly and Cuban operations are subject to many uncertainties. These uncertainties depend on political events, legal issues, business relationships, Cuban economic conditions, and a host of other risks. Overall, net income results suggested a low-risk loan opportunity, but the segment information reveals a high-risk situation.

Guidance Answers to **Quick Checks**

1. The five components are source documents, input devices, information processors, information storage, and output devices.
2. Information processors interpret, transform, and summarize the recorded accounting information so that it can be used in analysis, interpretation, and decision making.

General Ledger (Partial Listing)

Cash Acct. No. 101

Date	PR	Debit	Credit	Balance
Mar. 31	R3	187,140		187,140
31	D3		67,252	119,888

Accounts Receivable Acct. No. 106

Date	PR	Debit	Credit	Balance
Mar. 26	G2		600	(600)
31	S2	32,600		32,000
31	R3		27,000	5,000

Office Supplies Acct. No. 124

Date	PR	Debit	Credit	Balance
Mar. 31	P3	1,220		1,220

Store Equipment Acct. No. 165

Date	PR	Debit	Credit	Balance
Mar. 18	P3	22,850		22,850

Accounts Payable Acct. No. 201

Date	PR	Debit	Credit	Balance
Mar. 16	G2	200		(200)
31	P3		118,295	118,095
31	D3	52,400		65,695

Long-Term Notes Payable Acct. No. 251

Date	PR	Debit	Credit	Balance
Mar. 12	R3		26,000	26,000

Sales Acct. No. 413

Date	PR	Debit	Credit	Balance
Mar. 31	S2		32,600	32,600
31	R3		134,680	167,280

Sales Returns and Allowances Acct. No. 414

Date	PR	Debit	Credit	Balance
Mar. 26	G2	600		600

Sales Discounts Acct. No. 415

Date	PR	Debit	Credit	Balance
Mar. 31	R3	540		540

Purchases Acct. No. 505

Date	PR	Debit	Credit	Balance
Mar. 31	P3	94,225		94,225

Purchases Returns and Allowances Acct. No. 506

Date	PR	Debit	Credit	Balance
Mar. 16	G2		200	200

Purchases Discounts Acct. No. 507

Date	PR	Debit	Credit	Balance
Mar. 31	D3		1,048	1,048

Sales Salaries Expense Acct. No. 621

Date	PR	Debit	Credit	Balance
Mar. 31	D3	15,900		15,900

PEPPER COMPANY
Trial Balance (partial)
March 31

	Debit	Credit
Cash	$119,888	
Accounts receivable	5,000	
Office supplies	1,220	
Store equipment	22,850	
Accounts payable		$ 65,695
Long-term notes payable		26,000
Sales		167,280
Sales returns and allowances	600	
Sales discounts	540	
Purchases	94,225	
Purchases returns and allowances		200
Purchases discounts		1,048
Sales salaries expense	15,900	
Totals	$260,223	$260,223

PEPPER COMPANY
Schedule of Accounts Receivable
March 31

Marjorie Allen	$5,000
Total accounts receivable	$5,000

PEPPER COMPANY
Schedule of Accounts Payable
March 31

Mack Company	$ 1,220
Schmidt Supply	22,850
Welch Company	41,625
Total accounts payable	$65,695

Purchases Journal Page 3

Date	Account	Date of Invoice	Terms	PR	Accounts Payable Cr.	Purchases Dr.	Office Supplies Dr.	Other Accounts Dr.
Mar. 6	Office Supplies/Mack Co	3/3	n/30	✓	1,220		1,220	
11	Defore Industries	3/6	2/10, n/30	✓	52,600	52,600		
18	Store Equipment/Schmidt Supp	3/15	n/30	165/✓	22,850			22,850
22	Welch Company	3/18	2/10, n/30	✓	41,625	41,625		
31	Totals				118,295	94,225	1,220	22,850
					(201)	(505)	(124)	(x)

Cash Disbursements Journal Page 3

Date	Ck. No.	Payee	Account Debited	PR	Cash Cr.	Purchases Discount Cr.	Other Accounts Dr.	Accounts Payable Dr.
Mar. 21	516	Defore Industries	Defore Industries	✓	51,352	1,048		52,400
31	517	Payroll	Sales Salaries Expense	621	15,900		15,900	
31		Totals			67,252	1,048	15,900	52,400
					(101)	(507)	(x)	(201)

General Journal Page 2

Mar. 16	Accounts Payable—Defore Industries	201/✓	200	
	Purchases Returns and Allowances	506		200
	To record credit memorandum received.			
26	Sales Returns and Allowances	414	600	
	Accounts Receivable—Marjorie Allen	106/✓		600
	To record credit memorandum issued.			

Accounts Receivable Ledger

Marjorie Allen

Date	PR	Debit	Credit	Balance
Mar. 20	S2	5,600		5,600
26	G2		600	5,000

Dennie Hoskins

Date	PR	Debit	Credit	Balance
Mar. 6	S2	10,200		10,200
16	R3		10,200	0

Jennifer Nelson

Date	PR	Debit	Credit	Balance
Mar. 4	S2	16,800		16,800
14	R3		16,800	0

Accounts Payable Ledger

Defore Industries

Date	PR	Debit	Credit	Balance
Mar. 11	P3		52,600	52,600
16	G2	200		52,400
21	D3	52,400		0

Mack Company

Date	PR	Debit	Credit	Balance
Mar. 6	P3		1,220	1,220

Schmidt Supply

Date	PR	Debit	Credit	Balance
Mar. 18	P3		22,850	22,850

Welch Company

Date	PR	Debit	Credit	Balance
Mar. 22	P3		41,625	41,625

EXHIBIT 7A.1

Sales Journal—Periodic System

Sales Journal — Page 3

Date	Account Debited	Invoice Number	PR	Accounts Receivable Dr. Sales Cr.
Feb. 2	Jason Henry	307	✓	450
7	Albert Co.	308	✓	500
13	Kam Moore	309	✓	350
15	Paul Roth	310	✓	200
22	Jason Henry	311	✓	225
25	Frank Booth	312	✓	175
28	Albert Co.	313	✓	250
28	Total			2,150
				(106/413)

Cash Receipts Journal

The cash receipts journal using the periodic system is shown in Exhibit 7A.2. Note the absence of the column on the far right side to record debits to Cost of Goods Sold and credits to Inventory for the cost of merchandise sold (seen under the perpetual system). Consistent with the cash receipts journal shown in Exhibit 7.7, we show only the weekly (summary) cash sale entries.

EXHIBIT 7A.2

Cash Receipts Journal—Periodic System

Cash Receipts Journal — Page 2

Date	Account Credited	Explanation	PR	Cash Dr.	Sales Discount Dr.	Accounts Receivable Cr.	Sales Cr.	Other Accounts Cr.
Feb. 7	Sales	Cash sales	x	4,450			4,450	
12	Jason Henry	Invoice 307, 2/2	✓	441	9	450		
14	Sales	Cash sales	x	3,925			3,925	
17	Albert Co.	Invoice 308, 2/7	✓	490	10	500		
20	Notes Payable	Note to bank	245	750				750
21	Sales	Cash sales	x	4,700			4,700	
22	Interest revenue	Bank account	409	250				250
23	Kam Moore	Invoice 309, 2/13	✓	343	7	350		
25	Paul Roth	Invoice 310, 2/15	✓	196	4	200		
28	Sales	Cash sales	x	4,225			4,225	
28	Totals			19,770	30	1,500	17,300	1,000
				(101)	(415)	(106)	(413)	(x)

Purchases Journal

The purchases journal using the periodic system is shown in Exhibit 7A.3. This journal under a perpetual system included an Inventory column where the periodic system now has a Purchases column.

EXHIBIT 7A.3

Purchases Journal—Periodic System

Purchases Journal — Page 1

Date	Account	Date of Invoice	Terms	PR	Accounts Payable Cr.	Purchases Dr.	Office Supplies Dr.	Other Accounts Dr.
Feb. 3	Horning Supply Co.	2/2	n/30	✓	350	275	75	
5	Ace Mfg. Co.	2/5	2/10, n/30	✓	200	200		
13	Wynet and Co.	2/10	2/10, n/30	✓	150	150		
20	Smite Co.	2/18	2/10, n/30	✓	300	300		
25	Ace Mfg. Co.	2/24	2/10, n/30	✓	100	100		
28	Store Supplies/ITT Co.	2/28	n/30	125/✓	225	125	25	75
28	Totals				1,325	1,150	100	75
					(201)	(505)	(124)	(x)

Cash Disbursements Journal

The cash disbursements journal using a periodic system is shown in Exhibit 7A.4. This journal under the perpetual system included an Inventory column where the periodic system now has the Purchases Discounts column.

EXHIBIT 7A.4

Cash Disbursements Journal—Periodic System

Cash Disbursements Journal — Page 2

Date	Ck. No.	Payee	Account Debited	PR	Cash Cr.	Purchases Discounts Cr.	Other Accounts Dr.	Accounts Payable Dr.
Feb. 3	105	L. and N. Railroad	Purchases	505	15		15	
12	106	East Sales Co.	Purchases	505	25		25	
15	107	Ace Mfg. Co.	Ace Mfg. Co.	✓	196	4		200
15	108	Jerry Hale	Salaries Expense	622	250		250	
20	109	Wynet and Co.	Wynet and Co.	✓	147	3		150
28	110	Smite Co.	Smite Co.	✓	294	6		300
28		Totals			927	13	290	650
					(101)	(507)	(x)	(201)

Demonstration Problem—Periodic System

Refer to Pepper Company's selected transactions described under the Demonstration Problem—Perpetual System to fulfill the following requirements.

Required

1. Open the following selected general ledger accounts: Cash (101), Accounts Receivable (106), Office Supplies (124), Store Equipment (165), Accounts Payable (201), Long-Term Notes Payable (251), Sales (413), Sales Returns and Allowances (414), Sales Discounts (415), Purchases (505), Purchases Returns and Allowances (506), Purchases Discounts (507), and Sales Salaries Expense (621). Open the following accounts receivable ledger accounts: Marjorie Allen, Dennie Hoskins, and Jennifer Nelson. Open the following accounts payable ledger accounts: Defore Industries, Mack Company, Schmidt Supply, and Welch Company.
2. Enter the transactions using a sales journal, a purchases journal, a cash receipts journal, a cash disbursements journal, and a general journal similar to the ones illustrated in Appendix 7A. Regularly post to the individual customer and creditor accounts. Also, post any amounts that should be posted as individual amounts to general ledger accounts. Foot and crossfoot the journals and make the month-end postings. *Pepper Co. uses the periodic inventory system in this problem.*
3. Prepare a trial balance for the selected general ledger accounts in part 1 and prove the accuracy of subsidiary ledgers by preparing schedules of accounts receivable and accounts payable.

Solution to Demonstration Problem—Periodic System

Sales Journal — Page 2

Date	Account Debited	Invoice Number	PR	Accounts Receivable Dr. Sales Cr.
Mar. 4	Jennifer Nelson	954	✓	16,800
6	Dennie Hoskins	955	✓	10,200
20	Marjorie Allen	956	✓	5,600
31	Totals			32,600
				(106/413)

Cash Receipts Journal — Page 3

Date	Account Credited	Explanation	PR	Cash Dr.	Sales Discount Dr.	Accounts Receivable Cr.	Sales Cr.	Other Accounts Cr.
Mar. 12	L.T. Notes Payable	Note to bank	251	26,000				26,000
14	Jennifer Nelson	Invoice 954, 3/4	✓	16,464	336	16,800		
16	Dennie Hoskins	Invoice 955, 3/6	✓	9,996	204	10,200		
31	Sales	Cash sales	x	134,680			134,680	
31	Totals			187,140	540	27,000	134,680	26,000
				(101)	(415)	(106)	(413)	(x)

McGraw-Hill's HOMEWORK MANAGER® Available with McGraw-Hill's Homework Manager

For account titles and numbers, use the Chart of Accounts at the end of the book.

EXERCISES

Exercise 7-1
Sales journal—perpetual
P1

Levine Company uses a sales journal, a purchases journal, a cash receipts journal, a cash disbursement journal, and a general journal. The following transactions occur in the month of March.

Mar.	2	Sold merchandise costing $450 to R. Nagy for $675 cash, invoice no. 5703.
	5	Purchased $3,000 of merchandise on credit from Central Corp.
	7	Sold merchandise costing $1,215 to K. Anklam for $1,700, terms 2/10, n/30, invoice no. 5704.
	8	Borrowed $8,000 cash by signing a note payable to the bank.
	12	Sold merchandise costing $303 to B. Swanson for $484, terms n/30, invoice no. 5705.
	16	Received $1,666 cash from K. Anklam to pay for the purchase of March 7.
	19	Sold used store equipment for $900 cash to Algoma, Inc.
	25	Sold merchandise costing $500 to F. Sayers for $785, terms n/30, invoice no. 5706.

Prepare headings for a sales journal like the one in Exhibit 7.5. Journalize the March transactions that should be recorded in this sales journal.

Exercise 7-2
Identifying journal of entry
C3

Refer to Exercise 7-1 and for each of the March transactions identify the journal in which it would be recorded. Assume the company uses a sales journal, purchases journal, cash receipts journal, cash disbursements journal, and general journal as illustrated in this chapter.

Exercise 7-3^A
Sales journal—periodic
P3

Prepare headings for a sales journal like the one in Exhibit 7A.1. Journalize the March transactions shown in Exercise 7-1 that should be recorded in the sales journal assuming that the periodic inventory system is used.

Exercise 7-4
Cash receipts journal—perpetual
P1

Mizuno Co. uses a sales journal, a purchases journal, a cash receipts journal, a cash disbursements journal, and a general journal. The following transactions occur in the month of November.

Nov.	3	The company purchased $3,500 of merchandise on credit from Abbott Co., terms n/20.
	7	The company sold merchandise costing $923 on credit to E. Han for $1,015, subject to a $20 sales discount if paid by the end of the month.
	9	The company borrowed $3,375 cash by signing a note payable to the bank.
	13	I. Uno, the owner, contributed $4,675 cash to the company.
	18	The company sold merchandise costing $147 to C. Knapp for $261 cash.
	22	The company paid Abbott Co. $3,500 cash for the merchandise purchased on November 3.
	27	The company received $995 cash from E. Han in payment of the November 7 purchase.
	30	The company paid salaries of $1,750 in cash.

Prepare headings for a cash receipts journal like the one in Exhibit 7.7. Journalize the November transactions that should be recorded in the cash receipts journal.

Exercise 7-5
Identifying journal of entry
C3

Refer to Exercise 7-4 and for each of the November transactions identify the journal in which it would be recorded. Assume the company uses a sales journal, purchases journal, cash receipts journal, cash disbursements journal, and general journal as illustrated in this chapter.

Exercise 7-6^A
Cash receipts journal—periodic
P3

Prepare headings for a cash receipts journal like the one in Exhibit 7A.2. Journalize the November transactions shown in Exercise 7-4 that should be recorded in the cash receipts journal assuming that the periodic inventory system is used.

Exercise 7-7
Purchases journal—perpetual
P1

Altan Company uses a sales journal, a purchases journal, a cash receipts journal, a cash disbursements journal, and a general journal. The following transactions occur in the month of June.

June 1 Purchased $5,400 of merchandise on credit from Krause, Inc., terms n/30.
8 Sold merchandise costing $720 on credit to G. Seles for $1,080 subject to a $21 sales discount if paid by the end of the month.
14 Purchased $460 of store supplies from Chang Company on credit, terms n/30.
17 Purchased $480 of office supplies on credit from Monder Company, terms n/30.
24 Sold merchandise costing $272 to D. Lee for $432 cash.
28 Purchased store supplies from Porter's for $72 cash.
29 Paid Krause, Inc., $5,400 cash for the merchandise purchased on June 1.

Prepare headings for a purchases journal like the one in Exhibit 7.9. Journalize the June transactions that should be recorded in the purchases journal.

Exercise 7-8
Identifying journal of entry
C3

Refer to Exercise 7-7 and for each of the June transactions identify the journal in which it would be recorded. Assume the company uses a sales journal, purchases journal, cash receipts journal, cash disbursements journal, and general journal as illustrated in this chapter.

Exercise 7-9^A^
Purchases journal—periodic
P3

Prepare headings for a purchases journal like the one in Exhibit 7A.3. Journalize the June transactions from Exercise 7-7 that should be recorded in the purchases journal assuming the periodic inventory system is used.

Exercise 7-10
Cash disbursements journal—perpetual
P1

Louder Supply uses a sales journal, a purchases journal, a cash receipts journal, a cash disbursements journal, and a general journal. The following transactions occur in the month of April.

Apr. 3 Purchased merchandise for $2,700 on credit from Acco, Inc., terms 1/10, n/30.
9 Issued check no. 210 to Major Corp. to buy store supplies for $436.
12 Sold merchandise costing $486 on credit to N. Rogers for $816, terms n/30.
17 Issued check no. 211 for $1,500 to pay off a note payable to City Bank.
20 Purchased merchandise for $3,300 on credit from Factow, terms 1/10, n/30.
28 Issued check no. 212 to Factow to pay the amount due for the purchase of April 20, less the discount.
29 Paid salary of $1,675 to M. Robbins by issuing check no. 213.
30 Issued check no. 214 to Acco, Inc., to pay the amount due for the purchase of April 3.

Prepare headings for a cash disbursements journal like the one in Exhibit 7.11. Journalize the April transactions that should be recorded in the cash disbursements journal.

Exercise 7-11
Identifying journal of entry
C3

Refer to Exercise 7-10 and for each of the April transactions identify the journal in which it would be recorded. Assume the company uses a sales journal, purchases journal, cash receipts journal, cash disbursements journal, and general journal as illustrated in this chapter.

Exercise 7-12^A^
Cash disbursements journal—periodic P3

Prepare headings for a cash disbursements journal like the one in Exhibit 7A.4. Journalize the April transactions from Exercise 7-10 that should be recorded in the cash disbursements journal assuming that the periodic inventory system is used.

Exercise 7-13
Special journal transactions and error discovery
P1

Haver Pharmacy uses the following journals: sales journal, purchases journal, cash receipts journal, cash disbursements journal, and general journal. On June 5, Haver purchased merchandise priced at $14,000, subject to credit terms of 2/10, n/30. On June 14, the pharmacy paid the net amount due for the merchandise. In journalizing the payment, the pharmacy debited Accounts Payable for $14,000 but failed to record the cash discount on the purchases. Cash was properly credited for the actual $13,720 paid. (*a*) In what journals would the June 5 and the June 14 transactions be recorded? (*b*) What procedure is likely to discover the error in journalizing the June 14 transaction?

Exercise 7-14
Posting to subsidiary ledger accounts; preparing a schedule of accounts receivable

P1 P2

At the end of May, the sales journal of River View appears as follows.

Sales Journal — Page 2

Date	Account Debited	Invoice Number	PR	Accounts Receivable Dr. Sales Cr.	Cost of Goods Sold Dr. Inventory Cr.
May 6	Aaron Reckers	190		3,550	2,698
10	Sara Reed	191		2,610	2,153
17	Anna Page	192		1,161	682
25	Sara Reed	193		464	272
31	Totals			7,785	5,805

River View also recorded the return of defective merchandise with the following entry.

May 20	Sales Returns and Allowances	500	
	Accounts Receivable—Anna Page		500
	Customer returned (worthless) merchandise.		

Required

1. Open an accounts receivable subsidiary ledger that has a T-account for each customer listed in the sales journal. Post to the customer accounts the entries in the sales journal and any portion of the general journal entry that affects a customer's account.
2. Open a general ledger that has T-accounts for Accounts Receivable, Inventory, Sales, Sales Returns and Allowances, and Cost of Goods Sold. Post the sales journal and any portion of the general journal entry that affects these accounts.
3. Prepare a schedule of accounts receivable and prove that its total equals the balance in the Accounts Receivable controlling account.

Check (3) Ending Accounts Receivable, $7,285

Exercise 7-15
Accounts receivable ledger; posting from sales journal

P1 P2

Boyar Company posts its sales invoices directly and then binds them into a Sales Journal. Boyar had the following credit sales to these customers during June.

June 2	Joe Mack	$ 4,100
8	Eric Horner	6,929
10	Tess Wilson	15,252
14	Hong Jiang	23,329
20	Tess Wilson	11,400
29	Joe Mack	7,432
	Total credit sales	$68,442

Required

1. Open an accounts receivable subsidiary ledger having a T-account for each customer. Post the invoices to the subsidiary ledger.
2. Open an Accounts Receivable controlling T-account and a Sales T-account to reflect general ledger accounts. Post the end-of-month total from the sales journal to these accounts.
3. Prepare a schedule of accounts receivable and prove that its total equals the Accounts Receivable controlling account balance.

Exercise 7-16
Purchases journal and error identification

P1

A company that records credit purchases in a purchases journal and records purchases returns in a general journal made the following errors. Indicate when each error should be discovered.

1. Made an addition error in determining the balance of a creditor's subsidiary account.
2. Made an addition error in totaling the Office Supplies column of the purchases journal.
3. Posted a purchases return to the Accounts Payable account and to the creditor's subsidiary account but did not post the purchases return to the Inventory account.
4. Posted a purchases return to the Inventory account and to the Accounts Payable account but did not post to the creditor's subsidiary account.
5. Correctly recorded a $4,000 purchase in the purchases journal but posted it to the creditor's subsidiary account as a $400 purchase.

Exercise 7-17
Computing and analyzing segment return on assets
A1

Refer to Exhibit 7.13 and complete the segment return on assets table for Triton Company. Analyze your findings and identify the segment with the highest, and that with the lowest, segment return on assets.

Segment	Segment Operating Income (in $ mil.) 2009	Segment Operating Income (in $ mil.) 2008	Segment Assets (in $ mil.) 2009	Segment Assets (in $ mil.) 2008	Segment Return on Assets 2009
Specialty					
Skiing Group	$ 53	$ 47	$ 539	$398	
Skating Group	7	4	48	35	
Specialty Footwear	18	15	143	106	
Other Specialty	9	3	32	23	
Subtotal	87	69	762	562	
General Merchandise					
South America	26	29	281	207	
United States	6	6	45	33	
Europe	4	2	15	11	
Subtotal	36	37	341	251	
Total	$123	$106	$1,103	$813	

Check Europe segment return, 30.8%

Available with McGraw-Hill's Homework Manager

PROBLEM SET A

For account titles and numbers, use the Chart of Accounts at the end of the book.

Problem 7-1A
Special journals, subsidiary ledgers, and schedule of accounts receivable—perpetual
C4 P1 P2

Moore Company completes these transactions during April of the current year (the terms of all its credit sales are 2/10, n/30).

Apr. 2 Purchased $14,200 of merchandise on credit from Newt Company, invoice dated April 2, terms 2/10, n/60.
3 Sold merchandise on credit to Ty Afton, Invoice No. 760, for $5,200 (cost is $2,100).
3 Purchased $1,530 of office supplies on credit from Cray, Inc. Invoice dated April 2, terms n/10 EOM.
4 Issued Check No. 587 to *World View* for advertising expense, $879.
5 Sold merchandise on credit to Debra Kohn, Invoice No. 761, for $9,300 (cost is $7,600).
6 Received a $70 credit memorandum from Cray, Inc., for the return of some of the office supplies received on April 3.
9 Purchased $11,435 of store equipment on credit from Hafman Supply, invoice dated April 9, terms n/10 EOM.
11 Sold merchandise on credit to Pat Orlof, Invoice No 762, for $12,300 (cost is $7,300).
12 Issued Check No. 588 to Newt Company in payment of its April 2 invoice, less the discount.
13 Received payment from Ty Afton for the April 3 sale, less the discount.
13 Sold $6,900 of merchandise on credit to Ty Afton (cost is $3,600), Invoice No. 763.
14 Received payment from Debra Kohn for the April 5 sale, less the discount.
16 Issued Check No. 589, payable to Payroll, in payment of sales salaries expense for the first half of the month, $11,300. Cashed the check and paid employees.
16 Cash sales for the first half of the month are $54,240 (cost is $42,400). (Cash sales are recorded daily from cash register data but are recorded only twice in this problem to reduce repetitive entries.)
17 Purchased $12,850 of merchandise on credit from Dann Company, invoice dated April 17, terms 2/10, n/30.
18 Borrowed $55,000 cash from First State Bank by signing a long-term note payable.
20 Received payment from Pat Orlof for the April 11 sale, less the discount.
20 Purchased $1,000 of store supplies on credit from Hafman Supply, invoice dated April 19, terms n/10 EOM.
23 Received a $900 credit memorandum from Dann Company for the return of defective merchandise received on April 17.
23 Received payment from Ty Afton for the April 13 sale, less the discount.
25 Purchased $11,465 of merchandise on credit from Newt Company, invoice dated April 24, terms 2/10, n/60.

26 Issued Check No. 590 to Dann Company in payment of its April 17 invoice, less the return and the discount.
27 Sold $3,460 of merchandise on credit to Debra Kohn, Invoice No. 764 (cost is $2,470).
27 Sold $7,100 of merchandise on credit to Pat Orlof, Invoice No. 765 (cost is $4,895).
30 Issued Check No. 591, payable to Payroll, in payment of the sales salaries expense for the last half of the month, $11,000.
30 Cash sales for the last half of the month are $72,100 (cost is $61,500).

Required

1. Prepare a sales journal like that in Exhibit 7.5 and a cash receipts journal like that in Exhibit 7.7. Number both journal pages as page 3. Then review the transactions of Moore Company and enter those that should be journalized in the sales journal and those that should be journalized in the cash receipts journal. Ignore any transactions that should be journalized in a purchases journal, a cash disbursements journal, or a general journal.

2. Open the following general ledger accounts: Cash, Accounts Receivable, Inventory, Long-Term Notes Payable, Cost of Goods Sold, Sales, and Sales Discounts. Enter the March 31 balances for Cash ($85,000), Inventory ($152,000), Long-Term Notes Payable ($137,000), and B. Moore, Capital ($100,000). Also open accounts receivable subsidiary ledger accounts for Debra Kohn, Ty Afton, and Pat Orlof.

3. Verify that amounts that should be posted as individual amounts from the journals have been posted. (Such items are immediately posted.) Foot and crossfoot the journals and make the month-end postings.

4. Prepare a trial balance of the general ledger and prove the accuracy of the subsidiary ledger by preparing a schedule of accounts receivable.

Check Trial balance totals, $462,600

Analysis Component

5. Assume that the total for the schedule of Accounts Receivable does not equal the balance of the controlling account in the general ledger. Describe steps you would take to discover the error(s).

Problem 7-2A[A]
Special journals, subsidiary ledgers, and schedule of accounts receivable—periodic
C4 P2 P3

Assume that Moore Co. in Problem 7-1A uses the periodic inventory system.

Required

1. Prepare headings for a sales journal like the one in Exhibit 7A.1. Prepare headings for a cash receipts journal like the one in Exhibit 7A.2. Journalize the April transactions shown in Problem 7-1A that should be recorded in the sales journal and the cash receipts journal assuming the *periodic* inventory system is used.

2. Open the general ledger accounts with balances as shown in Problem 7-1A (do not open a Cost of Goods Sold ledger account). Also open accounts receivable subsidiary ledger accounts for Ty Afton, Debra Kohn, and Pat Orlof. Under the periodic system, an Inventory account exists but is inactive until its balance is updated to the correct inventory balance at year-end. In this problem, the Inventory account remains inactive but must be included to correctly complete the trial balance.

3. Complete parts 3, 4, and 5 of Problem 7-1A using the results of parts 1 and 2 of this problem.

Check Trial balance totals, $462,600

Problem 7-3A
Special journals, subsidiary ledgers, and schedule of accounts payable—perpetual
C4 P1 P2

The April transactions of Moore Company are described in Problem 7-1A.

Required

1. Prepare a general journal, a purchases journal like that in Exhibit 7.9, and a cash disbursements journal like that in Exhibit 7.11. Number all journal pages as page 3. Review the April transactions of Moore Company and enter those transactions that should be journalized in the general journal, the purchases journal, or the cash disbursements journal. Ignore any transactions that should be journalized in a sales journal or cash receipts journal.

2. Open the following general ledger accounts: Cash, Inventory, Office Supplies, Store Supplies, Store Equipment, Accounts Payable, Long-Term Notes Payable, Sales Salaries Expense, and Advertising Expense. Enter the March 31 balances of Cash ($85,000), Inventory ($152,000), Long-Term Notes Payable ($137,000), and B. Moore, Capital ($100,000). Also open accounts payable subsidiary ledger accounts for Hafman Supply, Newt Company, Dann Company, and Cray, Inc.

3. Verify that amounts that should be posted as individual amounts from the journals have been posted. (Such items are immediately posted.) Foot and crossfoot the journals and make the month-end postings.

Check Trial balance totals, $262,360

4. Prepare a trial balance of the general ledger and a schedule of accounts payable.

Problem 7-4A[A]
Special journals, subsidiary ledgers, and schedule of accounts payable—periodic
C4 P2 P3

Refer to Problem 7-1A and assume that Moore Co. uses the periodic inventory system.

Required

1. Prepare a general journal, a purchases journal like that in Exhibit 7A.3, and a cash disbursements journal like that in Exhibit 7A.4. Number all journal pages as page 3. Review the April transactions of Moore Company (Problem 7-1A) and enter those transactions that should be journalized in the general journal, the purchases journal, or the cash disbursements journal. Ignore any transaction that should be journalized in a sales journal or cash receipts journal.
2. Open the following general ledger accounts: Cash, Inventory, Office Supplies, Store Supplies, Store Equipment, Accounts Payable, Long-Term Notes Payable, Purchases, Purchases Returns and Allowances, Purchases Discounts, Sales Salaries Expense, and Advertising Expense. Enter the March 31 balances of Cash ($85,000), Inventory ($152,000), Long-Term Notes Payable ($137,000), and B. Moore, Capital ($100,000). Also open accounts payable subsidiary ledger accounts for Hafman Supply, Newt Company, Dann Company, and Cray, Inc.

Check Trial balance totals, $263,783

3. Complete parts 3 and 4 of Problem 7-3A using the results of parts 1 and 2 of this problem.

Problem 7-5A
Special journals, subsidiary ledgers, trial balance—perpetual
C4 P1 P2

eXcel
mhhe.com/wildFAP19e

Crystal Company completes these transactions and events during March of the current year (terms for all its credit sales are 2/10, n/30).

Mar. 1 Purchased $43,300 of merchandise from Value Industries, invoice dated March 1, terms 2/15, n/30.
2 Sold merchandise on credit to Chao Chu, Invoice No. 854, for $16,000 (cost is $8,050).
3 Purchased $1,300 of office supplies on credit from Glen Company, invoice dated March 3, terms n/10 EOM.
3 Sold merchandise on credit to Lance Wern, Invoice No. 855, for $9,500 (cost is $4,760).
6 Borrowed $72,000 cash from Federal Bank by signing a long-term note payable.
9 Purchased $21,000 of office equipment on credit from Simon Supply, invoice dated March 9, terms n/10 EOM.
10 Sold merchandise on credit to Jovita Altern, Invoice No. 856, for $4,700 (cost is $2,380).
12 Received payment from Chao Chu for the March 2 sale less the discount.
13 Sent Value Industries Check No. 416 in payment of the March 1 invoice less the discount.
13 Received payment from Lance Wern for the March 3 sale less the discount.
14 Purchased $32,200 of merchandise from the AJ Company, invoice dated March 13, terms 2/10, n/30.
15 Issued Check No. 417, payable to Payroll, in payment of sales salaries expense for the first half of the month, $17,700. Cashed the check and paid the employees.
15 Cash sales for the first half of the month are $67,570 (cost is $39,080). (Cash sales are recorded daily, but are recorded only twice here to reduce repetitive entries.)
16 Purchased $1,820 of store supplies on credit from Glen Company, invoice dated March 16, terms n/10 EOM.
17 Received a $2,500 credit memorandum from AJ Company for the return of unsatisfactory merchandise purchased on March 14.
19 Received a $630 credit memorandum from Simon Supply for office equipment received on March 9 and returned for credit.
20 Received payment from Jovita Altern for the sale of March 10 less the discount.
23 Issued Check No. 418 to AJ Company in payment of the invoice of March 13 less the March 17 return and the discount.
27 Sold merchandise on credit to Jovita Altern, Invoice No. 857, for $14,300 (cost is $6,285).
28 Sold merchandise on credit to Lance Wern, Invoice No. 858, for $5,400 (cost is $2,300).

31 Issued Check No. 419, payable to Payroll, in payment of sales salaries expense for the last half of the month, $17,700. Cashed the check and paid the employees.
31 Cash sales for the last half of the month are $77,625 (cost is $40,510).
31 Verify that amounts impacting customer and creditor accounts were posted and that any amounts that should have been posted as individual amounts to the general ledger accounts were posted. Foot and crossfoot the journals and make the month-end postings.

Required

1. Open the following general ledger accounts: Cash; Accounts Receivable; Inventory (March 1 beg. bal. is $50,000); Office Supplies; Store Supplies; Office Equipment; Accounts Payable; Long-Term Notes Payable; Z. Crystal, Capital (March 1 beg. bal. is $50,000); Sales; Sales Discounts; Cost of Goods Sold; and Sales Salaries Expense. Open the following accounts receivable subsidiary ledger accounts: Jovita Altern, Chao Chu, and Lance Wern. Open the following accounts payable subsidiary ledger accounts: Glen Company, Value Industries, Simon Supply, and AJ Company.

2. Enter these transactions in a sales journal like Exhibit 7.5, a purchases journal like Exhibit 7.9, a cash receipts journal like Exhibit 7.7, a cash disbursements journal like Exhibit 7.11, or a general journal. Number all journal pages as page 2.

3. Prepare a trial balance of the general ledger and prove the accuracy of the subsidiary ledgers by preparing schedules of both accounts receivable and accounts payable.

Check Trial balance totals, $340,585

Problem 7-6A^A
Special journals, subsidiary ledgers, trial balance—periodic
C4 P2 P3

excel
mhhe.com/wildFAP19e

Assume that Crystal Company in Problem 7-5A uses the periodic inventory system.

Required

1. Open the following general ledger accounts: Cash; Accounts Receivable; Inventory (March 1 beg. bal. is $50,000); Office Supplies; Store Supplies; Office Equipment; Accounts Payable; Long-Term Notes Payable; Z. Crystal, Capital (March 1 beg. bal. is $50,000); Sales; Sales Discounts; Purchases; Purchases Returns and Allowances; Purchases Discounts; and Sales Salaries Expense. Open the following accounts receivable subsidiary ledger accounts: Jovita Altern, Chao Chu, and Lance Wern. Open the following Accounts Payable subsidiary ledger accounts: Glen Company, Value Industries, Simon Supply, and AJ Company.

2. Enter the transactions from Problem 7-5A in a sales journal like that in Exhibit 7A.1, a purchases journal like that in Exhibit 7A.3, a cash receipts journal like that in Exhibit 7A.2, a cash disbursements journal like that in Exhibit 7A.4, or a general journal. Number journal pages as page 2.

3. Prepare a trial balance of the general ledger and prove the accuracy of the subsidiary ledgers by preparing schedules of both accounts receivable and accounts payable.

Check Trial balance totals, $344,545

For account titles and numbers, use the Chart of Accounts at the end of the book.

PROBLEM SET B

Problem 7-1B
Special journals, subsidiary ledgers, schedule of accounts receivable—perpetual
C4 P1 P2

Burns Industries completes these transactions during July of the current year (the terms of all its credit sales are 2/10, n/30).

July 1 Purchased $15,200 of merchandise on credit from Tryon Company, invoice dated June 30, terms 2/10, n/60.
3 Issued Check No. 300 to *The Weekly* for advertising expense, $890.
5 Sold merchandise on credit to Karen Noyes, Invoice No. 918, for $4,100 (cost is $3,300).
6 Sold merchandise on credit to Meg Azura, Invoice No. 919, for $9,200 (cost is $7,500).
7 Purchased $1,580 of store supplies on credit from Patton, Inc., invoice dated July 7, terms n/10 EOM.
8 Received a $90 credit memorandum from Patton, Inc., for the return of store supplies received on July 7.
9 Purchased $11,155 of store equipment on credit from Cheever Supply, invoice dated July 8, terms n/10 EOM.
10 Issued Check No. 301 to Tryon Company in payment of its June 30 invoice, less the discount.
13 Sold merchandise on credit to Tom Murphy, Invoice No. 920, for $13,600 (cost is $7,100).
14 Sold merchandise on credit to Karen Noyes, Invoice No. 921, for $6,500 (cost is $4,700).

15 Received payment from Karen Noyes for the July 5 sale, less the discount.
15 Issued Check No. 302, payable to Payroll, in payment of sales salaries expense for the first half of the month, \$39,250. Cashed the check and paid employees.
15 Cash sales for the first half of the month are \$59,920 (cost is \$42,900). (Cash sales are recorded daily using data from the cash registers but are recorded only twice in this problem to reduce repetitive entries.)
16 Received payment from Meg Azura for the July 6 sale, less the discount.
17 Purchased \$12,650 of merchandise on credit from Dart Company, invoice dated July 17, terms 2/10, n/30.
20 Purchased \$1,050 of office supplies on credit from Cheever Supply, invoice dated July 19, terms n/10 EOM.
21 Borrowed \$74,000 cash from College Bank by signing a long-term note payable.
23 Received payment from Tom Murphy for the July 13 sale, less the discount.
24 Received payment from Karen Noyes for the July 14 sale, less the discount.
24 Received a \$1,050 credit memorandum from Dart Company for the return of defective merchandise received on July 17.
26 Purchased \$11,635 of merchandise on credit from Tryon Company, invoice dated July 26, terms 2/10, n/60.
27 Issued Check No. 303 to Dart Company in payment of its July 17 invoice, less the return and the discount.
29 Sold merchandise on credit to Meg Azura, Invoice No. 922, for \$3,340 (cost is \$2,580).
30 Sold merchandise on credit to Tom Murphy, Invoice No. 923, for \$6,200 (cost is \$4,480).
31 Issued Check No. 304, payable to Payroll, in payment of the sales salaries expense for the last half of the month, \$39,250.
31 Cash sales for the last half of the month are \$74,200 (cost is \$67,400).

Required

1. Prepare a sales journal like that in Exhibit 7.5 and a cash receipts journal like that in Exhibit 7.7. Number both journals as page 3. Then review the transactions of Burns Industries and enter those transactions that should be journalized in the sales journal and those that should be journalized in the cash receipts journal. Ignore any transactions that should be journalized in a purchases journal, a cash disbursements journal, or a general journal.
2. Open the following general ledger accounts: Cash, Accounts Receivable, Inventory, Long-Term Notes Payable, Cost of Goods Sold, Sales, and Sales Discounts. Enter the June 30 balances for Cash (\$116,000), Inventory (\$150,000), Long-Term Notes Payable (\$166,000), and R. Burns, Capital (\$100,000). Also open accounts receivable subsidiary ledger accounts for Karen Noyes, Tom Murphy, and Meg Azura.
3. Verify that amounts that should be posted as individual amounts from the journals have been posted. (Such items are immediately posted.) Foot and crossfoot the journals and make the month-end postings.
4. Prepare a trial balance of the general ledger and prove the accuracy of the subsidiary ledger by preparing a schedule of accounts receivable.

Check Trial balance totals, \$517,060

Analysis Component

5. Assume that the total for the schedule of Accounts Receivable does not equal the balance of the controlling account in the general ledger. Describe steps you would take to discover the error(s).

Problem 7-2B[A]
Special journals, subsidiary ledgers, and schedule of accounts receivable—periodic
C4 P2 P3

Assume that Burns Industries in Problem 7-1B uses the periodic inventory system.

Required

1. Prepare headings for a sales journal like the one in Exhibit 7A.1. Prepare headings for a cash receipts journal like the one in Exhibit 7A.2. Journalize the July transactions shown in Problem 7-1B that should be recorded in the sales journal and the cash receipts journal assuming the periodic inventory system is used.
2. Open the general ledger accounts with balances as shown in Problem 7-1B (do not open a Cost of Goods Sold ledger account). Also open accounts receivable subsidiary ledger accounts for Meg Azura, Tom Murphy, and Karen Noyes. Under the periodic system, an Inventory account exists but is inactive

until its balance is updated to the correct inventory balance at year-end. In this problem, the Inventory account remains inactive but must be included to correctly complete the trial balance.

3. Complete parts 3, 4, and 5 of Problem 7-1B using the results of parts 1 and 2 of this problem.

Check Trial balance totals, $517,060

Problem 7-3B
Special journals, subsidiary ledgers, and schedule of accounts payable—perpetual
C4 P1 P2

The July transactions of Burns Industries are described in Problem 7-1B.

Required

1. Prepare a general journal, a purchases journal like that in Exhibit 7.9, and a cash disbursements journal like that in Exhibit 7.11. Number all journal pages as page 3. Review the July transactions of Burns Industries and enter those transactions that should be journalized in the general journal, the purchases journal, or the cash disbursements journal. Ignore any transactions that should be journalized in a sales journal or cash receipts journal.

2. Open the following general ledger accounts: Cash, Inventory, Office Supplies, Store Supplies, Store Equipment, Accounts Payable, Long-Term Notes Payable, Sales Salaries Expense, and Advertising Expense. Enter the June 30 balances of Cash ($116,000), Inventory ($150,000), Long-Term Notes Payable ($166,000), and R. Burns, Capital ($100,000). Also open accounts payable subsidiary ledger accounts for Cheever Supply, Tryon Company, Dart Company, and Patton, Inc.

3. Verify that amounts that should be posted as individual amounts from the journals have been posted. (Such items are immediately posted.) Foot and crossfoot the journals and make the month-end postings.

4. Prepare a trial balance of the general ledger and a schedule of accounts payable.

Check Trial balance totals, $291,330

Problem 7-4B[A]
Special journals, subsidiary ledgers, and schedule of accounts payable—periodic
C4 P2 P3

Refer to Problem 7-1B and assume that Burns uses the periodic inventory system.

Required

1. Prepare a general journal, a purchases journal like that in Exhibit 7A.3, and a cash disbursements journal like that in Exhibit 7A.4. Number all journal pages as page 3. Review the July transactions of Burns Company (Problem 7-1B) and enter those transactions that should be journalized in the general journal, the purchases journal, or the cash disbursements journal. Ignore any transaction that should be journalized in a sales journal or cash receipts journal.

2. Open the following general ledger accounts: Cash, Inventory, Office Supplies, Store Supplies, Store Equipment, Accounts Payable, Long-Term Notes Payable, Purchases, Purchases Returns and Allowances, Purchases Discounts, Sales Salaries Expense, and Advertising Expense. Enter the June 30 balances of Cash ($116,000), Inventory ($150,000), Long-Term Notes Payable ($166,000), and R. Burns, Capital ($100,000). Also open accounts payable subsidiary ledger accounts for Tryon Company, Patton, Inc., Cheever Supply, and Dart Company.

3. Complete parts 3 and 4 of Problem 7-3B using the results of parts 1 and 2 of this problem.

Check Trial balance totals, $292,916

Problem 7-5B
Special journals, subsidiary ledgers, trial balance—perpetual
C4 P2 P3

Madison Company completes these transactions during November of the current year (terms for all its credit sales are 2/10, n/30).

Nov. 1 Purchased $1,353 of office equipment on credit from Baxter Supply, invoice dated November 1, terms n/10 EOM.
2 Borrowed $72,000 cash from Wisconsin Bank by signing a long-term note payable.
4 Purchased $45,100 of merchandise from BLR Industries, invoice dated November 3, terms 2/15, n/30.
5 Purchased $21,874 of store supplies on credit from Gorton Company, invoice dated November 5, terms n/10 EOM.
8 Sold merchandise on credit to Cyd Ryan, Invoice No. 439, for $16,500 (cost is $8,340).
10 Sold merchandise on credit to Carlos Mantel, Invoice No. 440, for $9,900 (cost is $4,960).
11 Purchased $33,509 of merchandise from Ling Company, invoice dated November 10, terms 2/10, n/30.

12 Sent BLR Industries Check No. 633 in payment of its November 3 invoice less the discount.
15 Issued Check No. 634, payable to Payroll, in payment of sales salaries expense for the first half of the month, $13,900. Cashed the check and paid the employees.
15 Cash sales for the first half of the month are $174,537 (cost is $144,866). (Cash sales are recorded daily but are recorded only twice in this problem to reduce repetitive entries.)
15 Sold merchandise on credit to Tonya Will, Invoice No. 441, for $4,900 (cost is $2,480).
16 Purchased $1,873 of office supplies on credit from Gorton Company, invoice dated November 16, terms n/10 EOM.
17 Received a $2,659 credit memorandum from Ling Company for the return of unsatisfactory merchandise purchased on November 11.
18 Received payment from Cyd Ryan for the November 8 sale less the discount.
19 Received payment from Carlos Mantel for the November 10 sale less the discount.
19 Issued Check No. 635 to Ling Company in payment of its invoice of November 10 less the return and the discount.
22 Sold merchandise on credit to Carlos Mantel, Invoice No. 442, for $14,800 (cost is $6,540).
24 Sold merchandise on credit to Tonya Will, Invoice No. 443, for $5,600 (cost is $2,420).
25 Received payment from Tonya Will for the sale of November 15 less the discount.
26 Received a $256 credit memorandum from Baxter Supply for the return of office equipment purchased on November 1.
30 Issued Check No. 636, payable to Payroll, in payment of sales salaries expense for the last half of the month, $13,900. Cashed the check and paid the employees.
30 Cash sales for the last half of the month are $185,009 (cost is $111,398).
30 Verify that amounts impacting customer and creditor accounts were posted and that any amounts that should have been posted as individual amounts to the general ledger accounts were posted. Foot and crossfoot the journals and make the month-end postings.

Required

1. Open the following general ledger accounts: Cash; Accounts Receivable; Inventory (November 1 beg. bal. is $300,000); Office Supplies; Store Supplies; Office Equipment; Accounts Payable; Long-Term Notes Payable; O. Madison, Capital (Nov. 1 beg. bal. is $300,000); Sales; Sales Discounts; Cost of Goods Sold; and Sales Salaries Expense. Open the following accounts receivable subsidiary ledger accounts: Carlos Mantel, Tonya Will, and Cyd Ryan. Open the following accounts payable subsidiary ledger accounts: Gorton Company, BLR Industries, Baxter Supply, and Ling Company.
2. Enter these transactions in a sales journal like that in Exhibit 7.5, a purchases journal like that in Exhibit 7.9, a cash receipts journal like that in Exhibit 7.7, a cash disbursements journal like that in Exhibit 7.11, or a general journal. Number all journal pages as page 2.
3. Prepare a trial balance of the general ledger and prove the accuracy of the subsidiary ledgers by preparing schedules of both accounts receivable and accounts payable.

Check Trial balance totals, $808,090

Problem 7-6B[A]
Special journals, subsidiary ledgers, trial balance—periodic
C4 P2 P3

Assume that Madison Company in Problem 7-5B uses the periodic inventory system.

Required

1. Open the following general ledger accounts: Cash; Accounts Receivable; Inventory (November 1 beg. bal. is $300,000); Office Supplies; Store Supplies; Office Equipment; Accounts Payable; Long-Term Notes Payable; O. Madison, Capital (Nov. 1 beg. bal. is $300,000); Sales; Sales Discounts; Purchases; Purchases Returns and Allowances; Purchases Discounts; and Sales Salaries Expense. Open the following accounts receivable subsidiary ledger accounts: Carlos Mantel, Tonya Will, and Cyd Ryan. Open the following accounts payable subsidiary ledger accounts: Gorton Company, BLR Industries, Baxter Supply, and Ling Company.
2. Enter the transactions from Problem 7-5B in a sales journal like that in Exhibit 7A.1, a purchases journal like that in Exhibit 7A.3, a cash receipts journal like that in Exhibit 7A.2, a cash disbursements journal like that in Exhibit 7A.4, or a general journal. Number journal pages as page 2.
3. Prepare a trial balance of the general ledger and prove the accuracy of the subsidiary ledgers by preparing schedules of both accounts receivable and accounts payable.

Check Trial balance totals, $812,268

SERIAL PROBLEM

Success Systems

(This serial problem began in Chapter 1 and continues through most of the book. If previous chapter segments were not completed, the serial problem can begin at this point. It is helpful, but not necessary, to use the Working Papers that accompany the book.)

SP 7 Assume that A. Lopez expands Success Systems' accounting system to include special journals.

Required

1. Locate the transactions related to January through March 2010 for Success Systems in Chapter 5.

2. Enter the Success Systems transactions for January through March in a sales journal like that in Exhibit 7.5 (insert "n/a" in the Invoice column), a cash receipts journal like that in Exhibit 7.7, a purchases journal like that in Exhibit 7.9 (use Computer Supplies heading instead of Office Supplies), and a cash disbursements journal like that in Exhibit 7.11 (insert "n/a" in the Check Number column), or a general journal. Number journal pages as page 2. If the transaction does not specify the name of the payee, state "not specified" in the Payee column of the cash disbursements journal.

3. The transactions on the following dates should be journalized in the general journal: January 5, 11, 20, 24, and 29 (no entry required) and March 24. Do not record and post the adjusting entries for the end of March.

COMPREHENSIVE PROBLEM

Eureka Company

eXcel

mhhe.com/wildFAP19e

(If the Working Papers that accompany this book are not available, omit this comprehensive problem.) Assume it is Monday, May 1, the first business day of the month, and you have just been hired as the accountant for Eureka Company, which operates with monthly accounting periods. All of the company's accounting work is completed through the end of April and its ledgers show April 30 balances. During your first month on the job, the company experiences the following transactions and events (terms for all its credit sales are 2/10, n/30 unless stated differently):

May 1 Issued Check No. 3410 to J&K Management Co. in payment of the May rent, $3,710. (Use two lines to record the transaction. Charge 80% of the rent to Rent Expense—Selling Space and the balance to Rent Expense—Office Space.)

2 Sold merchandise on credit to Bowman Company, Invoice No. 8785, for $6,100 (cost is $4,100).

2 Issued a $175 credit memorandum to Knott Co., for defective (worthless) merchandise sold on April 28 and returned for credit. The total selling price (gross) was $4,725.

3 Received a $798 credit memorandum from Parker Products for the return of merchandise purchased on April 29.

4 Purchased the following on credit from Gates Supply Co.: merchandise, $37,072; store supplies, $574; and office supplies, $83. Invoice dated May 4, terms n/10 EOM.

5 Received payment from Knott Co., for the balance from the April 28 sale less the May 2 return and the discount.

8 Issued Check No. 3411 to Parker Products to pay for the $7,098 of merchandise purchased on April 29 less the May 3 return and a 2% discount.

9 Sold store supplies to the merchant next door at their cost of $350 cash.

10 Purchased $4,074 of office equipment on credit from Gates Supply Co., invoice dated May 10, terms n/10 EOM.

11 Received payment from Bowman Company for the May 2 sale less the discount.

11 Purchased $8,800 of merchandise from Gatsby, Inc., invoice dated May 10, terms 2/10, n/30.

12 Received an $854 credit memorandum from Gates Supply Co. for the return of defective office equipment received on May 10.

15 Issued Check No. 3412, payable to Payroll, in payment of sales salaries, $5,470, and office salaries, $3,000. Cashed the check and paid the employees.

15 Cash sales for the first half of the month are $55,220 (cost is $33,200). (Cash sales are recorded daily but are recorded only twice here to reduce repetitive entries.)

15 Post to the customer and creditor accounts. Also post individual items that are not included in column totals at the end of the month to the general ledger accounts. (Such items are posted daily but are posted only twice each month because they are few in number.)

16 Sold merchandise on credit to Bowman Company, Invoice No. 8786, for $3,990 (cost is $1,890).
17 Purchased $13,650 of merchandise from Joey Corp., invoice dated May 14, terms 2/10, n/60.
19 Issued Check No. 3413 to Gatsby, Inc., in payment of its May 10 invoice less the discount.
22 Sold merchandise to Karim Services, Invoice No. 8787, for $6,850 (cost is $4,990), terms 2/10, n/60.
23 Issued Check No. 3414 to Joey Corp. in payment of its May 14 invoice less the discount.
24 Purchased the following on credit from Gates Supply Co.: merchandise, $8,120; store supplies, $630; and office supplies, $280. Invoice dated May 24, terms n/10 EOM.
25 Purchased $3,080 of merchandise from Parker Products, invoice dated May 23, terms 2/10, n/30.
26 Sold merchandise on credit to Dexter Corp., Invoice No. 8788, for $14,210 (cost is $8,230).
26 Issued Check No. 3415 to Trinity Power in payment of the May electric bill, $1,283.
29 The owner of Eureka Company, Emlyn Eureka, used Check No. 3416 to withdraw $2,000 cash from the business for personal use.
30 Received payment from Karim Services for the May 22 sale less the discount.
30 Issued Check No. 3417, payable to Payroll, in payment of sales salaries, $5,320, and office salaries, $3,150. Cashed the check and paid the employees.
31 Cash sales for the last half of the month are $70,052 (cost is $45,500).
31 Post to the customer and creditor accounts. Also post individual items that are not included in column totals at the end of the month to the general ledger accounts. Foot and crossfoot the journals and make the month-end postings.

Required

1. Enter these transactions in a sales journal, a purchases journal, a cash receipts journal, a cash disbursements journal, or a general journal as illustrated in this chapter (number all journal pages as page 2). Post when instructed to do so. Assume a perpetual inventory system.

Check (2) Unadjusted trial balance totals, $545,020; Adjustments column totals, $2,657

2. Prepare a trial balance in the Trial Balance columns of the work sheet form provided with the working papers. Complete the work sheet using the following information for accounting adjustments.

a. Expired insurance, $403.

b. Ending store supplies inventory, $2,232.

c. Ending office supplies inventory, $504.

d. Depreciation of store equipment, $567.

e. Depreciation of office equipment, $329.

Prepare and post adjusting and closing entries.

(3) Net income, $33,397; Total assets, $392,541

3. Prepare a May 2010 multiple-step income statement, a May 2010 statement of owner's equity, and a May 31, 2010, classified balance sheet.

4. Prepare a post-closing trial balance. Also prove the accuracy of subsidiary ledgers by preparing schedules of both accounts receivable and accounts payable.

BEYOND THE NUMBERS

REPORTING IN ACTION

A1

BTN 7-1 Refer to **Best Buy**'s financial statements in Appendix A to answer the following.

1. Identify the note that reports on Best Buy's business segments.

2. Describe the focus and activities of each of Best Buy's business segments.

Fast Forward

3. Access Best Buy's annual report for fiscal years ending after March 3, 2007, from its Website (BestBuy.com) or the SEC's EDGAR database (www.SEC.gov). Has Best Buy changed its reporting policy regarding segment information? Explain.

BTN 7-2 Key figures for **Best Buy** and **Circuit City** follow ($ millions).

COMPARATIVE ANALYSIS

A1

Best Buy Segment	Current Year Segment Income	Current Year Segment Assets	One Year Prior Segment Income	One Year Prior Segment Assets	Two Years Prior Segment Income	Two Years Prior Segment Assets
Domestic	$1,889	$10,614	$1,588	$9,722	$1,393	$8,372
International	110	2,956	56	2,142	49	1,922

Circuit City Segment	Current Year Segment Income	Current Year Segment Assets	One Year Prior Segment Income	One Year Prior Segment Assets	Two Years Prior Segment Income	Two Years Prior Segment Assets
Domestic	$ 97	$3,658	$155	$3,594	$41	$3,405
International	(107)	350	(7)	475	16	435

Required

1. Compute the segment return on assets for each of the segments of Best Buy and Circuit City for each of the two most recent years shown.
2. Interpret and comment on your results of part 1.

BTN 7-3 Erica Gray, CPA, is a sole practitioner. She has been practicing as an auditor for 10 years. Recently a long-standing audit client asked Gray to design and implement an integrated computer-based accounting information system. The fees associated with this additional engagement with the client are very attractive. However, Gray wonders if she can remain objective on subsequent audits in her evaluation of the client's accounting system and its records if she was responsible for its design and implementation. Gray knows that professional auditing standards require her to remain independent in fact and appearance from her auditing clients.

ETHICS CHALLENGE

C5

Required

1. What do you believe auditing standards are mainly concerned with when they require independence in fact? In appearance?
2. Why is it important that auditors remain independent of their clients?
3. Do you think Gray can accept this engagement and remain independent? Justify your response.

BTN 7-4 Your friend, Wendy Geiger, owns a small retail store that sells candies and nuts. Geiger acquires her goods from a few select vendors. She generally makes purchase orders by phone and on credit. Sales are primarily for cash. Geiger keeps her own manual accounting system using a general journal and a general ledger. At the end of each business day, she records one summary entry for cash sales. Geiger recently began offering items in creative gift packages. This has increased sales substantially, and she is now receiving orders from corporate and other clients who order large quantities and prefer to buy on credit. As a result of increased credit transactions in both purchases and sales, keeping the accounting records has become extremely time consuming. Geiger wants to continue to maintain her own manual system and calls you for advice. Write a memo to her advising how she might modify her current manual accounting system to accommodate the expanded business activities. Geiger is accustomed to checking her ledger by using a trial balance. Your memo should explain the advantages of what you propose and of any other verification techniques you recommend.

COMMUNICATING IN PRACTICE

C3 C4

TAKING IT TO THE NET

A1

BTN 7-5 Access the October 30, 2007, filing of the fiscal 2007 10-K report for **Dell** (ticker DELL) at www.SEC.gov. Read its Note 10 that details Dell's segment information and answer the following.

1. Dell's operations are divided among which three geographic segments?

2. In fiscal year 2007, which geographic segment had the largest dollar amount of operating income? Which had the largest amount of assets?

3. Compute the return on assets for each segment for fiscal year 2007. Use operating income and average total assets by segment for your calculation. Which segment has the highest return on assets?

4. For what product groups does Dell provide segment data? What percent of Dell's net revenue is earned by each product group?

TEAMWORK IN ACTION

C4 P1 P2

BTN 7-6 Each member of the team is to assume responsibility for one of the following tasks:

a. Journalizing in the purchases journal.

b. Journalizing in the cash disbursements journal.

c. Maintaining and verifying the Accounts Payable ledger.

d. Journalizing in the sales journal and the general journal.

e. Journalizing in the cash receipts journal.

f. Maintaining and verifying the Accounts Receivable ledger.

The team should abide by the following procedures in carrying out responsibilities.

Required

1. After tasks *a–f* are assigned, each team member is to quickly read the list of transactions in Problem 7-5A, identifying with initials the journal in which each transaction is to be recorded. Upon completion, the team leader is to read transaction dates, and the appropriate team member is to vocalize responsibility. Any disagreement between teammates must be resolved.

2. Journalize and continually update subsidiary ledgers. Journal recorders should alert teammates assigned to subsidiary ledgers when an entry must be posted to their subsidiary.

3. Team members responsible for tasks *a*, *b*, *d*, and *e* are to summarize and prove journals; members responsible for tasks *c* and *f* are to prepare both payables and receivables schedules.

4. The team leader is to take charge of the general ledger, rotating team members to obtain amounts to be posted. The person responsible for a journal must complete posting references in that journal. Other team members should verify the accuracy of account balance computations. To avoid any abnormal account balances, post in the following order: P, S, G, R, D. (*Note:* Posting any necessary individual general ledger amounts is also done at this time.)

5. The team leader is to read out general ledger account balances while another team member fills in the trial balance form. Concurrently, one member should keep a running balance of debit account balance totals and another credit account balance totals. Verify the final total of the trial balance and the schedules. If necessary, the team must resolve any errors. Turn in the trial balance and schedules to the instructor.

ENTREPRENEURIAL DECISION

P1

BTN 7-7 Refer to the chapter's opening feature about Tom Szaky and his company, **TerraCycle**. His small manufacturing company deals with numerous suppliers and customers.

Required

1. Identify the special journals that TerraCycle would be likely to use in its operations. Also identify any subsidiary ledgers that TerraCycle would likely use.

2. TerraCycle hopes to double yearly sales within five years hence from its current $3 million annual amount. Assume that TerraCycle's sales growth projections are as follows.

Year	One Year Hence	Two Years Hence	Three Years Hence	Four Years Hence	Five Years Hence
Projected growth in sales	0%	20%	15%	25%	20%

Estimate TerraCycle's projected sales for each year (round to the nearest dollar). If this pattern of sales growth holds, will TerraCycle achieve its goal of doubling sales in five years?

GLOBAL DECISION

A1

DSG

BTN 7-8 Access and refer to the April 28, 2007 annual report for **DSG international plc** at www.DSGiplc.com.

Required

1. Identify its Note 2 (Segmental Analysis) to its financial statements and locate its information relating to DSG's geographic segments. Identify those four segments.
2. What financial figures does it disclose for each geographic segment?
3. Does DSG have a dominant segment? Explain.

ANSWERS TO MULTIPLE CHOICE QUIZ

1. a
2. e
3. d
4. b
5. a

A Look Back

Chapter 7 focused on accounting information systems. We explained the principles and components of information systems, the use of special journals and subsidiary ledgers, and technology-based systems.

A Look at This Chapter

This chapter extends our study of accounting to internal control and the analysis of cash. We describe procedures that are good for internal control. We also explain the control of and the accounting for cash, including control features of banking activities.

A Look Ahead

Chapter 9 focuses on receivables. We explain how to account and report on receivables and their related accounts. This includes estimating uncollectible receivables and computing interest earned.

8 Cash and Internal Controls

Chapter

Learning Objectives

CAP

Conceptual

C1 Define internal control and identify its purpose and principles. *(p. 314)*

C2 Define cash and cash equivalents and explain how to report them. *(p. 319)*

C3 Identify control features of banking activities. *(p. 326)*

Analytical

A1 Compute the days' sales uncollected ratio and use it to assess liquidity. *(p. 332)*

Procedural

P1 Apply internal control to cash receipts and disbursements. *(p. 320)*

P2 Explain and record petty cash fund transactions. *(p. 323)*

P3 Prepare a bank reconciliation. *(p. 329)*

P4 *Appendix 8A*—Describe the use of documentation and verification to control cash disbursements. *(p. 335)*

P5 *Appendix 8B—Apply the net method to control purchase discounts. (p. 338)*

LP8

Decision Feature

Sweet Success

"It's a creative outlet for me . . . it doesn't feel like work"—Dylan Lauren (Jeff Rubin on left)

NEW YORK—A 10-foot chocolate bunny named Jeffrey greets you as you enter the store—that should be warning enough! This elite designer candy store, christened **Dylan's Candy Bar (DylansCandyBar.com),** is the brainchild of co-founders Dylan Lauren and Jeff Rubin (the bunny is named for him). This sweet-lovers heaven offers more than 5,000 different choices of sweets from all over the world. It has become a hip hangout for locals and tourists—and it has made candy cool. Says Lauren, "Park Avenue women come in, and the first thing they ask for is Gummi bears. They love that it's very childhood, nostalgic."

Although marketing is an important part of its success, Lauren and Rubin's management of internal controls and cash is equally impressive. Several control procedures monitor its business activities and safeguard its assets. An example is the biometric time and attendance control system using fingerprint characteristics. Says Rubin, "There's no fooling the system! It is going to help us remotely manage our employees while eliminating human error and dishonesty. [It] is a cost-effective and important business management tool." Similar controls are applied throughout the store. Rubin asserts that such controls raise productivity and cut expenses.

The store's cash management practices are equally impressive, including controls over cash receipts, disbursements, and petty cash. The use of bank reconciliations further helps with the store's control and management of cash.

Internal controls are crucial when on a busy day its store brings in more than a thousand customers, and their cash. Moreover, expansion is already underway in Orlando and Houston. Through it all, Lauren says it is "totally fun."

[Sources: *Dylan's Candy Bar Website,* January 2009; *Entrepreneur,* June 2005; *USA Today,* October 26, 2001; *Duke Magazine,* January–February 2004; *CNN.com,* November 2005; *CandyAddict.com,* June 2007]

We all are aware of theft and fraud. They affect us in several ways: We lock doors, chain bikes, review sales receipts, and acquire alarm systems. A company also takes actions to safeguard, control, and manage what it owns. Experience tells us that small companies are most vulnerable, usually due to weak internal controls. It is management's responsibility to set up policies and procedures to safeguard a company's assets, especially cash. To do so, management *and* employees must understand and apply principles of internal control. This chapter describes these principles and how to apply them. It focuses special attention on cash because it is easily transferable and is often at high risk of loss.

Cash and Internal Controls

Internal Control
- Purpose of controls
- Principles of controls
- Technology and controls
- Limitations of controls

Control of Cash
- Cash, cash equivalents, and liquidity
- Control of receipts
- Control of disbursements

Banking Activities as Controls
- Basic bank services
- Bank statement
- Bank reconciliation

Internal Control

This section describes internal control and its fundamental principles. We also discuss the impact of technology on internal control and the limitations of control procedures.

Purpose of Internal Control

C1 Define internal control and identify its purpose and principles.

Managers (or owners) of small businesses often control the entire operation. These managers usually purchase all assets, hire and manage employees, negotiate all contracts, and sign all checks. They know from personal contact and observation whether the business is actually receiving the assets and services paid for. Most companies, however, cannot maintain this close personal supervision. They must delegate responsibilities and rely on formal procedures rather than personal contact in controlling business activities.

Managers use an internal control system to monitor and control business activities. An **internal control system** consists of the policies and procedures managers use to

- Protect assets.
- Ensure reliable accounting.
- Promote efficient operations.
- Urge adherence to company policies.

Video8.1

A properly designed internal control system is a key part of systems design, analysis, and performance. Managers place a high priority on internal control systems because they can prevent avoidable losses, help managers plan operations, and monitor company and employee performance. Internal controls do not provide guarantees, but they lower the company's risk of loss.

The **Sarbanes-Oxley Act (SOX)** requires the managers and auditors of companies whose stock is traded on an exchange (called *public companies*) to document and certify the system of internal controls. Following are some of the specific requirements:

- Auditors must evaluate internal controls and issue an internal control report.
- Auditors of a client are restricted as to what consulting services they can provide that client.
- The person leading an audit can serve no more than seven years without a two-year break.
- Auditors' work is overseen by the *Public Company Accounting Oversight Board* (PCAOB).
- Harsh penalties exist for violators—sentences up to 25 years in prison with severe fines.

SOX has markedly impacted companies, and the costs of its implementation are high. The benefits include greater confidence in accounting systems and their related reports. However, the public continues to debate the costs versus the benefits of SOX as nearly all business activities of these companies are impacted by SOX.

Principles of Internal Control

Internal control policies and procedures vary from company to company according to such factors as the nature of the business and its size. Certain fundamental internal control principles apply to all companies. The **principles of internal control** are to

1. Establish responsibilities.
2. Maintain adequate records.
3. Insure assets and bond key employees.
4. Separate recordkeeping from custody of assets.
5. Divide responsibility for related transactions.
6. Apply technological controls.
7. Perform regular and independent reviews.

Point: Sarbanes-Oxley Act (SOX) requires that each annual report contain an *internal control report,* which must: (1) state managers' responsibility for establishing and maintaining adequate internal controls for financial reporting; and (2) assess the effectiveness of those controls.

This section explains these seven principles and describes how internal control procedures minimize the risk of fraud and theft. These procedures also increase the reliability and accuracy of accounting records.

Establish Responsibilities Proper internal control means that responsibility for a task is clearly established and assigned to one person. When a problem occurs in a company where responsibility is not identified, determining who is at fault is difficult. For instance, if two salesclerks share the same cash register and there is a cash shortage, neither clerk can be held accountable. To prevent this problem, one clerk might be given responsibility for handling all cash sales. Alternately, a company can use a register with separate cash drawers for each clerk. Most of us have waited at a retail counter during a shift change while employees swap cash drawers.

Point: Many companies have a mandatory vacation policy for employees who handle cash. When another employee must cover for the one on vacation, it is more difficult to hide cash frauds.

Maintain Adequate Records Good recordkeeping is part of an internal control system. It helps protect assets and ensures that employees use prescribed procedures. Reliable records are also a source of information that managers use to monitor company activities. When detailed records of equipment are kept, for instance, items are unlikely to be lost or stolen without detection. Similarly, transactions are less likely to be entered in wrong accounts if a chart of accounts is set up and carefully used. Many preprinted forms and internal documents are also designed for use in a good internal control system. When sales slips are properly designed, for instance, sales personnel can record needed information efficiently with less chance of errors or delays to customers. When sales slips are prenumbered and controlled, each one issued is the responsibility of one salesperson, preventing the salesperson from pocketing cash by making a sale and destroying the sales slip. Computerized point-of-sale systems achieve the same control results.

Insure Assets and Bond Key Employees Good internal control means that assets are adequately insured against casualty and that employees handling large amounts of cash and easily transferable assets are bonded. An employee is *bonded* when a company purchases an insurance policy, or a bond, against losses from theft by that employee. Bonding reduces the risk of loss. It also discourages theft because bonded employees know an independent bonding company will be involved when theft is uncovered and is unlikely to be sympathetic with an employee involved in theft.

Point: The Association of Certified Fraud Examiners (cfenet.com) estimates that employee fraud costs small companies more than $100,000 per incident.

Decision Insight

Tag Control A novel technique exists for marking physical assets. It involves embedding a less than one-inch-square tag of fibers that creates a unique optical signature recordable by scanners. Manufacturers hope to embed tags in everything from compact discs and credit cards to designer clothes for purposes of internal control and efficiency.

Separate Recordkeeping from Custody of Assets A person who controls or has access to an asset must not keep that asset's accounting records. This principle reduces the risk of theft or waste of an asset because the person with control over it knows that another person keeps its records. Also, a recordkeeper who does not have access to the asset has no reason to falsify records. This means that to steal an asset and hide the theft from the records, two or more people must *collude*—or agree in secret to commit the fraud.

Divide Responsibility for Related Transactions Good internal control divides responsibility for a transaction or a series of related transactions between two or more individuals or departments. This is to ensure that the work of one individual acts as a check on the other. This principle, often called *separation of duties,* is not a call for duplication of work. Each employee or department should perform unduplicated effort. Examples of transactions with divided responsibility are placing purchase orders, receiving merchandise, and paying vendors. These tasks should not be given to one individual or department. Assigning responsibility for two or more of these tasks to one party increases mistakes and perhaps fraud. Having an independent person, for example, check incoming goods for quality and quantity encourages more care and attention to detail than having the person who placed the order do the checking. Added protection can result from identifying a third person to approve payment of the invoice. A company can even designate a fourth person with authority to write checks as another protective measure.

Point: There's a new security device—a person's ECG (electrocardiogram) reading—that is as unique as a fingerprint and a lot harder to lose or steal than a PIN. ECGs can be read through fingertip touches. An ECG also shows that a living person is actually there, whereas fingerprint and facial recognition software can be fooled.

Apply Technological Controls Cash registers, check protectors, time clocks, and personal identification scanners are examples of devices that can improve internal control. Technology often improves the effectiveness of controls. A cash register with a locked-in tape or electronic file makes a record of each cash sale. A check protector perforates the amount of a check into its face and makes it difficult to alter the amount. A time clock registers the exact time an employee both arrives at and departs from the job. Mechanical change and currency counters quickly and accurately count amounts, and personal scanners limit access to only authorized individuals. Each of these and other technological controls are an effective part of many internal control systems.

Decision Insight

About Face Face-recognition software snaps a digital picture of the face and converts key facial features—say, the distance between the eyes—into a series of numerical values. These can be stored on an ID or ATM card as a simple bar code to prohibit unauthorized access.

Perform Regular and Independent Reviews Changes in personnel, stress of time pressures, and technological advances present opportunities for shortcuts and lapses. To counter these factors, regular reviews of internal control systems are needed to ensure that procedures are followed. These reviews are preferably done by internal auditors not directly involved in the activities. Their impartial perspective encourages an evaluation of the efficiency as well as the effectiveness of the internal control system. Many companies also pay for audits by independent, external auditors. These external auditors test the company's financial records to give an opinion as to whether its financial statements are presented fairly. Before external auditors decide on how much testing is needed, they evaluate the effectiveness of the internal control system. This evaluation is often helpful to a client.

Decision Maker

Entrepreneur As owner of a start-up information services company, you hire a systems analyst. One of her first recommendations is to require all employees to take at least one week of vacation per year. Why would she recommend a "forced vacation" policy? [Answer—p. 340]

Technology and Internal Control

Point: Information on Internet fraud can be found at these Websites:
sec.gov/investor/pubs/cyberfraud.htm
ftc.gov/bcp/consumer.shtm
www.fraud.org

The fundamental principles of internal control are relevant no matter what the technological state of the accounting system, from purely manual to fully automated systems. Technology impacts an internal control system in several important ways. Perhaps the most obvious is that technology allows us quicker access to databases and information. Used effectively, technology greatly improves managers' abilities to monitor and control business activities. This section describes some technological impacts we must be alert to.

Reduced Processing Errors Technologically advanced systems reduce the number of errors in processing information. Provided the software and data entry are correct, the risk of mechanical and mathematical errors is nearly eliminated. However, we must remember that erroneous software or data entry does exist. Also, less human involvement in data processing can cause data entry errors to go undiscovered. Moreover, errors in software can produce consistent but erroneous processing of transactions. Continually checking and monitoring all types of systems are important.

Point: Evidence of any internal control failure for a company reduces user confidence in its financial statements.

More Extensive Testing of Records A company's review and audit of electronic records can include more extensive testing when information is easily and rapidly accessed. When accounting records are kept manually, auditors and others likely select only small samples of data to test. When data are accessible with computer technology, however, auditors can quickly analyze large samples or even the entire database.

Limited Evidence of Processing Many data processing steps are increasingly done by computer. Accordingly, fewer hard-copy items of documentary evidence are available for review. Yet technologically advanced systems can provide new evidence. They can, for instance, record who made the entries, the date and time, the source of the entry, and so on. Technology can also be designed to require the use of passwords or other identification before access to the system is granted. This means that internal control depends more on the design and operation of the information system and less on the analysis of its resulting documents.

Point: We look to several sources when assessing a company's internal controls. Sources include the auditor's report, management report on controls (if available), management discussion and analysis, and financial press.

Crucial Separation of Duties Technological advances in accounting information systems often yield some job eliminations or consolidations. While those who remain have the special skills necessary to operate advanced programs and equipment, a company with a reduced workforce risks losing its crucial separation of duties. The company must establish ways to control and monitor employees to minimize risk of error and fraud. For instance, the person who designs and programs the information system must not be the one who operates it. The company must also separate control over programs and files from the activities related to cash receipts and disbursements. For instance, a computer operator should not control checkwriting activities. Achieving acceptable separation of duties can be especially difficult and costly in small companies with few employees.

Increased E-Commerce Technology has encouraged the growth of e-commerce. **Amazon.com** and **eBay** are examples of companies that have successfully exploited e-commerce. Most companies have some e-commerce transactions. All such transactions involve at least three risks. (1) *Credit card number theft* is a risk of using, transmitting, and storing such data online. This increases the cost of e-commerce. (2) *Computer viruses* are malicious programs that attach themselves to innocent files for purposes of infecting and harming other files and programs. (3) *Impersonation* online can result in charges of sales to bogus accounts, purchases of inappropriate materials, and the unknowing giving up of confidential information to hackers. Companies use both firewalls and encryption to combat some of these risks—firewalls are points of entry to a system that require passwords to continue, and encryption is a mathematical process to rearrange contents that cannot be read without the process code. Nearly 5% of Americans already report being victims of identity theft, and roughly 10 million say their privacy has been compromised.

"Worst case of identity theft I've ever seen!"

Decision Insight

Cheery Fraud Victim Certified Fraud Examiners Website reports the following: Andrew Cameron stole Jacqueline Boanson's credit card. Cameron headed to the racetrack and promptly charged two bets for $150 on the credit card—winning $400. Unfortunately for Cameron the racetrack refused to pay him cash as its internal control policy is to credit winnings from bets made on a credit card to that same card. Cameron was later nabbed; and the racetrack let Ms. Boanson keep the winnings.

Limitations of Internal Control

All internal control policies and procedures have limitations that usually arise from either (1) the human element or (2) the cost–benefit principle.

Internal control policies and procedures are applied by people. This human element creates several potential limitations that we can categorize as either (1) human error or (2) human fraud. *Human error* can occur from negligence, fatigue, misjudgment, or confusion. *Human fraud* involves intent by people to defeat internal controls, such as *management override,* for personal gain. Fraud also includes collusion to thwart the separation of duties. The human element highlights the importance of establishing an *internal control environment* to convey management's commitment to internal control policies and procedures.

The second major limitation on internal control is the *cost–benefit principle,* which dictates that the costs of internal controls must not exceed their benefits. Analysis of costs and benefits must consider all factors, including the impact on morale. Most companies, for instance, have a legal right to read employees' e-mails, yet companies seldom exercise that right unless they are confronted with evidence of potential harm to the company. The same holds for drug testing, phone tapping, and hidden cameras. The bottom line is that managers must establish internal control policies and procedures with a net benefit to the company.

Point: Cybercrime.gov pursues computer and intellectual property crimes, including that of e-commerce.

Hacker's Guide to Cyberspace

Hacker's Guide to Cyberspace

Pharming Viruses attached to e-mails and Websites load software onto your PC that monitors keystrokes; when you sign on to financial Websites, it steals your passwords.

Phishing Hackers send e-mails to you posing as banks; you are asked for information using fake Websites where they reel in your passwords and personal data.

WI-Phishing Cybercrooks set up wireless networks hoping you use them to connect to the Web; your passwords and data are stolen as you use their network.

Bot-Networking Hackers send remote-control programs to your PC that take control to send out spam and viruses; they even rent your bot to other cybercrooks.

Typo-Squatting Hackers set up Websites with addresses similar to legit outfits; when you make a typo and hit their sites, they infect your PC with viruses or take them over as bots.

Quick Check

Answers—p. 340

1. Principles of internal control suggest that (choose one): (*a*) Responsibility for a series of related transactions (such as placing orders, receiving and paying for merchandise) should be assigned to one employee; (*b*) Responsibility for individual tasks should be shared by more than one employee so that one serves as a check on the other; or (*c*) Employees who handle considerable cash and easily transferable assets should be bonded.
2. What are some impacts of computing technology on internal control?

Control of Cash

Cash is a necessary asset of every company. Most companies also own *cash equivalents* (defined below), which are assets similar to cash. Cash and cash equivalents are the most liquid of all assets and are easily hidden and moved. An effective system of internal controls protects these assets and it should meet three basic guidelines:

Video8.1

1. Handling cash is separate from recordkeeping of cash.
2. Cash receipts are promptly deposited in a bank.
3. Cash disbursements are made by check.

The first guideline applies separation of duties to minimize errors and fraud. When duties are separated, two or more people must collude to steal cash and conceal this action in the accounting records. The second guideline uses immediate (say, daily) deposits of all cash receipts to produce a timely independent record of the cash received. It also reduces the likelihood of cash theft (or loss) and the risk that an employee could personally use the money before depositing it. The third guideline uses payments by check to develop an independent bank record of cash disbursements. This guideline also reduces the risk of cash theft (or loss).

This section begins with definitions of cash and cash equivalents. Discussion then focuses on controls and accounting for both cash receipts and disbursements. The exact procedures used to achieve control over cash vary across companies. They depend on factors such as company size, number of employees, volume of cash transactions, and sources of cash.

Cash, Cash Equivalents, and Liquidity

C2 Define cash and cash equivalents and explain how to report them.

Good accounting systems help in managing the amount of cash and controlling who has access to it. Cash is the usual means of payment when paying for assets, services, or liabilities. **Liquidity** refers to a company's ability to pay for its near-term obligations. Cash and similar assets are called **liquid assets** because they can be readily used to settle such obligations. A company needs liquid assets to effectively operate.

Cash includes currency and coins along with the amounts on deposit in bank accounts, checking accounts (called *demand deposits*), and many savings accounts (called *time deposits*). Cash also includes items that are acceptable for deposit in these accounts such as customer checks, cashier checks, certified checks, and money orders. **Cash equivalents** are short-term, highly liquid investment assets meeting two criteria: (1) readily convertible to a known cash amount and (2) sufficiently close to their due date so that their market value is not sensitive to interest rate changes. Only investments purchased within three months of their due date usually satisfy these criteria. Examples of cash equivalents are short-term investments in assets such as U.S. Treasury bills and money market funds. To increase their return, many companies invest idle cash in cash equivalents. Most companies combine cash equivalents with cash as a single item on the balance sheet.

Point: The most liquid assets are usually reported first on a balance sheet; the least liquid assets are reported last.

Point: **Google** reports cash and cash equivalents of $3,544 million in its balance sheet. This amount makes up nearly 20% of its total assets.

Cash Management

When companies fail, one of the most common causes is their inability to manage cash. Companies must plan both cash receipts and cash payments. The goals of cash management are twofold:

1. Plan cash receipts to meet cash payments when due.
2. Keep a minimum level of cash necessary to operate.

The *treasurer* of the company is responsible for cash management. Effective cash management involves applying the following cash management principles.

- **Encourage collection of receivables.** The more quickly customers and others pay the company, the more quickly that company can use the money. Some companies have cash-only sales policies. Others might offer discounts for payments received early.
- **Delay payment of liabilities.** The more delayed a company is in paying others, the more time it has to use the money. Some companies regularly wait until the last possible day required to pay its bills—although, a company must take care not to hurt its credit standing.
- **Keep only necessary levels of assets.** The less money tied up in idle assets, the more money to invest in productive assets. Some companies maintain *just-in-time* inventory; meaning they plan inventory to be available at the same time orders are filled. Others might lease out excess warehouse space or rent equipment instead of buying it.
- **Plan expenditures.** Money should be spent only when it is available. Companies must look at seasonal and business cycles to plan expenditures.
- **Invest excess cash.** Excess cash earns no return and should be invested. Excess cash from seasonal cycles can be placed in a bank account or other short-term investment for income. Excess cash beyond what's needed for regular business should be invested in productive assets like factories and inventories.

Decision Insight

Days' Cash Expense Coverage The ratio of *cash (and cash equivalents)* to *average daily cash expenses* indicates the number of days a company can operate without additional cash inflows. It reflects on company liquidity and on the potential of excess cash.

Control of Cash Receipts

P1 Apply internal control to cash receipts and disbursements.

Internal control of cash receipts ensures that cash received is properly recorded and deposited. Cash receipts can arise from transactions such as cash sales, collections of customer accounts, receipts of interest earned, bank loans, sales of assets, and owner investments. This section explains internal control over two important types of cash receipts: over-the-counter and by mail.

Over-the-Counter Cash Receipts For purposes of internal control, over-the-counter cash receipts from sales should be recorded on a cash register at the time of each sale. To help ensure that correct amounts are entered, each register should be located so customers can read the amounts entered. Clerks also should be required to enter each sale before wrapping merchandise and to give the customer a receipt for each sale. The design of each cash register should provide a permanent, locked-in record of each transaction. In many systems, the register is directly linked with computing and accounting services. Less advanced registers simply print a record of each transaction on a paper tape or electronic file locked inside the register.

Proper internal control prescribes that custody over cash should be separate from its recordkeeping. For over-the-counter cash receipts, this separation begins with the cash sale. The clerk who has access to cash in the register should not have access to its locked-in record. At the end of the clerk's work period, the clerk should count the cash in the register, record the amount, and turn over the cash and a record of its amount to the company cashier. The cashier, like the clerk, has access to the cash but should not have access to accounting records (or the register tape or file). A third employee, often a supervisor, compares the record of total register transactions (or the register tape or file) with the cash receipts reported by the cashier. This record is the basis for a journal entry recording over-the-counter cash receipts. The third employee has access to the records for cash but not to the actual cash. The clerk and the cashier have access to cash but not to the accounting records. None of them can make a mistake or divert cash without the difference being revealed—see the following diagram.

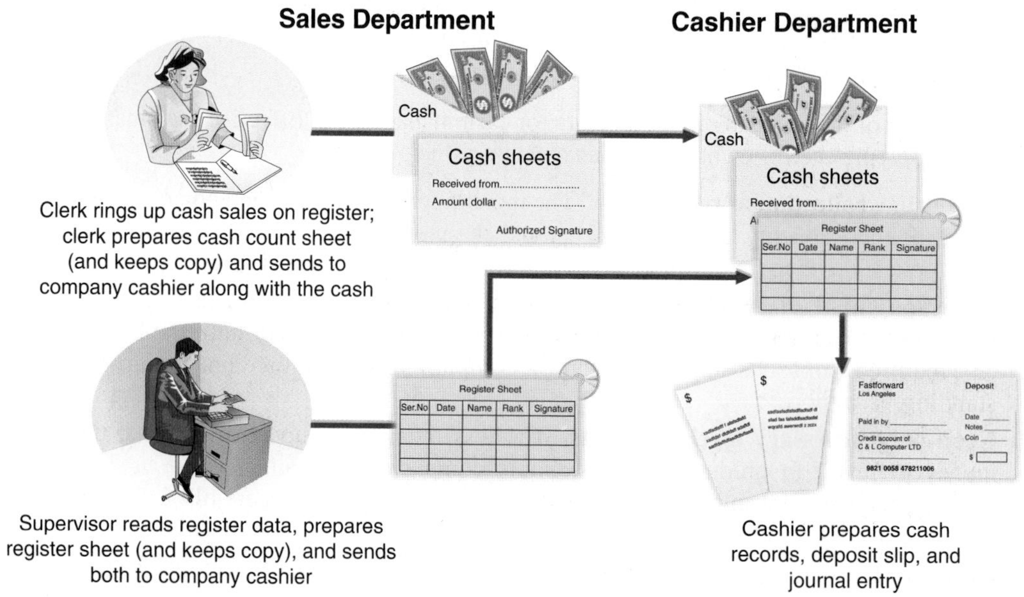

Point: Retailers often require cashiers to restrictively endorse checks immediately on receipt by stamping them "For deposit only."

Cash over and short. Sometimes errors in making change are discovered from differences between the cash in a cash register and the record of the amount of cash receipts. Although a clerk is careful, one or more customers can be given too much or too little change. This means that at the end of a work period, the cash in a cash register might not equal the record of cash receipts. This difference is reported in the **Cash Over and Short** account, also called *Cash Short and Over,* which is an income statement account recording the income effects of cash overages and cash shortages. To illustrate, if a cash register's record shows $550 but the count of cash in the register is $555, the entry to record cash sales and its overage is

Cash	555	
Cash Over and Short		5
Sales		550
To record cash sales and a cash overage.		

Assets = Liabilities + Equity
+555 + 5
+550

On the other hand, if a cash register's record shows $625 but the count of cash in the register is $621, the entry to record cash sales and its shortage is

Cash	621	
Cash Over and Short	4	
Sales		625
To record cash sales and a cash shortage.		

Assets = Liabilities + Equity
+621 − 4
+625

Since customers are more likely to dispute being shortchanged than being given too much change, the Cash Over and Short account usually has a debit balance at the end of an accounting period. A debit balance reflects an expense. It is reported on the income statement as part of general and administrative expenses. (Since the amount is usually small, it is often combined with other small expenses and reported as part of *miscellaneous expenses*—or as part of *miscellaneous revenues* if it has a credit balance.)

Point: Merchants begin a business day with a *change fund* in their cash register. The accounting for a change fund is similar to that for petty cash, including that for cash shortages or overages.

Cash Receipts by Mail Control of cash receipts that arrive through the mail starts with the person who opens the mail. Preferably, two people are assigned the task of, and are present for, opening the mail. In this case, theft of cash receipts by mail requires collusion between these two employees. Specifically, the person(s) opening the mail enters a list (in triplicate) of money received. This list should contain a record of each sender's name, the amount, and an explanation of why the money is sent. The first copy is sent with the money to the cashier. A second copy is sent to the recordkeeper in the accounting area. A third copy is kept by the clerk(s) who opened the mail. The cashier deposits the money in a bank, and the recordkeeper records the amounts received in the accounting records.

Point: Collusion implies that two or more individuals are knowledgeable or involved with the activities of the other(s).

This process reflects good internal control. That is, when the bank balance is reconciled by another person (explained later in the chapter), errors or acts of fraud by the mail clerks, the cashier, or the recordkeeper are revealed. They are revealed because the bank's record of cash deposited must agree with the records from each of the three. Moreover, if the mail clerks do not report all receipts correctly, customers will question their account balances. If the cashier does not deposit all receipts, the bank balance does not agree with the recordkeeper's cash balance. The recordkeeper and the person who reconciles the bank balance do not have access to cash and therefore have no opportunity to divert cash to themselves. This system makes errors and fraud highly unlikely. The exception is employee collusion.

Decision Insight

Perpetual Accounting Wal-Mart uses a network of information links with its point-of-sale cash registers to coordinate sales, purchases, and distribution. Its supercenters, for instance, ring up 15,000 separate sales on heavy days. By using cash register information, the company can fix pricing mistakes quickly and capitalize on sales trends.

Point: A petty cash fund is used only for business expenses.

When each cash disbursement is made, the person receiving payment should sign a prenumbered *petty cash receipt,* also called *petty cash ticket*—see Exhibit 8.2. The petty cash receipt is then placed in the petty cashbox with the remaining money. Under this system, the sum of all receipts plus the remaining cash equals the total fund amount. A $100 petty cash fund, for instance, contains any combination of cash and petty cash receipts that totals $100 (examples are $80 cash plus $20 in receipts, or $10 cash plus $90 in receipts). Each disbursement reduces cash and increases the amount of receipts in the petty cashbox.

EXHIBIT 8.2

Petty Cash Receipt

Z-Mart No. 9
PETTY CASH RECEIPT
For Freight charges
Date November 5, 2009
Charge to Merchandise Inventory
Amount $6.75
Approved by
Received by

Point: Petty cash receipts with either no signature or a forged signature usually indicate misuse of petty cash. Companies respond with surprise petty cash counts for verification.

The petty cash fund should be reimbursed when it is nearing zero and at the end of an accounting period when financial statements are prepared. For this purpose, the petty cashier sorts the paid receipts by the type of expense or account and then totals the receipts. The petty cashier presents all paid receipts to the company cashier, who stamps all receipts *paid* so they cannot be reused, files them for recordkeeping, and gives the petty cashier a check for their sum. When this check is cashed and the money placed in the cashbox, the total money in the cashbox is restored to its original amount. The fund is now ready for a new cycle of petty cash payments.

Illustrating a petty cash fund. To illustrate, assume Z-Mart establishes a petty cash fund on November 1 and designates one of its office employees as the petty cashier. A $75 check is drawn, cashed, and the proceeds given to the petty cashier. The entry to record the setup of this petty cash fund is

Assets = Liabilities + Equity
+75
−75

Nov. 1	Petty Cash.	75	
	Cash		75
	To establish a petty cash fund.		

Point: Reducing or eliminating a petty cash fund requires a credit to Petty Cash.

Point: Although *individual* petty cash disbursements are not evidenced by a check, the initial petty cash fund is evidenced by a check, and later petty cash expenditures are evidenced by a check to replenish them *in total.*

After the petty cash fund is established, the Petty Cash account is not debited or credited again unless the amount of the fund is changed. (A fund should be increased if it requires reimbursement too frequently. On the other hand, if the fund is too large, some of its money should be redeposited in the Cash account.)

Next, assume that Z-Mart's petty cashier makes several November payments from petty cash. Each person who received payment is required to sign a receipt. On November 27, after making a $26.50 cash payment for tile cleaning, only $3.70 cash remains in the fund. The petty cashier then summarizes and totals the petty cash receipts as shown in Exhibit 8.3.

EXHIBIT 8.3

Petty Cash Payments Report

Z-MART
Petty Cash Payments Report

Miscellaneous Expenses			
Nov. 2	Cleaning of LCD panels	$20.00	
Nov. 27	Tile cleaning	26.50	$ 46.50
Merchandise Inventory (transportation-in)			
Nov. 5	Transport of merchandise purchased	6.75	
Nov. 20	Transport of merchandise purchased	8.30	15.05
Delivery Expense			
Nov. 18	Customer's package delivered		5.00
Office Supplies Expense			
Nov. 15	Purchase of office supplies immediately used		4.75
Total			**$71.30**

Point: This report can also include receipt number and names of those who approved and received cash payment (see Demo Problem 2).

to accumulate information to control cash disbursements and to ensure that a transaction is properly recorded. This specific example begins with a *purchase requisition* and concludes with a *check* drawn against cash. Appendix 8A describes the documentation and verification necessary for a voucher system of control. It also describes the internal control objective served by each document.

A voucher system should be applied not only to purchases of inventory but to all expenditures. To illustrate, when a company receives a monthly telephone bill, it should review and verify the charges, prepare a voucher (file), and insert the bill. This transaction is then recorded with a journal entry. If the amount is currently due, a check is issued. If not, the voucher is filed for payment on its due date. If no voucher is prepared, verifying the invoice and its amount after several days or weeks can be difficult. Also, without records, a dishonest employee could collude with a dishonest supplier to get more than one payment for an obligation, payment for excessive amounts, or payment for goods and services not received. An effective voucher system helps prevent such frauds.

Point: A *voucher* is an internal document (or file).

Point: The basic purposes of paper and electronic documents are similar. However, the internal control system must change to reflect different risks, including confidential and competitive-sensitive information that is at greater risk in electronic systems.

Decision Insight

Cyber Setup The FTC is on the cutting edge of cybersleuthing. Opportunists in search of easy money are lured to WeMarket4U.net/netops. Take the bait and you get warned—and possibly targeted. The top 4 fraud complaints as compiled by the Internet Crime Complaint Center are shown to the right.

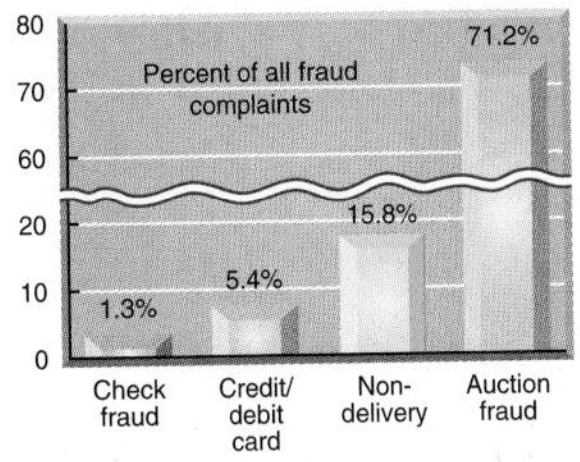

Quick Check

Answers—p. 340

3. Why must a company hold liquid assets?
4. Why does a company hold cash equivalent assets in addition to cash?
5. Identify at least two assets that are classified as cash equivalents.
6. Good internal control procedures for cash include which of the following? (*a*) All cash disbursements, other than those for very small amounts, are made by check; (*b*) One employee counts cash received from sales and promptly deposits cash receipts; or (*c*) Cash receipts by mail are opened by one employee who is then responsible for recording and depositing them.
7. Should all companies require a voucher system? At what point in a company's growth would you recommend a voucher system?

P2 Explain and record petty cash fund transactions.

Petty Cash System of Control A basic principle for controlling cash disbursements is that all payments must be made by check. An exception to this rule is made for *petty cash disbursements,* which are the small payments required for items such as postage, courier fees, minor repairs, and low-cost supplies. To avoid the time and cost of writing checks for small amounts, a company sets up a petty cash fund to make small payments. (**Petty cash** activities are part of an *imprest system,* which designates advance money to establish the fund, to withdraw from the fund, and to reimburse the fund.)

Operating a petty cash fund. Establishing a petty cash fund requires estimating the total amount of small payments likely to be made during a short period such as a week or month. A check is then drawn by the company cashier for an amount slightly in excess of this estimate. This check is recorded with a debit to the Petty Cash account (an asset) and a credit to Cash. The check is cashed, and the currency is given to an employee designated as the *petty cashier* or *petty cash custodian*. The petty cashier is responsible for keeping this cash safe, making payments from the fund, and keeping records of it in a secure place referred to as the *petty cashbox.*

Point: A petty cash fund is used only for business expenses.

When each cash disbursement is made, the person receiving payment should sign a prenumbered *petty cash receipt,* also called *petty cash ticket*—see Exhibit 8.2. The petty cash receipt is then placed in the petty cashbox with the remaining money. Under this system, the sum of all receipts plus the remaining cash equals the total fund amount. A $100 petty cash fund, for instance, contains any combination of cash and petty cash receipts that totals $100 (examples are $80 cash plus $20 in receipts, or $10 cash plus $90 in receipts). Each disbursement reduces cash and increases the amount of receipts in the petty cashbox.

EXHIBIT 8.2

Petty Cash Receipt

Z-Mart No. 9
PETTY CASH RECEIPT
For Freight charges
Date November 5, 2009
Charge to Merchandise Inventory
Amount $6.75
Approved by
Received by

Point: Petty cash receipts with either no signature or a forged signature usually indicate misuse of petty cash. Companies respond with surprise petty cash counts for verification.

The petty cash fund should be reimbursed when it is nearing zero and at the end of an accounting period when financial statements are prepared. For this purpose, the petty cashier sorts the paid receipts by the type of expense or account and then totals the receipts. The petty cashier presents all paid receipts to the company cashier, who stamps all receipts *paid* so they cannot be reused, files them for recordkeeping, and gives the petty cashier a check for their sum. When this check is cashed and the money placed in the cashbox, the total money in the cashbox is restored to its original amount. The fund is now ready for a new cycle of petty cash payments.

Illustrating a petty cash fund. To illustrate, assume Z-Mart establishes a petty cash fund on November 1 and designates one of its office employees as the petty cashier. A $75 check is drawn, cashed, and the proceeds given to the petty cashier. The entry to record the setup of this petty cash fund is

Assets = Liabilities + Equity
+75
−75

Nov. 1	Petty Cash.	75	
	Cash		75
	To establish a petty cash fund.		

Point: Reducing or eliminating a petty cash fund requires a credit to Petty Cash.

Point: Although *individual* petty cash disbursements are not evidenced by a check, the initial petty cash fund is evidenced by a check, and later petty cash expenditures are evidenced by a check to replenish them *in total.*

After the petty cash fund is established, the Petty Cash account is not debited or credited again unless the amount of the fund is changed. (A fund should be increased if it requires reimbursement too frequently. On the other hand, if the fund is too large, some of its money should be redeposited in the Cash account.)

Next, assume that Z-Mart's petty cashier makes several November payments from petty cash. Each person who received payment is required to sign a receipt. On November 27, after making a $26.50 cash payment for tile cleaning, only $3.70 cash remains in the fund. The petty cashier then summarizes and totals the petty cash receipts as shown in Exhibit 8.3.

EXHIBIT 8.3

Petty Cash Payments Report

Z-MART
Petty Cash Payments Report

Miscellaneous Expenses			
Nov. 2	Cleaning of LCD panels	$20.00	
Nov. 27	Tile cleaning	26.50	$ 46.50
Merchandise Inventory (transportation-in)			
Nov. 5	Transport of merchandise purchased	6.75	
Nov. 20	Transport of merchandise purchased	8.30	15.05
Delivery Expense			
Nov. 18	Customer's package delivered		5.00
Office Supplies Expense			
Nov. 15	Purchase of office supplies immediately used		4.75
Total			**$71.30**

Point: This report can also include receipt number and names of those who approved and received cash payment (see Demo Problem 2).

means that at the end of a work period, the cash in a cash register might not equal the record of cash receipts. This difference is reported in the **Cash Over and Short** account, also called *Cash Short and Over,* which is an income statement account recording the income effects of cash overages and cash shortages. To illustrate, if a cash register's record shows $550 but the count of cash in the register is $555, the entry to record cash sales and its overage is

Cash	555	
Cash Over and Short		5
Sales		550
To record cash sales and a cash overage.		

Assets = Liabilities + Equity
+555 + 5
+550

On the other hand, if a cash register's record shows $625 but the count of cash in the register is $621, the entry to record cash sales and its shortage is

Cash	621	
Cash Over and Short	4	
Sales.		625
To record cash sales and a cash shortage.		

Assets = Liabilities + Equity
+621 − 4
+625

Since customers are more likely to dispute being shortchanged than being given too much change, the Cash Over and Short account usually has a debit balance at the end of an accounting period. A debit balance reflects an expense. It is reported on the income statement as part of general and administrative expenses. (Since the amount is usually small, it is often combined with other small expenses and reported as part of *miscellaneous expenses*—or as part of *miscellaneous revenues* if it has a credit balance.)

Point: Merchants begin a business day with a *change fund* in their cash register. The accounting for a change fund is similar to that for petty cash, including that for cash shortages or overages.

Cash Receipts by Mail Control of cash receipts that arrive through the mail starts with the person who opens the mail. Preferably, two people are assigned the task of, and are present for, opening the mail. In this case, theft of cash receipts by mail requires collusion between these two employees. Specifically, the person(s) opening the mail enters a list (in triplicate) of money received. This list should contain a record of each sender's name, the amount, and an explanation of why the money is sent. The first copy is sent with the money to the cashier. A second copy is sent to the recordkeeper in the accounting area. A third copy is kept by the clerk(s) who opened the mail. The cashier deposits the money in a bank, and the recordkeeper records the amounts received in the accounting records.

Point: Collusion implies that two or more individuals are knowledgeable or involved with the activities of the other(s).

This process reflects good internal control. That is, when the bank balance is reconciled by another person (explained later in the chapter), errors or acts of fraud by the mail clerks, the cashier, or the recordkeeper are revealed. They are revealed because the bank's record of cash deposited must agree with the records from each of the three. Moreover, if the mail clerks do not report all receipts correctly, customers will question their account balances. If the cashier does not deposit all receipts, the bank balance does not agree with the recordkeeper's cash balance. The recordkeeper and the person who reconciles the bank balance do not have access to cash and therefore have no opportunity to divert cash to themselves. This system makes errors and fraud highly unlikely. The exception is employee collusion.

Decision Insight

Perpetual Accounting Wal-Mart uses a network of information links with its point-of-sale cash registers to coordinate sales, purchases, and distribution. Its supercenters, for instance, ring up 15,000 separate sales on heavy days. By using cash register information, the company can fix pricing mistakes quickly and capitalize on sales trends.

Control of Cash Disbursements

Control of cash disbursements is especially important as most large thefts occur from payment of fictitious invoices. One key to controlling cash disbursements is to require all expenditures to be made by check. The only exception is small payments made from petty cash. Another key is to deny access to the accounting records to anyone other than the owner who has the authority to sign checks. A small business owner often signs checks and knows from personal contact that the items being paid for are actually received. This arrangement is impossible in large businesses. Instead, internal control procedures must be substituted for personal contact. Such procedures are designed to assure the check signer that the obligations recorded are properly incurred and should be paid. This section describes these and other internal control procedures, including the voucher system and petty cash system. A method for management of cash disbursements for purchases is described in Appendix 8B.

Decision Insight

Cash Budget Projected cash receipts and cash disbursements are often summarized in a *cash budget.* Provided that sufficient cash exists for effective operations, companies wish to minimize the cash they hold because of its risk of theft and its low return versus other investment opportunities.

Voucher System of Control A **voucher system** is a set of procedures and approvals designed to control cash disbursements and the acceptance of obligations. The voucher system of control establishes procedures for

- Verifying, approving, and recording obligations for eventual cash disbursement.
- Issuing checks for payment of verified, approved, and recorded obligations.

A reliable voucher system follows standard procedures for every transaction. This applies even when multiple purchases are made from the same supplier.

A voucher system's control over cash disbursements begins when a company incurs an obligation that will result in payment of cash. A key factor in this system is that only approved departments and individuals are authorized to incur such obligations. The system often limits the type of obligations that a department or individual can incur. In a large retail store, for instance, only a purchasing department should be authorized to incur obligations for merchandise inventory. Another key factor is that procedures for purchasing, receiving, and paying for merchandise are divided among several departments (or individuals). These departments include the one requesting the purchase, the purchasing department, the receiving department, and the accounting department. To coordinate and control responsibilities of these departments, a company uses several different business documents. Exhibit 8.1 shows how documents are accumulated in a **voucher,** which is an internal document (or file) used

Point: MCI, formerly WorldCom, paid a whopping $500 million in SEC fines for accounting fraud. Among the charges were that it inflated earnings by as much as $10 billion. Its CEO, Bernard Ebbers, was sentenced to 25 years.

EXHIBIT 8.1

Document Flow in a Voucher System

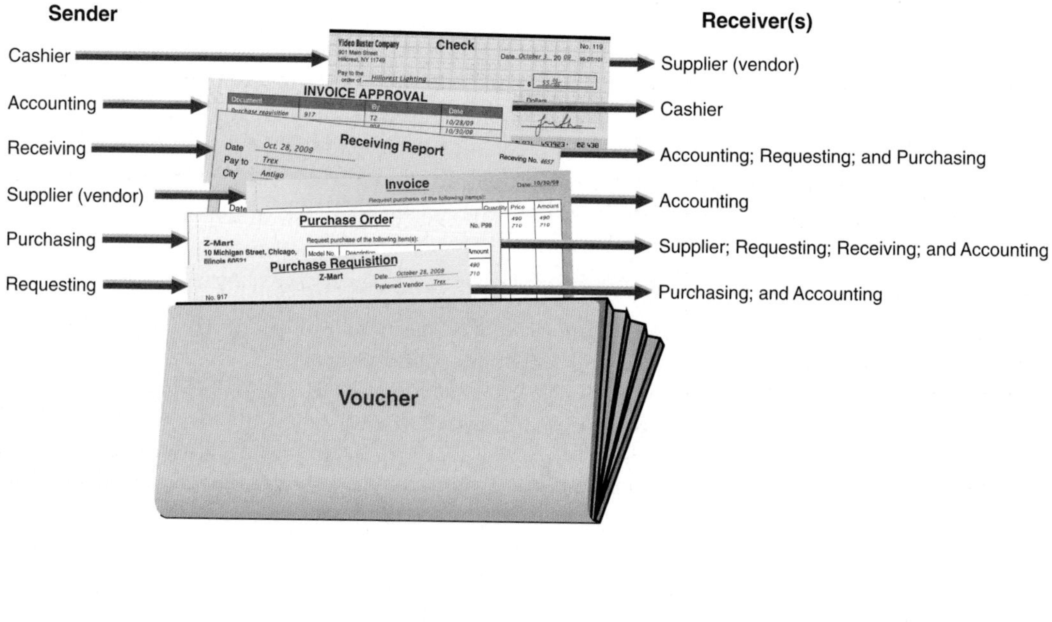

The petty cash payments report and all receipts are given to the company cashier in exchange for a $71.30 check to reimburse the fund. The petty cashier cashes the check and puts the $71.30 cash in the petty cashbox. The company records this reimbursement as follows.

Nov. 27	Miscellaneous Expenses	46.50	
	Merchandise Inventory	15.05	
	Delivery Expense	5.00	
	Office Supplies Expense	4.75	
	Cash		71.30
	To reimburse petty cash.		

Assets	= Liabilities	+ Equity
−71.30		−46.50
		−15.05
		− 5.00
		− 4.75

A petty cash fund is usually reimbursed at the end of an accounting period so that expenses are recorded in the proper period, even if the fund is not low on money. If the fund is not reimbursed at the end of a period, the financial statements would show both an overstated cash asset and understated expenses (or assets) that were paid out of petty cash. Some companies do not reimburse the petty cash fund at the end of each period under the notion that this amount is immaterial to users of financial statements.

Point: To avoid errors in recording petty cash reimbursement, follow these steps: (1) prepare payments report, (2) compute cash needed by subtracting cash remaining from total fund amount, (3) record entry, and (4) check "Dr. = Cr." in entry. Any difference is Cash Over and Short.

Increasing or decreasing a petty cash fund. A decision to increase or decrease a petty cash fund is often made when reimbursing it. To illustrate, assume Z-Mart decides to *increase* its petty cash fund from $75 to $100 on November 27 when it reimburses the fund. The entries required are to (1) reimburse the fund as usual (see the preceding November 27 entry) and (2) increase the fund amount as follows.

Nov. 27	Petty Cash	25	
	Cash		25
	To increase the petty cash fund amount.		

Event	Petty Cash	Cash	Expenses
Set up fund	Dr.	Cr.	—
Reimburse fund	—	Cr.	Dr.
Increase fund	Dr.	Cr.	—
Decrease fund	Cr.	Dr.	—

Alternatively, if Z-Mart *decreases* the petty cash fund from $75 to $55 on November 27, the entry is to (1) credit Petty Cash for $20 (decreasing the fund from $75 to $55) and (2) debit Cash for $20 (reflecting the $20 transfer from Petty Cash to Cash).

Cash over and short. Sometimes a petty cashier fails to get a receipt for payment or overpays for the amount due. When this occurs and the fund is later reimbursed, the petty cash payments report plus the cash remaining will not total to the fund balance. This mistake causes the fund to be *short*. This shortage is recorded as an expense in the reimbursing entry with a debit to the Cash Over and Short account. (An overage in the petty cash fund is recorded with a credit to Cash Over and Short in the reimbursing entry.) To illustrate, prepare the June 1 entry to reimburse a $200 petty cash fund when its payments report shows $178 in miscellaneous expenses and $15 cash remains.

$200 Petty Cash Fund

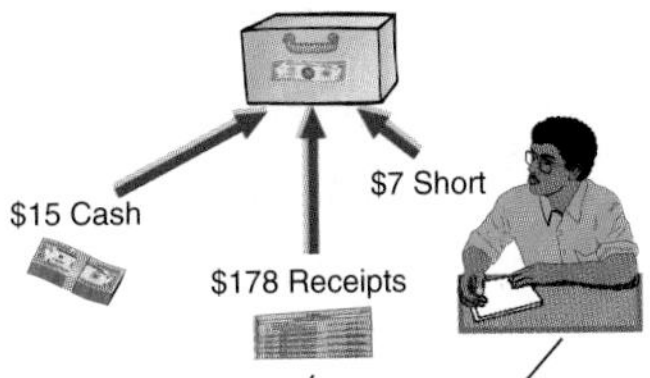

June 1	Miscellaneous Expenses	178	
	Cash Over and Short	7	
	Cash		185
	To reimburse petty cash.		

Decision Insight

Warning Signs There are clues to internal control violations. Warning signs from accounting include (1) an increase in customer refunds—could be fake, (2) missing documents—could be used for fraud, (3) differences between bank deposits and cash receipts—could be cash embezzled, and (4) delayed recording—could reflect fraudulent records. Warning signs from employees include (1) lifestyle change—could be embezzlement, (2) too close with suppliers—could signal fraudulent transactions, and (3) failure to leave job, even for vacations—could conceal fraudulent activities.

Quick Check Answers—p. 340

8. Why are some cash payments made from a petty cash fund and not by check?
9. Why should a petty cash fund be reimbursed at the end of an accounting period?
10. Identify at least two results of reimbursing a petty cash fund.

Banking Activities as Controls

Banks (and other financial institutions) provide many services, including helping companies control cash. Banks safeguard cash, provide detailed and independent records of cash transactions, and are a source of cash financing. This section describes these services and the documents provided by banking activities that increase managers' control over cash.

Basic Bank Services

C3 Identify control features of banking activities.

This section explains basic bank services—such as the bank account, the bank deposit, and checking—that contribute to the control of cash.

Bank Account, Deposit, and Check A *bank account* is a record set up by a bank for a customer. It permits a customer to deposit money for safekeeping and helps control withdrawals. To limit access to a bank account, all persons authorized to write checks on the account must sign a **signature card,** which bank employees use to verify signatures on checks. Many companies have more than one bank account to serve different needs and to handle special transactions such as payroll.

Point: Online banking services include the ability to stop payment on a check, move money between accounts, get up-to-date balances, and identify cleared checks and deposits.

Each bank deposit is supported by a **deposit ticket,** which lists items such as currency, coins, and checks deposited along with their corresponding dollar amounts. The bank gives the customer a copy of the deposit ticket or a deposit receipt as proof of the deposit. Exhibit 8.4 shows one type of deposit ticket.

EXHIBIT 8.4

Deposit Ticket

Front

Back

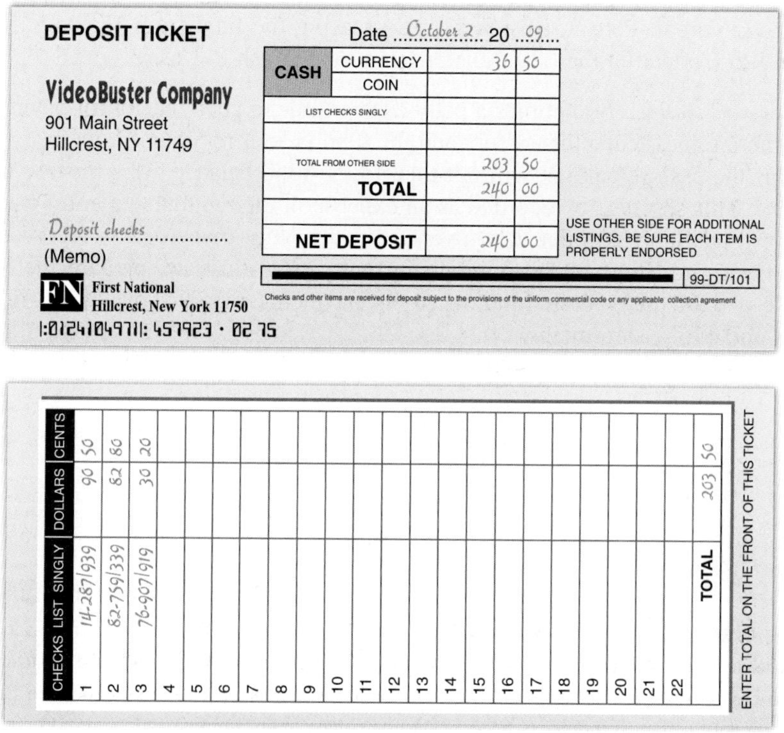
DEPOSIT TICKET

Date October 2 20 09

VideoBuster Company
901 Main Street
Hillcrest, NY 11749

CASH	CURRENCY	36	50
	COIN		
LIST CHECKS SINGLY			
TOTAL FROM OTHER SIDE		203	50
TOTAL		240	00
NET DEPOSIT		240	00

USE OTHER SIDE FOR ADDITIONAL LISTINGS. BE SURE EACH ITEM IS PROPERLY ENDORSED

Deposit checks
(Memo)

99-DT/101

FN First National
Hillcrest, New York 11750

Checks and other items are received for deposit subject to the provisions of the uniform commercial code or any applicable collection agreement

|:012410497|: 457923 · 02 75

CHECKS LIST SINGLY		DOLLARS	CENTS
1	14-287/939	90	50
2	82-759/339	82	80
3	76-907/919	30	20
4			
5			
6			
7			
8			
9			
10			
11			
12			
13			
14			
15			
16			
17			
18			
19			
20			
21			
22			
TOTAL		203	50

ENTER TOTAL ON THE FRONT OF THIS TICKET

To withdraw money from an account, the depositor can use a **check,** which is a document signed by the depositor instructing the bank to pay a specified amount of money to a designated recipient. A check involves three parties: a *maker* who signs the check, a *payee* who is the recipient, and a *bank* (or *payer*) on which the check is drawn. The bank provides a depositor the checks that are serially numbered and imprinted with the name and address of both the depositor and bank. Both checks and deposit tickets are imprinted with identification codes in magnetic ink for computer processing. Exhibit 8.5 shows one type of check. It is accompanied with an optional *remittance advice* explaining the payment. When a remittance advice is unavailable, the *memo* line is often used for a brief explanation.

EXHIBIT 8.5

Check with Remittance Advice

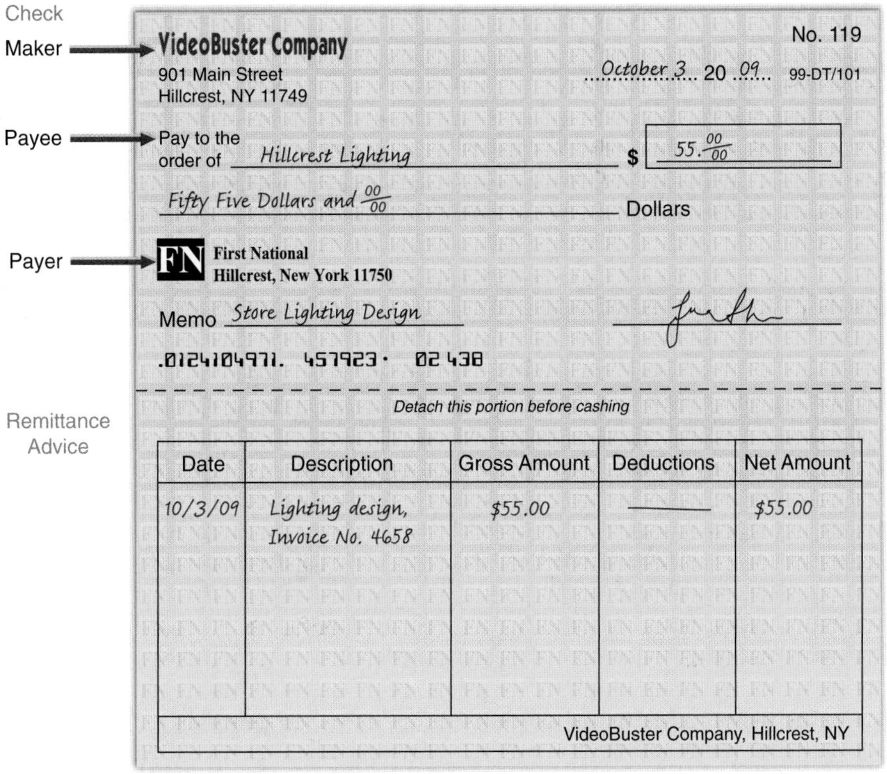

Electronic Funds Transfer **Electronic funds transfer (EFT)** is the electronic transfer of cash from one party to another. No paper documents are necessary. Banks simply transfer cash from one account to another with a journal entry. Companies are increasingly using EFT because of its convenience and low cost. For instance, it can cost up to 50 cents to process a check through the banking system, whereas EFT cost is near zero. We now commonly see items such as payroll, rent, utilities, insurance, and interest payments being handled by EFT. The bank statement lists cash withdrawals by EFT with the checks and other deductions. Cash receipts by EFT are listed with deposits and other additions. A bank statement is sometimes a depositor's only notice of an EFT. *Automated teller machines (ATMs)* are one form of EFT, which allows bank customers to deposit, withdraw, and transfer cash.

Bank Statement

Usually once a month, the bank sends each depositor a **bank statement** showing the activity in the account. Although a monthly statement is common, companies often regularly access information on its banking transactions. (Companies can choose to record any accounting adjustments required from the bank statement immediately or later, say, at the end of each day, week, month, or when reconciling a bank statement.) Different banks use different formats for their bank statements, but all of them include the following items of information:

Point: Good internal control is to deposit all cash receipts daily and make all payments for goods and services by check. This controls access to cash and creates an independent record of all cash activities.

1. Beginning-of-period balance of the depositor's account.
2. Checks and other debits decreasing the account during the period.
3. Deposits and other credits increasing the account during the period.
4. End-of-period balance of the depositor's account.

This information reflects the bank's records. Exhibit 8.6 shows one type of bank statement. Identify each of these four items in that statement. Part Ⓐ of Exhibit 8.6 summarizes changes in the account. Part Ⓑ lists paid checks along with other debits. Part Ⓒ lists deposits and credits to the account, and part Ⓓ shows the daily account balances.

EXHIBIT 8.6

Bank Statement

FN First National
Hillcrest, New York 11750

Member FDIC

Bank Statement

VideoBuster Company
901 Main Street
Hillcrest, NY 11749

October 31, 2009
Statement Date

494 504 2
Account Number

Ⓐ

Previous Balance	Total Checks and Debits	Total Deposits and Credits	Current Balance
1,609.58	723.00	1,163.42	2,050.00

Ⓑ **Checks and Debits**

Date	No.	Amount
10/03	119	55.00
10/09	120	200.00
10/10	121	120.00
10/12		23.00 DM
10/14	122	70.00
10/16	123	25.00
10/23	125	15.00
10/25		20.00 NSF
		10.00 DM
10/26	127	50.00
10/29	128	135.00

Ⓒ **Deposits and Credits**

Date	Amount
10/02	240.00
10/09	180.00
10/15	100.00
10/16	150.00
10/23	485.00 CM
10/31	8.42 IN

Ⓓ **Daily Balance**

Date	Amount
10/01	1,609.58
10/02	1,849.58
10/03	1,794.58
10/09	1,774.58
10/10	1,654.58
10/12	1,631.58
10/14	1,561.58
10/15	1,661.58
10/16	1,786.58
10/23	2,256.58
10/25	2,226.58
10/26	2,176.58
10/29	2,041.58
10/31	2,050.00

Symbols: **CM**–Credit Memo **EC**–Error Correction **NSF**–Non-Sufficient Funds **SC**–Service Charge **DM**–Debit Memo **IN**–Interest Earned **EFT**–Electronic Funds Transfer **OD**–Overdraft

< Reconcile the account immediately. >

Point: Many banks separately report other debits and credits apart from checks and deposits.

In reading a bank statement note that a depositor's account is a liability on the bank's records. This is so because the money belongs to the depositor, not the bank. When a depositor increases the account balance, the bank records it with a *credit* to that liability account. This means that debit memos from the bank produce *credits* on the depositor's books, and credit memos from the bank produce *debits* on the depositor's books.

Enclosed with a bank statement is a list of the depositor's canceled checks (or the actual canceled checks) along with any debit or credit memoranda affecting the account. Increasingly, banks are showing canceled checks electronically via online access to accounts. **Canceled checks** are checks the bank has paid and deducted from the customer's account during the period. Other deductions that can appear on a bank statement include (1) service charges and fees assessed by the bank, (2) checks deposited that are uncollectible, (3) corrections of previous errors, (4) withdrawals through automated teller machines (ATMs), and (5) periodic payments arranged in advance by a depositor. (Most company checking accounts do not allow ATM withdrawals because of the company's desire to make all disbursements by check.) Except for service charges, the bank notifies the depositor of each deduction with a debit memorandum when the bank reduces the balance. A copy of each debit memorandum is usually sent with the statement (again, this information is often available earlier via online access and notifications).

Global: If cash is in more than one currency, a company usually translates these amounts into U.S. dollars using the exchange rate as of the balance sheet date. Also, a company must disclose any restrictions on cash accounts located outside the U.S.

Transactions that increase the depositor's account include amounts the bank collects on behalf of the depositor and the corrections of previous errors. Credit memoranda notify the depositor of all increases when they are recorded. A copy of each credit memorandum is often sent with the bank statement. Banks that pay interest on checking accounts often compute the amount of interest earned on the average cash balance and credit it to the depositor's account each period. In Exhibit 8.6, the bank credits $8.42 of interest to the account.

Bank Reconciliation

When a company deposits all cash receipts and makes all cash payments (except petty cash) by check, it can use the bank statement for proving the accuracy of its cash records. This is done using a **bank reconciliation,** which is a report explaining any differences between the checking account balance according to the depositor's records and the balance reported on the bank statement.

P3 Prepare a bank reconciliation.

Purpose of Bank Reconciliation The balance of a checking account reported on the bank statement rarely equals the balance in the depositor's accounting records. This is usually due to information that one party has that the other does not. We must therefore prove the accuracy of both the depositor's records and those of the bank. This means we must *reconcile* the two balances and explain or account for any differences in them. Among the factors causing the bank statement balance to differ from the depositor's book balance are these:

- **Outstanding checks. Outstanding checks** are checks written (or drawn) by the depositor, deducted on the depositor's records, and sent to the payees but not yet received by the bank for payment at the bank statement date.
- **Deposits in transit** (also called **outstanding deposits**). **Deposits in transit** are deposits made and recorded by the depositor but not yet recorded on the bank statement. For example, companies can make deposits (in the night depository) at the end of a business day after the bank is closed. If such a deposit occurred on a bank statement date, it would not appear on this period's statement. The bank would record such a deposit on the next business day, and it would appear on the next period's bank statement. Deposits mailed to the bank near the end of a period also can be in transit and unrecorded when the statement is prepared.
- **Deductions for uncollectible items and for services.** A company sometimes deposits another party's check that is uncollectible (usually meaning the balance in that party's account is not large enough to cover the check). This check is called a *non-sufficient funds (NSF)* check. The bank would have initially credited the depositor's account for the amount of the check. When the bank learns the check is uncollectible, it debits (reduces) the depositor's account for the amount of that check. The bank may also charge the depositor a fee for processing an uncollectible check and notify the depositor of the deduction by sending a debit memorandum. The depositor should record each deduction when a debit memorandum is received, but an entry is sometimes not made until the bank reconciliation is prepared. Other possible bank charges to a depositor's account that are first reported on a bank statement include printing new checks and service fees.
- **Additions for collections and for interest.** Banks sometimes act as collection agents for their depositors by collecting notes and other items. Banks can also receive electronic funds transfers to the depositor's account. When a bank collects an item, it is added to the depositor's account, less any service fee. The bank also sends a credit memorandum to notify the depositor of the transaction. When the memorandum is received, the depositor should record it; yet it sometimes remains unrecorded until the bank reconciliation is prepared. The bank statement also includes a credit for any interest earned.
- **Errors.** Both banks and depositors can make errors. Bank errors might not be discovered until the depositor prepares the bank reconciliation. Also, depositor errors are sometimes discovered when the bank balance is reconciled. Error testing includes: (a) comparing deposits on the bank statement with deposits in the accounting records and (b) comparing canceled checks on the bank statement with checks recorded in the accounting records.

Forms of Check Fraud (CkFraud.org)

- Forged signatures—legitimate blank checks with fake payer signature
- Forged endorsements—stolen check that is endorsed and cashed by someone other than the payee
- Counterfeit checks—fraudulent checks with fake payer signature
- Altered checks—legitimate check altered (such as changed payee or amount) to benefit perpetrator
- Check kiting—deposit check from one bank account (without sufficient funds) into a second bank account

Point: Small businesses with few employees often allow recordkeepers to both write checks and keep the general ledger. If this is done, it is essential that the owner do the bank reconciliation.

Point: The person preparing the bank reconciliation should not be responsible for processing cash receipts, managing checks, or maintaining cash records.

Illustration of a Bank Reconciliation We follow nine steps in preparing the bank reconciliation. It is helpful to refer to the bank reconciliation in Exhibit 8.7 when studying steps 1 through 9.

EXHIBIT 8.7

Bank Reconciliation

VIDEOBUSTER
Bank Reconciliation
October 31, 2009

①	Bank statement balance		$ 2,050.00	⑤	Book balance		$ 1,404.58
②	Add			⑥	Add		
	Deposit of Oct. 31 in transit		145.00		Collect $500 note less $15 fee	$485.00	
			2,195.00		Interest earned	8.42	493.42
③	Deduct						1,898.00
	Outstanding checks			⑦	Deduct		
	No. 124	$150.00			Check printing charge	23.00	
	No. 126	200.00	350.00		NSF check plus service fee	30.00	53.00
④	**Adjusted bank balance**		**$1,845.00**	⑧	**Adjusted book balance**		**$1,845.00**

⑨ Balances are equal (reconciled)

1 Identify the bank statement balance of the cash account (*balance per bank*). VideoBuster's bank balance is $2,050.

2 Identify and list any unrecorded deposits and any bank errors understating the bank balance. Add them to the bank balance. VideoBuster's $145 deposit placed in the bank's night depository on October 31 is not recorded on its bank statement.

Point: Outstanding checks are identified by comparing canceled checks on the bank statement with checks recorded. This includes identifying any outstanding checks listed on the *previous* period's bank reconciliation that are not included in the canceled checks on this period's bank statement.

3 Identify and list any outstanding checks and any bank errors overstating the bank balance. Deduct them from the bank balance. VideoBuster's comparison of canceled checks with its books shows two checks outstanding: No. 124 for $150 and No. 126 for $200.

4 Compute the *adjusted bank balance,* also called the *corrected* or *reconciled balance.*

5 Identify the company's book balance of the cash account (*balance per book*). VideoBuster's book balance is $1,404.58.

6 Identify and list any unrecorded credit memoranda from the bank, any interest earned, and errors understating the book balance. Add them to the book balance. VideoBuster's bank statement includes a credit memorandum showing the bank collected a note receivable for the company on October 23. The note's proceeds of $500 (minus a $15 collection fee) are credited to the company's account. VideoBuster's bank statement also shows a credit of $8.42 for interest earned on the average cash balance. There was no prior notification of this item, and it is not yet recorded.

7 Identify and list any unrecorded debit memoranda from the bank, any service charges, and errors overstating the book balance. Deduct them from the book balance. Debits on VideoBuster's bank statement that are not yet recorded include (a) a $23 charge for check printing and (b) an NSF check for $20 plus a related $10 processing fee. (The NSF check is dated October 16 and was included in the book balance.)

8 Compute the *adjusted book balance,* also called *corrected* or *reconciled balance.*

Point: Adjusting entries can be combined into one compound entry.

9 Verify that the two adjusted balances from steps 4 and 8 are equal. If so, they are reconciled. If not, check for accuracy and missing data to achieve reconciliation.

Adjusting Entries from a Bank Reconciliation A bank reconciliation often identifies unrecorded items that need recording by the company. In VideoBuster's reconciliation, the adjusted balance of $1,845 is the correct balance as of October 31. But the company's accounting records show a $1,404.58 balance. We must prepare journal entries to adjust the book balance to the correct balance. It is important to remember that only the items reconciling the *book balance* require adjustment. A review of Exhibit 8.7 indicates that four entries are required for VideoBuster.

Collection of note. The first entry is to record the proceeds of its note receivable collected by the bank less the expense of having the bank perform that service.

Oct. 31	Cash	485	
	Collection Expense	15	
	Notes Receivable		500
	To record the collection fee and proceeds for a note collected by the bank.		

Assets = Liabilities + Equity
+485 −15
−500

Interest earned. The second entry records interest credited to its account by the bank.

Oct. 31	Cash	8.42	
	Interest Revenue		8.42
	To record interest earned on the cash balance in the checking account.		

Assets = Liabilities + Equity
+8.42 +8.42

Check printing. The third entry records expenses for the check printing charge.

Oct. 31	Miscellaneous Expenses	23	
	Cash		23
	Check printing charge.		

Assets = Liabilities + Equity
−23 −23

NSF check. The fourth entry records the NSF check that is returned as uncollectible. The $20 check was originally received from T. Woods in payment of his account and then deposited. The bank charged $10 for handling the NSF check and deducted $30 total from VideoBuster's account. This means the entry must reverse the effects of the original entry made when the check was received and must record (add) the $10 bank fee.

Point: The company will try to collect the entire NSF amount of $30.

Oct. 31	Accounts Receivable—T. Woods	30	
	Cash		30
	To charge Woods' account for $20 NSF check and $10 bank fee.		

Assets = Liabilities + Equity
+30
−30

After these four entries are recorded, the book balance of cash is adjusted to the correct amount of $1,845 (computed as $1,404.58 + $485 + $8.42 − $23 − $30). The Cash T-account to the side shows the same computation, where entries are keyed to the numerical codes in Exhibit 8.7.

Cash			
Unadj. bal.	1,404.58		
⑥	485.00	⑦	23.00
⑥	8.42	⑦	30.00
Adj. bal.	1,845.00		

Point: The Demo Problem 1 shows an adjusting entry for an error correction.

Decision Insight

IFRSs Internal controls are crucial to companies that convert from U.S. GAAP to IFRSs. Major risks include misstatement of financial information and fraud. Other risks are ineffective communication of the impact of this change for investors, creditors and others, and management's inability to certify the effectiveness of controls over financial reporting.

Quick Check

Answers—pp. 340–341

11. What is a bank statement?

12. What is the meaning of the phrase *to reconcile a bank balance?*

13. Why do we reconcile the bank statement balance of cash and the depositor's book balance of cash?

14. List at least two items affecting the bank balance side of a bank reconciliation and indicate whether the items are added or subtracted.

15. List at least three items affecting the book balance side of a bank reconciliation and indicate whether the items are added or subtracted.

Decision Analysis — Days' Sales Uncollected

A1 Compute the days' sales uncollected ratio and use it to assess liquidity.

An important part of cash management is monitoring the receipt of cash from receivables. If customers and others who owe money to a company are delayed in payment, then that company can find it difficult to pay its obligations when they are due. A company's customers are crucial partners in its cash management. Many companies attract customers by selling to them on credit. This means that cash receipts from customers are delayed until accounts receivable are collected.

One measure of how quickly a company can convert its accounts receivable into cash is the **days' sales uncollected,** also called *days' sales in receivables*. This measure is computed by dividing the current balance of receivables by net credit sales over the year just completed and then multiplying by 365 (number of days in a year). Since net credit sales usually are not reported to external users, the net sales (or revenues) figure is commonly used in the computation as in Exhibit 8.8.

EXHIBIT 8.8

Days' Sales Uncollected

$$\textbf{Days' sales uncollected} = \frac{\textbf{Accounts receivable}}{\textbf{Net sales}} \times 365$$

We use days' sales uncollected to estimate how much time is likely to pass before the current amount of accounts receivable is received in cash. For evaluation purposes, we need to compare this estimate to that for other companies in the same industry. We also make comparisons between current and prior periods.

To illustrate, we select data from the annual reports of two toy manufacturers, **Hasbro** and **Mattel**. Their days' sales uncollected figures are shown in Exhibit 8.9.

EXHIBIT 8.9

Analysis Using Days' Sales Uncollected

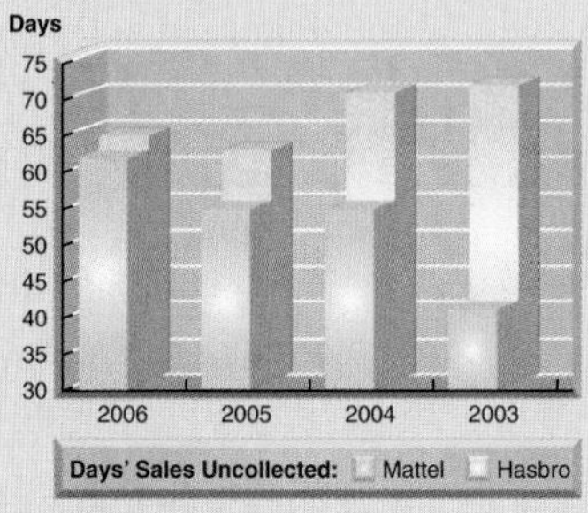

Company	Figure ($ millions)	2006	2005	2004	2003
Hasbro	Accounts receivable	$556	$523	$579	$608
	Net sales	$3,151	$3,088	$2,998	$3,139
	Days' sales uncollected	**64 days**	**62 days**	**70 days**	**71 days**
Mattel	Accounts receivable	$944	$761	$759	$544
	Net sales	$5,650	$5,179	$5,103	$4,960
	Days' sales uncollected	**61 days**	**54 days**	**54 days**	**40 days**

Days' sales uncollected for Hasbro in 2006 is computed as ($556/$3,151) × 365 days = 64 days. This means that it will take about 64 days to collect cash from ending accounts receivable. This number reflects one or more of the following factors: a company's ability to collect receivables, customer financial health, customer payment strategies, and discount terms. To further assess days' sales uncollected for Hasbro, we compare it to three prior years and to those of Mattel. We see that Hasbro's days' sales uncollected has generally improved over the past 4 years—from 71 days down to 64 days. In comparison, Mattel worsened on days' sales uncollected for each of those years—from 40 days to 61 days. Yet, for all years, Mattel is superior to Hasbro on this measure of cash management. The less time that money is tied up in receivables often translates into increased profitability.

Decision Maker

Sales Representative The sales staff is told to take action to help reduce days' sales uncollected for cash management purposes. What can you, a salesperson, do to reduce days' sales uncollected? [Answer—p. 340]

Demonstration Problem 1

Prepare a bank reconciliation for Jamboree Enterprises for the month ended November 30, 2009. The following information is available to reconcile Jamboree Enterprises' book balance of cash with its bank statement balance as of November 30, 2009:

a. After all posting is complete on November 30, the company's book balance of Cash has a $16,380 debit balance, but its bank statement shows a $38,520 balance.

b. Checks No. 2024 for $4,810 and No. 2026 for $5,000 are outstanding.

c. In comparing the canceled checks on the bank statement with the entries in the accounting records, it is found that Check No. 2025 in payment of rent is correctly drawn for $1,000 but is erroneously entered in the accounting records as $880.

d. The November 30 deposit of $17,150 was placed in the night depository after banking hours on that date, and this amount does not appear on the bank statement.

e. In reviewing the bank statement, a check written by Jumbo Enterprises in the amount of $160 was erroneously drawn against Jamboree's account.

f. A credit memorandum enclosed with the bank statement indicates that the bank collected a $30,000 note and $900 of related interest on Jamboree's behalf. This transaction was not recorded by Jamboree prior to receiving the statement.

g. A debit memorandum for $1,100 lists a $1,100 NSF check received from a customer, Marilyn Welch. Jamboree had not recorded the return of this check before receiving the statement.

h. Bank service charges for November total $40. These charges were not recorded by Jamboree before receiving the statement.

Planning the Solution

- Set up a bank reconciliation with a bank side and a book side (as in Exhibit 8.7). Leave room to both add and deduct items. Each column will result in a reconciled, equal balance.
- Examine each item *a* through *h* to determine whether it affects the book or the bank balance and whether it should be added or deducted from the bank or book balance.
- After all items are analyzed, complete the reconciliation and arrive at a reconciled balance between the bank side and the book side.
- For each reconciling item on the book side, prepare an adjusting entry. Additions to the book side require an adjusting entry that debits Cash. Deductions on the book side require an adjusting entry that credits Cash.

Solution to Demonstration Problem 1

JAMBOREE ENTERPRISES
Bank Reconciliation
November 30, 2009

Bank statement balance		$ 38,520	Book balance		$ 16,380
Add			Add		
Deposit of Nov. 30	$17,150		Collection of note	$30,000	
Bank error (Jumbo)	160	17,310	Interest earned	900	30,900
		55,830			47,280
Deduct			Deduct		
Outstanding checks			NSF check (M. Welch)	1,100	
No. 2024	4,810		Recording error (# 2025)	120	
No. 2026	5,000	9,810	Service charge	40	1,260
Adjusted bank balance		**$46,020**	**Adjusted book balance**		**$46,020**

Required Adjusting Entries for Jamboree

Nov. 30	Cash	30,900	
	Notes Receivable		30,000
	Interest Earned		900
	To record collection of note with interest.		
Nov. 30	Accounts Receivable—M. Welch	1,100	
	Cash		1,100
	To reinstate account due from an NSF check.		
Nov. 30	Rent Expense	120	
	Cash		120
	To correct recording error on check no. 2025.		

[continued on next page]

[continued from previous page]

Nov. 30	Bank Service Charges	40	
	Cash		40
	To record bank service charges.		

Demonstration Problem 2

Bacardi Company established a $150 petty cash fund with Dean Martin as the petty cashier. When the fund balance reached $19 cash, Martin prepared a petty cash payment report, which follows.

Petty Cash Payments Report

Receipt No.	Account Charged		Approved by	Received by
12	Delivery Expense	$ 29	Martin	A. Smirnoff
13	Merchandise Inventory	18	Martin	J. Daniels
15	(Omitted)	32	Martin	C. Carlsberg
16	Miscellaneous Expense	41	(Omitted)	J. Walker
	Total	$120		

Required

1. Identify four internal control weaknesses from the payment report.
2. Prepare general journal entries to record:
   a. Establishment of the petty cash fund.
   b. Reimbursement of the fund. (Assume for this part only that petty cash receipt no. 15 was issued for miscellaneous expenses.)
3. What is the Petty Cash account balance immediately before reimbursement? Immediately after reimbursement?

Solution to Demonstration Problem 2

1. Four internal control weaknesses are
   a. Petty cash ticket no. 14 is missing. Its omission raises questions about the petty cashier's management of the fund.
   b. The $19 cash balance means that $131 has been withdrawn ($150 − $19 = $131). However, the total amount of the petty cash receipts is only $120 ($29 + $18 + $32 + $41). The fund is $11 short of cash ($131 − $120 = $11). Was petty cash receipt no. 14 issued for $11? Management should investigate.
   c. The petty cashier (Martin) did not sign petty cash receipt no. 16. This omission could have been an oversight on his part or he might not have authorized the payment. Management should investigate.
   d. Petty cash receipt no. 15 does not indicate which account to charge. This omission could have been an oversight on the petty cashier's part. Management could check with C. Carlsberg and the petty cashier (Martin) about the transaction. Without further information, debit Miscellaneous Expense.
2. Petty cash general journal entries.
   a. Entry to establish the petty cash fund.

Petty Cash	150	
Cash		150

   b. Entry to reimburse the fund.

Delivery Expense	29	
Merchandise Inventory	18	
Miscellaneous Expense ($41 + $32)	73	
Cash Over and Short	11	
Cash		131

3. The Petty Cash account balance *always* equals its fund balance, in this case $150. This account balance does not change unless the fund is increased or decreased.

APPENDIX

Documentation and Verification

8A

This appendix describes the important business documents of a voucher system of control.

P4 Describe the use of documentation and verification to control cash disbursements.

Purchase Requisition Department managers are usually not allowed to place orders directly with suppliers for control purposes. Instead, a department manager must inform the purchasing department of its needs by preparing and signing a **purchase requisition,** which lists the merchandise needed and requests that it be purchased—see Exhibit 8A.1. Two copies of the purchase requisition are sent to the purchasing department, which then sends one copy to the accounting department. When the accounting department receives a purchase requisition, it creates and maintains a voucher for this transaction. The requesting department keeps the third copy.

EXHIBIT 8A.1

Purchase Requisition

Z-Mart

PURCHASE REQUISITION — No. 917

From: *Sporting Goods Department*
To: *Purchasing Department*

Date: *October 28, 2009*
Preferred Vendor: *Trex*

Request purchase of the following item(s):

MODEL NO.	DESCRIPTION	QUANTITY
CH 015	Challenger X7	1
SD 099	SpeedDemon	1

Reason for Request: *Replenish inventory*
Approval for Request: *T.Z.*

For Purchasing Department use only: Order Date *10/30/09* P.O. No. *P98*

Purchase Order A **purchase order** is a document the purchasing department uses to place an order with a **vendor** (seller or supplier). A purchase order authorizes a vendor to ship ordered merchandise at the stated price and terms—see Exhibit 8A.2. When the purchasing department receives a purchase requisition, it prepares at least five copies of a purchase order. The copies are distributed as follows: *copy 1* to the vendor as a purchase request and as authority to ship merchandise; *copy 2,* along with a copy of the purchase requisition, to the accounting department, where it is entered in the voucher and used in approving payment of the invoice; *copy 3* to the requesting department to inform its manager that action is being taken; *copy 4* to the receiving department without order quantity so it can compare with goods received and provide independent count of goods received; and *copy 5* retained on file by the purchasing department.

Point: It is important to note that a voucher system is designed to uniquely meet the needs of a specific business. Thus, you should read this appendix as one example of a common voucher system design, but *not* the only design.

Invoice An **invoice** is an itemized statement of goods prepared by the vendor listing the customer's name, items sold, sales prices, and terms of sale. An invoice is also a bill sent to the buyer from the supplier. From the vendor's point of view, it is a *sales invoice*. The buyer, or **vendee,** treats it as a *purchase invoice*. When receiving a purchase order, the vendor ships the ordered merchandise to the buyer and includes or mails a copy of the invoice covering the shipment to the buyer. The invoice is sent to the buyer's accounting department where it is placed in the voucher. (Refer back to Exhibit 5.5, which shows Z-Mart's purchase invoice.)

EXHIBIT 8A.2

Purchase Order

Z-Mart
10 Michigan Street
Chicago, Illinois 60521

PURCHASE ORDER

No. P98

To: Trex
W9797 Cherry Road
Antigo, Wisconsin 54409

Date	10/30/09
FOB	Destination
Ship by	As soon as possible
Terms	2/15, n/30

Request shipment of the following item(s):

Model No.	Description	Quantity	Price	Amount
CH 015	Challenger X7	1	490	490
SD 099	SpeedDemon	1	710	710

All shipments and invoices must include purchase order number

J.W.
ORDERED BY

Receiving Report Many companies maintain a separate department to receive all merchandise and purchased assets. When each shipment arrives, this receiving department counts the goods and checks them for damage and agreement with the purchase order. It then prepares four or more copies of a **receiving report,** which is used within the company to notify the appropriate persons that ordered goods have been received and to describe the quantities and condition of the goods. One copy is sent to accounting and placed in the voucher. Copies are also sent to the requesting department and the purchasing department to notify them that the goods have arrived. The receiving department retains a copy in its files.

Invoice Approval When a receiving report arrives, the accounting department should have copies of the following documents in the voucher: purchase requisition, purchase order, and invoice. With the information in these documents, the accounting department can record the purchase and approve its payment. In approving an invoice for payment, it checks and compares information across all documents. To facilitate this checking and to ensure that no step is omitted, it often uses an **invoice approval,** also called *check authorization*—see Exhibit 8A.3. An invoice approval is a checklist of steps necessary for approving an invoice for recording and payment. It is a separate document either filed in the voucher or preprinted (or stamped) on the voucher.

EXHIBIT 8A.3

Invoice Approval

INVOICE APPROVAL

DOCUMENT		BY	DATE
Purchase requisition	917	TZ	10/28/09
Purchase order	P98	JW	10/30/09
Receiving report	R85	SK	11/03/09
Invoice:	4657		11/12/09
Price		JK	11/12/09
Calculations		JK	11/12/09
Terms		JK	11/12/09
Approved for payment		BC	

Point: Recording a purchase is initiated by an invoice approval, not an invoice. An invoice approval verifies that the amount is consistent with that requested, ordered, and received. This controls and verifies purchases and related liabilities.

As each step in the checklist is approved, the person initials the invoice approval and records the current date. Final approval implies the following steps have occurred:

1. **Requisition check:** Items on invoice are requested per purchase requisition.
2. **Purchase order check:** Items on invoice are ordered per purchase order.
3. **Receiving report check:** Items on invoice are received per receiving report.
4. **Invoice check: Price:** Invoice prices are as agreed with the vendor.
   Calculations: Invoice has no mathematical errors.
   Terms: Terms are as agreed with the vendor.

Voucher Once an invoice has been checked and approved, the voucher is complete. A complete voucher is a record summarizing a transaction. Once the voucher certifies a transaction, it authorizes recording an obligation. A voucher also contains approval for paying the obligation on an appropriate date. The physical form of a voucher varies across companies. Many are designed so that the invoice and other related source documents are placed inside the voucher, which can be a folder.

Completion of a voucher usually requires a person to enter certain information on both the inside and outside of the voucher. Typical information required on the inside of a voucher is shown in Exhibit 8A.4, and that for the outside is shown in Exhibit 8A.5. This information is taken from the invoice and the supporting documents filed in the voucher. A complete voucher is sent to an authorized individual (often called an *auditor*). This person performs a final review, approves the accounts and amounts for debiting (called the *accounting distribution*), and authorizes recording of the voucher.

EXHIBIT 8A.4

Inside of a Voucher

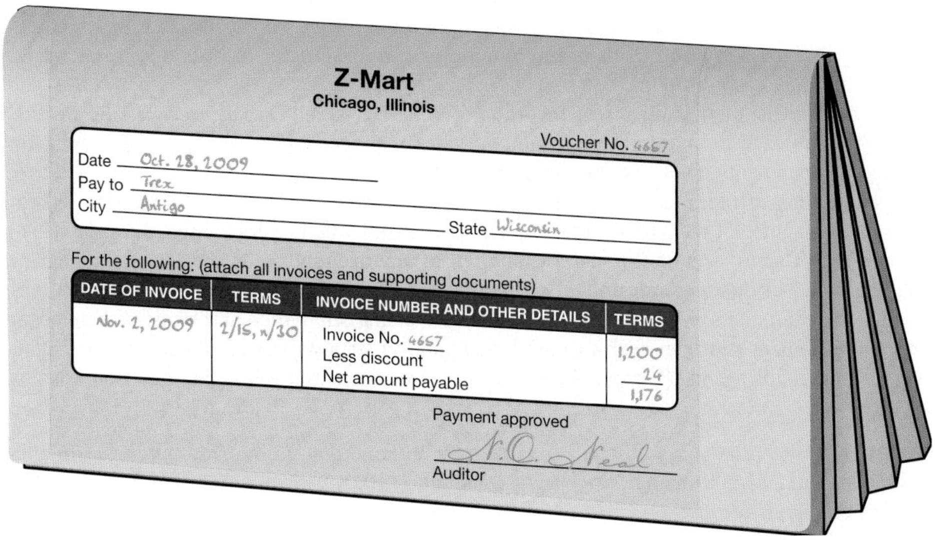

After a voucher is approved and recorded (in a journal called a **voucher register**), it is filed by its due date. A check is then sent on the payment date from the cashier, the voucher is marked "paid," and the voucher is sent to the accounting department and recorded (in a journal called the **check register**). The person issuing checks relies on the approved voucher and its signed supporting documents as proof that an obligation has been incurred and must be paid. The purchase requisition and purchase order confirm the purchase was authorized. The receiving report shows that items have been received, and the invoice approval form verifies that the invoice has been checked for errors. There is little chance for error and even less chance for fraud without collusion unless all the documents and signatures are forged.

EXHIBIT 8A.5

Outside of a Voucher

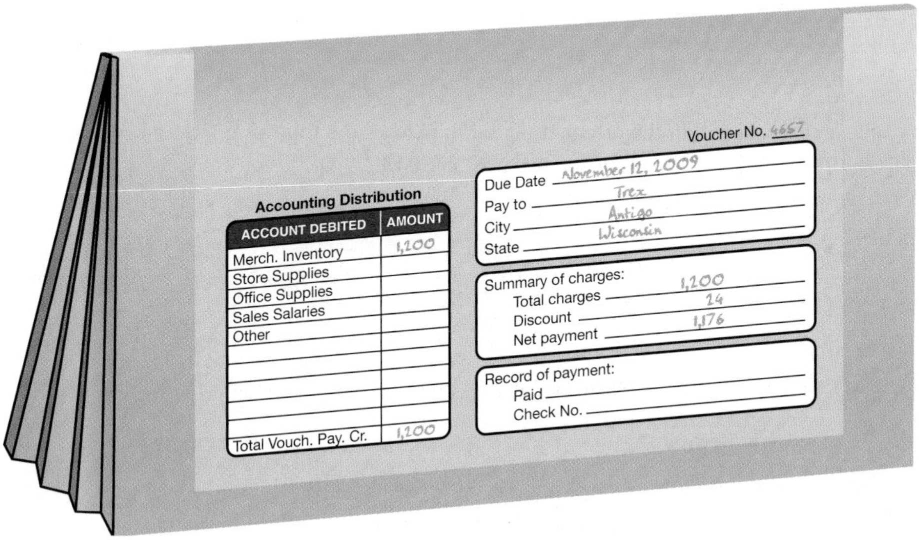

APPENDIX

8B Control of Purchase Discounts

P5 Apply the net method to control purchase discounts.

This appendix explains how a company can better control its cash *disbursements* to take advantage of favorable purchases discounts. Chapter 5 described the entries to record the receipt and payment of an invoice for a merchandise purchase with and without discount terms. Those entries were prepared under what is called the **gross method** of recording purchases, which initially records the invoice at its *gross* amount ignoring any cash discount.

The **net method** is another means of recording purchases, which initially records the invoice at its *net* amount of any cash discount. The net method gives management an advantage in controlling and monitoring cash payments involving purchase discounts.

To explain, when invoices are recorded at *gross* amounts, the amount of any discounts taken is deducted from the balance of the Merchandise Inventory account when cash payment is made. This means that the amount of any discounts lost is not reported in any account or on the income statement. Lost discounts recorded in this way are unlikely to come to the attention of management. When purchases are recorded at *net* amounts, a **Discounts Lost** expense account is recorded and brought to management's attention. Management can then seek to identify the reason for discounts lost such as oversight, carelessness, or unfavorable terms. (Chapter 5 explains how managers assess whether a discount is favorable or not.)

Perpetual Inventory System To illustrate, assume that a company purchases merchandise on November 2 at a $1,200 invoice price with terms of 2/10, n/30. Its November 2 entries under the gross and net methods are

Gross Method

Merchandise Inventory	1,200	
Accounts Payable		1,200

Net Method

Merchandise Inventory	1,176	
Accounts Payable		1,176

If the invoice is paid on November 12 within the discount period, it records the following:

Gross Method

Accounts Payable	1,200	
Merchandise Inventory		24
Cash		1,176

Net Method

Accounts Payable	1,176	
Cash		1,176

If the invoice is *not* paid within the discount period, it records the following November 12 entry (which is the date corresponding to the end of the discount period):

Gross Method

No entry		

Net Method

Discounts Lost	24	
Accounts Payable		24

Then, when the invoice is later paid on December 2, outside the discount period, it records the following:

Gross Method

Accounts Payable	1,200	
Cash		1,200

Net Method

Accounts Payable	1,200	
Cash		1,200

(The discount lost can be recorded when the cash payment is made with a single entry. However, in this case, when financial statements are prepared after a discount is lost and before the cash payment is made, an adjusting entry is required to recognize any unrecorded discount lost in the period when incurred.)

Periodic Inventory System The preceding entries assume a perpetual inventory system. If a company is using a *periodic system,* its November 2 entries under the gross and net methods are

Gross Method—Periodic

Purchases	1,200	
Accounts Payable		1,200

Net Method—Periodic

Purchases	1,176	
Accounts Payable		1,176

If the invoice is paid on November 12 within the discount period, it records the following:

Gross Method—Periodic

Accounts Payable	1,200	
Purchases Discounts		24
Cash		1,176

Net Method—Periodic

Accounts Payable	1,176	
Cash		1,176

If the invoice is *not* paid within the discount period, it records the following November 12 entry:

Gross Method—Periodic

No entry		

Net Method—Periodic

Discounts Lost	24	
Accounts Payable		24

Then, when the invoice is later paid on December 2, outside the discount period, it records the following:

Gross Method—Periodic

Accounts Payable	1,200	
Cash		1,200

Net Method—Periodic

Accounts Payable	1,200	
Cash		1,200

Summary

C1 **Define internal control and identify its purpose and principles.** An internal control system consists of the policies and procedures managers use to protect assets, ensure reliable accounting, promote efficient operations, and urge adherence to company policies. It can prevent avoidable losses and help managers both plan operations and monitor company and human performance. Principles of good internal control include establishing responsibilities, maintaining adequate records, insuring assets and bonding employees, separating recordkeeping from custody of assets, dividing responsibilities for related transactions, applying technological controls, and performing regular independent reviews.

C2 **Define cash and cash equivalents and explain how to report them.** Cash includes currency, coins, and amounts on (or acceptable for) deposit in checking and savings accounts. Cash equivalents are short-term, highly liquid investment assets readily convertible to a known cash amount and sufficiently close to their maturity date so that market value is not sensitive to interest rate changes. Cash and cash equivalents are liquid assets because they are readily converted into other assets or can be used to pay for goods, services, or liabilities.

C3 **Identify control features of banking activities.** Banks offer several services that promote the control and safeguarding of cash. A bank account is a record set up by a bank permitting a customer to deposit money for safekeeping and to draw checks on it. A bank deposit is money contributed to the account with a deposit ticket as proof. A check is a document signed by the depositor instructing the bank to pay a specified amount of money to a designated recipient.

A1 **Compute the days' sales uncollected ratio and use it to assess liquidity.** Many companies attract customers by selling to them on credit. This means that cash receipts from customers are delayed until accounts receivable are collected. Users want to know how quickly a company can convert its accounts receivable into cash. The days' sales uncollected ratio, one measure reflecting company liquidity, is computed by dividing the ending balance of receivables by annual net sales, and then multiplying by 365.

P1 Apply internal control to cash receipts and disbursements. Internal control of cash receipts ensures that all cash received is properly recorded and deposited. Attention focuses on two important types of cash receipts: over-the-counter and by mail. Good internal control for over-the-counter cash receipts includes use of a cash register, customer review, use of receipts, a permanent transaction record, and separation of the custody of cash from its recordkeeping. Good internal control for cash receipts by mail includes at least two people assigned to open mail and a listing of each sender's name, amount, and explanation.

P2 Explain and record petty cash fund transactions. Petty cash disbursements are payments of small amounts for items such as postage, courier fees, minor repairs, and supplies. A company usually sets up one or more petty cash funds. A petty fund cashier is responsible for safekeeping the cash, making payments from this fund, and keeping receipts and records. A Petty Cash account is debited only when the fund is established or increased in amount. When the fund is replenished, petty cash disbursements are recorded with debits to expense (or asset) accounts and a credit to cash.

P3 Prepare a bank reconciliation. A bank reconciliation proves the accuracy of the depositor's and the bank's records. The bank statement balance is adjusted for items such as outstanding checks and unrecorded deposits made on or before the bank statement date but not reflected on the statement. The book balance is adjusted for items such as service charges, bank collections for the depositor, and interest earned on the account.

P4[A] Describe the use of documentation and verification to control cash disbursements. A voucher system is a set of procedures and approvals designed to control cash disbursements and acceptance of obligations. The voucher system of control relies on several important documents, including the voucher and its supporting files. A key factor in this system is that only approved departments and individuals are authorized to incur certain obligations.

P5[B] Apply the net method to control purchase discounts. The net method aids management in monitoring and controlling purchase discounts. When invoices are recorded at gross amounts, the amount of discounts taken is deducted from the balance of the Inventory account. This means that the amount of any discounts lost is not reported in any account and is unlikely to come to the attention of management. When purchases are recorded at net amounts, a Discounts Lost account is brought to management's attention as an operating expense. Management can then seek to identify the reason for discounts lost, such as oversight, carelessness, or unfavorable terms.

Guidance Answers to **Decision Maker** and **Decision Ethics**

Entrepreneur A forced vacation policy is part of a good system of internal controls. When employees are forced to take vacations, their ability to hide any fraudulent behavior decreases because others must perform the vacationers' duties. A replacement employee potentially can uncover fraudulent behavior or falsified records. A forced vacation policy is especially important for employees in sensitive positions of handling money or in control of easily transferable assets.

Sales Representative A salesperson can take several steps to reduce days' sales uncollected. These include (1) decreasing the ratio of sales on account to total sales by encouraging more cash sales, (2) identifying customers most delayed in their payments and encouraging earlier payments or cash sales, and (3) applying stricter credit policies to eliminate credit sales to customers that never pay.

Guidance Answers to **Quick Checks**

1. (*c*)
2. Technology reduces processing errors. It also allows more extensive testing of records, limits the amount of hard evidence, and highlights the importance of separation of duties.
3. A company holds liquid assets so that it can purchase other assets, buy services, and pay obligations.
4. It owns cash equivalents because they yield a return greater than what cash earns (and are readily exchanged for cash).
5. Examples of cash equivalents are 90-day (or less) U.S. Treasury bills, money market funds, and commercial paper (notes).
6. (*a*)
7. A voucher system is used when an owner/manager can no longer control purchasing procedures through personal supervision and direct participation.
8. If all cash payments are made by check, numerous checks for small amounts must be written. Since this practice is expensive and time-consuming, a petty cash fund is often established for making small (immaterial) cash payments.
9. If the petty cash fund is not reimbursed at the end of an accounting period, the transactions involving petty cash are not yet recorded and the petty cash asset is overstated.
10. First, petty cash transactions are recorded when the petty cash fund is reimbursed. Second, reimbursement provides cash to allow the fund to continue being used. Third, reimbursement identifies any cash shortage or overage in the fund.
11. A bank statement is a report prepared by the bank describing the activities in a depositor's account.
12. To reconcile a bank balance means to explain the difference between the cash balance in the depositor's accounting records and the cash balance on the bank statement.

13. The purpose of the bank reconciliation is to determine whether the bank or the depositor has made any errors and whether the bank has entered any transactions affecting the account that the depositor has not recorded.

14. Unrecorded deposits—added
Outstanding checks—subtracted

15. Interest earned—added
Credit memos—added
Debit memos—subtracted
NSF checks—subtracted
Bank service charges—subtracted

Key Terms

mhhe.com/wildFAP19e

Key Terms are available at the book's Website for learning and testing in an online Flashcard Format.

Bank reconciliation (p. 329)
Bank statement (p. 327)
Canceled checks (p. 328)
Cash (p. 319)
Cash equivalents (p. 319)
Cash Over and Short (p. 321)
Check (p. 326)
Check register (p. 337)
Days' sales uncollected (p. 332)
Deposit ticket (p. 326)
Deposits in transit (p. 329)
Discounts lost (p. 338)
Electronic funds transfer (EFT) (p. 327)
Gross method (p. 338)
Internal control system (p. 314)
Invoice (p. 335)
Invoice approval (p. 336)
Liquid assets (p. 319)
Liquidity (p. 319)
Net method (p. 338)
Outstanding checks (p. 329)
Petty cash (p. 323)
Principles of internal control (p. 315)
Purchase order (p. 335)
Purchase requisition (p. 335)
Receiving report (p. 336)
Sarbanes-Oxley Act (p. 314)
Signature card (p. 326)
Vendee (p. 335)
Vendor (p. 335)
Voucher (p. 322)
Voucher register (p. 337)
Voucher system (p. 322)

Multiple Choice Quiz

Answers on p. 355

mhhe.com/wildFAP19e

Additional Quiz Questions are available at the book's Website.

Quiz8

1. A company needs to replenish its $500 petty cash fund. Its petty cash box has $75 cash and petty cash receipts of $420. The journal entry to replenish the fund includes
a. A debit to Cash for $75.
b. A credit to Cash for $75.
c. A credit to Petty Cash for $420.
d. A credit to Cash Over and Short for $5.
e. A debit to Cash Over and Short for $5.

2. The following information is available for Hapley Company:
- The November 30 bank statement shows a $1,895 balance.
- The general ledger shows a $1,742 balance at November 30.
- A $795 deposit placed in the bank's night depository on November 30 does not appear on the November 30 bank statement.
- Outstanding checks amount to $638 at November 30.
- A customer's $335 note was collected by the bank in November. A collection fee of $15 was deducted by the bank and the difference deposited in Hapley's account.
- A bank service charge of $10 is deducted by the bank and appears on the November 30 bank statement.

How will the customer's note appear on Hapley's November 30 bank reconciliation?
a. $320 appears as an addition to the book balance of cash.
b. $320 appears as a deduction from the book balance of cash.
c. $320 appears as an addition to the bank balance of cash.
d. $320 appears as a deduction from the bank balance of cash.
e. $335 appears as an addition to the bank balance of cash.

3. Using the information from question 2, what is the reconciled balance on Hapley's November 30 bank reconciliation?
a. $2,052
b. $1,895
c. $1,742
d. $2,201
e. $1,184

4. A company had net sales of $84,000 and accounts receivable of $6,720. Its days' sales uncollected is
a. 3.2 days
b. 18.4 days
c. 230.0 days
d. 29.2 days
e. 12.5 days

5.[B] A company records its purchases using the net method. On August 1, it purchases merchandise on account for $6,000 with terms of 2/10, n/30. The August 1 journal entry to record this transaction includes a
a. Debit to Merchandise Inventory for $6,000.
b. Debit to Merchandise Inventory for $5,880.
c. Debit to Merchandise Inventory for $120.
d. Debit to Accounts Payable for $5,880.
e. Credit to Accounts Payable for $6,000.

Superscript letter ^{A} (^{B}) denotes assignments based on Appendix 8A (8B).

Discussion Questions

1. List the seven broad principles of internal control.
2. Internal control procedures are important in every business, but at what stage in the development of a business do they become especially critical?
3. Why should responsibility for related transactions be divided among different departments or individuals?
4. Why should the person who keeps the records of an asset not be the person responsible for its custody?
5. When a store purchases merchandise, why are individual departments not allowed to directly deal with suppliers?
6. What are the limitations of internal controls?
7. Which of the following assets is most liquid? Which is least liquid? Inventory, building, accounts receivable, or cash.
8. What is a petty cash receipt? Who should sign it?
9. Why should cash receipts be deposited on the day of receipt?
10. **Best Buy**'s statement of cash flows in Appendix A describes changes in cash and cash equivalents for the year ended March 3, 2007. What amount is provided (used) by investing activities? What amount is provided (used) by financing activities?
11. Refer to **Circuit City**'s balance sheet in Appendix A. How does its cash compare with its other current assets (in both amount and percent) as of February 28, 2007? Compare and assess the cash amount at February 28, 2007, with its amount at February 28, 2006.
12. Refer to **RadioShack**'s financial statements in Appendix A. RadioShack's net income for the year ended December 31, 2006, was $73,400,000. Is its net income equal to the increase in cash and cash equivalents for the year? Explain the difference between net income and the increase in cash and cash equivalents.
13. **Apple**'s balance sheet in Appendix A reports that cash and equivalents increased during the fiscal year ended September 30, 2006. Identify at least three major causes of this change in cash and equivalents.

Denotes Discussion Questions that involve decision making.

Available with McGraw-Hill's Homework Manager

QUICK STUDY

QS 8-1
Internal control objectives
C1

An internal control system consists of all policies and procedures used to protect assets, ensure reliable accounting, promote efficient operations, and urge adherence to company policies.

1. What is the main objective of internal control procedures? How is that objective achieved?
2. Why should recordkeeping for assets be separated from custody over those assets?
3. Why should the responsibility for a transaction be divided between two or more individuals or departments?

QS 8-2
Cash and equivalents
C2

Good accounting systems help in managing cash and controlling who has access to it.

1. What items are included in the category of cash?
2. What items are included in the category of cash equivalents?
3. What does the term *liquidity* refer to?

QS 8-3
Cash, liquidity, and return
C1 C2

Good accounting systems help with the management and control of cash and cash equivalents.

1. Define and contrast the terms *liquid asset* and *cash equivalent.*
2. Why would companies invest their idle cash in cash equivalents?
3. Identify five principles of effective cash management.

QS 8-4
Internal control for cash
P1

A good system of internal control for cash provides adequate procedures for protecting both cash receipts and cash disbursements.

1. What are three basic guidelines that help achieve this protection?
2. Identify two control systems or procedures for cash disbursements.

QS 8-5
Petty cash accounting
P2

1. The petty cash fund of the Kaley Agency is established at $75. At the end of the current period, the fund contained $8.18 and had the following receipts: film rentals, $26.50, refreshments for meetings, $32.17 (both expenditures to be classified as Entertainment Expense); postage, $5.15; and printing, $3. Prepare journal entries to record (*a*) establishment of the fund and (*b*) reimbursement of the fund at the end of the current period.
2. Identify the two events that cause a Petty Cash account to be credited in a journal entry.

QS 8-6
Bank reconciliation
P3

1. For each of the following items, indicate whether its amount (i) affects the bank or book side of a bank reconciliation and (ii) represents an addition or a subtraction in a bank reconciliation.

a. Unrecorded deposits
b. Interest on cash balance
c. Bank service charges
d. Debit memos
e. Outstanding checks
f. Credit memos
g. NSF checks

2. Which of the items in part 1 require an adjusting journal entry?

QS 8-7
Bank reconciliation
P3

Madison Company deposits all cash receipts on the day when they are received and it makes all cash payments by check. At the close of business on July 31, 2009, its Cash account shows a $2,025 debit balance. Madison's July 31 bank statement shows $1,800 on deposit in the bank. Prepare a bank reconciliation for Madison Company using the following information.

a. The July 31 bank statement included a $30 debit memorandum for bank services; Madison has not yet recorded the cost of these services.

b. In reviewing the bank statement, a $90 check written by Madsen Company was mistakenly drawn against Madison's account.

c. July 31 cash receipts of $210 were placed in the bank's night depository after banking hours and were not recorded on the July 31 bank statement.

d. Outstanding checks as of July 31 total $100.

e. The bank statement included a $30 credit for interest earned on the cash in the bank.

QS 8-8
Days' sales uncollected
A1

The following annual account balances are taken from Mizuno Sports at December 31.

	2009	2008
Accounts receivable	$ 93,700	$ 90,450
Net sales	1,357,600	1,259,680

What is the change in the number of days' sales uncollected between years 2008 and 2009? According to this analysis, is the company's collection of receivables improving? Explain.

QS 8-9A
Documents in a voucher system
P4

Management uses a voucher system to help control and monitor cash disbursements. Identify and describe at least four key documents that are part of a voucher system of control.

QS 8-10B
Purchase discounts
P5

An important part of cash management is knowing when, and if, to take purchase discounts.

a. Which accounting method uses a Discounts Lost account?

b. What is the advantage of this method for management?

McGraw-Hill's HOMEWORK MANAGER® Available with McGraw-Hill's Homework Manager

EXERCISES

Exercise 8-1
Analyzing internal control
C1

Pacific Company is a rapidly growing start-up business. Its recordkeeper, who was hired one year ago, left town after the company's manager discovered that a large sum of money had disappeared over the past six months. An audit disclosed that the recordkeeper had written and signed several checks made payable to her fiancé and then recorded the checks as salaries expense. The fiancé, who cashed the checks but never worked for the company, left town with the recordkeeper. As a result, the company incurred an uninsured loss of $184,000. Evaluate Pacific's internal control system and indicate which principles of internal control appear to have been ignored.

Exercise 8-2
Control of cash receipts by mail
P1

Some of Chapman Company's cash receipts from customers are received by the company with the regular mail. Chapman's recordkeeper opens these letters and deposits the cash received each day. (*a*) Identify any internal control problem(s) in this arrangement. (*b*) What changes to its internal control system do you recommend?

Exercise 8-3
Internal control recommendations
C1

What internal control procedures would you recommend in each of the following situations?

1. A concession company has one employee who sells sunscreen, T-shirts, and sunglasses at the beach. Each day, the employee is given enough sunscreen, shirts, and sunglasses to last through the day and enough cash to make change. The money is kept in a box at the stand.

2. An antique store has one employee who is given cash and sent to garage sales each weekend. The employee pays cash for any merchandise acquired that the antique store resells.

Exercise 8-4
Petty cash fund accounting
P2

Check (2) Cr. Cash $210

Fresno Co. establishes a $350 petty cash fund on January 1. On January 8, the fund shows $140 in cash along with receipts for the following expenditures: postage, $67; transportation-in, $35; delivery expenses, $52; and miscellaneous expenses, $56. Fresno uses the perpetual system in accounting for merchandise inventory. Prepare journal entries to (1) establish the fund on January 1, (2) reimburse it on January 8, and (3) both reimburse the fund and increase it to $550 on January 8, assuming no entry in part 2. (*Hint*: Make two separate entries for part 3.)

Exercise 8-5
Petty cash fund with a shortage
P2

Check (2) Cr. Cash $216 and (3) Cr. Cash $50

Reichard Company establishes a $250 petty cash fund on September 9. On September 30, the fund shows $34 in cash along with receipts for the following expenditures: transportation-in, $47; postage expenses, $62; and miscellaneous expenses, $103. The petty cashier could not account for a $4 shortage in the fund. Reichard uses the perpetual system in accounting for merchandise inventory. Prepare (1) the September 9 entry to establish the fund, (2) the September 30 entry to reimburse the fund, and (3) an October 1 entry to increase the fund to $300.

Exercise 8-6
Bank reconciliation and adjusting entries
P3

Prepare a table with the following headings for a monthly bank reconciliation dated September 30.

Bank Balance		Book Balance			Not Shown on the Reconciliation
Add	Deduct	Add	Deduct	Adjust	

For each item 1 through 12, place an *x* in the appropriate column to indicate whether the item should be added to or deducted from the book or bank balance, or whether it should not appear on the reconciliation. If the book balance is to be adjusted, place a *Dr.* or *Cr.* in the Adjust column to indicate whether the Cash balance should be debited or credited. At the left side of your table, number the items to correspond to the following list.

1. NSF check from customer is returned on September 25 but not yet recorded by this company.
2. Interest earned on the September cash balance in the bank.
3. Deposit made on September 5 and processed by the bank on September 6.
4. Checks written by another depositor but charged against this company's account.
5. Bank service charge for September.
6. Checks outstanding on August 31 that cleared the bank in September.
7. Check written against the company's account and cleared by the bank; erroneously not recorded by the company's recordkeeper.
8. Principal and interest on a note receivable to this company is collected by the bank but not yet recorded by the company.
9. Checks written and mailed to payees on October 2.
10. Checks written by the company and mailed to payees on September 30.
11. Night deposit made on September 30 after the bank closed.
12. Special bank charge for collection of note in part 8 on this company's behalf.

Exercise 8-7
Voucher system
P1

The voucher system of control is designed to control cash disbursements and the acceptance of obligations.

1. The voucher system of control establishes procedures for what two processes?
2. What types of expenditures should be overseen by a voucher system of control?
3. When is the voucher initially prepared? Explain.

Exercise 8-8
Bank reconciliation
P3

Austin Clinic deposits all cash receipts on the day when they are received and it makes all cash payments by check. At the close of business on June 30, 2009, its Cash account shows a $15,671 debit balance. Austin Clinic's June 30 bank statement shows $15,382 on deposit in the bank. Prepare a bank reconciliation for Austin Clinic using the following information:

a. Outstanding checks as of June 30 total $2,700.
b. The June 30 bank statement included a $65 debit memorandum for bank services.

c. Check No. 919, listed with the canceled checks, was correctly drawn for $489 in payment of a utility bill on June 15. Austin Clinic mistakenly recorded it with a debit to Utilities Expense and a credit to Cash in the amount of $498.

d. The June 30 cash receipts of $2,933 were placed in the bank's night depository after banking hours and were not recorded on the June 30 bank statement.

Check Reconciled bal., $15,615

Exercise 8-9
Adjusting entries from bank reconciliation P3

Prepare the adjusting journal entries that Austin Clinic must record as a result of preparing the bank reconciliation in Exercise 8-8.

Exercise 8-10
Bank reconciliation
P3

Walsh Company deposits all cash receipts on the day when they are received and it makes all cash payments by check. At the close of business on May 31, 2009, its Cash account shows a $7,750 debit balance. Walsh's May 31 bank statement shows $6,900 on deposit in the bank. Prepare a bank reconciliation for Walsh Company using the following information.

a. May 31 cash receipts of $1,100 were placed in the bank's night depository after banking hours and were not recorded on the May 31 bank statement.

b. Outstanding checks as of May 31 total $800.

c. The May 31 bank statement included a $50 debit memorandum for bank services; Walsh has not yet recorded the cost of these services.

d. In reviewing the bank statement, a $200 check written by Wald Company was mistakenly drawn against Walsh's account.

e. A debit memorandum for $300 refers to a $300 NSF check from a customer; Walsh has not yet recorded this NSF check.

Check Reconciled bal., $7,400

Exercise 8-11
Liquid assets and accounts receivable
A1

Todd Co. reported annual net sales for 2008 and 2009 of $664,000 and $746,000, respectively. Its year-end balances of accounts receivable follow: December 31, 2008, $65,000; and December 31, 2009, $93,000. (*a*) Calculate its days' sales uncollected at the end of each year. (*b*) Evaluate and comment on any changes in the amount of liquid assets tied up in receivables.

Exercise 8-12[A]
Documents in a voucher system
P4

Match each document in a voucher system in column one with its description in column two.

Document

1. Purchase requisition
2. Purchase order
3. Invoice
4. Receiving report
5. Invoice approval
6. Voucher

Description

A. An itemized statement of goods prepared by the vendor listing the customer's name, items sold, sales prices, and terms of sale.

B. An internal file used to store documents and information to control cash disbursements and to ensure that a transaction is properly authorized and recorded.

C. A document used to place an order with a vendor that authorizes the vendor to ship ordered merchandise at the stated price and terms.

D. A checklist of steps necessary for the approval of an invoice for recording and payment; also known as a check authorization.

E. A document used by department managers to inform the purchasing department to place an order with a vendor.

F. A document used to notify the appropriate persons that ordered goods have arrived, including a description of the quantities and condition of goods.

Exercise 8-13[B]
Record invoices at gross or net amounts
P5

World Imports uses the perpetual system in accounting for merchandise inventory and had the following transactions during the month of October. Prepare entries to record these transactions assuming that World Imports records invoices (*a*) at gross amounts and (*b*) at net amounts.

Oct.	2	Purchased merchandise at a $5,600 price, invoice dated October 2, terms 1/10, n/30.
	10	Received a $900 credit memorandum (at full invoice price) for the return of merchandise that it purchased on October 2.
	17	Purchased merchandise at a $5,950 price, invoice dated October 16, terms 2/10, n/30.
	26	Paid for the merchandise purchased on October 17, less the discount.
	31	Paid for the merchandise purchased on October 2. Payment was delayed because the invoice was mistakenly filed for payment today. This error caused the discount to be lost.

PROBLEM SET A

For each of these five separate cases, identify the principle(s) of internal control that is violated. Recommend what the business should do to ensure adherence to principles of internal control.

Problem 8-1A
Analyzing internal control
C1

1. Chi Han records all incoming customer cash receipts for his employer and posts the customer payments to their respective accounts.
2. At Tico Company, Jenn and Kirsten alternate lunch hours. Jenn is the petty cash custodian, but if someone needs petty cash when she is at lunch, Kirsten fills in as custodian.
3. Nori Nozumi posts all patient charges and payments at the Hopeville Medical Clinic. Each night Nori backs up the computerized accounting system to a tape and stores the tape in a locked file at her desk.
4. Sanjay Shales prides himself on hiring quality workers who require little supervision. As office manager, Sanjay gives his employees full discretion over their tasks and for years has seen no reason to perform independent reviews of their work.
5. Cala Farah's manager has told her to reduce costs. Cala decides to raise the deductible on the plant's property insurance from $5,000 to $10,000. This cuts the property insurance premium in half. In a related move, she decides that bonding the plant's employees is a waste of money since the company has not experienced any losses due to employee theft. Cala saves the entire amount of the bonding insurance premium by dropping the bonding insurance.

Problem 8-2A
Establish, reimburse, and increase petty cash
P2

Beard Gallery had the following petty cash transactions in February of the current year.

Feb.	2	Wrote a $300 check, cashed it, and gave the proceeds and the petty cashbox to Reggie Gore, the petty cashier.
	5	Purchased bond paper for the copier for $14.55 that is immediately used.
	9	Paid $32.50 COD shipping charges on merchandise purchased for resale, terms FOB shipping point. Beard uses the perpetual system to account for merchandise inventory.
	12	Paid $7.85 postage to express mail a contract to a client.
	14	Reimbursed Jonny Carr, the manager, $66 for business mileage on her car.
	20	Purchased stationery for $67.67 that is immediately used.
	23	Paid a courier $23 to deliver merchandise sold to a customer, terms FOB destination.
	25	Paid $10.30 COD shipping charges on merchandise purchased for resale, terms FOB shipping point.
	27	Paid $55 for postage expenses.
	28	The fund had $20.82 remaining in the petty cash box. Sorted the petty cash receipts by accounts affected and exchanged them for a check to reimburse the fund for expenditures.
	28	The petty cash fund amount is increased by $100 to a total of $400.

Required

1. Prepare the journal entry to establish the petty cash fund.
2. Prepare a petty cash payments report for February with these categories: delivery expense, mileage expense, postage expense, merchandise inventory (for transportation-in), and office supplies expense. Sort the payments into the appropriate categories and total the expenditures in each category.
3. Prepare the journal entries for part 2 to both (*a*) reimburse and (*b*) increase the fund amount.

Check (3a) Cr. Cash $279.18

Problem 8-3A
Establish, reimburse, and adjust petty cash
P2

Dylan Co. set up a petty cash fund for payments of small amounts. The following transactions involving the petty cash fund occurred in May (the last month of the company's fiscal year).

May	1	Prepared a company check for $350 to establish the petty cash fund.
	15	Prepared a company check to replenish the fund for the following expenditures made since May 1.

a. Paid $109.20 for janitorial services.
b. Paid $89.15 for miscellaneous expenses.
c. Paid postage expenses of $60.90.
d. Paid $80.01 to *The County Gazette* (the local newspaper) for an advertisement.
e. Counted $16.84 remaining in the petty cash box.

16 Prepared a company check for $200 to increase the fund to $550.
31 The petty cashier reports that $390.27 cash remains in the fund. A company check is drawn to replenish the fund for the following expenditures made since May 15.
f. Paid postage expenses of $59.10.
g. Reimbursed the office manager for business mileage, $47.05.
h. Paid $48.58 to deliver merchandise to a customer, terms FOB destination.
31 The company decides that the May 16 increase in the fund was too large. It reduces the fund by $50, leaving a total of $500.

Required

1. Prepare journal entries to establish the fund on May 1, to replenish it on May 15 and on May 31, and to reflect any increase or decrease in the fund balance on May 16 and May 31.

Check (1) Cr. to Cash: May 15, $333.16; May 16, $200

Analysis Component

2. Explain how the company's financial statements are affected if the petty cash fund is not replenished and no entry is made on May 31.

Problem 8-4A
Prepare a bank reconciliation and record adjustments
P3 eXcel
mhhe.com/wildFAP19e

The following information is available to reconcile Hamilton Company's book balance of cash with its bank statement cash balance as of July 31, 2009.

a. On July 31, the company's Cash account has a $25,862 debit balance, but its July bank statement shows a $28,575 cash balance.

b. Check No. 3031 for $1,670 and Check No. 3040 for $827 were outstanding on the June 30 bank reconciliation. Check No. 3040 is listed with the July canceled checks, but Check No. 3031 is not. Also, Check No. 3065 for $611 and Check No. 3069 for $2,438, both written in July, are not among the canceled checks on the July 31 statement.

c. In comparing the canceled checks on the bank statement with the entries in the accounting records, it is found that Check No. 3056 for July rent was correctly written and drawn for $1,250 but was erroneously entered in the accounting records as $1,240.

d. A credit memorandum enclosed with the July bank statement indicates the bank collected $6,000 cash on a non-interest-bearing note for Hamilton, deducted a $30 collection fee, and credited the remainder to its account. Hamilton had not recorded this event before receiving the statement.

e. A debit memorandum for $805 lists a $795 NSF check plus a $10 NSF charge. The check had been received from a customer, Evan Shaw. Hamilton has not yet recorded this check as NSF.

f. Enclosed with the July statement is a $9 debit memorandum for bank services. It has not yet been recorded because no previous notification had been received.

g. Hamilton's July 31 daily cash receipts of $7,152 were placed in the bank's night depository on that date, but do not appear on the July 31 bank statement.

Required

1. Prepare the bank reconciliation for this company as of July 31, 2009.

2. Prepare the journal entries necessary to bring the company's book balance of cash into conformity with the reconciled cash balance as of July 31, 2009.

Check (1) Reconciled balance, $31,008; (2) Cr. Note Receivable $6,000

Analysis Component

3. Assume that the July 31, 2009, bank reconciliation for this company is prepared and some items are treated incorrectly. For each of the following errors, explain the effect of the error on (i) the adjusted bank statement cash balance and (ii) the adjusted cash account book balance.

a. The company's unadjusted cash account balance of $25,862 is listed on the reconciliation as $25,682.

b. The bank's collection of the $6,000 note less the $30 collection fee is added to the bank statement cash balance on the reconciliation.

Problem 8-5A
Prepare a bank reconciliation and record adjustments
P3

eXcel
mhhe.com/wildFAP19e

Madison Company most recently reconciled its bank statement and book balances of cash on August 31 and it reported two checks outstanding, No. 5888 for $1,089 and No. 5893 for $542. The following information is available for its September 30, 2009, reconciliation.

From the September 30 Bank Statement

PREVIOUS BALANCE	TOTAL CHECKS AND DEBITS	TOTAL DEPOSITS AND CREDITS	CURRENT BALANCE
18,500	9,799	11,463	20,164

CHECKS AND DEBITS			DEPOSITS AND CREDITS		DAILY BALANCE	
Date	No.	Amount	Date	Amount	Date	Amount
09/03	5888	1,089	09/05	1,145	08/31	18,500
09/04	5902	711	09/12	2,282	09/03	17,411
09/07	5901	1,805	09/21	4,072	09/04	16,700
09/17		631 NSF	09/25	2,323	09/05	17,845
09/20	5905	986	09/30	23 IN	09/07	16,040
09/22	5903	402	09/30	1,618 CM	09/12	18,322
09/22	5904	2,073			09/17	17,691
09/28	5907	213			09/20	16,705
09/29	5909	1,889			09/21	20,777
					09/22	18,302
					09/25	20,625
					09/28	20,412
					09/29	18,523
					09/30	20,164

From Madison Company's Accounting Records

Cash Receipts Deposited

Date			Cash Debit
Sept.	5		1,145
	12		2,282
	21		4,072
	25		2,323
	30		1,753
			11,575

Cash Disbursements

Check No.		Cash Credit
5901		1,805
5902		711
5903		402
5904		2,037
5905		986
5906		1,003
5907		213
5908		378
5909		1,889
		9,424

Cash Acct. No. 101

Date		Explanation	PR	Debit	Credit	Balance
Aug.	31	Balance				16,869
Sept.	30	Total receipts	R12	11,575		28,444
	30	Total disbursements	D23		9,424	19,020

Additional Information

Check No. 5904 is correctly drawn for $2,073 to pay for computer equipment; however, the recordkeeper misread the amount and entered it in the accounting records with a debit to Computer Equipment and a credit to Cash of $2,037. The NSF check shown in the statement was originally received from a customer, S. Nilson, in payment of her account. Its return has not yet been recorded by the company. The credit memorandum is from the collection of a $1,640 note for Madison Company by the bank. The bank deducted a $22 collection fee. The collection and fee are not yet recorded.

Required

1. Prepare the September 30, 2009, bank reconciliation for this company.
2. Prepare the journal entries to adjust the book balance of cash to the reconciled balance.

Check (1) Reconciled balance, $19,994 (2) Cr. Note Receivable $1,640

Analysis Component

3. The bank statement reveals that some of the prenumbered checks in the sequence are missing. Describe three situations that could explain this.

PROBLEM SET B

Problem 8-1B
Analyzing internal control

C1

For each of these five separate cases, identify the principle(s) of internal control that is violated. Recommend what the business should do to ensure adherence to principles of internal control.

1. Latisha Tally is the company's computer specialist and oversees its computerized payroll system. Her boss recently asked her to put password protection on all office computers. Latisha has put a password in place that allows only the boss access to the file where pay rates are changed and personnel are added or deleted from the payroll.
2. Marker Theater has a computerized order-taking system for its tickets. The system is active all week and backed up every Friday night.
3. Sutton Company has two employees handling acquisitions of inventory. One employee places purchase orders and pays vendors. The second employee receives the merchandise.
4. The owner of Super Pharmacy uses a check protector to perforate checks, making it difficult for anyone to alter the amount of the check. The check protector is on the owner's desk in an office that contains company checks and is normally unlocked.
5. Lavina Company is a small business that has separated the duties of cash receipts and cash disbursements. The employee responsible for cash disbursements reconciles the bank account monthly.

Problem 8-2B
Establish, reimburse, and increase petty cash

P2

Music City Center had the following petty cash transactions in March of the current year.

March	5	Wrote a $300 check, cashed it, and gave the proceeds and the petty cashbox to Abby Rode, the petty cashier.
	6	Paid $16.75 COD shipping charges on merchandise purchased for resale, terms FOB shipping point. Music City uses the perpetual system to account for merchandise inventory.
	11	Paid $44.50 delivery charges on merchandise sold to a customer, terms FOB destination.
	12	Purchased file folders for $7.95 that are immediately used.
	14	Reimbursed Alys Mingle, the manager, $68 for office supplies purchased and used.
	18	Purchased printer paper for $20 that is immediately used.
	27	Paid $11.60 COD shipping charges on merchandise purchased for resale, terms FOB shipping point.
	28	Paid postage expenses of $60.
	30	Reimbursed Mingle $56.80 for business car mileage.
	31	Cash of $16.81 remained in the fund. Sorted the petty cash receipts by accounts affected and exchanged them for a check to reimburse the fund for expenditures.
	31	The petty cash fund amount is increased by $50 to a total of $350.

Required

1. Prepare the journal entry to establish the petty cash fund.
2. Prepare a petty cash payments report for March with these categories: delivery expense, mileage expense, postage expense, merchandise inventory (for transportation-in), and office supplies expense. Sort the payments into the appropriate categories and total the expenses in each category.
3. Prepare the journal entries for part 2 to both (*a*) reimburse and (*b*) increase the fund amount.

Check (2) Total expenses $285.60

(3a) Cr. Cash $283.19

Problem 8-3B
Establishing, reimbursing, and adjusting petty cash
P2

Lansing Co. establishes a petty cash fund for payments of small amounts. The following transactions involving the petty cash fund occurred in January (the last month of the company's fiscal year).

Jan. 3 A company check for $150 is written and made payable to the petty cashier to establish the petty cash fund.

14 A company check is written to replenish the fund for the following expenditures made since January 3.

a. Purchased office supplies for $17.52 that are immediately used up.

b. Paid $20.50 COD shipping charges on merchandise purchased for resale, terms FOB shipping point. Lansing uses the perpetual system to account for inventory.

c. Paid $55.30 to All-Tech for minor repairs to a computer.

d. Paid $19.63 for items classified as miscellaneous expenses.

e. Counted $35.05 remaining in the petty cash box.

15 Prepared a company check for $50 to increase the fund to $200.

31 The petty cashier reports that $29.57 remains in the fund. A company check is written to replenish the fund for the following expenditures made since January 14.

f. Paid $52 to *The Smart Shopper* for an advertisement in January's newsletter.

g. Paid $55.61 for postage expenses.

h. Paid $65 to FedEx for delivery of merchandise, terms FOB destination.

31 The company decides that the January 15 increase in the fund was too little. It increases the fund by another $50, leaving a total of $250.

Required

Check (1) Cr. to Cash: Jan. 14, $114.95; Jan. 15, $50

1. Prepare journal entries to establish the fund on January 3, to replenish it on January 14 and January 31, and to reflect any increase or decrease in the fund balance on January 15 and 31.

Analysis Component

2. Explain how the company's financial statements are affected if the petty cash fund is not replenished and no entry is made on January 31.

Problem 8-4B
Prepare a bank reconciliation and record adjustments
P3

The following information is available to reconcile Gardenia Co.'s book balance of cash with its bank statement cash balance as of December 31, 2009.

a. The December 31 cash balance according to the accounting records is $13,599, and the bank statement cash balance for that date is $26,379.

b. Check No. 1273 for $1,800 and Check No. 1282 for $892, both written and entered in the accounting records in December, are not among the canceled checks. Two checks, No. 1231 for $676 and No. 1242 for $2,568, were outstanding on the most recent November 30 reconciliation. Check No. 1231 is listed with the December canceled checks, but Check No. 1242 is not.

c. When the December checks are compared with entries in the accounting records, it is found that Check No. 1267 had been correctly drawn for $1,230 to pay for office supplies but was erroneously entered in the accounting records as $1,320.

d. Two debit memoranda are enclosed with the statement and are unrecorded at the time of the reconciliation. One debit memorandum is for $805 and dealt with an NSF check for $795 received from a customer, Millard Industries, in payment of its account. The bank assessed a $10 fee for processing it. The second debit memorandum is a $99.00 charge for check printing. Gardenia did not record these transactions before receiving the statement.

e. A credit memorandum indicates that the bank collected $19,000 cash on a note receivable for the company, deducted a $14 collection fee, and credited the balance to the company's Cash account. Gardenia did not record this transaction before receiving the statement.

f. Gardenia's December 31 daily cash receipts of $10,652 were placed in the bank's night depository on that date, but do not appear on the December 31 bank statement.

Required

Check (1) Reconciled balance, $31,771; (2) Cr. Note Receivable $19,000

1. Prepare the bank reconciliation for this company as of December 31, 2009.

2. Prepare the journal entries necessary to bring the company's book balance of cash into conformity with the reconciled cash balance as of December 31, 2009.

Analysis Component

3. Explain the nature of the communications conveyed by a bank when the bank sends the depositor (*a*) a debit memorandum and (*b*) a credit memorandum.

Problem 8-5B
Prepare a bank reconciliation and record adjustments
P3

Tamzen Systems most recently reconciled its bank balance on April 30 and reported two checks outstanding at that time, No. 1771 for $1,037 and No. 1780 for $516. The following information is available for its May 31, 2009, reconciliation.

From the May 31 Bank Statement

PREVIOUS BALANCE	TOTAL CHECKS AND DEBITS	TOTAL DEPOSITS AND CREDITS	CURRENT BALANCE
18,500	8,041	11,611	22,070

CHECKS AND DEBITS			DEPOSITS AND CREDITS		DAILY BALANCE	
Date	No.	Amount	Date	Amount	Date	Amount
05/01	1771	1,037	05/04	1,109	04/30	18,500
05/02	1783	782	05/14	2,280	05/01	17,463
05/04	1782	1,801	05/22	4,304	05/02	16,681
05/11	1784	424	05/25	1,520 CM	05/04	15,989
05/18		688 NSF	05/26	2,398	05/11	15,565
05/25	1787	993			05/14	17,845
05/26	1785	2,056			05/18	17,157
05/29	1788	238			05/22	21,461
05/31		22 SC			05/25	21,998
					05/26	23,330
					05/29	22,092
					05/31	22,070

From Tamzen Systems' Accounting Records

Cash Receipts Deposited

Date			Cash Debit
May	4		1,109
	14		2,280
	22		4,304
	26		2,398
	31		1,716
			11,807

Cash Disbursements

Check No.		Cash Credit
1782		1,801
1783		782
1784		424
1785		2,056
1786		935
1787		993
1788		228
1789		371
		7,590

Cash — Acct. No. 101

Date		Explanation	PR	Debit	Credit	Balance
Apr.	30	Balance				16,947
May	31	Total receipts	R2	11,807		28,754
	31	Total disbursements	D23		7,590	21,164

Additional Information

Check No. 1788 is correctly drawn for $238 to pay for May utilities; however, the recordkeeper misread the amount and entered it in the accounting records with a debit to Utilities Expense and a credit to Cash for $228. The bank paid and deducted the correct amount. The NSF check shown in the statement was originally received from a customer, W. Sox, in payment of her account. The company has not yet recorded its return. The credit memorandum is from a $1,540 note that the bank collected for the company. The bank deducted a $20 collection fee and deposited the remainder in the company's account. The collection and fee have not yet been recorded.

Required

Check (1) Reconciled balance, $21,964; (2) Cr. Note Receivable $1,540

1. Prepare the May 31, 2009, bank reconciliation for Tamzen Systems.
2. Prepare the journal entries to adjust the book balance of cash to the reconciled balance.

Analysis Component

3. The bank statement reveals that some of the prenumbered checks in the sequence are missing. Describe three possible situations to explain this.

SERIAL PROBLEM

Success Systems

P3

(This serial problem began in Chapter 1 and continues through most of the book. If previous chapter segments were not completed, the serial problem can begin at this point. It is helpful, but not necessary, to use the Working Papers that accompany the book.)

SP 8 Adriana Lopez receives the March bank statement for Success Systems on April 11, 2010. The March 31 bank statement shows an ending cash balance of $77,354. A comparison of the bank statement with the general ledger Cash account, No. 101, reveals the following.

a. Lopez notices that the bank erroneously cleared a $500 check against her account in March that she did not issue. The check documentation included with the bank statement shows that this check was actually issued by a company named Sierra Systems.
b. On March 25, the bank issued a $50 debit memorandum for the safety deposit box that Success Systems agreed to rent from the bank beginning March 25.
c. On March 26, the bank issued a $102 debit memorandum for printed checks that Success Systems ordered from the bank.
d. On March 31, the bank issued a credit memorandum for $33 interest earned on Success Systems' checking account for the month of March.
e. Lopez notices that the check she issued for $128 on March 31, 2010, has not yet cleared the bank.
f. Lopez verifies that all deposits made in March do appear on the March bank statement.
g. The general ledger Cash account, No. 101, shows an ending cash balance per books of $77,845 as of March 31 (prior to any reconciliation).

Required

Check (1) Adj. bank bal. $77,726

1. Prepare a bank reconciliation for Success Systems for the month ended March 31, 2010.
2. Prepare any necessary adjusting entries. Use Miscellaneous Expenses, No. 677, for any bank charges. Use Interest Revenue, No. 404, for any interest earned on the checking account for the month of March.

BEYOND THE NUMBERS

REPORTING IN ACTION

C2 A1

BTN 8-1 Refer to **Best Buy**'s financial statements in Appendix A to answer the following.

1. For both fiscal year-ends March 3, 2007, and February 25, 2006, identify the total amount of cash and cash equivalents. Determine the percent this amount represents of total current assets, total current liabilities, total shareholders' equity, and total assets for both years. Comment on any trends.
2. For fiscal years ended March 3, 2007, and February 25, 2006, use the information in the statement of cash flows to determine the percent change between the beginning and ending year amounts of cash and cash equivalents.
3. Compute the days' sales uncollected as of March 3, 2007, and February 25, 2006. Has the collection of receivables improved? Are accounts receivable an important asset for Best Buy? Explain.

Fast Forward

4. Access Best Buy's financial statements for fiscal years ending after March 3, 2007, from its Website (BestBuy.com) or the SEC's EDGAR database (www.SEC.gov). Recompute its days' sales uncollected for fiscal years ending after March 3, 2007. Compare this to the days' sales uncollected for 2007 and 2006.

COMPARATIVE ANALYSIS

A1

BTN 8-2 Key comparative figures for **Best Buy**, **Circuit City**, and **RadioShack** follow.

($ millions)	Best Buy Current Year	Best Buy Prior Year	Circuit City Current Year	Circuit City Prior Year	RadioShack Current Year	RadioShack Prior Year
Accounts receivable	$ 548	$ 449	$ 383	$ 221	$ 248	$ 309
Net sales	35,934	30,848	12,430	11,514	4,778	5,082

Required

Compute days' sales uncollected for these companies for each of the two years shown. Comment on any trends for the companies. Which company has the largest percent change in days' sales uncollected?

ETHICS CHALLENGE

C1

BTN 8-3 Harriet Knox, Ralph Patton, and Marcia Diamond work for a family physician, Dr. Gwen Conrad, who is in private practice. Dr. Conrad is knowledgeable about office management practices and has segregated the cash receipt duties as follows. Knox opens the mail and prepares a triplicate list of money received. She sends one copy of the list to Patton, the cashier, who deposits the receipts daily in the bank. Diamond, the recordkeeper, receives a copy of the list and posts payments to patients' accounts. About once a month the office clerks have an expensive lunch they pay for as follows. First, Patton endorses a patient's check in Dr. Conrad's name and cashes it at the bank. Knox then destroys the remittance advice accompanying the check. Finally, Diamond posts payment to the customer's account as a miscellaneous credit. The three justify their actions by their relatively low pay and knowledge that Dr. Conrad will likely never miss the money.

Required

1. Who is the best person in Dr. Conrad's office to reconcile the bank statement?
2. Would a bank reconciliation uncover this office fraud?
3. What are some procedures to detect this type of fraud?
4. Suggest additional internal controls that Dr. Conrad could implement.

COMMUNICATING IN PRACTICE

P5

BTN 8-4[B] Assume you are a business consultant. The owner of a company sends you an e-mail expressing concern that the company is not taking advantage of its discounts offered by vendors. The company currently uses the gross method of recording purchases. The owner is considering a review of all invoices and payments from the previous period. Due to the volume of purchases, however, the owner recognizes that this is time-consuming and costly. The owner seeks your advice about monitoring purchase discounts in the future. Provide a response in memorandum form.

TAKING IT TO THE NET

C1 P1

BTN 8-5 Visit the Association of Certified Fraud Examiners Website at cfenet.com. Find and open the file "2006 Report to the Nation." Read the two-page Executive Summary and fill in the following blanks. (The report is under its *Fraud Resource Center* tab or under its *About ACFE* tab [under Press Room and under Fraud Statistics]; we can also use the *Search* tab.)

1. The median loss caused by occupational frauds was $________.
2. Nearly __________ of fraud cases caused at least $1 million in losses.
3. Companies lose ___% of their annual revenues to fraud; this figure translates to $______ billion in fraud losses.
4. The median length of fraud schemes was ____ months from the time the fraud began until it was detected.
5. Companies with anonymous fraud hotlines suffered a median loss of $_______, whereas those without hotlines had a median loss of $_______.

6. The median loss suffered by companies with fewer than 100 employees was $______ per scheme.
7. The most common frauds in small businesses involve employees ____________, ____________, and ____________.
8. Fewer than __% of small businesses had anonymous fraud reporting systems, and less than __% had internal audit departments, conducted surprise audits, or conducted fraud training.
9. Fewer than __% of the perpetrators had convictions prior to committing their frauds.

TEAMWORK IN ACTION

C1

BTN 8-6 Organize the class into teams. Each team must prepare a list of 10 internal controls a consumer could observe in a typical retail department store. When called upon, the team's spokesperson must be prepared to share controls identified by the team that have not been shared by another team's spokesperson.

ENTREPRENEURIAL DECISION

C1 P1

BTN 8-7 Review the opening feature of this chapter that highlights Dylan Lauren and Jeff Rubin, and their company **Dylan's Candy Bar**.

Required

1. List the seven principles of internal control and explain how Dylan and Jeff could implement each of them in their retail stores.
2. Do you believe that they will need to add controls as their business expands? Explain.

HITTING THE ROAD

C1

BTN 8-8 Visit an area of your college that serves the student community with either products or services. Some examples are food services, libraries, and bookstores. Identify and describe between four and eight internal controls being implemented.

GLOBAL DECISION

C2 A1

DSG

BTN 8-9 The following information is from **DSG international plc** (www.DSGiplc.com) financial statements.

(£ millions)	Current Year	Prior Year
Cash	441	618
Accounts receivable	393	370
Current assets	2,067	2,094
Total assets	3,977	4,120
Current liabilities	1,869	1,749
Shareholders' equity	1,304	1,424
Net sales	7,930	6,984

Required

1. For each year, compute the percentages that cash represents of current assets, total assets, current liabilities, and shareholders' equity. Comment on any trends in these percentages.
2. Determine the percentage change between the current and prior year cash balances.
3. Compute the days' sales uncollected at the end of both the current year and the prior year. Has the collection of receivables improved? Explain.

ANSWERS TO MULTIPLE CHOICE QUIZ

1. e; The entry follows.

Debits to expenses (or assets)	420	
Cash Over and Short	5	
Cash		425

2. a; recognizes cash collection of note by bank.

3. a; the bank reconciliation follows.

Bank Reconciliation
November 30

Balance per bank statement	$1,895	Balance per books	$1,742
Add: Deposit in transit	795	Add: Note collected less fee	320
Deduct: Outstanding checks	(638)	Deduct: Service charge	(10)
Reconciled balance	$2,052	Reconciled balance	$2,052

4. d; ($6,720/$84,000) × 365 = 29.2 days

5. b; The entry follows.

Merchandise Inventory*	5,880	
Accounts Payable		5,880

*$6,000 × 98%

A Look Back

Chapter 8 focused on internal control and reporting for cash. We described internal control procedures and the accounting for and management of cash.

A Look at This Chapter

This chapter emphasizes receivables. We explain that they are liquid assets and describe how companies account for and report them. We also discuss the importance of estimating uncollectibles.

A Look Ahead

Chapter 10 focuses on plant assets, natural resources, and intangible assets. We explain how to account for, report, and analyze these long-term assets.

Chapter 9 Accounting for Receivables

Learning Objectives

CAP

Conceptual

C1 Describe accounts receivable and how they occur and are recorded. *(p. 358)*

C2 Describe a note receivable and the computation of its maturity date and interest. *(p. 368)*

C3 Explain how receivables can be converted to cash before maturity. *(p. 371)*

Analytical

A1 Compute accounts receivable turnover and use it to help assess financial condition. *(p. 372)*

Procedural

P1 Apply the direct write-off and allowance methods to account for accounts receivable. *(p. 361)*

P2 Estimate uncollectibles using methods based on sales and accounts receivable. *(p. 364)*

P3 Record the receipt of a note receivable. *(p. 369)*

P4 Record the honoring and dishonoring of a note and adjustments for interest. *(p. 370)*

LP9

Decision Feature

Sweat Equity

"Create what the industry is missing . . . it is worth the hardships"—Kevin Plank (center)

BALTIMORE, MD—"There was a void in apparel and I decided to fill it," says Kevin Plank, the founder of **Under Armour (UnderArmour.com),** a manufacturer of athletic apparel using a polyester fabric that whisks perspiration away. He invested his life savings of $20,000 and began by working out of his grandma's basement.

As sales grew, Kevin partnered with a factory in Ohio and hit it off with the factory manager, Sal Fasciana. Sal spent many evenings and weekends teaching Kevin about accounting and costs. "I said, 'OK, kid. This is the way it's going to be done,'" recalls Sal. Attention to details carried over to where Kevin learned to monitor receivables. Decisions on credit sales and policies for extending credit can make or break a start-up.

Kevin applied well what Sal taught him. He ensured that credit sales were extended to customers in good credit standing. Kevin knows his customers, including who pays and when. Says Kevin, we understand our customers—inside and out—including cash payment patterns that allow us to estimate uncollectibles and minimize bad debts. His financial report says, "We make ongoing estimates relating to the collectibility of our accounts receivable and maintain a reserve for estimated losses resulting from the inability of our customers to make required payments."

A commitment to quality customers is propelling Under Armour's sales and shattering Kevin's most optimistic goals. "It's about educating consumers . . . investing in the product." Kevin has also issued notes receivable to select employees. Both accounts and notes receivables receive his attention. His financial report states that they "review the allowance for doubtful accounts monthly."

"When I first started . . . I was a young punk who thought he knew everything," explains Kevin. Although he admits that insight and ingenuity are vital, he knows accounting reports must show profits for long-term success. "Most people out there are saying we're going to trip up at some point," says Kevin. "Our job is to prove them wrong." He might also prove Thomas Edison right: genius is 99 percent perspiration and 1 percent inspiration.

[Sources: *Under Armour Website,* January 2009; *Under Armour 10-K Report,* Filed February 2007; *Entrepreneur,* November 2003; *FastCompany,* 2005 and 2002; *USA Today,* December 2004; *Inc.com,* 2003 and 2004; *All Headline News,* August 2005; *Entrepreneur's Journey,* November 2007]

This chapter focuses on accounts receivable and short-term notes receivable. We describe each of these assets, their uses, and how they are accounted for and reported in financial statements. This knowledge helps us use accounting information to make better business decisions. It can also help in predicting future company performance and financial condition as well as in managing one's own business.

Accounting for Receivables

Accounts Receivable
- Recognizing accounts receivable
- Valuing accounts receivable
- Estimating bad debts

Notes Receivable
- Computing maturity and interest
- Recognizing notes receivable
- Valuing and settling notes

Disposal of Receivables
- Selling receivables
- Pledging receivables

Accounts Receivable

Video9.1

A *receivable* is an amount due from another party. The two most common receivables are accounts receivable and notes receivable. Other receivables include interest receivable, rent receivable, tax refund receivable, and receivables from employees. **Accounts receivable** are amounts due from customers for credit sales. This section begins by describing how accounts receivable occur. It includes receivables that occur when customers use credit cards issued by third parties and when a company gives credit directly to customers. When a company does extend credit directly to customers, it (1) maintains a separate account receivable for each customer and (2) accounts for bad debts from credit sales.

Recognizing Accounts Receivable

C1 Describe accounts receivable and how they occur and are recorded.

Accounts receivable occur from credit sales to customers. The amount of credit sales has increased in recent years, reflecting several factors including an efficient financial system. Retailers such as **Limited Brands** and **Best Buy** hold millions of dollars in accounts receivable. Similar amounts are held by wholesalers such as **SUPERVALU** and **SYSCO**. Exhibit 9.1 shows recent dollar amounts of accounts receivable and their percent of total assets for four well-known companies.

EXHIBIT 9.1

Accounts Receivable for Selected Companies

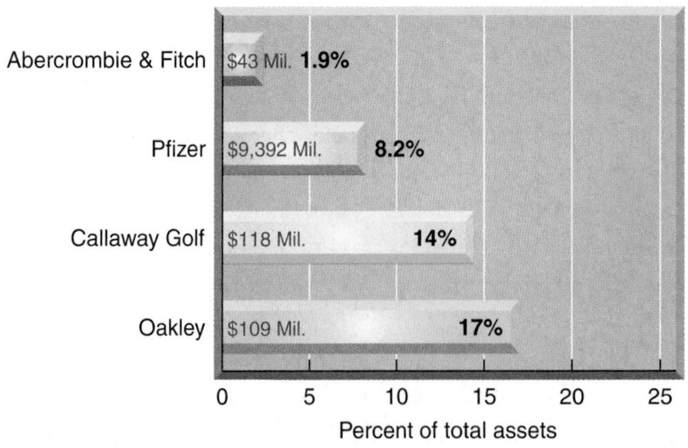

Sales on Credit Credit sales are recorded by increasing (debiting) Accounts Receivable. A company must also maintain a separate account for each customer that tracks how much that customer purchases, has already paid, and still owes. This information provides the basis for sending bills to customers and for other business analyses. To maintain this information, companies that extend credit directly to their customers keep a separate account receivable for each one of them.

The general ledger continues to have a single Accounts Receivable account along with the other financial statement accounts, but a supplementary record is created to maintain a separate account for each customer. This supplementary record is called the *accounts receivable ledger*.

Exhibit 9.2 shows the relation between the Accounts Receivable account in the general ledger and its individual customer accounts in the accounts receivable ledger for TechCom, a small electronics wholesaler. This exhibit reports a $3,000 ending balance of TechCom's accounts receivable for June 30. TechCom's transactions are mainly in cash, but it has two major credit customers: CompStore and RDA Electronics. Its *schedule of accounts receivable* shows that the $3,000 balance of the Accounts Receivable account in the general ledger equals the total of its two customers' balances in the accounts receivable ledger.

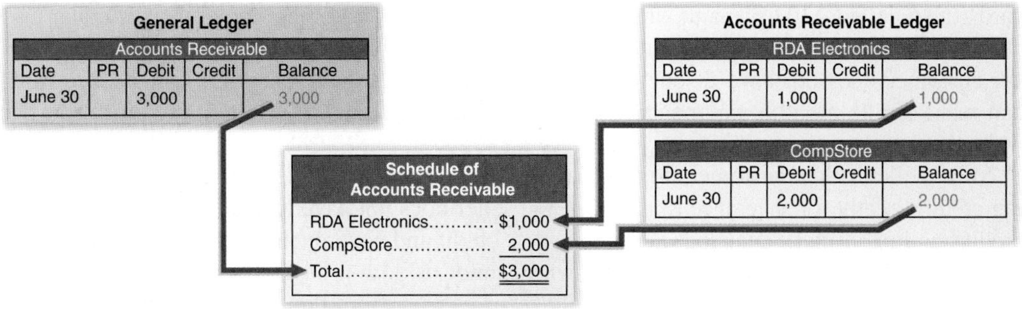

EXHIBIT 9.2

General Ledger and the Accounts Receivable Ledger (before July 1 transactions)

To see how accounts receivable from credit sales are recognized in the accounting records, we look at two transactions on July 1 between TechCom and its credit customers—see Exhibit 9.3. The first is a credit sale of $950 to CompStore. A credit sale is posted with both a debit to the Accounts Receivable account in the general ledger and a debit to the customer account in the accounts receivable ledger. The second transaction is a collection of $720 from RDA Electronics from a prior credit sale. Cash receipts from a credit customer are posted with a credit to the Accounts Receivable account in the general ledger and flow through to credit the customer account in the accounts receivable ledger. (Posting debits or credits to Accounts Receivable in two separate ledgers does not violate the requirement that debits equal credits. The equality of debits and credits is maintained in the general ledger. The accounts receivable ledger is a *supplementary* record providing information on each customer.)

EXHIBIT 9.3

Accounts Receivable Transactions

July 1	Accounts Receivable—CompStore	950	
	Sales.		950
	*To record credit sales**		
July 1	Cash	720	
	Accounts Receivable—RDA Electronics		720
	To record collection of credit sales.		

Assets = Liabilities + Equity
+ 950 +950

Assets = Liabilities + Equity
+720
−720

* We omit the entry to Dr. Cost of Sales and Cr. Merchandise Inventory to focus on sales and receivables.

Exhibit 9.4 shows the general ledger and the accounts receivable ledger after recording the two July 1 transactions. The general ledger shows the effects of the sale, the collection, and the resulting balance of $3,230. These events are also reflected in the individual customer accounts: RDA Electronics has an ending balance of $280, and CompStore's ending balance is

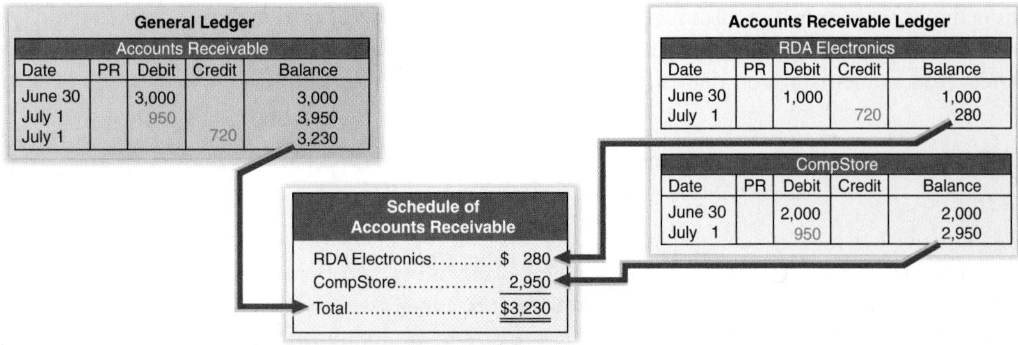

EXHIBIT 9.4

General Ledger and the Accounts Receivable Ledger (after July 1 transactions)

$2,950. The $3,230 sum of the individual accounts equals the debit balance of the Accounts Receivable account in the general ledger.

Like TechCom, many large retailers such as **Sears** and **JCPenney** sell on credit. Many also maintain their own credit cards to grant credit to approved customers and to earn interest on any balance not paid within a specified period of time. This allows them to avoid the fee charged by credit card companies. The entries in this case are the same as those for TechCom except for the possibility of added interest revenue. If a customer owes interest on a bill, we debit Interest Receivable and credit Interest Revenue for that amount.

Point: **Visa USA** now transacts more than $1 trillion from its credit, debit, and prepaid cards.

Credit Card Sales Many companies allow their customers to pay for products and services using third-party credit cards such as **Visa**, **MasterCard**, or **American Express**, and debit cards (also called ATM or bank cards). This practice gives customers the ability to make purchases without cash or checks. Once credit is established with a credit card company or bank, the customer does not have to open an account with each store. Customers using these cards can make single monthly payments instead of several payments to different creditors and can defer their payments.

Many sellers allow customers to use third-party credit cards and debit cards instead of granting credit directly for several reasons. First, the seller does not have to evaluate each customer's credit standing or make decisions about who gets credit and how much. Second, the seller avoids the risk of extending credit to customers who cannot or do not pay. This risk is transferred to the card company. Third, the seller typically receives cash from the card company sooner than had it granted credit directly to customers. Fourth, a variety of credit options for customers offers a potential increase in sales volume. **Sears** historically offered credit only to customers using a Sears card but later changed its policy to permit customers to charge purchases to third-party credit card companies in a desire to increase sales. It reported: "SearsCharge increased its share of Sears retail sales even as the company expanded the payment options available to its customers with the acceptance . . . of Visa, MasterCard, and American Express in addition to the [Sears] Card."

There are guidelines in how companies account for credit card and debit card sales. Some credit cards, but mostly debit cards, credit a seller's Cash account immediately upon deposit. In this case the seller deposits a copy of each card sales receipt in its bank account just as it deposits a customer's check. Some other cards require the seller to remit a copy (often electronically) of each receipt to the card company. Until payment is received, the seller has an account receivable from the card company. In both cases, the seller pays a fee for services provided by the card company, often ranging from 1% to 5% of card sales. This charge is deducted from the credit to the seller's account or the cash payment to the seller.

Decision Insight

Debit Card vs. Credit Card A buyer's debit card purchase reduces the buyer's cash account balance at the card company, which is often a bank. Since the buyer's cash account balance is a liability (with a credit balance) for the card company to the buyer, the card company would debit that account for a buyer's purchase—hence, the term *debit card.* A credit card reflects authorization by the card company of a line of credit for the buyer with preset interest rates and payment terms—hence, the term *credit card.* Most card companies waive interest charges if the buyer pays its balance each month.

Point: Web merchants pay twice as much in credit card association fees as other retailers because they suffer 10 times as much fraud.

The procedures used in accounting for credit card sales depend on whether cash is received immediately on deposit or cash receipt is delayed until the credit card company makes the payment. To illustrate, if TechCom has $100 of credit card sales with a 4% fee, and its $96 cash is received immediately on deposit, the entry is

Assets = Liabilities + Equity
+96 +100
−4

July 15	Cash	96	
	Credit Card Expense	4	
	Sales		100
	*To record credit card sales less a 4% credit card expense.**		

* We omit the entry to Dr. Cost of Sales and Cr. Merchandise Inventory to focus on credit card expense.

However, if instead TechCom must remit electronically the credit card sales receipts to the credit card company and wait for the $96 cash payment, the entry on the date of sale is

July 15	**Accounts Receivable—Credit Card Co.**	96	
	Credit Card Expense	4	
	Sales		100
	*To record credit card sales less 4% credit card expense.**		

Assets = Liabilities + Equity
+96 +100
−4

* We omit the entry to Dr. Cost of Sales and Cr. Merchandise Inventory to focus on credit card expense.

When cash is later received from the credit card company, usually through electronic funds transfer, the entry is

July 20	Cash	96	
	Accounts Receivable—Credit Card Co.		96
	To record cash receipt.		

Assets = Liabilities + Equity
+96
−96

Some firms report credit card expense in the income statement as a type of discount deducted from sales to get net sales. Other companies classify it as a selling expense or even as an administrative expense. Arguments can be made for each approach.

Point: Third-party credit card costs can be large. JCPenney recently reported third-party credit card costs exceeding $10 million.

Installment Sales and Receivables Many companies allow their credit customers to make periodic payments over several months. For example, **Ford Motor Company** reports more than $70 billion in installment receivables. The seller refers to such assets as *installment accounts receivable,* which are amounts owed by customers from credit sales for which payment is required in periodic amounts over an extended time period. Source documents for installment accounts receivable include sales slips or invoices describing the sales transactions. The customer is usually charged interest. Although installment accounts receivable can have credit periods of more than one year, they are classified as current assets if the seller regularly offers customers such terms.

Decision Maker

Entrepreneur As a small retailer, you are considering allowing customers to buy merchandise using credit cards. Until now, your store accepted only cash and checks. What analysis do you use to make this decision? [Answer—p. 376]

Quick Check

Answers—p. 376

1. In recording credit card sales, when do you debit Accounts Receivable and when do you debit Cash?
2. A company accumulates sales receipts and remits them to the credit card company for payment. When are the credit card expenses recorded? When are these expenses incurred?

Valuing Accounts Receivable—Direct Write-Off Method

P1 Apply the direct write-off and allowance methods to account for accounts receivable.

When a company directly grants credit to its customers, it expects that some customers will not pay what they promised. The accounts of these customers are *uncollectible accounts,* commonly called **bad debts.** The total amount of uncollectible accounts is an expense of selling on credit. Why do companies sell on credit if they expect some accounts to be uncollectible? The answer is that companies believe that granting credit will increase total sales and net income enough to offset bad debts. Companies use two methods to account for uncollectible accounts: (1) direct write-off method and (2) allowance method. We describe both.

Point: Managers realize that some portion of credit sales will be uncollectible, but which credit sales are uncollectible is unknown.

Recording and Writing Off Bad Debts The **direct write-off method** of accounting for bad debts records the loss from an uncollectible account receivable when it is determined to be uncollectible. No attempt is made to predict bad debts expense. To illustrate, if TechCom determines on January 23 that it cannot collect $520 owed to it by its customer J. Kent, it recognizes the loss using the direct write-off method as follows:

Assets = Liabilities + Equity
−520 −520

Jan. 23	Bad Debts Expense	520	
	Accounts Receivable—J. Kent		520
	To write off an uncollectible account.		

The debit in this entry charges the uncollectible amount directly to the current period's Bad Debts Expense account. The credit removes its balance from the Accounts Receivable account in the general ledger (and its subsidiary ledger).

Point: If a customer fails to pay within the credit period, most companies send out repeated billings and make other efforts to collect.

Recovering a Bad Debt Although uncommon, sometimes an account written off is later collected. This can be due to factors such as continual collection efforts or a customer's good fortune. If the account of J. Kent that was written off directly to Bad Debts Expense is later collected in full, the following two entries record this recovery.

Assets = Liabilities + Equity
+520 +520

Assets = Liabilities + Equity
+520
−520

Mar. 11	Accounts Receivable—J. Kent	520	
	Bad Debts Expense		520
	To reinstate account previously written off.		
Mar. 11	Cash	520	
	Accounts Receivable—J. Kent		520
	To record full payment of account.		

Assessing the Direct Write-Off Method Examples of companies that use the direct write-off method include **Rand Medical Billing**, **Gateway Distributors**, **Microwave Satellite Technologies**, **Frebon International**, **Slater Dome Properties**, **Interscope Technologies**, **On Line Payroll Services**, and **Sub Surface Waste Management**. The following disclosure by **Pharma-Bio Serv** is typical of the justification for this method: Bad debts are accounted for using the direct write-off method whereby an expense is recognized only when a specific account is determined to be uncollectible. The effect of using this method approximates that of the allowance method. Companies must weigh at least two accounting concepts when considering the use of the direct write-off method: the (1) matching principle and (2) materiality constraint.

Matching principle applied to bad debts. The **matching principle** requires expenses to be reported in the same accounting period as the sales they helped produce. This means that if extending credit to customers helped produce sales, the bad debts expense linked to those sales is matched and reported in the same period. The direct write-off method usually does *not* best match sales and expenses because bad debts expense is not recorded until an account becomes uncollectible, which often occurs in a period after that of the credit sale. To match bad debts expense with the sales it produces therefore requires a company to estimate future uncollectibles.

Point: **Oakley** reports $15 million of bad debts expense matched against $762 million of sales in a recent year.

Materiality constraint applied to bad debts. The **materiality constraint** states that an amount can be ignored if its effect on the financial statements is unimportant to users' business decisions. The materiality constraint permits the use of the direct write-off method when bad debts expenses are very small in relation to a company's other financial statement items such as sales and net income.

Valuing Accounts Receivable—Allowance Method

The **allowance method** of accounting for bad debts matches the *estimated* loss from uncollectible accounts receivable against the sales they helped produce. We must use estimated losses because when sales occur, management does not know which customers will not pay their bills. This means that at the end of each period, the allowance method requires an estimate of the total bad debts expected to result from that period's sales. This method has two advantages over the direct write-off method: (1) it records estimated bad debts expense in the period when the related sales are recorded and (2) it reports accounts receivable on the balance sheet at the estimated amount of cash to be collected.

Point: Under direct write-off, expense is recorded each time an account is written off. Under the allowance method, expense is recorded with an adjusting entry equal to the total estimated uncollectibles for that period's sales.

Recording Bad Debts Expense The allowance method estimates bad debts expense at the end of each accounting period and records it with an adjusting entry. TechCom, for instance, had credit sales of $300,000 during its first year of operations. At the end of the first year, $20,000 of credit sales remained uncollected. Based on the experience of similar businesses, TechCom estimated that $1,500 of its accounts receivable would be uncollectible. This estimated expense is recorded with the following adjusting entry.

Dec. 31	Bad Debts Expense	1,500	
	Allowance for Doubtful Accounts		1,500
	To record estimated bad debts.		

Assets = Liabilities + Equity
−1,500 −1,500

The estimated Bad Debts Expense of $1,500 is reported on the income statement (as either a selling expense or an administrative expense) and offsets the $300,000 credit sales it helped produce. The **Allowance for Doubtful Accounts** is a contra asset account. A contra account is used instead of reducing accounts receivable directly because at the time of the adjusting entry, the company does not know which customers will not pay. After the bad debts adjusting entry is posted, TechCom's account balances (in T-account form) for Accounts Receivable and its Allowance for Doubtful Accounts are as shown in Exhibit 9.5.

Point: Credit approval is usually not assigned to the selling dept. because its goal is to increase sales, and it may approve customers at the cost of increased bad debts. Instead, approval is assigned to a separate credit-granting or administrative dept.

EXHIBIT 9.5

General Ledger Entries after Bad Debts Adjusting Entry

Accounts Receivable				Allowance for Doubtful Accounts			
Dec. 31	20,000					Dec. 31	1,500

The Allowance for Doubtful Accounts credit balance of $1,500 has the effect of reducing accounts receivable to its estimated realizable value. **Realizable value** refers to the expected proceeds from converting an asset into cash. Although credit customers owe $20,000 to TechCom, only $18,500 is expected to be realized in cash collections from these customers. In the balance sheet, the Allowance for Doubtful Accounts is subtracted from Accounts Receivable and is often reported as shown in Exhibit 9.6.

Point: Bad Debts Expense is also called *Uncollectible Accounts Expense*. The Allowance for Doubtful Accounts is also called *Allowance for Uncollectible Accounts*.

EXHIBIT 9.6

Balance Sheet Presentation of the Allowance for Doubtful Accounts

Current assets		
Accounts receivable	**$20,000**	
Less allowance for doubtful accounts	**1,500**	**$18,500**

Sometimes the Allowance for Doubtful Accounts is not reported separately. This alternative presentation is shown in Exhibit 9.7 (also see Appendix A).

EXHIBIT 9.7

Alternative Presentation of the Allowance for Doubtful Accounts

Current assets	
Accounts receivable (net of $1,500 doubtful accounts)	**$18,500**

Writing Off a Bad Debt When specific accounts are identified as uncollectible, they are written off against the Allowance for Doubtful Accounts. To illustrate, TechCom decides that J. Kent's $520 account is uncollectible and makes the following entry to write it off.

Jan. 23	Allowance for Doubtful Accounts	520	
	Accounts Receivable—J. Kent		520
	To write off an uncollectible account.		

Assets = Liabilities + Equity
+520
−520

Posting this write-off entry to the Accounts Receivable account removes the amount of the bad debt from the general ledger (it is also posted to the accounts receivable subsidiary ledger). The general ledger accounts now appear as in Exhibit 9.8 (assuming no other transactions affecting these accounts).

Point: The Bad Debts Expense account is not debited in the write-off entry because it was recorded in the period when sales occurred.

EXHIBIT 9.8

General Ledger Entries after Write-Off

Accounts Receivable				Allowance for Doubtful Accounts			
Dec. 31	20,000					Dec. 31	1,500
		Jan. 23	520	Jan. 23	520		

Point: In posting a write-off, the ledger's Explanation column indicates the reason for this credit so it is not misinterpreted as payment in full.

The write-off does *not* affect the realizable value of accounts receivable as shown in Exhibit 9.9. Neither total assets nor net income is affected by the write-off of a specific account. Instead, both assets and net income are affected in the period when bad debts expense is predicted and recorded with an adjusting entry.

EXHIBIT 9.9

Realizable Value before and after Write-Off of a Bad Debt

	Before Write-Off	After Write-Off
Accounts receivable	$ 20,000	$ 19,480
Less allowance for doubtful accounts	1,500	980
Estimated realizable accounts receivable	**$18,500**	**$18,500**

Recovering a Bad Debt When a customer fails to pay and the account is written off as uncollectible, his or her credit standing is jeopardized. To help restore credit standing, a customer sometimes volunteers to pay all or part of the amount owed. A company makes two entries when collecting an account previously written off by the allowance method. The first is to reverse the write-off and reinstate the customer's account. The second entry records the collection of the reinstated account. To illustrate, if on March 11 Kent pays in full his account previously written off, the entries are

Assets = Liabilities + Equity
+520
−520

Assets = Liabilities + Equity
+520
−520

Mar. 11	Accounts Receivable—J. Kent	520	
	Allowance for Doubtful Accounts		520
	To reinstate account previously written off.		
Mar. 11	Cash	520	
	Accounts Receivable—J. Kent		520
	To record full payment of account.		

Example: If TechCom used a collection agency and paid a 35% commission on $520 collected from Kent, how is this recorded? *Answer:*

Cash	338	
Collection Expense	182	
Accts. Recble.—J. Kent		520

In this illustration, Kent paid the entire amount previously written off, but sometimes a customer pays only a portion of the amount owed. A question then arises as to whether the entire balance of the account or just the amount paid is returned to accounts receivable. This is a matter of judgment. If we believe this customer will later pay in full, we return the entire amount owed to accounts receivable, but if we expect no further collection, we return only the amount paid.

Decision Insight

PayPal PayPal is legally just a money transfer agent, but it is increasingly challenging big credit card brands—see chart. PayPal is successful because: (1) online credit card processing fees often exceed $0.15 per dollar, but PayPal's fees are under $0.10 per dollar. (2) PayPal's merchant fraud losses are under 0.2% of revenues, which compares to 1.8% for online merchants using credit cards.

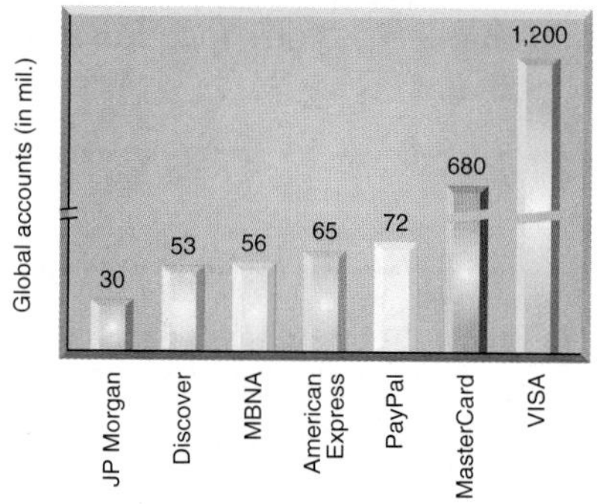

Estimating Bad Debts—Percent of Sales Method

P2 Estimate uncollectibles using methods based on sales and accounts receivable.

The allowance method requires an estimate of bad debts expense to prepare an adjusting entry at the end of each accounting period. There are two common methods. One is based on the income statement relation between bad debts expense and sales. The second is based on the balance sheet relation between accounts receivable and the allowance for doubtful accounts.

The *percent of sales method,* also referred to as the *income statement method,* is based on the idea that a given percent of a company's credit sales for the period are uncollectible. To illustrate, assume that Musicland has credit sales of $400,000 in year 2009. Based on past experience,

Musicland estimates 0.6% of credit sales to be uncollectible. This implies that Musicland expects \$2,400 of bad debts expense from its sales (computed as \$400,000 × 0.006). The adjusting entry to record this estimated expense is

Point: Focus is on *credit* sales because cash sales do not produce bad debts. If cash sales are a small or stable percent of credit sales, total sales can be used.

Dec. 31	Bad Debts Expense	2,400	
	Allowance for Doubtful Accounts.		2,400
	To record estimated bad debts.		

Assets = Liabilities + Equity
−2,400 −2,400

The allowance account ending balance on the balance sheet for this method would rarely equal the bad debts expense on the income statement. This is so because unless a company is in its first period of operations, its allowance account has a zero balance only if the prior amounts written off as uncollectible *exactly* equal the prior estimated bad debts expenses. (When computing bad debts expense as a percent of sales, managers monitor and adjust the percent so it is not too high or too low.)

Point: When using the *percent of sales method* for estimating uncollectibles, the estimate of bad debts is the number used in the adjusting entry.

Estimating Bad Debts—Percent of Receivables Method

The *accounts receivable methods,* also referred to as *balance sheet methods,* use balance sheet relations to estimate bad debts—mainly the relation between accounts receivable and the allowance amount. The goal of the bad debts adjusting entry for these methods is to make the Allowance for Doubtful Accounts balance equal to the portion of accounts receivable that is estimated to be uncollectible. The estimated balance for the allowance account is obtained in one of two ways: (1) computing the percent uncollectible from the total accounts receivable or (2) aging accounts receivable.

The *percent of accounts receivable method* assumes that a given percent of a company's receivables is uncollectible. This percent is based on past experience and is impacted by current conditions such as economic trends and customer difficulties. The total dollar amount of all receivables is multiplied by this percent to get the estimated dollar amount of uncollectible accounts—reported in the balance sheet as the Allowance for Doubtful Accounts.

To illustrate, assume that Musicland has \$50,000 of accounts receivable on December 31, 2009. Experience suggests 5% of its receivables are uncollectible. This means that *after* the adjusting entry is posted, we want the Allowance for Doubtful Accounts to show a \$2,500 credit balance (5% of \$50,000). We are also told that its beginning balance is \$2,200, which is 5% of the \$44,000 accounts receivable on December 31, 2008—see Exhibit 9.10.

Point: When using an accounts receivable method for estimating uncollectibles, the allowance account balance is adjusted to equal the estimate of uncollectibles.

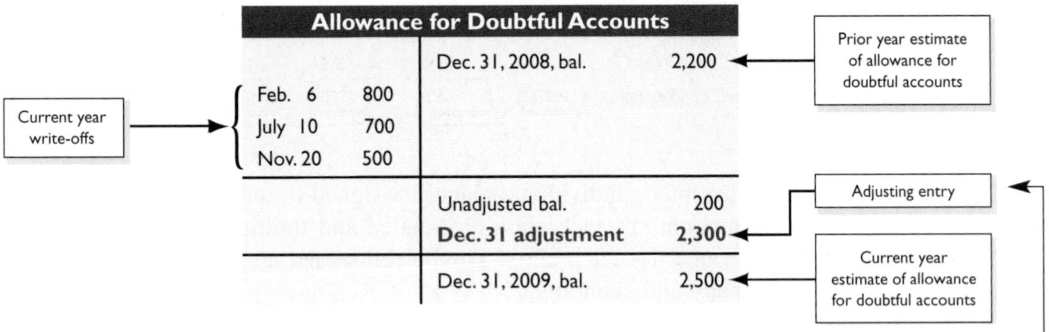

EXHIBIT 9.10

Allowance for Doubtful Accounts after Bad Debts Adjusting Entry

During 2009, accounts of customers are written off on February 6, July 10, and November 20. Thus, the account has a \$200 credit balance *before* the December 31, 2009, adjustment. The adjusting entry to give the allowance account the estimated \$2,500 balance is

Dec. 31	Bad Debts Expense	2,300	
	Allowance for Doubtful Accounts.		2,300
	To record estimated bad debts.		

Assets = Liabilities + Equity
−2,300 −2,300

Decision Insight

Aging Pains Experience shows that the longer a receivable is past due, the lower is the likelihood of its collection. An *aging schedule* uses this knowledge to estimate bad debts. The chart here is from a survey that reported estimates of bad debts for receivables grouped by how long they were past their due dates. Each company sets its own estimates based on its customers and its experiences with those customers' payment patterns.

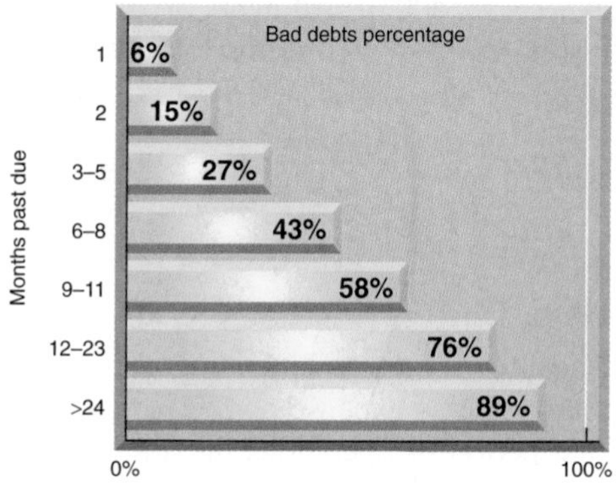

Estimating Bad Debts—Aging of Receivables Method

The **aging of accounts receivable** method uses both past and current receivables information to estimate the allowance amount. Specifically, each receivable is classified by how long it is past its due date. Then estimates of uncollectible amounts are made assuming that the longer an amount is past due, the more likely it is to be uncollectible. Classifications are often based on 30-day periods. After the amounts are classified (or aged), experience is used to estimate the percent of each uncollectible class. These percents are applied to the amounts in each class and then totaled to get the estimated balance of the Allowance for Doubtful Accounts. This computation is performed by setting up a schedule such as Exhibit 9.11.

EXHIBIT 9.11

Aging of Accounts Receivable

MUSICLAND
Schedule of Accounts Receivable by Age
December 31, 2009

Customer	Totals	Not Yet Due	1 to 30 Days Past Due	31 to 60 Days Past Due	61 to 90 Days Past Due	Over 90 Days Past Due
Carlie Abbott..............	$ 450	$ 450				
Jamie Allen................	710			$ 710		
Chavez Andres............	500	300	$ 200			
Balicia Company..........	740				$ 100	$ 640
Zamora Services.........	1,000	810	190			
Total receivables.......	$50,000	$37,000	$6,500	$3,700	$1,900	$ 900
Percent uncollectible.....		× 2%	× 5%	× 10%	× 25%	× 40%
Estimated uncollectible..	$ 2,270	$ 740	$ 325	$ 370	$ 475	$ 360

Each receivable is grouped by how long it is past its due date

Each age group is multiplied by its estimated bad debts percent

Estimated bad debts for each group are totaled

Exhibit 9.11 lists each customer's individual balances assigned to one of five classes based on its days past due. The amounts in each class are totaled and multiplied by the estimated percent of uncollectible accounts for each class. The percents used are regularly reviewed to reflect changes in the company and economy.

To explain, Musicland has $3,700 in accounts receivable that are 31 to 60 days past due. Its management estimates 10% of the amounts in this age class are uncollectible, or a total of $370 (computed as $3,700 × 10%). Similar analysis is done for each of the other four classes. The final total of $2,270 ($740 + $325 +370 + $475 + $360) shown in the first column is the estimated balance for the Allowance for Doubtful Accounts. Exhibit 9.12 shows that since the allowance

EXHIBIT 9.12

Computation of the Required Adjustment for the Accounts Receivable Method

Unadjusted balance	$ 200 credit
Estimated balance	2,270 credit
Required adjustment	**$2,070 credit**

account has an unadjusted credit balance of $200, the required adjustment to the Allowance for Doubtful Accounts is $2,070. This yields the following end-of-period adjusting entry.

Dec. 31	Bad Debts Expense	2,070	
	Allowance for Doubtful Accounts.		2,070
	To record estimated bad debts.		

Assets	= Liabilities	+ Equity
−2,070		−2,070

Alternatively, if the allowance account had an unadjusted *debit* balance of $500 (instead of the $200 credit balance), its required adjustment would be computed as follows.

Unadjusted balance	$ 500	debit
Estimated balance	2,270	credit ← Current year estimate of allowance for doubtful accounts
Required adjustment	**$ 2,770**	**credit**

Adjusting entry amount

The entry to record the end-of-period adjustment for this alternative case is

Dec. 31	Bad Debts Expense	2,770	
	Allowance for Doubtful Accounts.		2,770
	To record estimated bad debts.		

Assets	= Liabilities	+ Equity
−2,770		−2,770

The aging of accounts receivable method is an examination of specific accounts and is usually the most reliable of the estimation methods.

Estimating Bad Debts—Summary of Methods Exhibit 9.13 summarizes the principles guiding all three estimation methods and their focus of analysis. Percent of sales, with its income statement focus, does a good job at matching bad debts expense with sales. The accounts receivable methods, with their balance sheet focus, do a better job at reporting accounts receivable at realizable value.

EXHIBIT 9.13

Methods to Estimate Bad Debts

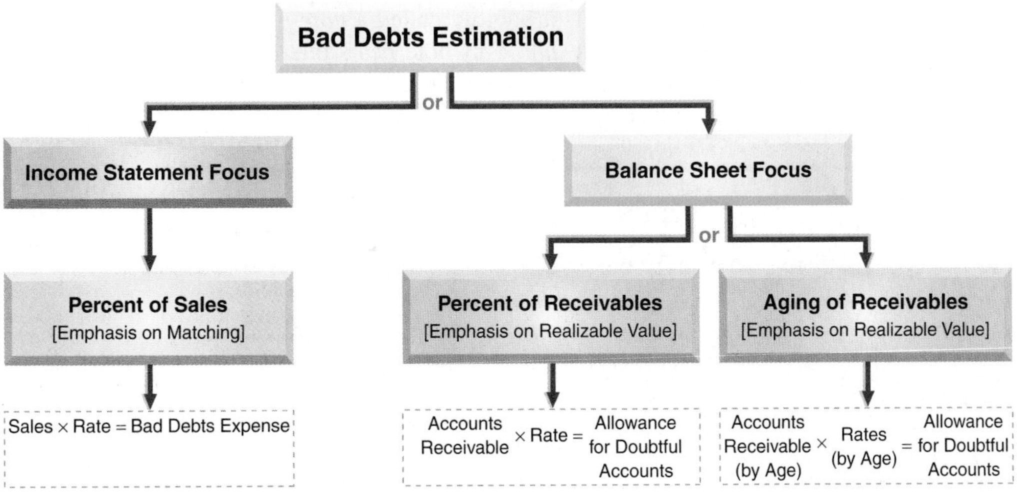

Decision Maker

Labor Union Chief One week prior to labor contract negotiations, financial statements are released showing no income growth. A 10% growth was predicted. Your analysis finds that the company increased its allowance for uncollectibles from 1.5% to 4.5% of receivables. Without this change, income would show a 9% growth. Does this analysis impact negotiations? [Answer—p. 376]

Quick Check

Answers—p. 376

3. Why must bad debts expense be estimated if such an estimate is possible?
4. What term describes the balance sheet valuation of Accounts Receivable less the Allowance for Doubtful Accounts?
5. Why is estimated bad debts expense credited to a contra account (Allowance for Doubtful Accounts) rather than to the Accounts Receivable account?
6. SnoBoard Company's year-end balance in its Allowance for Doubtful Accounts is a credit of $440. By aging accounts receivable, it estimates that $6,142 is uncollectible. Prepare SnoBoard's year-end adjusting entry for bad debts.
7. Record entries for these transactions assuming the allowance method is used:

   Jan. 10 The $300 account of customer Cool Jam is determined uncollectible.

   April 12 Cool Jam unexpectedly pays in full the account deemed uncollectible on Jan. 10.

Notes Receivable

C2 Describe a note receivable and the computation of its maturity date and interest.

A **promissory note** is a written promise to pay a specified amount of money, usually with interest, either on demand or at a definite future date. Promissory notes are used in many transactions, including paying for products and services, and lending and borrowing money. Sellers sometimes ask for a note to replace an account receivable when a customer requests additional time to pay a past-due account. For legal reasons, sellers generally prefer to receive notes when the credit period is long and when the receivable is for a large amount. If a lawsuit is needed to collect from a customer, a note is the buyer's written acknowledgment of the debt, its amount, and its terms.

Exhibit 9.14 shows a simple promissory note dated July 10, 2009. For this note, Julia Browne promises to pay TechCom or to its order (according to TechCom's instructions) a specified amount of money ($1,000), called the **principal of a note,** at a definite future date (October 8, 2009). As the one who signed the note and promised to pay it at maturity, Browne is the **maker of the note.** As the person to whom the note is payable, TechCom is the **payee of the note.** To Browne, the note is a liability called a *note payable*. To TechCom, the same note is an asset called a *note receivable*. This note bears interest at 12%, as written on the note. **Interest** is the charge for using the money until its due date. To a borrower, interest is an expense. To a lender, it is revenue.

EXHIBIT 9.14

Promissory Note

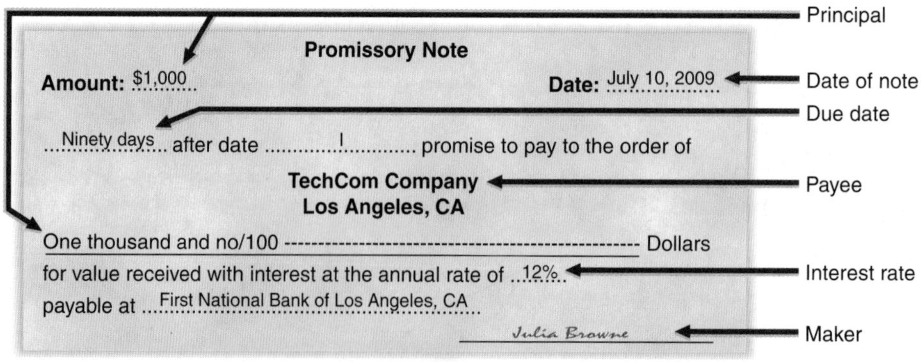

Computing Maturity and Interest

This section describes key computations for notes including the determination of maturity date, period covered, and interest computation.

Maturity Date and Period The **maturity date of a note** is the day the note (principal and interest) must be repaid. The *period* of a note is the time from the note's (contract) date to its maturity date. Many notes mature in less than a full year, and the period they cover is often expressed in days. When the time of a note is expressed in days, its maturity date is the specified number of days after the note's date. As an example, a five-day note dated June 15 matures and is due on June 20. A 90-day note dated July 10 matures on October 8. This October 8 due date is computed as shown in Exhibit 9.15. The period of a note is sometimes expressed in months or years. When months are used, the note matures and is payable in the month of its maturity on the *same day of the month* as its original date. A nine-month note dated July 10, for instance, is payable on April 10. The same analysis applies when years are used.

Video9.1

EXHIBIT 9.15

Maturity Date Computation

Days in July	31	
Minus the date of the note	10	
Days remaining in July	21	← July 11–31
Add days in August	31	← Aug. 1–31
Add days in September	30	← Sept. 1–30
Days to equal 90 days, or **maturity date of October 8**	8	← Oct. 1–8
Period of the note in days	90	

Interest Computation *Interest* is the cost of borrowing money for the borrower or, alternatively, the profit from lending money for the lender. Unless otherwise stated, the rate of interest on a note is the rate charged for the use of the principal for one year. The formula for computing interest on a note is shown in Exhibit 9.16.

EXHIBIT 9.16

Computation of Interest Formula

$$\text{Principal of the note} \times \text{Annual interest rate} \times \text{Time expressed in years} = \text{Interest}$$

To simplify interest computations, a year is commonly treated as having 360 days (called the *banker's rule* in the business world and widely used in commercial transactions). **We treat a year as having 360 days for interest computations in the examples and assignments.** Using the promissory note in Exhibit 9.14 where we have a 90-day, 12%, $1,000 note, the total interest is computed as follows.

$$\$1{,}000 \times 12\% \times \frac{90}{360} = \$1{,}000 \times 0.12 \times 0.25 = \$30$$

Recognizing Notes Receivable

P3 Record the receipt of a note receivable.

Notes receivable are usually recorded in a single Notes Receivable account to simplify recordkeeping. The original notes are kept on file, including information on the maker, rate of interest, and due date. (When a company holds a large number of notes, it sometimes sets up a controlling account and a subsidiary ledger for notes. This is similar to the handling of accounts receivable.) To illustrate the recording for the receipt of a note, we use the $1,000, 90-day, 12% promissory note in Exhibit 9.14. TechCom received this note at the time of a product sale to Julia Browne. This transaction is recorded as follows.

July 10*	Notes Receivable	1,000	
	Sales		1,000
	Sold goods in exchange for a 90-day, 12% note.		

Assets = Liabilities + Equity
+1,000 +1,000

* We omit the entry to Dr. Cost of Sales and Cr. Merchandise Inventory to focus on sales and receivables.

When a seller accepts a note from an overdue customer as a way to grant a time extension on a past-due account receivable, it will often collect part of the past-due balance in cash. This partial payment forces a concession from the customer, reduces the customer's debt (and the seller's risk), and produces a note for a smaller amount. To illustrate, assume that TechCom agreed to accept $232 in cash along with a $600, 60-day, 15% note from Jo Cook to settle

Point: Notes receivable often are a major part of a company's assets. Likewise, notes payable often are a large part of a company's liabilities.

her $832 past-due account. TechCom made the following entry to record receipt of this cash and note.

Assets = Liabilities + Equity
+232
+600
−832

Oct. 5	Cash	232	
	Notes Receivable	600	
	Accounts Receivable—J. Cook		832
	Received cash and note to settle account.		

Valuing and Settling Notes

P4 Record the honoring and dishonoring of a note and adjustments for interest.

Recording an Honored Note The principal and interest of a note are due on its maturity date. The maker of the note usually *honors* the note and pays it in full. To illustrate, when J. Cook pays the note above on its due date, TechCom records it as follows.

Assets = Liabilities + Equity
+615 +15
−600

Dec. 4	Cash	615	
	Notes Receivable		600
	Interest Revenue		15
	Collect note with interest of $600 × 15% × 60/360.		

Interest Revenue, also called *Interest Earned,* is reported on the income statement.

Recording a Dishonored Note When a note's maker is unable or refuses to pay at maturity, the note is *dishonored.* The act of dishonoring a note does not relieve the maker of the obligation to pay. The payee should use every legitimate means to collect. How do companies report this event? The balance of the Notes Receivable account should include only those notes that have not matured. Thus, when a note is dishonored, we remove the amount of this note from the Notes Receivable account and charge it back to an account receivable from its maker. To illustrate, TechCom holds an $800, 12%, 60-day note of Greg Hart. At maturity, Hart dishonors the note. TechCom records this dishonoring of the note as follows.

Point: When posting a dishonored note to a customer's account, an explanation is included so as not to misinterpret the debit as a sale on account.

Assets = Liabilities + Equity
+816 +16
−800

Oct. 14	Accounts Receivable—G. Hart	816	
	Interest Revenue		16
	Notes Receivable		800
	To charge account of G. Hart for a dishonored note and interest of $800 × 12% × 60/360.		

Point: Reporting the details of notes is consistent with the **full disclosure principle,** which requires financial statements (including footnotes) to report all relevant information.

Charging a dishonored note back to the account of its maker serves two purposes. First, it removes the amount of the note from the Notes Receivable account and records the dishonored note in the maker's account. Second, and more important, if the maker of the dishonored note applies for credit in the future, his or her account will reveal all past dealings, including the dishonored note. Restoring the account also reminds the company to continue collection efforts from Hart for both principal and interest. The entry records the full amount, including interest, to ensure that it is included in collection efforts.

Recording End-of-Period Interest Adjustment When notes receivable are outstanding at the end of a period, any accrued interest earned is computed and recorded. To illustrate, on December 16, TechCom accepts a $3,000, 60-day, 12% note from a customer in granting an extension on a past-due account. When TechCom's accounting period ends on December 31, $15 of interest has accrued on this note ($3,000 × 12% × 15/360). The following adjusting entry records this revenue.

Assets = Liabilities + Equity
+15 +15

Dec. 31	Interest Receivable	15	
	Interest Revenue		15
	To record accrued interest earned.		

Interest Revenue appears on the income statement, and Interest Receivable appears on the balance sheet as a current asset. When the December 16 note is collected on February 14, TechCom's entry to record the cash receipt is

Feb. 14	Cash	3,060	
	Interest Revenue		45
	Interest Receivable		15
	Notes Receivable		3,000
	Received payment of note and its interest.		

Assets	= Liabilities	+ Equity
+3,060		+45
−15		
−3,000		

Total interest earned on the 60-day note is $60. The $15 credit to Interest Receivable on February 14 reflects the collection of the interest accrued from the December 31 adjusting entry. The $45 interest earned reflects TechCom's revenue from holding the note from January 1 to February 14 of the current period.

Quick Check Answers—p. 376

8. Irwin purchases $7,000 of merchandise from Stamford on December 16, 2008. Stamford accepts Irwin's $7,000, 90-day, 12% note as payment. Stamford's accounting period ends on December 31, and it does not make reversing entries. Prepare entries for Stamford on December 16, 2008, and December 31, 2008.
9. Using the information in Quick Check 8, prepare Stamford's March 16, 2009, entry if Irwin dishonors the note.

Disposing of Receivables

Companies can convert receivables to cash before they are due. Reasons for this include the need for cash or the desire not to be involved in collection activities. Converting receivables is usually done either by (1) selling them or (2) using them as security for a loan. A recent survey shows that about 20% of companies obtain cash from either selling receivables or pledging them as security. In some industries such as textiles, apparel and furniture, this is common practice.

Selling Receivables

C3 Explain how receivables can be converted to cash before maturity.

A company can sell all or a portion of its receivables to a finance company or bank. The buyer, called a *factor,* charges the seller a *factoring fee* and then the buyer takes ownership of the receivables and receives cash when they come due. By incurring a factoring fee, the seller receives cash earlier and can pass the risk of bad debts to the factor. The seller can also choose to avoid costs of billing and accounting for the receivables. To illustrate, if TechCom sells $20,000 of its accounts receivable and is charged a 4% factoring fee, it records this sale as follows.

Global: Firms in export sales increasingly sell their receivables to factors.

Aug. 15	Cash	19,200	
	Factoring Fee Expense	800	
	Accounts Receivable		20,000
	Sold accounts receivable for cash, less 4% fee.		

Assets	= Liabilities	+ Equity
+19,200		−800
−20,000		

The accounting for sales of notes receivable is similar to that for accounts receivable. The detailed entries are covered in advanced courses.

Pledging Receivables

A company can raise cash by borrowing money and *pledging* its receivables as security for the loan. Pledging receivables does not transfer the risk of bad debts to the lender because the borrower retains ownership of the receivables. If the borrower defaults on the loan, the lender has a right to be paid from the cash receipts of the receivable when collected. To illustrate, when TechCom borrows $35,000 and pledges its receivables as security, it records this transaction as follows.

Assets	=	Liabilities	+	Equity
+35,000		+35,000		

Aug. 20	Cash	35,000	
	Notes Payable		35,000
	Borrowed money with a note secured by pledging receivables.		

Since pledged receivables are committed as security for a specific loan, the borrower's financial statements disclose the pledging of them. TechCom, for instance, includes the following note with its statements: Accounts receivable of $40,000 are pledged as security for a $35,000 note payable.

Decision Insight

What's the Proper Allowance? How can we assess whether a company has properly estimated its allowance for uncollectibles? One way is to compute the ratio of the allowance account to the gross accounts receivable. When this ratio is analyzed over several consecutive periods, trends often emerge that reflect on the adequacy of the allowance amount.

Decision Analysis — Accounts Receivable Turnover

A1 Compute accounts receivable turnover and use it to help assess financial condition.

For a company selling on credit, we want to assess both the quality and liquidity of its accounts receivable. *Quality* of receivables refers to the likelihood of collection without loss. Experience shows that the longer receivables are outstanding beyond their due date, the lower the likelihood of collection. *Liquidity* of receivables refers to the speed of collection. **Accounts receivable turnover** is a measure of both the quality and liquidity of accounts receivable. It indicates how often, on average, receivables are received and collected during the period. The formula for this ratio is shown in Exhibit 9.17.

EXHIBIT 9.17

Accounts Receivable Turnover

$$\textbf{Accounts receivable turnover} = \frac{\textbf{Net sales}}{\textbf{Average accounts receivable, net}}$$

Video9.1

We prefer to use net *credit* sales in the numerator because cash sales do not create receivables. However, since financial statements rarely report net credit sales, our analysis uses net sales. The denominator is the *average* accounts receivable balance, computed as (Beginning balance + Ending balance) ÷ 2. TechCom has an accounts receivable turnover of 5.1. This indicates its average accounts receivable balance is converted into cash 5.1 times during the period. Exhibit 9.18 shows graphically this turnover activity for TechCom.

EXHIBIT 9.18

Rate of Accounts Receivable Turnover for TechCom

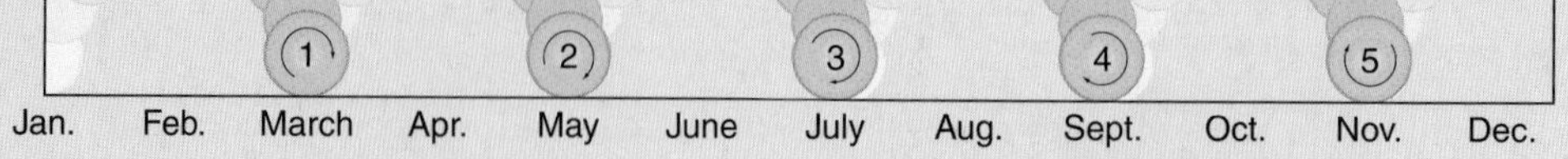

Accounts receivable turnover also reflects how well management is doing in granting credit to customers in a desire to increase sales. A high turnover in comparison with competitors suggests that management should consider using more liberal credit terms to increase sales. A low turnover suggests management should consider stricter credit terms and more aggressive collection efforts to avoid having its resources tied up in accounts receivable.

Point: Credit risk ratio is computed by dividing the Allowance for Doubtful Accounts by Accounts Receivable. The higher this ratio, the higher is credit risk.

To illustrate, we take data from two competitors: **Dell** and **Apple**. Exhibit 9.19 shows accounts receivable turnover for both companies.

Company	Figure ($ millions)	2006	2005	2004	2003
Dell	Net sales	$57,420	$55,788	$49,121	$41,327
	Average accounts receivable, net	$ 4,352	$ 3,826	$ 4,025	$ 3,111
	Accounts receivable turnover	**13.2**	**14.6**	**12.2**	**13.3**
Apple	Net sales	$19,315	$13,931	$ 8,279	$ 6,207
	Average accounts receivable, net	$ 1,074	$ 835	$ 770	$ 666
	Accounts receivable turnover	**18.0**	**16.7**	**10.8**	**9.3**

EXHIBIT 9.19

Analysis Using Accounts Receivable Turnover

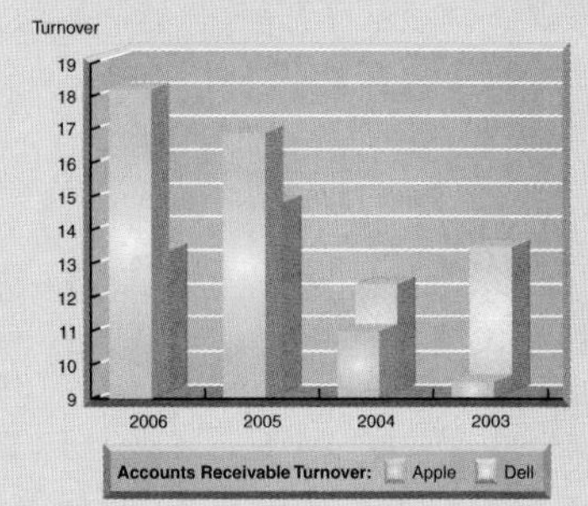

Dell's 2006 turnover is computed ($ millions) as $57,420/$4,352 = 13.2. This means that Dell's average accounts receivable balance was converted into cash 13.2 times in 2006. Its turnover declined in 2006, but is higher than that for 2004. Apple's turnover exceeds that for Dell in each of the past two years. Is either company's turnover too high? Since sales are markedly growing over this time period, each company's turnover rate does not appear to be too high. Instead, both Dell and Apple seem to be doing well in managing receivables. Turnover for competitors is generally in the range of 7 to 12 for this same period.[1]

Decision Maker

Family Physician Your medical practice is barely profitable, so you hire a health care analyst. The analyst highlights several points including the following: *"Accounts receivable turnover is too low. Tighter credit policies are recommended along with discontinuing service to those most delayed in payments."* How do you interpret these recommendations? What actions do you take? [Answer—p. 376]

Demonstration Problem

DP9

Clayco Company completes the following selected transactions during year 2009.

July 14 Writes off a $750 account receivable arising from a sale to Briggs Company that dates to 10 months ago. (Clayco Company uses the allowance method.)

30 Clayco Company receives a $1,000, 90-day, 10% note in exchange for merchandise sold to Sumrell Company (the merchandise cost $600).

Aug. 15 Receives $2,000 cash plus a $10,000 note from JT Co. in exchange for merchandise that sells for $12,000 (its cost is $8,000). The note is dated August 15, bears 12% interest, and matures in 120 days.

Nov. 1 Completed a $200 credit card sale with a 4% fee (the cost of sales is $150). The cash is received immediately from the credit card company.

3 Sumrell Company refuses to pay the note that was due to Clayco Company on October 28. Prepare the journal entry to charge the dishonored note plus accrued interest to Sumrell Company's accounts receivable.

5 Completed a $500 credit card sale with a 5% fee (the cost of sales is $300). The payment from the credit card company is received on Nov. 9.

15 Received the full amount of $750 from Briggs Company that was previously written off on July 14. Record the bad debts recovery.

Dec. 13 Received payment of principal plus interest from JT for the August 15 note.

Required

1. Prepare journal entries to record these transactions on Clayco Company's books.

2. Prepare an adjusting journal entry as of December 31, 2009, assuming the following:

a. Bad debts are estimated to be $20,400 by aging accounts receivable. The unadjusted balance of the Allowance for Doubtful Accounts is $1,000 debit.

[1] As an estimate of *average days' sales uncollected,* we compute how many days (*on average*) it takes to collect receivables as follows: 365 days ÷ accounts receivable turnover. An increase in this *average collection period* can signal a decline in customers' financial condition.

b. Alternatively, assume that bad debts are estimated using the percent of sales method. The Allowance for Doubtful Accounts had a $1,000 debit balance before adjustment, and the company estimates bad debts to be 1% of its credit sales of $2,000,000.

Planning the Solution

- Examine each transaction to determine the accounts affected, and then record the entries.
- For the year-end adjustment, record the bad debts expense for the two approaches.

Solution to Demonstration Problem

1.

July 14	Allowance for Doubtful Accounts	750	
	Accounts Receivable—Briggs Co.		750
	Wrote off an uncollectible account.		
July 30	Notes Receivable—Sumrell Co.	1,000	
	Sales		1,000
	Sold merchandise for a 90-day, 10% note.		
July 30	Cost of Goods Sold	600	
	Merchandise Inventory		600
	To record the cost of July 30 sale.		
Aug. 15	Cash	2,000	
	Notes Receivable—JT Co.	10,000	
	Sales		12,000
	Sold merchandise to customer for $2,000 cash and $10,000 note.		
Aug. 15	Cost of Goods Sold	8,000	
	Merchandise Inventory		8,000
	To record the cost of Aug. 15 sale.		
Nov. 1	Cash	192	
	Credit Card Expense	8	
	Sales		200
	To record credit card sale less a 4% credit card expense.		
Nov. 1	Cost of Goods Sold	150	
	Merchandise Inventory		150
	To record the cost of Nov. 1 sale.		
Nov. 3	Accounts Receivable—Sumrell Co.	1,025	
	Interest Revenue		25
	Notes Receivable—Sumrell Co.		1,000
	To charge account of Sumrell Company for a $1,000 dishonored note and interest of $1,000 × 10% × 90/360.		
Nov. 5	Accounts Receivable—Credit Card Co.	475	
	Credit Card Expense	25	
	Sales		500
	To record credit card sale less a 5% credit card expense.		
Nov. 5	Cost of Goods Sold	300	
	Merchandise Inventory		300
	To record the cost of Nov. 5 sale.		
Nov. 9	Cash	475	
	Accounts Receivable—Credit Card Co.		475
	To record cash receipt from Nov. 5 sale.		
Nov. 15	Accounts Receivable—Briggs Co.	750	
	Allowance for Doubtful Accounts		750
	To reinstate the account of Briggs Company previously written off.		

[continued on next page]

[continued from previous page]

Nov. 15	Cash	750	
	Accounts Receivable—Briggs Co.		750
	Cash received in full payment of account.		
Dec. 13	Cash	10,400	
	Interest Revenue		400
	Note Receivable—JT Co.		10,000
	Collect note with interest of $10,000 × 12% × 120/360.		

2a. Aging of accounts receivable method.

Dec. 31	Bad Debts Expense	21,400	
	Allowance for Doubtful Accounts		21,400
	To adjust allowance account from a $1,000 debit balance to a $20,400 credit balance.		

2b. Percent of sales method.*

Dec. 31	Bad Debts Expense	20,000	
	Allowance for Doubtful Accounts		20,000
	To provide for bad debts as 1% × $2,000,000 in credit sales.		

* For the income statement approach, which requires estimating bad debts as a percent of sales or credit sales, the Allowance account balance is *not* considered when making the adjusting entry.

Summary

C1 Describe accounts receivable and how they occur and are recorded. Accounts receivable are amounts due from customers for credit sales. A subsidiary ledger lists amounts owed by each customer. Credit sales arise from at least two sources: (1) sales on credit and (2) credit card sales. *Sales on credit* refers to a company's granting credit directly to customers. Credit card sales involve customers' use of third-party credit cards.

C2 Describe a note receivable and the computation of its maturity date and interest. A note receivable is a written promise to pay a specified amount of money at a definite future date. The maturity date is the day the note (principal and interest) must be repaid. Interest rates are normally stated in annual terms. The amount of interest on the note is computed by expressing time as a fraction of one year and multiplying the note's principal by this fraction and the annual interest rate.

C3 Explain how receivables can be converted to cash before maturity. Receivables can be converted to cash before maturity in three ways. First, a company can sell accounts receivable to a factor, who charges a factoring fee. Second, a company can borrow money by signing a note payable that is secured by pledging the accounts receivable. Third, notes receivable can be discounted at (sold to) a financial institution.

A1 Compute accounts receivable turnover and use it to help assess financial condition. Accounts receivable turnover is a measure of both the quality and liquidity of accounts receivable. The accounts receivable turnover measure indicates how often, on average, receivables are received and collected during the period. Accounts receivable turnover is computed as net sales divided by average accounts receivable.

P1 Apply the direct write-off and allowance methods to account for accounts receivable. The direct write-off method charges Bad Debts Expense when accounts are written off as uncollectible. This method is acceptable only when the amount of bad debts expense is immaterial. Under the allowance method, bad debts expense is recorded with an adjustment at the end of each accounting period that debits the Bad Debts Expense account and credits the Allowance for Doubtful Accounts. The uncollectible accounts are later written off with a debit to the Allowance for Doubtful Accounts.

P2 Estimate uncollectibles using methods based on sales and accounts receivable. Uncollectibles are estimated by focusing on either (1) the income statement relation between bad debts expense and credit sales or (2) the balance sheet relation between accounts receivable and the allowance for doubtful accounts. The first approach emphasizes the matching principle using the income statement. The second approach emphasizes realizable value of accounts receivable using the balance sheet.

P3 Record the receipt of a note receivable. A note received is recorded at its principal amount by debiting the Notes Receivable account. The credit amount is to the asset, product, or service provided in return for the note.

P4 Record the honoring and dishonoring of a note and adjustments for interest. When a note is honored, the payee debits the money received and credits both Notes Receivable and Interest Revenue. Dishonored notes are credited to Notes Receivable and debited to Accounts Receivable (to the account of the maker in an attempt to collect), and Interest Revenue is recorded for interest earned for the time the note is held.

Guidance Answers to **Decision Maker** and **Decision Ethics**

Entrepreneur Analysis of credit card sales should weigh the benefits against the costs. The primary benefit is the potential to increase sales by attracting customers who prefer the convenience of credit cards. The primary cost is the fee charged by the credit card company for providing this service. Analysis should therefore estimate the expected increase in dollar sales from allowing credit card sales and then subtract (1) the normal costs and expenses and (2) the credit card fees associated with this expected increase in dollar sales. If your analysis shows an increase in profit from allowing credit card sales, your store should probably accept them.

Labor Union Chief Yes, this information is likely to impact your negotiations. The obvious question is why the company markedly increased this allowance. The large increase in this allowance means a substantial increase in bad debts expense *and* a decrease in earnings. This change (coming immediately prior to labor contract discussions) also raises concerns since it reduces the union's bargaining power for increased compensation. You want to ask management for supporting documentation justifying this increase. You also want data for two or three prior years and similar data from competitors. These data should give you some sense of whether the change in the allowance for uncollectibles is justified.

Family Physician The recommendations are twofold. First, the analyst suggests more stringent screening of patients' credit standing. Second, the analyst suggests dropping patients who are most overdue in payments. You are likely bothered by both suggestions. They are probably financially wise recommendations, but you are troubled by eliminating services to those less able to pay. One alternative is to follow the recommendations while implementing a care program directed at patients less able to pay for services. This allows you to continue services to patients less able to pay and lets you discontinue services to patients able but unwilling to pay.

Guidance Answers to **Quick Checks**

1. If cash is immediately received when credit card sales receipts are deposited, the company debits Cash at the time of sale. If the company does not receive payment until after it submits receipts to the credit card company, it debits Accounts Receivable at the time of sale. (Cash is later debited when payment is received from the credit card company.)

2. Credit card expenses are usually *recorded* and *incurred* at the time of their related sales, not when cash is received from the credit card company.

3. If possible, bad debts expense must be matched with the sales that gave rise to the accounts receivable. This requires that companies estimate future bad debts at the end of each period before they learn which accounts are uncollectible.

4. Realizable value (also called *net realizable value*).

5. The estimated amount of bad debts expense cannot be credited to the Accounts Receivable account because the specific customer accounts that will prove uncollectible cannot yet be identified and removed from the accounts receivable subsidiary ledger. Moreover, if only the Accounts Receivable account is credited, its balance would not equal the sum of its subsidiary account balances.

6.

Dec. 31	Bad Debts Expense	5,702	
	Allowance for Doubtful Accounts		5,702

7.

Jan. 10	Allowance for Doubtful Accounts	300	
	Accounts Receivable—Cool Jam		300
Apr. 12	Accounts Receivable—Cool Jam	300	
	Allowance for Doubtful Accounts		300
Apr. 12	Cash	300	
	Accounts Receivable—Cool Jam		300

8.

Dec. 16	Note Receivable—Irwin	7,000	
	Sales		7,000
Dec. 31	Interest Receivable	35	
	Interest Revenue		35
	($7,000 × 12% × 15/360)		

9.

Mar. 16	Accounts Receivable—Irwin	7,210	
	Interest Revenue		175
	Interest Receivable		35
	Notes Receivable—Irwin		7,000

Key Terms

mhhe.com/wildFAP19e

Key Terms are available at the book's Website for learning and testing in an online Flashcard Format.

Accounts receivable (p. 358)
Accounts receivable turnover (p. 372)
Aging of accounts receivable (p. 366)
Allowance for Doubtful Accounts (p. 363)
Allowance method (p. 362)
Bad debts (p. 361)
Direct write-off method (p. 361)
Interest (p. 368)
Maker of the note (p. 368)
Matching principle (p. 362)
Materiality constraint (p. 362)
Maturity date of a note (p. 368)
Payee of the note (p. 368)
Principal of a note (p. 368)
Promissory note (or note) (p. 368)
Realizable value (p. 363)

Multiple Choice Quiz

Answers on p. 389 mhhe.com/wildFAP19e

Additional Quiz Questions are available at the book's Website.

Quiz9

1. A company's Accounts Receivable balance at its December 31 year-end is $125,650, and its Allowance for Doubtful Accounts has a credit balance of $328 before year-end adjustment. Its net sales are $572,300. It estimates that 4% of outstanding accounts receivable are uncollectible. What amount of Bad Debts Expense is recorded at December 31?
   a. $5,354
   b. $328
   c. $5,026
   d. $4,698
   e. $34,338
2. A company's Accounts Receivable balance at its December 31 year-end is $489,300, and its Allowance for Doubtful Accounts has a debit balance of $554 before year-end adjustment. Its net sales are $1,300,000. It estimates that 6% of outstanding accounts receivable are uncollectible. What amount of Bad Debts Expense is recorded at December 31?
   a. $29,912
   b. $28,804
   c. $78,000
   d. $29,358
   e. $554
3. Total interest to be earned on a $7,500, 5%, 90-day note is
   a. $93.75
   b. $375.00
   c. $1,125.00
   d. $31.25
   e. $125.00
4. A company receives a $9,000, 8%, 60-day note. The maturity value of the note is
   a. $120
   b. $9,000
   c. $9,120
   d. $720
   e. $9,720
5. A company has net sales of $489,600 and average accounts receivable of $40,800. What is its accounts receivable turnover?
   a. 0.08
   b. 30.41
   c. 1,341.00
   d. 12.00
   e. 111.78

Discussion Questions

1. How do sellers benefit from allowing their customers to use credit cards?
2. Why does the direct write-off method of accounting for bad debts usually fail to match revenues and expenses?
3. Explain the accounting constraint of materiality.
4. Explain why writing off a bad debt against the Allowance for Doubtful Accounts does not reduce the estimated realizable value of a company's accounts receivable.
5. Why does the Bad Debts Expense account usually not have the same adjusted balance as the Allowance for Doubtful Accounts?
6. Why might a business prefer a note receivable to an account receivable?
7. Refer to the financial statements of **Best Buy** in Appendix A. In its presentation of accounts receivable, Best Buy does not mention uncollectible accounts, nor does it list its receivables as "net." Why do you believe that Best Buy does not include information about uncollectible accounts?
8. Refer to the balance sheet of **Circuit City** in Appendix A. Does it use the direct write-off method or allowance method to account for doubtful accounts? What is the realizable value of its accounts receivable as of February 28, 2007?
9. Refer to the financial statements of **Apple** in Appendix A. What are Apple's gross accounts receivable at September 30, 2006? What percentage of its accounts receivable does Apple believe to be uncollectible at September 30, 2006?

Denotes Discussion Questions that involve decision making.

McGraw-Hill's HOMEWORK MANAGER® Available with McGraw-Hill's Homework Manager

QUICK STUDY

QS 9-1
Credit card sales
C1

Prepare journal entries for the following credit card sales transactions (the company uses the perpetual inventory system).

1. Sold $16,000 of merchandise, that cost $7,000, on MasterCard credit cards. The net cash receipts from sales are immediately deposited in the seller's bank account. MasterCard charges a 4% fee.
2. Sold $18,000 of merchandise, that cost $7,800, on an assortment of credit cards. Net cash receipts are received 5 days later, and a 3% fee is charged.

QS 9-2
Allowance method for bad debts
P1

Kordas Corp. uses the allowance method to account for uncollectibles. On October 31, it wrote off a $750 account of a customer, D. Elwick. On December 9, it receives a $400 payment from Elwick.

1. Prepare the journal entry or entries for October 31.
2. Prepare the journal entry or entries for December 9; assume no additional money is expected from Elwick.

QS 9-3
Percent of accounts receivable method
P1

Darius Company's year-end unadjusted trial balance shows accounts receivable of $95,000, allowance for doubtful accounts of $550 (credit), and sales of $350,000. Uncollectibles are estimated to be 1.5% of accounts receivable.

1. Prepare the December 31 year-end adjusting entry for uncollectibles.
2. What amount would have been used in the year-end adjusting entry if the allowance account had a year-end unadjusted debit balance of $150?

QS 9-4
Percent of sales method P2

Assume the same facts as in QS 9-3, except that Darius estimates uncollectibles as 0.5% of sales. Prepare the December 31 year-end adjusting entry for uncollectibles.

QS 9-5
Note receivable
P3 P4

On August 2, 2009, Passat Co. receives a $9,000, 90-day, 6% note from customer Dee Kissick as payment on her $9,000 account. Prepare Passat's journal entries for August 2 and for the note's maturity date assuming the note is honored by Kissick.

QS 9-6
Note receivable
C2 P4

Marlin Company's December 31 year-end unadjusted trial balance shows a ~~$24,000~~ 10,000 balance in Notes Receivable. This balance is from one 6% note dated December 1, with a period of 45 days. Prepare any necessary journal entries for December 31 and for the note's maturity date assuming it is honored.

QS 9-7
Accounts receivable turnover
A1

The following data are taken from the comparative balance sheets of Despina Company. Compute and interpret its accounts receivable turnover for year 2009 (competitors average a turnover of 7.5).

	2009	2008
Accounts receivable, net	$138,500	$153,400
Net sales	910,600	854,200

Available with McGraw-Hill's Homework Manager McGraw-Hill's HOMEWORK MANAGER®

EXERCISES

Exercise 9-1
Accounting for credit card sales
C1

Hue Company uses the perpetual inventory system and allows customers to use two credit cards in charging purchases. With the Omni Bank Card, Hue receives an immediate credit to its account when it deposits sales receipts. Omni assesses a 4% service charge for credit card sales. The second credit card that Hue accepts is the Continental Card. Hue sends its accumulated receipts to Continental on a weekly basis and is paid by Continental about a week later. Continental assesses a 2.5% charge on sales for using its card. Prepare journal entries to record the following selected credit card transactions of Hue Company.

Apr. 8 Sold merchandise for $5,600 (that had cost $4,138) and accepted the customer's Omni Bank Card. The Omni receipts are immediately deposited in Hue's bank account.
12 Sold merchandise for $6,000 (that had cost $4,400) and accepted the customer's Continental Card. Transferred $6,000 of credit card receipts to Continental, requesting payment.
20 Received Continental's check for the April 12 billing, less the service charge.

Exercise 9-2
Accounts receivable subsidiary ledger; schedule of accounts receivable
C1

Beachum Company recorded the following selected transactions during November 2009.

Nov. 5	Accounts Receivable—Ski Shop	5,817	
	Sales..................................		5,817
10	Accounts Receivable—Welcome Enterprises	1,774	
	Sales..................................		1,774
13	Accounts Receivable—Kit Ronin..............	1,040	
	Sales..................................		1,040
21	Sales Returns and Allowances	268	
	Accounts Receivable—Kit Ronin		268
30	Accounts Receivable—Ski Shop	3,698	
	Sales..................................		3,698

1. Open a general ledger having T-accounts for Accounts Receivable, Sales, and Sales Returns and Allowances. Also open an accounts receivable subsidiary ledger having a T-account for each customer. Post these entries to both the general ledger and the accounts receivable ledger.
2. Prepare a schedule of accounts receivable (see Exhibit 9.4) and compare its total with the balance of the Accounts Receivable controlling account as of November 30.

Check Accounts Receivable ending balance, $12,061

Exercise 9-3
Percent of sales method; write-off
P1 P2

At year-end (December 31), Terner Company estimates its bad debts as 0.6% of its annual credit sales of $858,000. Terner records its Bad Debts Expense for that estimate. On the following February 1, Terner decides that the $429 account of D. Fidel is uncollectible and writes it off as a bad debt. On June 5, Fidel unexpectedly pays the amount previously written off. Prepare the journal entries of Terner to record these transactions and events of December 31, February 1, and June 5.

Exercise 9-4
Percent of accounts receivable method
P1 P2

At each calendar year-end, Rivka Supply Co. uses the percent of accounts receivable method to estimate bad debts. On December 31, 2009, it has outstanding accounts receivable of $139,500, and it estimates that 2% will be uncollectible. Prepare the adjusting entry to record bad debts expense for year 2009 under the assumption that the Allowance for Doubtful Accounts has (*a*) a $2,371 credit balance before the adjustment and (*b*) a $487 debit balance before the adjustment.

Exercise 9-5
Aging of receivables method
P1 P2

Paloma Company estimates uncollectible accounts using the allowance method at December 31. It prepared the following aging of receivables analysis.

		Days Past Due				
	Total	0	1 to 30	31 to 60	61 to 90	Over 90
Accounts receivable	$95,000	$66,000	$15,000	$6,000	$3,000	$5,000
Percent uncollectible		1%	2%	4%	7%	12%

a. Estimate the balance of the Allowance for Doubtful Accounts using the aging of accounts receivable method.
b. Prepare the adjusting entry to record Bad Debts Expense using the estimate from part *a*. Assume the unadjusted balance in the Allowance for Doubtful Accounts is a $300 debit.
c. Prepare the adjusting entry to record Bad Debts Expense using the estimate from part *a*. Assume the unadjusted balance in the Allowance for Doubtful Accounts is a $200 credit.

Exercise 9-6
Percent of receivables method
P1 P2

Refer to the information in Exercise 9-5 to complete the following requirements.

a. Estimate the balance of the Allowance for Doubtful Accounts assuming the company uses 2% of total accounts receivable to estimate uncollectibles, instead of the aging of receivables method.
b. Prepare the adjusting entry to record Bad Debts Expense using the estimate from part *a*. Assume the unadjusted balance in the Allowance for Doubtful Accounts is a $300 debit.
c. Prepare the adjusting entry to record Bad Debts Expense using the estimate from part *a*. Assume the unadjusted balance in the Allowance for Doubtful Accounts is a $200 credit.

Exercise 9-7
Writing off receivables
P1 P2

Refer to the information in Exercise 9-5 to complete the following requirements.

a. On February 1 of the next period, the company determined that $950 in customer accounts is uncollectible; specifically, $200 for Laguna Co. and $750 for Malibu Co. Prepare the journal entry to write off those accounts.
b. On June 5 of that next period, the company unexpectedly received a $200 payment on a customer account, Laguna Company, that had previously been written off in part *a*. Prepare the entries necessary to reinstate the account and to record the cash received.

Exercise 9-8
Estimating bad debts
P1 P2

At December 31, Bowie Company reports the following results for its calendar-year.

Cash sales	$400,000
Credit sales	300,000

Its year-end unadjusted trial balance includes the following items.

Accounts receivable	$65,000 debit
Allowance for doubtful accounts	1,000 debit

Check Dr. Bad Debts Expense: (*a*) $6,000

(*c*) $6,200

a. Prepare the adjusting entry to record Bad Debts Expense assuming uncollectibles are estimated to be 2% of credit sales.

b. Prepare the adjusting entry to record Bad Debts Expense assuming uncollectibles are estimated to be 1% of total sales.

c. Prepare the adjusting entry to record Bad Debts Expense assuming uncollectibles are estimated to be 8% of year-end accounts receivable.

Exercise 9-9
Selling and pledging accounts receivable
C3

On June 30, Twain Co. has $145,600 of accounts receivable. Prepare journal entries to record the following selected July transactions. Also prepare any footnotes to the July 31 financial statements that result from these transactions. (The company uses the perpetual inventory system.)

July 4 Sold $7,160 of merchandise (that had cost $4,582) to customers on credit.
9 Sold $20,300 of accounts receivable to Main Bank. Main charges a 5% factoring fee.
17 Received $3,938 cash from customers in payment on their accounts.
27 Borrowed $11,000 cash from Main Bank, pledging $14,700 of accounts receivable as security for the loan.

Exercise 9-10
Honoring a note
P4

Prepare journal entries to record these selected transactions for Alvarez Company.

Nov. 1 Accepted a $15,000, 180-day, 7% note dated November 1 from Carlos Cruz in granting a time extension on his past-due account receivable.
Dec. 31 Adjusted the year-end accounts for the accrued interest earned on the Cruz note.
Apr. 30 Cruz honors his note when presented for payment; February has 28 days for the current year.

Exercise 9-11
Dishonoring a note
P4

Prepare journal entries to record the following selected transactions of Calio Company.

Mar. 21 Accepted a $17,200, 180-day, 7% note dated March 21 from James Penn in granting a time extension on his past-due account receivable.
Sept. 17 Penn dishonors his note when it is presented for payment.
Dec. 31 After exhausting all legal means of collection, Calio Company writes off Penn's account against the Allowance for Doubtful Accounts.

Exercise 9-12
Notes receivable transactions and entries
C2 P3 P4

Prepare journal entries for the following selected transactions of Hirona Company.

2008

Dec. 13 Accepted a $14,000, 60-day, 9% note dated December 13 in granting Allie Sumera a time extension on her past-due account receivable.
31 Prepared an adjusting entry to record the accrued interest on the Sumera note.

Check Dec. 31, Cr. Interest Revenue $63

2009

Feb. 11 Received Sumera's payment for principal and interest on the note dated December 13.
Mar. 3 Accepted a $10,000, 9%, 90-day note dated March 3 in granting a time extension on the past-due account receivable of Kudak Company.
17 Accepted a $9,000, 30-day, 8% note dated March 17 in granting Rod Burgess a time extension on his past-due account receivable.
Apr. 16 Burgess dishonors his note when presented for payment.
May 1 Wrote off the Burgess account against the Allowance for Doubtful Accounts.
June 1 Received the Kudak payment for principal and interest on the note dated March 3.

Feb. 11, Dr. Cash $14,210

June 1, Dr. Cash $10,225

Exercise 9-13
Accounts receivable turnover
A1

The following information is from the annual financial statements of Lucilla Company. Compute its accounts receivable turnover for 2008 and 2009. Compare the two years results and give a possible explanation for any change (competitors average a turnover of 7).

	2009	2008	2007
Net sales	$262,000	$193,000	$245,000
Accounts receivable, net (year-end)	42,700	40,500	37,200

McGraw-Hill's HOMEWORK MANAGER® Available with McGraw-Hill's Homework Manager

PROBLEM SET A

Problem 9-1A
Sales on account and credit card sales
C1

Bantay Co. allows select customers to make purchases on credit. Its other customers can use either of two credit cards: Zisa or Access. Zisa deducts a 3.5% service charge for sales on its credit card and credits the bank account of Bantay immediately when credit card receipts are deposited. Bantay deposits the Zisa credit card receipts each business day. When customers use Access credit cards, Bantay accumulates the receipts for several days before submitting them to Access for payment. Access deducts a 2.5% service charge and usually pays within one week of being billed. Bantay completes the following transactions in June. (The terms of all credit sales are 2/15, n/30, and all sales are recorded at the gross price.)

June	4	Sold $700 of merchandise (that had cost $220) on credit to Alfredia Bullaro.
	5	Sold $8,400 of merchandise (that had cost $4,300) to customers who used their Zisa cards.
	6	Sold $6,000 of merchandise (that had cost $3,680) to customers who used their Access cards.
	8	Sold $4,480 of merchandise (that had cost $2,600) to customers who used their Access cards.
	10	Submitted Access card receipts accumulated since June 6 to the credit card company for payment.
	13	Wrote off the account of Trenton Wanek against the Allowance for Doubtful Accounts. The $467 balance in Wanek's account stemmed from a credit sale in October of last year.
	17	Received the amount due from Access.
	18	Received Bullaro's check in full payment for the purchase of June 4.

Check June 17, Dr. Cash $10,218

Required

Prepare journal entries to record the preceding transactions and events. (The company uses the perpetual inventory system. Round amounts to the nearest dollar.)

Problem 9-2A
Accounts receivable transactions and bad debts adjustments
C1 P1 P2

Ming Company began operations on January 1, 2008. During its first two years, the company completed a number of transactions involving sales on credit, accounts receivable collections, and bad debts. These transactions are summarized as follows.

2008

a. Sold $1,347,700 of merchandise (that had cost $982,500) on credit, terms n/30.
b. Wrote off $20,676 of uncollectible accounts receivable.
c. Received $671,100 cash in payment of accounts receivable.
d. In adjusting the accounts on December 31, the company estimated that 1.3% of accounts receivable will be uncollectible.

Check (*d*) Dr. Bad Debts Expense $29,203

2009

e. Sold $1,517,800 of merchandise (that had cost $1,302,200) on credit, terms n/30.
f. Wrote off $32,624 of uncollectible accounts receivable.
g. Received $1,118,100 cash in payment of accounts receivable.
h. In adjusting the accounts on December 31, the company estimated that 1.3% of accounts receivable will be uncollectible.

(*h*) Dr. Bad Debts Expense $37,396

Required

Prepare journal entries to record Ming's 2008 and 2009 summarized transactions and its year-end adjustments to record bad debts expense. (The company uses the perpetual inventory system. Round amounts to the nearest dollar.)

2008

a. Sold $1,346,800 of merchandise (that had cost $980,300) on credit, terms n/30.

b. Received $666,300 cash in payment of accounts receivable.

c. Wrote off $21,000 of uncollectible accounts receivable.

Check (*d*) Dr. Bad Debts Expense $28,914

d. In adjusting the accounts on December 31, the company estimated that 1.2% of accounts receivable will be uncollectible.

2009

e. Sold $1,562,400 of merchandise (that had cost $1,339,300) on credit, terms n/30.

f. Received $1,168,400 cash in payment of accounts receivable.

g. Wrote off $30,400 of uncollectible accounts receivable.

(*h*) Dr. Bad Debts Expense $34,763

h. In adjusting the accounts on December 31, the company estimated that 1.2% of accounts receivable will be uncollectible.

Required

Prepare journal entries to record Freeman's 2008 and 2009 summarized transactions and its year-end adjusting entry to record bad debts expense. (The company uses the perpetual inventory system. Round amounts to the nearest dollar.)

Problem 9-3B
Estimating and reporting bad debts

P1 P2

At December 31, 2009, Tobie Company reports the following results for the year.

Cash sales	$1,600,000
Credit sales	2,926,000

In addition, its unadjusted trial balance includes the following items.

Accounts receivable	$886,000 debit
Allowance for doubtful accounts	2,300 credit

Required

1. Prepare the adjusting entry for Tobie Co. to recognize bad debts under each of the following independent assumptions.

a. Bad debts are estimated to be 1.2% of credit sales.

Check Bad debts expense: (1*b*) $31,682, (1*c*) $42,000

b. Bad debts are estimated to be 0.7% of total sales.

c. An aging analysis estimates that 5% of year-end accounts receivable are uncollectible.

2. Show how Accounts Receivable and the Allowance for Doubtful Accounts appear on its December 31, 2009, balance sheet given the facts in part 1*a*.

3. Show how Accounts Receivable and the Allowance for Doubtful Accounts appear on its December 31, 2009, balance sheet given the facts in part 1*c*.

Problem 9-4B
Aging accounts receivable and accounting for bad debts

P1 P2

Margrett Company has credit sales of $2.2 million for year 2009. At December 31, 2009, the company's Allowance for Doubtful Accounts has an unadjusted debit balance of $2,800. Margrett prepares a schedule of its December 31, 2009, accounts receivable by age. On the basis of past experience, it estimates the percent of receivables in each age category that will become uncollectible. This information is summarized here.

December 31, 2009 Accounts Receivable	Age of Accounts Receivable	Expected Percent Uncollectible
$616,000	Not yet due	0.90%
298,000	1 to 30 days past due	1.65
64,000	31 to 60 days past due	6.15
41,000	61 to 90 days past due	31.00
9,200	Over 90 days past due	64.00

2009

Feb. 14 Received Bakko's payment of principal and interest on the note dated December 16.

Mar. 2 Accepted an $8,000, 9%, 90-day note dated this day in granting a time extension on the past-due account receivable from Mayday Co.

17 Accepted a $2,200, 30-day, 6% note dated this day in granting Carrie Kadin a time extension on her past-due account receivable.

Apr. 16 Kadin dishonored her note when presented for payment.

June 2 Mayday Co. refuses to pay the note that was due to Chantay Co. on May 31. Prepare the journal entry to charge the dishonored note plus accrued interest to Mayday Co.'s accounts receivable.

July 17 Received payment from Mayday Co. for the maturity value of its dishonored note plus interest for 46 days beyond maturity at 9%.

Aug. 7 Accepted an $8,400, 90-day, 12% note dated this day in granting a time extension on the past-due account receivable of Trenton Co.

Sept. 3 Accepted a $3,335, 60-day, 9% note dated this day in granting Collin Marin a time extension on his past-due account receivable.

Nov. 2 Received payment of principal plus interest from Marin for the September 3 note.

Nov. 5 Received payment of principal plus interest from Trenton for the August 7 note.

Dec. 1 Wrote off the Carrie Kadin account against Allowance for Doubtful Accounts.

Check Feb. 14, Cr. Interest Revenue $144

June 2, Cr. Interest Revenue $180

Nov. 2, Cr. Interest Revenue $50

Required

1. Prepare journal entries to record these transactions and events. (Round amounts to the nearest dollar.)

Analysis Component

2. What reporting is necessary when a business pledges receivables as security for a loan and the loan is still outstanding at the end of the period? Explain the reason for this requirement and the accounting principle being satisfied.

PROBLEM SET B

Problem 9-1B

Sales on account and credit card sales

C1

Marbus Co. allows select customers to make purchases on credit. Its other customers can use either of two credit cards: Commerce Bank or Aztec. Commerce Bank deducts a 2% service charge for sales on its credit card and immediately credits the bank account of Marbus when credit card receipts are deposited. Marbus deposits the Commerce Bank credit card receipts each business day. When customers use the Aztec card, Marbus accumulates the receipts for several days and then submits them to Aztec for payment. Aztec deducts a 1% service charge and usually pays within one week of being billed. Marbus completed the following transactions in August (terms of all credit sales are 2/15, n/30; and all sales are recorded at the gross price).

Aug. 4 Sold $600 of merchandise (that had cost $470) on credit to Kirby Carpen.

10 Sold $6,100 of merchandise (that had cost $5,100) to customers who used their Commerce Bank credit cards.

11 Sold $7,200 of merchandise (that had cost $6,150) to customers who used their Aztec cards.

14 Received Carpen's check in full payment for the purchase of August 4.

15 Sold $4,900 of merchandise (that had cost $3,500) to customers who used their Aztec cards.

18 Submitted Aztec card receipts accumulated since August 11 to the credit card company for payment.

22 Wrote off the account of Rayvac Co. against the Allowance for Doubtful Accounts. The $568 balance in Rayvac's account stemmed from a credit sale in November of last year.

25 Received the amount due from Aztec.

Check Aug. 25, Dr. Cash $11,979

Required

Prepare journal entries to record the preceding transactions and events. (The company uses the perpetual inventory system. Round amounts to the nearest dollar.)

Problem 9-2B

Accounts receivable transactions and bad debts adjustments

C1 P1 P2

Freeman Co. began operations on January 1, 2008, and completed several transactions during 2008 and 2009 that involved sales on credit, accounts receivable collections, and bad debts. These transactions are summarized as follows.

2008

a. Sold $1,346,800 of merchandise (that had cost $980,300) on credit, terms n/30.

b. Received $666,300 cash in payment of accounts receivable.

c. Wrote off $21,000 of uncollectible accounts receivable.

Check (*d*) Dr. Bad Debts Expense $28,914

d. In adjusting the accounts on December 31, the company estimated that 1.2% of accounts receivable will be uncollectible.

2009

e. Sold $1,562,400 of merchandise (that had cost $1,339,300) on credit, terms n/30.

f. Received $1,168,400 cash in payment of accounts receivable.

g. Wrote off $30,400 of uncollectible accounts receivable.

(*h*) Dr. Bad Debts Expense $34,763

h. In adjusting the accounts on December 31, the company estimated that 1.2% of accounts receivable will be uncollectible.

Required

Prepare journal entries to record Freeman's 2008 and 2009 summarized transactions and its year-end adjusting entry to record bad debts expense. (The company uses the perpetual inventory system. Round amounts to the nearest dollar.)

Problem 9-3B
Estimating and reporting bad debts

P1 P2

At December 31, 2009, Tobie Company reports the following results for the year.

Cash sales	$1,600,000
Credit sales	2,926,000

In addition, its unadjusted trial balance includes the following items.

Accounts receivable	$886,000 debit
Allowance for doubtful accounts	2,300 credit

Required

1. Prepare the adjusting entry for Tobie Co. to recognize bad debts under each of the following independent assumptions.

a. Bad debts are estimated to be 1.2% of credit sales.

Check Bad debts expense: (1*b*) $31,682, (1*c*) $42,000

b. Bad debts are estimated to be 0.7% of total sales.

c. An aging analysis estimates that 5% of year-end accounts receivable are uncollectible.

2. Show how Accounts Receivable and the Allowance for Doubtful Accounts appear on its December 31, 2009, balance sheet given the facts in part 1*a*.

3. Show how Accounts Receivable and the Allowance for Doubtful Accounts appear on its December 31, 2009, balance sheet given the facts in part 1*c*.

Problem 9-4B
Aging accounts receivable and accounting for bad debts

P1 P2

Margrett Company has credit sales of $2.2 million for year 2009. At December 31, 2009, the company's Allowance for Doubtful Accounts has an unadjusted debit balance of $2,800. Margrett prepares a schedule of its December 31, 2009, accounts receivable by age. On the basis of past experience, it estimates the percent of receivables in each age category that will become uncollectible. This information is summarized here.

	December 31, 2009 Accounts Receivable	Age of Accounts Receivable	Expected Percent Uncollectible
3	$616,000	Not yet due	0.90%
4	298,000	1 to 30 days past due	1.65
5	64,000	31 to 60 days past due	6.15
6	41,000	61 to 90 days past due	31.00
7	9,200	Over 90 days past due	64.00
8			

Exercise 9-13
Accounts receivable turnover
A1

The following information is from the annual financial statements of Lucilla Company. Compute its accounts receivable turnover for 2008 and 2009. Compare the two years results and give a possible explanation for any change (competitors average a turnover of 7).

	2009	2008	2007
Net sales	$262,000	$193,000	$245,000
Accounts receivable, net (year-end)	42,700	40,500	37,200

McGraw-Hill's HOMEWORK MANAGER® Available with McGraw-Hill's Homework Manager

PROBLEM SET A

Problem 9-1A
Sales on account and credit card sales
C1

Bantay Co. allows select customers to make purchases on credit. Its other customers can use either of two credit cards: Zisa or Access. Zisa deducts a 3.5% service charge for sales on its credit card and credits the bank account of Bantay immediately when credit card receipts are deposited. Bantay deposits the Zisa credit card receipts each business day. When customers use Access credit cards, Bantay accumulates the receipts for several days before submitting them to Access for payment. Access deducts a 2.5% service charge and usually pays within one week of being billed. Bantay completes the following transactions in June. (The terms of all credit sales are 2/15, n/30, and all sales are recorded at the gross price.)

June 4 Sold $700 of merchandise (that had cost $220) on credit to Alfredia Bullaro.
5 Sold $8,400 of merchandise (that had cost $4,300) to customers who used their Zisa cards.
6 Sold $6,000 of merchandise (that had cost $3,680) to customers who used their Access cards.
8 Sold $4,480 of merchandise (that had cost $2,600) to customers who used their Access cards.
10 Submitted Access card receipts accumulated since June 6 to the credit card company for payment.
13 Wrote off the account of Trenton Wanek against the Allowance for Doubtful Accounts. The $467 balance in Wanek's account stemmed from a credit sale in October of last year.
17 Received the amount due from Access.
18 Received Bullaro's check in full payment for the purchase of June 4.

Check June 17, Dr. Cash $10,218

Required

Prepare journal entries to record the preceding transactions and events. (The company uses the perpetual inventory system. Round amounts to the nearest dollar.)

Problem 9-2A
Accounts receivable transactions and bad debts adjustments
C1 P1 P2

Ming Company began operations on January 1, 2008. During its first two years, the company completed a number of transactions involving sales on credit, accounts receivable collections, and bad debts. These transactions are summarized as follows.

2008

a. Sold $1,347,700 of merchandise (that had cost $982,500) on credit, terms n/30.
b. Wrote off $20,676 of uncollectible accounts receivable.
c. Received $671,100 cash in payment of accounts receivable.
d. In adjusting the accounts on December 31, the company estimated that 1.3% of accounts receivable will be uncollectible.

Check (d) Dr. Bad Debts Expense $29,203

2009

e. Sold $1,517,800 of merchandise (that had cost $1,302,200) on credit, terms n/30.
f. Wrote off $32,624 of uncollectible accounts receivable.
g. Received $1,118,100 cash in payment of accounts receivable.
h. In adjusting the accounts on December 31, the company estimated that 1.3% of accounts receivable will be uncollectible.

(h) Dr. Bad Debts Expense $37,396

Required

Prepare journal entries to record Ming's 2008 and 2009 summarized transactions and its year-end adjustments to record bad debts expense. (The company uses the perpetual inventory system. Round amounts to the nearest dollar.)

Problem 9-3A
Estimating and reporting bad debts
P1 P2

At December 31, 2009, Vizarro Company reports the following results for its calendar-year.

Cash sales	$2,184,700
Credit sales	3,720,000

In addition, its unadjusted trial balance includes the following items.

Accounts receivable	$1,127,500 debit
Allowance for doubtful accounts	29,030 debit

Required

1. Prepare the adjusting entry for Vizarro Co. to recognize bad debts under each of the following independent assumptions.
   a. Bad debts are estimated to be 1.5% of credit sales.
   b. Bad debts are estimated to be 1% of total sales.
   c. An aging analysis estimates that 3% of year-end accounts receivable are uncollectible.

Check Bad Debts Expense: (1*a*) $55,800, (1*c*) $62,855

2. Show how Accounts Receivable and the Allowance for Doubtful Accounts appear on its December 31, 2009, balance sheet given the facts in part 1*a*.

3. Show how Accounts Receivable and the Allowance for Doubtful Accounts appear on its December 31, 2009, balance sheet given the facts in part 1*c*.

Problem 9-4A
Aging accounts receivable and accounting for bad debts
P1 P2

Ghosh Company has credit sales of $2.8 million for year 2009. On December 31, 2009, the company's Allowance for Doubtful Accounts has an unadjusted credit balance of $22,800. Ghosh prepares a schedule of its December 31, 2009, accounts receivable by age. On the basis of past experience, it estimates the percent of receivables in each age category that will become uncollectible. This information is summarized here.

December 31, 2009 Accounts Receivable	Age of Accounts Receivable	Expected Percent Uncollectible
$784,000	Not yet due	1.25%
380,200	1 to 30 days past due	2.00
81,800	31 to 60 days past due	6.50
52,000	61 to 90 days past due	32.75
13,000	Over 90 days past due	68.00

Required

1. Estimate the required balance of the Allowance for Doubtful Accounts at December 31, 2009, using the aging of accounts receivable method.

Check (2) Dr. Bad Debts Expense $25,791

2. Prepare the adjusting entry to record bad debts expense at December 31, 2009.

Analysis Component

3. On June 30, 2010, Ghosh Company concludes that a customer's $4,750 receivable (created in 2009) is uncollectible and that the account should be written off. What effect will this action have on Ghosh's 2010 net income? Explain.

Problem 9-5A
Analyzing and journalizing notes receivable transactions
C2 C3 P3 P4

The following selected transactions are from Chantay Company.

2008

Dec. 16 Accepted a $14,400, 60-day, 8% note dated this day in granting Adam Bakko a time extension on his past-due account receivable.
31 Made an adjusting entry to record the accrued interest on the Bakko note.

Required

1. Compute the required balance of the Allowance for Doubtful Accounts at December 31, 2009, using the aging of accounts receivable method.

2. Prepare the adjusting entry to record bad debts expense at December 31, 2009.

Check (2) Dr. Bad Debts Expense $35,795

Analysis Component

3. On July 31, 2010, Margrett concludes that a customer's $3,455 receivable (created in 2009) is uncollectible and that the account should be written off. What effect will this action have on Margrett's 2010 net income? Explain.

Problem 9-5B
Analyzing and journalizing notes receivable transactions
C2 C3 P3 P4

The following selected transactions are from Castella Company.

2008

Nov.	1	Accepted a $13,560, 90-day, 10% note dated this day in granting Eric Merklin a time extension on his past-due account receivable.
Dec.	31	Made an adjusting entry to record the accrued interest on the Merklin note.

2009

Jan.	30	Received Merklin's payment for principal and interest on the note dated November 1.
Mar.	1	Accepted a $6,000, 8%, 30-day note dated this day in granting a time extension on the past-due account receivable from Zada Co.
Mar.	2	Accepted a $4,080, 60-day, 5% note dated this day in granting Shane Patru a time extension on his past-due account receivable.
	30	The Zada Co. dishonored its note when presented for payment.
May	1	Received payment of principal plus interest from S. Patru for the March 2 note.
June	15	Accepted a $9,000, 60-day, 11% note dated this day in granting a time extension on the past-due account receivable of Mary Braff.
	21	Accepted a $3,160, 90-day, 10% note dated this day in granting Harris Guam a time extension on his past-due account receivable.
Aug.	14	Received payment of principal plus interest from M. Braff for the note of June 15.
Sep.	19	Received payment of principal plus interest from H. Guam for the June 21 note.
Nov.	30	Wrote off Zada Co.'s account against Allowance for Doubtful Accounts.

Check Jan. 30, Cr. Interest Revenue $113

May 1, Cr. Interest Revenue $34

Sep. 19, Cr. Interest Revenue $79

Required

1. Prepare journal entries to record these transactions and events. (Round amounts to the nearest dollar.)

Analysis Component

2. What reporting is necessary when a business pledges receivables as security for a loan and the loan is still outstanding at the end of the period? Explain the reason for this requirement and the accounting principle being satisfied.

SERIAL PROBLEM

Success Systems

(This serial problem began in Chapter 1 and continues through most of the book. If previous chapter segments were not completed, the serial problem can begin at this point. It is helpful, but not necessary, to use the Working Papers that accompany the book.)

SP 9 Adriana Lopez, owner of Success Systems, realizes that she needs to begin accounting for bad debts expense. Assume that Success Systems has total revenues of $43,853 during the first three months of 2010, and that the Accounts Receivable balance on March 31, 2010, is $22,720.

Required

1. Prepare the adjusting entry needed for Success Systems to recognize bad debts expense on March 31, 2010, under each of the following independent assumptions (assume a zero unadjusted balance in the Allowance for Doubtful Accounts at March 31).

a. Bad debts are estimated to be 1% of total revenues. (Round amounts to the dollar.)

b. Bad debts are estimated to be 2% of accounts receivable. (Round amounts to the dollar.)

Check (2) Bad Debts Expense, $51

2. Assume that Success Systems' Accounts Receivable balance at June 30, 2010, is $20,250 and that one account of $100 has been written off against the Allowance for Doubtful Accounts since March 31, 2010. If Lopez uses the method prescribed in Part 1*b*, what adjusting journal entry must be made to recognize bad debts expense on June 30, 2010?

3. Should Lopez consider adopting the direct write-off method of accounting for bad debts expense rather than one of the allowance methods considered in part 1? Explain.

BEYOND THE NUMBERS

REPORTING IN ACTION

A1

BTN 9-1 Refer to **Best Buy**'s financial statements in Appendix A to answer the following.

1. What is the amount of Best Buy's accounts receivable as of March 3, 2007?

2. Compute Best Buy's accounts receivable turnover as of March 3, 2007.

3. How long does it take, *on average,* for Best Buy to collect receivables? Why is this period so short? Do you believe that customers actually pay the amounts due within this short period? Explain.

4. Best Buy's most liquid assets include (*a*) cash and cash equivalents, (*b*) short-term investments, and (*c*) receivables. Compute the percentage that these liquid assets make up of current liabilities as of March 3, 2007. Do the same computations for February 25, 2006. Comment on the company's ability to satisfy its current liabilities at the 2007 fiscal year-end compared to the 2006 fiscal year-end.

5. What criteria did Best Buy use to classify items as cash equivalents?

Fast Forward

6. Access Best Buy's financial statements for fiscal years after March 3, 2007, at its Website (www.BestBuy.com) or the SEC's EDGAR database (www.sec.gov). Recompute parts 2 and 4 and comment on any changes since March 3, 2007.

COMPARATIVE ANALYSIS

A1 P2

BTN 9-2 Comparative figures for **Best Buy**, **Circuit City**, and **RadioShack** follow.

	Best Buy			Circuit City			RadioShack		
($ millions)	Current Year	One Year Prior	Two Years Prior	Current Year	One Year Prior	Two Years Prior	Current Year	One Year Prior	Two Years Prior
Accounts receivable, net . . .	$ 548	$ 449	$ 375	$ 383	$ 221	$ 231	$ 248	$ 309	$ 241
Net sales	35,934	30,848	27,433	12,430	11,514	10,414	4,778	5,082	4,841

Required

1. Compute the accounts receivable turnover for Best Buy, Circuit City, and RadioShack for each of the two most recent years using the data shown.

Hint: Average collection period equals 365 divided by the accounts receivable turnover.

2. Using results from part 1, compute how many days it takes each company, *on average,* to collect receivables. Why are these periods so short? Do you believe that receivables are actually collected this quickly? Explain.

3. Which company is more efficient in collecting its accounts receivable? Explain.

BTN 9-3 Astin Blair is the manager of a medium-size company. A few years ago, Blair persuaded the owner to base a part of his compensation on the net income the company earns each year. Each December he estimates year-end financial figures in anticipation of the bonus he will receive. If the bonus is not as high as he would like, he offers several recommendations to the accountant for year-end adjustments. One of his favorite recommendations is for the controller to reduce the estimate of doubtful accounts.

ETHICS CHALLENGE

P1 P2

Required

1. What effect does lowering the estimate for doubtful accounts have on the income statement and balance sheet?
2. Do you believe Blair's recommendation to adjust the allowance for doubtful accounts is within his right as manager, or do you believe this action is an ethics violation? Justify your response.
3. What type of internal control(s) might be useful for this company in overseeing the manager's recommendations for accounting changes?

BTN 9-4 As the accountant for Pure-Air Distributing, you attend a sales managers' meeting devoted to a discussion of credit policies. At the meeting, you report that bad debts expense is estimated to be \$59,000 and accounts receivable at year-end amount to \$1,750,000 less a \$43,000 allowance for doubtful accounts. Sid Omar, a sales manager, expresses confusion over why bad debts expense and the allowance for doubtful accounts are different amounts. Write a one-page memorandum to him explaining why a difference in bad debts expense and the allowance for doubtful accounts is not unusual. The company estimates bad debts expense as 2% of sales.

COMMUNICATING IN PRACTICE

P1 P2

BTN 9-5 Access **eBay**'s, February 28, 2007, filing of its 10-K report for the year ended December 31, 2006, at www.sec.gov.

TAKING IT TO THE NET

C1

Required

1. What is the amount of eBay's net accounts receivable at December 31, 2006, and at December 31, 2005?
2. Note 7 to its financial statements lists eBay's gross accounts receivable, allowance for doubtful accounts, allowance for authorized credits, and net accounts receivable. For the two years ended December 31, 2006 and 2005, compute its allowance for doubtful accounts as a percent of gross accounts receivable.
3. Do you believe that these percentages are reasonable based on what you know about eBay? Explain.

BTN 9-6 Each member of a team is to participate in estimating uncollectibles using the aging schedule and percents shown in Problem 9-4A. The division of labor is up to the team. Your goal is to accurately complete this task as soon as possible. After estimating uncollectibles, check your estimate with the instructor. If the estimate is correct, the team then should prepare the adjusting entry and the presentation of accounts receivable (net) for the December 31, 2009, balance sheet.

TEAMWORK IN ACTION

P2

ENTREPRENEURIAL DECISION

C1

BTN 9-7 Kevin Plank of **Under Armour** is introduced in the chapter's opening feature. Kevin currently sells his products through multiple outlets. Assume that he is considering two new selling options.

Plan A. Under Armour would begin selling products online directly to customers. Online customers would use their credit cards. It currently has the capability of selling through its Website with no additional investment in hardware or software. Credit sales are expected to increase by $250,000 per year. Costs associated with this plan are: cost of these sales will be $135,500, credit card fees will be 4.75% of sales, and additional recordkeeping and shipping costs will be 6% of sales. These online sales will reduce the sales to stores by $35,000 because some customers will now purchase items online. Sales to stores have a 25% gross margin percentage.

Plan B. Under Armour would expand its market to more stores. It would make additional credit sales of $500,000 to those stores. Costs associated with those sales are: cost of sales will be $375,000, additional recordkeeping and shipping will be 4% of sales, and uncollectible accounts will be 6.2% of sales.

Required

Check (1b) Net income, $74,000

1. Compute the additional annual net income or loss expected under (a) Plan A and (b) Plan B.
2. Should Under Armour pursue either plan? Discuss both the financial and nonfinancial factors relevant to this decision.

HITTING THE ROAD

C1

BTN 9-8 Many commercials include comments similar to the following: "We accept **VISA**" or "We do not accept **American Express**." Conduct your own research by contacting at least five companies via interviews, phone calls, or the Internet to determine the reason(s) companies discriminate in their use of credit cards. Collect information on the fees charged by the different cards for the companies contacted. (The instructor can assign this as a team activity.)

GLOBAL DECISION

C1 P1 DSG

BTN 9-9 Key information from **DSG international plc** (DSGiplc.com) follows.

(£ millions)	Current Year	Prior Year
Accounts receivable, net	£ 393	£ 370
Sales	7,930	6,984

1. Compute the accounts receivable turnover for the current year.
2. How long does it take on average for DSG to collect receivables?
3. Refer to BTN 9-2. How does DSG compare to Best Buy, Circuit City, and RadioShack in terms of its accounts receivable turnover and its collection period?

ANSWERS TO MULTIPLE CHOICE QUIZ

1. d; Desired balance in Allowance for Doubtful Accounts = $ 5,026 cr.
($125,650 × 0.04)
Current balance in Allowance for Doubtful Accounts = (328) cr.
Bad Debts Expense to be recorded = $ 4,698

2. a; Desired balance in Allowance for Doubtful Accounts = $29,358 cr.
($489,300 × 0.06)
Current balance in Allowance for Doubtful Accounts = 554 dr.
Bad Debts Expense to be recorded = $29,912

3. a; $7,500 × 0.05 × 90/360 = $93.75

4. c; Principal amount $9,000
Interest accrued .... 120 ($9,000 × 0.08 × 60/360)
Maturity value $9,120

5. d; $489,600/$40,800 = 12

A Look Back

Chapters 8 and 9 focused on short-term assets: cash, cash equivalents, and receivables. We explained why they are known as liquid assets and described how companies account and report for them.

A Look at This Chapter

This chapter introduces us to long-term assets. We explain how to account for a long-term asset's cost, the allocation of an asset's cost to periods benefiting from it, the recording of additional costs after an asset is purchased, and the disposal of an asset.

A Look Ahead

Chapter 11 focuses on current liabilities. We explain how they are computed, recorded, and reported in financial statements. We also explain the accounting for company payroll and contingencies.

Chapter 10 Plant Assets, Natural Resources, and Intangibles

Learning Objectives

CAP

Conceptual

C1 Describe plant assets and issues in accounting for them. *(p. 392)*

C2 Explain depreciation and the factors affecting its computation. *(p. 395)*

C3 Explain depreciation for partial years and changes in estimates. *(p. 400)*

Analytical

A1 Compare and analyze alternative depreciation methods. *(p. 399)*

A2 Compute total asset turnover and apply it to analyze a company's use of assets. *(p. 410)*

Procedural

P1 Apply the cost principle to compute the cost of plant assets. *(p. 393)*

P2 Compute and record depreciation using the straight-line, units-of-production, and declining-balance methods. *(p. 396)*

P3 Distinguish between revenue and capital expenditures, and account for them. *(p. 402)*

P4 Account for asset disposal through discarding or selling an asset. *(p. 404)*

P5 Account for natural resource assets and their depletion. *(p. 406)*

P6 Account for intangible assets. *(p. 407)*

P7 *Appendix 10A*—Account for asset exchanges. *(p. 413)*

LP10

Decision Feature

Fruitful Assets

"The best way to predict the future is to create it"
—Jeremy Black (from left: E. Nichols, R. Black, T. Baumgardner, J. Black)

SAN CLEMENTE, CA—Surfing is the common bond for Ryan Black, Ed Nichols, and Jeremy Black. It also was the driving force for an excursion to ride the waves of Brazil. But what they encountered would change their lives forever.

The three surfers discovered beachgoers eating a purple berry called *acai* (ah-sigh-ee). "We too fell in love with it," says Ed. "We didn't want to leave Brazil without it." Adds Jeremy, "When people start eating acai, they want it . . . every day."

The three decided to become business missionaries and introduce acai to the masses. They launched **Sambazon (Sambazon.com),** short for Sustainable Management of the Brazilian Amazon, to manufacture and distribute acai. Scraping up just enough money, they started operations. Says Jeremy, "Financing our equipment, machinery, and other assets was a struggle as our operating cycle is long. We must pay cash to Brazilian acai growers, then pay for processing and shipping, and finally package and distribute acai products to buyers."

The power of the wave was with them. Sambazon now employs 120 workers, churns out numerous acai products, and generates nearly $20 million in annual sales. A continuing challenge is maintaining the right kind and amount of plant assets to meet demand and be profitable. Explains Jeremy, "Sambazon's success depends on monitoring and controlling plant asset costs, which range from bottling and packaging equipment to delivery vehicles, plant facilities, and land."

Sambazon must account for, manage, and recover all costs of long-term assets. "We built Sambazon on a triple bottom line business model . . . economic, environmental, and social," says Ryan. "[And we] recognize some things that are not just on our balance sheet."

Their success in asset management permits them to pursue other passions. "We've been given this incredible opportunity to make a lot of positive change with this berry," declares Jeremy. "It's not just a job . . . it's a mission!"

[Sources: *Sambazon Website,* January 2009; *The Wall Street Journal,* March 2007; *San Clemente Times,* March 2006; *CU Business Portfolio,* Spring 2007; *Entrepreneur,* November 2007]

This chapter focuses on long-term assets, which can be grouped into plant assets, natural resource assets, and intangible assets. Plant assets make up a large part of assets on most balance sheets, and they yield depreciation, often one of the largest expenses on income statements. The acquisition or building of a plant asset is often referred to as a *capital expenditure.* Capital expenditures are important events because they impact both the short- and long-term success of a company. Natural resource assets and intangible assets have similar impacts. This chapter describes the purchase and use of these assets. We also explain what distinguishes these assets from other types of assets, how to determine their cost, how to allocate their costs to periods benefiting from their use, and how to dispose of them.

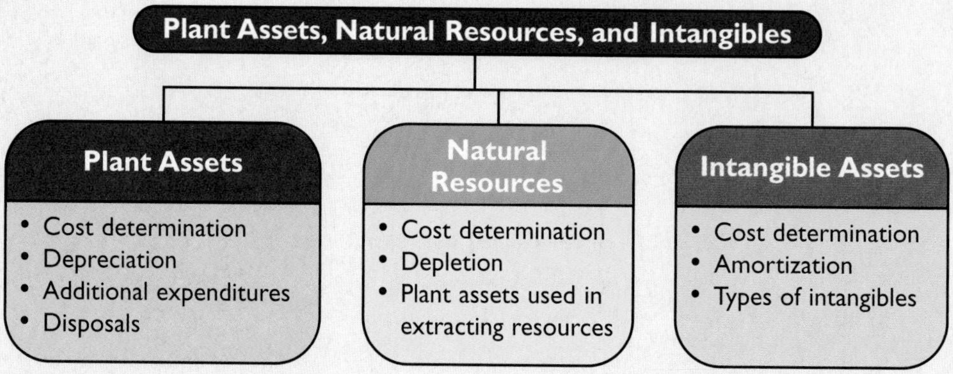

Section 1—Plant Assets

Plant assets are tangible assets used in a company's operations that have a useful life of more than one accounting period. Plant assets are also called *plant and equipment; property, plant, and equipment;* or *fixed assets.* For many companies, plant assets make up the single largest class of assets they own. Exhibit 10.1 shows plant assets as a percent of total assets for several companies. Not only do they make up a large percent of these companies' assets, but their dollar values are large. **McDonald's** plant assets, for instance, are reported at more than $20 billion, and **Wal-Mart** reports plant assets of more than $85 billion.

EXHIBIT 10.1

Plant Assets of Selected Companies

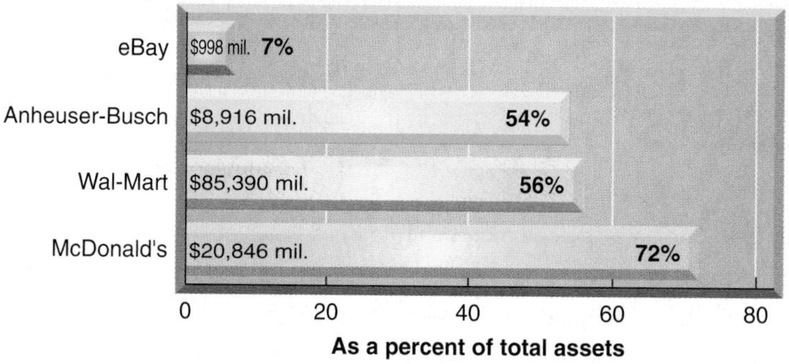

C1 Describe plant assets and issues in accounting for them.

Plant assets are set apart from other assets by two important features. First, *plant assets are used in operations.* This makes them different from, for instance, inventory that is held for sale and not used in operations. The distinctive feature here is use, not type of asset. A company that purchases a computer to resell it reports it on the balance sheet as inventory. If the same company purchases this computer to use in operations, however, it is a plant asset. Another example is land held for future expansion, which is reported as a long-term investment. However, if this land holds a factory used in operations, the land is part of plant assets. Another example is equipment held for use in the event of a breakdown or for peak periods of production, which is reported in plant assets. If this same equipment is removed from use and held for sale, however, it is not reported in plant assets.

The second important feature is that *plant assets have useful lives extending over more than one accounting period.* This makes plant assets different from current assets such as supplies that are normally consumed in a short time period after they are placed in use.

The accounting for plant assets reflects these two features. Since plant assets are used in operations, we try to match their costs against the revenues they generate. Also, since their useful lives extend over more than one period, our matching of costs and revenues must extend over several periods. Specifically, we value plant assets (balance sheet effect) and then, for many of them, we allocate their costs to periods benefiting from their use (income statement effect). An important exception is land; land cost is not allocated to expense when we expect it to have an indefinite life.

Point: It can help to view plant assets as prepaid expenses that benefit several future accounting periods.

Exhibit 10.2 shows four main issues in accounting for plant assets: (1) computing the costs of plant assets, (2) allocating the costs of most plant assets (less any salvage amounts) against revenues for the periods they benefit, (3) accounting for expenditures such as repairs and improvements to plant assets, and (4) recording the disposal of plant assets. The following sections discuss these issues.

EXHIBIT 10.2

Issues in Accounting for Plant Assets

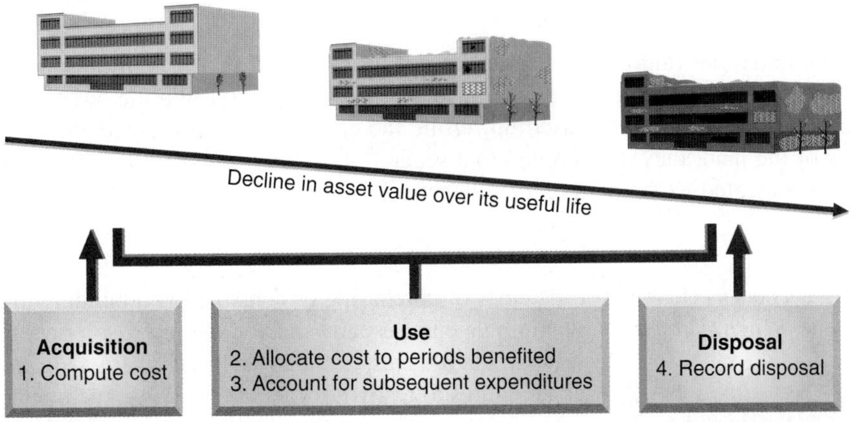

Cost Determination

Plant assets are recorded at cost when acquired. This is consistent with the *cost principle.* **Cost** includes all normal and reasonable expenditures necessary to get the asset in place and ready for its intended use. The cost of a factory machine, for instance, includes its invoice cost less any cash discount for early payment, plus any necessary freight, unpacking, assembling, installing, and testing costs. Examples are the costs of building a base or foundation for a machine, providing electrical hookups, and testing the asset before using it in operations.

Video10.1

To be recorded as part of the cost of a plant asset, an expenditure must be normal, reasonable, and necessary in preparing it for its intended use. If an asset is damaged during unpacking, the repairs are not added to its cost. Instead, they are charged to an expense account. Nor is a paid traffic fine for moving heavy machinery on city streets without a proper permit part of the machinery's cost; but payment for a proper permit is included in the cost of machinery. Charges are sometimes incurred to modify or customize a new plant asset. These charges are added to the asset's cost. We explain in this section how to determine the cost of plant assets for each of its four major classes.

Land

P1 Apply the cost principle to compute the cost of plant assets.

When land is purchased for a building site, its cost includes the total amount paid for the land, including any real estate commissions, title insurance fees, legal fees, and any accrued property taxes paid by the purchaser. Payments for surveying, clearing, grading, and draining also are included in the cost of land. Other costs include government assessments, whether incurred at the time of purchase or later, for items such as public roadways, sewers, and sidewalks. These assessments are included because they permanently add to the land's value. Land purchased as a building site sometimes includes structures that must be removed. In such cases, the total purchase price is charged to the Land account as is the cost of removing the structures, less any amounts recovered through sale of salvaged materials. To illustrate, assume that **Starbucks** paid $167,000 cash to acquire land for a retail store.

EXHIBIT 10.3

Computing Cost of Land

Cash price of land	$ 167,000
Net cost of garage removal	13,000
Closing costs	10,000
Cost of land	**$190,000**

This land had an old service garage that was removed at a net cost of $13,000 ($15,000 in costs less $2,000 proceeds from salvaged materials). Additional closing costs total $10,000, consisting of brokerage fees ($8,000), legal fees ($1,500), and title costs ($500). The cost of this land to Starbucks is $190,000 and is computed as shown in Exhibit 10.3.

Land Improvements

Land has an indefinite (unlimited) life and is not usually used up over time. **Land improvements** such as parking lot surfaces, driveways, fences, shrubs, and lighting systems, however, have limited useful lives and are used up. While the costs of these improvements increase the usefulness of the land, they are charged to a separate Land Improvement account so that their costs can be allocated to the periods they benefit.

Buildings

A Building account is charged for the costs of purchasing or constructing a building that is used in operations. When purchased, a building's costs usually include its purchase price, brokerage fees, taxes, title fees, and attorney fees. Its costs also include all expenditures to ready it for its intended use, including any necessary repairs or renovations such as wiring, lighting, flooring, and wall coverings. When a company constructs a building or any plant asset for its own use, its costs include materials and labor plus a reasonable amount of indirect overhead cost. Overhead includes the costs of items such as heat, lighting, power, and depreciation on machinery used to construct the asset. Costs of construction also include design fees, building permits, and insurance during construction. However, costs such as insurance to cover the asset *after* it is placed in use are operating expenses.

Machinery and Equipment

The costs of machinery and equipment consist of all costs normal and necessary to purchase them and prepare them for their intended use. These include the purchase price, taxes, transportation charges, insurance while in transit, and the installing, assembling, and testing of the machinery and equipment.

Lump-Sum Purchase

Example: If appraised values in Exhibit 10.4 are land, $24,000; land improvements, $12,000; and building, $84,000, what cost is assigned to the building? *Answer:*
(1) $24,000 + $12,000 + $84,000 = $120,000 (total appraisal)
(2) $84,000/$120,000 = 70% (building's percent of total)
(3) 70% × $90,000 = $63,000 (building's apportioned cost)

Plant assets sometimes are purchased as a group in a single transaction for a lump-sum price. This transaction is called a *lump-sum purchase,* or *group, bulk,* or *basket purchase.* When this occurs, we allocate the cost of the purchase among the different types of assets acquired based on their *relative market values,* which can be estimated by appraisal or by using the tax-assessed valuations of the assets. To illustrate, assume **Oakley** paid $90,000 cash to acquire a group of items consisting of land appraised at $30,000, land improvements appraised at $10,000, and a building appraised at $60,000. The $90,000 cost is allocated on the basis of these appraised values as shown in Exhibit 10.4.

EXHIBIT 10.4

Computing Costs in a Lump-Sum Purchase

	Appraised Value	Percent of Total	Apportioned Cost
Land	$ 30,000	30% ($30,000/$100,000)	**$27,000** ($90,000 × 30%)
Land improvements	10,000	10 ($10,000/$100,000)	**9,000** ($90,000 × 10%)
Building	60,000	60 ($60,000/$100,000)	**54,000** ($90,000 × 60%)
Totals	$100,000	100%	$ 90,000

Quick Check

Answers—p. 416

1. Identify the asset class for each of the following: (*a*) supplies, (*b*) office equipment, (*c*) inventory, (*d*) land for future expansion, and (*e*) trucks used in operations.
2. Identify the account charged for each of the following: (*a*) the purchase price of a vacant lot to be used in operations and (*b*) the cost of paving that same vacant lot.
3. Compute the amount recorded as the cost of a new machine given the following payments related to its purchase: gross purchase price, $700,000; sales tax, $49,000; purchase discount taken, $21,000; freight cost—terms FOB shipping point, $3,500; normal assembly costs, $3,000; cost of necessary machine platform, $2,500; cost of parts used in maintaining machine, $4,200.

Depreciation

Depreciation is the process of allocating the cost of a plant asset to expense in the accounting periods benefiting from its use. Depreciation does not measure the decline in the asset's market value each period, nor does it measure the asset's physical deterioration. Since depreciation reflects the cost of using a plant asset, depreciation charges are only recorded when the asset is actually in service. This section describes the factors we must consider in computing depreciation, the depreciation methods used, revisions in depreciation, and depreciation for partial periods.

Video10.1

Factors in Computing Depreciation

Factors that determine depreciation are (1) cost, (2) salvage value, and (3) useful life.

C2 Explain depreciation and the factors affecting its computation.

Cost The **cost** of a plant asset consists of all necessary and reasonable expenditures to acquire it and to prepare it for its intended use.

Salvage Value The total amount of depreciation to be charged off over an asset's benefit period equals the asset's cost minus its salvage value. **Salvage value,** also called *residual value* or *scrap value,* is an estimate of the asset's value at the end of its benefit period. This is the amount the owner expects to receive from disposing of the asset at the end of its benefit period. If the asset is expected to be traded in on a new asset, its salvage value is the expected trade-in value.

Point: If we expect additional costs in preparing a plant asset for disposal, the salvage value equals the expected amount from disposal less any disposal costs.

Useful Life The **useful life** of a plant asset is the length of time it is productively used in a company's operations. Useful life, also called *service life,* might not be as long as the asset's total productive life. For example, the productive life of a computer can be eight years or more. Some companies, however, trade in old computers for new ones every two years. In this case, these computers have a two-year useful life, meaning the cost of these computers (less their expected trade-in values) is charged to depreciation expense over a two-year period.

Point: Useful life and salvage value are estimates. Estimates require judgment based on all available information.

Several variables often make the useful life of a plant asset difficult to predict. A major variable is the wear and tear from use in operations. Two other variables, inadequacy and obsolescence, also require consideration. **Inadequacy** refers to the insufficient capacity of a company's plant assets to meet its growing productive demands. **Obsolescence** refers to a plant asset that is no longer useful in producing goods or services with a competitive advantage because of new inventions and improvements. Both inadequacy and obsolescence are difficult to predict because of demand changes, new inventions, and improvements. A company usually disposes of an inadequate or obsolete asset before it wears out.

A company is often able to better predict a new asset's useful life when it has past experience with a similar asset. When it has no such experience, a company relies on the experience of others or on engineering studies and judgment. In note 1 of its annual report, **Tootsie Roll**, a snack food manufacturer, reports the following useful lives:

Buildings	20–35 years
Machinery and Equipment	5–20 years

Decision Insight

Life Line Life expectancy of plant assets is often in the eye of the beholder. For instance, **Hershey Foods** and **Tootsie Roll** are competitors and apply similar manufacturing processes, yet their equipment's life expectancies are different. Hershey depreciates equipment over 3 to 15 years, but Tootsie Roll depreciates them over 5 to 20 years. Such differences markedly impact financial statements.

Depreciation Methods

Depreciation methods are used to allocate a plant asset's cost over the accounting periods in its useful life. The most frequently used method of depreciation is the straight-line method. Another common depreciation method is the units-of-production method. We explain both of these methods in this section. This section also describes accelerated depreciation methods, with a focus on the declining-balance method.

The computations in this section use information about a machine that inspects athletic shoes before packaging. Manufacturers such as **Converse**, **Reebok**, **Adidas**, and **Fila** use this machine. Data for this machine are in Exhibit 10.5.

EXHIBIT 10.5

Data for Athletic Shoe-Inspecting Machine

Cost	$10,000
Salvage value	1,000
Depreciable cost	$ 9,000
Useful life	
Accounting periods	5 years
Units inspected	36,000 shoes

P2 Compute and record depreciation using the straight-line, units-of-production, and declining-balance methods.

Straight-Line Method **Straight-line depreciation** charges the same amount of expense to each period of the asset's useful life. A two-step process is used. We first compute the *depreciable cost* of the asset, also called the *cost to be depreciated.* It is computed by subtracting the asset's salvage value from its total cost. Second, depreciable cost is divided by the number of accounting periods in the asset's useful life. The formula for straight-line depreciation, along with its computation for the inspection machine just described, is shown in Exhibit 10.6.

EXHIBIT 10.6

Straight-Line Depreciation Formula and Example

$$\frac{\textbf{Cost} - \textbf{Salvage value}}{\textbf{Useful life in periods}} = \frac{\$10{,}000 - \$1{,}000}{5 \text{ years}} = \$1{,}800 \text{ per year}$$

If this machine is purchased on December 31, 2008, and used throughout its predicted useful life of five years, the straight-line method allocates an equal amount of depreciation to each of the years 2009 through 2013. We make the following adjusting entry at the end of each of the five years to record straight-line depreciation of this machine.

Assets	=	Liabilities	+	Equity
−1,800				−1,800

Dec. 31	Depreciation Expense	1,800	
	Accumulated Depreciation—Machinery		1,800
	To record annual depreciation.		

Example: If the salvage value of the machine is $2,500, what is the annual depreciation? *Answer:* ($10,000 − $2,500)/5 years = $1,500

The $1,800 Depreciation Expense is reported on the income statement among operating expenses. The $1,800 Accumulated Depreciation is a contra asset account to the Machinery account in the balance sheet. The graph on the left in Exhibit 10.7 shows the $1,800 per year expenses reported in each of the five years. The graph on the right shows the amounts reported on each of the six December 31 balance sheets.

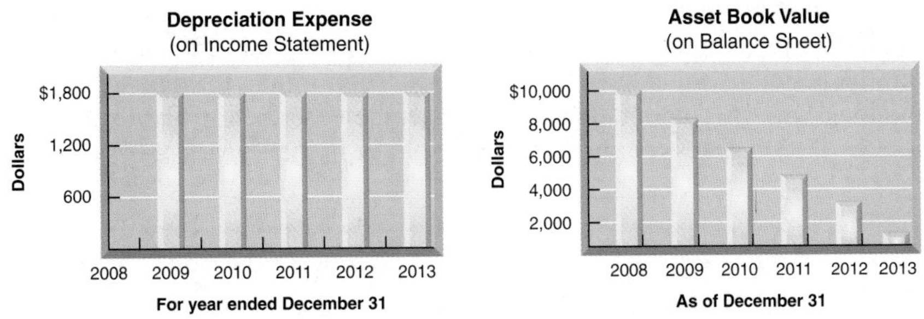

EXHIBIT 10.7

Financial Statement Effects of Straight-Line Depreciation

The net balance sheet amount is the **asset book value,** or simply *book value,* and is computed as the asset's total cost less its accumulated depreciation. For example, at the end of year 2 (December 31, 2010), its book value is $6,400 and is reported in the balance sheet as follows:

Machinery	$10,000	
Less accumulated depreciation	3,600	$6,400

The book value of this machine declines by $1,800 each year due to depreciation. From the graphs in Exhibit 10.7 we can see why this method is called straight-line.

We also can compute the *straight-line depreciation rate,* defined as 100% divided by the number of periods in the asset's useful life. For the inspection machine, this rate is 20% (100% ÷ 5 years, or 1/5 per period). We use this rate, along with other information, to compute the machine's *straight-line depreciation schedule* shown in Exhibit 10.8. Note three points in this exhibit. First, depreciation expense is the same each period. Second, accumulated depreciation is the sum of current and prior periods' depreciation expense. Third, book value declines each period until it equals salvage value at the end of the machine's useful life.

Point: Depreciation requires estimates for salvage value and useful life. Ethics are relevant when managers might be tempted to choose estimates to achieve desired results on financial statements.

EXHIBIT 10.8

Straight-Line Depreciation Schedule

	Depreciation for the Period			End of Period	
Annual Period	Depreciable Cost*	Depreciation Rate	Depreciation Expense	Accumulated Depreciation	Book Value†
2008	—	—	—	—	$10,000
2009	$9,000	20%	$1,800	$1,800	8,200
2010	9,000	20	1,800	3,600	6,400
2011	9,000	20	1,800	5,400	4,600
2012	9,000	20	1,800	7,200	2,800
2013	9,000	20	1,800	9,000	**1,000**

* $10,000 − $1,000. † Book value is total cost minus accumulated depreciation.

Units-of-Production Method The straight-line method charges an equal share of an asset's cost to each period. If plant assets are used up in about equal amounts each accounting period, this method produces a reasonable matching of expenses with revenues. However, the use of some plant assets varies greatly from one period to the next. A builder, for instance, might use a piece of construction equipment for a month and then not use it again for several months. When equipment use varies from period to period, the units-of-production depreciation method can better match expenses with revenues. **Units-of-production depreciation** charges a varying amount to expense for each period of an asset's useful life depending on its usage.

A two-step process is used to compute units-of-production depreciation. We first compute *depreciation per unit* by subtracting the asset's salvage value from its total cost and then dividing by the total number of units expected to be produced during its useful life. Units of production can be expressed in product or other units such as hours used or miles driven. The second step is to compute depreciation expense for the period by multiplying the units produced in the period by the depreciation per unit. The formula for units-of-production depreciation, along with its computation for the machine described in Exhibit 10.5, is shown in Exhibit 10.9. (7,000 shoes are inspected and sold in its first year.)

EXHIBIT 10.9

Units-of-Production Depreciation Formula and Example

Step 1

$$\textbf{Depreciation per unit} = \frac{\textbf{Cost} - \textbf{Salvage value}}{\textbf{Total units of production}} = \frac{\$10{,}000 - \$1{,}000}{36{,}000 \text{ shoes}} = \$0.25 \text{ per shoe}$$

Step 2

$$\textbf{Depreciation expense} = \textbf{Depreciation per unit} \times \textbf{Units produced in period}$$

$$\$0.25 \text{ per shoe} \times 7{,}000 \text{ shoes} = \$1{,}750$$

Using data on the number of shoes inspected by the machine, we can compute the *units-of-production depreciation schedule* shown in Exhibit 10.10. For example, depreciation for the first year is $1,750 (7,000 shoes at $0.25 per shoe). Depreciation for the second year is $2,000 (8,000 shoes at $0.25 per shoe). Other years are similarly computed. Exhibit 10.10 shows that (1) depreciation expense depends on unit output, (2) accumulated depreciation is the sum of current and prior periods' depreciation expense, and (3) book value declines each period until it equals salvage value at the end of the asset's useful life. **Boise Cascade** is one of many companies using the units-of-production depreciation method. It reports that most of its "paper and wood products manufacturing facilities determine depreciation by a units-of-production method." **Kimberly-Clark** also reports that much of its "depreciable property is depreciated on the . . . units-of-production method."

Example: Refer to Exhibit 10.10. If the number of shoes inspected in 2013 is 5,500, what is depreciation for 2013? *Answer:* $1,250 (never depreciate below salvage value)

EXHIBIT 10.10

Units-of-Production Depreciation Schedule

	Depreciation for the Period			End of Period	
Annual Period	**Number of Units**	**Depreciation per Unit**	**Depreciation Expense**	**Accumulated Depreciation**	**Book Value**
2008	—	—	—	—	$10,000
2009	7,000	$0.25	**$1,750**	$1,750	8,250
2010	8,000	0.25	**2,000**	3,750	6,250
2011	9,000	0.25	**2,250**	6,000	4,000
2012	7,000	0.25	**1,750**	7,750	2,250
2013	5,000	0.25	**1,250**	9,000	**1,000**

Declining-Balance Method An **accelerated depreciation method** yields larger depreciation expenses in the early years of an asset's life and less depreciation in later years. The most common accelerated method is the **declining-balance method** of depreciation, which uses a depreciation rate that is a multiple of the straight-line rate and applies it to the asset's beginning-of-period book value. The amount of depreciation declines each period because book value declines each period.

A common depreciation rate for the declining-balance method is double the straight-line rate. This is called the *double-declining-balance* (*DDB*) method. This method is applied in three steps: (1) compute the asset's straight-line depreciation rate, (2) double the straight-line rate, and (3) compute depreciation expense by multiplying this rate by the asset's beginning-of-period book value. To illustrate, let's return to the machine in Exhibit 10.5 and apply the double-declining-balance method to compute depreciation expense. Exhibit 10.11 shows the first-year depreciation computation for the machine. The three-step process is to (1) divide

Point: In the DDB method, *double* refers to the rate and *declining balance* refers to book value. The rate is applied to beginning book value each period.

100% by five years to determine the straight-line rate of 20%, or 1/5, per year, (2) double this 20% rate to get the declining-balance rate of 40%, or 2/5, per year, and (3) compute depreciation expense as 40%, or 2/5, multiplied by the beginning-of-period book value.

EXHIBIT 10.11

Double-Declining-Balance Depreciation Formula*

Step 1

Straight-line rate = 100% ÷ Useful life = 100% ÷ 5 years = 20%

Step 2

Double-declining-balance rate = 2 × Straight-line rate = 2 × 20% = 40%

Step 3

Depreciation expense = Double-declining-balance rate × Beginning-period book value

40% × $10,000 = $4,000 (for 2009)

* To simplify: DDB depreciation = (2 × Beginning-period book value)/Useful life.

The *double-declining-balance depreciation schedule* is shown in Exhibit 10.12. The schedule follows the formula except for year 2013, when depreciation expense is $296. This $296 is not equal to 40% × $1,296, or $518.40. If we had used the $518.40 for depreciation expense in 2013, the ending book value would equal $777.60, which is less than the $1,000 salvage value. Instead, the $296 is computed by subtracting the $1,000 salvage value from the $1,296 book value at the beginning of the fifth year (the year when DDB depreciation cuts into salvage value).

Example: What is the DDB depreciation expense in year 2012 if the salvage value is $2,000?
Answer: $2,160 − $2,000 = $160

EXHIBIT 10.12

Double-Declining-Balance Depreciation Schedule

	Depreciation for the Period			End of Period	
Annual Period	**Beginning of Period Book Value**	**Depreciation Rate**	**Depreciation Expense**	**Accumulated Depreciation**	**Book Value**
2008	—	—	—	—	$10,000
2009	$10,000	40%	**$4,000**	$4,000	6,000
2010	6,000	40	**2,400**	6,400	3,600
2011	3,600	40	**1,440**	7,840	2,160
2012	2,160	40	**864**	8,704	1,296
2013	1,296	40	**296***	9,000	**1,000**

* Year 2013 depreciation is $1,296 − $1,000 = $296 (never depreciate book value below salvage value).

Comparing Depreciation Methods Exhibit 10.13 shows depreciation expense for each year of the machine's useful life under each of the three depreciation methods. While depreciation expense per period differs for different methods, total depreciation expense of $9,000 is the same over the machine's useful life.

A1 Compare and analyze alternative depreciation methods.

EXHIBIT 10.13

Depreciation Expense for the Different Methods

Period	Straight-Line	Units-of-Production	Double-Declining-Balance
2009	$1,800	$1,750	$4,000
2010	1,800	2,000	2,400
2011	1,800	2,250	1,440
2012	1,800	1,750	864
2013	1,800	1,250	296
Totals	$9,000	$9,000	$9,000

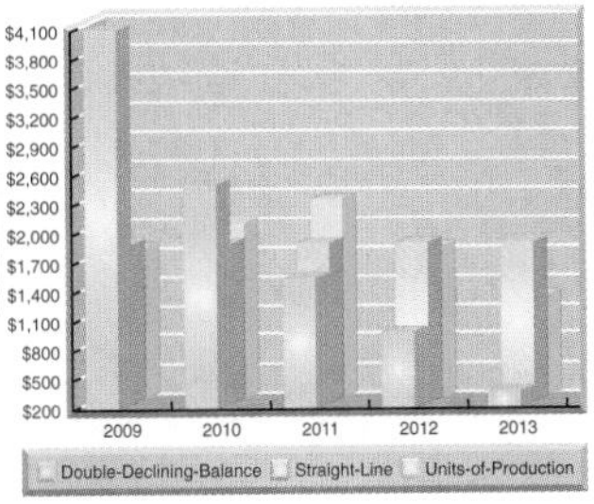

Each method starts with a total cost of $10,000 and ends with a salvage value of $1,000. The difference is the pattern in depreciation expense over the useful life. The book value of the asset when using straight-line is always greater than the book value from using double-declining-balance, except at the beginning and end of the asset's useful life, when it is the same.

Point: Depreciation is higher and income lower in the short run when using accelerated versus straight-line methods.

Also, the straight-line method yields a steady pattern of depreciation expense while the units-of-production depreciation depends on the number of units produced. Each of these methods is acceptable because it allocates cost in a systematic and rational manner.

Decision Insight

In Vogue About 85% of companies use straight-line depreciation for plant assets, 4% use units-of-production, and 4% use declining-balance. Another 7% use an unspecified accelerated method—most likely declining-balance.

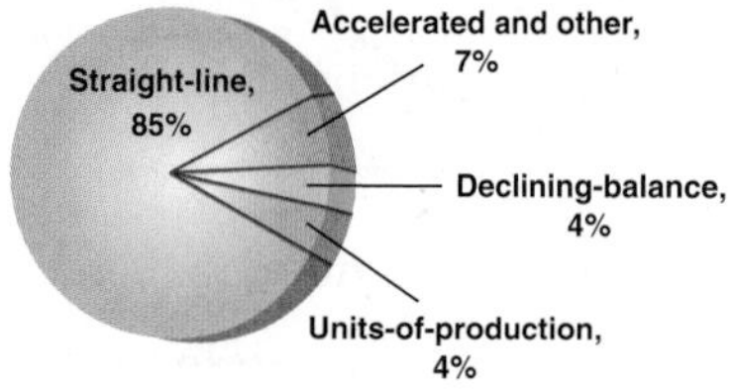

Depreciation for Tax Reporting The records a company keeps for financial accounting purposes are usually separate from the records it keeps for tax accounting purposes. This is so because financial accounting aims to report useful information on financial performance and position, whereas tax accounting reflects government objectives in raising revenues. Differences between these two accounting systems are normal and expected. Depreciation is a common example of how the records differ. For example, many companies use accelerated depreciation in computing taxable income. Reporting higher depreciation expense in the early years of an asset's life reduces the company's taxable income in those years and increases it in later years, when the depreciation expense is lower. The company's goal here is to *postpone* its tax payments.

Point: Understanding depreciation for financial accounting will help in learning MACRS for tax accounting. Rules for MACRS are available from www.IRS.gov.

The U.S. federal income tax law has rules for depreciating assets. These rules include the **Modified Accelerated Cost Recovery System (MACRS),** which allows straight-line depreciation for some assets but requires accelerated depreciation for most kinds of assets. MACRS separates depreciable assets into different classes and defines the depreciable life and rate for each class. MACRS is *not* acceptable for financial reporting because it often allocates costs over an arbitrary period that is less than the asset's useful life and it fails to estimate salvage value. Details of MACRS are covered in tax accounting courses.

Partial-Year Depreciation

C3 Explain depreciation for partial years and changes in estimates.

Plant assets are purchased and disposed of at various times. When an asset is purchased (or disposed of) at a time other than the beginning or end of an accounting period, depreciation is recorded for part of a year. This is done so that the year of purchase or the year of disposal is charged with its share of the asset's depreciation.

To illustrate, assume that the machine in Exhibit 10.5 is purchased and placed in service on October 8, 2008, and the annual accounting period ends on December 31. Since this machine is purchased and used for nearly three months in 2008, the calendar-year income statement should report depreciation expense on the machine for that part of the year. Normally, depreciation assumes that the asset is purchased on the first day of the month nearest the actual date of purchase. In this case, since the purchase occurred on October 8, we assume an October 1 purchase date. This means that three months' depreciation is recorded in 2008. Using straight-line depreciation, we compute three months' depreciation of $450 as follows.

$$\frac{\$10{,}000 - \$1{,}000}{5 \text{ years}} \times \frac{3}{12} = \$450$$

A similar computation is necessary when an asset disposal occurs during a period. To illustrate, assume that the machine is sold on June 24, 2013. Depreciation is recorded for the period January 1 through June 24 when it is disposed of. This partial year's depreciation, computed to the nearest whole month, is

$$\frac{\$10{,}000 - \$1{,}000}{5 \text{ years}} \times \frac{6}{12} = \$900$$

Example: If the machine's salvage value is zero and purchase occurs on Oct. 8, 2008, how much depreciation is recorded at Dec. 31, 2008? *Answer:* $10,000/5 × 3/12 = $500

Change in Estimates for Depreciation

Depreciation is based on estimates of salvage value and useful life. During the useful life of an asset, new information may indicate that these estimates are inaccurate. If our estimate of an asset's useful life and/or salvage value changes, what should we do? The answer is to use the new estimate to compute depreciation for current and future periods. This means that we revise the depreciation expense computation by spreading the cost yet to be depreciated over the remaining useful life. This approach is used for all depreciation methods.

Point: Remaining depreciable cost equals book value less revised salvage value at the point of revision.

Let's return to the machine described in Exhibit 10.8 using straight-line depreciation. At the beginning of this asset's third year, its book value is \$6,400, computed as \$10,000 minus \$3,600. Assume that at the beginning of its third year, the estimated number of years remaining in its useful life changes from three to four years *and* its estimate of salvage value changes from \$1,000 to \$400. Straight-line depreciation for each of the four remaining years is computed as shown in Exhibit 10.14.

Point: Income is overstated (and depreciation understated) when useful life is too high; when useful life is too low, the opposite results.

EXHIBIT 10.14

Computing Revised Straight-Line Depreciation

$$\frac{\textbf{Book value} - \textbf{Revised salvage value}}{\textbf{Revised remaining useful life}} = \frac{\$6{,}400 - \$400}{4 \text{ years}} = \$1{,}500 \text{ per year}$$

Thus, \$1,500 of depreciation expense is recorded for the machine at the end of the third through sixth years—each year of its remaining useful life. Since this asset was depreciated at \$1,800 per year for the first two years, it is tempting to conclude that depreciation expense was overstated in the first two years. However, these expenses reflected the best information available at that time. We do not go back and restate prior years' financial statements for this type of new information. Instead, we adjust the current and future periods' statements to reflect this new information. Revising an estimate of the useful life or salvage value of a plant asset is referred to as a **change in an accounting estimate** and is reflected in current and future financial statements, not in prior statements.

Example: If at the beginning of its second year the machine's remaining useful life changes from four to three years and salvage value from \$1,000 to \$400, how much straight-line depreciation is recorded in remaining years? *Answer:* Revised depreciation = (\$8,200 − \$400)/3 = \$2,600.

Reporting Depreciation

Both the cost and accumulated depreciation of plant assets are reported on the balance sheet or in its notes. **Dale Jarrett Racing Adventure**, for instance, reports the following.

Office furniture and equipment	\$ 45,386
Shop and track equipment	123,378
Race vehicles and other	775,363
Property and equipment, gross	944,127
Less accumulated depreciation	715,435
Property and equipment, net	\$228,692

Many companies also show plant assets on one line with the net amount of cost less accumulated depreciation. When this is done, the amount of accumulated depreciation is disclosed in a note. **Circuit City** reports only the net amount of its property and equipment in its balance sheet in Appendix A. To satisfy the full-disclosure principle, Circuit City describes its depreciation methods in its Note 2 and the amounts comprising plant assets in its Note 6—see its 10-K at www.SEC.gov.

Point: A company usually keeps records for each asset showing its cost and depreciation to date. The combined records for individual assets are a type of *plant asset subsidiary ledger.*

Reporting both the cost and accumulated depreciation of plant assets helps users compare the assets of different companies. For example, a company holding assets costing \$50,000 and accumulated depreciation of \$40,000 is likely in a situation different from a company with new assets costing \$10,000. While the net undepreciated cost of \$10,000 is the same in both cases, the first company may have more productive capacity available but likely is facing the need to replace older assets. These insights are not provided if the two balance sheets report only the \$10,000 book values.

Users must remember that plant assets are reported on a balance sheet at their undepreciated costs (book value), not at market values. This emphasis on costs rather than market values is based on the *going-concern assumption* described in Chapter 1. This assumption states that, unless there is evidence to the contrary, we assume that a company continues in business.

This implies that plant assets are held and used long enough to recover their cost through the sale of products and services. Since plant assets are not for sale, their market values are not reported. An exception is when there is a *permanent decline* in the market value of an asset relative to its book value, called an asset **impairment.** In this case the company writes the asset down to this market value (details for write-downs are in advanced courses).

Accumulated Depreciation is a contra asset account with a normal credit balance. It does *not* reflect funds accumulated to buy new assets when the assets currently owned are replaced. If a company has funds available to buy assets, the funds are shown on the balance sheet among liquid assets such as Cash or Investments.

Decision Ethics

Controller You are the controller for a struggling company. Its operations require regular investments in equipment, and depreciation is its largest expense. Its competitors frequently replace equipment—often depreciated over three years. The company president instructs you to revise useful lives of equipment from three to six years and to use a six-year life on all new equipment. What actions do you take? [Answer—p. 416]

Quick Check

Answers—p. 416

4. On January 1, 2009, a company pays $77,000 to purchase office furniture with a zero salvage value. The furniture's useful life is somewhere between 7 and 10 years. What is the year 2009 straight-line depreciation on the furniture using (*a*) a 7-year useful life and (*b*) a 10-year useful life?
5. What does the term *depreciation* mean in accounting?
6. A company purchases a machine for $96,000 on January 1, 2009. Its useful life is five years or 100,000 units of product, and its salvage value is $8,000. During 2009, 10,000 units of product are produced. Compute the book value of this machine on December 31, 2009, assuming (*a*) straight-line depreciation and (*b*) units-of-production depreciation.
7. In early January 2009, a company acquires equipment for $3,800. The company estimates this equipment to have a useful life of three years and a salvage value of $200. Early in 2011, the company changes its estimates to a total four-year useful life and zero salvage value. Using the straight-line method, what is depreciation for the year ended 2011?

Additional Expenditures

P3 Distinguish between revenue and capital expenditures, and account for them.

After a company acquires a plant asset and puts it into service, it often makes additional expenditures for that asset's operation, maintenance, repair, and improvement. In recording these expenditures, it must decide whether to capitalize or expense them (to capitalize an expenditure is to debit the asset account). The issue is whether these expenditures are reported as current period expenses or added to the plant asset's cost and depreciated over its remaining useful life.

Revenue expenditures, also called *income statement expenditures,* are additional costs of plant assets that do not materially increase the asset's life or productive capabilities. They are recorded as expenses and deducted from revenues in the current period's income statement. Examples of revenue expenditures are cleaning, repainting, adjustments, and lubricants. **Capital expenditures,** also called *balance sheet expenditures,* are additional costs of plant assets that provide benefits extending beyond the current period. They are debited to asset accounts and reported on the balance sheet. Capital expenditures increase or improve the type or amount of service an asset provides. Examples are roofing replacement, plant expansion, and major overhauls of machinery and equipment.

	Financial Statement Effect	
	Accounting	Expense Timing
Revenue expenditure	Income stmt. account debited	Expensed currently
Capital expenditure	Balance sheet account debited	Expensed in future

Financial statements are affected for several years by the accounting choice of recording costs as either revenue expenditures or capital expenditures. This decision is based on whether the expenditures are identified as ordinary repairs or as betterments and extraordinary repairs.

Ordinary Repairs

Ordinary repairs are expenditures to keep an asset in normal, good operating condition. They are necessary if an asset is to perform to expectations over its useful life. Ordinary repairs do not extend an asset's useful life beyond its original estimate or increase its productivity beyond original expectations. Examples are normal costs of cleaning, lubricating, adjusting, and replacing small parts of a machine. Ordinary repairs are treated as *revenue expenditures.* This means their costs are reported as expenses on the current period income statement. Following this rule, **Brunswick** reports that "maintenance and repair costs are expensed as incurred." If Brunswick's current year repair costs are $9,500, it makes the following entry.

Point: Many companies apply the *materiality constraint* to treat *low-cost plant assets* (say, less than $500) as revenue expenditures.

Dec. 31	Repairs Expense.	9,500	
	Cash		9,500
	To record ordinary repairs of equipment.		

Assets = Liabilities + Equity
−9,500 −9,500

Betterments and Extraordinary Repairs

Video10.1

Accounting for betterments and extraordinary repairs is similar—both are treated as *capital expenditures.*

Betterments (Improvements) **Betterments,** also called *improvements,* are expenditures that make a plant asset more efficient or productive. A betterment often involves adding a component to an asset or replacing one of its old components with a better one, and does not always increase an asset's useful life. An example is replacing manual controls on a machine with automatic controls. One special type of betterment is an *addition,* such as adding a new wing or dock to a warehouse. Since a betterment benefits future periods, it is debited to the asset account as a capital expenditure. The new book value (less salvage value) is then depreciated over the asset's remaining useful life. To illustrate, suppose a company pays $8,000 for a machine with an eight-year useful life and no salvage value. After three years and $3,000 of depreciation, it adds an automated control system to the machine at a cost of $1,800. This results in reduced labor costs in future periods. The cost of the betterment is added to the Machinery account with this entry.

Example: Assume a firm owns a Web server. Identify each cost as a revenue or capital expenditure: (1) purchase price, (2) necessary wiring, (3) platform for operation, (4) circuits to increase capacity, (5) cleaning after each month of use, (6) repair of a faulty switch, and (7) replaced a worn fan. *Answer:* Capital expenditures: 1, 2, 3, 4; revenue expenditures: 5, 6, 7.

Jan. 2	Machinery	1,800	
	Cash		1,800
	To record installation of automated system.		

Assets = Liabilities + Equity
+1,800
−1,800

After the betterment is recorded, the remaining cost to be depreciated is $6,800, computed as $8,000 − $3,000 + $1,800. Depreciation expense for the remaining five years is $1,360 per year, computed as $6,800/5 years.

Point: Both extraordinary repairs and betterments require revising future depreciation.

Extraordinary Repairs (Replacements) **Extraordinary repairs** are expenditures extending the asset's useful life beyond its original estimate. Extraordinary repairs are *capital expenditures* because they benefit future periods. Their costs are debited to the asset account (or to accumulated depreciation). For example, **America West Airlines** reports, "cost of major scheduled airframe, engine and certain component overhauls are capitalized (and expensed) . . . over the periods benefited."

Decision Maker

Entrepreneur Your start-up Internet services company needs cash, and you are preparing financial statements to apply for a short-term loan. A friend suggests that you treat as many expenses as possible as capital expenditures. What are the impacts on financial statements of this suggestion? What do you think is the aim of this suggestion? [Answer—p. 416]

Disposals of Plant Assets

Plant assets are disposed of for several reasons. Some are discarded because they wear out or become obsolete. Others are sold because of changing business plans. Regardless of the reason, disposals of plant assets occur in one of three basic ways: discarding, sale, or exchange. The general steps in accounting for a disposal of plant assets are described in Exhibit 10.15.

EXHIBIT 10.15

Accounting for Disposals of Plant Assets

1. Record depreciation up to the date of disposal—this also updates Accumulated Depreciation.
2. Record the removal of the disposed asset's account balances—including its Accumulated Depreciation.
3. Record any cash (and/or other assets) received or paid in the disposal.
4. Record any gain or loss—computed by comparing the disposed asset's book value with the market value of any assets received.*

* An exception to step 4 is the case of an exchange that lacks *commercial substance*—see Appendix 10A.

Discarding Plant Assets

P4 Account for asset disposal through discarding or selling an asset.

A plant asset is *discarded* when it is no longer useful to the company and it has no market value. To illustrate, assume that a machine costing $9,000 with accumulated depreciation of $9,000 is discarded. When accumulated depreciation equals the asset's cost, it is said to be *fully depreciated* (zero book value). The entry to record the discarding of this asset is

Assets = Liabilities + Equity
+9,000
−9,000

June 5	Accumulated Depreciation—Machinery	9,000	
	Machinery.		9,000
	To discard fully depreciated machinery.		

This entry reflects all four steps of Exhibit 10.15. Step 1 is unnecessary since the machine is fully depreciated. Step 2 is reflected in the debit to Accumulated Depreciation and credit to Machinery. Since no other asset is involved, step 3 is irrelevant. Finally, since book value is zero and no other asset is involved, no gain or loss is recorded in step 4.

How do we account for discarding an asset that is not fully depreciated or one whose depreciation is not up-to-date? To answer this, consider equipment costing $8,000 with accumulated depreciation of $6,000 on December 31 of the prior fiscal year-end. This equipment is being depreciated using the straight-line method over eight years with zero salvage. On July 1 of the current year it is discarded. Step 1 is to bring depreciation up-to-date.

Point: Recording depreciation expense up-to-date gives an up-to-date book value for determining gain or loss.

Assets = Liabilities + Equity
−500 −500

July 1	Depreciation Expense.	500	
	Accumulated Depreciation—Equipment		500
	To record 6 months' depreciation ($1,000 × 6/12).		

Steps 2 through 4 of Exhibit 10.15 are reflected in the second (and final) entry.

Assets = Liabilities + Equity
+6,500 −1,500
−8,000

July 1	Accumulated Depreciation—Equipment.	6,500	
	Loss on Disposal of Equipment	1,500	
	Equipment		8,000
	To discard equipment with a $1,500 book value.		

Point: Gain or loss is determined by comparing "value given" (book value) to "value received."

This loss is computed by comparing the equipment's $1,500 book value ($8,000 − $6,000 − $500) with the zero net cash proceeds. The loss is reported in the Other Expenses and Losses section of the income statement. Discarding an asset can sometimes require a cash payment that would increase the loss.

Selling Plant Assets

Companies often sell plant assets when they restructure or downsize operations. To illustrate the accounting for selling plant assets, we consider BTO's March 31 sale of equipment that cost $16,000 and has accumulated depreciation of $12,000 at December 31 of the prior calendar year-end. Annual depreciation on this equipment is $4,000 computed using straight-line depreciation. Step 1 of this sale is to record depreciation expense and update accumulated depreciation to March 31 of the current year.

March 31	Depreciation Expense	1,000	
	Accumulated Depreciation—Equipment		1,000
	To record 3 months' depreciation ($4,000 × 3/12).		

Assets = Liabilities + Equity
−1,000 −1,000

Steps 2 through 4 of Exhibit 10.15 can be reflected in one final entry that depends on the amount received from the asset's sale. We consider three different possibilities.

Sale at Book Value If BTO receives $3,000 cash, an amount equal to the equipment's book value as of March 31 (book value = $16,000 − $12,000 − $1,000), no gain or loss occurs on disposal. The entry is

March 31	Cash	3,000	
	Accumulated Depreciation—Equipment	13,000	
	Equipment		16,000
	To record sale of equipment for no gain or loss.		

Assets = Liabilities + Equity
+3,000
+13,000
−16,000

Sale above Book Value If BTO receives $7,000, an amount that is $4,000 above the equipment's $3,000 book value as of March 31, a gain on disposal occurs. The entry is

March 31	Cash	7,000	
	Accumulated Depreciation—Equipment	13,000	
	Gain on Disposal of Equipment		4,000
	Equipment		16,000
	To record sale of equipment for a $4,000 gain.		

Assets = Liabilities + Equity
+7,000 +4,000
+13,000
−16,000

Sale below Book Value If BTO receives $2,500, an amount that is $500 below the equipment's $3,000 book value as of March 31, a loss on disposal occurs. The entry is

March 31	Cash	2,500	
	Loss on Disposal of Equipment	500	
	Accumulated Depreciation—Equipment	13,000	
	Equipment		16,000
	To record sale of equipment for a $500 loss.		

Assets = Liabilities + Equity
+2,500 −500
+13,000
−16,000

Decision Insight

IFRSs Unlike U.S. GAAP, IFRSs require an annual review of useful life and salvage value estimates. IFRSs also permit revaluation of plant assets to market value if market value is reliably determined.

Quick Check

Answers—p. 416

8. Early in the fifth year of a machine's six-year useful life, it is overhauled, and its useful life is extended to nine years. This machine originally cost $108,000 and the overhaul cost is $12,000. Prepare the entry to record the overhaul cost.
9. Explain the difference between revenue expenditures and capital expenditures and how both are recorded.
10. What is a betterment? How is a betterment recorded?
11. A company acquires equipment on January 10, 2009, at a cost of $42,000. Straight-line depreciation is used with a five-year life and $7,000 salvage value. On June 27, 2010, the company sells this equipment for $32,000. Prepare the entry(ies) for June 27, 2010.

Section 2—Natural Resources

P5 Account for natural resource assets and their depletion.

Natural resources are assets that are physically consumed when used. Examples are standing timber, mineral deposits, and oil and gas fields. Since they are consumed when used, they are often called *wasting assets*. These assets represent soon-to-be inventories of raw materials that will be converted into one or more products by cutting, mining, or pumping. Until that conversion takes place, they are noncurrent assets and are shown in a balance sheet using titles such as timberlands, mineral deposits, or oil reserves. Natural resources are reported under either plant assets or their own separate category. **Alcoa**, for instance, reports its natural resources under the balance sheet title *Properties, plants and equipment.* In a note to its financial statements, Alcoa reports a separate amount for *Land and land rights, including mines.* **Weyerhaeuser**, on the other hand, reports its timber holdings in a separate balance sheet category titled *Timber and timberlands.*

Cost Determination and Depletion

Natural resources are recorded at cost, which includes all expenditures necessary to acquire the resource and prepare it for its intended use. **Depletion** is the process of allocating the cost of a natural resource to the period when it is consumed. Natural resources are reported on the balance sheet at cost less *accumulated depletion.* The depletion expense per period is usually based on units extracted from cutting, mining, or pumping. This is similar to units-of-production depreciation. **Exxon Mobil** uses this approach to amortize the costs of discovering and operating its oil wells.

To illustrate depletion of natural resources, let's consider a mineral deposit with an estimated 250,000 tons of available ore. It is purchased for $500,000, and we expect zero salvage value. The depletion charge per ton of ore mined is $2, computed as $500,000 ÷ 250,000 tons. If 85,000 tons are mined and sold in the first year, the depletion charge for that year is $170,000. These computations are detailed in Exhibit 10.16.

EXHIBIT 10.16

Depletion Formula and Example

Step 1

$$\textbf{Depletion per unit} = \frac{\textbf{Cost} - \textbf{Salvage value}}{\textbf{Total units of capacity}} = \frac{\$500{,}000 - \$0}{250{,}000 \text{ tons}} = \$2 \text{ per ton}$$

Step 2

$$\textbf{Depletion expense} = \textbf{Depletion per unit} \times \textbf{Units extracted and sold in period}$$
$$= \$2 \times 85{,}000 = \$170{,}000$$

Depletion expense for the first year is recorded as follows.

Assets	= Liabilities +	Equity
−170,000		−170,000

Dec. 31	Depletion Expense—Mineral Deposit	170,000	
	Accumulated Depletion—Mineral Deposit		170,000
	To record depletion of the mineral deposit.		

The period-end balance sheet reports the mineral deposit as shown in Exhibit 10.17.

EXHIBIT 10.17

Balance Sheet Presentation of Natural Resources

Mineral deposit	$500,000	
Less accumulated depletion	170,000	$330,000

Since all 85,000 tons of the mined ore are sold during the year, the entire $170,000 of depletion is reported on the income statement. If some of the ore remains unsold at year-end, however, the depletion related to the unsold ore is carried forward on the balance sheet and reported as Ore Inventory, a current asset. To illustrate, and continuing with our example, assume that 40,000 tons are mined in the second year, but only 34,000 tons are sold. We record depletion of $68,000 (34,000 tons × $2 depletion per unit) and the remaining Ore Inventory of $12,000 (6,000 tons × $2 depletion per unit) as follows.

Dec. 31	Depletion Expense—Mineral Deposit	68,000	
	Ore Inventory	12,000	
	Accumulated Depletion—Mineral Deposit		80,000
	To record depletion and inventory of mineral deposit.		

Assets	=	Liabilities	+	Equity
−80,000				−68,000
+12,000				

Plant Assets Used in Extracting

Video10.1

The conversion of natural resources by mining, cutting, or pumping usually requires machinery, equipment, and buildings. When the usefulness of these plant assets is directly related to the depletion of a natural resource, their costs are depreciated using the units-of-production method in proportion to the depletion of the natural resource. For example, if a machine is permanently installed in a mine and 10% of the ore is mined and sold in the period, then 10% of the machine's cost (less any salvage value) is allocated to depreciation expense. The same procedure is used when a machine is abandoned once resources have been extracted. If, however, a machine will be moved to and used at another site when extraction is complete, the machine is depreciated over its own useful life.

Section 3—Intangible Assets

P6 Account for intangible assets.

Intangible assets are nonphysical assets (used in operations) that confer on their owners long-term rights, privileges, or competitive advantages. Examples are patents, copyrights, licenses, leaseholds, franchises, goodwill, and trademarks. Lack of physical substance does not necessarily imply an intangible asset. Notes and accounts receivable, for instance, lack physical substance, but they are not intangibles. This section identifies the more common types of intangible assets and explains the accounting for them.

Cost Determination and Amortization

An intangible asset is recorded at cost when purchased. Intangibles are then separated into those with limited lives or indefinite lives. If an intangible has a **limited life,** its cost is systematically allocated to expense over its estimated useful life through the process of **amortization.** If an intangible asset has an **indefinite life**—meaning that no legal, regulatory, contractual, competitive, economic, or other factors limit its useful life—it should not be amortized. (If an intangible with an indefinite life is later judged to have a limited life, it is amortized over that limited life.) Amortization of intangible assets is similar to depreciation of plant assets and the depletion of natural resources in that it is a process of cost allocation. However, only the straight-line method is used for amortizing intangibles *unless* the company can show that another method is preferred. The effects of amortization are recorded in a contra account (Accumulated Amortization). The gross acquisition cost of intangible assets is disclosed in the balance sheet along with their accumulated amortization (these disclosures are new). The eventual disposal of an intangible asset involves removing its book value, recording any other asset(s) received or given up, and recognizing any gain or loss for the difference.

Many intangibles have limited lives due to laws, contracts, or other asset characteristics. Examples are patents, copyrights, and leaseholds. Other intangibles such as goodwill, trademarks, and trade names have lives that cannot be easily determined. The cost of intangible assets is amortized over the periods expected to benefit by their use, but in no case can this period be longer than the asset's legal existence. The values of some intangible assets such as goodwill continue indefinitely into the future and are not amortized. (An intangible asset that is not amortized is tested annually for **impairment**—if necessary, an impairment loss is recorded. Details for this test are in advanced courses.)

Point: The cost to acquire a Website address is an intangible asset.

Point: Goodwill is not amortized; instead, it is annually tested for impairment.

Intangible assets are often shown in a separate section of the balance sheet immediately after plant assets. **Callaway Golf**, for instance, follows this approach in reporting nearly $150 million of intangible assets in its balance sheet. Companies usually disclose their amortization periods for intangibles. The remainder of our discussion focuses on accounting for specific types of intangible assets.

Types of Intangibles

Patents The federal government grants patents to encourage the invention of new technology, mechanical devices, and production processes. A **patent** is an exclusive right granted to its owner to manufacture and sell a patented item or to use a process for 20 years. When patent rights are purchased, the cost to acquire the rights is debited to an account called Patents. If the owner engages in lawsuits to successfully defend a patent, the cost of lawsuits is debited to the Patents account. However, the costs of research and development leading to a new patent are expensed when incurred.

A patent's cost is amortized over its estimated useful life (not to exceed 20 years). If we purchase a patent costing $25,000 with a useful life of 10 years, we make the following adjusting entry at the end of each of the 10 years to amortize one-tenth of its cost.

Assets	=	Liabilities	+	Equity
−2,500				−2,500

Dec. 31	Amortization Expense—Patents	2,500	
	Accumulated Amortization—Patents		2,500
	To amortize patent costs over its useful life.		

The $2,500 debit to Amortization Expense appears on the income statement as a cost of the product or service provided under protection of the patent. The Accumulated Amortization—Patents account is a contra asset account to Patents.

Decision Insight

Mention "drug war" and most people think of illegal drug trade. But another drug war is under way: Brand-name drugmakers are fighting to stop generic copies of their products from hitting the market once patents expire. Delaying a generic rival can yield millions in extra sales.

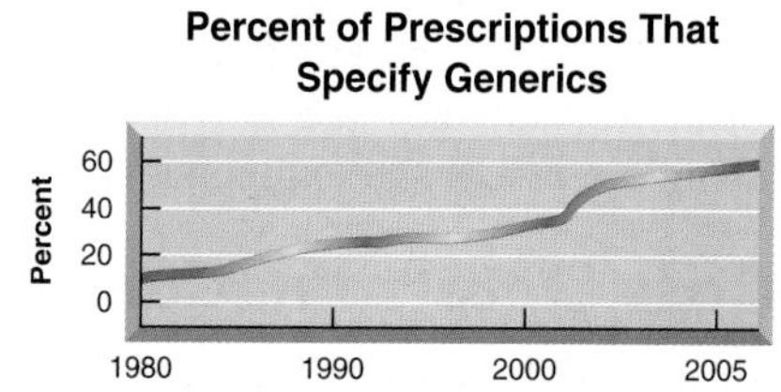

Copyrights A **copyright** gives its owner the exclusive right to publish and sell a musical, literary, or artistic work during the life of the creator plus 70 years, although the useful life of most copyrights is much shorter. The costs of a copyright are amortized over its useful life. The only identifiable cost of many copyrights is the fee paid to the Copyright Office of the federal government or international agency granting the copyright. If this fee is immaterial, it is charged directly to an expense account; but if the identifiable costs of a copyright are material, they are capitalized (recorded in an asset account) and periodically amortized by debiting an account called Amortization Expense—Copyrights.

Franchises and Licenses **Franchises** and **licenses** are rights that a company or government grants an entity to deliver a product or service under specified conditions. Many organizations grant franchise and license rights—**McDonald's**, **Pizza Hut**, and **Major League Baseball** are just a few examples. The costs of franchises and licenses are debited to a Franchises and Licenses asset account and are amortized over the lives of the agreements. If an agreement is for an indefinite or perpetual period, those costs are not amortized.

Trademarks and Trade Names Companies often adopt unique symbols or select unique names and brands in marketing their products. A **trademark** or **trade (brand) name** is a symbol, name, phrase, or jingle identified with a company, product, or service. Examples are Nike swoosh, Marlboro Man, Big Mac, Coca-Cola, and Corvette. Ownership and exclusive right to use a trademark or trade name is often established by showing that one company used it before another. Ownership is best established by registering a trademark or trade name with the government's Patent Office. The cost of developing, maintaining, or enhancing the value of a trademark or trade name (such as advertising) is charged to expense when incurred. If a trademark or trade name is purchased, however, its cost is debited to an asset account and then amortized over its expected life. If the company plans to renew indefinitely its right to the trademark or trade name, the cost is not amortized.

Point: McDonald's "golden arches" are one of the world's most valuable trademarks, yet this asset is not shown on McDonald's balance sheet.

Goodwill **Goodwill** has a specific meaning in accounting. Goodwill is the amount by which a company's value exceeds the value of its individual assets and liabilities. This usually implies that the company as a whole has certain valuable attributes not measured among its individual assets and liabilities. These can include superior management, skilled workforce, good supplier or customer relations, quality products or services, good location, or other competitive advantages.

To keep accounting information from being too subjective, goodwill is not recorded unless an entire company or business segment is purchased. Purchased goodwill is measured by taking the purchase price of the company and subtracting the market value of its individual net assets (excluding goodwill). For instance, **Yahoo!** paid nearly $3.0 billion to acquire **GeoCities**; about $2.8 of the $3.0 billion was for goodwill and other intangibles.

Goodwill is measured as the excess of the cost of an acquired entity over the value of the acquired net assets. Goodwill is recorded as an asset, and it is *not* amortized. Instead, goodwill is annually tested for impairment. If the book value of goodwill does not exceed its fair (market) value, goodwill is not impaired. However, if the book value of goodwill does exceed its fair value, an impairment loss is recorded equal to that excess. (Details of this test are in advanced courses.)

Point: Amortization of goodwill is different for financial accounting and tax accounting. The IRS requires the amortization of goodwill over 15 years.

Leaseholds Property is rented under a contract called a **lease.** The property's owner, called the **lessor,** grants the lease. The one who secures the right to possess and use the property is called the **lessee.** A **leasehold** refers to the rights the lessor grants to the lessee under the terms of the lease. A leasehold is an intangible asset for the lessee.

Certain leases require no advance payment from the lessee but require monthly rent payments. In this case, we do not set up a Leasehold account. Instead, the monthly payments are debited to a Rent Expense account. If a long-term lease requires the lessee to pay the final period's rent in advance when the lease is signed, the lessee records this advance payment with a debit to the Leasehold account. Since the advance payment is not used until the final period, the Leasehold account balance remains intact until that final period when its balance is transferred to Rent Expense. (Some long-term leases give the lessee essentially the same rights as a purchaser. This results in a tangible asset and a liability reported by the lessee. Chapter 14 describes these so-called *capital leases.*)

A long-term lease can increase in value when current rental rates for similar property rise while the required payments under the lease remain constant. This increase in value of a lease is not reported on the lessee's balance sheet. However, if the property is subleased and the new tenant makes a cash payment to the original lessee for the rights under the old lease, the new tenant debits this payment to a Leasehold account, which is amortized to Rent Expense over the remaining life of the lease.

Point: A leasehold account implies existence of future benefits that the lessee controls because of a prepayment. It also meets the definition of an asset.

Leasehold Improvements A lessee sometimes pays for alterations or improvements to the leased property such as partitions, painting, and storefronts. These alterations and improvements are called **leasehold improvements,** and the lessee debits these costs to a Leasehold Improvements account. Since leasehold improvements become part of the property and revert to the lessor at the end of the lease, the lessee amortizes these costs over the life of the lease or the life of the improvements, whichever is shorter. The amortization entry debits Amortization Expense—Leasehold Improvements and credits Accumulated Amortization—Leasehold Improvements.

Other Intangibles There are other types of intangible assets such as *software, noncompete covenants, customer lists,* and so forth. Our accounting for them is the same. First, we record the intangible asset's costs. Second, we determine whether the asset has a limited or indefinite life. If limited, we allocate its costs over that period. If indefinite, its costs are not amortized.

Quick Check

Answers—p. 416

12. Give an example of a natural resource and of an intangible asset.
13. A company pays $650,000 for an ore deposit. The deposit is estimated to have 325,000 tons of ore that will be mined over the next 10 years. During the first year, it mined, processed, and sold 91,000 tons. What is that year's depletion expense?
14. On January 6, 2009, a company pays $120,000 for a patent with a remaining 17-year legal life to produce a toy expected to be marketable for three years. Prepare entries to record its acquisition and the December 31, 2009, amortization entry.

Decision Analysis — Total Asset Turnover

A2 Compute total asset turnover and apply it to analyze a company's use of assets.

A company's assets are important in determining its ability to generate sales and earn income. Managers devote much attention to deciding what assets a company acquires, how much it invests in assets, and how to use assets most efficiently and effectively. One important measure of a company's ability to use its assets is **total asset turnover,** defined in Exhibit 10.18.

EXHIBIT 10.18

Total Asset Turnover

$$\textbf{Total asset turnover} = \frac{\textbf{Net sales}}{\textbf{Average total assets}}$$

The numerator reflects the net amounts earned from the sale of products and services. The denominator reflects the average total resources devoted to operating the company and generating sales.

To illustrate, let's look at total asset turnover in Exhibit 10.19 for two competing companies: **Molson Coors** and **Anheuser-Busch.**

EXHIBIT 10.19

Analysis Using Total Asset Turnover

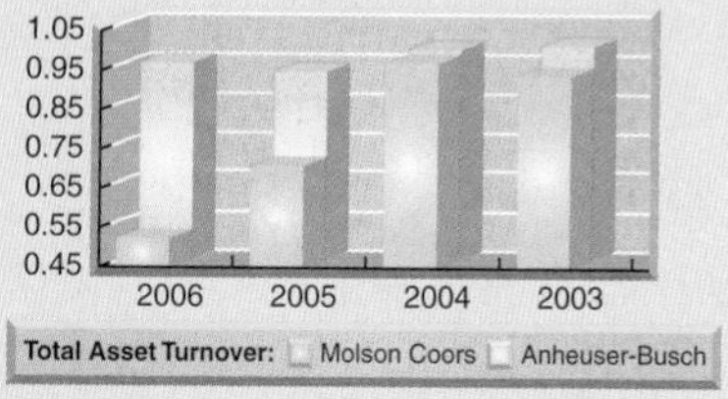

Company	Figure ($ millions)	2006	2005	2004	2003
Molson Coors	Net sales	$ 5,845	$ 5,507	$ 4,306	$ 4,000
	Average total assets	$11,701	$ 8,228	$ 4,551	$ 4,392
	Total asset turnover	**0.50**	**0.67**	**0.95**	**0.91**
Anheuser-Busch	Net sales	$15,717	$15,036	$14,934	$14,147
	Average total assets	$16,466	$16,362	$15,431	$14,405
	Total asset turnover	**0.95**	**0.92**	**0.97**	**0.98**

To show how we use total asset turnover, let's look at Molson Coors. We express Molson Coors's use of assets in generating net sales by saying "it turned its assets over 0.50 times during 2006." This means that each $1.00 of assets produced $0.50 of net sales. Is a total asset turnover of 0.50 good or bad? It is safe to say that all companies desire a high total asset turnover. Like many ratio analyses, however, a company's total asset turnover must be interpreted in comparison with those of prior years and of its competitors. Interpreting the total asset turnover also requires an understanding of the company's operations. Some operations are capital intensive, meaning that a relatively large amount is invested in assets to generate sales. This suggests a relatively lower total asset turnover. Other companies' operations are labor intensive, meaning that they generate sales more by the efforts of people than the use of assets. In that case, we expect a higher total asset turnover. Companies with low total asset turnover require higher profit margins (examples are hotels and real estate); companies with high total asset turnover can succeed with lower profit margins (examples are food stores and toy merchandisers). Molson Coors's turnover recently declined and is now much lower than that for Anheuser-Busch. Total asset turnover for Molson Coors's competitors, available in industry publications such as Dun & Bradstreet, is generally in the range of 0.7 to 1.0 over this same period. Overall, Molson Coors must improve relative to its competitors on total asset turnover.

Point: An estimate of **plant asset useful life** equals the plant asset cost divided by depreciation expense.

Point: The **plant asset age** is estimated by dividing accumulated depreciation by depreciation expense. Older plant assets can signal needed asset replacements; they may also signal less efficient assets.

Decision Maker

Environmentalist A paper manufacturer claims it cannot afford more environmental controls. It points to its low total asset turnover of 1.9 and argues that it cannot compete with companies whose total asset turnover is much higher. Examples cited are food stores (5.5) and auto dealers (3.8). How do you respond? [Answer—p. 416]

Demonstration Problem

DP10

On July 14, 2009, Tulsa Company pays $600,000 to acquire a fully equipped factory. The purchase involves the following assets and information.

Asset	Appraised Value	Salvage Value	Useful Life	Depreciation Method
Land	$160,000			Not depreciated
Land improvements	80,000	$ 0	10 years	Straight-line
Building	320,000	100,000	10 years	Double-declining-balance
Machinery	240,000	20,000	10,000 units	Units-of-production*
Total	$800,000			

* The machinery is used to produce 700 units in 2009 and 1,800 units in 2010.

Required

1. Allocate the total $600,000 purchase cost among the separate assets.
2. Compute the 2009 (six months) and 2010 depreciation expense for each asset, and compute the company's total depreciation expense for both years.
3. On the last day of calendar year 2011, Tulsa discarded machinery that had been on its books for five years. The machinery's original cost was $12,000 (estimated life of five years) and its salvage value was $2,000. No depreciation had been recorded for the fifth year when the disposal occurred. Journalize the fifth year of depreciation (straight-line method) and the asset's disposal.
4. At the beginning of year 2011, Tulsa purchased a patent for $100,000 cash. The company estimated the patent's useful life to be 10 years. Journalize the patent acquisition and its amortization for the year 2011.
5. Late in the year 2011, Tulsa acquired an ore deposit for $600,000 cash. It added roads and built mine shafts for an additional cost of $80,000. Salvage value of the mine is estimated to be $20,000. The company estimated 330,000 tons of available ore. In year 2011, Tulsa mined and sold 10,000 tons of ore. Journalize the mine's acquisition and its first year's depletion.
6. [A]On the first day of 2011, Tulsa exchanged machinery that was acquired on July 14, 2009, and $5,000 cash for machinery with a $210,000 market value. Journalize the exchange of these assets assuming the exchange lacked commercial substance.

Planning the Solution

- Complete a three-column table showing the following amounts for each asset: appraised value, percent of total value, and apportioned cost.
- Using allocated costs, compute depreciation for 2009 (only one-half year) and 2010 (full year) for each asset. Summarize those computations in a table showing total depreciation for each year.
- Remember that depreciation must be recorded up-to-date before discarding an asset. Calculate and record depreciation expense for the fifth year using the straight-line method. Since salvage value is not received at the end of a discarded asset's life, the amount of any salvage value becomes a loss on disposal. Record the loss on the disposal as well as the removal of the discarded asset and its related accumulated depreciation.
- Record the patent (an intangible asset) at its purchase price. Use straight-line amortization over its useful life to calculate amortization expense.
- Record the ore deposit (a natural resource asset) at its cost, including any added costs to ready the mine for use. Calculate depletion per ton using the depletion formula. Multiply the depletion per ton by the amount of tons mined and sold to calculate depletion expense for the year.
- Remember that gains and losses on asset exchanges that lack commercial substance are not recognized. Make a journal entry to add the acquired machinery to the books and to remove the old machinery, along with its accumulated depreciation, and to record the cash given in the exchange.

Solution to Demonstration Problem

1. Allocation of the total cost of $600,000 among the separate assets.

Asset	Appraised Value	Percent of Total Value	Apportioned Cost
Land	$160,000	20%	**$120,000** ($600,000 × 20%)
Land improvements	80,000	10	**60,000** ($600,000 × 10%)
Building	320,000	40	**240,000** ($600,000 × 40%)
Machinery	240,000	30	**180,000** ($600,000 × 30%)
Total	$800,000	100%	$ 600,000

2. Depreciation for each asset. (Land is not depreciated.)

Land Improvements	
Cost	$ 60,000
Salvage value	0
Depreciable cost	$ 60,000
Useful life	10 years
Annual depreciation expense ($60,000/10 years)	$ 6,000
2009 depreciation ($6,000 × 6/12)	**$ 3,000**
2010 depreciation	**$ 6,000**
Building	
Straight-line rate = 100%/10 years = 10%	
Double-declining-balance rate = 10% × 2 = 20%	
2009 depreciation ($240,000 × 20% × 6/12)	**$ 24,000**
2010 depreciation [($240,000 − $24,000) × 20%]	**$ 43,200**
Machinery	
Cost	$ 180,000
Salvage value	20,000
Depreciable cost	$ 160,000
Total expected units of production	10,000 units
Depreciation per unit ($160,000/10,000 units)	$ 16
2009 depreciation ($16 × 700 units)	**$ 11,200**
2010 depreciation ($16 × 1,800 units)	**$ 28,800**

Total depreciation expense for each year:

	2009	2010
Land improvements	$ 3,000	$ 6,000
Building	24,000	43,200
Machinery	11,200	28,800
Total	$38,200	$78,000

3. Record the depreciation up-to-date on the discarded asset.

Depreciation Expense—Machinery	2,000	
Accumulated Depreciation—Machinery		2,000
To record depreciation on date of disposal: ($12,000 − $2,000)/5		

Record the removal of the discarded asset and its loss on disposal.

Accumulated Depreciation—Machinery	10,000	
Loss on Disposal of Machinery	2,000	
Machinery		12,000
To record the discarding of machinery with a $2,000 book value.		

4.

Patent	100,000	
Cash		100,000
To record patent acquisition.		

Amortization Expense—Patent	10,000	
Accumulated Amortization—Patent		10,000
To record amortization expense: $100,000/10 years = $10,000.		

5.

Ore Deposit	680,000	
Cash		680,000
To record ore deposit acquisition and its related costs.		

Depletion Expense—Ore Deposit	20,000	
Accumulated Depletion—Ore Deposit		20,000
To record depletion expense: ($680,000 − $20,000)/330,000 tons = $2 per ton. 10,000 tons mined and sold × $2 = $20,000 depletion.		

6. Record the asset exchange: The book value on the exchange date is $180,000 (cost) − $40,000 (accumulated depreciation). The book value of the machinery given up in the exchange ($140,000) plus the $5,000 cash paid is less than the $210,000 value of the machine acquired. The entry to record this exchange of assets that lacks commercial substance does not recognize the $65,000 "gain."

Machinery (new)	145,000*	
Accumulated Depreciation—Machinery (old)	40,000	
Machinery (old)		180,000
Cash		5,000
To record asset exchange that lacks commercial substance.		

* Market value of the acquired asset of $210,000 minus $65,000 "gain."

APPENDIX

10A Exchanging Plant Assets

P7A Account for asset exchanges.

Many plant assets such as machinery, automobiles, and office equipment are disposed of by exchanging them for newer assets. In a typical exchange of plant assets, a *trade-in allowance* is received on the old asset and the balance is paid in cash. Accounting for the exchange of assets depends on whether the transaction has *commercial substance* (per *SFAS 153,* commercial substance implies that it alters the company's future cash flows). If an asset exchange has commercial substance, a gain or loss is recorded based on the difference between the book value of the asset(s) given up and the market value of the asset(s) received. If an asset exchange lacks commercial substance, no gain or loss is recorded, and the asset(s) received is recorded based on the book value of the asset(s) given up. An exchange has commercial substance if the company's future cash flows change as a result of the transaction. This section describes the accounting for the exchange of assets.

Exchange with Commercial Substance: A Loss A company acquires $42,000 in new equipment. In exchange, the company pays $33,000 cash and trades in old equipment. The old equipment originally cost $36,000 and has accumulated depreciation of $20,000, which implies a $16,000 book value at the time of exchange. We are told this exchange has commercial substance and that the old equipment has a trade-in allowance of $9,000. This exchange yields a loss as computed in the middle (Loss) columns of Exhibit 10A.1; the loss is computed as Asset received − Assets given = $42,000 − $49,000 = $(7,000). We can also compute the loss as Trade-in allowance − Book value of asset given = $9,000 − $16,000 = $(7,000).

Guidance Answers to **Decision Maker** and **Decision Ethics**

Controller The president's instructions may reflect an honest and reasonable prediction of the future. Since the company is struggling financially, the president may have concluded that the normal pattern of replacing assets every three years cannot continue. Perhaps the strategy is to avoid costs of frequent replacements and stretch use of equipment a few years longer until financial conditions improve. However, if you believe the president's decision is unprincipled, you might confront the president with your opinion that it is unethical to change the estimate to increase income. Another possibility is to wait and see whether the auditor will prohibit this change in estimate. In either case, you should insist that the statements be based on reasonable estimates.

Entrepreneur Treating an expense as a capital expenditure means that reported expenses will be lower and income higher in the short run. This is so because a capital expenditure is not expensed immediately but is spread over the asset's useful life. Treating an expense as a capital expenditure also means that asset and equity totals are reported at larger amounts in the short run. This continues until the asset is fully depreciated. Your friend is probably trying to help, but the suggestion is misguided. Only an expenditure benefiting future periods is a capital expenditure.

Environmentalist The paper manufacturer's comparison of its total asset turnover with food stores and auto dealers is misdirected. These other industries' turnovers are higher because their profit margins are lower (about 2%). Profit margins for the paper industry are usually 3% to 3.5%. You need to collect data from competitors in the paper industry to show that a 1.9 total asset turnover is about the norm for this industry. You might also want to collect data on this company's revenues and expenses, along with compensation data for its high-ranking officers and employees.

Guidance Answers to **Quick Checks**

1. **a.** Supplies—current assets
b. Office equipment—plant assets
c. Inventory—current assets
d. Land for future expansion—long-term investments
e. Trucks used in operations—plant assets

2. **a.** Land **b.** Land Improvements

3. $700,000 + $49,000 − $21,000 + $3,500 + $3,000 + $2,500 = $737,000

4. **a.** Straight-line with 7-year life: ($77,000/7) = $11,000
b. Straight-line with 10-year life: ($77,000/10) = $7,700

5. Depreciation is a process of allocating the cost of plant assets to the accounting periods that benefit from the assets' use.

6. **a.** Book value using straight-line depreciation:
$96,000 − [($96,000 − $8,000)/5] = $78,400
b. Book value using units of production:
$96,000 − [($96,000 − $8,000) × (10,000/100,000)] = $87,200

7. ($3,800 − $200)/3 = $1,200 (original depreciation per year)
$1,200 × 2 = $2,400 (accumulated depreciation)
($3,800 − $2,400)/2 = $700 (revised depreciation)

8.

Machinery	12,000	
Cash		12,000

9. A revenue expenditure benefits only the current period and should be charged to expense in the current period. A capital expenditure yields benefits that extend beyond the end of the current period and should be charged to an asset.

10. A betterment involves modifying an existing plant asset to make it more efficient, usually by replacing part of the asset with an improved or superior part. The cost of a betterment is debited to the asset account.

11.

Depreciation Expense	3,500	
Accumulated Depreciation		3,500
Cash	32,000	
Accumulated Depreciation	10,500	
Gain on Sale of Equipment		500
Equipment		42,000

12. Examples of natural resources are timberlands, mineral deposits, and oil reserves. Examples of intangible assets are patents, copyrights, leaseholds, leasehold improvements, goodwill, trademarks, and licenses.

13. ($650,000/325,000 tons) × 91,000 tons = $182,000

14.

Jan. 6	Patents	120,000	
	Cash		120,000
Dec. 31	Amortization Expense	40,000*	
	Accumulated Amortization—Patents		40,000

* $120,000/3 years = $40,000.

15.

(a) Equipment (new)	45,000	
Loss on Exchange of Assets	3,600	
Accumulated Depreciation—Equipment (old)	23,400	
Equipment (old)		30,000
Cash ($45,000 − $3,000)		42,000

(b) Equipment (new)*	44,600	
Accumulated Depreciation—Equipment (old)	23,400	
Equipment (old)		30,000
Cash ($45,000 − $7,000)		38,000

* Includes $400 unrecognized gain.

Quick Check

Answer—p. 416

15. A company trades an old Web server for a new one. The cost of the old server is $30,000, and its accumulated depreciation at the time of the trade is $23,400. The new server has a cash price of $45,000. Prepare entries to record the trade under two different assumptions where the company receives a trade-in allowance of (*a*) $3,000 and the exchange has commercial substance, and (*b*) $7,000 and the exchange lacks commercial substance.

Summary

C1 Describe plant assets and issues in accounting for them. Plant assets are tangible assets used in the operations of a company and have a useful life of more than one accounting period. Plant assets are set apart from other tangible assets by two important features: use in operations and useful lives longer than one period. The four main accounting issues with plant assets are (1) computing their costs, (2) allocating their costs to the periods they benefit, (3) accounting for subsequent expenditures, and (4) recording their disposal.

C2 Explain depreciation and the factors affecting its computation. *Depreciation* is the process of allocating to expense the cost of a plant asset over the accounting periods that benefit from its use. Depreciation does not measure the decline in a plant asset's market value or its physical deterioration. Three factors determine depreciation: cost, salvage value, and useful life. Salvage value is an estimate of the asset's value at the end of its benefit period. Useful (service) life is the length of time an asset is productively used.

C3 Explain depreciation for partial years and changes in estimates. Partial-year depreciation is often required because assets are bought and sold throughout the year. Depreciation is revised when changes in estimates such as salvage value and useful life occur. If the useful life of a plant asset changes, for instance, the remaining cost to be depreciated is spread over the remaining (revised) useful life of the asset.

A1 Compare and analyze alternative depreciation methods. The amount of depreciation expense per period is usually different for different methods, yet total depreciation expense over an asset's life is the same for all methods. Each method starts with the same total cost and ends with the same salvage value. The difference is in the pattern of depreciation expense over the asset's life. Common methods are straight-line, double-declining-balance, and units-of-production.

A2 Compute total asset turnover and apply it to analyze a company's use of assets. Total asset turnover measures a company's ability to use its assets to generate sales. It is defined as net sales divided by average total assets. While all companies desire a high total asset turnover, it must be interpreted in comparison with those for prior years and its competitors.

P1 Apply the cost principle to compute the cost of plant assets. Plant assets are recorded at cost when purchased. Cost includes all normal and reasonable expenditures necessary to get the asset in place and ready for its intended use. The cost of a lump-sum purchase is allocated among its individual assets.

P2 Compute and record depreciation using the straight-line, units-of-production, and declining-balance methods. The straight-line method divides cost less salvage value by the asset's useful life to determine depreciation expense per period. The units-of-production method divides cost less salvage value by the estimated number of units the asset will produce over its life to determine depreciation per unit. The declining-balance method multiplies the asset's beginning-of-period book value by a factor that is often double the straight-line rate.

P3 Distinguish between revenue and capital expenditures, and account for them. Revenue expenditures expire in the current period and are debited to expense accounts and matched with current revenues. Ordinary repairs are an example of revenue expenditures. Capital expenditures benefit future periods and are debited to asset accounts. Examples of capital expenditures are extraordinary repairs and betterments.

P4 Account for asset disposal through discarding or selling an asset. When a plant asset is discarded or sold, its cost and accumulated depreciation are removed from the accounts. Any cash proceeds from discarding or selling an asset are recorded and compared to the asset's book value to determine gain or loss.

P5 Account for natural resource assets and their depletion. The cost of a natural resource is recorded in a noncurrent asset account. Depletion of a natural resource is recorded by allocating its cost to depletion expense using the units-of-production method. Depletion is credited to an Accumulated Depletion account.

P6 Account for intangible assets. An intangible asset is recorded at the cost incurred to purchase it. The cost of an intangible asset with a definite useful life is allocated to expense using the straight-line method, and is called *amortization.* Goodwill and intangible assets with an indefinite useful life are not amortized—they are annually tested for impairment. Intangible assets include patents, copyrights, leaseholds, goodwill, and trademarks.

P7[A] Account for asset exchanges. For an asset exchange with commercial substance, a gain or loss is recorded based on the difference between the book value of the asset given up and the market value of the asset received. For an asset exchange without commercial substance, no gain or loss is recorded, and the asset received is recorded based on the book value of the asset given up.

Guidance Answers to **Decision Maker** and **Decision Ethics**

Controller The president's instructions may reflect an honest and reasonable prediction of the future. Since the company is struggling financially, the president may have concluded that the normal pattern of replacing assets every three years cannot continue. Perhaps the strategy is to avoid costs of frequent replacements and stretch use of equipment a few years longer until financial conditions improve. However, if you believe the president's decision is unprincipled, you might confront the president with your opinion that it is unethical to change the estimate to increase income. Another possibility is to wait and see whether the auditor will prohibit this change in estimate. In either case, you should insist that the statements be based on reasonable estimates.

Entrepreneur Treating an expense as a capital expenditure means that reported expenses will be lower and income higher in the short run. This is so because a capital expenditure is not expensed immediately but is spread over the asset's useful life. Treating an expense as a capital expenditure also means that asset and equity totals are reported at larger amounts in the short run. This continues until the asset is fully depreciated. Your friend is probably trying to help, but the suggestion is misguided. Only an expenditure benefiting future periods is a capital expenditure.

Environmentalist The paper manufacturer's comparison of its total asset turnover with food stores and auto dealers is misdirected. These other industries' turnovers are higher because their profit margins are lower (about 2%). Profit margins for the paper industry are usually 3% to 3.5%. You need to collect data from competitors in the paper industry to show that a 1.9 total asset turnover is about the norm for this industry. You might also want to collect data on this company's revenues and expenses, along with compensation data for its high-ranking officers and employees.

Guidance Answers to **Quick Checks**

1. a. Supplies—current assets
b. Office equipment—plant assets
c. Inventory—current assets
d. Land for future expansion—long-term investments
e. Trucks used in operations—plant assets

2. a. Land **b.** Land Improvements

3. $700,000 + $49,000 − $21,000 + $3,500 + $3,000 + $2,500 = $737,000

4. a. Straight-line with 7-year life: ($77,000/7) = $11,000
b. Straight-line with 10-year life: ($77,000/10) = $7,700

5. Depreciation is a process of allocating the cost of plant assets to the accounting periods that benefit from the assets' use.

6. a. Book value using straight-line depreciation:
$96,000 − [($96,000 − $8,000)/5] = $78,400
b. Book value using units of production:
$96,000 − [($96,000 − $8,000) × (10,000/100,000)] = $87,200

7. ($3,800 − $200)/3 = $1,200 (original depreciation per year)
$1,200 × 2 = $2,400 (accumulated depreciation)
($3,800 − $2,400)/2 = $700 (revised depreciation)

8.

Machinery	12,000	
Cash		12,000

9. A revenue expenditure benefits only the current period and should be charged to expense in the current period. A capital expenditure yields benefits that extend beyond the end of the current period and should be charged to an asset.

10. A betterment involves modifying an existing plant asset to make it more efficient, usually by replacing part of the asset with an improved or superior part. The cost of a betterment is debited to the asset account.

11.

Depreciation Expense	3,500	
Accumulated Depreciation		3,500
Cash	32,000	
Accumulated Depreciation	10,500	
Gain on Sale of Equipment		500
Equipment		42,000

12. Examples of natural resources are timberlands, mineral deposits, and oil reserves. Examples of intangible assets are patents, copyrights, leaseholds, leasehold improvements, goodwill, trademarks, and licenses.

13. ($650,000/325,000 tons) × 91,000 tons = $182,000

14.

Jan. 6	Patents	120,000	
	Cash		120,000
Dec. 31	Amortization Expense	40,000*	
	Accumulated Amortization—Patents		40,000

* $120,000/3 years = $40,000.

15.

(a) Equipment (new)	45,000	
Loss on Exchange of Assets	3,600	
Accumulated Depreciation—Equipment (old)	23,400	
Equipment (old)		30,000
Cash ($45,000 − $3,000)		42,000

(b) Equipment (new)*	44,600	
Accumulated Depreciation—Equipment (old)	23,400	
Equipment (old)		30,000
Cash ($45,000 − $7,000)		38,000

* Includes $400 unrecognized gain.

4.

Patent	100,000	
Cash		100,000
To record patent acquisition.		

Amortization Expense—Patent	10,000	
Accumulated Amortization—Patent		10,000
To record amortization expense: $100,000/10 years = $10,000.		

5.

Ore Deposit	680,000	
Cash		680,000
To record ore deposit acquisition and its related costs.		

Depletion Expense—Ore Deposit	20,000	
Accumulated Depletion—Ore Deposit		20,000
To record depletion expense: ($680,000 − $20,000)/330,000 tons = $2 per ton. 10,000 tons mined and sold × $2 = $20,000 depletion.		

6. Record the asset exchange: The book value on the exchange date is $180,000 (cost) − $40,000 (accumulated depreciation). The book value of the machinery given up in the exchange ($140,000) plus the $5,000 cash paid is less than the $210,000 value of the machine acquired. The entry to record this exchange of assets that lacks commercial substance does not recognize the $65,000 "gain."

Machinery (new)	145,000*	
Accumulated Depreciation—Machinery (old)	40,000	
Machinery (old)		180,000
Cash		5,000
To record asset exchange that lacks commercial substance.		

* Market value of the acquired asset of $210,000 minus $65,000 "gain."

APPENDIX

10A Exchanging Plant Assets

P7A Account for asset exchanges.

Many plant assets such as machinery, automobiles, and office equipment are disposed of by exchanging them for newer assets. In a typical exchange of plant assets, a *trade-in allowance* is received on the old asset and the balance is paid in cash. Accounting for the exchange of assets depends on whether the transaction has *commercial substance* (per *SFAS 153,* commercial substance implies that it alters the company's future cash flows). If an asset exchange has commercial substance, a gain or loss is recorded based on the difference between the book value of the asset(s) given up and the market value of the asset(s) received. If an asset exchange lacks commercial substance, no gain or loss is recorded, and the asset(s) received is recorded based on the book value of the asset(s) given up. An exchange has commercial substance if the company's future cash flows change as a result of the transaction. This section describes the accounting for the exchange of assets.

Exchange with Commercial Substance: A Loss A company acquires $42,000 in new equipment. In exchange, the company pays $33,000 cash and trades in old equipment. The old equipment originally cost $36,000 and has accumulated depreciation of $20,000, which implies a $16,000 book value at the time of exchange. We are told this exchange has commercial substance and that the old equipment has a trade-in allowance of $9,000. This exchange yields a loss as computed in the middle (Loss) columns of Exhibit 10A.1; the loss is computed as Asset received − Assets given = $42,000 − $49,000 = $(7,000). We can also compute the loss as Trade-in allowance − Book value of asset given = $9,000 − $16,000 = $(7,000).

EXHIBIT 10A.1

Computing Gain or Loss on Asset Exchange with Commercial Substance

Asset Exchange Has Commercial Substance		Loss		Gain
Market value of asset received		$42,000		$52,000
Book value of assets given:				
Equipment ($36,000 − $20,000)	$16,000		$16,000	
Cash	33,000	49,000	33,000	49,000
Gain (loss) on exchange		**$(7,000)**		**$ 3,000**

The entry to record this asset exchange is

Assets	= Liabilities +	Equity
+42,000		−7,000
+20,000		
−36,000		
−33,000		

Jan. 3	Equipment (**new**)	42,000	
	Loss on Exchange of Assets	7,000	
	Accumulated Depreciation—Equipment (**old**)	20,000	
	Equipment (**old**)		36,000
	Cash		33,000
	To record exchange (with commercial substance) of old equipment and cash for new equipment.		

Point: Parenthetical notes to "new" and "old" equipment are for illustration only. Both the debit and credit are to the same Equipment account.

Exchange with Commercial Substance: A Gain Let's assume the same facts as in the preceding asset exchange *except* that the new equipment received has a market value of $52,000 instead of $42,000. We are told that this exchange has commercial substance and that the old equipment has a trade-in allowance of $19,000. This exchange yields a gain as computed in the right-most (Gain) columns of Exhibit 10A.1; the gain is computed as Asset received − Assets given = $52,000 − $49,000 = $3,000. We can also compute the gain as Trade-in allowance − Book value of asset given = $19,000 − $16,000 = $3,000. The entry to record this asset exchange is

Assets	= Liabilities +	Equity
+52,000		+3,000
+20,000		
−36,000		
−33,000		

Jan. 3	Equipment (**new**)	52,000	
	Accumulated Depreciation—Equipment (**old**)	20,000	
	Equipment (**old**)		36,000
	Cash		33,000
	Gain on Exchange of Assets		3,000
	To record exchange (with commercial substance) of old equipment and cash for new equipment.		

Exchanges without Commercial Substance Let's assume the same facts as in the preceding asset exchange involving new equipment received with a market value of $52,000, but let's instead assume the transaction *lacks commercial substance.* The entry to record this asset exchange is

Assets	= Liabilities +	Equity
+49,000		
+20,000		
−36,000		
−33,000		

Jan. 3	Equipment (**new**)	49,000	
	Accumulated Depreciation—Equipment (**old**)	20,000	
	Equipment (**old**)		36,000
	Cash		33,000
	To record exchange (without commercial substance) of old equipment and cash for new equipment.		

Point: No gain or loss is recorded for exchanges *without* commercial substance.

The $3,000 gain recorded when the transaction has commercial substance is *not* recognized in this entry because of the rule prohibiting recording a gain or loss on asset exchanges without commercial substance. The $49,000 recorded for the new equipment equals its cash price ($52,000) less the unrecognized gain ($3,000) on the exchange. The $49,000 cost recorded is called the *cost basis* of the new machine. This cost basis is the amount we use to compute depreciation and its book value. The cost basis of the new asset also can be computed by summing the book values of the assets given up as shown in Exhibit 10A.2. The same analysis and approach are taken for a loss on an asset exchange without commercial substance.

EXHIBIT 10A.2

Cost Basis of New Asset When Gain Not Recorded on Asset Exchange without Commercial Substance

Cost of old equipment	$ 36,000
Less accumulated depreciation	20,000
Book value of old equipment	16,000
Cash paid in the exchange	33,000
Cost recorded for new equipment	**$49,000**

Key Terms

mhhe.com/wildFAP19e

Key Terms are available at the book's Website for learning and testing in an online Flashcard Format.

Accelerated depreciation method (p. 398)
Amortization (p. 407)
Asset book value (p. 397)
Betterments (p. 403)
Capital expenditures (p. 402)
Change in an accounting estimate (p. 401)
Copyright (p. 408)
Cost (p. 393, 395)
Declining-balance method (p. 398)
Depletion (p. 406)
Depreciation (p. 395)
Extraordinary repairs (p. 403)
Franchises (p. 408)
Goodwill (p. 409)
Impairment (p. 402, 407)
Inadequacy (p. 395)
Indefinite life (p. 407)
Intangible assets (p. 407)
Land improvements (p. 394)
Lease (p. 409)
Leasehold (p. 409)
Leasehold improvements (p. 409)
Lessee (p. 409)
Lessor (p. 409)
Licenses (p. 408)
Limited life (p. 407)
Modified Accelerated Cost Recovery System (MACRS) (p. 400)
Natural resources (p. 406)
Obsolescence (p. 395)
Ordinary repairs (p. 402)
Patent (p. 408)
Plant asset age (p. 410)
Plant assets (p. 392)
Plant asset useful life (p. 410)
Revenue expenditures (p. 402)
Salvage value (p. 395)
Straight-line depreciation (p. 396)
Total asset turnover (p. 410)
Trademark or **trade (brand) name** (p. 408)
Units-of-production depreciation (p. 397)
Useful life (p. 395)

Multiple Choice Quiz

Answers on p. 431

mhhe.com/wildFAP19e

Additional Quiz Questions are available at the book's Website.

Quiz10

1. A company paid $326,000 for property that included land, land improvements, and a building. The land was appraised at $175,000, the land improvements were appraised at $70,000, and the building was appraised at $105,000. What is the allocation of property costs to the three assets purchased?
   a. Land, $150,000; Land Improvements, $60,000; Building, $90,000
   b. Land, $163,000; Land Improvements, $65,200; Building, $97,800
   c. Land, $150,000; Land Improvements, $61,600; Building, $92,400
   d. Land, $159,000; Land Improvements, $65,200; Building, $95,400
   e. Land, $175,000; Land Improvements, $70,000; Building, $105,000

2. A company purchased a truck for $35,000 on January 1, 2009. The truck is estimated to have a useful life of four years and an estimated salvage value of $1,000. Assuming that the company uses straight-line depreciation, what is the depreciation expense on the truck for the year ended December 31, 2010?
   a. $8,750
   b. $17,500
   c. $8,500
   d. $17,000
   e. $25,500

3. A company purchased machinery for $10,800,000 on January 1, 2009. The machinery has a useful life of 10 years and an estimated salvage value of $800,000. What is the depreciation expense on the machinery for the year ended December 31, 2010, assuming that the double-declining-balance method is used?
   a. $2,160,000
   b. $3,888,000
   c. $1,728,000
   d. $2,000,000
   e. $1,600,000

4. A company sold a machine that originally cost $250,000 for $120,000 when accumulated depreciation on the machine was $100,000. The gain or loss recorded on the sale of this machine is
   a. $0 gain or loss.
   b. $120,000 gain.
   c. $30,000 loss.
   d. $30,000 gain.
   e. $150,000 loss.

5. A company had average total assets of $500,000, gross sales of $575,000, and net sales of $550,000. The company's total asset turnover is
   a. 1.15
   b. 1.10
   c. 0.91
   d. 0.87
   e. 1.05

Superscript letter A denotes assignments based on Appendix 10A.

Discussion Questions

1. What characteristics of a plant asset make it different from other assets?
2. What is the general rule for costs' inclusion for plant assets?
3. What is different between land and land improvements?
4. Why is the cost of a lump-sum purchase allocated to the individual assets acquired?
5. Does the balance in the Accumulated Depreciation—Machinery account represent funds to replace the machinery when it wears out? If not, what does it represent?
6. Why is the Modified Accelerated Cost Recovery System not generally accepted for financial accounting purposes?
7. What accounting concept justifies charging low-cost plant asset purchases immediately to an expense account?
8. What is the difference between ordinary repairs and extraordinary repairs? How should each be recorded?
9. Identify events that might lead to disposal of a plant asset.
10. What is the process of allocating the cost of natural resources to expense as they are used?
11. Is the declining-balance method an acceptable way to compute depletion of natural resources? Explain.
12. What are the characteristics of an intangible asset?
13. What general procedures are applied in accounting for the acquisition and potential cost allocation of intangible assets?
14. When do we know that a company has goodwill? When can goodwill appear in a company's balance sheet?
15. Assume that a company buys another business and pays for its goodwill. If the company plans to incur costs each year to maintain the value of the goodwill, must it also amortize this goodwill?
16. How is total asset turnover computed? Why would a financial statement user be interested in total asset turnover?
17. Refer to **Best Buy**'s balance sheet in Appendix A. What plant and equipment assets does Best Buy list on its balance sheet? What is the book value of its total plant and equipment assets at March 3, 2007?
18. Refer to **Circuit City**'s balance sheet in Appendix A. What does it title its plant assets? What is the book value of its plant assets at February 28, 2007?
19. **RadioShack** lists its plant assets as "Property, plant, and equipment, net." What does "net" mean in this title?
20. Refer to the September 30, 2006, balance sheet of **Apple** in Appendix A. What long-term assets discussed in this chapter are reported by the company?

Denotes Discussion Questions that involve decision making.

Available with McGraw-Hill's Homework Manager

QUICK STUDY

QS 10-1
Cost of plant assets
P1

Marlin Bowling installs automatic scorekeeping equipment with an invoice cost of $350,000. The electrical work required for the installation costs $10,000. Additional costs are $4,000 for delivery and $21,000 for sales tax. During the installation, a component of the equipment is carelessly left on a lane and hit by the automatic lane-cleaning machine. The cost of repairing the component is $4,200. What is the total recorded cost of the automatic scorekeeping equipment?

QS 10-2
Defining assets
C1

Identify the main difference between (1) plant assets and current assets, (2) plant assets and inventory, and (3) plant assets and long-term investments.

QS 10-3
Straight-line depreciation
P2

On January 2, 2009, the Deadra Band acquires sound equipment for concert performances at a cost of $32,500. The band estimates it will use this equipment for four years, during which time it anticipates performing about 200 concerts. It estimates that after four years it can sell the equipment for $2,500. During year 2009, the band performs 47 concerts. Compute the year 2009 depreciation using the straight-line method.

QS 10-4
Units-of-production depreciation
P2

Refer to the information in QS 10-3. Compute the year 2009 depreciation using the units-of-production method.

Refer to the facts in QS 10-3. Assume that the Deadra Band uses straight-line depreciation but realizes at the start of the second year that due to concert bookings beyond expectations, this equipment will last only a total of three years. The salvage value remains unchanged. Compute the revised depreciation for both the second and third years.

QS 10-5
Computing revised depreciation
C3

A fleet of refrigerated delivery trucks is acquired on January 5, 2009, at a cost of $1,200,000 with an estimated useful life of eight years and an estimated salvage value of $100,000. Compute the depreciation expense for the first three years using the double-declining-balance method.

QS 10-6
Double-declining-balance method
P2

1. Classify the following as either revenue or capital expenditures.
   a. Paid $40,000 cash to replace a compressor on a refrigeration system that extends its useful life by four years.
   b. Paid $200 cash per truck for the cost of their annual tune-ups.
   c. Paid $175 for the monthly cost of replacement filters on an air-conditioning system.
   d. Completed an addition to an office building for $225,000 cash.

2. Prepare the journal entries to record transactions *a* and *d* of part 1.

QS 10-7
Revenue and capital expenditures
P3

Tresler Co. owns equipment that cost $92,500, with accumulated depreciation of $54,000. Tresler sells the equipment for cash. Record the sale of the equipment assuming Tresler sells the equipment for (1) $42,000 cash, (2) $38,500 cash, and (3) $31,000 cash.

QS 10-8
Disposal of assets
P4

Crandon Company acquires an ore mine at a cost of $6,300,000. It incurs additional costs of $500,000 to access the mine, which is estimated to hold 1,000,000 tons of ore. The estimated value of the land after the ore is removed is $900,000.

1. Prepare the entry(ies) to record the cost of the ore mine.

2. Prepare the year-end adjusting entry if 125,000 tons of ore are mined and sold the first year.

QS 10-9
Natural resources and depletion
P5

Which of the following assets are reported on the balance sheet as intangible assets? Which are reported as natural resources? (*a*) Oil well, (*b*) trademark, (*c*) leasehold, (*d*) gold mine, (*e*) building, (*f*) copyright, (*g*) franchise, (*h*) timberland.

QS 10-10
Classify assets
P5 P6

On January 4 of this year, Brasen Boutique incurs a $275,000 cost to modernize its store. Improvements include new floors, ceilings, wiring, and wall coverings. These improvements are estimated to yield benefits for 10 years. Brasen leases its store and has eight years remaining on the lease. Prepare the entry to record (1) the cost of modernization and (2) amortization at the end of this current year.

QS 10-11
Intangible assets and amortization
P6

Camden Company reports the following ($ 000s): net sales of $14,880 for 2009 and $13,990 for 2008; end-of-year total assets of $15,869 for 2009 and $17,819 for 2008. Compute its total asset turnover for 2009, and assess its level if competitors average a total asset turnover of 2.0 times.

QS 10-12
Computing total asset turnover
A2

Gamma Co. owns a machine that costs $84,800 with accumulated depreciation of $36,800. Gamma exchanges the machine for a newer model that has a market value of $104,000. (1) Record the exchange assuming Gamma paid $60,000 cash and the exchange has commercial substance. (2) Record the exchange assuming Gamma pays $44,000 cash and the exchange lacks commercial substance.

QS 10-13A
Asset exchange
P7

McGraw-Hill's HOMEWORK MANAGER® Available with McGraw-Hill's Homework Manager

EXERCISES

Kruz Co. purchases a machine for $10,400, terms 1/10, n/60, FOB shipping point. The seller prepaid the $235 freight charges, adding the amount to the invoice and bringing its total to $10,635. The machine requires special steel mounting and power connections costing $719. Another $339 is paid to assemble the machine and get it into operation. In moving the machine to its steel mounting, $250 in damages occurred. Materials costing $40 are used in adjusting the machine to produce a satisfactory product. The adjustments are normal for this machine and are not the result of the damages. Compute the cost recorded for this machine. (Kruz pays for this machine within the cash discount period.)

Exercise 10-1
Cost of plant assets
P1

Exercise 10-2
Recording costs of assets
C1 P1

Fisk Manufacturing purchases a large lot on which an old building is located as part of its plans to build a new plant. The negotiated purchase price is $209,000 for the lot plus $104,000 for the old building. The company pays $40,400 to tear down the old building and $59,722 to fill and level the lot. It also pays a total of $1,663,150 in construction costs—this amount consists of $1,564,400 for the new building and $98,750 for lighting and paving a parking area next to the building. Prepare a single journal entry to record these costs incurred by Fisk, all of which are paid in cash.

Exercise 10-3
Lump-sum purchase of plant assets C1

Dillon Company pays $404,000 for real estate plus $21,500 in closing costs. The real estate consists of land appraised at $217,140; land improvements appraised at $83,160; and a building appraised at $161,700. Allocate the total cost among the three purchased assets and prepare the journal entry to record the purchase.

Exercise 10-4
Straight-line depreciation
P2

In early January 2009, Sanchez Builders purchases equipment for $102,000 to use in operating activities for the next five years. It estimates the equipment's salvage value at $21,000. Prepare a table showing depreciation and book value for each of the five years assuming straight-line depreciation.

Exercise 10-5
Double-declining-balance depreciation P2

Refer to the information in Exercise 10-4. Prepare a table showing depreciation and book value for each of the five years assuming double-declining-balance depreciation.

Exercise 10-6
Straight-line depreciation
P2

Sarita Company installs a computerized manufacturing machine in its factory at the beginning of the year at a cost of $67,000. The machine's useful life is estimated at 10 years, or 420,000 units of product, with a $4,000 salvage value. During its second year, the machine produces 29,900 units of product. Determine the machine's second-year depreciation under the straight-line method.

Exercise 10-7
Units-of-production depreciation
P2

Refer to the information in Exercise 10-6. Determine the machine's second-year depreciation using the units-of-production method.

Exercise 10-8
Double-declining-balance depreciation P2

Refer to the information in Exercise 10-6. Determine the machine's second-year depreciation using the double-declining-balance method.

Exercise 10-9
Straight-line, partial-year depreciation C3

On April 1, 2008, Bricen Backhoe Co. purchases a trencher for $253,000. The machine is expected to last five years and have a salvage value of $25,300. Compute depreciation expense for year 2009 assuming the company uses the straight-line method.

Exercise 10-10
Double-declining-balance, partial-year depreciation C3

Refer to the information in Exercise 10-9. Compute depreciation expense for year 2009 assuming the company uses the double-declining-balance method.

Exercise 10-11
Revising depreciation
C3

Check (2) $4,200

Siness Fitness Club uses straight-line depreciation for a machine costing $26,400, with an estimated four-year life and a $2,900 salvage value. At the beginning of the third year, Siness determines that the machine has three more years of remaining useful life, after which it will have an estimated $2,050 salvage value. Compute (1) the machine's book value at the end of its second year and (2) the amount of depreciation for each of the final three years given the revised estimates.

Exercise 10-12
Straight-line depreciation and income effects
A1

Echo Enterprises pays $274,900 for equipment that will last five years and have a $41,000 salvage value. By using the equipment in its operations for five years, the company expects to earn $86,800 annually, after deducting all expenses except depreciation. Prepare a table showing income before depreciation, depreciation expense, and net (pretax) income for each year and for the total five-year period, assuming straight-line depreciation.

Exercise 10-13
Double-declining-balance depreciation A1

Refer to the information in Exercise 10-12. Prepare a table showing income before depreciation, depreciation expense, and net (pretax) income for each year and for the total five-year period, assuming double-declining-balance depreciation is used.

Check Year 3 NI, $47,214

Exercise 10-14
Extraordinary repairs; plant asset age
P3

Horizon Company owns a building that appears on its prior year-end balance sheet at its original $620,000 cost less $496,000 accumulated depreciation. The building is depreciated on a straight-line basis assuming a 20-year life and no salvage value. During the first week in January of the current calendar year, major structural repairs are completed on the building at a $74,000 cost. The repairs extend its useful life for 7 years beyond the 20 years originally estimated.

1. Determine the building's age (plant asset age) as of the prior year-end balance sheet date.
2. Prepare the entry to record the cost of the structural repairs that are paid in cash.
3. Determine the book value of the building immediately after the repairs are recorded.
4. Prepare the entry to record the current calendar year's depreciation.

Check (3) $198,000

Exercise 10-15
Ordinary repairs, extraordinary repairs and betterments
P3

Bera Company pays $264,900 for equipment expected to last four years and have a $30,000 salvage value. Prepare journal entries to record the following costs related to the equipment.

1. During the second year of the equipment's life, $29,500 cash is paid for a new component expected to increase the equipment's productivity by 10% a year.
2. During the third year, $7,375 cash is paid for normal repairs necessary to keep the equipment in good working order.
3. During the fourth year, $22,450 is paid for repairs expected to increase the useful life of the equipment from four to five years.

Exercise 10-16
Disposal of assets
P4

Sydney Company owns a milling machine that cost $250,000 and has accumulated depreciation of $182,000. Prepare the entry to record the disposal of the milling machine on January 3 under each of the following independent situations.

1. The machine needed extensive repairs, and it was not worth repairing. Sydney disposed of the machine, receiving nothing in return.
2. Sydney sold the machine for $35,000 cash.
3. Sydney sold the machine for $68,000 cash.
4. Sydney sold the machine for $80,000 cash.

Exercise 10-17
Partial-year depreciation; disposal of plant asset
P4

Rayya Co. purchases and installs a machine on January 1, 2009, at a total cost of $94,000. Straight-line depreciation is taken each year for four years assuming an eight-year life and no salvage value. The machine is disposed of on July 1, 2013, during its fifth year of service. Prepare entries to record the partial year's depreciation on July 1, 2013, and to record the disposal under the following separate assumptions: (1) the machine is sold for $43,593 cash and (2) Rayya receives an insurance settlement of $39,480 resulting from the total destruction of the machine in a fire.

Exercise 10-18
Depletion of natural resources
P2 P5

On April 2, 2009, Mitzu Mining Co. pays $3,920,000 for an ore deposit containing 1,400,000 tons. The company installs machinery in the mine costing $210,000, with an estimated seven-year life and no salvage value. The machinery will be abandoned when the ore is completely mined. Mitzu begins mining on May 1, 2009, and mines and sells 178,200 tons of ore during the remaining eight months of 2009. Prepare the December 31, 2009, entries to record both the ore deposit depletion and the mining machinery depreciation. Mining machinery depreciation should be in proportion to the mine's depletion.

Exercise 10-19
Amortization of intangible assets
P6

Galvano Gallery purchases the copyright on an oil painting for $432,000 on January 1, 2009. The copyright legally protects its owner for 19 more years. However, the company plans to market and sell prints of the original for only 15 years. Prepare entries to record the purchase of the copyright on January 1, 2009, and its annual amortization on December 31, 2009.

Exercise 10-20
Goodwill
P6

On January 1, 2009, Jeffrey Company purchased Perrow Company at a price of $2,500,000. The fair market value of the net assets purchased equals $1,800,000.

1. What is the amount of goodwill that Jeffrey records at the purchase date?
2. Explain how Jeffrey would determine the amount of goodwill amortization for the year ended December 31, 2009.
3. Jeffrey Company believes that its employees provide superior customer service, and through their efforts, Jeffrey Company believes it has created $900,000 of goodwill. How would Jeffrey Company record this goodwill?

Exercise 10-21
Cash flows related to assets
C1

Refer to the statement of cash flows for **Circuit City** in Appendix A for the fiscal year ended February 28, 2007, to answer the following.

1. What amount of cash is used to purchase property and equipment?
2. How much depreciation and amortization are recorded?
3. What total amount of net cash is used in investing activities?

Exercise 10-22
Evaluating efficient use of assets
A2

Teridan Co. reports net sales of $4,796,000 for 2008 and $8,758,000 for 2009. End-of-year balances for total assets are 2007, $1,578,000; 2008, $1,824,000; and 2009, $1,946,000. (*a*) Compute Teridan's total asset turnover for 2008 and 2009. (*b*) Comment on Teridan's efficiency in using its assets if its competitors average a total asset turnover of 3.0.

Exercise 10-23[A]
Exchanging assets
P7

Corin Construction trades in an old tractor for a new tractor, receiving a $24,500 trade-in allowance and paying the remaining $71,750 in cash. The old tractor had cost $83,000, and straight-line accumulated depreciation of $45,000 had been recorded to date under the assumption that it would last eight years and have an $11,000 salvage value. Answer the following questions assuming the exchange has commercial substance.

1. What is the book value of the old tractor at the time of exchange?
2. What is the loss on this asset exchange?
3. What amount should be recorded (debited) in the asset account for the new tractor?

Check (2) $13,500

Exercise 10-24[A]
Recording plant asset disposals
P4 P7

On January 2, 2009, Bering Co. disposes of a machine costing $52,400 with accumulated depreciation of $28,227. Prepare the entries to record the disposal under each of the following separate assumptions.

1. The machine is sold for $20,274 cash.
2. The machine is traded in for a newer machine having a $68,900 cash price. A $24,953 trade-in allowance is received, and the balance is paid in cash. Assume the asset exchange lacks commercial substance.
3. The machine is traded in for a newer machine having a $68,900 cash price. An $18,714 trade-in allowance is received, and the balance is paid in cash. Assume the asset exchange has commercial substance.

Check (2) Dr. Machinery (new), $68,120

Available with McGraw-Hill's Homework Manager — McGraw-Hill's HOMEWORK MANAGER®

PROBLEM SET A

Problem 10-1A
Plant asset costs; depreciation methods
C1 C2 A1 P1 P2

eXcel
mhhe.com/wildFAP19e

Teness Construction negotiates a lump-sum purchase of several assets from a company that is going out of business. The purchase is completed on January 1, 2009, at a total cash price of $900,000 for a building, land, land improvements, and four vehicles. The estimated market values of the assets are building, $514,250; land, $271,150; land improvements, $65,450; and four vehicles, $84,150. The company's fiscal year ends on December 31.

Required

1. Prepare a table to allocate the lump-sum purchase price to the separate assets purchased. Prepare the journal entry to record the purchase.
2. Compute the depreciation expense for year 2009 on the building using the straight-line method, assuming a 15-year life and a $30,000 salvage value.
3. Compute the depreciation expense for year 2009 on the land improvements assuming a five-year life and double-declining-balance depreciation.

Check (2) $31,000
(3) $25,200

Analysis Component

4. Defend or refute this statement: Accelerated depreciation results in payment of less taxes over the asset's life.

Problem 10-2A
Asset cost allocation; straight-line depreciation
C1 C2 P1 P2

eXcel
mhhe.com/wildFAP19e

In January 2009, Solaris Co. pays $2,650,000 for a tract of land with two buildings on it. It plans to demolish Building 1 and build a new store in its place. Building 2 will be a company office; it is appraised at $692,530, with a useful life of 20 years and an $85,000 salvage value. A lighted parking lot near Building 1 has improvements (Land Improvements 1) valued at $451,650 that are expected to last another 12 years with no salvage value. Without the buildings and improvements, the tract of land is valued at $1,866,820. Solaris also incurs the following additional costs:

Cost to demolish Building 1	$ 342,400
Cost of additional land grading	193,400
Cost to construct new building (Building 3), having a useful life of 25 years and a $400,000 salvage value	2,282,000
Cost of new land improvements (Land Improvements 2) near Building 2 having a 20-year useful life and no salvage value	168,000

Required

1. Prepare a table with the following column headings: Land, Building 2, Building 3, Land Improvements 1, and Land Improvements 2. Allocate the costs incurred by Solaris to the appropriate columns and total each column.

Check (1) Land costs, $2,178,800; Building 2 costs, $609,500

2. Prepare a single journal entry to record all the incurred costs assuming they are paid in cash on January 1, 2009.

3. Using the straight-line method, prepare the December 31 adjusting entries to record depreciation for the 12 months of 2009 when these assets were in use.

(3) Depr.—Land Improv. 1 and 2, $33,125 and $8,400

Problem 10-3A
Computing and revising depreciation; revenue and capital expenditures
C3 P1 P3

Maxil Contractors completed the following transactions and events involving the purchase and operation of equipment in its business.

2008

Jan. 1 Paid $293,660 cash plus $11,740 in sales tax and $1,500 in transportation (FOB shipping point) for a new loader. The loader is estimated to have a four-year life and a $36,000 salvage value. Loader costs are recorded in the Equipment account.

Jan. 3 Paid $5,100 to enclose the cab and install air conditioning in the loader to enable operations under harsher conditions. This increased the estimated salvage value of the loader by another $1,000.

Dec. 31 Recorded annual straight-line depreciation on the loader.

Check Dec. 31, 2008, Dr. Depr. Expense—Equip., $68,750

2009

Jan. 1 Paid $4,500 to overhaul the loader's engine, which increased the loader's estimated useful life by two years.

Feb. 17 Paid $1,125 to repair the loader after the operator backed it into a tree.

Dec. 31 Recorded annual straight-line depreciation on the loader.

Check Dec. 31, 2009, Dr. Depr. Expense—Equip., $42,150

Required

Prepare journal entries to record these transactions and events.

Problem 10-4A
Computing and revising depreciation; selling plant assets
C3 P2 P4

Dakota Company completed the following transactions and events involving its delivery trucks.

2008

Jan. 1 Paid $25,015 cash plus $1,485 in sales tax for a new delivery truck estimated to have a five-year life and a $2,000 salvage value. Delivery truck costs are recorded in the Trucks account.

Dec. 31 Recorded annual straight-line depreciation on the truck.

2009

Dec. 31 Due to new information obtained earlier in the year, the truck's estimated useful life was changed from five to four years, and the estimated salvage value was increased to $2,700. Recorded annual straight-line depreciation on the truck.

Check Dec. 31, 2009, Dr. Depr. Expense—Trucks, $6,300

2010

Dec. 31, 2010, Dr. Loss on Disposal of Trucks, $3,400

Dec. 31 Recorded annual straight-line depreciation on the truck.
Dec. 31 Sold the truck for $5,600 cash.

Required

Prepare journal entries to record these transactions and events.

Problem 10-5A
Depreciation methods
A1 P2

A machine costing $320,000 with a four-year life and an estimated $33,000 salvage value is installed in Luther Company's factory on January 1. The factory manager estimates the machine will produce 512,500 units of product during its life. It actually produces the following units: year 1, 127,500; year 2, 129,000; year 3, 128,500; and year 4, 127,900. The total number of units produced by the end of year 4 exceeds the original estimate—this difference was not predicted. (The machine must not be depreciated below its estimated salvage value.)

Required

Prepare a table with the following column headings and compute depreciation for each year (and total depreciation of all years combined) for the machine under each depreciation method.

Check Year 4: units-of-production depreciation, $71,400; DDB depreciation, $7,000

Year	Straight-Line	Units-of-Production	Double-Declining-Balance

---

Problem 10-6A
Disposal of plant assets
P1 P2 P4

Platero Co. purchases a used machine for $198,750 cash on January 2 and readies it for use the next day at an $11,000 cost. On January 3, it is installed on a required operating platform costing $3,410, and it is further readied for operations. The company predicts the machine will be used for six years and have a $16,960 salvage value. Depreciation is to be charged on a straight-line basis. On December 31, at the end of its fifth year in operations, it is disposed of.

Required

1. Prepare journal entries to record the machine's purchase and the costs to ready and install it. Cash is paid for all costs incurred.

Check (2*b*) Depr. Exp., $32,700

2. Prepare journal entries to record depreciation of the machine at December 31 of (*a*) its first year in operations and (*b*) the year of its disposal.

(3*c*) Dr. Loss from Fire, $18,160

3. Prepare journal entries to record the machine's disposal under each of the following separate assumptions: (*a*) it is sold for $21,000 cash; (*b*) it is sold for $73,500 cash; and (*c*) it is destroyed in a fire and the insurance company pays $31,500 cash to settle the loss claim.

Problem 10-7A
Natural resources
P5

On July 23 of the current year, Serena Mining Co. pays $4,612,500 for land estimated to contain 5,125,000 tons of recoverable ore. It installs machinery costing $512,500 that has a 10-year life and no salvage value and is capable of mining the ore deposit in eight years. The machinery is paid for on July 25, seven days before mining operations begin. The company removes and sells 490,000 tons of ore during its first five months of operations ending on December 31. Depreciation of the machinery is in proportion to the mine's depletion as the machinery will be abandoned after the ore is mined.

Required

Check (*c*) Depletion, $441,000
(*d*) Depreciation, $49,000

Prepare entries to record (*a*) the purchase of the land, (*b*) the cost and installation of machinery, (*c*) the first five months' depletion assuming the land has a net salvage value of zero after the ore is mined, and (*d*) the first five months' depreciation on the machinery.

Analysis Component

Describe both the similarities and differences in amortization, depletion, and depreciation.

Problem 10-8A
Intangible assets
P6

On July 1, 2004, Harper Company signed a contract to lease space in a building for 15 years. The lease contract calls for annual (prepaid) rental payments of $80,000 on each July 1 throughout the life of the lease and for the lessee to pay for all additions and improvements to the leased property. On June 25, 2009, Harper decides to sublease the space to Bosio & Associates for the remaining 10 years of the lease—Bosio pays $260,000 to Harper for the right to sublease and it agrees to assume the obligation to pay the $80,000 annual rent to the building owner beginning July 1, 2009. After taking possession of the leased space, Bosio pays for improving the office portion of the leased space at a $160,000 cost. The improvements are paid for by Bosio on July 5, 2009, and are estimated to have a useful life equal to the 16 years remaining in the life of the building.

Required

1. Prepare entries for Bosio to record (*a*) its payment to Harper for the right to sublease the building space, (*b*) its payment of the 2009 annual rent to the building owner, and (*c*) its payment for the office improvements.

2. Prepare Bosio's year-end adjusting entries required at December 31, 2009, to (*a*) amortize the $260,000 cost of the sublease, (*b*) amortize the office improvements, and (*c*) record rent expense.

Check Dr. Rent Expense for (*2a*) $13,000, (*2c*) $40,000

PROBLEM SET B

Problem 10-1B
Plant asset costs; depreciation methods
C1 C2 A1 P1 P2

Clinton Company negotiates a lump-sum purchase of several assets from a contractor who is relocating. The purchase is completed on January 1, 2009, at a total cash price of $930,000 for a building, land, land improvements, and four trucks. The estimated market values of the assets are building, $469,200; land, $303,600; land improvements, $36,800; and four trucks, $110,400. The company's fiscal year ends on December 31.

Required

1. Prepare a table to allocate the lump-sum purchase price to the separate assets purchased. Prepare the journal entry to record the purchase.

2. Compute the depreciation expense for year 2009 on the building using the straight-line method, assuming a 15-year life and a $30,000 salvage value.

Check (2) $29,620

3. Compute the depreciation expense for year 2009 on the land improvements assuming a five-year life and double-declining-balance depreciation.

(3) $14,880

Analysis Component

4. Defend or refute this statement: Accelerated depreciation results in payment of more taxes over the asset's life.

Problem 10-2B
Asset cost allocation; straight-line depreciation
C1 C2 P1 P2

In January 2009, Boulware Co. pays $2,750,000 for a tract of land with two buildings. It plans to demolish Building A and build a new shop in its place. Building B will be a company office; it is appraised at $687,700, with a useful life of 20 years and an $85,000 salvage value. A lighted parking lot near Building B has improvements (Land Improvements B) valued at $478,400 that are expected to last another 10 years with no salvage value. Without the buildings and improvements, the tract of land is valued at $1,823,900. Boulware also incurs the following additional costs.

Cost to demolish Building A	$ 345,400
Cost of additional land grading	185,400
Cost to construct new building (Building C), having a useful life of 25 years and a $400,000 salvage value	2,282,000
Cost of new land improvements (Land Improvements C) near Building C, having a 20-year useful life and no salvage value	173,000

Required

1. Prepare a table with the following column headings: Land, Building B, Building C, Land Improvements B, and Land Improvements C. Allocate the costs incurred by Boulware to the appropriate columns and total each column.

Check (1) Land costs, $2,208,300; Building B costs, $632,500

2. Prepare a single journal entry to record all incurred costs assuming they are paid in cash on January 1, 2009.

3. Using the straight-line method, prepare the December 31 adjusting entries to record depreciation for the 12 months of 2009 when these assets were in use.

(3) Depr.—Land Improv. B and C, $44,000 and $8,650

Problem 10-3B
Computing and revising depreciation; revenue and capital expenditures
C3 P1 P3

Zander Delivery Service completed the following transactions and events involving the purchase and operation of equipment for its business.

2008

Jan. 1	Paid $58,000 cash plus $4,000 in sales tax for a new delivery van that was estimated to have a four-year life and a $3,000 salvage value. Van costs are recorded in the Equipment account.
Jan. 3	Paid $2,900 to install sorting racks in the van for more accurate and quicker delivery of packages. This increases the estimated salvage value of the van by another $200.
Dec. 31	Recorded annual straight-line depreciation on the van.

Check Dec. 31, 2008, Dr. Depr. Expense—Equip., $15,425

2009

Jan. 1	Paid $4,300 to overhaul the van's engine, which increased the van's estimated useful life by two years.
May 10	Paid $1,075 to repair the van after the driver backed it into a loading dock.
Dec. 31	Record annual straight-line depreciation on the van. (Round to the nearest dollar.)

Check Dec. 31, 2009, Dr. Depr. Expense—Equip., $10,115

Required

Prepare journal entries to record these transactions and events.

Problem 10-4B
Computing and revising depreciation; selling plant assets
C3 P2 P4

Walsh Instruments completed the following transactions and events involving its machinery.

2008

Jan. 1	Paid $20,515 cash plus $1,485 in sales tax for a new machine. The machine is estimated to have a five-year life and a $2,000 salvage value.
Dec. 31	Recorded annual straight-line depreciation on the machinery.

2009

Dec. 31	Due to new information obtained earlier in the year, the machine's estimated useful life was changed from five to four years, and the estimated salvage value was increased to $2,550. Recorded annual straight-line depreciation on the machinery.

Check Dec. 31, 2009, Dr. Depr. Expense—Machinery, $5,150

2010

Dec. 31	Recorded annual straight-line depreciation on the machinery.
Dec. 31	Sold the machine for $5,600 cash.

Dec. 31, 2010, Dr. Loss on Disposal of Machinery, $2,100

Required

Prepare journal entries to record these transactions and events.

Problem 10-5B
Depreciation methods
A1 P2

On January 2, Gillette Co. purchases and installs a new machine costing $360,000 with a five-year life and an estimated $33,000 salvage value. Management estimates the machine will produce 2,180,000 units of product during its life. Actual production of units is as follows: year 1, 425,000; year 2, 452,000; year 3, 445,000; year 4, 438,000; and year 5, 441,000. The total number of units produced by the end of year 5 exceeds the original estimate—this difference was not predicted. (The machine must not be depreciated below its estimated salvage value.)

Required

Prepare a table with the following column headings and compute depreciation for each year (and total depreciation of all years combined) for the machine under each depreciation method.

Check DDB Depreciation, Year 3, $51,840; U-of-P Depreciation, Year 4, $65,700

Year	Straight-Line	Units-of-Production	Double-Declining-Balance

Problem 10-6B
Disposal of plant assets
P1 P2 P4

On January 1, Ammons purchases a used machine for $238,500 and readies it for use the next day at a cost of $11,000. On January 4, it is mounted on a required operating platform costing $3,600, and it is further readied for operations. Management estimates the machine will be used for six years and have a $22,100 salvage value. Depreciation is to be charged on a straight-line basis. On December 31, at the end of its fifth year of use, the machine is disposed of.

Required

1. Prepare journal entries to record the machine's purchase and the costs to ready and install it. Cash is paid for all costs incurred.
2. Prepare journal entries to record depreciation of the machine at December 31 of (*a*) its first year in operations and (*b*) the year of its disposal.
3. Prepare journal entries to record the machine's disposal under each of the following separate assumptions: (*a*) it is sold for $20,500 cash; (*b*) it is sold for $71,750 cash; and (*c*) it is destroyed in a fire and the insurance company pays $31,000 cash to settle the loss claim.

Check (2*b*) Depr. Exp., $38,500
(3*c*) Dr. Loss from Fire, $29,600

Problem 10-7B
Natural resources
P5

On February 19 of the current year, Javier Co. pays $6,000,000 for land estimated to contain 4 million tons of recoverable ore. It installs machinery costing $480,000 that has a 16-year life and no salvage value and is capable of mining the ore deposit in 12 years. The machinery is paid for on March 21, seven days before mining operations begin. The company removes and sells 380,000 tons of ore during its first nine months of operations ending on December 31. Depreciation of the machinery is in proportion to the mine's depletion as the machinery will be abandoned after the ore is mined.

Required

Prepare entries to record (*a*) the purchase of the land, (*b*) the cost and installation of the machinery, (*c*) the first nine months' depletion assuming the land has a net salvage value of zero after the ore is mined, and (*d*) the first nine months' depreciation on the machinery.

Check (*c*) Depletion, $570,000; (*d*) Depreciation, $45,600

Analysis Component

Describe both the similarities and differences in amortization, depletion, and depreciation.

Problem 10-8B
Intangible assets
P6

On January 1, 2002, Palos Co. entered into a 12-year lease on a building. The lease contract requires (1) annual (prepaid) rental payments of $90,000 each January 1 throughout the life of the lease and (2) for the lessee to pay for all additions and improvements to the leased property. On January 1, 2009, Palos decides to sublease the space to Callahan Co. for the remaining five years of the lease—Callahan pays $200,000 to Palos for the right to sublease and agrees to assume the obligation to pay the $90,000 annual rent to the building owner beginning January 1, 2009. After taking possession of the leased space, Callahan pays for improving the office portion of the leased space at a $150,000 cost. The improvements are paid for by Callahan on January 3, 2009, and are estimated to have a useful life equal to the 13 years remaining in the life of the building.

Required

1. Prepare entries for Callahan to record (*a*) its payment to Palos for the right to sublease the building space, (*b*) its payment of the 2009 annual rent to the building owner, and (*c*) its payment for the office improvements.
2. Prepare Callahan's year-end adjusting entries required on December 31, 2009, to (*a*) amortize the $200,000 cost of the sublease, (*b*) amortize the office improvements, and (*c*) record rent expense.

Check Dr. Rent Expense: (2*a*) $40,000, (2*c*) $90,000

SERIAL PROBLEM

Success Systems

(This serial problem began in Chapter 1 and continues through most of the book. If previous chapter segments were not completed, the serial problem can begin at this point. It is helpful, but not necessary, to use the Working Papers that accompany the book.)

SP 10 Selected ledger account balances for Success Systems follow.

	For Three Months Ended December 31, 2009	For Three Months Ended March 31, 2010
Office equipment	$ 8,000	$ 8,000
Accumulated depreciation—Office equipment	400	800
Computer equipment	20,000	20,000
Accumulated depreciation—Computer equipment	1,250	2,500
Total revenue	31,284	43,853
Total assets	93,248	129,909

Required

1. Assume that Success Systems does not acquire additional office equipment or computer equipment in 2010. Compute the amounts for the year ended December 31, 2010, for Depreciation Expense—Office Equipment and for Depreciation Expense—Computer Equipment (assume use of the straight-line method).
2. Given the assumptions in part 1, what is the book value of both the office equipment and the computer equipment as of December 31, 2010?
3. Compute the three-month total asset turnover for Success Systems as of March 31, 2010. Use total revenue for the numerator and average the December 31, 2009, total assets and the March 31, 2010, total assets for the denominator. Interpret its total asset turnover if competitors average 2.5 for annual periods.

Check (3) Three-month (annual) turnover = 0.39 (1.56)

BEYOND THE NUMBERS

REPORTING IN ACTION

A1 A2

BTN 10-1 Refer to the financial statements of **Best Buy** in Appendix A to answer the following.

1. What percent of the original cost of Best Buy's property and equipment remain to be depreciated as of March 3, 2007, and at February 25, 2006? Assume these assets have no salvage value.
2. Over what length(s) of time is Best Buy amortizing its intangible assets?
3. What is the change in total property and equipment (before accumulated depreciation) for the year ended March 3, 2007? What is the amount of cash provided (used) by investing activities for property and equipment for the year ended March 3, 2007? What is one possible explanation for the difference between these two amounts?
4. Compute its total asset turnover for the year ended March 3, 2007, and the year ended February 25, 2006. Assume total assets at February 26, 2005, are $10,294 ($ millions).

Fast Forward

5. Access Best Buy's financial statements for the fiscal years ending after March 3, 2007, at its Website (BestBuy.com) or the SEC's EDGAR database (www.SEC.gov). Recompute Best Buy's total asset turnover for the additional years' data you collect. Comment on any differences relative to the turnover computed in part 4.

COMPARATIVE ANALYSIS

A2

BTN 10-2 Comparative figures for **Best Buy**, **Circuit City**, and **RadioShack** follow.

	Best Buy			Circuit City			RadioShack		
($ millions)	Current Year	One Year Prior	Two Years Prior	Current Year	One Year Prior	Two Years Prior	Current Year	One Year Prior	Two Years Prior
Total assets	$13,570	$11,864	$10,294	$ 4,007	$ 4,069	$ 3,840	$2,070	$2,205	$2,517
Net sales	35,934	30,848	27,433	12,430	11,514	10,414	4,778	5,082	4,841

Required

1. Compute the total asset turnover for the most recent two years for Best Buy, Circuit City, and RadioShack using the data shown.
2. Which company is more efficient in generating net sales given the total assets it employs? Assume an industry average of 2.6.

ETHICS CHALLENGE

C1 C2

BTN 10-3 Carmel Choi owns a small business and manages its accounting. Her company just finished a year in which a large amount of borrowed funds was invested in a new building addition as well as in equipment and fixture additions. Choi's banker requires her to submit semiannual financial statements so he can monitor the financial health of her business. He has warned her that if profit margins erode, he might raise the interest rate on the borrowed funds to reflect the increased loan risk from the bank's point of view. Choi knows profit margin is likely to decline this year. As she prepares year-end adjusting entries, she decides to apply the following depreciation rule: All asset additions are considered to be in use on the first day of the following month. (The previous rule assumed assets are in use on the first day of the month nearest to the purchase date.)

Required

1. Identify decisions that managers like Choi must make in applying depreciation methods.
2. Is Choi's rule an ethical violation, or is it a legitimate decision in computing depreciation?
3. How will Choi's new depreciation rule affect the profit margin of her business?

COMMUNICATING IN PRACTICE

A2

BTN 10-4 Teams are to select an industry, and each team member is to select a different company in that industry. Each team member is to acquire the financial statements (Form 10-K) of the company selected—see the company's Website or the SEC's EDGAR database (www.SEC.gov). Use the financial statements to compute total asset turnover. Communicate with teammates via a meeting, e-mail, or telephone to discuss the meaning of this ratio, how different companies compare to each other, and the industry norm. The team must prepare a one-page report that describes the ratios for each company and identifies the conclusions reached during the team's discussion.

TAKING IT TO THE NET

C1 P6

BTN 10-5 Access the **Yahoo!** (ticker: YHOO) 10-K report for the year ended December 31, 2006, filed on February 23, 2007, at www.SEC.gov.

Required

1. What amount of goodwill is reported on Yahoo!'s balance sheet? What percentage of total assets does its goodwill represent? Is goodwill a major asset for Yahoo!? Explain.
2. Locate Note 5 to its financial statements. Identify the change in goodwill from December 31, 2005, to December 31, 2006. Comment on the change in goodwill over this period.
3. Locate Note 6 to its financial statements. What are the three categories of intangible assets that Yahoo! reports at December 31, 2006? What proportion of total assets do the intangibles represent?
4. What does Yahoo! indicate is the life of "Trademark, trade name, and domain name" according to its Note 6? Comment on the difference between the estimated economic life and the legal life of Yahoo!'s trademark.

TEAMWORK IN ACTION

C2 A1 P2

Point: This activity can follow an overview of each method. Step 1 allows for three areas of expertise. Larger teams will have some duplication of areas, but the straight-line choice should not be duplicated. Expert teams can use the book and consult with the instructor.

BTN 10-6 Each team member is to become an expert on one depreciation method to facilitate teammates' understanding of that method. Follow these procedures:

a. Each team member is to select an area for expertise from one of the following depreciation methods: straight-line, units-of-production, or double-declining-balance.

b. Expert teams are to be formed from those who have selected the same area of expertise. The instructor will identify the location where each expert team meets.

c. Using the following data, expert teams are to collaborate and develop a presentation answering the requirements. Expert team members must write the presentation in a format they can show to their learning teams.

Data and Requirements On January 8, 2007, Whitewater Riders purchases a van to transport rafters back to the point of departure at the conclusion of the rafting adventures they operate. The cost of the van is $44,000. It has an estimated salvage value of $2,000 and is expected to be used for four years and driven 60,000 miles. The van is driven 12,000 miles in 2007, 18,000 miles in 2008, 21,000 in 2009, and 10,000 in 2010.

1. Compute the annual depreciation expense for each year of the van's estimated useful life.
2. Explain when and how annual depreciation is recorded.
3. Explain the impact on income of this depreciation method versus others over the van's life.
4. Identify the van's book value for each year of its life and illustrate the reporting of this amount for any one year.

d. Re-form original learning teams. In rotation, experts are to present to their teams the results from part *c*. Experts are to encourage and respond to questions.

ENTREPRENEURIAL DECISION

A2

BTN 10-7 Review the chapter's opening feature involving **Sambazon**. Assume that the company currently has net sales of $8,000,000, and that it is planning an expansion that will increase net sales by $4,000,000. To accomplish this expansion, Sambazon must increase its average total assets from $2,500,000 to $3,000,000.

Required

1. Compute the company's total asset turnover under (*a*) current conditions and (*b*) proposed conditions.
2. Evaluate and comment on the merits of the proposal given your analysis in part 1. Identify any concerns you would express about the proposal.

HITTING THE ROAD

C1 P5 P6

BTN 10-8 Team up with one or more classmates for this activity. Identify companies in your community or area that must account for at least one of the following assets: natural resource; patent; lease; leasehold improvement; copyright; trademark; or goodwill. You might find a company having more than one type of asset. Once you identify a company with a specific asset, describe the accounting this company uses to allocate the cost of that asset to the periods benefited from its use.

GLOBAL DECISION

A2

DSG

BTN 10-9 **DSG international**, **Best Buy**, **Circuit City**, and **RadioShack** are all competitors in the global marketplace. Comparative figures for these companies' recent annual accounting periods follow.

	DSG (£ millions)			Best Buy		Circuit City		RadioShack	
(in millions)	Current Year	Prior Year	Two Years Prior	Current Year	Prior Year	Current Year	Prior Year	Current Year	Prior Year
Total assets . .	£3,977	£4,120	£4,104	$13,570	$11,864	$ 4,007	$ 4,069	$2,070	$2,205
Net sales	7,930	6,984	6,983	35,934	30,848	12,430	11,514	4,778	5,082
Total asset turnover . . .	?	?	—	2.83	2.78	3.08	2.91	2.24	2.15

Required

1. Compute the total asset turnover for the most recent two years for DSG using the data shown.
2. Which company is most efficient in generating net sales given the total assets it employs?

ANSWERS TO MULTIPLE CHOICE QUIZ

1. b;

	Appraisal Value	%	Total Cost	Allocated
Land	$175,000	50%	$326,000	$163,000
Land improvements	70,000	20	326,000	65,200
Building	105,000	30	326,000	97,800
Totals	$350,000			$326,000

2. c; ($35,000 − $1,000)/4 years = $8,500 per year.

3. c; 2009: $10,800,000 × (2 × 10%) = $2,160,000
2010: ($10,800,000 − $2,160,000) × (2 × 10%) = $1,728,000

4. c;

Cost of machine	$250,000
Accumulated depreciation	100,000
Book value	150,000
Cash received	120,000
Loss on sale	$ 30,000

5. b; $550,000/$500,000 = 1.10

A Look Back

Chapter 10 focused on long-term assets including plant assets, natural resources, and intangibles. We showed how to account for and analyze those assets.

A Look at This Chapter

This chapter explains how to identify, compute, record, and report current liabilities in financial statements. We also analyze and interpret these liabilities, including those related to employee costs.

A Look Ahead

Chapter 12 explains the partnership form of organization. It also describes the accounting concepts and procedures for partnership transactions.

Chapter 11 Current Liabilities and Payroll Accounting

Learning Objectives

CAP

Conceptual

C1 Describe current and long-term liabilities and their characteristics. *(p. 434)*

C2 Identify and describe known current liabilities. *(p. 436)*

C3 Explain how to account for contingent liabilities. *(p. 445)*

Analytical

A1 Compute the times interest earned ratio and use it to analyze liabilities. *(p. 447)*

Procedural

P1 Prepare entries to account for short-term notes payable. *(p. 437)*

P2 Compute and record *employee* payroll deductions and liabilities. *(p. 439)*

P3 Compute and record *employer* payroll expenses and liabilities. *(p. 441)*

P4 Account for estimated liabilities, including warranties and bonuses. *(p. 443)*

P5 *Appendix 11A*—Identify and describe the details of payroll reports, records, and procedures. *(p. 450)*

LP11

Decision Feature

Granola Gurus

"Get a clear vision and stick to it"—Jason Osborn

NEW YORK—Jason Osborn never planned to be an entrepreneur. "It was sort of an accident," explains Osborn. "I was looking for a healthy snack food as an alternative to cookies and brownies." Osborn starting cooking with granola and his concoctions caught on. After sharing it with his buddy, Jason Wright, the two decided to launch **Feed Granola Company (FeedGranola.com),** a provider of granola snacks made with organic multi-grains.

"We started peddling it . . . to a few different coffee shops and one natural health food store," recalls Osborn. "That created a small demand and we realized we had a viable product." Adds Wright, "I had no idea that I would have a granola company one day!" Their commitment to healthy food carries over to the financial side. The two especially focus on the important task of managing liabilities for payroll, supplies, employee benefits, vacations, training, and taxes. Both insist that effective management of liabilities, especially payroll and employee benefits, is crucial to success. They stress that monitoring and controlling liabilities are a must.

To help control liabilities, Osborn describes how they began by trading their granola products for kitchen space. "We partnered with a meal delivery service and bartered to use their kitchen space," explains Osborn. "We'd bake our granola during the night when they weren't using it and we paid for the usage in granola. That's how we paid rent." Creative payment of liabilities can mean success or failure.

The two continue to monitor liabilities and their payment patterns. "Trying to balance receivables versus payables is always a big challenge," explains Wright. "When you are a small, growing company, cash flow is always a problem." The two insist that accounting for and monitoring liabilities are key to a successful startup. Their company now generates sufficient income to pay for liabilities and produces revenue growth for expansion. "We want to expand our product line," says Osborn. "[Soon] we'll be available in almost every region of the country."

[Sources: *Feed Granola Website,* January 2009; *BusinessWeek,* September 2007; *Inc.com,* July and October 2007; *The Wall Street Journal,* May 2008]

Previous chapters introduced liabilities such as accounts payable, notes payable, wages payable, and unearned revenues. This chapter further explains these liabilities and additional ones such as warranties, taxes, payroll, vacation pay, and bonuses. It also describes contingent liabilities and introduces long-term liabilities. The focus is on how to define, classify, measure, report, and analyze these liabilities so that this information is useful to business decision makers.

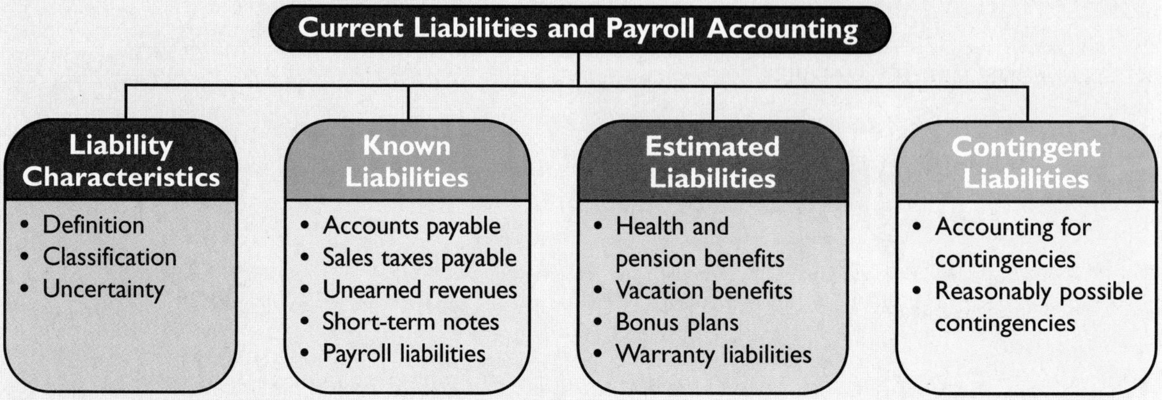

Characteristics of Liabilities

This section discusses important characteristics of liabilities and how liabilities are classified and reported.

Defining Liabilities

C1 Describe current and long-term liabilities and their characteristics.

A *liability* is a probable future payment of assets or services that a company is presently obligated to make as a result of past transactions or events. This definition includes three crucial factors:

1. A past transaction or event.
2. A present obligation.
3. A future payment of assets or services.

These three important elements are portrayed visually in Exhibit 11.1. Liabilities reported in financial statements exhibit those characteristics. No liability is reported when one or more of those characteristics is absent. For example, most companies expect to pay wages to their employees in upcoming months and years, but these future payments are *not* liabilities because no past event such as employee work resulted in a present obligation. Instead, such liabilities arise when employees perform their work and earn the wages.

EXHIBIT 11.1

Characteristics of a Liability

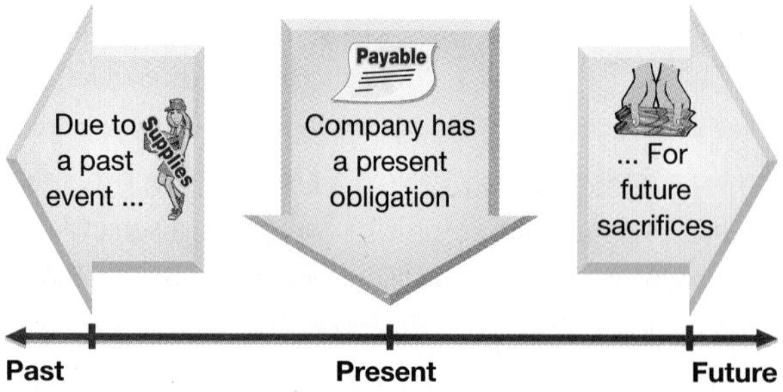

Classifying Liabilities

Video11.1

Information about liabilities is more useful when the balance sheet identifies them as either current or long term. Decision makers need to know when obligations are due so they can plan for them and take appropriate action.

Current Liabilities **Current liabilities,** also called *short-term liabilities,* are obligations due within one year or the company's operating cycle, whichever is longer. They are expected to be paid using current assets or by creating other current liabilities. Common examples of current liabilities are accounts payable, short-term notes payable, wages payable, warranty liabilities, lease liabilities, taxes payable, and unearned revenues.

Point: Improper classification of liabilities can distort ratios used in financial statement analysis and business decisions.

Current liabilities differ across companies because they depend on the type of company operations. **Univision Communications**, for instance, included the following current liabilities related to its Spanish-language media operations ($000s):

Music copyright and artist royalties	$53,054
Program rights obligations	15,658

Harley-Davidson reports a much different set of current liabilities. It discloses current liabilities made up of items such as warranty, recall, and dealer incentive liabilities.

Long-Term Liabilities A company's obligations not expected to be paid within the longer of one year or the company's operating cycle are reported as **long-term liabilities.** They can include long-term notes payable, warranty liabilities, lease liabilities, and bonds payable. They are sometimes reported on the balance sheet in a single long-term liabilities total or in multiple categories. **Domino's Pizza**, for instance, reports long-term liabilities of $982 million. They are reported after current liabilities. A single liability also can be divided between the current and noncurrent sections if a company expects to make payments toward it in both the short and long term. Domino's reports ($ millions) long-term debt, $789.9; and current portion of long-term debt, $1.5. The second item is reported in current liabilities. We sometimes see liabilities that do not have a fixed due date but instead are payable on the creditor's demand. These are reported as current liabilities because of the possibility of payment in the near term. Exhibit 11.2 shows amounts of current liabilities and as a percent of total liabilities for selected companies.

Point: The current ratio is overstated if a company fails to classify any portion of long-term debt due next period as a current liability.

EXHIBIT 11.2

Current Liabilities of Selected Companies

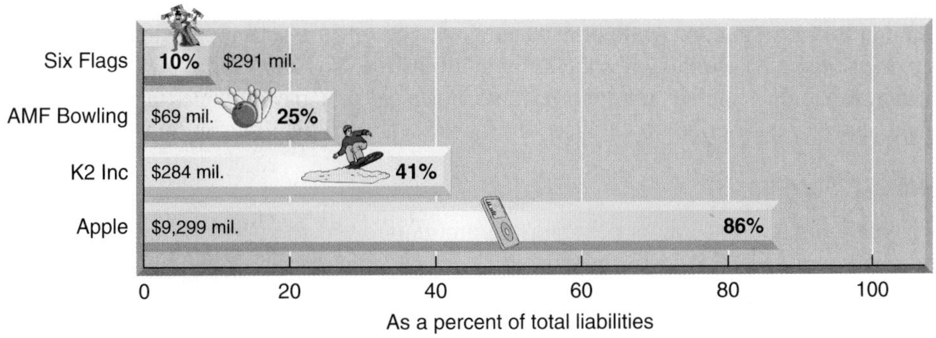

Uncertainty in Liabilities

Accounting for liabilities involves addressing three important questions: Whom to pay? When to pay? How much to pay? Answers to these questions are often decided when a liability is incurred. For example, if a company has a $100 account payable to a specific individual, payable on March 15, the answers are clear. The company knows whom to pay, when to pay, and how much to pay. However, the answers to one or more of these questions are uncertain for some liabilities.

Uncertainty in Whom to Pay Liabilities can involve uncertainty in whom to pay. For instance, a company can create a liability with a known amount when issuing a note that is payable to its holder. In this case, a specific amount is payable to the note's holder at a specified date, but the company does not know who the holder is until that date. Despite this uncertainty, the company reports this liability on its balance sheet.

Point: An *accrued expense* is an unpaid expense, and is also called an *accrued liability.*

Uncertainty in When to Pay A company can have an obligation of a known amount to a known creditor but not know when it must be paid. For example, a legal services firm can accept fees in advance from a client who plans to use the firm's services in the future. This means that the firm has a liability that it settles by providing services at an unknown future date. Although this uncertainty exists, the legal firm's balance sheet must report this liability. These types of obligations are reported as current liabilities because they are likely to be settled in the short term.

Uncertainty in How Much to Pay A company can be aware of an obligation but not know how much will be required to settle it. For example, a company using electrical power is billed only after the meter has been read. This cost is incurred and the liability created before a bill is received. A liability to the power company is reported as an estimated amount if the balance sheet is prepared before a bill arrives.

Decision Insight

IFRSs IFRSs record a contingent liability when an obligation exists from a past event if there is a 'probable' outflow of resources *and* the amount can be estimated reliably. However, IFRSs define probable as 'more likely than not' while U.S. GAAP defines it as 'likely to occur.'

Quick Check

Answers—p. 458

1. What is a liability? Identify its crucial characteristics.
2. Is every expected future payment a liability?
3. If a liability is payable in 15 months, is it classified as current or long term?

Known Liabilities

Video11.1

Most liabilities arise from situations with little uncertainty. They are set by agreements, contracts, or laws and are measurable. These liabilities are **known liabilities,** also called *definitely determinable liabilities.* Known liabilities include accounts payable, notes payable, payroll, sales taxes, unearned revenues, and leases. We describe how to account for these known liabilities in this section.

Accounts Payable

C2 Identify and describe known current liabilities.

Accounts payable, or trade accounts payable, are amounts owed to suppliers for products or services purchased on credit. Accounting for accounts payable is primarily explained and illustrated in our discussion of merchandising activities in Chapters 5 and 6.

Sales Taxes Payable

Nearly all states and many cities levy taxes on retail sales. Sales taxes are stated as a percent of selling prices. The seller collects sales taxes from customers when sales occur and remits these collections (often monthly) to the proper government agency. Since sellers currently owe these collections to the government, this amount is a current liability. **Home Depot**, for instance, reports sales taxes payable of $475 million in its recent annual report. To illustrate, if Home Depot sells materials on August 31 for $6,000 cash that are subject to a 5% sales tax, the revenue portion of this transaction is recorded as follows:

Assets	=	Liabilities	+	Equity
+6,300		+300		+6,000

Aug. 31	Cash	6,300	
	Sales.		6,000
	Sales Taxes Payable ($6,000 × 0.05).		300
	To record cash sales and 5% sales tax.		

Sales Taxes Payable is debited and Cash credited when it remits these collections to the government. Sales Taxes Payable is not an expense. It arises because laws require sellers to collect this cash from customers for the government.[1]

Unearned Revenues

Unearned revenues (also called *deferred revenues, collections in advance,* and *prepayments*) are amounts received in advance from customers for future products or services. Advance ticket sales for sporting events or music concerts are examples. **Bon Jovi**, for instance, has "deferred revenues" from advance ticket sales. To illustrate, assume that Bon Jovi sells $5 million in tickets for eight concerts; the entry is

Point: To *defer* a revenue means to postpone recognition of a revenue collected in advance until it is earned. Sport teams must defer recognition of ticket sales until games are played.

June 30	Cash	5,000,000	
	Unearned Ticket Revenue		5,000,000
	To record sale of concert tickets.		

Assets = Liabilities + Equity
+5,000,000 +5,000,000

When a concert is played, Bon Jovi would record revenue for the portion earned.

Oct. 31	Unearned Ticket Revenue	625,000	
	Ticket Revenue		625,000
	To record concert ticket revenues earned.		

Assets = Liabilities + Equity
−625,000 +625,000

Unearned Ticket Revenue is an unearned revenue account and is reported as a current liability. Unearned revenues also arise with airline ticket sales, magazine subscriptions, construction projects, hotel reservations, and custom orders.

Decision Insight

Reward Programs Gift card sales now exceed $100 billion annually, and reward (also called loyalty) programs are growing. There are no exact rules for how retailers account for rewards. When **Best Buy** launched its "Reward Zone," shoppers earned $5 on each $125 spent and had 90 days to spend it. Retailers make assumptions about how many reward program dollars will be spent and how to report it. Best Buy sets up a liability and reduces revenue by the same amount. **Talbots** does not reduce revenue but instead increases selling expense. **Men's Wearhouse** records rewards in cost of goods sold, whereas **Neiman Marcus** subtracts them from revenue. The FASB is reviewing reward programs.

Short-Term Notes Payable

P1 Prepare entries to account for short-term notes payable.

A **short-term note payable** is a written promise to pay a specified amount on a definite future date within one year or the company's operating cycle, whichever is longer. These promissory notes are negotiable (as are checks), meaning they can be transferred from party to party by endorsement. The written documentation provided by notes is helpful in resolving disputes and for pursuing legal actions involving these liabilities. Most notes payable bear interest to compensate for use of the money until payment is made. Short-term notes payable can arise from many transactions. A company that purchases merchandise on credit can sometimes extend the credit period by signing a note to replace an account payable. Such notes also can arise when money is borrowed from a bank. We describe both of these cases.

Point: Required characteristics for negotiability of a note: (1) unconditional promise, (2) in writing, (3) specific amount, and (4) definite due date.

---

[1] Sales taxes can be computed from total sales receipts when sales taxes are not separately identified on the register. To illustrate, assume a 5% sales tax and $420 in total sales receipts (which includes sales taxes). Sales are computed as follows:

$$\text{Sales} = \text{Total sales receipts}/(1 + \text{Sales tax percentage}) = \$420/1.05 = \$400$$

Thus, the sales tax amount equals total sales receipts minus sales, or $420 − $400 = $20.

Note Given to Extend Credit Period A company can replace an account payable with a note payable. A common example is a creditor that requires the substitution of an interest-bearing note for an overdue account payable that does not bear interest. A less common situation occurs when a debtor's weak financial condition motivates the creditor to accept a note, sometimes for a lesser amount, and to close the account to ensure that this customer makes no additional credit purchases.

To illustrate, let's assume that on August 23, Brady Company asks to extend its past-due $600 account payable to McGraw. After some negotiations, McGraw agrees to accept $100 cash and a 60-day, 12%, $500 note payable to replace the account payable. Brady records the transaction with this entry:

Assets	=	Liabilities	+	Equity
−100		−600		
		+500		

Aug. 23	Accounts Payable—McGraw	600	
	Cash		100
	Notes Payable—McGraw.		500
	Gave $100 cash and a 60-day, 12% note for payment on account.		

Point: Accounts payable are detailed in a subsidiary ledger, but notes payable are sometimes not. A file with copies of notes can serve as a subsidiary ledger.

Signing the note does not resolve Brady's debt. Instead, the form of debt is changed from an account payable to a note payable. McGraw prefers the note payable over the account payable because it earns interest and it is written documentation of the debt's existence, term, and amount. When the note comes due, Brady pays the note and interest by giving McGraw a check for $510. Brady records that payment with this entry:

Assets	=	Liabilities	+	Equity
−510		−500		−10

Oct. 22	Notes Payable—McGraw	500	
	Interest Expense	10	
	Cash		510
	Paid note with interest ($500 × 12% × 60/360).		

Point: Commercial companies commonly compute interest using a 360-day year. This is known as the *banker's rule.*

Interest expense is computed by multiplying the principal of the note ($500) by the annual interest rate (12%) for the fraction of the year the note is outstanding (60 days/360 days).

Note Given to Borrow from Bank A bank nearly always requires a borrower to sign a promissory note when making a loan. When the note matures, the borrower repays the note with an amount larger than the amount borrowed. The difference between the amount borrowed and the amount repaid is *interest.* This section considers a type of note whose signer promises to pay *principal* (the amount borrowed) plus interest. In this case, the *face value* of the note equals principal. Face value is the value shown on the face (front) of the note. To illustrate, assume that a company needs $2,000 for a project and borrows this money from a bank at 12% annual interest. The loan is made on September 30, 2009, and is due in 60 days. Specifically, the borrowing company signs a note with a face value equal to the amount borrowed. The note includes a statement similar to this: *"I promise to pay $2,000 plus interest at 12% within 60 days after September 30."* This simple note is shown in Exhibit 11.3.

Point: When money is borrowed from a bank, the loan is reported as an asset (receivable) on the bank's balance sheet.

EXHIBIT 11.3

Note with Face Value Equal to Amount Borrowed

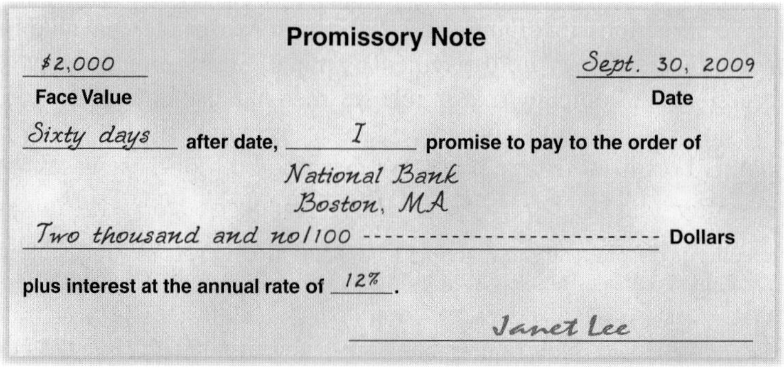
Promissory Note

$2,000 — Face Value

Sept. 30, 2009 — Date

Sixty days after date, I promise to pay to the order of

National Bank
Boston, MA

Two thousand and no/100 ------------------------ Dollars

plus interest at the annual rate of 12%.

Janet Lee

The borrower records its receipt of cash and the new liability with this entry:

Sept. 30	Cash	2,000	
	Notes Payable.		2,000
	Borrowed $2,000 cash with a 60-day, 12%, $2,000 note.		

Assets = Liabilities + Equity
+2,000 +2,000

When principal and interest are paid, the borrower records payment with this entry:

Nov. 29	Notes Payable	2,000	
	Interest Expense	40	
	Cash		2,040
	Paid note with interest ($2,000 × 12% × 60/360).		

Assets = Liabilities + Equity
−2,040 −2,000 −40

End-of-period interest adjustment. When the end of an accounting period occurs between the signing of a note payable and its maturity date, the *matching principle* requires us to record the accrued but unpaid interest on the note. To illustrate, let's return to the note in Exhibit 11.3, but assume that the company borrows $2,000 cash on December 16, 2009, instead of September 30. This 60-day note matures on February 14, 2010, and the company's fiscal year ends on December 31. Thus, we need to record interest expense for the final 15 days in December. This means that one-fourth (15 days/60 days) of the $40 total interest is an expense of year 2009. The borrower records this expense with the following adjusting entry:

2009			
Dec. 31	Interest Expense	10	
	Interest Payable		10
	To record accrued interest on note ($2,000 × 12% × 15/360).		

Assets = Liabilities + Equity
+10 −10

When this note matures on February 14, the borrower must recognize 45 days of interest expense for year 2010 and remove the balances of the two liability accounts:

Example: If this note is dated Dec. 1 instead of Dec. 16, how much expense is recorded on Dec. 31? *Answer:* $2,000 × 12% × 30/360 = $20

2010			
Feb. 14	Interest Expense*.	30	
	Interest Payable	10	
	Notes Payable	2,000	
	Cash		2,040
	*Paid note with interest. *($2,000 × 12% × 45/360)*		

Assets = Liabilities + Equity
−2,040 −10 −30
−2,000

Decision Insight

Many franchisors such as **Geeks on Call, Techs in a Sec,** and **Nerds on Site,** use notes to help entrepreneurs acquire their own franchises, including using notes to pay for the franchise fee and any equipment. Payments on these notes are usually collected monthly and often are secured by the franchisees' assets.

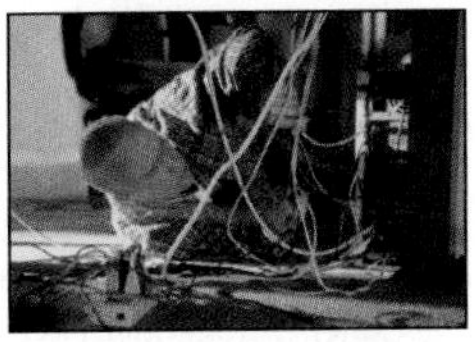

Payroll Liabilities

P2 Compute and record employee payroll deductions and liabilities.

An employer incurs several expenses and liabilities from having employees. These expenses and liabilities are often large and arise from salaries and wages earned, from employee benefits, and from payroll taxes levied on the employer. **Anheuser-Busch**, for instance, reports payroll-related current liabilities of more than $342.8 million from "accrued salaries, wages and benefits." We discuss payroll liabilities and related accounts in this section. The appendix to this chapter describes details about payroll reports, records, and procedures.

Point: Internal control is important for payroll accounting. Managers must monitor (1) employee hiring, (2) timekeeping, (3) payroll listings, and (4) payroll payments. Poor controls led the U.S. Army to pay nearly $10 million to deserters, fictitious soldiers, and other unauthorized entities.

Employee Payroll Deductions **Gross pay** is the total compensation an employee earns including wages, salaries, commissions, bonuses, and any compensation earned before deductions such as taxes. (*Wages* usually refer to payments to employees at an hourly rate. *Salaries* usually refer to payments to employees at a monthly or yearly rate.) **Net pay,** also called *take-home pay,* is gross pay less all deductions. **Payroll deductions,** commonly called *withholdings,* are amounts withheld from an employee's gross pay, either required or voluntary. Required deductions result from laws and include income taxes and Social Security taxes. Voluntary deductions, at an employee's option, include pension and health contributions, union dues, and charitable giving. Exhibit 11.4 shows the typical payroll deductions of an employee. The employer withholds payroll deductions from employees' pay and is obligated to transmit this money to the designated organization. The employer records payroll deductions as current liabilities until these amounts are transmitted. This section discusses the major payroll deductions.

EXHIBIT 11.4

Payroll Deductions

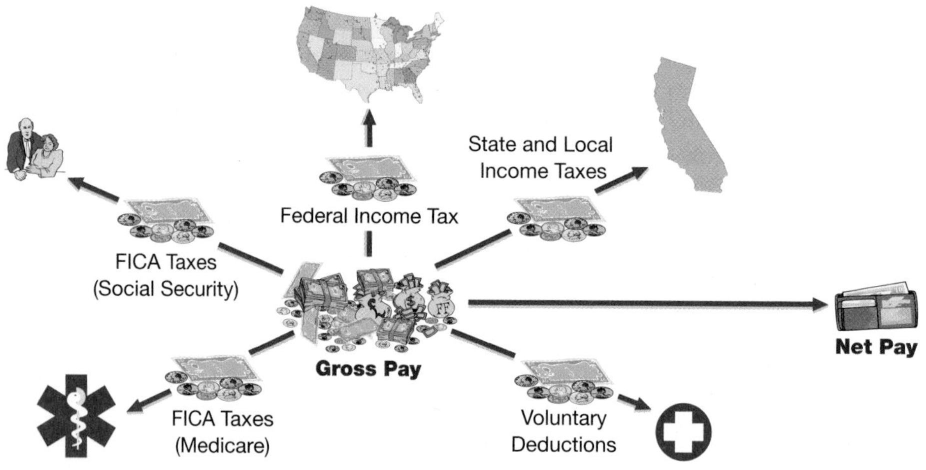

Employee FICA taxes. The federal Social Security system provides retirement, disability, survivorship, and medical benefits to qualified workers. Laws *require* employers to withhold **Federal Insurance Contributions Act (FICA) taxes** from employees' pay to cover costs of the system. Employers usually separate FICA taxes into two groups: (1) retirement, disability, and survivorship and (2) medical. For the first group, the Social Security system provides monthly cash payments to qualified retired workers for the rest of their lives. These payments are often called *Social Security benefits.* Taxes related to this group are often called *Social Security taxes.* For the second group, the system provides monthly payments to deceased workers' surviving families and to disabled workers who qualify for assistance. These payments are commonly called *Medicare benefits;* like those in the first group, they are paid with *Medicare taxes* (part of FICA taxes).

Law requires employers to withhold FICA taxes from each employee's salary or wages on each payday. The taxes for Social Security and Medicare are computed separately. For example, for the year 2008, the amount withheld from each employee's pay for Social Security tax was 6.2% of the first $102,000 the employee earns in the calendar year, or a maximum of $6,324. The Medicare tax was 1.45% of *all* amounts the employee earns; there is no maximum limit to Medicare tax.

Point: The sources of U.S. tax receipts are roughly as follows:

50%	Personal income tax
35	FICA and FUTA taxes
10	Corporate income tax
5	Other taxes

Employers must pay withheld taxes to the Internal Revenue Service (IRS) on specific filing dates during the year. Employers who fail to send the withheld taxes to the IRS on time can be assessed substantial penalties. Until all the taxes are sent to the IRS, they are included in employers' current liabilities. For any changes in rates or with the maximum earnings level, check the IRS Website at www.IRS.gov or the SSA Website at www.SSA.gov.

Point: Part-time employees may claim "exempt from withholding" if they did not have any income tax liability in the prior year and do not expect any in the current year.

Employee income tax. Most employers are required to withhold federal income tax from each employee's paycheck. The amount withheld is computed using tables published by the IRS. The amount depends on the employee's annual earnings rate and the number of *withholding allowances* the employee claims. Allowances reduce the amount of taxes one owes the government. The more allowances one claims, the less tax the employer will withhold. Employees can claim allowances for themselves and their dependents. They also can claim additional allowances if they expect major declines in their taxable income for medical expenses. (An employee who claims more allowances than appropriate is subject to a fine.) Most states and many local governments require employers to withhold income taxes from employees' pay and to remit them promptly to the proper government agency. Until they are paid, withholdings are reported as a current liability on the employer's balance sheet.

Point: IRS withholding tables are based on projecting weekly (or other period) pay into an annual figure.

Employee voluntary deductions. Beyond Social Security, Medicare, and income taxes, employers often withhold other amounts from employees' earnings. These withholdings arise from employee requests, contracts, unions, or other agreements. They can include amounts for charitable giving, medical insurance premiums, pension contributions, and union dues. Until they are paid, such withholdings are reported as part of employers' current liabilities.

Recording employee payroll deductions. Employers must accrue payroll expenses and liabilities at the end of each pay period. To illustrate, assume that an employee earns a salary of $2,000 per month. At the end of January, the employer's entry to accrue payroll expenses and liabilities for this employee is

Jan. 31	Salaries Expense	2,000	
	FICA—Social Security Taxes Payable (6.2%)		124
	FICA—Medicare Taxes Payable (1.45%)		29
	Employee Federal Income Taxes Payable*		213
	Employee Medical Insurance Payable*		85
	Employee Union Dues Payable*		25
	Salaries Payable		1,524
	To record accrued payroll for January.		

Assets	=	Liabilities	+	Equity
		+124		−2,000
		+29		
		+213		
		+85		
		+25		
		+1,524		

* Amounts taken from employer's accounting records.

Salaries Expense (debit) shows that the employee earns a gross salary of $2,000. The first five payables (credits) show the liabilities the employer owes on behalf of this employee to cover FICA taxes, income taxes, medical insurance, and union dues. The Salaries Payable account (credit) records the $1,524 net pay the employee receives from the $2,000 gross pay earned. When the employee is paid, another entry (or a series of entries) is required to record the check written and distributed (or funds transferred). The entry to record cash payment to this employee is to debit Salaries Payable and credit Cash for $1,524.

Decision Insight

A company's delay or failure to pay withholding taxes to the government has severe consequences. For example, a 100% penalty can be levied, with interest, on the unpaid balance. The government can even close a company, take its assets, and pursue legal actions against those involved.

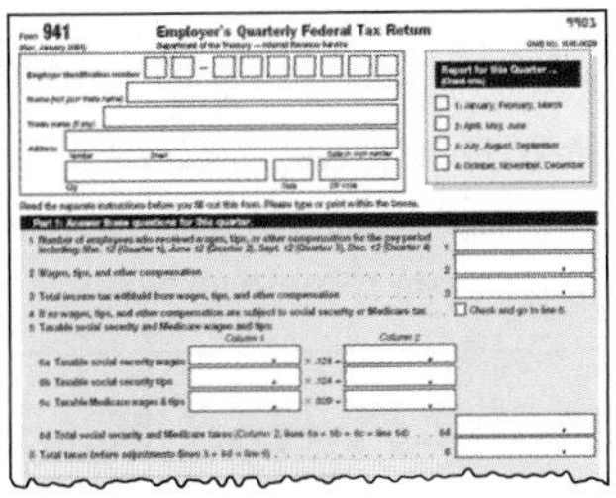

Employer Payroll Taxes

Employers must pay payroll taxes in addition to those required of employees. Employer taxes include FICA and unemployment taxes.

P3 Compute and record *employer* payroll expenses and liabilities.

Employer FICA tax. Employers must pay FICA taxes *equal in amount to* the FICA taxes withheld from their employees. An employer's tax is credited to the same FICA Taxes Payable accounts used to record the Social Security and Medicare taxes withheld from employees. (A self-employed person must pay both the employee and employer FICA taxes.)

Federal and state unemployment taxes. The federal government participates with states in a joint federal and state unemployment insurance program. Each state administers its program. These programs provide unemployment benefits to qualified workers. The federal government approves state programs and pays a portion of their administrative expenses.

Federal Unemployment Taxes (FUTA). Employers are subject to a federal unemployment tax on wages and salaries paid to their employees. For the year 2008, employers were required to pay FUTA taxes of as much as 6.2% of the first $7,000 earned by each employee. This federal tax can be reduced by a credit of up to 5.4% for taxes paid to a state program. As a result, the net federal unemployment tax is often only 0.8%.

State Unemployment Taxes (SUTA). All states support their unemployment insurance programs by placing a payroll tax on employers. (A few states require employees to make a contribution. In the book's assignments, we assume that this tax is only on the employer.) In most states, the base rate for SUTA taxes is 5.4% of the first $7,000 paid each employee. This base rate is adjusted according to an employer's merit rating. The state assigns a **merit rating** that reflects a company's stability or instability in employing workers. A good rating reflects stability in employment and means an employer can pay less than the 5.4% base rate. A low rating reflects high turnover or seasonal hirings and layoffs. To illustrate, an employer with 50 employees each of whom earns $7,000 or more per year saves $15,400 annually if it has a merit rating of 1.0% versus 5.4%. This is computed by comparing taxes of $18,900 at the 5.4% rate to only $3,500 at the 1.0% rate.

Recording employer payroll taxes. Employer payroll taxes are an added expense beyond the wages and salaries earned by employees. These taxes are often recorded in an entry separate from the one recording payroll expenses and deductions. To illustrate, assume that the $2,000 recorded salaries expense from the previous example is earned by an employee whose earnings have not yet reached $5,000 for the year. This means the entire salaries expense for this period is subject to tax because year-to-date pay is under $7,000. Also assume that the federal unemployment tax rate is 0.8% and the state unemployment tax rate is 5.4%. Consequently, the FICA portion of the employer's tax is $153, computed by multiplying both the 6.2% and 1.45% by the $2,000 gross pay. Moreover, state unemployment (SUTA) taxes are $108 (5.4% of the $2,000 gross pay), and federal unemployment (FUTA) taxes are $16 (0.8% of $2,000). The entry to record the employer's payroll tax expense and related liabilities is

Example: If the employer's merit rating in this example reduces its SUTA rate to 2.9%, what is its SUTA liability? *Answer:* SUTA payable = $2,000 × 2.9% = $58

Assets	=	Liabilities	+	Equity
		+124		−277
		+29		
		+108		
		+16		

Jan. 31	Payroll Taxes Expense	277	
	FICA—Social Security Taxes Payable (6.2%)		124
	FICA—Medicare Taxes Payable (1.45%)		29
	State Unemployment Taxes Payable		108
	Federal Unemployment Taxes Payable		16
	To record employer payroll taxes.		

Decision Ethics

Web Designer You take a summer job working for a family friend who runs a small IT service. On your first payday, the owner slaps you on the back, gives you full payment in cash, winks, and adds: "No need to pay those high taxes, eh." What action, if any, do you take? [Answer—p. 458]

Multi-Period Known Liabilities

Many known liabilities extend over multiple periods. These often include unearned revenues and notes payable. For example, if **Sports Illustrated** sells a four-year magazine subscription, it records amounts received for this subscription in an Unearned Subscription Revenues account. Amounts in this account are liabilities, but are they current or long term? They are *both.* The portion of the Unearned Subscription Revenues account that will be fulfilled in the next year is reported as a current liability. The remaining portion is reported as a long-term liability.

The same analysis applies to notes payable. For example, a borrower reports a three-year note payable as a long-term liability in the first two years it is outstanding. In the third year, the borrower reclassifies this note as a current liability since it is due within one year or the operating cycle, whichever is longer. The **current portion of long-term debt** refers to that part of long-term debt due within one year or the operating cycle, whichever is longer. Long-term debt is reported under long-term liabilities, but the *current portion due* is reported under current liabilities. To illustrate, assume that a $7,500 debt is paid in installments of $1,500 per year for five years. The $1,500 due within the year is reported as a current liability. No journal entry is necessary for this reclassification. Instead, we simply classify the amounts for debt as either current or long term when the balance sheet is prepared.

Some known liabilities are rarely reported in long-term liabilities. These include accounts payable, sales taxes, and wages and salaries.

Point: Alternatively, some accounting systems do make an entry to transfer the current amount due out of Long-Term Debt and into the Current Portion of Long-Term Debt.

Decision Insight

Liability Limits Probably the greatest number of frauds involve payroll. Companies must safeguard payroll activities. Controls include proper approvals and processes for employee additions, deletions, and pay rate changes. A common fraud is a manager adding a fictitious employee to the payroll and then cashing the fictitious employee's check.

Quick Check

Answers—p. 458

4. Why does a creditor prefer a note payable to a past-due account payable?
5. A company pays its one employee $3,000 per month. This company's FUTA rate is 0.8% on the first $7,000 earned; its SUTA rate is 4.0% on the first $7,000; its Social Security tax rate is 6.2% of the first $102,000; and its Medicare tax rate is 1.45% of all amounts earned. The entry to record this company's March payroll includes what amount for total payroll taxes expense?
6. Identify whether the employer or employee or both incurs each of the following: (*a*) FICA taxes, (*b*) FUTA taxes, (*c*) SUTA taxes, and (*d*) withheld income taxes.

Estimated Liabilities

An **estimated liability** is a known obligation that is of an uncertain amount but that can be reasonably estimated. Common examples are employee benefits such as pensions, health care and vacation pay, and warranties offered by a seller. We discuss each of these in this section. Other examples of estimated liabilities include property taxes and certain contracts to provide future services.

P4 Account for estimated liabilities, including warranties and bonuses.

Health and Pension Benefits

Many companies provide **employee benefits** beyond salaries and wages. An employer often pays all or part of medical, dental, life, and disability insurance. Many employers also contribute to *pension plans,* which are agreements by employers to provide benefits (payments) to employees after retirement. Many companies also provide medical care and insurance benefits to their retirees. When payroll taxes and charges for employee benefits are totaled, payroll cost often exceeds employees' gross earnings by 25% or more.

To illustrate, assume that an employer agrees to (1) pay an amount for medical insurance equal to $8,000 and (2) contribute an additional 10% of the employees' $120,000 gross salary to a retirement program. The entry to record these accrued benefits is

Dec. 31	Employee Benefits Expense	20,000	
	Employee Medical Insurance Payable		8,000
	Employee Retirement Program Payable		12,000
	To record costs of employee benefits.		

Assets	=	Liabilities	+	Equity
		+8,000		−20,000
		+12,000		

Decision Insight

Postgame Spoils Baseball was the first pro sport to set up a pension, originally up to $100 per month depending on years played. Many former players now take home six-figure pensions. Cal Ripken Jr.'s pension when he reaches 62 is estimated at $160,000 per year (he played 21 seasons). The requirement is only 43 games for a full pension and just one game for full medical benefits.

Vacation Benefits

Many employers offer paid vacation benefits, also called *paid absences*. To illustrate, assume that salaried employees earn 2 weeks' vacation per year. This benefit increases employers' payroll expenses because employees are paid for 52 weeks but work for only 50 weeks. Total annual salary is the same, but the cost per week worked is greater than the amount paid per week. For example, if an employee is paid $20,800 for 52 weeks but works only 50 weeks, the total weekly expense to the employer is $416 ($20,800/50 weeks) instead of the $400 cash paid weekly to the employee ($20,800/52 weeks). The $16 difference between these two amounts is recorded weekly as follows:

Assets = Liabilities + Equity
+16 −16

	Vacation Benefits Expense	16	
	Vacation Benefits Payable		16
	To record vacation benefits accrued.		

Vacation Benefits Expense is an operating expense, and Vacation Benefits Payable is a current liability. When the employee takes a vacation, the employer reduces (debits) the Vacation Benefits Payable and credits Cash (no additional expense is recorded).

Bonus Plans

Many companies offer bonuses to employees, and many of the bonuses depend on net income. To illustrate, assume that an employer offers a bonus to its employees equal to 5% of the company's annual net income (to be equally shared by all). The company's expected annual net income is $210,000. The year-end adjusting entry to record this benefit is

Assets = Liabilities + Equity
+10,000 −10,000

Dec. 31	Employee Bonus Expense*	10,000	
	Bonus Payable		10,000
	To record expected bonus costs.		

* Bonus Expense (B) equals 5% of net income, which equals $210,000 minus the bonus; this is computed as:

$$B = 0.05\ (\$210{,}000 - B)$$
$$B = \$10{,}500 - 0.05B$$
$$1.05B = \$10{,}500$$
$$\mathbf{B = \$10{,}500/1.05 = \$10{,}000}$$

When the bonus is paid, Bonus Payable is debited and Cash is credited for $10,000.

Warranty Liabilities

Point: Kodak recently reported $60 million in warranty obligations.

A **warranty** is a seller's obligation to replace or correct a product (or service) that fails to perform as expected within a specified period. Most new cars, for instance, are sold with a warranty covering parts for a specified period of time. **Ford Motor Company** reported more than $21.9 billion in "dealer and customer allowances and claims" in its annual report. To comply with the *full disclosure* and *matching principles,* the seller reports the expected warranty expense in the period when revenue from the sale of the product or service is reported. The seller reports this warranty obligation as a liability, although the existence, amount, payee, and date of future sacrifices are uncertain. This is because such warranty costs are probable and the amount can be estimated using, for instance, past experience with warranties.

To illustrate, a dealer sells a used car for $16,000 on December 1, 2009, with a maximum one-year or 12,000-mile warranty covering parts. This dealer's experience shows that warranty expense averages about 4% of a car's selling price, or $640 in this case ($16,000 × 4%). The dealer records the estimated expense and liability related to this sale with this entry:

Assets = Liabilities + Equity
+640 −640

2009			
Dec. 1	Warranty Expense	640	
	Estimated Warranty Liability		640
	To record estimated warranty expense.		

This entry alternatively could be made as part of end-of-period adjustments. Either way, the estimated warranty expense is reported on the 2009 income statement and the warranty liability on the 2009 balance sheet. To further extend this example, suppose the customer returns the car for warranty repairs on January 9, 2010. The dealer performs this work by replacing parts costing $200. The entry to record partial settlement of the estimated warranty liability is

Point: Recognition of warranty liabilities is necessary to comply with the matching and full disclosure principles.

2010			
Jan. 9	Estimated Warranty Liability	200	
	Auto Parts Inventory		200
	To record costs of warranty repairs.		

Assets = Liabilities + Equity
−200 −200

This entry reduces the balance of the estimated warranty liability. Warranty expense was previously recorded in 2009, the year the car was sold with the warranty. Finally, what happens if total warranty expenses are more or less than the estimated 4%, or $640? The answer is that management should monitor actual warranty expenses to see whether the 4% rate is accurate. If experience reveals a large difference from the estimate, the rate for current and future sales should be changed. Differences are expected, but they should be small.

Decision Insight

Guaranteed Profits **Best Buy** and **Circuit City** profit from sales of extended-warranty contracts with their electronics [*BusinessWeek*, 2004].

	Best Buy	Circuit City
Warranty contracts as a percentage of sales	4.0%	3.3%
Warranty contracts as a percentage of operating profit	45	100
Profit margin on warranty contracts	60	50

Multi-Period Estimated Liabilities

Estimated liabilities can be both current and long term. For example, pension liabilities to employees are long term to workers who will not retire within the next period. For employees who are retired or will retire within the next period, a portion of pension liabilities is current. Other examples include employee health benefits and warranties. Specifically, many warranties are for 30 or 60 days in length. Estimated costs under these warranties are properly reported in current liabilities. Many other automobile warranties are for three years or 36,000 miles. A portion of these warranties is reported as long term.

Quick Check

Answers—p. 458

7. Estimated liabilities involve an obligation to pay which of these? (*a*) An uncertain but reasonably estimated amount owed on a known obligation or (*b*) A known amount to a specific entity on an uncertain due date.
8. A car is sold for $15,000 on June 1, 2009, with a one-year warranty on parts. Warranty expense is estimated at 1.5% of selling price at each calendar year-end. On March 1, 2010, the car is returned for warranty repairs costing $135. The amount recorded as warranty expense on March 1 is (*a*) $0; (*b*) $60; (*c*) $75; (*d*) $135; (*e*) $225.

Contingent Liabilities

C3 Explain how to account for contingent liabilities.

A **contingent liability** is a potential obligation that depends on a future event arising from a past transaction or event. An example is a pending lawsuit. Here, a past transaction or event leads to a lawsuit whose result depends on the outcome of the suit. Future payment of a contingent liability depends on whether an uncertain future event occurs.

Accounting for Contingent Liabilities

Accounting for contingent liabilities depends on the likelihood that a future event will occur and the ability to estimate the future amount owed if this event occurs. Three different possibilities are identified in the following chart: record liability, disclose in notes, or no disclosure.

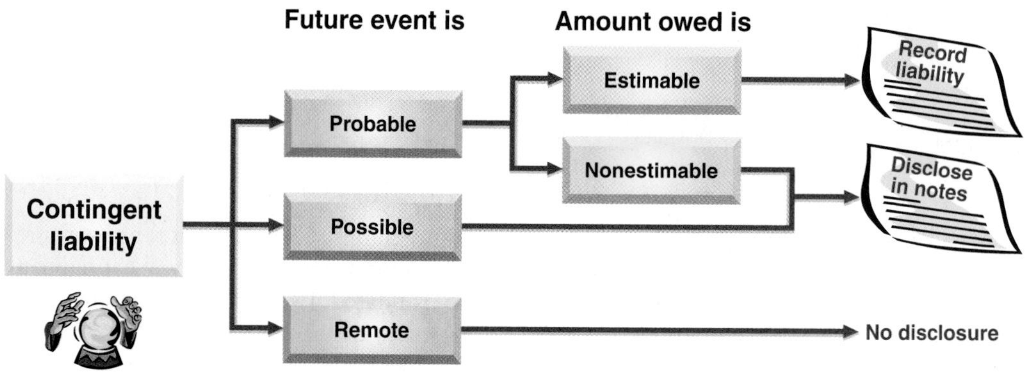

The conditions that determine each of these three possibilities follow:

1. The future event is *probable* (likely) and the amount owed can be *reasonably estimated.* We then record this amount as a liability. Examples are the estimated liabilities described earlier such as warranties, vacation pay, and income taxes.
2. The future event is *reasonably possible* (could occur). We disclose information about this type of contingent liability in notes to the financial statements.
3. The future event is *remote* (unlikely). We do not record or disclose information on remote contingent liabilities.

Point: A contingency is an *if.* Namely, if a future event occurs, then financial consequences are likely for the entity.

Reasonably Possible Contingent Liabilities

This section identifies and discusses contingent liabilities that commonly fall in the second category—when the future event is reasonably possible. Disclosing information about contingencies in this category is motivated by the *full-disclosure principle,* which requires information relevant to decision makers be reported and not ignored.

Potential Legal Claims Many companies are sued or at risk of being sued. The accounting issue is whether the defendant should recognize a liability on its balance sheet or disclose a contingent liability in its notes while a lawsuit is outstanding and not yet settled. The answer is that a potential claim is recorded in the accounts *only* if payment for damages is probable and the amount can be reasonably estimated. If the potential claim cannot be reasonably estimated or is less than probable but reasonably possible, it is disclosed. **Ford Motor Company**, for example, includes the following note in its annual report: "Various legal actions, governmental investigations and proceedings and claims are pending . . . arising out of alleged defects in our products."

Point: A sale of a note receivable is often a contingent liability. It becomes a liability if the original signer of the note fails to pay it at maturity.

Debt Guarantees Sometimes a company guarantees the payment of debt owed by a supplier, customer, or another company. The guarantor usually discloses the guarantee in its financial statement notes as a contingent liability. If it is probable that the debtor will default, the guarantor needs to record and report the guarantee in its financial statements as a liability. The **Boston Celtics** report a unique guarantee when it comes to coaches and players: "Certain of the contracts provide for guaranteed payments which must be paid even if the employee [player] is injured or terminated."

Other Contingencies Other examples of contingencies include environmental damages, possible tax assessments, insurance losses, and government investigations. **Sunoco**, for instance, reports that "federal, state and local laws . . . result in liabilities and loss contingencies. Sunoco accrues . . . cleanup costs [that] are probable and reasonably estimable. Management believes it is reasonably possible (i.e., less than probable but greater than remote) that additional . . . losses will be incurred." Many of Sunoco's contingencies are revealed only in notes.

Point: Auditors and managers often have different views about whether a contingency is recorded, disclosed, or omitted.

Decision Insight

Pricing Priceless What's it worth to see from one side of the Grand Canyon to the other? What's the cost when beaches are closed due to pollution? A method to measure environmental liabilities is *contingent valuation,* by which people answer such questions. Regulators use their answers to levy fines and assess punitive damages.

Uncertainties That Are Not Contingencies

All organizations face uncertainties from future events such as natural disasters and the development of new competing products or services. These uncertainties are not contingent liabilities because they are future events *not* arising from past transactions. Accordingly, they are not disclosed.

Quick Check

Answers—p. 458

9. A future payment is reported as a liability on the balance sheet if payment is contingent on a future event that (*a*) is reasonably possible but the payment cannot be reasonably estimated; (*b*) is probable and the payment can be reasonably estimated; or (*c*) is not probable but the payment is known.
10. Under what circumstances is a future payment reported in the notes to the financial statements as a contingent liability?

Times Interest Earned Ratio

Decision Analysis

A1 Compute the times interest earned ratio and use it to analyze liabilities.

A company incurs interest expense on many of its current and long-term liabilities. Examples extend from its short-term notes and the current portion of long-term liabilities to its long-term notes and bonds. Interest expense is often viewed as a *fixed expense* because the amount of these liabilities is likely to remain in one form or another for a substantial period of time. This means that the amount of interest is unlikely to vary due to changes in sales or other operating activities. While fixed expenses can be advantageous when a company is growing, they create risk. This risk stems from the possibility that a company might be unable to pay fixed expenses if sales decline. To illustrate, consider Diego Co.'s results for 2009 and two possible outcomes for year 2010 in Exhibit 11.5.

EXHIBIT 11.5

Actual and Projected Results

($ thousands)	2009	2010 Projections: Sales Increase	2010 Projections: Sales Decrease
Sales	$600	$900	$300
Expenses (75% of sales)	450	675	225
Income before interest	150	225	75
Interest expense (fixed)	60	60	60
Net income	$ 90	$165	$ 15

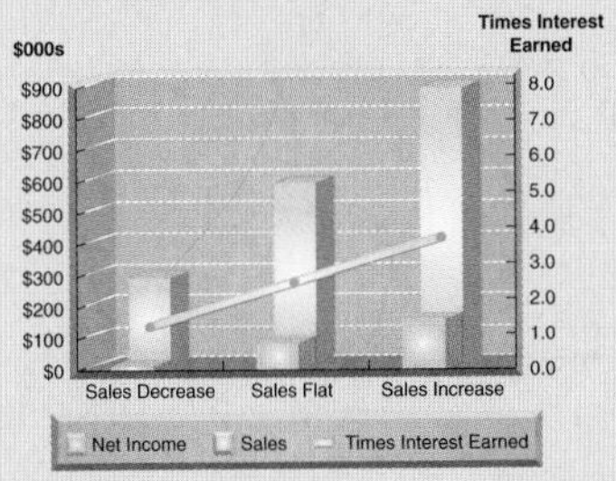

Expenses excluding interest are at, and expected to remain at, 75% of sales. Expenses such as these that change with sales volume are called *variable expenses.* However, interest expense is at, and expected to remain at, $60,000 per year due to its fixed nature.

The middle numerical column of Exhibit 11.5 shows that Diego's income increases by 83% to $165,000 if sales increase by 50% to $900,000. In contrast, the far right column shows that income decreases by 83% if sales decline by 50%. These results reveal that the amount of fixed interest expense affects a company's risk of its ability to pay interest, which is numerically reflected in the **times interest earned** ratio in Exhibit 11.6.

EXHIBIT 11.6

Times Interest Earned

$$\textbf{Times interest earned} = \frac{\textbf{Income before interest expense and income taxes}}{\textbf{Interest expense}}$$

For 2009, Diego's times interest earned is computed as $150,000/$60,000, or 2.5 times. This ratio suggests that Diego faces low to moderate risk because its sales must decline sharply before it would be unable to cover its interest expenses. (Diego is an LLC and does not pay income taxes.)

Experience shows that when times interest earned falls below 1.5 to 2.0 and remains at that level or lower for several periods, the default rate on liabilities increases sharply. This reflects increased risk for companies and their creditors. We also must interpret the times interest earned ratio in light of information about the variability of a company's income before interest. If income is stable from year to year or if it is growing, the company can afford to take on added risk by borrowing. If its income greatly varies from year to year, fixed interest expense can increase the risk that it will not earn enough income to pay interest.

Decision Maker

Entrepreneur You wish to invest in a franchise for either one of two national chains. Each franchise has an expected annual net income *after* interest and taxes of $100,000. Net income for the first franchise includes a regular fixed interest charge of $200,000. The fixed interest charge for the second franchise is $40,000. Which franchise is riskier to you if sales forecasts are not met? Does your decision change if the first franchise has more variability in its income stream? [Answer—p. 458]

Demonstration Problem

DP11

The following transactions and events took place at Kern Company during its recent calendar-year reporting period (Kern does not use reversing entries).

a. In September 2009, Kern sold $140,000 of merchandise covered by a 180-day warranty. Prior experience shows that costs of the warranty equal 5% of sales. Compute September's warranty expense and prepare the adjusting journal entry for the warranty liability as recorded at September 30. Also prepare the journal entry on October 8 to record a $300 cash expenditure to provide warranty service on an item sold in September.

b. On October 12, 2009, Kern arranged with a supplier to replace Kern's overdue $10,000 account payable by paying $2,500 cash and signing a note for the remainder. The note matures in 90 days and has a 12% interest rate. Prepare the entries recorded on October 12, December 31, and January 10, 2010, related to this transaction.

c. In late December, Kern learns it is facing a product liability suit filed by an unhappy customer. Kern's lawyer advises that although it will probably suffer a loss from the lawsuit, it is not possible to estimate the amount of damages at this time.

d. Sally Bline works for Kern. For the pay period ended November 30, her gross earnings are $3,000. Bline has $800 deducted for federal income taxes and $200 for state income taxes from each paycheck. Additionally, a $35 premium for her health care insurance and a $10 donation for the United Way are deducted. Bline pays FICA Social Security taxes at a rate of 6.2% and FICA Medicare taxes at a rate of 1.45%. She has not earned enough this year to be exempt from any FICA taxes. Journalize the accrual of salaries expense of Bline's wages by Kern.

e. On November 1, Kern borrows $5,000 cash from a bank in return for a 60-day, 12%, $5,000 note. Record the note's issuance on November 1 and its repayment with interest on December 31.

f.[B] Kern has estimated and recorded its quarterly income tax payments. In reviewing its year-end tax adjustments, it identifies an additional $5,000 of income tax expense that should be recorded. A portion of this additional expense, $1,000, is deferrable to future years. Record this year-end income taxes expense adjusting entry.

g. For this calendar-year, Kern's net income is $1,000,000, its interest expense is $275,000, and its income taxes expense is $225,000. Calculate Kern's times interest earned ratio.

Planning the Solution

- For *a,* compute the warranty expense for September and record it with an estimated liability. Record the October expenditure as a decrease in the liability.
- For *b,* eliminate the liability for the account payable and create the liability for the note payable. Compute interest expense for the 80 days that the note is outstanding in 2009 and record it as an additional liability. Record the payment of the note, being sure to include the interest for the 10 days in 2010.

- For *c,* decide whether the company's contingent liability needs to be disclosed or accrued (recorded) according to the two necessary criteria: probable loss and reasonably estimable.
- For *d,* set up payable accounts for all items in Bline's paycheck that require deductions. After deducting all necessary items, credit the remaining amount to Salaries Payable.
- For *e,* record the issuance of the note. Calculate 60 days' interest due using the 360-day convention in the interest formula.
- For *f,* determine how much of the income taxes expense is payable in the current year and how much needs to be deferred.
- For *g,* apply and compute times interest earned.

Solution to Demonstration Problem

a. Warranty expense = 5% × $140,000 = $7,000

Sept. 30	Warranty Expense	7,000	
	Estimated Warranty Liability		7,000
	To record warranty expense for the month.		
Oct. 8	Estimated Warranty Liability	300	
	Cash		300
	To record the cost of the warranty service.		

b. Interest expense for 2009 = 12% × $7,500 × 80/360 = $200

Interest expense for 2010 = 12% × $7,500 × 10/360 = $25

Oct. 12	Accounts Payable	10,000	
	Notes Payable		7,500
	Cash		2,500
	Paid $2,500 cash and gave a 90-day, 12% note to extend the due date on the account.		
Dec. 31	Interest Expense	200	
	Interest Payable		200
	To accrue interest on note payable.		
Jan. 10	Interest Expense	25	
	Interest Payable	200	
	Notes Payable	7,500	
	Cash		7,725
	Paid note with interest, including the accrued interest payable.		

c. Disclose the pending lawsuit in the financial statement notes. Although the loss is probable, no liability can be accrued since the loss cannot be reasonably estimated.

d.

Nov. 30	Salaries Expense	3,000.00	
	FICA—Social Security Taxes Payable (6.2%)		186.00
	FICA—Medicare Taxes Payable (1.45%)		43.50
	Employee Federal Income Taxes Payable		800.00
	Employee State Income Taxes Payable		200.00
	Employee Medical Insurance Payable		35.00
	Employee United Way Payable		10.00
	Salaries Payable		1,725.50
	To record Bline's accrued payroll.		

e.

Nov. 1	Cash	5,000	
	Notes Payable		5,000
	Borrowed cash with a 60-day, 12% note.		

When the note and interest are paid 60 days later, Kern Company records this entry:

Dec. 31	Notes Payable	5,000	
	Interest Expense	100	
	Cash		5,100
	Paid note with interest ($5,000 × 12% × 60/360).		

f.

Dec. 31	Income Taxes Expense	5,000	
	Income Taxes Payable		4,000
	Deferred Income Tax Liability		1,000
	To record added income taxes expense and the deferred tax liability.		

g. Times interest earned $= \dfrac{\$1{,}000{,}000 + \$275{,}000 + \$225{,}000}{\$275{,}000} = \underline{\underline{5.45 \text{ times}}}$

APPENDIX

11A Payroll Reports, Records, and Procedures

Understanding payroll procedures and keeping adequate payroll reports and records are essential to a company's success. This appendix focuses on payroll accounting and its reports, records, and procedures.

Payroll Reports

P5 Identify and describe the details of payroll reports, records, and procedures.

Most employees and employers are required to pay local, state, and federal payroll taxes. Payroll expenses involve liabilities to individual employees, to federal and state governments, and to other organizations such as insurance companies. Beyond paying these liabilities, employers are required to prepare and submit reports explaining how they computed these payments.

Reporting FICA Taxes and Income Taxes The Federal Insurance Contributions Act (FICA) requires each employer to file an Internal Revenue Service (IRS) **Form 941,** the *Employer's Quarterly Federal Tax Return,* within one month after the end of each calendar quarter. A sample Form 941 is shown in Exhibit 11A.1 for Phoenix Sales & Service, a landscape design company. Accounting information and software are helpful in tracking payroll transactions and reporting the accumulated information on Form 941. Specifically, the employer reports total wages subject to income tax withholding on line 2 of Form 941. (For simplicity, this appendix uses *wages* to refer to both wages and salaries.) The income tax withheld is reported on line 3. The combined amount of employee and employer FICA (Social Security) taxes for Phoenix Sales & Service is reported on line 5a (taxable Social Security wages, $36,599 × 12.4% = $4,538.28). The 12.4% is the sum of the Social Security tax withheld, computed as 6.2% tax withheld from the employee wages for the quarter plus the 6.2% tax levied on the employer. The combined amount of employee Medicare wages is reported on line 5c. The 2.9% is the sum of 1.45% withheld from employee wages for the quarter plus 1.45% tax levied on the employer. Total FICA taxes are reported on line 5d and are added to the total income taxes withheld of $3,056.47 to yield a total of $8,656.12. For this year, assume that income up to $102,000 is subject to Social Security tax. There is

EXHIBIT 11A.1

Form 941

Form **941** **Employer's QUARTERLY Federal Tax Return**

Department of the Treasury — Internal Revenue Service

(EIN) Employer identification number: 8 6 – 3 2 1 4 5 8 7

Name *(not your trade name)*: Phoenix Sales & Service

Trade name *(if any)*:

Address: 1214 Mill Road (Number, Street, Suite or room number)

Phoenix (City) AZ (State) 85621 (ZIP code)

Report for this Quarter ... (Check one.)

- ☐ 1: January, February, March
- ☐ 2: April, May, June
- ☐ 3: July, August, September
- ☒ 4: October, November, December

Part 1: Answer these questions for this quarter.

1 Number of employees who received wages, tips, or other compensation for the pay period including: *Mar. 12* (Quarter 1), *June 12* (Quarter 2), *Sept. 12* (Quarter 3), *Dec. 12* (Quarter 4)	1	1
2 Wages, tips, and other compensation	2	36,599.00
3 Total income tax withheld from wages, tips, and other compensation	3	3,056.47
4 If no wages, tips, and other compensation are subject to social security or Medicare tax		☐ Check and go to line 6.

5 Taxable social security and Medicare wages and tips:

	Column 1		Column 2
5a Taxable social security wages	36,599.00	× .124 =	4,538.28
5b Taxable social security tips	.	× .124 =	.
5c Taxable Medicare wages & tips	36,599.00	× .029 =	1,061.37

5d Total social security and Medicare taxes (*Column 2*, lines 5a + 5b + 5c = line 5d)	5d	5,599.65
6 Total taxes before adjustments (lines 3 + 5d = line 6)	6	8,656.12

7 TAX ADJUSTMENTS (Read the instructions for line 7 before completing lines 7a through 7h.):

7a Current quarter's fractions of cents	.
7b Current quarter's sick pay	.
7c Current quarter's adjustments for tips and group-term life insurance	.
7d Current year's income tax withholding (attach Form 941c)	.
7e Prior quarters' social security and Medicare taxes (attach Form 941c)	.
7f Special additions to federal income tax (attach Form 941c)	.
7g Special additions to social security and Medicare (attach Form 941c)	.

7h TOTAL ADJUSTMENTS (Combine all amounts: lines 7a through 7g.)	7h	0.00
8 Total taxes after adjustments (Combine lines 6 and 7h.)	8	8,656.12
9 Advance earned income credit (EIC) payments made to employees	9	.
10 Total taxes after adjustment for advance EIC (lines 8 – line 9 = line 10)	10	8,656.12
11 Total deposits for this quarter, including overpayment applied from a prior quarter	11	8,656.12
12 Balance due (If line 10 is more than line 11, write the difference here.) Make checks payable to *United States Treasury.*	12	0.00

13 Overpayment (If line 11 is more than line 10, write the difference here.) 0.00 Check one ☐ Apply to next return. ☐ Send a refund.

Part 2: Tell us about your deposit schedule and tax liability for this quarter.

If you are unsure about whether you are a monthly schedule depositor or a semiweekly schedule depositor, see *Pub. 15 (Circular E)*, section 11.

14 A Z Write the state abbreviation for the state where you made your deposits OR write "MU" if you made your deposits in *multiple* states.

15 Check one: ☐ Line 10 is less than $2,500. Go to Part 3.

☒ You were a monthly schedule depositor for the entire quarter. Fill out your tax liability for each month. Then go to Part 3.

Tax liability:	
Month 1	3,079.11
Month 2	2,049.77
Month 3	3,527.24
Total liability for quarter	8,656.12

Total must equal line 10.

☐ You were a semiweekly schedule depositor for any part of this quarter. Fill out *Schedule B (Form 941): Report of Tax Liability for Semiweekly Schedule Depositors,* and attach it to this form.

Part 3: Tell us about your business. If a question does NOT apply to your business, leave it blank.

16 If your business has closed or you stopped paying wages ☐ Check here, and enter the final date you paid wages / / .

17 If you are a seasonal employer and you do not have to file a return for every quarter of the year ☐ Check here.

Part 4: May we speak with your third-party designee?

Do you want to allow an employee, a paid preparer, or another person to discuss this return with the IRS? See the instructions for details.

☐ Yes. Designee's name

Phone ( ) – Personal Identification Number (PIN)

☒ No.

Part 5: Sign here. You MUST fill out both sides of this form and SIGN it.

Under penalties of perjury, I declare that I have examined this return, including accompanying schedules and statements, and to the best of my knowledge and belief, it is true, correct, and complete.

✗ Sign your name here

Print name and title

Date / / Phone ( ) –

no income limit on amounts subject to Medicare tax. Congress sets annual limits on the amount owed for Social Security tax.

Federal depository banks are authorized to accept deposits of amounts payable to the federal government. Deposit requirements depend on the amount of tax owed. For example, when the sum of FICA taxes plus the employee income taxes is less than $2,500 for a quarter, the taxes can be paid when Form 941 is filed. Companies with large payrolls are often required to pay monthly or even semiweekly.

Reporting FUTA Taxes and SUTA Taxes An employer's federal unemployment taxes (FUTA) are reported on an annual basis by filing an *Annual Federal Unemployment Tax Return,* IRS **Form 940.** It must be mailed on or before January 31 following the end of each tax year. Ten more days are allowed if all required tax deposits are filed on a timely basis and the full amount of tax is paid on or before January 31. FUTA payments are made quarterly to a federal depository bank if the total amount due exceeds $500. If $500 or less is due, the taxes are remitted annually. Requirements for paying and reporting state unemployment taxes (SUTA) vary depending on the laws of each state. Most states require quarterly payments and reports.

Reporting Wages and Salaries Employers are required to give each employee an annual report of his or her wages subject to FICA and federal income taxes along with the amounts of these taxes withheld. This report is called a *Wage and Tax Statement,* or **Form W-2.** It must be given to employees before January 31 following the year covered by the report. Exhibit 11A.2 shows Form W-2 for one of the employees at Phoenix Sales & Service. Copies of the W-2 Form must be sent to the Social Security Administration, where the amount of the employee's wages subject to FICA taxes and FICA taxes withheld are posted to each employee's Social Security account. These posted amounts become the basis for determining an employee's retirement and survivors' benefits. The Social Security Administration also transmits to the IRS the amount of each employee's wages subject to federal income taxes and the amount of taxes withheld.

Payroll Records

Employers must keep payroll records in addition to reporting and paying taxes. These records usually include a payroll register and an individual earnings report for each employee.

Payroll Register A **payroll register** usually shows the pay period dates, hours worked, gross pay, deductions, and net pay of each employee for each pay period. Exhibit 11A.3 shows a payroll register for Phoenix Sales & Service. It is organized into nine columns:

Col. 1 Employee identification (ID); Employee name; Social Security number (SS No.); Reference (check number); and Date (date check issued)
Col. 2 Pay Type (regular and overtime)
Col. 3 Pay Hours (number of hours worked as regular and overtime)
Col. 4 Gross Pay (amount of gross pay)[2]
Col. 5 FIT (federal income taxes withheld); FUTA (federal unemployment taxes)
Col. 6 SIT (state income taxes withheld); SUTA (state unemployment taxes)
Col. 7 FICA-SS_EE (social security taxes withheld, employee); FICA-SS_ER (social security taxes, employer)
Col. 8 FICA-Med_EE (medicare tax withheld, employee); FICA-Med_ER (medicare tax, employer)
Col. 9 Net pay (Gross pay less amounts withheld from employees)

Net pay for each employee is computed as gross pay minus the items on the first line of columns 5–8. The employer's payroll tax for each employee is computed as the sum of items on the third line of columns 5–8. A payroll register includes all data necessary to record payroll. In some software programs the entries to record payroll are made in a special *payroll journal.*

[2] The Gross Pay column shows regular hours worked on the first line multiplied by the regular pay rate—this equals regular pay. Overtime hours multiplied by the overtime premium rate equals overtime premium pay reported on the second line. If employers are engaged in interstate commerce, federal law sets a minimum overtime rate of pay to employees. For this company, workers earn 150% of their regular rate for hours in excess of 40 per week.

EXHIBIT 11A.2

Form W-2

Form **W-2** Wage and Tax Statement
Copy 1–For State, City, or Local Tax Department
Department of Treasury—Internal Revenue Service

a Control number: AR101 — 22222	OMB No. 1545-0006	
b Employer identification number (EIN): 86-3214587	1 Wages, tips, other compensation: 4,910.00	2 Federal income tax withheld: 333.37
c Employer's name, address and ZIP code: Phoenix Sales & Service, 1214 Mill Road, Phoenix, AZ 85621	3 Social security wages: 4,910.00	4 Social security tax withheld: 304.42
	5 Medicare wages and tips: 4,910.00	6 Medicare tax withheld: 71.20
	7 Social security tips	8 Allocated tips
d Employee's social security number: 333-22-9999	9 Advance EIC payment	10 Dependent care benefits
e Employee's first name and initial: Robert J. Last name: Austin	11 Nonqualified plans	12a Code
f Employee's address and ZIP code: 18 Roosevelt Blvd., Apt. C, Tempe, AZ 86322	13 Statutory employee / Retirement plan / Third-party sick pay	12b Code
	14 Other	12c Code
		12d Code

15 State	Employer's state ID number	16 State wages, tips, etc.	17 State income tax	18 Local wages, tips, etc.	19 Local income tax	20 Locality name
AZ	13-902319	4,910.00	26.68			

EXHIBIT 11A.3

Payroll Register

Accounting System: Exhibit A.3

File Edit Maintain Tasks Analysis Options Reports Window Help

Phoenix Sales & Service
Payroll Register
For Week Ended Oct. 8, 2009

Employee ID / Employee / SS No. / Refer., Date	Gross Pay: Pay Type	Pay Hours	Gross Pay	FIT / [blank] / FUTA	SIT / [blank] / SUTA	FICA-SS_EE / [blank] / FICA-SS_ER	FICA-Med_EE / [blank] / FICA-Med_ER	Net Pay
AR101	Regular	40.00	400.00	−28.99	−2.32	−24.80	−5.80	338.09
Robert Austin	Overtime	0.00	0.00					
333-22-9999			400.00	−3.20	−10.80	−24.80	−5.80	
9001, 10/8/09								
CJ102	Regular	40.00	560.00	−52.97	−4.24	−36.02	−8.42	479.35
Judy Cross	Overtime	1.00	21.00					
299-11-9201			581.00	−4.65	−15.69	−36.02	−8.42	
9002, 10/8/09								
DJ103	Regular	40.00	560.00	−48.33	−3.87	−37.32	−8.73	503.75
John Diaz	Overtime	2.00	42.00					
444-11-9090			602.00	−4.82	−16.25	−37.32	−8.73	
9003, 10/8/09								
KK104	Regular	40.00	560.00	−68.57	−5.49	−34.72	−8.12	443.10
Kay Keife	Overtime	0.00	0.00					
909-11-3344			560.00	−4.48	−15.12	−34.72	−8.12	
9004, 10/8/09								
ML105	Regular	40.00	560.00	−34.24	−2.74	−34.72	−8.12	480.18
Lee Miller	Overtime	0.00	0.00					
444-56-3211			560.00	−4.48	−15.12	−34.72	−8.12	
9005, 10/8/09								
SD106	Regular	40.00	560.00	−68.57	−5.49	−34.72	−8.12	443.10
Dale Sears	Overtime	0.00	0.00					
909-33-1234			560.00	−4.48	−15.12	−34.72	−8.12	
9006, 10/8/09								
Totals	Regular	240.00	3,200.00	−301.67	−24.15	−202.30	−47.31	2,687.57
	Overtime	3.00	63.00					
			3,263.00	−26.11	−88.10	−202.30	−47.31	

Sales Purchases General Ledger Payroll Inventory Company Analysis

Payroll Check Payment of payroll is usually done by check or electronic funds transfer. Exhibit 11A.4 shows a *payroll check* for a Phoenix employee. This check is accompanied with a detachable *statement of earnings* (at top) showing gross pay, deductions, and net pay.

EXHIBIT 11A.4

Check and Statement of Earnings

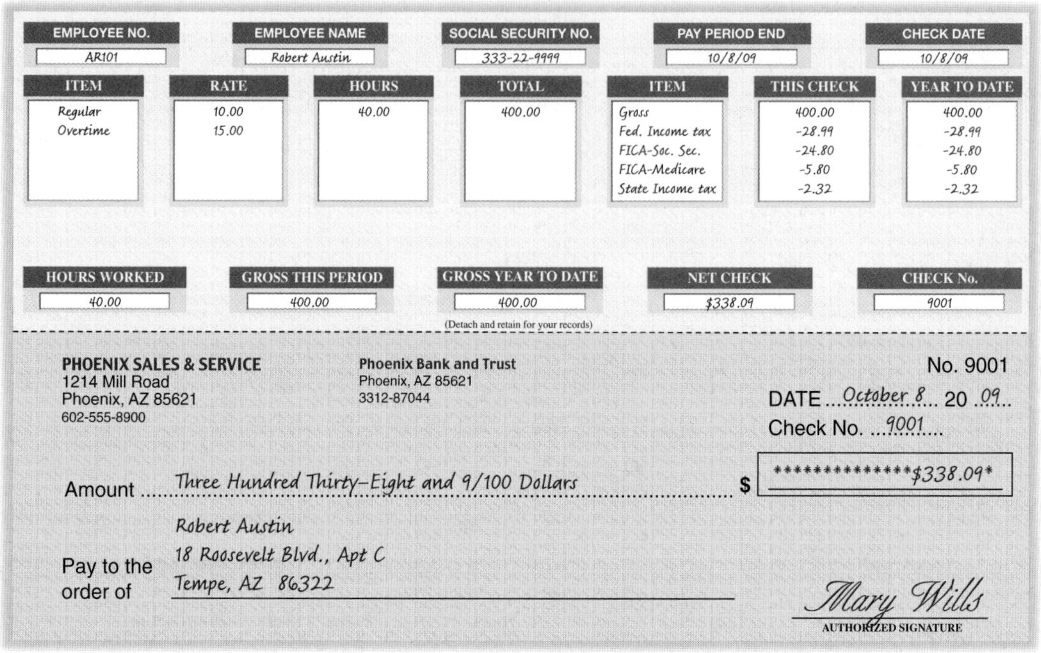

EMPLOYEE NO.	EMPLOYEE NAME	SOCIAL SECURITY NO.	PAY PERIOD END	CHECK DATE
AR101	Robert Austin	333-22-9999	10/8/09	10/8/09

ITEM	RATE	HOURS	TOTAL	ITEM	THIS CHECK	YEAR TO DATE
Regular	10.00	40.00	400.00	Gross	400.00	400.00
Overtime	15.00			Fed. Income tax	-28.99	-28.99
				FICA-Soc. Sec.	-24.80	-24.80
				FICA-Medicare	-5.80	-5.80
				State Income tax	-2.32	-2.32

HOURS WORKED	GROSS THIS PERIOD	GROSS YEAR TO DATE	NET CHECK	CHECK No.
40.00	400.00	400.00	$338.09	9001

(Detach and retain for your records)

PHOENIX SALES & SERVICE
1214 Mill Road
Phoenix, AZ 85621
602-555-8900

Phoenix Bank and Trust
Phoenix, AZ 85621
3312-87044

No. 9001
DATE ...October 8... 20 ..09..
Check No. ...9001....

Amount ....Three Hundred Thirty-Eight and 9/100 Dollars.... $ **************$338.09*

Pay to the order of
Robert Austin
18 Roosevelt Blvd., Apt C
Tempe, AZ 86322

Mary Wills
AUTHORIZED SIGNATURE

Employee Earnings Report An **employee earnings report** is a cumulative record of an employee's hours worked, gross earnings, deductions, and net pay. Payroll information on this report is taken from the payroll register. The employee earnings report for R. Austin at Phoenix Sales & Service is shown in Exhibit 11A.5. An employee earnings report accumulates information that can show when an employee's earnings reach the tax-exempt points for FICA, FUTA, and SUTA taxes. It also gives data an employer needs to prepare Form W-2.

Payroll Procedures

Employers must be able to compute federal income tax for payroll purposes. This section explains how we compute this tax and how to use a payroll bank account.

Computing Federal Income Taxes To compute the amount of taxes withheld from each employee's wages, we need to determine both the employee's wages earned and the employee's number of *withholding allowances.* Each employee records the number of withholding allowances claimed on a withholding allowance certificate, **Form W-4,** filed with the employer. When the number of withholding allowances increases, the amount of income taxes withheld decreases.

Employers often use a **wage bracket withholding table** similar to the one shown in Exhibit 11A.6 to compute the federal income taxes withheld from each employee's gross pay. The table in Exhibit 11A.6 is for a single employee paid weekly. Tables are also provided for married employees and for biweekly, semimonthly, and monthly pay periods (most payroll software includes these tables). When using a wage bracket withholding table to compute federal income tax withheld from an employee's gross wages, we need to locate an employee's wage bracket within the first two columns. We then find the amount withheld by looking in the withholding allowance column for that employee.

Payroll Bank Account Companies with few employees often pay them with checks drawn on the company's regular bank account. Companies with many employees often use a special **payroll bank account** to pay employees. When this account is used, a company either (1) draws one check for total payroll on the regular bank account and deposits it in the payroll bank account or (2) executes an *electronic funds transfer* to the payroll bank account. Individual payroll checks are then drawn on this payroll bank account. Since only one check for the total payroll is drawn on the regular bank account each payday, use of a special payroll bank account helps with internal control. It also helps in reconciling the

EXHIBIT 11A.5

Employee Earnings Report

Accounting System: Exhibit A.5

File Edit Maintain Tasks Analysis Options Reports Window Help

Phoenix Sales & Service
Employee Earnings Report
For Month Ended Dec. 31, 2009

Employee ID Employee SS No.	Date Reference	Gross Pay	FIT [blank] FUTA	SIT [blank] SUTA	FICA-SS_EE [blank] FICA-SS_ER	FICA-Med_EE [blank] FICA-Med_ER	Net Pay
Beginning Balance for Robert Austin		2,910.00	−188.42	−15.08	−180.42	−42.20	2,483.88
			−23.28	−78.57	−180.42	−42.20	
AR101 Robert Austin 333-22-9999	12/03/09 9049	400.00	−28.99	−2.32	−24.80	−5.80	338.09
			−3.20	−10.80	−24.80	−5.80	
AR101 Robert Austin 333-22-9999	12/10/09 9055	400.00	−28.99	−2.32	−24.80	−5.80	338.09
			−3.20	−10.80	−24.80	−5.80	
AR101 Robert Austin 333-22-9999	12/17/09 9061	400.00	−28.99	−2.32	−24.80	−5.80	338.09
			−3.20	−10.80	−24.80	−5.80	
AR101 Robert Austin 333-22-9999	12/24/09 9067	400.00	−28.99	−2.32	−24.80	−5.80	338.09
			−3.20	−10.80	−24.80	−5.80	
AR101 Robert Austin 333-22-9999	12/31/09 9073	400.00	−28.99	−2.32	−24.80	−5.80	338.09
			−3.20	−10.80	−24.80	−5.80	
Total 12/01/09 thru 12/31/09		2,000.00	−144.95	−11.60	−124.00	−29.00	1,690.45
			−16.00	−54.00	−124.00	−29.00	
Year-to-date Total for Robert Austin		4,910.00	−333.37	−26.68	−304.42	−71.20	4,174.33
			−39.28	−132.57	−304.42	−71.20	

Sales Purchases General Ledger Payroll Inventory Company Analysis

EXHIBIT 11A.6

Wage Bracket Withholding Table

SINGLE Persons—WEEKLY Payroll Period

If the wages are–		And the number of withholding allowances claimed is—										
At least	But less than	0	1	2	3	4	5	6	7	8	9	10
		The amount of income tax to be withheld is—										
$600	$610	$76	$67	$58	$49	$39	$30	$21	$12	$6	$0	$0
610	620	79	69	59	50	41	32	22	13	7	1	0
620	630	81	70	61	52	42	33	24	15	8	2	0
630	640	84	72	62	53	44	35	25	16	9	3	0
640	650	86	73	64	55	45	36	27	18	10	4	0
650	660	89	75	65	56	47	38	28	19	11	5	0
660	670	91	76	67	58	48	39	30	21	12	6	0
670	680	94	78	68	59	50	41	31	22	13	7	1
680	690	96	81	70	61	51	42	33	24	14	8	2
690	700	99	83	71	62	53	44	34	25	16	9	3
700	710	101	86	73	64	54	45	35	27	17	10	4
710	720	104	88	74	65	56	47	37	28	19	11	5
720	730	106	91	76	67	57	48	39	30	20	12	6
730	740	109	93	78	68	59	50	40	31	22	13	7
740	750	111	96	80	70	60	51	42	33	23	14	8

regular bank account. When companies use a payroll bank account, they usually include check numbers in the payroll register. The payroll register in Exhibit 11A.3 shows check numbers in column 1. For instance, Check No. 9001 is issued to Robert Austin. With this information, the payroll register serves as a supplementary record of wages earned by and paid to employees.

Who Pays What Payroll Taxes and Benefits

We conclude this appendix with the following table identifying who pays which payroll taxes and which common employee benefits such as medical, disability, pension, charitable, and union costs. Who pays which employee benefits, and what portion, is subject to agreements between companies and their workers. Also, self-employed workers must pay both the employer and employee FICA taxes for Social Security and Medicare.

Employer Payroll Taxes and Costs	Employee Payroll Deductions
• FICA—Social Security Taxes	• FICA—Social Security taxes
• FICA—Medicare Taxes	• FICA—Medicare taxes
• FUTA (Federal Unemployment Taxes)	• Federal Income taxes
• SUTA (State Unemployment Taxes)	• State and local income taxes
• Share of medical coverage, if any	• Share of medical coverage, if any
• Share of pension coverage, if any	• Share of pension coverage, if any
• Share of other benefits, if any	• Share of other benefits, if any

Quick Check

Answers—p. 458

11. What two items determine the amount deducted from an employee's wages for federal income taxes?
12. What amount of income tax is withheld from the salary of an employee who is single with three withholding allowances and earnings of $675 in a week? (*Hint:* Use the wage bracket withholding table in Exhibit 11A.6.)
13. Which of the following steps are executed when a company draws one check for total payroll and deposits it in a special payroll bank account? (*a*) Write a check to the payroll bank account for the total payroll and record it with a debit to Salaries Payable and a credit to Cash. (*b*) Deposit a check (or transfer funds) for the total payroll in the payroll bank account. (*c*) Issue individual payroll checks drawn on the payroll bank account. (*d*) All of the above.

APPENDIX

11B Corporate Income Taxes

This appendix explains current liabilities involving income taxes for corporations.

Income Tax Liabilities Corporations are subject to income taxes and must estimate their income tax liability when preparing financial statements. Since income tax expense is created by earning income, a liability is incurred when income is earned. This tax must be paid quarterly under federal regulations. To illustrate, consider a corporation that prepares monthly financial statements. Based on its income in January 2009, this corporation estimates that it owes income taxes of $12,100. The following adjusting entry records this estimate:

Assets = Liabilities + Equity
+12,100 −12,100

Jan. 31	Income Taxes Expense	12,100	
	Income Taxes Payable.		12,100
	To accrue January income taxes.		

The tax liability is recorded each month until the first quarterly payment is made. If the company's estimated taxes for this first quarter total $30,000, the entry to record its payment is

Apr. 10	Income Taxes Payable	30,000	
	Cash		30,000
	Paid estimated quarterly income taxes based on first quarter income.		

Assets = Liabilities + Equity
−30,000 −30,000

This process of accruing and then paying estimated income taxes continues through the year. When annual financial statements are prepared at year-end, the corporation knows its actual total income and the actual amount of income taxes it must pay. This information allows it to properly record income taxes expense for the fourth quarter so that the total of the four quarters' expense amounts equals the actual taxes paid to the government.

Deferred Income Tax Liabilities An income tax liability for corporations can arise when the amount of income before taxes that the corporation reports on its income statement is not the same as the amount of income reported on its income tax return. This difference occurs because income tax laws and GAAP measure income differently. (Differences between tax laws and GAAP arise because Congress uses tax laws to generate receipts, stimulate the economy, and influence behavior, whereas GAAP are intended to provide financial information useful for business decisions. Also, tax accounting often follows the cash basis, whereas GAAP follows the accrual basis.)

Some differences between tax laws and GAAP are temporary. *Temporary differences* arise when the tax return and the income statement report a revenue or expense in different years. As an example, companies are often able to deduct higher amounts of depreciation in the early years of an asset's life and smaller amounts in later years for tax reporting in comparison to GAAP. This means that in the early years, depreciation for tax reporting is often more than depreciation on the income statement. In later years, depreciation for tax reporting is often less than depreciation on the income statement. When temporary differences exist between taxable income on the tax return and the income before taxes on the income statement, corporations compute income taxes expense based on the income reported on the income statement. The result is that income taxes expense reported in the income statement is often different from the amount of income taxes payable to the government. This difference is the **deferred income tax liability.**

To illustrate, assume that in recording its usual quarterly income tax payments, a corporation computes $25,000 of income taxes expense. It also determines that only $21,000 is currently due and $4,000 is deferred to future years (a timing difference). The entry to record this end-of-period adjustment is

Dec. 31	Income Taxes Expense	25,000	
	Income Taxes Payable		21,000
	Deferred Income Tax Liability		4,000
	To record tax expense and deferred tax liability.		

Assets = Liabilities + Equity
+21,000 −25,000
+4,000

The credit to Income Taxes Payable reflects the amount currently due to be paid. The credit to Deferred Income Tax Liability reflects tax payments deferred until future years when the temporary difference reverses.

Temporary differences also can cause a company to pay income taxes *before* they are reported on the income statement as expense. If so, the company reports a *Deferred Income Tax Asset* on its balance sheet.

Summary

C1 **Describe current and long-term liabilities and their characteristics.** Liabilities are probable future payments of assets or services that past transactions or events obligate an entity to make. Current liabilities are due within one year or the operating cycle, whichever is longer. All other liabilities are long term.

C2 **Identify and describe known current liabilities.** Known (determinable) current liabilities are set by agreements or laws and are measurable with little uncertainty. They include accounts payable, sales taxes payable, unearned revenues, notes payable, payroll liabilities, and the current portion of long-term debt.

C3 **Explain how to account for contingent liabilities.** If an uncertain future payment depends on a probable future event and the amount can be reasonably estimated, the payment is recorded as a liability. The uncertain future payment is reported as a contingent liability (in the notes) if (*a*) the future event is reasonably possible but not probable or (*b*) the event is probable but the payment amount cannot be reasonably estimated.

A1 **Compute the times interest earned ratio and use it to analyze liabilities.** Times interest earned is computed by dividing a company's net income before interest expense and income taxes by the amount of interest expense. The times interest earned ratio reflects a company's ability to pay interest obligations.

P1 **Prepare entries to account for short-term notes payable.** Short-term notes payable are current liabilities; most bear interest. When a short-term note's face value equals the amount borrowed, it identifies a rate of interest to be paid at maturity.

P2 Compute and record *employee* payroll deductions and liabilities. Employee payroll deductions include FICA taxes, income taxes, and voluntary deductions such as for pensions and charities. They make up the difference between gross and net pay.

P3 Compute and record *employer* payroll expenses and liabilities. An employer's payroll expenses include employees' gross earnings, any employee benefits, and the payroll taxes levied on the employer. Payroll liabilities include employees' net pay amounts, withholdings from employee wages, any employer-promised benefits, and the employer's payroll taxes.

P4 Account for estimated liabilities, including warranties and bonuses. Liabilities for health and pension benefits, warranties, and bonuses are recorded with estimated amounts. These items are recognized as expenses when incurred and matched with revenues generated.

P5[A] Identify and describe the details of payroll reports, records, and procedures. Employers report FICA taxes and federal income tax withholdings using Form 941. FUTA taxes are reported on Form 940. Earnings and deductions are reported to each employee and the federal government on Form W-2. An employer's payroll records often include a payroll register for each pay period, payroll checks and statements of earnings, and individual employee earnings reports.

Guidance Answers to **Decision Maker** and **Decision Ethics**

Web Designer You need to be concerned about being an accomplice to unlawful payroll activities. Not paying federal and state taxes on wages earned is illegal and unethical. Such payments also will not provide the employee with Social Security and some Medicare credits. The best course of action is to request payment by check. If this fails to change the owner's payment practices, you must consider quitting this job.

Entrepreneur Risk is partly reflected by the times interest earned ratio. This ratio for the first franchise is 1.5 [($100,000 + $200,000)/$200,000], whereas the ratio for the second franchise is 3.5 [($100,000 + $40,000)/$40,000]. This analysis shows that the first franchise is more at risk of incurring a loss if its sales decline. The second question asks about variability of income. If income greatly varies, this increases the risk an owner will not earn sufficient income to cover interest. Since the first franchise has the greater variability, it is a riskier investment.

Guidance Answers to **Quick Checks**

1. A liability involves a probable future payment of assets or services that an entity is presently obligated to make as a result of past transactions or events.
2. No, an expected future payment is not a liability unless an existing obligation was created by a past event or transaction.
3. In most cases, a liability due in 15 months is classified as long term. It is classified as a current liability if the company's operating cycle is 15 months or longer.
4. A creditor prefers a note payable instead of a past-due account payable so as to (*a*) charge interest and/or (*b*) have evidence of the debt and its terms for potential litigation or disputes.
5. $1,000* × (.008) + $1,000* × (.04) + $3,000 × (.062) + $3,000 × (.0145) = $277.50

* $1,000 of the $3,000 March pay is subject to FUTA and SUTA—the entire $6,000 pay from January and February was subject to them.

6. (*a*) FICA taxes are incurred by both employee and employer.
   (*b*) FUTA taxes are incurred by the employer.
   (*c*) SUTA taxes are incurred by the employer.
   (*d*) Withheld income taxes are incurred by the employee.
7. (*a*)
8. (*a*) Warranty expense was previously estimated and recorded.
9. (*b*)
10. A future payment is reported in the notes as a contingent liability if (*a*) the uncertain future event is probable but the amount of payment cannot be reasonably estimated or (*b*) the uncertain future event is not probable but has a reasonable possibility of occurring.
11. An employee's marital status, gross earnings and number of withholding allowances determine the deduction for federal income taxes.
12. $59
13. (*d*)

Key Terms

mhhe.com/wildFAP19e

Key Terms are available at the book's Website for learning and testing in an online Flashcard Format.

Contingent liability (p. 445)
Current liabilities (p. 435)
Current portion of long-term debt (p. 442)
Deferred income tax liability (p. 457)
Employee benefits (p. 443)
Employee earnings report (p. 454)
Estimated liability (p. 443)
Federal depository bank (p. 452)
Federal Insurance Contributions Act (FICA) Taxes (p. 440)

Federal Unemployment Taxes (FUTA) (p. 442)
Form 940 (p. 452)
Form 941 (p. 450)
Form W-2 (p. 452)
Form W-4 (p. 454)
Gross pay (p. 440)
Known liabilities (p. 436)
Long-term liabilities (p. 435)
Merit rating (p. 442)
Net pay (p. 440)
Payroll bank account (p. 454)
Payroll deductions (p. 440)
Payroll register (p. 452)
Short-term note payable (p. 437)
State Unemployment Taxes (SUTA) (p. 442)
Times interest earned (p. 447)
Wage bracket withholding table (p. 454)
Warranty (p. 444)

Multiple Choice Quiz

Answers on p. 475

mhhe.com/wildFAP19e

Additional Quiz Questions are available at the book's Website.

Quiz11

1. On December 1, a company signed a $6,000, 90-day, 5% note payable, with principal plus interest due on March 1 of the following year. What amount of interest expense should be accrued at December 31 on the note?
   a. $300
   b. $25
   c. $100
   d. $75
   e. $0
2. An employee earned $50,000 during the year. FICA tax for social security is 6.2% and FICA tax for Medicare is 1.45%. The employer's share of FICA taxes is
   a. Zero, since the employee's pay exceeds the FICA limit.
   b. Zero, since FICA is not an employer tax.
   c. $3,100
   d. $725
   e. $3,825
3. Assume the FUTA tax rate is 0.8% and the SUTA tax rate is 5.4%. Both taxes are applied to the first $7,000 of an employee's pay. What is the total unemployment tax an employer must pay on an employee's annual wages of $40,000?
   a. $2,480
   b. $434
   c. $56
   d. $378
   e. Zero; the employee's wages exceed the $7,000 maximum.
4. A company sells big screen televisions for $3,000 each. Each television has a two-year warranty that covers the replacement of defective parts. It is estimated that 1% of all televisions sold will be returned under warranty at an average cost of $250 each. During July, the company sold 10,000 big screen televisions, and 80 were serviced under the warranty during July at a total cost of $18,000. The credit balance in the Estimated Warranty Liability account at July 1 was $26,000. What is the company's warranty expense for the month of July?
   a. $51,000
   b. $1,000
   c. $25,000
   d. $33,000
   e. $18,000
5. Employees earn vacation pay at the rate of 1 day per month. During October, 150 employees qualify for one vacation day each. Their average daily wage is $175 per day. What is the amount of vacation benefit expense for October?
   a. $26,250
   b. $175
   c. $2,100
   d. $63,875
   e. $150

Superscript letter A (B) denotes assignments based on Appendix 11A (11B).

Discussion Questions

1. What are the three important questions concerning the uncertainty of liabilities?
2. What is the difference between a current and a long-term liability?
3. What is an estimated liability?
4. If $988 is the total of a sale that includes its sales tax of 4%, what is the selling price of the item only?
5. What is the combined amount (in percent) of the employee and employer Social Security tax rate?
6. What is the current Medicare tax rate? This rate is applied to what maximum level of salary and wages?
7. What determines the amount deducted from an employee's wages for federal income taxes?
8. Which payroll taxes are the employee's responsibility and which are the employer's responsibility?
9. What is an employer's unemployment merit rating? How are these ratings assigned to employers?
10. Why are warranty liabilities usually recognized on the balance sheet as liabilities even when they are uncertain?
11. Suppose that a company has a facility located where disastrous weather conditions often occur. Should it report a probable loss from a future disaster as a liability on its balance sheet? Explain.

12.[A] What is a wage bracket withholding table?

13.[A] What amount of income tax is withheld from the salary of an employee who is single with two withholding allowances and earning $725 per week? What if the employee earned $625 and has no withholding allowances? (Use Exhibit 11A.6.)

14. Refer to **Best Buy**'s balance sheet in Appendix A. What payroll-related liability does Best Buy report at March 3, 2007?

15. Refer to **Circuit City**'s balance sheet in Appendix A. What accounts related to income taxes are on its balance sheet? Explain the meaning of each income tax account you identify.

16. Refer to **RadioShack**'s balance sheet in Appendix A. What is the amount of RadioShack's accounts payable as of December 31, 2006?

17. Refer to **Apple**'s balance sheet in Appendix A. List Apple's current liabilities as of September 30, 2006.

Denotes Discussion Questions that involve decision making.

Available with McGraw-Hill's Homework Manager

McGraw-Hill's HOMEWORK MANAGER®

QUICK STUDY

QS 11-1
Classifying liabilities C1

Which of the following items are normally classified as a current liability for a company that has a 15-month operating cycle?

1. Note payable due in 18 months.
2. Note payable maturing in 2 years.
3. Portion of long-term note due in 15 months.
4. Salaries payable.
5. FICA taxes payable.
6. Note payable due in 11 months.

QS 11-2
Unearned revenue C2

Tickets, Inc., receives $7,500,000 cash in advance ticket sales for a five-date tour of Bruce Springsteen. Record the advance ticket sales on October 31. Record the revenue earned for the first concert date of November 5, assuming it represents one-fifth of the advance ticket sales.

QS 11-3
Accounting for sales taxes
C2

Wheeling Computing sells merchandise for $12,000 cash on September 30 (cost of merchandise is $7,800). The sales tax law requires Wheeling to collect 6% sales tax on every dollar of merchandise sold. Record the entry for the $12,000 sale and its applicable sales tax. Also record the entry that shows the remittance of the 6% tax on this sale to the state government on October 15.

QS 11-4
Interest-bearing note transactions
P1

On November 7, 2009, Stockmann Company borrows $80,000 cash by signing a 90-day, 8% note payable with a face value of $80,000. (1) Compute the accrued interest payable on December 31, 2009, (2) prepare the journal entry to record the accrued interest expense at December 31, 2009, and (3) prepare the journal entry to record payment of the note at maturity.

QS 11-5
Record employer payroll taxes
P2 P3

DeNise Co. has five employees, each of whom earns $3,000 per month and has been employed since January 1. FICA Social Security taxes are 6.2% of the first $102,000 paid to each employee, and FICA Medicare taxes are 1.45% of gross pay. FUTA taxes are 0.8% and SUTA taxes are 5.4% of the first $7,000 paid to each employee. Prepare the March 31 journal entry to record the March payroll taxes expense.

QS 11-6
Accounting for vacations
P4

Chavez Co.'s salaried employees earn four weeks vacation per year. It pays $156,000 in total employee salaries for 52 weeks but its employees work only 48 weeks. This means Chavez's total weekly expense is $3,250 ($156,000/48 weeks) instead of the $3,000 cash paid weekly to the employees ($156,000/52 weeks). Record Chavez's weekly vacation benefits expense.

QS 11-7
Accounting for bonuses P4

Erik Company offers an annual bonus to employees if the company meets certain net income goals. Prepare the journal entry to record a $15,000 bonus owed to its workers (to be shared equally) at calendar year-end.

QS 11-8
Recording warranty repairs
P4

On September 11, 2008, Lawn Outfitters sells a mower for $750 with a one-year warranty that covers parts. Warranty expense is estimated at 3% of sales. On July 24, 2009, the mower is brought in for repairs covered under the warranty requiring $55 in materials taken from the Repair Parts Inventory. Prepare the July 24, 2009, entry to record the warranty repairs.

QS 11-9
Accounting for contingent liabilities
C3

The following legal claims exist for VanBeek Co. Identify the accounting treatment for each claim as either (*a*) a liability that is recorded or (*b*) an item described in notes to its financial statements.

1. VanBeek (defendant) estimates that a pending lawsuit could result in damages of $250,000; it is reasonably possible that the plaintiff will win the case.
2. VanBeek faces a probable loss on a pending lawsuit; the amount is not reasonably estimable.
3. VanBeek estimates damages in a case at $1,500,000 with a high probability of losing the case.

QS 11-10
Times interest earned
A1

Compute the times interest earned for Zelma Company, which reports income before interest expense and income taxes of $1,044,000, and interest expense of $145,000. Interpret its times interest earned (assume that its competitors average a times interest earned of 4.0).

QS 11-11[B]
Record deferred income tax liability
P4

Eastwood Corporation has made and recorded its quarterly income tax payments. After a final review of taxes for the year, the company identifies an additional $40,000 of income tax expense that should be recorded. A portion of this additional expense, $6,000, is deferred for payment in future years. Record Eastwood's year-end adjusting entry for income tax expense.

McGraw-Hill's HOMEWORK MANAGER® Available with McGraw-Hill's Homework Manager

EXERCISES

Exercise 11-1
Classifying liabilities
C1

The following items appear on the balance sheet of a company with a two-month operating cycle. Identify the proper classification of each item as follows: *C* if it is a current liability, *L* if it is a long-term liability, or *N* if it is not a liability.

_____	**1.** Notes payable (due in 120 days).	_____	**6.** Notes payable (mature in five years).
_____	**2.** Notes payable (due in 6 to 12 months).	_____	**7.** Current portion of long-term debt.
_____	**3.** Notes payable (due in 13 to 24 months).	_____	**8.** Sales taxes payable.
_____	**4.** Accounts receivable.	_____	**9.** Wages payable.
_____	**5.** FUTA taxes payable.	_____	**10.** Salaries payable.

Exercise 11-2
Adjusting entries for liabilities
C2 C3 P4

Prepare any necessary adjusting entries at December 31, 2009, for Madison Company's year-end financial statements for each of the following separate transactions and events.

1. During December, Madison Company sold 4,100 units of a product that carries a 60-day warranty. December sales for this product total $164,000. The company expects 6% of the units to need warranty repairs, and it estimates the average repair cost per unit will be $14.
2. A disgruntled employee is suing Madison Company. Legal advisers believe that the company will probably need to pay damages, but the amount cannot be reasonably estimated.
3. Employees earn vacation pay at a rate of one day per month. During December, 28 employees qualify for one vacation day each. Their average daily wage is $105 per employee.
4. Madison Company guarantees the $13,000 debt of a supplier. The supplier will probably not default on the debt.
5. Madison Company records an adjusting entry for $520,000 of previously unrecorded cash sales (costing $260,000) and its sales taxes at a rate of 7%.
6. The company earned $104,000 of $260,000 previously received in advance for services.

Exercise 11-3
Computing and recording bonuses C2

For the year ended December 31, 2009, Kava Company has implemented an employee bonus program equal to 4% of Kava's net income, which employees will share equally. Kava's net income (prebonus) is expected to be $1,300,000, and bonus expense is deducted in computing net income.

1. Compute the amount of the bonus payable to the employees at year-end (use the method described in the chapter and round to the nearest dollar).
2. Prepare the journal entry at December 31, 2009, to record the bonus due the employees.
3. Prepare the journal entry at January 19, 2010, to record payment of the bonus to employees.

Check (1) $50,000

Exercise 11-4
Accounting for note payable
P1

Check (2b) Interest expense, $6,165

Motora Systems borrows $137,000 cash on May 15, 2009, by signing a 180-day, 9% note.

1. On what date does this note mature?

2. Suppose the face value of the note equals $137,000, the principal of the loan. Prepare the journal entries to record (*a*) issuance of the note and (*b*) payment of the note at maturity.

Exercise 11-5
Interest-bearing notes payable with year-end adjustments
P1

Check (2) $4,000
(3) $8,000

Keshena Co. borrows $240,000 cash on November 1, 2009, by signing a 180-day, 10% note with a face value of $240,000.

1. On what date does this note mature? (February of 2009 has 28 days.)

2. How much interest expense results from this note in 2009? (Assume a 360-day year.)

3. How much interest expense results from this note in 2010? (Assume a 360-day year.)

4. Prepare journal entries to record (*a*) issuance of the note, (*b*) accrual of interest at the end of 2009, and (*c*) payment of the note at maturity.

Exercise 11-6
Computing payroll taxes
P2 P3

RNG Co. has one employee, and the company is subject to the following taxes.

Tax	Rate	Applied To
FICA—Social Security	6.20%	First $102,000
FICA—Medicare	1.45	All gross pay
FUTA	0.80	First $7,000
SUTA	2.90	First $7,000

Compute RNG's amounts for each of these four taxes as applied to the employee's gross earnings for September under each of three separate situations (*a*), (*b*), and (*c*).

Check (*a*) FUTA, $8.80; SUTA, $31.90

	Gross Pay through August	Gross Pay for September
a.	$ 5,900	$2,100
b.	17,700	2,500
c.	95,700	7,400

Exercise 11-7
Payroll-related journal entries
P2 P3

Using the data in situation *a* of Exercise 11-6, prepare the employer's September 30 journal entries to record (1) salary expense and its related payroll liabilities for this employee and (2) the employer's payroll taxes expense and its related liabilities. The employee's federal income taxes withheld by the employer are $250 for this pay period.

Exercise 11-8
Warranty expense and liability computations and entries
P4

Lee Co. sold a copier costing $6,500 with a two-year parts warranty to a customer on August 16, 2009, for $9,400 cash. Lee uses the perpetual inventory system. On November 22, 2010, the copier requires on-site repairs that are completed the same day. The repairs cost $125 for materials taken from the Repair Parts Inventory. These are the only repairs required in 2010 for this copier. Based on experience, Lee expects to incur warranty costs equal to 3% of dollar sales. It records warranty expense with an adjusting entry at the end of each year.

Check (1) $282

1. How much warranty expense does the company report in 2009 for this copier?

2. How much is the estimated warranty liability for this copier as of December 31, 2009?

3. How much warranty expense does the company report in 2010 for this copier?

(4) $157

4. How much is the estimated warranty liability for this copier as of December 31, 2010?

5. Prepare journal entries to record (*a*) the copier's sale; (*b*) the adjustment on December 31, 2009, to recognize the warranty expense; and (*c*) the repairs that occur in November 2010.

Exercise 11-9
Computing and interpreting times interest earned
A1

Use the following information from separate companies *a* through *f* to compute times interest earned. Which company indicates the strongest ability to pay interest expense as it comes due?

	Net Income (Loss)	Interest Expense	Income Taxes
a.	$122,000	$36,600	$30,500
b.	116,600	11,660	41,976
c.	125,100	7,506	60,048
d.	103,700	31,110	43,554
e.	79,300	9,516	30,134
f.	(34,160)	74,469	0

Check (b) 14.60

Exercise 11-10^A
Net pay and tax computations
P5

The payroll records of Simplex Software show the following information about Ken LeShon, an employee, for the weekly pay period ending September 30, 2009. LeShon is single and claims one allowance. Compute his Social Security tax (6.2%), Medicare tax (1.45%), federal income tax withholding, state income tax (0.5%), and net pay for the current pay period. The state income tax is 0.5 percent on the first $9,000 earned. (Use the withholding table in Exhibit 11A.6 and round tax amounts to the nearest cent.)

Total (gross) earnings for current pay period	$ 735
Cumulative earnings of previous pay periods	9,500

Check Net pay, $585.77

Exercise 11-11^A
Gross and net pay computation
P5

Tad Newbern, an unmarried employee, works 47 hours in the week ended January 12. His pay rate is $12 per hour, and his wages are subject to no deductions other than FICA—Social Security, FICA—Medicare, and federal income taxes. He claims two withholding allowances. Compute his regular pay, overtime pay (overtime premium is 50% of the regular rate for hours in excess of 40 per week), and gross pay. Then compute his FICA tax deduction (use 6.2% for the Social Security portion and 1.45% for the Medicare portion), income tax deduction (use the wage bracket withholding table of Exhibit 11A.6), total deductions, and net pay. (Round tax amounts to the nearest cent.)

Check Net pay, $501.64

Exercise 11-12^B
Accounting for income taxes
P4

Florita Corporation prepares financial statements for each month-end. As part of its accounting process, estimated income taxes are accrued each month for 34% of the current month's net income. The income taxes are paid in the first month of each quarter for the amount accrued for the prior quarter. The following information is available for the fourth quarter of year 2009. When tax computations are completed on January 20, 2010, Florita determines that the quarter's Income Taxes Payable account balance should be $46,693 on December 31, 2009 (its unadjusted balance is $42,364).

October 2009 net income	$45,200
November 2009 net income	29,400
December 2009 net income	50,000

1. Determine the amount of the accounting adjustment (dated as of December 31, 2009) to produce the proper ending balance in the Income Taxes Payable account.

Check (1) $4,329

2. Prepare journal entries to record (*a*) the December 31, 2009, adjustment to the Income Taxes Payable account and (*b*) the January 20, 2010, payment of the fourth-quarter taxes.

PROBLEM SET A

Problem 11-1A
Short-term notes payable transactions and entries
P1

Montag Co. entered into the following transactions involving short-term liabilities in 2008 and 2009.

2008

Apr. 20 Purchased $48,250 of merchandise on credit from Locust, terms are 1/10, n/30. Montag uses the perpetual inventory system.

May 19 Replaced the April 20 account payable to Locust with a 120-day, $39,000 note bearing 9% annual interest along with paying $9,250 in cash.

eXcel
mhhe.com/wildFAP19e

July 8	Borrowed $120,000 cash from National Bank by signing a 120-day, 8.5% interest-bearing note with a face value of $100,000.
?	Paid the amount due on the note to Locust at the maturity date.
?	Paid the amount due on the note to National Bank at the maturity date.
Nov. 28	Borrowed $60,000 cash from Fargo Bank by signing a 60-day, 8% interest-bearing note with a face value of $60,000.
Dec. 31	Recorded an adjusting entry for accrued interest on the note to Fargo Bank.

2009

?	Paid the amount due on the note to Fargo Bank at the maturity date.

Required

1. Determine the maturity date for each of the three notes described.
2. Determine the interest due at maturity for each of the three notes. (Assume a 360-day year.)
3. Determine the interest expense to be recorded in the adjusting entry at the end of 2008.
4. Determine the interest expense to be recorded in 2009.
5. Prepare journal entries for all the preceding transactions and events for years 2008 and 2009.

Check (2) Locust, $1,170
(3) $440
(4) $360

Problem 11-2A
Warranty expense and liability estimation
P4

On October 29, 2008, Bram Co. began operations by purchasing razors for resale. Bram uses the perpetual inventory method. The razors have a 90-day warranty that requires the company to replace any nonworking razor. When a razor is returned, the company discards it and mails a new one from Merchandise Inventory to the customer. The company's cost per new razor is $16 and its retail selling price is $60 in both 2008 and 2009. The manufacturer has advised the company to expect warranty costs to equal 7% of dollar sales. The following transactions and events occurred.

2008

Nov. 11	Sold 75 razors for $4,500 cash.
30	Recognized warranty expense related to November sales with an adjusting entry.
Dec. 9	Replaced 15 razors that were returned under the warranty.
16	Sold 210 razors for $12,600 cash.
29	Replaced 30 razors that were returned under the warranty.
31	Recognized warranty expense related to December sales with an adjusting entry.

2009

Jan. 5	Sold 130 razors for $7,800 cash.
17	Replaced 35 razors that were returned under the warranty.
31	Recognized warranty expense related to January sales with an adjusting entry.

Required

1. Prepare journal entries to record these transactions and adjustments for 2008 and 2009.
2. How much warranty expense is reported for November 2008 and for December 2008?
3. How much warranty expense is reported for January 2009?
4. What is the balance of the Estimated Warranty Liability account as of December 31, 2008?
5. What is the balance of the Estimated Warranty Liability account as of January 31, 2009?

Check (3) $546
(4) $477 Cr.
(5) $463 Cr.

Problem 11-3A
Computing and analyzing times interest earned
A1

Shown here are condensed income statements for two different companies (both are organized as LLCs and pay no income taxes).

Milo Company	
Sales	$1,450,000
Variable expenses (80%)	1,160,000
Income before interest	290,000
Interest expense (fixed)	60,000
Net income	$ 230,000

Warner Company	
Sales	$1,450,000
Variable expenses (60%)	870,000
Income before interest	580,000
Interest expense (fixed)	350,000
Net income	$ 230,000

Required

1. Compute times interest earned for Milo Company.
2. Compute times interest earned for Warner Company.
3. What happens to each company's net income if sales increase by 40%?
4. What happens to each company's net income if sales increase by 50%?
5. What happens to each company's net income if sales increase by 80%?
6. What happens to each company's net income if sales decrease by 20%?
7. What happens to each company's net income if sales decrease by 30%?
8. What happens to each company's net income if sales decrease by 40%?

Check (4) Milo net income, $375,000 (63% increase)

(6) Warner net income, $114,000 (50% decrease)

Analysis Component

9. Comment on the results from parts 3 through 8 in relation to the fixed-cost strategies of the two companies and the ratio values you computed in parts 1 and 2.

Problem 11-4A
Payroll expenses, withholdings, and taxes

P2 P3

mhhe.com/wildFAP19e

Pardee Co. pays its employees each week. Its employees' gross pay is subject to these taxes.

Tax	Rate	Applied To
FICA—Social Security	6.20%	First $102,000
FICA—Medicare	1.45	All gross pay
FUTA	0.80	First $7,000
SUTA	2.15	First $7,000

The company is preparing its payroll calculations for the week ended August 25. Payroll records show the following information for the company's four employees.

	Gross Pay	Current Week	
Name	through 8/18	Gross Pay	Income Tax Withholding
Dahlia	$100,500	$3,600	$450
Trey	31,850	1,275	140
Kiesha	6,260	1,440	173
Chee	1,000	400	36

In addition to gross pay, the company must pay one-half of the $22 per employee weekly health insurance; each employee pays the remaining one-half. The company also contributes an extra 8% of each employee's gross pay (at no cost to employees) to a pension fund.

Required

Compute the following for the week ended August 25 (round amounts to the nearest cent):

1. Each employee's FICA withholdings for Social Security.
2. Each employee's FICA withholdings for Medicare.
3. Employer's FICA taxes for Social Security.
4. Employer's FICA taxes for Medicare.
5. Employer's FUTA taxes.
6. Employer's SUTA taxes.
7. Each employee's net (take-home) pay.
8. Employer's total payroll-related expense for each employee.

Check (3) $286.13
(4) $97.37
(5) $9.12

(7) Total net pay, $5,488.50

Problem 11-5A^A
Entries for payroll transactions
P2 P3

On January 8, the end of the first weekly pay period of the year, Regal Company's payroll register showed that its employees earned $27,760 of office salaries and $70,240 of sales salaries. Withholdings from the employees' salaries include FICA Social Security taxes at the rate of 6.2%, FICA Medicare taxes at the rate of 1.45%, $13,360 of federal income taxes, $1,350 of medical insurance deductions, and $840 of union dues. No employee earned more than $7,000 in this first period.

Required

Check (1) Cr. Salaries Payable, $74,953.00

(2) Dr. Payroll Taxes Expense, $13,181.00

1. Calculate FICA Social Security taxes payable and FICA Medicare taxes payable. Prepare the journal entry to record Regal Company's January 8 (employee) payroll expenses and liabilities.

2. Prepare the journal entry to record Regal's (employer) payroll taxes resulting from the January 8 payroll. Regal's merit rating reduces its state unemployment tax rate to 5% of the first $7,000 paid each employee. The federal unemployment tax rate is 0.8%.

Problem 11-6A^A
Entries for payroll transactions
P2 P3 P5

Franco Company has 20 employees, each of whom earns $3,000 per month and is paid on the last day of each month. All 20 have been employed continuously at this amount since January 1. Franco uses a payroll bank account and special payroll checks to pay its employees. On March 1, the following accounts and balances exist in its general ledger:

a. FICA—Social Security Taxes Payable, $7,440; FICA—Medicare Taxes Payable, $1,740. (The balances of these accounts represent total liabilities for *both* the employer's and employees' FICA taxes for the February payroll only.)

b. Employees' Federal Income Taxes Payable, $5,250 (liability for February only).

c. Federal Unemployment Taxes Payable, $960 (liability for January and February together).

d. State Unemployment Taxes Payable, $4,800 (liability for January and February together).

During March and April, the company had the following payroll transactions.

Mar. 15 Issued check payable to Swift Bank, a federal depository bank authorized to accept employers' payments of FICA taxes and employee income tax withholdings. The $14,430 check is in payment of the February FICA and employee income taxes.

Check March 31: Cr. Salaries Payable, $50,160

31 Recorded the March payroll and transferred funds from the regular bank account to the payroll bank account. Issued checks payable to each employee in payment of the March payroll. The payroll register shows the following summary totals for the March pay period.

Salaries and Wages					
Office Salaries	Shop Wages	Gross Pay	FICA Taxes*	Federal Income Taxes	Net Pay
$24,000	$36,000	$60,000	$3,720 $ 870	$5,250	$50,160

* FICA taxes are Social Security and Medicare, respectively.

March 31: Dr. Payroll Taxes Expenses, $5,550

April 15: Cr. Cash, $14,430 (Swift Bank)

31 Recorded the employer's payroll taxes resulting from the March payroll. The company has a merit rating that reduces its state unemployment tax rate to 4.0% of the first $7,000 paid each employee. The federal rate is 0.8%.

Apr. 15 Issued check to Swift Bank in payment of the March FICA and employee income taxes.

15 Issued check to the State Tax Commission for the January, February, and March state unemployment taxes. Mailed the check and the first quarter tax return to the Commission.

30 Issued check payable to Swift Bank in payment of the employer's FUTA taxes for the first quarter of the year.

30 Mailed Form 941 to the IRS, reporting the FICA taxes and the employees' federal income tax withholdings for the first quarter.

Required

Prepare journal entries to record the transactions and events for both March and April.

PROBLEM SET B

Problem 11-1B
Short-term notes payable transactions and entries

P1

Nix Co. entered into the following transactions involving short-term liabilities in 2008 and 2009.

2008

Apr. 22	Purchased $6,000 of merchandise on credit from Wolf Products, terms are 1/10, n/30. Nix uses the perpetual inventory system.
May 23	Replaced the April 22 account payable to Wolf Products with a 60-day, $5,400 note bearing 8% annual interest along with paying $600 in cash.
July 15	Borrowed $8,500 cash from Autumn Bank by signing a 90-day, 8% interest-bearing note with a face value of $8,500.
?	Paid the amount due on the note to Wolf Products at maturity.
?	Paid the amount due on the note to Autumn Bank at maturity.
Dec. 6	Borrowed $9,600 cash from City Bank by signing a 90-day, 6% interest-bearing note with a face value of $9,600.
31	Recorded an adjusting entry for accrued interest on the note to City Bank.

2009

?	Paid the amount due on the note to City Bank at maturity. (February of 2009 has 28 days.)

Required

1. Determine the maturity date for each of the three notes described.
2. Determine the interest due at maturity for each of the three notes. (Assume a 360-day year.)
3. Determine the interest expense to be recorded in the adjusting entry at the end of 2008.
4. Determine the interest expense to be recorded in 2009.
5. Prepare journal entries for all the preceding transactions and events for years 2008 and 2009.

Check (2) Wolf, $72
(3) $40
(4) $104

Problem 11-2B
Warranty expense and liability estimation

P4

On November 10, 2009, Lorna Co. began operations by purchasing coffee grinders for resale. Lorna uses the perpetual inventory method. The grinders have a 90-day warranty that requires the company to replace any nonworking grinder. When a grinder is returned, the company discards it and mails a new one from Merchandise Inventory to the customer. The company's cost per new grinder is $15 and its retail selling price is $85 in both 2009 and 2010. The manufacturer has advised the company to expect warranty costs to equal 8% of dollar sales. The following transactions and events occurred.

2009

Nov. 16	Sold 50 grinders for $4,250 cash.
30	Recognized warranty expense related to November sales with an adjusting entry.
Dec. 12	Replaced 11 grinders that were returned under the warranty.
18	Sold 160 grinders for $13,600 cash.
28	Replaced 22 grinders that were returned under the warranty.
31	Recognized warranty expense related to December sales with an adjusting entry.

2010

Jan. 7	Sold 95 grinders for $8,075 cash.
21	Replaced 45 grinders that were returned under the warranty.
31	Recognized warranty expense related to January sales with an adjusting entry.

Required

1. Prepare journal entries to record these transactions and adjustments for 2009 and 2010.
2. How much warranty expense is reported for November 2009 and for December 2009?
3. How much warranty expense is reported for January 2010?
4. What is the balance of the Estimated Warranty Liability account as of December 31, 2009?
5. What is the balance of the Estimated Warranty Liability account as of January 31, 2010?

Check (3) $646
(4) $933 Cr.
(5) $904 Cr.

Problem 11-3B
Computing and analyzing times interest earned

A1

Shown here are condensed income statements for two different companies (both are organized as LLCs and pay no income taxes).

Ellis Company	
Sales	$250,000
Variable expenses (50%)	125,000
Income before interest	125,000
Interest expense (fixed)	75,000
Net income	$ 50,000

Seidel Company	
Sales	$250,000
Variable expenses (75%)	187,500
Income before interest	62,500
Interest expense (fixed)	12,500
Net income	$ 50,000

Required

1. Compute times interest earned for Ellis Company.
2. Compute times interest earned for Seidel Company.
3. What happens to each company's net income if sales increase by 40%?
4. What happens to each company's net income if sales increase by 50%?
5. What happens to each company's net income if sales increase by 80%?
6. What happens to each company's net income if sales decrease by 20%?
7. What happens to each company's net income if sales decrease by 30%?
8. What happens to each company's net income if sales decrease by 40%?

Check (3) Ellis net income, $100,000 (100% increase)

(6) Seidel net income, $37,500 (25% decrease)

Analysis Component

9. Comment on the results from parts 3 through 8 in relation to the fixed-cost strategies of the two companies and the ratio values you computed in parts 1 and 2.

Problem 11-4B
Payroll expenses, withholdings, and taxes

P2 P3

Fishing Guides Co. pays its employees each week. Employees' gross pay is subject to these taxes.

Tax	Rate	Applied To
FICA—Social Security	6.20%	First $102,000
FICA—Medicare	1.45	All gross pay
FUTA	0.80	First $7,000
SUTA	1.75	First $7,000

The company is preparing its payroll calculations for the week ended September 30. Payroll records show the following information for the company's four employees.

Name	Gross Pay through 9/23	Current Week Gross Pay	Current Week Income Tax Withholding
Ahmed	$99,500	$4,900	$613
Carlos	31,850	1,280	140
Jun	6,380	920	110
Marie	1,021	400	37

In addition to gross pay, the company must pay one-half of the $20 per employee weekly health insurance; each employee pays the remaining one-half. The company also contributes an extra 8% of each employee's gross pay (at no cost to employees) to a pension fund.

Required

Compute the following for the week ended September 30 (round amounts to the nearest cent):

1. Each employee's FICA withholdings for Social Security.
2. Each employee's FICA withholdings for Medicare.
3. Employer's FICA taxes for Social Security.
4. Employer's FICA taxes for Medicare.
5. Employer's FUTA taxes.
6. Employer's SUTA taxes.
7. Each employee's net (take-home) pay.
8. Employer's total payroll-related expense for each employee.

Check (3) $316.20
(4) $108.75
(5) $8.16
(7) Total net pay, $6,135.05

Problem 11-5B
Entries for payroll transactions
P2 P3

Ravello Company's first weekly pay period of the year ends on January 8. On that date, the column totals in Ravello's payroll register indicate its sales employees earned $20,160, its office employees earned $70,840, and its delivery employees earned $3,000. The employees are to have withheld from their wages FICA Social Security taxes at the rate of 6.2%, FICA Medicare taxes at the rate of 1.45%, $12,760 of federal income taxes, $1,350 of medical insurance deductions, and $820 of union dues. No employee earned more than $7,000 in the first pay period.

Required

1. Calculate FICA Social Security taxes payable and FICA Medicare taxes payable. Prepare the journal entry to record Ravello Company's January 8 (employee) payroll expenses and liabilities.
2. Prepare the journal entry to record Ravello's (employer) payroll taxes resulting from the January 8 payroll. Ravello's merit rating reduces its state unemployment tax rate to 2% of the first $7,000 paid each employee. The federal unemployment tax rate is 0.8%.

Check (1) Cr. Salaries Payable, $71,879.00
(2) Dr. Payroll Taxes Expense, $9,823.00

Problem 11-6B^A
Entries for payroll transactions
P2 P3 P5

JLS Company has 12 employees, each of whom earns $3,000 per month and is paid on the last day of each month. All 12 have been employed continuously at this amount since January 1. JLS uses a payroll bank account and special payroll checks to pay its employees. On March 1, the following accounts and balances exist in its general ledger:

a. FICA—Social Security Taxes Payable, $4,464; FICA—Medicare Taxes Payable, $1,044. (The balances of these accounts represent total liabilities for *both* the employer's and employees' FICA taxes for the February payroll only.)
b. Employees' Federal Income Taxes Payable, $4,050 (liability for February only).
c. Federal Unemployment Taxes Payable, $576 (liability for January and February together).
d. State Unemployment Taxes Payable, $3,600 (liability for January and February together).

During March and April, the company had the following payroll transactions.

March 15 Issued check payable to Security Bank, a federal depository bank authorized to accept employers' payments of FICA taxes and employee income tax withholdings. The $9,558 check is in payment of the February FICA and employee income taxes.

31 Recorded the March payroll and transferred funds from the regular bank account to the payroll bank account. Issued checks payable to each employee in payment of the March payroll. The payroll register shows the following summary totals for the March pay period.

Check Mar. 31: Cr. Salaries Payable, $29,196

Salaries and Wages					
Office Salaries	Shop Wages	Gross Pay	FICA Taxes*	Federal Income Taxes	Net Pay
$21,000	$15,000	$36,000	$2,232 $ 522	$4,050	$29,196

* FICA taxes are Social Security and Medicare, respectively.

Check March 31: Dr. Payroll Taxes Expenses, $3,450

April 15: Cr. Cash $9,558 (Security Bank)

31 Recorded the employer's payroll taxes resulting from the March payroll. The company has a merit rating that reduces its state unemployment tax rate to 5.0% of the first $7,000 paid each employee. The federal rate is 0.8%.

April 15 Issued check payable to Security Bank in payment of the March FICA and employee income taxes.

15 Issued check to the State Tax Commission for the January, February, and March state unemployment taxes. Mailed the check and the second quarter tax return to the State Tax Commission.

30 Issued check payable to Security Bank in payment of the employer's FUTA taxes for the first quarter of the year.

30 Mailed Form 941 to the IRS, reporting the FICA taxes and the employees' federal income tax withholdings for the first quarter.

Required

Prepare journal entries to record the transactions and events for both March and April.

SERIAL PROBLEM

Success Systems

(This serial problem began in Chapter 1 and continues through most of the book. If previous chapter segments were not completed, the serial problem can begin at this point. It is helpful, but not necessary, to use the Working Papers that accompany the book.)

SP 11 Review the February 26 and March 25 transactions for Success Systems (SP 5) from Chapter 5.

Required

1. Assume that Lyn Addie is an unmarried employee. Her $1,000 of wages are subject to no deductions other than FICA Social Security taxes, FICA Medicare taxes, and federal income taxes. Her federal income taxes for this pay period total $159. Compute her net pay for the eight days' work paid on February 26. (Round amounts to the nearest cent.)
2. Record the journal entry to reflect the payroll payment to Lyn Addie as computed in part 1.
3. Record the journal entry to reflect the (employer) payroll tax expenses for the February 26 payroll payment. Assume Lyn Addie has not met earnings limits for FUTA and SUTA—the FUTA rate is 0.8% and the SUTA rate is 4% for Success Systems. (Round amounts to the nearest cent.)
4. Record the entry(ies) for the merchandise sold on March 25 if a 4% sales tax rate applies.

COMPREHENSIVE PROBLEM

Bug-Off Exterminators (Review of Chapters 1–11)

CP 11 Bug-Off Exterminators provides pest control services and sells extermination products manufactured by other companies. The following six-column table contains the company's unadjusted trial balance as of December 31, 2009.

BUG-OFF EXTERMINATORS
December 31, 2009

	Unadjusted Trial Balance		Adjustments		Adjusted Trial Balance	
Cash	$ 17,000					
Accounts receivable	4,000					
Allowance for doubtful accounts		$ 828				
Merchandise inventory	11,700					
Trucks	32,000					
Accum. depreciation—Trucks		0				
Equipment	45,000					
Accum. depreciation—Equipment		12,200				
Accounts payable		5,000				
Estimated warranty liability		1,400				

[continued on next page]

[continued from previous page]

Unearned services revenue		0
Interest payable		0
Long-term notes payable		15,000
D. Buggs, Capital		59,700
D. Buggs, Withdrawals	10,000	
Extermination services revenue		60,000
Interest revenue		872
Sales (of merchandise)		71,026
Cost of goods sold	46,300	
Depreciation expense—Trucks	0	
Depreciation expense—Equipment	0	
Wages expense	35,000	
Interest expense	0	
Rent expense	9,000	
Bad debts expense	0	
Miscellaneous expense	1,226	
Repairs expense	8,000	
Utilities expense	6,800	
Warranty expense	0	
Totals	$226,026	$226,026

The following information in *a* through *h* applies to the company at the end of the current year.

a. The bank reconciliation as of December 31, 2009, includes the following facts.

Cash balance per bank	$15,100
Cash balance per books	17,000
Outstanding checks	1,800
Deposit in transit	2,450
Interest earned (on bank account)	52
Bank service charges (miscellaneous expense)	15

Reported on the bank statement is a canceled check that the company failed to record. (Information from the bank reconciliation allows you to determine the amount of this check, which is a payment on an account payable.)

b. An examination of customers' accounts shows that accounts totaling $679 should be written off as uncollectible. Using an aging of receivables, the company determines that the ending balance of the Allowance for Doubtful Accounts should be $700.

c. A truck is purchased and placed in service on January 1, 2009. Its cost is being depreciated with the straight-line method using the following facts and estimates.

Original cost	$32,000
Expected salvage value	8,000
Useful life (years)	4

d. Two items of equipment (a sprayer and an injector) were purchased and put into service in early January 2007. They are being depreciated with the straight-line method using these facts and estimates.

	Sprayer	Injector
Original cost	$27,000	$18,000
Expected salvage value	3,000	2,500
Useful life (years)	8	5

e. On August 1, 2009, the company is paid $3,840 cash in advance to provide monthly service for an apartment complex for one year. The company began providing the services in August. When the cash was received, the full amount was credited to the Extermination Services Revenue account.

f. The company offers a warranty for the services it sells. The expected cost of providing warranty service is 2.5% of the extermination services revenue of $57,760 for 2009. No warranty expense has been recorded for 2009. All costs of servicing warranties in 2009 were properly debited to the Estimated Warranty Liability account.

g. The $15,000 long-term note is an 8%, five-year, interest-bearing note with interest payable annually on December 31. The note was signed with First National Bank on December 31, 2009.

h. The ending inventory of merchandise is counted and determined to have a cost of $11,700. Bug-Off uses a perpetual inventory system.

Required

1. Use the preceding information to determine amounts for the following items.

Check (1*a*) Cash bal. $15,750
(1*b*) $551 credit

a. Correct (reconciled) ending balance of Cash, and the amount of the omitted check.
b. Adjustment needed to obtain the correct ending balance of the Allowance for Doubtful Accounts.
c. Depreciation expense for the truck used during year 2009.
d. Depreciation expense for the two items of equipment used during year 2009.
e. The adjusted 2009 ending balances of the Extermination Services Revenue and Unearned Services Revenue accounts.

(1*f*) Estim. warranty liability, $2,844 Cr.

f. The adjusted 2009 ending balances of the accounts for Warranty Expense and Estimated Warranty Liability.
g. The adjusted 2009 ending balances of the accounts for Interest Expense and Interest Payable. (Round amounts to nearest whole dollar.)

(2) Adjusted trial balance totals, $238,207

2. Use the results of part 1 to complete the six-column table by first entering the appropriate adjustments for items *a* through *g* and then completing the adjusted trial balance columns. (*Hint:* Item *b* requires two adjustments.)

3. Prepare journal entries to record the adjustments entered on the six-column table. Assume Bug-Off's adjusted balance for Merchandise Inventory matches the year-end physical count.

(4) Net income, $9,274; Total assets, $82,771

4. Prepare a single-step income statement, a statement of owner's equity (cash withdrawals during 2009 were $10,000), and a classified balance sheet.

BEYOND THE NUMBERS

REPORTING IN ACTION

A1 P4

BTN 11-1 Refer to the financial statements of **Best Buy** in Appendix A to answer the following.

1. Compute times interest earned for the fiscal years ended 2007, 2006, and 2005. Comment on Best Buy's ability to cover its interest expense for this period. Assume an industry average of 28.1.

2. Best Buy's current liabilities include "Unredeemed gift card liabilities." Explain how this liability is created and how Best Buy satisfies this liability.

3. Does Best Buy have any commitments or contingencies? Briefly explain them.

Fast Forward

4. Access Best Buy's financial statements for fiscal years ending after March 3, 2007, at its Website (BestBuy.com) or the SEC's EDGAR database (www.SEC.gov). Compute its times interest earned for years ending after March 3, 2007, and compare your results to those in part 1.

COMPARATIVE ANALYSIS

A1

BTN 11-2 Key figures for **Best Buy**, **Circuit City**, and **RadioShack** follow.

	Best Buy			Circuit City			RadioShack		
($ millions)	Current Year	One Year Prior	Two Years Prior	Current Year	One Year Prior	Two Years Prior	Current Year	One Year Prior	Two Years Prior
Net income	$1,377	$1,140	$984	$(8)	$140	$62	$73	$267	$337
Income taxes	752	581	509	31	86	36	38	52	205
Interest expense	31	30	44	2	3	4	44	45	30

Required

1. Compute times interest earned for the three years' data shown for each company.

2. Comment on which company appears stronger in its ability to pay interest obligations if income should decline. Assume an industry average of 28.1.

ETHICS CHALLENGE

P4

BTN 11-3 Connor Bly is a sales manager for an automobile dealership. He earns a bonus each year based on revenue from the number of autos sold in the year less related warranty expenses. Actual warranty expenses have varied over the prior 10 years from a low of 3% of an automobile's selling price to a high of 10%. In the past, Bly has tended to estimate warranty expenses on the high end to be conservative. He must work with the dealership's accountant at year-end to arrive at the warranty expense accrual for cars sold each year.

1. Does the warranty accrual decision create any ethical dilemma for Bly?

2. Since warranty expenses vary, what percent do you think Bly should choose for the current year? Justify your response.

COMMUNICATING IN PRACTICE

C3

BTN 11-4 Dustin Clemens is the accounting and finance manager for a manufacturer. At year-end, he must determine how to account for the company's contingencies. His manager, Madeline Pretti, objects to Clemens's proposal to recognize an expense and a liability for warranty service on units of a new product introduced in the fourth quarter. Pretti comments, "There's no way we can estimate this warranty cost. We don't owe anyone anything until a product fails and it is returned. Let's report an expense if and when we do any warranty work."

Required

Prepare a one-page memorandum for Clemens to send to Pretti defending his proposal.

TAKING IT TO THE NET

C1 A1

BTN 11-5 Access the February 26, 2007, filing of the December 31, 2006, annual 10-K report of **McDonald's Corporation** (Ticker: MCD), which is available from www.SEC.gov.

Required

1. Identify the current liabilities on McDonald's balance sheet as of December 31, 2006.

2. What portion (in percent) of McDonald's long-term debt matures within the next 12 months?

3. Use the consolidated statement of income for the year ended December 31, 2006, to compute McDonald's times interest earned ratio. Comment on the result. Assume an industry average of 7.9.

TEAMWORK IN ACTION

C2 P1

BTN 11-6 Assume that your team is in business and you must borrow $6,000 cash for short-term needs. You have been shopping banks for a loan, and you have the following two options.

A. Sign a $6,000, 90-day, 10% interest-bearing note dated June 1.

B. Sign a $6,000, 120-day, 8% interest-bearing note dated June 1.

Required

1. Discuss these two options and determine the best choice. Ensure that all teammates concur with the decision and understand the rationale.

2. Each member of the team is to prepare *one* of the following journal entries.

  a. Option A—at date of issuance.

  b. Option B—at date of issuance.

  c. Option A—at maturity date.

  d. Option B—at maturity date.

3. In rotation, each member is to explain the entry he or she prepared in part 2 to the team. Ensure that all team members concur with and understand the entries.

4. Assume that the funds are borrowed on December 1 (instead of June 1) and your business operates on a calendar-year reporting period. Each member of the team is to prepare *one* of the following entries.
   a. Option A—the year-end adjustment.
   b. Option B—the year-end adjustment.
   c. Option A—at maturity date.
   d. Option B—at maturity date.
5. In rotation, each member is to explain the entry he or she prepared in part 4 to the team. Ensure that all team members concur with and understand the entries.

ENTREPRENEURIAL DECISION

A1

BTN 11-7 Review the chapter's opening feature about Jason Osborn and Jason Wright, and their start-up company, **Feed Granola Company**. Assume that these young entrepreneurs are considering expanding their business to open an outlet in Europe. Assume their current income statement is as follows.

FEED GRANOLA COMPANY Income Statement For Year Ended December 31, 2009	
Sales	$1,000,000
Cost of goods sold (30%)	300,000
Gross profit	700,000
Operating expenses (25%)	250,000
Net income	$ 450,000

Feed Granola Company currently has no interest-bearing debt. If it expands to open a European location, it will require a $300,000 loan. Feed Granola Company has found a bank that will loan it the money on a 7% note payable. The company believes that, at least for the first few years, sales at its European location will be $250,000, and that all expenses (including cost of goods sold) will follow the same patterns as its current locations.

Required

1. Prepare an income statement (separately for current operations, European, and total) for Feed Granola Company assuming that it borrows the funds and expands to Europe. Annual revenues for current operations are expected to remain at $1,000,000.
2. Compute Feed Granola Company's times interest earned under the expansion assumptions in part 1.
3. Assume sales at its European location are $400,000. Prepare an income statement (separately for current operations, European, and total) for the company and compute times interest earned.
4. Assume sales at its European location are $100,000. Prepare an income statement (separately for current operations, European, and total) for the company and compute times interest earned.
5. Comment on your results from parts 1 through 4.

HITTING THE ROAD

P2

BTN 11-8 Check your phone book or the Social Security Administration Website (www.SSA.gov) to locate the Social Security office near you. Visit the office to request a personal earnings and estimate form. Fill out the form and mail according to the instructions. You will receive a statement from the Social Security Administration regarding your earnings history and future Social Security benefits you can receive. (Formerly the request could be made online. The online service has been discontinued and is now under review by the Social Security Administration due to security concerns.) It is good to request an earnings and benefit statement every 5 to 10 years to make sure you have received credit for all wages earned and for which you and your employer have paid taxes into the system.

BTN 11-9 **DSG international, Best Buy, Circuit City,** and **RadioShack** are all competitors in the global marketplace. Comparative figures for DSG (**DSGiplc.com**), along with selected figures from Best Buy, Circuit City, and RadioShack follow.

GLOBAL DECISION

A1

Key Figures	DSG (£ millions) Current Year	Prior Year	Best Buy Current Year	Prior Year	Circuit City Current Year	Prior Year	RadioShack Current Year	Prior Year
Net income	207	222	—	—	—	—	—	—
Income taxes	89	89	—	—	—	—	—	—
Interest expense*	73	65	—	—	—	—	—	—
Times interest earned	?	?	69.7	58.4	12.5	76.3	3.5	8.1

* Titled Finance costs for DSG.

Required

1. Compute the times interest earned ratio for the most recent two years for DSG using the data shown.
2. Which company of the four presented provides the best coverage of interest expense? Explain.

ANSWERS TO MULTIPLE CHOICE QUIZ

1. b; $6,000 × 0.05 × 30/360 = $25
2. e; $50,000 × (.062 + .0145) = $3,825
3. b; $7,000 × (.008 + .054) = $434
4. c; 10,000 television sets × .01 × $250 = $25,000
5. a; 150 employees × $175 per day × 1 vacation day earned = $26,250

A Look Back

Chapter 11 focused on how current liabilities are identified, computed, recorded, and reported. Attention was directed at notes, payroll, sales taxes, warranties, employee benefits, and contingencies.

A Look at This Chapter

This chapter explains the partnership form of organization. Important partnership characteristics are described along with the accounting concepts and procedures for its most fundamental transactions.

A Look Ahead

Chapter 13 extends our discussion to the corporate form of organization. We describe the accounting and reporting for stock issuances, dividends, and other equity transactions.

Chapter 12 Accounting for Partnerships

Learning Objectives

CAP

Conceptual

C1 Identify characteristics of partnerships and similar organizations. *(p. 478)*

Analytical

A1 Compute partner return on equity and use it to evaluate partnership performance. *(p. 490)*

Procedural

P1 Prepare entries for partnership formation. *(p. 481)*

P2 Allocate and record income and loss among partners. *(p. 481)*

P3 Account for the admission and withdrawal of partners. *(p. 484)*

P4 Prepare entries for partnership liquidation. *(p. 488)*

LP12

Decision Feature

A Fitting Pair

"Be your best, make a difference, and live with passion"—Samanta and Kelvin Joseph

NEW YORK—Business recipe: Take one information systems graduate, mix a bit of international flair, add an accountant, and stir. The result is **Samanta Shoes (SamantaShoes.com),** a start-up shoe manufacturer. Founded by Samanta and Kelvin Joseph, their partnership is aimed at providing "stylish, comfortable, and affordable" shoes, explains Samanta. "I design every shoe, and nothing less than the best material is used."

Kelvin's focus is on the accounting and financial side of Samanta Shoes. "The knowledge gained from my years at Ernst & Young LLP [a major accounting firm]," explains Kelvin, "has enabled me to be more helpful." Kelvin's knowledge of partnerships and their financial implications are important to Samanta's success. Both partners stress the importance of attending to partnership formation, partnership agreements, and financial reports to stay afloat. They refer to the partners' return on equity and the organizational form as key inputs to partnership success.

Success is causing their partnership to evolve, but the partners adhere to a quality first mentality. "It's all in the design," insists Samanta. "[A quality design] allows for more comfort and support." But quality also extends to style and uniqueness. "Women don't like other women having their shoe," explains Samanta. "We don't want to dilute our brand by being too mass market." Kelvin explains that the smallest manufacturing run they can have is 18 pairs of a special line. In a world of 6 billion people, that is unique.

The partners also continue to apply strict accounting fundamentals. "The partnership cannot survive," says Kelvin, "unless our business is profitable." They regularly review the accounting results and assess the partnership's costs and revenues. Although he adds, "money does not equal happiness." Samanta explains, "Live your dreams . . . make a difference . . . give back to your community"—advice that we can all live by. "If you're not enjoying it," continues Samanta, "there's no point to doing it."

[Sources: *Samanta Shoes Website,* January 2009; *New York Resident,* August 2004; *Caribbean Vibe,* August 2004; *Black Enterprise,* June 2006; *Regine Magazine,* Spring 2004; *Inc.com,* July 2007]

The three basic types of business organizations are proprietorships, partnerships, and corporations. Partnerships are similar to proprietorships, except they have more than one owner. This chapter explains partnerships and looks at several variations of them such as limited partnerships, limited liability partnerships, S corporations, and limited liability companies. Understanding the advantages and disadvantages of the partnership form of business organization is important for making informed business decisions.

Accounting for Partnerships

Partnership Organization
- Characteristics
- Organizations with partnership characteristics
- Choice of business form

Basic Partnership Accounting
- Organizing a partnership
- Dividing income or loss
- Partnership financial statements

Partner Admission and Withdrawal
- Admission of partner
- Withdrawal of partner
- Death of partner

Partnership Liquidation
- No capital deficiency
- Capital deficiency

Partnership Form of Organization

C1 Identify characteristics of partnerships and similar organizations.

A **partnership** is an unincorporated association of two or more people to pursue a business for profit as co-owners. Many businesses are organized as partnerships. They are especially common in small retail and service businesses. Many professional practitioners, including physicians, lawyers, investors, and accountants, also organize their practices as partnerships.

Characteristics of Partnerships

Partnerships are an important type of organization because they offer certain advantages with their unique characteristics. We describe these characteristics in this section.

Voluntary Association A partnership is a voluntary association between partners. Joining a partnership increases the risk to one's personal financial position. Some courts have ruled that partnerships are created by the actions of individuals even when there is no *express agreement* to form one.

Point: When a new partner is admitted, all parties usually must agree to the admission.

Partnership Agreement Forming a partnership requires that two or more legally competent people (who are of age and of sound mental capacity) agree to be partners. Their agreement becomes a **partnership contract,** also called *articles of copartnership.* Although it should be in writing, the contract is binding even if it is only expressed verbally. Partnership agreements normally include details of the partners' (1) names and contributions, (2) rights and duties, (3) sharing of income and losses, (4) withdrawal arrangement, (5) dispute procedures, (6) admission and withdrawal of partners, and (7) rights and duties in the event a partner dies.

Point: The end of a partnership is referred to as its *dissolution.*

Limited Life The life of a partnership is limited. Death, bankruptcy, or any event taking away the ability of a partner to enter into or fulfill a contract ends a partnership. Any one of the partners can also terminate a partnership at will.

Point: Partners are taxed on their share of partnership income, not on their withdrawals.

Taxation A partnership is not subject to taxes on its income. The income or loss of a partnership is allocated to the partners according to the partnership agreement, and it is included in determining the taxable income for each partner's tax return. Partnership income or loss is allocated each year whether or not cash is distributed to partners.

Mutual Agency **Mutual agency** implies that each partner is a fully authorized agent of the partnership. As its agent, a partner can commit or bind the partnership to any contract within the

scope of the partnership business. For instance, a partner in a merchandising business can sign contracts binding the partnership to buy merchandise, lease a store building, borrow money, or hire employees. These activities are all within the scope of a merchandising firm. A partner in a law firm, acting alone, however, cannot bind the other partners to a contract to buy snowboards for resale or rent an apartment for parties. These actions are outside the normal scope of a law firm's business. Partners also can agree to limit the power of any one or more of the partners to negotiate contracts for the partnership. This agreement is binding on the partners and on outsiders who know it exists. It is not binding on outsiders who do not know it exists. Outsiders unaware of the agreement have the right to assume each partner has normal agency powers for the partnership. Mutual agency exposes partners to the risk of unwise actions by any one partner.

Point: The majority of states adhere to the Uniform Partnership Act for the basic rules of partnership formation, operation, and dissolution.

Unlimited Liability **Unlimited liability** implies that each partner can be called on to pay a partnership's debts. When a partnership cannot pay its debts, creditors usually can apply their claims to partners' *personal* assets. If a partner does not have enough assets to meet his or her share of the partnership debt, the creditors can apply their claims to the assets of the other partners. A partnership in which all partners have *mutual agency* and *unlimited liability* is called a **general partnership.** Mutual agency and unlimited liability are two main reasons that most general partnerships have only a few members.

Point: Limited life, mutual agency, and unlimited liability are disadvantages of a partnership.

Co-Ownership of Property Partnership assets are owned jointly by all partners. Any investment by a partner becomes the joint property of all partners. Partners have a claim on partnership assets based on their capital account and the partnership contract.

Organizations with Partnership Characteristics

Organizations exist that combine certain characteristics of partnerships with other forms of organizations. We discuss several of these forms in this section.

Limited Partnerships Some individuals who want to invest in a partnership are unwilling to accept the risk of unlimited liability. Their needs can be met with a **limited partnership.** This type of organization is identified in its name with the words "Limited Partnership" or "Ltd." or "LP." A limited partnership has two classes of partners, general and limited. At least one partner must be a **general partner,** who assumes management duties and unlimited liability for the debts of the partnership. The **limited partners** have no personal liability beyond the amounts they invest in the partnership. Limited partners have no active role except as specified in the partnership agreement. A limited partnership agreement often specifies unique procedures for allocating income and losses between general and limited partners. The accounting procedures are similar for both limited and general partnerships.

Decision Insight

Nutty Partners The Hawaii-based **ML Macadamia Orchards LP** is one of the world's largest growers of macadamia nuts. It reported the following partners' capital balances ($ 000s) in its balance sheet:

General Partner	$ 81
Limited Partners	$43,297

Limited Liability Partnerships Most states allow individuals to form a **limited liability partnership.** This is identified in its name with the words "Limited Liability Partnership" or by "LLP." This type of partnership is designed to protect innocent partners from malpractice or negligence claims resulting from the acts of another partner. When a partner provides service resulting in a malpractice claim, that partner has personal liability for the claim. The remaining partners who were not responsible for the actions resulting in the claim are not personally liable for it. However, most states hold all partners personally liable for other partnership debts. Accounting for a limited liability partnership is the same as for a general partnership.

Point: Many accounting services firms are set up as LLPs.

S Corporations Certain corporations with 75 or fewer stockholders can elect to be treated as a partnership for income tax purposes. These corporations are called *Sub-Chapter S* or simply **S corporations.** This distinguishes them from other corporations, called *Sub-Chapter C* or simply **C corporations.** S corporations provide stockholders the same limited liability feature that C corporations do. The advantage of an S corporation is that it does not pay income taxes. If stockholders work for an S corporation, their salaries are treated as expenses of the corporation. The remaining income or loss of the corporation is allocated to stockholders for inclusion on their personal tax returns. Except for C corporations having to account for income tax expenses and liabilities, the accounting procedures are the same for both S and C corporations.

Point: The majority of proprietorships and partnerships that are organized today are set up as LLCs.

Limited Liability Companies A relatively new form of business organization is the **limited liability company.** The names of these businesses usually include the words "Limited Liability Company" or an abbreviation such as "LLC" or "LC." This form of business has certain features similar to a corporation and others similar to a limited partnership. The owners, who are called *members,* are protected with the same limited liability feature as owners of corporations. While limited partners cannot actively participate in the management of a limited partnership, the members of a limited liability company can assume an active management role. A limited liability company usually has a limited life. For income tax purposes, a limited liability company is typically treated as a partnership. This treatment depends on factors such as whether the members' equity interests are freely transferable and whether the company has continuity of life. A limited liability company's accounting system is designed to help management comply with the dictates of the articles of organization and company regulations adopted by its members. The accounting system also must provide information to support the company's compliance with state and federal laws, including taxation.

Point: Accounting for LLCs is similar to that for partnerships (and proprietorships). One difference is that Owner (Partner), Capital is usually called *Members, Capital* for LLCs.

Choosing a Business Form

Choosing the proper business form is crucial. Many factors should be considered, including taxes, liability risk, tax and fiscal year-end, ownership structure, estate planning, business risks, and earnings and property distributions. The following table summarizes several important characteristics of business organizations:

	Proprietorship	Partnership	LLP	LLC	S Corp.	Corporation
Business entity	Yes	Yes	Yes	Yes	Yes	Yes
Legal entity	No	No	No	Yes	Yes	Yes
Limited liability	No	No	Limited*	Yes	Yes	Yes
Business taxed	No	No	No	No	No	Yes
One owner allowed	Yes	No	No	Yes	Yes	Yes

* A partner's personal liability for LLP debts is limited. Most LLPs carry insurance to protect against malpractice.

Point: The Small Business Administration provides suggestions and information on setting up the proper form for your organization—see SBA.gov.

We must remember that this table is a summary, not a detailed list. Many details underlie each of these business forms, and several details differ across states. Also, state and federal laws change, and a body of law is still developing around LLCs. Business owners should look at these details and consider unique business arrangements such as organizing various parts of their businesses in different forms.

Quick Check Answers—p. 493

1. A partnership is terminated in the event (*a*) a partnership agreement is not in writing, (*b*) a partner dies, (*c*) a partner exercises mutual agency.
2. What does the term *unlimited liability* mean when applied to a general partnership?
3. Which of the following forms of organization do not provide limited liability to *all* of its owners? (*a*) S corporation, (*b*) limited liability company, (*c*) limited partnership.

Basic Partnership Accounting

Since ownership rights in a partnership are divided among partners, partnership accounting

- Uses a capital account for each partner.
- Uses a withdrawals account for each partner.
- Allocates net income or loss to partners according to the partnership agreement.

This section describes partnership accounting for organizing a partnership, distributing income and loss, and preparing financial statements.

Organizing a Partnership

P1 Prepare entries for partnership formation.

When partners invest in a partnership, their capital accounts are credited for the invested amounts. Partners can invest both assets and liabilities. Each partner's investment is recorded at an agreed-on value, normally the market values of the contributed assets and liabilities at the date of contribution. To illustrate, Kayla Zayn and Hector Perez organize a partnership on January 11 called BOARDS that offers year-round facilities for skateboarding and snowboarding. Zayn's initial net investment in BOARDS is $30,000, made up of cash ($7,000), boarding facilities ($33,000), and a note payable reflecting a bank loan for the new business ($10,000). Perez's initial investment is cash of $10,000. These amounts are the values agreed on by both partners. The entries to record these investments follow.

Zayn's Investment

Jan. 11	Cash	7,000	
	Boarding facilities	33,000	
	Note payable		10,000
	K. Zayn, Capital		30,000
	To record the investment of Zayn.		

Assets = Liabilities + Equity
+7,000 +10,000 +30,000
+33,000

Perez's Investment

Jan. 11	Cash	10,000	
	H. Perez, Capital		10,000
	To record the investment of Perez.		

Assets = Liabilities + Equity
+10,000 +10,000

In accounting for a partnership, the following additional relations hold true: (1) Partners' withdrawals are debited to their own separate withdrawals accounts. (2) Partners' capital accounts are credited (or debited) for their shares of net income (or net loss) when closing the accounts at the end of a period. (3) Each partner's withdrawals account is closed to that partner's capital account. Separate capital and withdrawals accounts are kept for each partner.

Point: Both equity and cash are reduced when a partner withdraws cash from a partnership.

Decision Insight

Broadway Partners **Big River Productions** is a partnership that owns the rights to the play *Big River*. The play is performed on tour and periodically on Broadway. For 2006, its Partners' Capital was **$288,640**, and it was distributed in its entirety to the partners.

Dividing Income or Loss

P2 Allocate and record income and loss among partners.

Partners are not employees of the partnership but are its owners. If partners devote their time and services to their partnership, they are understood to do so for profit, not for salary. This means there are no salaries to partners that are reported as expenses on the partnership income statement. However, when net income or loss of a partnership is allocated among partners, the partners can agree to allocate "salary allowances" reflecting the relative value of services provided. Partners also can agree to allocate "interest allowances" based on the amount invested. For instance, since Zayn contributes three times the investment of Perez, it is only fair that this be considered when allocating income between them. Like salary allowances, these interest allowances are not expenses on the income statement.

Partners can agree to any method of dividing income or loss. In the absence of an agreement, the law says that the partners share income or loss of a partnership equally. If partners agree on how to share income but say nothing about losses, they share losses the same way they share income. Three common methods to divide income or loss use (1) a stated ratio basis, (2) the ratio of capital balances, or (3) salary and interest allowances and any remainder according to a fixed ratio. We explain each of these methods in this section.

Point: Partners can agree on a ratio to divide income and another ratio to divide a loss.

Allocation on Stated Ratios The *stated ratio* (also called the *income-and-loss-sharing ratio,* the *profit and loss ratio,* or the *P&L ratio*) method of allocating partnership income or loss gives each partner a fraction of the total. Partners must agree on the fractional share each receives. To illustrate, assume the partnership agreement of K. Zayn and H. Perez says Zayn receives two-thirds and Perez one-third of partnership income and loss. If their partnership's net income is $60,000, it is allocated to the partners when the Income Summary account is closed as follows.

Point: The fractional basis can be stated as a proportion, ratio, or percent. For example, a 3:2 basis is the same as 3/5 and 2/5, or 60% and 40%.

Dec. 31	Income Summary	60,000	
	K. Zayn, Capital.		40,000
	H. Perez, Capital		20,000
	To allocate income and close Income Summary.		

Assets	=	Liabilities	+	Equity
				−60,000
				+40,000
				+20,000

Allocation on Capital Balances The *capital balances* method of allocating partnership income or loss assigns an amount based on the ratio of each partner's relative capital balance. If Zayn and Perez agree to share income and loss on the ratio of their beginning capital balances—Zayn's $30,000 and Perez's $10,000—Zayn receives three-fourths of any income or loss ($30,000/$40,000) and Perez receives one-fourth ($10,000/$40,000). The journal entry follows the same format as that using stated ratios (see the preceding entries).

Point: To determine the percent of income received by each partner, divide an individual partner's share by total net income.

Allocation on Services, Capital, and Stated Ratios The *services, capital, and stated ratio* method of allocating partnership income or loss recognizes that service and capital contributions of partners often are not equal. Salary allowances can make up for differences in service contributions. Interest allowances can make up for unequal capital contributions. Also, the allocation of income and loss can include *both* salary and interest allowances. To illustrate, assume that the partnership agreement of K. Zayn and H. Perez reflects differences in service and capital contributions as follows: (1) annual salary allowances of $36,000 to Zayn and $24,000 to Perez, (2) annual interest allowances of 10% of a partner's beginning-year capital balance, and (3) equal share of any remaining balance of income or loss. These salaries and interest allowances are *not* reported as expenses on the income statement. They are simply a means of dividing partnership income or loss. The remainder of this section provides two illustrations using this three-point allocation agreement.

Illustration when income exceeds allowance. If BOARDS has first-year net income of $70,000, and Zayn and Perez apply the three-point partnership agreement described in the prior paragraph, income is allocated as shown in Exhibit 12.1. Zayn gets $42,000 and Perez gets $28,000 of the $70,000 total.

Illustration when allowances exceed income. The sharing agreement between Zayn and Perez must be followed even if net income is less than the total of the allowances. For example, if BOARDS' first-year net income is $50,000 instead of $70,000, it is allocated to the partners as shown in Exhibit 12.2. Computations for salaries and interest are identical to those in Exhibit 12.1. However, when we apply the total allowances against income, the balance of income is negative. This $(14,000) negative balance is allocated equally to the partners per their sharing agreement. This means that a negative $(7,000) is allocated to each partner. In this case, Zayn ends up with $32,000 and Perez with $18,000. If BOARDS had experienced a net loss, Zayn and Perez would share it in the same manner as the $50,000 income. The only difference is that they would have begun with a negative amount because of the loss. Specifically, the partners

Point: When allowances exceed income, the amount of this negative balance often is referred to as a *sharing agreement loss* or *deficit.*

Point: Check to make sure the sum of the dollar amounts allocated to each partner equals net income or loss.

EXHIBIT 12.1

Dividing Income When Income Exceeds Allowances

	Zayn	Perez	Total
Net income			$70,000
Salary allowances			
Zayn	$ 36,000		
Perez		$ 24,000	
Interest allowances			
Zayn (10% × $30,000)	3,000		
Perez (10% × $10,000)		1,000	
Total salaries and interest	39,000	25,000	64,000
Balance of income			**6,000**
Balance allocated equally			
Zayn	3,000 ←		
Perez		3,000 ←	
Total allocated			6,000
Balance of income			$ 0
Income of each partner	$42,000	$28,000	

EXHIBIT 12.2

Dividing Income When Allowances Exceed Income

	Zayn	Perez	Total
Net income			$50,000
Salary allowances			
Zayn	$ 36,000		
Perez		$ 24,000	
Interest allowances			
Zayn (10% × $30,000)	3,000		
Perez (10% × $10,000)		1,000	
Total salaries and interest	39,000	25,000	64,000
Balance of income			**(14,000)**
Balance allocated equally			
Zayn	(7,000) ←		
Perez		(7,000) ←	
Total allocated			(14,000)
Balance of income			$ 0
Income of each partner	$32,000	$18,000	

would still have been allocated their salary and interest allowances, further adding to the negative balance of the loss. This *total* negative balance *after* salary and interest allowances would have been allocated equally between the partners. These allocations would have been applied against the positive numbers from any allowances to determine each partner's share of the loss.

Point: When a loss occurs, it is possible for a specific partner's capital to increase (when closing income summary) if that partner's allowance is in excess of his or her share of the negative balance. This implies that decreases to the capital balances of other partners exceed the partnership's loss amount.

Quick Check

Answers—p. 493

4. Denzel and Shantell form a partnership by contributing $70,000 and $35,000, respectively. They agree to an interest allowance equal to 10% of each partner's capital balance at the beginning of the year, with the remaining income shared equally. Allocate first-year income of $40,000 to each partner.

Partnership Financial Statements

Partnership financial statements are similar to those of other organizations. The **statement of partners' equity,** also called *statement of partners' capital,* is one exception. It shows *each* partner's beginning capital balance, additional investments, allocated income or loss, withdrawals, and ending capital balance. To illustrate, Exhibit 12.3 shows the statement of partners' equity for BOARDS prepared using the sharing agreement of Exhibit 12.1. Recall that BOARDS' income was $70,000; also, assume that Zayn withdrew $20,000 and Perez $12,000 at year-end.

EXHIBIT 12.3

Statement of Partners' Equity

BOARDS
Statement of Partners' Equity
For Year Ended December 31, 2009

	Zayn		Perez		Total
Beginning capital balances		$ 0		$ 0	$ 0
Plus					
Investments by owners		30,000		10,000	40,000
Net income					
Salary allowances	$36,000		$24,000		
Interest allowances	3,000		1,000		
Balance allocated	3,000		3,000		
Total net income		42,000		28,000	70,000
		72,000		38,000	110,000
Less partners' withdrawals		(20,000)		(12,000)	(32,000)
Ending capital balances		**$52,000**		**$26,000**	**$78,000**

The equity section of the balance sheet of a partnership usually shows the separate capital account balance of each partner. In the case of BOARDS, both K. Zayn, Capital, and H. Perez, Capital, are listed in the equity section along with their balances of $52,000 and $26,000, respectively.

Decision Insight

Gambling Partners **Trump Entertainment Resorts LP** and subsidiaries operate three casino hotel properties in Atlantic City: Trump Taj Mahal Casino Resort ("Trump Taj Mahal"), Trump Plaza Hotel and Casino ("Trump Plaza"), and Trump Marina Hotel Casino ("Trump Marina"). Its recent statement of partners' equity reports $979,000 in partners' withdrawals, leaving $594,230,000 in partners' capital balances.

Admission and Withdrawal of Partners

P3 Account for the admission and withdrawal of partners.

A partnership is based on a contract between individuals. When a partner is admitted or withdraws, the present partnership ends. Still, the business can continue to operate as a new partnership consisting of the remaining partners. This section considers how to account for the admission and withdrawal of partners.

Admission of a Partner

A new partner is admitted in one of two ways: by purchasing an interest from one or more current partners or by investing cash or other assets in the partnership.

Purchase of Partnership Interest The purchase of partnership interest is a *personal transaction between one or more current partners and the new partner.* To become a partner, the current partners must accept the purchaser. Accounting for the purchase of partnership interest involves reallocating current partners' capital to reflect the transaction. To illustrate, at the end of BOARDS' first year, H. Perez sells one-half of his partnership interest to Tyrell Rasheed for $18,000. This means that Perez gives up a $13,000 recorded interest ($26,000 × 1/2) in the partnership (see the ending capital balance in Exhibit 12.3). The partnership records this January 4 transaction as follows.

Assets = Liabilities + Equity
−13,000
+13,000

Jan. 4	H. Perez, Capital	13,000	
	T. Rasheed, Capital		13,000
	To record admission of Rasheed by purchase.		

After this entry is posted, BOARDS' equity shows K. Zayn, Capital; H. Perez, Capital; and T. Rasheed, Capital, and their respective balances of $52,000, $13,000, and $13,000.

Two aspects of this transaction are important. First, the partnership does *not* record the $18,000 Rasheed paid Perez. The partnership's assets, liabilities, and *total equity* are unaffected by this transaction among partners. Second, Zayn and Perez must agree that Rasheed is to become a partner. If they agree to accept Rasheed, a new partnership is formed and a new contract with a new income-and-loss-sharing agreement is prepared. If Zayn or Perez refuses to accept Rasheed as a partner, then (under the Uniform Partnership Act) Rasheed gets Perez's sold share of partnership income and loss. If the partnership is liquidated, Rasheed gets Perez's sold share of partnership assets. Rasheed gets no voice in managing the company unless Rasheed is admitted as a partner.

Point: Partners' withdrawals are not constrained by the partnership's annual income or loss.

Investing Assets in a Partnership Admitting a partner by accepting assets is a *transaction between the new partner and the partnership.* The invested assets become partnership property. To illustrate, if Zayn (with a $52,000 interest) and Perez (with a $26,000 interest) agree to accept Rasheed as a partner in BOARDS after an investment of $22,000 cash, this is recorded as follows.

Jan. 4	Cash	22,000	
	T. Rasheed, Capital.		22,000
	To record admission of Rasheed by investment.		

Assets	= Liabilities +	Equity
+22,000		+22,000

After this entry is posted, both assets (cash) and equity (T. Rasheed, Capital) increase by $22,000. Rasheed now has a 22% equity in the assets of the business, computed as $22,000 divided by the entire partnership equity ($52,000 + $26,000 + $22,000). Rasheed does not necessarily have a right to 22% of income. Dividing income and loss is a separate matter on which partners must agree.

Bonus to old partners. When the current value of a partnership is greater than the recorded amounts of equity, the partners usually require a new partner to pay a bonus for the privilege of joining. To illustrate, assume that Zayn and Perez agree to accept Rasheed as a partner with a 25% interest in BOARDS if Rasheed invests $42,000. Recall that the partnership's accounting records show that Zayn's recorded equity in the business is $52,000 and Perez's recorded equity is $26,000 (see Exhibit 12.3). Rasheed's equity is determined as follows.

Equities of existing partners ($52,000 + $26,000)	$ 78,000
Investment of new partner	42,000
Total partnership equity	$120,000
Equity of Rasheed (25% × $120,000)	$ 30,000

Although Rasheed invests $42,000, the equity attributed to Rasheed in the new partnership is only $30,000. The $12,000 difference is called a *bonus* and is allocated to existing partners (Zayn and Perez) according to their income-and-loss-sharing agreement. A bonus is shared in this way because it is viewed as reflecting a higher value of the partnership that is not yet reflected in income. The entry to record this transaction follows.

Jan. 4	Cash	42,000	
	T. Rasheed, Capital.		30,000
	K. Zayn, Capital ($12,000 × ½).		6,000
	H. Perez, Capital ($12,000 × ½)		6,000
	To record admission of Rasheed and bonus.		

Assets	= Liabilities +	Equity
+42,000		+30,000
		+6,000
		+6,000

Bonus to new partner. Alternatively, existing partners can grant a bonus to a new partner. This usually occurs when they need additional cash or the new partner has exceptional talents. The bonus to the new partner is in the form of a larger share of equity than the amount invested. To illustrate, assume that Zayn and Perez agree to accept Rasheed as a partner with a 25%

interest in the partnership, but they require Rasheed to invest only $18,000. Rasheed's equity is determined as follows.

Equities of existing partners ($52,000 + $26,000)	$78,000
Investment of new partner	18,000
Total partnership equity	$96,000
Equity of Rasheed (25% × $96,000)	$24,000

The old partners contribute the $6,000 bonus (computed as $24,000 minus $18,000) to Rasheed according to their income-and-loss-sharing ratio. Moreover, Rasheed's 25% equity does not necessarily entitle Rasheed to 25% of future income or loss. This is a separate matter for agreement by the partners. The entry to record the admission and investment of Rasheed is

Assets	= Liabilities +	Equity
+18,000		−3,000
		−3,000
		+24,000

Jan. 4	Cash	18,000	
	K. Zayn, Capital ($6,000 × ½)	3,000	
	H. Perez, Capital ($6,000 × ½)	3,000	
	T. Rasheed, Capital..................		24,000
	To record Rasheed's admission and bonus.		

Withdrawal of a Partner

A partner generally withdraws from a partnership in one of two ways. (1) First, the withdrawing partner can sell his or her interest to another person who pays for it in cash or other assets. For this, we need only debit the withdrawing partner's capital account and credit the new partner's capital account. (2) The second case is when cash or other assets of the partnership are distributed to the withdrawing partner in settlement of his or her interest. To illustrate these cases, assume that Perez withdraws from the partnership of BOARDS in some future period. The partnership shows the following capital balances at the date of Perez's withdrawal: K. Zayn, $84,000; H. Perez, $38,000; and T. Rasheed, $38,000. The partners (Zayn, Perez, and Rasheed) share income and loss equally. Accounting for Perez's withdrawal depends on whether a bonus is paid. We describe three possibilities.

No Bonus If Perez withdraws and takes cash equal to Perez's capital balance, the entry is

Assets	= Liabilities +	Equity
−38,000		−38,000

Oct. 31	H. Perez, Capital..................	38,000	
	Cash		38,000
	To record withdrawal of Perez from partnership with no bonus.		

Perez can take any combination of assets to which the partners agree to settle Perez's equity. Perez's withdrawal creates a new partnership between the remaining partners. A new partnership contract and a new income-and-loss-sharing agreement are required.

Bonus to Remaining Partners A withdrawing partner is sometimes willing to take less than the recorded value of his or her equity to get out of the partnership or because the recorded value is overstated. Whatever the reason, when this occurs, the withdrawing partner in effect gives the remaining partners a bonus equal to the equity left behind. The remaining partners share this unwithdrawn equity according to their income-and-loss-sharing ratio. To illustrate, if Perez withdraws and agrees to take $34,000 cash in settlement of Perez's capital balance, the entry is

Assets	= Liabilities +	Equity
−34,000		−38,000
		+2,000
		+2,000

Oct. 31	H. Perez, Capital..................	38,000	
	Cash		34,000
	K. Zayn, Capital..................		2,000
	T. Rasheed, Capital..................		2,000
	To record withdrawal of Perez and bonus to remaining partners.		

Perez withdrew $4,000 less than Perez's recorded equity of $38,000. This $4,000 is divided between Zayn and Rasheed according to their income-and-loss-sharing ratio.

Bonus to Withdrawing Partner A withdrawing partner may be able to receive more than his or her recorded equity for at least two reasons. First, the recorded equity may be understated. Second, the remaining partners may agree to remove this partner by giving assets of greater value than this partner's recorded equity. In either case, the withdrawing partner receives a bonus. The remaining partners reduce their equity by the amount of this bonus according to their income-and-loss-sharing ratio. To illustrate, if Perez withdraws and receives $40,000 cash in settlement of Perez's capital balance, the entry is

Oct. 31	H. Perez, Capital	38,000	
	K. Zayn, Capital	1,000	
	T. Rasheed, Capital	1,000	
	Cash		40,000
	To record Perez's withdrawal from partnership with a bonus to Perez.		

Assets	= Liabilities +	Equity
−40,000		−38,000
		−1,000
		−1,000

Falcon Cable Communications LLC set up a partnership withdrawal agreement. Falcon owns and operates cable television systems and had two managing general partners. The partnership agreement stated that either partner "can offer to sell to the other partner the offering partner's entire partnership interest . . . for a negotiated price. If the partner receiving such an offer rejects it, the offering partner may elect to cause [the partnership] . . . to be liquidated and dissolved."

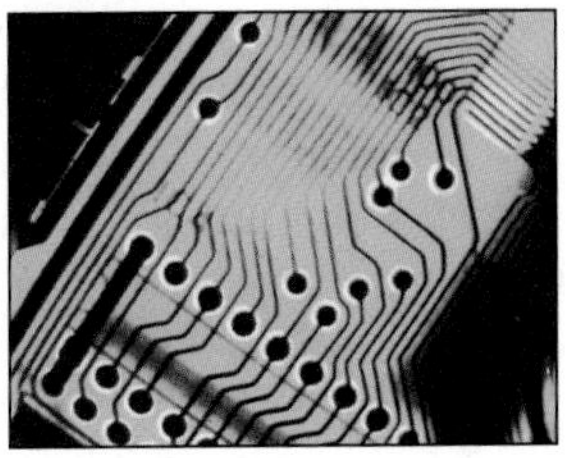

Death of a Partner

A partner's death dissolves a partnership. A deceased partner's estate is entitled to receive his or her equity. The partnership contract should contain provisions for settlement in this case. These provisions usually require (1) closing the books to determine income or loss since the end of the previous period and (2) determining and recording current market values for both assets and liabilities. The remaining partners and the deceased partner's estate then must agree to a settlement of the deceased partner's equity. This can involve selling the equity to remaining partners or to an outsider, or it can involve withdrawing assets.

Decision Ethics

Financial Planner You are hired by the two remaining partners of a three-member partnership after the third partner's death. The partnership agreement states that a deceased partner's estate is entitled to a "share of partnership assets equal to the partner's relative equity balance" (partners' equity balances are equal). The estate argues that it is entitled to one-third of the current value of partnership assets. The remaining partners say the distribution should use asset book values, which are 75% of current value. They also point to partnership liabilities, which equal 40% of total asset book value and 30% of current value. How would you resolve this situation? [Answer—p. 493]

Liquidation of a Partnership

When a partnership is liquidated, its business ends and four concluding steps are required.

1. Record the sale of noncash assets for cash and any gain or loss from their liquidation.
2. Allocate any gain or loss from liquidation of the assets in step 1 to the partners using their income-and-loss-sharing ratio.

3. Pay or settle all partner liabilities.
4. Distribute any remaining cash to partners based on their capital balances.

Partnership liquidation usually falls into one of two cases, as described in this section.

No Capital Deficiency

P4 Prepare entries for partnership liquidation.

No capital deficiency means that all partners have a zero or credit balance in their capital accounts for final distribution of cash. To illustrate, assume that Zayn, Perez, and Rasheed operate their partnership in BOARDS for several years, sharing income and loss equally. The partners then decide to liquidate. On the liquidation date, the current period's income or loss is transferred to the partners' capital accounts according to the sharing agreement. After that transfer, assume the partners' recorded equity balances (immediately prior to liquidation) are Zayn, $70,000; Perez, $66,000; and Rasheed, $62,000.

Next, assume that BOARDS sells its noncash assets for a net gain of $6,000. In a liquidation, gains or losses usually result from the sale of noncash assets, which are called *losses and gains from liquidation.* Partners share losses and gains from liquidation according to their income-and-loss-sharing agreement (equal for these partners) yielding the partners' revised equity balances of Zayn, $72,000; Perez, $68,000; and Rasheed, $64,000.[1] Then, after partnership assets are sold and any gain or loss is allocated, the liabilities must be paid. After creditors are paid, any remaining cash is divided among the partners according to their capital account balances. BOARDS' only liability at liquidation is $20,000 in accounts payable. The entries to record the payment to creditors and the final distribution of cash to partners follow.

Assets	= Liabilities +	Equity
−20,000	−20,000	

Assets	= Liabilities +	Equity
−204,000		−72,000
		−68,000
		−64,000

Jan. 15	Accounts Payable	20,000	
	Cash		20,000
	To pay claims of creditors.		
Jan. 15	K. Zayn, Capital	72,000	
	H. Perez, Capital	68,000	
	T. Rasheed, Capital	64,000	
	Cash		204,000
	To distribute remaining cash to partners.		

It is important to remember that the final cash payment is distributed to partners according to their capital account balances, whereas gains and losses from liquidation are allocated according to the income-and-loss-sharing ratio.

[1] The concepts behind these entries are not new. For example, assume that BOARDS has two noncash assets recorded as boarding facilities, $15,000, and land, $25,000. The entry to sell these assets for $46,000 is

Jan. 15	Cash	46,000	
	Boarding facilities		15,000
	Land		25,000
	Gain from liquidation		6,000
	Sold noncash assets at a gain.		

We then record the allocation of any loss or gain (a gain in this case) from liquidation according to the partners' income-and-loss-sharing agreement as follows.

Jan. 15	Gain from liquidation	6,000	
	K. Zayn, Capital		2,000
	H. Perez, Capital		2,000
	T. Rasheed, Capital		2,000
	To allocate liquidation gain to partners.		

Capital Deficiency

Capital deficiency means that at least one partner has a debit balance in his or her capital account at the point of final cash distribution. This can arise from liquidation losses, excessive withdrawals before liquidation, or recurring losses in prior periods. A partner with a capital deficiency must, if possible, cover the deficit by paying cash into the partnership.

To illustrate, assume that Zayn, Perez, and Rasheed operate their partnership in BOARDS for several years, sharing income and losses equally. The partners then decide to liquidate. Immediately prior to the final distribution of cash, the partners' recorded capital balances are Zayn, \$19,000; Perez, \$8,000; and Rasheed, \$(3,000). Rasheed's capital deficiency means that Rasheed owes the partnership \$3,000. Both Zayn and Perez have a legal claim against Rasheed's personal assets. The final distribution of cash in this case depends on how this capital deficiency is handled. Two possibilities exist.

Partner Pays Deficiency Rasheed is obligated to pay \$3,000 into the partnership to cover the deficiency. If Rasheed is willing and able to pay, the entry to record receipt of payment from Rasheed follows.

Jan. 15	Cash	3,000	
	T. Rasheed, Capital		3,000
	To record payment of deficiency by Rasheed.		

Assets = Liabilities + Equity
+3,000 +3,000

After the \$3,000 payment, the partners' capital balances are Zayn, \$19,000; Perez, \$8,000; and Rasheed, \$0. The entry to record the final cash distributions to partners is

Jan. 15	K. Zayn, Capital	19,000	
	H. Perez, Capital	8,000	
	Cash		27,000
	To distribute remaining cash to partners.		

Assets = Liabilities + Equity
−27,000 −19,000
−8,000

Partner Cannot Pay Deficiency The remaining partners with credit balances absorb any partner's unpaid deficiency according to their income-and-loss-sharing ratio. To illustrate, if Rasheed is unable to pay the \$3,000 deficiency, Zayn and Perez absorb it. Since they share income and loss equally, Zayn and Perez each absorb \$1,500 of the deficiency. This is recorded as follows.

Jan. 15	K. Zayn, Capital	1,500	
	H. Perez, Capital	1,500	
	T. Rasheed, Capital		3,000
	To transfer Rasheed deficiency to Zayn and Perez.		

Assets = Liabilities + Equity
−1,500
−1,500
+3,000

After Zayn and Perez absorb Rasheed's deficiency, the capital accounts of the partners are Zayn, \$17,500; Perez, \$6,500; and Rasheed, \$0. The entry to record the final cash distribution to the partners is

Jan. 15	K. Zayn, Capital	17,500	
	H. Perez, Capital	6,500	
	Cash		24,000
	To distribute remaining cash to partners.		

Assets = Liabilities + Equity
−24,000 −17,500
−6,500

Rasheed's inability to cover this deficiency does not relieve Rasheed of the liability. If Rasheed becomes able to pay at a future date, Zayn and Perez can each collect \$1,500 from Rasheed.

Decision Analysis — Partner Return on Equity

A1 Compute partner return on equity and use it to evaluate partnership performance.

An important role of partnership financial statements is to aid current and potential partners in evaluating partnership success compared with other opportunities. One measure of this success is the **partner return on equity** ratio:

$$\textbf{Partner return on equity} = \frac{\textbf{Partner net income}}{\textbf{Average partner equity}}$$

This measure is separately computed for each partner. To illustrate, Exhibit 12.4 reports selected data from the **Boston Celtics LP**. The return on equity for the *total* partnership is computed as \$216/[(\$84 + \$252)/2] = 128.6%. However, return on equity is quite different across the partners. For example, the **Boston Celtics LP I** partner return on equity is computed as \$44/[(\$122 + \$166)/2] = 30.6%, whereas the **Celtics LP** partner return on equity is computed as \$111/[(\$270 + \$333)/2] = 36.8%. Partner return on equity provides *each* partner an assessment of its return on its equity invested in the partnership. A specific partner often uses this return to decide whether additional investment or withdrawal of resources is best for that partner. Exhibit 12.4 reveals that the year shown produced good returns for all partners (the Boston Celtics LP II return is not computed because its average equity is negative due to an unusual and large distribution in the prior year).

EXHIBIT 12.4

Selected Data from Boston Celtics LP

($ thousands)	Total*	Boston Celtics LP I	Boston Celtics LP II	Celtics LP
Beginning-year balance	$ 84	$122	$(307)	$270
Net income (loss) for year	216	44	61	111
Cash distribution	(48)	—	—	(48)
Ending-year balance	$252	$166	$(246)	$333
Partner return on equity	**128.6%**	**30.6%**	**n.a.**	**36.8%**

* Totals may not add up due to rounding.

Demonstration Problem

DP12

The following transactions and events affect the partners' capital accounts in several successive partnerships. Prepare a table with six columns, one for each of the five partners along with a total column to show the effects of the following events on the five partners' capital accounts.

Part 1

4/13/2007 Ries and Bax create R&B Company. Each invests \$10,000, and they agree to share income and losses equally.

12/31/2007 R&B Co. earns \$15,000 in income for its first year. Ries withdraws \$4,000 from the partnership, and Bax withdraws \$7,000.

1/1/2008 Royce is made a partner in RB&R Company after contributing \$12,000 cash. The partners agree that a 10% interest allowance will be given on each partner's beginning-year capital balance. In addition, Bax and Royce are to receive \$5,000 salary allowances. The remainder of the income or loss is to be divided evenly.

12/31/2008 The partnership's income for the year is \$40,000, and withdrawals at year-end are Ries, \$5,000; Bax, \$12,500; and Royce, \$11,000.

1/1/2009 Ries sells her interest for \$20,000 to Murdock, whom Bax and Royce accept as a partner in the new BR&M Co. Income or loss is to be shared equally after Bax and Royce receive \$25,000 salary allowances.

12/31/2009 The partnership's income for the year is \$35,000, and year-end withdrawals are Bax, \$2,500, and Royce, \$2,000.

1/1/2010 Elway is admitted as a partner after investing \$60,000 cash in the new Elway & Associates partnership. He is given a 50% interest in capital after the other partners transfer \$3,000 to his account from each of theirs. A 20% interest allowance (on the beginning-year capital balances) will be used in sharing any income or loss, there will be no salary allowances, and Elway will receive 40% of the remaining balance—the other three partners will each get 20%.

12/31/2010 Elway & Associates earns $127,600 in income for the year, and year-end withdrawals are Bax, $25,000; Royce, $27,000; Murdock, $15,000; and Elway, $40,000.

1/1/2011 Elway buys out Bax and Royce for the balances of their capital accounts after a revaluation of the partnership assets. The revaluation gain is $50,000, which is divided in using a 1:1:1:2 ratio (Bax:Royce:Murdock:Elway). Elway pays the others from personal funds. Murdock and Elway will share income on a 1:9 ratio.

2/28/2011 The partnership earns $10,000 of income since the beginning of the year. Murdock retires and receives partnership cash equal to her capital balance. Elway takes possession of the partnership assets in his own name, and the partnership is dissolved.

Part 2

Journalize the events affecting the partnership for the year ended December 31, 2008.

Planning the Solution

- Evaluate each transaction's effects on the capital accounts of the partners.
- Each time a new partner is admitted or a partner withdraws, allocate any bonus based on the income-or-loss-sharing agreement.
- Each time a new partner is admitted or a partner withdraws, allocate subsequent net income or loss in accordance with the new partnership agreement.
- Prepare entries to (1) record Royce's initial investment; (2) record the allocation of interest, salaries, and remainder; (3) show the cash withdrawals from the partnership; and (4) close the withdrawal accounts on December 31, 2008.

Solution to Demonstration Problem

Part 1

Event	Ries	Bax	Royce	Murdock	Elway	Total
4/13/2007						
Initial investment	$10,000	$10,000				$ 20,000
12/31/2007						
Income (equal)	7,500	7,500				15,000
Withdrawals	(4,000)	(7,000)				(11,000)
Ending balance	$13,500	$10,500				$ 24,000
1/1/2008						
New investment			$12,000			$ 12,000
12/31/2008						
10% interest	1,350	1,050	1,200			3,600
Salaries		5,000	5,000			10,000
Remainder (equal)	8,800	8,800	8,800			26,400
Withdrawals	(5,000)	(12,500)	(11,000)			(28,500)
Ending balance	$18,650	$12,850	$16,000			$ 47,500
1/1/2009						
Transfer interest	(18,650)			$18,650		$ 0
12/31/2009						
Salaries		25,000	25,000			50,000
Remainder (equal)		(5,000)	(5,000)	(5,000)		(15,000)
Withdrawals		(2,500)	(2,000)			(4,500)
Ending balance	$ 0	$30,350	$34,000	$13,650		$ 78,000
1/1/2010						
New investment					$ 60,000	60,000
Bonuses to Elway		(3,000)	(3,000)	(3,000)	9,000	0
Adjusted balance		$27,350	$31,000	$10,650	$ 69,000	$138,000

[continued on next page]

[continued from previous page]

Event	Ries	Bax	Royce	Murdock	Elway	Total
12/31/2010						
20% interest		5,470	6,200	2,130	13,800	27,600
Remainder (1:1:1:2)		20,000	20,000	20,000	40,000	100,000
Withdrawals		(25,000)	(27,000)	(15,000)	(40,000)	(107,000)
Ending balance		$27,820	$30,200	$17,780	$ 82,800	$158,600
1/1/2011						
Gain (1:1:1:2)		10,000	10,000	10,000	20,000	50,000
Adjusted balance		$37,820	$40,200	$27,780	$102,800	$208,600
Transfer interests		(37,820)	(40,200)		78,020	0
Adjusted balance		$ 0	$ 0	$27,780	$180,820	$208,600
2/28/2011						
Income (1:9)				1,000	9,000	10,000
Adjusted balance				$28,780	$189,820	$218,600
Settlements				(28,780)	(189,820)	(218,600)
Final balance				$ 0	$ 0	$ 0

Part 2

2008			
Jan. 1	Cash	12,000	
	Royce, Capital		12,000
	To record investment of Royce.		
Dec. 31	Income Summary	40,000	
	Ries, Capital		10,150
	Bax, Capital		14,850
	Royce, Capital		15,000
	To allocate interest, salaries, and remainders.		
Dec. 31	Ries, Withdrawals	5,000	
	Bax, Withdrawals	12,500	
	Royce, Withdrawals	11,000	
	Cash		28,500
	To record cash withdrawals by partners.		
Dec. 31	Ries, Capital	5,000	
	Bax, Capital	12,500	
	Royce, Capital	11,000	
	Ries, Withdrawals		5,000
	Bax, Withdrawals		12,500
	Royce, Withdrawals		11,000
	To close withdrawal accounts.		

Summary

C1 Identify characteristics of partnerships and similar organizations. Partnerships are voluntary associations, involve partnership agreements, have limited life, are not subject to income tax, include mutual agency, and have unlimited liability. Organizations that combine selected characteristics of partnerships and corporations include limited partnerships, limited liability partnerships, S corporations, and limited liability companies.

A1 Compute partner return on equity and use it to evaluate partnership performance. Partner return on equity provides each partner an assessment of his or her return on equity invested in the partnership.

P1 Prepare entries for partnership formation. A partner's initial investment is recorded at the market value of the assets contributed to the partnership.

P2 Allocate and record income and loss among partners. A partnership agreement should specify how to allocate partnership income or loss among partners. Allocation can be based on a stated ratio, capital balances, or salary and interest allowances to compensate partners for differences in their service and capital contributions.

P3 Account for the admission and withdrawal of partners. When a new partner buys a partnership interest directly from one or more existing partners, the amount of cash paid from one partner to another does not affect the partnership total recorded equity. When a new partner purchases equity by investing additional assets in the partnership, the new partner's investment can yield a bonus either to existing partners or to the new partner. The entry to record a withdrawal can involve payment from either (1) the existing partners' personal assets or (2) partnership assets. The latter can yield a bonus to either the withdrawing or remaining partners.

P4 **Prepare entries for partnership liquidation.** When a partnership is liquidated, losses and gains from selling partnership assets are allocated to the partners according to their income-and-loss-sharing ratio. If a partner's capital account has a deficiency that the partner cannot pay, the other partners share the deficit according to their relative income-and-loss-sharing ratio.

Guidance Answers to **Decision Ethics**

Financial Planner The partnership agreement apparently fails to mention liabilities or use the term *net assets.* To give the estate one-third of total assets is not fair to the remaining partners because if the partner had lived and the partners had decided to liquidate, the liabilities would need to be paid out of assets before any liquidation. Also, a settlement based on the deceased partner's recorded equity would fail to recognize excess of current value over book value. This value increase would be realized if the partnership were liquidated. A fair settlement would seem to be a payment to the estate for the balance of the deceased partner's equity based on the *current value of net assets.*

Guidance Answers to **Quick Checks**

1. (*b*)

2. *Unlimited liability* means that the creditors of a partnership require each partner to be personally responsible for all partnership debts.

3. (*c*)

4.

	Denzel	Shantell	Total
Net income			$40,000
Interest allowance (10%)	$ 7,000	$ 3,500	10,500
Balance of income	↓	↓	**$29,500**
Balance allocated equally	14,750	14,750	29,500
Balance of income			$ 0
Income of partners	**$21,750**	**$18,250**	

Key Terms

mhhe.com/wildFAP19e

Key Terms are available at the book's Website for learning and testing in an online Flashcard Format.

C corporation (p. 480)
General partner (p. 479)
General partnership (p. 479)
Limited liability company (LLC) (p. 480)
Limited liability partnership (p. 479)
Limited partners (p. 479)
Limited partnership (p. 479)
Mutual agency (p. 478)
Partner return on equity (p. 490)
Partnership (p. 478)
Partnership contract (p. 478)
Partnership liquidation (p. 488)
S corporation (p. 480)
Statement of partners' equity (p. 483)
Unlimited liability (p. 479)

Multiple Choice Quiz

Answers on p. 503

mhhe.com/wildFAP19e

Additional Quiz Questions are available at the book's Website.

1. Stokely and Leder are forming a partnership. Stokely invests a building that has a market value of $250,000; and the partnership assumes responsibility for a $50,000 note secured by a mortgage on that building. Leder invests $100,000 cash. For the partnership, the amounts recorded for the building and for Stokely's Capital account are these:

a. Building, $250,000; Stokely, Capital, $250,000.
b. Building, $200,000; Stokely, Capital, $200,000.
c. Building, $200,000; Stokely, Capital, $100,000.
d. Building, $200,000; Stokely, Capital, $250,000.
e. Building, $250,000; Stokely, Capital, $200,000.

2. Katherine, Alliah, and Paulina form a partnership. Katherine contributes $150,000, Alliah contributes $150,000, and Paulina contributes $100,000. Their partnership agreement calls for the income or loss division to be based on the ratio of capital invested. If the partnership reports income of $90,000 for its first year of operations, what amount of income is credited to Paulina's capital account?
a. $22,500
b. $25,000
c. $45,000
d. $30,000
e. $90,000

3. Jamison and Blue form a partnership with capital contributions of $600,000 and $800,000, respectively. Their partnership agreement calls for Jamison to receive $120,000 per year in salary. Also, each partner is to receive an interest allowance equal to 10% of the partner's beginning capital contributions, with any remaining income or loss divided equally. If net income for its initial year is $270,000, then Jamison's and Blue's respective shares are
a. $135,000; $135,000.
b. $154,286; $115,714.
c. $120,000; $150,000.
d. $185,000; $85,000.
e. $85,000; $185,000.

4. Hansen and Fleming are partners and share equally in income or loss. Hansen's current capital balance in the partnership is $125,000 and Fleming's is $124,000. Hansen and Fleming agree to accept Black with a 20% interest. Black invests $75,000 in the partnership. The bonus granted to Hansen and Fleming equals
a. $13,000 each.
b. $5,100 each.
c. $4,000 each.
d. $5,285 to Hansen; $4,915 to Fleming.
e. $0; Hansen and Fleming grant a bonus to Black.

5. Mee Su is a partner in Hartford Partners, LLC. Her partnership capital balance at the beginning of the current year was $110,000, and her ending balance was $124,000. Her share of the partnership income is $10,500. What is her partner return on equity?
a. 8.97%
b. 1060.00%
c. 9.54%
d. 1047.00%
e. 8.47%

Discussion Questions

1. ♝ If a partnership contract does not state the period of time the partnership is to exist, when does the partnership end?

2. What does the term *mutual agency* mean when applied to a partnership?

3. ♝ Can partners limit the right of a partner to commit their partnership to contracts? Would such an agreement be binding (*a*) on the partners and (*b*) on outsiders?

4. ♝ Assume that Amey and Lacey are partners. Lacey dies, and her son claims the right to take his mother's place in the partnership. Does he have this right? Why or why not?

5. ♝ Assume that the Barnes and Ardmore partnership agreement provides for a two-third/one-third sharing of income but says nothing about losses. The first year of partnership operation resulted in a loss, and Barnes argues that the loss should be shared equally because the partnership agreement said nothing about sharing losses. Is Barnes correct? Explain.

6. Allocation of partnership income among the partners appears on what financial statement?

7. What does the term *unlimited liability* mean when it is applied to partnership members?

8. How does a general partnership differ from a limited partnership?

9. ♝ George, Burton, and Dillman have been partners for three years. The partnership is being dissolved. George is leaving the firm, but Burton and Dillman plan to carry on the business. In the final settlement, George places a $75,000 salary claim against the partnership. He contends that he has a claim for a salary of $25,000 for each year because he devoted all of his time for three years to the affairs of the partnership. Is his claim valid? Why or why not?

10. ♝ Kay, Kat, and Kim are partners. In a liquidation, Kay's share of partnership losses exceeds her capital account balance. Moreover, she is unable to meet the deficit from her personal assets, and her partners shared the excess losses. Does this relieve Kay of liability?

11. After all partnership assets have been converted to cash and all liabilities paid, the remaining cash should equal the sum of the balances of the partners' capital accounts. Why?

12. Assume a partner withdraws from a partnership and receives assets of greater value than the book value of his equity. Should the remaining partners share the resulting reduction in their equities in the ratio of their relative capital balances or according to their income-and-loss-sharing ratio?

♝ ***Denotes Discussion Questions that involve decision making.***

McGraw-Hill's HOMEWORK MANAGER® Available with McGraw-Hill's Homework Manager

QUICK STUDY

QS 12-1
Partnership liability
C1

Otis and Hunan are partners in operating a store. Without consulting Otis, Hunan enters into a contract to purchase merchandise for the store. Otis contends that he did not authorize the order and refuses to pay for it. The vendor sues the partners for the contract price of the merchandise. (*a*) Must the partnership pay for the merchandise? Why? (*b*) Does your answer differ if Otis and Hunan are partners in a public accounting firm? Explain.

QS 12-2
Partnership income allocation
P2

Ramona Stolton and Jerry Bright are partners in a business they started two years ago. The partnership agreement states that Stolton should receive a salary allowance of $30,000 and that Bright should receive a $40,000 salary allowance. Any remaining income or loss is to be shared equally. Determine each partner's share of the current year's net income of $104,000.

QS 12-3
Partnership income allocation
P2

Hiram and Tyrone are partners who agree that Hiram will receive a $50,000 salary allowance and that any remaining income or loss will be shared equally. If Tyrone's capital account is credited for $1,000 as her share of the net income in a given period, how much net income did the partnership earn in that period?

QS 12-4
Liability in limited partnerships
P1

Vernon organized a limited partnership and is the only general partner. Xavier invested $40,000 in the partnership and was admitted as a limited partner with the understanding that he would receive 10% of the profits. After two unprofitable years, the partnership ceased doing business. At that point, partnership liabilities were $170,000 larger than partnership assets. How much money can the partnership's creditors obtain from Xavier's personal assets to satisfy the unpaid partnership debts?

QS 12-5
Partner admission through purchase of interest P3

Dresden agrees to pay Choi and Amal $20,000 each for a one-third (33⅓%) interest in the Choi and Amal partnership. Immediately prior to Dresden's admission, each partner had a $60,000 capital balance. Make the journal entry to record Dresden's purchase of the partners' interest.

QS 12-6
Admission of a partner P3

Neal and Vanier are partners, each with $80,000 in their partnership capital accounts. Brantford is admitted to the partnership by investing $80,000 cash. Make the entry to show Brantford's admission to the partnership.

QS 12-7
Partner return on equity
A1

Paulson and Fleming's company is organized as a partnership. At the prior year-end, partnership equity totaled $300,000 ($200,000 from Paulson and $100,000 from Fleming). For the current year, partnership net income is $49,000 ($38,400 allocated to Paulson and $10,600 allocated to Fleming), and year-end total partnership equity is $400,000 ($280,000 from Paulson and $120,000 from Fleming). Compute the total partnership return on equity *and* the individual partner return on equity ratios.

McGraw-Hill's HOMEWORK MANAGER® Available with McGraw-Hill's Homework Manager

EXERCISES

Exercise 12-1
Characteristics of partnerships
C1

Next to the following list of eight characteristics of business organizations, enter a brief description of how each characteristic applies to general partnerships.

Characteristic	Application to General Partnerships
1. Life	
2. Owners' liability	
3. Legal status	
4. Tax status of income	
5. Owners' authority	
6. Ease of formation	
7. Transferability of ownership	
8. Ability to raise large amounts of capital	

Exercise 12-2
Forms of organization
C1

For each of the following separate cases, recommend a form of business organization. With each recommendation, explain how business income would be taxed if the owners adopt the form of organization recommended. Also list several advantages that the owners will enjoy from the form of business organization that you recommend.

a. Sharif, Henry, and Saanen are recent college graduates in computer science. They want to start a Website development company. They all have college debts and currently do not own any substantial computer equipment needed to get the company started.

b. Dr. LeBlanc and Dr. Liu are recent graduates from medical residency programs. Both are family practice physicians and would like to open a clinic in an underserved rural area. Although neither has any funds to bring to the new venture, a banker has expressed interest in making a loan to provide start-up funds for their practice.

c. Novato has been out of school for about five years and has become quite knowledgeable about the commercial real estate market. He would like to organize a company that buys and sells real estate. Novato believes he has the expertise to manage the company but needs funds to invest in commercial property.

Exercise 12-3
Journalizing partnership transactions
P2

On March 1, 2009, Eckert and Kelley formed a partnership. Eckert contributed $83,000 cash and Kelley contributed land valued at $66,400 and a building valued at $96,400. The partnership also assumed responsibility for Kelley's $77,800 long-term note payable associated with the land and building. The partners agreed to share income as follows: Eckert is to receive an annual salary allowance of $30,500, both are to receive an annual interest allowance of 11% of their beginning-year capital investment, and any remaining income or loss is to be shared equally. On October 20, 2009, Eckert withdrew $32,000 cash and Kelley withdrew $25,000 cash. After the adjusting and closing entries are made to the revenue and expense accounts at December 31, 2009, the Income Summary account had a credit balance of $86,000.

1. Prepare journal entries to record (*a*) the partners' initial capital investments, (*b*) their cash withdrawals, and (*c*) the December 31 closing of both the Withdrawals and Income Summary accounts.

2. Determine the balances of the partners' capital accounts as of December 31, 2009.

Check (2) Kelley, $87,860

Exercise 12-4
Income allocation in a partnership
P2

Daria and Farrah began a partnership by investing $64,000 and $58,000, respectively. During its first year, the partnership earned $175,000. Prepare calculations showing how the $175,000 income should be allocated to the partners under each of the following three separate plans for sharing income and loss: (1) the partners failed to agree on a method to share income; (2) the partners agreed to share income and loss in proportion to their initial investments (round amounts to the nearest dollar); and (3) the partners agreed to share income by granting a $52,000 per year salary allowance to Daria, a $42,000 per year salary allowance to Farrah, 8% interest on their initial capital investments, and the remaining balance shared equally.

Check Plan 3, Daria, $92,740

Exercise 12-5
Income allocation in a partnership
P2

Assume that the partners of Exercise 12-4 agreed to share net income and loss by granting annual salary allowances of $52,000 to Daria and $42,000 to Farrah, 8% interest allowances on their investments, and any remaining balance shared equally.

1. Determine the partners' shares of Daria and Farrah given a first-year net income of $98,800.

2. Determine the partners' shares of Daria and Farrah given a first-year net loss of $16,800.

Check (2) Daria, $(3,160)

Exercise 12-6
Sale of partnership interest P3

The partners in the Biz Partnership have agreed that partner Estella may sell her $111,000 equity in the partnership to Sean, for which Sean will pay Estella $88,800. Present the partnership's journal entry to record the sale of Estella's interest to Sean on September 30.

Exercise 12-7
Admission of new partner
P3

The Josetti Partnership has total partners' equity of $558,000, which is made up of Dopke, Capital, $392,000, and Hughes, Capital, $166,000. The partners share net income and loss in a ratio of 85% to Dopke and 15% to Hughes. On November 1, Nillsen is admitted to the partnership and given a 10% interest in equity and a 10% share in any income and loss. Prepare the journal entry to record the admission of Nillsen under each of the following separate assumptions: Nillsen invests cash of (1) $62,000; (2) $97,000; and (3) $32,000.

Exercise 12-8
Retirement of partner
P3

Edison, Delray, and West have been partners while sharing net income and loss in a 5:4:1 ratio. On January 31, the date West retires from the partnership, the equities of the partners are Edison, $330,000; Delray, $231,000; and West, $165,000. Present journal entries to record West's retirement under each of the following separate assumptions: West is paid for her equity using partnership cash of (1) $165,000; (2) $192,000; and (3) $129,000.

Exercise 12-9
Liquidation of partnership
P4

The Red, White & Blue partnership was begun with investments by the partners as follows: Red, $153,000; White, $183,000; and Blue, $180,000. The operations did not go well, and the partners eventually decided to liquidate the partnership, sharing all losses equally. On August 31, after all assets were converted to cash and all creditors were paid, only $39,000 in partnership cash remained.

1. Compute the capital account balance of each partner after the liquidation of assets and the payment of creditors.

Check (1) Red, $(6,000)

2. Assume that any partner with a deficit agrees to pay cash to the partnership to cover the deficit. Present the journal entries on August 31 to record (*a*) the cash receipt from the deficient partner(s) and (*b*) the final disbursement of cash to the partners.

3. Assume that any partner with a deficit is not able to reimburse the partnership. Present journal entries (*a*) to transfer the deficit of any deficient partners to the other partners and (*b*) to record the final disbursement of cash to the partners.

Exercise 12-10
Liquidation of partnership P4

Brewster, Conway, and Ogden are partners who share income and loss in a 1:5:4 ratio. After lengthy disagreements among the partners and several unprofitable periods, the partners decide to liquidate the partnership. Immediately before liquidation, the partnership balance sheet shows total assets, $117,000; total liabilities, $87,750; Brewster, Capital, $1,600; Conway, Capital, $11,600; and Ogden, Capital, $16,050. The cash proceeds from selling the assets were sufficient to repay all but $20,500 to the creditors. (*a*) Calculate the loss from selling the assets. (*b*) Allocate the loss to the partners. (*c*) Determine how much of the remaining liability should be paid by each partner.

Check (b) Ogden, Capital after allocation, $(3,850)

Exercise 12-11
Liquidation of limited partnership
P4

Assume that the Brewster, Conway, and Ogden partnership of Exercise 12-10 is a limited partnership. Brewster and Conway are general partners and Ogden is a limited partner. How much of the remaining $20,500 liability should be paid by each partner? (Round amounts to the nearest dollar.)

Exercise 12-12
Partner return on equity
A1

Hunt Sports Enterprises LP is organized as a limited partnership consisting of two individual partners: Soccer LP and Football LP. Both partners separately operate a minor league soccer team and a semipro football team. Compute partner return on equity for each limited partnership (and the total) for the year ended June 30, 2009, using the following selected data on partner capital balances from Hunt Sports Enterprises LP.

	Soccer LP	Football LP	Total
Balance at 6/30/2008	$331,000	$1,357,100	$1,688,100
Annual net income	35,405	725,803	761,208
Cash distribution	—	(65,000)	(65,000)
Balance at 6/30/2009	$366,405	$2,017,903	$2,384,308

McGraw-Hill's HOMEWORK MANAGER® Available with McGraw-Hill's Homework Manager

PROBLEM SET A

Problem 12-1A
Allocating partnership income
P2

Alex Jeffers, Jo Ford, and Rose Verne invested $32,500, $45,500, and $52,000, respectively, in a partnership. During its first calendar year, the firm earned $391,200.

Required

Prepare the entry to close the firm's Income Summary account as of its December 31 year-end and to allocate the $391,200 net income to the partners under each of the following separate assumptions: The partners (1) have no agreement on the method of sharing income and loss; (2) agreed to share income and loss in the ratio of their beginning capital investments; and (3) agreed to share income and loss by providing annual salary allowances of $40,000 to Jeffers, $35,000 to Ford, and $46,000 to Verne; granting 8% interest on the partners' beginning capital investments; and sharing the remainder equally.

Check (3) Verne, Capital, $136,760

Problem 12-2A
Allocating partnership income and loss; sequential years
P2

eXcel
mhhe.com/wildFAP19e

Jasmine Watts and Liz Thomas are forming a partnership to which Watts will devote one-half time and Thomas will devote full time. They have discussed the following alternative plans for sharing income and loss: (*a*) in the ratio of their initial capital investments, which they have agreed will be $30,000 for Watts and $45,000 for Thomas; (*b*) in proportion to the time devoted to the business; (*c*) a salary allowance of $3,000 per month to Thomas and the balance in accordance with the ratio of their initial capital investments; or (*d*) a salary allowance of $3,000 per month to Thomas, 10% interest on their initial capital investments, and the balance shared equally. The partners expect the business to perform as follows: year 1, $18,000 net loss; year 2, $45,000 net income; and year 3, $75,000 net income.

Required

Prepare three tables with the following column headings.

Income (Loss) Sharing Plan	Year ___ Calculations	Watts	Thomas

Complete the tables, one for each of the first three years, by showing how to allocate partnership income or loss to the partners under each of the four plans being considered. (Round answers to the nearest whole dollar.)

Check Plan d, year 1, Thomas's share, $9,750

Problem 12-3A
Partnership income allocation, statement of partners' equity, and closing entries
P2

eXcel
mhhe.com/wildFAP19e

Will Beck, Trevor Beck, and Barb Beck formed the BBB Partnership by making capital contributions of $142,500, $118,750, and $213,750, respectively. They predict annual partnership net income of $210,000 and are considering the following alternative plans of sharing income and loss: (*a*) equally; (*b*) in the ratio of their initial capital investments; or (*c*) salary allowances of $38,000 to Will, $28,000 to Trevor, and $43,000 to Barb; interest allowances of 10% on their initial capital investments; and the balance shared equally.

Required

1. Prepare a table with the following column headings.

Income (Loss) Sharing Plan	Calculations	Will	Trevor	Barb	Total

Use the table to show how to distribute net income of $210,000 for the calendar year under each of the alternative plans being considered. (Round answers to the nearest whole dollar.)

Check (2) Barb, Ending Capital, $221,125

2. Prepare a statement of partners' equity showing the allocation of income to the partners assuming they agree to use plan (*c*), that income earned is $87,500, and that Will, Trevor, and Barb withdraw $18,000, $25,000, and $34,000, respectively, at year-end.

3. Prepare the December 31 journal entry to close Income Summary assuming they agree to use plan (*c*) and that net income is $87,500. Also close the withdrawals accounts.

Problem 12-4A
Partner withdrawal and admission
P3

GL

Part 1. Meir, Zarcus, and Ross are partners and share income and loss in a 1:4:5 ratio. The partnership's capital balances are as follows: Meir, $43,000; Zarcus, $179,000; and Ross, $228,000. Zarcus decides to withdraw from the partnership, and the partners agree to not have the assets revalued upon Zarcus's retirement. Prepare journal entries to record Zarcus's February 1 withdrawal from the partnership under each of the following separate assumptions: Zarcus (*a*) sells her interest to Garcia for $160,000 after Meir and Ross approve the entry of Garcia as a partner; (*b*) gives her interest to a son-in-law, Fields, and thereafter Meir and Ross accept Fields as a partner; (*c*) is paid $179,000 in partnership cash for her equity; (*d*) is paid $215,000 in partnership cash for her equity; and (*e*) is paid $20,000 in partnership cash plus equipment recorded on the partnership books at $70,000 less its accumulated depreciation of $23,200.

Check (1e) Cr. Ross, Capital, $93,500

Part 2. Assume that Zarcus does not retire from the partnership described in Part 1. Instead, Potter is admitted to the partnership on February 1 with a 25% equity. Prepare journal entries to record Potter's entry into the partnership under each of the following separate assumptions: Potter invests (*a*) $150,000; (*b*) $110,000; and (*c*) $196,000.

(2c) Cr. Zarcus, Capital, $13,800

Problem 12-5A
Liquidation of a partnership
P4

Kendra, Cogley, and Mei share income and loss in a 3:2:1 ratio. The partners have decided to liquidate their partnership. On the day of liquidation their balance sheet appears as follows.

KENDRA, COGLEY, AND MEI
Balance Sheet
May 31

Assets		Liabilities and Equity	
Cash	$199,100	Accounts payable	$258,000
Inventory	548,400	Kendra, Capital	97,900
		Cogley, Capital	220,275
		Mei, Capital	171,325
Total assets	$747,500	Total liabilities and equity	$747,500

Required

Prepare journal entries for (*a*) the sale of inventory, (*b*) the allocation of its gain or loss, (*c*) the payment of liabilities at book value, and (*d*) the distribution of cash in each of the following separate cases: Inventory is sold for (1) $625,200; (2) $452,400; (3) $321,000 and any partners with capital deficits pay in the amount of their deficits; and (4) $249,000 and the partners have no assets other than those invested in the partnership. (Round to the nearest dollar.)

Check (4) Cash distribution: Mei, $104,158

PROBLEM SET B

Problem 12-1B
Allocating partnership income
P2

Erin Rock, Sal Arthur, and Chloe Binder invested $47,840, $64,400, and $71,760, respectively, in a partnership. During its first calendar year, the firm earned $361,800.

Required

Prepare the entry to close the firm's Income Summary account as of its December 31 year-end and to allocate the $361,800 net income to the partners under each of the following separate assumptions. (Round answers to whole dollars.) The partners (1) have no agreement on the method of sharing income and loss; (2) agreed to share income and loss in the ratio of their beginning capital investments; and (3) agreed to share income and loss by providing annual salary allowances of $33,000 to Rock, $28,000 to Arthur, and $40,000 to Binder; granting 10% interest on the partners' beginning capital investments; and sharing the remainder equally.

Check (3) Binder, Capital, $127,976

Problem 12-2B
Allocating partnership income and loss; sequential years
P2

Maria Selk and David Green are forming a partnership to which Selk will devote one-third time and Green will devote full time. They have discussed the following alternative plans for sharing income and loss: (*a*) in the ratio of their initial capital investments, which they have agreed will be $208,000 for Selk and $312,000 for Green; (*b*) in proportion to the time devoted to the business; (*c*) a salary allowance of $8,000 per month to Green and the balance in accordance with the ratio of their initial capital investments; or (*d*) a salary allowance of $8,000 per month to Green, 10% interest on their initial capital investments, and the balance shared equally. The partners expect the business to perform as follows: year 1, $72,000 net loss; year 2, $152,000 net income; and year 3, $376,000 net income.

Required

Prepare three tables with the following column headings.

Income (Loss) Sharing Plan	Calculations	Year____ Selk	Green

Check Plan d, year 1, Green's share, $17,200

Complete the tables, one for each of the first three years, by showing how to allocate partnership income or loss to the partners under each of the four plans being considered. (Round answers to the nearest whole dollar.)

Problem 12-3B
Partnership income allocation, statement of partners' equity, and closing entries

P2

Sally Cook, Lin Xi, and Sami Bruce formed the CXB Partnership by making capital contributions of $169,750, $121,250, and $194,000, respectively. They predict annual partnership net income of $270,000 and are considering the following alternative plans of sharing income and loss: (*a*) equally; (*b*) in the ratio of their initial capital investments; or (*c*) salary allowances of $40,000 to Cook, $29,000 to Xi, and $42,000 to Bruce; interest allowances of 12% on their initial capital investments; and the balance shared equally.

Required

1. Prepare a table with the following column headings.

Income (Loss) Sharing Plan	Calculations	Cook	Xi	Bruce	Total

Use the table to show how to distribute net income of $270,000 for the calendar year under each of the alternative plans being considered. (Round answers to the nearest whole dollar.)

Check (2) Bruce, Ending Capital, $208,380

2. Prepare a statement of partners' equity showing the allocation of income to the partners assuming they agree to use plan (*c*), that income earned is $124,500, and that Cook, Xi, and Bruce withdraw $19,000, $26,000, and $36,000, respectively, at year-end.

3. Prepare the December 31 journal entry to close Income Summary assuming they agree to use plan (*c*) and that net income is $124,500. Also close the withdrawals accounts.

Problem 12-4B
Partner withdrawal and admission

P3

Part 1. Davis, Brown, and Nell are partners and share income and loss in a 5:1:4 ratio. The partnership's capital balances are as follows: Davis, $303,000; Brown, $74,000; and Nell, $223,000. Davis decides to withdraw from the partnership, and the partners agree not to have the assets revalued upon Davis's retirement. Prepare journal entries to record Davis's April 30 withdrawal from the partnership under each of the following separate assumptions: Davis (*a*) sells her interest to Leer for $125,000 after Brown and Nell approve the entry of Leer as a partner; (*b*) gives her interest to a daughter-in-law, Gibson, and thereafter Brown and Nell accept Gibson as a partner; (*c*) is paid $303,000 in partnership cash for her equity; (*d*) is paid $175,000 in partnership cash for her equity; and (*e*) is paid $100,000 in partnership cash plus manufacturing equipment recorded on the partnership books at $269,000 less its accumulated depreciation of $168,000.

Check (1e) Cr. Nell, Capital, $81,600

Part 2. Assume that Davis does not retire from the partnership described in Part 1. Instead, McCann is admitted to the partnership on April 30 with a 20% equity. Prepare journal entries to record the entry of McCann under each of the following separate assumptions: McCann invests (*a*) $150,000; (*b*) $98,000; and (*c*) $213,000.

Check (2c) Cr. Brown, Capital, $5,040

Problem 12-5B
Liquidation of a partnership

P4

London, Ramirez, and Toney, who share income and loss in a 3:2:1 ratio, plan to liquidate their partnership. At liquidation, their balance sheet appears as follows.

LONDON, RAMIREZ, AND TONEY
Balance Sheet
January 18

Assets		Liabilities and Equity	
Cash	$179,500	Accounts payable	$241,500
Equipment	552,000	London, Capital	98,000
		Ramirez, Capital	220,500
		Toney, Capital	171,500
Total assets	$731,500	Total liabilities and equity	$731,500

Required

Prepare journal entries for (*a*) the sale of equipment, (*b*) the allocation of its gain or loss, (*c*) the payment of liabilities at book value, and (*d*) the distribution of cash in each of the following separate cases: Equipment is sold for (1) $605,400; (2) $474,000; (3) $301,200 and any partners with capital deficits pay in the amount of their deficits; and (4) $271,200 and the partners have no assets other than those invested in the partnership. (Round amounts to the nearest dollar.)

Check (4) Cash distribution: Ramirez, $98,633

SERIAL PROBLEM

Success Systems

(This serial problem began in Chapter 1 and continues through most of the book. If previous chapter segments were not completed, the serial problem can begin at this point. It is helpful, but not necessary, to use the Working Papers that accompany the book.)

SP 12 At the start of 2010, Adriana Lopez is considering adding a partner to her business. She envisions the new partner taking the lead in generating sales of both services and merchandise for Success Systems. Lopez's equity in Success Systems as of January 1, 2010, is reflected in the following capital balance.

A. Lopez, Capital	$90,148

Required

1. Lopez is evaluating whether the prospective partner should be an equal partner with respect to capital investment and profit sharing (1:1) or whether the agreement should be 4:1 with Lopez retaining four-fifths interest with rights to four-fifths of the net income or loss. What factors should she consider in deciding which partnership agreement to offer?

2. Prepare the January 1, 2010, journal entry(ies) necessary to admit a new partner to Success Systems through the purchase of a partnership interest for each of the following two separate cases: (*a*) 1:1 sharing agreement and (*b*) 4:1 sharing agreement.

3. Prepare the January 1, 2010, journal entry(ies) required to admit a new partner if the new partner invests cash of $22,537.

4. After posting the entry in part 3, what would be the new partner's equity percentage?

BEYOND THE NUMBERS

REPORTING IN ACTION

C1

BTN 12-1 Take a step back in time and imagine **Best Buy** in its infancy as a company. The year is 1966.

Required

1. Read the history of Best Buy at BestBuymedia.tekgroup.com. Can you determine from the history whether Best Buy was originally organized as a sole proprietorship, partnership, or corporation?

2. Assume that Best Buy was originally organized as a partnership. Best Buy's income statement in Appendix A varies in several key ways from what it would look like for a partnership. Identify at least two ways in which a corporate income statement differs from a partnership income statement.

3. Compare the Best Buy balance sheet in Appendix A to what a partnership balance sheet would have shown. Identify and explain any account differences you would anticipate.

COMPARATIVE ANALYSIS

C1

BTN 12-2 Over the years **Best Buy** and **Circuit City** have evolved into large corporations. Today it is difficult to imagine them as fledgling start-ups. Research each company's history online.

Required

1. Which company is older?

2. Which company started as a partnership?

3. In what years did each company first achieve $1,000,000 in sales?

4. In what years did each company have its first public offering of stock?

ETHICS CHALLENGE

P2

BTN 12-3 Doctors Maben, Orlando, and Clark have been in a group practice for several years. Maben and Orlando are family practice physicians, and Clark is a general surgeon. Clark receives many referrals for surgery from his family practice partners. Upon the partnership's original formation, the three doctors agreed to a two-part formula to share income. Every month each doctor receives a salary allowance of $3,000. Additional income is divided according to a percent of patient charges the doctors generate for the month. In the current month, Maben generated 10% of the billings, Orlando 30%, and Clark 60%. The group's income for this month is $50,000. Clark has expressed dissatisfaction with the income-sharing formula and asks that income be split entirely on patient charge percents.

Required

1. Compute the income allocation for the current month using the original agreement.
2. Compute the income allocation for the current month using Clark's proposed agreement.
3. Identify the ethical components of this partnership decision for the doctors.

COMMUNICATING IN PRACTICE

C1

BTN 12-4 Assume that you are studying for an upcoming accounting exam with a good friend. Your friend says that she has a solid understanding of general partnerships but is less sure that she understands organizations that combine certain characteristics of partnerships with other forms of business organization. You offer to make some study notes for your friend to help her learn about limited partnerships, limited liability partnerships, S corporations, and limited liability companies. Prepare a one-page set of well-organized, complete study notes on these four forms of business organization.

TAKING IT TO THE NET

P1 P2

BTN 12-5 Access the March 6, 2007, filing of the December 31, 2006, 10-K of **America First Tax Exempt Investors LP**. This company deals with tax-exempt mortgage revenue bonds that, among other things, finance student housing properties.

1. Locate its December 31, 2006, balance sheet and list the account titles reported in the equity section of the balance sheet.
2. Locate its statement of partners' capital and comprehensive income (loss). How many units of limited partnership (known as "beneficial unit certificate holders") are outstanding at December 31, 2006?
3. What is the partnership's largest asset and its amount at December 31, 2006?

TEAMWORK IN ACTION

P2

BTN 12-6 This activity requires teamwork to reinforce understanding of accounting for partnerships.

Required

1. Assume that Baker, Warner, and Rice form the BWR Partnership by making capital contributions of $200,000, $300,000, and $500,000, respectively. BWR predicts annual partnership net income of $600,000. The partners are considering various plans for sharing income and loss. Assign a different team member to compute how the projected $600,000 income would be shared under each of the following separate plans:
   - **a.** Shared equally.
   - **b.** In the ratio of the partners' initial capital investments.
   - **c.** Salary allowances of $50,000 to Baker, $60,000 to Warner, and $70,000 to Rice, with the remaining balance shared equally.
   - **d.** Interest allowances of 10% on the partners' initial capital investments, with the remaining balance shared equally.
2. In sequence, each member is to present his or her income-sharing calculations with the team.
3. As a team, identify and discuss at least one other possible way that income could be shared.

BTN 12-7 Recall the chapter's opening feature involving Samanta and Kelvin Joseph, and their company, **Samanta Shoes**. Assume that Samanta and Kelvin, partners in Samanta Shoes, decide to expand their business with the help of general partners.

ENTREPRENEURIAL DECISION

C1

Required

1. What details should Samanta, Kelvin, and their future partners specify in the general partnership agreements?
2. What advantages should Samanta, Kelvin, and their future partners be aware of with respect to organizing as a general partnership?
3. What disadvantages should Samanta, Kelvin, and their future partners be aware of with respect to organizing as a general partnership?

BTN 12-8 Access **DSG international**'s Website (www.DSGiplc.com) and research the company's history.

GLOBAL DECISION

C1

DSG

1. When was the company founded, and what was its original form of ownership?
2. Why did the company change its name from Dixons to DSG international?
3. What are some of the companies that are part of DSG international?

ANSWERS TO MULTIPLE CHOICE QUIZ

1. e; Capital = \$250,000 − \$50,000
2. a; \$90,000 × [\$100,000/(\$150,000 + \$150,000 + \$100,000)] = \$22,500
3. d;

	Jamison	Blue	Total
Net income			\$ 270,000
Salary allowance	\$120,000		(120,000)
Interest allowance	60,000	\$80,000	(140,000)
Balance of income			10,000
Balance divided equally	5,000	5,000	(10,000)
Totals	\$185,000	\$85,000	\$ 0

4. b; Total partnership equity = \$125,000 + \$124,000 + \$75,000 = \$324,000
   Equity of Black = \$324,000 × 20% = \$64,800
   Bonus to old partners = \$75,000 − \$64,800 = \$10,200, split equally
5. a; \$10,500/[(\$110,000 + \$124,000)/2] = 8.97%

A Look Back

Chapter 12 focused on the partnership form of organization. We described crucial characteristics of partnerships and the accounting and reporting of their important transactions.

A Look at This Chapter

This chapter emphasizes details of the corporate form of organization. The accounting concepts and procedures for equity transactions are explained. We also describe how to report and analyze income, earnings per share, and retained earnings.

A Look Ahead

Chapter 14 focuses on long-term liabilities. We explain how to value, record, amortize, and report these liabilities in financial statements.

Chapter 13 Accounting for Corporations

Learning Objectives

CAP

Conceptual

C1 Identify characteristics of corporations and their organization. *(p. 506)*

C2 Describe the components of stockholders' equity. *(p. 509)*

C3 Explain characteristics of common and preferred stock. *(p. 517)*

C4 Explain the items reported in retained earnings. *(p. 522)*

Analytical

A1 Compute earnings per share and describe its use. *(p. 524)*

A2 Compute price-earnings ratio and describe its use in analysis. *(p. 525)*

A3 Compute dividend yield and explain its use in analysis. *(p. 525)*

A4 Compute book value and explain its use in analysis. *(p. 526)*

Procedural

P1 Record the issuance of corporate stock. *(p. 510)*

P2 Record transactions involving cash dividends. *(p. 513)*

P3 Account for stock dividends and stock splits. *(p. 514)*

P4 Distribute dividends between common stock and preferred stock. *(p. 517)*

P5 Record purchases and sales of treasury stock and the retirement of stock. *(p. 520)*

LP13

Decision Feature

Breathing New Life

"We weren't planning on starting a company"
—Ali Perry

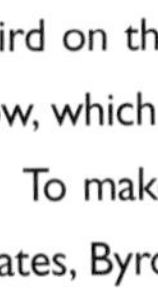

SANTA BARBARA, CA—"My grandma has COPD [chronic obstructive pulmonary disease] and she got put on oxygen," explains Ali Perry. "Her quality of life got destroyed because she couldn't go anywhere, she couldn't do anything. Everything was limited by how much she had in her bottles of compressed oxygen." Ali dreamed to help her grandma. She explains that COPD is the fourth leading cause of death, and is predicted to soon be third on that list. COPD is a disease where the airways of the lungs narrow, which limits the flow of air and causes shortness of breath.

To make her dream a reality, Ali enlisted the aid of two college classmates, Byron Myers and Brenton Taylor. The three of them designed a portable oxygen system, wrote a business plan, and set off to secure financing. Their company, named **Inogen**, which is a combination of the words innovation and oxygen **(Inogen.net),** soon had a portable oxygen supply unit whose sales exceed 10,000 units to date. "We worked really hard at the technology," explains Ali. "We saw the value of the company was in creating technology that was thought impossible in the marketplace."

The three founders insist that proper financing was a key to their success. To make it happen, says Ali, they needed equity (stock) financing. With their business plan and prototype, the three raised a whopping $4 million from a venture capital firm. Still, explains Ali, the focus is on helping folks, including her grandma. Adds Byron, "Oxygen users can now take off on a moment's notice, without having to watch the clock or guess at how long their oxygen will last."

Their equity financing "brings both opportunities and challenges," explains Byron. "New patients do not know anything about oxygen therapy. All they know is that their life has changed and they now need to have a supply of oxygen with them whenever and wherever." Inogen answers that call. Their focus on people continues to reap rewards as they recently secured another $22 million in equity financing. As Byron put it: "[Inogen] makes old ways of thinking and operating inadequate."

[Sources: *Inogen Website,* January 2009; *HME Business,* January 2006; *Daily Nexus,* January 2004; *Goleta Valley Voice,* December 2003; *Inc.com,* July 2007]

This chapter focuses on equity transactions. The first part of the chapter describes the basics of the corporate form of organization and explains the accounting for common and preferred stock. We then focus on several special financing transactions, including cash and stock dividends, stock splits, and treasury stock. The final section considers accounting for retained earnings, including prior period adjustments, retained earnings restrictions, and reporting guidelines.

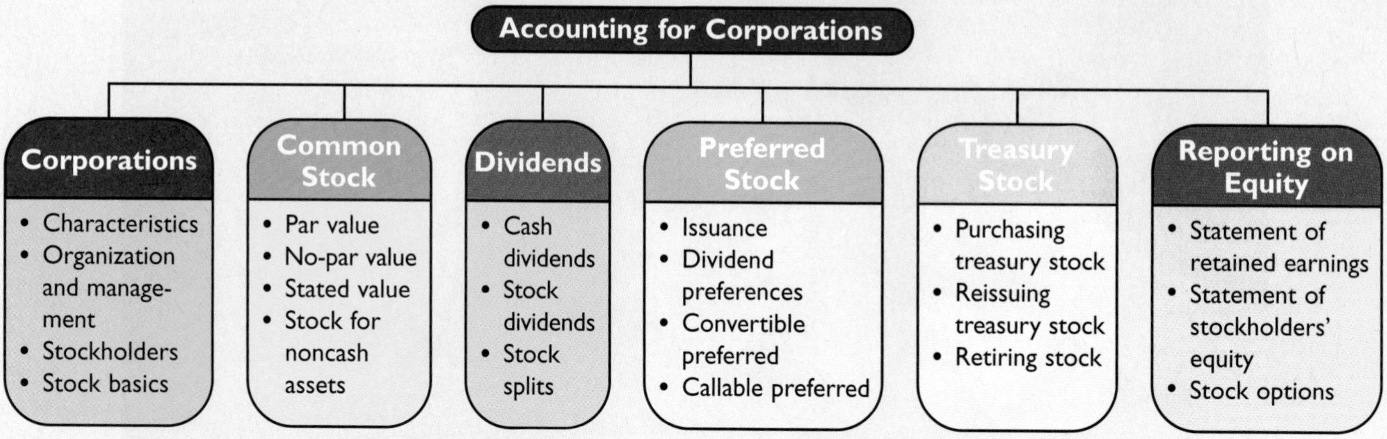

Corporate Form of Organization

Video13.1

A **corporation** is an entity created by law that is separate from its owners. It has most of the rights and privileges granted to individuals. Owners of corporations are called *stockholders* or *shareholders*. Corporations can be separated into two types. A *privately held* (or *closely held*) corporation does not offer its stock for public sale and usually has few stockholders. A *publicly held* corporation offers its stock for public sale and can have thousands of stockholders. *Public sale* usually refers to issuance and trading on an organized stock market.

Characteristics of Corporations

C1 Identify characteristics of corporations and their organization.

Corporations represent an important type of organization. Their unique characteristics offer advantages and disadvantages.

Advantages of Corporate Characteristics

- **Separate legal entity:** A corporation conducts its affairs with the same rights, duties, and responsibilities of a person. It takes actions through its agents, who are its officers and managers.
- **Limited liability of stockholders:** Stockholders are neither liable for corporate acts nor corporate debt.
- **Transferable ownership rights:** The transfer of shares from one stockholder to another usually has no effect on the corporation or its operations except when this causes a change in the directors who control or manage the corporation.
- **Continuous life:** A corporation's life continues indefinitely because it is not tied to the physical lives of its owners.
- **Lack of mutual agency for stockholders:** A corporation acts through its agents, who are its officers and managers. Stockholders, who are not its officers and managers, do not have the power to bind the corporation to contracts—referred to as *lack of mutual agency.*
- **Ease of capital accumulation:** Buying stock is attractive to investors because (1) stockholders are not liable for the corporation's acts and debts, (2) stocks usually are transferred easily, (3) the life of the corporation is unlimited, and (4) stockholders are not corporate agents. These advantages enable corporations to accumulate large amounts of capital from the combined investments of many stockholders.

Point: The *business entity assumption* requires a corporation to be accounted for separately from its owners (shareholders).

Global: U.S., U.K., and Canadian corporations finance much of their operations with stock issuances, but companies in countries such as France, Germany, and Japan finance mainly with note and bond issuances.

Disadvantages of Corporate Characteristics

- **Government regulation:** A corporation must meet requirements of a state's incorporation laws, which subject the corporation to state regulation and control. Proprietorships and partnerships avoid many of these regulations and governmental reports.
- **Corporate taxation:** Corporations are subject to the same property and payroll taxes as proprietorships and partnerships plus *additional* taxes. The most burdensome of these are federal and state income taxes that together can take 40% or more of corporate pretax income. Moreover, corporate income is usually taxed a second time as part of stockholders' personal income when they receive cash distributed as dividends. This is called *double taxation.* (The usual dividend tax is 15%; however, it is less than 15% for lower income taxpayers, and in some cases zero.)

Point: Proprietorships and partnerships are not subject to income taxes. Their income is taxed as the personal income of their owners.

Point: Double taxation is less severe when a corporation's owner-manager collects a salary that is taxed only once as part of his or her personal income.

Decision Insight

Stock Financing Marc Andreessen cofounded **Netscape** at age 22, only four months after earning his degree. One year later, he and friends issued Netscape shares to the public. The stock soared, making Andreessen a multimillionaire.

Corporate Organization and Management

This section describes the incorporation, costs, and management of corporate organizations.

Point: A corporation is not required to have an office in its state of incorporation.

Incorporation A corporation is created by obtaining a charter from a state government. A charter application usually must be signed by the prospective stockholders called *incorporators* or *promoters* and then filed with the proper state official. When the application process is complete and fees paid, the charter is issued and the corporation is formed. Investors then purchase the corporation's stock, meet as stockholders, and elect a board of directors. Directors oversee a corporation's affairs.

Organization Expenses **Organization expenses** (also called *organization costs*) are the costs to organize a corporation; they include legal fees, promoters' fees, and amounts paid to obtain a charter. The corporation records (debits) these costs to an expense account called *Organization Expenses*. Organization costs are expensed as incurred because it is difficult to determine the amount and timing of their future benefits.

Management of a Corporation The ultimate control of a corporation rests with stockholders who control a corporation by electing its *board of directors,* or simply, *directors.* Each stockholder usually has one vote for each share of stock owned. This control relation is shown in Exhibit 13.1. Directors are responsible for and have final authority for managing corporate activities. A board can act only as a collective body and usually limits its actions to setting general policy.

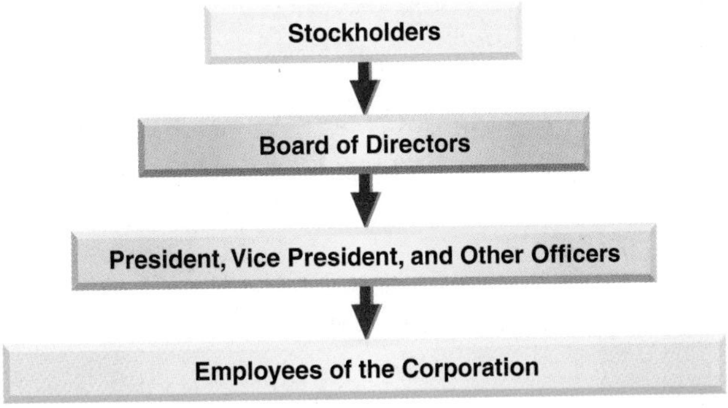

EXHIBIT 13.1

Corporate Structure

A corporation usually holds a stockholder meeting at least once a year to elect directors and transact business as its bylaws require. A group of stockholders owning or controlling votes of more than a 50% share of a corporation's stock can elect the board and control the corporation. Stockholders who do not attend stockholders' meetings must have an opportunity to delegate their voting rights to an agent by signing a **proxy,** a document that gives a designated agent the right to vote the stock.

Day-to-day direction of corporate business is delegated to executive officers appointed by the board. A corporation's chief executive officer (CEO) is often its president. Several vice

Point: *Bylaws* are guidelines that govern the behavior of individuals employed by and managing the corporation.

Global: Some corporate labels are:

Country	Label
United States	Inc.
France	SA
United Kingdom	
Public	PLC
Private	LTD
Germany	
Public	AG
Private	GmbH
Sweden	AB
Italy	SpA

presidents, who report to the president, are commonly assigned specific areas of management responsibility such as finance, production, and marketing. One person often has the dual role of chairperson of the board of directors and CEO. In this case, the president is usually designated the chief operating officer (COO).

Decision Insight

Seed Money Sources for start-up money include (1) "angel" investors such as family, friends, or anyone who believes in a company, (2) employees, investors, and even suppliers who can be paid with stock, and (3) venture capitalists (investors) who have a record of entrepreneurial success. See the National Venture Capital Association (**NVCA.org**) for information.

Stockholders of Corporations

This section explains stockholder rights, stock purchases and sales, and the role of registrar and transfer agents.

Rights of Stockholders When investors buy stock, they acquire all *specific* rights the corporation's charter grants to stockholders. They also acquire *general* rights granted stockholders by the laws of the state in which the company is incorporated. When a corporation has only one class of stock, it is identified as **common stock.** State laws vary, but common stockholders usually have the general right to

1. Vote at stockholders' meetings.
2. Sell or otherwise dispose of their stock.
3. Purchase their proportional share of any common stock later issued by the corporation. This **preemptive right** protects stockholders' proportionate interest in the corporation. For example, a stockholder who owns 25% of a corporation's common stock has the first opportunity to buy 25% of any new common stock issued.
4. Receive the same dividend, if any, on each common share of the corporation.
5. Share in any assets remaining after creditors and preferred stockholders are paid when, and if, the corporation is liquidated. Each common share receives the same amount.

Stockholders also have the right to receive timely financial reports.

Stock Certificates and Transfer Investors who buy a corporation's stock, sometimes receive a *stock certificate* as proof of share ownership. Many corporations issue only one certificate for each block of stock purchased. A certificate can be for any number of shares. Exhibit 13.2 shows a stock certificate of the **Green Bay Packers.** A certificate shows the company name, stockholder name, number of shares, and other crucial information. Issuance of certificates is becoming less common. Instead, many stockholders maintain accounts with the corporation or their stockbrokers and never receive actual certificates.

EXHIBIT 13.2

Stock Certificate

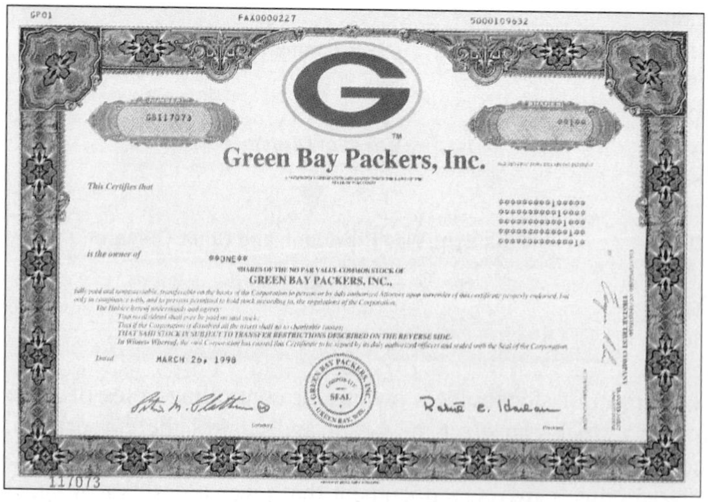

Registrar and Transfer Agents If a corporation's stock is traded on a major stock exchange, the corporation must have a registrar and a transfer agent. A *registrar* keeps stockholder records and prepares official lists of stockholders for stockholder meetings and dividend payments. A *transfer agent* assists with purchases and sales of shares by receiving and issuing certificates as necessary. Registrars and transfer agents are usually large banks or trust companies with computer facilities and staff to do this work.

Decision Insight

Pricing Stock A prospectus accompanies a stock's initial public offering (IPO), giving financial information about the company issuing the stock. A prospectus should help answer these questions to price an IPO: (1) Is the underwriter reliable? (2) Is there growth in revenues, profits, and cash flows? (3) What is management's view of operations? (4) Are current owners selling? (5) What are the risks?

Basics of Capital Stock

C2 Describe the components of stockholders' equity.

Capital stock is a general term that refers to any shares issued to obtain capital (owner financing). This section introduces terminology and accounting for capital stock.

Authorized Stock **Authorized stock** is the number of shares that a corporation's charter allows it to sell. The number of authorized shares usually exceeds the number of shares issued (and outstanding), often by a large amount. (*Outstanding stock* refers to issued stock held by stockholders.) No formal journal entry is required for stock authorization. A corporation must apply to the state for a change in its charter if it wishes to issue more shares than previously authorized. A corporation discloses the number of shares authorized in the equity section of its balance sheet or notes. **Best Buy**'s balance sheet in Appendix A reports 1 billion shares authorized as of the start of its 2008 fiscal year.

Subcategories of Authorized Stock

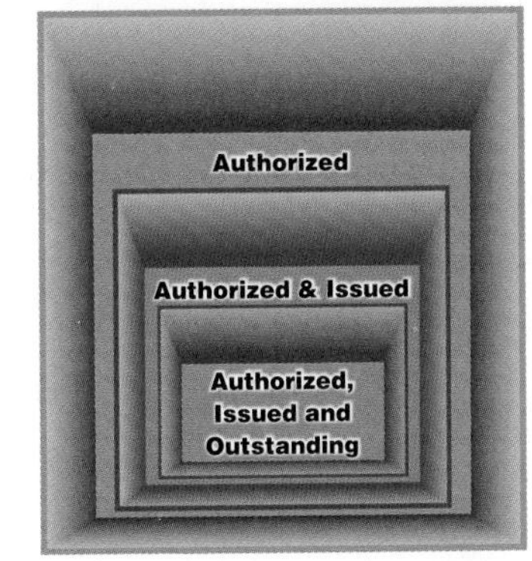

Selling (Issuing) Stock A corporation can sell stock directly or indirectly. To *sell directly,* it advertises its stock issuance to potential buyers. This type of issuance is most common with privately held corporations. To *sell indirectly,* a corporation pays a brokerage house (investment banker) to issue its stock. Some brokerage houses *underwrite* an indirect issuance of stock; that is, they buy the stock from the corporation and take all gains or losses from its resale.

Market Value of Stock **Market value per share** is the price at which a stock is bought and sold. Expected future earnings, dividends, growth, and other company and economic factors influence market value. Traded stocks' market values are available daily in newspapers such as *The Wall Street Journal* and online. The current market value of previously issued shares (for example, the price of stock in trades between investors) does not impact the issuing corporation's stockholders' equity.

Classes of Stock When all authorized shares have the same rights and characteristics, the stock is called *common stock.* A corporation is sometimes authorized to issue more than one class of stock, including preferred stock and different classes of common stock. **American Greetings**, for instance, has two types of common stock: Class A stock has 1 vote per share and Class B stock has 10 votes per share.

Par Value Stock **Par value stock** is stock that is assigned a **par value,** which is an amount assigned per share by the corporation in its charter. For example, Best Buy's common stock has a par value of $0.10. Other commonly assigned par values are $10, $5, $1 and $0.01. There is no restriction on the assigned par value. In many states, the par value of a stock establishes **minimum legal capital,** which refers to the least amount that the buyers of stock must contribute to the corporation or be subject to paying at a future date. For example, if a corporation issues 1,000 shares of $10 par value stock, the corporation's minimum legal capital in these states would be $10,000. Minimum legal capital is intended to protect a corporation's creditors. Since creditors cannot demand payment from stockholders' personal assets, their claims are limited to the corporation's assets and any minimum legal capital. At liquidation, creditor claims are paid before any amounts are distributed to stockholders.

Point: Managers are motivated to set a low par value when minimum legal capital or state issuance taxes are based on par value.

Point: Minimum legal capital was intended to protect creditors by requiring a minimum level of net assets.

No-Par Value Stock **No-par value stock,** or simply *no-par stock,* is stock *not* assigned a value per share by the corporate charter. Its advantage is that it can be issued at any price without the possibility of a minimum legal capital deficiency.

Point: Par, no-par, and stated value do *not* set the stock's market value.

EXHIBIT 13.3

Equity Composition

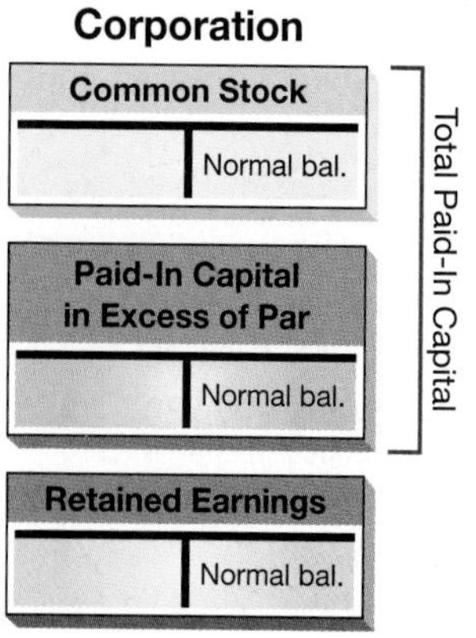

Point: Paid-in capital comes from stock-related transactions, whereas retained earnings comes from operations.

Stated Value Stock **Stated value stock** is no-par stock to which the directors assign a "stated" value per share. Stated value per share becomes the minimum legal capital per share in this case.

Stockholders' Equity A corporation's equity is known as **stockholders' equity,** also called *shareholders' equity* or *corporate capital.* Stockholders' equity consists of (1) paid-in (or contributed) capital and (2) retained earnings; see Exhibit 13.3. **Paid-in capital** is the total amount of cash and other assets the corporation receives from its stockholders in exchange for its stock. **Retained earnings** is the cumulative net income (and loss) not distributed as dividends to its stockholders.

Decision Insight

Stock Quote The **Best Buy** stock quote is interpreted as (left to right): **Hi,** highest price in past 52 weeks; **Lo,** lowest price in past 52 weeks; **Sym,** company exchange symbol; **Div,** dividends paid per share in past year; **Yld %,** dividend divided by closing price; **PE,** stock price per share divided by earnings per share; **Vol mil.,** number (in millions) of shares traded; **Hi,** highest price for the day; **Lo,** lowest price for the day; **Close,** closing price for the day; **Net Chg,** change in closing price from prior day.

52 Weeks				Yld		Vol				Net
Hi	Lo	Sym	Div	%	PE	mil.	Hi	Lo	Close	Chg
54.15	41.85	BBY	0.13	0.98	19	7.2	53.14	52.36	52.91	+0.20

Quick Check

Answers—p. 531

1. Which of the following is *not* a characteristic of the corporate form of business? (*a*) Ease of capital accumulation, (*b*) Stockholder responsibility for corporate debts, (*c*) Ease in transferability of ownership rights, or (*d*) Double taxation.
2. Why is a corporation's income said to be taxed twice?
3. What is a proxy?

Common Stock

P1 Record the issuance of corporate stock.

Video13.2

Accounting for the issuance of common stock affects only paid-in (contributed) capital accounts; no retained earnings accounts are affected.

Issuing Par Value Stock

Par value stock can be issued at par, at a premium (above par), or at a discount (below par). In each case, stock can be exchanged for either cash or noncash assets.

Issuing Par Value Stock at Par When common stock is issued at par value, we record amounts for both the asset(s) received and the par value stock issued. To illustrate, the entry to record Dillon Snowboards' issuance of 30,000 shares of $10 par value stock for $300,000 cash on June 5, 2009, follows.

Assets	= Liabilities +	Equity
+300,000		+300,000

June 5	Cash	300,000	
	Common Stock, $10 Par Value		300,000
	Issued 30,000 shares of $10 par value common stock at par.		

Exhibit 13.4 shows the stockholders' equity of Dillon Snowboards at year-end 2009 (its first year of operations) after income of $65,000 and no dividend payments.

EXHIBIT 13.4

Stockholders' Equity for Stock Issued at Par

Stockholders' Equity	
Common Stock—$10 par value; 50,000 shares authorized; 30,000 shares issued and outstanding	$300,000
Retained earnings	65,000
Total stockholders' equity	$365,000

Issuing Par Value Stock at a Premium A **premium on stock** occurs when a corporation sells its stock for more than par (or stated) value. To illustrate, if Dillon Snowboards issues its $10 par value common stock at $12 per share, its stock is sold at a $2 per share premium. The premium, known as **paid-in capital in excess of par value,** is reported as part of equity; it is not revenue and is not listed on the income statement. The entry to record Dillon Snowboards' issuance of 30,000 shares of $10 par value stock for $12 per share on June 5, 2009, follows

Point: A *premium* is the amount by which issue price exceeds par (or stated) value. It is recorded in the "Paid-In Capital in Excess of Par Value, Common Stock" account; also called "Additional Paid-In Capital, Common Stock."

June 5	Cash	360,000	
	Common Stock, $10 Par Value		300,000
	Paid-In Capital in Excess of Par Value, Common Stock		**60,000**
	Sold and issued 30,000 shares of $10 par value common stock at $12 per share.		

Assets	= Liabilities +	Equity
+360,000		+300,000
		+60,000

The Paid-In Capital in Excess of Par Value account is added to the par value of the stock in the equity section of the balance sheet as shown in Exhibit 13.5.

Point: The *Paid-In Capital* terminology is interchangeable with *Contributed Capital.*

EXHIBIT 13.5

Stockholders' Equity for Stock Issued at a Premium

Stockholders' Equity	
Common Stock—$10 par value; 50,000 shares authorized; 30,000 shares issued and outstanding	$300,000
Paid-in capital in excess of par value, common stock	**60,000**
Retained earnings	65,000
Total stockholders' equity	$425,000

Issuing Par Value Stock at a Discount A **discount on stock** occurs when a corporation sells its stock for less than par (or stated) value. Most states prohibit the issuance of stock at a discount. In states that allow stock to be issued at a discount, its buyers usually become contingently liable to creditors for the discount. If stock is issued at a discount, the amount by which issue price is less than par is debited to a *Discount on Common Stock* account, a contra to the common stock account, and its balance is subtracted from the par value of stock in the equity section of the balance sheet. This discount is not an expense and does not appear on the income statement.

Point: Retained earnings can be negative, reflecting accumulated losses. Amazon.com had an accumulated deficit of $1.8 billion at the start of 2007.

Issuing No-Par Value Stock

When no-par stock is issued and is not assigned a stated value, the amount the corporation receives becomes legal capital and is recorded as Common Stock. This means that the entire proceeds are credited to a no-par stock account. To illustrate, a corporation records its October 20 issuance of 1,000 shares of no-par stock for $40 cash per share as follows.

Oct. 20	Cash	40,000	
	Common Stock, No-Par Value		40,000
	Issued 1,000 shares of no-par value common stock at $40 per share.		

Assets	= Liabilities +	Equity
+40,000		+40,000

Frequency of Stock Types

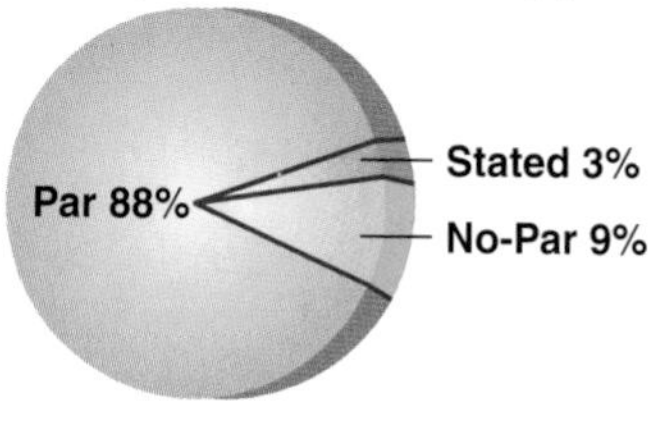

Issuing Stated Value Stock

When no-par stock is issued and assigned a stated value, its stated value becomes legal capital and is credited to a stated value stock account. Assuming that stated value stock is issued at an amount in excess of stated value (the usual case), the excess is credited to Paid-In Capital in Excess of Stated Value, Common Stock, which is reported in the stockholders' equity section. To illustrate, a corporation that issues 1,000 shares of no-par common stock having a stated value of $40 per share in return for $50 cash per share records this as follows.

Assets	= Liabilities +	Equity
+50,000		+40,000
		+10,000

Oct. 20	Cash	50,000	
	Common Stock, $40 Stated Value		40,000
	Paid-In Capital in Excess of Stated Value, Common Stock		10,000
	Issued 1,000 shares of $40 per share stated value stock at $50 per share.		

Issuing Stock for Noncash Assets

Point: Stock issued for noncash assets should be recorded at the market value of either the stock or the noncash asset, whichever is more clearly determinable.

A corporation can receive assets other than cash in exchange for its stock. (It can also assume liabilities on the assets received such as a mortgage on property received.) The corporation records the assets received at their market values as of the date of the transaction. The stock given in exchange is recorded at its par (or stated) value with any excess recorded in the Paid-In Capital in Excess of Par (or Stated) Value account. (If no-par stock is issued, the stock is recorded at the assets' market value.) To illustrate, the entry to record receipt of land valued at $105,000 in return for issuance of 4,000 shares of $20 par value common stock on June 10 is

Assets	= Liabilities +	Equity
+105,000		+80,000
		+25,000

June 10	Land	105,000	
	Common Stock, $20 Par Value		80,000
	Paid-In Capital in Excess of Par Value, Common Stock		25,000
	Exchanged 4,000 shares of $20 par value common stock for land.		

Point: Any type of stock can be issued for noncash assets.

A corporation sometimes gives shares of its stock to promoters in exchange for their services in organizing the corporation, which the corporation records as **Organization Expenses.** The entry to record receipt of services valued at $12,000 in organizing the corporation in return for 600 shares of $15 par value common stock on June 5 is

Assets	= Liabilities +	Equity
		−12,000
		+9,000
		+3,000

June 5	Organization Expenses	12,000	
	Common Stock, $15 Par Value		9,000
	Paid-In Capital in Excess of Par Value, Common Stock		3,000
	Gave promoters 600 shares of $15 par value common stock in exchange for their services.		

Quick Check

Answers—p. 531

4. A company issues 7,000 shares of its $10 par value common stock in exchange for equipment valued at $105,000. The entry to record this transaction includes a credit to (*a*) Paid-In Capital in Excess of Par Value, Common Stock, for $35,000. (*b*) Retained Earnings for $35,000. (*c*) Common Stock, $10 Par Value, for $105,000.
5. What is a premium on stock issuance?
6. Who is intended to be protected by minimum legal capital?

Dividends

This section describes both cash and stock dividend transactions.

P2 Record transactions involving cash dividends.

Video13.2

Cash Dividends

The decision to pay cash dividends rests with the board of directors and involves more than evaluating the amounts of retained earnings and cash. The directors, for instance, may decide to keep the cash to invest in the corporation's growth, to meet emergencies, to take advantage of unexpected opportunities, or to pay off debt. Alternatively, many corporations pay cash dividends to their stockholders at regular dates. These cash flows provide a return to investors and almost always affect the stock's market value.

Accounting for Cash Dividends Dividend payment involves three important dates: declaration, record, and payment. **Date of declaration** is the date the directors vote to declare and pay a dividend. This creates a legal liability of the corporation to its stockholders. **Date of record** is the future date specified by the directors for identifying those stockholders listed in the corporation's records to receive dividends. The date of record usually follows the date of declaration by at least two weeks. Persons who own stock on the date of record receive dividends. **Date of payment** is the date when the corporation makes payment; it follows the date of record by enough time to allow the corporation to arrange checks, money transfers, or other means to pay dividends.

Percent of Corporations Paying Dividends

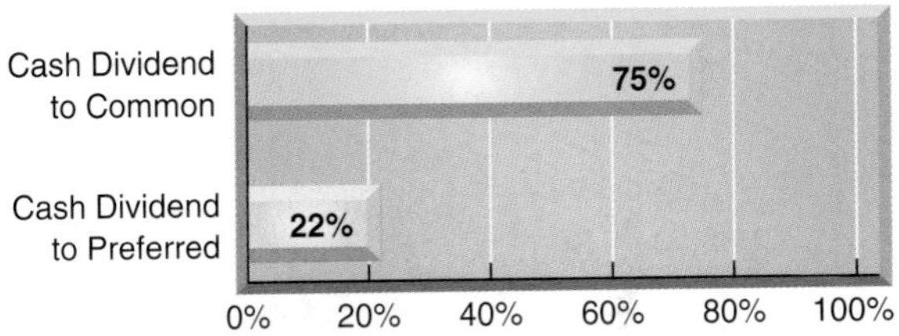

To illustrate, the entry to record a January 9 declaration of a $1 per share cash dividend by the directors of Z-Tech, Inc., with 5,000 outstanding shares is

Date of Declaration

Jan. 9	Retained Earnings	5,000	
	Common Dividend Payable		5,000
	Declared $1 per common share cash dividend.[1]		

Assets = Liabilities + Equity
+5,000 −5,000

Common Dividend Payable is a current liability. The date of record for the Z-Tech dividend is January 22. *No formal journal entry is needed on the date of record.* The February 1 date of payment requires an entry to record both the settlement of the liability and the reduction of the cash balance, as follows:

Date of Payment

Feb. 1	Common Dividend Payable	5,000	
	Cash		5,000
	Paid $1 per common share cash dividend.		

Assets = Liabilities + Equity
−5,000 −5,000

Deficits and Cash Dividends A corporation with a debit (abnormal) balance for retained earnings is said to have a **retained earnings deficit,** which arises when a company incurs cumulative losses and/or pays more dividends than total earnings from current and prior years. A deficit is reported as a deduction on the balance sheet, as shown in Exhibit 13.6. Most states prohibit a corporation with a deficit from paying a cash dividend to its stockholders. This legal restriction is designed to protect creditors by preventing distribution of assets to stockholders when the company may be in financial difficulty.

Point: It is often said a dividend is a distribution of retained earnings, but it is more precise to describe a dividend as a distribution of assets to satisfy stockholder claims.

Point: The Retained Earnings Deficit account is also called *Accumulated Deficit.*

[1] An alternative entry is to debit Dividends instead of Retained Earnings. The balance in Dividends is then closed to Retained Earnings at the end of the reporting period. The effect is the same: Retained Earnings is decreased and a Dividend Payable is increased. For simplicity, all assignments in this chapter use the Retained Earnings account to record dividend declarations.

EXHIBIT 13.6

Stockholders' Equity with a Deficit

Common stock—$10 par value, 5,000 shares authorized, issued, and outstanding	$50,000
Retained earnings deficit	**(6,000)**
Total stockholders' equity	$44,000

Some state laws allow cash dividends to be paid by returning a portion of the capital contributed by stockholders. This type of dividend is called a **liquidating cash dividend,** or simply *liquidating dividend,* because it returns a part of the original investment back to the stockholders. This requires a debit entry to one of the contributed capital accounts instead of Retained Earnings at the declaration date.

Point: Amazon.com has never declared a cash dividend.

Quick Check Answers—p. 531

7. What type of an account is the Common Dividend Payable account?
8. What three crucial dates are involved in the process of paying a cash dividend?
9. When does a dividend become a company's legal obligation?

Stock Dividends

P3 Account for stock dividends and stock splits.

A **stock dividend,** declared by a corporation's directors, is a distribution of additional shares of the corporation's own stock to its stockholders without the receipt of any payment in return. Stock dividends and cash dividends are different. A stock dividend does not reduce assets and equity but instead transfers a portion of equity from retained earnings to contributed capital.

Reasons for Stock Dividends Stock dividends exist for at least two reasons. First, directors are said to use stock dividends to keep the market price of the stock affordable. For example, if a corporation continues to earn income but does not issue cash dividends, the price of its common stock likely increases. The price of such a stock may become so high that it discourages some investors from buying the stock (especially in lots of 100 and 1,000). When a corporation has a stock dividend, it increases the number of outstanding shares and lowers the per share stock price. Another reason for a stock dividend is to provide evidence of management's confidence that the company is doing well and will continue to do well.

Accounting for Stock Dividends A stock dividend affects the components of equity by transferring part of retained earnings to contributed capital accounts, sometimes described as *capitalizing* retained earnings. Accounting for a stock dividend depends on whether it is a small or large stock dividend. A **small stock dividend** is a distribution of 25% or less of previously outstanding shares. It is recorded by capitalizing retained earnings for an amount equal to the market value of the shares to be distributed. A **large stock dividend** is a distribution of more than 25% of previously outstanding shares. A large stock dividend is recorded by capitalizing retained earnings for the minimum amount required by state law governing the corporation. Most states require capitalizing retained earnings equal to the par or stated value of the stock.

To illustrate stock dividends, we use the equity section of Quest's balance sheet shown in Exhibit 13.7 just *before* its declaration of a stock dividend on December 31.

EXHIBIT 13.7

Stockholders' Equity *before* Declaring a Stock Dividend

Stockholders' Equity (before dividend)	
Common stock—$10 par value, 15,000 shares authorized, 10,000 shares issued and outstanding	$100,000
Paid-in capital in excess of par value, common stock	8,000
Retained earnings	35,000
Total stockholders' equity	$143,000

Recording a small stock dividend. Assume that Quest's directors declare a 10% stock dividend on December 31. This stock dividend of 1,000 shares, computed as 10% of its 10,000 issued and outstanding shares, is to be distributed on January 20 to the stockholders of record on January 15. Since the market price of Quest's stock on December 31 is $15 per share, this small stock dividend declaration is recorded as follows:

Point: Small stock dividends are recorded at market value.

Date of Declaration

Dec. 31	Retained Earnings	15,000	
	Common Stock Dividend Distributable		10,000
	Paid-In Capital in Excess of Par Value, Common Stock		5,000
	Declared a 1,000-share (10%) stock dividend.		

Assets = Liabilities + Equity
−15,000
+10,000
+5,000

The $10,000 credit in the declaration entry equals the par value of the shares and is recorded in *Common Stock Dividend Distributable,* an equity account. Its balance exists only until the shares are issued. The $5,000 credit equals the amount by which market value exceeds par value. This amount increases the Paid-In Capital in Excess of Par Value account in anticipation of the issuance of shares. In general, the balance sheet changes in three ways when a stock dividend is declared. First, the amount of equity attributed to common stock increases; for Quest, from $100,000 to $110,000 for 1,000 additional declared shares. Second, paid-in capital in excess of par increases by the excess of market value over par value for the declared shares. Third, retained earnings decreases, reflecting the transfer of amounts to both common stock and paid-in capital in excess of par. The stockholders' equity of Quest is shown in Exhibit 13.8 *after* its 10% stock dividend is declared on December 31—the items impacted are in bold.

Point: The term *Distributable* (not *Payable*) is used for stock dividends. A stock dividend is never a liability because it never reduces assets.

Point: The credit to Paid-In Capital in Excess of Par Value is recorded when the stock dividend is declared. This account is not affected when stock is later distributed.

EXHIBIT 13.8

Stockholders' Equity *after* Declaring a Stock Dividend

Stockholders' Equity (after dividend)	
Common stock—$10 par value, 15,000 shares authorized, 10,000 shares issued and outstanding	$100,000
Common stock dividend distributable—1,000 shares	**10,000**
Paid-in capital in excess of par value, common stock	**13,000**
Retained earnings	**20,000**
Total stockholders' equity	$143,000

No entry is made on the date of record for a stock dividend. On January 20, the date of payment, Quest distributes the new shares to stockholders and records this entry:

Date of Payment

Jan. 20	Common Stock Dividend Distributable	10,000	
	Common Stock, $10 Par Value		10,000
	To record issuance of common stock dividend.		

Assets = Liabilities + Equity
−10,000
+10,000

The combined effect of these stock dividend entries is to transfer (or capitalize) $15,000 of retained earnings to paid-in capital accounts. The amount of capitalized retained earnings equals the market value of the 1,000 issued shares ($15 × 1,000 shares). A stock dividend has no effect on the ownership percent of individual stockholders.

Point: A stock dividend does not affect assets.

Recording a large stock dividend. A corporation capitalizes retained earnings equal to the minimum amount required by state law for a large stock dividend. For most states, this amount is the par or stated value of the newly issued shares. To illustrate, suppose Quest's board declares a stock dividend of 30% instead of 10% on December 31. Since this dividend is more

Point: Large stock dividends are recorded at par or stated value.

than 25%, it is treated as a large stock dividend. Thus, the par value of the 3,000 dividend shares is capitalized at the date of declaration with this entry:

Assets = Liabilities + Equity
−30,000
+30,000

Date of Declaration

Dec. 31	Retained Earnings.	30,000	
	Common Stock Dividend Distributable.		30,000
	Declared a 3,000-share (30%) stock dividend.		

This transaction decreases retained earnings and increases contributed capital by $30,000. On the date of payment the company debits Common Stock Dividend Distributable and credits Common Stock for $30,000. The effects from a large stock dividend on balance sheet accounts are similar to those for a small stock dividend except for the absence of any effect on paid-in capital in excess of par.

Before 5:1 Split: 1 share, $50 par

After 5:1 Split: 5 shares, $10 par

Point: Berkshire Hathaway has resisted a stock split. Its recent stock price was $150,000 per share.

Point: A **reverse stock split** is the opposite of a stock split. It increases both the market value per share and the par or stated value per share with a split ratio less than 1-for-1, such as 1-for-2. A reverse split results in fewer shares.

Stock Splits

A **stock split** is the distribution of additional shares to stockholders according to their percent ownership. When a stock split occurs, the corporation "calls in" its outstanding shares and issues more than one new share in exchange for each old share. Splits can be done in any ratio, including 2-for-1, 3-for-1, or higher. Stock splits reduce the par or stated value per share. The reasons for stock splits are similar to those for stock dividends.

To illustrate, CompTec has 100,000 outstanding shares of $20 par value common stock with a current market value of $88 per share. A 2-for-1 stock split cuts par value in half as it replaces 100,000 shares of $20 par value stock with 200,000 shares of $10 par value stock. Market value is reduced from $88 per share to about $44 per share. The split does not affect any equity amounts reported on the balance sheet or any individual stockholder's percent ownership. Both the Paid-In Capital and Retained Earnings accounts are unchanged by a split, and *no journal entry is made.* The only effect on the accounts is a change in the stock account description. CompTec's 2-for-1 split on its $20 par value stock means that after the split, it changes its stock account title to Common Stock, $10 Par Value. This stock's description on the balance sheet also changes to reflect the additional authorized, issued, and outstanding shares and the new par value.

The difference between stock splits and large stock dividends is often blurred. Many companies report stock splits in their financial statements without calling in the original shares by simply changing their par value. This type of "split" is really a large stock dividend and results in additional shares issued to stockholders by capitalizing retained earnings or transferring other paid-in capital to Common Stock. This approach avoids administrative costs of splitting the stock. **Harley-Davidson** recently declared a 2-for-1 stock split executed in the form of a 100% stock dividend.

Decision Maker

Entrepreneur A company you cofounded and own stock in announces a 50% stock dividend. Has the value of your stock investment increased, decreased, or remained the same? Would it make a difference if it was a 3-for-2 stock split executed in the form of a dividend? [Answer—p. 531]

Quick Check

Answers—p. 531

10. How does a stock dividend impact assets and retained earnings?
11. What distinguishes a large stock dividend from a small stock dividend?
12. What amount of retained earnings is capitalized for a small stock dividend?

Preferred Stock

A corporation can issue two basic kinds of stock, common and preferred. **Preferred stock** has special rights that give it priority (or senior status) over common stock in one or more areas. Special rights typically include a preference for receiving dividends and for the distribution of assets if the corporation is liquidated. Preferred stock carries all rights of common stock unless the corporate charter nullifies them. Most preferred stock, for instance, does not confer the right to vote. Exhibit 13.9 shows that preferred stock is issued by about one-fourth of large corporations. All corporations issue common stock.

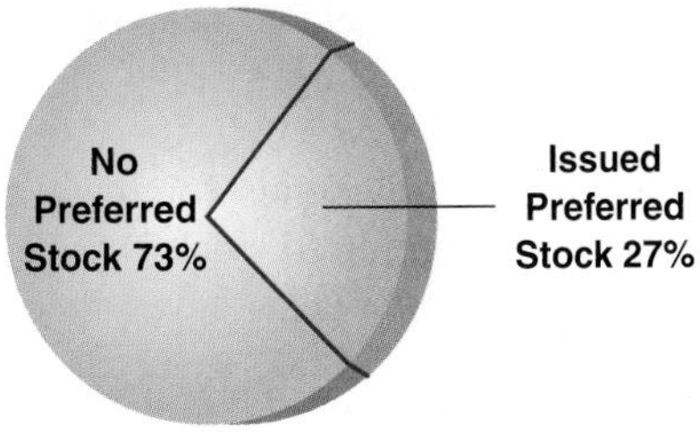

EXHIBIT 13.9

Corporations and Preferred Stock

Issuance of Preferred Stock

C3 Explain characteristics of common and preferred stock.

Preferred stock usually has a par value. Like common stock, it can be sold at a price different from par. Preferred stock is recorded in its own separate capital accounts. To illustrate, if Dillon Snowboards issues 50 shares of $100 par value preferred stock for $6,000 cash on July 1, 2009, the entry is

July 1	Cash	6,000	
	Preferred Stock, $100 Par Value		5,000
	Paid-In Capital in Excess of Par Value, Preferred Stock		1,000
	Issued preferred stock for cash.		

Assets = Liabilities + Equity
+6,000 +5,000
+1,000

The equity section of the year-end balance sheet for Dillon Snowboards, including preferred stock, is shown in Exhibit 13.10. (This exhibit assumes that common stock was issued at par.) Issuing no-par preferred stock is similar to issuing no-par common stock. Also, the entries for issuing preferred stock for noncash assets are similar to those for common stock.

EXHIBIT 13.10

Stockholders' Equity with Common and Preferred Stock

Stockholders' Equity	
Common stock—$10 par value; 50,000 shares authorized; 30,000 shares issued and outstanding	$300,000
Preferred stock—$100 par value; 1,000 shares authorized; 50 shares issued and outstanding	**5,000**
Paid-in capital in excess of par value, preferred stock	**1,000**
Retained earnings	65,000
Total stockholders' equity	$371,000

Dividend Preference of Preferred Stock

P4 Distribute dividends between common stock and preferred stock.

Preferred stock usually carries a preference for dividends, meaning that preferred stockholders are allocated their dividends before any dividends are allocated to common stockholders. The dividends allocated to preferred stockholders are usually expressed as a dollar amount per share or a percent applied to par value. A preference for dividends does *not* ensure dividends. If the directors do not declare a dividend, neither the preferred nor the common stockholders receive one.

Cumulative or Noncumulative Dividend Most preferred stocks carry a cumulative dividend right. **Cumulative preferred stock** has a right to be paid both the current and all prior periods' unpaid dividends before any dividend is paid to common stockholders. When preferred stock is cumulative and the directors either do not declare a dividend to preferred stockholders or declare one that does not cover the total amount of cumulative dividend, the unpaid dividend amount is called **dividend in arrears.** Accumulation of dividends in arrears on cumulative preferred stock does not guarantee they will be paid. **Noncumulative preferred stock** confers no right to prior periods' unpaid dividends if they were not declared in those prior periods.

Point: Dividend preference does not imply that preferred stockholders receive more dividends than common stockholders, nor does it guarantee a dividend.

To illustrate the difference between cumulative and noncumulative preferred stock, assume that a corporation's outstanding stock includes (1) 1,000 shares of $100 par, 9% preferred

Video13.2

stock—yielding $9,000 per year in potential dividends, and (2) 4,000 shares of $50 par value common stock. During 2008, the first year of operations, the directors declare cash dividends of $5,000. In year 2009, they declare cash dividends of $42,000. See Exhibit 13.11 for the allocation of dividends for these two years. Allocation of year 2009 dividends depends on whether the preferred stock is noncumulative or cumulative. With noncumulative preferred, the preferred stockholders never receive the $4,000 skipped in 2008. If the preferred stock is cumulative, the $4,000 in arrears is paid in 2009 before any other dividends are paid.

EXHIBIT 13.11

Allocation of Dividends (noncumulative vs. cumulative preferred stock)

	Preferred	Common
Preferred Stock Is Noncumulative		
Year 2008	$ 5,000	$ 0
Year 2009		
Step 1: Current year's preferred dividend	$ 9,000	
Step 2: Remainder to common		$33,000
Preferred Stock Is Cumulative		
Year 2008	$ 5,000	$ 0
Year 2009		
Step 1: Dividend in arrears	$ 4,000	
Step 2: Current year's preferred dividend	9,000	
Step 3: Remainder to common		$29,000
Totals for year 2009	$13,000	$29,000

Example: What dividends do cumulative preferred stockholders receive in 2009 if the corporation paid only $2,000 of dividends in 2008? How does this affect dividends to common stockholders in 2009? *Answers:* $16,000 ($7,000 dividends in arrears, plus $9,000 current preferred dividends). Dividends to common stockholders decrease to $26,000.

A liability for a dividend does not exist until the directors declare a dividend. If a preferred dividend date passes and the corporation's board fails to declare the dividend on its cumulative preferred stock, the dividend in arrears is not a liability. The *full-disclosure principle* requires a corporation to report (usually in a note) the amount of preferred dividends in arrears as of the balance sheet date.

Participating or Nonparticipating Dividend **Nonparticipating preferred stock** has a feature that limits dividends to a maximum amount each year. This maximum is often stated as a percent of the stock's par value or as a specific dollar amount per share. Once preferred stockholders receive this amount, the common stockholders receive any and all additional dividends. **Participating preferred stock** has a feature allowing preferred stockholders to share with common stockholders in any dividends paid in excess of the percent or dollar amount stated on the preferred stock. This participation feature does not apply until common stockholders receive dividends equal to the preferred stock's dividend percent. Many corporations are authorized to issue participating preferred stock but rarely do, and most managers never expect to issue it.[2]

Convertible Preferred Stock

Preferred stock is more attractive to investors if it carries a right to exchange preferred shares for a fixed number of common shares. **Convertible preferred stock** gives holders the option to

[2] Participating preferred stock is usually authorized as a defense against a possible corporate *takeover* by an "unfriendly" investor (or a group of investors) who intends to buy enough voting common stock to gain control. Taking a term from spy novels, the financial world refers to this type of plan as a *poison pill* that a company swallows if enemy investors threaten its capture. A poison pill usually works as follows: A corporation's common stockholders on a given date are granted the right to purchase a large amount of participating preferred stock at a very low price. This right to purchase preferred shares is *not* transferable. If an unfriendly investor buys a large block of common shares (whose right to purchase participating preferred shares does *not* transfer to this buyer), the board can issue preferred shares at a low price to the remaining common shareholders who retained the right to purchase. Future dividends are then divided between the newly issued participating preferred shares and the common shares. This usually transfers value from common shares to preferred shares, causing the unfriendly investor's common stock to lose much of its value and reduces the potential benefit of a hostile takeover.

exchange their preferred shares for common shares at a specified rate. When a company prospers and its common stock increases in value, convertible preferred stockholders can share in this success by converting their preferred stock into more valuable common stock.

Callable Preferred Stock

Callable preferred stock gives the issuing corporation the right to purchase (retire) this stock from its holders at specified future prices and dates. The amount paid to call and retire a preferred share is its **call price,** or *redemption value,* and is set when the stock is issued. The call price normally includes the stock's par value plus a premium giving holders additional return on their investment. When the issuing corporation calls and retires a preferred stock, the terms of the agreement often require it to pay the call price *and* any dividends in arrears.

Point: The issuing corporation has the right, or option, to retire its callable preferred stock.

Decision Insight

IFRSs Like U.S. GAAP, IFRSs require that preferred stock be classified as debt or equity based on analysis of the stock's contractual terms. However, IFRSs use different criteria for such classification.

Reasons for Issuing Preferred Stock

Corporations issue preferred stock for several reasons. One is to raise capital without sacrificing control. For example, suppose a company's organizers have $100,000 cash to invest and organize a corporation that needs $200,000 of capital to start. If they sell $200,000 worth of common stock (with $100,000 to the organizers), they would have only 50% control and would need to negotiate extensively with other stockholders in making policy. However, if they issue $100,000 worth of common stock to themselves and sell outsiders $100,000 of 8%, cumulative preferred stock with no voting rights, they retain control.

A second reason to issue preferred stock is to boost the return earned by common stockholders. To illustrate, suppose a corporation's organizers expect to earn an annual after-tax income of $24,000 on an investment of $200,000. If they sell and issue $200,000 worth of common stock, the $24,000 income produces a 12% return on the $200,000 of common stockholders' equity. However, if they issue $100,000 of 8% preferred stock to outsiders and $100,000 of common stock to themselves, their own return increases to 16% per year, as shown in Exhibit 13.12.

EXHIBIT 13.12

Return to Common Stockholders When Preferred Stock Is Issued

Net (after-tax) income	$24,000
Less preferred dividends at 8%	(8,000)
Balance to common stockholders	$16,000
Return to common stockholders ($16,000/$100,000)	16%

Common stockholders earn 16% instead of 12% because assets contributed by preferred stockholders are invested to earn $12,000 while the preferred dividend is only $8,000. Use of preferred stock to increase return to common stockholders is an example of **financial leverage** (also called *trading on the equity*). As a general rule, when the dividend rate on preferred stock is less than the rate the corporation earns on its assets, the effect of issuing preferred stock is to increase (or *lever)* the rate earned by common stockholders.

Point: Financial leverage also occurs when debt is issued and the interest rate paid on it is less than the rate earned from using the assets the creditors lend the company.

Other reasons for issuing preferred stock include its appeal to some investors who believe that the corporation's common stock is too risky or that the expected return on common stock is too low.

Decision Maker

Concert Organizer Assume that you alter your business strategy from organizing concerts targeted at under 1,000 people to those targeted at between 5,000 to 20,000 people. You also incorporate because of increased risk of lawsuits and a desire to issue stock for financing. It is important that you control the company for decisions on whom to schedule. What types of stock do you offer? [Answer—p. 531]

Quick Check Answers—p. 531

13. In what ways does preferred stock often have priority over common stock?
14. Increasing the return to common stockholders by issuing preferred stock is an example of (*a*) Financial leverage. (*b*) Cumulative earnings. (*c*) Dividend in arrears.
15. A corporation has issued and outstanding (i) 9,000 shares of $50 par value, 10% cumulative, nonparticipating preferred stock and (ii) 27,000 shares of $10 par value common stock. No dividends have been declared for the two prior years. During the current year, the corporation declares $288,000 in dividends. The amount paid to common shareholders is (*a*) $243,000. (*b*) $153,000. (*c*) $135,000.

Treasury Stock

P5 Record purchases and sales of treasury stock and the retirement of stock.

Corporations acquire shares of their own stock for several reasons: (1) to use their shares to acquire another corporation, (2) to purchase shares to avoid a hostile takeover of the company, (3) to reissue them to employees as compensation, and (4) to maintain a strong market for their stock or to show management confidence in the current price.

A corporation's reacquired shares are called **treasury stock,** which is similar to unissued stock in several ways: (1) neither treasury stock nor unissued stock is an asset, (2) neither receives cash dividends or stock dividends, and (3) neither allows the exercise of voting rights. However, treasury stock does differ from unissued stock in one major way: The corporation can resell treasury stock at less than par without having the buyers incur a liability, provided it was originally issued at par value or higher. Treasury stock purchases also require management to exercise ethical sensitivity because funds are being paid to specific stockholders instead of all stockholders. Managers must be sure the purchase is in the best interest of all stockholders. These concerns cause companies to fully disclose treasury stock transactions.

Corporations and Treasury Stock

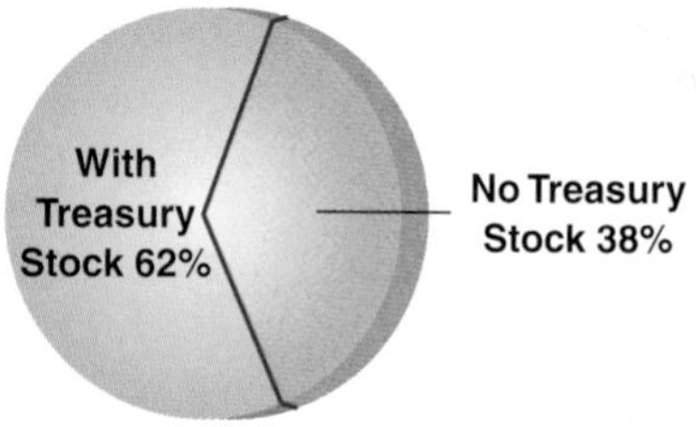

Purchasing Treasury Stock

Purchasing treasury stock reduces the corporation's assets and equity by equal amounts. (We describe the *cost method* of accounting for treasury stock, which is the most widely used method. The *par value* method is another method explained in advanced courses.) To illustrate, Exhibit 13.13 shows Cyber Corporation's account balances *before* any treasury stock purchase (Cyber has no liabilities).

EXHIBIT 13.13

Account Balances *before* Purchasing Treasury Stock

Assets		Stockholders' Equity	
Cash	$ 30,000	Common stock—$10 par; 10,000 shares	
Other assets	95,000	authorized, issued, and outstanding	$100,000
		Retained earnings	25,000
Total assets	$125,000	Total stockholders' equity	$125,000

Cyber then purchases 1,000 of its own shares for $11,500 on May 1, which is recorded as follows.

Assets	= Liabilities +	Equity
−11,500		−11,500

May 1	Treasury Stock, Common	11,500	
	Cash		11,500
	Purchased 1,000 treasury shares at $11.50 per share.		

This entry reduces equity through the debit to the Treasury Stock account, which is a contra equity account. Exhibit 13.14 shows account balances *after* this transaction.

EXHIBIT 13.14

Account Balances *after* Purchasing Treasury Stock

Assets		Stockholders' Equity	
Cash	$ 18,500	Common stock—$10 par; 10,000 shares authorized and issued; 1,000 shares in treasury	$100,000
Other assets	95,000	Retained earnings, $11,500 restricted by treasury stock purchase	25,000
		Less cost of treasury stock	**(11,500)**
Total assets	$113,500	Total stockholders' equity	$113,500

The treasury stock purchase reduces Cyber's cash, total assets, and total equity by $11,500 but does not reduce the balance of either the Common Stock or the Retained Earnings account. The equity reduction is reported by deducting the cost of treasury stock in the equity section. Also, two disclosures are evident. First, the stock description reveals that 1,000 issued shares are in treasury, leaving only 9,000 shares still outstanding. Second, the description for retained earnings reveals that it is partly restricted.

Point: The Treasury Stock account is *not* an asset. Treasury stock does not carry voting or dividend rights.

Point: A treasury stock purchase is also called a *stock buyback*.

Reissuing Treasury Stock

Treasury stock can be reissued by selling it at cost, above cost, or below cost.

Selling Treasury Stock at Cost If treasury stock is reissued at cost, the entry is the reverse of the one made to record the purchase. For instance, if on May 21 Cyber reissues 100 of the treasury shares purchased on May 1 at the same $11.50 per share cost, the entry is

May 21	Cash	1,150	
	Treasury Stock, Common		1,150
	Received $11.50 per share for 100 treasury shares costing $11.50 per share.		

Assets = Liabilities + Equity
+1,150 +1,150

Selling Treasury Stock *above* Cost If treasury stock is sold for more than cost, the amount received in excess of cost is credited to the Paid-In Capital, Treasury Stock account. This account is reported as a separate item in the stockholders' equity section. No gain is ever reported from the sale of treasury stock. To illustrate, if Cyber receives $12 cash per share for 400 treasury shares costing $11.50 per share on June 3, the entry is

Point: Treasury stock does not represent ownership. A company cannot own a part of itself.

June 3	Cash	4,800	
	Treasury Stock, Common		4,600
	Paid-In Capital, Treasury Stock		**200**
	Received $12 per share for 400 treasury shares costing $11.50 per share.		

Assets = Liabilities + Equity
+4,800 +4,600
+200

Selling Treasury Stock *below* Cost When treasury stock is sold below cost, the entry to record the sale depends on whether the Paid-In Capital, Treasury Stock account has a credit balance. If it has a zero balance, the excess of cost over the sales price is debited to Retained Earnings. If the Paid-In Capital, Treasury Stock account has a credit balance, it is debited for the excess of the cost over the selling price but not to exceed the balance in this account. When the credit balance in this paid-in capital account is eliminated, any remaining difference between the cost and selling price is debited to Retained Earnings. To illustrate, if Cyber sells its remaining 500 shares of treasury stock at $10 per share on July 10,

Point: The phrase *treasury stock* is believed to arise from the fact that reacquired stock is held in a corporation's treasury.

Point: The Paid-In Capital, Treasury Stock account can have a zero or credit balance but never a debit balance.

equity is reduced by $750 (500 shares × $1.50 per share excess of cost over selling price), as shown in this entry:

Assets	= Liabilities	+ Equity
+5,000		−200
		−550
		+5,750

July 10	Cash	5,000	
	Paid-In Capital, Treasury Stock	**200**	
	Retained Earnings	**550**	
	Treasury Stock, Common		5,750
	Received $10 per share for 500 treasury shares costing $11.50 per share.		

This entry eliminates the $200 credit balance in the paid-in capital account created on June 3 and then reduces the Retained Earnings balance by the remaining $550 excess of cost over selling price. A company never reports a loss (or gain) from the sale of treasury stock.

Retiring Stock

Point: Recording stock retirement results in canceling the equity from the original issuance of the shares.

A corporation can purchase its own stock and retire it. Retiring stock reduces the number of issued shares. Retired stock is the same as authorized and unissued shares. Purchases and retirements of stock are permissible under state law only if they do not jeopardize the interests of creditors and stockholders. When stock is purchased for retirement, we remove all capital amounts related to the retired shares. If the purchase price exceeds the net amount removed, this excess is debited to Retained Earnings. If the net amount removed from all capital accounts exceeds the purchase price, this excess is credited to the Paid-In Capital from Retirement of Stock account. A company's assets and equity are always reduced by the amount paid for the retiring stock.

Quick Check Answers—p. 531

16. Purchase of treasury stock (*a*) has no effect on assets; (*b*) reduces total assets and total equity by equal amounts; or (*c*) is recorded with a debit to Retained Earnings.
17. Southern Co. purchases shares of Northern Corp. Should either company classify these shares as treasury stock?
18. How does treasury stock affect the authorized, issued, and outstanding shares?
19. When a company purchases treasury stock, (*a*) retained earnings are restricted by the amount paid; (*b*) Retained Earnings is credited; or (*c*) it is retired.

Reporting of Equity

Statement of Retained Earnings

C4 Explain the items reported in retained earnings.

Retained earnings generally consist of a company's cumulative net income less any net losses and dividends declared since its inception. Retained earnings are part of stockholders' claims on the company's net assets, but this does *not* imply that a certain amount of cash or other assets is available to pay stockholders. For example, **Circuit City** has $1,336 million in retained earnings, but only $141 million in cash. This section describes events and transactions affecting retained earnings and how retained earnings are reported.

Video13.1

Restrictions and Appropriations The term **restricted retained earnings** refers to both statutory and contractual restrictions. A common *statutory* (or *legal*) *restriction* is to limit treasury stock purchases to the amount of retained earnings. The balance sheet in Exhibit 13.14 provides an example. A common *contractual restriction* involves loan agreements that restrict paying dividends beyond a specified amount or percent of retained earnings. Restrictions are usually described in the notes. The term **appropriated retained earnings** refers to a voluntary transfer of amounts from the Retained Earnings account to the Appropriated Retained Earnings account to inform users of special activities that require funds.

Prior Period Adjustments **Prior period adjustments** are corrections of material errors in prior period financial statements. These errors include arithmetic mistakes, unacceptable accounting, and missed facts. Prior period adjustments are reported in the *statement of retained earnings* (or the statement of stockholders' equity), net of any income tax effects. Prior period adjustments result in changing the beginning balance of retained earnings for events occurring prior to the earliest period reported in the current set of financial statements. To illustrate, assume that ComUS makes an error in a 2007 journal entry for the purchase of land by incorrectly debiting an expense account. When this is discovered in 2009, the statement of retained earnings includes a prior period adjustment, as shown in Exhibit 13.15. This exhibit also shows the usual format of the statement of retained earnings.

Point: If a year 2007 error is discovered in 2008, the company records the adjustment in 2008. But if the financial statements include 2007 and 2008 figures, the statements report the correct amounts for 2007, and a note describes the correction.

EXHIBIT 13.15

Statement of Retained Earnings with a Prior Period Adjustment

ComUS Statement of Retained Earnings For Year Ended December 31, 2009	
Retained earnings, Dec. 31, 2008, as previously reported	$4,745,000
Prior period adjustment	
Cost of land incorrectly expensed (net of $63,000 income taxes)	**147,000**
Retained earnings, Dec. 31, 2008, as adjusted	4,892,000
Plus net income	1,224,300
Less cash dividends declared	(301,800)
Retained earnings, Dec. 31, 2009	$5,814,500

Many items reported in financial statements are based on estimates. Future events are certain to reveal that some of these estimates were inaccurate even when based on the best data available at the time. These inaccuracies are *not* considered errors and are *not* reported as prior period adjustments. Instead, they are identified as **changes in accounting estimates** and are accounted for in current and future periods. To illustrate, we know that depreciation is based on estimated useful lives and salvage values. As time passes and new information becomes available, managers may need to change these estimates and the resulting depreciation expense for current and future periods.

Point: Accounting for changes in estimates is sometimes criticized as two wrongs to make a right. Consider a change in an asset's life. Depreciation neither before nor after the change is the amount computed if the revised estimate were originally selected. Regulators chose this approach to avoid restating prior period numbers.

Closing Process The closing process was explained earlier in the book as: (1) Close credit balances in revenue accounts to Income Summary, (2) Close debit balances in expense accounts to Income Summary, and (3) Close Income Summary to Retained Earnings. If dividends are recorded in a Dividends account, and not as an immediate reduction to Retained Earnings (as shown in this chapter), a fourth step is necessary to close the Dividends account to Retained Earnings.

Statement of Stockholders' Equity

Instead of a separate statement of retained earnings, companies commonly report a statement of stockholders' equity that includes changes in retained earnings. A **statement of stockholders' equity** lists the beginning and ending balances of key equity accounts and describes the changes that occur during the period. The companies in Appendix A report such a statement. The usual format is to provide a column for each component of equity and use the rows to describe events occurring in the period. Exhibit 13.16 shows a condensed statement for **Apple**.

Reporting Stock Options

The majority of corporations whose shares are publicly traded issue **stock options,** which are rights to purchase common stock at a fixed price over a specified period. As the stock's price rises, the option's value increases. **Starbucks** and **Home Depot** offer stock options to both full- and part-time employees. Stock options are said to motivate managers and employees to (1) focus on company performance, (2) take a long-run perspective, and (3) remain with

EXHIBIT 13.16

Statement of Stockholders' Equity

APPLE
Statement of Stockholders' Equity

($ millions, shares in thousands)	Common Stock Shares	Common Stock Amount	Retained Earnings	Other	Total Equity
Balance, Sept. 30, 2006	**855,263**	**$4,355**	**$5,607**	**$22**	**$9,984**
Net income	—	—	3,496	—	3,496
Issuance of Common Stock	17,066	364	(2)	—	362
Other	—	649	—	41	690
Cash Dividends ($0.00 per share)	—	—	—	—	—
Balance, Sept. 29, 2007	**872,329**	**$5,368**	**$9,101**	**$63**	**$14,532**

the company. A stock option is like having an investment with no risk ("a carrot with no stick").

To illustrate, Quantum grants each of its employees the option to purchase 100 shares of its $1 par value common stock at its current market price of $50 per share anytime within the next 10 years. If the stock price rises to $70 per share, an employee can exercise the option at a gain of $20 per share (acquire a $70 stock at the $50 option price). With 100 shares, a single employee would have a total gain of $2,000, computed as $20 × 100 shares. Companies report the cost of stock options in the income statement. Measurement of this cost is explained in advanced courses.

Video13.1

Decision Analysis — Earnings per Share, Price-Earnings Ratio, Dividend Yield, and Book Value per Share

Earnings per Share

A1 Compute earnings per share and describe its use.

The income statement reports **earnings per share,** also called *EPS* or *net income per share,* which is the amount of income earned per each share of a company's outstanding common stock. The **basic earnings per share** formula is shown in Exhibit 13.17. When a company has no preferred stock, then preferred dividends are zero. The weighted-average common shares outstanding is measured over the income reporting period; its computation is explained in advanced courses.

EXHIBIT 13.17

Basic Earnings per Share

$$\textbf{Basic earnings per share} = \frac{\textbf{Net income} - \textbf{Preferred dividends}}{\textbf{Weighted-average common shares outstanding}}$$

To illustrate, assume that Quantum Co. earns $40,000 net income in 2009 and declares dividends of $7,500 on its noncumulative preferred stock. (If preferred stock is *non*cumulative, the income available [numerator] is the current period net income less any preferred dividends *declared* in that same period. If preferred stock is cumulative, the income available [numerator] is the current period net income less the preferred dividends whether declared or not.) Quantum has 5,000 weighted-average common shares outstanding during 2009. Its basic EPS[3] is

$$\text{Basic earnings per share} = \frac{\$40{,}000 - \$7{,}500}{5{,}000 \text{ shares}} = \$6.50$$

[3] A corporation can be classified as having either a simple or complex capital structure. The term **simple capital structure** refers to a company with only common stock and nonconvertible preferred stock outstanding. The term **complex capital structure** refers to companies with dilutive securities. **Dilutive securities** include options, rights to purchase common stock, and any bonds or preferred stock that are convertible into common stock. A company with a complex capital structure must often report two EPS figures: basic and diluted. **Diluted earnings per share** is computed by adding all dilutive securities to the denominator of the basic EPS computation. It reflects the decrease in basic EPS *assuming* that all dilutive securities are converted into common shares.

Price-Earnings Ratio

A2 Compute price-earnings ratio and describe its use in analysis.

A stock's market value is determined by its *expected* future cash flows. A comparison of a company's EPS and its market value per share reveals information about market expectations. This comparison is traditionally made using a **price-earnings (or PE) ratio,** expressed also as *price earnings, price to earnings,* or *PE.* Some analysts interpret this ratio as what price the market is willing to pay for a company's current earnings stream. Price-earnings ratios can differ across companies that have similar earnings because of either higher or lower expectations of future earnings. The price-earnings ratio is defined in Exhibit 13.18.

Point: The average PE ratio of stocks in the 1950–2008 period is about 14.

EXHIBIT 13.18
Price-Earnings Ratio

$$\textbf{Price-earnings ratio} = \frac{\textbf{Market value (price) per share}}{\textbf{Earnings per share}}$$

This ratio is often computed using EPS from the most recent period (for Amazon, its PE is 31; for Altria, its PE is 13). However, many users compute this ratio using *expected* EPS for the next period.

Some analysts view stocks with high PE ratios (higher than 20 to 25) as more likely to be overpriced and stocks with low PE ratios (less than 5 to 8) as more likely to be underpriced. These investors prefer to sell or avoid buying stocks with high PE ratios and to buy or hold stocks with low PE ratios. However, investment decision making is rarely so simple as to rely on a single ratio. For instance, a stock with a high PE ratio can prove to be a good investment if its earnings continue to increase beyond current expectations. Similarly, a stock with a low PE ratio can prove to be a poor investment if its earnings decline below expectations.

Point: Average PE ratios for U.S. stocks increased over the past two decades. Some analysts interpret this as a signal the market is overpriced. But higher ratios can at least partly reflect accounting changes that have reduced reported earnings.

Decision Maker

Money Manager You plan to invest in one of two companies identified as having identical future prospects. One has a PE of 19 and the other a PE of 25. Which do you invest in? Does it matter if your *estimate* of PE for these two companies is 29 as opposed to 22? [Answer—p. 531]

Dividend Yield

A3 Compute dividend yield and explain its use in analysis.

Investors buy shares of a company's stock in anticipation of receiving a return from either or both cash dividends and stock price increases. Stocks that pay large dividends on a regular basis, called *income stocks,* are attractive to investors who want recurring cash flows from their investments. In contrast, some stocks pay little or no dividends but are still attractive to investors because of their expected stock price increases. The stocks of companies that distribute little or no cash but use their cash to finance expansion are called *growth stocks.* One way to help identify whether a stock is an income stock or a growth stock is to analyze its dividend yield. **Dividend yield,** defined in Exhibit 13.19, shows the annual amount of cash dividends distributed to common shares relative to their market value.

EXHIBIT 13.19
Dividend Yield

$$\textbf{Dividend yield} = \frac{\textbf{Annual cash dividends per share}}{\textbf{Market value per share}}$$

Dividend yield can be computed for current and prior periods using actual dividends and stock prices and for future periods using expected values. Exhibit 13.20 shows recent dividend and stock price data for **Amazon** and **Altria Group** to compute dividend yield.

EXHIBIT 13.20
Dividend and Stock Price Information

Company	Cash Dividends per Share	Market Value per Share	Dividend Yield
Amazon	$0.00	$90	0.0%
Altria Group	3.32	70	4.7

Point: The *payout ratio* equals cash dividends declared on common stock divided by net income. A low payout ratio suggests that a company is retaining earnings for future growth.

Dividend yield is zero for Amazon, implying it is a growth stock. An investor in Amazon would look for increases in stock prices (and eventual cash from the sale of stock). Altria has a dividend yield of 4.7%, implying it is an income stock for which dividends are important in assessing its value.

Book Value per Share

A4 Compute book value and explain its use in analysis.

Case 1: Common Stock (Only) Outstanding. **Book value per common share,** defined in Exhibit 13.21, reflects the amount of equity applicable to *common* shares on a per share basis. To illustrate, we use Dillon Snowboards' data from Exhibit 13.4. Dillon has 30,000 outstanding common shares, and the stockholders' equity applicable to common shares is $365,000. Dillon's book value per common share is $12.17, computed as $365,000 divided by 30,000 shares.

EXHIBIT 13.21

Book Value per Common Share

$$\textbf{Book value per common share} = \frac{\textbf{Stockholders' equity applicable to common shares}}{\textbf{Number of common shares outstanding}}$$

Point: Book value per share is also referred to as *stockholders' claim to assets on a per share basis.*

Case 2: Common and Preferred Stock Outstanding. To compute book value when both common and preferred shares are outstanding, we allocate total equity between the two types of shares. The **book value per preferred share** is computed first; its computation is shown in Exhibit 13.22.

EXHIBIT 13.22

Book Value per Preferred Share

$$\textbf{Book value per preferred share} = \frac{\textbf{Stockholders' equity applicable to preferred shares}}{\textbf{Number of preferred shares outstanding}}$$

The equity applicable to preferred shares equals the preferred share's call price (or par value if the preferred is not callable) plus any cumulative dividends in arrears. The remaining equity is the portion applicable to common shares. To illustrate, consider LTD's equity in Exhibit 13.23. Its preferred stock is callable at $108 per share, and two years of cumulative preferred dividends are in arrears.

EXHIBIT 13.23

Stockholders' Equity with Preferred and Common Stock

Stockholders' Equity	
Preferred stock—$100 par value, 7% cumulative, 2,000 shares authorized, 1,000 shares issued and outstanding	$100,000
Common stock—$25 par value, 12,000 shares authorized, 10,000 shares issued and outstanding	250,000
Paid-in capital in excess of par value, common stock	15,000
Retained earnings	82,000
Total stockholders' equity	$447,000

The book value computations are in Exhibit 13.24. Equity is first allocated to preferred shares before the book value of common shares is computed.

EXHIBIT 13.24

Computing Book Value per Preferred and Common Share

Total stockholders' equity		$447,000
Less equity applicable to preferred shares		
Call price (1,000 shares × $108)	$108,000	
Dividends in arrears ($100,000 × 7% × 2 years)	14,000	(122,000)
Equity applicable to common shares		$325,000
Book value per preferred share ($122,000/1,000 shares)		**$ 122.00**
Book value per common share ($325,000/10,000 shares)		**$ 32.50**

Book value per share reflects the value per share if a company is liquidated at balance sheet amounts. Book value is also the starting point in many stock valuation models, merger negotiations, price setting for public utilities, and loan contracts. The main limitation in using book value is the potential difference between recorded value and market value for assets and liabilities. Investors often adjust their analysis for estimates of these differences.

Decision Maker

Investor You are considering investing in **BMX**, whose book value per common share is $4 and price per common share on the stock exchange is $7. From this information, are BMX's net assets priced higher or lower than its recorded values? [Answer—p. 531]

Demonstration Problem 1

Barton Corporation began operations on January 1, 2008. The following transactions relating to stockholders' equity occurred in the first two years of the company's operations.

DP13

2008

Jan. 1 Authorized the issuance of 2 million shares of $5 par value common stock and 100,000 shares of $100 par value, 10% cumulative, preferred stock.

Jan. 2 Issued 200,000 shares of common stock for $12 cash per share.

Jan. 3 Issued 100,000 shares of common stock in exchange for a building valued at $820,000 and merchandise inventory valued at $380,000.

Jan. 4 Paid $10,000 cash to the company's founders for organization activities.

Jan. 5 Issued 12,000 shares of preferred stock for $110 cash per share.

2009

June 4 Issued 100,000 shares of common stock for $15 cash per share.

Required

1. Prepare journal entries to record these transactions.
2. Prepare the stockholders' equity section of the balance sheet as of December 31, 2008, and December 31, 2009, based on these transactions.
3. Prepare a table showing dividend allocations and dividends per share for 2008 and 2009 assuming Barton declares the following cash dividends: 2008, $50,000, and 2009, $300,000.
4. Prepare the January 2, 2008, journal entry for Barton's issuance of 200,000 shares of common stock for $12 cash per share assuming
   - a. Common stock is no-par stock without a stated value.
   - b. Common stock is no-par stock with a stated value of $10 per share.

Planning the Solution

- Record journal entries for the transactions for 2008 and 2009.
- Determine the balances for the 2008 and 2009 equity accounts for the balance sheet.
- Prepare the contributed capital portion of the 2008 and 2009 balance sheets.
- Prepare a table similar to Exhibit 13.11 showing dividend allocations for 2008 and 2009.
- Record the issuance of common stock under both specifications of no-par stock.

Solution to Demonstration Problem 1

1. Journal entries.

2008			
Jan. 2	Cash	2,400,000	
	Common Stock, $5 Par Value		1,000,000
	Paid-In Capital in Excess of Par Value, Common Stock		1,400,000
	Issued 200,000 shares of common stock.		
Jan. 3	Building	820,000	
	Merchandise Inventory	380,000	
	Common Stock, $5 Par Value		500,000
	Paid-In Capital in Excess of Par Value, Common Stock		700,000
	Issued 100,000 shares of common stock.		
Jan. 4	Organization Expenses	10,000	
	Cash		10,000
	Paid founders for organization costs.		

[continued on next page]

[continued from previous page]

Jan. 5	Cash	1,320,000	
	Preferred Stock, $100 Par Value		1,200,000
	Paid-In Capital in Excess of Par Value, Preferred Stock		120,000
	Issued 12,000 shares of preferred stock.		
2009			
June 4	Cash	1,500,000	
	Common Stock, $5 Par Value		500,000
	Paid-In Capital in Excess of Par Value, Common Stock		1,000,000
	Issued 100,000 shares of common stock.		

2. Balance sheet presentations (at December 31 year-end).

	2009	2008
Stockholders' Equity		
Preferred stock—$100 par value, 10% cumulative, 100,000 shares authorized, 12,000 shares issued and outstanding	$1,200,000	$1,200,000
Paid-in capital in excess of par value, preferred stock	120,000	120,000
Total paid-in capital by preferred stockholders	1,320,000	1,320,000
Common stock—$5 par value, 2,000,000 shares authorized, 300,000 shares issued and outstanding in 2008, and 400,000 shares issued and outstanding in 2009	2,000,000	1,500,000
Paid-in capital in excess of par value, common stock	3,100,000	2,100,000
Total paid-in capital by common stockholders	5,100,000	3,600,000
Total paid-in capital	$6,420,000	$4,920,000

3. Dividend allocation table.

	Common	Preferred
2008 ($50,000)		
Preferred—current year (12,000 shares × $10 = $120,000)	$ 0	$ 50,000
Common—remainder (300,000 shares outstanding)	0	0
Total for the year	$ 0	$ 50,000
2009 ($300,000)		
Preferred—dividend in arrears from 2008 ($120,000 − $50,000)	$ 0	$ 70,000
Preferred—current year	0	120,000
Common—remainder (400,000 shares outstanding)	110,000	0
Total for the year	$110,000	$190,000
Dividends per share		
2008	$ 0.00	$ 4.17
2009	$ 0.28	$ 15.83

4. Journal entries.

a. For 2008 (no-par stock without a stated value):

Jan. 2	Cash	2,400,000	
	Common Stock, No-Par Value		2,400,000
	Issued 200,000 shares of no-par common stock at $12 per share.		

b. For 2008 (no-par stock with a stated value):

Jan. 2	Cash	2,400,000	
	Common Stock, $10 Stated Value		2,000,000
	Paid-In Capital in Excess of Stated Value, Common Stock		400,000
	Issued 200,000 shares of $10 stated value common stock at $12 per share.		

Demonstration Problem 2

Precision Company began year 2008 with the following balances in its stockholders' equity accounts.

Common stock—$10 par, 500,000 shares authorized, 200,000 shares issued and outstanding	$2,000,000
Paid-in capital in excess of par, common stock	1,000,000
Retained earnings	5,000,000
Total	$8,000,000

All outstanding common stock was issued for $15 per share when the company was created. Prepare journal entries to account for the following transactions during year 2008.

Jan. 10	The board declared a $0.10 cash dividend per share to shareholders of record Jan. 28.
Feb. 15	Paid the cash dividend declared on January 10.
Mar. 31	Declared a 20% stock dividend. The market value of the stock is $18 per share.
May 1	Distributed the stock dividend declared on March 31.
July 1	Purchased 30,000 shares of treasury stock at $20 per share.
Sept. 1	Sold 20,000 treasury shares at $26 cash per share.
Dec. 1	Sold the remaining 10,000 shares of treasury stock at $7 cash per share.

Planning the Solution

- Calculate the total cash dividend to record by multiplying the cash dividend declared by the number of shares as of the date of record.
- Decide whether the stock dividend is a small or large dividend. Then analyze each event to determine the accounts affected and the appropriate amounts to be recorded.

Solution to Demonstration Problem 2

Jan. 10	Retained Earnings	20,000	
	Common Dividend Payable		20,000
	Declared a $0.10 per share cash dividend.		
Feb. 15	Common Dividend Payable	20,000	
	Cash		20,000
	Paid $0.10 per share cash dividend.		
Mar. 31	Retained Earnings	720,000	
	Common Stock Dividend Distributable		400,000
	Paid-In Capital in Excess of Par Value, Common Stock		320,000
	Declared a small stock dividend of 20% or 40,000 shares; market value is $18 per share.		

[continued on next page]

[continued from previous page]

May 1	Common Stock Dividend Distributable	400,000	
	Common Stock		400,000
	Distributed 40,000 shares of common stock.		
July 1	Treasury Stock, Common	600,000	
	Cash		600,000
	Purchased 30,000 common shares at $20 per share.		
Sept. 1	Cash	520,000	
	Treasury Stock, Common		400,000
	Paid-In Capital, Treasury Stock		120,000
	Sold 20,000 treasury shares at $26 per share.		
Dec. 1	Cash	70,000	
	Paid-In Capital, Treasury Stock	120,000	
	Retained Earnings	10,000	
	Treasury Stock, Common		200,000
	Sold 10,000 treasury shares at $7 per share.		

Summary

C1 **Identify characteristics of corporations and their organization.** Corporations are legal entities whose stockholders are not liable for its debts. Stock is easily transferred, and the life of a corporation does not end with the incapacity of a stock holder. A corporation acts through its agents, who are its officers and managers. Corporations are regulated and subject to income taxes.

C2 **Describe the components of stockholders' equity.** Authorized stock is the stock that a corporation's charter authorizes it to sell. Issued stock is the portion of authorized shares sold. Par value stock is a value per share assigned by the charter. No-par value stock is stock *not* assigned a value per share by the charter. Stated value stock is no-par stock to which the directors assign a value per share. Stockholders' equity is made up of (1) paid-in capital and (2) retained earnings. Paid-in capital consists of funds raised by stock issuances. Retained earnings consists of cumulative net income (losses) not distributed.

C3 **Explain characteristics of common and preferred stock.** Preferred stock has a priority (or senior status) relative to common stock in one or more areas, usually (1) dividends and (2) assets in case of liquidation. Preferred stock usually does not carry voting rights and can be convertible or callable. Convertibility permits the holder to convert preferred to common. Callability permits the issuer to buy back preferred stock under specified conditions.

C4 **Explain the items reported in retained earnings.** Many companies face statutory and contractual restrictions on retained earnings. Corporations can voluntarily appropriate retained earnings to inform others about their disposition. Prior period adjustments are corrections of errors in prior financial statements.

A1 **Compute earnings per share and describe its use.** A company with a simple capital structure computes basic EPS by dividing net income less any preferred dividends by the weighted-average number of outstanding common shares. A company with a complex capital structure must usually report both basic and diluted EPS.

A2 **Compute price-earnings ratio and describe its use in analysis.** A common stock's price-earnings (PE) ratio is computed by dividing the stock's market value (price) per share by its EPS. A stock's PE is based on expectations that can prove to be better or worse than eventual performance.

A3 **Compute dividend yield and explain its use in analysis.** Dividend yield is the ratio of a stock's annual cash dividends per share to its market value (price) per share. Dividend yield can be compared with the yield of other companies to determine whether the stock is expected to be an income or growth stock.

A4 **Compute book value and explain its use in analysis.** Book value per common share is equity applicable to common shares divided by the number of outstanding common shares. Book value per preferred share is equity applicable to preferred shares divided by the number of outstanding preferred shares.

P1 **Record the issuance of corporate stock.** When stock is issued, its par or stated value is credited to the stock account and any excess is credited to a separate contributed capital account. If a stock has neither par nor stated value, the entire proceeds are credited to the stock account. Stockholders must contribute assets equal to minimum legal capital or be potentially liable for the deficiency.

P2 **Record transactions involving cash dividends.** Cash dividends involve three events. On the date of declaration, the directors bind the company to pay the dividend. A dividend declaration reduces retained earnings and creates a current liability. On the date of record, recipients of the dividend are identified. On the date of payment, cash is paid to stockholders and the current liability is removed.

P3 **Account for stock dividends and stock splits.** Neither a stock dividend nor a stock split alters the value of the company. However, the value of each share is less due to the distribution of additional shares. The distribution of additional shares is according to individual stockholders' ownership percent. Small stock dividends ($\leq$25%) are recorded by capitalizing retained earnings equal to the market value of distributed shares. Large stock dividends (>25%) are recorded by capitalizing retained earnings equal to the par or stated value of distributed shares. Stock splits do not yield journal entries but do yield changes in the description of stock.

P4 **Distribute dividends between common stock and preferred stock.** Preferred stockholders usually hold the right to dividend distributions before common stockholders. When preferred stock is cumulative and in arrears, the amount in arrears must be distributed to preferred before any dividends are distributed to common.

P5 **Record purchases and sales of treasury stock and the retirement of stock.** When a corporation purchases its own previously issued stock, it debits the cost of these shares to Treasury Stock. Treasury stock is subtracted from equity in the balance sheet. If treasury stock is reissued, any proceeds in excess of cost are credited to Paid-In Capital, Treasury Stock. If the proceeds are less than cost, they are debited to Paid-In Capital, Treasury Stock to the extent a credit balance exists. Any remaining amount is debited to Retained Earnings. When stock is retired, all accounts related to the stock are removed.

Guidance Answers to Decision Maker and Decision Ethics

Entrepreneur The 50% stock dividend provides you no direct income. A stock dividend often reveals management's optimistic expectations about the future and can improve a stock's marketability by making it affordable to more investors. Accordingly, a stock dividend usually reveals "good news" and because of this, it likely increases (slightly) the market value for your stock. The same conclusions apply to the 3-for-2 stock split.

Concert Organizer You have two basic options: (1) different classes of common stock or (2) common and preferred stock. Your objective is to issue to yourself stock that has all or a majority of the voting power. The other class of stock would carry limited or no voting rights. In this way, you maintain control and are able to raise the necessary funds.

Money Manager Since one company requires a payment of $19 for each $1 of earnings, and the other requires $25, you would prefer the stock with the PE of 19; it is a better deal given identical prospects. You should make sure these companies' earnings computations are roughly the same, for example, no extraordinary items, unusual events, and so forth. Also, your PE estimates for these companies do matter. If you are willing to pay $29 for each $1 of earnings for these companies, you obviously expect both to exceed current market expectations.

Investor Book value reflects recorded values. BMX's book value is $4 per common share. Stock price reflects the market's expectation of net asset value (both tangible and intangible items). BMX's market value is $7 per common share. Comparing these figures suggests BMX's market value of net assets is higher than its recorded values (by an amount of $7 versus $4 per share).

Guidance Answers to Quick Checks

1. (*b*)
2. A corporation pays taxes on its income, and its stockholders normally pay personal income taxes (at the 15% rate or lower) on any cash dividends received from the corporation.
3. A proxy is a legal document used to transfer a stockholder's right to vote to another person.
4. (*a*)
5. A stock premium is an amount in excess of par (or stated) value paid by purchasers of newly issued stock.
6. Minimum legal capital intends to protect creditors of a corporation by obligating stockholders to some minimum level of equity financing and by constraining a corporation from excessive payments to stockholders.
7. Common Dividend Payable is a current liability account.
8. The date of declaration, date of record, and date of payment.
9. A dividend is a legal liability at the date of declaration, on which date it is recorded as a liability.
10. A stock dividend does not transfer assets to stockholders, but it does require an amount of retained earnings to be transferred to a contributed capital account(s).
11. A small stock dividend is 25% or less of the previous outstanding shares. A large stock dividend is more than 25%.
12. Retained earnings equal to the distributable shares' market value should be capitalized for a small stock dividend.
13. Typically, preferred stock has a preference in receipt of dividends and in distribution of assets.
14. (*a*)
15. (*b*)

Total cash dividend	$288,000
To preferred shareholders	135,000*
Remainder to common shareholders	$153,000

* 9,000 × $50 × 10% × 3 years = $135,000.

16. (*b*)
17. No. The shares are an investment for Southern Co. and are issued and outstanding shares for Northern Corp.
18. Treasury stock does not affect the number of authorized or issued shares, but it reduces the outstanding shares.
19. (*a*)

Key Terms

mhhe.com/wildFAP19e

Key Terms are available at the book's Website for learning and testing in an online Flashcard Format.

Appropriated retained earnings (p. 523)
Authorized stock (p. 509)
Basic earnings per share (p. 524)
Book value per common share (p. 526)
Book value per preferred share (p. 526)
Call price (p. 519)
Callable preferred stock (p. 519)
Capital stock (p. 509)
Changes in accounting estimates (p. 523)
Common stock (p. 508)
Complex capital structure (p. 524)
Convertible preferred stock (p. 518)
Corporation (p. 506)
Cumulative preferred stock (p. 517)
Date of declaration (p. 513)
Date of payment (p. 513)
Date of record (p. 513)
Diluted earnings per share (p. 524)
Dilutive securities (p. 524)
Discount on stock (p. 511)
Dividend in arrears (p. 517)
Dividend yield (p. 525)
Earnings per share (EPS) (p. 524)
Financial leverage (p. 519)
Large stock dividend (p. 514)
Liquidating cash dividend (p. 514)
Market value per share (p. 509)
Minimum legal capital (p. 509)
Noncumulative preferred stock (p. 517)
Nonparticipating preferred stock (p. 518)
No-par value stock (p. 509)
Organization expenses (pp. 507, 512)
Paid-in capital (p. 510)
Paid-in capital in excess of par value (p. 511)
Participating preferred stock (p. 518)
Par value (p. 509)
Par value stock (p. 509)
Preemptive right (p. 508)
Preferred stock (p. 516)
Premium on stock (p. 511)
Price-earnings (PE) ratio (p. 525)
Prior period adjustments (p. 523)
Proxy (p. 507)
Restricted retained earnings (p. 522)
Retained earnings (p. 510)
Retained earnings deficit (p. 513)
Reverse stock split (p. 516)
Simple capital structure (p. 524)
Small stock dividend (p. 514)
Stated value stock (p. 510)
Statement of stockholders' equity (p. 523)
Stock dividend (p. 514)
Stock options (p. 523)
Stock split (p. 516)
Stockholders' equity (p. 510)
Treasury stock (p. 520)

Multiple Choice Quiz

Answers on p. 547 mhhe.com/wildFAP19e

Additional Quiz Questions are available at the book's Website.

Quiz13

1. A corporation issues 6,000 shares of $5 par value common stock for $8 cash per share. The entry to record this transaction includes:
a. A debit to Paid-In Capital in Excess of Par Value for $18,000.
b. A credit to Common Stock for $48,000.
c. A credit to Paid-In Capital in Excess of Par Value for $30,000.
d. A credit to Cash for $48,000.
e. A credit to Common Stock for $30,000.

2. A company reports net income of $75,000. Its weighted-average common shares outstanding is 19,000. It has no other stock outstanding. Its earnings per share is:
a. $4.69
b. $3.95
c. $3.75
d. $2.08
e. $4.41

3. A company has 5,000 shares of $100 par preferred stock and 50,000 shares of $10 par common stock outstanding. Its total stockholders' equity is $2,000,000. Its book value per common share is:
a. $100.00
b. $ 10.00
c. $ 40.00
d. $ 30.00
e. $ 36.36

4. A company paid cash dividends of $0.81 per share. Its earnings per share is $6.95 and its market price per share is $45.00. Its dividend yield is:
a. 1.8%
b. 11.7%
c. 15.4%
d. 55.6%
e. 8.6%

5. A company's shares have a market value of $85 per share. Its net income is $3,500,000, and its weighted-average common shares outstanding is 700,000. Its price-earnings ratio is:
a. 5.9
b. 425.0
c. 17.0
d. 10.4
e. 41.2

Discussion Questions

1. What are organization expenses? Provide examples.
2. How are organization expenses reported?
3. Who is responsible for directing a corporation's affairs?
4. What is the preemptive right of common stockholders?
5. List the general rights of common stockholders.
6. What is the difference between authorized shares and outstanding shares?
7. Why would an investor find convertible preferred stock attractive?
8. What is the difference between the market value per share and the par value per share?
9. What is the difference between the par value and the call price of a share of preferred stock?
10. Identify and explain the importance of the three dates relevant to corporate dividends.
11. Why is the term *liquidating dividend* used to describe cash dividends debited against paid-in capital accounts?
12. How does declaring a stock dividend affect the corporation's assets, liabilities, and total equity? What are the effects of the eventual distribution of that stock?
13. What is the difference between a stock dividend and a stock split?
14. Courts have ruled that a stock dividend is not taxable income to stockholders. What justifies this decision?
15. How does the purchase of treasury stock affect the purchaser's assets and total equity?
16. Why do laws place limits on treasury stock purchases?
17. How are EPS results computed for a corporation with a simple capital structure?
18. What is a stock option?
19. How is book value per share computed for a corporation with no preferred stock? What is the main limitation of using book value per share to value a corporation?
20. Review the balance sheet for **Best Buy** in Appendix A and list the classes of stock that it has issued.
21. Refer to the balance sheet for **Circuit City** in Appendix A. What is the par value per share of its common stock? Suggest a rationale for the amount of par value it assigned.
22. Refer to **RadioShack**'s balance sheet in Appendix A. How many shares of common stock are authorized? How many shares of common stock are issued?
23. Refer to the financial statements for **Apple** in Appendix A. What are its cash proceeds from issuance of common stock and its cash repurchases of common stock for the year ended September 30, 2006? Explain.

Denotes Discussion Questions that involve decision making.

McGraw-Hill's HOMEWORK MANAGER® Available with McGraw-Hill's Homework Manager

QUICK STUDY

QS 13-1
Characteristics of corporations
C1

Of the following statements, which are true for the corporate form of organization?

1. Capital is more easily accumulated than with most other forms of organization.
2. Corporate income that is distributed to shareholders is usually taxed twice.
3. Owners have unlimited liability for corporate debts.
4. Ownership rights cannot be easily transferred.
5. Owners are not agents of the corporation.
6. It is a separate legal entity.
7. It has a limited life.

QS 13-2
Issuance of common stock
P1

Prepare the journal entry to record Miltone Company's issuance of 50,000 shares of \$1 par value common stock assuming the shares sell for:

a. \$1 cash per share.
b. \$3 cash per share.

QS 13-3
Issuance of par and stated value common stock
P1

Prepare the journal entry to record Katrick Company's issuance of 75,000 shares of its common stock assuming the shares have a:

a. \$5 par value and sell for \$12 cash per share.
b. \$5 stated value and sell for \$12 cash per share.

QS 13-4
Issuance of no-par common stock
P1

Prepare the journal entry to record Gaylord Company's issuance of 52,000 shares of no-par value common stock assuming the shares:

a. Sell for $30 cash per share.

b. Are exchanged for land valued at $1,560,000.

QS 13-5
Issuance of common stock
P1

Prepare the issuer's journal entry for each separate transaction. (*a*) On March 1, Atlantic Co. issues 37,500 shares of $5 par value common stock for $300,000 cash. (*b*) On April 1, BP Co. issues no-par value common stock for $90,000 cash. (*c*) On April 6, MPG issues 3,500 shares of $10 par value common stock for $20,000 of inventory, $130,000 of machinery, and acceptance of a $75,000 note payable.

QS 13-6
Issuance of preferred stock
C3

a. Prepare the journal entry to record Tamar Company's issuance of 6,000 shares of $100 par value 6% cumulative preferred stock for $102 cash per share.

b. Assuming the facts in part 1, if Tamar declares a year-end cash dividend, what is the amount of dividend paid to preferred shareholders? (Assume no dividends in arrears.)

QS 13-7
Accounting for cash dividends
P2

Prepare journal entries to record the following transactions for Forrest Corporation.

May 15 Declared a $32,000 cash dividend payable to common stockholders.
June 30 Paid the dividend declared on May 15.

QS 13-8
Accounting for small stock dividend
C2 P3

The stockholders' equity section of Atari Company's balance sheet as of April 1 follows. On April 2, Atari declares and distributes a 10% stock dividend. The stock's per share market value on April 2 is $18 (prior to the dividend). Prepare the stockholders' equity section immediately after the stock dividend.

Common stock—$5 par value, 375,000 shares authorized, 200,000 shares issued and outstanding	$1,000,000
Paid-in capital in excess of par value, common stock	600,000
Retained earnings	833,000
Total stockholders' equity	$2,433,000

QS 13-9
Dividend allocation between classes of shareholders
P4

Stockholders' equity of Marwick Company consists of 10,000 shares of $20 par value, 8% cumulative preferred stock and 400,000 shares of $1 par value common stock. Both classes of stock have been outstanding since the company's inception. Marwick did not declare any dividends in the prior year, but it now declares and pays a $92,000 cash dividend at the current year-end. Determine the amount distributed to each class of stockholders for this two-year-old company.

QS 13-10
Purchase and sale of treasury stock P5

On May 3, Winmac Corporation purchased 3,000 shares of its own stock for $45,000 cash. On November 4, Winmac reissued 850 shares of this treasury stock for $14,450. Prepare the May 3 and November 4 journal entries to record Winmac's purchase and reissuance of treasury stock.

QS 13-11
Accounting for changes in estimates; error adjustments
C4

Answer the following questions related to a company's activities for the current year:

1. A review of the notes payable files discovers that three years ago the company reported the entire amount of a payment (principal and interest) on an installment note payable as interest expense. This mistake had a material effect on the amount of income in that year. How should the correction be reported in the current year financial statements?

2. After using an expected useful life of seven years and no salvage value to depreciate its office equipment over the preceding three years, the company decided early this year that the equipment will last only two more years. How should the effects of this decision be reported in the current year financial statements?

QS 13-12 Basic earnings per share A1

Campbell Company reports net income of $840,000 for the year. It has no preferred stock, and its weighted-average common shares outstanding is 300,000 shares. Compute its basic earnings per share.

QS 13-13 Basic earnings per share A1

Epic Company earned net income of $950,000 this year. The number of common shares outstanding during the entire year was 400,000, and preferred shareholders received a $40,000 cash dividend. Compute Epic Company's basic earnings per share.

QS 13-14 Price-earnings ratio A2

Compute Tripp Company's price-earnings ratio if its common stock has a market value of $31.50 per share and its EPS is $3.75. Would an analyst likely consider this stock potentially over- or underpriced? Explain.

QS 13-15 Dividend yield A3

Payne Company expects to pay a $1.62 per share cash dividend this year on its common stock. The current market value of Payne stock is $22.50 per share. Compute the expected dividend yield on the Payne stock. Would you classify the Payne stock as a growth or an income stock? Explain.

QS 13-16 Book value per common share A4

The stockholders' equity section of Klaus Company's balance sheet follows. The preferred stock's call price is $25. Determine the book value per share of the common stock.

Preferred stock—5% cumulative, $10 par value, 20,000 shares authorized, issued and outstanding	$ 200,000
Common stock—$5 par value, 200,000 shares authorized, 150,000 shares issued and outstanding	750,000
Retained earnings	889,500
Total stockholders' equity	$1,839,500

McGraw-Hill's HOMEWORK MANAGER® Available with McGraw-Hill's Homework Manager

EXERCISES

Exercise 13-1 Characteristics of corporations C1

Describe how each of the following characteristics of organizations applies to corporations.

1. Owner authority and control	5. Duration of life
2. Ease of formation	6. Owner liability
3. Transferability of ownership	7. Legal status
4. Ability to raise large capital amounts	8. Tax status of income

Exercise 13-2 Accounting for par, stated, and no-par stock issuances P1

Rodriguez Corporation issues 12,000 shares of its common stock for $182,700 cash on February 20. Prepare journal entries to record this event under each of the following separate situations.

1. The stock has neither par nor stated value.

2. The stock has a $12 par value.

3. The stock has a $6 stated value.

Exercise 13-3 Recording stock issuances P1

Prepare journal entries to record the following four separate issuances of stock.

1. A corporation issued 2,500 shares of no-par common stock to its promoters in exchange for their efforts, estimated to be worth $43,500. The stock has no stated value.

2. A corporation issued 2,500 shares of no-par common stock to its promoters in exchange for their efforts, estimated to be worth $43,500. The stock has a $2 per share stated value.

3. A corporation issued 5,000 shares of $30 par value common stock for $180,000 cash.

4. A corporation issued 1,250 shares of $100 par value preferred stock for $168,500 cash.

Exercise 13-4 Stock issuance for noncash assets P1

Soku Company issues 12,000 shares of $9 par value common stock in exchange for land and a building. The land is valued at $75,000 and the building at $120,000. Prepare the journal entry to record issuance of the stock in exchange for the land and building.

Exercise 13-5
Identifying characteristics of preferred stock
C2 C3

Match each description 1 through 6 with the characteristic of preferred stock that it best describes by writing the letter of that characteristic in the blank next to each description.

A. Convertible **B.** Cumulative **C.** Noncumulative
D. Nonparticipating **E.** Participating **F.** Callable

_____ **1.** Holders of the stock are entitled to receive current and all past dividends before common stockholders receive any dividends.
_____ **2.** The issuing corporation can retire the stock by paying a prespecified price.
_____ **3.** Holders of the stock can receive dividends exceeding the stated rate under certain conditions.
_____ **4.** Holders of the stock are not entitled to receive dividends in excess of the stated rate.
_____ **5.** Holders of this stock can exchange it for shares of common stock.
_____ **6.** Holders of the stock lose any dividends that are not declared in the current year.

Exercise 13-6
Stock dividends and splits
P3

On June 30, 2009, Samson Corporation's common stock is priced at $30.50 per share before any stock dividend or split, and the stockholders' equity section of its balance sheet appears as follows.

Common stock—$8 par value, 80,000 shares authorized, 32,000 shares issued and outstanding	$256,000
Paid-in capital in excess of par value, common stock	100,000
Retained earnings	356,000
Total stockholders' equity	$712,000

1. Assume that the company declares and immediately distributes a 100% stock dividend. This event is recorded by capitalizing retained earnings equal to the stock's par value. Answer these questions about stockholders' equity as it exists *after* issuing the new shares.
a. What is the retained earnings balance?
b. What is the amount of total stockholders' equity?
c. How many shares are outstanding?

Check (1*b*) $712,000

2. Assume that the company implements a 2-for-1 stock split instead of the stock dividend in part 1. Answer these questions about stockholders' equity as it exists *after* issuing the new shares.
a. What is the retained earnings balance?
b. What is the amount of total stockholders' equity?
c. How many shares are outstanding?

(2*a*) $356,000

3. Explain the difference, if any, to a stockholder from receiving new shares distributed under a large stock dividend versus a stock split.

Exercise 13-7
Stock dividends and per share book values
P3

The stockholders' equity of Tyron Company at the beginning of the day on February 5 follows.

Common stock—$25 par value, 150,000 shares authorized, 64,000 shares issued and outstanding	$1,600,000
Paid-in capital in excess of par value, common stock	525,000
Retained earnings	671,800
Total stockholders' equity	$2,796,800

On February 5, the directors declare a 15% stock dividend distributable on February 28 to the February 15 stockholders of record. The stock's market value is $50 per share on February 5 before the stock dividend. The stock's market value is $43.60 per share on February 28.

1. Prepare entries to record both the dividend declaration and its distribution.
2. One stockholder owned 900 shares on February 5 before the dividend. Compute the book value per share and total book value of this stockholder's shares immediately before *and* after the stock dividend of February 5.

Check (2) Book value per share: before, $43.70; after, $38.00

3. Compute the total market value of the investor's shares in part 2 as of February 5 and February 28.

Exercise 13-8
Dividends on common and noncumulative preferred stock
P4

Norton's outstanding stock consists of (*a*) 13,000 shares of noncumulative 8% preferred stock with a $10 par value and (*b*) 32,500 shares of common stock with a $1 par value. During its first four years of operation, the corporation declared and paid the following total cash dividends.

2009	$ 8,000
2010	24,000
2011	120,000
2012	197,000

Determine the amount of dividends paid each year to each of the two classes of stockholders. Also compute the total dividends paid to each class for the four years combined.

Check Total paid to preferred, $39,200

Exercise 13-9
Dividends on common and cumulative preferred stock P4

Use the data in Exercise 13-8 to determine the amount of dividends paid each year to each of the two classes of stockholders assuming that the preferred stock is cumulative. Also determine the total dividends paid to each class for the four years combined.

Exercise 13-10
Recording and reporting treasury stock transactions
P5

On October 10, the stockholders' equity of Syntax Systems appears as follows.

Common stock—$10 par value, 72,000 shares authorized, issued, and outstanding	$ 720,000
Paid-in capital in excess of par value, common stock	216,000
Retained earnings	864,000
Total stockholders' equity	$1,800,000

1. Prepare journal entries to record the following transactions for Syntax Systems.
   a. Purchased 5,000 shares of its own common stock at $22 per share on October 11.
   b. Sold 1,000 treasury shares on November 1 for $28 cash per share.
   c. Sold all remaining treasury shares on November 25 for $17 cash per share.
2. Explain how the company's equity section changes after the October 11 treasury stock purchase, and prepare the revised equity section of its balance sheet at that date.

Check (1c) Dr. Retained Earnings, $14,000

Exercise 13-11
Preparing a statement of retained earnings
C4

The following information is available for Arturo Company for the year ended December 31, 2009.
a. Balance of retained earnings, December 31, 2008, prior to discovery of error, $1,375,000.
b. Cash dividends declared and paid during 2009, $43,000.
c. It neglected to record 2007 depreciation expense of $55,500, which is net of $4,500 in income taxes.
d. The company earned $126,000 in 2009 net income.
Prepare a 2009 statement of retained earnings for Arturo Company.

Exercise 13-12
Earnings per share
A1

Grossmont Company reports $1,375,500 of net income for 2009 and declares $192,500 of cash dividends on its preferred stock for 2009. At the end of 2009, the company had 350,000 weighted-average shares of common stock.
1. What amount of net income is available to common stockholders for 2009?
2. What is the company's basic EPS for 2009?

Check (2) $3.38

Exercise 13-13
Earnings per share
A1

Franklin Company reports $1,875,000 of net income for 2009 and declares $262,500 of cash dividends on its preferred stock for 2009. At the end of 2009, the company had 250,000 weighted-average shares of common stock.
1. What amount of net income is available to common stockholders for 2009?
2. What is the company's basic EPS for 2009?

Check (2) $6.45

Exercise 13-14
Price-earnings ratio computation and interpretation
A2

Compute the price-earnings ratio for each of these four separate companies. Which stock might an analyst likely investigate as being potentially undervalued by the market? Explain.

Company	Earnings per Share	Market Value per Share
1	$12.00	$145.20
2	11.00	116.60
3	7.80	74.10
4	43.20	60.48

Exercise 13-15
Dividend yield computation and interpretation
A3

Compute the dividend yield for each of these four separate companies. Which company's stock would probably *not* be classified as an income stock? Explain.

Company	Annual Cash Dividend per Share	Market Value per Share
1	$14.00	$229.51
2	11.00	110.00
3	5.52	60.00
4	1.90	118.75

Exercise 13-16
Book value per share
A4

The equity section of Westchester Corporation's balance sheet shows the following.

Preferred stock—6% cumulative, $30 par value, $35 call price, 10,000 shares issued and outstanding	$300,000
Common stock—$10 par value, 35,000 shares issued and outstanding	350,000
Retained earnings	267,500
Total stockholders' equity	$917,500

Determine the book value per share of the preferred and common stock under two separate situations.

1. No preferred dividends are in arrears.
2. Three years of preferred dividends are in arrears.

Check (1) Book value of common, $16.21

Available with McGraw-Hill's Homework Manager
McGraw-Hill's HOMEWORK MANAGER®

PROBLEM SET A

Problem 13-1A
Stockholders' equity transactions and analysis
C2 C3 P1

Keshena Co. is incorporated at the beginning of this year and engages in a number of transactions. The following journal entries impacted its stockholders' equity during its first year of operations.

a.	Cash	320,000	
	Common Stock, $25 Par Value		250,000
	Paid-In Capital in Excess of Par Value, Common Stock		70,000
b.	Organization Expenses	160,000	
	Common Stock, $25 Par Value		125,000
	Paid-In Capital in Excess of Par Value, Common Stock		35,000

[continued on next page]

[continued from previous page]

c.	Cash	45,500	
	Accounts Receivable	16,000	
	Building	82,000	
	Notes Payable		59,500
	Common Stock, $25 Par Value		50,000
	Paid-In Capital in Excess of Par Value, Common Stock		34,000
d.	Cash	123,000	
	Common Stock, $25 Par Value		75,000
	Paid-In Capital in Excess of Par Value, Common Stock		48,000

Required

1. Explain the transaction(s) underlying each journal entry (*a*) through (*d*).

2. How many shares of common stock are outstanding at year-end?

3. What is the amount of minimum legal capital (based on par value) at year-end?

4. What is the total paid-in capital at year-end?

5. What is the book value per share of the common stock at year-end if total paid-in capital plus retained earnings equals $785,000?

Check (2) 20,000 shares
(3) $500,000
(4) $687,000

Problem 13-2A
Cash dividends, treasury stock, and statement of retained earnings
C2 C4 P2 P5

Rocklin Corporation reports the following components of stockholders' equity on December 31, 2009.

Common stock—$25 par value, 100,000 shares authorized, 45,000 shares issued and outstanding	$1,125,000
Paid-in capital in excess of par value, common stock	60,000
Retained earnings	460,000
Total stockholders' equity	$1,645,000

In year 2010, the following transactions affected its stockholders' equity accounts.

Jan. 1 Purchased 4,500 shares of its own stock at $25 cash per share.
Jan. 5 Directors declared a $3 per share cash dividend payable on Feb. 28 to the Feb. 5 stockholders of record.
Feb. 28 Paid the dividend declared on January 5.
July 6 Sold 1,688 of its treasury shares at $29 cash per share.
Aug. 22 Sold 2,812 of its treasury shares at $22 cash per share.
Sept. 5 Directors declared a $3 per share cash dividend payable on October 28 to the September 25 stockholders of record.
Oct. 28 Paid the dividend declared on September 5.
Dec. 31 Closed the $388,000 credit balance (from net income) in the Income Summary account to Retained Earnings.

Required

1. Prepare journal entries to record each of these transactions for 2010.

2. Prepare a statement of retained earnings for the year ended December 31, 2010.

3. Prepare the stockholders' equity section of the company's balance sheet as of December 31, 2010.

Check (2) Retained earnings, Dec. 31, 2010, $589,816.

Problem 13-3A
Equity analysis—journal entries and account balances
P2 P3

At September 30, the end of Chan Company's third quarter, the following stockholders' equity accounts are reported.

Common stock, $10 par value	$420,000
Paid-in capital in excess of par value, common stock	100,000
Retained earnings	400,000

In the fourth quarter, the following entries related to its equity are recorded.

Oct. 2	Retained Earnings	63,000	
	Common Dividend Payable		63,000
Oct. 25	Common Dividend Payable	63,000	
	Cash		63,000
Oct. 31	Retained Earnings	92,400	
	Common Stock Dividend Distributable		42,000
	Paid-In Capital in Excess of Par Value, Common Stock		50,400
Nov. 5	Common Stock Dividend Distributable	42,000	
	Common Stock, $10 Par Value		42,000
Dec. 1	Memo—Change the title of the common stock account to reflect the new par value of $5.		
Dec. 31	Income Summary	230,000	
	Retained Earnings		230,000

Required

1. Explain the transaction(s) underlying each journal entry.

2. Complete the following table showing the equity account balances at each indicated date (include the balances from September 30).

	Oct. 2	Oct. 25	Oct. 31	Nov. 5	Dec. 1	Dec. 31
Common stock	$____	$____	$____	$____	$____	$____
Common stock dividend distributable	____	____	____	____	____	____
Paid-in capital in excess of par, common stock	____	____	____	____	____	____
Retained earnings	____	____	____	____	____	____
Total equity	$____	$____	$____	$____	$____	$____

Check Total equity: Oct. 2, $857,000; Dec. 31, $1,087,000

Problem 13-4A
Analysis of changes in stockholders' equity accounts
C4 P2 P3 P5

The equity sections from Sierra Group's 2009 and 2010 year-end balance sheets follow.

Stockholders' Equity (December 31, 2009)	
Common stock—$6 par value, 100,000 shares authorized, 45,000 shares issued and outstanding	$270,000
Paid-in capital in excess of par value, common stock	230,000
Retained earnings	340,000
Total stockholders' equity	$840,000

Stockholders' Equity (December 31, 2010)	
Common stock—$6 par value, 100,000 shares authorized, 53,200 shares issued, 4,000 shares in treasury	$319,200
Paid-in capital in excess of par value, common stock	262,800
Retained earnings ($60,000 restricted by treasury stock)	400,000
	982,000
Less cost of treasury stock	(60,000)
Total stockholders' equity	$922,000

The following transactions and events affected its equity during year 2010.

Jan. 5 Declared a $0.50 per share cash dividend, date of record January 10.
Mar. 20 Purchased treasury stock for cash.
Apr. 5 Declared a $0.50 per share cash dividend, date of record April 10.
July 5 Declared a $0.50 per share cash dividend, date of record July 10.
July 31 Declared a 20% stock dividend when the stock's market value is $10 per share.

Aug. 14 Issued the stock dividend that was declared on July 31.
Oct. 5 Declared a $0.50 per share cash dividend, date of record October 10.

Required

1. How many common shares are outstanding on each cash dividend date?
2. What is the total dollar amount for each of the four cash dividends?
3. What is the amount of the capitalization of retained earnings for the stock dividend?
4. What is the per share cost of the treasury stock purchased?
5. How much net income did the company earn during year 2010?

Check (3) $82,000
(4) $15
(5) $230,100

Problem 13-5A
Computation of book values and dividend allocations
C3 A4 P4

Folsom Corporation's common stock is currently selling on a stock exchange at $183 per share, and its current balance sheet shows the following stockholders' equity section.

Preferred stock—5% cumulative, $___ par value, 1,000 shares authorized, issued, and outstanding	$ 85,000
Common stock—$___ par value, 4,000 shares authorized, issued, and outstanding	200,000
Retained earnings	350,000
Total stockholders' equity	$635,000

Required

1. What is the current market value (price) of this corporation's common stock?
2. What are the par values of the corporation's preferred stock and its common stock?
3. If no dividends are in arrears, what are the book values per share of the preferred stock and the common stock?
4. If two years' preferred dividends are in arrears, what are the book values per share of the preferred stock and the common stock?
5. If two years' preferred dividends are in arrears and the preferred stock is callable at $95 per share, what are the book values per share of the preferred stock and the common stock?
6. If two years' preferred dividends are in arrears and the board of directors declares cash dividends of $24,750, what total amount will be paid to the preferred and to the common shareholders? What is the amount of dividends per share for the common stock?

Check (4) Book value of common, $135.38
(5) Book value of common, $132.88
(6) Dividends per common share, $3.00

Analysis Component

7. What are some factors that can contribute to a difference between the book value of common stock and its market value (price)?

PROBLEM SET B

Problem 13-1B
Stockholders' equity transactions and analysis
C2 C3 P1

Mayport Company is incorporated at the beginning of this year and engages in a number of transactions. The following journal entries impacted its stockholders' equity during its first year of operations.

a.	Cash	60,000	
	Common Stock, $1 Par Value		1,500
	Paid-In Capital in Excess of Par Value, Common Stock		58,500
b.	Organization Expenses	20,000	
	Common Stock, $1 Par Value		500
	Paid-In Capital in Excess of Par Value, Common Stock		19,500
c.	Cash	6,650	
	Accounts Receivable	4,000	
	Building	18,500	
	Notes Payable		9,150
	Common Stock, $1 Par Value		400
	Paid-In Capital in Excess of Par Value, Common Stock		19,600

[continued on next page]

[continued from previous page]

d.	Cash	30,000	
	Common Stock, $1 Par Value		600
	Paid-In Capital in Excess of Par Value, Common Stock		29,400

Required

Check (2) 3,000 shares
(3) $3,000
(4) $130,000

1. Explain the transaction(s) underlying each journal entry (*a*) through (*d*).
2. How many shares of common stock are outstanding at year-end?
3. What is the amount of minimum legal capital (based on par value) at year-end?
4. What is the total paid-in capital at year-end?
5. What is the book value per share of the common stock at year-end if total paid-in capital plus retained earnings equals $141,500?

Problem 13-2B
Cash dividends, treasury stock, and statement of retained earnings
C2 C4 P2 P5

San Marco Corp. reports the following components of stockholders' equity on December 31, 2009.

Common stock—$1 par value, 160,000 shares authorized, 100,000 shares issued and outstanding	$ 100,000
Paid-in capital in excess of par value, common stock	700,000
Retained earnings	1,080,000
Total stockholders' equity	$1,880,000

It completed the following transactions related to stockholders' equity in year 2010.

Jan. 10 Purchased 20,000 shares of its own stock at $12 cash per share.
Mar. 2 Directors declared a $1.50 per share cash dividend payable on March 31 to the March 15 stockholders of record.
Mar. 31 Paid the dividend declared on March 2.
Nov. 11 Sold 12,000 of its treasury shares at $13 cash per share.
Nov. 25 Sold 8,000 of its treasury shares at $9.50 cash per share.
Dec. 1 Directors declared a $2.50 per share cash dividend payable on January 2 to the December 10 stockholders of record.
Dec. 31 Closed the $536,000 credit balance (from net income) in the Income Summary account to Retained Earnings.

Required

Check (2) Retained earnings, Dec. 31, 2010, $1,238,000

1. Prepare journal entries to record each of these transactions for 2010.
2. Prepare a statement of retained earnings for the year ended December 31, 2010.
3. Prepare the stockholders' equity section of the company's balance sheet as of December 31, 2010.

Problem 13-3B
Equity analysis—journal entries and account balances
P2 P3

At December 31, the end of Santee Communication's third quarter, the following stockholders' equity accounts are reported.

Common stock, $10 par value	$480,000
Paid-in capital in excess of par value, common stock	192,000
Retained earnings	800,000

In the fourth quarter, the following entries related to its equity are recorded.

Jan. 17	Retained Earnings	48,000	
	Common Dividend Payable		48,000
Feb. 5	Common Dividend Payable	48,000	
	Cash		48,000

[continued on next page]

[continued from previous page]

Feb. 28	Retained Earnings	126,000	
	Common Stock Dividend Distributable		60,000
	Paid-In Capital in Excess of Par Value, Common Stock		66,000
Mar. 14	Common Stock Dividend Distributable	60,000	
	Common Stock, $10 Par Value		60,000
Mar. 25	Memo—Change the title of the common stock account to reflect the new par value of $5.		
Mar. 31	Income Summary	360,000	
	Retained Earnings		360,000

Required

1. Explain the transaction(s) underlying each journal entry.

2. Complete the following table showing the equity account balances at each indicated date (include the balances from December 31).

	Jan. 17	Feb. 5	Feb. 28	Mar. 14	Mar. 25	Mar. 31
Common stock	$____	$____	$____	$____	$____	$____
Common stock dividend distributable	____	____	____	____	____	____
Paid-in capital in excess of par, common stock	____	____	____	____	____	____
Retained earnings	____	____	____	____	____	____
Total equity	$____	$____	$____	$____	$____	$____

Check Total equity: Jan. 17, $1,424,000; Mar. 31, $1,784,000

Problem 13-4B
Analysis of changes in stockholders' equity accounts
C4 P2 P3 P5

The equity sections from Kiwa Corporation's 2009 and 2010 balance sheets follow.

Stockholders' Equity (December 31, 2009)

Common stock—$20 par value, 15,000 shares authorized, 8,500 shares issued and outstanding	$170,000
Paid-in capital in excess of par value, common stock	30,000
Retained earnings	135,000
Total stockholders' equity	$335,000

Stockholders' Equity (December 31, 2010)

Common stock—$20 par value, 15,000 shares authorized, 9,500 shares issued, 500 shares in treasury	$190,000
Paid-in capital in excess of par value, common stock	52,000
Retained earnings ($20,000 restricted by treasury stock)	147,600
	389,600
Less cost of treasury stock	(20,000)
Total stockholders' equity	$369,600

The following transactions and events affected its equity during year 2010.

Feb. 15 Declared a $0.40 per share cash dividend, date of record five days later.
Mar. 2 Purchased treasury stock for cash.
May 15 Declared a $0.40 per share cash dividend, date of record five days later.
Aug. 15 Declared a $0.40 per share cash dividend, date of record five days later.
Oct. 4 Declared a 12.5% stock dividend when the stock's market value is $42 per share.
Oct. 20 Issued the stock dividend that was declared on October 4.
Nov. 15 Declared a $0.40 per share cash dividend, date of record five days later.

Required

1. How many common shares are outstanding on each cash dividend date?
2. What is the total dollar amount for each of the four cash dividends?
3. What is the amount of the capitalization of retained earnings for the stock dividend?
4. What is the per share cost of the treasury stock purchased?
5. How much net income did the company earn during year 2010?

Check (3) $42,000
(4) $40
(5) $68,000

Problem 13-5B
Computation of book values and dividend allocations
C3 A4 P4

Hansen Company's common stock is currently selling on a stock exchange at $90 per share, and its current balance sheet shows the following stockholders' equity section.

Preferred stock—8% cumulative, $___ par value, 1,500 shares authorized, issued, and outstanding	$ 187,500
Common stock—$___ par value, 18,000 shares authorized, issued, and outstanding	450,000
Retained earnings	562,500
Total stockholders' equity	$1,200,000

Required

1. What is the current market value (price) of this corporation's common stock?
2. What are the par values of the corporation's preferred stock and its common stock?
3. If no dividends are in arrears, what are the book values per share of the preferred stock and the common stock?
4. If two years' preferred dividends are in arrears, what are the book values per share of the preferred stock and the common stock?
5. If two years' preferred dividends are in arrears and the preferred stock is callable at $140 per share, what are the book values per share of the preferred stock and the common stock?
6. If two years' preferred dividends are in arrears and the board of directors declares cash dividends of $50,000, what total amount will be paid to the preferred and to the common shareholders? What is the amount of dividends per share for the common stock?

Check (4) Book value of common, $54.58
(5) Book value of common, $53.33
(6) Dividends per common share, $0.28

Analysis Component

7. Discuss why the book value of common stock is not always a good estimate of its market value.

SERIAL PROBLEM

Success Systems

(This serial problem began in Chapter 1 and continues through most of the book. If previous chapter segments were not completed, the serial problem can begin at this point. It is helpful, but not necessary, to use the Working Papers that accompany the book.)

SP 13 Adriana Lopez created Success Systems on October 1, 2009. The company has been successful, and Adriana plans to expand her business. She believes that an additional $86,000 is needed and is investigating three funding sources.

a. Adriana's sister Cicely is willing to invest $86,000 in the business as a common shareholder. Since Adriana currently has about $129,000 invested in the business, Cicely's investment will mean that Adriana will maintain about 60% ownership, and Cicely will have 40% ownership of Success Systems.
b. Adriana's uncle Marcello is willing to invest $86,000 in the business as a preferred shareholder. Marcello would purchase 860 shares of $100 par value, 7% preferred stock.
c. Adriana's banker is willing to lend her $86,000 on a 7%, 10-year note payable. Adriana would make monthly payments of $1,000 per month for 10 years.

Required

1. Prepare the journal entry to reflect the initial $86,000 investment under each of the options (a), (b), and (c).

2. Evaluate the three proposals for expansion, providing the pros and cons of each option.

3. Which option do you recommend Adriana adopt? Explain.

BEYOND THE NUMBERS

REPORTING IN ACTION

C2 C3 A1 A4

BTN 13-1 Refer to **Best Buy**'s financial statements in Appendix A to answer the following.

1. How many shares of common stock are issued and outstanding at March 3, 2007, and February 25, 2006? How do these numbers compare with the basic weighted-average common shares outstanding at March 3, 2007, and February 25, 2006?

2. What is the book value of its entire common stock at March 3, 2007?

3. What is the total amount of cash dividends paid to common stockholders for the years ended March 3, 2007, and February 25, 2006?

4. Identify and compare basic EPS amounts across fiscal years 2007, 2006, and 2005. Identify and comment on any marked changes.

5. Does Best Buy hold any treasury stock as of March 3, 2007? As of February 25, 2006?

Fast Forward

6. Access Best Buy's financial statements for fiscal years ending after March 3, 2007, from its Website (BestBuy.com) or the SEC's EDGAR database (www.SEC.gov). Has the number of common shares outstanding increased since March 3, 2007? Has Best Buy increased the total amount of cash dividends paid compared to the total amount for fiscal year 2007?

COMPARATIVE ANALYSIS

A1 A2 A3 A4

BTN 13-2 Key comparative figures for **Best Buy**, **Circuit City**, and **RadioShack** follow.

Key Figures	Best Buy	Circuit City	RadioShack
Net income (in millions)	$1,377	$ (8)	$ 73
Cash dividends declared per common share	$ 0.36	$ 0.12	$ 0.25
Common shares outstanding (in millions)	481	171	136
Weighted-average common shares outstanding (in mil.)	482	170	136
Market value (price) per share	$46.35	$19.00	$16.78
Equity applicable to common shares (in millions)	$6,201	$1,791	$ 654

Required

1. Compute the book value per common share for each company using these data.

2. Compute the basic EPS for each company using these data.

3. Compute the dividend yield for each company using these data. Does the dividend yield of any of the companies characterize it as an income or growth stock? Explain.

4. Compute, compare, and interpret the price-earnings ratio for each company using these data.

ETHICS CHALLENGE

C4

BTN 13-3 Brianna Moore is an accountant for New World Pharmaceuticals. Her duties include tracking research and development spending in the new product development division. Over the course of the past six months, Brianna notices that a great deal of funds have been spent on a particular project for a new drug. She hears "through the grapevine" that the company is about to patent the drug and expects it to be a major advance in antibiotics. Brianna believes that this new drug will greatly improve company performance and will cause the company's stock to increase in value. Brianna decides to purchase shares of New World in order to benefit from this expected increase.

Required

What are Brianna's ethical responsibilities, if any, with respect to the information she has learned through her duties as an accountant for New World Pharmaceuticals? What are the implications to her planned purchase of New World shares?

COMMUNICATING IN PRACTICE

A1 A2

Hint: Make a transparency of each team's memo for a class discussion.

BTN 13-4 Teams are to select an industry, and each team member is to select a different company in that industry. Each team member then is to acquire the selected company's financial statements (or Form 10-K) from the SEC EDGAR site (**www.SEC.gov**). Use these data to identify basic EPS. Use the financial press (or **finance.yahoo.com**) to determine the market price of this stock, and then compute the price-earnings ratio. Communicate with teammates via a meeting, e-mail, or telephone to discuss the meaning of this ratio, how companies compare, and the industry norm. The team must prepare a single memorandum reporting the ratio for each company and identifying the team conclusions or consensus of opinion. The memorandum is to be duplicated and distributed to the instructor and teammates.

TAKING IT TO THE NET

C2

BTN 13-5 Access the February 26, 2007, filing of the 2006 calendar-year 10-K report of **McDonald's**, (ticker MCD) from **www.SEC.gov**.

Required

1. Review McDonald's balance sheet and identify how many classes of stock it has issued.
2. What are the par values, number of authorized shares, and issued shares of the classes of stock you identified in part 1?
3. Review its statement of cash flows and identify what total amount of cash it paid in 2006 to purchase treasury stock.
4. What amount did McDonald's pay out in common stock cash dividends for 2006?

TEAMWORK IN ACTION

P5

Hint: Instructor should be sure each team accurately completes part 1 before proceeding.

BTN 13-6 This activity requires teamwork to reinforce understanding of accounting for treasury stock.

1. Write a brief team statement (*a*) generalizing what happens to a corporation's financial position when it engages in a stock "buyback" and (*b*) identifying reasons that a corporation would engage in this activity.
2. Assume that an entity acquires 100 shares of its $100 par value common stock at a cost of $134 cash per share. Discuss the entry to record this acquisition. Next, assign *each* team member to prepare *one* of the following entries (assume each entry applies to all shares):
   a. Reissue treasury shares at cost.
   b. Reissue treasury shares at $150 per share.
   c. Reissue treasury shares at $120 per share; assume the paid-in capital account from treasury shares has a $1,500 balance.
   d. Reissue treasury shares at $120 per share; assume the paid-in capital account from treasury shares has a $1,000 balance.
   e. Reissue treasury shares at $120 per share; assume the paid-in capital account from treasury shares has a zero balance.
3. In sequence, each member is to present his/her entry to the team and explain the *similarities* and *differences* between that entry and the previous entry.

ENTREPRENEURIAL DECISION

C2 C3 P2

BTN 13-7 Assume that Ali Perry, Byron Myers, and Brenton Taylor of **Inogen** decide to launch a new retail chain to market their portable oxygen systems. This chain, named O-to-Go, requires $500,000 of start-up capital. The three contribute $375,000 of personal assets in return for 15,000 shares of common stock, but they need to raise another $125,000 in cash. There are two alternative plans for raising the additional cash. Plan A is to sell 3,750 shares of common stock to one or more investors for $125,000 cash. Plan B is to sell 1,250 shares of cumulative preferred stock to one or more investors for $125,000 cash (this preferred stock would have a $100 par value, an annual 8% dividend rate, and be issued at par).

1. If the new business is expected to earn $72,000 of after-tax net income in the first year, what rate of return on beginning equity will the three (as a group) earn under each alternative? Which plan will provide the higher expected return to them?
2. If the new business is expected to earn $16,800 of after-tax net income in the first year, what rate of return on beginning equity will the three (as a group) earn under each alternative? Which plan will provide the higher expected return to them?
3. Analyze and interpret the differences between the results for parts 1 and 2.

BTN 13-8 Watch 30 to 60 minutes of financial news programming on television. Take notes on companies that are catching analysts' attention. You might hear reference to over- and undervaluation of firms and to reports about PE ratios, dividend yields, and earnings per share. Be prepared to give a brief description to the class of your observations.

HITTING THE ROAD

A1 A2 A3

BTN 13-9 Financial information for **DSG international plc** (www.DSGiplc.com) follows.

GLOBAL DECISION

A1 C4

DSG

Net income (in millions)	£ 207
Cash dividends declared per share	£ 0.07
Number of shares outstanding (in millions)*	1,843
Equity applicable to shares (in millions)	£1,304

* Assume that the year-end number of shares outstanding approximates the weighted-average shares outstanding.

Required

1. Compute book value per share for DSG.
2. Compute earnings per share (EPS) for DSG.
3. Compare DSG's dividends per share with its EPS. Is DSG paying out a large or small amount of its income as dividends? Explain.

ANSWERS TO MULTIPLE CHOICE QUIZ

1. e; Entry to record this stock issuance is:

Cash (6,000 × $8)	48,000	
Common Stock (6,000 × $5)		30,000
Paid-In Capital in Excess of Par Value, Common Stock		18,000

2. b; $75,000/19,000 shares = $3.95 per share

3. d; Preferred stock = 5,000 × $100 = $500,000
   Book value per share = ($2,000,000 − $500,000)/50,000 shares = $30 per common share
4. a; $0.81/$45.00 = 1.8%
5. c; Earnings per share = $3,500,000/700,000 shares = $5 per share
   PE ratio = $85/$5 = 17.0

A Look Back

Chapter 13 focused on corporate equity transactions, including stock issuances and dividends. We also explained how to report and analyze income, earnings per share, and retained earnings.

A Look at This Chapter

This chapter describes the accounting for and analysis of bonds and notes. We explain their characteristics, payment patterns, interest computations, retirement, and reporting requirements. An appendix to this chapter introduces leases and pensions.

A Look Ahead

Chapter 15 focuses on how to classify, account for, and report investments in both debt and equity securities. We also describe accounting for transactions listed in a foreign currency.

Chapter 14 Long-Term Liabilities

Learning Objectives

CAP

Conceptual

C1 Explain the types and payment patterns of notes. *(p. 560)*

C2 *Appendix 14A*—Explain and compute the present value of an amount(s) to be paid at a future date(s). *(p. 567)*

C3 *Appendix 14C*—Describe the accrual of bond interest when bond payments do not align with accounting periods. *(p. 571)*

C4 *Appendix 14D*—Describe accounting for leases and pensions. *(p. 573)*

Analytical

A1 Compare bond financing with stock financing. *(p. 550)*

A2 Assess debt features and their implications. *(p. 563)*

A3 Compute the debt-to-equity ratio and explain its use. *(p. 563)*

LP14

Procedural

P1 Prepare entries to record bond issuance and bond interest expense. *(p. 552)*

P2 Compute and record amortization of bond discount. *(p. 553)*

P3 Compute and record amortization of bond premium. *(p. 556)*

P4 Record the retirement of bonds. *(p. 559)*

P5 Prepare entries to account for notes. *(p. 562)*

Decision Feature

Hip-Hop Financing

"I wanted to create a product that inner-city kids would relate to" — James Lindsay

PHILADELPHIA—James "Fly" Lindsay and his three sisters were raised by their mother in North Philadelphia. "We were poor," explains Lindsay, "but we were rich in the values that she [mother] set forth." One of those values was education—Lindsay was the first in his family to attend college—and another was the commitment to community. "You have everyone taking away, but you have to give back," insists Lindsay.

Lindsay decided to give back by launching his own business. "I wanted to have a chip company that kids from the hood could relate to," he explains. But Lindsay knew that success depended on securing financing and then planning for long-term liabilities. "Between family and friends," explains Lindsay, "we put our dollars together and made it happen." With $40,000 in financing, he launched **Rap Snacks [RapSnacks.com]**, a maker of snack foods with a twist: Lindsay would sell his snacks with rappers on the wrappers. The snacks would be targeted to urban youth immersed in hip-hop culture. The snack wrappers, importantly, would include positive messages to the kids such as "Stay in School," "Respect Yourself," and "Money equals Education." Lindsay hopes they instill a craving for success, commitment, and entrepreneurship.

Lindsay insists that urban youth need to learn about business and how it can help a community. Basic accounting principles and financing concepts such as bonds and notes are like another language to urban youth, he explains. Lindsay struggles to change that and more. "You can make money," says Lindsay, "but also have a social responsibility to where you came from." Actor and rapper Lil' Romeo has recently taken a lead in funding Rap Snacks.

Making investments in urban youth is a priority, says Lindsay. He continually works to convey knowledge of business financing, with the belief that urban youth can be successful. He manages his own company's long-term liabilities, interest payments, and collateral agreements, and is confident that urban youth can do the same. Understanding liabilities is not easy, says Lindsay, but the costs of not understanding are more severe—and more of the same—for the kids. "It feels good to make a difference," says Lindsay, "and set an example for the kids."

[Sources: *Rap Snacks Website*, January 2009; *Entrepreneur*, July 2003; *Philadelphia Inquirer*, October 2002; *Source Magazine*, June 2001; *Maxim*, March 2002; *Business Review*, September 2007; *PR Newswire*, September 2007]

Individuals, companies, and governments issue bonds to finance their activities. In return for financing, bonds promise to repay the lender with interest. This chapter explains the basics of bonds and the accounting for their issuance and retirement. The chapter also describes long-term notes as another financing source. We explain how present value concepts impact both the accounting for and reporting of bonds and notes. Appendixes to this chapter discuss present value concepts applicable to liabilities, effective interest amortization, and the accounting for leases and pensions.

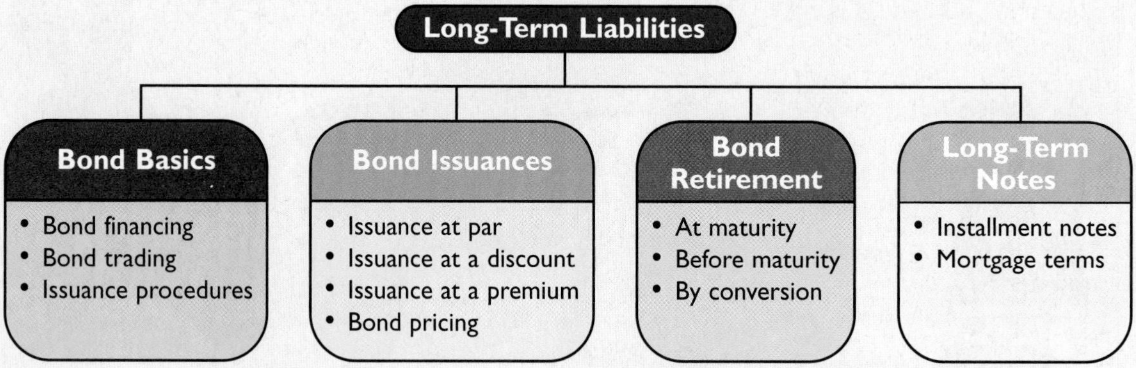

Basics of Bonds

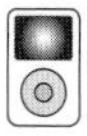

Video14.2

A1 Compare bond financing with stock financing.

This section explains the basics of bonds and a company's motivation for issuing them.

Bond Financing

Projects that demand large amounts of money often are funded from bond issuances. (Both for-profit and nonprofit companies, as well as governmental units, such as nations, states, cities, and school districts, issue bonds.) A **bond** is its issuer's written promise to pay an amount identified as the par value of the bond with interest. The **par value of a bond,** also called the *face amount* or *face value,* is paid at a specified future date known as the bond's *maturity date.* Most bonds also require the issuer to make semiannual interest payments. The amount of interest paid each period is determined by multiplying the par value of the bond by the bond's contract rate of interest. This section explains both advantages and disadvantages of bond financing.

Advantages of Bonds There are three main advantages of bond financing:

1. *Bonds do not affect owner control.* Equity financing reflects ownership in a company, whereas bond financing does not. A person who contributes $1,000 of a company's $10,000 equity financing typically controls one-tenth of all owner decisions. A person who owns a $1,000, 11%, 20-year bond has no ownership right. This person, or bondholder, is to receive from the bond issuer 11% interest, or $110, each year the bond is outstanding and $1,000 when it matures in 20 years.
2. *Interest on bonds is tax deductible.* Bond interest payments are tax deductible for the issuer, but equity payments (distributions) to owners are not. To illustrate, assume that a corporation with no bond financing earns $15,000 in income *before* paying taxes at a 40% tax rate, which amounts to $6,000 ($15,000 × 40%) in taxes. If a portion of its financing is in bonds, however, the resulting bond interest is deducted in computing taxable income. That is, if bond interest expense is $10,000, the taxes owed would be $2,000 ([$15,000 − $10,000] × 40%), which is less than the $6,000 owed with no bond financing.
3. *Bonds can increase return on equity.* A company that earns a higher return with borrowed funds than it pays in interest on those funds increases its return on equity. This process is called *financial leverage* or *trading on the equity.*

Point: Financial leverage reflects issuance of bonds, notes, or preferred stock.

To illustrate the third point, consider Magnum Co., which has $1 million in equity and is planning a $500,000 expansion to meet increasing demand for its product. Magnum predicts the

$500,000 expansion will yield $125,000 in additional income before paying any interest. It currently earns $100,000 per year and has no interest expense. Magnum is considering three plans. Plan A is to not expand. Plan B is to expand and raise $500,000 from equity financing. Plan C is to expand and issue $500,000 of bonds that pay 10% annual interest ($50,000). Exhibit 14.1 shows how these three plans affect Magnum's net income, equity, and return on equity (net income/equity). The owner(s) will earn a higher return on equity if expansion occurs. Moreover, the preferred expansion plan is to issue bonds. Projected net income under Plan C ($175,000) is smaller than under Plan B ($225,000), but the return on equity is larger because of less equity investment. Plan C has another advantage if income is taxable. This illustration reflects a general rule: *Return on equity increases when the expected rate of return from the new assets is higher than the rate of interest expense on the debt financing.*

Example: Compute return on equity for all three plans if Magnum currently earns $150,000 instead of $100,000.
Answer ($ 000s):
Plan A = 15% ($150/$1,000)
Plan B = 18.3% ($275/$1,500)
Plan C = 22.5% ($225/$1,000)

EXHIBIT 14.1

Financing with Bonds versus Equity

	Plan A: Do Not Expand	Plan B: Equity Financing	Plan C: Bond Financing
Income before interest expense	$ 100,000	$ 225,000	$ 225,000
Interest expense	—	—	(50,000)
Net income	**$ 100,000**	**$ 225,000**	**$ 175,000**
Equity	$1,000,000	$1,500,000	$1,000,000
Return on equity	**10.0%**	**15.0%**	**17.5%**

Disadvantages of Bonds The two main disadvantages of bond financing are these:

1. *Bonds can decrease return on equity.* When a company earns a lower return with the borrowed funds than it pays in interest, it decreases its return on equity. This downside risk of financial leverage is more likely to arise when a company has periods of low income or net losses.
2. *Bonds require payment of both periodic interest and the par value at maturity.* Bond payments can be especially burdensome when income and cash flow are low. Equity financing, in contrast, does not require any payments because cash withdrawals (dividends) are paid at the discretion of the owner (or board).

Point: Debt financing is desirable when interest is tax deductible, when owner control is preferred, and when return on equity exceeds the debt's interest rate.

A company must weigh the risks and returns of the disadvantages and advantages of bond financing when deciding whether to issue bonds to finance operations.

Bond Trading

Bonds are securities that can be readily bought and sold. A large number of bonds trade on both the New York Exchange and the American Exchange. A bond *issue* consists of a number of bonds, usually in denominations of $1,000 or $5,000, and is sold to many different lenders. After bonds are issued, they often are bought and sold by investors, meaning that any particular bond probably has a number of owners before it matures. Since bonds are exchanged (bought and sold) in the market, they have a market value (price). For convenience, bond market values are expressed as a percent of their par (face) value. For example, a company's bonds might be trading at 103½, meaning they can be bought or sold for 103.5% of their par value. Bonds can also trade below par value. For instance, if a company's bonds are trading at 95, they can be bought or sold at 95% of their par value.

Decision Insight

Bonds	Rate	Mat	Yld	Vol	Close	Chg
IBM	7	25	5.9	130	119¼	+1¼

Quotes The **IBM** bond quote here is interpreted (left to right) as **Bonds,** issuer name; **Rate,** contract interest rate (7%); **Mat,** matures in year 2025 when principal is paid; **Yld,** yield rate (5.9%) of bond at current price; **Vol,** daily dollar worth ($130,000) of trades (in 1,000s); **Close,** closing price (119.25) for the day as percentage of par value; **Chg,** change (+1.25) in closing price from prior day's close.

Bond-Issuing Procedures

State and federal laws govern bond issuances. Bond issuers also want to ensure that they do not violate any of their existing contractual agreements when issuing bonds. Authorization of bond issuances includes the number of bonds authorized, their par value, and the contract interest rate. The legal document identifying the rights and obligations of both the bondholders and the issuer is called the **bond indenture,** which is the legal contract between the issuer and the bondholders. A bondholder may also receive a bond certificate as evidence of the company's debt. A **bond certificate,** such as that shown in Exhibit 14.2, includes specifics such as the issuer's name, the par value, the contract interest rate, and the maturity date. Many companies reduce costs by not issuing paper certificates to bondholders.[1]

EXHIBIT 14.2

Bond Certificate

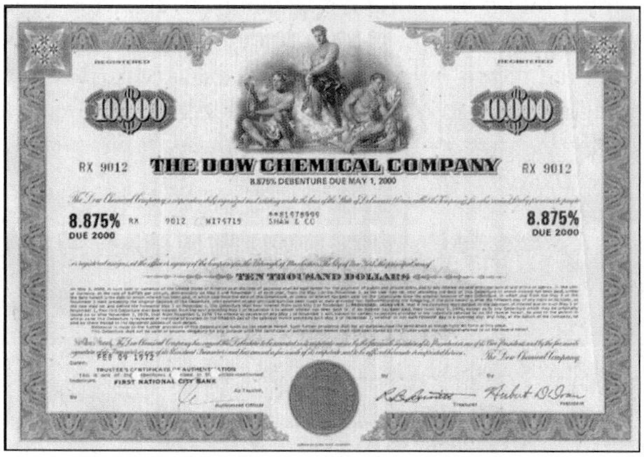

Point: *Indenture* refers to a bond's legal contract; *debenture* refers to an unsecured bond.

Bond Issuances

Video14.2

This section explains accounting for bond issuances at par, below par (discount), and above par (premium). It also describes how to amortize a discount or premium and record bonds issued between interest payment dates.

Issuing Bonds at Par

P1 Prepare entries to record bond issuance and bond interest expense.

To illustrate an issuance of bonds at par value, suppose a company receives authorization to issue $800,000 of 9%, 20-year bonds dated January 1, 2009, that mature on December 31, 2028, and pay interest semiannually on each June 30 and December 31. After accepting the bond indenture on behalf of the bondholders, the trustee can sell all or a portion of the bonds to an underwriter. If all bonds are sold at par value, the issuer records the sale as follows.

Assets	= Liabilities	+ Equity
+800,000	+800,000	

2009			
Jan. 1	Cash	800,000	
	Bonds Payable.		800,000
	Sold bonds at par.		

This entry reflects increases in the issuer's cash *and* long-term liabilities.

The issuer records the first semiannual interest payment as follows.

Assets	= Liabilities	+ Equity
−36,000		−36,000

2009			
June 30	Bond Interest Expense	36,000	
	Cash		36,000
	Paid semiannual interest (9% × $800,000 × ½ year).		

[1] The issuing company normally sells its bonds to an investment firm called an *underwriter,* which resells them to the public. An issuing company can also sell bonds directly to investors. When an underwriter sells bonds to a large number of investors, a *trustee* represents and protects the bondholders' interests. The trustee monitors the issuer to ensure that it complies with the obligations in the bond indenture. Most trustees are large banks or trust companies. The trustee writes and accepts the terms of a bond indenture before it is issued. When bonds are offered to the public, called *floating an issue,* they must be registered with the Securities and Exchange Commission (SEC). SEC registration requires the issuer to file certain financial information. Most company bonds are issued in par value units of $1,000 or $5,000. *A baby bond* has a par value of less than $1,000, such as $100.

Point: The *spread* between the dealer's cost and what buyers pay can be huge. Dealers earn more than $25 billion in annual spread revenue.

Global: In the United Kingdom, government bonds are called *gilts*—short for gilt-edged investments.

The issuer pays and records its semiannual interest obligation every six months until the bonds mature. When they mature, the issuer records its payment of principal as follows.

2028			
Dec. 31	Bonds Payable	800,000	
	Cash		800,000
	Paid bond principal at maturity.		

Assets = Liabilities + Equity
−800,000 −800,000

Bond Discount or Premium

The bond issuer pays the interest rate specified in the indenture, the **contract rate,** also referred to as the *coupon rate, stated rate,* or *nominal rate*. The annual interest paid is determined by multiplying the bond par value by the contract rate. The contract rate is usually stated on an annual basis, even if interest is paid semiannually. For example, if a company issues a $1,000, 8% bond paying interest semiannually, it pays annual interest of $80 (8% × $1,000) in two semiannual payments of $40 each.

The contract rate sets the amount of interest the issuer pays in *cash,* which is not necessarily the *bond interest expense* actually incurred by the issuer. Bond interest expense depends on the bond's market value at issuance, which is determined by market expectations of the risk of lending to the issuer. The bond's **market rate** of interest is the rate that borrowers are willing to pay and lenders are willing to accept for a particular bond and its risk level. As the risk level increases, the rate increases to compensate purchasers for the bonds' increased risk. Also, the market rate is generally higher when the time period until the bond matures is longer due to the risk of adverse events occurring over a longer time period.

Many bond issuers try to set a contract rate of interest equal to the market rate they expect as of the bond issuance date. When the contract rate and market rate are equal, a bond sells at par value, but when they are not equal, a bond does not sell at par value. Instead, it is sold at a *premium* above par value or at a *discount* below par value. Exhibit 14.3 shows the relation between the contract rate, market rate, and a bond's issue price.

EXHIBIT 14.3

Relation between Bond Issue Price, Contract Rate, and Market Rate

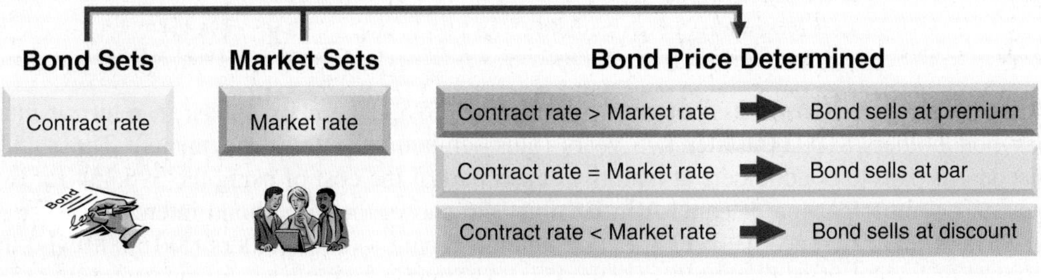

Quick Check Answers—p. 576

1. Unsecured bonds backed only by the issuer's general credit standing are called (*a*) serial bonds, (*b*) debentures, (*c*) registered bonds, or (*d*) convertible bonds.
2. How do you compute the amount of interest a bond issuer pays in cash each year?
3. When the contract rate is above the market rate, do bonds sell at a premium or a discount? Do purchasers pay more or less than the par value of the bonds?

Issuing Bonds at a Discount

P2 Compute and record amortization of bond discount.

A **discount on bonds payable** occurs when a company issues bonds with a contract rate less than the market rate. This means that the issue price is less than par value. To illustrate, assume that **Fila** announces an offer to issue bonds with a $100,000 par value, an 8% annual contract rate (paid semiannually), and a two-year life. Also assume that the market rate for Fila

Point: The difference between the contract rate and the market rate of interest on a new bond issue is usually a fraction of a percent. We use a difference of 2% to emphasize the effects.

bonds is 10%. These bonds then will sell at a discount since the contract rate is less than the market rate. The exact issue price for these bonds is stated as 96.454 (implying 96.454% of par value, or $96,454); we show how to compute this issue price later in the chapter. These bonds obligate the issuer to pay two separate types of future cash flows:

1. Par value of $100,000 cash at the end of the bonds' two-year life.
2. Cash interest payments of $4,000 (4% × $100,000) at the end of each semiannual period during the bonds' two-year life.

The exact pattern of cash flows for the Fila bonds is shown in Exhibit 14.4.

EXHIBIT 14.4

Cash Flows for Fila Bonds

				$100,000
	$4,000	**$4,000**	**$4,000**	**$4,000**
0	6 mo.	12 mo.	18 mo.	24 mo.

When Fila accepts $96,454 cash for its bonds on the issue date of December 31, 2009, it records the sale as follows.

Assets	=	Liabilities	+	Equity
+96,454		+100,000		
		−3,546		

Dec. 31	Cash	96,454	
	Discount on Bonds Payable.	3,546	
	Bonds Payable.		100,000
	Sold bonds at a discount on their issue date.		

Point: Book value at issuance always equals the issuer's cash borrowed.

These bonds are reported in the long-term liability section of the issuer's December 31, 2009, balance sheet as shown in Exhibit 14.5. A discount is deducted from the par value of bonds to yield the **carrying (book) value of bonds.** Discount on Bonds Payable is a contra liability account.

EXHIBIT 14.5

Balance Sheet Presentation of Bond Discount

Long-term liabilities		
Bonds payable, 8%, due December 31, 2011	$100,000	
Less discount on bonds payable	3,546	$96,454

Point: *Zero-coupon bonds* do not pay periodic interest (contract rate is zero). These bonds always sell at a discount because their 0% contract rate is always below the market rate.

Video14.2

Amortizing a Bond Discount Fila receives $96,454 for its bonds; in return it must pay bondholders $100,000 after two years (plus semiannual interest payments). The $3,546 discount is paid to bondholders at maturity and is part of the cost of using the $96,454 for two years. The upper portion of panel A in Exhibit 14.6 shows that total bond interest expense of $19,546 is the difference between the total amount repaid to bondholders ($116,000) and the amount borrowed from bondholders ($96,454). Alternatively, we can compute total bond interest expense as the sum of the four interest payments and the bond discount. This alternative computation is shown in the lower portion of panel A.

The total $19,546 bond interest expense must be allocated across the four semiannual periods in the bonds' life, and the bonds' carrying value must be updated at each balance sheet date. This is accomplished using the straight-line method (or the effective interest method in Appendix 14B). Both methods systematically reduce the bond discount to zero over the two-year life. This process is called *amortizing a bond discount.*

Straight-Line Method The **straight-line bond amortization** method allocates an equal portion of the total bond interest expense to each interest period. To apply the straight-line method to Fila's bonds, we divide the total bond interest expense of $19,546 by 4 (the number of semiannual periods in the bonds' life). This gives a bond interest expense of $4,887 per period, which is $4,886.5 rounded to the nearest dollar per period (all computations, including those for assignments, are rounded to the nearest whole dollar). Alternatively, we can find this number by first dividing the $3,546 discount by 4, which yields the $887 amount of discount to be amortized each interest period. When the $887 is added to the $4,000 cash payment, the

EXHIBIT 14.6

Interest Computation and Entry for Bonds Issued at a Discount

Panel A: Interest Computations

Amount repaid to bondholders	
Four interest payments of $4,000	$ 16,000
Par value at maturity	100,000
Total repaid to bondholders	116,000
Less amount borrowed from bondholders	(96,454)
Total bond interest expense	**$ 19,546**
Alternative Computation	
Four payments of $4,000	$ 16,000
Plus discount	3,546
Total bond interest expense	**$ 19,546**

Equal

$$\frac{\text{Bond interest expense}}{\text{(per interest period)}} = \frac{\text{Total bond interest expense}}{\text{Number of interest periods}} = \frac{\$19,546}{4} = \$4,887$$

Panel B: Entry to Record Interest Payment and Amortization

2010–2011			
June 30 and Dec. 31	Bond Interest Expense	4,887	
	Discount on Bonds Payable		887
	Cash		4,000
	To record semiannual interest and discount amortization (straight-line method).		

Discount ÷ periods

Par value × contract rate

bond interest expense for each period is $4,887. Panel B of Exhibit 14.6 shows how the issuer records bond interest expense and updates the balance of the bond liability account at the end of *each* of the four semiannual interest periods (June 30, 2010, through December 31, 2011).

Exhibit 14.7 shows the pattern of decreases in the Discount on Bonds Payable account and the pattern of increases in the bonds' carrying value. The following points summarize the discount bonds' straight-line amortization:

1. At issuance, the $100,000 par value consists of the $96,454 cash received by the issuer plus the $3,546 discount.
2. During the bonds' life, the (unamortized) discount decreases each period by the $887 amortization ($3,546/4), and the carrying value (par value less unamortized discount) increases each period by $887.
3. At maturity, the unamortized discount equals zero, and the carrying value equals the $100,000 par value that the issuer pays the holder.

EXHIBIT 14.7

Straight-Line Amortization of Bond Discount

Semiannual Period-End	Unamortized Discount*	Carrying Value†
(0) 12/31/2009	$3,546	$ 96,454
(1) 6/30/2010	2,659	97,341
(2) 12/31/2010	1,772	98,228
(3) 6/30/2011	885	99,115
(4) **12/31/2011**	**0‡**	**100,000**

* Total bond discount (of $3,546) less accumulated periodic amortization ($887 per semiannual interest period).

† Bond par value (of $100,000) less unamortized discount.

‡ Adjusted for rounding.

The two columns always sum to par value for a discount bond.

We see that the issuer incurs a $4,887 bond interest expense each period but pays only $4,000 cash. The $887 unpaid portion of this expense is added to the bonds' carrying value. (The total $3,546 unamortized discount is "paid" when the bonds mature; $100,000 is paid at maturity but only $96,454 was received at issuance.)

Decision Insight

Ratings Game Many bond buyers rely on rating services to assess bond risk. The best known are **Standard & Poor's** and **Moody's.** These services focus on the issuer's financial statements and other factors in setting ratings. Standard & Poor's ratings, from best quality to default, are AAA, AA, A, BBB, BB, B, CCC, CC, C, and D. Ratings can include a plus (+) or minus (−) to show relative standing within a category.

Quick Check

Answers—p. 576

Five-year, 6% bonds with a $100,000 par value are issued at a price of $91,893. Interest is paid semiannually, and the bonds' market rate is 8% on the issue date. Use this information to answer the following questions:

4. Are these bonds issued at a discount or a premium? Explain your answer.
5. What is the issuer's journal entry to record the issuance of these bonds?
6. What is the amount of bond interest expense recorded at the first semiannual period using the straight-line method?

Issuing Bonds at a Premium

P3 Compute and record amortization of bond premium.

When the contract rate of bonds is higher than the market rate, the bonds sell at a price higher than par value. The amount by which the bond price exceeds par value is the **premium on bonds.** To illustrate, assume that **Adidas** issues bonds with a $100,000 par value, a 12% annual contract rate, semiannual interest payments, and a two-year life. Also assume that the market rate for Adidas bonds is 10% on the issue date. The Adidas bonds will sell at a premium because the contract rate is higher than the market rate. The issue price for these bonds is stated as 103.546 (implying 103.546% of par value, or $103,546); we show how to compute this issue price later in the chapter. These bonds obligate the issuer to pay out two separate future cash flows:

1. Par value of $100,000 cash at the end of the bonds' two-year life.
2. Cash interest payments of $6,000 (6% × $100,000) at the end of each semiannual period during the bonds' two-year life.

The exact pattern of cash flows for the Adidas bonds is shown in Exhibit 14.8.

EXHIBIT 14.8

Cash Flows for Adidas Bonds

				$100,000
	$6,000	**$6,000**	**$6,000**	**$6,000**
0	6 mo.	12 mo.	18 mo.	24 mo.

When Adidas accepts $103,546 cash for its bonds on the issue date of December 31, 2009, it records this transaction as follows.

Assets = Liabilities + Equity
+103,546 +100,000
+3,546

Dec. 31	Cash	103,546	
	Premium on Bonds Payable		3,546
	Bonds Payable		100,000
	Sold bonds at a premium on their issue date.		

These bonds are reported in the long-term liability section of the issuer's December 31, 2009, balance sheet as shown in Exhibit 14.9. A premium is added to par value to yield the carrying (book) value of bonds. Premium on Bonds Payable is an adjunct (also called *accretion*) liability account.

EXHIBIT 14.9

Balance Sheet Presentation of Bond Premium

Long-term liabilities		
Bonds payable, 12%, due December 31, 2011	$100,000	
Plus premium on bonds payable	3,546	$103,546

Amortizing a Bond Premium Adidas receives $103,546 for its bonds; in return, it pays bondholders $100,000 after two years (plus semiannual interest payments). The $3,546 premium not repaid to issuer's bondholders at maturity goes to reduce the issuer's expense of using the $103,546 for two years. The upper portion of panel A of Exhibit 14.10 shows that total bond interest expense of $20,454 is the difference between the total amount repaid to bondholders ($124,000) and the amount borrowed from bondholders ($103,546). Alternatively, we can compute

EXHIBIT 14.10

Interest Computation and Entry for Bonds Issued at a Premium

Panel A: Interest Computations

Amount repaid to bondholders	
Four interest payments of $6,000	$ 24,000
Par value at maturity	100,000
Total repaid to bondholders	124,000
Less amount borrowed from bondholders	(103,546)
Total bond interest expense	**$ 20,454**
Alternative Computation	
Four payments of $6,000	$ 24,000
Less premium	(3,546)
Total bond interest expense	**$ 20,454**

(Equal)

$$\frac{\text{Bond interest expense}}{\text{(per interest period)}} = \frac{\text{Total bond interest expense}}{\text{Number of interest periods}} = \frac{\$20{,}454}{4} = \$5{,}113$$

Panel B: Entry to Record Interest Payment and Amortization

2010–2011				
June 30 and Dec. 31	Bond Interest Expense	5,113		
	Premium on Bonds Payable	887		Premium ÷ periods
	Cash		6,000	Par value × contract rate
	To record semiannual interest and premium amortization (straight-line method).			

total bond interest expense as the sum of the four interest payments less the bond premium. The premium is subtracted because it will not be paid to bondholders when the bonds mature; see the lower portion of panel A. Total bond interest expense must be allocated over the four semiannual periods using the straight-line method (or the effective interest method in Appendix 14B).

Straight-Line Method The straight-line method allocates an equal portion of total bond interest expense to each of the bonds' semiannual interest periods. To apply this method to Adidas bonds, we divide the two years' total bond interest expense of $20,454 by 4 (the number of semiannual periods in the bonds' life). This gives a total bond interest expense of $5,113 per period, which is $5,113.5 rounded down so that the journal entry balances and for simplicity in presentation (alternatively, one could carry cents). Panel B of Exhibit 14.10 shows how the issuer records bond interest expense and updates the balance of the bond liability account for *each* semiannual period (June 30, 2010, through December 31, 2011).

Point: A premium decreases Bond Interest Expense; a discount increases it.

EXHIBIT 14.11

Straight-Line Amortization of Bond Premium

Semiannual Period-End	Unamortized Premium*	Carrying Value†
(0) 12/31/2009	$3,546	$103,546
(1) 6/30/2010	2,659	102,659
(2) 12/31/2010	1,772	101,772
(3) 6/30/2011	885	100,885
(4) 12/31/2011	**0‡**	**100,000**

* Total bond premium (of $3,546) less accumulated periodic amortization ($887 per semiannual interest period).

† Bond par value (of $100,000) plus unamortized premium.

‡ Adjusted for rounding.

During the bond life, carrying value is adjusted to par and the amortized premium to zero.

Exhibit 14.11 shows the pattern of decreases in the unamortized Premium on Bonds Payable account and in the bonds' carrying value. The following points summarize straight-line amortization of the premium bonds:

1. At issuance, the $100,000 par value plus the $3,546 premium equals the $103,546 cash received by the issuer.
2. During the bonds' life, the (unamortized) premium decreases each period by the $887 amortization ($3,546/4), and the carrying value decreases each period by the same $887.
3. At maturity, the unamortized premium equals zero, and the carrying value equals the $100,000 par value that the issuer pays the holder.

The next section describes bond pricing. An instructor can choose to cover bond pricing or not. Assignments requiring the next section are Quick Study 14-4, Exercises 14-9 & 14-10, and Problems 14-1A & 14-1B and 14-4A & 14-4B.

Bond Pricing

Prices for bonds traded on an organized exchange are often published in newspapers and through online services. This information normally includes the bond price (called *quote*), its contract rate, and its current market (called *yield*) rate. However, only a fraction of bonds are traded on organized exchanges. To compute the price of a bond, we apply present value concepts. This section explains how to use *present value concepts* to price the Fila discount bond and the Adidas premium bond described earlier.

Point: InvestingInBonds.com is a bond research and learning source.

Present Value of a Discount Bond The issue price of bonds is found by computing the present value of the bonds' cash payments, discounted at the bonds' market rate. When computing the present value of the Fila bonds, we work with *semiannual* compounding periods because this is the time between interest payments; the annual market rate of 10% is considered a semiannual rate of 5%. Also, the two-year bond life is viewed as four semiannual periods. The price computation is twofold: (1) Find the present value of the $100,000 par value paid at maturity and (2) find the present value of the series of four semiannual payments of $4,000 each; see Exhibit 14.4. These present values can be found by using *present value tables.* Appendix B at the end of this book shows present value tables and describes their use. Table B.1 at the end of Appendix B is used for the single $100,000 maturity payment, and Table B.3 in Appendix B is used for the $4,000 series of interest payments. Specifically, we go to Table B.1, row 4, and across to the 5% column to identify the present value factor of 0.8227 for the maturity payment. Next, we go to Table B.3, row 4, and across to the 5% column, where the present value factor is 3.5460 for the series of interest payments. We compute bond price by multiplying the cash flow payments by their corresponding present value factors and adding them together; see Exhibit 14.12.

Point: A bond's market value (price) at issuance equals the present value of its future cash payments, where the interest (discount) rate used is the bond's market rate.

Point: Many calculators have present value functions for computing bond prices.

EXHIBIT 14.12

Computing Issue Price for the Fila Discount Bonds

Cash Flow	Table	Present Value Factor		Amount		Present Value
$100,000 par (maturity) value	B.1	0.8227	×	$100,000	=	$ 82,270
$4,000 interest payments	B.3	3.5460	×	4,000	=	14,184
Price of bond						**$96,454**

Present Value of a Premium Bond We find the issue price of the Adidas bonds by using the market rate to compute the present value of the bonds' future cash flows. When computing the present value of these bonds, we again work with *semiannual* compounding periods because this is the time between interest payments. The annual 10% market rate is applied as a semiannual rate of 5%, and the two-year bond life is viewed as four semiannual periods. The computation is twofold: (1) Find the present value of the $100,000 par value paid at maturity and (2) find the present value of the series of four payments of $6,000 each; see Exhibit 14.8. These present values can be found by using present value tables. First, go to Table B.1, row 4, and across to the 5% column where the present value factor is 0.8227 for the maturity payment. Second, go to Table B.3, row 4, and across to the 5% column, where the present value factor is 3.5460 for the series of interest payments. The bonds' price is computed by multiplying the cash flow payments by their corresponding present value factors and adding them together; see Exhibit 14.13.

Point: There are nearly 5 million individual U.S. bond issues, ranging from huge treasuries to tiny municipalities. This compares to about 12,000 individual U.S. stocks that are traded.

EXHIBIT 14.13

Computing Issue Price for the Adidas Premium Bonds

Cash Flow	Table	Present Value Factor		Amount		Present Value
$100,000 par (maturity) value	B.1	0.8227	×	$100,000	=	$ 82,270
$6,000 interest payments	B.3	3.5460	×	6,000	=	21,276
Price of bond						**$103,546**

Quick Check Answers—p. 576

On December 31, 2008, a company issues 16%, 10-year bonds with a par value of $100,000. Interest is paid on June 30 and December 31. The bonds are sold to yield a 14% annual market rate at an issue price of $110,592. Use this information to answer questions 7 through 9:

7. Are these bonds issued at a discount or a premium? Explain your answer.
8. Using the straight-line method to allocate bond interest expense, the issuer records the second interest payment (on December 31, 2009) with a debit to Premium on Bonds Payable in the amount of (*a*) $7,470, (*b*) $530, (*c*) $8,000, or (*d*) $400.
9. How are these bonds reported in the long-term liability section of the issuer's balance sheet as of December 31, 2009?

Bond Retirement

This section describes the retirement of bonds (1) at maturity, (2) before maturity, and (3) by conversion to stock.

Bond Retirement at Maturity

P4 Record the retirement of bonds.

The carrying value of bonds at maturity always equals par value. For example, both Exhibits 14.7 (a discount) and 14.11 (a premium) show that the carrying value of bonds at the end of their lives equals par value ($100,000). The retirement of these bonds at maturity, assuming interest is already paid and entered, is recorded as follows:

2011			
Dec. 31	Bonds Payable	100,000	
	Cash		100,000
	To record retirement of bonds at maturity.		

Assets	= Liabilities	+ Equity
−100,000	−100,000	

Bond Retirement before Maturity

Issuers sometimes wish to retire some or all of their bonds prior to maturity. For instance, if interest rates decline greatly, an issuer may wish to replace high-interest-paying bonds with new low-interest bonds. Two common ways to retire bonds before maturity are to (1) exercise a call option or (2) purchase them on the open market. In the first instance, an issuer can reserve the right to retire bonds early by issuing callable bonds. The bond indenture can give the issuer an option to *call* the bonds before they mature by paying the par value plus a *call premium* to bondholders. In the second case, the issuer retires bonds by repurchasing them on the open market at their current price. Whether bonds are called or repurchased, the issuer is unlikely to pay a price that exactly equals their carrying value. When a difference exists between the bonds' carrying value and the amount paid, the issuer records a gain or loss equal to the difference.

Point: Bond retirement is also referred to as *bond redemption.*

Point: Gains and losses from retiring bonds were *previously* reported as extraordinary items. New standards require that they now be judged by the "unusual and infrequent" criteria for reporting purposes.

To illustrate the accounting for retiring callable bonds, assume that a company issued callable bonds with a par value of $100,000. The call option requires the issuer to pay a call premium of $3,000 to bondholders in addition to the par value. Next, assume that after the June 30, 2009, interest payment, the bonds have a carrying value of $104,500. Then on July 1, 2009, the issuer calls these bonds and pays $103,000 to bondholders. The issuer recognizes a $1,500 gain from the difference between the bonds' carrying value of $104,500 and the retirement price of $103,000. The issuer records this bond retirement as follows.

July 1	Bonds Payable	100,000	
	Premium on Bonds Payable	4,500	
	Gain on Bond Retirement		1,500
	Cash		103,000
	To record retirement of bonds before maturity.		

Assets	= Liabilities	+ Equity
−103,000	−100,000	+1,500
	−4,500	

An issuer usually must call all bonds when it exercises a call option. However, to retire as many or as few bonds as it desires, an issuer can purchase them on the open market. If it retires less than the entire class of bonds, it recognizes a gain or loss for the difference between the carrying value of those bonds retired and the amount paid to acquire them.

Bond Retirement by Conversion

Convertible Bond

Holders of convertible bonds have the right to convert their bonds to stock. When conversion occurs, the bonds' carrying value is transferred to equity accounts and no gain or loss is recorded. (We further describe convertible bonds in the Decision Analysis section of this chapter.)

To illustrate, assume that on January 1 the $100,000 par value bonds of **Converse**, with a carrying value of $100,000, are converted to 15,000 shares of $2 par value common stock. The entry to record this conversion follows (the market prices of the bonds and stock are *not* relevant to this entry; the material in Chapter 13 is helpful in understanding this transaction):

Assets	= Liabilities	+ Equity
	−100,000	+30,000
		+70,000

Jan. 1	Bonds Payable	100,000	
	Common Stock		30,000
	Paid-In Capital in Excess of Par Value		70,000
	To record retirement of bonds by conversion.		

Decision Insight

Junk Bonds Junk bonds are company bonds with low credit ratings due to a higher than average likelihood of default. On the upside, the high risk of junk bonds can yield high returns if the issuer survives and repays its debt.

Quick Check

Answer—p. 576

10. Six years ago, a company issued $500,000 of 6%, eight-year bonds at a price of 95. The current carrying value is $493,750. The company decides to retire 50% of these bonds by buying them on the open market at a price of 102½. What is the amount of gain or loss on the retirement of these bonds?

Long-Term Notes Payable

Video14.1

Like bonds, notes are issued to obtain assets such as cash. Unlike bonds, notes are typically transacted with a *single* lender such as a bank. An issuer initially records a note at its selling price—that is, the note's face value minus any discount or plus any premium. Over the note's life, the amount of interest expense allocated to each period is computed by multiplying the market rate (at issuance of the note) by the beginning-of-period note balance. The note's carrying (book) value at any time equals its face value minus any unamortized discount or plus any unamortized premium; carrying value is also computed as the present value of all remaining payments, discounted using the market rate at issuance.

Installment Notes

C1 Explain the types and payment patterns of notes.

An **installment note** is an obligation requiring a series of payments to the lender. Installment notes are common for franchises and other businesses when lenders and borrowers agree to spread payments over several periods. To illustrate, assume that Foghog borrows $60,000 from a bank to purchase equipment. It signs an 8% installment note requiring six annual payments of principal plus interest and it records the note's issuance at January 1, 2009, as follows.

Assets	= Liabilities	+ Equity
+60,000	+60,000	

Jan. 1	Cash	60,000	
	Notes Payable		60,000
	Borrowed $60,000 by signing an 8%, six-year installment note.		

Payments on an installment note normally include the accrued interest expense plus a portion of the amount borrowed (the *principal*). This section describes an installment note with equal payments.

The equal total payments pattern consists of changing amounts of both interest and principal. To illustrate, assume that Foghog borrows $60,000 by signing a $60,000 note that requires six *equal payments* of $12,979 at the end of each year. (The present value of an annuity of six annual payments of $12,979, discounted at 8%, equals $60,000; we show this computation in footnote 2 on the next page.) The $12,979 includes both interest and principal, the amounts of which change with each payment. Exhibit 14.14 shows the pattern of equal total payments and its two parts, interest and principal. Column A shows the note's beginning balance. Column B shows accrued interest for each year at 8% of the beginning note balance. Column C shows the impact on the note's principal, which equals the difference between the total payment in column D and the interest expense in column B. Column E shows the note's year-end balance.

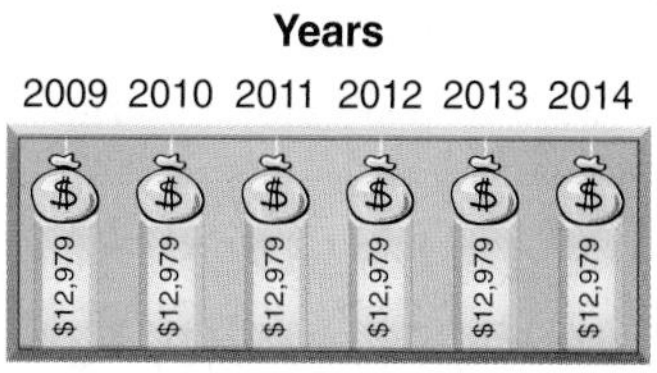

Point: Most consumer notes are installment notes that require equal total payments.

EXHIBIT 14.14

Installment Note: Equal Total Payments

Period Ending Date	(A) Beginning Balance		Payments			(E) Ending Balance (A) − (C)
		(B) *Debit* Interest Expense 8% × (A)	+ (C) *Debit* Notes Payable (D) − (B)	=	(D) *Credit* Cash (computed)	
(1) **12/31/2009**	**$60,000**	**$ 4,800**	**$ 8,179**		**$12,979**	**$51,821**
(2) 12/31/2010	51,821	4,146	8,833		12,979	42,988
(3) 12/31/2011	42,988	3,439	9,540		12,979	33,448
(4) 12/31/2012	33,448	2,676	10,303		12,979	23,145
(5) 12/31/2013	23,145	1,852	11,127		12,979	12,018
(6) 12/31/2014	12,018	961	12,018		12,979	0
		$17,874	**$60,000**		**$77,874**	

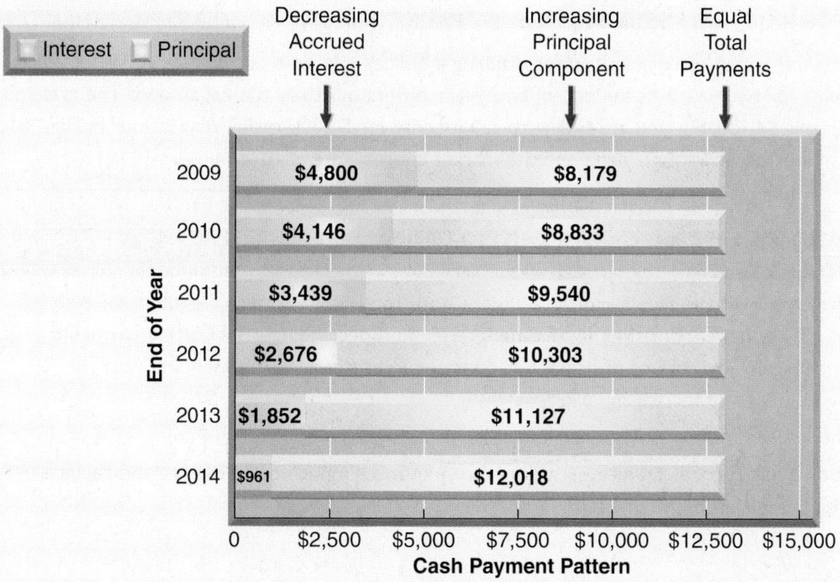

Although the six cash payments are equal, accrued interest decreases each year because the principal balance of the note declines. As the amount of interest decreases each year, the portion of each payment applied to principal increases. This pattern is graphed in the lower part

Point: The Truth-in-Lending Act requires lenders to provide information about loan costs including finance charges and interest rate.

P5 Prepare entries to account for notes.

of Exhibit 14.14. Foghog uses the amounts in Exhibit 14.14 to record its first two payments (for years 2009 and 2010) as follows:

Assets	= Liabilities	+ Equity
−12,979	−8,179	−4,800

2009			
Dec. 31	Interest Expense	4,800	
	Notes Payable	8,179	
	Cash		12,979
	To record first installment payment.		

Assets	= Liabilities	+ Equity
−12,979	−8,833	−4,146

2010			
Dec. 31	Interest Expense	4,146	
	Notes Payable	8,833	
	Cash		12,979
	To record second installment payment.		

Foghog records similar entries but with different amounts for each of the remaining four payments. After six years, the Notes Payable account balance is zero.[2]

Mortgage Notes and Bonds

A **mortgage** is a legal agreement that helps protect a lender if a borrower fails to make required payments on notes or bonds. A mortgage gives the lender a right to be paid from the cash proceeds of the sale of a borrower's assets identified in the mortgage. A legal document, called a *mortgage contract,* describes the mortgage terms.

Mortgage notes carry a mortgage contract pledging title to specific assets as security for the note. Mortgage notes are especially popular in the purchase of homes and the acquisition of plant assets. Less common *mortgage bonds* are backed by the issuer's assets. Accounting for mortgage notes and bonds is similar to that for unsecured notes and bonds, except that the mortgage agreement must be disclosed. For example, **Musicland** reports that its "mortgage note payable is collateralized by land, buildings and certain fixtures."

Global: Countries vary in the preference given to debtholders vs. stockholders when a company is in financial distress. Some countries such as Germany, France, and Japan give preference to stockholders over debtholders.

Decision Maker

Entrepreneur You are an electronics retailer planning a holiday sale on a custom stereo system that requires no payments for two years. At the end of two years, buyers must pay the full amount. The system's suggested retail price is $4,100, but you are willing to sell it today for $3,000 cash. What is your holiday sale price if payment will not occur for two years and the market interest rate is 10%? [Answer—p. 576]

Quick Check

Answers—p. 576

11. Which of the following is true for an installment note requiring a series of equal total cash payments? (*a*) Payments consist of increasing interest and decreasing principal; (*b*) payments consist of changing amounts of principal but constant interest; or (*c*) payments consist of decreasing interest and increasing principal.
12. How is the interest portion of an installment note payment computed?
13. When a borrower records an interest payment on an installment note, how are the balance sheet and income statement affected?

[2] Table B.3 in Appendix B is used to compute the dollar amount of the six payments that equal the initial note balance of $60,000 at 8% interest. We go to Table B.3, row 6, and across to the 8% column, where the present value factor is 4.6229. The dollar amount is then computed by solving this relation:

Table	Present Value Factor		Dollar Amount		Present Value
B.3	4.6229	×	?	=	$60,000

The dollar amount is computed by dividing $60,000 by 4.6229, yielding $12,979.

Example: Suppose the $60,000 installment loan has an 8% interest rate with eight equal annual payments. What is the annual payment? *Answer* (using Table B.3): $60,000/5.7466 = $10,441

Debt Features and the Debt-to-Equity Ratio

Decision Analysis

Collateral agreements can reduce the risk of loss for both bonds and notes. Unsecured bonds and notes are riskier because the issuer's obligation to pay interest and principal has the same priority as all other unsecured liabilities in the event of bankruptcy. If a company is unable to pay its debts in full, the unsecured creditors (including the holders of debentures) lose all or a portion of their balances. These types of legal agreements and other characteristics of long-term liabilities are crucial for effective business decisions. The first part of this section describes the different types of features sometimes included with bonds and notes. The second part explains and applies the debt-to-equity ratio.

Features of Bonds and Notes

A2 Assess debt features and their implications.

This section describes common features of debt securities.

Secured or Unsecured **Secured bonds** (and notes) have specific assets of the issuer pledged (or *mortgaged*) as collateral. This arrangement gives holders added protection against the issuer's default. If the issuer fails to pay interest or par value, the secured holders can demand that the collateral be sold and the proceeds used to pay the obligation. **Unsecured bonds** (and notes), also called *debentures,* are backed by the issuer's general credit standing. Unsecured debt is riskier than secured debt. *Subordinated debentures* are liabilities that are not repaid until the claims of the more senior, unsecured (and secured) liabilities are settled.

Secured Debt

Unsecured Debt

Term or Serial **Term bonds** (and notes) are scheduled for maturity on one specified date. **Serial bonds** (and notes) mature at more than one date (often in series) and thus are usually repaid over a number of periods. For instance, $100,000 of serial bonds might mature at the rate of $10,000 each year from 6 to 15 years after they are issued. Many bonds are **sinking fund bonds,** which to reduce the holder's risk require the issuer to create a *sinking fund* of assets set aside at specified amounts and dates to repay the bonds.

Registered or Bearer Bonds issued in the names and addresses of their holders are **registered bonds.** The issuer makes bond payments by sending checks (or cash transfers) to registered holders. A registered holder must notify the issuer of any ownership change. Registered bonds offer the issuer the practical advantage of not having to actually issue bond certificates. Bonds payable to whoever holds them (the *bearer*) are called **bearer bonds** or *unregistered bonds.* Sales or exchanges might not be recorded, so the holder of a bearer bond is presumed to be its rightful owner. As a result, lost bearer bonds are difficult to replace. Many bearer bonds are also **coupon bonds.** This term reflects interest coupons that are attached to the bonds. When each coupon matures, the holder presents it to a bank or broker for collection. At maturity, the holder follows the same process and presents the bond certificate for collection. Issuers of coupon bonds cannot deduct the related interest expense for taxable income. This is to prevent abuse by taxpayers who own coupon bonds but fail to report interest income on their tax returns.

Convertible and/or Callable **Convertible bonds** (and notes) can be exchanged for a fixed number of shares of the issuing corporation's common stock. Convertible debt offers holders the potential to participate in future increases in stock price. Holders still receive periodic interest while the debt is held and the par value if they hold the debt to maturity. In most cases, the holders decide whether and when to convert debt to stock. **Callable bonds** (and notes) have an option exercisable by the issuer to retire them at a stated dollar amount before maturity.

Convertible Debt

Callable Debt

Decision Insight

Munis More than a million municipal bonds, or "munis," exist, and many are tax exempt. Munis are issued by state, city, town, and county governments to pay for public projects including schools, libraries, roads, bridges, and stadiums.

Debt-to-Equity Ratio

A3 Compute the debt-to-equity ratio and explain its use.

Beyond assessing different characteristics of debt as just described, we want to know the level of debt, especially in relation to total equity. Such knowledge helps us assess the risk of a company's financing structure. A company financed mainly with debt is more risky because liabilities must be repaid—usually with periodic interest—whereas equity financing does not. A measure to assess the risk of a company's financing structure is the **debt-to-equity ratio** (see Exhibit 14.15).

EXHIBIT 14.15

Debt-to-Equity Ratio

$$\textbf{Debt-to-equity} = \frac{\textbf{Total liabilities}}{\textbf{Total equity}}$$

The debt-to-equity ratio varies across companies and industries. Industries that are more variable tend to have lower ratios, while more stable industries are less risky and tend to have higher ratios. To apply the debt-to-equity ratio, let's look at this measure for **Six Flags** in Exhibit 14.16.

EXHIBIT 14.16

Six Flags' Debt-to-Equity Ratio

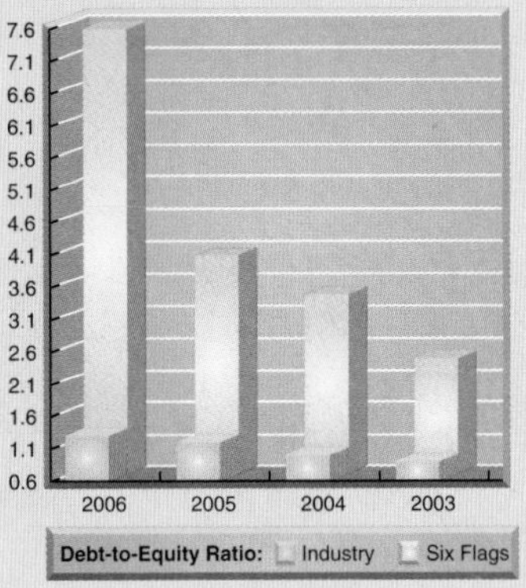

($ millions)	2006	2005	2004	2003
Total liabilities	$2,811	$2,799	$2,816	$3,321
Total equity	$ 376	$ 694	$ 826	$1,362
Debt-to-equity	**7.5**	**4.0**	**3.4**	**2.4**
Industry debt-to-equity	1.2	1.1	0.9	0.8

Six Flags' 2006 debt-to-equity ratio was 7.5, meaning that debtholders contributed $7.5 for each $1 contributed by equityholders. This implies a fairly risky financing structure for Six Flags. A similar concern is drawn from a comparison of Six Flags with its competitors, where the 2006 industry ratio was 1.2. Analysis across the years shows that Six Flags' financing structure has grown increasingly risky in recent years. Given its sluggish revenues and increasing operating expenses in recent years (see its annual report), Six Flags is increasingly at risk of financial distress.

Decision Maker

Bond Investor You plan to purchase debenture bonds from one of two companies in the same industry that are similar in size and performance. The first company has $350,000 in total liabilities, and $1,750,000 in equity. The second company has $1,200,000 in total liabilities, and $1,000,000 in equity. Which company's debenture bonds are less risky based on the debt-to-equity ratio? [Answer—p. 576]

Demonstration Problem

DP14

Water Sports Company (WSC) patented and successfully test-marketed a new product. To expand its ability to produce and market the new product, WSC needs to raise $800,000 of financing. On January 1, 2009, the company obtained the money in two ways:

a. WSC signed a $400,000, 10% installment note to be repaid with five equal annual installments to be made on December 31 of 2009 through 2013.

b. WSC issued five-year bonds with a par value of $400,000. The bonds have a 12% annual contract rate and pay interest on June 30 and December 31. The bonds' annual market rate is 10% as of January 1, 2009.

Required

1. For the installment note, (*a*) compute the size of each annual payment, (*b*) prepare an amortization table such as Exhibit 14.14, and (*c*) prepare the journal entry for the first payment.

2. For the bonds, (*a*) compute their issue price; (*b*) prepare the January 1, 2009, journal entry to record their issuance; (*c*) prepare an amortization table using the straight-line method; (*d*) prepare the June 30, 2009, journal entry to record the first interest payment; and (*e*) prepare a journal entry to record retiring the bonds at a $416,000 call price on January 1, 2011.

3.[B] Redo parts 2(*c*), 2(*d*), and 2(*e*) assuming the bonds are amortized using the effective interest method.

Planning the Solution

- For the installment note, divide the borrowed amount by the annuity factor (from Table B.3) using the 10% rate and five payments to compute the amount of each payment. Prepare a table similar to Exhibit 14.14 and use the numbers in the table's first line for the journal entry.
- Compute the bonds' issue price by using the market rate to find the present value of their cash flows (use tables found in Appendix B). Then use this result to record the bonds' issuance. Next, prepare an amortization table like Exhibit 14.11 (and Exhibit 14B.2) and use it to get the numbers needed for the journal entry. Also use the table to find the carrying value as of the date of the bonds' retirement that you need for the journal entry.

Solution to Demonstration Problem

Part 1: Installment Note

a. Annual payment = Note balance/Annuity factor = $400,000/3.7908 = $105,519 (The annuity factor is for five payments and a rate of 10%.)

b. An amortization table follows.

Annual Period Ending	(a) Beginning Balance	(b) Debit Interest Expense	+	(c) Debit Notes Payable	=	(d) Credit Cash	(e) Ending Balance
(1) 12/31/2009	$400,000	$ 40,000		$ 65,519		$105,519	$334,481
(2) 12/31/2010	334,481	33,448		72,071		105,519	262,410
(3) 12/31/2011	262,410	26,241		79,278		105,519	183,132
(4) 12/31/2012	183,132	18,313		87,206		105,519	95,926
(5) 12/31/2013	95,926	9,593		95,926		105,519	0
		$127,595		$400,000		$527,595	

(Columns (b), (c) and (d) are grouped under "Payments".)

c. Journal entry for December 31, 2009, payment.

Dec. 31	Interest Expense	40,000	
	Notes Payable	65,519	
	Cash		105,519
	To record first installment payment.		

Part 2: Bonds (Straight-Line Amortization)

a. Compute the bonds' issue price.

Cash Flow	Table	Present Value Factor*	Amount	Present Value
Par (maturity) value	B.1 in App. B (PV of 1)	0.6139	× 400,000	= $245,560
Interest payments	B.3 in App. B (PV of annuity)	7.7217	× 24,000	= 185,321
Price of bond				$430,881

* Present value factors are for 10 payments using a semiannual market rate of 5%.

b. Journal entry for January 1, 2009, issuance.

Jan. 1	Cash	430,881	
	Premium on Bonds Payable		30,881
	Bonds Payable		400,000
	Sold bonds at a premium.		

c. Straight-line amortization table for premium bonds.

Semiannual Period-End	Unamortized Premium	Carrying Value
(0) 1/1/2009	$30,881	$430,881
(1) 6/30/2009	27,793	427,793
(2) 12/31/2009	24,705	424,705
(3) 6/30/2010	21,617	421,617
(4) 12/31/2010	18,529	418,529
(5) 6/30/2011	15,441	415,441
(6) 12/31/2011	12,353	412,353
(7) 6/30/2012	9,265	409,265
(8) 12/31/2012	6,177	406,177
(9) 6/30/2013	3,089	403,089
(10) 12/31/2013	0*	400,000

* Adjusted for rounding.

d. Journal entry for June 30, 2009, bond payment.

June 30	Bond Interest Expense	20,912	
	Premium on Bonds Payable	3,088	
	Cash		24,000
	Paid semiannual interest on bonds.		

e. Journal entry for January 1, 2011, bond retirement.

Jan. 1	Bonds Payable	400,000	
	Premium on Bonds Payable	18,529	
	Cash		416,000
	Gain on Retirement of Bonds		2,529
	To record bond retirement (carrying value as of Dec. 31, 2010).		

Part 3: Bonds (Effective Interest Amortization)[B]

c. The effective interest amortization table for premium bonds.

Semiannual Interest Period	(A) Cash Interest Paid 6% × $400,000	(B) Interest Expense 5% × Prior (E)	(C) Premium Amortization (A) − (B)	(D) Unamortized Premium Prior (D) − (C)	(E) Carrying Value $400,000 + (D)
(0) 1/1/2009				$30,881	$430,881
(1) 6/30/2009	$ 24,000	$ 21,544	$ 2,456	28,425	428,425
(2) 12/31/2009	24,000	21,421	2,579	25,846	425,846
(3) 6/30/2010	24,000	21,292	2,708	23,138	423,138
(4) 12/31/2010	24,000	21,157	2,843	20,295	420,295
(5) 6/30/2011	24,000	21,015	2,985	17,310	417,310
(6) 12/31/2011	24,000	20,866	3,134	14,176	414,176
(7) 6/30/2012	24,000	20,709	3,291	10,885	410,885
(8) 12/31/2012	24,000	20,544	3,456	7,429	407,429
(9) 6/30/2013	24,000	20,371	3,629	3,800	403,800
(10) 12/31/2013	24,000	20,200*	3,800	0	400,000
	$240,000	$209,119	$30,881		

* Adjusted for rounding

d. Journal entry for June 30, 2009, bond payment.

June 30	Bond Interest Expense	21,544	
	Premium on Bonds Payable	2,456	
	Cash		24,000
	Paid semiannual interest on bonds.		

e. Journal entry for January 1, 2011, bond retirement.

Jan. 1	Bonds Payable	400,000	
	Premium on Bonds Payable	20,295	
	Cash		416,000
	Gain on Retirement of Bonds		4,295
	To record bond retirement (carrying value as of December 31, 2010).		

APPENDIX

Present Values of Bonds and Notes

14A

This appendix explains how to apply present value techniques to measure a long-term liability when it is created and to assign interest expense to the periods until it is settled. Appendix B at the end of the book provides additional discussion of present value concepts.

Present Value Concepts

C2 Explain and compute the present value of an amount(s) to be paid at a future date(s).

The basic present value concept is that cash paid (or received) in the future has less value now than the same amount of cash paid (or received) today. To illustrate, if we must pay $1 one year from now, its present value is less than $1. To see this, assume that we borrow $0.9259 today that must be paid back in one year with 8% interest. Our interest expense for this loan is computed as $0.9259 × 8%, or $0.0741. When the $0.0741 interest is added to the $0.9259 borrowed, we get the $1 payment necessary to repay our loan with interest. This is formally computed in Exhibit 14A.1. The $0.9259 borrowed is the present value of the $1 future payment. More generally, an amount borrowed equals the present value of the future payment. (This same interpretation applies to an investment. If $0.9259 is invested at 8%, it yields $0.0741 in revenue after one year. This amounts to $1, made up of principal and interest.)

EXHIBIT 14A.1

Components of a One-Year Loan

Amount borrowed	**$0.9259**
Interest for one year at 8%	0.0741
Amount owed after 1 year	$ 1.0000

To extend this example, assume that we owe $1 two years from now instead of one year, and the 8% interest is compounded annually. *Compounded* means that interest during the second period is based on the total of the amount borrowed plus the interest accrued from the first period. The second period's interest is then computed as 8% multiplied by the sum of the amount borrowed plus interest earned in the first period. Exhibit 14A.2 shows how we compute the present value of $1 to be paid in two years. This amount is $0.8573. The first year's interest of $0.0686 is added to the principal so that the second year's interest is based on $0.9259. Total interest for this two-year period is $0.1427, computed as $0.0686 plus $0.0741.

Point: Benjamin Franklin is said to have described compounding as "the money, money makes, makes more money."

EXHIBIT 14A.2

Components of a Two-Year Loan

Amount borrowed	**$0.8573**
Interest for first year ($0.8573 × 8%)	0.0686
Amount owed after 1 year	0.9259
Interest for second year ($0.9259 × 8%)	0.0741
Amount owed after 2 years	$ 1.0000

Present Value Tables

The present value of $1 that we must repay at some future date can be computed by using this formula: $1/(1 + i)^n$. The symbol i is the interest rate per period and n is the number of periods until the future payment must be made. Applying this formula to our two-year loan, we get $\$1/(1.08)^2$, or $0.8573. This is the same value shown in Exhibit 14A.2. We can use this formula to find any present value. However, a simpler method is to use a *present value table,* which lists present values computed with this formula for various interest rates and time periods. Many people find it helpful in learning present value concepts to first work with the table and then move to using a calculator.

EXHIBIT 14A.3

Present Value of 1

	Rate		
Periods	6%	8%	10%
1	0.9434	**0.9259**	0.9091
2	0.8900	**0.8573**	0.8264
3	0.8396	0.7938	0.7513
4	0.7921	0.7350	0.6830
5	0.7473	0.6806	0.6209
6	0.7050	0.6302	0.5645
7	0.6651	0.5835	0.5132
8	0.6274	0.5403	0.4665
9	0.5919	0.5002	0.4241
10	0.5584	0.4632	0.3855

Exhibit 14A.3 shows a present value table for a future payment of 1 for up to 10 periods at three different interest rates. Present values in this table are rounded to four decimal places. This table is drawn from the larger and more complete Table B.1 in Appendix B at the end of the book. Notice that the first value in the 8% column is 0.9259, the value we computed earlier for the present value of a $1 loan for one year at 8% (see Exhibit 14A.1). Go to the second row in the same 8% column and find the present value of 1 discounted at 8% for two years, or 0.8573. This $0.8573 is the present value of our obligation to repay $1 after two periods at 8% interest (see Exhibit 14A.2).

Example: Use Exhibit 14A.3 to find the present value of $1 discounted for 2 years at 6%. *Answer:* $0.8900

Applying a Present Value Table

To illustrate how to measure a liability using a present value table, assume that a company plans to borrow cash and repay it as follows: $2,000 after one year, $3,000 after two years, and $5,000 after three years. How much does this company receive today if the interest rate on this loan is 10%? To answer, we need to compute the present value of the three future payments, discounted at 10%. This computation is shown in Exhibit 14A.4 using present values from Exhibit 14A.3. The company can borrow $8,054 today at 10% interest in exchange for its promise to make these three payments at the scheduled dates.

EXHIBIT 14A.4

Present Value of a Series of Unequal Payments

Periods	Payments	Present Value of 1 at 10%	Present Value of Payments
1	$2,000	0.9091	$ 1,818
2	3,000	0.8264	2,479
3	5,000	0.7513	3,757
Present value of all payments			**$8,054**

Present Value of an Annuity

The $8,054 present value for the loan in Exhibit 14A.4 equals the sum of the present values of the three payments. When payments are not equal, their combined present value is best computed by adding the individual present values as shown in Exhibit 14A.4. Sometimes payments follow an **annuity,** which is a series of *equal* payments at equal time intervals. The present value of an annuity is readily computed.

To illustrate, assume that a company must repay a 6% loan with a $5,000 payment at each year-end for the next four years. This loan amount equals the present value of the four payments discounted at 6%. Exhibit 14A.5 shows how to compute this loan's present value of $17,326 by multiplying each payment by its matching present value factor taken from Exhibit 14A.3.

EXHIBIT 14A.5

Present Value of a Series of Equal Payments (Annuity) by Discounting Each Payment

Periods	Payments	Present Value of 1 at 6%	Present Value of Payments
1	$5,000	0.9434	$ 4,717
2	5,000	0.8900	4,450
3	5,000	0.8396	4,198
4	5,000	0.7921	3,961
Present value of all payments		**3.4651**	**$17,326**

However, the series of $5,000 payments is an annuity, so we can compute its present value with either of two shortcuts. First, the third column of Exhibit 14A.5 shows that the sum of the present values of 1 at 6% for periods 1 through 4 equals 3.4651. One shortcut is to multiply this total of 3.4651 by the $5,000 annual payment to get the combined present value of $17,326. It requires one multiplication instead of four.

The second shortcut uses an *annuity table* such as the one shown in Exhibit 14A.6, which is drawn from the more complete Table B.3 in Appendix B. We go directly to the annuity table to get the present value factor for a specific number of payments and interest rate. We then multiply this factor by the amount of the payment to find the present value of the annuity. Specifically, find the row for four periods and go across to the 6% column, where the factor is 3.4651. This factor equals the present value of an annuity with four payments of 1, discounted at 6%. We then multiply 3.4651 by $5,000 to get the $17,326 present value of the annuity.

EXHIBIT 14A.6

Present Value of an Annuity of 1

	Rate		
Periods	**6%**	**8%**	**10%**
1	0.9434	0.9259	0.9091
2	1.8334	1.7833	1.7355
3	2.6730	2.5771	2.4869
4	**3.4651**	3.3121	3.1699
5	4.2124	3.9927	3.7908
6	4.9173	4.6229	4.3553
7	5.5824	5.2064	4.8684
8	6.2098	5.7466	5.3349
9	6.8017	6.2469	5.7590
10	7.3601	6.7101	6.1446

Example: Use Exhibit 14A.6 to find the present value of an annuity of eight $15,000 payments with an 8% interest rate. *Answer:* $15,000 × 5.7466 = $86,199

Compounding Periods Shorter Than a Year

The present value examples all involved periods of one year. In many situations, however, interest is compounded over shorter periods. For example, the interest rate on bonds is usually stated as an annual rate but interest is often paid every six months (semiannually). This means that the present value of interest payments from such bonds must be computed using interest periods of six months.

Assume that a borrower wants to know the present value of a series of 10 *semiannual payments* of $4,000 made over five years at an *annual interest rate* of 12%. The interest rate is stated as an annual rate of 12%, but it is actually a rate of 6% per semiannual interest period. To compute the present value of this series of $4,000 payments, go to row 10 of Exhibit 14A.6 and across to the 6% column to find the factor 7.3601. The present value of this annuity is $29,440 (7.3601 × $4,000).

Appendix B further describes present value concepts and includes more complete present value tables and assignments.

Example: If this borrower makes five semiannual payments of $8,000, what is the present value of this annuity at a 12% rate? *Answer:* 4.2124 × $8,000 = $33,699

Quick Check

Answers—p. 576

14. A company enters into an agreement to make four annual year-end payments of $1,000 each, starting one year from now. The annual interest rate is 8%. The present value of these four payments is (*a*) $2,923, (*b*) $2,940, or (*c*) $3,312.

15. Suppose a company has an option to pay either (*a*) $10,000 after one year or (*b*) $5,000 after six months and another $5,000 after one year. Which choice has the lower present value?

APPENDIX

Effective Interest Amortization 14B

Effective Interest Amortization of a Discount Bond

The straight-line method yields changes in the bonds' carrying value while the amount for bond interest expense remains constant. This gives the impression of a changing interest rate when users divide a constant bond interest expense over a changing carrying value. As a result, accounting standards allow use of the straight-line method only when its results do not differ materially from those obtained using the effective interest method. The **effective interest method,** or simply *interest method,* allocates total bond interest expense over the bonds' life in a way that yields a constant rate of interest. This constant rate of interest is the market rate at the issue date. Thus, bond interest expense for a period equals the carrying value of the bond at the beginning of that period multiplied by the market rate when issued.

Point: The effective interest method computes bond interest expense using the market rate at issuance. This rate is applied to a changing carrying value.

Exhibit 14B.1 shows an effective interest amortization table for the Fila bonds (as described in Exhibit 14.4). The key difference between the effective interest and straight-line methods lies in computing bond interest expense. Instead of assigning an equal amount of bond interest expense to each period, the effective interest method assigns a bond interest expense amount that increases over the life of a discount bond. **Both methods allocate the *same* $19,546 of total bond interest expense to the bonds' life, but in different patterns.** Specifically, the amortization table in Exhibit 14B.1 shows that the balance of the discount (column D) is amortized until it reaches zero. Also, the bonds' carrying value (column E) changes each period until it equals par value at maturity. Compare columns D and E to the corresponding columns in Exhibit 14.7 to see the amortization patterns. Total bond interest expense is $19,546, consisting of $16,000 of semiannual cash payments and $3,546 of the original bond discount, the same for both methods.

EXHIBIT 14B.1

Effective Interest Amortization of Bond Discount

Bonds: $100,000 Par Value, Semiannual Interest Payments, Two-Year Life, 4% Semiannual Contract Rate, 5% Semiannual Market Rate

Semiannual Interest Period-End	(A) Cash Interest Paid	(B) Bond Interest Expense	(C) Discount Amortization	(D) Unamortized Discount	(E) Carrying Value
(0) 12/31/2009				$3,546	$ 96,454
(1) 6/30/2010	$4,000	$4,823	$ 823	2,723	97,277
(2) 12/31/2010	4,000	4,864	864	1,859	98,141
(3) 6/30/2011	4,000	4,907	907	952	99,048
(4) 12/31/2011	4,000	4,952	952	0	100,000
	$16,000	$19,546	$3,546		

Column (**A**) is the par value ($100,000) multiplied by the semiannual contract rate (4%).
Column (**B**) is the prior period's carrying value multiplied by the semiannual market rate (5%).
Column (**C**) is the difference between interest paid and bond interest expense, or [(B) − (A)].
Column (**D**) is the prior period's unamortized discount less the current period's discount amortization.
Column (**E**) is the par value less unamortized discount, or [$100,000 − (D)].

Except for differences in amounts, journal entries recording the expense and updating the liability balance are the same under the effective interest method and the straight-line method. We can use the numbers in Exhibit 14B.1 to record each semiannual entry during the bonds' two-year life (June 30, 2010, through December 31, 2011). For instance, we record the interest payment at the end of the first semiannual period as follows:

Assets	=	Liabilities	+	Equity
−4,000		+823		−4,823

2010			
June 30	Bond Interest Expense	4,823	
	Discount on Bonds Payable		823
	Cash		4,000
	To record semiannual interest and discount amortization (effective interest method).		

Effective Interest Amortization of a Premium Bond

Exhibit 14B.2 shows the amortization table using the effective interest method for the Adidas bonds (as described in Exhibit 14.8). Column A lists the semiannual cash payments. Column B shows the amount of bond interest expense, computed as the 5% semiannual market rate at issuance multiplied by the beginning-of-period carrying value. The amount of cash paid in column A is larger than the bond interest expense because the cash payment is based on the higher 6% semiannual contract rate. The excess cash payment over the interest expense reduces the principal. These amounts are shown in column C. Column E

EXHIBIT 14B.2

Effective Interest Amortization of Bond Premium

Bonds: $100,000 Par Value, Semiannual Interest Payments, Two-Year Life, 6% Semiannual Contract Rate, 5% Semiannual Market Rate					
	(A)	(B)	(C)	(D)	(E)
Semiannual Interest Period-End	Cash Interest Paid	Bond Interest Expense	Premium Amortization	Unamortized Premium	Carrying Value
(0) 12/31/2009				$3,546	$103,546
(1) 6/30/2010	$6,000	$5,177	$ 823	2,723	102,723
(2) 12/31/2010	6,000	5,136	864	1,859	101,859
(3) 6/30/2011	6,000	5,093	907	952	100,952
(4) 12/31/2011	6,000	5,048	952	0	100,000
	$24,000	$20,454	$3,546		

Column (**A**) is the par value ($100,000) multiplied by the semiannual contract rate (6%).
Column (**B**) is the prior period's carrying value multiplied by the semiannual market rate (5%).
Column (**C**) is the difference between interest paid and bond interest expense, or [(A) − (B)].
Column (**D**) is the prior period's unamortized premium less the current period's premium amortization.
Column (**E**) is the par value plus unamortized premium, or [$100,000 + (D)].

shows the carrying value after deducting the amortized premium in column C from the prior period's carrying value. Column D shows the premium's reduction by periodic amortization. When the issuer makes the first semiannual interest payment, the effect of premium amortization on bond interest expense and bond liability is recorded as follows:

2010			
June 30	Bond Interest Expense	5,177	
	Premium on Bonds Payable	823	
	Cash		6,000
	To record semiannual interest and premium amortization (effective interest method).		

Assets	=	Liabilities	+	Equity
−6,000		−823		−5,177

Similar entries with different amounts are recorded at each payment date until the bond matures at the end of 2011. The effective interest method yields decreasing amounts of bond interest expense and increasing amounts of premium amortization over the bonds' life.

Decision Insight

IFRSs Unlike U.S. GAAP, IFRSs require that interest expense be computed using the effective interest method with *no exemptions.*

APPENDIX

Issuing Bonds between Interest Dates

14C

C3 Describe the accrual of bond interest when bond payments do not align with accounting periods.

An issuer can sell bonds at a date other than an interest payment date. When this occurs, the buyers normally pay the issuer the purchase price plus any interest accrued since the prior interest payment date. This accrued interest is then repaid to these buyers on the next interest payment date. To illustrate, suppose **Avia** sells $100,000 of its 9% bonds at par on March 1, 2009, 60 days after the stated issue date. The interest on Avia bonds is payable semiannually on each June 30 and December 31. Since 60 days have passed, the issuer collects accrued interest from the buyers at the time of issuance. This amount is \$1,500 (\$100,000 × 9% × 60/360 year). This case is reflected in Exhibit 14C.1.

EXHIBIT 14C.1

Accruing Interest between Interest Payment Dates

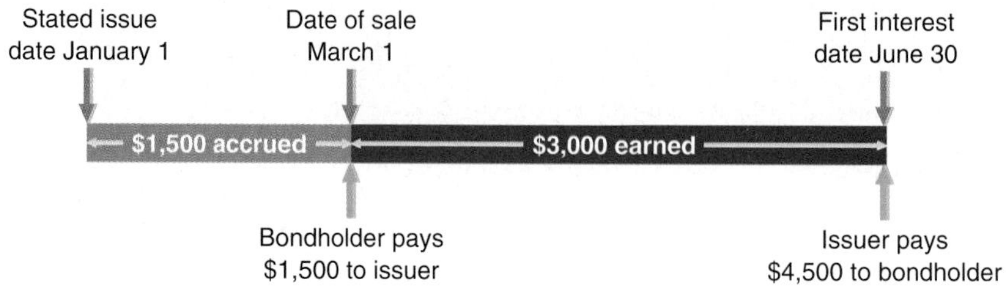

Avia records the issuance of these bonds on March 1, 2009, as follows:

Assets	=	Liabilities	+	Equity
+101,500		+100,000		
		+1,500		

Mar. 1	Cash	101,500	
	Interest Payable		1,500
	Bonds Payable		100,000
	Sold bonds at par with accrued interest.		

Example: How much interest is collected from a buyer of \$50,000 of Avia bonds sold at par 150 days after the contract issue date? *Answer:* \$1,875 (computed as \$50,000 × 9% × 150/360 year)

Liabilities for interest payable and bonds payable are recorded in separate accounts. When the June 30, 2009, semiannual interest date arrives, Avia pays the full semiannual interest of \$4,500 (\$100,000 × 9% × ½ year) to the bondholders. This payment includes the four months' interest of \$3,000 earned by the bondholders from March 1 to June 30 *plus* the repayment of the 60 days' accrued interest collected by Avia when the bonds were sold. Avia records this first semiannual interest payment as follows:

Assets	=	Liabilities	+	Equity
−4,500		−1,500		−3,000

June 30	Interest Payable	1,500	
	Bond Interest Expense	3,000	
	Cash		4,500
	Paid semiannual interest on the bonds.		

The practice of collecting and then repaying accrued interest with the next interest payment is to simplify the issuer's administrative efforts. To explain, suppose an issuer sells bonds on 15 or 20 different dates between the stated issue date and the first interest payment date. If the issuer does not collect accrued interest from buyers, it needs to pay different amounts of cash to each of them according to the time that passed after purchasing the bonds. The issuer needs to keep detailed records of buyers and the dates they bought bonds. Issuers avoid this recordkeeping by having each buyer pay accrued interest at purchase. Issuers then pay the full semiannual interest to all buyers, regardless of when they bought bonds.

Accruing Bond Interest Expense

If a bond's interest period does not coincide with the issuer's accounting period, an adjusting entry is needed to recognize bond interest expense accrued since the most recent interest payment. To illustrate, assume that the stated issue date for Adidas bonds described in Exhibit 14.10 is September 1, 2009, instead of December 31, 2009, and that the bonds are sold on September 1, 2009. As a result, four months' interest (and premium amortization) accrue before the end of the 2009 calendar year. Interest for this period equals \$3,409, or 4/6 of the first six months' interest of \$5,113. Also, the premium amortization is \$591, or 4/6 of the first six months' amortization of \$887. The sum of the bond interest expense and the amortization is \$4,000 (\$3,409 + \$591), which equals 4/6 of the \$6,000 cash payment due on February 28, 2010. Adidas records these effects with an adjusting entry at December 31, 2009.

Point: Computation of accrued bond interest may use months instead of days for simplicity purposes. For example, the accrued interest computation for the Adidas bonds is based on months.

Assets	=	Liabilities	+	Equity
		−591		−3,409
		+4,000		

Dec. 31	Bond Interest Expense	3,409	
	Premium on Bonds Payable	591	
	Interest Payable		4,000
	To record four months' accrued interest and premium amortization.		

Similar entries are made on each December 31 throughout the bonds' two-year life. When the \$6,000 cash payment occurs on each February 28 interest payment date, Adidas must recognize bond interest expense and amortization for January and February. It must also eliminate the interest payable liability created by the December 31 adjusting entry. For example, Adidas records its payment on February 28, 2010, as follows:

Feb. 28	Interest Payable	4,000	
	Bond Interest Expense ($5,113 × $\frac{2}{6}$)	1,705	
	Premium on Bonds Payable ($887 × $\frac{2}{6}$)	295*	
	Cash		6,000
	To record 2 months' interest and amortization, and eliminate accrued interest liability.		

Assets	=	Liabilities	+	Equity
−6,000		−4,000		−1,705
		−295		

*Adjusted for rounding.

The interest payments made each August 31 are recorded as usual because the entire six-month interest period is included within this company's calendar-year reporting period.

Decision Maker

Bond Rater You must assign a rating to a bond that reflects its risk to bondholders. Identify factors you consider in assessing bond risk. Indicate the likely levels (relative to the norm) for the factors you identify for a bond that sells at a discount. [Answer—p. 576]

Quick Check

Answer—p. 576

16. On May 1, a company sells 9% bonds with a $500,000 par value that pay semiannual interest on each January 1 and July 1. The bonds are sold at par plus interest accrued since January 1. The issuer records the first semiannual interest payment on July 1 with (*a*) a debit to Interest Payable for $15,000, (*b*) a debit to Bond Interest Expense for $22,500, or (*c*) a credit to Interest Payable for $7,500.

APPENDIX

Leases and Pensions

14D

This appendix briefly explains the accounting and analysis for both leases and pensions.

Lease Liabilities

A **lease** is a contractual agreement between a *lessor* (asset owner) and a *lessee* (asset renter or tenant) that grants the lessee the right to use the asset for a period of time in return for cash (rent) payments. Nearly one-fourth of all equipment purchases are financed with leases. The advantages of lease financing include the lack of an immediate large cash payment and the potential to deduct rental payments in computing taxable income. From an accounting perspective, leases can be classified as either operating or capital leases.

C4 Describe accounting for leases and pensions.

Operating Leases **Operating leases** are short-term (or cancelable) leases in which the lessor retains the risks and rewards of ownership. Examples include most car and apartment rental agreements. The lessee records such lease payments as expenses; the lessor records them as revenue. The lessee does not report the leased item as an asset or a liability (it is the lessor's asset). To illustrate, if an employee of Amazon leases a car for $300 at an airport while on company business, Amazon (lessee) records this cost as follows:

Point: Home Depot reports that its rental expenses from operating leases total more than $900 million.

July 4	Rental Expense	300	
	Cash		300
	To record lease rental payment.		

Assets	=	Liabilities	+	Equity
−300				−300

Capital Leases **Capital leases** are long-term (or noncancelable) leases by which the lessor transfers substantially all risks and rewards of ownership to the lessee.[3] Examples include most leases of airplanes and department store buildings. The lessee records the leased item as its own asset along with a lease liability at the start of the lease term; the amount recorded equals the present value of all lease payments. To illustrate, assume that K2 Co. enters into a six-year lease of a building in which it will sell sporting equipment. The lease transfers all building ownership risks and rewards to K2 (the present value of its $12,979 annual lease payments is $60,000). K2 records this transaction as follows:

Assets	= Liabilities	+ Equity
+60,000	+60,000	

2009			
Jan. 1	Leased Asset—Building	60,000	
	Lease Liability		60,000
	To record leased asset and lease liability.		

Point: Home Depot reports *"certain locations . . . are leased under capital leases."* The net present value of this Lease Liability is about $400 million.

K2 reports the leased asset as a plant asset and the lease liability as a long-term liability. The portion of the lease liability expected to be paid in the next year is reported as a current liability.[4] At each year-end, K2 records depreciation on the leased asset (assume straight-line depreciation, six-year lease term, and no salvage value) as follows:

Assets	= Liabilities	+ Equity
−10,000		−10,000

Dec. 31	Depreciation Expense—Building	10,000	
	Accumulated Depreciation—Building		10,000
	To record depreciation on leased asset.		

K2 also accrues interest on the lease liability at each year-end. Interest expense is computed by multiplying the remaining lease liability by the interest rate on the lease. Specifically, K2 records its annual interest expense as part of its annual lease payment ($12,979) as follows (for its first year):

Assets	= Liabilities	+ Equity
−12,979	−8,179	−4,800

2009			
Dec. 31	Interest Expense	4,800	
	Lease Liability	8,179	
	Cash		12,979
	*To record first annual lease payment.**		

* These numbers are computed from a *lease payment schedule.* For simplicity, we use the same numbers from Exhibit 14.14 for this lease payment schedule—with different headings as follows:

		Payments			
	(A)	(B) *Debit*	(C) *Debit*	(D) *Credit*	(E)
Period Ending Date	Beginning Balance of Lease Liability	Interest on Lease Liability 8% × (A)	+ Lease Liability (D) − (B)	= Cash Lease Payment	Ending Balance of Lease Liability (A) − (C)
12/31/2009	**$60,000**	**$ 4,800**	**$ 8,179**	**$12,979**	**$51,821**
12/31/2010	51,821	4,146	8,833	12,979	42,988
12/31/2011	42,988	3,439	9,540	12,979	33,448
12/31/2012	33,448	2,676	10,303	12,979	23,145
12/31/2013	23,145	1,852	11,127	12,979	12,018
12/31/2014	12,018	961	12,018	12,979	0
		$17,874	**$60,000**	**$77,874**	

[3] A *capital lease* meets any one or more of four criteria: (1) transfers title of leased asset to lessee, (2) contains a bargain purchase option, (3) has a lease term that is 75% or more of the leased asset's useful life, or (4) has a present value of lease payments that is 90% or more of the leased asset's market value.

[4] Most lessees try to keep leased assets and lease liabilities off their balance sheets by failing to meet any one of the four criteria of a capital lease. This is because a lease liability increases a company's total liabilities, making it more difficult to obtain additional financing. The acquisition of assets without reporting any related liabilities (or other asset outflows) on the balance sheet is called **off-balance-sheet financing.**

Pension Liabilities

A **pension plan** is a contractual agreement between an employer and its employees for the employer to provide benefits (payments) to employees after they retire. Most employers pay the full cost of the pension, but sometimes employees pay part of the cost. An employer records its payment into a pension plan with a debit to Pension Expense and a credit to Cash. A *plan administrator* receives payments from the employer, invests them in pension assets, and makes benefit payments to *pension recipients* (retired employees). Insurance and trust companies often serve as pension plan administrators.

Point: Fringe benefits are often 40% or more of salaries and wages, and pension benefits make up nearly 15% of fringe benefits.

Many pensions are known as *defined benefit plans* that define future benefits; the employer's contributions vary, depending on assumptions about future pension assets and liabilities. Several disclosures are necessary in this case. Specifically, a pension liability is reported when the accumulated benefit obligation is *more than* the plan assets, a so-called *underfunded plan.* The accumulated benefit obligation is the present value of promised future pension payments to retirees. *Plan assets* refer to the market value of assets the plan administrator holds. A pension asset is reported when the accumulated benefit obligation is *less than* the plan assets, a so-called *overfunded plan.* An employer reports pension expense when it receives the benefits from the employees' services, which is sometimes decades before it pays pension benefits to employees. (*Other Postretirement Benefits* refer to nonpension benefits such as health care and life insurance benefits. Similar to a pension, costs of these benefits are estimated and liabilities accrued when the employees earn them.)

Point: Two types of pension plans are (1) *defined benefit plan*—the retirement benefit is defined and the employer estimates the contribution necessary to pay these benefits—and (2) *defined contribution plan*—the pension contribution is defined and the employer and/or employee contributes amounts specified in the pension agreement.

Summary

C1 Explain the types and payment patterns of notes. Notes repaid over a period of time are called *installment notes* and usually follow one of two payment patterns: (1) decreasing payments of interest plus equal amounts of principal or (2) equal total payments. Mortgage notes also are common.

C2[A] Explain and compute the present value of an amount(s) to be paid at a future date(s). The basic concept of present value is that an amount of cash to be paid or received in the future is worth less than the same amount of cash to be paid or received today. Another important present value concept is that interest is compounded, meaning interest is added to the balance and used to determine interest for succeeding periods. An annuity is a series of equal payments occurring at equal time intervals. An annuity's present value can be computed using the present value table for an annuity (or a calculator).

C3[C] Describe the accrual of bond interest when bond payments do not align with accounting periods. Issuers and buyers of debt record the interest accrued when issue dates or accounting periods do not coincide with debt payment dates.

C4[D] Describe accounting for leases and pensions. A lease is a rental agreement between the lessor and the lessee. When the lessor retains the risks and rewards of asset ownership (an *operating lease*), the lessee debits Rent Expense and credits Cash for its lease payments. When the lessor substantially transfers the risks and rewards of asset ownership to the lessee (a *capital lease*), the lessee capitalizes the leased asset and records a lease liability. Pension agreements can result in either pension assets or pension liabilities.

A1 Compare bond financing with stock financing. Bond financing is used to fund business activities. Advantages of bond financing versus stock include (1) no effect on owner control, (2) tax savings, and (3) increased earnings due to financial leverage. Disadvantages include (1) interest and principal payments and (2) amplification of poor performance.

A2 Assess debt features and their implications. Certain bonds are secured by the issuer's assets; other bonds, called *debentures,* are unsecured. Serial bonds mature at different points in time; term bonds mature at one time. Registered bonds have each bondholder's name recorded by the issuer; bearer bonds are payable to the holder. Convertible bonds are exchangeable for shares of the issuer's stock. Callable bonds can be retired by the issuer at a set price. Debt features alter the risk of loss for creditors.

A3 Compute the debt-to-equity ratio and explain its use. Both creditors and equity holders are concerned about the relation between the amount of liabilities and the amount of equity. A company's financing structure is at less risk when the debt-to-equity ratio is lower, as liabilities must be paid and usually with periodic interest.

P1 Prepare entries to record bond issuance and bond interest expense. When bonds are issued at par, Cash is debited and Bonds Payable is credited for the bonds' par value. At bond interest payment dates (usually semiannual), Bond Interest Expense is debited and Cash credited—the latter for an amount equal to the bond par value multiplied by the bond contract rate.

P2 Compute and record amortization of bond discount. Bonds are issued at a discount when the contract rate is less than the market rate, making the issue (selling) price less than par. When this occurs, the issuer records a credit to Bonds Payable (at par) and debits both Discount on Bonds Payable and Cash. The amount of bond interest expense assigned to each period is computed using either the straight-line or effective interest method.

P3 Compute and record amortization of bond premium. Bonds are issued at a premium when the contract rate is higher than the market rate, making the issue (selling) price greater than par. When this occurs, the issuer records a debit to Cash and credits both Premium on Bonds Payable and Bonds Payable (at par). The amount of bond interest expense assigned to each period is computed using either the straight-line or effective interest method. The Premium on Bonds Payable is allocated to reduce bond interest expense over the life of the bonds.

P4 Record the retirement of bonds. Bonds are retired at maturity with a debit to Bonds Payable and a credit to Cash at par value. The issuer can retire the bonds early by exercising a call option or purchasing them in the market. Bondholders can also retire bonds early by exercising a conversion feature on convertible bonds. The issuer recognizes a gain or loss for the difference between the amount paid and the bond carrying value.

P5 **Prepare entries to account for notes.** Interest is allocated to each period in a note's life by multiplying its beginning-period carrying value by its market rate at issuance. If a note is repaid with equal payments, the payment amount is computed by dividing the borrowed amount by the present value of an annuity factor (taken from a present value table) using the market rate and the number of payments.

Guidance Answers to **Decision Maker**

Entrepreneur This is a "present value" question. The market interest rate (10%) and present value ($3,000) are known, but the payment required two years later is unknown. This amount ($3,630) can be computed as $3,000 × 1.10 × 1.10. Thus, the sale price is $3,630 when no payments are received for two years. The $3,630 received two years from today is equivalent to $3,000 cash today.

Bond Investor The debt-to-equity ratio for the first company is 0.2 ($350,000/$1,750,000) and for the second company is 1.2 ($1,200,000/$1,000,000), suggesting that the financing structure of the second company is more risky than that of the first company. Consequently, as a buyer of unsecured debenture bonds, you prefer the first company (all else equal).

Bond Rater Bonds with longer repayment periods (life) have higher risk. Also, bonds issued by companies in financial difficulties or facing higher than normal uncertainties have higher risk. Moreover, companies with higher than normal debt and large fluctuations in earnings are considered of higher risk. Discount bonds are more risky on one or more of these factors.

Guidance Answers to **Quick Checks**

1. (*b*)

2. Multiply the bond's par value by its contract rate of interest.

3. Bonds sell at a premium when the contract rate exceeds the market rate and the purchasers pay more than their par value.

4. The bonds are issued at a discount, meaning that issue price is less than par value. A discount occurs because the bond contract rate (6%) is less than the market rate (8%).

5.

Cash	91,893	
Discount on Bonds Payable	8,107	
Bonds Payable		100,000

6. $3,811 (total bond interest expense of $38,107 divided by 10 periods; or the $3,000 semiannual cash payment plus the $8,107 discount divided by 10 periods).

7. The bonds are issued at a premium, meaning issue price is higher than par value. A premium occurs because the bonds' contract rate (16%) is higher than the market rate (14%).

8. (*b*) For each semiannual period: $10,592/20 periods = $530 premium amortization.

9.

Bonds payable, 16%, due 12/31/2018	$100,000	
Plus premium on bonds payable	9,532*	$109,532

* Original premium balance of $10,592 less $530 and $530 amortized on 6/30/2009 and 12/31/2009, respectively.

10. $9,375 loss, computed as the difference between the repurchase price of $256,250 [50% of ($500,000 × 102.5%)] and the carrying value of $246,875 (50% of $493,750).

11. (*c*)

12. The interest portion of an installment payment equals the period's beginning loan balance multiplied by the market interest rate at the time of the note's issuance.

13. On the balance sheet, the account balances of the related liability (note payable) and asset (cash) accounts are decreased. On the income statement, interest expense is recorded.

14. (*c*), computed as 3.3121 × $1,000 = $3,312.

15. The option of paying $10,000 after one year has a lower present value. It postpones paying the first $5,000 by six months. More generally, the present value of a further delayed payment is always lower than a less delayed payment.

16. (*a*) Reflects payment of accrued interest recorded back on May 1; $500,000 × 9% × 4/12 = $15,000.

Key Terms

mhhe.com/wildFAP19e

Key Terms are available at the book's Website for learning and testing in an online Flashcard Format.

Pension plan (p. 575)
Premium on bonds (p. 556)
Registered bonds (p. 563)
Secured bonds (p. 563)
Serial bonds (p. 563)
Sinking fund bonds (p. 563)
Straight-line bond amortization (p. 554)
Term bonds (p. 563)
Unsecured bonds (p. 563)

Multiple Choice Quiz

Answers on p. 589

mhhe.com/wildFAP19e

Additional Quiz Questions are available at the book's Website.

Quiz14

1. A bond traded at 97½ means that
a. The bond pays 97½% interest.
b. The bond trades at $975 per $1,000 bond.
c. The market rate of interest is below the contract rate of interest for the bond.
d. The bonds can be retired at $975 each.
e. The bond's interest rate is 2½%.

2. A bondholder that owns a $1,000, 6%, 15-year bond has
a. The right to receive $1,000 at maturity.
b. Ownership rights in the bond issuing entity.
c. The right to receive $60 per month until maturity.
d. The right to receive $1,900 at maturity.
e. The right to receive $600 per year until maturity.

3. A company issues 8%, 20-year bonds with a par value of $500,000. The current market rate for the bonds is 8%. The amount of interest owed to the bondholders for each semiannual interest payment is
a. $40,000.
b. $0.
c. $20,000.
d. $800,000.
e. $400,000.

4. A company issued 5-year, 5% bonds with a par value of $100,000. The company received $95,735 for the bonds. Using the straight-line method, the company's interest expense for the first semiannual interest period is
a. $2,926.50.
b. $5,853.00.
c. $2,500.00.
d. $5,000.00.
e. $9,573.50.

5. A company issued 8-year, 5% bonds with a par value of $350,000. The company received proceeds of $373,745. Interest is payable semiannually. The amount of premium amortized for the first semiannual interest period, assuming straight-line bond amortization, is
a. $2,698.
b. $23,745.
c. $8,750.
d. $9,344.
e. $1,484.

Superscript letter ^{B} ($^{C, D}$) denotes assignments based on Appendix 14B (14C, 14D).

Discussion Questions

1. What is the main difference between a bond and a share of stock?

2. What is the main difference between notes payable and bonds payable?

3. What is the advantage of issuing bonds instead of obtaining financing from the company's owners?

4. What are the duties of a trustee for bondholders?

5. What is a bond indenture? What provisions are usually included in it?

6. What are the *contract* rate and the *market* rate for bonds?

7. What factors affect the market rates for bonds?

8.^{B} Does the straight-line or effective interest method produce an interest expense allocation that yields a constant rate of interest over a bond's life? Explain.

9.^{C} Why does a company that issues bonds between interest dates collect accrued interest from the bonds' purchasers?

10. If you know the par value of bonds, the contract rate, and the market rate, how do you compute the bonds' price?

11. What is the issue price of a $2,000 bond sold at 98¼? What is the issue price of a $6,000 bond sold at 101½?

12. Describe the debt-to-equity ratio and explain how creditors and owners would use this ratio to evaluate a company's risk.

13. What obligation does an entrepreneur (owner) have to investors that purchase bonds to finance the business?

14. Refer to **Best Buy**'s annual report in Appendix A. Is there any indication that Best Buy has issued bonds?

15. Refer to the statement of cash flows for **Circuit City** in Appendix A. For the year ended February 28, 2007, what was the amount of principal payments on long-term debt?

16. Did **RadioShack**'s long-term debt increase or decrease during 2006?

17. Refer to the annual report for **Apple** in Appendix A. For the year ended September 30, 2006, did it raise more cash by issuing stock or debt?

18.^{D} When can a lease create both an asset and a liability for the lessee?

19.^{D} Compare and contrast an operating lease with a capital lease.

20.^{D} Describe the two basic types of pension plans.

Denotes Discussion Questions that involve decision making.

QUICK STUDY

Round dollar amounts to the nearest whole dollar.

QS 14-1
Bond computations—straight-line P1 P2

Randell Company issues 7%, 10-year bonds with a par value of $150,000 and semiannual interest payments. On the issue date, the annual market rate for these bonds is 8%, which implies a selling price of 93¼. The straight-line method is used to allocate interest expense.

1. What are the issuer's cash proceeds from issuance of these bonds?
2. What total amount of bond interest expense will be recognized over the life of these bonds?
3. What is the amount of bond interest expense recorded on the first interest payment date?

QS 14-2^B
Bond computations—effective interest
P1 P3

Elton Company issues 7%, 15-year bonds with a par value of $350,000 and semiannual interest payments. On the issue date, the annual market rate for these bonds is 6%, which implies a selling price of 109¾. The effective interest method is used to allocate interest expense.

1. What are the issuer's cash proceeds from issuance of these bonds?
2. What total amount of bond interest expense will be recognized over the life of these bonds?
3. What amount of bond interest expense is recorded on the first interest payment date?

QS 14-3
Journalize bond issuance P1

Prepare the journal entries for the issuance of the bonds in both QS 14-1 and QS 14-2. Assume that both bonds are issued for cash on January 1, 2009.

QS 14-4
Computing bond price P2 P3

Using the bond details in both QS 14-1 and QS 14-2, confirm that the bonds' selling prices given in each problem are approximately correct. Use the present value tables B.1 and B.3 in Appendix B.

QS 14-5
Recording bond issuance and discount amortization P1 P2

Boulware Company issues 8%, five-year bonds, on December 31, 2008, with a par value of $100,000 and semiannual interest payments. Use the following straight-line bond amortization table and prepare journal entries to record (*a*) the issuance of bonds on December 31, 2008; (*b*) the first interest payment on June 30, 2009; and (*c*) the second interest payment on December 31, 2009.

Semiannual Period-End	Unamortized Discount	Carrying Value
(0) 12/31/2008	$7,723	$92,277
(1) 6/30/2009	6,951	93,049
(2) 12/31/2009	6,179	93,821

QS 14-6
Bond retirement by call option
P4

On July 1, 2009, Teller Company exercises a $4,000 call option (plus par value) on its outstanding bonds that have a carrying value of $208,000 and par value of $200,000. The company exercises the call option after the semiannual interest is paid on June 30, 2009. Record the entry to retire the bonds.

QS 14-7
Bond retirement by stock conversion P4

On January 1, 2009, the $1,000,000 par value bonds of Staten Company with a carrying value of $1,000,000 are converted to 500,000 shares of $1.00 par value common stock. Record the entry for the conversion of the bonds.

QS 14-8
Computing payments for an installment note C1

Jordyn Company borrows $600,000 cash from a bank and in return signs an installment note for five annual payments of equal amount, with the first payment due one year after the note is signed. Use Table B.3 in Appendix B to compute the amount of the annual payment for each of the following annual market rates: (*a*) 4%, (*b*) 6%, and (*c*) 8%.

QS 14-9
Bond features and terminology
A2

Enter the letter of the description *A* through *H* that best fits each term or phrase 1 through 8.

A. Records and tracks the bondholders' names.
B. Is unsecured; backed only by the issuer's credit standing.
C. Has varying maturity dates for amounts owed.
D. Identifies rights and responsibilities of the issuer and the bondholders.
E. Can be exchanged for shares of the issuer's stock.
F. Is unregistered; interest is paid to whoever possesses them.
G. Maintains a separate asset account from which bondholders are paid at maturity.

H. Pledges specific assets of the issuer as collateral.

1. _______ Convertible bond
2. _______ Bond indenture
3. _______ Sinking fund bond
4. _______ Debenture
5. _______ Registered bond
6. _______ Serial bond
7. _______ Secured bond
8. _______ Bearer bond

QS 14-10
Debt-to-equity ratio
A2

Compute the debt-to-equity ratio for each of the following companies. Which company appears to have a riskier financing structure? Explain.

	NLF Company	ABL Company
Total liabilities	$615,000	$ 480,000
Total equity	820,000	1,500,000

QS 14-11[C]
Issuing bonds between interest dates
P1

Knapp Company plans to issue 6% bonds on January 1, 2009, with a par value of $2,000,000. The company sells $1,800,000 of the bonds on January 1, 2009. The remaining $200,000 sells at par on March 1, 2009. The bonds pay interest semiannually as of June 30 and December 31. Record the entry for the March 1 cash sale of bonds.

QS 14-12[D]
Recording operating leases C4

Lu Villena, an employee of ETrain.com, leases a car at O'Hare airport for a three-day business trip. The rental cost is $400. Prepare the entry by ETrain.com to record Lu Villena's short-term car lease cost.

QS 14-13[D]
Recording capital leases C4

Artel, Inc., signs a five-year lease for office equipment with Office Solutions. The present value of the lease payments is $13,500. Prepare the journal entry that Artel records at the inception of this capital lease.

McGraw-Hill's HOMEWORK MANAGER® Available with McGraw-Hill's Homework Manager

Round dollar amounts to the nearest whole dollar. Assume no reversing entries are used.

EXERCISES

Exercise 14-1
Recording bond issuance and interest
P1

On January 1, 2009, Bartel Enterprises issues bonds that have a $3,650,000 par value, mature in 20 years, and pay 10% interest semiannually on June 30 and December 31. The bonds are sold at par.

1. How much interest will Bartel pay (in cash) to the bondholders every six months?
2. Prepare journal entries to record (*a*) the issuance of bonds on January 1, 2009; (*b*) the first interest payment on June 30, 2009; and (*c*) the second interest payment on December 31, 2009.
3. Prepare the journal entry for issuance assuming the bonds are issued at (*a*) 98 and (*b*) 105.

Exercise 14-2
Straight-line amortization of bond discount
P2

Sears issues bonds with a par value of $175,000 on January 1, 2009. The bonds' annual contract rate is 4%, and interest is paid semiannually on June 30 and December 31. The bonds mature in three years. The annual market rate at the date of issuance is 6%, and the bonds are sold for $165,523.

1. What is the amount of the discount on these bonds at issuance?
2. How much total bond interest expense will be recognized over the life of these bonds?
3. Prepare an amortization table like the one in Exhibit 14.7 for these bonds; use the straight-line method to amortize the discount.

Exercise 14-3[B]
Effective interest amortization of bond discount
P2

Ritter issues bonds dated January 1, 2009, with a par value of $300,000. The bonds' annual contract rate is 9%, and interest is paid semiannually on June 30 and December 31. The bonds mature in three years. The annual market rate at the date of issuance is 12%, and the bonds are sold for $277,872.

1. What is the amount of the discount on these bonds at issuance?
2. How much total bond interest expense will be recognized over the life of these bonds?
3. Prepare an amortization table like the one in Exhibit 14B.1 for these bonds; use the effective interest method to amortize the discount.

Exercise 14-4
Straight-line amortization of bond premium P3

Dell Co. issues bonds dated January 1, 2009, with a par value of $450,000. The bonds' annual contract rate is 9%, and interest is paid semiannually on June 30 and December 31. The bonds mature in three years. The annual market rate at the date of issuance is 8%, and the bonds are sold for $461,795.

1. What is the amount of the premium on these bonds at issuance?
2. How much total bond interest expense will be recognized over the life of these bonds?
3. Prepare an amortization table like the one in Exhibit 14.11 for these bonds; use the straight-line method to amortize the premium.

Exercise 14-5B
Effective interest amortization of bond premium P3

Refer to the bond details in Exercise 14-4 and prepare an amortization table like the one in Exhibit 14B.2 for these bonds using the effective interest method to amortize the premium.

Exercise 14-6
Recording bond issuance and premium amortization
P1 P3

Anna Company issues 8%, five-year bonds, on December 31, 2008, with a par value of $100,000 and semiannual interest payments. Use the following straight-line bond amortization table and prepare journal entries to record (*a*) the issuance of bonds on December 31, 2008; (*b*) the first interest payment on June 30, 2009; and (*c*) the second interest payment on December 31, 2009.

Semiannual Period-End	Unamortized Premium	Carrying Value
(0) 12/31/2008	$7,720	$107,720
(1) 6/30/2009	6,948	106,948
(2) 12/31/2009	6,176	106,176

Exercise 14-7
Recording bond issuance and discount amortization
P1 P2

St. Charles Company issues 10%, four-year bonds, on December 31, 2009, with a par value of $100,000 and semiannual interest payments. Use the following straight-line bond amortization table and prepare journal entries to record (*a*) the issuance of bonds on December 31, 2009; (*b*) the first interest payment on June 30, 2010; and (*c*) the second interest payment on December 31, 2010.

Semiannual Period-End	Unamortized Discount	Carrying Value
(0) 12/31/2009	$8,000	$92,000
(1) 6/30/2010	7,000	93,000
(2) 12/31/2010	6,000	94,000

Exercise 14-8
Recording bond issuance and discount amortization
P1 P2

Zander Company issues 6%, two-year bonds, on December 31, 2009, with a par value of $100,000 and semiannual interest payments. Use the following straight-line bond amortization table and prepare journal entries to record (*a*) the issuance of bonds on December 31, 2009; (*b*) the first through fourth interest payments on each June 30 and December 31; and (*c*) the maturity of the bond on December 31, 2011.

Semiannual Period-End	Unamortized Discount	Carrying Value
(0) 12/31/2009	$4,000	$ 96,000
(1) 6/30/2010	3,000	97,000
(2) 12/31/2010	2,000	98,000
(3) 6/30/2011	1,000	99,000
(4) 12/31/2011	0	100,000

Exercise 14-9
Computing bond interest and price; recording bond issuance
P2

Target Company issues bonds with a par value of $950,000 on their stated issue date. The bonds mature in 15 years and pay 10% annual interest in semiannual payments. On the issue date, the annual market rate for the bonds is 12%.

1. What is the amount of each semiannual interest payment for these bonds?
2. How many semiannual interest payments will be made on these bonds over their life?
3. Use the interest rates given to determine whether the bonds are issued at par, at a discount, or at a premium.
4. Compute the price of the bonds as of their issue date.
5. Prepare the journal entry to record the bonds' issuance.

Check (4) $819,223

Exercise 14-10
Computing bond interest and price; recording bond issuance
P3

Boston Company issues bonds with a par value of $160,000 on their stated issue date. The bonds mature in six years and pay 8% annual interest in semiannual payments. On the issue date, the annual market rate for the bonds is 6%.

1. What is the amount of each semiannual interest payment for these bonds?
2. How many semiannual interest payments will be made on these bonds over their life?
3. Use the interest rates given to determine whether the bonds are issued at par, at a discount, or at a premium.
4. Compute the price of the bonds as of their issue date.
5. Prepare the journal entry to record the bonds' issuance.

Check (4) $175,930

Exercise 14-11
Bond computations, straight-line amortization, and bond retirement
P2 P4

On January 1, 2009, Seldon issues $450,000 of 10%, 15-year bonds at a price of 93¼. Six years later, on January 1, 2015, Seldon retires 20% of these bonds by buying them on the open market at 109¾. All interest is accounted for and paid through December 31, 2014, the day before the purchase. The straight-line method is used to amortize any bond discount.

1. How much does the company receive when it issues the bonds on January 1, 2009?
2. What is the amount of the discount on the bonds at January 1, 2009?
3. How much amortization of the discount is recorded on the bonds for the entire period from January 1, 2009, through December 31, 2014?
4. What is the carrying (book) value of the bonds as of the close of business on December 31, 2014? What is the carrying value of the 20% soon-to-be-retired bonds on this same date?
5. How much did the company pay on January 1, 2015, to purchase the bonds that it retired?
6. What is the amount of the recorded gain or loss from retiring the bonds?
7. Prepare the journal entry to record the bond retirement at January 1, 2015.

Check (6) $12,420 loss

Exercise 14-12C
Recording bond issuance with accrued interest
C4 P1

On May 1, 2009, Bradley Enterprises issues bonds dated January 1, 2009, that have a $1,950,000 par value, mature in 20 years, and pay 8% interest semiannually on June 30 and December 31. The bonds are sold at par plus four months' accrued interest.

1. How much accrued interest do the bond purchasers pay Bradley on May 1, 2009?
2. Prepare Bradley's journal entries to record (*a*) the issuance of bonds on May 1, 2009; (*b*) the first interest payment on June 30, 2009; and (*c*) the second interest payment on December 31, 2009.

Check (1) $52,000

Exercise 14-13
Straight-line amortization and accrued bond interest expense
P1 P2

Stockton Co. issues four-year bonds with a $50,000 par value on June 1, 2009, at a price of $47,850. The annual contract rate is 8%, and interest is paid semiannually on November 30 and May 31.

1. Prepare an amortization table like the one in Exhibit 14.7 for these bonds. Use the straight-line method of interest amortization.
2. Prepare journal entries to record the first two interest payments and to accrue interest as of December 31, 2009.

Exercise 14-14
Installment note with equal total payments C1 P5

On January 1, 2009, American Eagle borrows $90,000 cash by signing a four-year, 5% installment note. The note requires four equal total payments of accrued interest and principal on December 31 of each year from 2009 through 2012.

1. Compute the amount of each of the four equal total payments.
2. Prepare an amortization table for this installment note like the one in Exhibit 14.14.

Check (1) $25,381

Exercise 14-15
Installment note entries P5

Use the information in Exercise 14-14 to prepare the journal entries for American Eagle to record the loan on January 1, 2009, and the four payments from December 31, 2009, through December 31, 2012.

Exercise 14-16
Applying debt-to-equity ratio
A3

Motin Company is considering a project that will require a $250,000 loan. It presently has total liabilities of $110,000, and total assets of $310,000.

1. Compute Motin's (*a*) present debt-to-equity ratio and (*b*) the debt-to-equity ratio assuming it borrows $250,000 to fund the project.
2. Evaluate and discuss the level of risk involved if Motin borrows the funds to pursue the project.

Exercise 14-17^D
Identifying capital and operating leases
C4

Indicate whether the company in each separate case 1 through 3 has entered into an operating lease or a capital lease.

1. The lessor retains title to the asset, and the lease term is three years on an asset that has a five-year useful life.
2. The title is transferred to the lessee, the lessee can purchase the asset for $1 at the end of the lease, and the lease term is five years. The leased asset has an expected useful life of six years.
3. The present value of the lease payments is 95% of the leased asset's market value, and the lease term is 70% of the leased asset's useful life.

Exercise 14-18^D
Accounting for capital lease
C4

Hartel (lessee) signs a five-year capital lease for office equipment with a $21,000 annual lease payment. The present value of the five annual lease payments is $88,460, based on a 6% interest rate.

1. Prepare the journal entry Hartel will record at inception of the lease.
2. If the leased asset has a five-year useful life with no salvage value, prepare the journal entry Hartel will record each year to recognize depreciation expense related to the leased asset.

Exercise 14-19^D
Analyzing lease options
C2 C3 C4

General Motors advertised three alternatives for a 25-month lease on a new Blazer: (1) zero dollars down and a lease payment of $2,522 per month for 25 months, (2) $5,000 down and $2,240 per month for 25 months, or (3) $55,000 down and no payments for 25 months. Use the present value Table B.3 in Appendix B to determine which is the best alternative (assume you have enough cash to accept any alternative and the annual interest rate is 12% compounded monthly).

PROBLEM SET A

Round dollar amounts to the nearest whole dollar. Assume no reversing entries are used.

Problem 14-1A
Computing bond price and recording issuance
P1 P2 P3

Check (1) Premium, $4,760

(3) Discount, $4,223

Harvard Research issues bonds dated January 1, 2009, that pay interest semiannually on June 30 and December 31. The bonds have a $45,000 par value and an annual contract rate of 6%, and they mature in six years.

Required

For each of the following three separate situations, (*a*) determine the bonds' issue price on January 1, 2009, and (*b*) prepare the journal entry to record their issuance.

1. The market rate at the date of issuance is 4%.
2. The market rate at the date of issuance is 6%.
3. The market rate at the date of issuance is 8%.

Problem 14-2A
Straight-line amortization of bond discount and bond premium
P1 P2 P3

eXcel
mhhe.com/wildFAP19e

Check (3) $4,676,000

(4) 12/31/2010 carrying value, $3,087,468

Braeburn issues $3,500,000 of 8%, 15-year bonds dated January 1, 2009, that pay interest semiannually on June 30 and December 31. The bonds are issued at a price of $3,024,000.

Required

1. Prepare the January 1, 2009, journal entry to record the bonds' issuance.
2. For each semiannual period, compute (*a*) the cash payment, (*b*) the straight-line discount amortization, and (*c*) the bond interest expense.
3. Determine the total bond interest expense to be recognized over the bonds' life.
4. Prepare the first two years of an amortization table like Exhibit 14.7 using the straight-line method.
5. Prepare the journal entries to record the first two interest payments.
6. Assume that the bonds are issued at a price of $4,284,000. Repeat parts 1 through 5.

Problem 14-3A
Straight-line amortization of bond premium
P1 P3

eXcel
mhhe.com/wildFAP19e

Check (2) 6/30/2009 carrying value, $234,644

Jules issues 4.5%, five-year bonds dated January 1, 2009, with a $230,000 par value. The bonds pay interest on June 30 and December 31 and are issued at a price of $235,160. The annual market rate is 4% on the issue date.

Required

1. Calculate the total bond interest expense over the bonds' life.
2. Prepare a straight-line amortization table like Exhibit 14.11 for the bonds' life.
3. Prepare the journal entries to record the first two interest payments.

Refer to the bond details in Problem 14-3A.

Problem 14-4A[B]
Effective interest amortization of bond premium; computing bond price P1 P3

Required

1. Compute the total bond interest expense over the bonds' life.
2. Prepare an effective interest amortization table like the one in Exhibit 14B.2 for the bonds' life.
3. Prepare the journal entries to record the first two interest payments.
4. Use the market rate at issuance to compute the present value of the remaining cash flows for these bonds as of December 31, 2011. Compare your answer with the amount shown on the amortization table as the balance for that date (from part 2) and explain your findings.

Check (2) 6/30/2011 carrying value, $232,704
(4) $232,179

Legacy issues $345,000 of 5%, four-year bonds dated January 1, 2009, that pay interest semiannually on June 30 and December 31. They are issued at $332,888 and their market rate is 6% at the issue date.

Problem 14-5A
Straight-line amortization of bond discount
P1 P2

Required

1. Prepare the January 1, 2009, journal entry to record the bonds' issuance.
2. Determine the total bond interest expense to be recognized over the bonds' life.
3. Prepare a straight-line amortization table like the one in Exhibit 14.7 for the bonds' first two years.
4. Prepare the journal entries to record the first two interest payments.

Check (2) $81,112
(3) 12/31/2010 carrying value, $338,944

Analysis Component

5. Assume the market rate on January 1, 2009, is 4% instead of 6%. Without providing numbers, describe how this change affects the amounts reported on Legacy's financial statements.

Refer to the bond details in Problem 14-5A.

Problem 14-6A[B]
Effective interest amortization of bond discount P1 P2

Required

1. Prepare the January 1, 2009, journal entry to record the bonds' issuance.
2. Determine the total bond interest expense to be recognized over the bonds' life.
3. Prepare an effective interest amortization table like the one in Exhibit 14B.1 for the bonds' first two years.
4. Prepare the journal entries to record the first two interest payments.

Check (2) $81,112
(3) 12/31/2010 carrying value, $338,586

eXcel
mhhe.com/wildFAP19e

Shopko issues $185,000 of 12%, three-year bonds dated January 1, 2009, that pay interest semiannually on June 30 and December 31. They are issued at $189,620. Their market rate is 11% at the issue date.

Problem 14-7A[B]
Effective interest amortization of bond premium; retiring bonds
P1 P3 P4

Required

1. Prepare the January 1, 2009, journal entry to record the bonds' issuance.
2. Determine the total bond interest expense to be recognized over the bonds' life.
3. Prepare an effective interest amortization table like Exhibit 14B.2 for the bonds' first two years.
4. Prepare the journal entries to record the first two interest payments.
5. Prepare the journal entry to record the bonds' retirement on January 1, 2011, at 97.

Check (3) 6/30/2010 carrying value, $187,494
(5) $7,256 gain

Analysis Component

6. Assume that the market rate on January 1, 2009, is 13% instead of 11%. Without presenting numbers, describe how this change affects the amounts reported on Shopko's financial statements.

eXcel
mhhe.com/wildFAP19e

On November 1, 2009, Norwood borrows $700,000 cash from a bank by signing a five-year installment note bearing 7% interest. The note requires equal total payments each year on October 31.

Problem 14-8A
Installment notes
C1 P5

Required

1. Compute the total amount of each installment payment.
2. Complete an amortization table for this installment note similar to the one in Exhibit 14.14.
3. Prepare the journal entries in which Norwood records (*a*) accrued interest as of December 31, 2009 (the end of its annual reporting period), and (*b*) the first annual payment on the note.

Check (2) 10/31/2013 ending balance, $159,556

Problem 14-9A
Applying the debt-to-equity ratio
A3

At the end of the current year, the following information is available for both the Pulaski Company and the Scott Company.

	Pulaski Company	Scott Company
Total assets	$1,800,000	$900,000
Total liabilities	723,600	478,800
Total equity	1,080,000	420,000

Required

1. Compute the debt-to-equity ratios for both companies.
2. Comment on your results and discuss the riskiness of each company's financing structure.

Problem 14-10A[D]
Capital lease accounting
C4

Thomas Company signs a five-year capital lease with Universal Company for office equipment. The annual lease payment is $14,000, and the interest rate is 8%.

Required

Check (1) $55,898

1. Compute the present value of Thomas's five-year lease payments.
2. Prepare the journal entry to record Thomas's capital lease at its inception.

(3) Year 3 ending balance, $24,966

3. Complete a lease payment schedule for the five years of the lease with the following headings. Assume that the beginning balance of the lease liability (present value of lease payments) is $55,898. (*Hint:* To find the amount allocated to interest in year 1, multiply the interest rate by the beginning-of-year lease liability. The amount of the annual lease payment not allocated to interest is allocated to principal. Reduce the lease liability by the amount allocated to principal to update the lease liability at each year-end.)

Period Ending Date	Beginning Balance of Lease Liability	Interest on Lease Liability	Reduction of Lease Liability	Cash Lease Payment	Ending Balance of Lease Liability

4. Use straight-line depreciation and prepare the journal entry to depreciate the leased asset at the end of year 1. Assume zero salvage value and a five-year life for the office equipment.

PROBLEM SET B

Round dollar amounts to the nearest whole dollar. Assume no reversing entries are used.

Problem 14-1B
Computing bond price and recording issuance
P1 P2 P3

Fortune Systems issues bonds dated January 1, 2009, that pay interest semiannually on June 30 and December 31. The bonds have a $35,000 par value and an annual contract rate of 4%, and they mature in four years.

Required

For each of the following three separate situations, (*a*) determine the bonds' issue price on January 1, 2009, and (*b*) prepare the journal entry to record their issuance.

Check (1) Premium, $2,679

1. The market rate at the date of issuance is 2%.
2. The market rate at the date of issuance is 4%.

(3) Discount, $2,457

3. The market rate at the date of issuance is 6%.

Problem 14-2B
Straight-line amortization of bond discount and bond premium
P1 P2 P3

Long Beach issues $4,500,000 of 8%, 15-year bonds dated January 1, 2009, that pay interest semiannually on June 30 and December 31. The bonds are issued at a price of $3,888,000.

Required

1. Prepare the January 1, 2009, journal entry to record the bonds' issuance.
2. For each semiannual period, compute (*a*) the cash payment, (*b*) the straight-line discount amortization, and (*c*) the bond interest expense.

Check (3) $6,012,000

(4) 6/30/2010 carrying value, $3,949,200

3. Determine the total bond interest expense to be recognized over the bonds' life.
4. Prepare the first two years of an amortization table like Exhibit 14.7 using the straight-line method.
5. Prepare the journal entries to record the first two interest payments.
6. Assume that the bonds are issued at a price of $5,508,000. Repeat parts 1 through 5.

San Mateo Company issues 7%, five-year bonds dated January 1, 2009, with a $220,000 par value. The bonds pay interest on June 30 and December 31 and are issued at a price of $229,385. Their annual market rate is 6% on the issue date.

Problem 14-3B
Straight-line amortization of bond premium
P1 P3

Required

1. Calculate the total bond interest expense over the bonds' life.
2. Prepare a straight-line amortization table like Exhibit 14.11 for the bonds' life.
3. Prepare the journal entries to record the first two interest payments.

Check (2) 12/31/2011 carrying value, $223,751

Refer to the bond details in Problem 14-3B.

Problem 14-4B[B]
Effective interest amortization of bond premium; computing bond price P1 P3

Required

1. Compute the total bond interest expense over the bonds' life.
2. Prepare an effective interest amortization table like the one in Exhibit 14B.2 for the bonds' life.
3. Prepare the journal entries to record the first two interest payments.
4. Use the market rate at issuance to compute the present value of the remaining cash flows for these bonds as of December 31, 2011. Compare your answer with the amount shown on the amortization table as the balance for that date (from part 2) and explain your findings.

Check (2) 6/30/2011 carrying value, $225,041

(4) $224,092

Kelly issues $315,000 of 4%, 15-year bonds dated January 1, 2009, that pay interest semiannually on June 30 and December 31. They are issued at $253,263, and their market rate is 6% at the issue date.

Problem 14-5B
Straight-line amortization of bond discount
P1 P2

Required

1. Prepare the January 1, 2009, journal entry to record the bonds' issuance.
2. Determine the total bond interest expense to be recognized over the life of the bonds.
3. Prepare a straight-line amortization table like the one in Exhibit 14.7 for the bonds' first two years.
4. Prepare the journal entries to record the first two interest payments.

Check (2) $250,737

(3) 6/30/2010 carrying value, $259,437

Refer to the bond details in Problem 14-5B.

Problem 14-6B[B]
Effective interest amortization of bond discount
P1 P2

Required

1. Prepare the January 1, 2009, journal entry to record the bonds' issuance.
2. Determine the total bond interest expense to be recognized over the bonds' life.
3. Prepare an effective interest amortization table like the one in Exhibit 14B.1 for the bonds' first two years.
4. Prepare the journal entries to record the first two interest payments.

Check (2) $250,737;
(3) 6/30/2010 carrying value, $257,275

Kendall issues $175,000 of 11%, three-year bonds dated January 1, 2009, that pay interest semiannually on June 30 and December 31. They are issued at $179,439, and their market rate is 10% at the issue date.

Problem 14-7B[B]
Effective interest amortization of bond premium; retiring bonds
P1 P3 P4

Required

1. Prepare the January 1, 2009, journal entry to record the bonds' issuance.
2. Determine the total bond interest expense to be recognized over the bonds' life.
3. Prepare an effective interest amortization table like the one in Exhibit 14B.2 for the bonds' first two years.
4. Prepare the journal entries to record the first two interest payments.
5. Prepare the journal entry to record the bonds' retirement on January 1, 2011, at 105.

Check (3) 6/30/2010 carrying value, $177,380

(5) $7,126 loss

Analysis Component

6. Assume that the market rate on January 1, 2009, is 12% instead of 10%. Without presenting numbers, describe how this change affects the amounts reported on Kendall's financial statements.

Problem 14-8B
Installment notes

C1 P5

On October 1, 2009, Miami Enterprises borrows $200,000 cash from a bank by signing a three-year installment note bearing 7% interest. The note requires equal total payments each year on September 30.

Required

1. Compute the total amount of each installment payment.

2. Complete an amortization table for this installment note similar to the one in Exhibit 14.14.

3. Prepare the journal entries to record (*a*) accrued interest as of December 31, 2009 (the end of its annual reporting period) and (*b*) the first annual payment on the note.

Check (2) 9/30/2011 ending balance, $71,223

Problem 14-9B
Applying the debt-to-equity ratio

A3

At the end of the current year, the following information is available for both Caesar Company and Delta Company.

	Caesar Company	Delta Company
Total assets	$360,000	$1,500,000
Total liabilities	162,360	1,125,000
Total equity	198,000	375,000

Required

1. Compute the debt-to-equity ratios for both companies.

2. Comment on your results and discuss what they imply about the relative riskiness of these companies.

Problem 14-10B[D]
Capital lease accounting

C4

Allan Company signs a five-year capital lease with Vortal Company for office equipment. The annual lease payment is $13,000, and the interest rate is 8%.

Required

1. Compute the present value of Allan's lease payments.

2. Prepare the journal entry to record Allan's capital lease at its inception.

3. Complete a lease payment schedule for the five years of the lease with the following headings. Assume that the beginning balance of the lease liability (present value of lease payments) is $51,905. (*Hint:* To find the amount allocated to interest in year 1, multiply the interest rate by the beginning-of-year lease liability. The amount of the annual lease payment not allocated to interest is allocated to principal. Reduce the lease liability by the amount allocated to principal to update the lease liability at each year-end.)

Period Ending Date	Beginning Balance of Lease Liability	Interest on Lease Liability	Reduction of Lease Liability	Cash Lease Payment	Ending Balance of Lease Liability

4. Use straight-line depreciation and prepare the journal entry to depreciate the leased asset at the end of year 1. Assume zero salvage value and a five-year life for the office equipment.

Check (1) $51,905

(3) Year 3 ending balance, $23,182

SERIAL PROBLEM

Success Systems

(This serial problem began in Chapter 1 and continues through most of the book. If previous chapter segments were not completed, the serial problem can begin at this point. It is helpful, but not necessary, to use the Working Papers that accompany the book.)

SP 14 Adriana Lopez has consulted with her local banker and is considering financing an expansion of her business by obtaining a long-term bank loan. Selected account balances at March 31, 2010, for Success Systems follow.

Total assets	$129,909	Total liabilities	$875	Total equity	$129,034

Required

1. The bank has offered a long-term secured note to Success Systems. The bank's loan procedures require that a client's debt-to-equity ratio not exceed 0.8. As of March 31, 2010, what is the maximum amount that Success Systems could borrow from this bank (rounded to nearest dollar)?
2. If Success Systems borrows the maximum amount allowed from the bank, what percentage of assets would be financed (*a*) by debt and (*b*) by equity?
3. What are some factors Lopez should consider before borrowing the funds?

Check (1) $102,352

BEYOND THE NUMBERS

REPORTING IN ACTION

A1 A2

BTN 14-1 Refer to **Best Buy**'s financial statements in Appendix A to answer the following.

1. Identify the items that make up Best Buy's long-term debt at March 3, 2007. (*Hint:* See note 5.)
2. How much annual cash interest must Best Buy pay on its 2.25% convertible subordinated debt?
3. Did it have any additions to long-term debt that provided cash for the year ending March 3, 2007?

Fast Forward

4. Access Best Buy's financial statements for the years ending after March 3, 2007, from its Website (BestBuy.com) or the SEC's EDGAR database (www.SEC.gov). Has it issued additional long-term debt since the year-end March 3, 2007? If yes, identify the amount(s).

COMPARATIVE ANALYSIS

A3

BTN 14-2 Key figures for **Best Buy**, **Circuit City**, and **RadioShack** follow.

	Best Buy		Circuit City		RadioShack	
($ millions)	Current Year	Prior Year	Current Year	Prior Year	Current Year	Prior Year
Total assets	$13,570	$11,864	$4,007	$4,069	$2,070	$2,205
Total liabilities	7,369	6,607	2,216	2,114	1,416	1,616
Total equity	6,201	5,257	1,791	1,955	654	589

Required

1. Compute the debt-to-equity ratios for Best Buy, Circuit City, and RadioShack for both the current year and the prior year.
2. Use the ratios you computed in part 1 to determine which company's financing structure is least risky. Assume an industry average of 0.24 for debt-to-equity.

ETHICS CHALLENGE

C4 A1

BTN 14-3 Brevard County needs a new county government building that would cost $24 million. The politicians feel that voters will not approve a municipal bond issue to fund the building since it would increase taxes. They opt to have a state bank issue $24 million of tax-exempt securities to pay for the building construction. The county then will make yearly lease payments (of principal and interest) to repay the obligation. Unlike conventional municipal bonds, the lease payments are not binding obligations on the county and, therefore, require no voter approval.

Required

1. Do you think the actions of the politicians and the bankers in this situation are ethical?
2. How do the tax-exempt securities used to pay for the building compare in risk to a conventional municipal bond issued by Brevard County?

COMMUNICATING IN PRACTICE

P3

BTN 14-4 Your business associate mentions that she is considering investing in corporate bonds currently selling at a premium. She says that since the bonds are selling at a premium, they are highly valued and her investment will yield more than the going rate of return for the risk involved. Reply with a memorandum to confirm or correct your associate's interpretation of premium bonds.

TAKING IT TO THE NET

A2

BTN 14-5 Access the March 29, 2007, filing of the 10-K report of **Home Depot** for the year ended January 28, 2007, from www.SEC.gov (Ticker: HD). Refer to Home Depot's balance sheet, including its note 4 (on debt).

Required

1. Identify Home Depot's long-term liabilities and the amounts for those liabilities from Home Depot's balance sheet at January 28, 2007.
2. Review Home Depot's note 4. The note reports that it "issued \$3.0 billion of 5.875% senior notes due December 16, 2036, at a discount of \$42 million with interest payable semiannually on June 16 and December 16 each year."
   a. Why would Home Depot issue \$3.0 billion of its notes for only \$2.958 billion?
   b. How much cash interest must Home Depot pay each June 16 and December 16 on these notes?

TEAMWORK IN ACTION

P2 P3

BTN 14-6[B] Break into teams and complete the following requirements related to effective interest amortization for a premium bond.

1. Each team member is to independently prepare a blank table with proper headings for amortization of a bond premium. When all have finished, compare tables and ensure that all are in agreement.

Parts 2 and 3 require use of these facts: On January 1, 2008, BC issues \$100,000, 9%, five-year bonds at 104.1. The market rate at issuance is 8%. BC pays interest semiannually on June 30 and December 31.

2. In rotation, *each* team member must explain how to complete *one* line of the bond amortization table, including all computations for his or her line. (Round amounts to the nearest dollar.) All members are to fill in their tables during this process. You need not finish the table; stop after all members have explained a line.
3. In rotation, *each* team member is to identify a separate column of the table and indicate what the final number in that column will be and explain the reasoning.
4. Reach a team consensus as to what the total bond interest expense on this bond issue will be if the bond is not retired before maturity.
5. As a team, prepare a list of similarities and differences between the amortization table just prepared and the amortization table if the bond had been issued at a discount.

Hint: Rotate teams to report on parts 4 and 5. Consider requiring entries for issuance and interest payments.

ENTREPRENEURIAL DECISION

A1

BTN 14-7 James Lindsay is the founder of **Rap Snacks**. Assume that his company currently has \$250,000 in equity, and he is considering a \$100,000 expansion to meet increased demand. The \$100,000 expansion would yield \$16,000 in additional annual income before interest expense. Assume that the business currently earns \$40,000 annual income before interest expense of \$10,000, yielding a return on equity of 12% (\$30,000/\$250,000). To fund the expansion, he is considering the issuance of a 10-year, \$100,000 note with annual interest payments (the principal due at the end of 10 years).

Required

1. Using return on equity as the decision criterion, show computations to support or reject the expansion if interest on the \$100,000 note is (*a*) 10%, (*b*) 15%, (*c*) 16%, (*d*) 17%, and (*e*) 20%.
2. What general rule do the results in part 1 illustrate?

HITTING THE ROAD

A1

BTN 14-8 Visit your city or county library. Ask the librarian to help you locate the recent financial records of your city or county government. Examine those records.

Required

1. Determine the amount of long-term bonds and notes currently outstanding.
2. Read the supporting information to your municipality's financial statements and record
   a. The market interest rate(s) when the bonds and/or notes were issued.
   b. The date(s) when the bonds and/or notes will mature.
   c. Any rating(s) on the bonds and/or notes received from **Moody's**, **Standard & Poor's**, or another rating agency.

BTN 14-9 DSG international plc (www.DSGiplc.com), Best Buy, Circuit City, and RadioShack are competitors in the global marketplace. Selected results from these companies follow.

GLOBAL DECISION

A3

DSG

BEST BUY

circuit city

RadioShack.

	DSG (£ millions)		Best Buy ($ millions)		Circuit City ($ millions)		RadioShack ($ millions)	
Key Figures	Current Year	Prior Year	Current Year	Prior Year	Current Year	Prior Year	Current Year	Prior Year
Total assets	£3,977	£4,120	$13,570	$11,864	$4,007	$4,069	$2,070	$2,205
Total liabilities	2,673	2,696	7,369	6,607	2,216	2,114	1,416	1,616
Total equity	1,304	1,424	6,201	5,257	1,791	1,955	654	589
Debt-to-equity ratio	?	?	1.2	1.3	1.2	1.1	2.2	2.7

Required

1. Compute DSG's debt-to-equity ratios for the current year and the prior year.
2. Use the data provided and the ratios you computed in part 1 to determine which company's financing structure is least risky.

ANSWERS TO MULTIPLE CHOICE QUIZ

1. b
2. a
3. c; $500,000 × 0.08 × ½ year = $20,000
4. a; Cash interest paid = $100,000 × 5% × ½ year = $2,500
   Discount amortization = ($100,000 − $95,735)/10 periods = $426.50
   Interest expense = $2,500.00 + $426.50 = $2,926.50
5. e; ($373,745 − $350,000)/16 periods = $1,484

A Look Back

Chapter 14 focused on long-term liabilities—a main part of most companies' financing. We explained how to value, record, amortize, and report these liabilities in financial statements.

A Look at This Chapter

This chapter focuses on investments in securities. We explain how to identify, account for, and report investments in both debt and equity securities. We also explain accounting for transactions listed in a foreign currency.

A Look Ahead

Chapter 16 focuses on reporting and analyzing a company's cash flows. Special emphasis is directed at the statement of cash flows reported under the indirect method.

Chapter 15 Investments and International Operations

Learning Objectives

CAP

Conceptual

C1 Distinguish between debt and equity securities and between short-term and long-term investments. *(p. 592)*

C2 Identify and describe the different classes of investments in securities. *(p. 593)*

C3 Describe how to report equity securities with controlling influence. *(p. 599)*

C4 *Appendix 15A*—Explain foreign exchange rates between currencies. *(p. 605)*

Analytical

A1 Compute and analyze the components of return on total assets. *(p. 600)*

LP15

Procedural

P1 Account for trading securities. *(p. 595)*

P2 Account for held-to-maturity securities. *(p. 596)*

P3 Account for available-for-sale securities. *(p. 596)*

P4 Account for equity securities with significant influence. *(p. 598)*

P5 *Appendix 15A*—Record transactions listed in a foreign currency. *(p. 606)*

Decision Feature

Designing Business

"It's a wonderful insanity"—Amy Smilovic

NEW YORK—Amy Smilovic loves business. But after a job transfer by her husband to Hong Kong, she quit her job and looked for her next inspiration. Within weeks, and inspired by the colorful and comfortable clothing she saw, Amy jumped into the designing business of clothes. Her company, **Tibi (Tibi.com),** experienced quick success. "I really kind of just did it," explains Amy. "I tried not to over-think it."

What Amy did was design a clothing line that appeals to the masses. "Just design for yourself, someone will identify with it," insists Amy. "You'll find a group of people who want to dress like you." Amy has been so successful that this group of people extends to many countries. She now has showrooms in Milan and London, and locations in Australia, Hong Kong, Indonesia, Japan, Korea, Malaysia, New Zealand, and Singapore.

This broad reach became what she calls her biggest challenge: investments and international operations. "I didn't know what custom regulations were," explains Amy. "I didn't know how to set up a U.S. base and distribute . . . I was buying books on customs and international shipping laws." Her investments in international operations require Amy to translate their performance into U.S. dollars for financial reports. It also requires conducting international transactions and doing currency translations. Those tasks require knowledge of accounting and reporting requirements for investments, including investments in securities of other companies.

Amy's continued success is sure to include more investments and further international operations. She views her business background and focus as key to that success. "People always ask me, 'How are you a designer without a design background,'" laughs Amy. "I always wonder, 'How are you a designer without a business background?' It's really a business at the end of the day."

[Sources: *Tibi Website,* January 2009, *Entrepreneur,* October 2007; *Fashion Week,* 2008; *Ladies Who Launch,* 2008; *New York Social Diary,* April 2007]

This chapter's main focus is investments in securities. Many companies have investments, and many of these are in the form of debt and equity securities issued by other companies. We describe investments in these securities and how to account for them. An increasing number of companies also invest in international operations. We explain how to account for and report international transactions listed in foreign currencies.

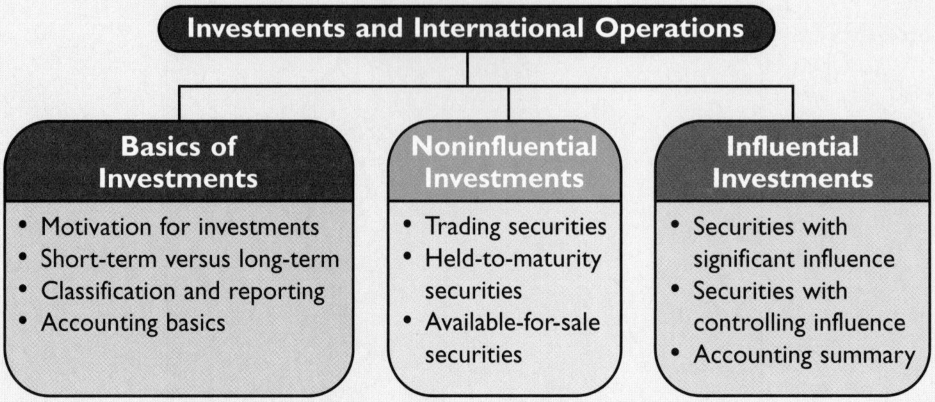

Basics of Investments

C1 Distinguish between debt and equity securities and between short-term and long-term investments.

This section describes the motivation for investments, the distinction between short- and long-term investments, and the different classes of investments.

Motivation for Investments

Companies make investments for at least three reasons. First, companies transfer *excess cash* into investments to produce higher income. Second, some entities, such as mutual funds and pension funds, are set up to produce income from investments. Third, companies make investments for strategic reasons. Examples are investments in competitors, suppliers, and even customers. Exhibit 15.1 shows short-term (S-T) and long-term (L-T) investments as a percent of total assets for several companies.

EXHIBIT 15.1

Investments of Selected Companies

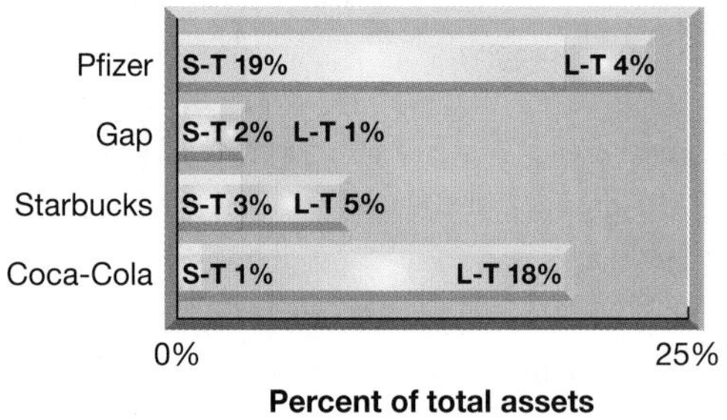

Short-Term versus Long-Term

Cash equivalents are investments that are both readily converted to known amounts of cash and mature within three months. Many investments, however, mature between 3 and 12 months. These investments are **short-term investments,** also called *temporary investments* and *marketable securities*. Specifically, short-term investments are securities that (1) management intends to convert to cash within one year or the operating cycle, whichever is longer, and (2) are readily convertible to cash. Short-term investments are reported under current assets and serve a purpose similar to cash equivalents.

Long-term investments in securities are defined as those securities that are not readily convertible to cash or are not intended to be converted into cash in the short term. Long-term investments can also include funds earmarked for a special purpose, such as bond sinking funds and investments in land or other assets not used in the company's operations. Long-term investments are reported in the noncurrent section of the balance sheet, often in its own separate line titled *Long-Term Investments*.

Investments in securities can include both debt and equity securities. *Debt securities* reflect a creditor relationship such as investments in notes, bonds, and certificates of deposit; they are issued by governments, companies, and individuals. *Equity securities* reflect an owner relationship such as shares of stock issued by companies.

Classification and Reporting

C2 Identify and describe the different classes of investments in securities.

Accounting for investments in securities depends on three factors: (1) security type, either debt or equity, (2) the company's intent to hold the security either short term or long term, and (3) the company's (investor's) percent ownership in the other company's (investee's) equity securities. Exhibit 15.2 identifies five classes of securities using these three factors. It describes each of these five classes of securities and the standard reporting required under each class.

EXHIBIT 15.2

Investments in Securities

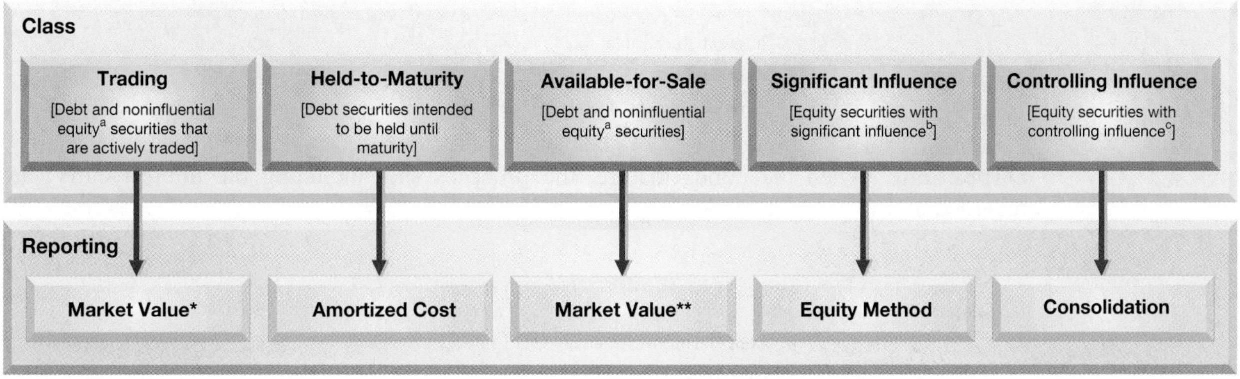

[a] Holding less than 20% of voting stock (equity securities only). [b] Holding 20% or more, but not more than 50%, of voting stock.
[c] Holding more than 50% of voting stock.
* Unrealized gains and losses reported on the income statement.
** Unrealized gains and losses reported in the equity section of the balance sheet and in comprehensive income.

Accounting Basics for Debt Securities

This section explains the accounting basics for *debt securities,* including that for acquisition, disposition, and any interest.

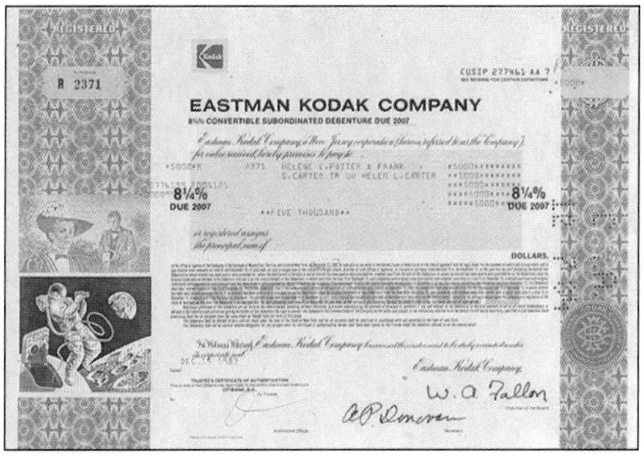

Acquisition. Debt securities are recorded at cost when purchased. To illustrate, assume that Music City paid \$29,500 plus a \$500 brokerage fee on September 1, 2008, to buy Dell's 7%, two-year bonds payable with a \$30,000 par value. The bonds pay interest semiannually on August 31 and February 28. Music City intends to hold the bonds until they mature on August 31, 2010; consequently, they are classified as held-to-maturity (HTM) securities. The entry to record this purchase follows. (If the maturity of the securities was short term, and management's intent was to hold them until they mature, then they would be classified as Short-Term Investments—HTM.)

2008			
Sept. 1	Long-Term Investments—HTM (Dell)	30,000	
	Cash		30,000
	Purchased bonds to be held to maturity.		

Assets = Liabilities + Equity
+30,000
−30,000

Interest earned. Interest revenue for investments in debt securities is recorded when earned. To illustrate, on December 31, 2008, at the end of its accounting period, Music City accrues interest receivable as follows.

Dec. 31	Interest Receivable	700	
	Interest Revenue		700
	Accrued interest earned (\$30,000 × 7% × 4/12).		

Assets = Liabilities + Equity
+700 +700

The \$700 reflects 4/6 of the semiannual cash receipt of interest—the portion Music City earned as of December 31. Relevant sections of Music City's financial statements at December 31, 2008, are shown in Exhibit 15.3.

EXHIBIT 15.3

Financial Statement Presentation of Debt Securities

On the income statement for year 2008:	
Interest revenue	**$ 700**
On the December 31, 2008, balance sheet:	
Long-term investments—Held-to-maturity securities (at amortized cost)	**$30,000**

On February 28, 2009, Music City records receipt of semiannual interest.

Assets = Liabilities + Equity
+1,050 +350
−700

Feb. 28	Cash	1,050	
	Interest Receivable		700
	Interest Revenue		350
	Received six months' interest on Dell bonds.		

Disposition. When the bonds mature, the proceeds (not including the interest entry) are recorded as:

Assets = Liabilities + Equity
+30,000
−30,000

2010			
Aug. 31	Cash	30,000	
	Long-Term Investments—HTM (Dell)		30,000
	Received cash from matured bonds.		

The cost of a debt security can be either higher or lower than its maturity value. When the investment is long term, the difference between cost and maturity value is amortized over the remaining life of the security. We assume for ease of computations that the cost of a long-term debt security equals its maturity value.

Example: What is cost per share? *Answer:* Cost per share is the total cost of acquisition, including broker fees, divided by number of shares acquired.

Accounting Basics for Equity Securities

This section explains the accounting basics for *equity securities,* including that for acquisition, dividends, and disposition.

Acquisition. Equity securities are recorded at cost when acquired, including commissions or brokerage fees paid. To illustrate, assume that Music City purchases 1,000 shares of Intex common stock at par value for $86,000 on October 10, 2008. It records this purchase of available-for-sale (AFS) securities as follows.

Assets = Liabilities + Equity
+86,000
−86,000

Oct. 10	Long-Term Investments—AFS (Intex)	86,000	
	Cash		86,000
	Purchased 1,000 shares of Intex.		

Dividend earned. Any cash dividends received are credited to Dividend Revenue and reported in the income statement. To illustrate, on November 2, Music City receives a $1,720 quarterly cash dividend on the Intex shares, which it records as:

Assets = Liabilities + Equity
+1,720 +1,720

Nov. 2	Cash	1,720	
	Dividend Revenue		1,720
	Received dividend of $1.72 per share.		

Disposition. When the securities are sold, sale proceeds are compared with the cost, and any gain or loss is recorded. To illustrate, on December 20, Music City sells 500 of the Intex shares for $45,000 cash and records this sale as:

Assets = Liabilities + Equity
+45,000 +2,000
−43,000

Dec. 20	Cash	45,000	
	Long-Term Investments—AFS (Intex)		43,000
	Gain on Sale of Long-Term Investments		2,000
	Sold 500 Intex shares ($86,000 × 500/1,000).		

Reporting of *Non*influential Investments

Companies must value and report most noninfluential investments at *fair market value,* or simply *market value.* The exact reporting requirements depend on whether the investments are classified as (1) trading, (2) held-to-maturity, or (3) available-for-sale.

P1 Account for trading securities.

Trading Securities

Trading securities are *debt and equity securities* that the company intends to actively manage and trade for profit. Frequent purchases and sales are expected and are made to earn profits on short-term price changes. Trading securities are *always* reported as current assets.

Valuing and reporting trading securities. The entire portfolio of trading securities is reported at its market value; this requires a "market adjustment" from the cost of the portfolio. The term *portfolio* refers to a group of securities. Any **unrealized gain (or loss)** from a change in the market value of the portfolio of trading securities is reported on the income statement. Most users believe accounting reports are more useful when changes in market value for trading securities are reported in income.

To illustrate, TechCom's portfolio of trading securities had a total cost of $11,500 and a market value of $13,000 on December 31, 2008, the first year it held trading securities. The difference between the $11,500 cost and the $13,000 market value reflects a $1,500 gain. It is an unrealized gain because it is not yet confirmed by actual sales. The market adjustment for trading securities is recorded with an adjusting entry at the end of each period to equal the difference between the portfolio's cost and its market value. TechCom records this gain as follows.

Point: *'Unrealized gain (or loss)'* refers to a change in market value that is not yet realized through actual sale.

Point: 'Market Adjustment—Trading' is a *permanent account,* shown as a deduction or addition to 'Short-Term Investments—Trading.'

Dec. 31	Market Adjustment—Trading.	1,500	
	Unrealized Gain—Income		1,500
	To reflect an unrealized gain in market values of trading securities.		

Assets = Liabilities + Equity
+1,500 +1,500

The Unrealized Gain (or Loss) is reported in the Other Revenues and Gains (or Expenses and Losses) section on the income statement. Unrealized Gain (or Loss)—Income is a *temporary* account that is closed to Income Summary at the end of each period. Market Adjustment—Trading is a *permanent* account, which adjusts the reported value of the trading securities portfolio from its prior period market value to the current period market value. The total cost of the trading securities portfolio is maintained in one account, and the market adjustment is recorded in a separate account. For example, TechCom's investment in trading securities is reported in the current assets section of its balance sheet as follows.

Example: If TechCom's trading securities have a cost of $14,800 and a market of $16,100 at Dec. 31, 2009, its adjusting entry is
Unrealized Loss—Income 200
Market Adj.—Trading 200
This is computed as: $1,500 Beg. Dr. bal. + $200 Cr. = $1,300 End. Dr. bal.

Current Assets		
Short-term investments—Trading (at cost)	$11,500	
Market adjustment—Trading	1,500	
Short-term investments—Trading (at market)		$13,000
or simply		
Short-term investments—Trading (at market; cost is $11,500)		$13,000

Selling trading securities. When individual trading securities are sold, the difference between the net proceeds (sale price less fees) and the cost of the individual trading securities that are sold is recognized as a gain or a loss. Any prior period market adjustment to the portfolio is *not* used to compute the gain or loss from sale of individual trading securities. For example, if TechCom sold some of its trading securities that had cost $1,000 for $1,200 cash on January 9, 2009, it would record the following.

Point: Reporting securities at market value is referred to as *mark-to-market* accounting.

Assets = Liabilities + Equity
+1,200 +200
−1,000

Jan. 9	Cash	1,200	
	Short-Term Investments—Trading		1,000
	Gain on Sale of Short-Term Investments		200
	Sold trading securities costing $1,000 for $1,200 cash.		

A gain is reported in the Other Revenues and Gains section on the income statement, whereas a loss is shown in Other Expenses and Losses. When the period-end market adjustment for the portfolio of trading securities is computed, it excludes the cost and market value of any securities sold.

Held-to-Maturity Securities

P2 Account for held-to-maturity securities.

Held-to-maturity (HTM) securities are *debt* securities a company intends and is able to hold until maturity. They are reported in current assets if their maturity dates are within one year or the operating cycle, whichever is longer. HTM securities are reported in long-term assets when the maturity dates extend beyond one year or the operating cycle, whichever is longer. All HTM securities are recorded at cost when purchased, and interest revenue is recorded when earned.

The portfolio of HTM securities is usually reported at (amortized) cost, which is explained in advanced courses. There is no market adjustment to the portfolio of HTM securities—neither to the short-term nor long-term portfolios. The basics of accounting for HTM securities were described earlier in this chapter.

Point: Only debt securities can be classified as *held-to-maturity;* equity securities have no maturity date.

Decision Maker

Money Manager You expect interest rates to sharply fall within a few weeks and remain at this lower rate. What is your strategy for holding investments in fixed-rate bonds and notes? [Answer—p. 608]

Available-for-Sale Securities

P3 Account for available-for-sale securities.

Available-for-sale (AFS) securities are *debt and equity securities* not classified as trading or held-to-maturity securities. AFS securities are purchased to yield interest, dividends, or increases in market value. They are not actively managed like trading securities. If the intent is to sell AFS securities within the longer of one year or operating cycle, they are classified as short-term investments. Otherwise, they are classified as long-term.

Valuing and reporting available-for-sale securities. As with trading securities, companies adjust the cost of the portfolio of AFS securities to reflect changes in market value. This is done with a market adjustment to its total portfolio cost. However, any unrealized gain or loss for the portfolio of AFS securities is *not* reported on the income statement. Instead, it is reported in the equity section of the balance sheet (and is part of *comprehensive income,* explained later). To illustrate, assume that Music City had no prior period investments in available-for-sale securities other than those purchased in the current period. Exhibit 15.4 shows both the cost and market value of those investments on December 31, 2008, the end of its reporting period.

Example: If market value in Exhibit 15.4 is $70,000 (instead of $74,550), what entry is made? *Answer:*
Unreal. Loss—Equity . . . 3,000
Market Adj.—AFS 3,000

EXHIBIT 15.4

Cost and Market Value of Available-for-Sale Securities

	Cost	Market Value	Unrealized Gain (Loss)
Improv bonds	$30,000	$29,050	$ (950)
Intex common stock, 500 shares	43,000	45,500	2,500
Total	$73,000	$74,550	$1,550

The year-end adjusting entry to record the market value of these investments follows.

Assets = Liabilities + Equity
+1,550 +1,550

Dec. 31	Market Adjustment—Available-for-Sale (LT)	1,550	
	Unrealized Gain—Equity		1,550
	To record adjustment to market value of available-for-sale securities.		

Exhibit 15.5 shows the December 31, 2008, balance sheet presentation—it assumes these investments are long term, but they can also be short term. It is also common to combine the cost of investments with the balance in the Market Adjustment account and report the net as a single amount.

Point: 'Unrealized Loss—Equity' and 'Unrealized Gain—Equity' are *permanent* (balance sheet) equity *accounts.*

EXHIBIT 15.5

Balance Sheet Presentation of Available-for-Sale Securities

Assets		
Long-term investments—Available-for-sale (at cost)	$73,000	
Market adjustment— Available-for-sale	1,550	
Long-term investments—Available-for-sale (at market)		$74,550
or simply		
Long-term investments—Available-for-sale (at market; cost is $73,000)		$74,550
Equity		
... consists of usual equity accounts ...		
Add unrealized gain on available-for-sale securities*		$ 1,550

(Reconciled)

* Often included under the caption Accumulated Other Comprehensive Income.

Let's extend this illustration and assume that at the end of its next calendar year (December 31, 2009), Music City's portfolio of long-term AFS securities has an $81,000 cost and an $82,000 market value. It records the adjustment to market value as follows.

Point: Income can be window-dressed upward by selling AFS securities with unrealized gains; income is reduced by selling those with unrealized losses.

Dec. 31	Unrealized Gain—Equity	550	
	Market Adjustment—Available-for-Sale (LT)		550
	To record adjustment to market value of available-for-sale securities.		

Assets = Liabilities + Equity
−550 −550

The effects of the 2008 and 2009 securities transactions are reflected in the following T-accounts.

Example: If cost is $83,000 and market is $82,000 at Dec. 31, 2009, it records the following adjustment:
Unreal. Gain—Equity . . . 1,550
Unreal. Loss—Equity . . . 1,000
Mkt. Adj.—AFS 2,550

Unrealized Gain—Equity			
Adj. 12/31/09	550	Bal. 12/31/08	1,550
		Bal. 12/31/09	**1,000**

Market Adjustment—Available-for-Sale (LT)			
Bal. 12/31/08	1,550	Adj. 12/31/09	550
Bal. 12/31/09	**1,000**		

Amounts reconcile.

Selling available-for-sale securities. Accounting for the sale of individual AFS securities is identical to that described for the sale of trading securities. When individual AFS securities are sold, the difference between the cost of the individual securities sold and the net proceeds (sale price less fees) is recognized as a gain or loss.

Point: 'Market Adjustment—Available-for-Sale' is a permanent account, shown as a deduction or addition to the Investment account.

Quick Check

Answers—p. 608

1. How are short-term held-to-maturity securities reported (valued) on the balance sheet?
2. How are trading securities reported (valued) on the balance sheet?
3. Where are unrealized gains and losses on available-for-sale securities reported?
4. Where are unrealized gains and losses on trading securities reported?

Alert *The FASB released FAS 157 and FAS 159 that permit companies to use market value in reporting financial assets (referred to as the fair value option). This option allows companies to report any financial asset at fair market value and recognize value changes in income. This method was previously reserved only for trading securities, but would now be an option for available-for-sale and held-to-maturity securities (and other 'financial assets and liabilities' such as accounts and notes receivable, accounts and notes payable, and bonds). These standards also set a 3-level system to determine fair value:*
—Level 1: Use quoted market values
—Level 2: Use observable values from related assets or liabilities
—Level 3: Use unobservable values from estimates or assumptions
To date, a fairly small set of companies has chosen to broadly apply the fair value option—but, we continue to monitor its use...

Reporting of Influential Investments

Investment in Securities with Significant Influence

P4 Account for equity securities with significant influence.

A long-term investment classified as **equity securities with significant influence** implies that the investor can exert significant influence over the investee. An investor that owns 20% or more (but not more than 50%) of a company's voting stock is usually presumed to have a significant influence over the investee. In some cases, however, the 20% test of significant influence is overruled by other, more persuasive, evidence. This evidence can either lower the 20% requirement or increase it. The **equity method** of accounting and reporting is used for long-term investments in equity securities with significant influence, which is explained in this section.

Long-term investments in equity securities with significant influence are recorded at cost when acquired. To illustrate, Micron Co. records the purchase of 3,000 shares (30%) of Star Co. common stock at a total cost of $70,650 on January 1, 2008, as follows.

Assets = Liabilities + Equity
+70,650
−70,650

Jan. 1	Long-Term Investments—Star	70,650	
	Cash		70,650
	To record purchase of 3,000 Star shares.		

The investee's (Star) earnings increase both its net assets and the claim of the investor (Micron) on the investee's net assets. Thus, when the investee reports its earnings, the investor records its share of those earnings in its investment account. To illustrate, assume that Star reports net income of $20,000 for 2008. Micron then records its 30% share of those earnings as follows.

Assets = Liabilities + Equity
+6,000 +6,000

Dec. 31	Long-Term Investments—Star	6,000	
	Earnings from Long-Term Investment		6,000
	To record 30% equity in investee earnings.		

The debit reflects the increase in Micron's equity in Star. The credit reflects 30% of Star's net income. Earnings from Long-Term Investment is a *temporary* account (closed to Income Summary at each period-end) and is reported on the investor's (Micron's) income statement. If the investee incurs a net loss instead of a net income, the investor records its share of the loss and reduces (credits) its investment account. The investor closes this earnings or loss account to Income Summary.

The receipt of cash dividends is not revenue under the equity method because the investor has already recorded its share of the investee's earnings. Instead, cash dividends received by an investor from an investee are viewed as a conversion of one asset to another; that is, dividends reduce the balance of the investment account. To illustrate, Star declares and pays $10,000 in cash dividends on its common stock. Micron records its 30% share of these dividends received on January 9, 2009, as:

Assets = Liabilities + Equity
+3,000
−3,000

Jan. 9	Cash	3,000	
	Long-Term Investments—Star.		3,000
	To record share of dividend paid by Star.		

The book value of an investment under the equity method equals the cost of the investment plus (minus) the investor's equity in the *undistributed* (*distributed*) earnings of the investee. Once Micron records these transactions, its Long-Term Investments account appears as in Exhibit 15.6.

EXHIBIT 15.6

Investment in Star Common Stock (Ledger Account)

Date	Explanation	Debit	Credit	Balance
2008				
Jan. 1	Investment acquisition	70,650		70,650
Dec. 31	Share of earnings	6,000		76,650
2009				
Jan. 9	Share of dividend		3,000	73,650

Micron's account balance on January 9, 2009, for its investment in Star is $73,650. This is the investment's cost *plus* Micron's equity in Star's earnings since its purchase *less* Micron's equity in Star's cash dividends since its purchase. When an investment in equity securities is sold, the gain or loss is computed by comparing proceeds from the sale with the book value of the investment on the date of sale. If Micron sells its Star stock for $80,000 on January 10, 2009, it records the sale as:

Point: Security prices are sometimes listed in fractions. For example, a debt security with a price of $22\frac{1}{4}$, is the same as $22.25.

Jan. 10	Cash	80,000	
	Long-Term Investments—Star		73,650
	Gain on Sale of Investment		6,350
	Sold 3,000 shares of stock for $80,000.		

Assets	=	Liabilities	+	Equity
+80,000				+6,350
−73,650				

Investment in Securities with Controlling Influence

C3 Describe how to report equity securities with controlling influence.

A long-term investment classified as **equity securities with controlling influence** implies that the investor can exert a controlling influence over the investee. An investor who owns more than 50% of a company's voting stock has control over the investee. This investor can dominate all other shareholders in electing the corporation's board of directors and has control over the investee's management. In some cases, controlling influence can extend to situations of less than 50% ownership. Exhibit 15.7 summarizes the accounting for investments in equity securities based on an investor's ownership in the stock.

EXHIBIT 15.7

Accounting for Equity Investments by Percent of Ownership

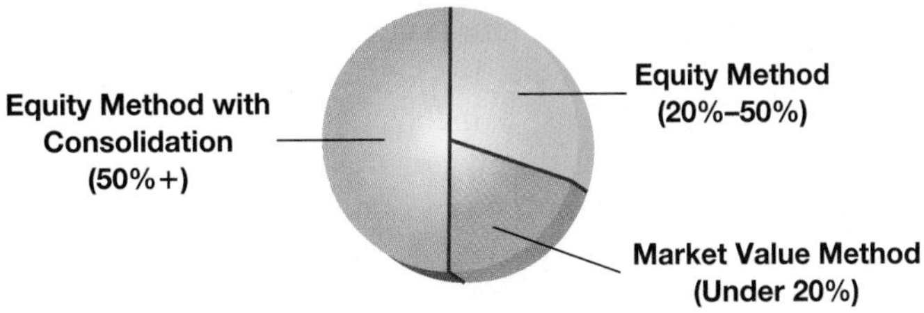

The *equity method with consolidation* is used to account for long-term investments in equity securities with controlling influence. The investor reports *consolidated financial statements* when owning such securities. The controlling investor is called the **parent,** and the investee is called the **subsidiary.** Many companies are parents with subsidiaries. Examples are (1) **McGraw-Hill**, the parent of *BusinessWeek,* Standard & Poor's, and Compustat; (2) **Gap, Inc.**, the parent of Gap, Old Navy, and Banana Republic; and (3) **Brunswick**, the parent of Mercury Marine, Sea Ray, and U.S. Marine. A company owning all the outstanding stock of a subsidiary can, if it desires, take over the subsidiary's assets, retire the subsidiary's stock, and merge the subsidiary into the parent. However, there often are financial, legal, and tax advantages if a business operates as a parent controlling one or more subsidiaries. When a company operates as a parent with subsidiaries, each entity maintains separate accounting records. From a legal viewpoint, the parent and each subsidiary are separate entities with all rights, duties, and responsibilities of individual companies.

Consolidated financial statements show the financial position, results of operations, and cash flows of all entities under the parent's control, including all subsidiaries. These statements are prepared as if the business were organized as one entity. The parent uses the equity method in its accounts, but the investment account is *not* reported on the parent's financial statements. Instead, the individual assets and liabilities of the parent and its subsidiaries are combined on one balance sheet. Their revenues and expenses also are combined on one income statement, and their cash flows are combined on one statement of cash flows. The procedures for preparing consolidated financial statements are in advanced courses.

Decision Insight

IFRSs Unlike U.S. GAAP, IFRSs require uniform accounting policies be used throughout the group of consolidated subsidiaries. Also, unlike U.S. GAAP, IFRSs offer no detailed guidance on valuation procedures.

Accounting Summary for Investments in Securities

Exhibit 15.8 summarizes the standard accounting for investments in securities. Recall that many investment securities are classified as either short term or long term depending on management's

EXHIBIT 15.8

Accounting for Investments in Securities

Classification	Accounting
Short-Term Investment in Securities	
Held-to-maturity (debt) securities	**Cost** (without any discount or premium amortization)
Trading (debt and equity) securities	**Market value** (with market adjustment to income)
Available-for-sale (debt and equity) securities	**Market value** (with market adjustment to equity)
Long-Term Investment in Securities	
Held-to-maturity (debt) securities	**Cost** (with any discount or premium amortization)
Available-for-sale (debt and equity) securities	**Market value** (with market adjustment to equity)
Equity securities with significant influence	Equity method
Equity securities with controlling influence	Equity method (with consolidation)

intent and ability to convert them in the future. Understanding the accounting for these investments enables us to draw better conclusions from financial statements in making business decisions.

Comprehensive Income The term **comprehensive income** refers to all changes in equity for a period except those due to investments and distributions to owners. This means that it includes (1) the revenues, gains, expenses, and losses reported in net income *and* (2) the gains and losses that bypass net income but affect equity. An example of an item that bypasses net income is unrealized gains and losses on available-for-sale securities. These items make up *other comprehensive income* and are usually reported as a part of the statement of stockholders' equity. (Two other options are as a second separate income statement or as a combined income statement of comprehensive income; these less common options are described in advanced courses.) Most often this simply requires one additional column for Other Comprehensive Income in the usual columnar form of the statement of stockholders' equity (the details of this are left for advanced courses). The FASB encourages, but does *not* require, other comprehensive income items to be grouped under the caption *Accumulated Other Comprehensive Income* in the equity section of the balance sheet, which would include unrealized gains and losses on available-for-sale securities. For instructional benefits, we use actual account titles for these items in the equity section instead of this general, less precise caption.

Point: Some users believe that since AFS securities are not actively traded, reporting market value changes in income would unnecessarily increase income variability and decrease usefulness.

Quick Check

Answers—p. 608

5. Give at least two examples of assets classified as long-term investments.
6. What are the requirements for an equity security to be listed as a long-term investment?
7. Identify similarities and differences in accounting for long-term investments in debt securities that are held-to-maturity versus those available-for-sale.
8. What are the three possible classifications of long-term equity investments? Describe the criteria for each class and the method used to account for each.

Decision Analysis — Components of Return on Total Assets

A1 Compute and analyze the components of return on total assets.

A company's **return on total assets** (or simply *return on assets*) is important in assessing financial performance. The return on total assets can be separated into two components, profit margin and total asset turnover, for additional analyses. Exhibit 15.9 shows how these two components determine return on total assets.

EXHIBIT 15.9

Components of Return on Total Assets

Return on total assets = Profit margin × Total asset turnover

$$\frac{\text{Net income}}{\text{Average total assets}} = \frac{\text{Net income}}{\text{Net sales}} \times \frac{\text{Net sales}}{\text{Average total assets}}$$

Profit margin reflects the percent of net income in each dollar of net sales. Total asset turnover reflects a company's ability to produce net sales from total assets. All companies desire a high return on total assets.

By considering these two components, we can often discover strengths and weaknesses not revealed by return on total assets alone. This improves our ability to assess future performance and company strategy.

To illustrate, consider return on total assets and its components for **Gap Inc.** in Exhibit 15.10.

EXHIBIT 15.10

Gap's Components of Return on Total Assets

Fiscal Year	Return on Total Assets	=	Profit Margin	×	Total Asset Turnover
2007	9.0%	=	4.9%	×	1.84
2006	11.8	=	6.9	×	1.70
2005	11.1	=	7.1	×	1.57

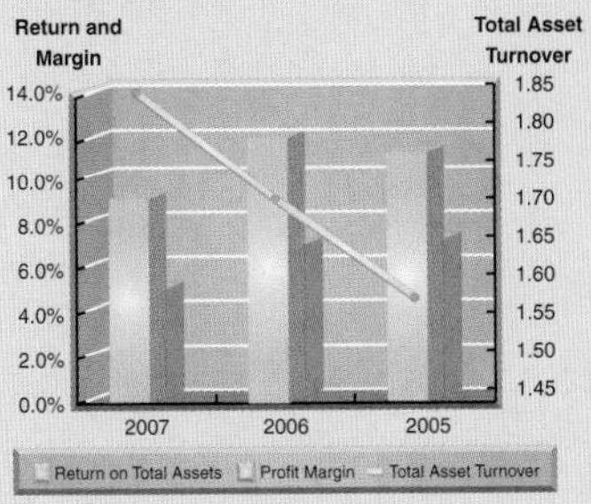

At least three findings emerge. First, Gap's return on total assets improved from 11.1% in 2005 to 11.8% in 2006, but then declined to 9.0% in 2007. Second, total asset turnover has markedly improved from 1.57 to 1.70 to 1.84 over this period. Third, Gap's profit margin steadily declined from 7.1% to 6.9%, and then to 4.9% over this period. These components reveal the dual role of profit margin and total asset turnover in determining return on total assets. They also reveal that the driver of Gap's recent decline is not total asset turnover but profit margin.

Generally, if a company is to maintain or improve its return on total assets, it must meet any decline in either profit margin or total asset turnover with an increase in the other. If not, return on assets will decline. Companies consider these components in planning strategies. A component analysis can also reveal where a company is weak and where changes are needed, especially in a competitor analysis. If asset turnover is lower than the industry norm, for instance, a company should focus on raising asset turnover at least to the norm. The same applies to profit margin.

Decision Maker

Retailer You are an entrepreneur and owner of a retail sporting goods store. The store's recent annual performance reveals (industry norms in parentheses): return on total assets = 11% (11.2%); profit margin = 4.4% (3.5%); and total asset turnover = 2.5 (3.2). What does your analysis of these figures reveal? [Answer—p. 608]

Demonstration Problem—1

DP15

Garden Company completes the following selected transactions related to its short-term investments during 2008.

May 8 Purchased 300 shares of FedEx stock as a short-term investment in available-for-sale securities at $40 per share plus $975 in broker fees.

Sept. 2 Sold 100 shares of its investment in FedEx stock at $47 per share and held the remaining 200 shares; broker's commission was $225.

Oct. 2 Purchased 400 shares of Ajay stock for $60 per share plus $1,600 in commissions. The stock is held as a short-term investment in available-for-sale securities.

Required

1. Prepare journal entries for the above transactions of Garden Company for 2008.
2. Prepare an adjusting journal entry as of December 31, 2008, if the market prices of the equity securities held by Garden Company are $48 per share for FedEx and $55 per share for Ajay. (Year 2008 is the first year Garden Company acquired short-term investments.)

Solution to Demonstration Problem—1

1.

May 8	Short-Term Investments—AFS (FedEx)	12,975	
	Cash		12,975
	Purchased 300 shares of FedEx stock (300 × $40) + $975.		

[continued on next page]

[continued from previous page]

Sept. 2	Cash	4,475	
	Gain on Sale of Short-Term Investment		150
	Short-Term Investments—AFS (FedEx)		4,325
	Sold 100 shares of FedEx for $47 per share less a $225 commission. The original cost is ($12,975 × 100/300).		
Oct. 2	Short-Term Investments—AFS (Ajay)	25,600	
	Cash		25,600
	Purchased 400 shares of Ajay for $60 per share plus $1,600 in commissions.		

2. Computation of unrealized gain or loss follows.

Short-Term Investments in Available-for-Sale Securities	Shares	Cost per Share	Total Cost	Market Value per Share	Total Market Value	Unrealized Gain (Loss)
FedEx	200	$43.25	$ 8,650	$48.00	$ 9,600	
Ajay	400	64.00	25,600	55.00	22,000	
Totals			$34,250		$31,600	$(2,650)

The adjusting entry follows.

Dec. 31	Unrealized Loss—Equity	2,650	
	Market Adjustment—Available-for-Sale (ST)		2,650
	To reflect an unrealized loss in market values of available-for-sale securities.		

Demonstration Problem—2

The following transactions relate to Brown Company's long-term investments during 2008 and 2009. Brown did not own any long-term investments prior to 2008. Show (1) the appropriate journal entries and (2) the relevant portions of each year's balance sheet and income statement that reflect these transactions for both 2008 and 2009.

2008

Sept. 9 Purchased 1,000 shares of Packard, Inc., common stock for $80,000 cash. These shares represent 30% of Packard's outstanding shares.

Oct. 2 Purchased 2,000 shares of AT&T common stock for $60,000 cash. These shares represent less than a 1% ownership in AT&T.

17 Purchased as a long-term investment 1,000 shares of Apple Computer common stock for $40,000 cash. These shares are less than 1% of Apple's outstanding shares.

Nov. 1 Received $5,000 cash dividend from Packard.

30 Received $3,000 cash dividend from AT&T.

Dec. 15 Received $1,400 cash dividend from Apple.

31 Packard's net income for this year is $70,000.

31 Market values for the investments in equity securities are Packard, $84,000; AT&T, $48,000; and Apple Computer, $45,000.

31 For preparing financial statements, note the following post-closing account balances: Common Stock, $500,000, and Retained Earnings, $350,000.

2009

Jan. 1 Sold Packard, Inc., shares for $108,000 cash.

May 30 Received $3,100 cash dividend from AT&T.

June 15 Received $1,600 cash dividend from Apple.

Aug. 17 Sold the AT&T stock for $52,000 cash.
19 Purchased 2,000 shares of Coca-Cola common stock for $50,000 cash as a long-term investment. The stock represents less than a 5% ownership in Coca-Cola.
Dec. 15 Received $1,800 cash dividend from Apple.
31 Market values of the investments in equity securities are Apple, $39,000, and Coca-Cola, $48,000.
31 For preparing financial statements, note the following post-closing account balances: Common Stock, $500,000, and Retained Earnings, $410,000.

Planning the Solution

- Account for the investment in Packard under the equity method.
- Account for the investments in AT&T, Apple, and Coca-Cola as long-term investments in available-for-sale securities.
- Prepare the information for the two years' balance sheets by including the appropriate asset and equity accounts.

Solution to Demonstration Problem—2

1. Journal entries for 2008.

Sept. 9	Long-Term Investments—Packard	80,000	
	Cash		80,000
	Acquired 1,000 shares, representing a 30% equity in Packard.		
Oct. 2	Long-Term Investments—AFS (AT&T)	60,000	
	Cash		60,000
	Acquired 2,000 shares as a long-term investment in available-for-sale securities.		
Oct. 17	Long-Term Investments—AFS (Apple)	40,000	
	Cash		40,000
	Acquired 1,000 shares as a long-term investment in available-for-sale securities.		
Nov. 1	Cash	5,000	
	Long-Term Investments—Packard		5,000
	Received dividend from Packard.		
Nov. 30	Cash	3,000	
	Dividend Revenue		3,000
	Received dividend from AT&T.		
Dec. 15	Cash	1,400	
	Dividend Revenue		1,400
	Received dividend from Apple.		
Dec. 31	Long-Term Investments—Packard	21,000	
	Earnings from Investment (Packard)		21,000
	To record 30% share of Packard's annual earnings of $70,000.		
Dec. 31	Unrealized Loss—Equity	7,000	
	Market Adjustment—Available-for-Sale (LT)*		7,000
	To record change in market value of long-term available-for-sale securities.		

* Market adjustment computations:

	Cost	Market Value	Unrealized Gain (Loss)
AT&T	$ 60,000	$48,000	$(12,000)
Apple	40,000	45,000	5,000
Total	$100,000	$93,000	$ (7,000)

Required balance of the Market Adjustment—Available-for-Sale (LT) account (credit)	$(7,000)
Existing balance	0
Necessary adjustment (credit)	$(7,000)

2. The December 31, 2008, selected balance sheet items appear as follows.

Assets	
Long-term investments	
Available-for-sale securities (at market; cost is $100,000)	$ 93,000
Investment in equity securities	96,000
Total long-term investments	189,000
Stockholders' Equity	
Common stock	500,000
Retained earnings	350,000
Unrealized loss—Equity	(7,000)

The relevant income statement items for the year ended December 31, 2008, follow.

Dividend revenue	$ 4,400
Earnings from investment	21,000

1. Journal entries for 2009.

Jan. 1	Cash	108,000	
	Long-Term Investments—Packard		96,000
	Gain on Sale of Long-Term Investments		12,000
	Sold 1,000 shares for cash.		
May 30	Cash	3,100	
	Dividend Revenue		3,100
	Received dividend from AT&T.		
June 15	Cash	1,600	
	Dividend Revenue		1,600
	Received dividend from Apple.		
Aug. 17	Cash	52,000	
	Loss on Sale of Long-Term Investments	8,000	
	Long-Term Investments—AFS (AT&T)		60,000
	Sold 2,000 shares for cash.		
Aug. 19	Long-Term Investments—AFS (Coca-Cola)	50,000	
	Cash		50,000
	Acquired 2,000 shares as a long-term investment in available-for-sale securities.		
Dec. 15	Cash	1,800	
	Dividend Revenue		1,800
	Received dividend from Apple.		
Dec. 31	Market Adjustment—Available-for-Sale (LT)*	4,000	
	Unrealized Loss—Equity		4,000
	To record change in market value of long-term available-for-sale securities.		

* Market adjustment computations:

	Cost	Market Value	Unrealized Gain (Loss)
Apple	$40,000	$39,000	$(1,000)
Coca-Cola	50,000	48,000	(2,000)
Total	$90,000	$87,000	$(3,000)

Required balance of the Market Adjustment—Available-for-Sale (LT) account (credit)	$(3,000)
Existing balance (credit)	(7,000)
Necessary adjustment (debit)	$ 4,000

2. The December 31, 2009, balance sheet items appear as follows.

Assets	
Long-term investments	
Available-for-sale securities (at market; cost is $90,000)	$ 87,000
Stockholders' Equity	
Common stock	500,000
Retained earnings	410,000
Unrealized loss—Equity	(3,000)

The relevant income statement items for the year ended December 31, 2009, follow.

Dividend revenue	$ 6,500
Gain on sale of long-term investments	12,000
Loss on sale of long-term investments	(8,000)

APPENDIX

Investments in International Operations

15A

Many entities from small entrepreneurs to large corporations conduct business internationally. Some entities' operations occur in so many different countries that the companies are called **multinationals.** Many of us think of **Coca-Cola** and **McDonald's**, for example, as primarily U.S. companies, but most of their sales occur outside the United States. Exhibit 15A.1 shows the percent of international sales and income for selected U.S. companies. Managing and accounting for multinationals present challenges. This section describes some of these challenges and how to account for and report these activities.

Two major accounting challenges that arise when companies have international operations relate to transactions that involve more than one currency. The first is to account for sales and purchases listed in a foreign currency. The second is to prepare consolidated financial statements with international subsidiaries. For ease in this discussion, we use companies with a U.S. base of operations and assume the need to prepare financial statements in U.S. dollars. This means the *reporting currency* of these companies is the U.S. dollar.

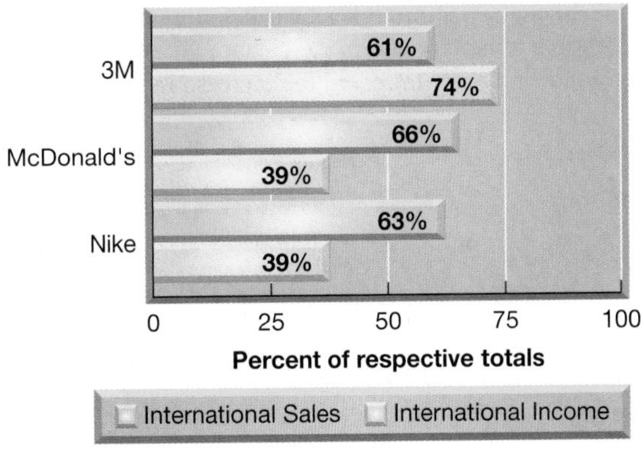

EXHIBIT 15A.1

International Sales and Income as a Percent of Their Totals

Point: Transactions *listed* or *stated* in a foreign currency are said to be *denominated* in that currency.

Exchange Rates between Currencies

C4 Explain foreign exchange rates between currencies.

Markets for the purchase and sale of foreign currencies exist all over the world. In these markets, U.S. dollars can be exchanged for Canadian dollars, British pounds, Japanese yen, Euros, or any other legal currencies. The price of one currency stated in terms of another currency is called a **foreign exchange rate.** Exhibit 15A.2 lists recent exchange rates for selected currencies. The exchange rate for British pounds and U.S. dollars is $1.8054, meaning 1 British pound could be purchased for $1.8054. On that same day, the exchange rate between Mexican pesos and U.S. dollars is $0.0925, or 1 Mexican peso can be purchased for $0.0925. Exchange rates fluctuate due to changing economic and political conditions, including the supply and demand for currencies and expectations about future events.

Point: To convert currency, see XE.com

Decision Insight

Rush to Russia Investors are still eager to buy Russian equities even in the face of rampant crime, corruption, and slow economic growth. Why? Many argue Russia remains a bargain-priced, if risky, bet on future growth. Some analysts argue that natural-resource-rich Russia is one of the least expensive emerging markets.

EXHIBIT 15A.2

Foreign Exchange Rates for Selected Currencies*

Source (unit)	Price in $U.S.	Source (unit)	Price in $U.S.
Britain (pound)	$1.8980	Canada (dollar)	$0.9793
Mexico (peso)	0.0925	Japan (yen)	0.0090
Taiwan (dollar)	0.0305	Europe (Euro)	1.2920

* Rates will vary over time based on economic, political, and other changes.

Sales and Purchases Listed in a Foreign Currency

P5 Record transactions listed in a foreign currency.

When a U.S. company makes a credit sale to an international customer, accounting for the sale and the account receivable is straightforward if sales terms require the international customer's payment in U.S. dollars. If sale terms require (or allow) payment in a foreign currency, however, the U.S. company must account for the sale and the account receivable in a different manner.

Sales in a Foreign Currency To illustrate, consider the case of the U.S.-based manufacturer Boston Company, which makes credit sales to London Outfitters, a British retail company. A sale occurs on December 12, 2008, for a price of £10,000 with payment due on February 10, 2009. Boston Company keeps its accounting records in U.S. dollars. To record the sale, Boston Company must translate the sales price from pounds to dollars. This is done using the exchange rate on the date of the sale. Assuming the exchange rate on December 12, 2008, is $1.80, Boston records this sale as follows.

Assets = Liabilities + Equity
+18,000 +18,000

Dec. 12	Accounts Receivable—London Outfitters	18,000	
	Sales*		18,000
	To record a sale at £10,000, when the exchange rate equals $1.80. * (£10,000 × $1.80)		

When Boston Company prepares its annual financial statements on December 31, 2008, the current exchange rate is $1.84. Thus, the current dollar value of Boston Company's receivable is $18,400 (10,000 × $1.84). This amount is $400 higher than the amount recorded on December 12. Accounting principles require a receivable to be reported in the balance sheet at its current dollar value. Thus, Boston Company must make the following entry to record the increase in the dollar value of this receivable at year-end.

Assets = Liabilities + Equity
+400 +400

Dec. 31	Accounts Receivable—London Outfitters	400	
	Foreign Exchange Gain		400
	To record the increased value of the British pound for the receivable.		

Point: Foreign exchange gains are credits, and foreign exchange losses are debits.

On February 10, 2009, Boston Company receives London Outfitters' payment of £10,000. It immediately exchanges the pounds for U.S. dollars. On this date, the exchange rate for pounds is $1.78. Thus, Boston Company receives only $17,800 (£10,000 × $1.78). It records the cash receipt and the loss associated with the decline in the exchange rate as follows.

Assets = Liabilities + Equity
+17,800 −600
−18,400

Feb. 10	Cash	17,800	
	Foreign Exchange Loss	600	
	Accounts Receivable—London Outfitters		18,400
	Received foreign currency payment of an account and converted it into dollars.		

Gains and losses from foreign exchange transactions are accumulated in the Foreign Exchange Gain (or Loss) account. After year-end adjustments, the balance in the Foreign Exchange Gain (or Loss) account is reported on the income statement and closed to the Income Summary account.

Example: Assume that a U.S. company makes a credit purchase from a British company for £10,000 when the exchange rate is $1.62. At the balance sheet date, this rate is $1.72. Does this imply a gain or loss for the U.S. company? *Answer:* A loss.

Purchases in a Foreign Currency Accounting for credit purchases from an international seller is similar to the case of a credit sale to an international customer. In particular, if the U.S. company is required to make payment in a foreign currency, the account payable must be translated into dollars before the U.S. company can record it. If the exchange rate is different when preparing financial statements and when paying for the purchase, the U.S. company must recognize a foreign exchange gain or loss at those dates. To illustrate, assume NC Imports, a U.S. company, purchases products costing

€20,000 (euros) from Hamburg Brewing on January 15, when the exchange rate is $1.20 per euro. NC records this transaction as follows.

Jan. 15	Inventory.	24,000	
	Accounts Payable—Hamburg Brewing.		24,000
	To record a €20,000 purchase when exchange rate is $1.20 (€20,000 × $1.20)		

Assets = Liabilities + Equity
+24,000 +24,000

NC Imports makes payment in full on February 14 when the exchange rate is $1.25 per euro, which is recorded as follows.

Feb. 14	Accounts Payable—Hamburg Brewing	24,000	
	Foreign Exchange Loss	1,000	
	Cash		25,000
	To record cash payment towards €20,000 account when exchange rate is $1.25 (€20.000 × $1.25).		

Assets = Liabilities + Equity
−25,000 −24,000 −1,000

Decision Insight

Global Greenback What do changes in foreign exchange rates mean? A decline in the price of the U.S. dollar against other currencies usually yields increased international sales for U.S. companies, without hiking prices or cutting costs, and puts them on a stronger competitive footing abroad. At home, they can raise prices without fear that foreign rivals will undercut them.

Consolidated Statements with International Subsidiaries

A second challenge in accounting for international operations involves preparing consolidated financial statements when the parent company has one or more international subsidiaries. Consider a U.S.-based company that owns a controlling interest in a French subsidiary. The reporting currency of the U.S. parent is the dollar. The French subsidiary maintains its financial records in euros. Before preparing consolidated statements, the parent must translate financial statements of the French company into U.S. dollars. After this translation is complete (including that for accounting differences), it prepares consolidated statements the same as for domestic subsidiaries. Procedures for translating an international subsidiary's account balances depend on the nature of the subsidiary's operations. The process requires the parent company to select appropriate foreign exchange rates and to apply those rates to the foreign subsidiary's account balances. This is described in advanced courses.

Global: A weaker U.S. dollar often increases global sales for U.S. companies.

Decision Maker

Entrepreneur You are a U.S. home builder that purchases lumber from mills in both the U.S. and Canada. The price of the Canadian dollar in terms of the U.S. dollar jumps from US$0.70 to US$0.80. Are you now more or less likely to buy lumber from Canadian or U.S. mills? [Answer—p. 608]

Summary

C1 Distinguish between debt and equity securities and between short-term and long-term investments. *Debt securities* reflect a creditor relationship and include investments in notes, bonds, and certificates of deposit. *Equity securities* reflect an owner relationship and include shares of stock issued by other companies. Short-term investments in securities are current assets that meet two criteria: (1) They are expected to be converted into cash within one year or the current operating cycle of the business, whichever is longer and (2) they are readily convertible to cash, or *marketable*. All other investments in securities are long-term. Long-term investments also include assets not used in operations and those held for special purposes, such as land for expansion.

C2 Identify and describe the different classes of investments in securities. Investments in securities are classified into one of five groups: (1) trading securities, which are always short-term, (2) debt securities held-to-maturity, (3) debt and equity securities available-for-sale, (4) equity securities in which an investor has a significant influence over the investee, and (5) equity securities in which an investor has a controlling influence over the investee.

C3 Describe how to report equity securities with controlling influence. If an investor owns more than 50% of another company's voting stock and controls the investee, the investor's financial reports are prepared on a consolidated basis. These reports are prepared as if the company were organized as one entity.

C4[A] **Explain foreign exchange rates between currencies.** A foreign exchange rate is the price of one currency stated in terms of another. An entity with transactions in a foreign currency when the exchange rate changes between the transaction dates and their settlement will experience exchange gains or losses.

A1 **Compute and analyze the components of return on total assets.** Return on total assets has two components: profit margin and total asset turnover. A decline in one component must be met with an increase in another if return on assets is to be maintained. Component analysis is helpful in assessing company performance compared to that of competitors and its own past.

P1 **Account for trading securities.** Investments are initially recorded at cost, and any dividend or interest from these investments is recorded in the income statement. Investments classified as trading securities are reported at market value. Unrealized gains and losses on trading securities are reported in income. When investments are sold, the difference between the net proceeds from the sale and the cost of the securities is recognized as a gain or loss.

P2 **Account for held-to-maturity securities.** Debt securities held-to-maturity are reported at cost when purchased. Interest revenue is recorded as it accrues. The cost of long-term held-to-maturity securities is adjusted for the amortization of any difference between cost and maturity value.

P3 **Account for available-for-sale securities.** Debt and equity securities available-for-sale are recorded at cost when purchased. Available-for-sale securities are reported at their market values on the balance sheet with unrealized gains or losses shown in the equity section. Gains and losses realized on the sale of these investments are reported in the income statement.

P4 **Account for equity securities with significant influence.** The equity method is used when an investor has a significant influence over an investee. This usually exists when an investor owns 20% or more of the investee's voting stock but not more than 50%. The equity method means an investor records its share of investee earnings with a debit to the investment account and a credit to a revenue account. Dividends received reduce the investment account balance.

P5[A] **Record transactions listed in a foreign currency.** When a company makes a credit sale to a foreign customer and sales terms call for payment in a foreign currency, the company must translate the foreign currency into dollars to record the receivable. If the exchange rate changes before payment is received, exchange gains or losses are recognized in the year they occur. The same treatment is used when a company makes a credit purchase from a foreign supplier and is required to make payment in a foreign currency.

Guidance Answers to **Decision Maker**

Money Manager If you have investments in fixed-rate bonds and notes when interest rates fall, the value of your investments increases. This is so because the bonds and notes you hold continue to pay the same (high) rate while the market is demanding a new lower interest rate. Your strategy is to continue holding your investments in bonds and notes, and, potentially, to increase these holdings through additional purchases.

Retailer Your store's return on assets is 11%, which is similar to the industry norm of 11.2%. However, disaggregation of return on assets reveals that your store's profit margin of 4.4% is much higher than the norm of 3.5%, but your total asset turnover of 2.5 is much lower than the norm of 3.2. These results suggest that, as compared with competitors, you are less efficient in using assets. You need to focus on increasing sales or reducing assets. You might consider reducing prices to increase sales, provided such a strategy does not reduce your return on assets. For instance, you could reduce your profit margin to 4% to increase sales. If total asset turnover increases to more than 2.75 when profit margin is lowered to 4%, your overall return on assets is improved.

Entrepreneur You are now less likely to buy Canadian lumber because it takes more U.S. money to buy a Canadian dollar (and lumber). For instance, the purchase of lumber from a Canadian mill with a \$1,000 (Canadian dollars) price would have cost the U.S. builder \$700 (U.S. dollars, computed as C\$1,000 × US\$0.70) before the rate change, and \$800 (US dollars, computed as C\$1,000 × US\$0.80) after the rate change.

Guidance Answers to **Quick Checks**

1. Short-term held-to-maturity securities are reported at cost.
2. Trading securities are reported at market value.
3. The equity section of the balance sheet (and in comprehensive income).
4. The income statement.
5. Long-term investments include (1) long-term funds earmarked for a special purpose, (2) debt and equity securities that do not meet current asset requirements, and (3) long-term assets not used in the regular operations of the business.
6. An equity investment is classified as long term if it is not marketable or, if marketable, it is not held as an available source of cash to meet the needs of current operations.
7. Debt securities held-to-maturity and debt securities available-for-sale are both recorded at cost. Also, interest on both is accrued as earned. However, only long-term securities held-to-maturity require amortization of the difference between cost and maturity value. In addition, only securities available-for-sale require a period-end adjustment to market value.
8. Long-term equity investments are placed in one of three categories and accounted for as follows: (a) **available-for-sale** (noninfluential, less than 20% of outstanding stock)—market value; (b) **significant influence** (20% to 50% of outstanding stock)—equity method; and (c) **controlling influence** (holding more than 50% of outstanding stock)—equity method with consolidation.

Key Terms

mhhe.com/wildFAP19e

Key Terms are available at the book's Website for learning and testing in an online Flashcard Format.

Available-for-sale (AFS) securities (p. 596)
Comprehensive income (p. 600)
Consolidated financial statements (p. 599)
Equity method (p. 598)
Equity securities with controlling influence (p. 599)
Equity securities with significant influence (p. 598)
Foreign exchange rate (p. 605)
Held-to-maturity (HTM) securities (p. 596)
Long-term investments (p. 592)
Multinational (p. 605)
Parent (p. 599)
Return on total assets (p. 600)
Short-term investments (p. 592)
Subsidiary (p. 599)
Trading securities (p. 595)
Unrealized gain (loss) (p. 595)

Multiple Choice Quiz

Answers on p. 625

mhhe.com/wildFAP19e

Additional Quiz Questions are available at the book's Website.

1. A company purchased $30,000 of 5% bonds for investment purposes on May 1. The bonds pay interest on February 1 and August 1. The amount of interest revenue accrued at December 31 (the company's year-end) is:
a. $1,500
b. $1,375
c. $1,000
d. $625
e. $300

2. Earlier this period, Amadeus Co. purchased its only available-for-sale investment in the stock of Bach Co. for $83,000. The period-end market value of this stock is $84,500. Amadeus records a:
a. Credit to Unrealized Gain—Equity for $1,500
b. Debit to Unrealized Loss—Equity for $1,500
c. Debit to Investment Revenue for $1,500
d. Credit to Market Adjustment—Available-for-Sale for $3,500
e. Credit to Cash for $1,500

3. Mozart Co. owns 35% of Melody Inc. Melody pays $50,000 in cash dividends to its shareholders for the period. Mozart's entry to record the Melody dividend includes a:
a. Credit to Investment Revenue for $50,000.
b. Credit to Long-Term Investments for $17,500.
c. Credit to Cash for $17,500.
d. Debit to Long-Term Investments for $17,500.
e. Debit to Cash for $50,000.

4. A company has net income of $300,000, net sales of $2,500,000, and total assets of $2,000,000. Its return on total assets equals:
a. 6.7%
b. 12.0%
c. 8.3%
d. 80.0%
e. 15.0%

5. A company had net income of $80,000, net sales of $600,000, and total assets of $400,000. Its profit margin and total asset turnover are:

	Profit Margin	Total Asset Turnover
a.	1.5%	13.3
b.	13.3%	1.5
c.	13.3%	0.7
d.	7.0%	13.3
e.	10.0%	26.7

Superscript A denotes assignments based on Appendix 15A.

Discussion Questions

1. Under what two conditions should investments be classified as current assets?

2. On a balance sheet, what valuation must be reported for short-term investments in trading securities?

3. If a short-term investment in available-for-sale securities costs $6,780 and is sold for $7,500, how should the difference between these two amounts be recorded?

4. Identify the three classes of noninfluential and two classes of influential investments in securities.

5. Under what conditions should investments be classified as current assets? As long-term assets?

6. If a company purchases its only long-term investments in available-for-sale debt securities this period and their market value is below cost at the balance sheet date, what entry is required to recognize this unrealized loss?

7. On a balance sheet, what valuation must be reported for debt securities classified as available-for-sale?

EXERCISES

Exercise 15-1
Accounting for transactions in short-term securities
C2 P1 P2 P3

Check (c) Dr. Cash $173,400

(f) Dr. Cash $13,025

Prepare journal entries to record the following transactions involving the short-term securities investments of Bolton Co., all of which occurred during year 2009.

a. On February 15, paid $170,000 cash to purchase ACC's 90-day short-term debt securities ($170,000 principal), dated February 15, that pay 8% interest (categorized as held-to-maturity securities).

b. On March 22, purchased 850 shares of Ross Company stock at $21 per share plus a $100 brokerage fee. These shares are categorized as trading securities.

c. On May 16, received a check from ACC in payment of the principal and 90 days' interest on the debt securities purchased in transaction *a*.

d. On August 1, paid $70,000 cash to purchase Nita Co.'s 11% debt securities ($70,000 principal), dated July 30, 2009, and maturing January 30, 2010 (categorized as available-for-sale securities).

e. On September 1, received a $1.10 per share cash dividend on the Ross Company stock purchased in transaction *b*.

f. On October 8, sold 425 shares of Ross Co. stock for $31 per share, less a $150 brokerage fee.

g. On October 30, received a check from Nita Co. for 90 days' interest on the debt securities purchased in transaction *d*.

Exercise 15-2
Accounting for trading securities
C1 P1

Check (3) Gain, $2,250

Borchert Co. purchases various investments in trading securities at a cost of $76,000 on December 27, 2009. (This is its first and only purchase of such securities.) At December 31, 2009, these securities had a market value of $85,000.

1. Prepare the December 31, 2009, year-end adjusting entry for the trading securities' portfolio.
2. Explain how each account in the entry of part 1 is reported in financial statements.
3. Prepare the January 3, 2010, entry when Borchert sells a portion of its trading securities (that had originally cost $38,000) for $40,250.

Exercise 15-3
Adjusting available-for-sale securities to market
C2 P3

Check Unrealized loss, $392

On December 31, 2009, Tagert Company held the following short-term investments in its portfolio of available-for-sale securities. Tagert had no short-term investments in its prior accounting periods. Prepare the December 31, 2009, adjusting entry to report these investments at market value.

	Cost	Market Value
Verrizano Corporation bonds payable	$ 81,400	$92,000
Porter Corporation notes payable	54,900	47,928
Laverne Company common stock	100,500	96,480

Exercise 15-4
Transactions in short-term and long-term investments
C1 C2

Prepare journal entries to record the following transactions involving both the short-term and long-term investments of Corveau Corp., all of which occurred during calendar year 2009. Use the account Short-Term Investments for any transactions that you determine are short term.

a. On February 15, paid $100,000 cash to purchase Anthem's 90-day short-term notes at par, which are dated February 15 and pay 6% interest (classified as held-to-maturity).

b. On March 22, bought 600 shares of Frain Industries common stock at $43 cash per share plus a $140 brokerage fee (classified as long-term available-for-sale securities).

c. On May 15, received a check from Anthem in payment of the principal and 90 days' interest on the notes purchased in transaction *a*.

d. On July 30, paid $30,000 cash to purchase Moto Electronics' 5% notes at par, dated July 30, 2009, and maturing on January 30, 2010 (classified as trading securities).

e. On September 1, received a $0.40 per share cash dividend on the Frain Industries common stock purchased in transaction *b*.

f. On October 8, sold 300 shares of Frain Industries common stock for $49 cash per share, less a $120 brokerage fee.

g. On October 30, received a check from Moto Electronics for three months' interest on the notes purchased in transaction *d*.

c. They can include investments in trading securities.
d. They can include debt securities held-to-maturity.
e. They are always easily sold and therefore qualify as being marketable.
f. They can include debt and equity securities available-for-sale.
g. They can include bonds and stocks not intended to serve as a ready source of cash.

QS 15-6
Describing investments in securities
C1 C2 C3

Complete the following descriptions by filling in the blanks.

1. Equity securities giving an investor significant influence are accounted for using the ____ ____.
2. Trading securities are classified as ____ assets.
3. Accrual of interest on bonds held as long-term investments requires a credit to ____ ____.
4. The controlling investor (more than 50% ownership) is called the ____, and the investee company is called the ____.
5. Available-for-sale debt securities are reported on the balance sheet at ____ ____.

QS 15-7
Debt securities transactions
C2 P2

On February 1, 2009, Garzon purchased 6% bonds issued by Integal Utilities at a cost of $80,000, which is their par value. The bonds pay interest semiannually on July 31 and January 31. For 2009, prepare entries to record Garzon's July 31 receipt of interest and its December 31 year-end interest accrual.

QS 15-8
Recording equity securities
C2 P3

On May 20, 2009, Chiu Co. paid $1,500,000 to acquire 25,000 common shares (10%) of BBE Corp. as a long-term investment. On August 5, 2010, Chiu sold one-half of these shares for $937,500. What valuation method should be used to account for this stock investment? Prepare entries to record both the acquisition and the sale of these shares.

QS 15-9
Equity method transactions
C2 P4

Assume the same facts as in QS 15-8 except that the stock acquired represents 40% of BBE Corp.'s outstanding stock. Also assume that BBE Corp. paid a $150,000 dividend on November 1, 2009, and reported a net income of $1,050,000 for 2009. Prepare the entries to record (*a*) the receipt of the dividend and (*b*) the December 31, 2009, year-end adjustment required for the investment account.

QS 15-10
Recording market adjustment for securities
P3

During the current year, Marketplace Consulting Group acquired long-term available-for-sale securities at an $85,000 cost. At its December 31 year-end, these securities had a market value of $62,000. This is the first and only time the company purchased such securities.

1. Prepare the necessary year-end adjusting entry related to these securities.
2. Explain how each account used in part 1 is reported in the financial statements.

QS 15-11
Return on total assets A1

The return on total assets is the focus of analysts, creditors, and other users of financial statements.

1. How is the return on total assets computed?
2. What does this important ratio reflect?

QS 15-12
Component return on total assets A1

Return on total assets can be separated into two important components.

1. Write the formula to separate the return on total assets into its two basic components.
2. Explain how these components of the return on total assets are helpful to financial statement users for business decisions.

QS 15-13^A
Foreign currency transactions
P5

A U.S. company sells a product to a British company with the transaction listed in British pounds. On the date of the sale, the transaction total of $40,600 is billed as £20,000, reflecting an exchange rate of 2.03 (that is, $2.03 per pound). Prepare the entry to record (1) the sale and (2) the receipt of payment in pounds when the exchange rate is 1.95.

QS 15-14^A
Foreign currency transactions
P5

On March 1, 2009, a U.S. company made a credit sale requiring payment in 30 days from a Malaysian company, Hamac Sdn. Bhd., in 20,000 Malaysian ringgits. Assuming the exchange rate between Malaysian ringgits and U.S. dollars is $0.2963 on March 1 and $0.3005 on March 31, prepare the entries to record the sale on March 1 and the cash receipt on March 31.

EXERCISES

Exercise 15-1
Accounting for transactions in short-term securities
C2 P1 P2 P3

Check (c) Dr. Cash $173,400

(f) Dr. Cash $13,025

Prepare journal entries to record the following transactions involving the short-term securities investments of Bolton Co., all of which occurred during year 2009.

a. On February 15, paid $170,000 cash to purchase ACC's 90-day short-term debt securities ($170,000 principal), dated February 15, that pay 8% interest (categorized as held-to-maturity securities).

b. On March 22, purchased 850 shares of Ross Company stock at $21 per share plus a $100 brokerage fee. These shares are categorized as trading securities.

c. On May 16, received a check from ACC in payment of the principal and 90 days' interest on the debt securities purchased in transaction *a*.

d. On August 1, paid $70,000 cash to purchase Nita Co.'s 11% debt securities ($70,000 principal), dated July 30, 2009, and maturing January 30, 2010 (categorized as available-for-sale securities).

e. On September 1, received a $1.10 per share cash dividend on the Ross Company stock purchased in transaction *b*.

f. On October 8, sold 425 shares of Ross Co. stock for $31 per share, less a $150 brokerage fee.

g. On October 30, received a check from Nita Co. for 90 days' interest on the debt securities purchased in transaction *d*.

Exercise 15-2
Accounting for trading securities
C1 P1

Check (3) Gain, $2,250

Borchert Co. purchases various investments in trading securities at a cost of $76,000 on December 27, 2009. (This is its first and only purchase of such securities.) At December 31, 2009, these securities had a market value of $85,000.

1. Prepare the December 31, 2009, year-end adjusting entry for the trading securities' portfolio.

2. Explain how each account in the entry of part 1 is reported in financial statements.

3. Prepare the January 3, 2010, entry when Borchert sells a portion of its trading securities (that had originally cost $38,000) for $40,250.

Exercise 15-3
Adjusting available-for-sale securities to market
C2 P3

Check Unrealized loss, $392

On December 31, 2009, Tagert Company held the following short-term investments in its portfolio of available-for-sale securities. Tagert had no short-term investments in its prior accounting periods. Prepare the December 31, 2009, adjusting entry to report these investments at market value.

	Cost	Market Value
Verrizano Corporation bonds payable	$ 81,400	$92,000
Porter Corporation notes payable	54,900	47,928
Laverne Company common stock	100,500	96,480

Exercise 15-4
Transactions in short-term and long-term investments
C1 C2

Prepare journal entries to record the following transactions involving both the short-term and long-term investments of Corveau Corp., all of which occurred during calendar year 2009. Use the account Short-Term Investments for any transactions that you determine are short term.

a. On February 15, paid $100,000 cash to purchase Anthem's 90-day short-term notes at par, which are dated February 15 and pay 6% interest (classified as held-to-maturity).

b. On March 22, bought 600 shares of Frain Industries common stock at $43 cash per share plus a $140 brokerage fee (classified as long-term available-for-sale securities).

c. On May 15, received a check from Anthem in payment of the principal and 90 days' interest on the notes purchased in transaction *a*.

d. On July 30, paid $30,000 cash to purchase Moto Electronics' 5% notes at par, dated July 30, 2009, and maturing on January 30, 2010 (classified as trading securities).

e. On September 1, received a $0.40 per share cash dividend on the Frain Industries common stock purchased in transaction *b*.

f. On October 8, sold 300 shares of Frain Industries common stock for $49 cash per share, less a $120 brokerage fee.

g. On October 30, received a check from Moto Electronics for three months' interest on the notes purchased in transaction *d*.

Key Terms

mhhe.com/wildFAP19e

Key Terms are available at the book's Website for learning and testing in an online Flashcard Format.

Available-for-sale (AFS) securities (p. 596)
Comprehensive income (p. 600)
Consolidated financial statements (p. 599)
Equity method (p. 598)
Equity securities with controlling influence (p. 599)
Equity securities with significant influence (p. 598)
Foreign exchange rate (p. 605)
Held-to-maturity (HTM) securities (p. 596)
Long-term investments (p. 592)
Multinational (p. 605)
Parent (p. 599)
Return on total assets (p. 600)
Short-term investments (p. 592)
Subsidiary (p. 599)
Trading securities (p. 595)
Unrealized gain (loss) (p. 595)

Multiple Choice Quiz

Answers on p. 625 mhhe.com/wildFAP19e

Additional Quiz Questions are available at the book's Website.

1. A company purchased $30,000 of 5% bonds for investment purposes on May 1. The bonds pay interest on February 1 and August 1. The amount of interest revenue accrued at December 31 (the company's year-end) is:
   a. $1,500
   b. $1,375
   c. $1,000
   d. $625
   e. $300
2. Earlier this period, Amadeus Co. purchased its only available-for-sale investment in the stock of Bach Co. for $83,000. The period-end market value of this stock is $84,500. Amadeus records a:
   a. Credit to Unrealized Gain—Equity for $1,500
   b. Debit to Unrealized Loss—Equity for $1,500
   c. Debit to Investment Revenue for $1,500
   d. Credit to Market Adjustment—Available-for-Sale for $3,500
   e. Credit to Cash for $1,500
3. Mozart Co. owns 35% of Melody Inc. Melody pays $50,000 in cash dividends to its shareholders for the period. Mozart's entry to record the Melody dividend includes a:
   a. Credit to Investment Revenue for $50,000.
   b. Credit to Long-Term Investments for $17,500.
   c. Credit to Cash for $17,500.
   d. Debit to Long-Term Investments for $17,500.
   e. Debit to Cash for $50,000.
4. A company has net income of $300,000, net sales of $2,500,000, and total assets of $2,000,000. Its return on total assets equals:
   a. 6.7%
   b. 12.0%
   c. 8.3%
   d. 80.0%
   e. 15.0%
5. A company had net income of $80,000, net sales of $600,000, and total assets of $400,000. Its profit margin and total asset turnover are:

	Profit Margin	Total Asset Turnover
a.	1.5%	13.3
b.	13.3%	1.5
c.	13.3%	0.7
d.	7.0%	13.3
e.	10.0%	26.7

Superscript A denotes assignments based on Appendix 15A.

Discussion Questions

1. Under what two conditions should investments be classified as current assets?
2. On a balance sheet, what valuation must be reported for short-term investments in trading securities?
3. If a short-term investment in available-for-sale securities costs $6,780 and is sold for $7,500, how should the difference between these two amounts be recorded?
4. Identify the three classes of noninfluential and two classes of influential investments in securities.
5. Under what conditions should investments be classified as current assets? As long-term assets?
6. If a company purchases its only long-term investments in available-for-sale debt securities this period and their market value is below cost at the balance sheet date, what entry is required to recognize this unrealized loss?
7. On a balance sheet, what valuation must be reported for debt securities classified as available-for-sale?

8. Under what circumstances are long-term investments in debt securities reported at cost and adjusted for amortization of any difference between cost and maturity value?

9. For investments in available-for-sale securities, how are unrealized (holding) gains and losses reported?

10. In accounting for investments in equity securities, when should the equity method be used?

11. Under what circumstances does a company prepare consolidated financial statements?

12. [A] What are two major challenges in accounting for international operations?

13. [A] Assume a U.S. company makes a credit sale to a foreign customer that is required to make payment in its foreign currency. In the current period, the exchange rate is $1.40 on the date of the sale and is $1.30 on the date the customer pays the receivable. Will the U.S. company record an exchange gain or loss?

14. [A] If a U.S. company makes a credit sale to a foreign customer required to make payment in U.S. dollars, can the U.S. company have an exchange gain or loss on this sale?

15. Refer to **Best Buy**'s statement of changes in shareholders' equity in Appendix A. What is the amount of foreign currency translation adjustment for the year ended March 3, 2007? Is this adjustment an unrealized gain or an unrealized loss?

16. Refer to the balance sheet of **Circuit City** in Appendix A. How can you tell that Circuit City uses the consolidated method of accounting?

17. Refer to **RadioShack**'s statement of stockholders' equity. What was the amount of its 2006 unrealized gain or loss on securities?

18. Refer to the financial statements of **Apple** in Appendix A. Compute its return on total assets for the year ended September 30, 2006.

Denotes Discussion Questions that involve decision making.

QUICK STUDY

QS 15-1
Short-term equity investments C2 P1

On April 18, Rollo Co. made a short-term investment in 600 common shares of TXT Co. The purchase price is $84 per share and the broker's fee is $500. The intent is to actively manage these shares for profit. On May 30, Rollo Co. receives $0.75 per share from TXT in dividends. Prepare the April 18 and May 30 journal entries to record these transactions.

QS 15-2
Available-for-sale securities
C2 P3

Malox Co. purchased short-term investments in available-for-sale securities at a cost of $100,000 on November 25, 2009. At December 31, 2009, these securities had a market value of $94,000. This is the first and only time the company has purchased such securities.

1. Prepare the December 31, 2009, year-end adjusting entry for the securities' portfolio.
2. For each account in the entry for part 1, explain how it is reported in financial statements.
3. Prepare the April 6, 2010, entry when Malox sells one-fourth of these securities for $27,000.

QS 15-3
Available-for-sale securities
C2 P3

Prepare Vikon Company's journal entries to reflect the following transactions for the current year.

May 7 Purchases 200 shares of Felton stock as a short-term investment in available-for-sale securities at a cost of $100 per share plus $400 in broker fees.
June 6 Sells 200 shares of its investment in Felton stock at $112 per share. The broker's commission on this sale is $250.

QS 15-4
Available-for-sale securities
C2 P3

Texar Company completes the following transactions during the current year.

May 9 Purchases 400 shares of Crayton stock as a short-term investment in available-for-sale securities at a cost of $30 per share plus $200 in broker fees.
June 2 Sells 200 shares of its investment in Crayton stock at $32 per share. The broker's commission on this sale is $120.
Dec. 31 The closing market price of the Crayton stock is $28 per share.

Prepare the May 9 and June 2 journal entries and the December 31 adjusting entry. This is the first and only time the company purchased such securities.

QS 15-5
Identifying long-term investments
C1

Which of the following statements are true of long-term investments?

a. They are held as an investment of cash available for current operations.
b. They can include funds earmarked for a special purpose, such as bond sinking funds.

On December 31, 2009, Loren Co. held the following short-term available-for-sale securities.

Exercise 15-5
Market adjustment to available-for-sale securities
P3

	Cost	Market Value
Nintendo Co. common stock	$64,500	$70,305
Unilever bonds payable	25,800	23,994
Kellogg Co. notes payable	46,440	43,654
McDonald's Corp. common stock	87,075	82,721

Loren had no short-term investments prior to the current period. Prepare the December 31, 2009, year-end adjusting entry to record the market adjustment for these securities.

Patica Co. began operations in 2008. The cost and market values for its long-term investments portfolio in available-for-sale securities are shown below. Prepare Patica's December 31, 2009, adjusting entry to reflect any necessary market adjustment for these investments.

Exercise 15-6
Market adjustment to available-for-sale securities
P3

	Cost	Market Value
December 31, 2008	$67,842	$61,736
December 31, 2009	73,479	77,888

Basil Services began operations in 2007 and maintains long-term investments in available-for-sale securities. The year-end cost and market values for its portfolio of these investments follow. Prepare journal entries to record each year-end market adjustment for these securities.

Exercise 15-7
Multi-year market adjustments to available-for-sale securities
P3

	Cost	Market Value
December 31, 2007	$392,900	$381,113
December 31, 2008	447,906	474,780
December 31, 2009	609,152	720,627
December 31, 2010	919,820	818,640

Information regarding Seaton Company's individual investments in securities during its calendar-year 2009, along with the December 31, 2009, market values, follows.

Exercise 15-8
Classifying investments in securities; recording market values
C1 C2 P2 P3 P4

a. Investment in Beeman Company bonds: $443,150 cost, $481,704 market value. Seaton intends to hold these bonds until they mature in 2014.

b. Investment in Baybridge common stock: 29,500 shares; $352,304 cost; $382,954 market value. Seaton owns 32% of Baybridge's voting stock and has a significant influence over Baybridge.

c. Investment in Carroll common stock: 12,000 shares; $181,692 cost; $195,864 market value. This investment amounts to 3% of Carroll's outstanding shares, and Seaton's goal with this investment is to earn dividends over the next few years.

d. Investment in Newtech common stock: 3,500 shares; $101,038 cost; $99,320 market value. Seaton's goal with this investment is to reap an increase in market value of the stock over the next three to five years. Newtech has 30,000 common shares outstanding.

e. Investment in Flock common stock: 16,300 shares; $110,788 cost; $117,657 market value. This stock is marketable and is held as an investment of cash available for operations.

Required

1. Identify whether each investment should be classified as a short-term or long-term investment. For each long-term investment, indicate in which of the long-term investment classifications it should be placed.

2. Prepare a journal entry dated December 31, 2009, to record the market value adjustment of the long-term investments in available-for-sale securities. Seaton had no long-term investments prior to year 2009.

Check (2) Unrealized gain, $12,454

Exercise 15-9
Securities transactions; equity method
P4 C2

Prepare journal entries to record the following transactions and events of Kareen Company.

2009

Jan. 2 Purchased 55,000 shares of Altus Co. common stock for $374,000 cash plus a broker's fee of $2,650 cash. Altus has 137,500 shares of common stock outstanding and its policies will be significantly influenced by Kareen.
Sept. 1 Altus declared and paid a cash dividend of $3.05 per share.
Dec. 31 Altus announced that net income for the year is $1,106,900.

2010

June 1 Altus declared and paid a cash dividend of $3.30 per share.
Dec. 31 Altus announced that net income for the year is $1,240,900.
Dec. 31 Kareen sold 11,000 shares of Altus for $294,250 cash.

Exercise 15-10
Return on total assets
A1

The following information is available from the financial statements of Interstate Industries. Compute Interstate's return on total assets for 2009 and 2010. (Round returns to one-tenth of a percent.) Comment on the company's efficiency in using its assets in 2009 and 2010.

		2008	2009	2010
1		2008	2009	2010
2	Total assets, December 31	$148,000	$252,000	$592,000
3	Net income	22,200	28,600	45,998
4				

Exercise 15-11^A
Foreign currency transactions
P5

Leigh of New York sells its products to customers in the United States and the United Kingdom. On December 16, 2009, Leigh sold merchandise on credit to Berton Ltd. of London at a price of 20,000 pounds. The exchange rate on that day for £1 was $2.0325. On December 31, 2009, when Leigh prepared its financial statements, the rate was £1 for $2.0292. Berton paid its bill in full on January 15, 2010, at which time the exchange rate was £1 for $2.0340. Leigh immediately exchanged the 20,000 pounds for U.S. dollars. Prepare Leigh's journal entries on December 16, December 31, and January 15 (round to the nearest dollar).

Exercise 15-12^A
Computing foreign exchange gains and losses on receivables
C4 P5

On May 8, 2009, Jett Company (a U.S. company) made a credit sale to Munoz (a Mexican company). The terms of the sale required Munoz to pay 850,000 pesos on February 10, 2010. Jett prepares quarterly financial statements on March 31, June 30, September 30, and December 31. The exchange rates for pesos during the time the receivable is outstanding follow.

May 8, 2009	$0.0932
June 30, 2009	0.0941
September 30, 2009	0.0952
December 31, 2009	0.0935
February 10, 2010	0.0974

Compute the foreign exchange gain or loss that Jett should report on each of its quarterly income statements for the last three quarters of 2009 and the first quarter of 2010. Also compute the amount reported on Jett's balance sheets at the end of each of its last three quarters of 2009.

Available with McGraw-Hill's Homework Manager — McGraw-Hill's HOMEWORK MANAGER®

PROBLEM SET A

Problem 15-1A
Recording transactions and market adjustments for trading securities
C2 P1

Protom Company, which began operations in 2009, invests its idle cash in trading securities. The following transactions are from its short-term investments in its trading securities.

2009

Jan. 20 Purchased 800 shares of Ford Motor Co. at $26 per share plus a $120 commission.
Feb. 9 Purchased 2,600 shares of Lucent at $39 per share plus a $578 commission.
Oct. 12 Purchased 800 shares of Z-Seven at $7.50 per share plus a $200 commission.

2010

Apr. 15 Sold 800 shares of Ford Motor Co. at $30 per share less a $300 commission.
July 5 Sold 800 shares of Z-Seven at $11 per share less a $103 commission.
July 22 Purchased 2,000 shares of Hunt Corp. at $39 per share plus a $444 commission.
Aug. 19 Purchased 1,600 shares of Donna Karan at $19.50 per share plus a $290 commission.

2011

Feb. 27 Purchased 3,500 shares of HCA at $31 per share plus a $420 commission.
Mar. 3 Sold 2,000 shares of Hunt at $35 per share less a $250 commission.
June 21 Sold 2,600 shares of Lucent at $36.75 per share less a $420 commission.
June 30 Purchased 1,300 shares of Black & Decker at $47.50 per share plus a $595 commission.
Nov. 1 Sold 1,600 shares of Donna Karan at $19.50 per share less a $309 commission.

Required

1. Prepare journal entries to record these short-term investment activities for the years shown. (Ignore any year-end adjusting entries.)

2. On December 31, 2011, prepare the adjusting entry to record any necessary market adjustment for the portfolio of trading securities when HCA's share price is $33 and Black & Decker's share price is $43.50. (Assume the Market Adjustment—Trading account had an unadjusted balance of zero.)

Check (2) Dr. Market Adjustment—Trading $785

Problem 15-2A
Recording, adjusting, and reporting short-term available-for-sale securities
C2 P3

Freema Company had no short-term investments prior to year 2009. It had the following transactions involving short-term investments in available-for-sale securities during 2009.

Apr. 16 Purchased 8,000 shares of Gem Co. stock at $29.75 per share plus a $440 brokerage fee.
May 1 Paid $125,000 to buy 90-day U.S. Treasury bills (debt securities): $125,000 principal amount, 4% interest, securities dated May 1.
July 7 Purchased 4,000 shares of PepsiCo stock at $47.75 per share plus a $410 brokerage fee.
20 Purchased 2,000 shares of Xerox stock at $19.75 per share plus a $490 brokerage fee.
Aug. 3 Received a check for principal and accrued interest on the U.S. Treasury bills that matured on July 29.
15 Received a $0.90 per share cash dividend on the Gem Co. stock.
28 Sold 4,000 shares of Gem Co. stock at $36.50 per share less a $250 brokerage fee.
Oct. 1 Received a $1.75 per share cash dividend on the PepsiCo shares.
Dec. 15 Received a $1.05 per share cash dividend on the remaining Gem Co. shares.
31 Received a $1.30 per share cash dividend on the PepsiCo shares.

Required

1. Prepare journal entries to record the preceding transactions and events.

2. Prepare a table to compare the year-end cost and market values of Freema's short-term investments in available-for-sale securities. The year-end market values per share are: Gem Co., $32.00; PepsiCo, $45.00; and Xerox, $16.75.

Check (2) Cost = $350,620

3. Prepare an adjusting entry, if necessary, to record the year-end market adjustment for the portfolio of short-term investments in available-for-sale securities.

(3) Dr. Unrealized Loss—Equity $9,120

Analysis Component

4. Explain the balance sheet presentation of the market adjustment for Freema's short-term investments.

5. How do these short-term investments affect Freema's (*a*) income statement for year 2009 and (*b*) the equity section of its balance sheet at year-end 2009?

Problem 15-3A
Recording, adjusting, and reporting long-term available-for-sale securities
C2 P3

Tennant Security, which began operations in 2009, invests in long-term available-for-sale securities. Following is a series of transactions and events determining its long-term investment activity.

2009

Jan. 20 Purchased 1,200 shares of Johnson & Johnson at $20.50 per share plus a $240 commission.
Feb. 9 Purchased 1,000 shares of Sony at $46.20 per share plus a $220 commission.
June 12 Purchased 1,700 shares of Mattel at $28 per share plus a $195 commission.
Dec. 31 Per share market values for stocks in the portfolio are Johnson & Johnson, $21.50; Mattel, $26.50; Sony, $38.

2010

Apr. 15 Sold 1,200 shares of Johnson & Johnson at $23.50 per share less a $525 commission.
July 5 Sold 1,700 shares of Mattel at $26.50 per share less a $235 commission.
July 22 Purchased 500 shares of Sara Lee at $22.50 per share plus a $420 commission.
Aug. 19 Purchased 900 shares of Eastman Kodak at $14 per share plus a $198 commission.
Dec. 31 Per share market values for stocks in the portfolio are: Kodak, $16.25; Sara Lee, $20.00; Sony, $35.00.

2011

Feb. 27 Purchased 3,000 shares of Microsoft at $65 per share plus a $520 commission.
June 21 Sold 1,000 shares of Sony at $48.00 per share less an $880 commission.
June 30 Purchased 1,500 shares of Black & Decker at $38 per share plus a $435 commission.
Aug. 3 Sold 500 shares of Sara Lee at $16.25 per share less a $435 commission.
Nov. 1 Sold 900 shares of Eastman Kodak at $19.75 per share less a $625 commission.
Dec. 31 Per share market values for stocks in the portfolio are: Black & Decker, $41; Microsoft, $67.

Required

1. Prepare journal entries to record these transactions and events and any year-end market adjustments to the portfolio of long-term available-for-sale securities.

Check (2b) Market adjustment bal.: 12/31/09, $(10,205); 12/31/10; $(11,263)

2. Prepare a table that summarizes the (*a*) total cost, (*b*) total market adjustment, and (*c*) total market value of the portfolio of long-term available-for-sale securities at each year-end.

(3b) Unrealized Gain at 12/31/2011, $9,545

3. Prepare a table that summarizes (*a*) the realized gains and losses and (*b*) the unrealized gains or losses for the portfolio of long-term available-for-sale securities at each year-end.

Problem 15-4A
Long-term investment transactions; unrealized and realized gains and losses
C2 C3 P3 P4

Elevant Co.'s long-term available-for-sale portfolio at December 31, 2008, consists of the following.

Available-for-Sale Securities	Cost	Market Value
40,000 shares of Company A common stock	$535,300	$500,000
7,000 shares of Company B common stock	159,380	151,000
17,500 shares of Company C common stock	662,600	640,938

Elevant enters into the following long-term investment transactions during year 2009.

Jan. 29 Sold 3,500 shares of Company B common stock for $79,100 less a brokerage fee of $1,400.
Apr. 17 Purchased 9,900 shares of Company W common stock for $197,500 plus a brokerage fee of $2,300. The shares represent a 30% ownership in Company W.
July 6 Purchased 4,200 shares of Company X common stock for $118,125 plus a brokerage fee of $1,650. The shares represent a 10% ownership in Company X.
Aug. 22 Purchased 50,000 shares of Company Y common stock for $375,000 plus a brokerage fee of $1,100. The shares represent a 51% ownership in Company Y.
Nov. 13 Purchased 8,300 shares of Company Z common stock for $261,596 plus a brokerage fee of $2,350. The shares represent a 5% ownership in Company Z.
Dec. 9 Sold 40,000 shares of Company A common stock for $515,000 less a brokerage fee of $4,000.

The market values of its investments at December 31, 2009, are: B, $81,375; C, $610,312; W, $191,250; X, $110,250; Y, $531,250; and Z, $272,240.

Required

1. Determine the amount Elevant should report on its December 31, 2009, balance sheet for its long-term investments in available-for-sale securities.

Check (2) Cr. Unrealized Loss—Equity, $13,508

2. Prepare any necessary December 31, 2009, adjusting entry to record the market value adjustment for the long-term investments in available-for-sale securities.

3. What amount of gains or losses on transactions relating to long-term investments in available-for-sale securities should Elevant report on its December 31, 2009, income statement?

Problem 15-5A
Accounting for long-term investments in securities; with and without significant influence
C2 P3 P4

Selk Steel Co., which began operations on January 4, 2009, had the following subsequent transactions and events in its long-term investments.

2009

Jan. 5	Selk purchased 50,000 shares (20% of total) of Wulf's common stock for $1,567,000.
Oct. 23	Wulf declared and paid a cash dividend of $3.20 per share.
Dec. 31	Wulf's net income for 2009 is $1,164,000, and the market value of its stock at December 31 is $34 per share.

2010

Oct. 15	Wulf declared and paid a cash dividend of $2.50 per share.
Dec. 31	Wulf's net income for 2010 is $1,476,000, and the market value of its stock at December 31 is $36.00 per share.

2011

Jan. 2	Selk sold all of its investment in Wulf for $1,895,500 cash.

Part 1

Assume that Selk has a significant influence over Wulf with its 20% share of stock.

Required

1. Prepare journal entries to record these transactions and events for Selk.
2. Compute the carrying (book) value per share of Selk's investment in Wulf common stock as reflected in the investment account on January 1, 2011.
3. Compute the net increase or decrease in Selk's equity from January 5, 2009, through January 2, 2011, resulting from its investment in Wulf.

Check (2) Carrying value per share, $36.20

Part 2

Assume that although Selk owns 20% of Wulf's outstanding stock, circumstances indicate that it does not have a significant influence over the investee and that it is classified as an available-for-sale security investment.

Required

1. Prepare journal entries to record the preceding transactions and events for Selk. Also prepare an entry dated January 2, 2011, to remove any balance related to the market adjustment.
2. Compute the cost per share of Selk's investment in Wulf common stock as reflected in the investment account on January 1, 2011.
3. Compute the net increase or decrease in Selk's equity from January 5, 2009, through January 2, 2011, resulting from its investment in Wulf.

(1) 1/2/2011 Dr. Unrealized Gain—Equity $233,000

(3) Net increase, $613,500

Problem 15-6A^A
Foreign currency transactions
C4 P5

Patriot Company, a U.S. corporation with customers in several foreign countries, had the following selected transactions for 2009 and 2010.

2009

Apr. 8	Sold merchandise to Salinas & Sons of Mexico for $27,456 cash. The exchange rate for pesos is $0.0932 on this day.
July 21	Sold merchandise on credit to Sumito Corp. in Japan. The price of 2.7 million yen is to be paid 120 days from the date of sale. The exchange rate for yen is $0.0082 on this day.
Oct. 14	Sold merchandise for 18,000 pounds to Smithers Ltd. of Great Britain, payment in full to be received in 90 days. The exchange rate for pounds is $2.0330 on this day.
Nov. 18	Received Sumito's payment in yen for its July 21 purchase and immediately exchanged the yen for dollars. The exchange rate for yen is $0.0079 on this day.
Dec. 20	Sold merchandise for 20,000 ringgits to Hamid Albar of Malaysia, payment in full to be received in 30 days. On this day, the exchange rate for ringgits is $0.2963.

Dec. 31 Recorded adjusting entries to recognize exchange gains or losses on Patriot's annual financial statements. Rates for exchanging foreign currencies on this day follow.

Pesos (Mexico)	$0.0937
Yen (Japan)	0.0075
Pounds (Britain)	2.0345
Ringgits (Malaysia)	0.2949

2010

Jan. 12 Received full payment in pounds from Smithers for the October 14 sale and immediately exchanged the pounds for dollars. The exchange rate for pounds is $2.0355 on this day.

Jan. 19 Received Hamid Albar's full payment in ringgits for the December 20 sale and immediately exchanged the ringgits for dollars. The exchange rate for ringgits is $0.2936 on this day.

Required

1. Prepare journal entries for the Patriot transactions and adjusting entries (round amounts to the nearest dollar).

2. Compute the foreign exchange gain or loss to be reported on Patriot's 2009 income statement.

Check (2) 2009 total foreign exchange loss, $811

Analysis Component

3. What actions might Patriot consider to reduce its risk of foreign exchange gains or losses?

PROBLEM SET B

Problem 15-1B
Recording transactions and market adjustments for trading securities
C2 P1

Harter Company, which began operations in 2009, invests its idle cash in trading securities. The following transactions relate to its short-term investments in its trading securities.

2009

Mar. 10 Purchased 900 shares of Timex at $28.00 per share plus a $125 commission.
May 7 Purchased 2,500 shares of MTV at $37.00 per share plus a $578 commission.
Sept. 1 Purchased 780 shares of UPS at $7.00 per share plus a $200 commission.

2010

Apr. 26 Sold 2,500 shares of MTV at $35.50 per share less a $295 commission.
Apr. 27 Sold 780 shares of UPS at $10.50 per share less a $103 commission.
June 2 Purchased 1,600 shares of SPW at $34.00 per share plus a $444 commission.
June 14 Purchased 1,600 shares of Wal-Mart at $20.00 per share plus a $290 commission.

2011

Jan. 28 Purchased 3,400 shares of PepsiCo at $38.00 per share plus a $400 commission.
Jan. 31 Sold 1,600 shares of SPW at $29.00 per share less a $250 commission.
Aug. 22 Sold 900 shares of Timex at $26.25 per share less a $420 commission.
Sept. 3 Purchased 1,500 shares of Vodaphone at $47.50 per share plus a $600 commission.
Oct. 9 Sold 1,600 shares of Wal-Mart at $22.50 per share less a $309 commission.

Required

1. Prepare journal entries to record these short-term investment activities for the years shown. (Ignore any year-end adjusting entries.)

2. On December 31, 2011, prepare the adjusting entry to record any necessary market adjustment for the portfolio of trading securities when PepsiCo's share price is $36.00 and Vodaphone's share price is $44.00. (Assume the Market Adjustment—Trading account had an unadjusted balance of zero.)

Check (2) Cr. Market Adjustment—Trading $13,050

SP Systems had no short-term investments prior to 2009. It had the following transactions involving short-term investments in available-for-sale securities during 2009.

Problem 15-2B
Recording, adjusting, and reporting short-term available-for-sale securities

C2 P3

Feb.	6	Purchased 6,000 shares of Nokia stock at $24.75 per share plus a $400 brokerage fee.
	15	Paid $250,000 to buy six-month U.S. Treasury bills (debt securities): $250,000 principal amount, 4% interest, securities dated February 15.
Apr.	7	Purchased 3,000 shares of Dell Co. stock at $49.25 per share plus a $370 brokerage fee.
June	2	Purchased 1,500 shares of Merck stock at $18.25 per share plus a $450 brokerage fee.
	30	Received a $0.19 per share cash dividend on the Nokia shares.
Aug.	11	Sold 1,500 shares of Nokia stock at $29.50 per share less a $490 brokerage fee.
	16	Received a check for principal and accrued interest on the U.S. Treasury bills purchased February 15.
	24	Received a $0.16 per share cash dividend on the Dell shares.
Nov.	9	Received a $0.20 per share cash dividend on the remaining Nokia shares.
Dec.	18	Received a $0.21 per share cash dividend on the Dell shares.

Required

1. Prepare journal entries to record the preceding transactions and events.

2. Prepare a table to compare the year-end cost and market values of the short-term investments in available-for-sale securities. The year-end market values per share are: Nokia, $23.50; Dell, $55.50; and Merck, $15.25.

Check (2) Cost = $287,620

3. Prepare an adjusting entry, if necessary, to record the year-end market adjustment for the portfolio of short-term investments in available-for-sale securities.

(3) Cr. Unrealized Gain—Equity, $7,505

Analysis Component

4. Explain the balance sheet presentation of the market adjustment to SP's short-term investments.

5. How do these short-term investments affect (*a*) its income statement for year 2009 and (*b*) the equity section of its balance sheet at the 2009 year-end?

Bleeker Enterprises, which began operations in 2009, invests in long-term available-for-sale securities. Following is a series of transactions and events involving its long-term investment activity.

Problem 15-3B
Recording, adjusting, and reporting long-term available-for-sale securities

C2 P3

2009

Mar. 10	Purchased 1,000 shares of Apple at $23.00 per share plus $240 commission.
Apr. 7	Purchased 1,300 shares of Ford at $46.20 per share plus $225 commission.
Sept. 1	Purchased 1,500 shares of Polaroid at $25.00 per share plus $195 commission.
Dec. 31	Per share market values for stocks in the portfolio are: Apple, $24.00; Ford, $42.00; Polaroid, $27.00.

2010

Apr. 26	Sold 1,300 shares of Ford at $44.00 per share less a $250 commission.
June 2	Purchased 1,800 shares of Duracell at $19.25 per share plus a $235 commission.
June 14	Purchased 600 shares of Sears at $22.50 per share plus a $470 commission.
Nov. 27	Sold 1,500 shares of Polaroid at $29 per share less a $198 commission.
Dec. 31	Per share market values for stocks in the portfolio are: Apple, $26.00; Duracell, $18.00; Sears, $25.00.

2011

Jan. 28	Purchased 2,000 shares of Coca-Cola Co. at $69 per share plus a $530 commission.
Aug. 22	Sold 1,000 shares of Apple at $20.00 per share less a $280 commission.
Sept. 3	Purchased 2,000 shares of Motorola at $36 per share plus a $435 commission.
Oct. 9	Sold 600 shares of Sears at $26.25 per share less a $435 commission.
Oct. 31	Sold 1,800 shares of Duracell at $15.00 per share less a $425 commission.
Dec. 31	Per share market values for stocks in the portfolio are: Coca-Cola, $75.00; Motorola, $32.00.

Required

1. Prepare journal entries to record these transactions and events and any year-end market adjustments to the portfolio of long-term available-for-sale securities.

2. Prepare a table that summarizes the (*a*) total cost, (*b*) total market adjustment, and (*c*) total market value for the portfolio of long-term available-for-sale securities at each year-end.

3. Prepare a table that summarizes (*a*) the realized gains and losses and (*b*) the unrealized gains or losses for the portfolio of long-term available-for-sale securities at each year-end.

Check (2b) Market adjustment bal.: 12/31/09, $(2,120); 12/31/10, $1,305

(3b) Unrealized Gain at 12/31/2011, $3,035

Problem 15-4B

Long-term investment transactions; unrealized and realized gains and losses

C2 C3 P3 P4

Chavez's long-term available-for-sale portfolio at December 31, 2008, consists of the following.

Available-for-Sale Securities	Cost	Market Value
55,000 shares of Company R common stock	$1,118,250	$1,198,000
17,000 shares of Company S common stock	600,600	586,500
22,000 shares of Company T common stock	294,590	303,600

Chavez enters into the following long-term investment transactions during year 2009.

Jan. 13 Sold 4,250 shares of Company S stock for $145,500 less a brokerage fee of $650.

Mar. 24 Purchased 31,000 shares of Company U common stock for $565,750 plus a brokerage fee of $1,980. The shares represent a 62% ownership interest in Company U.

Apr. 5 Purchased 85,000 shares of Company V common stock for $267,750 plus a brokerage fee of $1,125. The shares represent a 10% ownership in Company V.

Sept. 2 Sold 22,000 shares of Company T common stock for $313,500 less a brokerage fee of $2,700.

Sept. 27 Purchased 5,000 shares of Company W common stock for $101,000 plus a brokerage fee of $350. The shares represent a 25% ownership interest in Company W.

Oct. 30 Purchased 10,000 shares of Company X common stock for $97,500 plus a brokerage fee of $300. The shares represent a 13% ownership interest in Company X.

The market values of its investments at December 31, 2009, are: R, $1,136,250; S, $420,750; U, $545,600; V, $269,876; W, $109,378; and X, $91,250.

Required

1. Determine the amount Chavez should report on its December 31, 2009, balance sheet for its long-term investments in available-for-sale securities.

2. Prepare any necessary December 31, 2009, adjusting entry to record the market value adjustment of the long-term investments in available-for-sale securities.

3. What amount of gains or losses on transactions relating to long-term investments in available-for-sale securities should Chavez report on its December 31, 2009, income statement?

Check (2) Dr. Unrealized Gain—Equity, $74,660; Cr. Market Adjustment, $91,909

Problem 15-5B

Accounting for long-term investments in securities; with and without significant influence

C2 P3 P4

Devin Company, which began operations on January 3, 2009, had the following subsequent transactions and events in its long-term investments.

2009

Jan. 5 Devin purchased 25,000 shares (25% of total) of Bloch's common stock for $401,000.

Aug. 1 Bloch declared and paid a cash dividend of $1.10 per share.

Dec. 31 Bloch's net income for 2009 is $164,000, and the market value of its stock is $17.50 per share.

2010

Aug. 1 Bloch declared and paid a cash dividend of $1.30 per share.

Dec. 31 Bloch's net income for 2010 is $156,000, and the market value of its stock is $19.25 per share.

2011

Jan. 8 Devin sold all of its investment in Bloch for $550,000 cash.

Part 1

Assume that Devin has a significant influence over Bloch with its 25% share.

Required

1. Prepare journal entries to record these transactions and events for Devin.
2. Compute the carrying (book) value per share of Devin's investment in Bloch common stock as reflected in the investment account on January 7, 2011.
3. Compute the net increase or decrease in Devin's equity from January 5, 2009, through January 8, 2011, resulting from its investment in Bloch.

Check (2) Carrying value per share, $16.84

Part 2

Assume that although Devin owns 25% of Bloch's outstanding stock, circumstances indicate that it does not have a significant influence over the investee and that it is classified as an available-for-sale security investment.

Required

1. Prepare journal entries to record these transactions and events for Devin. Also prepare an entry dated January 8, 2011, to remove any balance related to the market adjustment.
2. Compute the cost per share of Devin's investment in Bloch common stock as reflected in the investment account on January 7, 2011.
3. Compute the net increase or decrease in Devin's equity from January 5, 2009, through January 8, 2011, resulting from its investment in Bloch.

(1) 1/8/2011 Dr. Unrealized Gain—Equity $80,250

(3) Net increase, $209,000

Problem 15-6B[A]
Foreign currency transactions
C4 P5

Kitna, a U.S. corporation with customers in several foreign countries, had the following selected transactions for 2009 and 2010.

2009

May 26 Sold merchandise for 5.5 million yen to Fuji Company of Japan, payment in full to be received in 60 days. On this day, the exchange rate for yen is $0.0088.

June 1 Sold merchandise to Fordham Ltd. of Great Britain for $73,500 cash. The exchange rate for pounds is $2.0331 on this day.

July 25 Received Fuji's payment in yen for its May 26 purchase and immediately exchanged the yen for dollars. The exchange rate for yen is $0.0087 on this day.

Oct. 15 Sold merchandise on credit to Martinez Brothers of Mexico. The price of 425,000 pesos is to be paid 90 days from the date of sale. On this day, the exchange rate for pesos is $0.0932.

Dec. 6 Sold merchandise for 300,000 yuans to Chi-Ying Company of China, payment in full to be received in 30 days. The exchange rate for yuans is $0.1335 on this day.

Dec. 31 Recorded adjusting entries to recognize exchange gains or losses on Kitna's annual financial statements. Rates of exchanging foreign currencies on this day follow.

Yen (Japan)	$0.0089
Pounds (Britain)	2.0402
Pesos (Mexico)	0.0994
Yuans (China)	0.1351

2010

Jan. 5 Received Chi-Ying's full payment in yuans for the December 6 sale and immediately exchanged the yuans for dollars. The exchange rate for yuans is $0.1372 on this day.

Jan. 13 Received full payment in pesos from Martinez for the October 15 sale and immediately exchanged the pesos for dollars. The exchange rate for pesos is $0.0960 on this day.

Required

1. Prepare journal entries for the Kitna transactions and adjusting entries.
2. Compute the foreign exchange gain or loss to be reported on Kitna's 2009 income statement.

Check 2009 total foreign exchange gain, $2,565

Analysis Component

3. What actions might Kitna consider to reduce its risk of foreign exchange gains or losses?

SERIAL PROBLEM

Success Systems

(This serial problem began in Chapter 1 and continues through most of the book. If previous chapter segments were not completed, the serial problem can begin at this point. It is helpful, but not necessary, to use the Working Papers that accompany the book.)

SP 15 While reviewing the March 31, 2010, balance sheet of Success Systems, Adriana Lopez notes that the business has built a large cash balance of $77,845. Its most recent bank money market statement shows that the funds are earning an annualized return of 0.75%. Lopez decides to make several investments with the desire to earn a higher return on the idle cash balance. Accordingly, in April 2010, Success Systems makes the following investments in trading securities:

April 16 Purchases 400 shares of Johnson & Johnson stock at $50 per share plus $300 commission.
April 30 Purchases 200 shares of Starbucks Corporation at $22 per share plus $250 commission.

On June 30, 2010, the per share market price of the Johnson & Johnson shares is $55 and the Starbucks shares is $19.

Required

1. Prepare journal entries to record the April purchases of trading securities by Success Systems.
2. On June 30, 2010, prepare the adjusting entry to record any necessary market adjustment to its portfolio of trading securities.

BEYOND THE NUMBERS

REPORTING IN ACTION

C3 C4 A1

BEST BUY

BTN 15-1 Refer to **Best Buy**'s financial statements in Appendix A to answer the following.

1. Are Best Buy's financial statements consolidated? How can you tell?
2. What is Best Buy's *comprehensive income* for the year ended March 3, 2007?
3. Does Best Buy have any foreign operations? How can you tell?
4. Compute Best Buy's return on total assets for the year ended March 3, 2007.

Fast Forward

5. Access Best Buy's annual report for a fiscal year ending after March 3, 2007, from either its Website (BestBuy.com) or the SEC's EDGAR database (www.SEC.gov). Recompute Best Buy's return on total assets for the years subsequent to March 3, 2007.

COMPARATIVE ANALYSIS

A1

BEST BUY Circuit City RadioShack

BTN 15-2 Key figures for **Best Buy**, **Circuit City**, and **RadioShack** follow.

	Best Buy			Circuit City			RadioShack		
($ millions)	Current Year	1 Year Prior	2 Years Prior	Current Year	1 Year Prior	2 Years Prior	Current Year	1 Year Prior	2 Years Prior
Net income	$ 1,377	$ 1,140	$ 984	$ (8)	$ 140	$ 62	$ 73	$ 267	$ 337
Net sales	35,934	30,848	27,433	12,430	11,514	10,414	4,778	5,082	4,841
Total assets	13,570	11,864	10,294	4,007	4,069	3,840	2,070	2,205	2,517

Required

1. Compute return on total assets for Best Buy, Circuit City, and RadioShack for the two most recent years.
2. Separate the return on total assets computed in part 1 into its components for all three companies and both years according to the formula in Exhibit 15.9.
3. Which company has the highest total return on assets? The highest profit margin? The highest total asset turnover? What does this comparative analysis reveal? (Assume an industry average of 8.2% for return on assets.)

ETHICS CHALLENGE

C2 P2 P3

BTN 15-3 Kaylee Wecker is the controller for Wildcat Company, which has numerous long-term investments in debt securities. Wildcat's investments are mainly in 10-year bonds. Wecker is preparing its year-end financial statements. In accounting for long-term debt securities, she knows that each long-term investment must be designated as a held-to-maturity or an available-for-sale security. Interest rates rose sharply this past year causing the portfolio's market value to substantially decline. The company does not intend to hold the bonds for the entire 10 years. Wecker also earns a bonus each year, which is computed as a percent of net income.

Required

1. Will Wecker's bonus depend in any way on the classification of the debt securities? Explain.
2. What criteria must Wecker use to classify the securities as held-to-maturity or available-for-sale?
3. Is there likely any company oversight of Wecker's classification of the securities? Explain.

COMMUNICATING IN PRACTICE

C2 P4

BTN 15-4 Assume that you are Jackson Company's accountant. Company owner Abel Terrio has reviewed the 2009 financial statements you prepared and questions the $6,000 loss reported on the sale of its investment in Blackhawk Co. common stock. Jackson acquired 50,000 shares of Blackhawk's common stock on December 31, 2007, at a cost of $500,000. This stock purchase represented a 40% interest in Blackhawk. The 2008 income statement reported that earnings from all investments were $126,000. On January 3, 2009, Jackson Company sold the Blackhawk stock for $575,000. Blackhawk did not pay any dividends during 2008 but reported a net income of $202,500 for that year. Terrio believes that because the Blackhawk stock purchase price was $500,000 and was sold for $575,000, the 2009 income statement should report a $75,000 gain on the sale.

Required

Draft a one-half page memorandum to Terrio explaining why the $6,000 loss on sale of Blackhawk stock is correctly reported.

TAKING IT TO THE NET

C1 C2

BTN 15-5 Access the August 3, 2007, 10-K filing (for year-end June 30, 2007) of **Microsoft** (MSFT) at www.SEC.gov. Review its note 3, "Investments."

Required

1. How does the cost-basis total for its investments as of June 30, 2007, compare to the prior year-end amount?
2. Identify at least eight types of short-term investments held by Microsoft as of June 30, 2007.
3. What were Microsoft's unrealized gains and its unrealized losses from its investments for 2007?
4. Was the cost or market ("recorded") value of the investments higher as of June 30, 2007?

TEAMWORK IN ACTION

C1 C2 C3 P1 P2 P3 P4

BTN 15-6 Each team member is to become an expert on a specific classification of long-term investments. This expertise will be used to facilitate other teammates' understanding of the concepts and procedures relevent to the classification chosen.

1. Each team member must select an area for expertise by choosing one of the following classifications of long-term investments.
   - **a.** Held-to-maturity debt securities
   - **b.** Available-for-sale debt and equity securities
   - **c.** Equity securities with significant influence
   - **d.** Equity securities with controlling influence
2. Learning teams are to disburse and expert teams are to be formed. Expert teams are made up of those who select the same area of expertise. The instructor will identify the location where each expert team will meet.
3. Expert teams will collaborate to develop a presentation based on the following requirements. Students must write the presentation in a format they can show to their learning teams in part (4).

Requirements for Expert Presentation

- **a.** Write a transaction for the acquisition of this type of investment security. The transaction description is to include all necessary data to reflect the chosen classification.
- **b.** Prepare the journal entry to record the acquisition.

  [*Note:* The expert team on equity securities with controlling influence will substitute requirements (*d*) and (*e*) with a discussion of the reporting of these investments.]
- **c.** Identify information necessary to complete the end-of-period adjustment for this investment.
- **d.** Assuming that this is the only investment owned, prepare any necessary year-end entries.
- **e.** Present the relevant balance sheet section(s).

4. Re-form learning teams. In rotation, experts are to present to their teams the presentations they developed in part 3. Experts are to encourage and respond to questions.

ENTREPRENEURIAL DECISION

C4 P5

BTN 15-7[A] Refer to the opening feature in this chapter about Amy Smilovic and her company, **Tibi**. Assume that Amy must acquire the Japanese rights to certain clothing designs that will then be produced for sale to U.S. consumers. Amy acquires those rights on January 1, 2008, from a Japanese distributor and agrees to pay 12,000,000 yen per year for those rights. Quarterly payments are due March 31, June 30, September 30, and December 31 each year. On January 1, 2008, the yen is worth $0.00891.

Required

1. Prepare the journal entry to record the rights purchased on January 1, 2008.

2. Prepare the journal entries to record the payments on March 31, June 30, September 30, and December 31, 2008. The value of the yen on those dates follows.

March 31	$0.00893
June 30	0.00901
September 30	0.00902
December 31	0.00897

3. How can Amy protect herself from unanticipated gains and losses from currency translation if all of her payments are specified to be paid in yen?

HITTING THE ROAD C4

BTN 15-8[A] Assume that you are planning a spring break trip to Europe. Identify three locations where you can find exchange rates for the dollar relative to the Euro or other currencies.

GLOBAL DECISION

A1

DSG

RadioShack

BTN 15-9 **DSG international**, **Best Buy**, **Circuit City**, and **RadioShack** are competitors in the global marketplace. Following are selected data from each company.

	DSG (£ millions)			Best Buy		Circuit City		RadioShack	
Key Figure	Current Year	One Year Prior	Two Years Prior	Current Year	Prior Year	Current Year	Prior Year	Current Year	Prior Year
Net income . . .	£ 18	£ 256	£ 212	—	—	—	—	—	—
Total assets . . .	3,977	4,120	4,104	—	—	—	—	—	—
Net sales	7,930	6,984	7,072	—	—	—	—	—	—
Profit margin . .	?	?	—	3.8%	3.7%	(0.1)%	1.2%	1.5%	5.3%
Total asset turnover	?	?	—	2.8	2.8	3.1	2.9	2.2	2.2

Required

1. Compute DSG's return on total assets for the most recent two years using the data provided.
2. Which of these four companies has the highest return on total assets? Highest profit margin? Highest total asset turnover?

ANSWERS TO MULTIPLE CHOICE QUIZ

1. d; $\$30,000 \times 5\% \times 5/12 = \$625$
2. a; Unrealized gain = $\$84,500 - \$83,000 = \$1,500$
3. b; $\$50,000 \times 35\% = \$17,500$
4. e; $\$300,000/\$2,000,000 = 15\%$
5. b; Profit margin = $\$80,000/\$600,000 = 13.3\%$
   Total asset turnover = $\$600,000/\$400,000 = 1.5$

A Look Back

Chapter 15 focused on how to identify, account for, and report investments in securities. We also accounted for transactions listed in a foreign currency.

A Look at This Chapter

This chapter focuses on reporting and analyzing cash inflows and cash outflows. We emphasize how to prepare and interpret the statement of cash flows.

A Look Ahead

Chapter 17 focuses on tools to help us analyze financial statements. We also describe comparative analysis and the application of ratios for financial analysis.

Chapter 16 Reporting the Statement of Cash Flows

Learning Objectives

CAP

Conceptual

C1 Explain the purpose and importance of cash flow information. *(p. 628)*

C2 Distinguish between operating, investing, and financing activities. *(p. 629)*

C3 Identify and disclose noncash investing and financing activities. *(p. 631)*

C4 Describe the format of the statement of cash flows. *(p. 631)*

Analytical

A1 Analyze the statement of cash flows. *(p. 645)*

A2 Compute and apply the cash flow on total assets ratio. *(p. 646)*

LP16

Procedural

P1 Prepare a statement of cash flows. *(p. 632)*

P2 Compute cash flows from operating activities using the indirect method. *(p. 635)*

P3 Determine cash flows from both investing and financing activities. *(p. 641)*

P4 *Appendix 16A*—Illustrate use of a spreadsheet to prepare a statement of cash flows. *(p. 649)*

P5 *Appendix 16B*—Compute cash flows from operating activities using the direct method. *(p. 652)*

Decision Feature

Wizard of Odd

"If you put enough energy into your dream, you can make anything happen" —Jim Bonaminio

FAIRFIELD, OH—Jim Bonaminio built his roadside produce stand while living in an abandoned gas station. "I would get up and leave at 4 in the morning to buy everything fresh [and] my wife opened the market at 8 a.m.," recalls Jim. "By 10 o'clock at night, we'd be sitting on the bed balancing the register receipts . . . we worked seven days a week." The fruit of those early efforts is **Jungle Jim's International Market (JungleJims.com).**

Jungle Jim's is no Wal-Mart wannabe, but it is arguably America's wackiest supermarket. Instead of trying to beat the big chains at the price-squeezing game, Jim's is a funhouse maze of a store. A seven-foot Elvis lion sings "Jailhouse Rock," an antique fire engine rests atop cases of hot sauce, port-a-potties lead to fancy restrooms, and Robin Hood greets customers with English food set within a 30-foot-tall Sherwood Forest. This is just a sampling.

"If you don't go out on a limb, then you're just like everybody else," insists Jim. "The stuff I've collected—all sorts of weird stuff—gets reused." Despite the wackiness, Jim is first and foremost a businessman. He learned firsthand about the importance of monitoring cash inflows and cash outflows. In the early days, recalls Jim, it was all about sales and profits. Then inventory and asset growth yielded negative cash flows, and Jim was in a pinch. That's when he realized that tracking cash flows was important, explains Jim.

Jim eventually learned how to monitor and control cash flows for each of his operating, investing, and financing activities. Today, says Jim, "I hire professional people to [help me monitor cash] . . . and to look for ways to make money." Yet Jim explains that he always reviews the statement of cash flows and the individual cash inflows and outflows.

Cash management has not curtailed Jim's fun-loving approach to business. "I'm trying to create something that has never been done," laughs Jim. "I just want to see if I can do it and have fun."

[Sources: *Jungle Jim's Website,* January 2009; *BusinessWeek,* April 2005; *Country Living,* November 2004; *Miamian,* Summer 2004; *Plain Dealer,* November 2004; *Supermarket News,* September 2006; *Cintas,* August 2007]

A company cannot achieve or maintain profits without carefully managing cash. Managers and other users of information pay attention to a company's cash position and the events and transactions affecting cash. This chapter explains how we prepare, analyze, and interpret a statement of cash flows. It also discusses the importance of cash flow information for predicting future performance and making managerial decisions. More generally, effectively using the statement of cash flows is crucial for managing and analyzing the operating, investing, and financing activities of businesses.

Reporting the Statement of Cash Flows

Basics of Cash Flow Reporting
- Purpose
- Importance
- Measurement
- Classification
- Noncash activities
- Format and preparation

Cash Flows from Operating
- Indirect and direct methods of reporting
- Application of indirect method of reporting
- Summary of indirect method adjustments

Cash Flows from Investing
- Three-stage process of analysis
- Analysis of noncurrent assets
- Analysis of other assets

Cash Flows from Financing
- Three-stage process of analysis
- Analysis of noncurrent liabilities
- Analysis of equity

Basics of Cash Flow Reporting

This section describes the basics of cash flow reporting, including its purpose, measurement, classification, format, and preparation.

Purpose of the Statement of Cash Flows

C1 Explain the purpose and importance of cash flow information.

The purpose of the **statement of cash flows** is to report cash receipts (inflows) and cash payments (outflows) during a period. This includes separately identifying the cash flows related to operating, investing, and financing activities. The statement of cash flows does more than simply report changes in cash. It is the detailed disclosure of individual cash flows that makes this statement useful to users. Information in this statement helps users answer questions such as these:

- How does a company obtain its cash?
- Where does a company spend its cash?
- What explains the change in the cash balance?

Point: Internal users rely on the statement of cash flows to make investing and financing decisions. External users rely on this statement to assess the amount and timing of a company's cash flows.

The statement of cash flows addresses important questions such as these by summarizing, classifying, and reporting a company's cash inflows and cash outflows for each period.

Importance of Cash Flows

Information about cash flows can influence decision makers in important ways. For instance, we look more favorably at a company that is financing its expenditures with cash from operations than one that does it by selling its assets. Information about cash flows helps users decide whether a company has enough cash to pay its existing debts as they mature. It is also relied upon to evaluate a company's ability to meet unexpected obligations and pursue unexpected opportunities. External information users especially want to assess a company's ability to take advantage of new business opportunities. Internal users such as managers use cash flow information to plan day-to-day operating activities and make long-term investment decisions.

Macy's striking turnaround is an example of how analysis and management of cash flows can lead to improved financial stability. Several years ago Macy's obtained temporary protection from bankruptcy, at which time it desperately needed to improve its cash flows. It did so by engaging in aggressive cost-cutting measures. As a result, Macy's annual cash flow rose to $210 million, up from a negative cash flow of $38.9 million in the prior year. Macy's eventually met its financial obligations and then successfully merged with **Federated Department Stores**.

The case of **W. T. Grant Co.** is a classic example of the importance of cash flow information in predicting a company's future performance and financial strength. Grant reported net income of more than $40 million per year for three consecutive years. At that same time, it was experiencing an alarming decrease in cash provided by operations. For instance, net cash outflow was more than $90 million by the end of that three-year period. Grant soon went bankrupt. Users who relied solely on Grant's income numbers were unpleasantly surprised. This reminds us that cash flows as well as income statement and balance sheet information are crucial in making business decisions.

Video16.1

Decision Insight

Cash Savvy "A lender must have a complete understanding of a borrower's cash flows to assess both the borrowing needs and repayment sources. This requires information about the major types of cash inflows and outflows. I have seen many companies, whose financial statements indicate good profitability, experience severe financial problems because the owners or managers lacked a good understanding of cash flows."—Mary E. Garza, **Bank of America**

Measurement of Cash Flows

Cash flows are defined to include both *cash* and *cash equivalents*. The statement of cash flows explains the difference between the beginning and ending balances of cash and cash equivalents. We continue to use the phrases *cash flows* and the *statement of cash flows,* but we must remember that both phrases refer to cash and cash equivalents. Recall that a cash equivalent must satisfy two criteria: (1) be readily convertible to a known amount of cash and (2) be sufficiently close to its maturity so its market value is unaffected by interest rate changes. In most cases, a debt security must be within three months of its maturity to satisfy these criteria. Companies must disclose and follow a clear policy for determining cash and cash equivalents and apply it consistently from period to period. **American Express**, for example, defines its cash equivalents as "time deposits and other highly liquid investments with original maturities of 90 days or less."

Classification of Cash Flows

C2 Distinguish between operating, investing, and financing activities.

Since cash and cash equivalents are combined, the statement of cash flows does not report transactions between cash and cash equivalents such as cash paid to purchase cash equivalents and cash received from selling cash equivalents. However, all other cash receipts and cash payments are classified and reported on the statement as operating, investing, or financing activities. Individual cash receipts and payments for each of these three categories are labeled to identify their originating transactions or events. A net cash inflow (source) occurs when the receipts in a category exceed the payments. A net cash outflow (use) occurs when the payments in a category exceed the receipts.

Operating Activities **Operating activities** include those transactions and events that determine net income. Examples are the production and purchase of merchandise, the sale of goods and services to customers, and the expenditures to administer the business. Not all items in income, such as unusual gains and losses, are operating activities (we discuss these exceptions later in the chapter). Exhibit 16.1 lists the more common cash inflows and outflows from operating activities. (Although cash receipts and cash payments from buying and selling trading

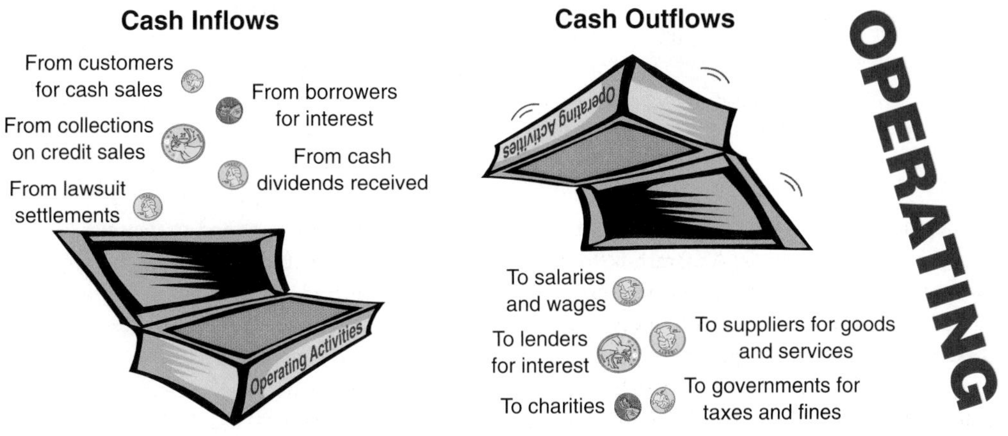

EXHIBIT 16.1

Cash Flows from Operating Activities

securities are often reported under operating activities, new standards require that these receipts and payments be classified based on the nature and purpose of those securities.)

Investing Activities **Investing activities** generally include those transactions and events that affect long-term assets—namely, the purchase and sale of long-term assets. They also include (1) the purchase and sale of short-term investments in the securities of other entities, other than cash equivalents and trading securities and (2) lending and collecting money for notes receivable. Exhibit 16.2 lists examples of cash flows from investing activities. Proceeds from collecting the principal amounts of notes deserve special mention. If the note results from sales to customers, its cash receipts are classed as operating activities whether short-term or long-term. If the note results from a loan to another party apart from sales, however, the cash receipts from collecting the note principal are classed as an investing activity. The FASB requires that the collection of interest on loans be reported as an operating activity.

Point: The FASB requires that *cash dividends received* and *cash interest received* be reported as operating activities.

EXHIBIT 16.2

Cash Flows from Investing Activities

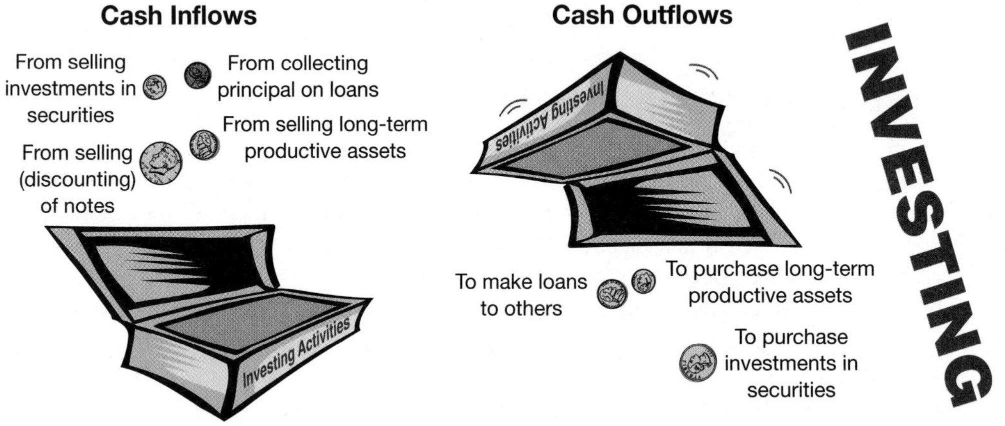

Financing Activities **Financing activities** include those transactions and events that affect long-term liabilities and equity. Examples are (1) obtaining cash from issuing debt and repaying the amounts borrowed and (2) receiving cash from or distributing cash to owners. These activities involve transactions with a company's owners and creditors. They also often involve borrowing and repaying principal amounts relating to both short- and long-term debt. GAAP requires that payments of interest expense be classified as operating activities. Also, cash payments to settle credit purchases of merchandise, whether on account or by note, are operating activities. Exhibit 16.3 lists examples of cash flows from financing activities.

EXHIBIT 16.3

Cash Flows from Financing Activities

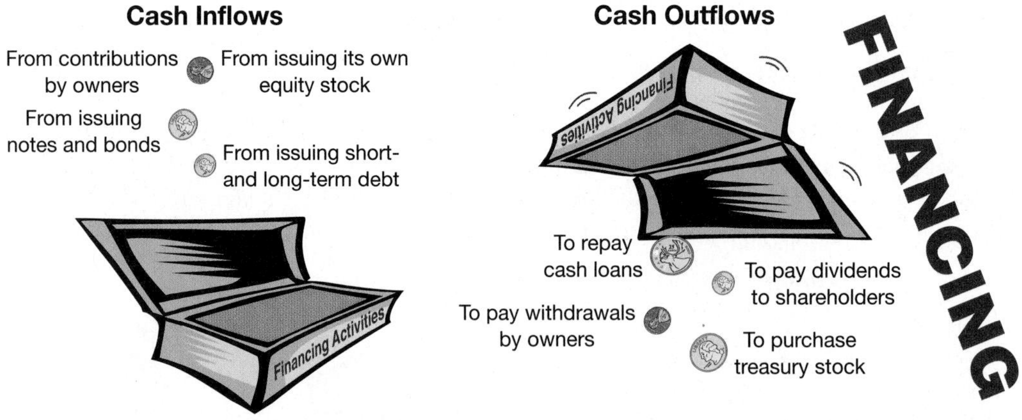

Point: Interest payments on a loan are classified as operating activities, but payments of loan principal are financing activities.

Decision Insight

Cash Reporting Cash flows can be delayed or accelerated at the end of a period to improve or reduce current period cash flows. Also, cash flows can be misclassified. Cash outflows reported under operations are interpreted as expense payments. However, cash outflows reported under investing activities are interpreted as a positive sign of growth potential. Thus, managers face incentives to misclassify cash flows. For these reasons, cash flow reporting warrants our scrutiny.

Noncash Investing and Financing

C3 Identify and disclose noncash investing and financing activities.

When important investing and financing activities do not affect cash receipts or payments, they are still disclosed at the bottom of the statement of cash flows or in a note to the statement because of their importance and the *full-disclosure principle*. One example of such a transaction is the purchase of long-term assets using a long-term note payable (loan). This transaction involves both investing and financing activities but does not affect any cash inflow or outflow and is not reported in any of the three sections of the statement of cash flows. This disclosure rule also extends to transactions with partial cash receipts or payments.

To illustrate, assume that Goorin purchases land for $12,000 by paying $5,000 cash and trading in used equipment worth $7,000. The investing section of the statement of cash flows reports only the $5,000 cash outflow for the land purchase. The $12,000 investing transaction is only partially described in the body of the statement of cash flows, yet this information is potentially important to users because it changes the makeup of assets. Goorin could either describe the transaction in a footnote or include information at the bottom of its statement that lists the $12,000 land purchase along with the cash financing of $5,000 and a $7,000 trade-in of equipment. As another example, Borg Co. acquired $900,000 of assets in exchange for $200,000 cash and a $700,000 long-term note, which should be reported as follows:

Point: A stock dividend transaction involving a transfer from retained earnings to common stock or a credit to contributed capital is *not* considered a noncash investing and financing activity because the company receives no consideration for shares issued.

Fair value of assets acquired	$900,000
Less cash paid	200,000
Liabilities incurred or assumed	$700,000

Exhibit 16.4 lists transactions commonly disclosed as noncash investing and financing activities.

EXHIBIT 16.4

Examples of Noncash Investing and Financing Activities

- Retirement of debt by issuing equity stock.
- Conversion of preferred stock to common stock.
- Lease of assets in a capital lease transaction.
- Purchase of long-term assets by issuing a note or bond.
- Exchange of noncash assets for other noncash assets.
- Purchase of noncash assets by issuing equity or debt.

Format of the Statement of Cash Flows

C4 Describe the format of the statement of cash flows.

Accounting standards require companies to include a statement of cash flows in a complete set of financial statements. This statement must report information about a company's cash receipts and cash payments during the period. Exhibit 16.5 shows the usual format. A company must report cash flows from three activities: operating, investing, and financing. The statement explains how transactions and events impact the prior period-end cash (and cash equivalents) balance to produce its current period-end balance.

EXHIBIT 16.5

Format of the Statement of Cash Flows

COMPANY NAME
Statement of Cash Flows
For *period* Ended *date*

Cash flows from operating activities	
[List of individual inflows and outflows]	
Net cash provided (used) by operating activities	$ #
Cash flows from investing activities	
[List of individual inflows and outflows]	
Net cash provided (used) by investing activities	#
Cash flows from financing activities	
[List of individual inflows and outflows]	
Net cash provided (used) by financing activities	#
Net increase (decrease) in cash	$ #
Cash (and equivalents) balance at prior period-end	#
Cash (and equivalents) balance at current period-end	$ #

Separate schedule or note disclosure of any "noncash investing and financing transactions" is required.

Decision Maker

Entrepreneur You are considering purchasing a start-up business that recently reported a $110,000 annual net loss and a $225,000 annual net cash inflow. How are these results possible? [Answer—p. 658]

Quick Check

Answers—p. 658

1. Does a statement of cash flows report the cash payments to purchase cash equivalents? Does it report the cash receipts from selling cash equivalents?
2. Identify the three categories of cash flows reported separately on the statement of cash flows.
3. Identify the cash activity category for each transaction: (*a*) purchase equipment for cash, (*b*) cash payment of wages, (*c*) sale of common stock for cash, (*d*) receipt of cash dividends from stock investment, (e) cash collection from customers, (*f*) notes issued for cash.

Preparing the Statement of Cash Flows

P1 Prepare a statement of cash flows.

Preparing a statement of cash flows involves five steps: (1) compute the net increase or decrease in cash; (2) compute and report the net cash provided or used by operating activities (using either the direct or indirect method; both are explained); (3) compute and report the net cash provided or used by investing activities; (4) compute and report the net cash provided or used by financing activities; and (5) compute the net cash flow by combining net cash provided or used by operating, investing, and financing activities and then *prove it* by adding it to the beginning cash balance to show that it equals the ending cash balance.

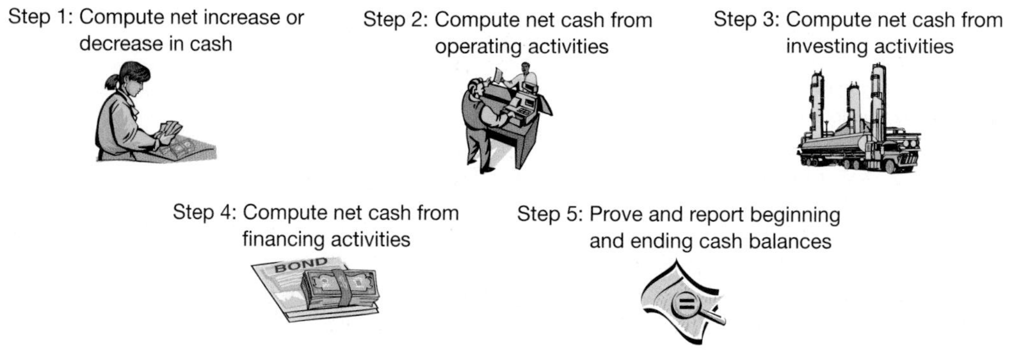

Computing the net increase or net decrease in cash is a simple but crucial computation. It equals the current period's cash balance minus the prior period's cash balance. This is the *bottom-line* figure for the statement of cash flows and is a check on accuracy. The information we need to prepare a statement of cash flows comes from various sources including comparative balance sheets at the beginning and end of the period, and an income statement for the period. There are two alternative approaches to preparing the statement: (1) analyzing the Cash account and (2) analyzing noncash accounts.

Analyzing the Cash Account A company's cash receipts and cash payments are recorded in the Cash account in its general ledger. The Cash account is therefore a natural place to look for information about cash flows from operating, investing, and financing activities. To illustrate, review the summarized Cash T-account of Genesis, Inc., in Exhibit 16.6. Individual cash transactions are summarized in this Cash account according to the major types of cash receipts and cash payments. For instance, only the total of cash receipts from all customers is listed. Individual cash transactions underlying these totals can number in the thousands. Accounting software is available to provide summarized cash accounts.

Preparing a statement of cash flows from Exhibit 16.6 requires determining whether an individual cash inflow or outflow is an operating, investing, or financing activity, and then listing each by

EXHIBIT 16.6

Summarized Cash Account

Accounting System:

File Edit Maintain Tasks Analysis Options Reports Window Help

Cash

Balance, Dec. 31, 2008	12,000		
Receipts from customers	570,000	Payments for merchandise	319,000
Receipts from asset sales	12,000	Payments for wages and operating expenses	218,000
Receipts from stock issuance	15,000	Payments for interest	8,000
		Payments for taxes	5,000
		Payments for assets	10,000
		Payments for notes retirement	18,000
		Payments for dividends	14,000
Balance, Dec. 31, 2009	17,000		

Sales Purchases General Ledger Payroll Inventory Company Analysis

activity. This yields the statement shown in Exhibit 16.7. However, preparing the statement of cash flows from an analysis of the summarized Cash account has two limitations. First, most companies have many individual cash receipts and payments, making it difficult to review them all. Accounting software minimizes this burden, but it is still a task requiring professional judgment for many transactions. Second, the Cash account does not usually carry an adequate description of each cash transaction, making assignment of all cash transactions according to activity difficult.

Point: View the change in cash as a *target* number that we will fully explain and prove in the statement of cash flows.

EXHIBIT 16.7

Statement of Cash Flows—Direct Method

GENESIS
Statement of Cash Flows
For Year Ended December 31, 2009

Cash flows from operating activities		
Cash received from customers	$570,000	
Cash paid for merchandise	(319,000)	
Cash paid for wages and other operating expenses	(218,000)	
Cash paid for interest	(8,000)	
Cash paid for taxes	(5,000)	
Net cash provided by operating activities		$20,000
Cash flows from investing activities		
Cash received from sale of plant assets	12,000	
Cash paid for purchase of plant assets	(10,000)	
Net cash provided by investing activities		2,000
Cash flows from financing activities		
Cash received from issuing stock	15,000	
Cash paid to retire notes	(18,000)	
Cash paid for dividends	(14,000)	
Net cash used in financing activities		(17,000)
Net increase in cash		$ 5,000
Cash balance at prior year-end		12,000
Cash balance at current year-end		$17,000

Analyzing Noncash Accounts A second approach to preparing the statement of cash flows is analyzing noncash accounts. This approach uses the fact that when a company records cash inflows and outflows with debits and credits to the Cash account (see Exhibit 16.6), it also records credits and debits in noncash accounts (reflecting double-entry accounting). Many of these noncash accounts are balance sheet accounts—for instance, from the sale of land for cash. Others are revenue and expense accounts that are closed to equity. For instance, the sale of services for cash yields a credit to Services Revenue that is closed to Retained Earnings for a corporation. In sum, *all cash transactions eventually affect noncash balance sheet accounts*. Thus, we can determine cash inflows and outflows by analyzing changes in noncash balance sheet accounts.

Exhibit 16.8 uses the accounting equation to show the relation between the Cash account and the noncash balance sheet accounts. This exhibit starts with the accounting equation at the top. It is then expanded in line (2) to separate cash from noncash asset accounts. Line (3) moves noncash asset accounts to the right-hand side of the equality where they are subtracted. This shows that cash equals the sum of the liability and equity accounts *minus* the noncash asset accounts. Line (4) points

EXHIBIT 16.8

Relation between Cash and Noncash Accounts

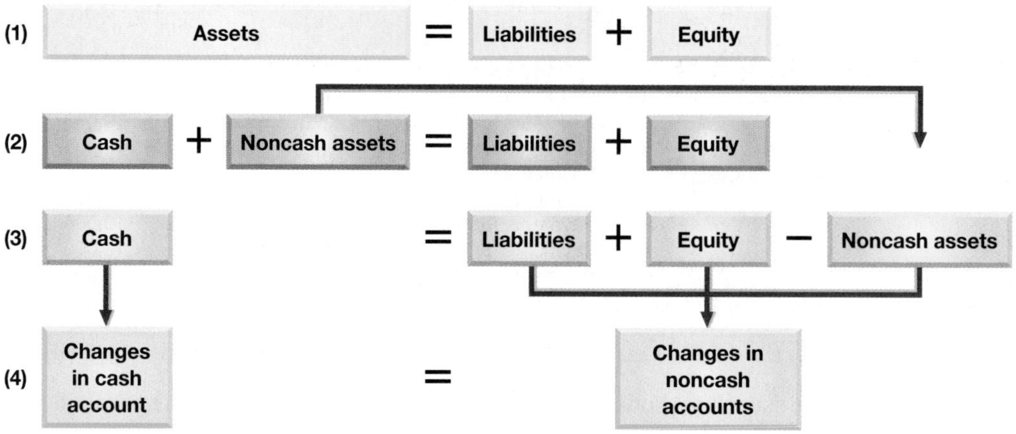

out that *changes* on one side of the accounting equation equal *changes* on the other side. It shows that we can explain changes in cash by analyzing changes in the noncash accounts consisting of liability accounts, equity accounts, and noncash asset accounts. By analyzing noncash balance sheet accounts and any related income statement accounts, we can prepare a statement of cash flows.

Information to Prepare the Statement Information to prepare the statement of cash flows usually comes from three sources: (1) comparative balance sheets, (2) the current income statement, and (3) additional information. Comparative balance sheets are used to compute changes in noncash accounts from the beginning to the end of the period. The current income statement is used to help compute cash flows from operating activities. Additional information often includes details on transactions and events that help explain both the cash flows and noncash investing and financing activities.

Decision Insight

e-Cash Every credit transaction on the Net leaves a trail that a hacker or a marketer can pick up. Enter e-cash—or digital money. The encryption of e-cash protects your money from snoops and thieves and cannot be traced, even by the issuing bank.

Cash Flows from Operating

Indirect and Direct Methods of Reporting

Cash flows provided (used) by operating activities are reported in one of two ways: the *direct method* or the *indirect method.* **These two different methods apply only to the operating activities section.**

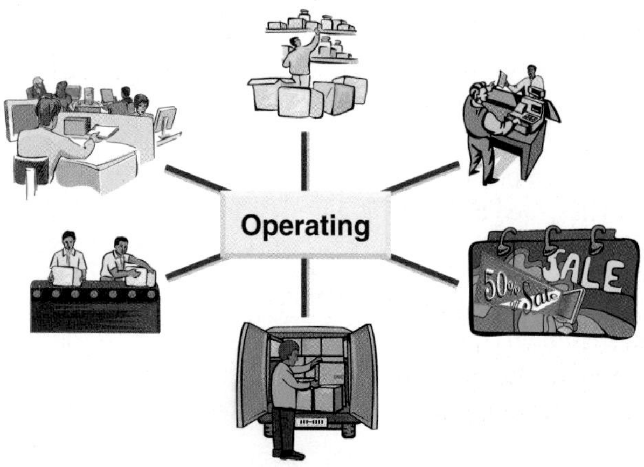

The **direct method** separately lists each major item of operating cash receipts (such as cash received from customers) and each major item of operating cash payments (such as cash paid for merchandise). The cash payments are subtracted from cash receipts to determine the net cash provided (used) by operating activities. The operating activities section of Exhibit 16.7 reflects the direct method of reporting operating cash flows.

The **indirect method** reports net income and then adjusts it for items necessary to obtain net cash provided or used by operating activities. It does *not* report individual items of cash inflows and cash outflows from operating activities. Instead, the indirect method reports the necessary adjustments to reconcile net income to net cash provided or used by operating activities. The operating activities section for Genesis prepared under the indirect method is shown in Exhibit 16.9.

EXHIBIT 16.9

Operating Activities Section—Indirect Method

Cash flows from operating activities		
Net income	$ 38,000	
Adjustments to reconcile net income to net cash provided by operating activities		
Increase in accounts receivable	(20,000)	
Increase in merchandise inventory	(14,000)	
Increase in prepaid expenses	(2,000)	
Decrease in accounts payable	(5,000)	
Decrease in interest payable	(1,000)	
Increase in income taxes payable	10,000	
Depreciation expense	24,000	
Loss on sale of plant assets	6,000	
Gain on retirement of notes	(16,000)	
Net cash provided by operating activities		**$20,000**

The net cash amount provided by operating activities is *identical* under both the direct and indirect methods. This equality always exists. The difference in these methods is with the computation and presentation of this amount. The FASB recommends the direct method, but because it is not required and the indirect method is arguably easier to compute, nearly all companies report operating cash flows using the indirect method.

Point: To better understand the direct and indirect methods of reporting operating cash flows, identify similarities and differences between Exhibits 16.7 and 16.11.

To illustrate, we prepare the operating activities section of the statement of cash flows for Genesis. Exhibit 16.10 shows the December 31, 2008 and 2009, balance sheets of Genesis along with its 2009 income statement. We use this information to prepare a statement of cash flows that explains the $5,000 increase in cash for 2009 as reflected in its balance sheets. This $5,000 is computed as Cash of $17,000 at the end of 2009 minus Cash of $12,000 at the end of 2008. Genesis discloses additional information on its 2009 transactions:

Video16.1

a. The accounts payable balances result from merchandise inventory purchases.

b. Purchased $70,000 in plant assets by paying $10,000 cash and issuing $60,000 of notes payable.

c. Sold plant assets with an original cost of $30,000 and accumulated depreciation of $12,000 for $12,000 cash, yielding a $6,000 loss.

d. Received $15,000 cash from issuing 3,000 shares of common stock.

e. Paid $18,000 cash to retire notes with a $34,000 book value, yielding a $16,000 gain.

f. Declared and paid cash dividends of $14,000.

The next section describes the indirect method. Appendix 16B describes the direct method. An instructor can choose to cover either one or both methods. Neither section depends on the other.

Application of the Indirect Method of Reporting

P2 Compute cash flows from operating activities using the indirect method.

Net income is computed using accrual accounting, which recognizes revenues when earned and expenses when incurred. Revenues and expenses do not necessarily reflect the receipt and payment of cash. The indirect method of computing and reporting net cash flows from operating activities involves adjusting the net income figure to obtain the net cash provided or used by operating activities. This includes subtracting noncash increases (credits) from net income and adding noncash charges (debits) back to net income.

To illustrate, the indirect method begins with Genesis's net income of $38,000 and adjusts it to obtain net cash provided by operating activities of $20,000. Exhibit 16.11 shows the results of the indirect method of reporting operating cash flows, which adjusts net income for three types of adjustments. There are adjustments ① to reflect changes in noncash current assets and current liabilities related to operating activities, ② to income statement items involving operating activities that do not affect cash inflows or outflows, and ③ to eliminate gains and losses resulting from investing and financing activities (not part of operating activities). This section describes each of these adjustments.

Point: *Noncash credits* refer to revenue amounts reported on the income statement that are *not collected in cash* this period. *Noncash charges* refer to *expense* amounts reported on the income statement that are *not paid* this period.

EXHIBIT 16.10

Financial Statements

GENESIS
Income Statement
For Year Ended December 31, 2009

Sales		$590,000
Cost of goods sold	$300,000	
Wages and other operating expenses	216,000	
Interest expense	7,000	
Depreciation expense	24,000	(547,000)
		43,000
Other gains (losses)		
Gain on retirement of notes	16,000	
Loss on sale of plant assets	(6,000)	10,000
Income before taxes		53,000
Income taxes expense		(15,000)
Net income		$ 38,000

GENESIS
Balance Sheets
December 31, 2009 and 2008

	2009	2008
Assets		
Current assets		
Cash	$ 17,000	$ 12,000
Accounts receivable	60,000	40,000
Merchandise inventory	84,000	70,000
Prepaid expenses	6,000	4,000
Total current assets	167,000	126,000
Long-term assets		
Plant assets	250,000	210,000
Accumulated depreciation	(60,000)	(48,000)
Total assets	$357,000	$288,000
Liabilities		
Current liabilities		
Accounts payable	$ 35,000	$ 40,000
Interest payable	3,000	4,000
Income taxes payable	22,000	12,000
Total current liabilities	60,000	56,000
Long-term notes payable	90,000	64,000
Total liabilities	150,000	120,000
Equity		
Common stock, $5 par	95,000	80,000
Retained earnings	112,000	88,000
Total equity	207,000	168,000
Total liabilities and equity	$357,000	$288,000

① Adjustments for Changes in Current Assets and Current Liabilities This section describes adjustments for changes in noncash current assets and current liabilities.

Point: Operating activities are typically those that determine income, which are often reflected in changes in current assets and current liabilities.

Adjustments for changes in noncash current assets. Changes in noncash current assets normally result from operating activities. Examples are sales affecting accounts receivable and building usage affecting prepaid rent. Decreases in noncash current assets yield the following adjustment:

Decreases in noncash current assets are added to net income.

To see the logic for this adjustment, consider that a decrease in a noncash current asset such as accounts receivable suggests more available cash at the end of the period compared to the beginning. This is so because a decrease in accounts receivable implies higher cash receipts than reflected in sales. We add these higher cash receipts (from decreases in noncash current assets) to net income when computing cash flow from operations.

In contrast, an increase in noncash current assets such as accounts receivable implies less cash receipts than reflected in sales. As another example, an increase in prepaid rent indicates that more cash is paid for rent than is deducted as rent expense. Increases in noncash current assets yield the following adjustment:

Increases in noncash current assets are subtracted from net income.

To illustrate, these adjustments are applied to the noncash current assets in Exhibit 16.10.

Accounts receivable. Accounts receivable *increase* $20,000, from a beginning balance of $40,000 to an ending balance of $60,000. This increase implies that Genesis collects less cash than is reported in sales. That is, some of these sales were in the form of accounts receivable and that amount increased during the period. To see this it is helpful to use *account analysis.* This usually involves setting up a T-account and reconstructing its major entries to compute cash receipts or payments. The following reconstructed Accounts Receivable T-account reveals that cash receipts are less than sales:

Numbers in black are taken from Exhibit 16.10. The red number is the computed (plug) figure.

Accounts Receivable			
Bal., Dec. 31, 2008	40,000		
Sales	590,000	**Cash receipts =**	**570,000**
Bal., Dec. 31, 2009	60,000		

We see that sales are $20,000 greater than cash receipts. This $20,000—as reflected in the $20,000 increase in Accounts Receivable—is subtracted from net income when computing cash provided by operating activities (see Exhibit 16.11).

Merchandise inventory. Merchandise inventory *increases* by $14,000, from a $70,000 beginning balance to an $84,000 ending balance. This increase implies that Genesis had greater cash purchases than cost of goods sold. This larger amount of cash purchases is in the form of inventory, as reflected in the following account analysis:

Merchandise Inventory			
Bal., Dec. 31, 2008	70,000		
Purchases =	**314,000**	Cost of goods sold	300,000
Bal., Dec. 31, 2009	84,000		

EXHIBIT 16.11

Statement of Cash Flows—Indirect Method

GENESIS Statement of Cash Flows For Year Ended December 31, 2009			
Cash flows from operating activities			
Net income		$ 38,000	
Adjustments to reconcile net income to net cash provided by operating activities			
①	Increase in accounts receivable	(20,000)	
	Increase in merchandise inventory	(14,000)	
	Increase in prepaid expenses	(2,000)	
	Decrease in accounts payable	(5,000)	
	Decrease in interest payable	(1,000)	
	Increase in income taxes payable	10,000	
②	Depreciation expense	24,000	
③	Loss on sale of plant assets	6,000	
	Gain on retirement of notes	(16,000)	
Net cash provided by operating activities			$20,000
Cash flows from investing activities			
Cash received from sale of plant assets		12,000	
Cash paid for purchase of plant assets		(10,000)	
Net cash provided by investing activities			2,000
Cash flows from financing activities			
Cash received from issuing stock		15,000	
Cash paid to retire notes		(18,000)	
Cash paid for dividends		(14,000)	
Net cash used in financing activities			(17,000)
Net increase in cash			$ 5,000
Cash balance at prior year-end			12,000
Cash balance at current year-end			$17,000

Point: Refer to Exhibit 16.10 and identify the $5,000 change in cash. This change is what the statement of cash flows explains; it serves as a check.

The amount by which purchases exceed cost of goods sold—as reflected in the $14,000 increase in inventory—is subtracted from net income when computing cash provided by operating activities (see Exhibit 16.11).

Prepaid expenses. Prepaid expenses *increase* $2,000, from a $4,000 beginning balance to a $6,000 ending balance, implying that Genesis's cash payments exceed its recorded prepaid expenses. These higher cash payments increase the amount of Prepaid Expenses, as reflected in its reconstructed T-account:

Prepaid Expenses			
Bal., Dec. 31, 2008	4,000		
Cash payments =	**218,000**	Wages and other operating exp.	216,000
Bal., Dec. 31, 2009	6,000		

The amount by which cash payments exceed the recorded operating expenses—as reflected in the $2,000 increase in Prepaid Expenses—is subtracted from net income when computing cash provided by operating activities (see Exhibit 16.11).

Adjustments for changes in current liabilities. Changes in current liabilities normally result from operating activities. An example is a purchase that affects accounts payable. Increases in current liabilities yield the following adjustment to net income when computing operating cash flows:

Increases in current liabilities are added to net income.

To see the logic for this adjustment, consider that an increase in the Accounts Payable account suggests that cash payments are less than the related (cost of goods sold) expense. As another example, an increase in wages payable implies that cash paid for wages is less than the recorded wages expense. Since the recorded expense is greater than the cash paid, we add the increase in wages payable to net income to compute net cash flow from operations.

Conversely, when current liabilities decrease, the following adjustment is required:

Decreases in current liabilities are subtracted from net income.

To illustrate, these adjustments are applied to the current liabilities in Exhibit 16.10.

Accounts payable. Accounts payable *decrease* $5,000, from a beginning balance of $40,000 to an ending balance of $35,000. This decrease implies that cash payments to suppliers exceed purchases by $5,000 for the period, which is reflected in the reconstructed Accounts Payable T-account:

Accounts Payable			
		Bal., Dec. 31, 2008	40,000
Cash payments =	**319,000**	Purchases	314,000
		Bal., Dec. 31, 2009	35,000

The amount by which cash payments exceed purchases—as reflected in the $5,000 decrease in Accounts Payable—is subtracted from net income when computing cash provided by operating activities (see Exhibit 16.11).

Interest payable. Interest payable *decreases* $1,000, from a $4,000 beginning balance to a $3,000 ending balance. This decrease indicates that cash paid for interest exceeds interest expense by $1,000, which is reflected in the Interest Payable T-account:

Interest Payable			
		Bal., Dec. 31, 2008	4,000
Cash paid for interest =	**8,000**	Interest expense	7,000
		Bal., Dec. 31, 2009	3,000

The amount by which cash paid exceeds recorded expense—as reflected in the $1,000 decrease in Interest Payable—is subtracted from net income (see Exhibit 16.11).

Income taxes payable. Income taxes payable *increase* $10,000, from a $12,000 beginning balance to a $22,000 ending balance. This increase implies that reported income taxes exceed the cash paid for taxes, which is reflected in the Income Taxes Payable T-account:

Income Taxes Payable			
		Bal., Dec. 31, 2008	12,000
Cash paid for taxes =	5,000	Income taxes expense	15,000
		Bal., Dec. 31, 2009	22,000

The amount by which cash paid falls short of the reported taxes expense—as reflected in the $10,000 increase in Income Taxes Payable—is added to net income when computing cash provided by operating activities (see Exhibit 16.11).

Summary Adjustments for Changes in Current Assets and Current Liabilities

Account	Increases	Decreases
Noncash current assets	Deduct from NI	Add to NI
Current liabilities	Add to NI	Deduct from NI

② Adjustments for Operating Items Not Providing or Using Cash The income statement usually includes some expenses that do not reflect cash outflows in the period. Examples are depreciation, amortization, depletion, and bad debts expense. The indirect method for reporting operating cash flows requires that

Expenses with no cash outflows are added back to net income.

To see the logic of this adjustment, recall that items such as depreciation, amortization, depletion, and bad debts originate from debits to expense accounts and credits to noncash accounts. These entries have *no* cash effect, and we add them back to net income when computing net cash flows from operations. Adding them back cancels their deductions.

Similarly, when net income includes revenues that do not reflect cash inflows in the period, the indirect method for reporting operating cash flows requires that

Revenues with no cash inflows are subtracted from net income.

We apply these adjustments to the Genesis operating items that do not provide or use cash.

Depreciation. Depreciation expense is the only Genesis operating item that has no effect on cash flows in the period. We must add back the $24,000 depreciation expense to net income when computing cash provided by operating activities. (We later explain that any cash outflow to acquire a plant asset is reported as an investing activity.)

③ Adjustments for Nonoperating Items Net income often includes losses that are not part of operating activities but are part of either investing or financing activities. Examples are a loss from the sale of a plant asset and a loss from retirement of notes payable. The indirect method for reporting operating cash flows requires that

Nonoperating losses are added back to net income.

To see the logic, consider that items such as a plant asset sale and a notes retirement are normally recorded by recognizing the cash, removing all plant asset or notes accounts, and recognizing any loss or gain. The cash received or paid is not part of operating activities but is part of either investing or financing activities. *No* operating cash flow effect occurs. However, because the nonoperating loss is a deduction in computing net income, we need to add it back to net income when computing cash flow from operations. Adding it back cancels the deduction.

Point: An income statement reports revenues, gains, expenses, and losses on an accrual basis. The statement of cash flows reports cash received and cash paid for operating, financing, and investing activities.

Similarly, when net income includes gains not part of operating activities, the indirect method for reporting operating cash flows requires that

Nonoperating gains are subtracted from net income.

To illustrate these adjustments, we consider the nonoperating items of Genesis.

Loss on sale of plant assets. Genesis reports a $6,000 loss on sale of plant assets as part of net income. This loss is a proper deduction in computing income, but it is *not part of operating activities.* Instead, a sale of plant assets is part of investing activities. Thus, the $6,000 nonoperating loss is added back to net income (see Exhibit 16.11). Adding it back cancels the loss. We later explain how to report the cash inflow from the asset sale in investing activities.

Gain on retirement of debt. A $16,000 gain on retirement of debt is properly included in net income, but it is *not part of operating activities.* This means the $16,000 nonoperating gain must be subtracted from net income to obtain net cash provided by operating activities (see Exhibit 16.11). Subtracting it cancels the recorded gain. We later describe how to report the cash outflow to retire debt.

Summary of Adjustments for Indirect Method

Exhibit 16.12 summarizes the most common adjustments to net income when computing net cash provided or used by operating activities under the indirect method.

EXHIBIT 16.12

Summary of Selected Adjustments for Indirect Method

Net Income	
+Decrease in noncash current asset	① Adjustments for changes in current assets and current liabilities
−Increase in noncash current asset	
+Increase in current liability*	
−Decrease in current liability*	
+Depreciation, depletion, and amortization	② Adjustments for operating items not providing or using cash
+Losses from disposal of long-term assets and retirement of debt	③ Adjustments for nonoperating items
−Gains from disposal of long-term assets and retirement of debt	
Net cash provided (used) by operating activities	

* Excludes current portion of long-term debt and any (nonsales-related) short-term notes payable—both are financing activities.

The computations in determining cash provided or used by operating activities are different for the indirect and direct methods, but the result is identical. Both methods yield the same $20,000 figure for cash from operating activities for Genesis; see Exhibits 16.7 and 16.11.

Decision Insight

Cash or Income The difference between net income and operating cash flows can be large and sometimes reflects on the quality of earnings. This bar chart shows the net income and operating cash flows of three companies. Operating cash flows can be either higher or lower than net income.

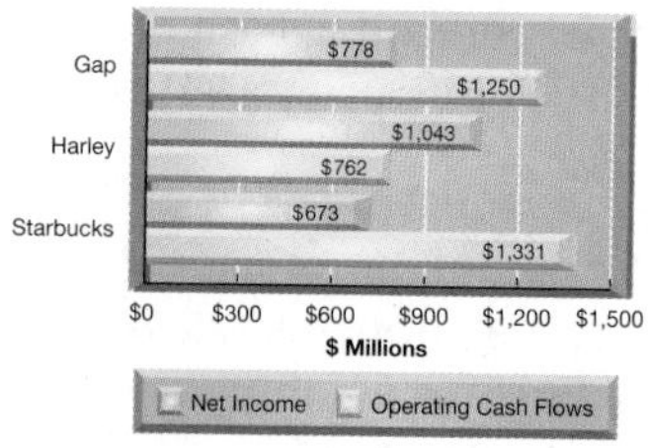

Quick Check

Answers—p. 658

4. Determine the net cash provided or used by operating activities using the following data: net income, $74,900; decrease in accounts receivable, $4,600; increase in inventory, $11,700; decrease in accounts payable, $1,000; loss on sale of equipment, $3,400; payment of cash dividends, $21,500.
5. Why are expenses such as depreciation and amortization added to net income when cash flow from operating activities is computed by the indirect method?
6. A company reports net income of $15,000 that includes a $3,000 gain on the sale of plant assets. Why is this gain subtracted from net income in computing cash flow from operating activities using the indirect method?

Cash Flows from Investing

The third major step in preparing the statement of cash flows is to compute and report cash flows from investing activities. We normally do this by identifying changes in (1) all noncurrent asset accounts and (2) the current accounts for both notes receivable and investments in securities (excluding trading securities). We then analyze changes in these accounts to determine their effect, if any, on cash and report the cash flow effects in the investing activities section of the statement of cash flows. **Reporting of investing activities is identical under the direct method and indirect method.**

Three-Stage Process of Analysis

Video16.1

Information to compute cash flows from investing activities is usually taken from beginning and ending balance sheets and the income statement. We use a three-stage process to determine cash provided or used by investing activities: (1) identify changes in investing-related accounts, (2) explain these changes using reconstruction analysis, and (3) report their cash flow effects.

Analysis of Noncurrent Assets

P3 Determine cash flows from both investing and financing activities.

Information about the Genesis transactions provided earlier reveals that the company both purchased and sold plant assets during the period. Both transactions are investing activities and are analyzed for their cash flow effects in this section.

Plant Asset Transactions The first stage in analyzing the Plant Assets account and its related Accumulated Depreciation is to identify any changes in these accounts from comparative balance sheets in Exhibit 16.10. This analysis reveals a $40,000 increase in plant assets from $210,000 to $250,000 and a $12,000 increase in accumulated depreciation from $48,000 to $60,000.

Point: Investing activities include (1) purchasing and selling long-term assets, (2) lending and collecting on notes receivable, and (3) purchasing and selling short-term investments other than cash equivalents and trading securities.

The second stage is to explain these changes. Items *b* and *c* of the additional information for Genesis (page 635) are relevant in this case. Recall that the Plant Assets account is affected by both asset purchases and sales, while its Accumulated Depreciation account is normally increased from depreciation and decreased from the removal of accumulated depreciation in asset sales. To explain changes in these accounts and to identify their cash flow effects, we prepare *reconstructed entries* from prior transactions; *they are not the actual entries by the preparer.*

Point: Financing and investing info is available in ledger accounts to help explain changes in comparative balance sheets. Post references lead to relevant entries and explanations.

To illustrate, item *b* reports that Genesis purchased plant assets of $70,000 by issuing $60,000 in notes payable to the seller and paying $10,000 in cash. The reconstructed entry for analysis of item *b* follows:

Reconstruction	Plant Assets	70,000	
	Notes Payable		60,000
	Cash		**10,000**

This entry reveals a $10,000 cash outflow for plant assets and a $60,000 noncash investing and financing transaction involving notes exchanged for plant assets.

Next, item *c* reports that Genesis sold plant assets costing $30,000 (with $12,000 of accumulated depreciation) for $12,000 cash, resulting in a $6,000 loss. The reconstructed entry for analysis of item *c* follows:

Reconstruction	**Cash**	**12,000**	
	Accumulated Depreciation	12,000	
	Loss on Sale of Plant Assets	6,000	
	Plant Assets		30,000

This entry reveals a $12,000 cash inflow from assets sold. The $6,000 loss is computed by comparing the asset book value to the cash received and does not reflect any cash inflow or outflow. We also reconstruct the entry for Depreciation Expense using information from the income statement.

Reconstruction	Depreciation Expense	24,000	
	Accumulated Depreciation		24,000

This entry shows that Depreciation Expense results in no cash flow effect. These three reconstructed entries are reflected in the following plant asset and related T-accounts.

Plant Assets			
Bal., Dec. 31, 2008	210,000		
Purchase	**70,000**	**Sale**	**30,000**
Bal., Dec. 31, 2009	250,000		

Accumulated Depreciation—Plant Assets			
		Bal., Dec. 31, 2008	48,000
Sale	**12,000**	**Depr. expense**	**24,000**
		Bal., Dec. 31, 2009	60,000

Example: If a plant asset costing $40,000 with $37,000 of accumulated depreciation is sold at a $1,000 loss, what is the cash flow? What is the cash flow if this asset is sold at a gain of $3,000? *Answers:* +$2,000; +$6,000.

This reconstruction analysis is complete in that the change in plant assets from $210,000 to $250,000 is fully explained by the $70,000 purchase and the $30,000 sale. Also, the change in accumulated depreciation from $48,000 to $60,000 is fully explained by depreciation expense of $24,000 and the removal of $12,000 in accumulated depreciation from an asset sale. (Preparers of the statement of cash flows have the entire ledger and additional information at their disposal, but for brevity reasons only the information needed for reconstructing accounts is given.)

The third stage looks at the reconstructed entries for identification of cash flows. The two identified cash flow effects are reported in the investing section of the statement as follows (also see Exhibit 16.7 or 16.11):

Cash flows from investing activities	
Cash received from sale of plant assets	$12,000
Cash paid for purchase of plant assets	(10,000)

The $60,000 portion of the purchase described in item *b* and financed by issuing notes is a noncash investing and financing activity. It is reported in a note or in a separate schedule to the statement as follows:

Noncash investing and financing activity	
Purchased plant assets with issuance of notes	$60,000

Analysis of Other Assets

Many other asset transactions (including those involving current notes receivable and investments in certain securities) are considered investing activities and can affect a company's cash flows. Since Genesis did not enter into other investing activities impacting assets, we do not need to extend our analysis to these other assets. If such transactions did exist, we would analyze them using the same three-stage process illustrated for plant assets.

Quick Check

Answer—p. 658

7. Equipment costing $80,000 with accumulated depreciation of $30,000 is sold at a loss of $10,000. What is the cash receipt from this sale? In what section of the statement of cash flows is this transaction reported?

Cash Flows from Financing

The fourth major step in preparing the statement of cash flows is to compute and report cash flows from financing activities. We normally do this by identifying changes in all noncurrent liability accounts (including the current portion of any notes and bonds) and the equity accounts. These accounts include long-term debt, notes payable, bonds payable, common stock, and retained earnings. Changes in these accounts are then analyzed using available information to determine their effect, if any, on cash. Results are reported in the financing activities section of the statement. **Reporting of financing activities is identical under the direct method and indirect method.**

Three-Stage Process of Analysis

Video16.1

We again use a three-stage process to determine cash provided or used by financing activities: (1) identify changes in financing-related accounts, (2) explain these changes using reconstruction analysis, and (3) report their cash flow effects.

Analysis of Noncurrent Liabilities

Information about Genesis provided earlier reveals two transactions involving noncurrent liabilities. We analyzed one of those, the $60,000 issuance of notes payable to purchase plant assets. This transaction is reported as a significant noncash investing and financing activity in a footnote or a separate schedule to the statement of cash flows. The other remaining transaction involving noncurrent liabilities is the cash retirement of notes payable.

Point: Financing activities generally refer to changes in the noncurrent liability and the equity accounts. Examples are (1) receiving cash from issuing debt or repaying amounts borrowed and (2) receiving cash from or distributing cash to owners.

Notes Payable Transactions The first stage in analysis of notes is to review the comparative balance sheets from Exhibit 16.10. This analysis reveals an increase in notes payable from $64,000 to $90,000.

The second stage explains this change. Item *e* of the additional information for Genesis (page 635) reports that notes with a carrying value of $34,000 are retired for $18,000 cash, resulting in a $16,000 gain. The reconstructed entry for analysis of item *e* follows:

Reconstruction	Notes Payable	34,000	
	Gain on retirement of debt		16,000
	Cash		**18,000**

This entry reveals an $18,000 cash outflow for retirement of notes and a $16,000 gain from comparing the notes payable carrying value to the cash received. This gain does not reflect any cash inflow or outflow. Also, item *b* of the additional information reports that Genesis purchased plant assets costing $70,000 by issuing $60,000 in notes payable to the seller and paying $10,000 in cash. We reconstructed this entry when analyzing investing activities: It showed a $60,000 increase to notes payable that is reported as a noncash investing and financing transaction. The Notes Payable account reflects (and is fully explained by) these reconstructed entries as follows:

Notes Payable			
		Bal., Dec. 31, 2008	64,000
Retired notes	**34,000**	**Issued notes**	**60,000**
		Bal., Dec. 31, 2009	90,000

The third stage is to report the cash flow effect of the notes retirement in the financing section of the statement as follows (also see Exhibit 16.7 or 16.11):

Cash flows from financing activities	
Cash paid to retire notes	$(18,000)

Analysis of Equity

The Genesis information reveals two transactions involving equity accounts. The first is the issuance of common stock for cash. The second is the declaration and payment of cash dividends. We analyze both.

Common Stock Transactions The first stage in analyzing common stock is to review the comparative balance sheets from Exhibit 16.10, which reveals an increase in common stock from $80,000 to $95,000.

The second stage explains this change. Item *d* of the additional information (page 635) reports that 3,000 shares of common stock are issued at par for $5 per share. The reconstructed entry for analysis of item *d* follows:

Reconstruction	**Cash**	**15,000**	
	Common Stock		15,000

This entry reveals a $15,000 cash inflow from stock issuance and is reflected in (and explains) the Common Stock account as follows:

Common Stock			
		Bal., Dec. 31, 2008	80,000
		Issued stock	**15,000**
		Bal., Dec. 31, 2009	95,000

The third stage discloses the cash flow effect from stock issuance in the financing section of the statement as follows (also see Exhibit 16.7 or 16.11):

Cash flows from financing activities	
Cash received from issuing stock	$15,000

Retained Earnings Transactions The first stage in analyzing the Retained Earnings account is to review the comparative balance sheets from Exhibit 16.10. This reveals an increase in retained earnings from $88,000 to $112,000.

The second stage explains this change. Item *f* of the additional information (page 635) reports that cash dividends of $14,000 are paid. The reconstructed entry follows:

Reconstruction	Retained Earnings	14,000	
	Cash		**14,000**

This entry reveals a $14,000 cash outflow for cash dividends. Also see that the Retained Earnings account is impacted by net income of $38,000. (Net income was analyzed under the operating section of the statement of cash flows.) The reconstructed Retained Earnings account follows:

Retained Earnings			
		Bal., Dec. 31, 2008	88,000
Cash dividend	**14,000**	**Net income**	**38,000**
		Bal., Dec. 31, 2009	112,000

Point: Financing activities not affecting cash flow include *declaration* of a cash dividend, *declaration* of a stock dividend, payment of a stock dividend, and a stock split.

The third stage reports the cash flow effect from the cash dividend in the financing section of the statement as follows (also see Exhibit 16.7 or 16.11):

Cash flows from financing activities	
Cash paid for dividends	$(14,000)

Global: There are no requirements to separate domestic and international cash flows, leading some users to ask, "Where in the world is cash flow?"

We now have identified and explained all of the Genesis cash inflows and cash outflows and one noncash investing and financing transaction. Specifically, our analysis has reconciled changes in all noncash balance sheet accounts.

Proving Cash Balances

The fifth and final step in preparing the statement is to report the beginning and ending cash balances and prove that the *net change in cash* is explained by operating, investing, and financing cash flows. This step is shown here for Genesis.

Net cash provided by operating activities	$20,000
Net cash provided by investing activities	2,000
Net cash used in financing activities	(17,000)
Net increase in cash	**$ 5,000**
Cash balance at 2008 year-end	12,000
Cash balance at 2009 year-end	$17,000

The preceding table shows that the $5,000 net increase in cash, from $12,000 at the beginning of the period to $17,000 at the end, is reconciled by net cash flows from operating ($20,000 inflow), investing ($2,000 inflow), and financing ($17,000 outflow) activities. This is formally reported at the bottom of the statement of cash flows as shown in both Exhibits 16.7 and 16.11.

Decision Maker

Reporter Management is in labor contract negotiations and grants you an interview. It highlights a recent $600,000 net loss that involves a $930,000 extraordinary loss and a total net cash outflow of $550,000 (which includes net cash outflows of $850,000 for investing activities and $350,000 for financing activities). What is your assessment of this company? [Answer—p. 658]

Cash Flow Analysis

Decision Analysis

Analyzing Cash Sources and Uses

A1 Analyze the statement of cash flows.

Most managers stress the importance of understanding and predicting cash flows for business decisions. Creditors evaluate a company's ability to generate cash before deciding whether to lend money. Investors also assess cash inflows and outflows before buying and selling stock. Information in the statement of cash flows helps address these and other questions such as (1) How much cash is generated from or used in operations? (2) What expenditures are made with cash from operations? (3) What is the source of cash for debt payments? (4) What is the source of cash for distributions to owners? (5) How is the increase in investing activities financed? (6) What is the source of cash for new plant assets? (7) Why is cash flow from operations different from income? (8) How is cash from financing used?

To effectively answer these questions, it is important to separately analyze investing, financing, and operating activities. To illustrate, consider data from three different companies in Exhibit 16.13. These companies operate in the same industry and have been in business for several years.

EXHIBIT 16.13

Cash Flows of Competing Companies

($ thousands)	BMX	ATV	Trex
Cash provided (used) by operating activities	$90,000	$40,000	$(24,000)
Cash provided (used) by investing activities			
Proceeds from sale of plant assets			26,000
Purchase of plant assets	(48,000)	(25,000)	
Cash provided (used) by financing activities			
Proceeds from issuance of debt			13,000
Repayment of debt	(27,000)		
Net increase (decrease) in cash	$15,000	$15,000	$ 15,000

Each company generates an identical $15,000 net increase in cash, but its sources and uses of cash flows are very different. BMX's operating activities provide net cash flows of $90,000, allowing it to purchase plant assets of $48,000 and repay $27,000 of its debt. ATV's operating activities provide $40,000 of cash flows, limiting its purchase of plant assets to $25,000. Trex's $15,000 net cash increase is due to selling plant assets and incurring additional debt. Its operating activities yield a net cash outflow of $24,000.

Overall, analysis of these cash flows reveals that BMX is more capable of generating future cash flows than is ATV or Trex.

Decision Insight

Free Cash Flows Many investors use cash flows to value company stock. However, cash-based valuation models often yield different stock values due to differences in measurement of cash flows. Most models require cash flows that are "free" for distribution to shareholders. These *free cash flows* are defined as cash flows available to shareholders after operating asset reinvestments and debt payments. Knowledge of the statement of cash flows is key to proper computation of free cash flows. A company's growth and financial flexibility depend on adequate free cash flows.

Cash Flow on Total Assets

A2 Compute and apply the cash flow on total assets ratio.

Cash flow information has limitations, but it can help measure a company's ability to meet its obligations, pay dividends, expand operations, and obtain financing. Users often compute and analyze a cash-based ratio similar to return on total assets except that its numerator is net cash flows from operating activities. The **cash flow on total assets** ratio is in Exhibit 16.14.

EXHIBIT 16.14

Cash Flow on Total Assets

$$\textbf{Cash flow on total assets} = \frac{\textbf{Cash flow from operations}}{\textbf{Average total assets}}$$

This ratio reflects actual cash flows and is not affected by accounting income recognition and measurement. It can help business decision makers estimate the amount and timing of cash flows when planning and analyzing operating activities.

To illustrate, the 2007 cash flow on total assets ratio for **Nike** is 18.3%—see Exhibit 16.15. Is an 18.3% ratio good or bad? To answer this question, we compare this ratio with the ratios of prior years (we could also compare its ratio with those of its competitors and the market). Nike's cash flow on total assets ratio for several prior years is in the second column of Exhibit 16.15. Results show that its 18.3% return is the median of the prior years' returns.

EXHIBIT 16.15

Nike's Cash Flow on Total Assets

Year	Cash Flow on Total Assets	Return on Total Assets
2007	18.3%	14.5%
2006	17.9	14.9
2005	18.8	14.5
2004	20.6	12.8
2003	13.9	7.1

As an indicator of *earnings quality,* some analysts compare the cash flow on total assets ratio to the return on total assets ratio. Nike's return on total assets is provided in the third column of Exhibit 16.15. Nike's cash flow on total assets ratio exceeds its return on total assets in each of the five years, leading some analysts to infer that Nike's earnings quality is high for that period because more earnings are realized in the form of cash.

Decision Insight

Cash Flow Ratios Analysts use various other cash-based ratios, including the following two:

(1) $$\textbf{Cash coverage of growth} = \frac{\textbf{Operating cash flow}}{\textbf{Cash outflow for plant assets}}$$

where a low ratio (less than 1) implies cash inadequacy to meet asset growth, whereas a high ratio implies cash adequacy for asset growth.

(2) $$\textbf{Operating cash flow to sales} = \frac{\textbf{Operating cash flow}}{\textbf{Net sales}}$$

When this ratio substantially and consistently differs from the operating income to net sales ratio, the risk of accounting improprieties increases.

Point: The following ratio helps assess whether operating cash flow is adequate to meet long-term obligations: **Cash coverage of debt** = Cash flow from operations ÷ Noncurrent liabilities. A low ratio suggests a higher risk of insolvency; a high ratio suggests a greater ability to meet long-term obligations.

Demonstration Problem

Umlauf's comparative balance sheets, income statement, and additional information follow.

DP16

UMLAUF COMPANY
Balance Sheets
December 31, 2009 and 2008

	2009	2008
Assets		
Cash	$ 43,050	$ 23,925
Accounts receivable	34,125	39,825
Merchandise inventory	156,000	146,475
Prepaid expenses	3,600	1,650
Equipment	135,825	146,700
Accum. depreciation—Equipment	(61,950)	(47,550)
Total assets	$310,650	$311,025
Liabilities and Equity		
Accounts payable	$ 28,800	$ 33,750
Income taxes payable	5,100	4,425
Dividends payable	0	4,500
Bonds payable	0	37,500
Common stock, $10 par	168,750	168,750
Retained earnings	108,000	62,100
Total liabilities and equity	$310,650	$311,025

UMLAUF COMPANY
Income Statement
For Year Ended December 31, 2009

Sales		$446,100
Cost of goods sold	$222,300	
Other operating expenses	120,300	
Depreciation expense	25,500	(368,100)
		78,000
Other gains (losses)		
Loss on sale of equipment	3,300	
Loss on retirement of bonds	825	(4,125)
Income before taxes		73,875
Income taxes expense		(13,725)
Net income		$ 60,150

Additional Information

a. Equipment costing $21,375 with accumulated depreciation of $11,100 is sold for cash.

b. Equipment purchases are for cash.

c. Accumulated Depreciation is affected by depreciation expense and the sale of equipment.

d. The balance of Retained Earnings is affected by dividend declarations and net income.

e. All sales are made on credit.

f. All merchandise inventory purchases are on credit.

g. Accounts Payable balances result from merchandise inventory purchases.

h. Prepaid expenses relate to "other operating expenses."

Required

1. Prepare a statement of cash flows using the indirect method for year 2009.

2.[B] Prepare a statement of cash flows using the direct method for year 2009.

Planning the Solution

- Prepare two blank statements of cash flows with sections for operating, investing, and financing activities using the (1) indirect method format and (2) direct method format.
- Compute the cash paid for equipment and the cash received from the sale of equipment using the additional information provided along with the amount for depreciation expense and the change in the balances of equipment and accumulated depreciation. Use T-accounts to help chart the effects of the sale and purchase of equipment on the balances of the Equipment account and the Accumulated Depreciation account.
- Compute the effect of net income on the change in the Retained Earnings account balance. Assign the difference between the change in retained earnings and the amount of net income to dividends declared. Adjust the dividends declared amount for the change in the Dividends Payable balance.
- Compute cash received from customers, cash paid for merchandise, cash paid for other operating expenses, and cash paid for taxes as illustrated in the chapter.
- Enter the cash effects of reconstruction entries to the appropriate section(s) of the statement.
- Total each section of the statement, determine the total net change in cash, and add it to the beginning balance to get the ending balance of cash.

Solution to Demonstration Problem

Supporting computations for cash receipts and cash payments.

(1)	*Cost of equipment sold	$ 21,375
	Accumulated depreciation of equipment sold	(11,100)
	Book value of equipment sold	10,275
	Loss on sale of equipment	(3,300)
	Cash received from sale of equipment	**$ 6,975**
	Cost of equipment sold	$ 21,375
	Less decrease in the equipment account balance	(10,875)
	Cash paid for new equipment	**$ 10,500**
(2)	Loss on retirement of bonds	$ 825
	Carrying value of bonds retired	37,500
	Cash paid to retire bonds	**$ 38,325**
(3)	Net income	$ 60,150
	Less increase in retained earnings	45,900
	Dividends declared	14,250
	Plus decrease in dividends payable	4,500
	Cash paid for dividends	**$ 18,750**
(4)[B]	Sales	$ 446,100
	Add decrease in accounts receivable	5,700
	Cash received from customers	**$451,800**
(5)[B]	Cost of goods sold	$ 222,300
	Plus increase in merchandise inventory	9,525
	Purchases	231,825
	Plus decrease in accounts payable	4,950
	Cash paid for merchandise	**$236,775**
(6)[B]	Other operating expenses	$ 120,300
	Plus increase in prepaid expenses	1,950
	Cash paid for other operating expenses	**$122,250**
(7)[B]	Income taxes expense	$ 13,725
	Less increase in income taxes payable	(675)
	Cash paid for income taxes	**$ 13,050**

* Supporting T-account analysis for part 1 follows:

Equipment

Debit		Credit	
Bal., Dec. 31, 2008	146,700		
Cash purchase	10,500	Sale	21,375
Bal., Dec. 31, 2009	135,825		

Accumulated Depreciation—Equipment

Debit		Credit	
		Bal., Dec. 31, 2008	47,550
Sale	11,100	Depr. expense	25,500
		Bal., Dec. 31, 2009	61,950

UMLAUF COMPANY
Statement of Cash Flows (Indirect Method)
For Year Ended December 31, 2009

Cash flows from operating activities		
Net income	$60,150	
Adjustments to reconcile net income to net cash provided by operating activities		
Decrease in accounts receivable	5,700	
Increase in merchandise inventory	(9,525)	
Increase in prepaid expenses	(1,950)	
Decrease in accounts payable	(4,950)	
Increase in income taxes payable	675	
Depreciation expense	25,500	
Loss on sale of plant assets	3,300	
Loss on retirement of bonds	825	
Net cash provided by operating activities		$79,725

[continued on next page]

[continued from previous page]

Cash flows from investing activities		
Cash received from sale of equipment	6,975	
Cash paid for equipment	(10,500)	
Net cash used in investing activities		(3,525)
Cash flows from financing activities		
Cash paid to retire bonds payable	(38,325)	
Cash paid for dividends	(18,750)	
Net cash used in financing activities		(57,075)
Net increase in cash		$19,125
Cash balance at prior year-end		23,925
Cash balance at current year-end		$43,050

UMLAUF COMPANY
Statement of Cash Flows (Direct Method)
For Year Ended December 31, 2009

Cash flows from operating activities		
Cash received from customers	$451,800	
Cash paid for merchandise	(236,775)	
Cash paid for other operating expenses	(122,250)	
Cash paid for income taxes	(13,050)	
Net cash provided by operating activities		$79,725
Cash flows from investing activities		
Cash received from sale of equipment	6,975	
Cash paid for equipment	(10,500)	
Net cash used in investing activities		(3,525)
Cash flows from financing activities		
Cash paid to retire bonds payable	(38,325)	
Cash paid for dividends	(18,750)	
Net cash used in financing activities		(57,075)
Net increase in cash		$19,125
Cash balance at prior year-end		23,925
Cash balance at current year-end		$43,050

APPENDIX

Spreadsheet Preparation of the Statement of Cash Flows

16A

This appendix explains how to use a spreadsheet to prepare the statement of cash flows under the indirect method.

Preparing the Indirect Method Spreadsheet

P4 Illustrate use of a spreadsheet to prepare a statement of cash flows.

Analyzing noncash accounts can be challenging when a company has a large number of accounts and many operating, investing, and financing transactions. A *spreadsheet,* also called *work sheet* or *working paper,* can help us organize the information needed to prepare a statement of cash flows. A spreadsheet also makes it easier to check the accuracy of our work. To illustrate, we return to the comparative balance sheets and income statement shown in Exhibit 16.10. We use the following identifying letters *a* through *g* to code changes in accounts, and letters *h* through *m* for additional information, to prepare the statement of cash flows:

a. Net income is $38,000.
b. Accounts receivable increase by $20,000.
c. Merchandise inventory increases by $14,000.
d. Prepaid expenses increase by $2,000.
e. Accounts payable decrease by $5,000.
f. Interest payable decreases by $1,000.
g. Income taxes payable increase by $10,000.
h. Depreciation expense is $24,000.
i. Plant assets costing $30,000 with accumulated depreciation of $12,000 are sold for $12,000 cash. This yields a loss on sale of assets of $6,000.
j. Notes with a book value of $34,000 are retired with a cash payment of $18,000, yielding a $16,000 gain on retirement.
k. Plant assets costing $70,000 are purchased with a cash payment of $10,000 and an issuance of notes payable for $60,000.
l. Issued 3,000 shares of common stock for $15,000 cash.
m. Paid cash dividends of $14,000.

Exhibit 16A.1 shows the indirect method spreadsheet for Genesis. We enter both beginning and ending balance sheet amounts on the spreadsheet. We also enter information in the Analysis of Changes columns (keyed to the additional information items *a* through *m*) to explain changes in the accounts and determine the cash flows for operating, investing, and financing activities. Information about noncash investing and financing activities is reported near the bottom.

Entering the Analysis of Changes on the Spreadsheet

The following sequence of procedures is used to complete the spreadsheet after the beginning and ending balances of the balance sheet accounts are entered:

① Enter net income as the first item in the Statement of Cash Flows section for computing operating cash inflow (debit) and as a credit to Retained Earnings.

② In the Statement of Cash Flows section, adjustments to net income are entered as debits if they increase cash flows and as credits if they decrease cash flows. Applying this same rule, adjust net income for the change in each noncash current asset and current liability account related to operating activities. For each adjustment to net income, the offsetting debit or credit must help reconcile the beginning and ending balances of a current asset or current liability account.

③ Enter adjustments to net income for income statement items not providing or using cash in the period. For each adjustment, the offsetting debit or credit must help reconcile a noncash balance sheet account.

④ Adjust net income to eliminate any gains or losses from investing and financing activities. Because the cash from a gain must be excluded from operating activities, the gain is entered as a credit in the operating activities section. Losses are entered as debits. For each adjustment, the related debit and/or credit must help reconcile balance sheet accounts and involve reconstructed entries to show the cash flow from investing or financing activities.

⑤ After reviewing any unreconciled balance sheet accounts and related information, enter the remaining reconciling entries for investing and financing activities. Examples are purchases of plant assets, issuances of long-term debt, stock issuances, and dividend payments. Some of these may require entries in the noncash investing and financing section of the spreadsheet (reconciled).

⑥ Check accuracy by totaling the Analysis of Changes columns and by determining that the change in each balance sheet account has been explained (reconciled).

Point: Analysis of the changes on the spreadsheet are summarized here:

1. Cash flows from operating activities generally affect net income, current assets, and current liabilities.
2. Cash flows from investing activities generally affect noncurrent asset accounts.
3. Cash flows from financing activities generally affect noncurrent liability and equity accounts.

We illustrate these steps in Exhibit 16A.1 for Genesis:

Step	Entries
①.........	(*a*)
②.........	(*b*) through (*g*)
③.........	(*h*)
④.........	(*i*) through (*j*)
⑤.........	(*k*) through (*m*)

EXHIBIT 16A.1

Spreadsheet for Preparing Statement of Cash Flows—Indirect Method

GENESIS
Spreadsheet for Statement of Cash Flows—Indirect Method
For Year Ended December 31, 2009

	Dec. 31, 2008	Analysis of Changes	Debit		Credit	Dec. 31, 2009
Balance Sheet—Debits						
Cash	$ 12,000					$ 17,000
Accounts receivable	40,000	(b)	$ 20,000			60,000
Merchandise inventory	70,000	(c)	14,000			84,000
Prepaid expenses	4,000	(d)	2,000			6,000
Plant assets	210,000	(k1)	70,000	(i)	$ 30,000	250,000
	$336,000					$417,000
Balance Sheet—Credits						
Accumulated depreciation	$ 48,000	(i)	12,000	(h)	24,000	$ 60,000
Accounts payable	40,000	(e)	5,000			35,000
Interest payable	4,000	(f)	1,000			3,000
Income taxes payable	12,000			(g)	10,000	22,000
Notes payable	64,000	(j)	34,000	(k2)	60,000	90,000
Common stock, $5 par value	80,000			(l)	15,000	95,000
Retained earnings	88,000	(m)	14,000	(a)	38,000	112,000
	$336,000					$417,000
Statement of Cash Flows						
Operating activities						
Net income		(a)	38,000			
Increase in accounts receivable				(b)	20,000	
Increase in merchandise inventory				(c)	14,000	
Increase in prepaid expenses				(d)	2,000	
Decrease in accounts payable				(e)	5,000	
Decrease in interest payable				(f)	1,000	
Increase in income taxes payable		(g)	10,000			
Depreciation expense		(h)	24,000			
Loss on sale of plant assets		(i)	6,000			
Gain on retirement of notes				(j)	16,000	
Investing activities						
Receipts from sale of plant assets		(i)	12,000			
Payment for purchase of plant assets				(k1)	10,000	
Financing activities						
Payment to retire notes				(j)	18,000	
Receipts from issuing stock		(l)	15,000			
Payment of cash dividends				(m)	14,000	
Noncash Investing and Financing Activities						
Purchase of plant assets with notes		(k2)	60,000	(k1)	60,000	
			$337,000		$337,000	

Since adjustments *i*, *j*, and *k* are more challenging, we show them in the following debit and credit format. These entries are for purposes of our understanding; they are *not* the entries actually made in the journals. Changes in the Cash account are identified as sources or uses of cash.

i.	Loss from sale of plant assets	6,000	
	Accumulated depreciation	12,000	
	Receipt from sale of plant assets **(source of cash)**	12,000	
	Plant assets		30,000
	To describe sale of plant assets.		

[continued on next page]

[continued from previous page]

j.	Notes payable	34,000	
	Payments to retire notes **(use of cash)**		18,000
	Gain on retirement of notes		16,000
	To describe retirement of notes.		
k1.	Plant assets	70,000	
	Payment to purchase plant assets **(use of cash)**		10,000
	Purchase of plant assets financed by notes		60,000
	To describe purchase of plant assets.		
k2.	Purchase of plant assets financed by notes	60,000	
	Notes payable		60,000
	To issue notes for purchase of assets.		

APPENDIX

16B Direct Method of Reporting Operating Cash Flows

P5 Compute cash flows from operating activities using the direct method.

We compute cash flows from operating activities under the direct method by adjusting accrual-based income statement items to the cash basis. The usual approach is to adjust income statement accounts related to operating activities for changes in their related balance sheet accounts as follows:

Revenue or expense	+ or −	Adjustments for changes in related balance sheet accounts	=	Cash receipts or cash payments

The framework for reporting cash receipts and cash payments for the operating section of the cash flow statement under the direct method is shown in Exhibit 16B.1. We consider cash receipts first and then cash payments.

EXHIBIT 16B.1

Major Classes of Operating Cash Flows

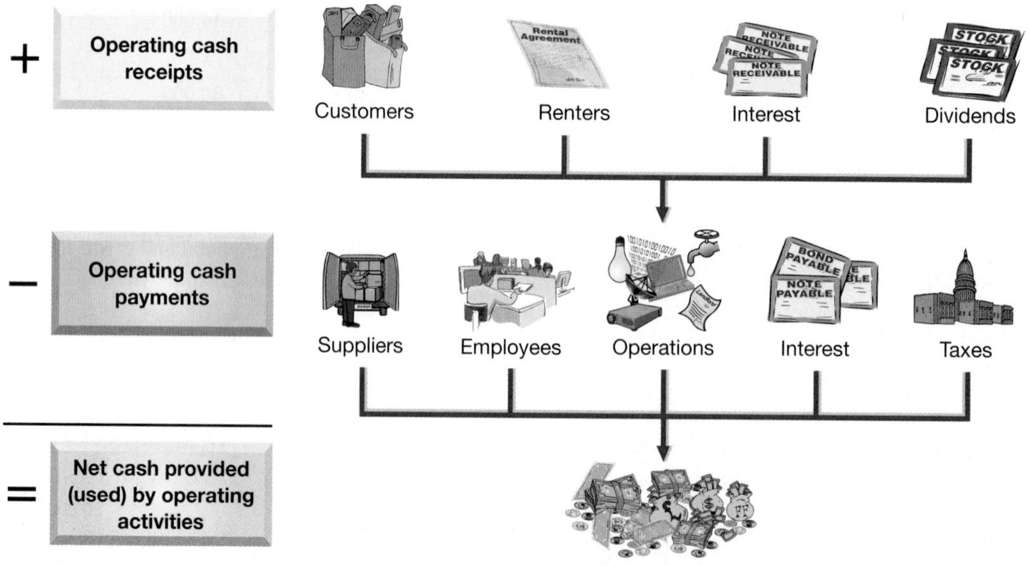

Operating Cash Receipts

A review of Exhibit 16.10 and the additional information reported by Genesis suggests only one potential cash receipt: sales to customers. This section, therefore, starts with sales to customers as reported on the income statement and then adjusts it as necessary to obtain cash received from customers to report on the statement of cash flows.

Cash Received from Customers If all sales are for cash, the amount received from customers equals the sales reported on the income statement. When some or all sales are on account, however, we must adjust the amount of sales for the change in Accounts Receivable. It is often helpful to use *account analysis* to do this. This usually involves setting up a T-account and reconstructing its major entries, with emphasis on cash receipts and payments. To illustrate, we use a T-account that includes accounts receivable balances for Genesis on December 31, 2008 and 2009. The beginning balance is $40,000 and the ending balance is $60,000. Next, the income statement shows sales of $590,000, which we enter on the debit side of this account. We now can reconstruct the Accounts Receivable account to determine the amount of cash received from customers as follows:

Point: An accounts receivable increase implies that cash received from customers is less than sales (the converse is also true).

Accounts Receivable			
Bal., Dec. 31, 2008	40,000		
Sales	590,000	**Cash receipts =**	**570,000**
Bal., Dec. 31, 2009	60,000		

This T-account shows that the Accounts Receivable balance begins at $40,000 and increases to $630,000 from sales of $590,000, yet its ending balance is only $60,000. This implies that cash receipts from customers are $570,000, computed as $40,000 + $590,000 − [?] = $60,000. This computation can be rearranged to express cash received as equal to sales of $590,000 minus a $20,000 increase in accounts receivable. This computation is summarized as a general rule in Exhibit 16B.2. The statement of cash flows in Exhibit 16.7 reports the $570,000 cash received from customers as a cash inflow from operating activities.

Example: If the ending balance of accounts receivable is $20,000 (instead of $60,000), what is cash received from customers? *Answer:* $610,000

EXHIBIT 16B.2

Formula to Compute Cash Received from Customers—Direct Method

$$\text{Cash received from customers} = \text{Sales} \begin{cases} + \text{ Decrease in accounts receivable} \\ \text{or} \\ - \text{ Increase in accounts receivable} \end{cases}$$

Other Cash Receipts While Genesis's cash receipts are limited to collections from customers, we often see other types of cash receipts, most commonly cash receipts involving rent, interest, and dividends. We compute cash received from these items by subtracting an increase in their respective receivable or adding a decrease. For instance, if rent receivable increases in the period, cash received from renters is less than rent revenue reported on the income statement. If rent receivable decreases, cash received is more than reported rent revenue. The same logic applies to interest and dividends. The formulas for these computations are summarized later in this appendix.

Point: Net income is measured using accrual accounting. Cash flows from operations are measured using cash basis accounting.

Operating Cash Payments

A review of Exhibit 16.10 and the additional Genesis information shows four operating expenses: cost of goods sold; wages and other operating expenses; interest expense; and taxes expense. We analyze each expense to compute its cash amounts for the statement of cash flows. (We then examine depreciation and the other losses and gains.)

Cash Paid for Merchandise We compute cash paid for merchandise by analyzing both cost of goods sold and merchandise inventory. If all merchandise purchases are for cash and the ending balance of Merchandise Inventory is unchanged from the beginning balance, the amount of cash paid for merchandise equals cost of goods sold—an uncommon situation. Instead, there normally is some change in the Merchandise Inventory balance. Also, some or all merchandise purchases are often made on credit, and this yields changes in the Accounts Payable balance. When the balances of both Merchandise Inventory and Accounts Payable change, we must adjust the cost of goods sold for changes in both accounts to compute cash paid for merchandise. This is a two-step adjustment.

Available with McGraw-Hill's Homework Manager McGraw-Hill's HOMEWORK MANAGER®

QUICK STUDY

QS 16-1
Statement of cash flows
C1 C2 C3

The statement of cash flows is one of the four primary financial statements.

1. Describe the content and layout of a statement of cash flows, including its three sections.
2. List at least three transactions classified as investing activities in a statement of cash flows.
3. List at least three transactions classified as financing activities in a statement of cash flows.
4. List at least three transactions classified as significant noncash financing and investing activities in the statement of cash flows.

QS 16-2
Transaction classification by activity
C2

Classify the following cash flows as operating, investing, or financing activities.

1. Sold long-term investments for cash.
2. Received cash payments from customers.
3. Paid cash for wages and salaries.
4. Purchased inventories for cash.
5. Paid cash dividends.
6. Issued common stock for cash.
7. Received cash interest on a note.
8. Paid cash interest on outstanding notes.
9. Received cash from sale of land at a loss.
10. Paid cash for property taxes on building.

QS 16-3
Computing cash from operations (indirect)
P2

Use the following information to determine this company's cash flows from operating activities using the indirect method.

LOLLAND COMPANY
Selected Balance Sheet Information
December 31, 2009 and 2008

	2009	2008
Current assets		
Cash	$169,300	$ 53,600
Accounts receivable	50,000	64,000
Inventory	120,000	108,200
Current liabilities		
Accounts payable	60,800	51,400
Income taxes payable	4,100	4,400

LOLLAND COMPANY
Income Statement
For Year Ended December 31, 2009

Sales		$1,030,000
Cost of goods sold		663,200
Gross profit		366,800
Operating expenses		
Depreciation expense	$ 72,000	
Other expenses	243,000	315,000
Income before taxes		51,800
Income taxes expense		15,400
Net income		$ 36,400

QS 16-4
Computing cash from asset sales
P3

The following selected information is from Manning Company's comparative balance sheets.

At December 31	2009	2008
Furniture	$ 264,000	$ 369,000
Accumulated depreciation—Furniture	(174,400)	(221,400)

The income statement reports depreciation expense for the year of $36,000. Also, furniture costing $105,000 was sold for its book value. Compute the cash received from the sale of furniture.

QS 16-5
Computing financing cash flows
P3

The following selected information is from the Tanner Company's comparative balance sheets.

At December 31	2009	2008
Common stock, $10 par value	$ 210,000	$200,000
Paid-in capital in excess of par	1,134,000	684,000
Retained earnings	627,000	575,000

The company's net income for the year ended December 31, 2009, was $96,000.

1. Compute the cash received from the sale of its common stock during 2009.
2. Compute the cash paid for dividends during 2009.

a. $23,550 used by operating activities
b. $23,550 provided by operating activities
c. $15,550 provided by operating activities
d. $42,400 provided by operating activities
e. $20,850 provided by operating activities

2. A machine with a cost of $175,000 and accumulated depreciation of $94,000 is sold for $87,000 cash. The amount reported as a source of cash under cash flows from investing activities is
a. $81,000.
b. $6,000.
c. $87,000.
d. Zero; this is a financing activity.
e. Zero; this is an operating activity.

3. A company settles a long-term note payable plus interest by paying $68,000 cash toward the principal amount and $5,440 cash for interest. The amount reported as a use of cash under cash flows from financing activities is
a. Zero; this is an investing activity.
b. Zero; this is an operating activity.
c. $73,440.
d. $68,000.
e. $5,440.

4. The following information is available regarding a company's annual salaries and wages. What amount of cash is paid for salaries and wages?

Salaries and wages expense	$255,000
Salaries and wages payable, prior year-end	8,200
Salaries and wages payable, current year-end	10,900

a. $252,300
b. $257,700
c. $255,000
d. $274,100
e. $235,900

5. The following information is available for a company. What amount of cash is paid for merchandise for the current year?

Cost of goods sold	$545,000
Merchandise inventory, prior year-end	105,000
Merchandise inventory, current year-end	112,000
Accounts payable, prior year-end	98,500
Accounts payable, current year-end	101,300

a. $545,000
b. $554,800
c. $540,800
d. $535,200
e. $549,200

Superscript letter ^{A}(^{B}) denotes assignments based on Appendix 16A (16B).

Discussion Questions

1. What is the reporting purpose of the statement of cash flows? Identify at least two questions that this statement can answer.

2. Describe the direct method of reporting cash flows from operating activities.

3. When a statement of cash flows is prepared using the direct method, what are some of the operating cash flows?

4. Describe the indirect method of reporting cash flows from operating activities.

5. What are some investing activities reported on the statement of cash flows?

6. What are some financing activities reported on the statement of cash flows?

7. Where on the statement of cash flows is the payment of cash dividends reported?

8. Assume that a company purchases land for $100,000, paying $20,000 cash and borrowing the remainder with a long-term note payable. How should this transaction be reported on a statement of cash flows?

9. On June 3, a company borrows $50,000 cash by giving its bank a 160-day, interest-bearing note. On the statement of cash flows, where should this be reported?

10. If a company reports positive net income for the year, can it also show a net cash outflow from operating activities? Explain.

11. Is depreciation a source of cash flow?

12. Refer to **Best Buy**'s statement of cash flows in Appendix A. (*a*) Which method is used to compute its net cash provided by operating activities? (*b*) While its balance sheet shows an increase in receivables from fiscal years 2006 to 2007, why is this increase in receivables subtracted when computing net cash provided by operating activities for the year ended March 3, 2007?

13. Refer to **Circuit City**'s statement of cash flows in Appendix A. What are its cash flows from financing activities for the year ended February 28, 2007? List items and amounts.

14. Refer to **RadioShack**'s statement of cash flows in Appendix A. List its cash flows from operating activities, investing activities, and financing activities.

15. Refer to **Apple**'s statement of cash flows in Appendix A. What investing activities result in cash outflows for the year ended September 30, 2006? List items and amounts.

Denotes Discussion Questions that involve decision making.

QUICK STUDY

QS 16-1
Statement of cash flows
C1 C2 C3

The statement of cash flows is one of the four primary financial statements.

1. Describe the content and layout of a statement of cash flows, including its three sections.
2. List at least three transactions classified as investing activities in a statement of cash flows.
3. List at least three transactions classified as financing activities in a statement of cash flows.
4. List at least three transactions classified as significant noncash financing and investing activities in the statement of cash flows.

QS 16-2
Transaction classification by activity
C2

Classify the following cash flows as operating, investing, or financing activities.

1. Sold long-term investments for cash.
2. Received cash payments from customers.
3. Paid cash for wages and salaries.
4. Purchased inventories for cash.
5. Paid cash dividends.
6. Issued common stock for cash.
7. Received cash interest on a note.
8. Paid cash interest on outstanding notes.
9. Received cash from sale of land at a loss.
10. Paid cash for property taxes on building.

QS 16-3
Computing cash from operations (indirect)
P2

Use the following information to determine this company's cash flows from operating activities using the indirect method.

LOLLAND COMPANY
Selected Balance Sheet Information
December 31, 2009 and 2008

	2009	2008
Current assets		
Cash	$169,300	$ 53,600
Accounts receivable	50,000	64,000
Inventory	120,000	108,200
Current liabilities		
Accounts payable	60,800	51,400
Income taxes payable	4,100	4,400

LOLLAND COMPANY
Income Statement
For Year Ended December 31, 2009

Sales		$1,030,000
Cost of goods sold		663,200
Gross profit		366,800
Operating expenses		
Depreciation expense	$ 72,000	
Other expenses	243,000	315,000
Income before taxes		51,800
Income taxes expense		15,400
Net income		$ 36,400

QS 16-4
Computing cash from asset sales
P3

The following selected information is from Manning Company's comparative balance sheets.

At December 31	2009	2008
Furniture	$ 264,000	$ 369,000
Accumulated depreciation—Furniture	(174,400)	(221,400)

The income statement reports depreciation expense for the year of $36,000. Also, furniture costing $105,000 was sold for its book value. Compute the cash received from the sale of furniture.

QS 16-5
Computing financing cash flows
P3

The following selected information is from the Tanner Company's comparative balance sheets.

At December 31	2009	2008
Common stock, $10 par value	$ 210,000	$200,000
Paid-in capital in excess of par	1,134,000	684,000
Retained earnings	627,000	575,000

The company's net income for the year ended December 31, 2009, was $96,000.

1. Compute the cash received from the sale of its common stock during 2009.
2. Compute the cash paid for dividends during 2009.

when we can explain changes in these accounts from the beginning to the end of the period.

$P4^A$ Illustrate use of a spreadsheet to prepare a statement of cash flows. A spreadsheet is a useful tool in preparing a statement of cash flows. Six key steps (see Appendix 16A) are applied when using the spreadsheet to prepare the statement.

$P5^B$ Compute cash flows from operating activities using the direct method. The direct method for reporting net cash provided or used by operating activities lists major operating cash inflows less cash outflows to yield net cash inflow or outflow from operations.

Guidance Answers to **Decision Maker**

Entrepreneur Several factors might explain an increase in net cash flows when a net loss is reported, including (1) early recognition of expenses relative to revenues generated (such as research and development), (2) cash advances on long-term sales contracts not yet recognized in income, (3) issuances of debt or equity for cash to finance expansion, (4) cash sale of assets, (5) delay of cash payments, and (6) cash prepayment on sales. Analysis needs to focus on the components of both the net loss and the net cash flows and their implications for future performance.

Reporter Your initial reaction based on the company's $600,000 loss with a $550,000 decrease in net cash flows is not positive. However, closer scrutiny reveals a more positive picture of this company's performance. Cash flow from operating activities is $650,000, computed as [?] − $850,000 − $350,000 = $(550,000). You also note that net income *before* the extraordinary loss is $330,000, computed as [?] − $930,000 = $(600,000).

Guidance Answers to **Quick Checks**

1. No to both. The statement of cash flows reports changes in the sum of cash plus cash equivalents. It does not report transfers between cash and cash equivalents.
2. The three categories of cash inflows and outflows are operating activities, investing activities, and financing activities.
3. **a.** Investing **c.** Financing **e.** Operating
   b. Operating **d.** Operating **f.** Financing
4. $74,900 + $4,600 − $11,700 − $1,000 + $3,400 = $70,200
5. Expenses such as depreciation and amortization do not require current cash outflows. Therefore, adding these expenses back to net income eliminates these noncash items from the net income number, converting it to a cash basis.
6. A gain on the sale of plant assets is subtracted from net income because a sale of plant assets is not an operating activity; it is an investing activity for the amount of cash received from its sale. Also, such a gain yields no cash effects.
7. $80,000 − $30,000 − $10,000 = $40,000 cash receipt. The $40,000 cash receipt is reported as an investing activity.
8. $590,000 + ($120,000 − $90,000) = $620,000
9. $168,000 − ($32,000 − $28,000) − $2,400 = $161,600
10. $112,000 + ($4,200 − $1,200) − $5,600 = $109,400

Key Terms

mhhe.com/wildFAP19e

Key Terms are available at the book's Website for learning and testing in an online Flashcard Format.

Cash flow on total assets (p. 646)
Direct method (p. 634)
Financing activities (p. 630)
Indirect method (p. 634)
Investing activities (p. 630)
Operating activities (p. 629)
Statement of cash flows (p. 628)

Multiple Choice Quiz

Answers on p. 677

mhhe.com/wildFAP19e

Additional Quiz Questions are available at the book's Website.

Quiz16

1. A company uses the indirect method to determine its cash flows from operating activities. Use the following information to determine its net cash provided or used by operating activities.

Net income	$15,200
Depreciation expense	10,000
Cash payment on note payable	8,000
Gain on sale of land	3,000
Increase in inventory	1,500
Increase in accounts payable	2,850

Direct Method Format of Operating Activities Section

Exhibit 16.7 shows the Genesis statement of cash flows using the direct method. Major items of cash inflows and cash outflows are listed separately in the operating activities section. The format requires that operating cash outflows be subtracted from operating cash inflows to get net cash provided (used) by operating activities. The FASB recommends that the operating activities section of the statement of cash flows be reported using the direct method, which is considered more useful to financial statement users. *However, the FASB requires a reconciliation of net income to net cash provided (used) by operating activities when the direct method is used* (which can be reported in the notes). This reconciliation is similar to preparation of the operating activities section of the statement of cash flows using the indirect method.

Point: Some preparers argue that it is easier to prepare a statement of cash flows using the indirect method. This likely explains its greater frequency in financial statements.

Decision Insight

IFRSs Like U.S. GAAP, IFRSs allow cash flows from operating activities to be reported using either the indirect method or the direct method.

Quick Check

Answers—p. 658

8. Net sales in a period are $590,000, beginning accounts receivable are $120,000, and ending accounts receivable are $90,000. What cash amount is collected from customers in the period?
9. The Merchandise Inventory account balance decreases in the period from a beginning balance of $32,000 to an ending balance of $28,000. Cost of goods sold for the period is $168,000. If the Accounts Payable balance increases $2,400 in the period, what is the cash amount paid for merchandise inventory?
10. This period's wages and other operating expenses total $112,000. Beginning-of-period prepaid expenses totaled $1,200, and its ending balance is $4,200. There were no beginning-of-period accrued liabilities, but end-of-period wages payable equal $5,600. How much cash is paid for wages and other operating expenses?

Summary

C1 Explain the purpose and importance of cash flow information. The main purpose of the statement of cash flows is to report the major cash receipts and cash payments for a period. This includes identifying cash flows as relating to operating, investing, or financing activities. Most business decisions involve evaluating activities that provide or use cash.

C2 Distinguish between operating, investing, and financing activities. Operating activities include transactions and events that determine net income. Investing activities include transactions and events that mainly affect long-term assets. Financing activities include transactions and events that mainly affect long-term liabilities and equity.

C3 Identify and disclose noncash investing and financing activities. Noncash investing and financing activities must be disclosed in either a note or a separate schedule to the statement of cash flows. Examples are the retirement of debt by issuing equity and the exchange of a note payable for plant assets.

C4 Describe the format of the statement of cash flows. The statement of cash flows separates cash receipts and cash payments into operating, investing, or financing activities.

A1 Analyze the statement of cash flows. To understand and predict cash flows, users stress identification of the sources and uses of cash flows by operating, investing, and financing activities. Emphasis is on operating cash flows since they derive from continuing operations.

A2 Compute and apply the cash flow on total assets ratio. The cash flow on total assets ratio is defined as operating cash flows divided by average total assets. Analysis of current and past values for this ratio can reflect a company's ability to yield regular and positive cash flows. It is also viewed as a measure of earnings quality.

P1 Prepare a statement of cash flows. Preparation of a statement of cash flows involves five steps: (1) Compute the net increase or decrease in cash; (2) compute net cash provided or used by operating activities (*using either the direct or indirect method*); (3) compute net cash provided or used by investing activities; (4) compute net cash provided or used by financing activities; and (5) report the beginning and ending cash balance and prove that it is explained by net cash flows. Noncash investing and financing activities are also disclosed.

P2 Compute cash flows from operating activities using the indirect method. The indirect method for reporting net cash provided or used by operating activities starts with net income and then adjusts it for three items: (1) changes in noncash current assets and current liabilities related to operating activities, (2) revenues and expenses not providing or using cash, and (3) gains and losses from investing and financing activities.

P3 Determine cash flows from both investing and financing activities. Cash flows from both investing and financing activities are determined by identifying the cash flow effects of transactions and events affecting each balance sheet account related to these activities. All cash flows from these activities are identified

EXHIBIT 16B.5

Formulas to Compute Cash Paid for Both Interest and Taxes—Direct Method

Cash paid for interest = Interest expense — [+ Decrease in interest payable or − Increase in interest payable]

Cash paid for taxes = Income taxes expenses — [+ Decrease in income taxes payable or − Increase in income taxes payable]

Analysis of Additional Expenses, Gains, and Losses Genesis has three additional items reported on its income statement: depreciation, loss on sale of assets, and gain on retirement of debt. We must consider each for its potential cash effects.

Depreciation Expense Depreciation expense is $24,000. It is often called a *noncash expense* because depreciation has no cash flows. Depreciation expense is an allocation of an asset's depreciable cost. The cash outflow with a plant asset is reported as part of investing activities when it is paid for. Thus, depreciation expense is *never* reported on a statement of cash flows using the direct method; nor is depletion or amortization expense.

Loss on Sale of Assets Sales of assets frequently result in gains and losses reported as part of net income, but the amount of recorded gain or loss does *not* reflect any cash flows in these transactions. Asset sales result in cash inflow equal to the cash amount received, regardless of whether the asset was sold at a gain or a loss. This cash inflow is reported under investing activities. Thus, the loss or gain on a sale of assets is *never* reported on a statement of cash flows using the direct method.

Gain on Retirement of Debt Retirement of debt usually yields a gain or loss reported as part of net income, but that gain or loss does *not* reflect cash flow in this transaction. Debt retirement results in cash outflow equal to the cash paid to settle the debt, regardless of whether the debt is retired at a gain or loss. This cash outflow is reported under financing activities; the loss or gain from retirement of debt is *never* reported on a statement of cash flows using the direct method.

Point: The direct method is usually viewed as *user friendly* because less accounting knowledge is required to understand and use it.

Summary of Adjustments for Direct Method

Exhibit 16B.6 summarizes common adjustments for net income to yield net cash provided (used) by operating activities under the direct method.

EXHIBIT 16B.6

Summary of Selected Adjustments for Direct Method

Item	From Income Statement	Adjustments to Obtain Cash Flow Numbers
Receipts		
From sales	Sales Revenue	+Decrease in Accounts Receivable −Increase in Accounts Receivable
From rent	Rent Revenue	+Decrease in Rent Receivable −Increase in Rent Receivable
From interest	Interest Revenue	+Decrease in Interest Receivable −Increase in Interest Receivable
From dividends	Dividend Revenue	+Decrease in Dividends Receivable −Increase in Dividends Receivable
Payments		
To suppliers	Cost of Goods Sold	+Increase in Inventory −Decrease in Inventory — +Decrease in Accounts Payable −Increase in Accounts Payable
For operations	Operating Expense	+Increase in Prepaids −Decrease in Prepaids — +Decrease in Accrued Liabilities −Increase in Accrued Liabilities
To employees	Wages (Salaries) Expense	+Decrease in Wages (Salaries) Payable −Increase in Wages (Salaries) Payable
For interest	Interest Expense	+Decrease in Interest Payable −Increase in Interest Payable
For taxes	Income Tax Expense	+Decrease in Income Tax Payable −Increase in Income Tax Payable

Exhibit 16.10. The balance sheets show prepaid expenses but no accrued liabilities. Thus, the adjustment is limited to the change in prepaid expenses. The amount of adjustment is computed by assuming that all cash paid for wages and other operating expenses is initially debited to Prepaid Expenses. This assumption allows us to reconstruct the Prepaid Expenses account:

Prepaid Expenses			
Bal., Dec. 31, 2008	4,000		
Cash payments =	**218,000**	Wages and other operating exp.	216,000
Bal., Dec. 31, 2009	6,000		

Prepaid Expenses increase by $2,000 in the period, meaning that cash paid for wages and other operating expenses exceeds the reported expense by $2,000. Alternatively, we can express cash paid for wages and other operating expenses as equal to its reported expenses of $216,000 plus the $2,000 increase in prepaid expenses.[1]

Point: A decrease in prepaid expenses implies that reported expenses include an amount(s) that did not require a cash outflow in the period.

Exhibit 16B.4 summarizes the adjustments to wages (including salaries) and other operating expenses. The Genesis balance sheet did not report accrued liabilities, but we include them in the formula to explain the adjustment to cash when they do exist. A decrease in accrued liabilities implies that we paid cash for more goods or services than received this period, so we add the decrease in accrued liabilities to the expense amount to obtain cash paid for these goods or services. An increase in accrued liabilities implies that we paid cash for less than what was acquired, so we subtract this increase in accrued liabilities from the expense amount to get cash paid.

EXHIBIT 16B.4

Formula to Compute Cash Paid for Wages and Operating Expenses—Direct Method

Cash paid for wages and other operating expenses	=	Wages and other operating expenses	+ Increase in prepaid expenses or − Decrease in prepaid expenses	+ Decrease in accrued liabilities or − Increase in accrued liabilities

Cash Paid for Interest and Income Taxes Computing operating cash flows for interest and taxes is similar to that for operating expenses. Both require adjustments to their amounts reported on the income statement for changes in their related balance sheet accounts. We begin with the Genesis income statement showing interest expense of $7,000 and income taxes expense of $15,000. To compute the cash paid, we adjust interest expense for the change in interest payable and then the income taxes expense for the change in income taxes payable. These computations involve reconstructing both liability accounts:

Interest Payable			
		Bal., Dec. 31, 2008	4,000
Cash paid for interest =	**8,000**	Interest expense	7,000
		Bal., Dec. 31, 2009	3,000

Income Taxes Payable			
		Bal., Dec. 31, 2008	12,000
Cash paid for taxes =	**5,000**	Income taxes expense	15,000
		Bal., Dec. 31, 2009	22,000

These accounts reveal cash paid for interest of $8,000 and cash paid for income taxes of $5,000. The formulas to compute these amounts are in Exhibit 16B.5. Both of these cash payments are reported as operating cash outflows on the statement of cash flows in Exhibit 16.7.

[1] The assumption that all cash payments for wages and operating expenses are initially debited to Prepaid Expenses is not necessary for our analysis to hold. If cash payments are debited directly to the expense account, the total amount of cash paid for wages and other operating expenses still equals the $216,000 expense plus the $2,000 increase in Prepaid Expenses (which arise from end-of-period adjusting entries).

Operating Cash Receipts

A review of Exhibit 16.10 and the additional information reported by Genesis suggests only one potential cash receipt: sales to customers. This section, therefore, starts with sales to customers as reported on the income statement and then adjusts it as necessary to obtain cash received from customers to report on the statement of cash flows.

Cash Received from Customers If all sales are for cash, the amount received from customers equals the sales reported on the income statement. When some or all sales are on account, however, we must adjust the amount of sales for the change in Accounts Receivable. It is often helpful to use *account analysis* to do this. This usually involves setting up a T-account and reconstructing its major entries, with emphasis on cash receipts and payments. To illustrate, we use a T-account that includes accounts receivable balances for Genesis on December 31, 2008 and 2009. The beginning balance is $40,000 and the ending balance is $60,000. Next, the income statement shows sales of $590,000, which we enter on the debit side of this account. We now can reconstruct the Accounts Receivable account to determine the amount of cash received from customers as follows:

Point: An accounts receivable increase implies that cash received from customers is less than sales (the converse is also true).

Accounts Receivable			
Bal., Dec. 31, 2008	40,000		
Sales	590,000	**Cash receipts =**	**570,000**
Bal., Dec. 31, 2009	60,000		

This T-account shows that the Accounts Receivable balance begins at $40,000 and increases to $630,000 from sales of $590,000, yet its ending balance is only $60,000. This implies that cash receipts from customers are $570,000, computed as $40,000 + $590,000 − [?] = $60,000. This computation can be rearranged to express cash received as equal to sales of $590,000 minus a $20,000 increase in accounts receivable. This computation is summarized as a general rule in Exhibit 16B.2. The statement of cash flows in Exhibit 16.7 reports the $570,000 cash received from customers as a cash inflow from operating activities.

Example: If the ending balance of accounts receivable is $20,000 (instead of $60,000), what is cash received from customers? *Answer:* $610,000

EXHIBIT 16B.2

Formula to Compute Cash Received from Customers—Direct Method

Cash received from customers = Sales	+ Decrease in accounts receivable	
	or	
	− Increase in accounts receivable	

Other Cash Receipts While Genesis's cash receipts are limited to collections from customers, we often see other types of cash receipts, most commonly cash receipts involving rent, interest, and dividends. We compute cash received from these items by subtracting an increase in their respective receivable or adding a decrease. For instance, if rent receivable increases in the period, cash received from renters is less than rent revenue reported on the income statement. If rent receivable decreases, cash received is more than reported rent revenue. The same logic applies to interest and dividends. The formulas for these computations are summarized later in this appendix.

Point: Net income is measured using accrual accounting. Cash flows from operations are measured using cash basis accounting.

Operating Cash Payments

A review of Exhibit 16.10 and the additional Genesis information shows four operating expenses: cost of goods sold; wages and other operating expenses; interest expense; and taxes expense. We analyze each expense to compute its cash amounts for the statement of cash flows. (We then examine depreciation and the other losses and gains.)

Cash Paid for Merchandise We compute cash paid for merchandise by analyzing both cost of goods sold and merchandise inventory. If all merchandise purchases are for cash and the ending balance of Merchandise Inventory is unchanged from the beginning balance, the amount of cash paid for merchandise equals cost of goods sold—an uncommon situation. Instead, there normally is some change in the Merchandise Inventory balance. Also, some or all merchandise purchases are often made on credit, and this yields changes in the Accounts Payable balance. When the balances of both Merchandise Inventory and Accounts Payable change, we must adjust the cost of goods sold for changes in both accounts to compute cash paid for merchandise. This is a two-step adjustment.

First, we use the change in the account balance of Merchandise Inventory, along with the cost of goods sold amount, to compute cost of purchases for the period. An increase in merchandise inventory implies that we bought more than we sold, and we add this inventory increase to cost of goods sold to compute cost of purchases. A decrease in merchandise inventory implies that we bought less than we sold, and we subtract the inventory decrease from cost of goods sold to compute purchases. We illustrate the *first step* by reconstructing the Merchandise Inventory account of Genesis:

Merchandise Inventory			
Bal., Dec. 31, 2008	70,000		
Purchases =	**314,000**	Cost of goods sold	300,000
Bal., Dec. 31, 2009	84,000		

The beginning balance is $70,000, and the ending balance is $84,000. The income statement shows that cost of goods sold is $300,000, which we enter on the credit side of this account. With this information, we determine the amount for cost of purchases to be $314,000. This computation can be rearranged to express cost of purchases as equal to cost of goods sold of $300,000 plus the $14,000 increase in inventory.

The second step uses the change in the balance of Accounts Payable, and the amount of cost of purchases, to compute cash paid for merchandise. A decrease in accounts payable implies that we paid for more goods than we acquired this period, and we would then add the accounts payable decrease to cost of purchases to compute cash paid for merchandise. An increase in accounts payable implies that we paid for less than the amount of goods acquired, and we would subtract the accounts payable increase from purchases to compute cash paid for merchandise. The *second step* is applied to Genesis by reconstructing its Accounts Payable account:

Accounts Payable			
		Bal., Dec. 31, 2008	40,000
Cash payments =	**319,000**	Purchases	314,000
		Bal., Dec. 31, 2009	35,000

Example: If the ending balances of Inventory and Accounts Payable are $60,000 and $50,000, respectively (instead of $84,000 and $35,000), what is cash paid for merchandise? *Answer:* $280,000

Its beginning balance of $40,000 plus purchases of $314,000 minus an ending balance of $35,000 yields cash paid of $319,000 (or $40,000 + $314,000 − [?] = $35,000). Alternatively, we can express cash paid for merchandise as equal to purchases of $314,000 plus the $5,000 decrease in accounts payable. The $319,000 cash paid for merchandise is reported on the statement of cash flows in Exhibit 16.7 as a cash outflow under operating activities.

We summarize this two-step adjustment to cost of goods sold to compute cash paid for merchandise inventory in Exhibit 16B.3.

EXHIBIT 16B.3

Two Steps to Compute Cash Paid for Merchandise—Direct Method

Step 1

Purchases = Cost of goods sold { + Increase in merchandise inventory or − Decrease in merchandise inventory }

Step 2

Cash paid for merchandise = Purchases { + Decrease in accounts payable or − Increase in accounts payable }

Cash Paid for Wages and Operating Expenses (Excluding Depreciation) The income statement of Genesis shows wages and other operating expenses of $216,000 (see Exhibit 16.10). To compute cash paid for wages and other operating expenses, we adjust this amount for any changes in their related balance sheet accounts. We begin by looking for any prepaid expenses and accrued liabilities related to wages and other operating expenses in the balance sheets of Genesis in

Use the following balance sheets and income statement to answer QS 16-6 through QS 16-11.

QS 16-6
Computing cash from operations (indirect) P2

Use the indirect method to prepare the cash provided or used from operating activities section only of the statement of cash flows for this company.

AMMONS, INC.
Comparative Balance Sheets
December 31, 2009

	2009	2008
Assets		
Cash	$189,600	$ 48,000
Accounts receivable, net	82,000	102,000
Inventory	171,600	191,600
Prepaid expenses	10,800	8,400
Furniture	218,000	238,000
Accum. depreciation—Furniture	(34,000)	(18,000)
Total assets	$638,000	$570,000
Liabilities and Equity		
Accounts payable	$ 30,000	$ 42,000
Wages payable	18,000	10,000
Income taxes payable	2,800	5,200
Notes payable (long-term)	58,000	138,000
Common stock, $5 par value	458,000	358,000
Retained earnings	71,200	16,800
Total liabilities and equity	$638,000	$570,000

AMMONS, INC.
Income Statement
For Year Ended December 31, 2009

Sales		$976,000
Cost of goods sold		628,000
Gross profit		348,000
Operating expenses		
Depreciation expense	$ 75,200	
Other expenses	178,200	253,400
Income before taxes		94,600
Income taxes expense		34,600
Net income		$ 60,000

QS 16-7
Computing cash from asset sales P3

Refer to the data in QS 16-6.
Furniture costing $110,000 is sold at its book value in 2009. Acquisitions of furniture total $90,000 cash, on which no depreciation is necessary because it is acquired at year-end. What is the cash inflow related to the sale of furniture?

QS 16-8
Computing financing cash outflows P3

Refer to the data in QS 16-6.
1. Assume that all common stock is issued for cash. What amount of cash dividends is paid during 2009?
2. Assume that no additional notes payable are issued in 2009. What cash amount is paid to reduce the notes payable balance in 2009?

QS 16-9B
Computing cash received from customers P5

Refer to the data in QS 16-6.
1. How much cash is received from sales to customers for year 2009?
2. What is the net increase or decrease in cash for year 2009?

QS 16-10B
Computing operating cash outflows P5

Refer to the data in QS 16-6.
1. How much cash is paid to acquire merchandise inventory during year 2009?
2. How much cash is paid for operating expenses during year 2009?

QS 16-11B
Computing cash from operations (direct) P5

Refer to the data in QS 16-6.
Use the direct method to prepare the cash provided or used from operating activities section only of the statement of cash flows for this company.

QS 16-12
Analyses of sources and uses of cash A1 A2

Financial data from three competitors in the same industry follow.
1. Which of the three competitors is in the strongest position as shown by its statement of cash flows?
2. Analyze and compare the strength of Peña's cash flow on total assets ratio to that of Garcia.

($ thousands)	Peña	Garcia	Piniella
Cash provided (used) by operating activities	$ 140,000	$ 120,000	$ (48,000)
Cash provided (used) by investing activities			
Proceeds from sale of operating assets			52,000
Purchase of operating assets	(56,000)	(68,000)	
Cash provided (used) by financing activities			
Proceeds from issuance of debt			46,000
Repayment of debt	(12,000)		
Net increase (decrease) in cash	$ 72,000	$ 52,000	$ 50,000
Average total assets	$ 1,580,000	$ 1,250,000	$ 600,000

QS 16-13^A
Noncash accounts on a spreadsheet P4

When a spreadsheet for a statement of cash flows is prepared, all changes in noncash balance sheet accounts are fully explained on the spreadsheet. Explain how these noncash balance sheet accounts are used to fully account for cash flows on a spreadsheet.

QS 16-14
Computing cash flows from operations (indirect)
P2

For each of the following separate cases, compute cash flows from operations. The list includes all balance sheet accounts related to operating activities.

	Case A	Case B	Case C
Net income	$ 8,000	$200,000	$144,000
Depreciation expense	60,000	16,000	48,000
Accounts receivable increase (decrease)	80,000	40,000	(8,000)
Inventory increase (decrease)	(40,000)	(20,000)	21,000
Accounts payable increase (decrease)	48,000	(44,000)	28,000
Accrued liabilities increase (decrease)	(88,000)	24,000	(16,000)

QS 16-15
Computing cash flows from investing
P3

Compute cash flows from investing activities using the following company information.

Sale of short-term investments	$12,000
Cash collections from customers	32,000
Purchase of used equipment	10,000
Depreciation expense	4,000

QS 16-16
Computing cash flows from financing
P3

Compute cash flows from financing activities using the following company information.

Additional short-term borrowings	$40,000
Purchase of short-term investments	10,000
Cash dividends paid	32,000
Interest paid	16,000

Available with McGraw-Hill's Homework Manager McGraw-Hill's HOMEWORK MANAGER®

EXERCISES

Exercise 16-1
Cash flow from operations (indirect)
P2

Hehman Company reports net income of $530,000 for the year ended December 31, 2009. It also reports $95,400 depreciation expense and a $4,000 gain on the sale of machinery. Its comparative balance sheets reveal a $42,400 increase in accounts receivable, $21,730 increase in accounts payable, $11,660 decrease in prepaid expenses, and $16,430 decrease in wages payable.

Required

Prepare only the operating activities section of the statement of cash flows for 2009 using the *indirect method.*

Exercise 16-2
Cash flow classification (indirect) C2 C3 P2

The following transactions and events occurred during the year. Assuming that this company uses the *indirect method* to report cash provided by operating activities, indicate where each item would appear on its statement of cash flows by placing an *x* in the appropriate column.

	Statement of Cash Flows			Noncash Investing and Financing Activities	Not Reported on Statement or in Notes
	Operating Activities	Investing Activities	Financing Activities		
a. Paid cash to purchase inventory.	____	____	____	____	____
b. Purchased land by issuing common stock.	____	____	____	____	____
c. Accounts receivable decreased in the year.	____	____	____	____	____
d. Sold equipment for cash, yielding a loss.	____	____	____	____	____
e. Recorded depreciation expense.	____	____	____	____	____
f. Income taxes payable increased in the year.	____	____	____	____	____
g. Declared and paid a cash dividend.	____	____	____	____	____
h. Accounts payable decreased in the year	____	____	____	____	____
i. Paid cash to settle notes payable	____	____	____	____	____
j. Prepaid expenses increased in the year	____	____	____	____	____

Exercise 16-3^B
Cash flow classification (direct) C2 C3 P5

The following transactions and events occurred during the year. Assuming that this company uses the *direct method* to report cash provided by operating activities, indicate where each item would appear on the statement of cash flows by placing an *x* in the appropriate column.

	Statement of Cash Flows			Noncash Investing and Financing Activities	Not Reported on Statement or in Notes
	Operating Activities	Investing Activities	Financing Activities		
a. Retired long-term notes payable by issuing common stock	____	____	____	____	____
b. Recorded depreciation expense.	____	____	____	____	____
c. Paid cash dividend that was declared in a prior period.	____	____	____	____	____
d. Sold inventory for cash.	____	____	____	____	____
e. Borrowed cash from bank by signing a nine-month note payable.	____	____	____	____	____
f. Paid cash to purchase a patent.	____	____	____	____	____
g. Accepted six-month note receivable in exchange for plant assets.	____	____	____	____	____
h. Paid cash toward accounts payable.	____	____	____	____	____
i. Collected cash from sales.	____	____	____	____	____
j. Paid cash to acquire treasury stock.	____	____	____	____	____

Exercise 16-4
Cash flows from operating activities (indirect)

P2

Zander Company's calendar-year 2009 income statement shows the following: Net Income, $395,000; Depreciation Expense, $48,980; Amortization Expense, $9,875; Gain on Sale of Plant Assets, $4,900. An examination of the company's current assets and current liabilities reveals the following changes (all from operating activities): Accounts Receivable decrease, $7,600; Merchandise Inventory decrease, $22,040; Prepaid Expenses increase, $2,000; Accounts Payable decrease, $5,000; Other Payables increase, $760. Use the *indirect method* to compute cash flow from operating activities.

Exercise 16-5[B]
Computation of cash flows (direct)
P5

For each of the following three separate cases, use the information provided about the calendar-year 2010 operations of Kowa Company to compute the required cash flow information.

Case A: Compute cash received from customers:	
Sales	$590,000
Accounts receivable, December 31, 2009	38,000
Accounts receivable, December 31, 2010	52,440
Case B: Compute cash paid for rent:	
Rent expense	$117,400
Rent payable, December 31, 2009	6,700
Rent payable, December 31, 2010	5,561
Case C: Compute cash paid for merchandise:	
Cost of goods sold	$651,000
Merchandise inventory, December 31, 2009	201,810
Accounts payable, December 31, 2009	84,760
Merchandise inventory, December 31, 2010	165,484
Accounts payable, December 31, 2010	105,102

Exercise 16-6
Cash flows from operating activities (indirect)
P2

Use the following income statement and information about changes in noncash current assets and current liabilities to prepare only the cash flows from operating activities section of the statement of cash flows using the *indirect* method.

SEYMOUR COMPANY
Income Statement
For Year Ended December 31, 2009

Sales		$2,175,000
Cost of goods sold		1,065,750
Gross profit		1,109,250
Operating expenses		
Salaries expense	$297,975	
Depreciation expense	52,200	
Rent expense	58,725	
Amortization expenses—Patents	6,525	
Utilities expense	23,925	439,350
		669,900
Gain on sale of equipment		8,700
Net income		$ 678,600

Changes in current asset and current liability accounts for the year that relate to operations follow.

Accounts receivable	$45,300 increase	Accounts payable	$10,075 decrease
Merchandise inventory	35,150 increase	Salaries payable	4,750 decrease

Exercise 16-7[B]
Cash flows from operating activities (direct) P5

Refer to the information about Seymour Company in Exercise 16-6.
Use the *direct method* to prepare only the cash provided or used by operating activities section of the statement of cash flows for this company.

Exercise 16-8
Cash flows from investing activities
P3

Use the following information to determine this company's cash flows from investing activities.

a. Equipment with a book value of $72,500 and an original cost of $158,000 was sold at a loss of $22,000.
b. Paid $95,000 cash for a new truck.
c. Sold land costing $315,000 for $400,000 cash, yielding a gain of $15,000.
d. Long-term investments in stock were sold for $94,700 cash, yielding a gain of $5,750.

Exercise 16-9
Cash flows from financing activities
P3

Use the following information to determine this company's cash flows from financing activities.

a. Net income was $53,000.
b. Issued common stock for $75,000 cash.
c. Paid cash dividend of $13,000.
d. Paid $90,000 cash to settle a note payable at its $90,000 maturity value.
e. Paid $18,000 cash to acquire its treasury stock.
f. Purchased equipment for $67,000 cash.

Exercise 16-10
Preparation of statement of cash flows (indirect)
C2 A2 P1 P2 P3

Use the following financial statements and additional information to (1) prepare a statement of cash flows for the year ended June 30, 2009, using the *indirect method,* and (2) compute the company's cash flow on total assets ratio for its fiscal year 2009.

BOULWARE INC.
Comparative Balance Sheets
June 30, 2009 and 2008

	2009	2008
Assets		
Cash	$ 84,663	$ 49,494
Accounts receivable, net	65,720	56,952
Inventory	62,620	106,107
Prepaid expenses	4,960	5,763
Equipment	118,387	131,532
Accum. depreciation—Equipment	(26,350)	(10,848)
Total assets	$310,000	$339,000
Liabilities and Equity		
Accounts payable	$ 24,490	$ 35,256
Wages payable	6,510	17,628
Income taxes payable	2,170	4,068
Notes payable (long term)	31,953	76,953
Common stock, $5 par value	208,000	158,000
Retained earnings	36,877	47,095
Total liabilities and equity	$310,000	$339,000

BOULWARE INC.
Income Statement
For Year Ended June 30, 2009

Sales		$976,600
Cost of goods sold		625,024
Gross profit		351,576
Operating expenses		
Depreciation expense	$ 88,753	
Other expenses	101,879	
Total operating expenses		190,632
		160,944
Other gains (losses)		
Gain on sale of equipment		3,125
Income before taxes		164,069
Income taxes expense		56,604
Net income		$107,465

Additional Information

a. A $45,000 note payable is retired at its carrying (book) value in exchange for cash.
b. The only changes affecting retained earnings are net income and cash dividends paid.
c. New equipment is acquired for $85,000 cash.
d. Received cash for the sale of equipment that had cost $98,145, yielding a $3,125 gain.
e. Prepaid Expenses and Wages Payable relate to Other Expenses on the income statement.
f. All purchases and sales of merchandise inventory are on credit.

Exercise 16-11[B]
Preparation of statement of cash flows (direct) C2 P1 P3 P5

Refer to the data in Exercise 16-10.
Using the *direct method,* prepare the statement of cash flows for the year ended June 30, 2009.

Exercise 16-12[B]
Preparation of statement of cash flows (direct) and supporting note
C2 C3 C4 P1

Use the following information about the cash flows of Valencia Company to prepare a complete statement of cash flows (*direct method*) for the year ended December 31, 2009. Use a note disclosure for any noncash investing and financing activities.

Cash and cash equivalents balance, December 31, 2008	$ 43,000
Cash and cash equivalents balance, December 31, 2009	120,916
Cash received as interest	4,300
Cash paid for salaries	124,700
Bonds payable retired by issuing common stock (no gain or loss on retirement)	180,000
Cash paid to retire long-term notes payable	215,000
Cash received from sale of equipment	105,350
Cash received in exchange for six-month note payable	43,000
Land purchased by issuing long-term note payable	104,400
Cash paid for store equipment	40,850
Cash dividends paid	25,800
Cash paid for other expenses	68,800
Cash received from customers	834,200
Cash paid for merchandise	433,784

Exercise 16-13[B]
Preparation of statement of cash flows (direct) from Cash T-account
C2 A1 P1 P3 P5

The following summarized Cash T-account reflects the total debits and total credits to the Cash account of Clarett Corporation for calendar year 2009.

(1) Use this information to prepare a complete statement of cash flows for year 2009. The cash provided or used by operating activities should be reported using the *direct method.*

(2) Refer to the statement of cash flows prepared for part 1 to answer the following questions *a* through *d*: (*a*) Which section—operating, investing, or financing—shows the largest cash (i) inflow and (ii) outflow? (*b*) What is the largest individual item among the investing cash outflows? (*c*) Are the cash proceeds larger from issuing notes or issuing stock? (*d*) Does the company have a net cash inflow or outflow from borrowing activities?

Accounting System:
File Edit Maintain Tasks Analysis Options Reports Window Help

Cash			
Balance, Dec. 31, 2008	251,700		
Receipts from customers	7,074,800	Payments for merchandise	2,934,822
Receipts from dividends	876,180	Payments for wages	1,018,882
Receipts from land sale	397,676	Payments for rent	586,964
Receipts from machinery sale	606,826	Payments for interest	398,693
Receipts from issuing stock	2,846,224	Payments for taxes	830,610
Receipts from borrowing	1,795,388	Payments for machinery	3,130,900
		Payments for long-term investments	2,295,200
		Payments for note payable	905,787
		Payments for dividends	519,208
		Payments for treasury stock	398,693
Balance, Dec. 31, 2009	$?		

Sales Purchases General Ledger Payroll Inventory Company Analysis

Exercise 16-14
Reporting cash flows from operations (indirect)
C4 P2

Woodlock Company reports the following information for its recent calendar year.

Sales	$80,000
Expenses	
Cost of goods sold	50,000
Salaries expense	12,000
Depreciation expense	6,000
Net income	$12,000
Accounts receivable increase	$ 5,000
Inventory decrease	8,000
Salaries payable increase	500

Required

Prepare the operating activities section of the statement of cash flows for Woodlock Company using the indirect method.

Exercise 16-15
Reporting and interpreting cash flows from operations (indirect)
C4 P2

Portland Company disclosed the following information for its recent calendar year.

Revenues	$200,000
Expenses	
Salaries expense	168,000
Utilities expense	28,000
Depreciation expense	29,200
Other expenses	6,800
Net loss	$ (32,000)
Accounts receivable decrease	$ 48,000
Purchased a machine	20,000
Salaries payable increase	36,000
Other accrued liabilities decrease	16,000

Required

1. Prepare the operating activities section of the statement of cash flows using the indirect method.
2. What were the major reasons that this company was able to report a net loss but positive cash flow from operations?
3. Of the potential causes of differences between cash flow from operations and net income, which are the most important to investors?

McGraw-Hill's HOMEWORK MANAGER® Available with McGraw-Hill's Homework Manager

PROBLEM SET A

Problem 16-1A
Statement of cash flows (indirect method)
C2 C3 A1 P1 P2 P3

Georgia Company, a merchandiser, recently completed its calendar-year 2009 operations. For the year, (1) all sales are credit sales, (2) all credits to Accounts Receivable reflect cash receipts from customers, (3) all purchases of inventory are on credit, (4) all debits to Accounts Payable reflect cash payments for inventory, and (5) Other Expenses are paid in advance and are initially debited to Prepaid Expenses. The company's balance sheets and income statement follow.

GEORGIA COMPANY
Comparative Balance Sheets
December 31, 2009 and 2008

	2009	2008
Assets		
Cash	$ 49,800	$ 73,500
Accounts receivable	65,840	56,000
Merchandise inventory	277,000	252,000
Prepaid expenses	1,000	1,500
Equipment	158,500	107,500
Accum. depreciation—Equipment	(43,000)	(52,000)
Total assets	$509,140	$438,500
Liabilities and Equity		
Accounts payable	$ 42,965	$113,000
Short-term notes payable	10,000	7,000
Long-term notes payable	70,000	48,000
Common stock, $5 par value	162,750	151,000
Paid-in capital in excess of par, common stock	35,250	0
Retained earnings	188,175	119,500
Total liabilities and equity	$509,140	$438,500

GEORGIA COMPANY
Income Statement
For Year Ended December 31, 2009

Sales		$584,500
Cost of goods sold		281,000
Gross profit		303,500
Operating expenses		
Depreciation expense	$ 20,000	
Other expenses	132,800	152,800
Other gains (losses)		
Loss on sale of equipment		5,875
Income before taxes		144,825
Income taxes expense		24,250
Net income		$120,575

Additional Information on Year 2009 Transactions

a. The loss on the cash sale of equipment was $5,875 (details in *b*).

b. Sold equipment costing $46,500, with accumulated depreciation of $29,000, for $11,625 cash.

c. Purchased equipment costing $97,500 by paying $35,000 cash and signing a long-term note payable for the balance.

d. Borrowed $3,000 cash by signing a short-term note payable.

e. Paid $40,500 cash to reduce the long-term notes payable.

f. Issued 2,350 shares of common stock for $20 cash per share.

g. Declared and paid cash dividends of $51,900.

Required

Check Cash from operating activities, $42,075

1. Prepare a complete statement of cash flows; report its operating activities using the *indirect method.* Disclose any noncash investing and financing activities in a note.

Analysis Component

2. Analyze and discuss the statement of cash flows prepared in part 1, giving special attention to the wisdom of the cash dividend payment.

Problem 16-2A[A]

Cash flows spreadsheet (indirect method)

P1 P2 P3 P4

Refer to the information reported about Georgia Company in Problem 16-1A.

Required

Prepare a complete statement of cash flows using a spreadsheet as in Exhibit 16A.1; report its operating activities using the indirect method. Identify the debits and credits in the Analysis of Changes columns with letters that correspond to the following list of transactions and events.

a. Net income was $120,575.

b. Accounts receivable increased.

c. Merchandise inventory increased.

d. Prepaid expenses decreased.

e. Accounts payable decreased.

f. Depreciation expense was $20,000.

g. Sold equipment costing $46,500, with accumulated depreciation of $29,000, for $11,625 cash. This yielded a loss of $5,875.

h. Purchased equipment costing $97,500 by paying $35,000 cash and **(i.)** by signing a long-term note payable for the balance.

j. Borrowed $3,000 cash by signing a short-term note payable.

k. Paid $40,500 cash to reduce the long-term notes payable.

l. Issued 2,350 shares of common stock for $20 cash per share.

m. Declared and paid cash dividends of $51,900.

Check Analysis of Changes column totals, $594,850

Problem 16-3A[B]

Statement of cash flows (direct method) C3 P1 P3 P5

Check Cash used in financing activities, $(42,400)

Refer to Georgia Company's financial statements and related information in Problem 16-1A.

Required

Prepare a complete statement of cash flows; report its operating activities according to the *direct method.* Disclose any noncash investing and financing activities in a note.

Problem 16-4A

Statement of cash flows (indirect method) C3 P1 P2 P3

eXcel

mhhe.com/wildFAP19e

Memphis Corp., a merchandiser, recently completed its 2009 operations. For the year, (1) all sales are credit sales, (2) all credits to Accounts Receivable reflect cash receipts from customers, (3) all purchases of inventory are on credit, (4) all debits to Accounts Payable reflect cash payments for inventory, (5) Other Expenses are all cash expenses, and (6) any change in Income Taxes Payable reflects the accrual and cash payment of taxes. The company's balance sheets and income statement follow.

PROBLEM SET B

Problem 16-1B (40 minutes)

Part 1

WILSON CORPORATION Statement of Cash Flows For Year Ended December 31, 2009		
Cash flows from operating activities		
Net income	$116,125	
Adjustments to reconcile net income to net cash provided by operating activities		
Increase in accounts receivable ($65,830 - $55,000)	(10,830)	
Increase in inventory ($277,000 - $252,000)	(25,000)	
Decrease in prepaid expenses ($1,600 - $1,250)	350	
Decrease in accounts payable ($112,000 - $55,380)	(56,620)	
Depreciation expense	20,000	
Loss on disposal of equipment	5,625	
Net cash provided by operating activities		$ 49,650
Cash flows from investing activities		
Cash received from sale of equipment	11,500	
Cash paid for equipment	(25,000)	
Net cash used in investing activities		(13,500)
Cash flows from financing activities		
Cash borrowed on short-term note	2,000	
Cash paid on long-term note	(50,750)	
Cash received from issuing stock (2,350 x $20)	47,000	
Cash paid for dividends	(59,000)	
Net cash used in financing activities		(60,750)
Net decrease in cash		$ (24,600)
Cash balance at December 31, 2008		74,000
Cash balance at December 31, 2009		$ 49,400

inc dec
curr. asset - +
liab + -

FORTEN COMPANY
Statement of Cash Flows
For Year Ended December 31, 2008

Cash flows from operating activities			from I/S
Net income	$114,975		
Adjustments to reconcile net income to net cash provided by operating activities:			day to day – longest sect.
Increase in accounts receivable ($65,810- $50,625)	(15,185)		U - cust. owes ↑#
Increase in inventory ($275,656 - $251,800)	(23,856)		U - # out to buy invet
Decrease in prepaid expenses ($1,875 - $1,250)	625		S - no # out · asset - using up, not buying more
Decrease in accounts payable ($114,675 - $53,141)	(61,534)		U - # pd out to ↓ acc pay
Depreciation expense	20,750		S - always
Loss on disposal of equipment	5,125		S - no cash out
Net cash provided by operating activities		$ 40,900	must use words; or "used" if neg.
Cash flows from investing activities			growing or contracting bus
Cash received from sale of equipment	11,625		S - cash ↑
Cash paid for equipment	(30,000)		U - cash ↓ purch.
Net cash used in investing activities		(18,375)	
Cash flows from financing activities			
Cash borrowed on short-term note	4,000		S - cash ↑
Cash paid on long-term note	(50,125)		U - cash ↓ to pay
Cash received from issuing stock (2,500 x $20)	50,000		S - cash ↑
Cash paid for dividends	(50,100)		U - cash ↓ payments
Net cash used in financing activities		(46,225)	
Net decrease in cash		$(23,700)	
Cash balance at December 31, 2007		73,500	must net to #
Cash balance at December 31, 2008		$ 49,800	

beg of this yr is same # as ending last yr.

bal. this yr cash

gives knowledge of those things that made cash ↑ or ↓

FORTEN COMPANY Statement of Cash Flows For Year Ended December 31, 2008		
Cash flows from operating activities		
Net income	$114,975	
Adjustments to reconcile net income to net cash provided by operating activities:		
Increase in accounts receivable ($65,810- $50,625)	(15,185)	
Increase in inventory ($275,656 - $251,800)	(23,856)	
Decrease in prepaid expenses ($1,875 - $1,250)	625	
Decrease in accounts payable ($114,675 - $53,141)	(61,534)	
Depreciation expense	20,750	
Loss on disposal of equipment	5,125	
Net cash provided by operating activities		$ 40,900
Cash flows from investing activities		
Cash received from sale of equipment	11,625	
Cash paid for equipment	(30,000)	
Net cash used in investing activities		(18,375)
Cash flows from financing activities		
Cash borrowed on short-term note	4,000	
Cash paid on long-term note	(50,125)	
Cash received from issuing stock (2,500 x $20)	50,000	
Cash paid for dividends	(50,100)	
Net cash used in financing activities		(46,225)
Net decrease in cash		$(23,700)
Cash balance at December 31, 2007		73,500
Cash balance at December 31, 2008		$ 49,800

FORTEN COMPANY
Statement of Cash Flows
For Year Ended December 31, 2008

Cash flows from operating activities		
Net income	$114,975	
Adjustments to reconcile net income to net cash provided by operating activities:		
Increase in accounts receivable ($65,810- $50,625)	(15,185)	
Increase in inventory ($275,656 - $251,800)	(23,856)	
Decrease in prepaid expenses ($1,875 - $1,250)	625	
Decrease in accounts payable ($114,675 - $53,141)	(61,534)	
Depreciation expense	20,750	
Loss on disposal of equipment	5,125	
Net cash provided by operating activities		$ 40,900
Cash flows from investing activities		
Cash received from sale of equipment	11,625	
Cash paid for equipment	(30,000)	
Net cash used in investing activities		(18,375)
Cash flows from financing activities		
Cash borrowed on short-term note	4,000	
Cash paid on long-term note	(50,125)	
Cash received from issuing stock (2,500 x $20)	50,000	
Cash paid for dividends	(50,100)	
Net cash used in financing activities		(46,225)
Net decrease in cash		$(23,700)
Cash balance at December 31, 2007		73,500
Cash balance at December 31, 2008		$ 49,800

MEMPHIS CORPORATION
Comparative Balance Sheets
December 31, 2009 and 2008

	2009	2008
Assets		
Cash	$ 165,000	$137,000
Accounts receivable	82,000	74,000
Merchandise inventory	620,000	525,000
Equipment	345,000	240,000
Accum. depreciation—Equipment	(159,000)	(102,000)
Total assets	$1,053,000	$874,000
Liabilities and Equity		
Accounts payable	$ 160,000	$ 96,000
Income taxes payable	22,000	19,000
Common stock, $2 par value	588,000	560,000
Paid-in capital in excess of par value, common stock	201,000	159,000
Retained earnings	82,000	40,000
Total liabilities and equity	$1,053,000	$874,000

MEMPHIS CORPORATION
Income Statement
For Year Ended December 31, 2009

Sales		$1,794,000
Cost of goods sold		1,088,000
Gross profit		706,000
Operating expenses		
Depreciation expense	$ 57,000	
Other expenses	500,000	557,000
Income before taxes		149,000
Income taxes expense		22,000
Net income		$ 127,000

Additional Information on Year 2009 Transactions

a. Purchased equipment for $105,000 cash.
b. Issued 14,000 shares of common stock for $5 cash per share.
c. Declared and paid $85,000 in cash dividends.

Required

Prepare a complete statement of cash flows; report its cash inflows and cash outflows from operating activities according to the *indirect method.*

Check Cash from operating activities, $148,000

Problem 16-5A^A
Cash flows spreadsheet (indirect method)
P1 P2 P3 P4
eXcel
mhhe.com/wildFAP19e

Refer to the information reported about Memphis Corporation in Problem 16-4A.

Required

Prepare a complete statement of cash flows using a spreadsheet as in Exhibit 16A.1; report operating activities under the indirect method. Identify the debits and credits in the Analysis of Changes columns with letters that correspond to the following list of transactions and events.

a. Net income was $127,000.
b. Accounts receivable increased.
c. Merchandise inventory increased.
d. Accounts payable increased.
e. Income taxes payable increased.
f. Depreciation expense was $57,000.
g. Purchased equipment for $105,000 cash.
h. Issued 14,000 shares at $5 cash per share.
i. Declared and paid $85,000 of cash dividends.

Check Analysis of Changes column totals, $614,000

Problem 16-6A^B
Statement of cash flows (direct method) P1 P3 P5
eXcel
mhhe.com/wildFAP19e

Refer to Memphis Corporation's financial statements and related information in Problem 16-4A.

Required

Prepare a complete statement of cash flows; report its cash flows from operating activities according to the *direct method.*

Check Cash used in financing activities, $(15,000)

Problem 16-7A
Computing cash flows from operations (indirect)
C4 P2

Rawling Company's 2009 income statement and selected balance sheet data at December 31, 2008 and 2009, follow ($ thousands).

RAWLING COMPANY
Income Statement

Sales revenue		$48,600
Expenses		
Cost of goods sold		21,000
Depreciation expense		6,000
Salaries expense		9,000
Rent expense		4,500
Insurance expense		1,900
Interest expense		1,800
Utilities expense		1,400
Net income		$ 3,000

RAWLING COMPANY
Selected Balance Sheet Accounts

At December 31	2009	2008
Accounts receivable	$280	$290
Inventory	99	77
Accounts payable	220	230
Salaries payable	44	35
Utilities payable	11	8
Prepaid insurance	13	14
Prepaid rent	11	9

Required

Prepare the cash flows from operating activities section only of the company's 2009 statement of cash flows using the indirect method.

Check Cash from operating activities, $8,989

Problem 16-8A[B]
Computing cash flows from operations (direct)
C4 P5

Refer to the information in Problem 16-7A.

Required

Prepare the cash flows from operating activities section only of the company's 2009 statement of cash flows using the direct method.

PROBLEM SET B

Problem 16-1B
Statement of cash flows (indirect method)
C2 C3 A1 P1 P2 P3

Wilson Corporation, a merchandiser, recently completed its calendar-year 2009 operations. For the year, (1) all sales are credit sales, (2) all credits to Accounts Receivable reflect cash receipts from customers, (3) all purchases of inventory are on credit, (4) all debits to Accounts Payable reflect cash payments for inventory, and (5) Other Expenses are paid in advance and are initially debited to Prepaid Expenses. The company's balance sheets and income statement follow.

WILSON CORPORATION
Comparative Balance Sheets
December 31, 2009 and 2008

	2009	2008
Assets		
Cash	$ 49,400	$ 74,000
Accounts receivable	65,830	55,000
Merchandise inventory	277,000	252,000
Prepaid expenses	1,250	1,600
Equipment	158,500	107,500
Accum. depreciation—Equipment	(36,625)	(46,000)
Total assets	$515,355	$444,100
Liabilities and Equity		
Accounts payable	$ 55,380	$112,000
Short-term notes payable	9,000	7,000
Long-term notes payable	70,000	48,250
Common stock, $5 par	162,500	150,750
Paid-in capital in excess of par, common stock	35,250	0
Retained earnings	183,225	126,100
Total liabilities and equity	$515,355	$444,100

WILSON CORPORATION
Income Statement
For Year Ended December 31, 2009

Sales		$585,000
Cost of goods sold		285,000
Gross profit		300,000
Operating expenses		
Depreciation expense	$ 20,000	
Other expenses	134,000	
Total operating expenses		154,000
		146,000
Other gains (losses)		
Loss on sale of equipment		5,625
Income before taxes		140,375
Income taxes expense		24,250
Net income		$116,125

Additional Information on Year 2009 Transactions

a. The loss on the cash sale of equipment was $5,625 (details in *b*).

b. Sold equipment costing $46,500, with accumulated depreciation of $29,375, for $11,500 cash.

c. Purchased equipment costing $97,500 by paying $25,000 cash and signing a long-term note payable for the balance.

d. Borrowed $2,000 cash by signing a short-term note payable.

e. Paid $50,750 cash to reduce the long-term notes payable.

f. Issued 2,350 shares of common stock for $20 cash per share.

g. Declared and paid cash dividends of $59,000.

Required

1. Prepare a complete statement of cash flows; report its operating activities using the *indirect method*. Disclose any noncash investing and financing activities in a note.

Check Cash from operating activities, $49,650

Analysis Component

2. Analyze and discuss the statement of cash flows prepared in part 1, giving special attention to the wisdom of the cash dividend payment.

Problem 16-2B[A]
Cash flows spreadsheet (indirect method)
P1 P2 P3 P4

Refer to the information reported about Wilson Corporation in Problem 16-1B.

Required

Prepare a complete statement of cash flows using a spreadsheet as in Exhibit 16A.1; report its operating activities using the *indirect method.* Identify the debits and credits in the Analysis of Changes columns with letters that correspond to the following list of transactions and events.

a. Net income was $116,125.

b. Accounts receivable increased.

c. Merchandise inventory increased.

d. Prepaid expenses decreased.

e. Accounts payable decreased.

f. Depreciation expense was $20,000.

g. Sold equipment costing $46,500, with accumulated depreciation of $29,375, for $11,500 cash. This yielded a loss of $5,625.

h. Purchased equipment costing $97,500 by paying $25,000 cash and **(i.)** by signing a long-term note payable for the balance.

j. Borrowed $2,000 cash by signing a short-term note payable.

k. Paid $50,750 cash to reduce the long-term notes payable.

l. Issued 2,350 shares of common stock for $20 cash per share.

m. Declared and paid cash dividends of $59,000.

Check Analysis of Changes column totals, $604,175

Problem 16-3B[B]
Statement of cash flows (direct method) C3 P1 P3 P5

Refer to Wilson Corporation's financial statements and related information in Problem 16-1B.

Required

Prepare a complete statement of cash flows; report its operating activities according to the *direct method.* Disclose any noncash investing and financing activities in a note.

Check Cash used in financing activities, $(60,750)

Problem 16-4B
Statement of cash flows (indirect method)
C3 P1 P2 P3

Prius Company, a merchandiser, recently completed its 2009 operations. For the year, (1) all sales are credit sales, (2) all credits to Accounts Receivable reflect cash receipts from customers, (3) all purchases of inventory are on credit, (4) all debits to Accounts Payable reflect cash payments for inventory, (5) Other Expenses are cash expenses, and (6) any change in Income Taxes Payable reflects the accrual and cash payment of taxes. The company's balance sheets and income statement follow.

PRIUS COMPANY
Comparative Balance Sheets
December 31, 2009 and 2008

	2009	2008
Assets		
Cash	$ 164,000	$ 131,000
Accounts receivable	82,000	70,000
Merchandise inventory	605,000	515,000
Equipment	350,000	276,000
Accum. depreciation—Equipment	(157,000)	(102,000)
Total assets	$1,044,000	$ 890,000
Liabilities and Equity		
Accounts payable	$ 173,000	$ 119,000
Income taxes payable	20,000	17,000
Common stock, $2 par value	580,000	560,000
Paid-in capital in excess of par, common stock	193,000	163,000
Retained earnings	78,000	31,000
Total liabilities and equity	$1,044,000	$ 890,000

PRIUS COMPANY
Income Statement
For Year Ended December 31, 2009

Sales		$1,792,000
Cost of goods sold		1,087,000
Gross profit		705,000
Operating expenses		
Depreciation expense	$ 55,000	
Other expenses	494,000	549,000
Income before taxes		156,000
Income taxes expense		24,000
Net income		$ 132,000

Additional Information on Year 2009 Transactions

a. Purchased equipment for $74,000 cash.

b. Issued 10,000 shares of common stock for $5 cash per share.

c. Declared and paid $85,000 of cash dividends.

Required

Prepare a complete statement of cash flows; report its cash inflows and cash outflows from operating activities according to the *indirect method.*

Check Cash from operating activities, $142,000

Problem 16-5B[A]
Cash flows spreadsheet (indirect method)
P1 P2 P3 P4

Refer to the information reported about Prius Company in Problem 16-4B.

Required

Prepare a complete statement of cash flows using a spreadsheet as in Exhibit 16A.1; report operating activities under the *indirect method.* Identify the debits and credits in the Analysis of Changes columns with letters that correspond to the following list of transactions and events.

a. Net income was $132,000.

b. Accounts receivable increased.

c. Merchandise inventory increased.

d. Accounts payable increased.

e. Income taxes payable increased.

f. Depreciation expense was $55,000.

g. Purchased equipment for $74,000 cash.

h. Issued 10,000 shares at $5 cash per share.

i. Declared and paid $85,000 of cash dividends.

Check Analysis of Changes column totals, $555,000

Problem 16-6B[B]
Statement of cash flows (direct method) P1 P3 P5

Refer to Prius Company's financial statements and related information in Problem 16-4B.

Required

Prepare a complete statement of cash flows; report its cash flows from operating activities according to the *direct method.*

Check Cash used by financing activities, $(35,000)

Problem 16-7B
Computing cash flows from operations (indirect)
C4 P2

Kodak Company's 2009 income statement and selected balance sheet data at December 31, 2008 and 2009, follow ($ thousands).

KODAK COMPANY Income Statement	
Sales revenue	$312,000
Expenses	
Cost of goods sold	144,000
Depreciation expense	64,000
Salaries expense	40,000
Rent expense	10,000
Insurance expense	5,200
Interest expense	4,800
Utilities expense	4,000
Net income	$ 40,000

KODAK COMPANY
Selected Balance Sheet Accounts

At December 31	2009	2008
Accounts receivable	$720	$600
Inventory	172	196
Accounts payable	480	520
Salaries payable	180	120
Utilities payable	40	0
Prepaid insurance	28	36
Prepaid rent	20	40

Required

Prepare the cash flows from operating activities section only of the company's 2009 statement of cash flows using the indirect method.

Check Cash from operating activities, $103,992

Problem 16-8B[B]
Computing cash flows from operations (direct)
C4 P5

Refer to the information in Problem 16-7B.

Required

Prepare the cash flows from operating activities section only of the company's 2009 statement of cash flows using the direct method.

SERIAL PROBLEM

Success Systems

(This serial problem began in Chapter 1 and continues through most of the book. If previous chapter segments were not completed, the serial problem can begin at this point. It is helpful, but not necessary, to use the Working Papers that accompany the book.)

SP 16 Adriana Lopez, owner of Success Systems, decides to prepare a statement of cash flows for her business. (Although the serial problem allowed for various ownership changes in earlier chapters, we will prepare the statement of cash flows using the following financial data.)

SUCCESS SYSTEMS
Income Statement
For Three Months Ended March 31, 2010

Computer services revenue		$25,160
Net sales		18,693
Total revenue		43,853
Cost of goods sold	$14,052	
Depreciation expense—Office equipment	400	
Depreciation expense—Computer equipment	1,250	
Wages expense	3,250	
Insurance expense	555	
Rent expense	2,475	
Computer supplies expense	1,305	
Advertising expense	600	
Mileage expense	320	
Repairs expense—Computer	960	
Total expenses		25,167
Net income		$18,686

SUCCESS SYSTEMS
Comparative Balance Sheets
December 31, 2009, and March 31, 2010

	2010	2009
Assets		
Cash	$ 77,845	$58,160
Accounts receivable	22,720	5,668
Merchandise inventory	704	0
Computer supplies	2,005	580
Prepaid insurance	1,110	1,665
Prepaid rent	825	825
Office equipment	8,000	8,000
Accumulated depreciation—Office equipment	(800)	(400)
Computer equipment	20,000	20,000
Accumulated depreciation—Computer equipment	(2,500)	(1,250)
Total assets	$129,909	$93,248
Liabilities and Equity		
Accounts payable	$ 0	$ 1,100
Wages payable	875	500
Unearned computer service revenue	0	1,500
Common stock	108,000	83,000
Retained earnings	21,034	7,148
Total liabilities and equity	$129,909	$93,248

Required

Prepare a statement of cash flows for Success Systems using the *indirect method* for the three months ended March 31, 2010. Recall that the owner Adriana Lopez contributed $25,000 to the business in exchange for additional stock in the first quarter of 2010 and has received $4,800 in cash dividends.

Check Cash flows used by operations: $(515)

BEYOND THE NUMBERS

REPORTING IN ACTION

C4 A1

BTN 16-1 Refer to **Best Buy**'s financial statements in Appendix A to answer the following.

1. Is Best Buy's statement of cash flows prepared under the direct method or the indirect method? How do you know?
2. For each fiscal year 2007, 2006, and 2005, is the amount of cash provided by operating activities more or less than the cash paid for dividends?
3. What is the largest amount in reconciling the difference between net income and cash flow from operating activities in 2007? In 2006? In 2005?
4. Identify the largest cash flows for investing and for financing activities in 2007 and in 2006.

Fast Forward

5. Obtain Best Buy's financial statements for a fiscal year ending after March 3, 2007, from either its Website (BestBuy.com) or the SEC's EDGAR database (www.sec.gov). Since March 3, 2007, what are Best Buy's largest cash outflows and cash inflows in the investing and in the financing sections of its statement of cash flow?

BTN 16-2 Key figures for **Best Buy**, **Circuit City**, and **RadioShack** follow.

COMPARATIVE ANALYSIS

A1 A2

($ millions)	Best Buy Current Year	Best Buy 1 Year Prior	Best Buy 2 Years Prior	Circuit City Current Year	Circuit City 1 Year Prior	Circuit City 2 Years Prior	RadioShack Current Year	RadioShack 1 Year Prior	RadioShack 2 Years Prior
Operating cash flows	$ 1,762	$ 1,740	$ 1,981	$ 316	$ 365	$ 389	$ 315	$ 363	$ 353
Total assets	13,570	11,864	10,294	4,007	4,069	3,840	2,070	2,205	2,517

Required

1. Compute the recent two years' cash flow on total assets ratios for Best Buy, Circuit City, and RadioShack.
2. What does the cash flow on total assets ratio measure?
3. Which company has the highest cash flow on total assets ratio for the periods shown?
4. Does the cash flow on total assets ratio reflect on the quality of earnings? Explain.

BTN 16-3 Kaelyn Gish is preparing for a meeting with her banker. Her business is finishing its fourth year of operations. In the first year, it had negative cash flows from operations. In the second and third years, cash flows from operations were positive. However, inventory costs rose significantly in year 4, and cash flows from operations will probably be down 25%. Gish wants to secure a line of credit from her banker as a financing buffer. From experience, she knows the banker will scrutinize operating cash flows for years 1 through 4 and will want a projected number for year 5. Gish knows that a steady progression upward in operating cash flows for years 1 through 4 will help her case. She decides to use her discretion as owner and considers several business actions that will turn her operating cash flow in year 4 from a decrease to an increase.

ETHICS CHALLENGE

C1 C2 A1

Required

1. Identify two business actions Gish might take to improve cash flows from operations.
2. Comment on the ethics and possible consequences of Gish's decision to pursue these actions.

BTN 16-4 Your friend, Hanna Willard, recently completed the second year of her business and just received annual financial statements from her accountant. Willard finds the income statement and balance sheet informative but does not understand the statement of cash flows. She says the first section is especially confusing because it contains a lot of additions and subtractions that do not make sense to her. Willard adds, "The income statement tells me the business is more profitable than last year and that's most important. If I want to know how cash changes, I can look at comparative balance sheets."

COMMUNICATING IN PRACTICE

C1 C4

Required

Write a half-page memorandum to your friend explaining the purpose of the statement of cash flows. Speculate as to why the first section is so confusing and how it might be rectified.

BTN 16-5 Access the April 19, 2007, filing of the 10-K report (for fiscal year ending February 3, 2007) of **J. Crew Group, Inc.**, at www.SEC.gov.

TAKING IT TO THE NET

A1

Required

1. Does J. Crew use the direct or indirect method to construct its consolidated statement of cash flows?
2. For the fiscal year ended February 3, 2007, what is the largest item in reconciling the net income to net cash provided by operating activities?
3. In the recent three years, has the company been more successful in generating operating cash flows or in generating net income? Identify the figures to support the answer.
4. In the year ended February 3, 2007, what was the largest cash outflow for investing activities and for financing activities?
5. What item(s) does J. Crew report as supplementary cash flow information?
6. Does J. Crew report any noncash financing activities for fiscal year 2007? Identify them, if any.

TEAMWORK IN ACTION

C1 C4 A1 P2 P5

BTN 16-6 Team members are to coordinate and independently answer one question within each of the following three sections. Team members should then report to the team and confirm or correct teammates' answers.

1. Answer *one* of the following questions about the statement of cash flows.
   a. What are this statement's reporting objectives?
   b. What two methods are used to prepare it? Identify similarities and differences between them.
   c. What steps are followed to prepare the statement?
   d. What types of analyses are often made from this statement's information?

2. Identify and explain the adjustment from net income to obtain cash flows from operating activities using the indirect method for *one* of the following items.
   a. Noncash operating revenues and expenses.
   b. Nonoperating gains and losses.
   c. Increases and decreases in noncash current assets.
   d. Increases and decreases in current liabilities.

3.[B]Identify and explain the formula for computing cash flows from operating activities using the direct method for *one* of the following items.
   a. Cash receipts from sales to customers.
   b. Cash paid for merchandise inventory.
   c. Cash paid for wages and operating expenses.
   d. Cash paid for interest and taxes.

Note: For teams of more than four, some pairing within teams is necessary. Use as an in-class activity or as an assignment. If used in class, specify a time limit on each part. Conclude with reports to the entire class, using team rotation. Each team can prepare responses on a transparency.

ENTREPRENEURIAL DECISION

C1 A1

BTN 16-7 Review the chapter's opener involving **Jungle Jim's International Market**.

Required

1. In a business such as Jungle Jim's, monitoring cash flow is always a priority. Even though Jungle Jim's now has thousands in annual sales and earns a positive net income, explain how cash flow can lag behind earnings.

2. Jungle Jim's is a closely held corporation. What are potential sources of financing for its future expansion?

C2 A1

BTN 16-8 Jenna and Matt Wilder are completing their second year operating Mountain High, a downhill ski area and resort. Mountain High reports a net loss of $(10,000) for its second year, which includes an $85,000 extraordinary loss from fire. This past year also involved major purchases of plant assets for renovation and expansion, yielding a year-end total asset amount of $800,000. Mountain High's net cash outflow for its second year is $(5,000); a summarized version of its statement of cash flows follows:

Net cash flow provided by operating activities	$295,000
Net cash flow used by investing activities	(310,000)
Net cash flow provided by financing activities	10,000

Required

Write a one-page memorandum to the Wilders evaluating Mountain High's current performance and assessing its future. Give special emphasis to cash flow data and their interpretation.

HITTING THE ROAD

C1

BTN 16-9 Visit **The Motley Fool**'s Website (**Fool.com**). Click on the sidebar link titled *Fool's School* (or *Fool.com/School*). Identify and select the link *How to Value Stocks.*

Required

1. Click on *Introduction to Valuation,* and then *Cash-Flow-Based Valuations.* How does the Fool's school define cash flow? What is the school's reasoning for this definition?

2. Per the school's instruction, why do analysts focus on earnings before interest and taxes (EBIT)?

3. Visit other links at this Website that interest you such as "How to Read a Balance Sheet," or find out what the "Fool's Ratio" is. Write a half-page report on what you find.

BTN 16-10 Key comparative information for **DSG international plc (DSGiplc.com)** follows.

GLOBAL DECISION

C1 C2 C4

DSG

(£ millions)	Current Year	1 Year Prior	2 Years Prior
Operating cash flows	£ 207	£ 338	£ 375
Total assets	3,977	4,120	4,104

Required

1. Compute the recent two years' cash flow on total assets ratio for DSG.

2. How does DSG's ratio compare to Best Buy's, Circuit City's, and RadioShack's ratios from BTN 16-2?

ANSWERS TO MULTIPLE CHOICE QUIZ

1. b;

Net income	$15,200
Depreciation expense	10,000
Gain on sale of land	(3,000)
Increase in inventory	(1,500)
Increase in accounts payable	2,850
Net cash provided by operations	$23,550

2. c; cash received from sale of machine is reported as an investing activity.

3. d; FASB requires cash interest paid to be reported under operating.

4. a; Cash paid for salaries and wages = $255,000 + $8,200 − $10,900 = $252,300

5. e; Increase in inventory = $112,000 − $105,000 = $7,000
Increase in accounts payable = $101,300 − $98,500 = $2,800
Cash paid for merchandise = $545,000 + $7,000 − $2,800 = $549,200

A Look Back

Chapter 16 focused on reporting and analyzing cash inflows and cash outflows. We explained how to prepare, analyze, and interpret the statement of cash flows.

A Look at This Chapter

This chapter emphasizes the analysis and interpretation of financial statement information. We learn to apply horizontal, vertical, and ratio analyses to better understand company performance and financial condition.

Chapter 17 Analysis of Financial Statements

Learning Objectives

CAP

Conceptual

C1 Explain the purpose of analysis. *(p. 680)*

C2 Identify the building blocks of analysis. *(p. 681)*

C3 Describe standards for comparisons in analysis. *(p. 682)*

C4 Identify the tools of analysis. *(p. 682)*

Analytical

A1 Summarize and report results of analysis. *(p. 700)*

A2 *Appendix 17A*—Explain the form and assess the content of a complete income statement. *(p. 703)*

LP17

Procedural

P1 Explain and apply methods of horizontal analysis. *(p. 682)*

P2 Describe and apply methods of vertical analysis. *(p. 687)*

P3 Define and apply ratio analysis. *(p. 690)*

Decision Feature

Motley Fool

"What goes on at The Motley Fool . . . is similar to what goes on in a library"
—Tom Gardner (David Gardner on left)

ALEXANDRIA, VA—In Shakespeare's Elizabethan comedy *As You Like It,* only the fool could speak truthfully to the King without getting his head lopped off. Inspired by Shakespeare's stage character, Tom and David Gardner vowed to become modern-day fools who tell it like it is. With under $10,000 in start-up money, the brothers launched **The Motley Fool (Fool.com).** And befitting of a Shakespearean play, the two say they are "dedicated to educating, amusing, and enriching individuals in search of the truth."

The Gardners do not fear the wrath of any King, real or fictional. They are intent on exposing the truth, as they see it, "that the financial world preys on ignorance and fear." As Tom explains, "There is such a great need in the general populace for financial information." Who can argue, given their brilliant success through practically every medium; including their Website, radio shows, newspaper columns, online store, investment newsletters, and global expansion.

Despite the brothers' best efforts, however, ordinary people still do not fully use information contained in financial statements. For instance, discussions keep appearing on The Motley Fool's online bulletin board that can be easily resolved using reliable and available accounting data. So, it would seem that the Fools must continue their work of "educating and enriching" individuals.

Resembling The Motley Fools' objectives, this chapter introduces horizontal and vertical analyses—tools used to reveal crucial trends and insights from financial information. It also expands on ratio analysis, which gives insight into a company's financial condition and performance. By arming ourselves with the information contained in this chapter and the investment advice of The Motley Fool, *we* can be sure to not play the fool in today's financial world.

[Sources: *Motley Fool Website,* January 2009; *Entrepreneur,* July 1997; *What to Do with Your Money Now,* June 2002; *USA Weekend,* July 2004; *Washington Post,* November 2007; *Money after 40,* April 2007]

This chapter shows how we use financial statements to evaluate a company's financial performance and condition. We explain financial statement analysis, its basic building blocks, the information available, standards for comparisons, and tools of analysis. Three major analysis tools are presented: horizontal analysis, vertical analysis, and ratio analysis. We apply each of these tools using **Best Buy**'s financial statements, and we introduce comparative analysis using **Circuit City** and **RadioShack**. This chapter expands and organizes the ratio analyses introduced at the end of each chapter.

Analysis of Financial Statements

Basics of Analysis
- Purpose
- Building blocks
- Information
- Standards for comparisons
- Tools

Horizontal Analysis
- Comparative balance sheets
- Comparative income statements
- Trend analysis

Vertical Analysis
- Common-size balance sheet
- Common-size income statement
- Common-size graphics

Ratio Analysis
- Liquidity and efficiency
- Solvency
- Profitability
- Market prospects
- Ratio summary

Basics of Analysis

Video17.1

Financial statement analysis applies analytical tools to general-purpose financial statements and related data for making business decisions. It involves transforming accounting data into more useful information. Financial statement analysis reduces our reliance on hunches, guesses, and intuition as well as our uncertainty in decision making. It does not lessen the need for expert judgment; instead, it provides us an effective and systematic basis for making business decisions. This section describes the purpose of financial statement analysis, its information sources, the use of comparisons, and some issues in computations.

Purpose of Analysis

C1 Explain the purpose of analysis.

Internal users of accounting information are those involved in strategically managing and operating the company. They include managers, officers, internal auditors, consultants, budget directors, and market researchers. The purpose of financial statement analysis for these users is to provide strategic information to improve company efficiency and effectiveness in providing products and services.

External users of accounting information are *not* directly involved in running the company. They include shareholders, lenders, directors, customers, suppliers, regulators, lawyers, brokers, and the press. External users rely on financial statement analysis to make better and more informed decisions in pursuing their own goals.

Point: Financial statement analysis tools are also used for personal financial investment decisions.

We can identify other uses of financial statement analysis. Shareholders and creditors assess company prospects to make investing and lending decisions. A board of directors analyzes financial statements in monitoring management's decisions. Employees and unions use financial statements in labor negotiations. Suppliers use financial statement information in establishing credit terms. Customers analyze financial statements in deciding whether to establish supply relationships. Public utilities set customer rates by analyzing financial statements. Auditors use financial statements in assessing the "fair presentation" of their clients' financial results. Analyst services such as **Dun & Bradstreet**, **Moody's**, and **Standard & Poor's** use financial statements in making buy-sell recommendations and in setting credit ratings. The common goal of these users is to evaluate company performance and financial condition. This includes evaluating (1) past and current performance, (2) current financial position, and (3) future performance and risk.

Point: Financial statement analysis is a topic on the CPA, CMA, CIA, and CFA exams.

Building Blocks of Analysis

C2 Identify the building blocks of analysis.

Financial statement analysis focuses on one or more elements of a company's financial condition or performance. Our analysis emphasizes four areas of inquiry—with varying degrees of importance. These four areas are described and illustrated in this chapter and are considered the *building blocks* of financial statement analysis:

- **Liquidity** and **efficiency**—ability to meet short-term obligations and to efficiently generate revenues.
- **Solvency**—ability to generate future revenues and meet long-term obligations.
- **Profitability**—ability to provide financial rewards sufficient to attract and retain financing.
- **Market prospects**—ability to generate positive market expectations.

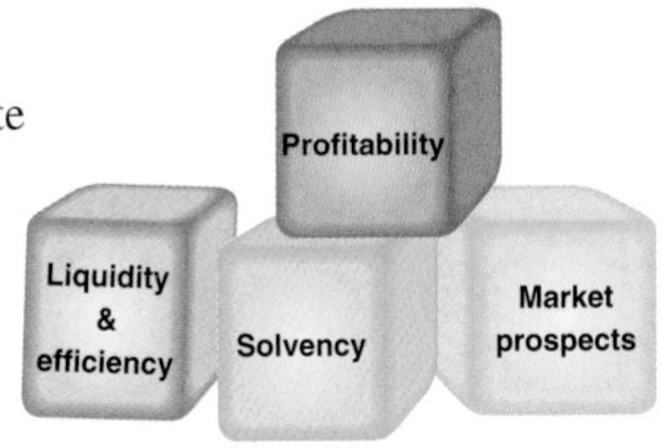

Applying the building blocks of financial statement analysis involves determining (1) the objectives of analysis and (2) the relative emphasis among the building blocks. We distinguish among these four building blocks to emphasize the different aspects of a company's financial condition or performance, yet we must remember that these areas of analysis are interrelated. For instance, a company's operating performance is affected by the availability of financing and short-term liquidity conditions. Similarly, a company's credit standing is not limited to satisfactory short-term liquidity but depends also on its profitability and efficiency in using assets. Early in our analysis, we need to determine the relative emphasis of each building block. Emphasis and analysis can later change as a result of evidence collected.

Decision Insight

Chips and Brokers The phrase *blue chips* refers to stock of big, profitable companies. The phrase comes from poker; where the most valuable chips are blue. The term *brokers* refers to those who execute orders to buy or sell stock. The term comes from wine retailers—individuals who broach (break) wine casks.

Information for Analysis

Some users, such as managers and regulatory authorities, are able to receive special financial reports prepared to meet their analysis needs. However, most users must rely on **general-purpose financial statements** that include the (1) income statement, (2) balance sheet, (3) statement of stockholders' equity (or statement of retained earnings), (4) statement of cash flows, and (5) notes to these statements.

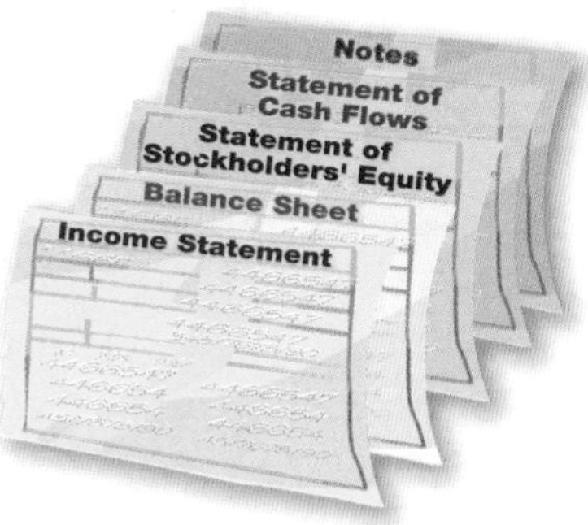

Financial reporting refers to the communication of financial information useful for making investment, credit, and other business decisions. Financial reporting includes not only general-purpose financial statements but also information from SEC 10-K or other filings, press releases, shareholders' meetings, forecasts, management letters, auditors' reports, and Webcasts.

Management's Discussion and Analysis (MD&A) is one example of useful information outside traditional financial statements. **Best Buy**'s MD&A (available at **BestBuy.com**), for example, begins with an overview and strategic initiatives. It then discusses operating results followed by liquidity and capital resources—roughly equivalent to investing and financing. The final few parts discuss special financing arrangements, key accounting policies, interim results, and the next year's outlook. The MD&A is an excellent starting point in understanding a company's business activities.

Decision Insight

Analysis Online Many Websites offer free access and screening of companies by key numbers such as earnings, sales, and book value. For instance, **Standard & Poor's** has information for more than 10,000 stocks (**StandardPoor.com**).

Standards for Comparisons

C3 Describe standards for comparisons in analysis.

When interpreting measures from financial statement analysis, we need to decide whether the measures indicate good, bad, or average performance. To make such judgments, we need standards (benchmarks) for comparisons that include the following:

- *Intracompany*—The company under analysis can provide standards for comparisons based on its own prior performance and relations between its financial items. **Best Buy**'s current net income, for instance, can be compared with its prior years' net income and in relation to its revenues or total assets.
- *Competitor*—One or more direct competitors of the company being analyzed can provide standards for comparisons. **Coca-Cola**'s profit margin, for instance, can be compared with **PepsiCo**'s profit margin.
- *Industry*—Industry statistics can provide standards of comparisons. Such statistics are available from services such as **Dun & Bradstreet**, **Standard & Poor's**, and **Moody's**.
- *Guidelines (rules of thumb)*—General standards of comparisons can develop from experience. Examples are the 2:1 level for the current ratio or 1:1 level for the acid-test ratio. Guidelines, or rules of thumb, must be carefully applied because context is crucial.

Point: Each chapter's *Reporting in Action* problems engage students in *intracompany* analysis, whereas *Comparative Analysis* problems require competitor analysis (Best Buy vs. Circuit City).

All of these comparison standards are useful when properly applied, yet measures taken from a selected competitor or group of competitors are often best. Intracompany and industry measures are also important. Guidelines or rules of thumb should be applied with care, and then only if they seem reasonable given past experience and industry norms.

Tools of Analysis

C4 Identify the tools of analysis.

Three of the most common tools of financial statement analysis are

1. **Horizontal analysis**—Comparison of a company's financial condition and performance across time.
2. **Vertical analysis**—Comparison of a company's financial condition and performance to a base amount.
3. **Ratio analysis**—Measurement of key relations between financial statement items.

The remainder of this chapter describes these analysis tools and how to apply them.

Quick Check

Answers—p. 706

1. Who are the intended users of general-purpose financial statements?
2. General-purpose financial statements consist of what information?
3. Which of the following is *least* useful as a basis for comparison when analyzing ratios? (*a*) Company results from a different economic setting. (*b*) Standards from past experience. (*c*) Rule-of-thumb standards. (*d*) Industry averages.
4. What is the preferred basis of comparison for ratio analysis?

Horizontal Analysis

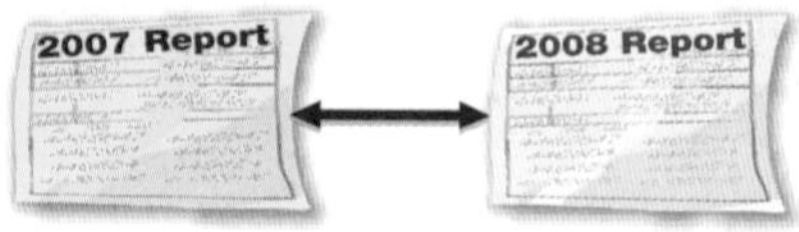

Analysis of any single financial number is of limited value. Instead, much of financial statement analysis involves identifying and describing relations between numbers, groups of numbers, and changes in those numbers. Horizontal analysis refers to examination of financial statement data *across time*. [The term *horizontal analysis* arises from the left-to-right (or right-to-left) movement of our eyes as we review comparative financial statements across time.]

Comparative Statements

P1 Explain and apply methods of horizontal analysis.

Comparing amounts for two or more successive periods often helps in analyzing financial statements. **Comparative financial statements** facilitate this comparison by showing financial amounts in side-by-side columns on a single statement, called a *comparative format*. Using figures from **Best Buy**'s financial statements, this section explains how to compute dollar changes and percent changes for comparative statements.

Video17.1

Computation of Dollar Changes and Percent Changes Comparing financial statements over relatively short time periods—two to three years—is often done by analyzing changes in line items. A change analysis usually includes analyzing absolute dollar amount changes and percent changes. Both analyses are relevant because dollar changes can yield large percent changes inconsistent with their importance. For instance, a 50% change from a base figure of $100 is less important than the same percent change from a base amount of $100,000 in the same statement. Reference to dollar amounts is necessary to retain a proper perspective and to assess the importance of changes. We compute the *dollar change* for a financial statement item as follows:

Example: What is a more significant change, a 70% increase on a $1,000 expense or a 30% increase on a $400,000 expense? *Answer:* The 30% increase.

$$\textbf{Dollar change} = \textbf{Analysis period amount} - \textbf{Base period amount}$$

Analysis period is the point or period of time for the financial statements under analysis, and *base period* is the point or period of time for the financial statements used for comparison purposes. The prior year is commonly used as a base period. We compute the *percent change* by dividing the dollar change by the base period amount and then multiplying this quantity by 100 as follows:

$$\textbf{Percent change (\%)} = \frac{\textbf{Analysis period amount} - \textbf{Base period amount}}{\textbf{Base period amount}} \times 100$$

We can always compute a dollar change, but we must be aware of a few rules in working with percent changes. To illustrate, look at four separate cases in this chart:

Case	Analysis Period	Base Period	Change Analysis Dollar	Change Analysis Percent
A	$ 1,500	$(4,500)	$ 6,000	—
B	(1,000)	2,000	(3,000)	—
C	8,000	—	8,000	—
D	0	10,000	(10,000)	(100%)

When a negative amount appears in the base period and a positive amount in the analysis period (or vice versa), we cannot compute a meaningful percent change; see cases A and B. Also, when no value is in the base period, no percent change is computable; see case C. Finally, when an item has a value in the base period and zero in the analysis period, the decrease is 100 percent; see case D.

Example: When there is a value in the base period and zero in the analysis period, the decrease is 100%. Why isn't the reverse situation an increase of 100%? *Answer:* A 100% increase of zero is still zero.

It is common when using horizontal analysis to compare amounts to either average or median values from prior periods (average and median values smooth out erratic or unusual fluctuations).[1] We also commonly round percents and ratios to one or two decimal places, but practice on this matter is not uniform. Computations are as detailed as necessary, which is judged by whether rounding potentially affects users' decisions. Computations should not be excessively detailed so that important relations are lost among a mountain of decimal points and digits.

Comparative Balance Sheets Comparative balance sheets consist of balance sheet amounts from two or more balance sheet dates arranged side by side. Its usefulness is often improved by showing each item's dollar change and percent change to highlight large changes.

[1] *Median* is the middle value in a group of numbers. For instance, if five prior years' incomes are (in 000s) $15, $19, $18, $20, and $22, the median value is $19. When there are two middle numbers, we can take their average. For instance, if four prior years' sales are (in 000s) $84, $91, $96, and $93, the median is $92 (computed as the average of $91 and $93).

Point: Spreadsheet programs can help with horizontal, vertical, and ratio analyses, including graphical depictions of financial relations.

Point: Business consultants use comparative statement analysis to provide management advice.

Analysis of comparative financial statements begins by focusing on items that show large dollar or percent changes. We then try to identify the reasons for these changes and, if possible, determine whether they are favorable or unfavorable. We also follow up on items with small changes when we expected the changes to be large.

Exhibit 17.1 shows comparative balance sheets for **Best Buy**. A few items stand out. Many asset categories substantially increase, which is probably not surprising because Best Buy is a growth company. Much of the increase in current assets is from the 20.7% increase in merchandise inventories. The long-term assets of property, equipment, and goodwill also increased. Of course, its sizeable total asset growth of 14.4% must be accompanied by future income to validate Best Buy's growth strategy.

We likewise see substantial increases on the financing side, the most notable ones being accounts payable and long-term debt totaling about $1,112 million. The increase in payables is related to the increase in cash levels, and the increase in debt is partly explained by the increase in long-term assets. Best Buy also reinvested much of its income as reflected in the $1,203 million increase in retained earnings. Again, we must monitor these increases in

EXHIBIT 17.1

Comparative Balance Sheets

BEST BUY
Comparative Balance Sheets
March 3, 2007, and February 25, 2006

(in millions)	2007	2006	Dollar Change	Percent Change
Assets				
Cash and cash equivalents	$ 1,205	$ 748	$ 457	61.1%
Short-term investments	2,588	3,041	(453)	(14.9)
Receivables, net	548	449	99	22.0
Merchandise inventories	4,028	3,338	690	20.7
Other current assets	712	409	303	74.1
Total current assets	9,081	7,985	1,096	13.7
Property and equipment	4,904	4,836	68	1.4
Less accumulated depreciation	1,966	2,124	(158)	(7.4)
Net property and equipment	2,938	2,712	226	8.3
Goodwill	919	557	362	65.0
Tradenames	81	44	37	84.1
Long-term investments	318	218	100	45.9
Other long-term assets	233	348	(115)	(33.0)
Total assets	$13,570	$11,864	$1,706	14.4
Liabilities				
Accounts payable	$ 3,934	$ 3,234	$ 700	21.6%
Unredeemed gift card liabilities	496	469	27	5.8
Accrued compensation and related expenses	332	354	(22)	(6.2)
Accrued liabilities	990	878	112	12.8
Accrued income taxes	489	703	(214)	(30.4)
Short-term debt	41	0	41	—
Current portion of long-term debt	19	418	(399)	(95.5)
Total current liabilities	6,301	6,056	245	4.0
Long-term liabilities	443	373	70	18.8
Long-term debt	590	178	412	231.5
Minority interests	35	0	35	—
Stockholders' Equity				
Common stock	48	49	(1)	(2.0)
Additional paid-in capital	430	643	(213)	(33.1)
Retained earnings	5,507	4,304	1,203	28.0
Accumulated other comprehensive income	216	261	(45)	(17.2)
Total stockholders' equity	6,201	5,257	944	18.0
Total liabilities and stockholders' equity	$13,570	$11,864	$1,706	14.4

investing and financing activities to be sure they are reflected in increased operating performance.

Comparative Income Statements Comparative income statements are prepared similarly to comparative balance sheets. Amounts for two or more periods are placed side by side, with additional columns for dollar and percent changes. Exhibit 17.2 shows Best Buy's comparative income statements.

EXHIBIT 17.2

Comparative Income Statements

BEST BUY
Comparative Income Statements
For Years Ended March 3, 2007, and February 25, 2006

(in millions, except per share data)	2007	2006	Dollar Change	Percent Change
Revenues	$35,934	$30,848	$5,086	16.5%
Cost of goods sold	27,165	23,122	4,043	17.5
Gross profit	8,769	7,726	1,043	13.5
Selling, general, and administrative expenses	6,770	6,082	688	11.3
Operating income	1,999	1,644	355	21.6
Net interest income (expense)	111	77	34	44.2
Gain on investments	20	0	20	—
Earnings from continuing operations before income taxes	2,130	1,721	409	23.8
Income tax expense	752	581	171	29.4
Minority interest in earnings	1	0	1	—
Net earnings	$ 1,377	$ 1,140	$ 237	20.8
Basic earnings per share	$ 2.86	$ 2.33	$ 0.53	22.7
Diluted earnings per share	$ 2.79	$ 2.27	$ 0.52	22.9

Best Buy has substantial revenue growth of 16.5% in 2007. This finding helps support management's growth strategy as reflected in the comparative balance sheets. Best Buy also reveals some ability to control cost of sales and general and administrative expenses, which increased 17.5% and 11.3%, respectively. Best Buy's net income growth of 20.8% on revenue growth of 16.5% is impressive.

Point: Percent change can also be computed by dividing the current period by the prior period and subtracting 1.0. For example, the 16.5% revenue increase of Exhibit 17.2 is computed as: ($35,934/$30,848) − 1.

Trend Analysis

Trend analysis, also called *trend percent analysis* or *index number trend analysis,* is a form of horizontal analysis that can reveal patterns in data across successive periods. It involves computing trend percents for a series of financial numbers and is a variation on the use of percent changes. The difference is that trend analysis does not subtract the base period amount in the numerator. To compute trend percents, we do the following:

1. Select a *base period* and assign each item in the base period a weight of 100%.
2. Express financial numbers as a percent of their base period number.

Specifically, a *trend percent,* also called an *index number,* is computed as follows:

Point: *Index* refers to the comparison of the analysis period to the base period. Percents determined for each period are called *index numbers.*

$$\textbf{Trend percent (\%)} = \frac{\textbf{Analysis period amount}}{\textbf{Base period amount}} \times 100$$

To illustrate trend analysis, we use the **Best Buy** data shown in Exhibit 17.3.

EXHIBIT 17.3

Revenues and Expenses

(in millions)	2007	2006	2005	2004	2003
Revenues	$35,934	$30,848	$27,433	$24,548	$20,943
Cost of goods sold	27,165	23,122	20,938	18,677	15,998
Selling, general & administrative expenses	6,770	6,082	5,053	4,567	3,935

These data are from Best Buy's *Selected Financial Data* section. The base period is 2003 and the trend percent is computed in each subsequent year by dividing that year's amount by its 2003 amount. For instance, the revenue trend percent for 2007 is 171.6%, computed as $35,934/$20,943. The trend percents—using the data from Exhibit 17.3—are shown in Exhibit 17.4.

EXHIBIT 17.4

Trend Percents for Revenues and Expenses

	2007	2006	2005	2004	2003
Revenues	171.6%	147.3%	131.0%	117.2%	100.0%
Cost of goods sold	169.8	144.5	130.9	116.7	100.0
Selling, general & administrative expenses	172.0	154.6	128.4	116.1	100.0

Point: Trend analysis expresses a percent of base, not a percent of change.

Graphical depictions often aid analysis of trend percents. Exhibit 17.5 shows the trend percents from Exhibit 17.4 in a *line graph,* which can help us identify trends and detect changes in direction or magnitude. It reveals that the trend line for revenues consistently exceeds that for cost of goods sold. Moreover, the magnitude of that difference has slightly grown. This result bodes well for Best Buy because its cost of goods sold are by far its largest cost, and the company shows an ability to control these expenses as it expands. The line graph also reveals a consistent increase in each of these accounts, which is typical of growth companies. The trend line for selling, general and administrative expenses is less encouraging because it exceeds the revenue trend line in 2006–2007. The good news is that nearly all of that upward shift in costs occured in one year (2006). In other years, management appears to have limited those costs to not exceed revenue growth.

EXHIBIT 17.5

Trend Percent Lines for Revenues and Expenses of Best Buy

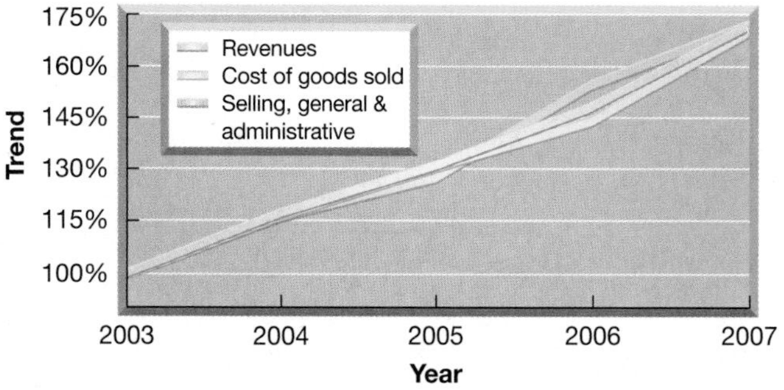

Exhibit 17.6 compares **Best Buy**'s revenue trend line to that of **Circuit City** and **RadioShack** for this same period. Best Buy's revenues sharply increased over this time period while those of Circuit City exhibited less growth, and those for RadioShack were flat. These data indicate that Best Buy's products and services have met with considerable consumer acceptance.

EXHIBIT 17.6

Trend Percent Lines—Best Buy, Circuit City, and RadioShack

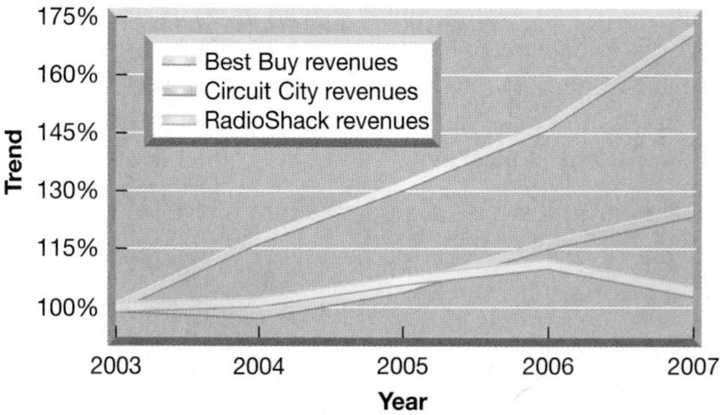

Trend analysis of financial statement items can include comparisons of relations between items on different financial statements. For instance, Exhibit 17.7 compares Best Buy's revenues and total assets. The rate of increase in total assets (176.4%) is greater than the increase in revenues (171.6%) since 2003. Is this result favorable or not? It suggests that Best Buy was slightly less efficient in using its assets in 2007. Management apparently is expecting future years' revenues to compensate for this asset growth.

Overall we must remember that an important role of financial statement analysis is identifying questions and areas of interest, which often direct us to important factors bearing

EXHIBIT 17.7

Revenue and Asset Data for Best Buy

($ millions)	2007	2003	Trend Percent (2007 vs. 2003)
Revenues	$35,934	$20,943	171.6%
Total assets	13,570	7,694	176.4

on a company's future. Accordingly, financial statement analysis should be seen as a continuous process of refining our understanding and expectations of company performance and financial condition.

Decision Maker

Auditor Your tests reveal a 3% increase in sales from $200,000 to $206,000 and a 4% decrease in expenses from $190,000 to $182,400. Both changes are within your "reasonableness" criterion of ±5%, and thus you don't pursue additional tests. The audit partner in charge questions your lack of follow-up and mentions the *joint relation* between sales and expenses. To what is the partner referring? [Answer—p. 706]

Vertical Analysis

Vertical analysis is a tool to evaluate individual financial statement items or a group of items in terms of a specific base amount. We usually define a key aggregate figure as the base, which for an income statement is usually revenue and for a balance sheet is usually total assets. This section explains vertical analysis and applies it to Best Buy. [The term *vertical analysis* arises from the up-down (or down-up) movement of our eyes as we review common-size financial statements. Vertical analysis is also called *common-size analysis*.]

Income Statement	
Sales	10,000
Expenses	6,000
Income	4,000

Common-Size Statements

P2 Describe and apply methods of vertical analysis.

The comparative statements in Exhibits 17.1 and 17.2 show the change in each item over time, but they do not emphasize the relative importance of each item. We use **common-size financial statements** to reveal changes in the relative importance of each financial statement item. All individual amounts in common-size statements are redefined in terms of common-size percents. A *common-size percent* is measured by dividing each individual financial statement amount under analysis by its base amount:

$$\textbf{Common-size percent (\%)} = \frac{\textbf{Analysis amount}}{\textbf{Base amount}} \times 100$$

Common-Size Balance Sheets Common-size statements express each item as a percent of a *base amount*, which for a common-size balance sheet is usually total assets. The base amount is assigned a value of 100%. (This implies that the total amount of liabilities plus equity equals 100% since this amount equals total assets.) We then compute a common-size percent for each asset, liability, and equity item using total assets as the base amount. When we present a company's successive balance sheets in this way, changes in the mixture of assets, liabilities, and equity are apparent.

Exhibit 17.8 shows common-size comparative balance sheets for Best Buy. Some relations that stand out on both a magnitude and percentage basis include (1) a 41% increase in cash and equivalents, (2) a 6.5% decline in short-term investments as a percentage of assets, (3) a 1.2% decrease in net property and equipment as a percentage of assets, (4) a 1.7% increase in the percentage of accounts payable, (5) a 3.4% decline in the current portion of long-term debt, and (6) a marked increase in retained earnings. Most of these changes are characteristic of a successful growth/stable company. The concern, if any, is whether Best Buy can continue to generate sufficient revenues and income to support its asset buildup within a very competitive industry.

Point: The *base* amount in common-size analysis is an *aggregate* amount from that period's financial statement.

Point: Common-size statements often are used to compare two or more companies in the same industry.

Point: Common-size statements are also useful in comparing firms that report in different currencies.

EXHIBIT 17.8

Common-Size Comparative Balance Sheets

BEST BUY
Common-Size Comparative Balance Sheets
March 3, 2007, and February 25, 2006

(in millions)	2007	2006	Common-Size Percents* 2007	Common-Size Percents* 2006
Assets				
Cash and cash equivalents	$ 1,205	$ 748	8.9%	6.3%
Short-term investments	2,588	3,041	19.1	25.6
Receivables, net	548	449	4.0	3.8
Merchandise inventories	4,028	3,338	29.7	28.1
Other current assets	712	409	5.2	3.4
Total current assets	9,081	7,985	66.9	67.3
Property and equipment	4,904	4,836	36.1	40.8
Less accumulated depreciation	1,966	2,124	14.5	17.9
Net property and equipment	2,938	2,712	21.7	22.9
Goodwill	919	557	6.8	4.7
Tradenames	81	44	0.6	0.4
Long-term investments	318	218	2.3	1.8
Other long-term assets	233	348	1.7	2.9
Total assets	$13,570	$11,864	100.0%	100.0%
Liabilities				
Accounts payable	$ 3,934	$ 3,234	29.0%	27.3%
Unredeemed gift card liabilities	496	469	3.7	4.0
Accrued compensation and related expenses	332	354	2.4	3.0
Accrued liabilities	990	878	7.3	7.4
Accrued income taxes	489	703	3.6	5.9
Short-term debt	41	0	0.3	0.0
Current portion of long-term debt	19	418	0.1	3.5
Total current liabilities	6,301	6,056	46.4	51.0
Long-term liabilities	443	373	3.3	3.1
Long-term debt	590	178	4.3	1.5
Minority interests	35	0	0.3	0.0
Stockholders' Equity				
Common stock	48	49	0.4	0.4
Additional paid-in capital	430	643	3.2	5.4
Retained earnings	5,507	4,304	40.6	36.3
Accumulated other comprehensive income	216	261	1.6	2.2
Total stockholders' equity	6,201	5,257	45.7	44.3
Total liabilities and stockholders' equity	$13,570	$11,864	100.0%	100.0%

* Percents are rounded to tenths and thus may not exactly sum to totals and subtotals.

Global: International companies sometimes disclose "convenience" financial statements, which are statements translated in other languages and currencies. However, these statements rarely adjust for differences in accounting principles across countries.

Common-Size Income Statements Analysis also benefits from use of a common-size income statement. Revenues is usually the base amount, which is assigned a value of 100%. Each common-size income statement item appears as a percent of revenues. If we think of the 100% revenues amount as representing one sales dollar, the remaining items show how each revenue dollar is distributed among costs, expenses, and income.

Exhibit 17.9 shows common-size comparative income statements for each dollar of Best Buy's revenues. The past two years' common-size numbers are similar. The good news is that Best Buy has been able to squeeze an extra 0.1 cent in earnings per revenue dollar—evidenced by the 3.7% to 3.8% rise in earnings as a percentage of revenues. This implies that management is effectively controlling costs and/or the company is reaping growth benefits, so-called *economies of scale*. The bad news is that gross profit lost 0.6 cent per revenue dollar—evidenced by the 25.0% to 24.4% decline in gross profit as a percentage of revenues. This is a concern given the price-competitive

EXHIBIT 17.9

Common-Size Comparative Income Statements

BEST BUY Common-Size Comparative Income Statements For Years Ended March 3, 2007, and February 25, 2006			Common-Size Percents*	
($ millions)	2007	2006	2007	2006
Revenues	$35,934	$30,848	100.0%	100.0%
Cost of goods sold	27,165	23,122	75.6	75.0
Gross profit	8,769	7,726	24.4	25.0
Selling, general, and administrative expenses	6,770	6,082	18.8	19.7
Operating income	1,999	1,644	5.6	5.3
Net interest income (expense)	111	77	0.3	0.2
Gain on investments	20	0	0.1	0.0
Earnings from continuing operations before income taxes	2,130	1,721	5.9	5.6
Income tax expense	752	581	2.1	1.9
Minority interest in earnings	1	0	0.0	0.0
Net earnings	$ 1,377	$ 1,140	3.8%	3.7%

* Percents are rounded to tenths and thus may not exactly sum to totals and subtotals.

electronics market. Analysis here shows that common-size percents for successive income statements can uncover potentially important changes in a company's expenses. Evidence of no changes, especially when changes are expected, is also informative.

Common-Size Graphics

Two of the most common tools of common-size analysis are trend analysis of common-size statements and graphical analysis. The trend analysis of common-size statements is similar to that of comparative statements discussed under vertical analysis. It is not illustrated here because the only difference is the substitution of common-size percents for trend percents. Instead, this section discusses graphical analysis of common-size statements.

An income statement readily lends itself to common-size graphical analysis. This is so because revenues affect nearly every item in an income statement. Exhibit 17.10 shows **Best Buy**'s 2007 common-size income statement in graphical form. This pie chart highlights the contribution of each component of revenues for net earnings.

EXHIBIT 17.10

Common-Size Graphic of Income Statement

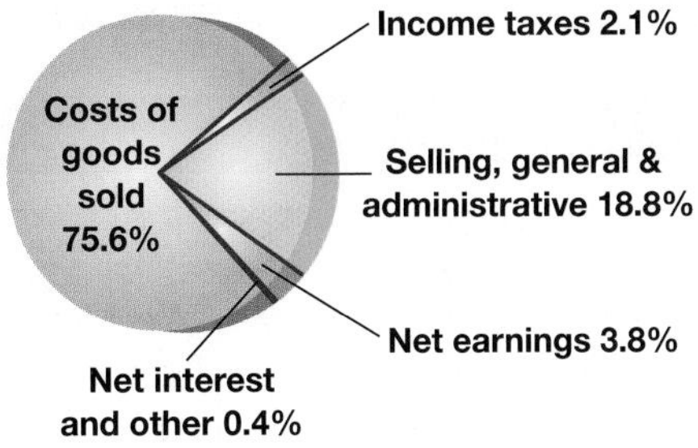

Exhibit 17.11 previews more complex graphical analyses available and the insights they provide. The data for this exhibit are taken from **Best Buy**'s *Segments* footnote. Best Buy has two reportable segments: domestic and international.

EXHIBIT 17.11

Revenue and Operating Income Breakdown by Segment

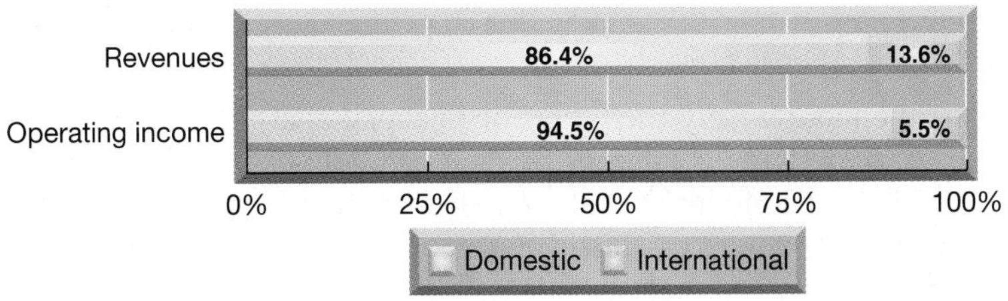

EXHIBIT 17.12

Common-Size Graphic of Asset Components

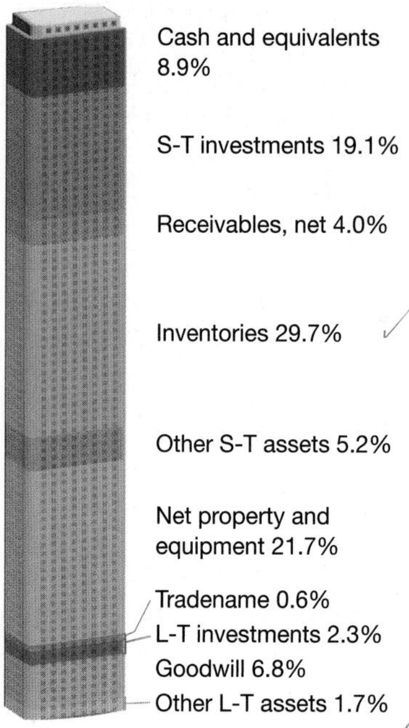

The upper bar in Exhibit 17.11 shows the percent of revenues from each segment. The major revenue source is Domestic (86.4%). The lower bar shows the percent of operating income from each segment. Although International provides 13.6% of revenues, it provides only 5.5% of operating income. This type of information can help users in determining strategic analyses and actions.

Graphical analysis is also useful in identifying (1) sources of financing including the distribution among current liabilities, noncurrent liabilities, and equity capital and (2) focuses of investing activities, including the distribution among current and noncurrent assets. As illustrative, Exhibit 17.12 shows a common-size graphical display of Best Buy's assets. Common-size balance sheet analysis can be extended to examine the composition of these subgroups. For instance, in assessing liquidity of current assets, knowing what proportion of current assets consists of inventories is usually important, and not simply what proportion inventories are of total assets.

Common-size financial statements are also useful in comparing different companies. Exhibit 17.13 shows common-size graphics of Best Buy, Circuit City, and RadioShack on financing sources. This graphic highlights the larger percent of equity financing for Best Buy and Circuit City than for RadioShack. It also highlights the much larger noncurrent (debt) financing of RadioShack. Comparison of a company's common-size statements with competitors' or industry common-size statistics alerts us to differences in the structure or distribution of its financial statements but not to their dollar magnitude.

EXHIBIT 17.13

Common-Size Graphic of Financing Sources—Competitor Analysis

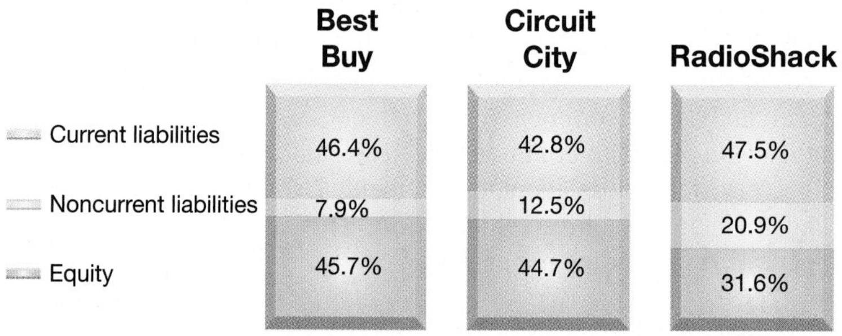

Quick Check

Answers—p. 706

5. Which of the following is true for common-size comparative statements? (*a*) Each item is expressed as a percent of a base amount. (*b*) Total assets often are assigned a value of 100%. (*c*) Amounts from successive periods are placed side by side. (*d*) All are true. (*e*) None is true.
6. What is the difference between the percents shown on a comparative income statement and those shown on a common-size comparative income statement?
7. Trend percents are (*a*) shown on comparative income statements and balance sheets, (*b*) shown on common-size comparative statements, or (*c*) also called *index numbers*.

Ratio Analysis

P3 Define and apply ratio analysis.

Ratios are among the more widely used tools of financial analysis because they provide clues to and symptoms of underlying conditions. A ratio can help us uncover conditions and trends difficult to detect by inspecting individual components making up the ratio. Ratios, like other analysis tools, are usually future oriented; that is, they are often adjusted for their probable future trend and magnitude, and their usefulness depends on skillful interpretation.

A ratio expresses a mathematical relation between two quantities. It can be expressed as a percent, rate, or proportion. For instance, a change in an account balance from \$100 to \$250 can be expressed as (1) 150%, (2) 2.5 times, or (3) 2.5 to 1 (or 2.5:1). Computation of a ratio is a simple arithmetic operation, but its interpretation is not. To be meaningful, a ratio must refer to an economically important relation. For example, a direct and crucial relation exists between an item's sales price and its cost. Accordingly, the ratio of cost of goods sold to sales is meaningful. In contrast, no obvious relation exists between freight costs and the balance of long-term investments.

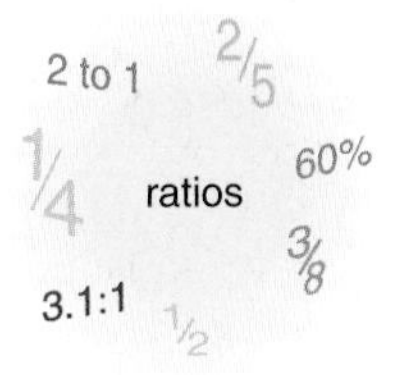

This section describes an important set of financial ratios and its application. The selected ratios are organized into the four building blocks of financial statement analysis: (1) liquidity and efficiency, (2) solvency, (3) profitability, and (4) market prospects. All of these ratios were explained at relevant points in prior chapters. The purpose here is to organize and apply them under a summary framework. We use four common standards, in varying degrees, for comparisons: intracompany, competitor, industry, and guidelines.

Point: Some sources for industry norms are *Annual Statement Studies* by Robert Morris Associates, *Industry Norms & Key Business Ratios* by Dun & Bradstreet, *Standard & Poor's Industry Surveys*, and Reuters.com/finance.

Liquidity and Efficiency

Liquidity refers to the availability of resources to meet short-term cash requirements. It is affected by the timing of cash inflows and outflows along with prospects for future performance. Analysis of liquidity is aimed at a company's funding requirements. *Efficiency* refers to how productive a company is in using its assets. Efficiency is usually measured relative to how much revenue is generated from a certain level of assets.

Both liquidity and efficiency are important and complementary. If a company fails to meet its current obligations, its continued existence is doubtful. Viewed in this light, all other measures of analysis are of secondary importance. Although accounting measurements assume the company's continued existence, our analysis must always assess the validity of this assumption using liquidity measures. Moreover, inefficient use of assets can cause liquidity problems. A lack of liquidity often precedes lower profitability and fewer opportunities. It can foretell a loss of owner control. To a company's creditors, lack of liquidity can yield delays in collecting interest and principal payments or the loss of amounts due them. A company's customers and suppliers of goods and services also are affected by short-term liquidity problems. Implications include a company's inability to execute contracts and potential damage to important customer and supplier relationships. This section describes and illustrates key ratios relevant to assessing liquidity and efficiency.

Working Capital and Current Ratio The amount of current assets less current liabilities is called **working capital,** or *net working capital.* A company needs adequate working capital to meet current debts, to carry sufficient inventories, and to take advantage of cash discounts. A company that runs low on working capital is less likely to meet current obligations or to continue operating. When evaluating a company's working capital, we must not only look at the dollar amount of current assets less current liabilities, but also at their ratio. The *current ratio* is defined as follows (see Chapter 3 for additional explanation):

$$\textbf{Current ratio} = \frac{\textbf{Current assets}}{\textbf{Current liabilities}}$$

Drawing on information in Exhibit 17.1, **Best Buy**'s working capital and current ratio for both 2007 and 2006 are shown in Exhibit 17.14. **Circuit City** (1.68), **RadioShack** (1.63), and the Industry's current ratio of 1.6 is shown in the margin. Best Buy's 2007 ratio (1.44) is lower than any of the comparison ratios, but it does not appear in danger of defaulting on loan payments. A high current ratio suggests a strong liquidity position and an ability to meet current obligations. A company can, however, have a current ratio that is too high. An excessively high current ratio means that the company has invested too much in current assets compared to its current obligations. An

EXHIBIT 17.14

Best Buy's Working Capital and Current Ratio

($ millions)	2007	2006
Current assets	\$ 9,081	\$ 7,985
Current liabilities	6,301	6,056
Working capital	**\$2,780**	**\$1,929**
Current ratio		
\$9,081/\$6,301	**1.44 to 1**	
\$7,985/\$6,056		**1.32 to 1**

Current ratio
Circuit City = 1.68
RadioShack = 1.63
Industry = 1.6

excessive investment in current assets is not an efficient use of funds because current assets normally generate a low return on investment (compared with long-term assets).

Many users apply a guideline of 2:1 (or 1.5:1) for the current ratio in helping evaluate a company's debt-paying ability. A company with a 2:1 or higher current ratio is generally thought to be a good credit risk in the short run. Such a guideline or any analysis of the current ratio must recognize at least three additional factors: (1) type of business, (2) composition of current assets, and (3) turnover rate of current asset components.

Type of business. A service company that grants little or no credit and carries few inventories can probably operate on a current ratio of less than 1:1 if its revenues generate enough cash to pay its current liabilities. On the other hand, a company selling high-priced clothing or furniture requires a higher ratio because of difficulties in judging customer demand and cash receipts. For instance, if demand falls, inventory may not generate as much cash as expected. Accordingly, analysis of the current ratio should include a comparison with ratios from successful companies in the same industry and from prior periods. We must also recognize that a company's accounting methods, especially choice of inventory method, affect the current ratio. For instance, when costs are rising, a company using LIFO tends to report a smaller amount of current assets than when using FIFO.

Point: When a firm uses LIFO in a period of rising costs, the standard for an adequate current ratio usually is lower than if it used FIFO.

Composition of current assets. The composition of a company's current assets is important to an evaluation of short-term liquidity. For instance, cash, cash equivalents, and short-term investments are more liquid than accounts and notes receivable. Also, short-term receivables normally are more liquid than inventory. Cash, of course, can be used to immediately pay current debts. Items such as accounts receivable and inventory, however, normally must be converted into cash before payment is made. An excessive amount of receivables and inventory weakens a company's ability to pay current liabilities. The acid-test ratio (see below) can help with this assessment.

Turnover rate of assets. Asset turnover measures a company's efficiency in using its assets. One relevant measure of asset efficiency is the revenue generated. A measure of total asset turnover is revenues divided by total assets, but evaluation of turnover for individual assets is also useful. We discuss both receivables turnover and inventory turnover on the next page.

Decision Maker

Banker A company requests a one-year, $200,000 loan for expansion. This company's current ratio is 4:1, with current assets of $160,000. Key competitors carry a current ratio of about 1.9:1. Using this information, do you approve the loan application? Does your decision change if the application is for a 10-year loan? [Answer—p. 706]

Acid-Test Ratio Quick assets are cash, short-term investments, and current receivables. These are the most liquid types of current assets. The *acid-test ratio,* also called *quick ratio,* and introduced in Chapter 5, reflects on a company's short-term liquidity.

$$\textbf{Acid-test ratio} = \frac{\textbf{Cash + Short-term investments + Current receivables}}{\textbf{Current liabilities}}$$

Best Buy's acid-test ratio is computed in Exhibit 17.15. Best Buy's 2007 acid-test ratio (0.69) is between that for Circuit City (0.65) and RadioShack (0.73), and less than the 1:1 common

EXHIBIT 17.15

Acid-Test Ratio

($ millions)	2007	2006
Cash and equivalents	$1,205	$ 748
Short-term investments	2,588	3,041
Current receivables	548	449
Total quick assets	$4,341	$4,238
Current liabilities	$6,301	$6,056
Acid-test ratio		
$4,341/$6,301	**0.69 to 1**	
$4,238/$6,056		**0.70 to 1**

Acid-test ratio
Circuit City = 0.65
RadioShack = 0.73
Industry = 0.7

guideline for an acceptable acid-test ratio; each of these ratios is similar to the 0.7 industry ratio. As with analysis of the current ratio, we need to consider other factors. For instance, the frequency with which a company converts its current assets into cash affects its working capital requirements. This implies that analysis of short-term liquidity should also include an analysis of receivables and inventories, which we consider next.

Global: Ratio analysis helps overcome currency translation problems, but it does *not* overcome differences in accounting principles.

Accounts Receivable Turnover We can measure how frequently a company converts its receivables into cash by computing the *accounts receivable turnover*. This ratio is defined as follows (see Chapter 9 for additional explanation):

$$\textbf{Accounts receivable turnover} = \frac{\textbf{Net sales}}{\textbf{Average accounts receivable, net}}$$

Short-term receivables from customers are often included in the denominator along with accounts receivable. Also, accounts receivable turnover is more precise if credit sales are used for the numerator, but external users generally use net sales (or net revenues) because information about credit sales is typically not reported. Best Buy's 2007 accounts receivable turnover is computed as follows ($ millions).

Point: Some users prefer using gross accounts receivable (before subtracting the allowance for doubtful accounts) to avoid the influence of a manager's bad debts estimate.

$$\frac{\$35{,}934}{(\$548 + \$449)/2} = 72.1 \text{ times}$$

Accounts receivable turnover
Circuit City = 41.2
RadioShack = 17.1

Best Buy's value of 72.1 is larger than Circuit City's 41.2 and RadioShack's 17.1. Accounts receivable turnover is high when accounts receivable are quickly collected. A high turnover is favorable because it means the company need not commit large amounts of funds to accounts receivable. However, an accounts receivable turnover can be too high; this can occur when credit terms are so restrictive that they negatively affect sales volume.

Point: Ending accounts receivable can be substituted for the average balance in computing accounts receivable turnover if the difference between ending and average receivables is small.

Inventory Turnover How long a company holds inventory before selling it will affect working capital requirements. One measure of this effect is *inventory turnover,* also called *merchandise turnover* or *merchandise inventory turnover,* which is defined as follows (see Chapter 6 for additional explanation):

$$\textbf{Inventory turnover} = \frac{\textbf{Cost of goods sold}}{\textbf{Average inventory}}$$

Using Best Buy's cost of goods sold and inventories information, we compute its inventory turnover for 2007 as follows (if the beginning and ending inventories for the year do not represent the usual inventory amount, an average of quarterly or monthly inventories can be used).

$$\frac{\$27{,}165}{(\$4{,}028 + \$3{,}338)/2} = 7.38 \text{ times}$$

Inventory turnover
Circuit City = 5.70
RadioShack = 2.96
Industry = 4.5

Best Buy's inventory turnover of 7.38 is higher than Circuit City's 5.70, RadioShack's 2.96, and the industry's 4.5. A company with a high turnover requires a smaller investment in inventory than one producing the same sales with a lower turnover. Inventory turnover can be too high, however, if the inventory a company keeps is so small that it restricts sales volume.

Days' Sales Uncollected Accounts receivable turnover provides insight into how frequently a company collects its accounts. Days' sales uncollected is one measure of this activity, which is defined as follows (Chapter 8 provides additional explanation):

$$\textbf{Days' sales uncollected} = \frac{\textbf{Accounts receivable, net}}{\textbf{Net sales}} \times \textbf{365}$$

Any short-term notes receivable from customers are normally included in the numerator.

Best Buy's 2007 days' sales uncollected follows.

Day's sales uncollected
Circuit City = 11.23
RadioShack = 18.94

$$\frac{\$548}{\$35{,}934} \times 365 = 5.57 \text{ days}$$

Both Circuit City's days' sales uncollected of 11.23 days and RadioShack's 18.94 days are longer than the 5.57 days for Best Buy. Days' sales uncollected is more meaningful if we know company credit terms. A rough guideline states that days' sales uncollected should not exceed $1\frac{1}{3}$ times the days in its (1) credit period, *if* discounts are not offered or (2) discount period, *if* favorable discounts are offered.

Days' Sales in Inventory *Days' sales in inventory* is a useful measure in evaluating inventory liquidity. Days' sales in inventory is linked to inventory in a way that days' sales uncollected is linked to receivables. We compute days' sales in inventory as follows (Chapter 6 provides additional explanation).

$$\textbf{Days' sales in inventory} = \frac{\textbf{Ending inventory}}{\textbf{Cost of goods sold}} \times \textbf{365}$$

Best Buy's days' sales in inventory for 2007 follows.

Days' sales in inventory
Circuit City = 62.9
RadioShack = 107.9

$$\frac{\$4{,}028}{\$27{,}165} \times 365 = 54.1 \text{ days}$$

Point: *Average collection period* is estimated by dividing 365 by the accounts receivable turnover ratio. For example, 365 divided by an accounts receivable turnover of 6.1 indicates a 60-day average collection period.

If the products in Best Buy's inventory are in demand by customers, this formula estimates that its inventory will be converted into receivables (or cash) in 54.1 days. If all of Best Buy's sales were credit sales, the conversion of inventory to receivables in 54.1 days *plus* the conversion of receivables to cash in 5.57 days implies that inventory will be converted to cash in about 59.67 days (54.1 + 5.57).

Total Asset Turnover *Total asset turnover* reflects a company's ability to use its assets to generate sales and is an important indication of operating efficiency. The definition of this ratio follows (Chapter 10 offers additional explanation).

$$\textbf{Total asset turnover} = \frac{\textbf{Net sales}}{\textbf{Average total assets}}$$

Best Buy's total asset turnover for 2007 follows and is less than Circuit City's, but greater than that for RadioShack.

Total asset turnover
Circuit City = 3.08
RadioShack = 2.24

$$\frac{\$35{,}934}{(\$13{,}570 + \$11{,}864)/2} = 2.83 \text{ times}$$

Quick Check

Answers—p. 706

8. Information from Paff Co. at Dec. 31, 2008, follows: cash, \$820,000; accounts receivable, \$240,000; inventories, \$470,000; plant assets, \$910,000; accounts payable, \$350,000; and income taxes payable, \$180,000. Compute its (*a*) current ratio and (*b*) acid-test ratio.
9. On Dec. 31, 2009, Paff Company (see question 8) had accounts receivable of \$290,000 and inventories of \$530,000. During 2009, net sales amounted to \$2,500,000 and cost of goods sold was \$750,000. Compute (*a*) accounts receivable turnover, (*b*) days' sales uncollected, (*c*) inventory turnover, and (*d*) days' sales in inventory.

Solvency

Solvency refers to a company's long-run financial viability and its ability to cover long-term obligations. All of a company's business activities—financing, investing, and operating—affect its solvency. Analysis of solvency is long term and uses less precise but more encompassing measures than liquidity. One of the most important components of solvency analysis is the composition of a company's capital structure. *Capital structure* refers to a company's financing sources. It ranges from relatively permanent equity financing to riskier or more temporary short-term financing. Assets represent security for financiers, ranging from loans secured by specific assets to the assets available as general security to unsecured creditors. This section describes the tools of solvency analysis. Our analysis focuses on a company's ability to both meet its obligations and provide security to its creditors *over the long run*. Indicators of this ability include *debt* and *equity* ratios, the relation between *pledged assets and secured liabilities,* and the company's capacity to earn sufficient income to *pay fixed interest charges*.

Debt and Equity Ratios One element of solvency analysis is to assess the portion of a company's assets contributed by its owners and the portion contributed by creditors. This relation is reflected in the debt ratio (also described in Chapter 2). The *debt ratio* expresses total liabilities as a percent of total assets. The **equity ratio** provides complementary information by expressing total equity as a percent of total assets. **Best Buy**'s debt and equity ratios follow.

Point: For analysis purposes, Minority Interest is usually included in equity.

($ millions)	2007	Ratios	
Total liabilities	$ 7,369	54.3%	[Debt ratio]
Total equity	6,201	45.7	[Equity ratio]
Total liabilities and equity	$13,570	100.0%	

Debt ratio :: Equity ratio
Circuit City = 55.3% :: 44.7%
RadioShack = 68.4% :: 31.6%

Best Buy's financial statements reveal more debt than equity. A company is considered less risky if its capital structure (equity and long-term debt) contains more equity. One risk factor is the required payment for interest and principal when debt is outstanding. Another factor is the greater the stockholder financing, the more losses a company can absorb through equity before the assets become inadequate to satisfy creditors' claims. From the stockholders' point of view, if a company earns a return on borrowed capital that is higher than the cost of borrowing, the difference represents increased income to stockholders. The inclusion of debt is described as *financial leverage* because debt can have the effect of increasing the return to stockholders. Companies are said to be highly leveraged if a large portion of their assets is financed by debt.

Point: Bank examiners from the FDIC and other regulatory agencies use debt and equity ratios to monitor compliance with regulatory capital requirements imposed on banks and S&Ls.

Debt-to-Equity Ratio The ratio of total liabilities to equity is another measure of solvency. We compute the ratio as follows (Chapter 14 offers additional explanation).

$$\textbf{Debt-to-equity ratio} = \frac{\textbf{Total liabilities}}{\textbf{Total equity}}$$

Best Buy's debt-to-equity ratio for 2007 is

$$\$7{,}369/\$6{,}201 = 1.19$$

Debt-to-equity
Circuit City = 1.24
RadioShack = 2.17
Industry = 0.99

Best Buy's 1.19 debt-to-equity ratio is less than the 1.24 ratio for Circuit City and the 2.17 for RadioShack, but greater than the industry ratio of 0.99. Consistent with our inferences from the debt ratio, Best Buy's capital structure has more debt than equity, which increases risk. Recall that debt must be repaid with interest, while equity does not. These debt requirements can be burdensome when the industry and/or the economy experience a downturn. A larger debt-to-equity ratio also implies less opportunity to expand through use of debt financing.

Times Interest Earned The amount of income before deductions for interest expense and income taxes is the amount available to pay interest expense. The following

Point: The times interest earned ratio and the debt and equity ratios are of special interest to bank lending officers.

times interest earned ratio reflects the creditors' risk of loan repayments with interest (see Chapter 11 for additional explanation).

$$\textbf{Times interest earned} = \frac{\textbf{Income before interest expense and income taxes}}{\textbf{Interest expense}}$$

The larger this ratio, the less risky is the company for creditors. One guideline says that creditors are reasonably safe if the company earns its fixed interest expense two or more times each year. Best Buy's times interest earned ratio follows; its value suggests that its creditors have little risk of nonrepayment.

Times interest earned
Circuit City = 12.5
RadioShack = 3.5

$$\frac{\$1{,}377 + \$31 \text{ (see Best Buy note \#7)} + \$752}{\$31} = 69.7$$

Decision Insight

Bears and Bulls A *bear market* is a declining market. The phrase comes from bear-skin jobbers who often sold the skins before the bears were caught. The term *bear* was then used to describe investors who sold shares they did not own in anticipation of a price decline. A *bull market* is a rising market. This phrase comes from the once popular sport of bear and bull baiting. The term *bull* came to mean the opposite of *bear.*

Profitability

We are especially interested in a company's ability to use its assets efficiently to produce profits (and positive cash flows). *Profitability* refers to a company's ability to generate an adequate return on invested capital. Return is judged by assessing earnings relative to the level and sources of financing. Profitability is also relevant to solvency. This section describes key profitability measures and their importance to financial statement analysis.

Profit Margin A company's operating efficiency and profitability can be expressed by two components. The first is *profit margin,* which reflects a company's ability to earn net income from sales (Chapter 3 offers additional explanation). It is measured by expressing net income as a percent of sales (*sales* and *revenues* are similar terms). **Best Buy**'s profit margin follows.

Profit margin
Circuit City = −0.1%
RadioShack = 1.5%

$$\textbf{Profit margin} = \frac{\textbf{Net income}}{\textbf{Net sales}} = \frac{\$1{,}377}{\$35{,}934} = 3.8\%$$

To evaluate profit margin, we must consider the industry. For instance, an appliance company might require a profit margin between 10% and 15%; whereas a retail supermarket might require a profit margin of 1% or 2%. Both profit margin and *total asset turnover* make up the two basic components of operating efficiency. These ratios reflect on management because managers are ultimately responsible for operating efficiency. The next section explains how we use both measures to analyze return on total assets.

Return on Total Assets *Return on total assets* is defined as follows.

$$\textbf{Return on total assets} = \frac{\textbf{Net income}}{\textbf{Average total assets}}$$

Best Buy's 2007 return on total assets is

Return on total assets
Circuit City = −0.2%
RadioShack = 3.4%
Industry = 3.0

$$\frac{\$1{,}377}{(\$13{,}570 + \$11{,}864)/2} = 10.8\%$$

Best Buy's 10.8% return on total assets is lower than that for many businesses but is higher than RadioShack's return of 3.4% and the industry's 3.0% return. We also should evaluate any trend in the rate of return.

Point: Many analysts add back *Interest expense* × *(1 − Tax rate)* to net income in computing return on total assets.

The following equation shows the important relation between profit margin, total asset turnover, and return on total assets.

$$\textbf{Profit margin} \times \textbf{Total asset turnover} = \textbf{Return on total assets}$$

or

$$\frac{\textbf{Net income}}{\textbf{Net sales}} \times \frac{\textbf{Net sales}}{\textbf{Average total assets}} = \frac{\textbf{Net income}}{\textbf{Average total assets}}$$

Both profit margin and total asset turnover contribute to overall operating efficiency, as measured by return on total assets. If we apply this formula to Best Buy, we get

$$3.8\% \times 2.83 = 10.8\%$$

Circuit City: $-0.1\% \times 3.08 = -0.2\%$
RadioShack: $1.5\% \times 2.24 = 3.4\%$ **(with rounding)**

This analysis shows that Best Buy's superior return on assets versus that of Circuit City and RadioShack is driven mainly by its higher profit margin.

Return on Common Stockholders' Equity Perhaps the most important goal in operating a company is to earn net income for its owner(s). *Return on common stockholders' equity* measures a company's success in reaching this goal and is defined as follows.

$$\textbf{Return on common stockholders' equity} = \frac{\textbf{Net income} - \textbf{Preferred dividends}}{\textbf{Average common stockholders' equity}}$$

Best Buy's 2007 return on common stockholders' equity is computed as follows:

$$\frac{\$1{,}377 - \$0}{(\$6{,}236 + \$5{,}257)/2} = 24.0\%$$

Return on common equity
Circuit City = −0.4%
RadioShack = 11.8%

The denominator in this computation is the book value of common equity (including minority interest). In the numerator, the dividends on cumulative preferred stock are subtracted whether they are declared or are in arrears. If preferred stock is noncumulative, its dividends are subtracted only if declared.

Decision Insight

Wall Street *Wall Street* is synonymous with financial markets, but its name comes from the street location of the original New York Stock Exchange. The street's name derives from stockades built by early settlers to protect New York from pirate attacks.

Market Prospects

Market measures are useful for analyzing corporations with publicly traded stock. These market measures use stock price, which reflects the market's (public's) expectations for the company. This includes expectations of both company return and risk—as the market perceives it.

Price-Earnings Ratio Computation of the *price-earnings ratio* follows (Chapter 13 provides additional explanation).

$$\textbf{Price-earnings ratio} = \frac{\textbf{Market price per common share}}{\textbf{Earnings per share}}$$

Point: PE ratio can be viewed as an indicator of the market's expected growth and risk for a stock. High expected risk suggests a low PE ratio. High expected growth suggests a high PE ratio.

Predicted earnings per share for the next period is often used in the denominator of this computation. Reported earnings per share for the most recent period is also commonly used. In both cases, the ratio is used as an indicator of the future growth and risk of a company's earnings as perceived by the stock's buyers and sellers.

The market price of Best Buy's common stock at the start of fiscal year 2008 was $46.35. Using Best Buy's $2.86 basic earnings per share, we compute its price-earnings ratio as follows (some analysts compute this ratio using the median of the low and high stock price).

PE (year-end)
Circuit City = −380.0
RadioShack = 31.1

$$\frac{\$46.35}{\$2.86} = 16.2$$

Point: Some investors avoid stocks with high PE ratios under the belief they are "overpriced." Alternatively, some investors *sell these stocks short*—hoping for price declines.

Best Buy's price-earnings ratio is less than that for RadioShack, but is slightly higher than the norm. (Circuit City's ratio is negative due to its abnormally low earnings.) Best Buy's middle-of-the-pack ratio likely reflects investors' expectations of continued growth but normal earnings.

Dividend Yield *Dividend yield* is used to compare the dividend-paying performance of different investment alternatives. We compute dividend yield as follows (Chapter 13 offers additional explanation).

$$\textbf{Dividend yield} = \frac{\textbf{Annual cash dividends per share}}{\textbf{Market price per share}}$$

Best Buy's dividend yield, based on its fiscal year-end market price per share of $46.35 and its policy of $0.36 cash dividends per share, is computed as follows.

Dividend yield
Circuit City = 0.6%
RadioShack = 1.5%

$$\frac{\$0.36}{\$46.35} = 0.8\%$$

Some companies do not declare and pay dividends because they wish to reinvest the cash.

Point: Corporate PE ratios and dividend yields are found in daily stock market quotations listed in *The Wall Street Journal, Investor's Business Daily,* or other publications and Web services.

Summary of Ratios

Exhibit 17.16 summarizes the major financial statement analysis ratios illustrated in this chapter and throughout the book. This summary includes each ratio's title, its formula, and the purpose for which it is commonly used.

Decision Insight

Ticker Prices *Ticker prices* refer to a band of moving data on a monitor carrying up-to-the-minute stock prices. The phrase comes from *ticker tape,* a 1-inch-wide strip of paper spewing stock prices from a printer that ticked as it ran. Most of today's investors have never seen actual ticker tape, but the phrase survives.

Quick Check

Answers—p. 706

10. Which ratio best reflects a company's ability to meet immediate interest payments? (*a*) Debt ratio. (*b*) Equity ratio. (*c*) Times interest earned.
11. Which ratio best measures a company's success in earning net income for its owner(s)? (*a*) Profit margin. (*b*) Return on common stockholders' equity. (*c*) Price-earnings ratio. (*d*) Dividend yield.
12. If a company has net sales of $8,500,000, net income of $945,000, and total asset turnover of 1.8 times, what is its return on total assets?

EXHIBIT 17.16

Financial Statement Analysis Ratios*

Ratio	Formula	Measure of
Liquidity and Efficiency		
Current ratio	$= \frac{\text{Current assets}}{\text{Current liabilities}}$	Short-term debt-paying ability
Acid-test ratio	$= \frac{\text{Cash + Short-term investments + Current receivables}}{\text{Current liabilities}}$	Immediate short-term debt-paying ability
Accounts receivable turnover	$= \frac{\text{Net sales}}{\text{Average accounts receivable, net}}$	Efficiency of collection
Inventory turnover	$= \frac{\text{Cost of goods sold}}{\text{Average inventory}}$	Efficiency of inventory management
Days' sales uncollected	$= \frac{\text{Accounts receivable, net}}{\text{Net sales}} \times 365$	Liquidity of receivables
Days' sales in inventory	$= \frac{\text{Ending inventory}}{\text{Cost of goods sold}} \times 365$	Liquidity of inventory
Total asset turnover	$= \frac{\text{Net sales}}{\text{Average total assets}}$	Efficiency of assets in producing sales
Solvency		
Debt ratio	$= \frac{\text{Total liabilities}}{\text{Total assets}}$	Creditor financing and leverage
Equity ratio	$= \frac{\text{Total equity}}{\text{Total assets}}$	Owner financing
Debt-to-equity ratio	$= \frac{\text{Total liabilities}}{\text{Total equity}}$	Debt versus equity financing
Times interest earned	$= \frac{\text{Income before interest expense and income taxes}}{\text{Interest expense}}$	Protection in meeting interest payments
Profitability		
Profit margin ratio	$= \frac{\text{Net income}}{\text{Net sales}}$	Net income in each sales dollar
Gross margin ratio	$= \frac{\text{Net sales} - \text{Cost of goods sold}}{\text{Net sales}}$	Gross margin in each sales dollar
Return on total assets	$= \frac{\text{Net income}}{\text{Average total assets}}$	Overall profitability of assets
Return on common stockholders' equity	$= \frac{\text{Net income} - \text{Preferred dividends}}{\text{Average common stockholders' equity}}$	Profitability of owner investment
Book value per common share	$= \frac{\text{Shareholders' equity applicable to common shares}}{\text{Number of common shares outstanding}}$	Liquidation at reported amounts
Basic earnings per share	$= \frac{\text{Net income} - \text{Preferred dividends}}{\text{Weighted-average common shares outstanding}}$	Net income per common share
Market Prospects		
Price-earnings ratio	$= \frac{\text{Market price per common share}}{\text{Earnings per share}}$	Market value relative to earnings
Dividend yield	$= \frac{\text{Annual cash dividends per share}}{\text{Market price per share}}$	Cash return per common share

* Additional ratios also examined in previous chapters included credit risk ratio; plant asset useful life; plant asset age; days' cash expense coverage; cash coverage of growth; cash coverage of debt; free cash flow; cash flow on total assets; and payout ratio.

Decision Analysis

Analysis Reporting

A1 Summarize and report results of analysis.

Understanding the purpose of financial statement analysis is crucial to the usefulness of any analysis. This understanding leads to efficiency of effort, effectiveness in application, and relevance in focus. The purpose of most financial statement analyses is to reduce uncertainty in business decisions through a rigorous and sound evaluation. A *financial statement analysis report* helps by directly addressing the building blocks of analysis and by identifying weaknesses in inference by requiring explanation: It forces us to organize our reasoning and to verify its flow and logic. A report also serves as a communication link with readers, and the writing process reinforces our judgments and vice versa. Finally, the report helps us (re)evaluate evidence and refine conclusions on key building blocks. A good analysis report usually consists of six sections:

1. **Executive summary**—brief focus on important analysis results and conclusions.
2. **Analysis overview**—background on the company, its industry, and its economic setting.
3. **Evidential matter**—financial statements and information used in the analysis, including ratios, trends, comparisons, statistics, and all analytical measures assembled; often organized under the building blocks of analysis.
4. **Assumptions**—identification of important assumptions regarding a company's industry and economic environment, and other important assumptions for estimates.
5. **Key factors**—list of important favorable and unfavorable factors, both quantitative and qualitative, for company performance; usually organized by areas of analysis.
6. **Inferences**—forecasts, estimates, interpretations, and conclusions drawing on all sections of the report.

We must remember that the user dictates relevance, meaning that the analysis report should include a brief table of contents to help readers focus on those areas most relevant to their decisions. All irrelevant matter must be eliminated. For example, decades-old details of obscure transactions and detailed miscues of the analysis are irrelevant. Ambiguities and qualifications to avoid responsibility or hedging inferences must be eliminated. Finally, writing is important. Mistakes in grammar and errors of fact compromise the report's credibility.

Decision Insight

Short Selling *Short selling* refers to selling stock before you buy it. Here's an example: You borrow 100 shares of Nike stock, sell them at $40 each, and receive money from their sale. You then wait. You hope that Nike's stock price falls to, say, $35 each and you can replace the borrowed stock for less than you sold it for, reaping a profit of $5 each less any transaction costs.

Demonstration Problem

DP17

Use the following financial statements of Precision Co. to complete these requirements.

1. Prepare comparative income statements showing the percent increase or decrease for year 2009 in comparison to year 2008.
2. Prepare common-size comparative balance sheets for years 2009 and 2008.
3. Compute the following ratios as of December 31, 2009, or for the year ended December 31, 2009, and identify its building block category for financial statement analysis.
   a. Current ratio
   b. Acid-test ratio
   c. Accounts receivable turnover
   d. Days' sales uncollected
   e. Inventory turnover
   f. Debt ratio
   g. Debt-to-equity ratio
   h. Times interest earned
   i. Profit margin ratio
   j. Total asset turnover
   k. Return on total assets
   l. Return on common stockholders' equity

PRECISION COMPANY Comparative Balance Sheets December 31, 2009 and 2008	2009	2008
Assets		
Current assets		
Cash	$ 79,000	$ 42,000
Short-term investments	65,000	96,000
Accounts receivable, net	120,000	100,000
Merchandise inventory	250,000	265,000
Total current assets	514,000	503,000
Plant assets		
Store equipment, net	400,000	350,000
Office equipment, net	45,000	50,000
Buildings, net	625,000	675,000
Land	100,000	100,000
Total plant assets	1,170,000	1,175,000
Total assets	$1,684,000	$1,678,000
Liabilities		
Current liabilities		
Accounts payable	$ 164,000	$ 190,000
Short-term notes payable	75,000	90,000
Taxes payable	26,000	12,000
Total current liabilities	265,000	292,000
Long-term liabilities		
Notes payable (secured by mortgage on buildings)	400,000	420,000
Total liabilities	665,000	712,000
Stockholders' Equity		
Common stock, $5 par value	475,000	475,000
Retained earnings	544,000	491,000
Total stockholders' equity	1,019,000	966,000
Total liabilities and equity	$1,684,000	$1,678,000

PRECISION COMPANY Comparative Income Statements For Years Ended December 31, 2009 and 2008	2009	2008
Sales	$2,486,000	$2,075,000
Cost of goods sold	1,523,000	1,222,000
Gross profit	963,000	853,000
Operating expenses		
Advertising expense	145,000	100,000
Sales salaries expense	240,000	280,000
Office salaries expense	165,000	200,000
Insurance expense	100,000	45,000
Supplies expense	26,000	35,000
Depreciation expense	85,000	75,000
Miscellaneous expenses	17,000	15,000
Total operating expenses	778,000	750,000
Operating income	185,000	103,000
Interest expense	44,000	46,000
Income before taxes	141,000	57,000
Income taxes	47,000	19,000
Net income	$ 94,000	$ 38,000
Earnings per share	$ 0.99	$ 0.40

Planning the Solution

- Set up a four-column income statement; enter the 2009 and 2008 amounts in the first two columns and then enter the dollar change in the third column and the percent change from 2008 in the fourth column.
- Set up a four-column balance sheet; enter the 2009 and 2008 year-end amounts in the first two columns and then compute and enter the amount of each item as a percent of total assets.
- Compute the required ratios using the data provided. Use the average of beginning and ending amounts when appropriate (see Exhibit 17.16 for definitions).

Solution to Demonstration Problem

1.

PRECISION COMPANY Comparative Income Statements For Years Ended December 31, 2009 and 2008			Increase (Decrease) in 2009	
	2009	2008	Amount	Percent
Sales	$2,486,000	$2,075,000	$411,000	19.8%
Cost of goods sold	1,523,000	1,222,000	301,000	24.6
Gross profit	963,000	853,000	110,000	12.9
Operating expenses				
Advertising expense	145,000	100,000	45,000	45.0
Sales salaries expense	240,000	280,000	(40,000)	(14.3)
Office salaries expense	165,000	200,000	(35,000)	(17.5)

[continued on next page]

[continued from previous page]

Insurance expense	100,000	45,000	55,000	122.2
Supplies expense	26,000	35,000	(9,000)	(25.7)
Depreciation expense	85,000	75,000	10,000	13.3
Miscellaneous expenses	17,000	15,000	2,000	13.3
Total operating expenses	778,000	750,000	28,000	3.7
Operating income	185,000	103,000	82,000	79.6
Interest expense	44,000	46,000	(2,000)	(4.3)
Income before taxes	141,000	57,000	84,000	147.4
Income taxes	47,000	19,000	28,000	147.4
Net income	$ 94,000	$ 38,000	$ 56,000	147.4
Earnings per share	$ 0.99	$ 0.40	$ 0.59	147.5

2.

PRECISION COMPANY
Common-Size Comparative Balance Sheets
December 31, 2009 and 2008

	December 31		Common-Size Percents	
	2009	2008	2009*	2008*
Assets				
Current assets				
Cash	$ 79,000	$ 42,000	4.7%	2.5%
Short-term investments	65,000	96,000	3.9	5.7
Accounts receivable, net	120,000	100,000	7.1	6.0
Merchandise inventory	250,000	265,000	14.8	15.8
Total current assets	514,000	503,000	30.5	30.0
Plant Assets				
Store equipment, net	400,000	350,000	23.8	20.9
Office equipment, net	45,000	50,000	2.7	3.0
Buildings, net	625,000	675,000	37.1	40.2
Land	100,000	100,000	5.9	6.0
Total plant assets	1,170,000	1,175,000	69.5	70.0
Total assets	$1,684,000	$1,678,000	100.0	100.0
Liabilities				
Current liabilities				
Accounts payable	$ 164,000	$ 190,000	9.7%	11.3%
Short-term notes payable	75,000	90,000	4.5	5.4
Taxes payable	26,000	12,000	1.5	0.7
Total current liabilities	265,000	292,000	15.7	17.4
Long-term liabilities				
Notes payable (secured by mortgage on buildings)	400,000	420,000	23.8	25.0
Total liabilities	665,000	712,000	39.5	42.4
Stockholders' Equity				
Common stock, $5 par value	475,000	475,000	28.2	28.3
Retained earnings	544,000	491,000	32.3	29.3
Total stockholders' equity	1,019,000	966,000	60.5	57.6
Total liabilities and equity	$1,684,000	$1,678,000	100.0	100.0

* Columns do not always exactly add to 100 due to rounding.

3. Ratios for 2009:

a. Current ratio: $514,000/$265,000 = 1.9:1 (liquidity and efficiency)

b. Acid-test ratio: ($79,000 + $65,000 + $120,000)/$265,000 = 1.0:1 (liquidity and efficiency)

c. Average receivables: ($120,000 + $100,000)/2 = $110,000
Accounts receivable turnover: $2,486,000/$110,000 = 22.6 times (liquidity and efficiency)

d. Days' sales uncollected: ($120,000/$2,486,000) × 365 = 17.6 days (liquidity and efficiency)

e. Average inventory: ($250,000 + $265,000)/2 = $257,500
Inventory turnover: $1,523,000/$257,500 = 5.9 times (liquidity and efficiency)

f. Debt ratio: $665,000/$1,684,000 = 39.5% (solvency)

g. Debt-to-equity ratio: $665,000/$1,019,000 = 0.65 (solvency)

h. Times interest earned: $185,000/$44,000 = 4.2 times (solvency)

i. Profit margin ratio: $94,000/$2,486,000 = 3.8% (profitability)

j. Average total assets: ($1,684,000 + $1,678,000)/2 = $1,681,000
Total asset turnover: $2,486,000/$1,681,000 = 1.48 times (liquidity and efficiency)

k. Return on total assets: $94,000/$1,681,000 = 5.6% or 3.8% × 1.48 = 5.6% (profitability)

l. Average total common equity: ($1,019,000 + $966,000)/2 = $992,500
Return on common stockholders' equity: $94,000/$992,500 = 9.5% (profitability)

APPENDIX

17A

Sustainable Income

A2 Explain the form and assess the content of a complete income statement.

When a company's revenue and expense transactions are from normal, continuing operations, a simple income statement is usually adequate. When a company's activities include income-related events not part of its normal, continuing operations, it must disclose information to help users understand these events and predict future performance. To meet these objectives, companies separate the income statement into continuing operations, discontinued segments, extraordinary items, comprehensive income, and earnings per share. For illustration, Exhibit 17A.1 shows such an income statement for ComUS. These separate distinctions help us measure *sustainable income,* which is the income level most likely to continue into the future. Sustainable income is commonly used in PE ratios and other market-based measures of performance.

Continuing Operations

The first major section (①) shows the revenues, expenses, and income from continuing operations. Users especially rely on this information to predict future operations. Many users view this section as the most important. Earlier chapters explained the items comprising income from continuing operations.

Discontinued Segments

A **business segment** is a part of a company's operations that serves a particular line of business or class of customers. A segment has assets, liabilities, and financial results of operations that can be distinguished from those of other parts of the company. A company's gain or loss from selling or closing down a segment is separately reported. Section ② of Exhibit 17A.1 reports both (1) income from operating the discontinued segment for the current period prior to its disposal and (2) the loss from disposing of the segment's net assets. The income tax effects of each are reported separately from the income taxes expense in section ①.

Extraordinary Items

Section ③ reports **extraordinary gains and losses,** which are those that are *both unusual* and *infrequent.* An **unusual gain or loss** is abnormal or otherwise unrelated to the company's regular activities and environment. An **infrequent gain or loss** is not expected to recur given the company's operating environment. Reporting extraordinary items in a separate category helps users predict future performance, absent the effects of extraordinary items. Items usually considered extraordinary include (1) expropriation (taking away) of property by a foreign government, (2) condemning of property by a domestic government body, (3) prohibition against using an asset by a newly enacted law, and (4) losses and gains from an unusual and infrequent calamity ("act of God"). Items *not* considered extraordinary include (1) write-downs

EXHIBIT 17A.1

Income Statement (all-inclusive) for a Corporation

ComUS Income Statement For Year Ended December 31, 2009			
①	Net sales		$8,478,000
	Operating expenses		
	Cost of goods sold	$5,950,000	
	Depreciation expense	35,000	
	Other selling, general, and administrative expenses	515,000	
	Interest expense	20,000	
	Total operating expenses		(6,520,000)
	Other gains (losses)		
	Loss on plant relocation		(45,000)
	Gain on sale of surplus land		72,000
	Income from continuing operations before taxes		1,985,000
	Income taxes expense		(595,500)
	Income from continuing operations		1,389,500
②	**Discontinued segment**		
	Income from operating Division A (net of $180,000 taxes)	420,000	
	Loss on disposal of Division A (net of $66,000 tax benefit)	(154,000)	266,000
	Income before extraordinary items		1,655,500
③	**Extraordinary items**		
	Gain on land expropriated by state (net of $85,200 taxes)	198,800	
	Loss from earthquake damage (net of $270,000 tax benefit)	(630,000)	(431,200)
	Net income		$1,224,300
④	**Earnings per common share (200,000 outstanding shares)**		
	Income from continuing operations		$ 6.95
	Discontinued operations		1.33
	Income before extraordinary items		8.28
	Extraordinary items		(2.16)
	Net income (basic earnings per share)		$ 6.12

of inventories and write-offs of receivables, (2) gains and losses from disposing of segments, and (3) financial effects of labor strikes.

Gains and losses that are neither unusual nor infrequent are reported as part of continuing operations. Gains and losses that are *either* unusual *or* infrequent, but *not* both, are reported as part of continuing operations *but* after the normal revenues and expenses.

Decision Maker

Small Business Owner You own an orange grove near Jacksonville, Florida. A bad frost destroys about one-half of your oranges. You are currently preparing an income statement for a bank loan. Can you claim the loss of oranges as extraordinary? [Answer—p. 706]

Earnings per Share

The final section ④ of the income statement in Exhibit 17A.1 reports earnings per share for each of the three subcategories of income (continuing operations, discontinued segments, and extraordinary items) when they exist. Earnings per share is discussed in Chapter 13.

Changes in Accounting Principles

Point: Changes in principles are sometimes required when new accounting standards are issued.

The *consistency concept* directs a company to apply the same accounting principles across periods. Yet a company can change from one acceptable accounting principle (such as FIFO, LIFO, or weighted-average) to another as long as the change improves the usefulness of information in its financial statements. A footnote would describe the accounting change and why it is an improvement.

Changes in accounting principles require retrospective application to prior periods' financial statements. *Retrospective application* involves applying a different accounting principle to prior periods as if that principle had always been used. Retrospective application enhances the consistency of financial information between periods, which improves the usefulness of information, especially with comparative analyses. (Prior to 2005, the cumulative effect of changes in accounting principles was recognized in net income in the period of the change.) Accounting standards also require that *a change in depreciation, amortization, or depletion method for long-term operating assets is accounted for as a change in accounting estimate*—that is, prospectively over current and future periods. This reflects the notion that an entity should change its depreciation, amortization, or depletion method only with changes in estimated asset benefits, the pattern of benefit usage, or information about those benefits.

Comprehensive Income

Comprehensive income is net income plus certain gains and losses that bypass the income statement. These items are recorded directly to equity. Specifically, comprehensive income equals the change in equity for the period, excluding investments from and distributions (dividends) to its stockholders. For **Best Buy**, it is computed as follows ($ millions):

Net income	$1,377
Accumulated other comprehensive income (loss)	(45)
Comprehensive income	$1,332

The most common items included in *accumulated other comprehensive income,* or *AOCI,* are unrealized gains and losses on available-for-sale securities and foreign currency translation adjustments. (Detailed computations for these items are in advanced courses.) Analysts disagree on how to treat these items. Some analysts believe that AOCI items should not be considered when predicting future performance, and some others believe AOCI items should be considered as they reflect on company and managerial performance. Whatever our position, we must be familiar with what AOCI items are as they are commonly reported in financial statements. Best Buy reports its comprehensive income in its statement of shareholders' equity (see Appendix A).

Quick Check

Answers—p. 706

13. Which of the following is an extraordinary item? (*a*) a settlement paid to a customer injured while using the company's product, (*b*) a loss to a plant from damages caused by a meteorite, or (*c*) a loss from selling old equipment.

14. Identify the four major sections of an income statement that are potentially reportable.

15. A company using FIFO for the past 15 years decides to switch to LIFO. The effect of this event on prior years' net income is (*a*) reported as if the new method had always been used; (*b*) ignored because it is a change in an accounting estimate; or (*c*) reported on the current year income statement.

Summary

C1 Explain the purpose of analysis. The purpose of financial statement analysis is to help users make better business decisions. Internal users want information to improve company efficiency and effectiveness in providing products and services. External users want information to make better and more informed decisions in pursuing their goals. The common goals of all users are to evaluate a company's (1) past and current performance, (2) current financial position, and (3) future performance and risk.

C2 Identify the building blocks of analysis. Financial statement analysis focuses on four "building blocks" of analysis: (1) liquidity and efficiency—ability to meet short-term obligations and efficiently generate revenues; (2) solvency—ability to generate future revenues and meet long-term obligations; (3) profitability—ability to provide financial rewards sufficient to attract and retain financing; and (4) market prospects—ability to generate positive market expectations.

C3 Describe standards for comparisons in analysis. Standards for comparisons include (1) intracompany—prior performance and relations between financial items for the company under analysis; (2) competitor—one or more direct competitors of the company; (3) industry—industry statistics; and (4) guidelines (rules of thumb)—general standards developed from past experiences and personal judgments.

C4 Identify the tools of analysis. The three most common tools of financial statement analysis are (1) horizontal analysis—comparing a company's financial condition and performance across time; (2) vertical analysis—comparing a company's financial condition and performance to a base amount such as revenues or total assets; and (3) ratio analysis—using and quantifying key relations among financial statement items.

A1 Summarize and report results of analysis. A financial statement analysis report is often organized around the building blocks of analysis. A good report separates interpretations and conclusions of analysis from the information underlying them. An analysis report often consists of six sections: (1) executive summary, (2) analysis overview, (3) evidential matter, (4) assumptions, (5) key factors, and (6) inferences.

A2[A] Explain the form and assess the content of a complete income statement. An income statement has four *potential* sections: (1) continuing operations, (2) discontinued segments, (3) extraordinary items, and (4) earnings per share.

P1 Explain and apply methods of horizontal analysis. Horizontal analysis is a tool to evaluate changes in data across time. Two important tools of horizontal analysis are comparative statements and trend analysis. Comparative statements show amounts for two or more successive periods, often with changes disclosed in both absolute and percent terms. Trend analysis is used to reveal important changes occurring from one period to the next.

P2 Describe and apply methods of vertical analysis. Vertical analysis is a tool to evaluate each financial statement item or group of items in terms of a base amount. Two tools of vertical analysis are common-size statements and graphical analyses. Each item in common-size statements is expressed as a percent of a base amount. For the balance sheet, the base amount is usually total assets, and for the income statement, it is usually sales.

P3 Define and apply ratio analysis. Ratio analysis provides clues to and symptoms of underlying conditions. Ratios, properly interpreted, identify areas requiring further investigation. A ratio expresses a mathematical relation between two quantities such as a percent, rate, or proportion. Ratios can be organized into the building blocks of analysis: (1) liquidity and efficiency, (2) solvency, (3) profitability, and (4) market prospects.

Guidance Answers to **Decision Maker**

Auditor The *joint relation* referred to is the combined increase in sales and the decrease in expenses yielding more than a 5% increase in income. Both *individual* accounts (sales and expenses) yield percent changes within the ±5% acceptable range. However, a joint analysis suggests a different picture. For example, consider a joint analysis using the profit margin ratio. The client's profit margin is 11.46% ($206,000 − $182,400/$206,000) for the current year compared with 5.0% ($200,000 − $190,000/$200,000) for the prior year—yielding a 129% increase in profit margin! This is what concerns the partner, and it suggests expanding audit tests to verify or refute the client's figures.

Banker Your decision on the loan application is positive for at least two reasons. First, the current ratio suggests a strong ability to meet short-term obligations. Second, current assets of $160,000 and a current ratio of 4:1 imply current liabilities of $40,000 (one-fourth of current assets) and a working capital excess of $120,000. This working capital excess is 60% of the loan amount. However, if the application is for a 10-year loan, our decision is less optimistic. The current ratio and working capital suggest a good safety margin, but indications of inefficiency in operations exist. In particular, a 4:1 current ratio is more than double its key competitors' ratio. This is characteristic of inefficient asset use.

Small Business Owner The frost loss is probably not extraordinary. Jacksonville experiences enough recurring frost damage to make it difficult to argue this event is both unusual and infrequent. Still, you want to highlight the frost loss and hope the bank views this uncommon event separately from continuing operations.

Guidance Answers to **Quick Checks**

1. General-purpose financial statements are intended for a variety of users interested in a company's financial condition and performance—users without the power to require specialized financial reports to meet their specific needs.
2. General-purpose financial statements include the income statement, balance sheet, statement of stockholders' (owner's) equity, and statement of cash flows plus the notes related to these statements.
3. *a*
4. Data from one or more direct competitors are usually preferred for comparative purposes.
5. *d*
6. Percents on comparative income statements show the increase or decrease in each item from one period to the next. On common-size comparative income statements, each item is shown as a percent of net sales for that period.
7. *c*
8. (*a*) ($820,000 + $240,000 + $470,000)/($350,000 + $180,000) = 2.9 to 1.
   (*b*) ($820,000 + $240,000)/($350,000 + $180,000) = 2:1.
9. (*a*) $2,500,000/[($290,000 + $240,000)/2] = 9.43 times.
   (*b*) ($290,000/$2,500,000) × 365 = 42 days.
   (*c*) $750,000/[($530,000 + $470,000)/2] = 1.5 times.
   (*d*) ($530,000/$750,000) × 365 = 258 days.
10. *c*
11. *b*
12. $$\text{Profit margin} \times \frac{\text{Total asset}}{\text{turnover}} = \frac{\text{Return on}}{\text{total assets}}$$
    $$\frac{\$945{,}000}{\$8{,}500{,}000} \times 1.8 = 20\%$$
13. (*b*)
14. The four (potentially reportable) major sections are income from continuing operations, discontinued segments, extraordinary items, and earnings per share.
15. (*a*); known as retrospective application.

Key Terms

mhhe.com/wildFAP19e

Key Terms are available at the book's Website for learning and testing in an online Flashcard Format.

Business segment (p. 703)
Common-size financial statement (p. 687)
Comparative financial statements (p. 682)
Efficiency (p. 681)
Equity ratio (p. 695)
Extraordinary gains and losses (p. 703)
Financial reporting (p. 681)
Financial statement analysis (p. 680)
General-purpose financial statements (p. 681)
Horizontal analysis (p. 682)
Infrequent gain or loss (p. 703)
Liquidity (p. 681)
Market prospects (p. 681)
Profitability (p. 681)
Ratio analysis (p. 682)
Solvency (p. 681)
Unusual gain or loss (p. 703)
Vertical analysis (p. 682)
Working capital (p. 691)

Multiple Choice Quiz

Answers on p. 723

mhhe.com/wildFAP19e

Additional Quiz Questions are available at the book's Website.

Quiz17

1. A company's sales in 2008 were $300,000 and in 2009 were $351,000. Using 2008 as the base year, the sales trend percent for 2009 is:
a. 17%
b. 85%
c. 100%
d. 117%
e. 48%

Use the following information for questions 2 through 5.

GALLOWAY COMPANY
Balance Sheet
December 31, 2009

Assets	
Cash	$ 86,000
Accounts receivable	76,000
Merchandise inventory	122,000
Prepaid insurance	12,000
Long-term investments	98,000
Plant assets, net	436,000
Total assets	$830,000
Liabilities and Equity	
Current liabilities	$124,000
Long-term liabilities	90,000
Common stock	300,000
Retained earnings	316,000
Total liabilities and equity	$830,000

2. What is Galloway Company's current ratio?
a. 0.69
b. 1.31
c. 3.88
d. 6.69
e. 2.39

3. What is Galloway Company's acid-test ratio?
a. 2.39
b. 0.69
c. 1.31
d. 6.69
e. 3.88

4. What is Galloway Company's debt ratio?
a. 25.78%
b. 100.00%
c. 74.22%
d. 137.78%
e. 34.74%

5. What is Galloway Company's equity ratio?
a. 25.78%
b. 100.00%
c. 34.74%
d. 74.22%
e. 137.78%

Superscript letter A denotes assignments based on Appendix 17A.

Discussion Questions

1. What is the difference between comparative financial statements and common-size comparative statements?

2. Which items are usually assigned a 100% value on (*a*) a common-size balance sheet and (*b*) a common-size income statement?

3. Explain the difference between financial reporting and financial statements.

4. What three factors would influence your evaluation as to whether a company's current ratio is good or bad?

5. Suggest several reasons why a 2:1 current ratio might not be adequate for a particular company.
6. Why is working capital given special attention in the process of analyzing balance sheets?
7. What does the number of days' sales uncollected indicate?
8. What does a relatively high accounts receivable turnover indicate about a company's short-term liquidity?
9. Why is a company's capital structure, as measured by debt and equity ratios, important to financial statement analysts?
10. How does inventory turnover provide information about a company's short-term liquidity?
11. What ratios would you compute to evaluate management performance?
12. Why would a company's return on total assets be different from its return on common stockholders' equity?
13. Where on the income statement does a company report an unusual gain not expected to occur more often than once every two years or so?
14. Use **Best Buy**'s financial statements in Appendix A to compute its return on total assets for the years ended March 3, 2007, and February 25, 2006. Total assets at February 26, 2005, were $10,294 (in millions).
15. Refer to **Circuit City**'s financial statements in Appendix A to compute its equity ratio as of February 28, 2007, and February 28, 2006.
16. Refer to **RadioShack**'s financial statements in Appendix A. Compute its debt ratio as of December 31, 2006, and December 31, 2005.
17. Refer to **Apple**'s financial statements in Appendix A. Compute its profit margin for the fiscal year ended September 30, 2006.

Denotes Discussion Questions that involve decision making.

Available with McGraw-Hill's Homework Manager

QUICK STUDY

QS 17-1
Financial reporting C1

Which of the following items (1) through (9) are part of financial reporting but are *not* included as part of general-purpose financial statements? (1) stock price information and analysis, (2) statement of cash flows, (3) management discussion and analysis of financial performance, (4) income statement, (5) company news releases, (6) balance sheet, (7) financial statement notes, (8) statement of shareholders' equity, (9) prospectus.

QS 17-2
Standard of comparison C3

What are four possible standards of comparison used to analyze financial statement ratios? Which of these is generally considered to be the most useful? Which one is least likely to provide a good basis for comparison?

QS 17-3
Common-size and trend percents
P1 P2

Use the following information for Owens Corporation to determine (1) the 2008 and 2009 common-size percents for cost of goods sold using net sales as the base and (2) the 2008 and 2009 trend percents for net sales using 2008 as the base year.

($ thousands)	2009	2008
Net sales	$101,400	$58,100
Cost of goods sold	55,300	30,700

QS 17-4
Horizontal analysis
P1

Compute the annual dollar changes and percent changes for each of the following accounts.

	2009	2008
Short-term investments	$110,000	$80,000
Accounts receivable	22,000	25,000
Notes payable	30,000	0

QS 17-5
Building blocks of analysis
C2 C4 P3

Match the ratio to the building block of financial statement analysis to which it best relates.

A. Liquidity and efficiency
B. Solvency
C. Profitability
D. Market prospects

1. ______ Gross margin ratio
2. ______ Acid-test ratio
3. ______ Equity ratio
4. ______ Return on total assets
5. ______ Dividend yield
6. ______ Book value per common share
7. ______ Days' sales in inventory
8. ______ Accounts receivable turnover
9. ______ Debt-to-equity
10. ______ Times interest earned

QS 17-6
Identifying financial ratios
C4 P3

1. Which two short-term liquidity ratios measure how frequently a company collects its accounts?
2. What measure reflects the difference between current assets and current liabilities?
3. Which two ratios are key components in measuring a company's operating efficiency? Which ratio summarizes these two components?

QS 17-7
Ratio interpretation
P3

For each ratio listed, identify whether the change in ratio value from 2008 to 2009 is usually regarded as favorable or unfavorable.

Ratio	2009	2008	Ratio	2009	2008
1. Profit margin	10%	9%	5. Accounts receivable turnover	6.7	5.5
2. Debt ratio	43%	39%	6. Basic earnings per share	$1.25	$1.10
3. Gross margin	32%	44%	7. Inventory turnover	3.4	3.6
4. Acid-test ratio	1.20	1.05	8. Dividend yield	4%	3.2%

QS 17-8A
Error adjustments
A2

A review of the notes payable files discovers that three years ago the company reported the entire amount of a payment (principal and interest) on an installment note payable as interest expense. This mistake had a material effect on the amount of income in that year. How should the correction be reported in the current year financial statements?

McGraw-Hill's HOMEWORK MANAGER® Available with McGraw-Hill's Homework Manager

EXERCISES

Exercise 17-1
Computation and analysis of trend percents
P1

Compute trend percents for the following accounts, using 2007 as the base year. State whether the situation as revealed by the trends appears to be favorable or unfavorable for each account.

	2011	2010	2009	2008	2007
Sales	$282,700	$270,700	$252,500	$234,460	$150,000
Cost of goods sold	128,100	121,980	115,180	106,340	67,000
Accounts receivable	18,000	17,200	16,300	15,100	9,000

Exercise 17-2
Determination of income effects from common-size and trend percents
P1 P2

Common-size and trend percents for Danian Company's sales, cost of goods sold, and expenses follow. Determine whether net income increased, decreased, or remained unchanged in this three-year period.

	Common-Size Percents			Trend Percents		
	2010	2009	2008	2010	2009	2008
Sales	100.0%	100.0%	100.0%	104.9%	103.7%	100.0%
Cost of goods sold	67.7	61.2	58.4	102.5	108.6	100.0
Total expenses	14.4	13.9	14.2	106.5	101.5	100.0

Exercise 17-3
Common-size percent computation and interpretation
P2

Express the following comparative income statements in common-size percents and assess whether or not this company's situation has improved in the most recent year.

MULAN CORPORATION
Comparative Income Statements
For Years Ended December 31, 2009 and 2008

	2009	2008
Sales	$657,386	$488,400
Cost of goods sold	427,301	286,202
Gross profit	230,085	202,198
Operating expenses	138,051	94,750
Net income	$ 92,034	$107,448

Exercise 17-4
Analysis of short-term financial condition

A1 P3

The following information is available for Orkay Company and Lowes Company, similar firms operating in the same industry. Write a half-page report comparing Orkay and Lowes using the available information. Your discussion should include their ability to meet current obligations and to use current assets efficiently.

Team Project: Assume that the two companies apply for a one-year loan from the team. Identify additional information the companies must provide before the team can make a loan decision.

	Orkay			Lowes		
	2010	2009	2008	2010	2009	2008
Current ratio	1.6	1.7	2.0	3.1	2.6	1.8
Acid-test ratio	0.9	1.0	1.1	2.7	2.4	1.5
Accounts receivable turnover	29.5	24.2	28.2	15.4	14.2	15.0
Merchandise inventory turnover	23.2	20.9	16.1	13.5	12.0	11.6
Working capital	$60,000	$48,000	$42,000	$121,000	$93,000	$68,000

Exercise 17-5
Analysis of efficiency and financial leverage

A1 P3

Caren Company and Revlon Company are similar firms that operate in the same industry. Revlon began operations in 2009 and Caren in 2006. In 2011, both companies pay 7% interest on their debt to creditors. The following additional information is available.

	Caren Company			Revlon Company		
	2011	2010	2009	2011	2010	2009
Total asset turnover	3.0	2.7	2.9	1.6	1.4	1.1
Return on total assets	8.9%	9.5%	8.7%	5.8%	5.5%	5.2%
Profit margin ratio	2.3%	2.4%	2.2%	2.7%	2.9%	2.8%
Sales	$400,000	$370,000	$386,000	$200,000	$160,000	$100,000

Write a half-page report comparing Caren and Revlon using the available information. Your analysis should include their ability to use assets efficiently to produce profits. Also comment on their success in employing financial leverage in 2011.

Exercise 17-6
Common-size percents

P2

Nabisco Company's year-end balance sheets follow. Express the balance sheets in common-size percents. Round amounts to the nearest one-tenth of a percent. Analyze and comment on the results.

At December 31	2010	2009	2008
Assets			
Cash	$ 36,229	$ 42,780	$ 44,562
Accounts receivable, net	106,073	76,377	57,087
Merchandise inventory	137,408	98,929	62,038
Prepaid expenses	11,548	11,003	4,903
Plant assets, net	335,317	311,062	272,710
Total assets	$626,575	$540,151	$441,300
Liabilities and Equity			
Accounts payable	$157,577	$ 94,024	$ 57,087
Long-term notes payable secured by mortgages on plant assets	116,618	127,962	99,478
Common stock, $10 par value	163,500	163,500	163,500
Retained earnings	188,880	154,665	121,235
Total liabilities and equity	$626,575	$540,151	$441,300

Exercise 17-7
Liquidity analysis
P3

Refer to Nabisco Company's balance sheets in Exercise 17-6. Analyze its year-end short-term liquidity position at the end of 2010, 2009, and 2008 by computing (1) the current ratio and (2) the acid-test ratio. Comment on the ratio results. (Round ratio amounts to two decimals.)

Exercise 17-8
Liquidity analysis and interpretation
P3

Refer to the Nabisco Company information in Exercise 17-6. The company's income statements for the years ended December 31, 2010 and 2009, follow. Assume that all sales are on credit and then compute: (1) days' sales uncollected, (2) accounts receivable turnover, (3) inventory turnover, and (4) days' sales in inventory. Comment on the changes in the ratios from 2009 to 2010. (Round amounts to one decimal.)

For Year Ended December 31	2010		2009	
Sales		$685,000		$557,000
Cost of goods sold	$417,850		$356,265	
Other operating expenses	207,282		141,971	
Interest expense	8,175		8,960	
Income taxes	12,900		12,450	
Total costs and expenses		646,207		519,646
Net income		$ 38,793		$ 37,354
Earnings per share		$ 2.37		$ 2.28

Exercise 17-9
Risk and capital structure analysis
P3

Refer to the Nabisco Company information in Exercises 17-6 and 17-8. Compare the company's long-term risk and capital structure positions at the end of 2010 and 2009 by computing these ratios: (1) debt and equity ratios, (2) debt-to-equity ratio, and (3) times interest earned. Comment on these ratio results.

Exercise 17-10
Efficiency and profitability analysis P3

Refer to Nabisco Company's financial information in Exercises 17-6 and 17-8. Evaluate the company's efficiency and profitability by computing the following for 2010 and 2009: (1) profit margin ratio, (2) total asset turnover, and (3) return on total assets. Comment on these ratio results.

Exercise 17-11
Profitability analysis
P3

Refer to Nabisco Company's financial information in Exercises 17-6 and 17-8. Additional information about the company follows. To help evaluate the company's profitability, compute and interpret the following ratios for 2010 and 2009: (1) return on common stockholders' equity, (2) price-earnings ratio on December 31, and (3) dividend yield.

Common stock market price, December 31, 2010	$30.00
Common stock market price, December 31, 2009	28.00
Annual cash dividends per share in 2010	0.28
Annual cash dividends per share in 2009	0.24

Exercise 17-12[A]
Income statement categories
A2

In 2009, Simplon Merchandising, Inc., sold its interest in a chain of wholesale outlets, taking the company completely out of the wholesaling business. The company still operates its retail outlets. A listing of the major sections of an income statement follows:

A. Income (loss) from continuing operations

B. Income (loss) from operating, or gain (loss) from disposing, a discontinued segment

C. Extraordinary gain (loss)

Indicate where each of the following income-related items for this company appears on its 2009 income statement by writing the letter of the appropriate section in the blank beside each item.

Section	Item	Debit	Credit
_____	1. Net sales		$3,000,000
_____	2. Gain on state's condemnation of company property (net of tax)		330,000
_____	3. Cost of goods sold	$1,580,000	
_____	4. Income taxes expense	117,000	
_____	5. Depreciation expense	332,500	
_____	6. Gain on sale of wholesale business segment (net of tax)		875,000
_____	7. Loss from operating wholesale business segment (net of tax)	544,000	
_____	8. Salaries expense	740,000	

Exercise 17-13A
Income statement presentation
A2

Use the financial data for Simplon Merchandising, Inc., in Exercise 17-12 to prepare its income statement for calendar year 2009. (Ignore the earnings per share section.)

Available with McGraw-Hill's Homework Manager

McGraw-Hill's HOMEWORK MANAGER®

PROBLEM SET A

Problem 17-1A
Ratios, common-size statements, and trend percents
P1 P2 P3

excel
mhhe.com/wildFAP19e

Selected comparative financial statements of Astalon Company follow.

ASTALON COMPANY
Comparative Income Statements
For Years Ended December 31, 2010, 2009, and 2008

	2010	2009	2008
Sales	$526,304	$403,192	$279,800
Cost of goods sold	316,835	255,624	179,072
Gross profit	209,469	147,568	100,728
Selling expenses	74,735	55,640	36,934
Administrative expenses	47,367	35,481	23,223
Total expenses	122,102	91,121	60,157
Income before taxes	87,367	56,447	40,571
Income taxes	16,250	11,572	8,236
Net income	$ 71,117	$ 44,875	$ 32,335

ASTALON COMPANY
Comparative Balance Sheets
December 31, 2010, 2009, and 2008

	2010	2009	2008
Assets			
Current assets	$ 48,242	$ 38,514	$ 51,484
Long-term investments	0	800	3,620
Plant assets, net	92,405	97,259	58,047
Total assets	$140,647	$136,573	$113,151
Liabilities and Equity			
Current liabilities	$ 20,534	$ 20,349	$ 19,801
Common stock	69,000	69,000	51,000
Other paid-in capital	8,625	8,625	5,667
Retained earnings	42,488	38,599	36,683
Total liabilities and equity	$140,647	$136,573	$113,151

Required

1. Compute each year's current ratio. (Round ratio amounts to one decimal.)

2. Express the income statement data in common-size percents. (Round percents to two decimals.)

3. Express the balance sheet data in trend percents with 2008 as the base year. (Round percents to two decimals.)

Check (3) 2010, Total assets trend, 124.30%

Analysis Component

4. Comment on any significant relations revealed by the ratios and percents computed.

Problem 17-2A
Calculation and analysis of trend percents
A1 P1

Selected comparative financial statements of Adobe Company follow.

ADOBE COMPANY
Comparative Income Statements
For Years Ended December 31, 2010–2004

($ thousands)	2010	2009	2008	2007	2006	2005	2004
Sales	$2,431	$2,129	$1,937	$1,776	$1,657	$1,541	$1,263
Cost of goods sold	1,747	1,421	1,223	1,070	994	930	741
Gross profit	684	708	714	706	663	611	522
Operating expenses	521	407	374	276	239	236	196
Net income	$ 163	$ 301	$ 340	$ 430	$ 424	$ 375	$ 326

ADOBE COMPANY
Comparative Balance Sheets
December 31, 2010–2004

($ thousands)	2010	2009	2008	2007	2006	2005	2004
Assets							
Cash	$ 163	$ 216	$ 224	$ 229	$ 238	$ 235	$ 242
Accounts receivable, net	1,173	1,232	1,115	855	753	714	503
Merchandise inventory	4,244	3,090	2,699	2,275	2,043	1,735	1,258
Other current assets	109	98	60	108	91	93	48
Long-term investments	0	0	0	334	334	334	334
Plant assets, net	5,192	5,172	4,526	2,553	2,639	2,345	2,015
Total assets	$10,881	$9,808	$8,624	$6,354	$6,098	$5,456	$4,400
Liabilities and Equity							
Current liabilities	$ 2,734	$2,299	$1,509	$1,255	$1,089	$1,030	$ 664
Long-term liabilities	2,924	2,547	2,478	1,151	1,176	1,273	955
Common stock	1,980	1,980	1,980	1,760	1,760	1,540	1,540
Other paid-in capital	495	495	495	440	440	385	385
Retained earnings	2,748	2,487	2,162	1,748	1,633	1,228	856
Total liabilities and equity	$10,881	$9,808	$8,624	$6,354	$6,098	$5,456	$4,400

Required

1. Compute trend percents for all components of both statements using 2004 as the base year. (Round percents to one decimal.)

Check (1) 2010, Total assets trend, 247.3%

Analysis Component

2. Analyze and comment on the financial statements and trend percents from part 1.

Problem 17-3A
Transactions, working capital, and liquidity ratios
P3

eXcel
mhhe.com/wildFAP19e

Page Corporation began the month of May with $884,000 of current assets, a current ratio of 2.6:1, and an acid-test ratio of 1.5:1. During the month, it completed the following transactions (the company uses a perpetual inventory system).

May 2 Purchased $70,000 of merchandise inventory on credit.
8 Sold merchandise inventory that cost $60,000 for $130,000 cash.
10 Collected $30,000 cash on an account receivable.
15 Paid $31,000 cash to settle an account payable.

Check May 22: Current ratio, 2.23; Acid-test ratio, 1.37

May 29: Current ratio, 2.00; Working capital, $462,000

17 Wrote off a $5,000 bad debt against the Allowance for Doubtful Accounts account.
22 Declared a $1 per share cash dividend on its 67,000 shares of outstanding common stock.
26 Paid the dividend declared on May 22.
27 Borrowed $85,000 cash by giving the bank a 30-day, 10% note.
28 Borrowed $100,000 cash by signing a long-term secured note.
29 Used the $185,000 cash proceeds from the notes to buy new machinery.

Required

Prepare a table showing Page's (1) current ratio, (2) acid-test ratio, and (3) working capital, after each transaction. Round ratios to two decimals.

Problem 17-4A
Calculation of financial statement ratios
P3

excel
mhhe.com/wildFAP19e

Selected year-end financial statements of Cadet Corporation follow. (All sales were on credit; selected balance sheet amounts at December 31, 2008, were inventory, $56,900; total assets, $219,400; common stock, $85,000; and retained earnings, $52,348.)

CADET CORPORATION
Income Statement
For Year Ended December 31, 2009

Sales	$456,600
Cost of goods sold	297,450
Gross profit	159,150
Operating expenses	99,400
Interest expense	3,900
Income before taxes	55,850
Income taxes	22,499
Net income	$ 33,351

CADET CORPORATION
Balance Sheet
December 31, 2009

Assets		Liabilities and Equity	
Cash	$ 20,000	Accounts payable	$ 21,500
Short-term investments	8,200	Accrued wages payable	4,400
Accounts receivable, net	29,400	Income taxes payable	3,700
Notes receivable (trade)*	7,000	Long-term note payable, secured by mortgage on plant assets	67,400
Merchandise inventory	34,150	Common stock	85,000
Prepaid expenses	2,700	Retained earnings	66,750
Plant assets, net	147,300	Total liabilities and equity	$248,750
Total assets	$248,750		

* These are short-term notes receivable arising from customer (trade) sales.

Check Acid-test ratio, 2.2 to 1; Inventory turnover, 6.5

Required

Compute the following: (1) current ratio, (2) acid-test ratio, (3) days' sales uncollected, (4) inventory turnover, (5) days' sales in inventory, (6) debt-to-equity ratio, (7) times interest earned, (8) profit margin ratio, (9) total asset turnover, (10) return on total assets, and (11) return on common stockholders' equity.

Problem 17-5A
Comparative ratio analysis A1 P3

Summary information from the financial statements of two companies competing in the same industry follows.

	Karto Company	Bryan Company		Karto Company	Bryan Company
Data from the current year-end balance sheets			**Data from the current year's income statement**		
Assets			Sales	$790,000	$897,200
Cash	$ 19,500	$ 36,000	Cost of goods sold	588,100	634,500
Accounts receivable, net	36,400	53,400	Interest expense	7,600	19,000
Current notes receivable (trade)	9,400	7,600	Income tax expense	15,185	24,769
Merchandise inventory	84,740	134,500	Net income	$179,115	$218,931
Prepaid expenses	6,200	7,250	Basic earnings per share	$ 4.71	$ 5.58
Plant assets, net	350,000	307,400			
Total assets	$506,240	$546,150			
			Beginning-of-year balance sheet data		
Liabilities and Equity			Accounts receivable, net	$ 26,800	$ 51,200
Current liabilities	$ 63,340	$ 73,819	Current notes receivable (trade)	0	0
Long-term notes payable	82,485	99,000	Merchandise inventory	55,600	107,400
Common stock, $5 par value	190,000	196,000	Total assets	408,000	422,500
Retained earnings	170,415	177,331	Common stock, $5 par value	190,000	196,000
Total liabilities and equity	$506,240	$546,150	Retained earnings	124,300	95,600

Required

1. For both companies compute the (*a*) current ratio, (*b*) acid-test ratio, (*c*) accounts (including notes) receivable turnover, (*d*) inventory turnover, (*e*) days' sales in inventory, and (*f*) days' sales uncollected. Identify the company you consider to be the better short-term credit risk and explain why.

Check (1) Bryan: Accounts receivable turnover, 16.0; Inventory turnover, 5.2

2. For both companies compute the (*a*) profit margin ratio, (*b*) total asset turnover, (*c*) return on total assets, and (*d*) return on common stockholders' equity. Assuming that each company paid cash dividends of $3.50 per share and each company's stock can be purchased at $85 per share, compute their (*e*) price-earnings ratios and (*f*) dividend yields. Identify which company's stock you would recommend as the better investment and explain why.

(2) Karto: Profit margin, 22.7%; PE, 18.0

Problem 17-6A[A]
Income statement computations and format
A2

Selected account balances from the adjusted trial balance for Lindo Corporation as of its calendar year-end December 31, 2009, follow.

	Debit	Credit
a. Interest revenue		$ 15,000
b. Depreciation expense—Equipment	$ 35,000	
c. Loss on sale of equipment	26,850	
d. Accounts payable		45,000
e. Other operating expenses	107,400	
f. Accumulated depreciation—Equipment		72,600
g. Gain from settlement of lawsuit		45,000
h. Accumulated depreciation—Buildings		175,500
i. Loss from operating a discontinued segment (pretax)	19,250	
j. Gain on insurance recovery of tornado damage (pretax and extraordinary)		30,120
k. Net sales		999,500
l. Depreciation expense—Buildings	53,000	
m. Correction of overstatement of prior year's sales (pretax)	17,000	
n. Gain on sale of discontinued segment's assets (pretax)		35,000
o. Loss from settlement of lawsuit	24,750	
p. Income taxes expense	?	
q. Cost of goods sold	483,500	

Required

Answer each of the following questions by providing supporting computations.

1. Assume that the company's income tax rate is 30% for all items. Identify the tax effects and after-tax amounts of the four items labeled pretax.

2. What is the amount of income from continuing operations before income taxes? What is the amount of the income taxes expense? What is the amount of income from continuing operations?

3. What is the total amount of after-tax income (loss) associated with the discontinued segment?

4. What is the amount of income (loss) before the extraordinary items?

5. What is the amount of net income for the year?

Check (3) $11,025
(4) $241,325
(5) $262,409

PROBLEM SET B

Selected comparative financial statement information of Danno Corporation follows.

Problem 17-1B
Ratios, common-size statements, and trend percents
P1 P2 P3

DANNO CORPORATION
Comparative Income Statements
For Years Ended December 31, 2010, 2009, and 2008

	2010	2009	2008
Sales	$392,000	$300,304	$208,400
Cost of goods sold	235,984	190,092	133,376
Gross profit	156,016	110,212	75,024
Selling expenses	55,664	41,442	27,509
Administrative expenses	35,280	26,427	17,297
Total expenses	90,944	67,869	44,806
Income before taxes	65,072	42,343	30,218
Income taxes	12,103	8,680	6,134
Net income	$ 52,969	$ 33,663	$ 24,084

DANNO CORPORATION
Comparative Balance Sheets
December 31, 2010, 2009, and 2008

	2010	2009	2008
Assets			
Current assets	$ 53,776	$ 42,494	$ 55,118
Long-term investments	0	400	4,110
Plant assets, net	99,871	106,303	64,382
Total assets	$153,647	$149,197	$123,610
Liabilities and Equity			
Current liabilities	$ 22,432	$ 22,230	$ 21,632
Common stock	70,000	70,000	52,000
Other paid-in capital	8,750	8,750	5,778
Retained earnings	52,465	48,217	44,200
Total liabilities and equity	$153,647	$149,197	$123,610

Required

1. Compute each year's current ratio. (Round ratio amounts to one decimal.)

2. Express the income statement data in common-size percents. (Round percents to two decimals.)

3. Express the balance sheet data in trend percents with 2008 as the base year. (Round percents to two decimals.)

Check (3) 2010, Total assets trend, 124.30%

Analysis Component

4. Comment on any significant relations revealed by the ratios and percents computed.

Problem 17-2B
Calculation and analysis of trend percents
A1 P1

Selected comparative financial statements of Park Company follow.

PARK COMPANY
Comparative Income Statements
For Years Ended December 31, 2010–2004

($ thousands)	2010	2009	2008	2007	2006	2005	2004
Sales	$570	$620	$640	$690	$750	$780	$870
Cost of goods sold	286	300	304	324	350	360	390
Gross profit	284	320	336	366	400	420	480
Operating expenses	94	114	122	136	150	154	160
Net income	$190	$206	$214	$230	$250	$266	$320

PARK COMPANY
Comparative Balance Sheets
December 31, 2010–2004

($ thousands)	2010	2009	2008	2007	2006	2005	2004
Assets							
Cash	$ 54	$ 56	$ 62	$ 64	$ 70	$ 72	$ 78
Accounts receivable, net	140	146	150	154	160	164	170
Merchandise inventory	176	182	188	190	196	200	218
Other current assets	44	44	46	48	48	50	50
Long-term investments	46	40	36	120	120	120	120
Plant assets, net	520	524	530	422	430	438	464
Total assets	$980	$992	$1,012	$998	$1,024	$1,044	$1,100
Liabilities and Equity							
Current liabilities	$158	$166	$ 196	$200	$ 220	$ 270	$ 290
Long-term liabilities	102	130	152	158	204	224	270
Common stock	180	180	180	180	180	180	180
Other paid-in capital	80	80	80	80	80	80	80
Retained earnings	460	436	404	380	340	290	280
Total liabilities and equity	$980	$992	$1,012	$998	$1,024	$1,044	$1,100

Required

1. Compute trend percents for all components of both statements using 2004 as the base year. (Round percents to one decimal.)

Check (1) 2010, Total assets trend, 89.1%

Analysis Component

2. Analyze and comment on the financial statements and trend percents from part 1.

Problem 17-3B
Transactions, working capital, and liquidity ratios
P3

Menardo Corporation began the month of June with $600,000 of current assets, a current ratio of 2.5:1, and an acid-test ratio of 1.4:1. During the month, it completed the following transactions (the company uses a perpetual inventory system).

June 1 Sold merchandise inventory that cost $150,000 for $240,000 cash.
3 Collected $176,000 cash on an account receivable.
5 Purchased $300,000 of merchandise inventory on credit.
7 Borrowed $200,000 cash by giving the bank a 60-day, 8% note.
10 Borrowed $240,000 cash by signing a long-term secured note.
12 Purchased machinery for $550,000 cash.
15 Declared a $1 per share cash dividend on its 160,000 shares of outstanding common stock.
19 Wrote off a $10,000 bad debt against the Allowance for Doubtful Accounts account.
22 Paid $24,000 cash to settle an account payable.
30 Paid the dividend declared on June 15.

Check June 3: Current ratio, 2.88; Acid-test ratio, 2.40

June 30: Working capital, $(20,000); Current ratio, 0.97

Required

Prepare a table showing the company's (1) current ratio, (2) acid-test ratio, and (3) working capital after each transaction. Round ratios to two decimals.

Required

1. Compute common-sized percents for DSG using the data provided. (Round percents to one decimal.)

2. Compare the results with Best Buy, Circuit City, and RadioShack from BTN 17-2.

ANSWERS TO MULTIPLE CHOICE QUIZ

1. d; ($351,000/$300,000) × 100 = 117%

2. e; ($86,000 + $76,000 + $122,000 + $12,000)/$124,000 = 2.39

3. c; ($86,000 + $76,000)/$124,000 = 1.31

4. a; ($124,000 + $90,000)/$830,000 = 25.78%

5. d; ($300,000 + $316,000)/$830,000 = 74.22%

ENTREPRENEURIAL DECISION

A1 P1 P2 P3

BTN 17-7 Assume that David and Tom Gardner of **The Motley Fool** (Fool.com) have impressed you since you first heard of their rather improbable rise to prominence in financial circles. You learn of a staff opening at The Motley Fool and decide to apply for it. Your resume is successfully screened from the thousands received and you advance to the interview process. You learn that the interview consists of analyzing the following financial facts and answering analysis questions. (*Note:* The data are taken from a small merchandiser in outdoor recreational equipment.)

	2008	2007	2006
Sales trend percents	137.0%	125.0%	100.0%
Selling expenses to sales	9.8%	13.7%	15.3%
Sales to plant assets ratio	3.5 to 1	3.3 to 1	3.0 to 1
Current ratio	2.6 to 1	2.4 to 1	2.1 to 1
Acid-test ratio	0.8 to 1	1.1 to 1	1.2 to 1
Merchandise inventory turnover	7.5 times	8.7 times	9.9 times
Accounts receivable turnover	6.7 times	7.4 times	8.2 times
Total asset turnover	2.6 times	2.6 times	3.0 times
Return on total assets	8.8%	9.4%	11.1%
Return on equity	9.75%	11.50%	12.25%
Profit margin ratio	3.3%	3.5%	3.7%

Required

Use these data to answer each of the following questions with explanations.

1. Is it becoming easier for the company to meet its current liabilities on time and to take advantage of any available cash discounts? Explain.
2. Is the company collecting its accounts receivable more rapidly? Explain.
3. Is the company's investment in accounts receivable decreasing? Explain.
4. Is the company's investment in plant assets increasing? Explain.
5. Is the owner's investment becoming more profitable? Explain.
6. Did the dollar amount of selling expenses decrease during the three-year period? Explain.

HITTING THE ROAD

C1 P3

BTN 17-8 You are to devise an investment strategy to enable you to accumulate $1,000,000 by age 65. Start by making some assumptions about your salary. Next compute the percent of your salary that you will be able to save each year. If you will receive any lump-sum monies, include those amounts in your calculations. Historically, stocks have delivered average annual returns of 10–11%. Given this history, you should probably not assume that you will earn above 10% on the money you invest. It is not necessary to specify exactly what types of assets you will buy for your investments; just assume a rate you expect to earn. Use the future value tables in Appendix B to calculate how your savings will grow. Experiment a bit with your figures to see how much less you have to save if you start at, for example, age 25 versus age 35 or 40. (For this assignment, do not include inflation in your calculations.)

GLOBAL DECISION

A1

BTN 17-9 **DSG international plc** (www.DSGiplc.com), **Best Buy**, **Circuit City**, and **RadioShack** are competitors in the global marketplace. Key figures for DSG follow (in millions).

Cash and equivalents	£ 441
Accounts receivable, net	393
Inventories	1,031
Retained earnings	1,490
Cost of sales	7,285
Revenues	7,930
Total assets	3,977

After the meeting, the company's CEO holds a press conference with analysts in which she mentions the following ratios.

	2009	2008	2007
Sales trend percent	147.0%	135.0%	100.0%
Selling expenses to sales	10.1%	14.0%	15.6%
Sales to plant assets ratio	3.8 to 1	3.6 to 1	3.3 to 1
Current ratio	2.9 to 1	2.7 to 1	2.4 to 1

Required

1. Why do you think the CEO decided to report 4 ratios instead of the 11 prepared?

2. Comment on the possible consequences of the CEO's reporting of the ratios selected.

COMMUNICATING IN PRACTICE

C2 A1 P3

BTN 17-4 Each team is to select a different industry, and each team member is to select a different company in that industry and acquire its financial statements. Use those statements to analyze the company, including at least one ratio from each of the four building blocks of analysis. When necessary, use the financial press to determine the market price of its stock. Communicate with teammates via a meeting, e-mail, or telephone to discuss how different companies compare to each other and to industry norms. The team is to prepare a single one-page memorandum reporting on its analysis and the conclusions reached.

TAKING IT TO THE NET

C4 P3

BTN 17-5 Access the February 23, 2007, filing of the 2006 10-K report of the **Hershey Foods Corporation** (ticker HSY) at www.SEC.gov and complete the following requirements.

Required

Compute or identify the following profitability ratios of Hershey for its years ending December 31, 2006, *and* December 31, 2005. Interpret its profitability using the results obtained for these two years.

1. Profit margin ratio.

2. Gross profit ratio.

3. Return on total assets. (Total assets in 2004 were $3,794,750,000.)

4. Return on common stockholders' equity. (Total shareholders' equity in 2004 was $1,137,103,000.)

5. Basic earnings per common share.

TEAMWORK IN ACTION

C2 P1 P2 P3

BTN 17-6 A team approach to learning financial statement analysis is often useful.

Required

1. Each team should write a description of horizontal and vertical analysis that all team members agree with and understand. Illustrate each description with an example.

2. *Each* member of the team is to select *one* of the following categories of ratio analysis. Explain what the ratios in that category measure. Choose one ratio from the category selected, present its formula, and explain what it measures.

   a. Liquidity and efficiency **c.** Profitability

   b. Solvency **d.** Market prospects

3. Each team member is to present his or her notes from part 2 to teammates. Team members are to confirm or correct other teammates' presentation.

Hint: Pairing within teams may be necessary for part 2. Use as an in-class activity or as an assignment. Consider presentations to the entire class using team rotation with transparencies.

Required

1. Compute the gross margin ratio (both with and without services revenue) and net profit margin ratio.
2. Compute the current ratio and acid-test ratio.
3. Compute the debt ratio and equity ratio.
4. What percent of its assets are current? What percent are long term?

BEYOND THE NUMBERS

REPORTING IN ACTION

A1 P1 P2

BTN 17-1 Refer to **Best Buy**'s financial statements in Appendix A to answer the following.

1. Using fiscal 2005 as the base year, compute trend percents for fiscal years 2005, 2006, and 2007 for revenues, cost of sales, selling general and administrative expenses, income taxes, and net income. (Round to the nearest whole percent.)
2. Compute common-size percents for fiscal years 2007 and 2006 for the following categories of assets: (*a*) total current assets, (*b*) property and equipment, net, and (*c*) intangible assets. (Round to the nearest tenth of a percent.)
3. Comment on any significant changes across the years for the income statement trends computed in part 1 and the balance sheet percents computed in part 2.

Fast Forward

4. Access Best Buy's financial statements for fiscal years ending after March 3, 2007, from Best Buy's Website (**BestBuy.com**) or the SEC database (**www.SEC.gov**). Update your work for parts 1, 2, and 3 using the new information accessed.

COMPARATIVE ANALYSIS

C3 P2

BTN 17-2 Key figures for **Best Buy**, **Circuit City**, and **RadioShack** follow.

($ millions)	Best Buy	Circuit City	RadioShack
Cash and equivalents	$ 1,205	$ 141	$ 472
Accounts receivable, net	548	383	248
Inventories	4,028	1,637	752
Retained earnings	5,507	1,336	1,781
Cost of sales	27,165	9,501	2,544
Revenues	35,934	12,430	4,778
Total assets	13,570	4,007	2,070

Required

1. Compute common-size percents for each of the companies using the data provided. (Round percents to one decimal.)
2. Which company retains a higher portion of cumulative net income in the company?
3. Which company has a higher gross margin ratio on sales?
4. Which company holds a higher percent of its total assets as inventory?

ETHICS CHALLENGE

A1

BTN 17-3 As Beacon Company controller, you are responsible for informing the board of directors about its financial activities. At the board meeting, you present the following information.

	2009	2008	2007
Sales trend percent	147.0%	135.0%	100.0%
Selling expenses to sales	10.1%	14.0%	15.6%
Sales to plant assets ratio	3.8 to 1	3.6 to 1	3.3 to 1
Current ratio	2.9 to 1	2.7 to 1	2.4 to 1
Acid-test ratio	1.1 to 1	1.4 to 1	1.5 to 1
Inventory turnover	7.8 times	9.0 times	10.2 times
Accounts receivable turnover	7.0 times	7.7 times	8.5 times
Total asset turnover	2.9 times	2.9 times	3.3 times
Return on total assets	10.4%	11.0%	13.2%
Return on stockholders' equity	10.7%	11.5%	14.1%
Profit margin ratio	3.6%	3.8%	4.0%

Required

1. For both companies compute the (*a*) current ratio, (*b*) acid-test ratio, (*c*) accounts (including notes) receivable turnover, (*d*) inventory turnover, (*e*) days' sales in inventory, and (*f*) days' sales uncollected. Identify the company you consider to be the better short-term credit risk and explain why.

2. For both companies compute the (*a*) profit margin ratio, (*b*) total asset turnover, (*c*) return on total assets, and (*d*) return on common stockholders' equity. Assuming that each company paid cash dividends of $1.10 per share and each company's stock can be purchased at $25 per share, compute their (*e*) price-earnings ratios and (*f*) dividend yields. Identify which company's stock you would recommend as the better investment and explain why.

Check (1) Crisco: Accounts receivable turnover, 4.8; Inventory turnover, 3.0

(2) Silas: Profit margin, 9.4%; PE, 13.6

Problem 17-6B[A]
Income statement computations and format
A2

Selected account balances from the adjusted trial balance for Harton Corp. as of its calendar year-end December 31, 2009, follow.

	Debit	Credit
a. Accumulated depreciation—Buildings		$ 410,000
b. Interest revenue		30,000
c. Net sales		2,650,000
d. Income taxes expense	$?	
e. Loss on hurricane damage (pretax and extraordinary)	74,000	
f. Accumulated depreciation—Equipment		230,000
g. Other operating expenses	338,000	
h. Depreciation expense—Equipment	110,000	
i. Loss from settlement of lawsuit	46,000	
j. Gain from settlement of lawsuit		78,000
k. Loss on sale of equipment	34,000	
l. Loss from operating a discontinued segment (pretax)	130,000	
m. Depreciation expense—Buildings	166,000	
n. Correction of overstatement of prior year's expense (pretax)		58,000
o. Cost of goods sold	1,050,000	
p. Loss on sale of discontinued segment's assets (pretax)	190,000	
q. Accounts payable		142,000

Required

Answer each of the following questions by providing supporting computations.

1. Assume that the company's income tax rate is 25% for all items. Identify the tax effects and after-tax amounts of the four items labeled pretax.

2. What is the amount of income from continuing operations before income taxes? What is the amount of income taxes expense? What is the amount of income from continuing operations?

3. What is the total amount of after-tax income (loss) associated with the discontinued segment?

4. What is the amount of income (loss) before the extraordinary items?

5. What is the amount of net income for the year?

Check (3) $(240,000)
(4) $520,500
(5) $465,000

SERIAL PROBLEM

Success Systems

(This serial problem began in Chapter 1 and continues through most of the book. If previous chapter segments were not completed, the serial problem can begin at this point. It is helpful, but not necessary, to use the Working Papers that accompany the book.)

SP 17 Use the following selected data from Success Systems' income statement for the three months ended March 31, 2010, and from its March 31, 2010, balance sheet to complete the requirements below: computer services revenue, $25,160; net sales (of goods), $18,693; total sales and revenue, $43,853; cost of goods sold, $14,052; net income, $18,686; quick assets, $100,205; current assets, $105,209; total assets, $129,909; current liabilities, $875; total liabilities, $875; and total equity, $129,034.

Problem 17-2B
Calculation and analysis of trend percents
A1 P1

Selected comparative financial statements of Park Company follow.

PARK COMPANY
Comparative Income Statements
For Years Ended December 31, 2010–2004

($ thousands)	2010	2009	2008	2007	2006	2005	2004
Sales	$570	$620	$640	$690	$750	$780	$870
Cost of goods sold	286	300	304	324	350	360	390
Gross profit	284	320	336	366	400	420	480
Operating expenses	94	114	122	136	150	154	160
Net income	$190	$206	$214	$230	$250	$266	$320

PARK COMPANY
Comparative Balance Sheets
December 31, 2010–2004

($ thousands)	2010	2009	2008	2007	2006	2005	2004
Assets							
Cash	$ 54	$ 56	$ 62	$ 64	$ 70	$ 72	$ 78
Accounts receivable, net	140	146	150	154	160	164	170
Merchandise inventory	176	182	188	190	196	200	218
Other current assets	44	44	46	48	48	50	50
Long-term investments	46	40	36	120	120	120	120
Plant assets, net	520	524	530	422	430	438	464
Total assets	$980	$992	$1,012	$998	$1,024	$1,044	$1,100
Liabilities and Equity							
Current liabilities	$158	$166	$ 196	$200	$ 220	$ 270	$ 290
Long-term liabilities	102	130	152	158	204	224	270
Common stock	180	180	180	180	180	180	180
Other paid-in capital	80	80	80	80	80	80	80
Retained earnings	460	436	404	380	340	290	280
Total liabilities and equity	$980	$992	$1,012	$998	$1,024	$1,044	$1,100

Required

1. Compute trend percents for all components of both statements using 2004 as the base year. (Round percents to one decimal.)

Check (1) 2010, Total assets trend, 89.1%

Analysis Component

2. Analyze and comment on the financial statements and trend percents from part 1.

Problem 17-3B
Transactions, working capital, and liquidity ratios
P3

Check June 3: Current ratio, 2.88; Acid-test ratio, 2.40

Menardo Corporation began the month of June with $600,000 of current assets, a current ratio of 2.5:1, and an acid-test ratio of 1.4:1. During the month, it completed the following transactions (the company uses a perpetual inventory system).

June 1 Sold merchandise inventory that cost $150,000 for $240,000 cash.
3 Collected $176,000 cash on an account receivable.
5 Purchased $300,000 of merchandise inventory on credit.
7 Borrowed $200,000 cash by giving the bank a 60-day, 8% note.
10 Borrowed $240,000 cash by signing a long-term secured note.
12 Purchased machinery for $550,000 cash.
15 Declared a $1 per share cash dividend on its 160,000 shares of outstanding common stock.
19 Wrote off a $10,000 bad debt against the Allowance for Doubtful Accounts account.
22 Paid $24,000 cash to settle an account payable.
30 Paid the dividend declared on June 15.

June 30: Working capital, $(20,000); Current ratio, 0.97

Required

Prepare a table showing the company's (1) current ratio, (2) acid-test ratio, and (3) working capital after each transaction. Round ratios to two decimals.

Problem 17-4B
Calculation of financial statement ratios
P3

Selected year-end financial statements of Steele Corporation follow. (All sales were on credit; selected balance sheet amounts at December 31, 2008, were inventory, $55,900; total assets, $249,400; common stock, $105,000; and retained earnings, $17,748.)

STEELE CORPORATION Income Statement For Year Ended December 31, 2009	
Sales	$447,600
Cost of goods sold	298,150
Gross profit	149,450
Operating expenses	98,500
Interest expense	4,600
Income before taxes	46,350
Income taxes	18,672
Net income	$ 27,678

STEELE CORPORATION Balance Sheet December 31, 2009			
Assets		**Liabilities and Equity**	
Cash	$ 8,000	Accounts payable	$ 25,500
Short-term investments	8,000	Accrued wages payable	3,000
Accounts receivable, net	28,800	Income taxes payable	4,000
Notes receivable (trade)*	8,000	Long-term note payable, secured	
Merchandise inventory	34,150	by mortgage on plant assets	63,400
Prepaid expenses	2,750	Common stock, $5 par value	105,000
Plant assets, net	150,300	Retained earnings	39,100
Total assets	$240,000	Total liabilities and equity	$240,000

* These are short-term notes receivable arising from customer (trade) sales.

Required

Check Acid-test ratio, 1.6 to 1; Inventory turnover, 6.6

Compute the following: (1) current ratio, (2) acid-test ratio, (3) days' sales uncollected, (4) inventory turnover, (5) days' sales in inventory, (6) debt-to-equity ratio, (7) times interest earned, (8) profit margin ratio, (9) total asset turnover, (10) return on total assets, and (11) return on common stockholders' equity.

Problem 17-5B
Comparative ratio analysis A1 P3

Summary information from the financial statements of two companies competing in the same industry follows.

	Crisco Company	Silas Company		Crisco Company	Silas Company
Data from the current year-end balance sheets			**Data from the current year's income statement**		
Assets			Sales	$394,600	$668,500
Cash	$ 21,000	$ 37,500	Cost of goods sold	291,600	481,000
Accounts receivable, net	78,100	71,500	Interest expense	6,900	13,300
Current notes receivable (trade)	12,600	10,000	Income tax expense	6,700	14,300
Merchandise inventory	87,800	83,000	Net income	34,850	62,700
Prepaid expenses	10,700	11,100	Basic earnings per share	1.16	1.84
Plant assets, net	177,900	253,300			
Total assets	$388,100	$466,400			
			Beginning-of-year balance sheet data		
Liabilities and Equity			Accounts receivable, net	$ 73,200	$ 74,300
Current liabilities	$100,500	$ 98,000	Current notes receivable (trade)	0	0
Long-term notes payable	85,650	62,400	Merchandise inventory	106,100	81,500
Common stock, $5 par value	150,000	170,000	Total assets	384,400	444,000
Retained earnings	51,950	136,000	Common stock, $5 par value	150,000	170,000
Total liabilities and equity	$388,100	$466,400	Retained earnings	50,100	110,700

A Financial Statement Information

This appendix includes financial information for (1) **Best Buy**, (2) **Circuit City**, (3) **RadioShack**, and (4) **Apple**. This information is taken from their annual 10-K reports filed with the SEC. An **annual report** is a summary of a company's financial results for the year along with its current financial condition and future plans. This report is directed to external users of financial information, but it also affects the actions and decisions of internal users.

A company uses an annual report to showcase itself and its products. Many annual reports include attractive photos, diagrams, and illustrations related to the company. The primary objective of annual reports, however, is the *financial section,* which communicates much information about a company, with most data drawn from the accounting information system. The layout of an annual report's financial section is fairly established and typically includes the following:

- Letter to Shareholders
- Financial History and Highlights
- Management Discussion and Analysis
- Management's Report on Financial Statements and on Internal Controls
- Report of Independent Accountants (Auditor's Report) and on Internal Controls
- Financial Statements
- Notes to Financial Statements
- List of Directors and Officers

This appendix provides the financial statements for Best Buy (plus selected notes), Circuit City, RadioShack, and Apple. The appendix is organized as follows:

Many assignments at the end of each chapter refer to information in this appendix. We encourage readers to spend time with these assignments; they are especially useful in showing the relevance and diversity of financial accounting and reporting.

> *Special note:* The SEC maintains the EDGAR (**E**lectronic **D**ata **G**athering, **A**nalysis, and **R**etrieval) database at www.sec.gov. The **Form 10-K** is the annual report form for most companies. It provides electronically accessible information. The **Form 10-KSB** is the annual report form filed by small businesses. It requires slightly less information than the Form 10-K. One of these forms must be filed within 90 days after the company's fiscal year-end. (Forms 10-K405, 10-KT, 10-KT405, and 10-KSB405 are slight variations of the usual form due to certain regulations or rules.)

Financial Report

Selected Financial Data

The following table presents our selected financial data. In fiscal 2004, we sold our interest in Musicland. All fiscal years presented reflect the classification of Musicland's financial results as discontinued operations.

Five-Year Financial Highlights

$ in millions, except per share amounts

Fiscal Year	2007[1]	2006	2005	2004	2003
Consolidated Statements of Earnings Data					
Revenue	$35,934	$30,848	$27,433	$24,548	$20,943
Operating income	1,999	1,644	1,442	1,304	1,010
Earnings from continuing operations	1,377	1,140	934	800	622
Loss from discontinued operations, net of tax	—	—	—	(29)	(441)
Gain (loss) on disposal of discontinued operations, net of tax	—	—	50	(66)	—
Cumulative effect of change in accounting principles, net of tax	—	—	—	—	(82)
Net earnings	1,377	1,140	984	705	99
Per Share Data					
Continuing operations	$ 2.79	$ 2.27	$ 1.86	$ 1.61	$ 1.27
Discontinued operations	—	—	—	(0.06)	(0.89)
Gain (loss) on disposal of discontinued operations	—	—	0.10	(0.13)	—
Cumulative effect of accounting changes	—	—	—	—	(0.16)
Net earnings	2.79	2.27	1.96	1.42	0.20
Cash dividends declared and paid	0.36	0.31	0.28	0.27	—
Common stock price:					
High	59.50	56.00	41.47	41.80	35.83
Low	43.51	31.93	29.25	17.03	11.33
Operating Statistics					
Comparable store sales gain	5.0%	4.9%	4.3%	7.1%	2.4%
Gross profit rate	24.4%	25.0%	23.7%	23.9%	23.6%
Selling, general and administrative expenses rate	18.8%	19.7%	18.4%	18.6%	18.8%
Operating income rate	5.6%	5.3%	5.3%	5.3%	4.8%
Year-End Data					
Current ratio	1.4	1.3	1.4	1.3	1.3
Total assets	$13,570	$11,864	$10,294	$ 8,652	$ 7,694
Debt, including current portion	650	596	600	850	834
Total shareholders' equity	6,201	5,257	4,449	3,422	2,730
Number of stores					
Domestic	868	774	694	631	567
International	304	167	144	127	112
Total	1,172	941	838	758	679
Retail square footage (000s)					
Domestic	33,959	30,826	28,465	26,640	24,432
International	7,926	3,564	3,139	2,800	2,375
Total	41,885	34,390	31,604	29,440	26,807

(1) Fiscal 2007 included 53 weeks. All other periods presented included 52 weeks.

Consolidated Balance Sheets
$ in millions, except per share amounts

	March 3, 2007	February 25, 2006
Assets		
Current Assets		
Cash and cash equivalents	$ 1,205	$ 748
Short-term investments	2,588	3,041
Receivables	548	449
Merchandise inventories	4,028	3,338
Other current assets	712	409
Total current assets	9,081	7,985
Property and Equipment		
Land and buildings	705	580
Leasehold improvements	1,540	1,325
Fixtures and equipment	2,627	2,898
Property under capital lease	32	33
	4,904	4,836
Less accumulated depreciation	1,966	2,124
Net property and equipment	2,938	2,712
Goodwill	919	557
Tradenames	81	44
Long-Term Investments	318	218
Other Assets	233	348
Total Assets	$13,570	$11,864
Liabilities and Shareholders' Equity		
Current Liabilities		
Accounts payable	$ 3,934	$ 3,234
Unredeemed gift card liabilities	496	469
Accrued compensation and related expenses	332	354
Accrued liabilities	990	878
Accrued income taxes	489	703
Short-term debt	41	—
Current portion of long-term debt	19	418
Total current liabilities	6,301	6,056
Long-Term Liabilities	443	373
Long-Term Debt	590	178
Minority Interests	35	—
Shareholders' Equity		
Preferred stock, $1.00 par value: Authorized — 400,000 shares; Issued and outstanding — none	—	—
Common stock, $.10 par value: Authorized — 1 billion shares; Issued and outstanding — 480,655,000 and 485,098,000 shares, respectively	48	49
Additional paid-in capital	430	643
Retained earnings	5,507	4,304
Accumulated other comprehensive income	216	261
Total shareholders' equity	6,201	5,257
Total Liabilities and Shareholders' Equity	$13,570	$11,864

Consolidated Statements of Earnings
$ in millions, except per share amounts

Fiscal Years Ended	March 3, 2007	February 25, 2006	February 26, 2005
Revenue	$35,934	$30,848	$27,433
Cost of goods sold	27,165	23,122	20,938
Gross profit	8,769	7,726	6,495
Selling, general and administrative expenses	6,770	6,082	5,053
Operating income	1,999	1,644	1,442
Net interest income	111	77	1
Gain on investments	20	—	—
Earnings from continuing operations before income tax expense	2,130	1,721	1,443
Income tax expense	752	581	509
Minority interest in earnings	1	—	—
Earnings from continuing operations	1,377	1,140	934
Gain on disposal of discontinued operations, net of tax	—	—	50
Net earnings	$ 1,377	$ 1,140	$ 984
Basic earnings per share:			
Continuing operations	$ 2.86	$ 2.33	$ 1.91
Gain on disposal of discontinued operations	—	—	0.10
Basic earnings per share	$ 2.86	$ 2.33	$ 2.01
Diluted earnings per share:			
Continuing operations	$ 2.79	$ 2.27	$ 1.86
Gain on disposal of discontinued operations	—	—	0.10
Diluted earnings per share	$ 2.79	$ 2.27	$ 1.96
Basic weighted-average common shares outstanding (in millions)	482.1	490.3	488.9
Diluted weighted-average common shares outstanding (in millions)	496.2	504.8	505.0

Consolidated Statements of Changes in Shareholders' Equity
$ and shares in millions

	Common Shares	Common Stock	Additional Paid-In Capital	Retained Earnings	Accumulated Other Comprehensive Income	Total
Balances at February 28, 2004	**487**	**$49**	**$819**	**$ 2,468**	**$ 86**	**$3,422**
Net earnings	—	—	—	984	—	984
Other comprehensive income, net of tax:						
Foreign currency translation adjustments	—	—	—	—	59	59
Other	—	—	—	—	4	4
Total comprehensive income						1,047
Stock options exercised	10	1	219	—	—	220
Tax benefit from stock options exercised and employee stock purchase plan	—	—	60	—	—	60
Issuance of common stock under employee stock purchase plan	2	—	36	—	—	36
Vesting of restricted stock awards	—	—	1	—	—	1
Common stock dividends, $0.28 per share	—	—	—	(137)	—	(137)
Repurchase of common stock	(6)	(1)	(199)	—	—	(200)
Balances at February 26, 2005	**493**	**49**	**936**	**3,315**	**149**	**4,449**
Net earnings	—	—	—	1,140	—	1,140
Other comprehensive income, net of tax:						
Foreign currency translation adjustments	—	—	—	—	101	101
Other	—	—	—	—	11	11
Total comprehensive income						1,252
Stock options exercised	9	1	256	—	—	257
Tax benefit from stock options exercised and employee stock purchase plan	—	—	55	—	—	55
Issuance of common stock under employee stock purchase plan	1	—	35	—	—	35
Stock-based compensation	—	—	132	—	—	132
Common stock dividends, $0.31 per share	—	—	—	(151)	—	(151)
Repurchase of common stock	(18)	(1)	(771)	—	—	(772)
Balances at February 25, 2006	**485**	**49**	**643**	**4,304**	**261**	**5,257**
Net earnings	—	—	—	1,377	—	1,377
Other comprehensive loss, net of tax:						
Foreign currency translation adjustments	—	—	—	—	(33)	(33)
Other	—	—	—	—	(12)	(12)
Total comprehensive income						1,332
Stock options exercised	7	1	167	—	—	168
Tax benefit from stock options exercised and employee stock purchase plan	—	—	47	—	—	47
Issuance of common stock under employee stock purchase plan	1	—	49	—	—	49
Stock-based compensation	—	—	121	—	—	121
Common stock dividends, $0.36 per share	—	—	—	(174)	—	(174)
Repurchase of common stock	(12)	(2)	(597)	—	—	(599)
Balances at March 3, 2007	**481**	**$48**	**$430**	**$5,507**	**$216**	**$6,201**

Consolidated Statements of Cash Flows
$ in millions

Fiscal Years Ended	March 3, 2007	February 25, 2006	February 26, 2005
Operating Activities			
Net earnings	$1,377	$1,140	$ 984
Gain from disposal of discontinued operations, net of tax	—	—	(50)
Earnings from continuing operations	1,377	1,140	934
Adjustments to reconcile earnings from continuing operations to total cash provided by operating activities from continuing operations:			
Depreciation	509	456	459
Asset impairment charges	32	4	22
Stock-based compensation	121	132	(1)
Deferred income taxes	82	(151)	(28)
Excess tax benefits from stock-based compensation	(50)	(55)	—
Other, net	(11)	(3)	24
Changes in operating assets and liabilities, net of acquired assets and liabilities:			
Receivables	(70)	(43)	(30)
Merchandise inventories	(550)	(457)	(240)
Other assets	(47)	(11)	(50)
Accounts payable	320	385	347
Other liabilities	185	165	243
Accrued income taxes	(136)	178	301
Total cash provided by operating activities from continuing operations	1,762	1,740	1,981
Investing Activities			
Additions to property and equipment, net of $75 and $117 noncash capital expenditures in fiscal 2006 and 2005, respectively	(733)	(648)	(502)
Purchases of available-for-sale securities	(4,541)	(4,319)	(8,517)
Sales of available-for-sale securities	4,886	4,187	7,730
Acquisitions of businesses, net of cash acquired	(421)	—	—
Proceeds from disposition of investments	24	—	—
Change in restricted assets	—	(20)	(140)
Other, net	5	46	7
Total cash used in investing activities from continuing operations	(780)	(754)	(1,422)
Financing Activities			
Repurchase of common stock	(599)	(772)	(200)
Issuance of common stock under employee stock purchase plan and for the exercise of stock options	217	292	256
Dividends paid	(174)	(151)	(137)
Repayments of debt	(84)	(69)	(371)
Proceeds from issuance of debt	96	36	—
Excess tax benefits from stock-based compensation	50	55	—
Other, net	(19)	(10)	(7)
Total cash used in financing activities from continuing operations	(513)	(619)	(459)
Effect of Exchange Rate Changes on Cash	(12)	27	9
Increase in Cash and Cash Equivalents	457	394	109
Cash and Cash Equivalents at Beginning of Year	748	354	245
Cash and Cash Equivalents at End of Year	$1,205	$ 748	$ 354
Supplemental Disclosure of Cash Flow Information			
Income taxes paid	$ 804	$ 547	$ 241
Interest paid	14	16	35

SELECTED Notes to Consolidated Financial Statements

$ in millions, except per share amounts

1. Summary of Significant Accounting Policies

Description of Business

Best Buy Co., Inc. is a specialty retailer of consumer electronics, home-office products, entertainment software, appliances and related services, with fiscal 2007 revenue from continuing operations of $35.9 billion.

We operate two reportable segments: Domestic and International. The Domestic segment is comprised of all U.S. store and online operations of Best Buy, Geek Squad, Magnolia Audio Video and Pacific Sales Kitchen and Bath Centers, Inc. ("Pacific Sales"). We acquired Pacific Sales on March 7, 2006. U.S. Best Buy stores offer a wide variety of consumer electronics, home-office products, entertainment software, appliances and related services through 822 stores at the end of fiscal 2007. Geek Squad provides residential and commercial computer repair, support and installation services in all U.S. Best Buy stores and at 12 stand-alone stores at the end of fiscal 2007. Magnolia Audio Video stores offer high-end audio and video products and related services through 20 stores at the end of fiscal 2007. Pacific Sales stores offer high-end home-improvement products, appliances and related services through 14 stores at the end of fiscal 2007.

Fiscal Year

Our fiscal year ends on the Saturday nearest the end of February. Fiscal 2007 included 53 weeks and fiscal 2006 and 2005 each included 52 weeks.

Cash and Cash Equivalents

Cash primarily consists of cash on hand and bank deposits. Cash equivalents primarily consist of money market accounts and other highly liquid investments with an original maturity of three months or less when purchased. We carry these investments at cost, which approximates market value. The amounts of cash equivalents at March 3, 2007, and February 25, 2006, were $695 and $350, respectively, and the weighted-average interest rates were 4.8% and 3.3%, respectively.

Outstanding checks in excess of funds on deposit ("book overdrafts") totaled $183 and $230 at March 3, 2007, and February 25, 2006, respectively, and are reflected as current liabilities in our consolidated balance sheets.

Merchandise Inventories

Merchandise inventories are recorded at the lower of average cost or market. In-bound freight-related costs from our vendors are included as part of the net cost of merchandise inventories. Also included in the cost of inventory are certain vendor allowances that are not a reimbursement of specific, incremental and identifiable costs to promote a vendor's products. Other costs associated with acquiring, storing and transporting merchandise inventories to our retail stores are expensed as incurred and included in cost of goods sold.

Our inventory loss reserve represents anticipated physical inventory losses (e.g., theft) that have occurred since the last physical inventory date. Independent physical inventory counts are taken on a regular basis to ensure that the inventory reported in our consolidated financial statements is properly stated. During the interim period between physical inventory counts, we reserve for anticipated physical inventory losses on a location-by-location basis.

Property and Equipment

Property and equipment are recorded at cost. We compute depreciation using the straight-line method over the estimated useful lives of the assets. Leasehold improvements are depreciated over the shorter of their estimated useful lives or the period from the date the assets are placed in service to the end of the initial lease term. Leasehold improvements made significantly after the initial lease term are depreciated over the shorter of their estimated useful lives or the remaining lease term, including renewal periods, if reasonably assured.

$ in millions, except per share amounts

Accelerated depreciation methods are generally used for income tax purposes.

When property is fully depreciated, retired or otherwise disposed of, the cost and accumulated depreciation are removed from the accounts and any resulting gain or loss is reflected in the consolidated statement of earnings.

Repairs and maintenance costs are charged directly to expense as incurred. Major renewals or replacements that substantially extend the useful life of an asset are capitalized and depreciated.

Estimated useful lives by major asset category are as follows:

Asset	Life (in years)
Buildings	30–40
Leasehold improvements	3–25
Fixtures and equipment	3–20
Property under capital lease	3–20

Impairment of Long-Lived Assets

We account for the impairment or disposal of long-lived assets in accordance with SFAS No. 144, *Accounting for the Impairment* or *Disposal of Long-Lived Assets,* which requires long-lived assets, such as property and equipment, to be evaluated for impairment whenever events or changes in circumstances indicate the carrying value of an asset may not be recoverable. Factors considered important that could result in an impairment review include, but are not limited to, significant underperformance relative to historical or planned operating results, significant changes in the manner of use of the assets or significant changes in our business strategies. An impairment loss is recognized when the estimated undiscounted cash flows expected to result from the use of the asset plus net proceeds expected from disposition of the asset (if any) are less than the carrying value of the asset. When an impairment loss is recognized, the carrying amount of the asset is reduced to its estimated fair value based on quoted market prices or other valuation techniques.

Leases

We conduct the majority of our retail and distribution operations from leased locations. The leases require payment of real estate taxes, insurance and common area maintenance, in addition to rent. The terms of our lease agreements generally range from 10 to 20 years. Most of the leases contain renewal options and escalation clauses, and certain store leases require contingent rents based on factors such as specified percentages of revenue or the consumer price index. Other leases contain covenants related to the maintenance of financial ratios.

Goodwill and Intangible Assets

Goodwill

Goodwill is the excess of the purchase price over the fair value of identifiable net assets acquired in business combinations accounted for under the purchase method. We do not amortize goodwill but test it for impairment annually, or when indications of potential impairment exist, utilizing a fair value approach at the reporting unit level. A reporting unit is the operating segment, or a business unit one level below that operating segment, for which discrete financial information is prepared and regularly reviewed by segment management.

Tradenames

We have an indefinite-lived intangible asset related to our Pacific Sales tradename which is included in the Domestic segment. We also have indefinite-lived intangible assets related to our Future Shop and Five Star tradenames which are included in the International segment.

We determine fair values utilizing widely accepted valuation techniques, including discounted cash flows and market multiple analyses. During the fourth quarter of fiscal 2007, we completed our annual impairment testing of our goodwill and tradenames, using the valuation techniques as described above, and determined there was no impairment.

Lease Rights

Lease rights represent costs incurred to acquire the lease of a specific commercial property. Lease rights are recorded at cost and are amortized to rent expense over the remaining lease term, including renewal periods, if reasonably assured. Amortization periods range up to 16 years, beginning with the date we take possession of the property.

$ in millions, except per share amounts

Investments

Short-term and long-term investments are comprised of municipal and United States government debt securities as well as auction-rate securities and variable-rate demand notes. In accordance with SFAS No. 115, *Accounting for Certain Investments in Debt and Equity Securities,* and based on our ability to market and sell these instruments, we classify auction-rate securities, variable-rate demand notes and other investments in debt securities as available-for-sale and carry them at amortized cost, which approximates fair value. Auction-rate securities and variable-rate demand notes are similar to short-term debt instruments because their interest rates are reset periodically. Investments in these securities can be sold for cash on the auction date. We classify auction-rate securities and variable-rate demand notes as short-term or long-term investments based on the reset dates.

We also hold investments in marketable equity securities and classify them as available-for-sale. Investments in marketable equity securities are included in other assets in our consolidated balance sheets. Investments in marketable equity securities are reported at fair value, based on quoted market prices when available. All unrealized holding gains or losses are reflected net of tax in accumulated other comprehensive income in shareholders' equity.

We review the key characteristics of our debt and marketable equity securities portfolio and their classification in accordance with GAAP on an annual basis, or when indications of potential impairment exist. If a decline in the fair value of a security is deemed by management to be other than temporary, the cost basis of the investment is written down to fair value, and the amount of the write-down is included in the determination of net earnings.

Income Taxes

We account for income taxes under the liability method. Under this method, deferred tax assets and liabilities are recognized for the estimated future tax consequences attributable to differences between the financial statement carrying amounts of existing assets and liabilities and their respective tax bases, and operating loss and tax credit carryforwards. Deferred tax assets and liabilities are measured using enacted income tax rates in effect for the year in which those temporary differences are expected to be recovered or settled. The effect on deferred tax assets and liabilities of a change in income tax rates is recognized in our consolidated statement of earnings in the period that includes the enactment date. A valuation allowance is recorded to reduce the carrying amounts of deferred tax assets if it is more likely than not that such assets will not be realized.

Long-Term Liabilities

The major components of long-term liabilities at March 3, 2007, and February 25, 2006, included long-term rent-related liabilities, deferred compensation plan liabilities, self-insurance reserves and advances received under vendor alliance programs.

Foreign Currency

Foreign currency denominated assets and liabilities are translated into U.S. dollars using the exchange rates in effect at our consolidated balance sheet date. Results of operations and cash flows are translated using the average exchange rates throughout the period. The effect of exchange rate fluctuations on translation of assets and liabilities is included as a component of shareholders' equity in accumulated other comprehensive income. Gains and losses from foreign currency transactions, which are included in SG&A, have not been significant.

Revenue Recognition

We recognize revenue when the sales price is fixed or determinable, collectibility is reasonably assured and the customer takes possession of the merchandise, or in the case of services, at the time the service is provided.

$ in millions, except per share amounts

Amounts billed to customers for shipping and handling are included in revenue. Revenue is reported net of estimated sales returns and excludes sales taxes.

We estimate our sales returns reserve based on historical return rates. We initially established our sales returns reserve in the fourth quarter of fiscal 2005. Our sales returns reserve was $104 and $78, at March 3, 2007, and February 25, 2006, respectively.

We sell extended service contracts on behalf of an unrelated third party. In jurisdictions where we are not deemed to be the obligor on the contract, commissions are recognized in revenue at the time of sale. In jurisdictions where we are deemed to be the obligor on the contract, commissions are recognized in revenue ratably over the term of the service contract. Commissions represented 2.2%, 2.5% and 2.6% of revenues in fiscal 2007, 2006 and 2005, respectively.

For revenue transactions that involve multiple deliverables, we defer the revenue associated with any undelivered elements. The amount of revenue deferred in connection with the undelivered elements is determined using the relative fair value of each element, which is generally based on each element's relative retail price. See additional information regarding our customer loyalty program in *Sales Incentives* below.

Gift Cards

We sell gift cards to our customers in our retail stores, through our Web sites, and through selected third parties. We do not charge administrative fees on unused gift cards and our gift cards do not have an expiration date. We recognize income from gift cards when: (i) the gift card is redeemed by the customer; or (ii) the likelihood of the gift card being redeemed by the customer is remote ("gift card breakage") and we determine that we do not have a legal obligation to remit the value of unredeemed gift cards to the relevant jurisdictions. We determine our gift card breakage rate based upon historical redemption patterns. Based on our historical information, the likelihood of a gift card remaining unredeemed can be determined 24 months after the gift card is issued. At that time, we recognize breakage income for those cards for which the likelihood of redemption is deemed remote and we do not have a legal obligation to remit the value of such unredeemed gift cards to the relevant jurisdictions. Gift card breakage income is included in revenue in our consolidated statements of earnings.

We began recognizing gift card breakage income during the third quarter of fiscal 2006. Gift card breakage income was as follows in fiscal 2007, 2006 and 2005:

	2007[(1)]	2006[(1)]	2005
Gift card breakage income	$46	$43	$ —

(1) Due to the resolution of certain legal matters associated with gift card liabilities, we recognized $19 and $27 of gift card breakage income in fiscal 2007 and 2006, respectively, that related to prior fiscal years.

Sales Incentives

We frequently offer sales incentives that entitle our customers to receive a reduction in the price of a product or service. Sales incentives include discounts, coupons and other offers that entitle a customer to receive a reduction in the price of a product or service by submitting a claim for a refund or rebate. For sales incentives issued to a customer in conjunction with a sale of merchandise or services, for which we are the obligor, the reduction in revenue is recognized at the time of sale, based on the retail value of the incentive expected to be redeemed.

Customer Loyalty Program

We have a customer loyalty program which allows members to earn points for each qualifying purchase. Points earned enable members to receive a certificate that may be redeemed on future purchases at U.S. Best Buy stores.

$ in millions, except per share amounts

Cost of Goods Sold and Selling, General and Administrative Expenses

The following table illustrates the primary costs classified in each major expense category:

Cost of Goods Sold

- Total cost of products sold including:
  —Freight expenses associated with moving merchandise inventories from our vendors to our distribution centers;
  —Vendor allowances that are not a reimbursement of specific, incremental and identifiable costs to promote a vendor's products; and
  —Cash discounts on payments to vendors;
- Cost of services provided including:
  —Payroll and benefits costs for services employees; and
  —Cost of replacement parts and related freight expenses;
- Physical inventory losses;
- Markdowns;
- Customer shipping and handling expenses;
- Costs associated with operating our distribution network, including payroll and benefit costs, occupancy costs, and depreciation;
- Freight expenses associated with moving merchandise inventories from our distribution centers to our retail stores; and
- Promotional financing costs.

SG&A

- Payroll and benefit costs for retail and corporate employees;
- Occupancy costs of retail, services and corporate facilities;
- Depreciation related to retail, services and corporate assets;
- Advertising;
- Vendor allowances that are a reimbursement of specific, incremental and identifiable costs to promote a vendor's products;
- Charitable contributions;
- Outside service fees;
- Long-lived asset impairment charges; and
- Other administrative costs, such as credit card service fees, supplies, and travel and lodging.

Advertising Costs

Advertising costs, which are included in SG&A, are expensed the first time the advertisement runs. Advertising costs consist primarily of print and television advertisements as well as promotional events. Net advertising expenses were $692, $644 and $597 in fiscal 2007, 2006 and 2005, respectively. Allowances received from vendors for advertising of $140, $123 and $115, in fiscal 2007, 2006 and 2005, respectively, were classified as reductions of advertising expenses.

$ in millions, except per share amounts

4. Investments

Short-Term and Long-Term Investments

The following table presents the amortized principal amounts, related weighted-average interest rates, maturities and major security types for our investments:

	March 3, 2007		Feb. 25, 2006	
	Amortized Principal Amount	Weighted-Average Interest Rate	Amortized Principal Amount	Weighted-Average Interest Rate
Short-term investments (less than one year)	$2,588	5.68%	$3,041	4.76%
Long-term investments (one to three years)	318	5.68%	218	4.95%
Total	$2,906		$3,259	
Municipal debt securities	$2,840		$3,155	
Auction-rate and asset-backed securities	66		97	
Debt securities issued by U.S. Treasury and other U.S. government entities	—		7	
Total	$2,906		$3,259	

The carrying value of our investments approximated fair value at March 3, 2007, and February 25, 2006, due to the rapid turnover of our portfolio and the highly liquid nature of these investments. Therefore, there were no significant realized or unrealized gains or losses.

Marketable Equity Securities

The carrying values of our investments in marketable equity securities at March 3, 2007, and February 25, 2006, were $4 and $28, respectively. Net unrealized (loss)/gain, net of tax, included in accumulated other comprehensive income was ($1) and $12 at March 3, 2007, and February 25, 2006, respectively.

$ in millions, except per share amounts

5. Debt

Short-term debt consisted of the following:

	March 3, 2007	Feb. 25, 2006
Notes payable to banks, secured, interest rates ranging from 3.5% to 6.7%	$ 21	$ —
Revolving credit facility, secured, variable interest rate of 5.6% at March 3, 2007	20	—
Total short-term debt	$ 41	$ —
Weighted-average interest rate	5.3%	—

Long-term debt consisted of the following:

	March 3, 2007	Feb. 25, 2006
Convertible subordinated debentures, unsecured, due 2022, interest rate 2.25%	$402	$ 402
Financing lease obligations, due 2009 to 2023, interest rates ranging from 3.0% to 6.5%	171	157
Capital lease obligations, due 2008 to 2026, interest rates ranging from 1.8% to 8.0%	24	27
Other debt, due 2010, interest rate 8.8%	12	10
Total debt	609	596
Less: current portion[(1)]	(19)	(418)
Total long-term debt	$590	$ 178

(1) Since holders of our debentures due in 2022 could have required us to purchase all or a portion of their debentures on January 15, 2007, we classified our debentures in the current portion of long-term debt at February 25, 2006. However, no holders of our debentures exercised this put option on January 15, 2007. The next time the holders of our debentures could require us to purchase all or a portion of their debentures is January 15, 2012. Therefore, we classified our debentures as long-term debt at March 3, 2007.

Certain debt is secured by property and equipment with a net book value of $80 and $41 at March 3, 2007, and February 25, 2006, respectively.

Convertible Debentures

In January 2002, we sold convertible subordinated debentures having an aggregate principal amount of $402. The proceeds from the offering, net of $6 in offering expenses, were $396. The debentures mature in 2022 and are callable at par, at our option, for cash on or after January 15, 2007.

Holders may require us to purchase all or a portion of their debentures on January 15, 2012, and January 15, 2017, at a purchase price equal to 100% of the principal amount of the debentures plus accrued and unpaid interest up to but not including the date of purchase. We have the option to settle the purchase price in cash, stock, or a combination of cash and stock.

$ in millions, except per share amounts

Other

The fair value of debt approximated $683 and $693 at March 3, 2007, and February 25, 2006, respectively, based on the ask prices quoted from external sources, compared with carrying values of $650 and $596, respectively.

At March 3, 2007, the future maturities of long-term debt, including capitalized leases, consisted of the following:

Fiscal Year	
2008	$ 19
2009	18
2010	27
2011	18
2012	420
Thereafter	107
	$609

Earnings per Share

Our basic earnings per share calculation is computed based on the weighted-average number of common shares outstanding. Our diluted earnings per share calculation is computed based on the weighted-average number of common shares outstanding adjusted by the number of additional shares that would have been outstanding had the potentially dilutive common shares been issued. Potentially dilutive shares of common stock include stock options, nonvested share awards and shares issuable under our ESPP, as well as common shares that would have resulted from the assumed conversion of our convertible debentures. Since the potentially dilutive shares related to the convertible debentures are included in the calculation, the related interest expense, net of tax, is added back to earnings from continuing operations, as the interest would not have been paid if the convertible debentures had been converted to common stock. Nonvested market-based share awards and nonvested performance-based share awards are included in the average diluted shares outstanding each period if established market or performance criteria have been met at the end of the respective periods.

The following table presents a reconciliation of the numerators and denominators of basic and diluted earnings per share from continuing operations in fiscal 2007, 2006 and 2005:

	2007	2006	2005
Numerator:			
Earnings from continuing operations, basic	$1,377	$1,140	$ 934
Adjustment for assumed dilution:			
Interest on convertible debentures due in 2022, net of tax	7	7	7
Earnings from continuing operations, diluted	$1,384	$1,147	$ 941
Denominator (in millions):			
Weighted-average common shares outstanding	482.1	490.3	488.9
Effect of potentially dilutive securities:			
Shares from assumed conversion of convertible debentures	8.8	8.8	8.8
Stock options and other	5.3	5.7	7.3
Weighted-average common shares outstanding, assuming dilution	496.2	504.8	505.0
Basic earnings per share — continuing operations	$ 2.86	$ 2.33	$ 1.91
Diluted earnings per share — continuing operations	$ 2.79	$ 2.27	$ 1.86

$ in millions, except per share amounts

Comprehensive Income

Comprehensive income is computed as net earnings plus certain other items that are recorded directly to shareholders' equity. In addition to net earnings, the significant components of comprehensive income include foreign currency translation adjustments and unrealized gains and losses, net of tax, on available-for-sale marketable equity securities. Foreign currency translation adjustments do not include a provision for income tax expense when earnings from foreign operations are considered to be indefinitely reinvested outside the United States. Comprehensive income was $1,332, $1,252 and $1,047 in fiscal 2007, 2006 and 2005, respectively.

7. Net Interest Income

Net interest income was comprised of the following in fiscal 2007, 2006 and 2005:

	2007	2006	2005
Interest income	$142	$103	$ 45
Interest expense	(31)	(30)	(44)
Dividend income	—	4	—
Net interest income	$111	$ 77	$ 1

8. Leases

The composition of net rent expense for all operating leases, including leases of property and equipment, was as follows in fiscal 2007, 2006 and 2005:

	2007	2006	2005
Minimum rentals	$679	$569	$516
Contingent rentals	1	1	1
Total rent expense	680	570	517
Less: sublease income	(20)	(18)	(16)
Net rent expense	$660	$552	$501

$ in millions, except per share amounts

The future minimum lease payments under our capital, financing and operating leases by fiscal year (not including contingent rentals) at March 3, 2007, were as follows:

Fiscal Year	Capital Leases	Financing Leases	Operating Leases
2008	$ 6	$ 23	$ 741
2009	4	23	715
2010	4	23	672
2011	3	23	632
2012	1	23	592
Thereafter	17	112	3,316
Subtotal	35	227	$6,668
Less: imputed interest	(11)	(56)	
Present value of lease obligations	$24	$171	

Total minimum lease payments have not been reduced by minimum sublease rent income of approximately $119 due under future noncancelable subleases.

10. Income Taxes

The following is a reconciliation of the federal statutory income tax rate to income tax expense from continuing operations in fiscal 2007, 2006 and 2005:

	2007	2006	2005
Federal income tax at the statutory rate	$ 747	$ 603	$ 505
State income taxes, net of federal benefit	38	34	29
Benefit from foreign operations	(36)	(37)	(7)
Non-taxable interest income	(34)	(28)	(22)
Other	37	9	4
Income tax expense	$ 752	$ 581	$ 509
Effective income tax rate	35.3%	33.7%	35.3%

Income tax expense was comprised of the following in fiscal 2007, 2006 and 2005:

	2007	2006	2005
Current:			
Federal	$609	$640	$502
State	45	78	36
Foreign	16	14	(1)
	670	732	537
Deferred:			
Federal	51	(131)	(4)
State	19	(14)	(20)
Foreign	12	(6)	(4)
	82	(151)	(28)
Income tax expense	$752	$581	$509

Deferred taxes are the result of differences between the bases of assets and liabilities for financial reporting and income tax purposes.

$ in millions, except per share amounts

11. Segment and Geographic Information

Segment Information

We operate two reportable segments: Domestic and International. The Domestic segment is comprised of U.S. store and online operations, including Best Buy, Geek Squad, Magnolia Audio Video and Pacific Sales. The International segment is comprised of all Canada store and online operations, including Best Buy, Future Shop and Geek Squad, as well as our Five Star and Best Buy retail and online operations in China.

The following tables present our business segment information for continuing operations in fiscal 2007, 2006 and 2005:

	2007	2006	2005
Revenue			
Domestic	$31,031	$27,380	$24,616
International	4,903	3,468	2,817
Total revenue	$35,934	$30,848	$27,433
Operating Income			
Domestic	$ 1,889	$ 1,588	$ 1,393
International	110	56	49
Total operating income	1,999	1,644	1,442
Net interest income	111	77	1
Gain on investments	20	—	—
Earnings from continuing operations before income tax expense	$ 2,130	$ 1,721	$ 1,443
Assets			
Domestic	$10,614	$ 9,722	$ 8,372
International	2,956	2,142	1,922
Total assets	$13,570	$11,864	$10,294

12. Contingencies and Commitments

Contingencies

On December 8, 2005, a purported class action lawsuit captioned, *Jasmen Holloway, et cl. v. Best Buy Co., Inc.*, was filed in the U.S. District Court for the Northern District of California alleging we discriminate against women and minority individuals on the basis of gender, race, color and/or national origin with respect to our employment policies and practices. The action seeks an end to discriminatory policies and practices, an award of back and front pay, punitive damages and injunctive relief, including rightful place relief for all class members. As of March 3, 2007, no accrual had been established as it was not possible to estimate the possible loss or range of loss because this matter had not advanced to a stage where we could make any such estimate. We believe the allegations are without merit and intend to defend this action vigorously.

We are involved in various other legal proceedings arising in the normal course of conducting business. We believe the amounts provided in our consolidated financial statements, as prescribed by GAAP, are adequate in light of the probable and estimable liabilities. The resolution of those other proceedings is not expected to have a material impact on our results of operations or financial condition.

Commitments

We engage Accenture LLP ("Accenture") to assist us with improving our operational capabilities and reducing our costs in the information systems, procurement and human resources areas. Our future contractual obligations to Accenture are expected to range from $76 to $334 per year through 2012, the end of the contract period. Prior to our engagement of Accenture, a significant portion of these costs were incurred as part of normal operations.

We had outstanding letters of credit for purchase obligations with a fair value of $85 at March 3, 2007.

At March 3, 2007, we had commitments for the purchase and construction of facilities valued at approximately $69. Also, at March 3, 2007, we had entered into lease commitments for land and buildings for 115 future locations. These lease commitments with real estate developers provide for minimum rentals ranging from seven to 20 years, which if consummated based on current cost estimates, will approximate $84 annually over the initial lease terms. These minimum rentals have been included in the future minimum lease payments included in Note 8, Leases.

Financial Reports

CIRCUIT CITY STORES, INC.

Circuit City Stores, Inc.
CONSOLIDATED BALANCE SHEETS

(Amounts in thousands except share data)	At February 28 2007	2006
ASSETS		
CURRENT ASSETS:		
Cash and cash equivalents	**$ 141,141**	$ 315,970
Short-term investments	**598,341**	521,992
Accounts receivable, net of allowance for doubtful accounts	**382,555**	220,869
Merchandise inventory	**1,636,507**	1,698,026
Deferred income taxes	**34,868**	29,598
Income tax receivable	**42,722**	5,571
Prepaid expenses and other current assets	**47,378**	41,315
TOTAL CURRENT ASSETS	**2,883,512**	2,833,341
Property and equipment, net of accumulated depreciation	**921,027**	839,356
Deferred income taxes	**31,910**	97,889
Goodwill	**121,774**	223,999
Other intangible assets, net of accumulated amortization	**19,285**	30,372
Other assets	**29,775**	44,087
TOTAL ASSETS	**$4,007,283**	$4,069,044
LIABILITIES AND STOCKHOLDERS' EQUITY		
CURRENT LIABILITIES:		
Merchandise payable	**$ 922,205**	$ 850,359
Expenses payable	**281,709**	202,300
Accrued expenses and other current liabilities	**404,444**	379,768
Accrued compensation	**98,509**	84,743
Accrued income taxes	**–**	75,909
Short-term debt	**–**	22,003
Current installments of long-term debt	**7,162**	7,248
TOTAL CURRENT LIABILITIES	**1,714,029**	1,622,330
Long-term debt, excluding current installments	**50,487**	51,985
Accrued straight-line rent and deferred rent credits	**277,636**	256,120
Accrued lease termination costs	**76,326**	79,091
Other liabilities	**97,561**	104,885
TOTAL LIABILITIES	**2,216,039**	2,114,411
Commitments and contingent liabilities		
STOCKHOLDERS' EQUITY:		
Common stock, $0.50 par value; 525,000,000 shares authorized; 170,689,406 shares issued and outstanding (174,789,390 in 2006)	**85,345**	87,395
Additional paid-in capital	**344,144**	458,211
Retained earnings	**1,336,317**	1,364,740
Accumulated other comprehensive income	**25,438**	44,287
TOTAL STOCKHOLDERS' EQUITY	**1,791,244**	1,954,633
TOTAL LIABILITIES AND STOCKHOLDERS' EQUITY	**$4,007,283**	$4,069,044

Circuit City Stores, Inc.
CONSOLIDATED STATEMENTS OF OPERATIONS

(Amounts in thousands except per share data)	2007	%	2006	%	2005	%
	Years Ended February 28					
NET SALES	**$12,429,754**	100.0	$11,514,151	100.0	$10,413,524	100.0
Cost of sales, buying and warehousing	**9,501,438**	76.4	8,703,683	75.6	7,861,364	75.5
GROSS PROFIT	**2,928,316**	23.6	2,810,468	24.4	2,552,160	24.5
Selling, general and administrative expenses	**2,841,619**	22.9	2,595,706	22.5	2,470,712	23.7
Impairment of goodwill	**92,000**	0.7	–	–	–	–
Finance income	**–**	**–**	–	–	5,564	0.1
OPERATING (LOSS) INCOME	**(5,303)**	–	214,762	1.9	87,012	0.8
Interest income	**27,150**	0.2	21,826	0.2	14,404	0.1
Interest expense	**1,519**	–	3,143	–	4,451	–
Earnings from continuing operations before income taxes	**20,328**	0.2	233,445	2.0	96,965	0.9
Income tax expense	**30,510**	0.2	85,996	0.7	36,396	0.3
NET (LOSS) EARNINGS FROM CONTINUING OPERATIONS	**(10,182)**	(0.1)	147,449	1.3	60,569	0.6
EARNINGS (LOSS) FROM DISCONTINUED OPERATIONS, NET OF TAX	**128**	**–**	(5,350)	–	1,089	–
CUMULATIVE EFFECT OF CHANGE IN ACCOUNTING PRINCIPLES, NET OF TAX	**1,773**	–	(2,353)	–	–	–
NET (LOSS) EARNINGS	**$ (8,281)**	(0.1)	$ 139,746	1.2	$ 61,658	0.6

	2007	2006	2005
Weighted average common shares:			
Basic	**170,448**	177,456	193,466
Diluted	**170,448**	180,653	196,227
(LOSS) EARNINGS PER SHARE:			
Basic:			
Continuing operations	**$ (0.06)**	$ 0.83	$ 0.31
Discontinued operations	**$ –**	$ (0.03)	$ 0.01
Cumulative effect of change in accounting principles	**$ 0.01**	$ (0.01)	$ –
Basic (loss) earnings per share	**$ (0.05)**	$ 0.79	$ 0.32
Diluted:			
Continuing operations	**$ (0.06)**	$ 0.82	$ 0.31
Discontinued operations	**$ –**	$ (0.03)	$ 0.01
Cumulative effect of change in accounting principles	**$ 0.01**	$ (0.01)	$ –
Diluted (loss) earnings per share	**$ (0.05)**	$ 0.77	$ 0.31

Circuit City Stores, Inc.

CONSOLIDATED STATEMENTS OF STOCKHOLDERS' EQUITY AND COMPREHENSIVE INCOME

(Amounts in thousands except per share data)	Common Stock Shares	Common Stock Amount	Additional Paid-in Capital	Retained Earnings	Accumulated Other Comprehensive Income	Total
BALANCE AT FEBRUARY 29, 2004	203,899	$101,950	$922,600	$1,191,904	$ –	$2,216,454
Comprehensive income:						
Net earnings	–	–	–	61,658	–	61,658
Other comprehensive income, net of taxes:						
Foreign currency translation adjustment (net of deferred taxes of $13,707)	–	–	–	–	25,100	25,100
Comprehensive income						86,758
Repurchases of common stock	(19,163)	(9,582)	(250,250)	–	–	(259,832)
Compensation for stock awards	–	–	18,305	–	–	18,305
Exercise of common stock options	3,489	1,745	26,761	–	–	28,506
Shares issued under stock-based incentive plans, net of cancellations, and other	(75)	(38)	(1,312)	–	–	(1,350)
Tax effect from stock issued	–	–	(1,564)	–	–	(1,564)
Shares issued in acquisition of InterTAN, Inc.	–	–	6,498	–	–	6,498
Dividends – common stock ($0.07 per share)	–	–	–	(13,848)	–	(13,848)
BALANCE AT FEBRUARY 28, 2005	188,150	94,075	721,038	1,239,714	25,100	2,079,927
Comprehensive income:						
Net earnings	–	–	–	139,746	–	139,746
Other comprehensive income (loss), net of taxes:						
Foreign currency translation adjustment (net of deferred taxes of $11,316)	–	–	–	–	19,500	19,500
Minimum pension liability adjustment (net of deferred taxes of $182)	–	–	–	–	(313)	(313)
Comprehensive income						158,933
Repurchases of common stock	(19,396)	(9,698)	(328,778)	–	–	(338,476)
Compensation for stock awards	–	–	24,386	–	–	24,386
Exercise of common stock options	3,830	1,915	36,752	–	–	38,667
Shares issued under stock-based incentive plans, net of cancellations, and other	2,205	1,103	(2,160)	–	–	(1,057)
Tax effect from stock issued	–	–	6,973	–	–	6,973
Redemption of preferred share purchase rights	–	–	–	(1,876)	–	(1,876)
Dividends – common stock ($0.07 per share)	–	–	–	(12,844)	–	(12,844)
BALANCE AT FEBRUARY 28, 2006	174,789	87,395	458,211	1,364,740	44,287	1,954,633
Comprehensive loss:						
Net loss	–	–	–	(8,281)	–	(8,281)
Other comprehensive (loss) income, net of taxes:						
Foreign currency translation adjustment (net of deferred taxes of $3,630)	–	–	–	–	(7,793)	(7,793)
Unrealized gain on available-for-sale securities (net of deferred taxes of $219)	–	–	–	–	377	377
Minimum pension liability adjustment (net of deferred taxes of $136)	–	–	–	–	(229)	(229)
Comprehensive loss						(15,926)
Adjustment to initially apply SFAS No. 158 (net of deferred taxes of $6,628)	–	–	–	–	(11,204)	(11,204)
Repurchases of common stock	(10,032)	(5,016)	(232,187)	–	–	(237,203)
Compensation for stock awards	–	–	26,727	–	–	26,727
Adjustment to initially apply SFAS No. 123(R)	–	–	(2,370)	–	–	(2,370)
Exercise of common stock options, net	5,767	2,883	86,228	–	–	89,111
Shares issued under stock-based incentive plans, net of cancellations, and other	165	83	(1,027)	–	–	(944)
Tax effect from stock issued	–	–	8,562	–	–	8,562
Dividends – common stock ($0.115 per share)	–	–	–	(20,142)	–	(20,142)
BALANCE AT FEBRUARY 28, 2007	170,689	$85,345	$344,144	$1,336,317	$25,438	$1,791,244

Circuit City Stores, Inc.

CONSOLIDATED STATEMENTS OF CASH FLOWS

(Amounts in thousands)	Years Ended February 28 **2007**	2006	2005(a)
OPERATING ACTIVITIES:			
Net (loss) earnings	$ **(8,281)**	$ 139,746	$ 61,658
Adjustments to reconcile net (loss) earnings to net cash provided by operating activities of continuing operations:			
Net (earnings) loss from discontinued operations	**(128)**	5,350	(1,089)
Depreciation expense	**177,828**	160,608	151,597
Amortization expense	**3,645**	2,618	1,851
Impairment of goodwill	**92,000**	–	–
Stock-based compensation expense	**26,727**	24,386	18,305
(Gain) loss on dispositions of property and equipment	**(1,439)**	2,370	(206)
Provision for deferred income taxes	**72,717**	(14,252)	(116,300)
Cumulative effect of change in accounting principles	**(1,773)**	2,353	–
Other	**1,689**	(1,726)	–
Changes in operating assets and liabilities:			
Accounts receivable, net	**(133,152)**	16,552	(58,738)
Retained interests in securitized receivables	**–**	–	32,867
Merchandise inventory	**49,352**	(231,114)	160,037
Prepaid expenses and other current assets	**(9,580)**	(17,341)	7,207
Other assets	**535**	(3,061)	3,816
Merchandise payable	**73,317**	211,362	28,199
Expenses payable	**55,722**	40,921	(17,372)
Accrued expenses and other current liabilities, and accrued income taxes	**(81,364)**	43,202	54,021
Other long-term liabilities	**(1,474)**	(17,032)	63,494
NET CASH PROVIDED BY OPERATING ACTIVITIES OF CONTINUING OPERATIONS	**316,341**	364,942	389,347
INVESTING ACTIVITIES:			
Purchases of property and equipment	**(285,725)**	(254,451)	(261,461)
Proceeds from sales of property and equipment	**38,620**	55,421	106,369
Purchases of investment securities	**(2,002,123)**	(1,409,760)	(125,325)
Sales and maturities of investment securities	**1,926,086**	1,014,910	–
Other investing activities	**(11,567)**	–	–
Proceeds from the sale of the private-label finance operation	**–**	–	475,857
Acquisitions, net of cash acquired of $30,615	**–**	–	(262,320)
NET CASH USED IN INVESTING ACTIVITIES OF CONTINUING OPERATIONS	**(334,709)**	(593,880)	(66,880)
FINANCING ACTIVITIES:			
Proceeds from short-term borrowings	**35,657**	73,954	12,329
Principal payments on short-term borrowings	**(56,912)**	(53,893)	(13,458)
Proceeds from long-term debt	**1,216**	1,032	–
Principal payments on long-term debt	**(6,724)**	(1,829)	(28,008)
Changes in overdraft balances	**19,347**	(22,540)	36,329
Repurchases of common stock	**(237,203)**	(338,476)	(259,832)
Issuances of common stock	**89,662**	38,038	27,156
Dividends paid	**(20,126)**	(12,844)	(13,848)
Excess tax benefit from stock-based payments	**15,729**	–	–
Redemption of preferred share purchase rights	**–**	(1,876)	–
Other financing activities	**(1,424)**	–	–
NET CASH USED IN FINANCING ACTIVITIES OF CONTINUING OPERATIONS	**(160,778)**	(318,434)	(239,332)
DISCONTINUED OPERATIONS:			
Operating cash flows	**3,310**	(9,884)	(7,193)
Investing cash flows	**2,958**	(8,089)	(6,615)
Financing cash flows	**(592)**	–	(724)
NET CASH PROVIDED BY (USED IN) DISCONTINUED OPERATIONS	**5,676**	(17,973)	(14,532)
EFFECT OF EXCHANGE RATE CHANGES ON CASH	**(1,359)**	1,655	2,016
(Decrease) increase in cash and cash equivalents	**(174,829)**	(563,690)	70,619
Cash and cash equivalents at beginning of year	**315,970**	879,660	809,041
CASH AND CASH EQUIVALENTS AT END OF YEAR	$ **141,141**	$ 315,970	$879,660

CIRCUIT CITY

Alabama Albertville, Alexander City, Andalusia, Arab, Ardmore, Athens, Atmore, Attalla, Bay Minette, Bayou La Batre, Bessemer, Birmingham, Butler, Calera, Camden, Center Point, Centre, Childersburg, Clanton,
Daphne, Decatur, Demopolis, Dothan, Enterprise, Fairfield, Fairhope, Florence, Foley, Fort Payne, Gadsden, Gardendale, Gulf Shores, Guntersville, Haleyville, Hamilton, Hartselle, Hoover, Huntsville, Jackson, Jaspe
Linden, Luverne, Madison, Marion, Mobile, Montgomery, Moulton, Northport, Opelika, Opp, Oxford, Pelham, Pell City, Phenix City, Piedmont, Prattville, Robertsdale, Rogersville, Russellville, Saraland, Scottsboro
Sumiton, Sylacauga, Tallassee, Thomasville, Troy, Tuscaloosa *Alaska* Anchorage, Bethel, Cordova, Craig, Eagle River, Fairbanks, Glennallen, Haines, Homer, Juneau, Kenai, Ketchikan, Kodiak, Petersburg, Sewar
Skagway, Soldotna, Valdez, Wasilla *Arizona* Ajo, Apache Junction, Avondale, Benson, Bullhead City, Camp Verde, Casa Grande, Chandler, Chino Valley, Colorado City, Coolidge, Cottonwood, Douglas, Flagstaff,
Fort Mohave, Fountain Hills, Gilbert, Glendale, Greenvalley, Heber, Holbrook, Kayenta, Kingman, Lake Havasu, Lakeside, Maricopa, Mesa, Miami, Morenci, New River, Nogales, Oro Valley, Parker, Payson, Peoria,
Prescott, Prescott Valley, Quartzsite, Safford, San Manuel, Scottsdale, Sedona, Show Low, Sierra Vista, Springerville, St. Johns, Sun City, Surprise, Taylor, Tempe, Thatcher, Tuba City, Tucson, Wickenburg, Willco
Arkansas Arkadelphia, Ash Flat, Batesville, Beebe, Benton, Bentonville, Berryville, Brinkley, Bryant, Cabot, Camden, Cave City, Clarksville, Clinton, Conway, Danville, De Queen, De Witt, Dumas, El Dorado, Fayetteville
Forrest City, Fort Smith, Glenwood, Harrison, Heber Springs, Hope, Hot Springs, Jacksonville, Jasper, Jonesboro, Little Rock, Magnolia, Malvern, Mammoth Springs, Marshall, Melbourne, Mena, Mountain Home, M
View, North Little Rock, Nashville, Newport, Paragould, Paris, Pine Bluff, Prescott, Rogers, Russellville, Salem, Searcy, Sheridan, Siloam Springs, Springdale, Star City, Stuttgart, Van Buren, West Helena, West M
Wynne *California* Agoura, Alameda, Albany, Alhambra, Alta Loma, Alturas, American Canyon, Anaheim, Anaheim Hills, Anderson, Angels Camp, Antioch, Apple Valley, Arcadia, Arcata, Arnold, Arroyo Grande, Ata
Atwater, Auburn, Avalon, Azusa, Bakersfield, Baldwin Park, Barstow, Beaumont, Bell, Belmont, Benicia, Berkeley, Beverly Hills, Big Bear Lake, Bishop, Blue Jay, Blythe, Brawley, Brea, Buellton, Buena Park,
Burlingame, Calexico, California City, Camarillo, Canoga Park, Canyon Country, Capitola, Carlsbad, Carmichael, Carpinteria, Carson, Castro Valley, Cathedral City, Cerritos, Chatsworth, Chico, Chino, Chino Hills, Chu
Citrus Heights, City of Industry, Clearlake, Cloverdale, Clovis, Coachella, Coalinga, Colton, Colusa, Compton, Concord, Corcoran, Corning, Corona, Corte Madera, Costa Mesa, Covina, Crescent City, Crestline, Cu
Cupertino, Cypress, Daly City, Dana Point, Danville, Davis, Del Mar, Delano, Desert Hot Springs, Diamond Bar, Dinuba, Downey, Duarte, Dublin, E Los Angeles, El Cajon, El Centro, El Cerrito, El Monte, Elk Grove, Em
Encinitas, Encino, Escondido, Eureka, Fairfield, Fall River Mills, Fallbrook, Folsom, Fontana, Foothill Ranch, Fortuna, Foster City, Fountain Valley, Freedom, Fremont, Fresno, Fort Bragg, Fullerton, Garberville, Garde
Gardena, Gilroy, Glendale, Glendora, Goleta, Gonzales, Granada Hills, Grass Valley, Greenfield, Grover Beach, Hanford, Harbor City, Hawthorne, Hayward, Hemet, Hercules, Hesperia, Highland, Hollister, Ho
Huntington Beach, Huntington Park, Indio, Inglewood, Irvine, Jackson, King City, La Habra, La Jolla, La Mesa, La Mirada, La Puente, La Quinta, La Verne, Lafayette, Laguna Hills, Laguna Niguel, Lake Elsinore, Lake
Lakeport, Lakewood, Lancaster, Lawndale, Lemoore, Lincoln Heights, Livermore, Lodi, Lompoc, Long Beach, Los Alamitos, Los Angeles, Los Banos, Los Gatos, Los Osos, Lynwood, Madera, Malibu, Mammot
Manhattan Beach, Manteca, Marina Del Rey, Martinez, Marysville, Maywood, Merced, Milpitas, Mission Hills, Modesto, Mojave, Monrovia, Montclair, Montebello, Monterey, Monterey Park, Montrose, Moorpark,
Valley, Morgan Hill, Morro Bay, Mountain View, Mount Shasta, Murrieta, Napa, National City, Newbury Park, Newhall, Newport Beach, North Highlands, North Hollywood, Northridge, Norwalk, Novato, Oakdale, C
Oakland, Oakley, Oceanside, Ojai, Ontario, Orange, Orangevale, Orland, Oroville, Oxnard, Pacifica, Palm Desert, Palm Springs, Palmdale, Palo Alto, Panorama City, Paradise, Paramount, Pasadena, Paso Robles, Pa
Perris, Petaluma, Phelan, Pico Rivera, Pinole, Pittsburg, Placentia, Placerville, Pleasant Hill, Pleasanton, Pollock Pines, Pomona, Porterville, Poway, Quincy, Ramona, Rancho Cordova, Rancho Cucamonga, Ranch
Margarita, Red Bluff, Redding, Redlands, Redondo Beach, Redwood City, Reedley, Rialto, Ridgecrest, Rio Vista, Riverbank, Riverside, Rocklin, Rohnert Park, Rolling Hills, Rosamond, Rosemead, Roseville, Rowland
Sacramento, Salinas, San Bernardino, San Bruno, San Clemente, San Diego, San Dimas, San Francisco, San Jose, San Leandro, San Luis Obispo, San Marcos, San Mateo, San Pablo, San Pedro, San Rafael, San
Sanger, Santa Ana, Santa Barbara, Santa Clara, Santa Cruz, Santa Maria, Santa Monica, Santa Paula, Santa Rosa, Santee, Saugus, Scotts Valley, Seal Beach, Seaside, Sebastopol, Selma, Sherman Oaks, Signal H
San Juan Capistrano, Soledad, Sonoma, Sonora, South Gate, South Lake Tahoe, South Pasadena, South San Francisco, Spring Valley, Stockton, Studio City, Sun Valley, Sunnyvale, Susanville, Sylmar, Taft, Te
Temecula, Temple City, Thousand Oaks, Torrance, Tracy, Truckee, Tujunga, Tulare, Turlock, Tustin, Twentynine Palms, Ukiah, Union City, Upland, Vacaville, Valencia, Vallejo, Valley Springs, Van Nuys, Venice,
Victorville, Visalia, Vista, Walnut Creek, Wasco, Watsonville, Weaverville, West Covina, West Hollywood, West Los Angeles, West Sacramento, Westchester, Westminster, Whittier, Willits, Willows, Wilmington,
Woodland, Woodland Hills, Yorba Linda, Yreka, Yuba City, Yucaipa, Yucca Valley *Colorado* Alamosa, Arvada, Aspen, Aurora, Avon, Bayfield, Bennett, Boulder, Brighton, Broomfield, Buena Vista, Burlington, Canon Cit
Rock, Castle Rock, Centennial, Center, Colorado Springs, Conifer, Cortez, Craig, Crested Butte, Denver, Durango, Elizabeth, Englewood, Estes Park, Evergreen, Flagler, Fort Collins, Fountain, Fraser, Frisco, Glenwood
Golden, Grand Junction, Greeley, Greenwood Village, Gunnison, Highlands Ranch, Holyoke, Idaho Springs, La Junta, Lafayette, Lakewood, Lamar, Limon, Littleton, Longmont, Loveland, Meeker, Monte Vista, M
Monument, Northglenn, Pagosa Springs, Paonia, Parachute, Parker, Pueblo, Rifle, Salida, Springfield, Steamboat Springs, Sterling, Thornton, Westminster, Woodland Park, Wray, Yuma *Connecticut* Avon, Bark
Bloomfield, Branford, Bridgeport, Bristol, Canaan, Cheshire, Clinton, Cos Cob, Cromwell, Danbury, Derby, East Haven, Enfield, Fairfield, Farmington, Glastonbury, Groton, Guilford, Hamden, Hartford, Manchester,
Middletown, Milford, Naugatuck, New Britain, New Canaan, New Haven, New London, New Milford, Newington, Newtown, North Haven, Norwalk, Norwich, Old Saybrook, Orange, Plainfield, Putnam, Ridgefield, R
Southbury, Southington, Stamford, Torrington, Trumbull, Vernon, Wallingford, Waterbury, Waterford, Watertown, West Hartford, Westport, Wethersfield, Willimantic, Wilton, Windsor, *D.C.* Washington *Delawa*
Claymont, Dover, Georgetown, Middletown, Milford, New Castle, Newark, Rehoboth Beach, Seaford, Smyrna, Wilmington *Florida* Alachua, Altamonte, Altamonte Springs, Apopka, Arcadia, Atlantic Beach, Auburnda
Park, Bartow, Bayonet Point, Belle Glade, Belleview, Big Pine Key, Boca Raton, Bonita Springs, Boynton Beach, Bradenton, Brandon, Branford, Brooksville, Callaway, Cape Coral, Casselberry, Century, Chiefland,
Clearwater, Clermont, Clewiston, Cocoa, Cocoa Beach, Cooper City, Coral Gables, Coral Springs, Crawfordville, Crestview, Crystal River, Davie, Daytona Beach, Deerfield, Deerfield Beach, Defuniak Springs, Delan
Beach, Deltona, Destin, Dunnellon, Englewood, Fernandina Beach, Florida City, Fort Lauderdale, Fort Myers, Fort Pierce, Fort Walton Beach, Gainesville, Greenacres, Gulf Breeze, Haines City, Hialeah, Hilliard,
Hollywood, Homestead, Homosassa, Immokalee, Indiantown, Inverness, Jacksonville, Jensen Beach, Jupiter, Key Largo, Key West, Keystone Heights, Kissimmee, Lady Lake, Lake City, Lake Mary, Lake Placid, Lak
Lake Worth, Lakeland, Lantana, Largo, Lauderdale Lakes, Lauderhill, Leesburg, Lehigh Acres, Live Oak, Longwood, Lutz, Macclenny, Madison, Marathon, Marco Island, Margate, Marianna, Mary Esther, Melbourne
Island, Miami, Miami Beach, Milton, Miramar, Monticello, Mount Dora, North Fort Myers, North Miami Beach, Naples, Navarre, New Port Richey, New Smyrna Beach, Niceville, Oakland Park, Ocala, Ocoee, Okee
Orange City, Orange Park, Orlando, Ormond Beach, Oviedo, Palatka, Palm Bay, Palm Beach Garden, Palm Coast, Palm Harbor, Panama City, Pembroke Pines, Pensacola, Perry, Plant City, Plantation, Pompano Bea
Charlotte, Port Orange, Port Richey, Port St. Joe, Port St. Lucie, Punta Gorda, Riverview, Royal Palm Beach, Ruskin, Sanford, Santa Rosa Beach, Sarasota, Satellite Beach, Sebastian, Sebring, Seffner, Seminol
Daytona, Spring Hill, St. Augustine, St. Cloud, St. Petersburg, Starke, Stuart, Sunrise, Tallahassee, Tampa, Tarpon Springs, Temple Terrace, Tequesta, Titusville, Venice, Vero Beach, Wauchula, Wellington, West Paln
Weston, Wildwood, Wilton Manors, Winter Haven, Winter Park, Winter Springs, Zephyrhills *Georgia* Adel, Albany, Alpharetta, Americus, Athens, Atlanta, Augusta, Austell, Bainbridge, Barnesville, Baxley, Blairsville,
Blue Ridge, Brunswick, Buford, Cairo, Calhoun, Canton, Carrollton, Cartersville, Cedartown, Centerville, Chamblee, Chatsworth, Clayton, Cleveland, Columbus, Commerce, Conyers, Cordele, Cornelia, Covington, Cu
Cuthbert, Dahlonega, Dalton, Dawson, Dawsonville, Decatur, Donalsonville, Douglas, Douglasville, Dublin, Duluth, East Ellijay, Elberton, Fayetteville, Fitzgerald, Folkston, Forest Park, Forsyth, Fort Gaines, Fort Ogl
Fort Valley, Gainesville, Griffin, Hampton, Hartwell, Hazlehurst, Hiawassee, Hinesville, Hiram, Homerville, Jackson, Jasper, Jesup, Kennesaw, Lafayette, Lagrange, Lawrenceville, Lilburn, Lincolnton, Lithonia,
Madison, Marietta, Martinez, Mc Rae, McDonough, Metter, Milledgeville, Monroe, Monticello, Morrow, Moultrie, Nashville, Newnan, Norcross, Oakwood, Peachtree City, Perry, Quitman, Richmond Hill, Riverdale, Ro
Rome, Roswell, Royston, Savannah, Smyrna, Snellville, St. Marys, St. Simons Island, Statesboro, Stockbridge, Stone Mountain, Summerville, Suwanee, Sylvania, Sylvester, Thomaston, Thomasville, Thomson, Tifton,
Trenton, Union City, Valdosta, Vidalia, Villa Rica, Warner Robins, Washington, Waycross, Winder, Woodbury, Woodstock *Hawaii* Aiea, Ewa Beach, Haleiwa, Hilo, Honolulu, Kahului, Kailua, Kailua-Kona, Kamuela, K
Kapolei, Kihei, Lahaina, Lihue, Mililani, Wahiawa, Waianae, Waipahu *Idaho* American Falls, Blackfoot, Boise, Bonners Ferry, Buhl, Burley, Caldwell, Chubbuck, Coeur d'Alene, Cottonwood, Driggs, Emmett, Grangeville
Idaho Falls, Lewiston, McCall, Meridian, Montpelier, Moscow, Mountain Home, Nampa, Orofino, Pocatello, Post Falls, Rexburg, Rigby, Salmon, Sandpoint, Twin Falls, Wendell *Illinois* Aledo, Alton, Anna, Antioch
Arlington Heights, Arthur, Aurora, Bartlett, Batavia, Belleville, Belvidere, Bensenville, Benton, Berwyn, Bloomingdale, Bloomington, Blue Island, Bolingbrook, Bourbonnais, Burbank, Calumet City, Canton, Car
Carlinville, Carmi, Centralia, Champaign, Channahon, Chester, Chicago, Chicago Heights, Cicero, Collinsville, Crystal Lake, Danville, Decatur, Des Plaines, Dixon, Dolton, Downers Grove, Du Quoin, Dwight, East Peo
St Louis, Effingham, El Paso, Elgin, Elk Grove Village, Eureka, Evanston, Fairbury, Fairfield, Fairview Heights, Flora, Fox Lake, Frankfort, Freeport, Galesburg, Geneseo, Gibson City, Glen Carbon, Glen Ellyn, Glencoe, G
Granite City, Greenville, Gurnee, Harrisburg, Havana, Highland, Highland Park, Hoffman Estates, Homer Glen, Homewood, Hoopeston, Jacksonville, Jerseyville, Joliet, Kankakee, Kewanee, La Grange, Lake Zurich,
Lemont, Lincoln, Litchfield, Lake in the Hills, Lombard, Machesney Park, Macomb, Marengo, Marion, Markham, Mascoutah, Matteson, Mattoon, McHenry, Melrose Park, Mendota, Midlothian, Moline, Montgomery
Mount Vernon, Mundelein, Naperville, Nashville, Niles, Norridge, North Riverside, Oak Lawn, Oak Park, Olney, Ottawa, Palatine, Palos Heights, Paris, Pekin, Peoria, Peru, Petersburg, Pontiac, Princeton, Quincy, R
Rochelle, Rockford, Round Lake Beach, Salem, Sandwich, Savanna, Savoy, Schaumburg, Seneca, Shiloh, Skokie, South Elgin, South Holland, Sparta, Springfield, St. Charles, Staunton, Sterling, Streator, Sullivan, Sy
Tinley Park, Tuscola, Urbana, Vernon Hills, Villa Park, Virden, Waterloo, Watseka, Waukegan, West Dundee, Wheaton, Wheeling, Willowbrook, Wilmington, Wood River, Yorkville, Zion *Indiana* Anderson, Angola
Auburn, Aurora, Avon, Batesville, Bedford, Berne, Bicknell, Bloomington, Bluffton, Brazil, Bremen, Brook, Brookville, Brownsburg, Brownstown, Cannelton, Carmel, Clarksville, Columbia City, Columbus, Corydon, Co
Crawfordsville, Crown Point, Decatur, Demotte, Elkhart, Elwood, Evansville, Fishers, Fort Wayne, Fowler, Frankfort, Franklin, Gary, Goshen, Greencastle, Greenfield, Greensburg, Greenwood, Griffith, Hammond,
Huntington, Indianapolis, Jasper, Kendallville, Knox, Kokomo, La Porte, Lafayette, Lagrange, Lebanon, Ligonier, Linton, Madison, Marion, Martinsville, Merrillville, Michigan City, Mishawaka, Monticello, Mooresville,
Munster, Nappanee, New Albany, New Carlisle, New Castle, New Haven, Noblesville, North Manchester, North Vernon, Paoli, Peru, Petersburg, Plainfield, Plymouth, Portage, Portland, Princeton, Rensselaer, Ri
Rising Sun, Rochester, Rockport, Rockville, Rushville, Schererville, Seymour, Shelbyville, South Bend, Syracuse, Terre Haute, Tipton, Valparaiso, Vincennes, W Lafayette, Wabash, Warsaw, Washington, Winamac, Wi
Iowa Adel, Altoona, Ames, Ankeny, Atlantic, Belle Plaine, Boone, Carroll, Cedar Falls, Cedar Rapids, Chariton, Charles City, Cherokee, Clarinda, Clinton, Coralville, Council Bluffs, Cresco, Creston, Davenport,
Denison, Des Moines, Dubuque, Dyersville, Eagle Grove, Estherville, Fairfield, Fort Dodge, Fort Madison, Garner, Glenwood, Greenfield, Grinnell, Hampton, Harlan, Humboldt, Independence, Iowa City, Iowa Falls, Je
Keokuk, Knoxville, Le Mars, Logan, Manchester, Maquoketa, Marengo, Marshalltown, Mason City, Mount Pleasant, Muscatine, New Hampton, Newton, Orange City, Osage, Osceola, Ottumwa, Pella, Perry, Pocahon
Oak, Rock Valley, Sac City, Sheldon, Sioux Center, Sioux City, Spencer, Spirit Lake, Stuart, Vinton, Washington, Waterloo, Webster City, West Burlington, West Des Moines, West Union, Winterset *Kansas* Abilene,
Arkansas City, Atchison, Atwood, Bonner Springs, Burlington, Chanute, Clay Center, Colby, Columbus, Concordia, Derby, Dodge City, El Dorado, Ellsworth, Emporia, Fort Scott, Garden City, Garnett, Girard, Goodlar
Bend, Hays, Hillsboro, Horton, Hutchinson, Independence, Iola, Junction City, Kansas City, Lawrence ... Lenexa, Liberal, Manhattan, McPherson, Mission, Newton, Oakley, Olathe, Osage City, Osav
Ottawa, Overland Park, Parsons, Pittsburg, Pratt, Salina, Scott City, Seneca, Shawnee Mission ... Wellington, Wichita, Winfield *Kentucky* Alexandria, Ashland, Barbourville, Bardstown, B
Beaver Dam, Berea, Bowling Green, Brandenburg, Cadiz, Campbellsville, Campton, Carrollt ... al City, Columbia, ... a, Danville, Dry Ridge, Elizabethtown, Erlanger, Falmouth, Flemingsburg, Florence, F
Franklin, Georgetown, Glasgow, Grayson, Hazard, Henderson, Hopkinsville, Jackson, ... er, La Grange, Latonia, Leba ... exington, London, Louisville, Madisonville, Mayfield, Maysville, Middlesboro, Mo
Morehead, Morgantown, Mount Sterling, Mount Vernon, Murray, Newport, Nicho ... e, Owensboro, Paducah, Paris, Pike ... Pineville, Prestonsburg, Princeton, Radcliff, Richmond, Russell Springs, Rus
Salyersville, Scottsville, Shelbyville, Somerset, South Williamson, Stanton, Taylorsvil ... arsaw, West Liberty, Whitley City, Williams ... Winchester *Louisiana* Abbeville, Alexandria, Bastrop, Baton Rouge, Bogalusa
City, Boutte, Crowley, Cut Off, Denham Springs, Deridder, Eunice, Franklinton, G ... ies, Hammond, Harahan, Harvey, Houma, Jea ... te, Jena, Jennings, Kenner, Kentwood, La Place, Lafayette, Lake Charles, L
Mandeville, Mansfield, Many, Metairie, Minden, Monroe, Morgan City, Natchit ... s, New Iberia, New Orleans, New Roads, Oakdale ... elousas, Pineville, Plaquemine, Rayne, Ruston, Shreveport, Slidell, Sprin
Francisville, Sulphur, Thibodaux, Ville Platte, West Monroe, Westwego, Winfiel ... innsboro, Zachary *Maine* Auburn, Augusta, Bangor, B ... arbor, Belfast, Biddeford, Boothbay Harbor, Brunswick, Bucksport, Dama
Dover-Foxcroft, Ellsworth, Falmouth, Farmington, Fort Kent, Lewiston, Ma ... s, Madawaska, Mexico, Millinocket, Oxford, Portland, P ... ue Isle, Rockland, Sanford, Skowhegan, South Portland, Standish, T
Waterville, Wells, Windham *Maryland* Aberdeen, Annapolis, Baltimore, Bel ... Beltsville. Bethesda. Bowie. Burtonsville, Cambridge, Cator ... le, Charlotte Hall, Chestertown, Clinton, Cockeysville, College Park, C
Denton, Derwood, Dunkirk, Easton, Edgewood, Eldersburg, Elkton, Ellicot ... y, F ... rederick, Gaithersburg, Gan ... ls, Germantown, Glen Burnie, Greenbelt, Hagerstown, Hampstead,
Hyattsville, Kensington, La Plata, La Vale, Largo, Laurel, Leonardtown, Lexi ... on Park, M ... ights, M ... Mount Airy, Oakland, Ocea ... ity, Odenton, Olney, Owings Mills, Oxon Hill, Oxon Hill, Pasadena, Po
City, Potomac, Prince Fredrick, Randallstown, Reisterstown, Rockville, S ... bury, Seat ... , Severna ... er Spring, Stevensville, ... oma Park, Towson, Waldorf, Westminster, Wheaton *Massachusett*
Andover, Ashland, Athol, Auburn, Bedford, Beverly, Billerica, Boston, Bra ... ee, Bridge ... ckton, Br ... rlington, Cambridge, Che ... sford, Chicopee, Danvers, Dedham, Dorchester, East Boston, East
East Wareham, Fairhaven, Fall River, Falmouth, Fitchburg, Foxboro, Fra ... , Gardner, ... r, Greenfi ... Barrington, Hadley, Hano ... Haverhill, Holyoke, Hyannis, Kingston, Lanesborough, Lenox, Leo
Lowell, Lynn, Malden, Marlborough, Marshfield, Medford, Milford, Nan ... ket, Natick, ... ford, New ... Newton, North Adams, N ... Attleboro, North Dartmouth, Northampton, Orleans, Peabody, P
Plymouth, Quincy, Raynham, Revere, Roslindale, Saugus, South Attle ... o, South B ... uth Denni ... Easton, South Lawrence, ... th Yarmouth, Southbridge, Springfield, Stoneham, Stoughton,
Swampscott, Swansea, Taunton, Vineyard Haven, Waltham, Watertow ... Webster, We ... field, We ... n, Westfield, Westford, Whi ... sville, Wilmington, Woburn, Worcester *Michigan* Adrian, Albion,
Alpena, Ann Arbor, Auburn Hills, Bad Axe, Battle Creek, Bay City, Bellaire ... lleville, Ben ... ig Rapids, Birmingham, Bloomfie ... Boyne City, Brighton, Brooklyn, Brown City, Burton, Byron Center,
Canton, Caro, Carson City, Cass City, Center Line, Charlevoix, Cheboygan ... esaning, C ... n Township, Clio, Coldwater, Co ... erce, Davison, Dearborn, Dearborn Heights, Detroit, Dowagiac, Eas
Eaton Rapids, Escanaba, Evart, Farmington Hills, Farmington, Fenton, Fe ... ale, Flint, F ... t, Fra ... Fremont, Gaylord, Grand Bla ... Grand Haven, Grand Rapids, Grayling, Greenville, Grosse Pointe, H
Hemlock, Highland Park, Holland, Houghton Lake, Howell, Imlay City, Ion ... ron Mount ... ood, Is ... ackson, Jenison, Jonesville ... lamazoo, Kalkaska, Kentwood, Lake Orion, L'Anse, Lansing, Lapeer
Park, Livonia, Ludington, Madison Heights, Manistee, Manistique, Marin ... ty, Marqu ... hall, Mi ... ord, Monroe, Mount Pleas ... , Munising, Muskegon, Newberry, Niles, Novi, Oak Park, Okemos,
Owosso, Petoskey, Pinconning, Plainwell, Pontiac, Port Huron, Portage, Re ... d, Reed C ... ond, Roc ... s, Rogers City, Roseville, ... al Oak, Saginaw, Sandusky, Sault St. Marie, Shelby, South Haven, So
Southgate, St. Ignace, St. Johns, Standish, Stanton, Sturgis, Suttons Bay, ... as City, ... ee Oaks, ... rs, Traverse City, Troy, ... a, Vassar, Washington Township, Waterford, Wayne, Westland, Whit
White Pigeon, Whitehall, Woodhaven, Wyoming, Ypsilanti *Minnesota* Ada, ... n, Alba ... Lea, Alex ... ple Valley, Austin, Ba ... e, Baxter, Bemidji, Benson, Blaine, Bloomington, Brooklyn Center, B
Cambridge, Chanhassen, Coon Rapids, Cottage Grove, Crystal, Detroit Lakes, ... uth, D ... gan, Eden ... na, Elk River, Erskine ... irmont, Faribault, Fergus Falls, Forest Lake, Golden Valley, Grand Mara
Rapids, Hibbing, Hilltop, Hutchinson, International Falls, Jackson, Lake City, ... ueur ... Little Fall ... airie, Mankato, Ma ... Grove, Marshall, Minneapolis, Minnetonka, Montevideo, Monticello, M
Moose Lake, Mora, Morris, New Ulm, North Branch, Ortonville, Owatonna, Pa ... pids, Pi ... eton, Red W ... Redwood Falls, Richfield, Rochester, Roseau, Roseville, Saint Cloud, Sa
Savage, Shakopee, Sleepy Eye, St. Cloud, St. James, St. Louis Park, St. Paul, S ... ter, Stillwater, Thief River Falls, Vadnais Height ... rginia, Walker, Warroad, Waseca, Wayzata, Willmar, Windom, Winona, W
Worthington, Young America *Mississippi* Amory, Batesville, Biloxi, Booneville, Bro ... ven, Canton, Carthage, Clarksdale, Clevel ... Clinton, Columbia, Columbus, Corinth, Crystal Springs, D'Iberville, Flora, G
Greenwood, Grenada, Gulfport, Hattiesburg, Houston, Jackson, Laurel, Lucedale, Mag ... McComb, Mendenhall, Meridian, Mont ... , Morton, Natchez, New Albany, Ocean Springs, Olive Branch, Oxford, Pascagou
Philadelphia, Picayune, Pontotoc, Poplarville, Prentiss, Purvis, Quitman, Ridgeland, Se ... , Southaven, Starkville, Tupel ... rtown, Vicksburg, Waynesboro, West Point, Wiggins, Yazoo City *Missouri* Alton,

RADIOSHACK

RadioShack.

RadioShack Corporation | **Financial Reports**

CONSOLIDATED BALANCE SHEETS
RadioShack Corporation and Subsidiaries

	December 31, 2006	December 31, 2005
(In millions, except for share amounts)		
Assets		
Current assets:		
Cash and cash equivalents	$ 472.0	$ 224.0
Accounts and notes receivable, net	247.9	309.4
Inventories	752.1	964.9
Other current assets	127.6	129.0
Total current assets	1,599.6	1,627.3
Property, plant and equipment, net	386.3	476.2
Other assets, net	84.1	101.6
Total assets	$ 2,070.0	$ 2,205.1
Liabilities and Stockholders' Equity		
Current liabilities:		
Short-term debt, including current maturities of long-term debt	$ 194.9	$ 40.9
Accounts payable	254.5	490.9
Accrued expenses and other current liabilities	442.2	379.5
Income taxes payable	92.6	75.0
Total current liabilities	984.2	986.3
Long-term debt, excluding current maturities	345.8	494.9
Other non-current liabilities	86.2	135.1
Total liabilities	1,416.2	1,616.3
Commitments and contingent liabilities		
Stockholders' equity:		
Preferred stock, no par value, 1,000,000 shares authorized:		
Series A junior participating, 300,000 shares designated and none issued	—	—
Common stock, $1 par value, 650,000,000 shares authorized; 191,033,000 shares issued	191.0	191.0
Additional paid-in capital	92.6	87.7
Retained earnings	1,780.9	1,741.4
Treasury stock, at cost; 55,196,000 and 56,071,000 shares, respectively	(1,409.1)	(1,431.6)
Accumulated other comprehensive (loss) income	(1.6)	0.3
Total stockholders' equity	653.8	588.8
Total liabilities and stockholders' equity	$ 2,070.0	$ 2,205.1

CONSOLIDATED STATEMENTS OF INCOME
RadioShack Corporation and Subsidiaries

	Year Ended December 31,					
	2006		2005		2004	
(In millions, except per share amounts)	**Dollars**	**% of Revenues**	**Dollars**	**% of Revenues**	**Dollars**	**% of Revenues**
Net sales and operating revenues	$ 4,777.5	100.0%	$ 5,081.7	100.0%	$ 4,841.2	100.0%
Cost of products sold	2,544.4	53.3	2,706.3	53.3	2,406.7	49.7
Gross profit	2,233.1	46.7	2,375.4	46.7	2,434.5	50.3
Operating expenses:						
Selling, general and administrative	1,903.7	39.8	1,901.7	37.4	1,774.8	36.7
Depreciation and amortization	128.2	2.7	123.8	2.4	101.4	2.1
Impairment of long-lived assets and other charges	44.3	0.9	—	—	—	—
Total operating expenses	2,076.2	43.4	2,025.5	39.8	1,876.2	38.8
Operating income	156.9	3.3	349.9	6.9	558.3	11.5
Interest income	7.4	0.1	5.9	0.1	11.4	0.2
Interest expense	(44.3)	(0.9)	(44.5)	(0.8)	(29.6)	(0.5)
Other (loss) income	(8.6)	(0.2)	10.2	0.2	2.0	—
Income before income taxes	111.4	2.3	321.5	6.4	542.1	11.2
Income tax provision	38.0	0.8	51.6	1.0	204.9	4.2
Income before cumulative effect of change in accounting principle	73.4	1.5	269.9	5.4	337.2	7.0
Cumulative effect of change in accounting principle, net of $1.8 million tax benefit in 2005	—	—	(2.9)	(0.1)	—	—
Net income	$ 73.4	1.5%	$ 267.0	5.3%	$ 337.2	7.0%
Net income per share						
Basic:						
Income before cumulative effect of change in accounting principle	$ 0.54		$ 1.82		$ 2.09	
Cumulative effect of change in accounting principle, net of taxes	—		(0.02)		—	
Basic income per share	$ 0.54		$ 1.80		$ 2.09	
Assuming dilution:						
Income before cumulative effect of change in accounting principle	$ 0.54		$ 1.81		$ 2.08	
Cumulative effect of change in accounting principle, net of taxes	—		(0.02)		—	
Diluted income per share	$ 0.54		$ 1.79		$ 2.08	
Shares used in computing income per share:						
Basic	136.2		148.1		161.0	
Diluted	136.2		148.8		162.5	

CONSOLIDATED STATEMENTS OF STOCKHOLDERS' EQUITY AND COMPREHENSIVE INCOME
RadioShack Corporation and Subsidiaries

	Shares at December 31,			Dollars at December 31,		
(In millions)	2006	2005	2004	2006	2005	2004
Common stock						
Beginning and end of year	191.0	191.0	191.0	$ 191.0	$ 191.0	$ 191.0
Treasury stock						
Beginning of year	(56.0)	(32.8)	(28.5)	$ (1,431.6)	$ (859.4)	$ (707.2)
Purchase of treasury stock	—	(25.3)	(8.0)	—	(625.8)	(246.9)
Issuance of common stock	0.6	1.2	1.3	18.6	31.8	33.8
Exercise of stock options and grant of stock awards	0.2	0.9	2.4	3.9	21.8	60.9
End of year	(55.2)	(56.0)	(32.8)	$ (1,409.1)	$ (1,431.6)	$ (859.4)
Additional paid-in capital						
Beginning of year				$ 87.7	$ 82.7	$ 75.2
Issuance of common stock				(5.7)	3.5	5.7
Exercise of stock options and grant of stock awards				(1.7)	(5.0)	(9.5)
Stock option compensation				12.0	—	—
Stock option income tax benefits				0.3	6.5	11.3
End of year				$ 92.6	$ 87.7	$ 82.7
Retained earnings						
Beginning of year				$ 1,741.4	$ 1,508.1	$ 1,210.6
Net income				73.4	267.0	337.2
Common stock cash dividends declared				(33.9)	(33.7)	(39.7)
End of year				$ 1,780.9	$ 1,741.4	$ 1,508.1
Accumulated other comprehensive (loss) income						
Beginning of year				$ 0.3	$ (0.3)	$ (0.3)
Pension adjustments, net of tax				(1.0)	—	—
Other comprehensive (loss) income				(0.9)	0.6	—
End of year				$ (1.6)	$ 0.3	$ (0.3)
Total stockholders' equity				$ 653.8	$ 588.8	$ 922.1
Comprehensive income						
Net income				$ 73.4	$ 267.0	$ 337.2
Other comprehensive income, net of tax:						
Foreign currency translation adjustments				0.3	(0.4)	0.1
Amortization of gain on cash flow hedge				(0.1)	(0.1)	(0.1)
Unrealized (loss) gain on securities				(1.1)	1.1	—
Other comprehensive (loss) income				(0.9)	0.6	—
Comprehensive income				$ 72.5	$ 267.6	$ 337.2

CONSOLIDATED STATEMENTS OF CASH FLOWS
RadioShack Corporation and Subsidiaries

(In millions)	Year Ended December 31, 2006	2005	2004
Cash flows from operating activities:			
Net income	$ 73.4	$ 267.0	$ 337.2
Adjustments to reconcile net income to net cash provided by operating activities:			
Depreciation and amortization	128.2	123.8	101.4
Cumulative effect of change in accounting principle	—	4.7	—
Impairment of long-lived assets and other charges	44.3	—	—
Stock option compensation	12.0	—	—
Deferred income taxes and other items	(27.6)	(76.9)	50.2
Provision for credit losses and bad debts	0.4	0.1	(0.3)
Changes in operating assets and liabilities, excluding acquisitions:			
Accounts and notes receivable	61.8	(68.2)	(53.0)
Inventories	212.8	38.8	(234.2)
Other current assets	2.5	28.5	(7.5)
Accounts payable, accrued expenses, income taxes payable and other	(193.0)	45.1	158.7
Net cash provided by operating activities	314.8	362.9	352.5
Cash flows from investing activities:			
Additions to property, plant and equipment	(91.0)	(170.7)	(229.4)
Proceeds from sale of property, plant and equipment	11.1	226.0	2.5
Purchase of kiosk business	—	—	(59.1)
Other investing activities	0.6	(16.0)	(4.2)
Net cash (used in) provided by investing activities	(79.3)	39.3	(290.2)
Cash flows from financing activities:			
Purchases of treasury stock	—	(625.8)	(251.1)
Sale of treasury stock to employee benefit plans	10.5	30.1	35.4
Proceeds from exercise of stock options	1.7	17.4	50.4
Payments of dividends	(33.9)	(33.7)	(39.7)
Changes in short-term borrowings and outstanding checks in excess of cash balances, net	42.2	(4.0)	(14.0)
Reductions of long-term borrowings	(8.0)	(0.1)	(40.1)
Net cash provided by (used in) financing activities	12.5	(616.1)	(259.1)
Net increase (decrease) in cash and cash equivalents	248.0	(213.9)	(196.8)
Cash and cash equivalents, beginning of period	224.0	437.9	634.7
Cash and cash equivalents, end of period	$ 472.0	$ 224.0	$ 437.9
Supplemental cash flow information:			
Interest paid	$ 44.0	$ 43.4	$ 29.3
Income taxes paid	52.9	158.5	182.7

RADIOSHACK

Apple Financial Report

APPLE

CONSOLIDATED BALANCE SHEETS
(In millions, except share amounts)

	September 30, 2006	September 24, 2005
ASSETS		
Current assets:		
Cash and cash equivalents	$ 6,392	$ 3,491
Short-term investments	3,718	4,770
Accounts receivable, less allowances of $52 and $46, respectively	1,252	895
Inventories	270	165
Deferred tax assets	607	331
Other current assets	2,270	648
Total current assets	14,509	10,300
Property, plant, and equipment, net	1,281	817
Goodwill	38	69
Acquired intangible assets, net	139	27
Other assets	1,238	303
Total assets	$17,205	$11,516
LIABILITIES AND SHAREHOLDERS' EQUITY		
Current liabilities:		
Accounts payable	$ 3,390	$ 1,779
Accrued expenses	3,081	1,708
Total current liabilities	6,471	3,487
Noncurrent liabilities	750	601
Total liabilities	7,221	4,088
Commitments and contingencies		
Shareholders' equity:		
Common stock, no par value; 1,800,000,000 shares authorized; 855,262,568 and 835,019,364 shares issued and outstanding, respectively	4,355	3,564
Deferred stock compensation	—	(61)
Retained earnings	5,607	3,925
Accumulated other comprehensive income	22	—
Total shareholders' equity	9,984	7,428
Total liabilities and shareholders' equity	$17,205	$11,516

APPLE

CONSOLIDATED STATEMENTS OF OPERATIONS
(In millions, except share and per share amounts)

Three fiscal years ended September 30, 2006	2006	2005	2004
Net sales	$ 19,315	$ 13,931	$ 8,279
Cost of sales	13,717	9,889	6,022
Gross margin	5,598	4,042	2,257
Operating expenses:			
Research and development	712	535	491
Selling, general, and administrative	2,433	1,864	1,430
Restructuring costs	—	—	23
Total operating expenses	3,145	2,399	1,944
Operating income	2,453	1,643	313
Other income and expense	365	165	57
Income before provision for income taxes	2,818	1,808	370
Provision for income taxes	829	480	104
Net income	$ 1,989	$ 1,328	$ 266
Earnings per common share:			
Basic	$ 2.36	$ 1.64	$ 0.36
Diluted	$ 2.27	$ 1.55	$ 0.34
Shares used in computing earnings per share (in thousands):			
Basic	844,058	808,439	743,180
Diluted	877,526	856,878	774,776

CONSOLIDATED STATEMENTS OF SHAREHOLDERS' EQUITY
(In millions, except share amounts which are in thousands)

	Common Stock Shares	Common Stock Amount	Deferred Stock Compensation	Retained Earnings	Accumulated Other Comprehensive Income (Loss)	Total Shareholders' Equity
Balances as of September 27, 2003 as previously reported	733,454	$1,926	$ (62)	$2,394	$(35)	$4,223
Adjustments to opening shareholders' equity	—	85	(22)	(63)	—	—
Balance as of September 27, 2003 as restated	733,454	$2,011	$ (84)	$2,331	$(35)	$4,223
Components of comprehensive income:						
Net income	—	—	—	266	—	266
Change in foreign currency translation	—	—	—	—	13	13
Change in unrealized gain on available-for-sale securities, net of tax	—	—	—	—	(5)	(5)
Change in unrealized loss on derivative investments, net of tax	—	—	—	—	12	12
Total comprehensive income						286
Issuance of stock-based compensation awards	—	63	(63)	—	—	—
Adjustment to common stock related to a prior year acquisition	(159)	(2)	—	—	—	(2)
Stock-based compensation	—	—	46	—	—	46
Common stock issued under stock plans	49,592	427	—	—	—	427
Tax benefit related to stock options	—	83	—	—	—	83
Balances as of September 25, 2004	782,887	$2,582	$(101)	$2,597	$(15)	$5,063
Components of comprehensive income:						
Net income	—	—	—	1,328	—	1,328
Change in foreign currency translation	—	—	—	—	7	7
Change in unrealized gain on derivative investments, net of tax	—	—	—	—	8	8
Total comprehensive income						1,343
Issuance of stock-based compensation awards	—	7	(7)	—	—	—
Stock-based compensation	—	—	47	—	—	47
Common stock issued under stock plans	52,132	547	—	—	—	547
Tax benefit related to stock options	—	428	—	—	—	428
Balances as of September 24, 2005	835,019	$3,564	$ (61)	$3,925	$ —	$7,428
Components of comprehensive income:						
Net income	—	—	—	1,989	—	1,989
Change in foreign currency translation	—	—	—	—	19	19
Change in unrealized gain on available-for-sale securities, net of tax	—	—	—	—	4	4
Change in unrealized loss on derivative investments, net of tax	—	—	—	—	(1)	(1)
Total comprehensive income						2,011
Common stock repurchased	(4,574)	(48)	—	(307)	—	(355)
Stock-based compensation	—	163	—	—	—	163
Deferred compensation	—	(61)	61	—	—	—
Common stock issued under stock plans	24,818	318	—	—	—	318
Tax benefit related to stock-based compensation	—	419	—	—	—	419
Balances as of September 30, 2006	855,263	$4,355	$ —	$5,607	$ 22	$9,984

APPLE

CONSOLIDATED STATEMENTS OF CASH FLOWS
(In millions)

Three fiscal years ended September 30, 2006	2006	2005	2004
Cash and cash equivalents, beginning of the year	$ 3,491	$ 2,969	$ 3,396
Operating Activities:			
Net income	1,989	1,328	266
Adjustments to reconcile net income to cash generated by operating activities:			
Depreciation, amortization and accretion	225	179	150
Stock-based compensation expense	163	49	46
Provision for deferred income taxes	53	50	19
Excess tax benefits from stock options	—	428	83
Gain on sale of PowerSchool net assets	(4)	—	—
Loss on disposition of property, plant, and equipment	15	9	7
Gains on sales of investments, net	—	—	(5)
Changes in operating assets and liabilities:			
Accounts receivable	(357)	(121)	(8)
Inventories	(105)	(64)	(45)
Other current assets	(1,626)	(150)	(176)
Other assets	(1,040)	(35)	(25)
Accounts payable	1,611	328	297
Other liabilities	1,296	534	325
Cash generated by operating activities	2,220	2,535	934
Investing Activities:			
Purchases of short-term investments	(7,255)	(11,470)	(3,270)
Proceeds from maturities of short-term investments	7,226	8,609	1,141
Proceeds from sales of investments	1,086	586	806
Purchases of long-term investments	(25)	—	—
Proceeds from sale of PowerSchool net assets	40	—	—
Purchases of property, plant, and equipment	(657)	(260)	(176)
Other	(58)	(21)	11
Cash generated by (used for) investing activities	357	(2,556)	(1,488)
Financing Activities:			
Payment of long-term debt	—	—	(300)
Proceeds from issuance of common stock	318	543	427
Excess tax benefits from stock-based compensation	361	—	—
Repurchases of common stock	(355)	—	—
Cash generated by financing activities	324	543	127
Increase (decrease) in cash and cash equivalents	2,901	522	(427)
Cash and cash equivalents, end of the year	$ 6,392	$ 3,491	$ 2,969
Supplemental cash flow disclosures:			
Cash paid during the year for interest	$ —	$ —	$ 10
Cash paid (received) for income taxes, net	$ 194	$ 17	$ (7)

B Time Value of Money

Learning Objectives

CAP

Conceptual

C1 Describe the earning of interest and the concepts of present and future values. *(p. B-1)*

Procedural

P1 Apply present value concepts to a single amount by using interest tables. *(p. B-3)*

P2 Apply future value concepts to a single amount by using interest tables. *(p. B-4)*

P3 Apply present value concepts to an annuity by using interest tables. *(p. B-5)*

P4 Apply future value concepts to an annuity by using interest tables. *(p. B-6)*

The concepts of present and future values are important to modern business, including the preparation and analysis of financial statements. The purpose of this appendix is to explain, illustrate, and compute present and future values. This appendix applies these concepts with reference to both business and everyday activities.

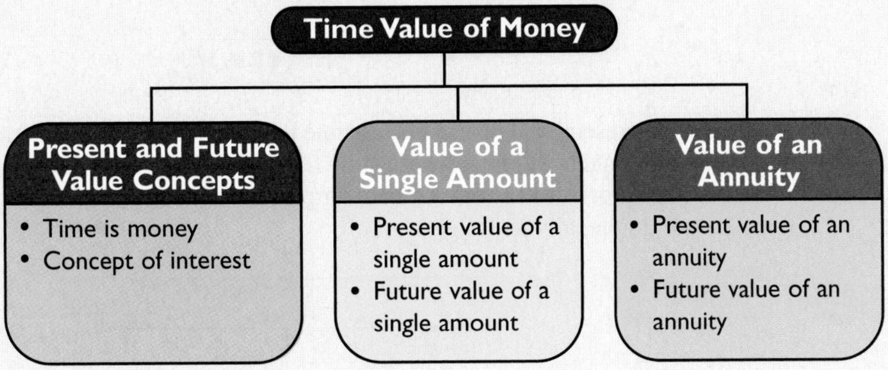

Present and Future Value Concepts

C1 Describe the earning of interest and the concepts of present and future values.

The old saying "Time is money" reflects the notion that as time passes, the values of our assets and liabilities change. This change is due to *interest,* which is a borrower's payment to the owner of an asset for its use. The most common example of interest is a savings account asset. As we keep a balance of cash in the account, it earns interest that the financial institution pays us. An example of a liability is a car loan. As we carry the balance of the loan, we accumulate interest costs on it. We must ultimately repay this loan with interest.

Present and future value computations enable us to measure or estimate the interest component of holding assets or liabilities over time. The present value computation is important when we want to know the value of future-day assets *today.* The future value computation is important when we want to know the value of present-day assets *at a future date.* The first section focuses on the present value of a single amount. The second section focuses on the future value of a single amount. Then both the present and future values of a series of amounts (called an *annuity*) are defined and explained.

Decision Insight

Keep That Job Lottery winners often never work again. Kenny Dukes, a recent Georgia lottery winner, doesn't have that option. He is serving parole for burglary charges, and Georgia requires its parolees to be employed (or in school). For his lottery winnings, Dukes had to choose between $31 million in 30 annual payments or $16 million in one lump sum ($10.6 million after-tax); he chose the latter.

Present Value of a Single Amount

We graphically express the present value, called p, of a single future amount, called f, that is received or paid at a future date in Exhibit B.1.

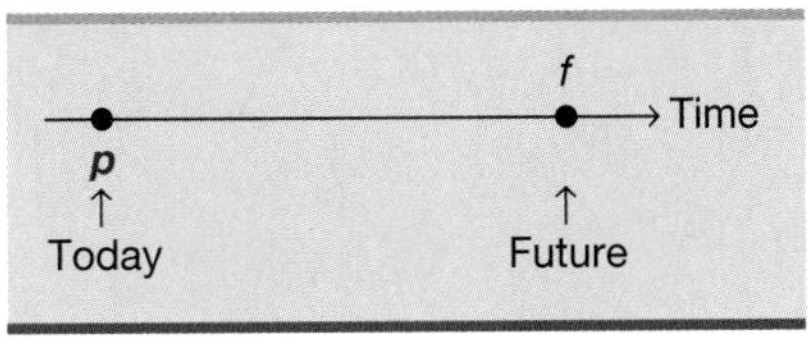

EXHIBIT B.1

Present Value of a Single Amount Diagram

The formula to compute the present value of a single amount is shown in Exhibit B.2, where p = present value; f = future value; i = rate of interest per period; and n = number of periods. (Interest is also called the *discount,* and an interest rate is also called the *discount rate.*)

EXHIBIT B.2

Present Value of a Single Amount Formula

$$p = \frac{f}{(1 + i)^n}$$

To illustrate present value concepts, assume that we need \$220 one period from today. We want to know how much we must invest now, for one period, at an interest rate of 10% to provide for this \$220. For this illustration, the p, or present value, is the unknown amount—the specifics are shown graphically as follows:

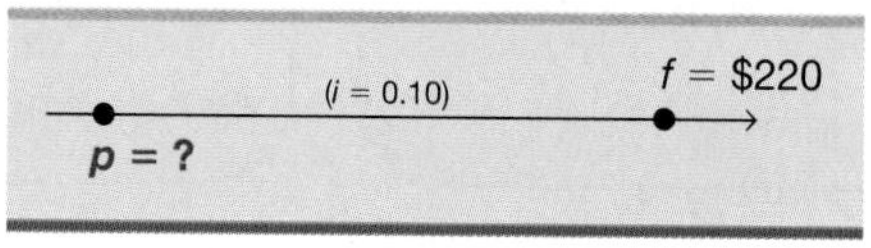

Conceptually, we know p must be less than \$220. This is obvious from the answer to this question: Would we rather have \$220 today or \$220 at some future date? If we had \$220 today, we could invest it and see it grow to something more than \$220 in the future. Therefore, we would prefer the \$220 today. This means that if we were promised \$220 in the future, we would take less than \$220 today. But how much less? To answer that question, we compute an estimate of the present value of the \$220 to be received one period from now using the formula in Exhibit B.2 as follows:

$$p = \frac{f}{(1 + i)^n} = \frac{\$220}{(1 + 0.10)^1} = \$200$$

We interpret this result to say that given an interest rate of 10%, we are indifferent between \$200 today or \$220 at the end of one period.

We can also use this formula to compute the present value for *any number of periods.* To illustrate, consider a payment of \$242 at the end of two periods at 10% interest. The present value of this \$242 to be received two periods from now is computed as follows:

$$p = \frac{f}{(1 + i)^n} = \frac{\$242}{(1 + 0.10)^2} = \$200$$

Together, these results tell us we are indifferent between \$200 today, or \$220 one period from today, or \$242 two periods from today given a 10% interest rate per period.

The number of periods (n) in the present value formula does not have to be expressed in years. Any period of time such as a day, a month, a quarter, or a year can be used. Whatever period is used, the interest rate (i) must be compounded for the same period. This means that if a situation expresses n in months and i equals 12% per year, then i is transformed into interest earned per month (or 1%). In this case, interest is said to be *compounded monthly.*

A present value table helps us with present value computations. It gives us present values (factors) for a variety of both interest rates (i) and periods (n). Each present value in a present value table assumes that the future value (f) equals 1. When the future value (f) is different from 1, we simply multiply the present value (p) from the table by that future value to give us the estimate. The formula used to construct a table of present values for a single future amount of 1 is shown in Exhibit B.3.

EXHIBIT B.3

Present Value of 1 Formula

$$p = \frac{1}{(1 + i)^n}$$

This formula is identical to that in Exhibit B.2 except that f equals 1. Table B.1 at the end of this appendix is such a present value table. It is often called a **present value of 1 table.** A present value table involves three factors: p, i, and n. Knowing two of these three factors allows us to compute the third. (A fourth is f, but as already explained, we need only multiply the 1 used in the formula by f.) To illustrate the use of a present value table, consider three cases.

P1 Apply present value concepts to a single amount by using interest tables.

Case 1 (solve for p when knowing i and n). To show how we use a present value table, let's look again at how we estimate the present value of \$220 (the f value) at the end of one period ($n = 1$) where the interest rate (i) is 10%. To solve this case, we go to the present value table (Table B.1) and look in the row for 1 period and in the column for 10% interest. Here we find a present value (p) of 0.9091 based on a future value of 1. This means, for instance, that \$1 to be received one period from today at 10% interest is worth \$0.9091 today. Since the future value in this case is not \$1 but \$220, we multiply the 0.9091 by \$220 to get an answer of \$200.

Case 2 (solve for n when knowing p and i). To illustrate, assume a \$100,000 future value (f) that is worth \$13,000 today (p) using an interest rate of 12% (i) but where n is unknown. In particular, we want to know how many periods (n) there are between the present value and the future value. To put this in context, it would fit a situation in which we want to retire with \$100,000 but currently have only \$13,000 that is earning a 12% return and we will be unable to save any additional money. How long will it be before we can retire? To answer this, we go to Table B.1 and look in the 12% interest column. Here we find a column of present values (p) based on a future value of 1. To use the present value table for this solution, we must divide \$13,000 (p) by \$100,000 (f), which equals 0.1300. This is necessary because *a present value table defines* f *equal to 1, and* p *as a fraction of 1.* We look for a value nearest to 0.1300 (p), which we find in the row for 18 periods (n). This means that the present value of \$100,000 at the end of 18 periods at 12% interest is \$13,000; alternatively stated, we must work 18 more years.

Case 3 (solve for i when knowing p and n). In this case, we have, say, a \$120,000 future value (f) worth \$60,000 today (p) when there are nine periods (n) between the present and future values, but the interest rate is unknown. As an example, suppose we want to retire with \$120,000, but we have only \$60,000 and we will be unable to save any additional money, yet we hope to retire in nine years. What interest rate must we earn to retire with \$120,000 in nine years? To answer this, we go to the present value table (Table B.1) and look in the row for nine periods. To use the present value table, we must divide \$60,000 (p) by \$120,000 (f), which equals 0.5000. Recall that this step is necessary because a present value table defines f equal to 1 and p as a fraction of 1. We look for a value in the row for nine periods that is nearest to 0.5000 (p), which we find in the column for 8% interest (i). This means that the present value of \$120,000 at the end of nine periods at 8% interest is \$60,000 or, in our example, we must earn 8% annual interest to retire in nine years.

Quick Check Answer—p. B-7

1. A company is considering an investment expected to yield \$70,000 after six years. If this company demands an 8% return, how much is it willing to pay for this investment?

Future Value of a Single Amount

We must modify the formula for the present value of a single amount to obtain the formula for the future value of a single amount. In particular, we multiply both sides of the equation in Exhibit B.2 by $(1 + i)^n$ to get the result shown in Exhibit B.4.

EXHIBIT B.4

Future Value of a Single Amount Formula

$$f = p \times (1 + i)^n$$

The future value (f) is defined in terms of p, i, and n. We can use this formula to determine that \$200 (p) invested for 1 (n) period at an interest rate of 10% (i) yields a future value of

$220 as follows:

$$f = p \times (1 + i)^n$$
$$= \$200 \times (1 + 0.10)^1$$
$$= \$220$$

P2 Apply future value concepts to a single amount by using interest tables.

This formula can also be used to compute the future value of an amount for *any number of periods* into the future. To illustrate, assume that $200 is invested for three periods at 10%. The future value of this $200 is $266.20, computed as follows:

$$f = p \times (1 + i)^n$$
$$= \$200 \times (1 + 0.10)^3$$
$$= \$266.20$$

A future value table makes it easier for us to compute future values (f) for many different combinations of interest rates (i) and time periods (n). Each future value in a future value table assumes the present value (p) is 1. As with a present value table, if the future amount is something other than 1, we simply multiply our answer by that amount. The formula used to construct a table of future values (factors) for a single amount of 1 is in Exhibit B.5.

EXHIBIT B.5

Future Value of 1 Formula

$$f = (1 + i)^n$$

Table B.2 at the end of this appendix shows a table of future values for a current amount of 1. This type of table is called a **future value of 1 table**.

There are some important relations between Tables B.1 and B.2. In Table B.2, for the row where $n = 0$, the future value is 1 for each interest rate. This is so because no interest is earned when time does not pass. We also see that Tables B.1 and B.2 report the same information but in a different manner. In particular, one table is simply the *inverse* of the other. To illustrate this inverse relation, let's say we invest $100 for a period of five years at 12% per year. How much do we expect to have after five years? We can answer this question using Table B.2 by finding the future value (f) of 1, for five periods from now, compounded at 12%. From that table we find $f = 1.7623$. If we start with $100, the amount it accumulates to after five years is $176.23 ($100 × 1.7623). We can alternatively use Table B.1. Here we find that the present value (p) of 1, discounted five periods at 12%, is 0.5674. Recall the inverse relation between present value and future value. This means that $p = 1/f$ (or equivalently, $f = 1/p$). We can compute the future value of $100 invested for five periods at 12% as follows: $f = \$100 \times (1/0.5674) = \$176.24$ (which equals the $176.23 just computed, except for a 1 cent rounding difference).

A future value table involves three factors: f, i, and n. Knowing two of these three factors allows us to compute the third. To illustrate, consider these three possible cases.

Case 1 (solve for f when knowing i and n). Our preceding example fits this case. We found that $100 invested for five periods at 12% interest accumulates to $176.24.

Case 2 (solve for n when knowing f and i). In this case, we have, say, $2,000 ($p$) and we want to know how many periods (n) it will take to accumulate to $3,000 ($f$) at 7% ($i$) interest. To answer this, we go to the future value table (Table B.2) and look in the 7% interest column. Here we find a column of future values (f) based on a present value of 1. To use a future value table, we must divide $3,000 ($f$) by $2,000 ($p$), which equals 1.500. This is necessary because *a future value table defines* p *equal to 1, and* f *as a multiple of 1.* We look for a value nearest to 1.50 (f), which we find in the row for six periods (n). This means that $2,000 invested for six periods at 7% interest accumulates to $3,000.

Case 3 (solve for i when knowing f and n). In this case, we have, say, $2,001 ($p$), and in nine years ($n$) we want to have $4,000 ($f$). What rate of interest must we earn to accomplish this? To answer that, we go to Table B.2 and search in the row for nine periods. To use a future value table, we must divide $4,000 ($f$) by $2,001 ($p$), which equals 1.9990. Recall that this is necessary because a future value table defines p equal to 1 and f as a multiple of 1. We look for a value nearest to 1.9990 (f), which we find in the column for 8% interest (i). This means that $2,001 invested for nine periods at 8% interest accumulates to $4,000.

Quick Check Answer—p. B-7

2. Assume that you win a $150,000 cash sweepstakes. You decide to deposit this cash in an account earning 8% annual interest, and you plan to quit your job when the account equals $555,000. How many years will it be before you can quit working?

Present Value of an Annuity

An *annuity* is a series of equal payments occurring at equal intervals. One example is a series of three annual payments of $100 each. An *ordinary annuity* is defined as equal end-of-period payments at equal intervals. An ordinary annuity of $100 for three periods and its present value (p) are illustrated in Exhibit B.6.

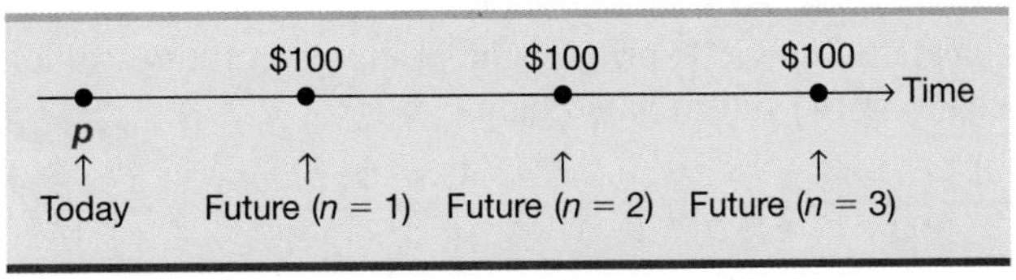

EXHIBIT B.6

Present Value of an Ordinary Annuity Diagram

P3 Apply present value concepts to an annuity by using interest tables.

One way to compute the present value of an ordinary annuity is to find the present value of each payment using our present value formula from Exhibit B.3. We then add each of the three present values. To illustrate, let's look at three $100 payments at the end of each of the next three periods with an interest rate of 15%. Our present value computations are

$$p = \frac{\$100}{(1+0.15)^1} + \frac{\$100}{(1+0.15)^2} + \frac{\$100}{(1+0.15)^3} = \$228.32$$

This computation is identical to computing the present value of each payment (from Table B.1) and taking their sum or, alternatively, adding the values from Table B.1 for each of the three payments and multiplying their sum by the $100 annuity payment.

A more direct way is to use a present value of annuity table. Table B.3 at the end of this appendix is one such table. This table is called a **present value of an annuity of 1 table**. If we look at Table B.3 where $n = 3$ and $i = 15\%$, we see the present value is 2.2832. This means that the present value of an annuity of 1 for three periods, with a 15% interest rate, equals 2.2832.

A present value of an annuity formula is used to construct Table B.3. It can also be constructed by adding the amounts in a present value of 1 table. To illustrate, we use Tables B.1 and B.3 to confirm this relation for the prior example:

From Table B.1		From Table B.3	
$i = 15\%, n = 1$	0.8696		
$i = 15\%, n = 2$	0.7561		
$i = 15\%, n = 3$	0.6575		
Total	2.2832	$i = 15\%, n = 3$	2.2832

We can also use business calculators or spreadsheet programs to find the present value of an annuity.

Decision Insight

Better Lucky Than Good "I don't have good luck—I'm blessed," proclaimed Andrew "Jack" Whittaker, 55, a sewage treatment contractor, after winning the largest ever undivided jackpot in a U.S. lottery. Whittaker had to choose between $315 million in 30 annual installments or $170 million in one lump sum ($112 million after-tax).

Quick Check

Answer—p. B-7

3. A company is considering an investment paying $10,000 every six months for three years. The first payment would be received in six months. If this company requires an 8% annual return, what is the maximum amount it is willing to pay for this investment?

Future Value of an Annuity

The future value of an *ordinary annuity* is the accumulated value of each annuity payment with interest as of the date of the final payment. To illustrate, let's consider the earlier annuity of three annual payments of $100. Exhibit B.7 shows the point in time for the future value (f). The first payment is made two periods prior to the point when future value is determined, and the final payment occurs on the future value date.

EXHIBIT B.7

Future Value of an Ordinary Annuity Diagram

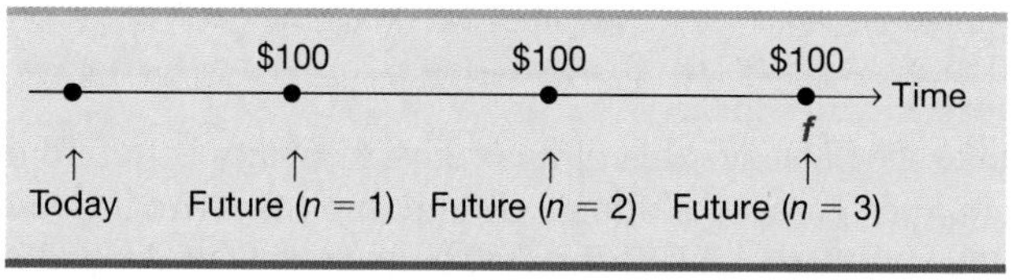

One way to compute the future value of an annuity is to use the formula to find the future value of *each* payment and add them. If we assume an interest rate of 15%, our calculation is

$$f = \$100 \times (1 + 0.15)^2 + \$100 \times (1 + 0.15)^1 + \$100 \times (1 + 0.15)^0 = \$347.25$$

This is identical to using Table B.2 and summing the future values of each payment, or adding the future values of the three payments of 1 and multiplying the sum by $100.

P4 Apply future value concepts to an annuity by using interest tables.

A more direct way is to use a table showing future values of annuities. Such a table is called a **future value of an annuity of 1 table**. Table B.4 at the end of this appendix is one such table. Note that in Table B.4 when $n = 1$, the future values equal 1 ($f = 1$) for all rates of interest. This is so because such an annuity consists of only one payment and the future value is determined on the date of that payment—no time passes between the payment and its future value. The future value of an annuity formula is used to construct Table B.4. We can also construct it by adding the amounts from a future value of 1 table. To illustrate, we use Tables B.2 and B.4 to confirm this relation for the prior example:

From Table B.2		From Table B.4	
$i = 15\%, n = 0$	1.0000		
$i = 15\%, n = 1$	1.1500		
$i = 15\%, n = 2$	1.3225		
Total	3.4725	$i = 15\%, n = 3$	3.4725

Note that the future value in Table B.2 is 1.0000 when $n = 0$, but the future value in Table B.4 is 1.0000 when $n = 1$. Is this a contradiction? No. When $n = 0$ in Table B.2, the future value is determined on the date when a single payment occurs. This means that no interest is earned because no time has passed, and the future value equals the payment. Table B.4 describes annuities with equal payments occurring at the end of each period. When $n = 1$, the annuity has one payment, and its future value equals 1 on the date of its final and only payment. Again, no time passes between the payment and its future value date.

Quick Check

Answer—p. B-7

4. A company invests $45,000 per year for five years at 12% annual interest. Compute the value of this annuity investment at the end of five years.

Summary

C1 Describe the earning of interest and the concepts of present and future values. Interest is payment by a borrower to the owner of an asset for its use. Present and future value computations are a way for us to estimate the interest component of holding assets or liabilities over a period of time.

P1 Apply present value concepts to a single amount by using interest tables. The present value of a single amount received at a future date is the amount that can be invested now at the specified interest rate to yield that future value.

P2 Apply future value concepts to a single amount by using interest tables. The future value of a single amount invested at a specified rate of interest is the amount that would accumulate by the future date.

P3 Apply present value concepts to an annuity by using interest tables. The present value of an annuity is the amount that can be invested now at the specified interest rate to yield that series of equal periodic payments.

P4 Apply future value concepts to an annuity by using interest tables. The future value of an annuity invested at a specific rate of interest is the amount that would accumulate by the date of the final payment.

Guidance Answers to **Quick Checks**

1. $70,000 × 0.6302 = $44,114 (use Table B.1, i = 8%, n = 6).
2. $555,000/$150,000 = 3.7000; Table B.2 shows this value is not achieved until after 17 years at 8% interest.
3. $10,000 × 5.2421 = $52,421 (use Table B.3, i = 4%, n = 6).
4. $45,000 × 6.3528 = $285,876 (use Table B.4, i = 12%, n = 5).

McGraw-Hill's HOMEWORK MANAGER® Available with McGraw-Hill's Homework Manager

QUICK STUDY

QS B-1 Identifying interest rates in tables C1

Assume that you must make future value estimates using the *future value of 1 table* (Table B.2). Which interest rate column do you use when working with the following rates?

1. 8% compounded quarterly
2. 12% compounded annually
3. 6% compounded semiannually
4. 12% compounded monthly

QS B-2 Interest rate on an investment P1

Ken Francis is offered the possibility of investing $2,745 today and in return to receive $10,000 after 15 years. What is the annual rate of interest for this investment? (Use Table B.1.)

QS B-3 Number of periods of an investment P1

Megan Brink is offered the possibility of investing $6,651 today at 6% interest per year in a desire to accumulate $10,000. How many years must Brink wait to accumulate $10,000? (Use Table B.1.)

QS B-4 Present value of an amount P1

Flaherty is considering an investment that, if paid for immediately, is expected to return $140,000 five years from now. If Flaherty demands a 9% return, how much is she willing to pay for this investment?

QS B-5 Future value of an amount P2

CII, Inc., invests $630,000 in a project expected to earn a 12% annual rate of return. The earnings will be reinvested in the project each year until the entire investment is liquidated 10 years later. What will the cash proceeds be when the project is liquidated?

QS B-6
Present value of an annuity P3

Beene Distributing is considering a project that will return $150,000 annually at the end of each year for six years. If Beene demands an annual return of 7% and pays for the project immediately, how much is it willing to pay for the project?

QS B-7
Future value of an annuity P4

Claire Fitch is planning to begin an individual retirement program in which she will invest $1,500 at the end of each year. Fitch plans to retire after making 30 annual investments in the program earning a return of 10%. What is the value of the program on the date of the last payment?

EXERCISES

Exercise B-1
Number of periods of an investment P2

Bill Thompson expects to invest $10,000 at 12% and, at the end of a certain period, receive $96,463. How many years will it be before Thompson receives the payment? (Use Table B.2.)

Exercise B-2
Interest rate on an investment P2

Ed Summers expects to invest $10,000 for 25 years, after which he wants to receive $108,347. What rate of interest must Summers earn? (Use Table B.2.)

Exercise B-3
Interest rate on an investment P3

Jones expects an immediate investment of $57,466 to return $10,000 annually for eight years, with the first payment to be received one year from now. What rate of interest must Jones earn? (Use Table B.3.)

Exercise B-4
Number of periods of an investment P3

Keith Riggins expects an investment of $82,014 to return $10,000 annually for several years. If Riggins earns a return of 10%, how many annual payments will he receive? (Use Table B.3.)

Exercise B-5
Interest rate on an investment P4

Algoe expects to invest $1,000 annually for 40 years to yield an accumulated value of $154,762 on the date of the last investment. For this to occur, what rate of interest must Algoe earn? (Use Table B.4.)

Exercise B-6
Number of periods of an investment P4

Kate Beckwith expects to invest $10,000 annually that will earn 8%. How many annual investments must Beckwith make to accumulate $303,243 on the date of the last investment? (Use Table B.4.)

Exercise B-7
Present value of an annuity P3

Sam Weber finances a new automobile by paying $6,500 cash and agreeing to make 40 monthly payments of $500 each, the first payment to be made one month after the purchase. The loan bears interest at an annual rate of 12%. What is the cost of the automobile?

Exercise B-8
Present value of bonds
P1 P3

Spiller Corp. plans to issue 10%, 15-year, $500,000 par value bonds payable that pay interest semiannually on June 30 and December 31. The bonds are dated December 31, 2008, and are issued on that date. If the market rate of interest for the bonds is 8% on the date of issue, what will be the total cash proceeds from the bond issue?

Exercise B-9
Present value of an amount P1

McAdams Company expects to earn 10% per year on an investment that will pay $606,773 six years from now. Use Table B.1 to compute the present value of this investment. (Round the amount to the nearest dollar.)

Exercise B-10
Present value of an amount and of an annuity P1 P3

Compute the amount that can be borrowed under each of the following circumstances:

1. A promise to repay $90,000 seven years from now at an interest rate of 6%.
2. An agreement made on February 1, 2008, to make three separate payments of $20,000 on February 1 of 2009, 2010, and 2011. The annual interest rate is 10%.

Exercise B-11
Present value of an amount P1

On January 1, 2008, a company agrees to pay $20,000 in three years. If the annual interest rate is 10%, determine how much cash the company can borrow with this agreement.

Exercise B-12
Present value of an amount P1

Find the amount of money that can be borrowed today with each of the following separate debt agreements *a* through *f*. (Round amounts to the nearest dollar.)

Case	Single Future Payment	Number of Periods	Interest Rate
a.	$40,000	3	4%
b.	75,000	7	8
c.	52,000	9	10
d.	18,000	2	4
e.	63,000	8	6
f.	89,000	5	2

Exercise B-13
Present values of annuities P3

C&H Ski Club recently borrowed money and agrees to pay it back with a series of six annual payments of $5,000 each. C&H subsequently borrows more money and agrees to pay it back with a series of four annual payments of $7,500 each. The annual interest rate for both loans is 6%.

1. Use Table B.1 to find the present value of these two separate annuities. (Round amounts to the nearest dollar.)

2. Use Table B.3 to find the present value of these two separate annuities. (Round amounts to the nearest dollar.)

Exercise B-14
Present value with semiannual compounding C1 P3

Otto Co. borrows money on April 30, 2008, by promising to make four payments of $13,000 each on November 1, 2008; May 1, 2009; November 1, 2009; and May 1, 2010.

1. How much money is Otto able to borrow if the interest rate is 8%, compounded semiannually?

2. How much money is Otto able to borrow if the interest rate is 12%, compounded semiannually?

3. How much money is Otto able to borrow if the interest rate is 16%, compounded semiannually?

Exercise B-15
Future value of an amount P2

Mark Welsch deposits $7,200 in an account that earns interest at an annual rate of 8%, compounded quarterly. The $7,200 plus earned interest must remain in the account 10 years before it can be withdrawn. How much money will be in the account at the end of 10 years?

Exercise B-16
Future value of an annuity P4

Kelly Malone plans to have $50 withheld from her monthly paycheck and deposited in a savings account that earns 12% annually, compounded monthly. If Malone continues with her plan for two and one-half years, how much will be accumulated in the account on the date of the last deposit?

Exercise B-17
Future value of an amount plus an annuity P2 P4

Starr Company decides to establish a fund that it will use 10 years from now to replace an aging production facility. The company will make a $100,000 initial contribution to the fund and plans to make quarterly contributions of $50,000 beginning in three months. The fund earns 12%, compounded quarterly. What will be the value of the fund 10 years from now?

Exercise B-18
Future value of an amount P2

Catten, Inc., invests $163,170 today earning 7% per year for nine years. Use Table B.2 to compute the future value of the investment nine years from now. (Round the amount to the nearest dollar.)

Exercise B-19
Using present and future value tables C1 P1 P2 P3 P4

For each of the following situations, identify (1) the case as either (*a*) a present or a future value and (*b*) a single amount or an annuity, (2) the table you would use in your computations (but do not solve the problem), and (3) the interest rate and time periods you would use.

a. You need to accumulate $10,000 for a trip you wish to take in four years. You are able to earn 8% compounded semiannually on your savings. You plan to make only one deposit and let the money accumulate for four years. How would you determine the amount of the one-time deposit?

b. Assume the same facts as in part (*a*) except that you will make semiannual deposits to your savings account.

c. You want to retire after working 40 years with savings in excess of $1,000,000. You expect to save $4,000 a year for 40 years and earn an annual rate of interest of 8%. Will you be able to retire with more than $1,000,000 in 40 years? Explain.

d. A sweepstakes agency names you a grand prize winner. You can take $225,000 immediately or elect to receive annual installments of $30,000 for 20 years. You can earn 10% annually on any investments you make. Which prize do you choose to receive?

TABLE B.1

Present Value of 1

$$p = 1/(1 + i)^n$$

	Rate											
Periods	**1%**	**2%**	**3%**	**4%**	**5%**	**6%**	**7%**	**8%**	**9%**	**10%**	**12%**	**15%**
1	0.9901	0.9804	0.9709	0.9615	0.9524	0.9434	0.9346	0.9259	0.9174	0.9091	0.8929	0.8696
2	0.9803	0.9612	0.9426	0.9246	0.9070	0.8900	0.8734	0.8573	0.8417	0.8264	0.7972	0.7561
3	0.9706	0.9423	0.9151	0.8890	0.8638	0.8396	0.8163	0.7938	0.7722	0.7513	0.7118	0.6575
4	0.9610	0.9238	0.8885	0.8548	0.8227	0.7921	0.7629	0.7350	0.7084	0.6830	0.6355	0.5718
5	0.9515	0.9057	0.8626	0.8219	0.7835	0.7473	0.7130	0.6806	0.6499	0.6209	0.5674	0.4972
6	0.9420	0.8880	0.8375	0.7903	0.7462	0.7050	0.6663	0.6302	0.5963	0.5645	0.5066	0.4323
7	0.9327	0.8706	0.8131	0.7599	0.7107	0.6651	0.6227	0.5835	0.5470	0.5132	0.4523	0.3759
8	0.9235	0.8535	0.7894	0.7307	0.6768	0.6274	0.5820	0.5403	0.5019	0.4665	0.4039	0.3269
9	0.9143	0.8368	0.7664	0.7026	0.6446	0.5919	0.5439	0.5002	0.4604	0.4241	0.3606	0.2843
10	0.9053	0.8203	0.7441	0.6756	0.6139	0.5584	0.5083	0.4632	0.4224	0.3855	0.3220	0.2472
11	0.8963	0.8043	0.7224	0.6496	0.5847	0.5268	0.4751	0.4289	0.3875	0.3505	0.2875	0.2149
12	0.8874	0.7885	0.7014	0.6246	0.5568	0.4970	0.4440	0.3971	0.3555	0.3186	0.2567	0.1869
13	0.8787	0.7730	0.6810	0.6006	0.5303	0.4688	0.4150	0.3677	0.3262	0.2897	0.2292	0.1625
14	0.8700	0.7579	0.6611	0.5775	0.5051	0.4423	0.3878	0.3405	0.2992	0.2633	0.2046	0.1413
15	0.8613	0.7430	0.6419	0.5553	0.4810	0.4173	0.3624	0.3152	0.2745	0.2394	0.1827	0.1229
16	0.8528	0.7284	0.6232	0.5339	0.4581	0.3936	0.3387	0.2919	0.2519	0.2176	0.1631	0.1069
17	0.8444	0.7142	0.6050	0.5134	0.4363	0.3714	0.3166	0.2703	0.2311	0.1978	0.1456	0.0929
18	0.8360	0.7002	0.5874	0.4936	0.4155	0.3503	0.2959	0.2502	0.2120	0.1799	0.1300	0.0808
19	0.8277	0.6864	0.5703	0.4746	0.3957	0.3305	0.2765	0.2317	0.1945	0.1635	0.1161	0.0703
20	0.8195	0.6730	0.5537	0.4564	0.3769	0.3118	0.2584	0.2145	0.1784	0.1486	0.1037	0.0611
25	0.7798	0.6095	0.4776	0.3751	0.2953	0.2330	0.1842	0.1460	0.1160	0.0923	0.0588	0.0304
30	0.7419	0.5521	0.4120	0.3083	0.2314	0.1741	0.1314	0.0994	0.0754	0.0573	0.0334	0.0151
35	0.7059	0.5000	0.3554	0.2534	0.1813	0.1301	0.0937	0.0676	0.0490	0.0356	0.0189	0.0075
40	0.6717	0.4529	0.3066	0.2083	0.1420	0.0972	0.0668	0.0460	0.0318	0.0221	0.0107	0.0037

TABLE B.2

Future Value of 1

$$f = (1 + i)^n$$

	Rate											
Periods	**1%**	**2%**	**3%**	**4%**	**5%**	**6%**	**7%**	**8%**	**9%**	**10%**	**12%**	**15%**
0	1.0000	1.0000	1.0000	1.0000	1.0000	1.0000	1.0000	1.0000	1.0000	1.0000	1.0000	1.0000
1	1.0100	1.0200	1.0300	1.0400	1.0500	1.0600	1.0700	1.0800	1.0900	1.1000	1.1200	1.1500
2	1.0201	1.0404	1.0609	1.0816	1.1025	1.1236	1.1449	1.1664	1.1881	1.2100	1.2544	1.3225
3	1.0303	1.0612	1.0927	1.1249	1.1576	1.1910	1.2250	1.2597	1.2950	1.3310	1.4049	1.5209
4	1.0406	1.0824	1.1255	1.1699	1.2155	1.2625	1.3108	1.3605	1.4116	1.4641	1.5735	1.7490
5	1.0510	1.1041	1.1593	1.2167	1.2763	1.3382	1.4026	1.4693	1.5386	1.6105	1.7623	2.0114
6	1.0615	1.1262	1.1941	1.2653	1.3401	1.4185	1.5007	1.5869	1.6771	1.7716	1.9738	2.3131
7	1.0721	1.1487	1.2299	1.3159	1.4071	1.5036	1.6058	1.7138	1.8280	1.9487	2.2107	2.6600
8	1.0829	1.1717	1.2668	1.3686	1.4775	1.5938	1.7182	1.8509	1.9926	2.1436	2.4760	3.0590
9	1.0937	1.1951	1.3048	1.4233	1.5513	1.6895	1.8385	1.9990	2.1719	2.3579	2.7731	3.5179
10	1.1046	1.2190	1.3439	1.4802	1.6289	1.7908	1.9672	2.1589	2.3674	2.5937	3.1058	4.0456
11	1.1157	1.2434	1.3842	1.5395	1.7103	1.8983	2.1049	2.3316	2.5804	2.8531	3.4785	4.6524
12	1.1268	1.2682	1.4258	1.6010	1.7959	2.0122	2.2522	2.5182	2.8127	3.1384	3.8960	5.3503
13	1.1381	1.2936	1.4685	1.6651	1.8856	2.1329	2.4098	2.7196	3.0658	3.4523	4.3635	6.1528
14	1.1495	1.3195	1.5126	1.7317	1.9799	2.2609	2.5785	2.9372	3.3417	3.7975	4.8871	7.0757
15	1.1610	1.3459	1.5580	1.8009	2.0789	2.3966	2.7590	3.1722	3.6425	4.1772	5.4736	8.1371
16	1.1726	1.3728	1.6047	1.8730	2.1829	2.5404	2.9522	3.4259	3.9703	4.5950	6.1304	9.3576
17	1.1843	1.4002	1.6528	1.9479	2.2920	2.6928	3.1588	3.7000	4.3276	5.0545	6.8660	10.7613
18	1.1961	1.4282	1.7024	2.0258	2.4066	2.8543	3.3799	3.9960	4.7171	5.5599	7.6900	12.3755
19	1.2081	1.4568	1.7535	2.1068	2.5270	3.0256	3.6165	4.3157	5.1417	6.1159	8.6128	14.2318
20	1.2202	1.4859	1.8061	2.1911	2.6533	3.2071	3.8697	4.6610	5.6044	6.7275	9.6463	16.3665
25	1.2824	1.6406	2.0938	2.6658	3.3864	4.2919	5.4274	6.8485	8.6231	10.8347	17.0001	32.9190
30	1.3478	1.8114	2.4273	3.2434	4.3219	5.7435	7.6123	10.0627	13.2677	17.4494	29.9599	66.2118
35	1.4166	1.9999	2.8139	3.9461	5.5160	7.6861	10.6766	14.7853	20.4140	28.1024	52.7996	133.1755
40	1.4889	2.2080	3.2620	4.8010	7.0400	10.2857	14.9745	21.7245	31.4094	45.2593	93.0510	267.8635

$$p = \left[1 - \frac{1}{(1+i)^n}\right] / i$$

TABLE B.3

Present Value of an Annuity of 1

	Rate											
Periods	1%	2%	3%	4%	5%	6%	7%	8%	9%	10%	12%	15%
1	0.9901	0.9804	0.9709	0.9615	0.9524	0.9434	0.9346	0.9259	0.9174	0.9091	0.8929	0.8696
2	1.9704	1.9416	1.9135	1.8861	1.8594	1.8334	1.8080	1.7833	1.7591	1.7355	1.6901	1.6257
3	2.9410	2.8839	2.8286	2.7751	2.7232	2.6730	2.6243	2.5771	2.5313	2.4869	2.4018	2.2832
4	3.9020	3.8077	3.7171	3.6299	3.5460	3.4651	3.3872	3.3121	3.2397	3.1699	3.0373	2.8550
5	4.8534	4.7135	4.5797	4.4518	4.3295	4.2124	4.1002	3.9927	3.8897	3.7908	3.6048	3.3522
6	5.7955	5.6014	5.4172	5.2421	5.0757	4.9173	4.7665	4.6229	4.4859	4.3553	4.1114	3.7845
7	6.7282	6.4720	6.2303	6.0021	5.7864	5.5824	5.3893	5.2064	5.0330	4.8684	4.5638	4.1604
8	7.6517	7.3255	7.0197	6.7327	6.4632	6.2098	5.9713	5.7466	5.5348	5.3349	4.9676	4.4873
9	8.5660	8.1622	7.7861	7.4353	7.1078	6.8017	6.5152	6.2469	5.9952	5.7590	5.3282	4.7716
10	9.4713	8.9826	8.5302	8.1109	7.7217	7.3601	7.0236	6.7101	6.4177	6.1446	5.6502	5.0188
11	10.3676	9.7868	9.2526	8.7605	8.3064	7.8869	7.4987	7.1390	6.8052	6.4951	5.9377	5.2337
12	11.2551	10.5753	9.9540	9.3851	8.8633	8.3838	7.9427	7.5361	7.1607	6.8137	6.1944	5.4206
13	12.1337	11.3484	10.6350	9.9856	9.3936	8.8527	8.3577	7.9038	7.4869	7.1034	6.4235	5.5831
14	13.0037	12.1062	11.2961	10.5631	9.8986	9.2950	8.7455	8.2442	7.7862	7.3667	6.6282	5.7245
15	13.8651	12.8493	11.9379	11.1184	10.3797	9.7122	9.1079	8.5595	8.0607	7.6061	6.8109	5.8474
16	14.7179	13.5777	12.5611	11.6523	10.8378	10.1059	9.4466	8.8514	8.3126	7.8237	6.9740	5.9542
17	15.5623	14.2919	13.1661	12.1657	11.2741	10.4773	9.7632	9.1216	8.5436	8.0216	7.1196	6.0472
18	16.3983	14.9920	13.7535	12.6593	11.6896	10.8276	10.0591	9.3719	8.7556	8.2014	7.2497	6.1280
19	17.2260	15.6785	14.3238	13.1339	12.0853	11.1581	10.3356	9.6036	8.9501	8.3649	7.3658	6.1982
20	18.0456	16.3514	14.8775	13.5903	12.4622	11.4699	10.5940	9.8181	9.1285	8.5136	7.4694	6.2593
25	22.0232	19.5235	17.4131	15.6221	14.0939	12.7834	11.6536	10.6748	9.8226	9.0770	7.8431	6.4641
30	25.8077	22.3965	19.6004	17.2920	15.3725	13.7648	12.4090	11.2578	10.2737	9.4269	8.0552	6.5660
35	29.4086	24.9986	21.4872	18.6646	16.3742	14.4982	12.9477	11.6546	10.5668	9.6442	8.1755	6.6166
40	32.8347	27.3555	23.1148	19.7928	17.1591	15.0463	13.3317	11.9246	10.7574	9.7791	8.2438	6.6418

$$f = [(1+i)^n - 1] / i$$

TABLE B.4

Future Value of an Annuity of 1

	Rate											
Periods	1%	2%	3%	4%	5%	6%	7%	8%	9%	10%	12%	15%
1	1.0000	1.0000	1.0000	1.0000	1.0000	1.0000	1.0000	1.0000	1.0000	1.0000	1.0000	1.0000
2	2.0100	2.0200	2.0300	2.0400	2.0500	2.0600	2.0700	2.0800	2.0900	2.1000	2.1200	2.1500
3	3.0301	3.0604	3.0909	3.1216	3.1525	3.1836	3.2149	3.2464	3.2781	3.3100	3.3744	3.4725
4	4.0604	4.1216	4.1836	4.2465	4.3101	4.3746	4.4399	4.5061	4.5731	4.6410	4.7793	4.9934
5	5.1010	5.2040	5.3091	5.4163	5.5256	5.6371	5.7507	5.8666	5.9847	6.1051	6.3528	6.7424
6	6.1520	6.3081	6.4684	6.6330	6.8019	6.9753	7.1533	7.3359	7.5233	7.7156	8.1152	8.7537
7	7.2135	7.4343	7.6625	7.8983	8.1420	8.3938	8.6540	8.9228	9.2004	9.4872	10.0890	11.0668
8	8.2857	8.5830	8.8923	9.2142	9.5491	9.8975	10.2598	10.6366	11.0285	11.4359	12.2997	13.7268
9	9.3685	9.7546	10.1591	10.5828	11.0266	11.4913	11.9780	12.4876	13.0210	13.5795	14.7757	16.7858
10	10.4622	10.9497	11.4639	12.0061	12.5779	13.1808	13.8164	14.4866	15.1929	15.9374	17.5487	20.3037
11	11.5668	12.1687	12.8078	13.4864	14.2068	14.9716	15.7836	16.6455	17.5603	18.5312	20.6546	24.3493
12	12.6825	13.4121	14.1920	15.0258	15.9171	16.8699	17.8885	18.9771	20.1407	21.3843	24.1331	29.0017
13	13.8093	14.6803	15.6178	16.6268	17.7130	18.8821	20.1406	21.4953	22.9534	24.5227	28.0291	34.3519
14	14.9474	15.9739	17.0863	18.2919	19.5986	21.0151	22.5505	24.2149	26.0192	27.9750	32.3926	40.5047
15	16.0969	17.2934	18.5989	20.0236	21.5786	23.2760	25.1290	27.1521	29.3609	31.7725	37.2797	47.5804
16	17.2579	18.6393	20.1569	21.8245	23.6575	25.6725	27.8881	30.3243	33.0034	35.9497	42.7533	55.7175
17	18.4304	20.0121	21.7616	23.6975	25.8404	28.2129	30.8402	33.7502	36.9737	40.5447	48.8837	65.0751
18	19.6147	21.4123	23.4144	25.6454	28.1324	30.9057	33.9990	37.4502	41.3013	45.5992	55.7497	75.8364
19	20.8109	22.8406	25.1169	27.6712	30.5390	33.7600	37.3790	41.4463	46.0185	51.1591	63.4397	88.2118
20	22.0190	24.2974	26.8704	29.7781	33.0660	36.7856	40.9955	45.7620	51.1601	57.2750	72.0524	102.4436
25	28.2432	32.0303	36.4593	41.6459	47.7271	54.8645	63.2490	73.1059	84.7009	98.3471	133.3339	212.7930
30	34.7849	40.5681	47.5754	56.0849	66.4388	79.0582	94.4608	113.2832	136.3075	164.4940	241.3327	434.7451
35	41.6603	49.9945	60.4621	73.6522	90.3203	111.4348	138.2369	172.3168	215.7108	271.0244	431.6635	881.1702
40	48.8864	60.4020	75.4013	95.0255	120.7998	154.7620	199.6351	259.0565	337.8824	442.5926	767.0914	1,779.0903

Glossary

Absorption costing Costing method that assigns both variable and fixed costs to products.

Accelerated depreciation method Method that produces larger depreciation charges in the early years of an asset's life and smaller charges in its later years. *(p. 398)*

Account Record within an accounting system in which increases and decreases are entered and stored in a specific asset, liability, equity, revenue, or expense. *(p. 49)*

Account balance Difference between total debits and total credits (including the beginning balance) for an account. *(p. 53)*

Account form balance sheet Balance sheet that lists assets on the left side and liabilities and equity on the right. *(p. 18)*

Account payable Liability created by buying goods or services on credit; backed by the buyer's general credit standing. *(p. 50)*

Accounting Information and measurement system that identifies, records, and communicates relevant information about a company's business activities. *(p. 4)*

Accounting cycle Recurring steps performed each accounting period, starting with analyzing transactions and continuing through the post-closing trial balance (or reversing entries). *(p. 144)*

Accounting equation Equality involving a company's assets, liabilities, and equity; Assets = Liabilities + Equity; also called *balance sheet equation. (p. 12)*

Accounting information system People, records, and methods that collect and process data from transactions and events, organize them in useful forms, and communicate results to decision makers. *(p. 268)*

Accounting period Length of time covered by financial statements; also called *reporting period. (p. 92)*

Accounting rate of return Rate used to evaluate the acceptability of an investment; equals the after-tax periodic income from a project divided by the average investment in the asset; also called *rate of return on average investment. (p. 1027)*

Accounts payable ledger Subsidiary ledger listing individual creditor (supplier) accounts. *(p. 273)*

Accounts receivable Amounts due from customers for credit sales; backed by the customer's general credit standing. *(p. 358)*

Accounts receivable ledger Subsidiary ledger listing individual customer accounts. *(p. 273)*

Accounts receivable turnover Measure of both the quality and liquidity of accounts receivable; indicates how often receivables are received and collected during the period; computed by dividing net sales by average accounts receivable. *(p. 372)*

Accrual basis accounting Accounting system that recognizes revenues when earned and expenses when incurred; the basis for GAAP. *(p. 93)*

Accrued expenses Costs incurred in a period that are both unpaid and unrecorded; adjusting entries for recording accrued expenses involve increasing expenses and increasing liabilities. *(p. 99)*

Accrued revenues Revenues earned in a period that are both unrecorded and not yet received in cash (or other assets); adjusting entries for recording accrued revenues involve increasing assets and increasing revenues. *(p. 101)*

Accumulated depreciation Cumulative sum of all depreciation expense recorded for an asset. *(p. 97)*

Acid-test ratio Ratio used to assess a company's ability to settle its current debts with its most liquid assets; defined as quick assets (cash, short-term investments, and current receivables) divided by current liabilities. *(p. 193)*

Activity-based budgeting (ABB) Budget system based on expected activities. *(p. 953)*

Activity-based costing (ABC) Cost allocation method that focuses on activities performed; traces costs to activities and then assigns them to cost objects. *(p. 854)*

Activity cost driver Variable that causes an activity's cost to go up or down; a causal factor. *(p. 855)*

Activity cost pool Temporary account that accumulates costs a company incurs to support an activity. *(p. 855)*

Adjusted trial balance List of accounts and balances prepared after period-end adjustments are recorded and posted. *(p. 104)*

Adjusting entry Journal entry at the end of an accounting period to bring an asset or liability account to its proper amount and update the related expense or revenue account. *(p. 94)*

Aging of accounts receivable Process of classifying accounts receivable by how long they are past due for purposes of estimating uncollectible accounts. *(p. 366)*

Allowance for Doubtful Accounts Contra asset account with a balance approximating uncollectible accounts receivable; also called *Allowance for Uncollectible Accounts. (p. 363)*

Allowance method Procedure that (a) estimates and matches bad debts expense with its sales for the period and/or (b) reports accounts receivable at estimated realizable value. *(p. 362)*

Amortization Process of allocating the cost of an intangible asset to expense over its estimated useful life. *(p. 407)*

Annual financial statements Financial statements covering a one-year period; often based on a calendar year, but any consecutive 12-month (or 52-week) period is acceptable. *(p. 92)*

Annual report Summary of a company's financial results for the year with its current financial condition and future plans; directed to external users of financial information. *(p. A-1)*

Annuity Series of equal payments at equal intervals. *(p. 568)*

Appropriated retained earnings Retained earnings separately reported to inform stockholders of funding needs. *(p. 523)*

Asset book value (See *book value.*)

Assets Resources a business owns or controls that are expected to provide current and future benefits to the business. *(p. 13)*

Audit Analysis and report of an organization's accounting system, its records, and its reports using various tests. *(p. 11)*

Auditors Individuals hired to review financial reports and information systems. *Internal auditors* of a company are employed to assess and evaluate its system of internal controls, including the resulting reports. *External auditors* are independent of a company and are hired to assess and evaluate the "fairness" of financial statements (or to perform other contracted financial services) *(p. 11).*

Authorized stock Total amount of stock that a corporation's charter authorizes it to issue. *(p. 509)*

Available-for-sale (AFS) securities Investments in debt and equity securities that are not classified as trading securities or held-to-maturity securities. *(p. 596)*

Average cost See *weighted average. (p. 230)*

Avoidable expense Expense (or cost) that is relevant for decision making; expense that is not incurred if a department, product, or service is eliminated. *(p. 1041)*

Bad debts Accounts of customers who do not pay what they have promised to pay; an expense of selling on credit; also called *uncollectible accounts. (p. 361)*

Balance column account Account with debit and credit columns for recording entries and another column for showing the balance of the account after each entry. *(p. 56)*

Balance sheet Financial statement that lists types and dollar amounts of assets, liabilities, and equity at a specific date. *(p. 18)*

Balance sheet equation (See *accounting equation.*)

Bank reconciliation Report that explains the difference between the book (company) balance of cash and the cash balance reported on the bank statement. *(p. 329)*

Bank statement Bank report on the depositor's beginning and ending cash balances, and a listing of its changes, for a period. *(p. 327)*

Basic earnings per share Net income less any preferred dividends and then divided by weighted-average common shares outstanding. *(p. 524)*

Batch processing Accumulating source documents for a period of time and then processing them all at once such as once a day, week, or month. *(p. 282)*

Bearer bonds Bonds made payable to whoever holds them (the *bearer*); also called *unregistered bonds. (p. 563)*

Benchmarking Practice of comparing and analyzing company financial performance or position with other companies or standards.

Betterments Expenditures to make a plant asset more efficient or productive; also called *improvements. (p. 403)*

Bond Written promise to pay the bond's par (or face) value and interest at a stated contract rate; often issued in denominations of $1,000. *(p. 550)*

Bond certificate Document containing bond specifics such as issuer's name, bond par value, contract interest rate, and maturity date. *(p. 552)*

Bond indenture Contract between the bond issuer and the bondholders; identifies the parties' rights and obligations. *(p. 552)*

Book value Asset's acquisition costs less its accumulated depreciation (or depletion, or amortization); also sometimes used synonymously as the *carrying value* of an account. *(p. 98)*

Book value per common share Recorded amount of equity applicable to common shares divided by the number of common shares outstanding. *(p. 526)*

Book value per preferred share Equity applicable to preferred shares (equals its call price [or par value if it is not callable] plus any cumulative dividends in arrears) divided by the number of preferred shares outstanding. *(p. 526)*

Bookkeeping (See *recordkeeping.*)

Break-even point Output level at which sales equals fixed plus variable costs; where income equals zero. *(p. 909)*

Break-even time (BET) Time-based measurement used to evaluate the acceptability of an investment; equals the time expected to pass before the present value of the net cash flows from an investment equals its initial cost. *(p. 1043)*

Budget Formal statement of future plans, usually expressed in monetary terms. *(p. 940)*

Budget report Report comparing actual results to planned objectives; sometimes used as a progress report. *(p. 980)*

Budgetary control Management use of budgets to monitor and control company operations. *(p. 980)*

Budgeted balance sheet Accounting report that presents predicted amounts of the company's assets, liabilities, and equity balances as of the end of the budget period. *(p. 952)*

Budgeted income statement Accounting report that presents predicted amounts of the company's revenues and expenses for the budget period. *(p. 952)*

Budgeting Process of planning future business actions and expressing them as formal plans. *(p. 940)*

Business An organization of one or more individuals selling products and/or services for profit. *(p. 10)*

Business entity assumption Principle that requires a business to be accounted for separately from its owner(s) and from any other entity. *(p. 10)*

Business segment Part of a company that can be separately identified by the products or services that it provides or by the geographic markets that it serves; also called *segment. (p. 703)*

C corporation Corporation that does not qualify for nor elect to be treated as a proprietorship or partnership for income tax purposes and therefore is subject to income taxes; also called *C corp. (p. 480)*

Call price Amount that must be paid to call and retire a callable preferred stock or a callable bond. *(p. 519)*

Callable bonds Bonds that give the issuer the option to retire them at a stated amount prior to maturity. *(p. 563)*

Callable preferred stock Preferred stock that the issuing corporation, at its option, may retire by paying the call price plus any dividends in arrears. *(p. 519)*

Canceled checks Checks that the bank has paid and deducted from the depositor's account. *(p. 328)*

Capital budgeting Process of analyzing alternative investments and deciding which assets to acquire or sell. *(p. 1024)*

Capital expenditures Additional costs of plant assets that provide material benefits extending beyond the current period; also called *balance sheet expenditures. (p. 402)*

Capital expenditures budget Plan that lists dollar amounts to be both received from disposal of plant assets and spent to purchase plant assets. *(p. 949)*

Capital leases Long-term leases in which the lessor transfers substantially all risk and rewards of ownership to the lessee. *(p. 574)*

Capital stock General term referring to a corporation's stock used in obtaining capital (owner financing). *(p. 509)*

Capitalize Record the cost as part of a permanent account and allocate it over later periods. *(p. 402)*

Carrying (book) value of bonds Net amount at which bonds are reported on the balance sheet; equals the par value of the bonds less any unamortized discount or plus any unamortized premium; also called *carrying amount* or *book value. (p. 554)*

Cash Includes currency, coins, and amounts on deposit in bank checking or savings accounts. *(p. 319)*

Cash basis accounting Accounting system that recognizes revenues when cash is received and records expenses when cash is paid. *(p. 93)*

Cash budget Plan that shows expected cash inflows and outflows during the budget period, including receipts from loans needed to maintain a minimum cash balance and repayments of such loans. *(p. 950)*

Cash disbursements journal Special journal normally used to record all payments of cash; also called *cash payments journal. (p. 280)*

Cash discount Reduction in the price of merchandise granted by a seller to a buyer when payment is made within the discount period. *(p. 181)*

Cash equivalents Short-term, investment assets that are readily convertible to a known cash amount or sufficiently close to their maturity date (usually within 90 days) so that market value is not sensitive to interest rate changes. *(p. 319)*

Cash flow on total assets Ratio of operating cash flows to average total assets; not sensitive to income recognition and measurement; partly reflects earnings quality. *(p. 646)*

Cash Over and Short Income statement account used to record cash overages and cash shortages arising from errors in cash receipts or payments. *(p. 321)*

Cash receipts journal Special journal normally used to record all receipts of cash. *(p. 277)*

Change in an accounting estimate Change in an accounting estimate that results from new information, subsequent developments, or improved judgment that impacts current and future periods. *(pp. 401 & 523)*

Chart of accounts List of accounts used by a company; includes an identification number for each account. *(p. 52)*

Check Document signed by a depositor instructing the bank to pay a specified amount to a designated recipient. *(p. 326)*

Check register Another name for a cash disbursements journal when the journal has a column for check numbers. *(pp. 280 & 337)*

Classified balance sheet Balance sheet that presents assets and liabilities in relevant subgroups, including current and noncurrent classifications. *(p. 145)*

Clock card Source document used to record the number of hours an employee works and to determine the total labor cost for each pay period. *(p. 776)*

Closing entries Entries recorded at the end of each accounting period to transfer end-of-period balances in revenue, gain, expense, loss, and withdrawal (dividend for a corporation) accounts to the capital account (to retained earnings for a corporation). *(p. 141)*

Closing process Necessary end-of-period steps to prepare the accounts for recording the transactions of the next period. *(p. 140)*

Columnar journal Journal with more than one column. *(p. 274)*

Common stock Corporation's basic ownership share; also generically called *capital stock. (pp. 11 & 508)*

Common-size financial statement Statement that expresses each amount as a percent of a base amount. In the balance sheet, total assets is usually the base and is expressed as 100%. In the income statement, net sales is usually the base. *(p. 687)*

Comparative financial statement Statement with data for two or more successive periods placed in side-by-side columns, often with changes shown in dollar amounts and percents. *(p. 682)*

Compatibility principle Information system principle that prescribes an accounting system to conform with a company's activities, personnel, and structure. *(p. 269)*

Complex capital structure Capital structure that includes outstanding rights or options to purchase common stock, or securities that are convertible into common stock. *(p. 524)*

Components of accounting systems Five basic components of accounting systems are source documents, input devices, information processors, information storage, and output devices. *(p. 269)*

Composite unit Generic unit consisting of a specific number of units of each product; unit comprised in proportion to the expected sales mix of its products. *(p. 916)*

Compound journal entry Journal entry that affects at least three accounts. *(p. 61)*

Comprehensive income Net change in equity for a period, excluding owner investments and distributions. *(p. 600)*

Computer hardware Physical equipment in a computerized accounting information system.

Computer network Linkage giving different users and different computers access to common databases and programs. *(p. 283)*

Computer software Programs that direct operations of computer hardware.

Conservatism constraint Principle that prescribes the less optimistic estimate when two estimates are about equally likely. *(p. 234)*

Consignee Receiver of goods owned by another who holds them for purposes of selling them for the owner. *(p. 224)*

Consignor Owner of goods who ships them to another party who will sell them for the owner. *(p. 224)*

Consistency concept Principle that prescribes use of the same accounting method(s) over time so that financial statements are comparable across periods. *(p. 233)*

Consolidated financial statements Financial statements that show all (combined) activities under the parent's control, including those of any subsidiaries. *(p. 599)*

Contingent liability Obligation to make a future payment if, and only if, an uncertain future event occurs. *(p. 445)*

Continuous budgeting Practice of preparing budgets for a selected number of future periods and revising those budgets as each period is completed. *(p. 942)*

Continuous improvement Concept requiring every manager and employee continually to look to improve operations. *(p. 730)*

Contra account Account linked with another account and having an opposite normal balance; reported as a subtraction from the other account's balance. *(p. 97)*

Contract rate Interest rate specified in a bond indenture (or note); multiplied by the par value to determine the interest paid each period; also called *coupon rate, stated rate,* or *nominal rate. (p. 553)*

Contributed capital Total amount of cash and other assets received from stockholders in exchange for stock; also called *paid-in capital. (p. 13)*

Contributed capital in excess of par value Difference between the par value of stock and its issue price when issued at a price above par.

Contribution margin Sales revenue less total variable costs.

Contribution margin income statement Income statement that separates variable and fixed costs; highlights the contribution margin, which is sales less variable expenses.

Contribution margin per unit Amount that the sale of one unit contributes toward recovering fixed costs and earning profit; defined as sales price per unit minus variable expense per unit. *(p. 908)*

Contribution margin ratio Product's contribution margin divided by its sale price. *(p. 908)*

Control Process of monitoring planning decisions and evaluating the organization's activities and employees. *(p. 727)*

Control principle Information system principle that prescribes an accounting system to aid managers in controlling and monitoring business activities. *(p. 268)*

Controllable costs Costs that a manager has the power to control or at least strongly influence. *(pp. 733 & 870)*

Controllable variance Combination of both overhead spending variances (variable and fixed) and the variable overhead efficiency variance. *(p. 993)*

Controlling account General ledger account, the balance of which (after posting) equals the sum of the balances in its related subsidiary ledger. *(p. 273)*

Conversion costs Expenditures incurred in converting raw materials to finished goods; includes direct labor costs and overhead costs. *(p. 738)*

Convertible bonds Bonds that bondholders can exchange for a set number of the issuer's shares. *(p. 563)*

Convertible preferred stock Preferred stock with an option to exchange it for common stock at a specified rate. *(p. 518)*

Copyright Right giving the owner the exclusive privilege to publish and sell musical, literary, or artistic work during the creator's life plus 70 years. *(p. 408)*

Corporation Business that is a separate legal entity under state or federal laws with owners called *shareholders* or *stockholders. (pp. 11 & 506)*

Cost All normal and reasonable expenditures necessary to get an asset in place and ready for its intended use. *(p. 393)*

Cost accounting system Accounting system for manufacturing activities based on the perpetual inventory system. *(p. 770)*

Cost-benefit principle Information system principle that prescribes the benefits from an activity in an accounting system to outweigh the costs of that activity. *(p. 269)*

Cost center Department that incurs costs but generates no revenues; common example is the accounting or legal department. *(p. 858)*

Cost object Product, process, department, or customer to which costs are assigned. *(p. 732)*

Cost of goods available for sale Consists of beginning inventory plus net purchases of a period.

Cost of goods manufactured Total manufacturing costs (direct materials, direct labor, and factory overhead) for the period plus beginning goods in process less ending goods in process; also called *net cost of goods manufactured* and *cost of goods completed. (p. 821)*

Cost of goods sold Cost of inventory sold to customers during a period; also called *cost of sales. (p. 178)*

Cost principle Accounting principle that prescribes financial statement information to be based on actual costs incurred in business transactions. *(p. 9)*

Cost variance Difference between the actual incurred cost and the standard cost. *(p. 986)*

Cost-volume-profit (CVP) analysis Planning method that includes predicting the volume of activity, the costs incurred, sales earned, and profits received. *(p. 902)*

Cost-volume-profit (CVP) chart Graphic representation of cost-volume-profit relations. *(p. 910)*

Coupon bonds Bonds with interest coupons attached to their certificates; bondholders detach coupons when they mature and present them to a bank or broker for collection. *(p. 563)*

Credit Recorded on the right side; an entry that decreases asset and expense accounts, and increases liability, revenue, and most equity accounts; abbreviated Cr. *(p. 53)*

Credit memorandum Notification that the sender has credited the recipient's account in the sender's records. *(p. 187)*

Credit period Time period that can pass before a customer's payment is due. *(p. 181)*

Credit terms Description of the amounts and timing of payments that a buyer (debtor) agrees to make in the future. *(p. 181)*

Creditors Individuals or organizations entitled to receive payments. *(p. 50)*

Cumulative preferred stock Preferred stock on which undeclared dividends accumulate until paid; common stockholders cannot receive dividends until cumulative dividends are paid. *(p. 517)*

Current assets Cash and other assets expected to be sold, collected, or used within one year or the company's operating cycle, whichever is longer. *(p. 146)*

Current liabilities Obligations due to be paid or settled within one year or the company's operating cycle, whichever is longer. *(pp. 147 & 435)*

Current portion of long-term debt Portion of long-term debt due within one year or the operating cycle, whichever is longer; reported under current liabilities. *(p. 442)*

Current ratio Ratio used to evaluate a company's ability to pay its short-term obligations, calculated by dividing current assets by current liabilities. *(p. 147)*

Curvilinear cost Cost that changes with volume but not at a constant rate. *(p. 904)*

Customer orientation Company position that its managers and employees be in tune with the changing wants and needs of consumers. *(p. 729)*

Cycle efficiency (CE) A measure of production efficiency, which is defined as value-added (process) time divided by total cycle time. *(p. 743)*

Cycle time (CT) A measure of the time to produce a product or service, which is the sum of process time, inspection time, move time, and wait time; also called *throughput time. (p. 742)*

Date of declaration Date the directors vote to pay a dividend. *(p. 513)*

Date of payment Date the corporation makes the dividend payment. *(p. 513)*

Date of record Date directors specify for identifying stockholders to receive dividends. *(p. 513)*

Days' sales in inventory Estimate of number of days needed to convert inventory into receivables or cash; equals ending inventory divided by cost of goods sold and then multiplied by 365; also called *days' stock on hand. (p. 237)*

Days' sales uncollected Measure of the liquidity of receivables computed by dividing the current balance of receivables by the annual credit (or net) sales and then multiplying by 365; also called *days' sales in receivables. (p. 332)*

Debit Recorded on the left side; an entry that increases asset and expense accounts, and decreases liability, revenue, and most equity accounts; abbreviated Dr. *(p. 53)*

Debit memorandum Notification that the sender has debited the recipient's account in the sender's records. *(p. 182)*

Debt ratio Ratio of total liabilities to total assets; used to reflect risk associated with a company's debts. *(p. 67)*

Debt-to-equity ratio Defined as total liabilities divided by total equity; shows the proportion of a company financed by non-owners (creditors) in comparison with that financed by owners. *(p. 564)*

Debtors Individuals or organizations that owe money. *(p. 49)*

Declining-balance method Method that determines depreciation charge for the period by multiplying a depreciation rate (often twice the straight-line rate) by the asset's beginning-period book value. *(p. 398)*

Deferred income tax liability Corporation income taxes that are deferred until future years because of temporary differences between GAAP and tax rules. *(p. 457)*

Degree of operating leverage (DOL) Ratio of contribution margin divided by pretax income; used to assess the effect on income of changes in sales. *(p. 918)*

Departmental accounting system Accounting system that provides information useful in evaluating the profitability or cost effectiveness of a department. *(p. 858)*

Departmental contribution to overhead Amount by which a department's revenues exceed its direct expenses. *(p. 866)*

Depletion Process of allocating the cost of natural resources to periods when they are consumed and sold. *(p. 406)*

Deposit ticket Lists items such as currency, coins, and checks deposited and their corresponding dollar amounts. *(p. 326)*

Deposits in transit Deposits recorded by the company but not yet recorded by its bank. *(p. 329)*

Depreciable cost Cost of a plant asset less its salvage value.

Depreciation Expense created by allocating the cost of plant and equipment to periods in which they are used; represents the expense of using the asset. *(pp. 97 & 395)*

Diluted earnings per share Earnings per share calculation that requires dilutive securities be added to the denominator of the basic EPS calculation. *(p. 524)*

Dilutive securities Securities having the potential to increase common shares outstanding; examples are options, rights, convertible bonds, and convertible preferred stock. *(p. 524)*

Direct costs Costs incurred for the benefit of one specific cost object. *(p. 732)*

Direct expenses Expenses traced to a specific department (object) that are incurred for the sole benefit of that department. *(p. 859)*

Direct labor Efforts of employees who physically convert materials to finished product. *(p. 738)*

Direct labor costs Wages and salaries for direct labor that are separately and readily traced through the production process to finished goods. *(p. 738)*

Direct material Raw material that physically becomes part of the product and is clearly identified with specific products or batches of product. *(p. 738)*

Direct material costs Expenditures for direct material that are separately and readily traced through the production process to finished goods. *(p. 738)*

Direct method Presentation of net cash from operating activities for the statement of cash flows that lists major operating cash receipts less major operating cash payments. *(p. 634)*

Direct write-off method Method that records the loss from an uncollectible account receivable at the time it is determined to be uncollectible; no attempt is made to estimate bad debts. *(p. 361)*

Discount on bonds payable Difference between a bond's par value and its lower issue price or carrying value; occurs when the contract rate is less than the market rate. *(p. 553)*

Discount on note payable Difference between the face value of a note payable and the (lesser) amount borrowed; reflects the added interest to be paid on the note over its life.

Discount on stock Difference between the par value of stock and its issue price when issued at a price below par value. *(p. 511)*

Discount period Time period in which a cash discount is available and the buyer can make a reduced payment. *(p. 181)*

Discount rate Expected rate of return on investments; also called *cost of capital, hurdle rate,* or *required rate of return. (p. B-2)*

Discounts lost Expenses resulting from not taking advantage of cash discounts on purchases. *(p. 338)*

Dividend in arrears Unpaid dividend on cumulative preferred stock; must be paid before any regular dividends on preferred stock and before any dividends on common stock. *(p. 517)*

Dividend yield Ratio of the annual amount of cash dividends distributed to common shareholders relative to the common stock's market value (price). *(p. 525)*

Dividends Corporation's distributions of assets to its owners.

Double-declining-balance (DDB) depreciation Depreciation equals beginning book value multiplied by 2 times the straight-line rate.

Double-entry accounting Accounting system in which each transaction affects at least two accounts and has at least one debit and one credit. *(p. 53)*

Double taxation Corporate income is taxed and then its later distribution through dividends is normally taxed again for shareholders. *(p. 11)*

Earnings (See *net income.*)

Earnings per share (EPS) Amount of income earned by each share of a company's outstanding common stock; also called *net income per share. (p. 524)*

Effective interest method Allocates interest expense over the bond life to yield a constant rate of interest; interest expense for a period is found by multiplying the balance of the liability at the beginning of the period by the bond market rate at issuance; also called *interest method. (p. 569)*

Efficiency Company's productivity in using its assets; usually measured relative to how much revenue a certain level of assets generates. *(p. 681)*

Efficiency variance Difference between the actual quantity of an input and the standard quantity of that input. *(p. 993)*

Electronic funds transfer (EFT) Use of electronic communication to transfer cash from one party to another. *(p. 327)*

Employee benefits Additional compensation paid to or on behalf of employees, such as premiums for medical, dental, life, and disability insurance, and contributions to pension plans. *(p. 443)*

Employee earnings report Record of an employee's net pay, gross pay, deductions, and year-to-date payroll information. *(p. 454)*

Enterprise resource planning (ERP) software Programs that manage a company's vital operations, which range from order taking to production to accounting. *(p. 283)*

Entity Organization that, for accounting purposes, is separate from other organizations and individuals. *(p. 10)*

EOM Abbreviation for *end of month;* used to describe credit terms for credit transactions. *(p. 181)*

Equity Owner's claim on the assets of a business; equals the residual interest in an entity's assets after deducting liabilities; also called *net assets. (p. 13)*

Equity method Accounting method used for long-term investments when the investor has "significant influence" over the investee. *(p. 598)*

Equity ratio Portion of total assets provided by equity, computed as total equity divided by total assets. *(p. 695)*

Equity securities with controlling influence Long-term investment when the investor is able to exert controlling influence over the investee; investors owning 50% or more of voting stock are presumed to exert controlling influence. *(p. 599)*

Equity securities with significant influence Long-term investment when the investor is able to exert significant influence over the investee; investors owning 20 percent or more (but less than 50 percent) of voting stock are presumed to exert significant influence. *(p. 598)*

Equivalent units of production (EUP) Number of units that would be completed if all effort during a period had been applied to units that were started and finished. *(p. 815)*

Estimated liability Obligation of an uncertain amount that can be reasonably estimated. *(p. 443)*

Estimated line of cost behavior Line drawn on a graph to visually fit the relation between cost and sales. *(p. 906)*

Ethics Codes of conduct by which actions are judged as right or wrong, fair or unfair, honest or dishonest. *(pp. 8, 731)*

Events Happenings that both affect an organization's financial position and can be reliably measured. *(p. 14)*

Expanded accounting equation Assets = Liabilities + Equity; Equity equals [Owner capital − Owner withdrawals + Revenues − Expenses] for a noncorporation; Equity equals [Contributed capital + Retained earnings + Revenues − Expenses] for a corporation where dividends are subtracted from retained earnings. *(p. 13)*

Expenses Outflows or using up of assets as part of operations of a business to generate sales. *(p. 13)*

External transactions Exchanges of economic value between one entity and another entity. *(p. 13)*

External users Persons using accounting information who are not directly involved in running the organization. *(p. 5)*

Extraordinary gains or losses Gains or losses reported separately from continuing operations because they are both unusual and infrequent. *(p. 703)*

Extraordinary repairs Major repairs that extend the useful life of a plant asset beyond prior expectations; treated as a capital expenditure. *(p. 403)*

Factory overhead Factory activities supporting the production process that are not direct material or direct labor; also called *overhead* and *manufacturing overhead. (p. 738)*

Factory overhead costs Expenditures for factory overhead that cannot be separately or readily traced to finished goods; also called *overhead costs*. *(p. 738)*

Favorable variance Difference in actual revenues or expenses from the budgeted amount that contributes to a higher income. *(p. 981)*

Federal depository bank Bank authorized to accept deposits of amounts payable to the federal government. *(p. 452)*

Federal Insurance Contributions Act (FICA) Taxes Taxes assessed on both employers and employees; for Social Security and Medicare programs. *(p. 440)*

Federal Unemployment Taxes (FUTA) Payroll taxes on employers assessed by the federal government to support its unemployment insurance program. *(p. 442)*

FIFO method (See *first-in, first-out.*)

Financial accounting Area of accounting mainly aimed at serving external users. *(p. 5)*

Financial Accounting Standards Board (FASB) Independent group of full-time members responsible for setting accounting rules. *(p. 9)*

Financial leverage Earning a higher return on equity by paying dividends on preferred stock or interest on debt at a rate lower than the return earned with the assets from issuing preferred stock or debt; also called *trading on the equity*. *(p. 519)*

Financial reporting Process of communicating information relevant to investors, creditors, and others in making investment, credit, and business decisions. *(p. 681)*

Financial statement analysis Application of analytical tools to general-purpose financial statements and related data for making business decisions. *(p. 680)*

Financial statements Includes the balance sheet, income statement, statement of owner's (or stockholders') equity, and statement of cash flows. *(p. 17)*

Financing activities Transactions with owners and creditors that include obtaining cash from issuing debt, repaying amounts borrowed, and obtaining cash from or distributing cash to owners. *(p. 630)*

Finished goods inventory Account that controls the finished goods files, which acts as a subsidiary ledger (of the Inventory account) in which the costs of finished goods that are ready for sale are recorded. *(pp. 736 & 772)*

First-in, first-out (FIFO) Method to assign cost to inventory that assumes items are sold in the order acquired; earliest items purchased are the first sold. *(pp. 229, 827)*

Fiscal year Consecutive 12-month (or 52-week) period chosen as the organization's annual accounting period. *(p. 93)*

Fixed budget Planning budget based on a single predicted amount of volume; unsuitable for evaluations if the actual volume differs from predicted volume. *(p. 981)*

Fixed budget performance report Report that compares actual revenues and costs with fixed budgeted amounts and identifies the differences as favorable or unfavorable variances. *(p. 981)*

Fixed cost Cost that does not change with changes in the volume of activity. *(p. 732)*

Flexibility principle Information system principle that prescribes an accounting system be able to adapt to changes in the company, its operations, and needs of decision makers. *(p. 269)*

Flexible budget Budget prepared (using actual volume) once a period is complete that helps managers evaluate past performance; uses fixed and variable costs in determining total costs. *(p. 982)*

Flexible budget performance report Report that compares actual revenues and costs with their variable budgeted amounts based on actual sales volume (or other level of activity) and identifies the differences as variances. *(p. 958)*

FOB Abbreviation for *free on board;* the point when ownership of goods passes to the buyer; *FOB shipping point* (or *factory*) means the buyer pays shipping costs and accepts ownership of goods when the seller transfers goods to carrier; *FOB destination* means the seller pays shipping costs and buyer accepts ownership of goods at the buyer's place of business. *(p. 183)*

Foreign exchange rate Price of one currency stated in terms of another currency. *(p. 605)*

Form 940 IRS form used to report an employer's federal unemployment taxes (FUTA) on an annual filing basis. *(p. 452)*

Form 941 IRS form filed to report FICA taxes owed and remitted. *(p. 450)*

Form 10-K (or 10-KSB) Annual report form filed with SEC by businesses (small businesses) with publicly traded securities. *(p. A-1)*

Form W-2 Annual report by an employer to each employee showing the employee's wages subject to FICA and federal income taxes along with amounts withheld. *(p. 452)*

Form W-4 Withholding allowance certificate, filed with the employer, identifying the number of withholding allowances claimed. *(p. 454)*

Franchises Privileges granted by a company or government to sell a product or service under specified conditions. *(p. 408)*

Full disclosure principle Principle that prescribes financial statements (including notes) to report all relevant information about an entity's operations and financial condition. *(p. 10)*

GAAP (See *generally accepted accounting principles.*)

General accounting system Accounting system for manufacturing activities based on the *periodic* inventory system. *(p. 770)*

General and administrative expenses Expenses that support the operating activities of a business. *(p. 191)*

General and administrative expense budget Plan that shows predicted operating expenses not included in the selling expenses budget. *(p. 948)*

General journal All-purpose journal for recording the debits and credits of transactions and events. *(pp. 54 & 272)*

General ledger (See *ledger.*)

General partner Partner who assumes unlimited liability for the debts of the partnership; responsible for partnership management. *(p. 479)*

General partnership Partnership in which all partners have mutual agency and unlimited liability for partnership debts. *(p. 479)*

Generally accepted accounting principles (GAAP) Rules that specify acceptable accounting practices. *(p. 8)*

Generally accepted auditing standards (GAAS) Rules that specify acceptable auditing practices.

General-purpose financial statements Statements published periodically for use by a variety of interested parties; includes the income statement, balance sheet, statement of owner's equity (or statement of retained earnings for a corporation), statement of cash flows, and notes to these statements. *(p. 681)*

Going-concern assumption Principle that prescribes financial statements to reflect the assumption that the business will continue operating. *(p. 10)*

Goods in process inventory Account in which costs are accumulated for products that are in the process of being produced but are not yet complete; also called *work in process inventory*. *(pp. 736 & 772)*

Goodwill Amount by which a company's (or a segment's) value exceeds the value of its individual assets less its liabilities. *(p. 409)*

Gross margin (See *gross profit.*)

Gross margin ratio Gross margin (net sales minus cost of goods sold) divided by net sales; also called *gross profit ratio*. *(p. 193)*

Gross method Method of recording purchases at the full invoice price without deducting any cash discounts. *(p. 338)*

Gross pay Total compensation earned by an employee. *(p. 440)*

Gross profit Net sales minus cost of goods sold; also called *gross margin*. *(p. 178)*

Gross profit method Procedure to estimate inventory when the past gross profit rate is used to estimate cost of goods sold, which is then subtracted from the cost of goods available for sale. *(p. 248)*

Held-to-maturity (HTM) securities Debt securities that a company has the intent and ability to hold until they mature. *(p. 596)*

High-low method Procedure that yields an estimated line of cost behavior by graphically connecting costs associated with the highest and lowest sales volume. *(p. 906)*

Horizontal analysis Comparison of a company's financial condition and performance across time. *(p. 682)*

Hurdle rate Minimum acceptable rate of return (set by management) for an investment. *(pp. 868 & 1033)*

Impairment Diminishment of an asset value. *(pp. 402 & 407)*

Imprest system Method to account for petty cash; maintains a constant balance in the fund, which equals cash plus petty cash receipts.

Inadequacy Condition in which the capacity of plant assets is too small to meet the company's production demands. *(p. 395)*

Income (See *net income.*)

Income statement Financial statement that subtracts expenses from revenues to yield a net income or loss over a specified period of time; also includes any gains or losses. *(p. 17)*

Income Summary Temporary account used only in the closing process to which the balances of revenue and expense accounts (including any gains or losses) are transferred; its balance is transferred to the capital account (or retained earnings for a corporation). *(p. 141)*

Incremental cost Additional cost incurred only if a company pursues a specific course of action. *(p. 1036)*

Indefinite life Asset life that is not limited by legal, regulatory, contractual, competitive, economic, or other factors. *(p. 407)*

Indirect costs Costs incurred for the benefit of more than one cost object. *(p. 732)*

Indirect expenses Expenses incurred for the joint benefit of more than one department (or cost object). *(p. 859)*

Indirect labor Efforts of production employees who do not work specifically on converting direct materials into finished products and who are not clearly identified with specific units or batches of product. *(p. 738)*

Indirect labor costs Labor costs that cannot be physically traced to production of a product or service; included as part of overhead. *(p. 738)*

Indirect material Material used to support the production process but not clearly identified with products or batches of product. *(p. 735)*

Indirect method Presentation that reports net income and then adjusts it by adding and subtracting items to yield net cash from operating activities on the statement of cash flows. *(p. 634)*

Information processor Component of an accounting system that interprets, transforms, and summarizes information for use in analysis and reporting. *(p. 270)*

Information storage Component of an accounting system that keeps data in a form accessible to information processors. *(p. 270)*

Infrequent gain or loss Gain or loss not expected to recur given the operating environment of the business. *(p. 703)*

Input device Means of capturing information from source documents that enables its transfer to information processors. *(p. 270)*

Installment note Liability requiring a series of periodic payments to the lender. *(p. 560)*

Institute of Management Accountants (IMA) A professional association of management accountants. *(p. 731)*

Intangible assets Long-term assets (resources) used to produce or sell products or services; usually lack physical form and have uncertain benefits. *(pp. 147 & 407)*

Interest Charge for using money (or other assets) loaned from one entity to another. *(p. 368)*

Interim financial statements Financial statements covering periods of less than one year; usually based on one-, three-, or six-month periods. *(pp. 92 & 247)*

Internal controls or **Internal control system** All policies and procedures used to protect assets, ensure reliable accounting, promote efficient operations, and urge adherence to company policies. *(pp. 268 & 314)*

Internal rate of return (IRR) Rate used to evaluate the acceptability of an investment; equals the rate that yields a net present value of zero for an investment. *(p. 1031)*

Internal transactions Activities within an organization that can affect the accounting equation. *(p. 13)*

Internal users Persons using accounting information who are directly involved in managing the organization. *(p. 6)*

International Accounting Standards Board (IASB) Group that identifies preferred accounting practices and encourages global acceptance; issues International Financial Reporting Standards (IFRS). *(p. 9)*

Inventory Goods a company owns and expects to sell in its normal operations. *(p. 179)*

Inventory turnover Number of times a company's average inventory is sold during a period; computed by dividing cost of goods sold by average inventory; also called *merchandise turnover*. *(p. 236)*

Investing activities Transactions that involve purchasing and selling of long-term assets, includes making and collecting notes receivable and investments in other than cash equivalents. *(p. 630)*

Investment center Center of which a manager is responsible for revenues, costs, and asset investments. *(p. 858)*

Investment center residual income The net income an investment center earns above a target return on average invested assets. *(p. 867)*

Investment center return on total assets Center net income divided by average total assets for the center. *(p. 867)*

Investment turnover The efficiency with which a company generates sales from its available assets; computed as sales divided by average invested assets. *(p. 872)*

Invoice Itemized record of goods prepared by the vendor that lists the customer's name, items sold, sales prices, and terms of sale. *(p. 335)*

Invoice approval Document containing a checklist of steps necessary for approving the recording and payment of an invoice; also called *check authorization*. *(p. 336)*

Job Production of a customized product or service. *(p. 770)*

Job cost sheet Separate record maintained for each job. *(p. 772)*

Job lot Production of more than one unit of a customized product or service. *(p. 771)*

Job order cost accounting system Cost accounting system to determine the cost of producing each job or job lot. *(pp. 772 & 811)*

Job order production Production of special-order products; also called *customized production*. *(p. 770)*

Joint cost Cost incurred to produce or purchase two or more products at the same time. *(p. 877)*

Journal Record in which transactions are entered before they are posted to ledger accounts; also called *book of original entry*. *(p. 54)*

Journalizing Process of recording transactions in a journal. *(p. 54)*

Just-in-time (JIT) manufacturing Process of acquiring or producing inventory only when needed. *(p. 730)*

Known liabilities Obligations of a company with little uncertainty; set by agreements, contracts, or laws; also called *definitely determinable liabilities*. *(p. 436)*

Land improvements Assets that increase the benefits of land, have a limited useful life, and are depreciated. *(p. 394)*

Large stock dividend Stock dividend that is more than 25% of the previously outstanding shares. *(p. 514)*

Last-in, first-out (LIFO) Method to assign cost to inventory that assumes costs for the most recent items purchased are sold first and charged to cost of goods sold. *(p. 229)*

Lean business model Practice of eliminating waste while meeting customer needs and yielding positive company returns. *(p. 730)*

Lease Contract specifying the rental of property. *(pp. 409 & 573)*

Leasehold Rights the lessor grants to the lessee under the terms of a lease. *(p. 409)*

Leasehold improvements Alterations or improvements to leased property such as partitions and storefronts. *(p. 409)*

Least-squares regression Statistical method for deriving an estimated line of cost behavior that is more precise than the high-low method and the scatter diagram. *(p. 907)*

Ledger Record containing all accounts (with amounts) for a business; also called *general ledger*. *(p. 49)*

Lessee Party to a lease who secures the right to possess and use the property from another party (the lessor). *(p. 409)*

Lessor Party to a lease who grants another party (the lessee) the right to possess and use its property. *(p. 409)*

Liabilities Creditors' claims on an organization's assets; involves a probable future payment of assets, products, or services that a company is obligated to make due to past transactions or events. *(p. 12)*

Licenses (See *franchises*.) *(p. 408)*

Limited liability Owner can lose no more than the amount invested. *(p. 11)*

Limited liability company Organization form that combines select features of a corporation and a limited partnership; provides limited liability to its members (owners), is free of business tax, and allows members to actively participate in management. *(p. 480)*

Limited liability partnership Partnership in which a partner is not personally liable for malpractice or negligence unless that partner is responsible for providing the service that resulted in the claim. *(p. 479)*

Limited life (See *useful life*.)

Limited partners Partners who have no personal liability for partnership debts beyond the amounts they invested in the partnership. *(p. 479)*

Limited partnership Partnership that has two classes of partners, limited partners and general partners. *(p. 479)*

Liquid assets Resources such as cash that are easily converted into other assets or used to pay for goods, services, or liabilities. *(p. 319)*

Liquidating cash dividend Distribution of assets that returns part of the original investment to stockholders; deducted from contributed capital accounts. *(p. 514)*

Liquidation Process of going out of business; involves selling assets, paying liabilities, and distributing remainder to owners.

Liquidity Availability of resources to meet short-term cash requirements. *(pp. 319 & 681)*

List price Catalog (full) price of an item before any trade discount is deducted. *(p. 180)*

Long-term investments Long-term assets not used in operating activities such as notes receivable and investments in stocks and bonds. *(pp. 147 & 592)*

Long-term liabilities Obligations not due to be paid within one year or the operating cycle, whichever is longer. *(pp. 147 & 435)*

Lower of cost or market (LCM) Required method to report inventory at market replacement cost when that market cost is lower than recorded cost. *(p. 233)*

Maker of the note Entity who signs a note and promises to pay it at maturity. *(p. 368)*

Management by exception Management process to focus on significant variances and give less attention to areas where performance is close to the standard. *(p. 996)*

Managerial accounting Area of accounting mainly aimed at serving the decision-making needs of internal users; also called *management accounting. (pp. 6 & 726)*

Manufacturer Company that uses labor and operating assets to convert raw materials to finished goods. *(p. 13)*

Manufacturing budget Plan that shows the predicted costs for direct materials, direct labor, and overhead to be incurred in manufacturing units in the production budget. *(p. 959)*

Manufacturing statement Report that summarizes the types and amounts of costs incurred in a company's production process for a period; also called *cost of goods manufacturing statement. (p. 740)*

Margin of safety Excess of expected sales over the level of break-even sales. *(p. 914)*

Market prospects Expectations (both good and bad) about a company's future performance as assessed by users and other interested parties. *(p. 681)*

Market rate Interest rate that borrowers are willing to pay and lenders are willing to accept for a specific lending agreement given the borrowers' risk level. *(p. 553)*

Market value per share Price at which stock is bought or sold. *(p. 509)*

Master budget Comprehensive business plan that includes specific plans for expected sales, product units to be produced, merchandise (or materials) to be purchased, expenses to be incurred, plant assets to be purchased, and amounts of cash to be borrowed or loans to be repaid, as well as a budgeted income statement and balance sheet. *(p. 944)*

Matching principle Prescribes expenses to be reported in the same period as the revenues that were earned as a result of the expenses. *(pp. 10 & 362)*

Materiality constraint Prescribes that accounting for items that significantly impact financial statement and any inferences from them adhere strictly to GAAP. *(p. 362)*

Materials consumption report Document that summarizes the materials a department uses during a reporting period; replaces materials requisitions. *(p. 812)*

Materials ledger card Perpetual record updated each time units are purchased or issued for production use. *(p. 773)*

Materials requisition Source document production managers use to request materials for production; used to assign materials costs to specific jobs or overhead. *(p. 774)*

Maturity date of a note Date when a note's principal and interest are due. *(p. 368)*

Merchandise (See *merchandise inventory.*)

Merchandise inventory Goods that a company owns and expects to sell to customers; also called *merchandise* or *inventory. (p. 179)*

Merchandise purchases budget Plan that shows the units or costs of merchandise to be purchased by a merchandising company during the budget period. *(p. 947)*

Merchandiser Entity that earns net income by buying and selling merchandise. *(p. 178)*

Merit rating Rating assigned to an employer by a state based on the employer's record of employment. *(p. 442)*

Minimum legal capital Amount of assets defined by law that stockholders must (potentially) invest in a corporation; usually defined as par value of the stock; intended to protect creditors. *(p. 509)*

Mixed cost Cost that behaves like a combination of fixed and variable costs. *(p. 903)*

Modified Accelerated Cost Recovery System (MACRS) Depreciation system required by federal income tax law. *(p. 400)*

Monetary unit assumption Principle that assumes transactions and events can be expressed in money units. *(p. 10)*

Mortgage Legal loan agreement that protects a lender by giving the lender the right to be paid from the cash proceeds from the sale of a borrower's assets identified in the mortgage. *(p. 562)*

Multinational Company that operates in several countries. *(p. 605)*

Multiple-step income statement Income statement format that shows subtotals between sales and net income, categorizes expenses, and often reports the details of net sales and expenses. *(p. 191)*

Mutual agency Legal relationship among partners whereby each partner is an agent of the partnership and is able to bind the partnership to contracts within the scope of the partnership's business. *(p. 478)*

Natural business year Twelve-month period that ends when a company's sales activities are at their lowest point. *(p. 93)*

Natural resources Assets physically consumed when used; examples are timber, mineral deposits, and oil and gas fields; also called *wasting assets. (p. 406)*

Net assets (See *equity.*)

Net income Amount earned after subtracting all expenses necessary for and matched with sales for a period; also called *income, profit,* or *earnings. (p. 13)*

Net loss Excess of expenses over revenues for a period. *(p. 18)*

Net method Method of recording purchases at the full invoice price less any cash discounts. *(p. 338)*

Net pay Gross pay less all deductions; also called *take-home pay. (p. 440)*

Net present value (NPV) Dollar estimate of an asset's value that is used to evaluate the acceptability of an investment; computed by discounting future cash flows from the investment at a satisfactory rate and then subtracting the initial cost of the investment. *(p. 1029)*

Net realizable value Expected selling price (value) of an item minus the cost of making the sale. *(p. 224)*

Noncumulative preferred stock Preferred stock on which the right to receive dividends is lost for any period when dividends are not declared. *(p. 517)*

Noninterest-bearing note Note with no stated (contract) rate of interest; interest is implicitly included in the note's face value.

Nonparticipating preferred stock Preferred stock on which dividends are limited to a maximum amount each year. *(p. 518)*

No-par value stock Stock class that has not been assigned a par (or stated) value by the corporate charter. *(p. 509)*

Nonsufficient funds (NSF) check Maker's bank account has insufficient money to pay the check; also called *hot check.*

Non-value-added time The portion of cycle time that is not directed at producing a product or service; equals the sum of inspection time, move time, and wait time. *(p. 743)*

Not controllable costs Costs that a manager does not have the power to control or strongly influence. *(p. 733)*

Note (See promissory note.)

Note payable Liability expressed by a written promise to pay a definite sum of money on demand or on a specific future date(s).

Note receivable Asset consisting of a written promise to receive a definite sum of money on demand or on a specific future date(s).

Objectivity principle Principle that prescribes independent, unbiased evidence to support financial statement information. *(p. 9)*

Obsolescence Condition in which, because of new inventions and improvements, a plant asset can no longer be used to produce goods or services with a competitive advantage. *(p. 395)*

Off-balance-sheet financing Acquisition of assets by agreeing to liabilities not reported on the balance sheet. *(p. 574)*

Online processing Approach to inputting data from source documents as soon as the information is available. *(p. 282)*

Operating activities Activities that involve the production or purchase of merchandise and the sale of goods or services to customers, including expenditures related to administering the business. *(p. 629)*

Operating cycle Normal time between paying cash for merchandise or employee services and receiving cash from customers. *(p. 145)*

Operating leases Short-term (or cancelable) leases in which the lessor retains risks and rewards of ownership. *(p. 573)*

Operating leverage Extent, or relative size, of fixed costs in the total cost structure. *(p. 918)*

Opportunity cost Potential benefit lost by choosing a specific action from two or more alternatives. *(p. 733)*

Ordinary repairs Repairs to keep a plant asset in normal, good operating condition; treated as a revenue expenditure and immediately expensed. *(p. 402)*

Organization expenses (costs) Costs such as legal fees and promoter fees to bring an entity into existence. *(pp. 507 & 512)*

Out-of-pocket cost Cost incurred or avoided as a result of management's decisions. *(p. 733)*

Output devices Means by which information is taken out of the accounting system and made available for use. *(p. 271)*

Outsourcing Manager decision to buy a product or service from another entity; part of a *make-or-buy* decision; also called *make or buy.*

Outstanding checks Checks written and recorded by the depositor but not yet paid by the bank at the bank statement date. *(p. 329)*

Outstanding stock Corporation's stock held by its shareholders.

Overapplied overhead Amount by which the overhead applied to production in a period using the predetermined overhead rate exceeds the actual overhead incurred in a period. *(p. 782)*

Overhead cost variance Difference between the total overhead cost applied to products and the total overhead cost actually incurred. *(p. 992)*

Owner, Capital Account showing the owner's claim on company assets; equals owner investments plus net income (or less net losses) minus owner withdrawals since the company's inception; also referred to as *equity. (p. 13)*

Owner investment Assets put into the business by the owner. *(p. 13)*

Owner's equity (See *equity.*)

Owner, Withdrawals Account used to record asset distributions to the owner. (See also *withdrawals.*) *(pp. 13 & 51)*

Paid-in capital (See *contributed capital.*) *(p. 510)*

Paid-in capital in excess of par value Amount received from issuance of stock that is in excess of the stock's par value. *(p. 511)*

Par value Value assigned a share of stock by the corporate charter when the stock is authorized. *(p. 509)*

Par value of a bond Amount the bond issuer agrees to pay at maturity and the amount on which cash interest payments are based; also called *face amount* or *face value* of a bond. *(p. 550)*

Par value stock Class of stock assigned a par value by the corporate charter. *(p. 509)*

Parent Company that owns a controlling interest in a corporation (requires more than 50% of voting stock). *(p. 599)*

Participating preferred stock Preferred stock that shares with common stockholders any dividends paid in excess of the percent stated on preferred stock. *(p. 518)*

Partner return on equity Partner net income divided by average partner equity for the period. *(p. 490)*

Partnership Unincorporated association of two or more persons to pursue a business for profit as co-owners. *(pp. 10 & 478)*

Partnership contract Agreement among partners that sets terms under which the affairs of the partnership are conducted; also called *articles of partnership. (p. 478)*

Partnership liquidation Dissolution of a partnership by (1) selling noncash assets and allocating any gain or loss according to partners' income-and-loss ratio, (2) paying liabilities, and (3) distributing any remaining cash according to partners' capital balances. *(p. 488)*

Patent Exclusive right granted to its owner to produce and sell an item or to use a process for 17 years. *(p. 408)*

Payback period (PBP) Time-based measurement used to evaluate the acceptability of an investment; equals the time expected to pass before an investment's net cash flows equal its initial cost. *(p. 1025)*

Payee of the note Entity to whom a note is made payable. *(p. 368)*

Payroll bank account Bank account used solely for paying employees; each pay period an amount equal to the total employees' net pay is deposited in it and the payroll checks are drawn on it. *(p. 454)*

Payroll deductions Amounts withheld from an employee's gross pay; also called *withholdings. (p. 440)*

Payroll register Record for a pay period that shows the pay period dates, regular and overtime hours worked, gross pay, net pay, and deductions. *(p. 452)*

Pension plan Contractual agreement between an employer and its employees for the employer to provide benefits to employees after they retire; expensed when incurred. *(p. 575)*

Period costs Expenditures identified more with a time period than with finished products costs; includes selling and general administrative expenses. *(p. 733)*

Periodic inventory system Method that records the cost of inventory purchased but does not continuously track the quantity available or sold to customers; records are updated at the end of each period to reflect the physical count and costs of goods available. *(p. 180)*

Permanent accounts Accounts that reflect activities related to one or more future periods; balance sheet accounts whose balances are not closed; also called *real accounts. (p. 140)*

Perpetual inventory system Method that maintains continuous records of the cost of inventory available and the cost of goods sold. *(p. 180)*

Petty cash Small amount of cash in a fund to pay minor expenses; accounted for using an imprest system. *(p. 323)*

Planning Process of setting goals and preparing to achieve them. *(p. 726)*

Plant assets Tangible long-lived assets used to produce or sell products and services; also called *property, plant and equipment (PP&E)* or *fixed assets. (p. 403)*

Pledged assets to secured liabilities Ratio of the book value of a company's pledged assets to the book value of its secured liabilities.

Post-closing trial balance List of permanent accounts and their balances from the ledger after all closing entries are journalized and posted. *(p. 144)*

Posting Process of transferring journal entry information to the ledger; computerized systems automate this process. *(p. 54)*

Posting reference (PR) column A column in journals in which individual ledger account numbers are entered when entries are posted to those ledger accounts. *(p. 56)*

Predetermined overhead rate Rate established prior to the beginning of a period that relates estimated overhead to another variable, such as estimated direct labor, and is used to assign overhead cost to production. *(p. 778)*

Preemptive right Stockholders' right to maintain their proportionate interest in a corporation with any additional shares issued. *(p. 508)*

Preferred stock Stock with a priority status over common stockholders in one or more ways, such as paying dividends or distributing assets. *(p. 516)*

Premium on bonds Difference between a bond's par value and its higher carrying value; occurs when the contract rate is higher than the market rate; also called *bond premium. (p. 556)*

Premium on stock (See *contributed capital in excess of par value.*) *(p. 511)*

Prepaid expenses Items paid for in advance of receiving their benefits; classified as assets. *(p. 95)*

Price-earnings (PE) ratio Ratio of a company's current market value per share to its earnings per share; also called *price-to-earnings. (p. 525)*

Price variance Difference between actual and budgeted revenue or cost caused by the difference between the actual price per unit and the budgeted price per unit. *(p. 984)*

Prime costs Expenditures directly identified with the production of finished goods; include direct materials costs and direct labor costs. *(p. 738)*

Principal of a note Amount that the signer of a note agrees to pay back when it matures, not including interest. *(p. 368)*

Principles of internal control Principles prescribing management to establish responsibility, maintain records, insure assets, separate recordkeeping from custody of assets, divide responsibility for related transactions, apply technological controls, and perform reviews. *(p. 315)*

Prior period adjustment Correction of an error in a prior year that is reported in the statement of retained earnings (or statement of stockholders' equity) net of any income tax effects. *(p. 523)*

Pro forma financial statements Statements that show the effects of proposed transactions and events as if they had occurred. *(p. 140)*

Process cost accounting system System of assigning direct materials, direct labor, and overhead to specific processes; total costs associated with each process are then divided by the number of units passing through that process to determine the cost per equivalent unit. *(p. 811)*

Process cost summary Report of costs charged to a department, its equivalent units of production achieved, and the costs assigned to its output. *(p. 820)*

Process operations Processing of products in a continuous (sequential) flow of steps; also called *process manufacturing* or *process production. (p. 808)*

Product costs Costs that are capitalized as inventory because they produce benefits expected to have future value; include direct materials, direct labor, and overhead. *(p. 733)*

Production budget Plan that shows the units to be produced each period. *(p. 959)*

Profit (See *net income.*)

Profit center Business unit that incurs costs and generates revenues. *(p. 858)*

Profit margin Ratio of a company's net income to its net sales; the percent of income in each dollar of revenue; also called *net profit margin. (pp. 106 & 872)*

Profitability Company's ability to generate an adequate return on invested capital. *(p. 681)*

Profitability index A measure of the relation between the expected benefits of a project and its investment, computed as the present value of expected future cash flows from the investment divided by the cost of the investment; a higher value indicates a more desirable investment, and a value below 1 indicates an unacceptable project. *(p. 1031)*

Promissory note (or **note**) Written promise to pay a specified amount either on demand or at a definite future date; is a *note receivable* for the lender but a *note payable* for the lendee. *(p. 368)*

Proprietorship (See *sole proprietorship.*)

Proxy Legal document giving a stockholder's agent the power to exercise the stockholder's voting rights. *(p. 507)*

Purchase discount Term used by a purchaser to describe a cash discount granted to the purchaser for paying within the discount period. *(p. 181)*

Purchase order Document used by the purchasing department to place an order with a seller (vendor). *(p. 335)*

Purchase requisition Document listing merchandise needed by a department and requesting it be purchased. *(p. 335)*

Purchases journal Journal normally used to record all purchases on credit. *(p. 279)*

Quantity variance Difference between actual and budgeted revenue or cost caused by the difference between the actual number of units and the budgeted number of units. *(p. 984)*

Ratio analysis Determination of key relations between financial statement items as reflected in numerical measures. *(p. 682)*

Raw materials inventory Goods a company acquires to use in making products. *(p. 735)*

Realizable value Expected proceeds from converting an asset into cash. *(p. 363)*

Receiving report Form used to report that ordered goods are received and to describe their quantity and condition. *(p. 336)*

Recordkeeping Part of accounting that involves recording transactions and events, either manually or electronically; also called *bookkeeping. (p. 4)*

Registered bonds Bonds owned by investors whose names and addresses are recorded by the issuer; interest payments are made to the registered owners. *(p. 563)*

Relevance principle Information system principle prescribing that its reports be useful, understandable, timely, and pertinent for decision making. *(p. 268)*

Relevant benefits Additional or incremental revenue generated by selecting a particular course of action over another. *(p. 1035)*

Relevant range of operations Company's normal operating range; excludes extremely high and low volumes not likely to occur. *(p. 911)*

Report form balance sheet Balance sheet that lists accounts vertically in the order of assets, liabilities, and equity. *(p. 18)*

Responsibility accounting budget Report of expected costs and expenses under a manager's control. *(p. 870)*

Responsibility accounting performance report Responsibility report that compares actual costs and expenses for a department with budgeted amounts. *(p. 870)*

Responsibility accounting system System that provides information that management can use to evaluate the performance of a department's manager. *(p. 858)*

Restricted retained earnings Retained earnings not available for dividends because of legal or contractual limitations. *(p. 510)*

Retail inventory method Method to estimate ending inventory based on the ratio of the amount of goods for sale at cost to the amount of goods for sale at retail. *(p. 247)*

Retailer Intermediary that buys products from manufacturers or wholesalers and sells them to consumers. *(p. 178)*

Retained earnings Cumulative income less cumulative losses and dividends. *(p. 510)*

Retained earnings deficit Debit (abnormal) balance in Retained Earnings; occurs when cumulative losses and dividends exceed cumulative income; also called *accumulated deficit. (p. 513)*

Return Monies received from an investment; often in percent form. *(p. 23)*

Return on assets (See *return on total assets*) *(p. 20)*

Return on equity Ratio of net income to average equity for the period.

Return on total assets Ratio reflecting operating efficiency; defined as net income divided by average total assets for the period; also called *return on assets* or *return on investment. (p. 600)*

Revenue expenditures Expenditures reported on the current income statement as an expense because they do not provide benefits in future periods. *(p. 402)*

Revenue recognition principle The principle prescribing that revenue is recognized when earned. *(p. 10)*

Revenues Gross increase in equity from a company's business activities that earn income; also called *sales. (p. 13)*

Reverse stock split Occurs when a corporation calls in its stock and replaces each share with less than one new share; increases both market value per share and any par or stated value per share. *(p. 516)*

Reversing entries Optional entries recorded at the beginning of a period that prepare the accounts for the usual journal entries as if adjusting entries had not occurred in the prior period. *(p. 151)*

Risk Uncertainty about an expected return. *(p. 24)*

Rolling budget New set of budgets a firm adds for the next period (with revisions) to replace the ones that have lapsed. *(p. 942)*

S corporation Corporation that meets special tax qualifications so as to be treated like a partnership for income tax purposes. *(p. 480)*

Safety stock Quantity of inventory or materials over the minimum needed to satisfy budgeted demand. *(p. 947)*

Sales (See *revenues.*)

Sales budget Plan showing the units of goods to be sold or services to be provided; the starting point in the budgeting process for most departments. *(p. 946)*

Sales discount Term used by a seller to describe a cash discount granted to buyers who pay within the discount period. *(p. 181)*

Sales journal Journal normally used to record sales of goods on credit. *(p. 274)*

Sales mix Ratio of sales volumes for the various products sold by a company. *(p. 915)*

Salvage value Estimate of amount to be recovered at the end of an asset's useful life; also called *residual value* or *scrap value. (p. 395)*

Sarbanes-Oxley Act (SOX) Created the Public *Company Accounting Oversight Board*, regulates analyst conflicts, imposes corporate governance requirements, enhances accounting and control disclosures, impacts insider transactions and executive loans, establishes new types of criminal conduct, and expands penalties for violations of federal securities laws. *(pp. 11 & 314)*

Scatter diagram Graph used to display data about past cost behavior and sales as points on a diagram. *(p. 905)*

Schedule of accounts payable List of the balances of all accounts in the accounts payable ledger and their total. *(p. 280)*

Schedule of accounts receivable List of the balances for all accounts in the accounts receivable ledger and their total. *(p. 275)*

Secured bonds Bonds that have specific assets of the issuer pledged as collateral. *(p. 563)*

Securities and Exchange Commission (SEC) Federal agency Congress has charged to set reporting rules for organizations that sell ownership shares to the public. *(p. 9)*

Segment return on assets Segment operating income divided by segment average (identifiable) assets for the period. *(p. 284)*

Selling expense budget Plan that lists the types and amounts of selling expenses expected in the budget period. *(p. 948)*

Selling expenses Expenses of promoting sales, such as displaying and advertising merchandise, making sales, and delivering goods to customers. *(p. 191)*

Serial bonds Bonds consisting of separate amounts that mature at different dates. *(p. 563)*

Service company Organization that provides services instead of tangible products.

Shareholders Owners of a corporation; also called *stockholders. (p. 11)*

Shares Equity of a corporation divided into ownership units; also called *stock. (p. 11)*

Short-term investments Debt and equity securities that management expects to convert to cash within the next 3 to 12 months (or the operating cycle if longer); also called *temporary investments* or *marketable securities. (p. 592)*

Short-term note payable Current obligation in the form of a written promissory note. *(p. 437)*

Shrinkage Inventory losses that occur as a result of theft or deterioration. *(p. 188)*

Signature card Includes the signatures of each person authorized to sign checks on the bank account. *(p. 326)*

Simple capital structure Capital structure that consists of only common stock and nonconvertible preferred stock; consists of no dilutive securities. *(p. 524)*

Single-step income statement Income statement format that includes cost of goods sold as an expense and shows only one subtotal for total expenses. *(p. 192)*

Sinking fund bonds Bonds that require the issuer to make deposits to a separate account; bondholders are repaid at maturity from that account. *(p. 563)*

Small stock dividend Stock dividend that is 25% or less of a corporation's previously outstanding shares. *(p. 514)*

Social responsibility Being accountable for the impact that one's actions might have on society. *(p. 8)*

Sole proprietorship Business owned by one person that is not organized as a corporation; also called *proprietorship. (p. 10)*

Solvency Company's long-run financial viability and its ability to cover long-term obligations. *(p. 681)*

Source documents Source of information for accounting entries that can be in either paper or electronic form; also called *business papers. (p. 49)*

Special journal Any journal used for recording and posting transactions of a similar type. *(p. 272)*

Specific identification Method to assign cost to inventory when the purchase cost of each item in inventory is identified and used to compute cost of inventory. *(p. 227)*

Spending variance Difference between the actual price of an item and its standard price. *(p. 993)*

Spreadsheet Computer program that organizes data by means of formulas and format; also called *electronic work sheet.*

Standard costs Costs that should be incurred under normal conditions to produce a product or component or to perform a service. *(p. 985)*

State Unemployment Taxes (SUTA) State payroll taxes on employers to support its unemployment programs. *(p. 442)*

Stated value stock No-par stock assigned a stated value per share; this amount is recorded in the stock account when the stock is issued. *(p. 510)*

Statement of cash flows A financial statement that lists cash inflows (receipts) and cash outflows (payments) during a period; arranged by operating, investing, and financing. *(p. 628)*

Statement of owner's equity Report of changes in equity over a period; adjusted for increases (owner investment and net income) and for decreases (withdrawals and net loss). *(p. 17)*

Statement of partners' equity Financial statement that shows total capital balances at the beginning of the period, any additional investment by partners, the income or loss of the period, the partners' withdrawals, and the partners' ending capital balances; also called *statement of partners' capital. (p. 483)*

Statement of retained earnings Report of changes in retained earnings over a period; adjusted for increases (net income), for decreases (dividends and net loss), and for any prior period adjustment. *(p. 7)*

Statement of stockholders' equity Financial statement that lists the beginning and ending balances of each major equity account and describes all changes in those accounts. *(p. 523)*

Statements of Financial Accounting Standards (SFAS) FASB publications that establish U.S. GAAP. *(p. 9)*

Step-wise cost Cost that remains fixed over limited ranges of volumes but changes by a lump sum when volume changes occur outside these limited ranges. *(p. 904).*

Stock (See *shares.*)

Stock dividend Corporation's distribution of its own stock to its stockholders without the receipt of any payment. *(p. 514)*

Stock options Rights to purchase common stock at a fixed price over a specified period of time. *(p. 523)*

Stock split Occurs when a corporation calls in its stock and replaces each share with more than one new share; decreases both the market value per share and any par or stated value per share. *(p. 516)*

Stock subscription Investor's contractual commitment to purchase unissued shares at future dates and prices.

Stockholders (See *shareholders.*) *(p. 11)*

Stockholders' equity A corporation's equity; also called *shareholders' equity* or *corporate capital. (p. 510)*

Straight-line depreciation Method that allocates an equal portion of the depreciable cost of plant asset (cost minus salvage) to each accounting period in its useful life. *(pp. 97 & 396)*

Straight-line bond amortization Method allocating an equal amount of bond interest expense to each period of the bond life. *(p. 554)*

Subsidiary Entity controlled by another entity (parent) in which the parent owns more than 50% of the subsidiary's voting stock. *(p. 599)*

Subsidiary ledger List of individual sub-accounts and amounts with a common characteristic; linked to a controlling account in the general ledger. *(p. 272)*

Sunk cost Cost already incurred and cannot be avoided or changed. *(p. 733)*

Supplementary records Information outside the usual accounting records; also called *supplemental records. (p. 184)*

Supply chain Linkages of services or goods extending from suppliers, to the company itself, and on to customers.

T-account Tool used to show the effects of transactions and events on individual accounts. *(p. 53)*

Target cost Maximum allowable cost for a product or service; defined as expected selling price less the desired profit. *(p. 771)*

Temporary accounts Accounts used to record revenues, expenses, and withdrawals (dividends for a corporation); they are closed at the end of each period; also called *nominal accounts. (p. 140)*

Term bonds Bonds scheduled for payment (maturity) at a single specified date. *(p. 563)*

Throughput time (See *cycle time.*)

Time period assumption Assumption that an organization's activities can be divided into specific time periods such as months, quarters, or years. *(p. 92)*

Time ticket Source document used to report the time an employee spent working on a job or on overhead activities and then to determine the amount of direct labor to charge to the job or the amount of indirect labor to charge to overhead. *(p. 776)*

Times interest earned Ratio of income before interest expense (and any income taxes) divided by interest expense; reflects risk of covering interest commitments when income varies. *(p. 447)*

Total asset turnover Measure of a company's ability to use its assets to generate sales; computed by dividing net sales by average total assets. *(p. 410)*

Total quality management (TQM) Concept calling for all managers and employees at all stages of operations to strive toward higher standards and reduce number of defects. *(p. 730)*

Trade discount Reduction from a list or catalog price that can vary for wholesalers, retailers, and consumers. *(p. 180)*

Trademark or **Trade (Brand) name** Symbol, name, phrase, or jingle identified with a company, product, or service. *(p. 408)*

Trading on the equity (See *financial leverage.*)

Trading securities Investments in debt and equity securities that the company intends to actively trade for profit. *(p. 595)*

Transaction Exchange of economic consideration affecting an entity's financial position that can be reliably measured. *(p. 13)*

Treasury stock Corporation's own stock that it reacquired and still holds. *(p. 520)*

Trial balance List of accounts and their balances at a point in time; total debit balances equal total credit balances. *(p. 63)*

Unadjusted trial balance List of accounts and balances prepared before accounting adjustments are recorded and posted. *(p. 104)*

Unavoidable expense Expense (or cost) that is not relevant for business decisions; an expense that would continue even if a department, product, or service is eliminated. *(p. 1041)*

Unclassified balance sheet Balance sheet that broadly groups assets, liabilities, and equity accounts. *(p. 145)*

Uncontrollable costs Costs that a manager does not have the power to determine or strongly influence. *(p. 870)*

Underapplied overhead Amount by which overhead incurred in a period exceeds the overhead applied to that period's production using the predetermined overhead rate. *(p. 781)*

Unearned revenue Liability created when customers pay in advance for products or services; earned when the products or services are later delivered. *(pp. 50 & 98)*

Unfavorable variance Difference in revenues or costs, when the actual amount is compared to the budgeted amount, that contributes to a lower income. *(p. 981)*

Unit contribution margin Amount a product's unit selling price exceeds its total unit variable cost.

Units-of-production depreciation Method that charges a varying amount to depreciation expense for each period of an asset's useful life depending on its usage. *(p. 397)*

Unlimited liability Legal relationship among general partners that makes each of them responsible for partnership debts if the other partners are unable to pay their shares. *(p. 479)*

Unrealized gain (loss) Gain (loss) not yet realized by an actual transaction or event such as a sale. *(p. 595)*

Unsecured bonds Bonds backed only by the issuer's credit standing; almost always riskier than secured bonds; also called *debentures. (p. 563)*

Unusual gain or loss Gain or loss that is abnormal or unrelated to the company's ordinary activities and environment. *(p. 703)*

Useful life Length of time an asset will be productively used in the operations of a business; also called *service life* or *limited life. (p. 395)*

Value-added time The portion of cycle time that is directed at producing a product or service; equals process time. *(p. 743)*

Value chain Sequential activities that add value to an entity's products or services; includes design, production, marketing, distribution, and service. *(p. 740)*

Variable cost Cost that changes in proportion to changes in the activity output volume. *(p. 732)*

Variance analysis Process of examining differences between actual and budgeted revenues or costs and describing them in terms of price and quantity differences. *(p. 984)*

Vendee Buyer of goods or services. *(p. 335)*

Vendor Seller of goods or services. *(p. 335)*

Vertical analysis Evaluation of each financial statement item or group of items in terms of a specific base amount. *(p. 682)*

Volume variance Difference between two dollar amounts of fixed overhead cost; one amount is the total budgeted overhead cost, and the other is the overhead cost allocated to products using the predetermined fixed overhead rate. *(p. 993)*

Voucher Internal file used to store documents and information to control cash disbursements and to ensure that a transaction is properly authorized and recorded. *(p. 322)*

Voucher register Journal (referred to as *book of original entry*) in which all vouchers are recorded after they have been approved. *(p. 337)*

Voucher system Procedures and approvals designed to control cash disbursements and acceptance of obligations. *(p. 322)*

Wage bracket withholding table Table of the amounts of income tax withheld from employees' wages. *(p. 454)*

Warranty Agreement that obligates the seller to correct or replace a product or service when it fails to perform properly within a specified period. *(p. 444)*

Weighted average Method to assign inventory cost to sales; the cost of available-for-sale units is divided by the number of units available to determine per unit cost prior to each sale that is then multiplied by the units sold to yield the cost of that sale. *(pp. 230, 245 & 818)*

Weighted-average method (See *weighted average.*)

Wholesaler Intermediary that buys products from manufacturers or other wholesalers and sells them to retailers or other wholesalers. *(p. 178)*

Withdrawals Payment of cash or other assets from a proprietorship or partnership to its owner or owners. *(p. 13)*

Work sheet Spreadsheet used to draft an unadjusted trial balance, adjusting entries, adjusted trial balance, and financial statements. *(p. 136)*

Working capital Current assets minus current liabilities at a point in time. *(p. 691)*

Working papers Analyses and other informal reports prepared by accountants and managers when organizing information for formal reports and financial statements. *(p. 136)*

Credits

Chapter 1
Page 3 Allison Shirreffs/Courtesy of Life is good, Inc.
Page 6 Seth Wenig/Reuters/Landov
Page 9 © Mel Curtis/Getty Images
Page 10 © Joe Robbins/Getty Images
Page 13 © Sam Sharpe/Corbis

Chapter 2
Page 47 Courtesy of Spanx
Page 50 Courtesy of Spanx
Page 51 © Jonathan Daniel/Getty Images
Page 52 Copyright 2007 NBAE. Photo by Joe Murphy/NBAE via Getty Images

Chapter 3
Page 91 Courtesy of PopCap Games, Inc.
Page 93 © Henny Ray Abrams/AFP/Getty Images

Chapter 4
Page 135 Courtesy of Kathryn Kerrigan
Page 145 © Brian Bahr/Getty Images

Chapter 5
Page 177 Courtesy www.bigbadtoystore.com
Page 183 © Anne-Marie Weber/Getty Images/Taxi
Page 187 © Michael Newman/PhotoEdit

Chapter 6
Page 223 Courtesy of Beauty Encounter, Photo: Larry Atil Content: Jacquelyn Tran
Page 225 © Sam Ogden/Photo Researchers, Inc.

Chapter 7
Page 267 Courtesy of TerraCycle, Inc.
Page 270 AP Images/Eric Risberg
Page 271 © Royalty-Free/CORBIS
Page 273 © Jody Dole/Getty Images/The Image Bank
Page 278 AP Images/Topeka Capital-Journal, David Eulitt
Page 282 © Nick Koudis/Getty Images/PhotoDisc
Page 283 © Sonda Dawes/The Image Works

Chapter 8
Page 313 Courtesy of Dylan's Candy Bar
Page 315 © Lawrence Lawry/Getty Images/Photodisc
Page 321 © Bob Daemmrich/The Image Works

Chapter 9
Page 357 AP Images/Nick Wass
Page 360 AP Images/Mark Lennihan
Page 361 © Car Culture/Corbis

Chapter 10
Page 391 Courtesy of Sambazon.com
Page 393 © David M. Grossman/The Image Works
Page 394 © Lester Lefkowitz/Getty Images/The Image Bank
Page 396 © Ilene MacDonald/Alamy
Page 401 © George Tiedemann/GT Images/Corbis
Page 406 © Digital Vision/Getty Images
Page 408 © Scott Halleran/Getty Images

Chapter 11
Page 433 Courtesy of Feed Granola Company
Page 437 © Michael Loccisano/FilmMagic/Getty Images
Page 439 © JUPITERIMAGES/Thinkstock/Alamy
Page 443 © Stephen Jaffe/AFP/Getty Images
Page 447 © John Burcham/National Geographic/Getty Images

Chapter 12
Page 477 Courtesy of Samantashoes.com
Page 479 © David R. Frazier Photolibrary, Inc./Alamy
Page 481 © Erik Freeland/Corbis
Page 484 © Bill Bachmann/Alamy
Page 487 © James Doberman/Getty Images/Iconica

Chapter 13
Page 505 Courtesy of Inogen, Inc.
Page 508 Courtesy of Green Bay Packers, Inc.

Chapter 14
Page 549 © James Wasserman
Page 552 Courtesy of Dow Chemicals

Chapter 15
Page 591 Courtesy of Tibi.com
Page 593 Courtesy of Scripophily.com
Page 595 AP Images/Richard Drew

Chapter 16
Page 627 Courtesy of Jungle Jim's International Market
Page 628 AP Images/Brian Kersey
Page 634 © Corbis Super RF/Alamy

Chapter 17
Page 679 © Dirck Halstead/Liaison/Getty Images
Page 693 AP Images/Ben Margot
Page 698 AP Images/Chuck Burton

Index

Note: Page numbers followed by *n* indicate material in footnotes.

Chart of Accounts

Following is a typical chart of accounts. Each company has its own unique accounts and numbering system.

Assets

Current Assets

101 Cash
102 Petty cash
103 Cash equivalents
104 Short-term investments
105 Market adjustment, _______ securities (S-T)
106 Accounts receivable
107 Allowance for doubtful accounts
108 Legal fees receivable
109 Interest receivable
110 Rent receivable
111 Notes receivable
119 Merchandise inventory
120 _________ inventory
121 _________ inventory
124 Office supplies
125 Store supplies
126 _______ supplies
128 Prepaid insurance
129 Prepaid interest
131 Prepaid rent
132 Raw materials inventory
133 Goods in process inventory, _______
134 Goods in process inventory, _______
135 Finished goods inventory

Long-Term Investments

141 Long-term investments
142 Market adjustment, _______ securities (L-T)
144 Investment in _______
145 Bond sinking fund

Plant Assets

151 Automobiles
152 Accumulated depreciation—Automobiles
153 Trucks
154 Accumulated depreciation—Trucks
155 Boats
156 Accumulated depreciation—Boats
157 Professional library
158 Accumulated depreciation—Professional library
159 Law library
160 Accumulated depreciation—Law library
161 Furniture
162 Accumulated depreciation—Furniture
163 Office equipment
164 Accumulated depreciation—Office equipment
165 Store equipment
166 Accumulated depreciation—Store equipment
167 _______ equipment
168 Accumulated depreciation—_______ equipment
169 Machinery
170 Accumulated depreciation—Machinery
173 Building _______
174 Accumulated depreciation—Building _______
175 Building _______
176 Accumulated depreciation—Building _______
179 Land improvements _______
180 Accumulated depreciation—Land improvements _______
181 Land improvements _______
182 Accumulated depreciation—Land improvements _______
183 Land

Natural Resources

185 Mineral deposit
186 Accumulated depletion—Mineral deposit

Intangible Assets

191 Patents
192 Leasehold
193 Franchise
194 Copyrights
195 Leasehold improvements
196 Licenses
197 Accumulated amortization—_______

Liabilities

Current Liabilities

201 Accounts payable
202 Insurance payable
203 Interest payable
204 Legal fees payable
207 Office salaries payable
208 Rent payable
209 Salaries payable
210 Wages payable
211 Accrued payroll payable
214 Estimated warranty liability
215 Income taxes payable
216 Common dividend payable
217 Preferred dividend payable
218 State unemployment taxes payable
219 Employee federal income taxes payable
221 Employee medical insurance payable
222 Employee retirement program payable
223 Employee union dues payable
224 Federal unemployment taxes payable
225 FICA taxes payable
226 Estimated vacation pay liability

Unearned Revenues

230 Unearned consulting fees
231 Unearned legal fees
232 Unearned property management fees
233 Unearned _______ fees
234 Unearned _______ fees
235 Unearned janitorial revenue
236 Unearned _______ revenue
238 Unearned rent

Notes Payable

240 Short-term notes payable
241 Discount on short-term notes payable
245 Notes payable
251 Long-term notes payable
252 Discount on long-term notes payable

Long-Term Liabilities

253 Long-term lease liability
255 Bonds payable
256 Discount on bonds payable
257 Premium on bonds payable
258 Deferred income tax liability

Equity

Owner's Equity

301 ____________, Capital
302 ____________, Withdrawals
303 ____________, Capital
304 ____________, Withdrawals
305 ____________, Capital
306 ____________, Withdrawals

Paid-In Capital

307 Common stock, $ _______ par value
308 Common stock, no-par value
309 Common stock, $ _______ stated value
310 Common stock dividend distributable
311 Paid-in capital in excess of par value, Common stock
312 Paid-in capital in excess of stated value, No-par common stock
313 Paid-in capital from retirement of common stock
314 Paid-in capital, Treasury stock
315 Preferred stock
316 Paid-in capital in excess of par value, Preferred stock

Retained Earnings

318 Retained earnings
319 Cash dividends (or Dividends)
320 Stock dividends

Other Equity Accounts

321 Treasury stock, Common
322 Unrealized gain—Equity
323 Unrealized loss—Equity

Revenues

401 ____________ fees earned
402 ____________ fees earned
403 ____________ services revenue
404 ____________ services revenue
405 Commissions earned
406 Rent revenue (or Rent earned)
407 Dividends revenue (or Dividends earned)
408 Earnings from investment in ______
409 Interest revenue (or Interest earned)
410 Sinking fund earnings
413 Sales
414 Sales returns and allowances
415 Sales discounts

Cost of Sales

Cost of Goods Sold

502 Cost of goods sold
505 Purchases
506 Purchases returns and allowances
507 Purchases discounts
508 Transportation-in

Manufacturing

520 Raw materials purchases
521 Freight-in on raw materials
530 Factory payroll
531 Direct labor
540 Factory overhead
541 Indirect materials
542 Indirect labor
543 Factory insurance expired
544 Factory supervision
545 Factory supplies used
546 Factory utilities
547 Miscellaneous production costs
548 Property taxes on factory building
549 Property taxes on factory equipment
550 Rent on factory building
551 Repairs, factory equipment
552 Small tools written off
560 Depreciation of factory equipment
561 Depreciation of factory building

Standard Cost Variance

580 Direct material quantity variance
581 Direct material price variance
582 Direct labor quantity variance
583 Direct labor price variance
584 Factory overhead volume variance
585 Factory overhead controllable variance

Expenses

Amortization, Depletion, and Depreciation

601 Amortization expense—______
602 Amortization expense—______
603 Depletion expense—______
604 Depreciation expense—Boats
605 Depreciation expense—Automobiles
606 Depreciation expense—Building ______
607 Depreciation expense—Building ______
608 Depreciation expense—Land improvements ______
609 Depreciation expense—Land improvements ______
610 Depreciation expense—Law library
611 Depreciation expense—Trucks
612 Depreciation expense—______ equipment
613 Depreciation expense—______ equipment
614 Depreciation expense—______
615 Depreciation expense—______

Employee-Related Expenses

620 Office salaries expense
621 Sales salaries expense
622 Salaries expense
623 ______ wages expense
624 Employees' benefits expense
625 Payroll taxes expense

Financial Expenses

630 Cash over and short
631 Discounts lost
632 Factoring fee expense
633 Interest expense

Insurance Expenses

635 Insurance expense—Delivery equipment
636 Insurance expense—Office equipment
637 Insurance expense—______

Rental Expenses

640 Rent expense
641 Rent expense—Office space
642 Rent expense—Selling space
643 Press rental expense
644 Truck rental expense
645 ______ rental expense

Supplies Expenses

650 Office supplies expense
651 Store supplies expense
652 ______ supplies expense
653 ______ supplies expense

Miscellaneous Expenses

655 Advertising expense
656 Bad debts expense
657 Blueprinting expense
658 Boat expense
659 Collection expense
661 Concessions expense
662 Credit card expense
663 Delivery expense
664 Dumping expense
667 Equipment expense
668 Food and drinks expense
671 Gas and oil expense
672 General and administrative expense
673 Janitorial expense
674 Legal fees expense
676 Mileage expense
677 Miscellaneous expenses
678 Mower and tools expense
679 Operating expense
680 Organization expense
681 Permits expense
682 Postage expense
683 Property taxes expense
684 Repairs expense—______
685 Repairs expense—______
687 Selling expense
688 Telephone expense
689 Travel and entertainment expense
690 Utilities expense
691 Warranty expense
695 Income taxes expense

Gains and Losses

701 Gain on retirement of bonds
702 Gain on sale of machinery
703 Gain on sale of investments
704 Gain on sale of trucks
705 Gain on ______
706 Foreign exchange gain or loss
801 Loss on disposal of machinery
802 Loss on exchange of equipment
803 Loss on exchange of ______
804 Loss on sale of notes
805 Loss on retirement of bonds
806 Loss on sale of investments
807 Loss on sale of machinery
808 Loss on ______
809 Unrealized gain—Income
810 Unrealized loss—Income

Clearing Accounts

901 Income summary
902 Manufacturing summary

A Rose by Any Other Name

The same financial statement sometimes receives different titles. Following are some of the more common aliases.*

Balance Sheet	Statement of Financial Position Statement of Financial Condition
Income Statement	Statement of Income Operating Statement Statement of Operations Statement of Operating Activity Earnings Statement Statement of Earnings Profit and Loss (P&L) Statement
Statement of Cash Flows	Statement of Cash Flow Cash Flows Statement Statement of Changes in Cash Position Statement of Changes in Financial Position
Statement of Owner's Equity	Statement of Changes in Owner's Equity Statement of Changes in Owner's Capital Statement of Shareholders' Equity† Statement of Changes in Shareholders' Equity† Statement of Stockholders' Equity and Comprehensive Income† Statement of Changes in Capital Accounts†

* The term **Consolidated** often precedes or follows these statement titles to reflect the combination of different entities, such as a parent company and its subsidiaries.
† Corporation only.

We thank Dr. Louella Moore from Arkansas State University for suggesting this listing.

MANAGERIAL ANALYSES AND REPORTS

① Cost Types

Variable costs: Total cost changes in proportion to volume of activity
Fixed costs: Total cost does not change in proportion to volume of activity
Mixed costs: Cost consists of both a variable and a fixed element

② Cost Sources

Direct materials: Raw materials costs directly linked to finished product
Direct labor: Employee costs directly linked to finished product
Overhead: Costs indirectly linked to finished product

③ Costing Systems

Job order costing: Costs assigned to each unique unit or batch of units
Process costing: Costs assigned to similar products that are mass-produced in a continuous manner

④ Costing Ratios

Contribution margin ratio = (Net sales − Variable costs)/Net sales
Predetermined overhead rate = Estimated overhead costs/Estimated activity base
Break-even point in units = Total fixed costs/Contribution margin per unit

⑤ Planning and Control Metrics

Cost variance = Actual cost − Standard (budgeted) cost
Sales (revenue) variance = Actual sales − Standard (budgeted) sales

⑥ Capital Budgeting

Payback period = Time expected to recover investment cost
Accounting rate of return = Expected annual net income/Average annual investment
Net present value (NPV) = Present value of future cash flows − Investment cost
NPV rule: 1. Compute net present value (NPV in $)
2. If NPV ≥ 0, then accept project; If NPV < 0, then reject project
Internal rate of return rule: 1. Compute internal rate of return (IRR in %)
2. If IRR ≥ hurdle rate, accept project; If IRR < hurdle rate, reject project

⑦ Costing Terminology

Relevant range: Organization's normal range of operating activity.
Direct cost: Cost incurred for the benefit of one cost object.
Indirect cost: Cost incurred for the benefit of more than one cost object.
Product cost: Cost that is necessary and integral to finished products.
Period cost: Cost identified more with a time period than with finished products.
Overhead cost: Cost not separately or directly traceable to a cost object.
Relevant cost: Cost that is pertinent to a decision.
Opportunity cost: Benefit lost by choosing an action from two or more alternatives.
Sunk cost: Cost already incurred that cannot be avoided or changed.
Standard cost: Cost computed using standard price and standard quantity.
Cost variance: Difference between actual cost and budgeted (standard) cost.
Budget: Formal statement of an organization's future plans.
Break-even point: Sales level at which an organization earns zero profit.
Incremental cost: Cost incurred only if the organization undertakes certain action.
Transfer price: Price on transactions between divisions within a company.

⑧ Standard Cost Variances

Total materials variance = Materials price variance + Materials quantity variance

Total labor variance = Labor (rate) variance + Labor efficiency (quantity) variance

Total overhead variance = Overhead controllable variance + Fixed overhead volume variance

Variable overhead variance = Variable overhead spending variance + Variable overhead efficiency variance
Fixed overhead variance = Fixed overhead spending variance + Fixed overhead volume variance
} = Total overhead variance

Overhead controllable variance = Variable overhead spending variance + Variable overhead efficiency variance + Fixed overhead spending variance

Materials price variance = [AQ × AP] − [AQ × SP]

Materials quantity variance = [AQ × SP] − [SQ × SP]

Labor (rate) variance = [AH × AR] − [AH × SR]

Labor efficiency (quantity) variance = [AH × SR] − [SH × SR]

Variable overhead spending variance = [AH × AVR] − [AH × SVR]

Variable overhead efficiency variance = [AH × SVR] − [SH × SVR]

Fixed overhead spending variance = Actual overhead − Budgeted overhead

Fixed overhead volume variance = Budgeted overhead − Applied overhead

where
AQ is actual quantity of materials; AP is actual price of materials; AH is actual hours of labor; AR is actual rate of wages; AVR is actual variable rate of overhead; SQ is standard quantity of materials; SP is standard price of materials; SH is standard hours of labor; SR is standard rate of wages; SVR is standard variable rate of overhead.

Manufacturing Statement
For _period_ Ended _date_

Direct materials	
Raw materials inventory, Beginning	$ #
Raw materials purchases	#
Raw materials available for use	#
Raw materials inventory, Ending	(#)
Direct materials used	#
Direct labor	#
Overhead costs	
Total overhead costs	#
Total manufacturing costs	#
Add goods in process inventory, Beginning	#
Total cost of goods in process	#
Deduct goods in process inventory, Ending	(#)
Cost of goods manufactured	$ #

Contribution Margin Income Statement
For _period_ Ended _date_

Net sales (revenues)	$ #
Total variable costs	#
Contribution margin	#
Total fixed costs	#
Net income	$ #

Flexible Budget
For _period_ Ended _date_

	Flexible Budget: Variable Amount per Unit	Flexible Budget: Fixed Cost	Flexible Budget for Unit Sales of #
Sales (revenues)	$ #		$ #
Variable costs			
Examples: Direct materials, Direct labor, Other variable costs	#		#
Total variable costs	#		#
Contribution margin	$ #		#
Fixed costs			
Examples: Depreciation, Manager		$ #	#
salaries, Administrative salaries		#	#
Total fixed costs		$ #	#
Income from operations			$ #

Fixed Budget Performance Report
For _period_ Ended _date_

	Fixed Budget	Actual Performance	Variances[†]
Sales: In units	#	#	
In dollars	$ #	$ #	$ # F or U
Cost of sales			
Direct costs	#	#	# F or U
Indirect costs	#	#	# F or U
Selling expenses			
Examples: Commissions,	#	#	# F or U
Shipping expenses	#	#	# F or U
General and administrative expenses			
Examples: Administrative salaries	#	#	# F or U
Total expenses	$ #	$ #	$ # F or U
Income from operations	$ #	$ #	$ # F or U

[†] *F = Favorable variance; U = Unfavorable variance.*

Master Budget Sequence

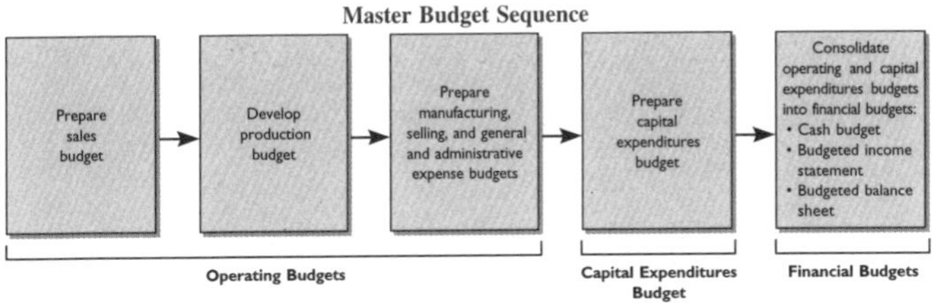

FUNDAMENTALS

① Accounting Equation

Assets		=	Liabilities		+	Equity	
↑ Debit for increases	↓ Credit for decreases		↓ Debit for decreases	↑ Credit for increases		↓ Debit for decreases	↑ Credit for increases

Owner's Capital*		−	Owner's Withdrawals*		+	Revenues		−	Expenses	
↓ Dr. for decreases	↑ Cr. for increases		↑ Dr. for increases	↓ Cr. for decreases		↓ Dr. for decreases	↑ Cr. for increases		↑ Dr. for increases	↓ Cr. for decreases

[shaded] Indicates normal balance.

*Comparable corporate accounts are Common Stock (Paid-In Capital) and Dividends.

② Accounting Cycle

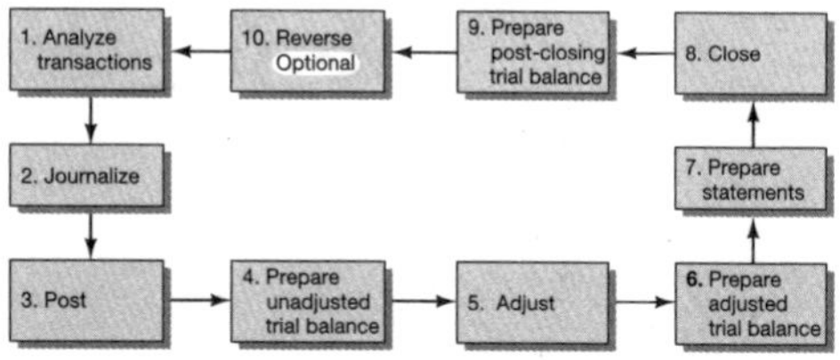

③ Adjustments and Entries

Type	Adjusting Entry	
Prepaid Expenses	Dr. Expense	Cr. Asset*
Unearned Revenues	Dr. Liability	Cr. Revenue
Accrued Expenses	Dr. Expense	Cr. Liability
Accrued Revenues	Dr. Asset	Cr. Revenue

*For depreciation, credit Accumulated Depreciation (contra asset).

④ 4-Step Closing Process

1. Transfer revenue and gain account balances to Income Summary.
2. Transfer expense and loss account balances to Income Summary.
3. Transfer Income Summary balance to Owner's Capital.
4. Transfer Withdrawals balance to Owner's Capital.

⑤ Accounting Concepts

Characteristics	Assumptions	Principles	Constraints
Relevance	Business entity	Historical cost	Cost-benefit
Reliability	Going concern	Revenue recognition	Materiality
Comparability	Monetary unit	Matching	Industry practice
Consistency	Periodicity	Full disclosure	Conservatism

⑥ Ownership of Inventory

	Ownership Transfers When Goods Passed To	Transportation Costs Paid By
FOB Shipping Point	Carrier	Buyer
FOB Destination	Buyer	Seller

⑦ Inventory Costing Methods

Specific Identification
First-In, First-Out (FIFO)
Weighted-Average
Last-In, First-Out (LIFO)

⑧ Depreciation and Depletion

Straight-Line: $\frac{\text{Cost} - \text{Salvage value}}{\text{Useful life in periods}} \times \text{Periods expired}$

Units-of-Production: $\frac{\text{Cost} - \text{Salvage value}}{\text{Useful life in units}} \times \text{Units produced}$

Declining-Balance: Rate* × Beginning-of-period book value

*Rate is often double the straight-line rate, or 2 × (1/Useful life)

Depletion: $\frac{\text{Cost} - \text{Salvage value}}{\text{Total capacity in units}} \times \text{Units extracted}$

⑨ Interest Computation

Interest = Principal (face) × Rate × Time

⑩ Accounting for Investment Securities

Trading (debt and equity) securities	Market value (with market adjustment to income)
Held-to-maturity (debt) securities*	
Short-term	Cost (without any discount or premium amortization)
Long-term	Cost (with any discount or premium amortization)
Available-for-sale (debt and equity) securities*	Market value (with market adjustment to equity)
Equity securities with significant influence	Equity method

*A *fair value option* allows companies to report these securities much like trading securities.

ANALYSES

① Liquidity and Efficiency

Current ratio $= \frac{\text{Current assets}}{\text{Current liabilities}}$	p. 148
Working capital = Current assets − Current liabilities	p. 691
Acid-test ratio $= \frac{\text{Cash} + \text{Short-term investments} + \text{Current receivables}}{\text{Current liabilities}}$	p. 193
Accounts receivable turnover $= \frac{\text{Net sales}}{\text{Average accounts receivable, net}}$	p. 372
Credit risk ratio $= \frac{\text{Allowance for doubtful accounts}}{\text{Accounts receivable, net}}$	p. 372
Inventory turnover $= \frac{\text{Cost of goods sold}}{\text{Average inventory}}$	p. 236
Days' sales uncollected $= \frac{\text{Accounts receivable, net}}{\text{Net sales}} \times 365^*$	p. 332
Days' sales in inventory $= \frac{\text{Ending inventory}}{\text{Cost of goods sold}} \times 365^*$	p. 237
Total asset turnover $= \frac{\text{Net sales}}{\text{Average total assets}}$	p. 410
Plant asset useful life $= \frac{\text{Plant asset cost}}{\text{Depreciation expense}}$	p. 410
Plant asset age $= \frac{\text{Accumulated depreciation}}{\text{Depreciation expense}}$	p. 410
Days' cash expense coverage $= \frac{\text{Cash and cash equivalents}}{\text{Average daily cash expenses}}$	p. 320

*360 days is also commonly used.

② Solvency

Debt ratio $= \frac{\text{Total liabilities}}{\text{Total assets}}$ Equity ratio $= \frac{\text{Total equity}}{\text{Total assets}}$	pp. 67 & 695
Debt-to-equity $= \frac{\text{Total liabilities}}{\text{Total equity}}$	p. 564
Times interest earned $= \frac{\text{Income before interest expense and income taxes}}{\text{Interest expense}}$	p. 447
Cash coverage of growth $= \frac{\text{Cash flow from operations}}{\text{Cash outflow for plant assets}}$	p. 646
Cash coverage of debt $= \frac{\text{Cash flow from operations}}{\text{Total noncurrent liabilities}}$	p. 646

③ Profitability

Profit margin ratio $= \frac{\text{Net income}}{\text{Net sales}}$	p. 106
Gross margin ratio $= \frac{\text{Net sales} - \text{Cost of goods sold}}{\text{Net sales}}$	p. 193
Return on total assets $= \frac{\text{Net income}}{\text{Average total assets}}$	p. 20
= Profit margin ratio × Total asset turnover	p. 697
Return on common stockholders' equity $= \frac{\text{Net income} - \text{Preferred dividends}}{\text{Average common stockholders' equity}}$	p. 697
Book value per common share $= \frac{\text{Stockholders' equity applicable to common shares}}{\text{Number of common shares outstanding}}$	p. 526
Basic earnings per share $= \frac{\text{Net income} - \text{Preferred dividends}}{\text{Weighted-average common shares outstanding}}$	p. 524
Cash flow on total assets $= \frac{\text{Cash flow from operations}}{\text{Average total assets}}$	p. 646
Payout ratio $= \frac{\text{Cash dividends declared on common stock}}{\text{Net income}}$	p. 525

④ Market

Price-earnings ratio $= \frac{\text{Market value (price) per share}}{\text{Earnings per share}}$	p. 525
Dividend yield $= \frac{\text{Annual cash dividends per share}}{\text{Market price per share}}$	p. 525

Residual income = Net income − Target net income